The Laghusiddhāntakaumudī of Varadarāja

A Primer of Pāṇini's Grammar

The Laghusiddhāntakaumudī of Varadarāja

A Primer of Pāṇini's Grammar

Translated & Elucidated by
KANSHI RAM

Edited by
MITHILESH CHATURVEDI

Volume I

MOTILAL BANARSIDASS PUBLISHERS
PRIVATE LIMITED • DELHI

Reprint : Delhi, 2011
First Edition : Delhi, 2010

ISBN : 978-81-208-3451-4

MOTILAL BANARSIDASS
41 U.A. Bungalow Road, Jawahar Nagar, Delhi 110007
8 Mahalaxmi Chamber, 22 Bhulabhai Desai Road, Mumbai 400026
203 Royapettah High Road, Mylapore, Chennai 600004
236, 9th Main III Block, Jayanagar, Bangalore 560011
Sanas Plaza, 1302 Baji Rao Road, Pune 411002
8 Camac Street, Kolkata 700017
Ashok Rajpath, Patna 800004
Chowk, Varanasi 221001

Printed in India
By Jainendra Prakash Jain at Shri Jainendra Press,
A-45, Naraina, Phase-I, New Delhi 110028
and Published by Narendra Prakash Jain for
Motilal Banarsidass Publishers Private Limited,
Bungalow Road, Delhi 110007

Dedicated to
Baba Mastaramji, who showered his grace upon me, and with his enlightening discourses filled the spiritual vacuum within me at a time when I most needed this act of kindness.

Contents

A Note on Transliteration

a	अ
ā	आ
i	इ
ī	ई
u	उ
ū	ऊ
ṛ	ऋ
ṝ	ॠ
ḷ	ऌ
e	ए
ai	ऐ
o	ओ
au	औ
aṁ	अं
aḥ	अः

क्	ख्	ग्	घ्	ङ्
k	kh	g	gh	ṅ
च्	छ्	ज्	झ्	ञ्
c	ch	j	jh	ñ
ट्	ठ्	ड्	ढ्	ण्
ṭ	ṭh	ḍ	ḍh	ṇ
त्	थ्	द्	ध्	न्
t	th	d	dh	n
प्	फ्	ब्	भ्	म्
p	ph	b	bh	m

य्	र्	ल्	व्
y	r	l	v

ym̐	यँ्
vm̐	वँ्
lm̐	लँ्

श्	ष्	स्	ह्
ś	ṣ	s	h
क्ष्	त्र्	ज्ञ्	
kṣ	tr	jñ	

Acknowledgements

I pay homage to my guru, Baba Mastaramji, whose incomparable grace has enabled me to complete this volume. The opening verse of his hymn to Ātman - The Ātmacintanam - forms the invocation of this work.

I would like to acknowledge the help of my spiritual sister, Naniji, disciple of Baba Mastaramji and Trustee of Ganga Prem Hospice, Rishikesh. She went through the manuscript very carefully and gave me invaluable suggestions for improvement both in form and content. I have no words to thank her. I also want to express my gratitude to Swami Radha Ramana, disciple of Baba Mastaramji who was always ready to help me in solving difficult issues of the Śāstras.

I take this opportunity to express my gratitude to those who helped me in studying Pāṇini's grammar. Prof. Satyavrat Shastri taught us the tiṅanta-prakaraṇa of the Siddhāntakaumudī in 1966-67. The late Prof. Harshanath Mishra gladly helped me with cogent solutions whenever I came across problems while teaching the Siddhāntakaumudī at the University level. If the problem was not addressed satisfactorily on the spur of the moment, he always took care to write long letters explaining the intricate problems of grammar and offering solutions. I also attended classes at the Motinath Sanskrit Mahavidyalaya, Ramesh Nagar, Delhi and listened attentively while the late Pt. Vedananda Jha taught Prauḍhamanoramā, Laghuśabdenduśekhara, Nyāyasiddhāntamuktāvalī, Vyāptipañcaka, Citsukhī, etc. in 1983-1986 when I was on a three-year study leave. Prof. George Cardona enlightened me on the subtle points of Pāṇini's grammar through long e-mails whenever I approached him with my problems. I owe a deep debt of gratitude to all of them.

Both Shri Narendra Prakash Jain (Prakashji), Director, Motilal Banarsidass, and I respectively sent the saṁjñā prakaraṇa to Professor Madhav M. Deshpande and Professor George Cardona for their opinion. Prof. Deshpande kindly went through it and sent me an encouraging message through Prakashji. He drew my attention to one omission saying that I did not say anything on Varadarāja's provision for distinct internal efforts for the sibilants and vowels as īṣadvivṛta and vivṛta respectively since this makes Pāṇini's rule *nājjhalau* Pā. 1. 1. 10 purposeless. Consequent upon his suggestion, I have added footnote 2 on page 14. Prof. George Cardona also went through the saṁjñā-prakaraṇa thoroughly and made several significant suggestions. I emended this chapter in the light of his suggestions. I express my gratefulness to these stalwarts in the field of Pāṇinian studies.

It is generally good students who contribute to the making of a teacher worth the name. I am fortunate enough to have had good students who, with their penetrating queries, kept me constantly busy finding solutions to their problems in grammar. Omnath Bimali, Satya Pal Singh, P. S. Roodurmun, Sandhya Rathore, Ranjeet Kumar Mishra, Avanish Kumar, Dolamani, Jag Mohan, etc. have been some such students. Most of them are now teaching in various institutions of Delhi University and other universities. Omnath Bimali and Sandhya Rathore read the manuscript thoroughly and helped improve it significantly. For this they richly deserve my thanks and blessings. Dr. A. K. Monga also read the first chapter and gave useful suggestions for which I thank him.

Authors of works on the grammar of Pāṇini, such as Bhimasena Shastri, S. M. Katre, S. D. Joshi, Rama Nath Sharma, S. C. Vasu, J. R. Ballantyne, to name but a few, have, through their works, been instrumental in my completing the present volume. I take this opportunity to pay my deep regards to them and other scholars whose works have been included in the bibliography.

Dr. Mithilesh Chaturvedi, Department of Sanskrit, Delhi University, took upon himself the onerous task of editing this work. He did his job sincerely and I thank him for it. Morevoer, the suggestions given by him have gone a long way in making the elucidation student-friendly. Prakashji took personal interest in the preparation of the first volume of this three-volume project and arranged for everything which I requested him to provide.

Finally, I take this opportunity to acknowledge the support of my wife, Kesar, who was always ready to take care of me while I was doing this job.

Introduction

The Aṣṭādhyāyī of Pāṇini is the culmination of a long grammatical tradition. It has been acclaimed as a 'monumental work of human intelligence' and the best descriptive model of a language which was the mother tongue of Pāṇini[1] in the middle of the fifth century B. C.[2] Pāṇini ably blended his originality with careful and ingenious borrowings from the texts of the old grammarians to compose the Aṣṭādhyāyī. The extensive recognition of this perfect grammatical work consisting of 3983 sūtras[3] (aphorisms) is evidenced by the near extinction of the pre-Pāṇinian works of grammar and by the enormity of commentarial literature written on it. Probably in the fourth century B. C. Kātyāyana composed about four thousand vārttikas which proposed the correction, completion and explanation of the aphorisms of the Aṣṭādhyāyī.[4] These vārttikas as well as the sūtras of the Aṣṭādhyāyī became the focal point for Patañjali to author the great commentary called Mahābhāṣya in the second century B. C. The Mahābhāṣya stands distinguished from other bhāṣya texts and hence is called the Mahābhāṣya. The reason is that it also assumed the role of the Aṣṭādhyāyī by proposing iṣṭis (*bhāṣyasūtras*) to describe Sanskrit language.[5]

The grammatical literature composed by the reputed triad of grammarians came to be known by the appellation *trimuni vyākaraṇam*. It is indeed the encyclopedic Mahābhāṣya that has discussed thoroughly almost all grammatical issues and has laid down such principles as

---

1. Cf. Bloomfield, p. 11.

2. See V. S. Agrawal, pp. 456-75 and Kanshi Ram, p. 48.

3. *alpākṣaram asandigdhaṁ sāravad viśvatomukham, astobham anavadyaṁ ca sūtraṁ sūtravido viduḥ* : A sūtra is defined as an unambiguous pithy statement which contains essence, is capable of several interpretations, contains nothing meaningless and has nothing unfit to be stated. It is of six kinds : 1. saṁjñā (rules defining technical terms), 2. paribhāṣā (interpretive rules), 3. vidhi (operational rules), 4. niyama (restrictive rules), 5. atideśa (extension rules) and 6. adhikāra (heading rules). There are also other types of rules, namely, pratiṣedha (negation rules), vibhāṣā (optional rules) and nipātana (ad hoc rules). Cf. *saṁjñā ca paribhāṣā ca vidhir niyama eva ca, atideśo 'dhikāraś ca ṣaḍvidhaṁ sūtralakṣaṇam.* Nyāyakośa, p. 1031.

4. *uktānuktaduruktānāṁ cintā yatra pravartate,*
taṁ granthaṁ vārttikaṁ prāhur vārttikajñā manīṣiṇaḥ. Dictionary, s. v. vārttika.

5. Mbh. P., p. 4 line 3. Also cf. *sarvanyāyabījahetutvād eva mahacchabdena mahābhāṣyam ityucyate loke*. PR, p. 189.

have become the last and final word in all places of doubt. It would not be out of plaçe to say that it is Patañjali who, through his magnum opus, raised the grammatical issues to the level of philosophy. After a gap of nearly six centuries, Bhartṛhari made the theoretical isssues of grammar a focal point of study and wrote an authoritative and scholarly siddhānta text, the Vākyapadīya, on the philosophical tenets of grammar as well as his Mahābhāṣyadīpikā (....ṭīkā : at present available up to seven āhnikas).

The grammatical apparatus set up by Pāṇini regarding the structural aspect of Sanskrit attracted the attention of Jayāditya and Vāmana who wrote the Kāśikāvṛtti in the seventh century A. D. It is the only extant full-length commentary on the sūtras of the Aṣṭādhyāyī. According to Haradatta the term *vṛtti* means 'a work in which the meaning of a sūtra is given primacy'.[1] Although the title of the commentary on the Aṣṭādhyāyī written by Jayāditya and Vāmana is the Kāśikāvṛtti, it contains more than the meaning of a sūtra as is clear from its opening verses. Jayāditya and Vāmana describe it as being a summary of the significant views that are found scattered in the vṛttis of Kuṇi, Cūllibhaṭṭi, Nallūra, etc.[2] on the Aṣṭādhyāyī, the Mahābhāṣya of Patañjali, the Dhātupārāyaṇa, Nāmapārāyaṇa, etc. It also has iṣṭis (desirable proposals by Patañjali in the Mahābhāṣya), upasaṅkhyānas (emending statements made by Kātyāyana on the sūtras of the Aṣṭādhyāyī), edited lists of gaṇas, unravelling of the deeper significance of difficult sūtras and derivational details of word-forms constituting illustrations.[3] So, the Kāśikā is more than a vṛtti.

Jinendrabuddhi, a Buddhist grammarian of the eighth century, wrote an easy but illuminating gloss on the Kāśikā. It is known as Nyāsa or Kāśikāvivaraṇapañjikā. In the twelfth century, Haradatta, another famous grammarian of Southern India, wrote a very learned and scholarly commentary on the Kāśikāvṛtti, known as the Padamañjarī. Both these works together propagated and popularized the study of the Aṣṭādhyāyī. Jinendrabuddhi's work is a great aid in getting at the meaning of the sūtras of Pāṇini in a considerably comprehensible way and presents the derivational details lucidly, whereas the work of Haradatta contains everything important that is propounded in the Mahābhāṣya, which is implied from the popular saying : If the

1. *sūtrārthapradhāno grantho vṛttiḥ*. KP, I, p. 4.
2. KN, I, p. 4.
3. *vṛttau bhāṣye tathā dhātunāmapārāyaṇādiṣu,*
viprakīrṇasya tantrasya kriyate sārasaṅgrahaḥ.
iṣṭyupasaṅkhyānavatī śuddhagaṇā vivṛtagūḍhasūtrārthā,
vyutpannarūpasiddhir vṛttir iyam kāśikā nāma. Kāśikā, p. 1.

Mahābhāṣya has been studied, then it is no use studying the Padamañjarī.[1]

Puruṣottamadeva wrote the commentary Bhāṣāvṛtti in the twelfth century. He made use of the Kāśikā in preparing his commentary. As the title suggests, it was only on those sūtras of the Aṣṭādhyāyī which deal with bhāṣā 'classical language'. His exposition was brief and straightforward. He did not pay any attention to the theoretical aspect of the Pāṇinian system. Nonetheless, the examples which he has provided in the Bhāṣāvṛtti are varied and have been chosen for clarity of structure and frequency in usage.

With the advent of the Rūpāvatāra of Dharmakīrti in the eleventh century, the focus of study in the Pāṇinian system of grammar shifted from interpretation to application. The Rūpāvatāra of Dharmakīrti is the oldest extant text of the prakriyā tradition. Its goal was to facilitate the understanding of beginners. Accordingly, the number of sūtras which are discussed by Dharmakīrti is limited. Dharmakīrti commented on 2664 sūtras only, as he did not include the rules on accent and Vedic Sanskrit but the number of illustrations used is manifold. Because there was a shift in emphasis, the order of the sūtras of the Aṣṭādhyāyī was given up. The rules were taken up as and when they were required by the stage of derivational process of the illustrations which were selected purely for derivational reasons. So, the focus for this commentary was the application of grammar in chosen examples. Despite being a successful attempt, the Rūpāvatāra of Dharmakīrti did not gain much popularity due to its over-simplified approach to the treatment of the sūtras of the Aṣṭādhyāyī and their frequent repetition.

Rāmacandra, a grammarian of the fourteenth century,[2] wrote the Prakriyākaumudī and thereby improved upon the prakriyā method initiated by Dharmakīrti and standardized it. He too focussed on those sūtras which dealt with classical Sanskrit. However, at the end, he included a small section dealing with the Vedic prakriyā. Many Vedic rules have also been included elsewhere in the Prakriyākaumudī according to the context. His treatment of the verbal paradigms with reference to the grouping of roots, their categorization and arrangement became standard for later prakriyā texts. These two prakriyā works did not match the depth with which the Kāśikāvṛtti was written. Nonetheless, they did usher in the prakriyā tradition which gradually gained popularity.

The prakriyā method, which laid emphasis on the applied aspect of Pāṇini's grammar, reached its culmination in the Vaiyākaraṇasiddhānta-

1. *adhīte hi mahābhāṣye vyarthā sā padamañjarī*. Dictionary, p. 235.

2. Yudhiṣṭhira Mīmāṁsaka, I, p. 485.

kaumudī of Bhaṭṭoji Dīkṣita in the first half of the seventeenth century (Dictionary, p. 289). This prakriyā work is popularly known as the Siddhānta-kaumudī. Although it follows the organizational format of the Prakriyākaumudī, its scope is much wider since it comments on every sūtra of the Aṣṭādhyāyī. Its scholarly interpretation of the rules of Pāṇini's grammar with examples and counter-examples accompanied by paṅktis (pithy statements containing the gist of the principles of grammar as discussed in the Mahābhāṣya) overshadowed not only the Rūpāvatāra and Prakriyākaumudī but also the Kāśikā and other commentaries. At several places Bhaṭṭoji Dīkṣita does not accept the interpretation of the sūtras of the Aṣṭādhyāyī by Haradatta, Mādhava, Rāmacandra, etc. if it is not in consonance with the interpretation of the Mahābhāṣya. He also criticizes the Kāśikā whenever he finds in it something inconsistent with the Mahābhāṣya.

A perusal of the Siddhāntakaumudī shows that it is undoubtedly helpful in understanding the Mahābhāṣya. This is also clear from the popular saying *kaumudī yadi kaṇṭhasthā vṛthā bhāṣye pariśramaḥ, kaumudī yadyakaṇṭhasthā vṛthā bhāṣye pariśramaḥ* : 'if you have mastered the Siddhāntakaumudī, it is no use studying the Mahābhāṣya and if you have not mastered it, it is futile to study the Mahābhāṣya'. This means that the study of the Siddhāntakaumudī enables you to comprehend the gist of grammatical principles that have been discussed in the Mahābhāṣya even without studying the latter. On the other hand, if you have not properly studied the Siddhāntakaumudī, it would be very difficult to grasp what the Mahābhāṣya has got to say regarding the grammar of Pāṇini. In both ways it is indispensable to study the Siddhāntakaumudī.

Bhaṭṭoji himself wrote the commentary Prauḍhamanoramā on the Siddhāntakaumudī to elaborate it in a scholarly manner. In the eighteenth century, Nāgeśa wrote two elaborate glosses on the Siddhāntakaumudī : Bṛhacchabdenduśekhara and its shorter version Laghuśabdenduśekhara. Of the two, it is the latter which became popular and is taught nowadays at traditional pāṭhaśālās in courses on Navya-vyākaraṇa. The meticulous and precise presentation of the principles of grammar in the Laghuśabdenduśekhara speaks volumes for Nāgeśa's mastery of the Mahābhāṣya. At every step, whenever he critically examines the views of Bhaṭṭoji, whether in the Siddhāntakaumudī or in the Prauḍhamanoramā, he invariably supports his own view by quoting from the Mahābhāṣya. It is this reason that Nāgeśa became the most reputed scholar of Pāṇini's grammar in his time and was approached by everybody who wanted to gain proficiency in the grammar of Pāṇini.

It is true that the approach of the Prakriyā tradition was pedagogical but Bhaṭṭoji's goal was not exactly the same. It cannot be denied that he shared the responsibility of shifting the focus from the theory of grammar to the derivational process and from the order of rules of the Aṣṭādhyāyī to the order conducive to that process. Nonetheless, it cannot be gainsaid that the phase of grammar that started with Bhaṭṭoji and continued up to Nageśa did contribute to the understanding of Pāṇini's grammar. This could be fairly assessed by visualizing the Siddhānta-kaumudī rearranged in the Aṣṭādhyāyī order.

Varadarāja, a disciple of Bhaṭṭoji Dīkṣita, composed three separate short versions of the Siddhāntakaumudī : 1. Madhyasiddhāntakaumudī (medium version), 2. Laghusiddhāntakaumudī (short version) more popularly called Laghukaumudī, 3. Sārasiddhāntakaumudī (abridged version of the Laghukaumudī). Out of the three, it is particularly the Laghukaumudī which is the most valuable and helpful to those who want to be initiated into the grammar of Pāṇini. It covers topics which are common to the Siddhāntakaumudī but they are fewer and arranged in a different order. This will be clear from the following description. The Siddhānta-kaumudī has been organized into two parts : Pūrvārdha and Uttarārdha. The arrangement of the topics of the Siddhāntakaumudī in these two parts is as follows : saṁjñā, paribhāṣā, sandhi, ṣaḍliṅga or subanta, avyaya, strīpratyaya, kāraka, samāsa, taddhita, dviruktaprakriyā (pūrvārddha); tiṅanta, lakārārtha, kṛdanta with uṇādisūtras, vaidika-prakaraṇa, svaraprakaraṇa with phiṭsūtras and liṅgānuśāsana (uttarārddha).[1] The arrangement of the topics in the Laghukaumudī is as follows : saṁjñā, sandhi, ṣaḍliṅga or subanta, avyaya, tiṅanta, kṛdanta, vibhaktyartha, samāsa, taddhita and strīpratyaya.

The Laghusiddhāntakaumudī has 1270 sūtras. Various editions have different numbers of sūtras. The GP and NS editions repeat nine and eight sūtras respectively. Bhimasena Shastri repeats six sūtras but counts them separately. Thus the number of sūtras in his edition comes to 1276. These sūtras are : 1. *visarjanīyasya saḥ* (Bhaimī, I, 96 and 103), 2. *ata ut sārvadhātuke* (Bhaimī, II, 572 and 677), 3. *tanādikṛñbhya uḥ* (Bhaimī, II, 571 and 673), 4. *na bhakurchurām* (Bhaimī, II, 678 and Bhaimī V, 1133), 5. *svatantraḥ kartā* (Bhaimī, II, 698 and Bhaimī, III, 893) and 6. *anuśatikādīnāṁ ca* (Bhaimī, V, 1095 and 1146). With the exclusion of the sūtras which are repeated, the number of the sūtras expounded in the Laghu comes to 1270. Without numbering a repeated sūtra, I have given it with an asterisk or have made such a sūtra a part of the vṛtti.

1. For a detailed description of the structure of the Siddhāntakaumudī, see Rama Nath Sharma, Vol. I, pp. 26-31.

The reading of the vārttikas that occur in the Laghu sometimes differs significantly from that available in the Mahābhāṣya. Most of them are in the form of paraphrases of the vārttikas as they are found in the Mahābhāṣya. At some places, the iṣṭis of the Mahābhāṣya have been made into vārttikas. To exemplify, the first vārttika *ṛḷvarṇayor mithaḥ sāvarṇyaṁ vācyam* in the Laghukaumudī is a paraphrase of *ṛḷkārayoḥ savarṇavidhiḥ*, Mbh 1. 1. 9 vtk 9 and the eighteenth vārttika *gatikārakeṭara-pūrvapadasya yaṇ neṣyate* is given in the Mahābhāṣya in the form of an iṣṭi on Pā. 6. 4. 82.

While preparing an abridged version of the Siddhāntakaumudī, Varadarāja has kept in mind that he is writing it for beginners. In the beginning itself he gives the sūtra *halantyam* (1) and comments on it in a simple way without resorting to iteration (*āvṛtti*) which Bhaṭṭoji Dīkṣita has done in the Siddhāntakaumudī (see infra p. 5) to avoid the defect of mutual dependence. He does not follow Bhaṭṭoji while making provision for distinct internal efforts for the sibilants and vowels as Īṣadvivṛta and vivṛta respectively. This dispenses with the need of *nājjhalau* Pā. 1. 1. 10 (see p. 14 fn. 2). He makes Pāṇini's position untenable when he interprets the rule *śeṣe lopaḥ* (312) as *etayoṣṭilopaḥ* (see pp. 430-31). This interpretation by Varadarāja does not satisfactorily explain why Pāṇini has enunciated the augment *ām* with *suṭ* in the sūtra *sāma ākam* (327). I have given my point of view while elucidating this aphorism (see pp. 443-45). Even in the case of anuvṛttis, significant things seem to go unheeded. To explain, he does not mention in his commentary on *anaci ca* Pā. 8. 4. 47 that this rule occurs in the governing domain of *saṁhitāyām* by virtue of the sūtra *tayoryvāvaci saṁhitāyām* Pā. 8. 2. 108, whereas the rule *iko yaṇaci* occurs in the domain of the governing rule *saṁhitāyām* Pā. 6. 1. 72. Both the governing domains should have been distinctly mentioned. Again it appears inexplicable why Varadarāja does not carry over the term *vibhaktau* into the sūtra *aci ra ṛtaḥ* Pā. 7. 2. 100 from *aṣṭana ā vibhaktau* Pā. 7. 2. 84, whereas the anuvṛtti of the term *vibhaktau* has been shown in the preceding sūtra *tricaturoḥ striyāṁ tisṛcatasṛ* Pā. 7. 2. 99. Bhimasena Shastri also does not take note of this omission. Such an omission adds to the antagonistic attitude that is generally harboured against the Kaumudī tradition that the prakriyā method carries a reader far away from the Aṣṭādhyāyī tradition and makes things difficult for him to understand. On the other hand by following the Aṣṭādhyāyī method a reader is enabled to make a small and elliptical sūtra into a complete sentence with the help of anuvṛtti. It is obvious that learning the sūtras by heart in the order in which they are given in the Aṣṭādhyāyī makes it easy to make an elliptical rule into a complete sentence since in this way the carrying over of missing words into following sūtras is made easier. For this to happen, we have endeavoured to carry over the missing words and have shown them in the 'Elucidation'.

There are several commentaries in Hindi on the Laghusiddhānta-kaumudī, e. g. by Śrīdharānanda Śāstrī, Mahesh Singh Kushwaha, Govind Prasad Sharma, etc. but the commentary (Bhaimī) by Bhimasena Shastri is by far the best of all the commentaries that have been written on the Laghu so far. Bhimasena Shastri's method of presentation is elaborate and lucid. He disjoins the padas of the sūtra and shows in which case-endings they are. Then he gives the meaning of the sūtra. In the vyākhyā portion, he shows the carrying over of the padas from the preceding rules and by using these padas, he makes the elliptical sūtra into a complete sentence. After this, he elaborately discusses the significance of the constituting padas as well as other important grammatical points. His commentary abounds in useful illustrations from literary sources and exercises. If I am making some critical observations about it in the following, the credit goes to the Bhaimī vyākhyā since I started studying Sanskrit grammar with its help in 1962 when only the first part was available. Nonetheless, when we closely read it, we come to know that Bhimasena Shastri takes many things for granted. He does not give complete references to important quotes that he makes in his vyākhyā, e. g., *chandovat sūtrāṇi bhavanti* (Bhaimī, I, pp. 7, 391), *apavādo vacanaprāmāṇyāt* (Bhaimī, I, pp. 100, 351, 416), *yaḥ śiṣyate sa lupyamānārthābhidhāyī* (Bhaimī, I, p. 169), *chandovat kavayaḥ kurvanti* (Bhaimī, I, p. 236), *kvibantā dhātutvaṁ na jahati* (Bhaimī, I, p. 270), *ḍittvābhāve 'mi siddhe 'pi sāvaniṣṭaṁ prasajyate, dakāre vā takāre vā sambuddhau tatsthitiḥ kutaḥ* (Bhaimī, I, p. 330), *nimittāpāye naimittika-syāpyapāyaḥ* (355), *aṅgavṛtte punarvṛttau avidhir niṣṭhitasya* (Bhaimī, I, p. 428, fn. 2), etc. The commentary teems with such referenceless quotes.

Bhimasena Shastri mainly follows the Bālamanoramā of Vāsudeva Dīkṣita in commenting on the sūtras of the Laghu. This becomes clear when we come across his analysis of the compounds and other relevant grammatical annotations. However, I have tried to trace and quote the original source as far as possible to drive home the point which I am making while commenting on a particular sūtra. At one place, I have followed the sequence of the sūtras as given in the GP edition since its sequence accords with that of the Aṣṭādhyāyī, whereas Bhimasena Shastri follows the NS edition in this respect. I see no point in changing the sequence of the Aṣṭādhyāyī. The sequence of the sūtras as given in the Bhaimī vyākhyā is as follows: (84) *ḍaḥ si dhuṭ* (85) *ādyantau ṭakitau*

(86) *ṅṇoḥ kukṭuk śari*. The order that is followed in the present edition is: (84) *ādyantau ṭakitau* (85) *ṅṇoḥ kukṭuk śari* (86) *ḍaḥ si dhuṭ*.

At one place in the vṛtti I have spotted that the punctuation in the Bhaimī vyākhyā differs from that given in the GP and NS editions and the Sārasiddhāntakaumudī of Varadarāja (p. 54). If we retain the reading given in the above two editions and the Sāra, then the vṛtti, split in two sentences, reads well and makes sense while Varadarāja's vṛtti in a single sentence, as given in the Bhaimī, without a full stop after the term *pare* (after *sarvanāmasthāne* in Sāra), does not make the sense clear. I am referring to Varadarāja's vṛtti on the sūtra *tṛjvatkroṣṭuḥ* [(203) in the Bhaimī and (202) in the present edition]. At another place, Bhimasena Shastri interprets the sūtra *vā 'vasāne* (145) in a different manner from Nāgeśa, Jñānendra Sarasvatī and Vāsudeva Dīkṣita. He considers the rule *jhalāṁ jaśo 'nte* (67) to be nitya and firmly holds the view that its application should precede that of the rule *vā 'vasāne* (145). On the other hand I think that the rule *vā 'vasāne* (145) is an exception. I have shown that the paribhāṣā *yena nāprāpte yo vidhir ārabhyate sa tasya bādhako bhavati* (Abhyankar, 57) applies here. Jñānendra Sarasvatī and Vāsudeva Dīkṣita endorse this view. Nāgeśa (LS, p. 315) too supports the view that the rule *vā 'vasāne* is an exception to *jhalāṁ jaśo 'nte* (67). Being an exception, *vā 'vasāne* should apply prior to the latter in accordance with the paribhāṣā *pūrvaparanityāntaraṅgāpavādānām uttarottaraṁ balīyaḥ* (Abhyankar, 38). However, keeping in view the nature of the Laghu, I have applied *jhalāṁ jaśo 'nte* (67) before *vā 'vasāne* in describing the derivational process where I considered that the prior application of *vā-'vasāne* (145) would add to the complexity in the derivational process.

The Laghukaumudī of Varadarāja was translated into English for the first time by James R. Ballantyne in 1849. It is a simple translation of both the sūtras and Varadarāja's vṛtti on them making very brief references to the sūtras which are required to be shown in the derivational process. In 1928, V. V. Mirashi published the Laghu-siddhāntakaumudī, part I comprising sections on saṁjñā, sandhi, kṛt affixes, senses of case-endings and compounds. It consists of an original commentary in Sanskrit and an English translation with explanatory notes. The second part comprising the rest of the Laghu never saw the light of the day. Of these two translations, the former is available but the latter is out of print. Evidently, there is a compelling need for a detailed commentary on the Laghusiddhāntakaumudī in English and I felt this need when I taught it to some foreign students at University level.

Although the Laghusiddhāntakaumudī has been composed for beginners, the present work is not meant only for beginners in schools since nowadays the Laghu is generally prescribed at the University level in Sanskrit curriculum. So, I think it proper to expose such grown up students to a little higher level of detailed grammatical comments on the sūtras of the Laghu. If a motivated student reads this book sincerely, I am hopeful that he will acquire, in the real sense, the kind of ability that is required to have access to Pāṇini's Aṣṭādhyāyī as Varadarāja claims in the invocatory verse of the Laghu.

Let us now address ourselves to the scheme that I have adopted in preparing the present gloss of Varadarāja's Laghukaumudī. I have first given the sūtras of the Aṣṭādhyāyī in the Devanāgarī script, which are prefaced by a sequential number in parentheses. Since this number, which is given to a sūtra as it comes in the Laghu, is different from that generally given in other editions, I am appending a list of all the 1270 sūtras of the Laghu for easy reference. The sūtra of Laghu in Devanāgarī is followed by its transliterated form. It is accompanied by the number as it occurs in the Aṣṭādhyāyī. The Aṣṭādhyāyī number is based on the Kāśikā edited by Vijayapala. The text of the Laghukaumudī in the Devanāgarī comes next and is followed by its transliteration. Then follows the English translation. The translation is not literal. I have only tried to make the sense of the sūtra clear. Therefore each and every sentence of the vṛtti of Varadarāja is not translated. Only that portion of the vṛtti has been translated which makes the sense of the sūtra clear. The rest of the vṛtti is explained in the 'Elucidation' part.

The translation is followed by the 'paraphrased' sūtra in which padas are kept in non-sandhi form and in which the carried over padas have been shown in two ways : 1. without parentheses and 2. within parentheses. The padas, given without parentheses, are taken into consideration when I translate the vṛtti on the sūtra. The terms which are shown in parentheses are also carried over into the sūtra under discussion but are not taken into consideration for the purpose of translation and comments. In showing the carried over padas in the 'paraphrase' I have followed by and large the Kāśikāvṛtti of Jayāditya and Vāmana. The paraphrase is immediately followed by the 'Elucidation'. In the 'Elucidation' I have tried to give the sūtra with the sequential number of the Aṣṭādhyāyī from which a particular pada is made to recur in the sūtra under discussion so that we do not become oblivious to the fact that we are actually reading an abridged version of the Aṣṭādhyāyī of Pāṇini with a different arrangement and also so that we do not lose sight of the real objective of studying Sanskrit grammar. I have also tried to explain why the number or case-ending of a particular carried over term is changed to suit the context, using the technical process of vacana-vipariṇāma or vibhakti-vipariṇāma. This kind of training does help in inculcating in the reader an ability to gain an access to the Aṣṭādhyāyī, which is the main purpose for which the Lahgukaumudī has been composed.

While elucidating the sūtra and the vṛtti, I have taken care to introduce the reader to such grammatical devices as are responsible for such a precise and brief presentation as is available in the Aṣṭādhyāyī. The device of implication (*jñāpana*), anuvṛtti, nirdeśa, praśleṣa, niyama (restriction), atideśa (extension), utsarga (general), apavāda (exception), etc. which have been used by Pāṇini are discussed in the relevant contexts. Whenever I find an opportunity to introduce the reader to grammatical polemics, I do not hesitate to do that. For example, I have disagreed with Bhimasena Shastri when, following the Bālamanoramā of Vāsudeva Dīkṣita, he says that the locative case-ending in the term *aci* in the aphorism *iko yaṇaci* (15) is sati-saptamī or bhāva-saptamī according to the rule *yasya ca bhāvena bhāvalakṣṇanam* Pā. 2. 3. 37. I have shown how this approach leads to a problem and then, how it is solved by interpreting the locative as aupaśleṣika adhikaraṇa in the present context (see Bhaimī, I, p. 34, fn 2 and the present commentary, p. 24). It is hoped that this kind of exercise will help the reader acquire a logical ability to comprehend the grammatical nuances with ease.

The derivational description shows how the finished word passes through different stages of the derivation. Each derivational stage is accompanied by the relevant sūtras that are required even though they have got to be repeated. Whenever there is a sequential clash between two rules, I have tried to explain the precedence of one rule over the other. In such a situation, I take into consideration the paribhāṣā *pūrvaparanityāntaraṅgāpavādānām uttarottaraṁ balīyaḥ* to determine the sequential status of the rule to be applied in the derivational process. If a rule of the tripādī has relevance in the instances of determining sequential status, we take into consideration the importance of the two divisions of the Aṣṭādhyāyī on the basis of the rule *pūrvatrāsiddham* Pā. 8. 2. 1. Such instances have been pointed out in the 'Elucidation'.

Normally I have italicised only those Sanskrit words which are given in parentheses for their English equivalents and which have been used to denote their own form (*śabdasvarūpa*). The sūtras, vārttikas, paribhāṣās, pratyāhāras and quotations from Sanskrit commentaries such as the Kāśikā, the Padamañjarī, the Mahābhāṣya, etc. are italicised. The words that are likely to be confused with English words such as *it, iṭ, ṭi,* etc. have been put in italics. Names of Sanskrit works are italicised only when they occur as titles in the bibliography.

Abbreviations

Abhyankar : see Paribhāṣenduśekhara of Nāgojibhaṭṭa
Bh. G. : Śrīmadbhagavadgītā
Bhāg. Pu. : Bhāgavata Purāṇa
Bhāmv. : Bhāminīvilāsa
Bhaimī : see Bhimsena Shastri
Bloomfield : see Bloomfield, Leonard
BM : Bālamanoramā of Vāsudeva Dīkṣita, see Vaiyākaraṇasiddhāntakaumudī of Bhāṭṭoji Dīkṣita
Bṛh. Up. : Bṛhadāraṇyakopaniṣad
Ch. U. : Chāndogyopaniṣad
Dictionary : see Abhyankar, K. V.
Dīpikā : see Mahābhāṣyadīpikā of Bhartṛhari
Eluc. : Elucidation
Gaṇaratna : Gaṇaratnamahodadhi of Vardhamāna
GP : Gita Press Gorakhpur
Kāśikā : see Kāśikā ed. by Vijayapāla
Kielhorn : see Kielhorn, F., Paribhāṣenduśekhara of Nāgojibhaṭṭa, part II
Kirāta : Kirātārjunīya of Bhāravi
KN : Jinendrabuddhi's Nyāsa on Kāśikā : see Kāśikāvṛtti of Vāmana and Jayāditya with the commentaries, Jinendrabuddhi's Nyāsa and Haradatta's Padamañjarī
KP : Haradatta' s Padamañjarī : see Kāśikāvṛtti of Vāmana and Jayāditya with the commentaries, Jinendrabuddhi's Nyāsa and Haradatta's Padamañjarī
Kumāra : Kumārasambhava of Kālidāsa
Laghu : Laghusiddhāntakaumudī.
LS : Laghuśabdenduśekhara of Nāgeśa
Manu : Manusmṛti
Mālvikā : Mālvikāgnimitra of Kālidāsa
Mā. Pu. : Mārkaṇḍeya Purāṇa

Mbh : Mahābhāṣya : see The Vyākaraṇamahābhāṣya of Patañjali
Mbh. Puc. : Mahābhāṣyapradīpa-udyota-chāyā : see The Vyākaraṇa-mahābhāṣya of Patañjali with Bhāṣyapradīpa-udyota
Mbh. U. : Mahābhāṣya Udyota : see The Vyākaraṇa-mahābhāṣya of Patañjali with Bhāṣyapradīpa-udyota
Megha : Meghadūta of Kālidāsa
Mu. Up. : Muṇḍakopaniṣad
Naiṣadha : Naiṣadhacarita of Śrīharṣa
NB : Nyāyabhāṣyam
NS : Nirnaya Sagar
Pā. : Aṣṭādhyāyī of Pāṇini, see Kāśikā, ed. by Vijayapāla
PP : Paraphrased sūtra
PR : Puṇyarāja's commentary on VP II, see Vākyapadīya of Bhartṛhari Kāṇḍa II.
PS : Paribhāṣāsaṅgraha
Raghu : Raghuvaṁśa of Kālidāsa
Śākuntala : Abhijñānaśākuntala of Kālidāsa
Sāra : Sārasiddhāntakaumudī of Varadarāja
Svapna : Svapnavāsavadattam of Bhāsa
Śiśu : Śiśupālavadha of Māgha
TB : Tattvabodhinī, see Vaiyākaraṇasiddhānta-kaumudī of Bhaṭṭoji Dīkṣita with Bālamanoramā of Vāsudeva Dīkṣita and Jñānendra Sarasvatī's Tattvabodhinī.
Trans. : Translation
US : Uṇādi Sūtra
Uttara : Uttararāmacarita of Bhavabhūti
VP : Vākyapadīya of Bhartṛhari
Vyā. cand. : see Charudeva Shastri
vtk : vārttika.
Vyā. Sudhā. : Vyākaraṇasiddhānatasudhānidhi

ॐ नमोऽनन्ताय नित्याय निरस्ताध्यस्तधर्मिणे।
पुरुषायाप्रमेयाय नमस्ते हेतुहेतवे ॥*

लघुसिद्धान्तकौमुदी
Laghusiddhāntakaumudī

संज्ञाप्रकरणम्
Technical Terms

लघुसिद्धान्तकौमुदी - नत्वा सरस्वतीं देवीं शुद्धां गुण्यां करोम्यहम्।
पाणिनीयप्रवेशाय लघुसिद्धान्तकौमुदीम् ॥

natvā sarasvatīṁ devīṁ śuddhāṁ guṇyāṁ karomyaham,
pāṇinīyapraveśāya laghusiddhāntakaumudīm.

Translation : Paying obeisance to Goddess Sarasvatī who is pure and endowed with virtues,[1] I compose Laghusiddhāntakaumudī so that (ability to gain) an access to Pāṇini's grammar may be acquired.

Elucidation : In the beginning Varadarāja invokes Goddess Sarasvatī and pays obeisance to Her so that the work which he has undertaken may be completed without any obstacle and may grow and continue to be of advantage to those desirous of studying the grammar of Pāṇini.

---

* "Salutations to the Supreme Spirit dwelling in the cave of the heart (*puruṣa*), the Infinite, the Eternal, the One devoid of superimpositions, the Immeasurable; salutations to You who are the cause of even the primary cause (*prakṛti*)." The principle of brevity based on the statement *na karmadhārayānmatvarthīyo bahuvrīhiścet tadarthapratipattikaraḥ* requires that the possessive affix *ini* should not be added to the compound *nirastādhyastadharma*. However, Patañjali's use of the possessive affix *matup* in *asubvataḥ* (Mbh 7. 3. 44) shows that the statement quoted above is not universally applicable. The present form *nirastādhyastadharmiṇe* in the invocation can be explained on the same anaiogy. Cf. Prauḍhamanoramā, p. 741 and its commentaries Śabdaratna and Bhairavī, pp. 741-43.

1. The qualifications could as well apply to the Laghusiddhāntakaumudī.

प्रत्याहारसूत्राणि

अ इ उण्। ऋ ऌक्। ए ओङ्। ऐ औच्। ह य व रट्। लण्। ञ म ङ ण नम्। झ भञ्। घ ढ धष्। ज ब ग ड दश्। ख फ छ ठ थ च ट तव्। क पय्। श ष सर्। हल्। *a i uṇ. ṛ ḷk. e oṅ. ai auc. ha ya va raṭ. laṇ. ña ma ṅa ṇa nam. jha bhañ. gha ḍha dhaṣ. ja ba ga ḍa daś. kha pha cha ṭha tha ca ṭa tav. ka pay. śa ṣa sar. hal.*

लघु० – इति माहेश्वराणि सूत्राण्यणादिसंज्ञार्थानि। एषामन्त्या इतः। हकारादिष्वकार उच्चारणार्थः। लण्मध्ये तु इत्संज्ञकः। *iti māheśvarāṇi sūtrāṇyaṇādisaṁjñārthāni. eṣāmantyā itaḥ. hakārādiṣvakāra uccāraṇārthaḥ. laṇmadhye tu itsaṁjñakaḥ.*

Trans. : These are the sūtras that emanated from Lord Maheśvara. They are meant for the formation of pratyāhāras such as *aṇ* and the like. The consonantal sounds occurring at the end of pratyāhārasūtras are called *it*s. (The vowel) *a* has been used in *ha* and so on to facilitate their pronunciation but *a* within *laṇ* pratyāhāra has the designation *it*.

Eluc. : It is traditionally believed that the great Lord Śiva sounded his drum (*ḍhakkā*) fourteen times and thereby revealed these fourteen groups of sounds or phonemes. Nandikeśvara mentions this in the first verse of his Kāśikā, known as Nandikeśvara-Kāśikā, which he wrote on the philosophical significance of these pratyāhārasūtras :

nṛttāvasāne naṭarājarājo nanāda ḍhakkāṁ navapañcavāram,
uddhartukāmaḥ sanakādisiddhān etadvimarśe śivasūtrajālam.

The word *śivasūtrajālam* occurring at the end of the above verse means the group of śivasūtras which obviously refer to these pratyāhārasūtras. The word Māheśvara mentioned by Varadarāja in his vṛtti is formed with the taddhita affix *aṇ* in accordance with the sūtra *tata āgataḥ* Pā. 4. 3. 74. This also endorses the view that these sūtras were revealed by the grace of Lord Maheśvara. The importance of these sūtras cannot be overemphasized so far as the precision and brevity of the Aṣṭādhyāyī are concerned. Pāṇini has used 41 pratyāhāras (abbreviations) in all in the Aṣṭādhyāyī which are based on this repertory of phonemes.

The fourteen consonants occurring at the end of pratyāhārasūtras are technically called *it*s. Pāṇini has defined and delineated *it* in the Aṣṭādhyāyī in the sūtras ranging from 1.3.2 to 1.3.8. In the pratyāhārasūtras, *it*s serve the purpose of forming the pratyāhāras.

The method of the formation of pratyāhāra is spelt out in the sūtra *ādirantyena sahetā* (4). The anubandhas (*it*s) in the first four pratyāhārasūtras are not enunciated in a manner that they are included in *ac* (vowels). Had this been the case, Pāṇini would have shown the change of *ik* into *yaṇ* in the sūtras, such as *upadeśe 'janunāsika it, uṇādayo bahulam*, etc. In the former sūtra *i* followed by *k* and in the latter *u* followed by *ṇ* are not changed into *yaṇ*. The enunciation of these sūtras in this form implies that Pāṇini does not intend them to be included in the list of the phonemes denoted by *ac* pratyāhāra. That the *it*s are used to form the pratyāhāras such as *aṇ, ak*, etc. means that they serve the purpose of others, that is, *aṇ, ak*, etc. So they are not independent or pradhāna but *a, i, u*, etc. are not like them and stand for themselves. Hence they are indepedent or pradhāna. Since this is not the case with the markers (*it*s), they are treated as subordinate. This is the reason why *it*s are not denoted by the pratyāhāras. The third ground why they are not included in the pratyāhāras is that their elision is intended to be primary. The ācāryas have used them only as markers. Pāṇini has enjoined their elision by *tasya lopaḥ* (3). That is why the pratyāhāra *ac* formed with the beginning *a* of the pratyāhārasūtra *a i uṇ* and the ending *c* of the pratyāhārasūtra *ai auc* does not signify *ṇ, k* and *ṅ*.

A consonant is not pronounced without the help of a vowel {*nāntareṇācaṁ vyañjanasyoccāraṇaṁ bhavati* (BM, I, p. 5)}. Consequently, *a* has been used in the phonemes beginning with *h* and so on to facilitate their pronunciation.

According to Bhartṛhari (Dīpikā, p. 35), Kāśikā (p. 3) and Bhaṭṭoji Dīkṣita (SK, I, p. 4), *a* within *laṇ* is nasal and hence *it* in accordance with the sūtra *upadeśe 'janunāsika it* (28). With the help of this *a*, the *ra*-pratyāhāra is formed which denotes both repha and lakāra. Nāgeśa does not subscribe to this view. We will discuss this under the rule *uraṇ raparaḥ* (29).

Two points are worth mentioning with regard to the pratyāhārasūtras. The consonant *ṇ* as *it* and *h* have been used twice. The purpose of the repetition of *ṇ* is different from that of *h*. According to Patañjali, the ambiguity arising out of the repetition of *ṇ* should not be allowed to render inauthentic what Pāṇini has enunciated. He says that the repetition of *ṇ*, apparently being redundant, implies the paribhāṣā : *vyākhyānato viśeṣapratipattiḥ, na hi sandehād alakṣaṇam*. This means that it is the interpretation given by the learned that decides the exact meaning of an apparently ambiguous statement of Pāṇini and that ambiguity must not be allowed to lead to the conclusion that the statement is inauthentic. In this context it has been further clarified by Patañjali that the pratyāhāra *aṇ* used in Pā. 1. 1. 69 is formed with the latter *ṇ* and elsewhere it has been formed with *ṇ* occurring in the pratyāhārasūtra *a i uṇ* {see under (11)}.

The consonant *h* also occurs twice in the above pratyāhārasūtras, first in sūtra five and then in the last sūtra. The object of the first *h* is to include it in the pratyāhāras *aṭ, aś, haś* and *iṇ* whereas the purpose of the second *h* is that it is included in the pratyāhāras *val, ral, jhal* and *śal*.

(1) हलन्त्यम्। *halantyam.* 1. 3. 3

लघु० - उपदेशेऽन्त्यं हलित् स्यात्। उपदेश आद्योच्चारणम्। सूत्रेष्वदृष्टं पदं सूत्रान्तरादनुवर्तनीयं सर्वत्र। *upadeśe 'ntyaṁ hal it syāt. upadeśa ādyoccāraṇam. sūtreṣvadṛṣṭaṁ padaṁ sūtrāntarād anuvartanīyaṁ sarvatra.*

Trans. : Let the last *hal* (consonant) at the end of a (grammatical) enunciation be designated as *it* (marker). Upadeśa is the (grammatical) enunciation of the initial preceptors (of Grammar). The word which is missing in the sūtras is to be carried over from other sūtras (in order to make the sūtra a complete sentence).

Paraphrase (PP) : *upadeśe hal antyam it (syāt).*

Eluc. : Upadeśa means either an initial enunciation (LS, p. 29) in grammar (*vyākaraṇa*) or the grammatical citations of Pāṇini, Kātyāyana and Patañjali. These grammatical enunciations, called Upadeśas, are enlisted in the following śloka :

pratyayāḥ śivasūtrāṇi, ādeśā āgamāstathā,
dhātupāṭho gaṇe pāṭhaḥ, upadeśāḥ prakīrtitāḥ. (Bhaimī, I, p. 8, fn 1,)

The affixes, pratyāhārasūtras, substitutes, augments, the lists of roots and nominal stems are known as Upadeśas.

The Aṣṭādhyāyī was composed by Pāṇini in eight chapters each containing four quarters. It contains 3983 sūtras. The number of sūtras which has been given here is on the basis of Cardona (1997) and the Kāśikā edited by Vijayapāla and differs from that given by Bhimasena Shastri (see Bhaimī, I, ātma-nivedanam, p. 10). The numerical scheme of the Aṣṭādhyāyī adopted here is like this : The first numerical figure in it denotes the number of the chapter. The second numerical figure indicates the number of the quarter-chapter, while the third figure indicates the serial number of the sūtra in that quarter. The sūtra under discussion is numbered 1. 3. 3, which means that this is the third sūtra of the third quarter (pāda) of the first chapter (adhyāya) of the Aṣṭādhyāyī.

We have already said that the words which are missing in a particular sūtra are generally carried over from the preceding sūtras to make the sense complete. This device of carrying over (*anuvṛtti*) is not a new thing peculiar to the Aṣṭādhyāyī. It is also used in ordinary language. We make use of an elliptical sentence after a complete sentence. Something said in a previous sentence is understood in a subsequent sentence. Take, for example, this sentence : "Give a white horse to Mohan." Now in this context if we make use of an elliptical sentence like this : "Black to Sohan", then the words 'give' and 'horse' are to be understood from the previous sentence. In the same manner the sūtra *halantyam* (1) is also an elliptical sentence. Hence two missing words *upadeśe* and *it* are to be carried over into this sūtra from the sūtra *upadeśe-'janunāsika it* Pā. 1. 3. 2, which just precedes the present sūtra in the Aṣṭādhyāyī. Then the sūtra under discussion with the addition of the third person singular optative verbal form of the root *as* will make a complete sentence as given by Varadarāja in his vṛtti : *upadeśe 'ntyaṁ hal it syāt*. We have to use this device of carrying over the missing words from other sūtras throughout the Aṣṭādhyāyī so that the apparently elliptical sūtras may be made into complete sentences. Therefore we will provide the "Paraphrased sūtra" with the carried over words just before "Elucidation".

We have explained above that a *hal* at the end of a grammatical enunciation is *it*. Here we have obviously taken *hal* as a pratyāhāra, but actually we have to know first what an *it* is before we are able to form a pratyāhāra. The knowledge of *it* depends on the knowledge of *hal* as pratyāhāra and the knowledge of *hal* as pratyāhāra rests upon the knowledge of what an *it* is. As a consequence, there is a defect of mutual dependence. In order to solve this problem this sūtra has been explained by Bhaṭṭoji, etc. in two ways by taking recourse to the tantra[1] technique in which a single term is used once but is understood as repeated. In pursuance of this technique, Bhaṭṭoji advocates iteration (*āvṛtti*) of the present sūtra. In accordance with the first iterated sūtra, the explanation would be as follows : In the 14th pratyāhārasūtra *hal*, the last phoneme '*l*' is *it*. Now taking this '*l*' as *it* we can form the *hal* pratyāhāra beginning with *h* of the pratyāhārasūtra *ha ya va raṭ* with the help of the sūtra *ādirantyena sahetā* (4). Taking *hal* as pratyāhāra, which now includes all consonants, we can explain that the last *hal* (consonant) at the end of initial enunciations is *it*. This is the second explanation. In this way the defect of mutual dependence can be removed.

---

1. Cf. Nāgeśa's Udyota on the Mahābhāṣya on *ekaśeṣanirdeśād vā* Pā. 1. 3. 3 vārttika 5.

(2) अदर्शनं लोपः । *adarśanaṁ lopaḥ*. 1. 1. 60

लघु०– प्रसक्तस्यादर्शनं लोपसंज्ञं स्यात् । *prasaktasyādarśanaṁ lopa-saṁjñaṁ syāt.*

Trans. : Let the non-perception of what is given be designated as *lopa*. (Let zero-replacement be called *lopa)*.

PP. *sthānasya adarśanam lopaḥ.*

Eluc. : The word *sthāne* in the locative case has been carried over from the sūtra *sthāne 'ntaratamaḥ* (17). This has been changed into *sthānasya* by the process of vibhaktivipariṇāma which consists in supposing for the purpose of interpretation a different case-ending in the place of that which is actually stated (cf. *arthavaśād vibhaktivipariṇāmaḥ*, Abhyankar, Paribhāṣāsaṅgraha, p. 28, p. 268, etc.). Varadarāja has interpreted *sthānasya* as *prasaktasya* which, in accordance with *ṣaṣṭhī sthāneyogā* Pā. 1. 1. 48, means 'in place of what exists'. The word *darśana* means simply a cognition which in *śabdānuśāsana* stands for the auditory cognition. The whole sūtra then means as follows : The term *lopa* consists in the auditory non-perception of what is given. It should be borne in mind here that lopa is the designation of the meaning of the word *adarśana* (non-perception) and not of the word *adarśana*.

Thus the term *lopa* is arthasaṁjñā and not śabdasaṁjñā in consonance with the sūtra *svaṁ rūpaṁ śabdasyāśabdasaṁjñā* Pā. 1. 1. 68 which means 'a word, other than the one which is a technical term in grammar, denotes its form only'. We arrive at this meaning by the word *iti* which has been carried over from the sūtra *na veti vibhāṣā* Pā. 1. 1. 44 into this sūtra in the manner of the leap of a frog *(maṇḍūkapluti)*, that is, it recurs in this sūtra without recurring in the intervening sūtras. The technical term *vibhāṣā* is also arthasaṁjñā since this applies to the meanings of the words *na* (negation) and *vā* (optionality) put together and not to the words themselves because of the use of the word *iti*. Similarly, when the word *iti* is read into the sūtra under discussion, it would then read *adarśanamiti lopaḥ* and yield lopa as arthasaṁjñā.

(3) तस्य लोपः । *tasya lopaḥ*. 1. 3. 9

लघु० – तस्येतो लोपः स्यात् । णादयोऽणाद्यर्थाः । *tasyeto lopaḥ syāt. ṇādayo 'ṇādyarthāḥ.*

Trans. : Let that to which the class name *it* has been assigned be replaced by lopa. (The anubandhas) *ṇ*, etc. are meant to form *aṇ*, etc.

PP. *tasya itaḥ lopaḥ.*

Eluc. : The term *it* has been defined and delineated in the preceding seven sūtras of the Aṣṭādhyāyī. In other words these seven sūtras have explained that certain elements are called *it*. The pronoun *tasya* in the present sūtra refers to the word *it* which has been carried over from the sūtra *upadeśe 'janunāsika it* Pā. 1. 3. 2. Although the carried over *it* is in the nominative case, it is transformed into the genitive case so that it may syntactically agree with the pronoun *tasya*. The purpose of the pronoun *tasya* is also to make it clear that the whole of that, which is assigned the class name *it*, is to be elided and not only the phoneme which comes at the end of *it* as enjoined by the sūtra *alo 'ntyasya* (21). This grammatical operation, i.e. the elision of the last phoneme, could be applicable in such roots as *ñimidā snehane, ḍukṛñ karaṇe* where *ñi* and *ḍu* are *it*s by virtue of the sūtra *ādirñiṭuḍavaḥ* Pā. 1. 3. 5 and contain two phonemes each. As a consequence only the elision of the last phonemes of these two *it*s, that is, of *i* and *u* respectively becomes applicable by *alo 'ntyasya* as they are the last phonemes of these two *it*s. The term *tasya* is meant to avoid such an eventuality. In this context, one more point requires clarification. By the present sūtra, the elision of all *it*s in the pratyāhārasūtras is applicable. This is the reason why Varadarāja clarifies that the purpose of *it*s in the pratyāhārasūtras is to form the pratyāhāras such as *aṇ, ak, ik, ac, hal, śal* and the like. Precisely for this reason, *it*s in these pratyāhāras are not to undergo zero-substitution; these are not to be elided (Bhaimī, I, p. 9).

(4) आदिरन्त्येन सहेता । *ādirantyena sahetā*. 1. 1. 71

लघु० – अन्त्येनेता सहित आदिर्मध्यगानां स्वस्य च संज्ञा स्यात्। यथाण् इति अ इ उ इति वर्णानां संज्ञा । एवमच् हल् अल् इत्यादयः । *antyenetā sahita ādir madhyagānāṁ svasya ca saṁjñā syāt. yathā aṇ iti a i u iti varṇānāṁ saṁjñā. evam ac hal al ityādayaḥ.*

Trans. : Let an initial phoneme together with a final *it* be a name (*saṁjñā*) for the intervening phonemes and for itself. To illustrate, *aṇ* denotes the vowels *a i u* . (Other pratyāhāras) such as *ac hal al*, etc. will (also) denote in the same manner.

PP. *ādiḥ antyena itā saha svasya.*

Eluc. : This is a saṁjñā sūtra. It tells us the method of how to form a pratyāhāra. The word *svam* is lent into this sūtra from *svaṁ rūpaṁ śabdasyāśabdasaṁjñā* Pā. 1. 1. 68. The word *svam* changes into the genitive and refers to the principal. The reason is that the word *svaṁ*, being a pronoun, will refer to it, and not to the secondary. In the present sūtra the final *it* is in the instrumental case and therefore secondary according to *sahayukte 'pradhāne* Pā. 2. 3 .19. Thus the sūtra finally means : The initial phoneme accompanied by the last *it* forms a pratyāhāra which denotes itself and the intervening phonemes. Why the intervening *its* are not included in pratyāhāras has been explained earlier (p. 3). These pratyāhāras number forty-one which are as follows :

aṇ ak ik uk eṅ ac ic ec aic aṭ aṇ iṇ yaṇ am yam ṅam yañ jhaṣ bhaṣ aś haś vaś jaś jhaś baś chav yay may jhay khay yar jhar khar car śar al hal val ral jhal śal.

Besides, there are three more pratyāhāras : *ñam, cay* and *ra*. The pratyāhāras *ñam* and *cay* occur in *ñamantāḍḍaḥ*, Uṇādi Sūtra 1. 111 and *cayo dvitīyāḥ śari pauṣkarasādeḥ*, Mbh 8. 4. 48, vārttika 3 respectively. There is a controversy about the *ra* pratyāhāra which we have already pointed out. Together with these three, the number of pratyāhāras comes to forty-four.

(5) ऊकालोऽज्झ्रस्वदीर्घप्लुतः । *ūkālo 'jjhrasvadīrghaplutaḥ* 1. 2. 27.

लघु० – उश्च ऊश्च ऊ३श्च वः, वां काल इव कालो यस्य सोऽच् क्रमाद्ध्रस्वदीर्घप्लुतसंज्ञः स्यात्। स प्रत्येकमुदात्तादिभेदेन त्रिधा । *uś ca ūś ca ū3ś ca vaḥ, vāṁ kala iva kalo yasya so 'c kramāddhrasva-dīrgha-pluta-saṁjñaḥ syāt. sa pratyekam udāttādibhedena tridhā.*

Trans. : Let a vowel (*ac*) having time-duration equivalent to *u, ū* and *ū3* be respectively called short, long and prolated. Each such vowel (*ac*) is again divided into three types having high (*udātta*), low (*anudātta*) and combined pitch (*svarita*).

PP. *ūkālaḥ ac hrasvadīrghaplutaḥ.*

Eluc. : The nominative plural of *u, ū* and *ū3* is *vaḥ* and the genitive plural is *vām* as shown in the vṛtti. Each of these ukāras metaphorically means the time-duration which is required to pronounce each of these vowels (BM, I, p. 12 & TB, I, p. 13). Thus *u* requires a single mora, *ū*, two morae and *ū3*, three. The time-duration which is required for one mora may be understood as equivalent to one second. Consequently *u*, which requires one second for its pronunciation, is called short (*hrasva*), *ū*, which needs two seconds, is called long (*dīrgha*) and *ū3*, which requires 3 seconds, is called prolated or extra-long (*pluta*).

There are two significant points which deserve mention in connection with this sūtra : 1. Why has ukāra been singled out by Pāṇini to describe the different types of vowels as hrasva, dīrgha and pluta? 2. Why has masculine been used in the word *hrasvadīrghaplutaḥ*, occurring in the sūtra, which, being a samāhāradvandva compound, should have been used in the neuter gender?

Pāṇini has used *ūkālaḥ* in the sūtra since the pronunciation of this vowel resembles the crowing of a cock which could be easily understood in those days. Vāsudeva Dīkṣita seems to endorse this view when he says that the short, long and pluta ukāra resembles the ascending note of a cock {*ūśabdasyātra ekamātradvimātratrimātrakukkuṭarutānukaraṇatvāt* (BM, I, p. 13)}. Pāṇini must have had this in his mind. Otherwise he could have used *ākālaḥ* instead of *ūkālaḥ*. With regard to the use of the samāhāradvandva compound in the masculine, Jñānendra Sarasvatī says that the use in the masculine is peculiar to the sūtra only {*samāhāre sautraṁ puṁstvam* (TB, p. 12)}. Had it been used in the spoken language (*bhāṣā*), it would have normally been in the neuter gender. (Cf. *chandasi 'vyatyayo bahulam' iti liṅgavyatyaya uktaḥ. 'chandovat sūtrāṇi bhavanti' ityaviruddhāsya pulṁliṅgatā*, KN, I, p. 302).

(6) उच्चैरुदात्तः । *uccair udāttaḥ*. 1. 2. 29

Trans. : A vowel with the property of high pitch be called *udātta*.

(7) नीचैरनुदात्तः । *nīcair anudāttaḥ*. 1. 2. 30

Trans. : A vowel with the property of low pitch be called *anudātta*.

(8) समाहारः स्वरितः । *samāhāraḥ svaritaḥ*. 1. 2. 31

Trans. : A vowel with the combination of high and low pitches be called *svarita*.

PP. *udāttasya anudāttasya samāhāraḥ svaritaḥ*.

Eluc. : The words *udāttaḥ* and *anudāttaḥ* are carried over from the preceding two sūtras and have been changed into the genitive singular by the process of vibhaktivipariṇāma. Vāsudeva Dīkṣita says that the word *uccaiḥ*, in the sūtra *uccairudāttaḥ* 1. 2. 29, does not mean loud pronunciation of the vowels. Otherwise the definition of udātta would not cover those vowels which are pronounced in a very low voice just as in a prayer uttered in a low voice (BM, I, p. 13). The full *traisvarya* system was still in force in the bhāṣā that Pāṇini described, but this was a regular feature of the Vedic language. "A svarita vowel has high-pitched segment at its beginning for the length equivalent to that of half a short vowel. That is, the first half-mora of a vowel is high-pitched, its remainder low-pitched" (Cardona 1997 : pp. 17-18). A vowel with the property of high pitch carries no accent mark. A vowel with a low pitch (*anudātta*) carries a horizontal bar beneath it whereas that with a combination of both the pitches (*svarita*) carries a vertical bar above it :

अ इ उ

अ॒ इ॒ उ॒

अ॑ इ॑ उ॑

(9) मुखनासिकावचनोऽनुनासिकः। ***mukhanāsikāvacano 'nunāsikaḥ*. 1. 1. 8**

लघु० - तदित्थम् अ इ उ ऋ एषां वर्णानां प्रत्येकमष्टादश भेदाः। लृवर्णस्य द्वादश दीर्घाभावात्। एचामपि द्वादश तेषां ह्रस्वाभावात्। *tad ittham - a i u ṛ eṣāṁ varṇānāṁ pratyekam aṣṭādaśa bhedāḥ. ḷvarṇasya dvādaśa dīrghābhāvāt. ecām api dvādaśa teṣāṁ hrasvābhāvāt.*

Trans. : Let a phoneme uttered through both oral and nasal passages be called *anunāsika*. In this way, the vowels *a, i, u* and *ṛ* have each eighteen forms. The vowel *ḷ* has twelve forms since it does not have any long counterpart. Also the vowels denoted by *ec* have each twelve forms because they do not have any short form.

PP. *mukhanāsikāvacanaḥ anunāsikaḥ.*

Eluc. : The word *mukhanāsikā-vacanaḥ* means that which is pronounced simultaneously by the mouth and the nose. The nasal stops *ṅ, ñ, ṇ, n* and *m* are pronounced in this manner. Hence they are called *anunāsika*. Similarly, the vowels which are pronounced by the mouth and the nose are also called *anunāsika*. The phonemes which are pronounced by the mouth only are called *niranunāsika*.

By now we have come to know that there are three factors which are responsible for a homogeneous vowel to have eighteen or twelve varieties. These factors are : 1. Temporal factor 2. Pitch-factor and 3. Nasal factor. For example, if we take the vowel *i*, it will have three different forms due to difference in temporal duration required in its pronunciation. If it has one-mora duration, it is called short (*hrasva*). If it has two-mora duration, it is called long (*dīrgha*). In case it has three-mora-duration, it is called prolated (*pluta*). These three forms of *i*, have each three varieties on account of the property of the pitch. High pitch, low pitch and their blend render them each udātta, anudātta and svarita respectively. Thus the vowel *i* has nine (3×3) forms. When the nasal factor plays its role, each of the nine varieties comes to have two further varieties : anunāsika and niranunāsika. Thus nine multiplied by two becomes eighteen. This is true in the case of *a, i, u* and *ṛ*, but it is not true in case of *ḷ* since it does not have any long homogeneous counterpart having two morae. Similarly in the case of the denotata of *ec*, they have twelve forms due to their having no short form of one mora. The eighteen different forms of *a* can be demonstrated as follows :

hrasva :	अँ	अ	अँ॒	अ॒	अँ॑	अ॑
dīrgha :	आँ	आ	आँ॒	आ॒	आ॑	आ॑
pluta :	आँ३	आ३	आँ३॒	आ३॒	आँ३॑	आ३॑

(10) तुल्यास्यप्रयत्नं सवर्णम् । *tulyāsyaprayatnaṁ savarṇam*. 1. 1. 9

लघु० - ताल्वादिस्थानमाभ्यन्तरप्रयत्नश्चेत्येतद् द्वयं यस्य येन तुल्यं तन्मिथः सवर्णसंज्ञं स्यात् । *tālvādisthānam ābhyantaraprayatnaścetyetad dvayaṁ yasya yena tulyaṁ tanmithaḥ savarṇasaṁjñaṁ syāt.*

Trans. : Let the phonemes produced at the same place of pronunciation and with the same articulatory (*ābhyantara)* effort, such as the palate, etc. be called mutually homogeneous (*savarṇa*).

PP. *tulyāsyaprayatnam savarṇam.*

Eluc. : The word *āsya* formed with the taddhita affix *yat* means 'occurring in the mouth (oral cavity)'. The word *prayatna,* because of the prefix *pra,* excludes the external effort which takes place when the phoneme is being actually pronounced. It means that the 'articulatory effort' occurs in the oral cavity before the phonemes are articulated. The word *tulyāsyaprayatnam* is a bahuvrīhi compound which qualifies the word *savarṇam*. Homogeneity conveyed by the word *savarṇa* obtains at least between two elements. Therefore the condition for homogeneity between two phonemes can be explained like this : If two phonemes are produced with the same articulatory effort at the same place of pronunciation such as the velum, palate, etc., they can be called homogeneous with each other. Right from the Kāśikā, the word *āsya* in the sūtra has been interpreted as 'within the mouth', i. e. *tālvādisthānam* whereas the initial place in the mouth where the phonemes are produced/pronounced is the velum which is near the soft palate. It may be accepted as such without going into unnecessary and intricate details regarding the dissolving of the compound *tālvādi* in a manner so that the velum (throat) may be arrived at as the meaning. The word *ādi* may indicate the other places of pronunciation including the velum/throat in the oral cavity.

In this context it may be pointed out that the two phonemes can be called homogeneous only when there is complete similarity between the articulatory effort and the place of pronunciation of these two. The phonemes *u* and *o* cannot be called homogeneous. Although the lips are involved in the pronunciation of both these vowels, *o* is gutturo-labial and thus requires the additional place, throat, in the oral cavity, for its production. In the absence of complete similarity, they cannot be called homogeneous (*savarṇa*). However, although there is an absence of complete similarity from the point of view of pronunciation between *k* and *ṅ*, they are called homogeneous. The problem of *k* and *ṅ* being homogeneous can be solved by the fact that, although in the pronunciation of *ṅ*, the nasal passage is required more than the velum required in the pronunciation of *k*, the nose which is required additionally in the pronunciation of *ṅ* falls outside the mouth. Thus the nose does not exist within the oral cavity. Hence it is not *āsya*, which is the condition laid down by the present sūtra. It can consequently be left out as a condition for homogeneity between *k* and *ṅ*. Thus there is no problem in respect of *k* and *ṅ* being homogeneous.

It should also be borne in mind that both *e* and *ai* have the same articulatory effort and the same place of pronunciation. Even then they cannot be called homogeneous since Pāṇini enunciated them separately in the pratyāhārasūtras. Had Pāṇini intended them to be homogeneous, he would not have mentioned them separately as *e* would have denoted *ai* by virtue of the sūtra *aṇudit savarṇasya cāpratyayaḥ* (11).

1. वार्त्तिक - ऋऌवर्णयोर्मिथः सावर्ण्यं वाच्यम्। *ṛḷvarṇayormithaḥ sāvarṇyaṁ vācyam*. (Cf. *ṛḷkārayoḥ savarṇavidhiḥ*. Mbh 1. 1. 9 vtk 9).

Trans. : Homogeneity between *ṛ* and *ḷ* should be stated.

Eluc. : Although there is no complete similarity between these two vowels from the point of view of pronunciation and articulatory effort, they are to be treated as homogeneous in deference to the present vārttika of Kātyāyana.

Varadarāja now enumerates the places of pronunciation :

लघु० – अकुहविसर्जनीयानां कण्ठः । *akuhavisarjanīyānāṁ kaṇṭhaḥ.*

Trans. : (The place of production) for *a, ku* =kavarga : *k kh g gh ṅ, h* and *visarga* is the velar area. Hence they are called *kaṇṭhya.*

लघु० – इचुयशानां तालु । *icuyaśānāṁ tālu.*

Trans. : *i, cu*=cavarga: *c ch j jh ñ, y* and *ś* are palatal (*tālavya*) since they are produced at the hard palate.

लघु० – ऋटुरषाणां मूर्धा । *ṛṭuraṣāṇāṁ mūrdhā.*

Trans. : *ṛ, ṭu*= ṭavarga : *ṭ ṭh ḍ ḍh ṇ, r* and *ṣ* are retroflex (*mūrdhanya*).

लघु० – ऌतुलसानां दन्ताः । *ḷtulasānāṁ dantāḥ.*

Trans. : *ḷ, tu*=tavarga: *t th d dh n, l* and *s* are dental (*dantya*).

लघु० – उपूपध्मानीयानामोष्ठौ । *upūpadhmānīyānāmoṣṭhau.*

Trans. : *u, pu*=pavarga: *p ph b bh m* and *upadhmānīya* are labial (*oṣṭhya*)

लघु० – ञमङणनानां नासिका च । *ñamaṅaṇanānāṁ nāsikā ca.*

Trans. : *ñ m ṅ ṇ n* are pronounced through the nasal passage in addition to their places of pronunciation where their homogeneous class sounds are produced.

लघु० –एदैतोः कण्ठतालु । *edaitoḥ kaṇṭhatālu.*

Trans. : *e* and *ai* are gutturo-palatal (*kaṇṭhatālavya*)

लघु० – ओदौतोः कण्ठोष्ठम् । *odautoḥ kaṇṭhoṣṭham.*

Trans. : *o* and *au* are gutturo-labial (*kaṇṭhoṣṭhya*).

लघु० – वकारस्य दन्तोष्ठम्। *vakārasya dantoṣṭham.*

Trans. : *v* is denti-labial (*dantoṣṭhya*)

लघु० – जिह्वामूलीयस्य जिह्वामूलम्। *jihvāmūlīyasya jihvāmūlam.*

Trans. : *jihvāmūlīya* is produced at the root of the tongue.

लघु० – नासिकाऽनुस्वारस्य। *nāsikā 'nusvārasya.*

Trans. : The anusvāra (*ṁ*) is pronounced through the nasal passage only.[1]

लघु० – इति स्थानानि। *iti sthānāni.*

Trans. : These are the places of pronunciation.

लघु० – यत्नो द्विधा आभ्यन्तरो बाह्यश्च। आद्यः पञ्चधा स्पृष्टेषत्स्पृष्टेषद्विवृतविवृतसंवृतभेदात्। तत्र स्पृष्टं प्रयतनं स्पर्शानाम्। ईषत्स्पृष्टमन्तःस्थानाम्। ईषद्विवृतमूष्मणाम्। विवृतं स्वराणाम्। ह्रस्वस्यावर्णस्य प्रयोगे संवृतम्। प्रक्रियादशायां तु विवृतमेव। *yatno dvidhā ābhyantaro bāhyaś ca. ādyaḥ pañcadhā spṛṣṭeṣatspṛṣṭeṣadvivṛtavivṛtasaṁvṛtabhedāt. tatra spṛṣṭaṁ prayatanaṁ sparśānām. īṣatspṛṣṭam antaḥsthānām. īṣadvivṛtam ūṣmaṇām. vivṛtaṁ svarāṇām. hrasvasyāvarṇasya prayoge saṁvṛtam. prakriyādaśāyāṁ tu vivṛtameva.*

Trans. : The effort (that we make in order to articulate phonemes) is of two kinds: 1. Internal and 2. External. The first has five kinds[2] : 1. spṛṣṭa 2. īṣatspṛṣṭa 3. īṣadvivṛta 4. vivṛta 5. saṁvṛta. The effort called *spṛṣṭa* (contact) belongs to the stops (*sparśa*). The effort called *īṣatspṛṣṭa* (in which the contact is partial) belongs to semi-vowels (*antaḥstha*). The effort called *īṣadvivṛta* belongs to *ś*, *ṣ*, *s* and *h* (*ūṣma*). The internal effort known as *vivṛta* belongs to the vowels. The last effort, called *saṁvṛta*, takes place when *a* is used in spoken language, but during grammatical operation it is treated as vivṛta.

---

1. Besides, *kn*, *khn*, *gn*, etc. which are called *yama*s are also articulated or produced by the nose. These are included among ayogavāhas.

2. Varadarāja's provision for distinct internal efforts for the sibilants and vowels as Īṣadvivṛta and vivṛta respectively makes Pāṇini's rule *nājjhalau* Pā. 1. 1. 10 purposeless. Pāṇini most likely held that they had the same internal effort. This is probably the reason why he enunciated the sūtra *nājjhalau*.

Eluc. : The internal effort takes place just before we articulate the phonemes. Probably it is called internal since this effort consists in bringing closer the organ of pronunciation to some part of the tongue or a part of the tongue to some other organ of pronunciation before a phoneme is articulated. It is in contradistinction to the other effort (*bāhya*) which occurs during the process of actual articulation. Before *k c ṭ t* or any of the phonemes of these groups is attempted to be pronounced, the tongue is brought in contact with the velum (*kaṇṭha*), palate, cerebrum or teeth respectively. For *p ph b* etc. lips come in contact with each other. In the same manner in attempting to pronounce *y r l v*, the tongue and the respective organs are brought in contact, but this contact is partial. That is the reason why this is called slight-contact-effort (*īṣatspṛṣṭa*). Before we produce vowel sounds, we keep separate the tongue and other organs of pronunciation. This effort is vivṛta. However, this separation is less in the case of attempting to pronounce the consonants *ś*, *ṣ*, *s* and *h*. Hence this is called *īṣadvivṛta*. The last internal effort is saṁvṛta. This is with reference to the short *a* of the spoken language. The effort that we make by contracting the cavity of the throat before we actually pronounce it, is called *saṁvṛta*. It is only when the grammatical operations have to be performed that a short *a* is to be understood as pronounced with a vivṛta effort. For if, in these grammatical operations, we accept the saṁvṛta effort, then a short *a* will have an internal effort different from that of a long *ā*. Short *a* and long *ā* will then cease to be homogeneous. Thus there will be no sandhi between these two akāras as obtaining between *daṇḍa* + *āghāta*. The last *a* of *daṇḍa* is saṁvṛta and the initial *ā* of the word *āghāta* is vivṛta. The internal efforts of these vowels being dissimilar, they would not be homogeneous. Hence there will be no sandhi by *akaḥ savarṇe dīrghaḥ* (42). The last sūtra *a a* Pā. 8. 4. 68 of the Aṣṭādhyāyī enjoins that the short *a* with a vivṛta *prayatna* should be treated as *saṁvṛta*. The last sūtra is deemed to have performed no grammatical operation with reference to the whole of Aṣṭādhyāyī by virtue of the sūtra *pūrvatrāsiddham* Pā. 8. 2. 1.

लघु० – बाह्यप्रयत्नस्त्वेकादशधा । विवारः संवारः श्वासो नादोऽघोषो घोषोऽल्पप्राणो महाप्राण उदातोऽनुदात्तः स्वरितश्चेति । खरो विवाराः श्वासा अघोषाश्च । हशः संवारा नादा घोषाश्च । वर्गाणां प्रथमतृतीयपञ्चमा यणश्चाल्पप्राणाः । वर्गाणां द्वितीयचतुर्थौ शलश्च महाप्राणाः ।
bāhyayatnas tvekādaśadhā. vivāraḥ saṁvāraḥ śvāso nādo 'ghoṣo ghoṣo-'lpaprāṇo mahāprāṇa udāto 'nudāttaḥ svaritaś ceti. kharo vivārāḥ śvāsā aghoṣāś ca. haśaḥ saṁvārā nādā ghoṣāś ca. vargāṇāṁ prathama-tṛtīyapañcamā yaṇaś cālpaprāṇāḥ. vargāṇāṁ dvitīyacaturthau śalaś ca mahāprāṇāḥ.

Trans. : The external effort is of eleven kinds : vivāra, saṁvāra, śvāsa, nāda, aghoṣa, ghoṣa, alpaprāṇa, mahāprāṇa, udātta, anudātta and svarita. The three external efforts vivāra, śvāsa and aghoṣa belong to *khar*, that is, *kh ph ch ṭh th c ṭ t k p ś ṣ* and *s* (during the process of their being pronounced). The efforts known as saṁvāra, nāda and ghoṣa belong to the elements denoted by *haś*, that is, *h y v r l ñ m ṅ ṇ n jh bh gh ḍh dh j b g ḍ* and *d*. The first, third and fifth stops of the class groups, and *yaṇ* (*y v r l*) have alpaprāṇa effort whereas the second and fourth of the class groups and *śal* (*ś ṣ s* and *h*) have mahāprāṇa effort.

Eluc. : The external effort known as vivāra consists in keeping the glottis open and is witnessed when the process of articulating the elements denoted by *khar* is on. The saṁvāra effort consists in contracting the glottis while pronouncing the *haś* phonemes. In śvāsa effort comparatively more breath is exhaled as is seen while pronouncing the *khar* elements. The external effort nāda consists in creating some resonance as while pronouncing the *haś* phonemes. The efforts ghoṣa and aghoṣa belong to voiced (*haś*) and voiceless (*khar*) consonants respectively. The former have the depth of the tone, whereas the latter don't have it. The first, third and fifth of the five group classes and *yaṇ* require comparatively less breath from the mouth for their utterance. Hence they belong to alpaprāṇa (non-aspirate) category. Under mahāprāṇa (aspirate) category fall the second and fourth stops of the group classes and *śal* fricatives since they have aspirate characteristic and require more prāṇa while being pronounced. The udātta, anudāta and svarita vowels have already been explained under (6), (7) and (8).

लघु० – कादयो मावसानाः स्पर्शाः। यणोऽन्तःस्थाः। शल ऊष्माणः। अचः स्वराः। ×क ×ख इति कखाभ्यां प्रागर्धविसर्गसदृशो जिह्वामूलीयः। ×प ×फ इति पफाभ्यां प्रागर्धविसर्गसदृश उपध्मानीयः। अं अः इत्यचः परावनुस्वारविसर्गौ। *kādayo māvasānāḥ sparśāḥ. yaṇo 'ntasthāḥ. śala ūṣmāṇaḥ. acaḥ svarāḥ.×ka×kha iti kakhābhyāṁ prāgardhavisargasadṛśo jihvāmūlīyaḥ. ×pa×pha iti paphābhyāṁ prāgardhavisargasadṛśa upadhmānīyaḥ. aṁ aḥ ityacaḥ parāvanusvāravisargau.*

Trans. : The class sounds beginning with *k* and ending with *m* are called stops (*sparśa*). The phonemes denoted by *yaṇ* are semivowels (*antaḥstha*). The *śal* fricatives are known as spirants (*ūṣma*). The phonemes denoted by *ac* pratyāhāra are designated as *svaras* (vowels). The symbol preceding *k* and *kh* which somewhat resembles half-visarga is called *jihvāmūlīya*. The same symbol used before either *p* or *ph* is called *upadhmānīya*. 'अं अः' – here the dot above अ and two dots immediately following it respectively represent anusvāra (*ṁ*) and visarga (*ḥ*).

Eluc. : There is no obstruction in the way of the pulmonary air (prāṇa) coming out of the mouth when vowels are uttered. When we attempt to pronounce the vowels, we keep the throat and mouth open and they remain so when the vowels are being produced. This is the reason that they are called *vivṛta*. On the other hand there is obstruction when consonants are being articulated as there is contact between some part of the tongue and that of the organ of pronunciation. As an illustration, take cavarga stops *c, ch,* etc. When we attempt to articulate these stops, the front portion of the tongue touches the hard palate and thus the air coming out is obstructed. When we attempt to pronounce the vowels, there is no such obstruction. The five group classes of the consonants beginning with *k* and ending with *m* are called stops or *sparśa* since, when we articulate them, there is contact of some portion of the tongue with some other part of the mouth. When we articulate the labial stops, both lips come in contact with each other to obstruct the pulmonary air.

This contact is slightly less in case of the semi-vowels, that is, *yaṇ* (*antaḥstha*). As such the internal effort used in producing these semi-vowels is called *īṣatspṛṣṭa*. Uvaṭa calls them *antaḥsthā* in the feminine and explains that they are so called because they are placed between the stops (*sparśa*) and the spirants (*ūṣma*). The *śal* are called *ūṣma* as there is an exhalation of breath while producing these sounds.

The visarga, when followed either by *k* or *kh,* is replaced by the symbol ⨯ which represents jihvāmūlīya. The visarga is produced in the throat. When it is immediately followed by *k* or *kh,* it is produced at the root of the tongue. As such it is called (*jihvāmūlīya*) which means articulated at the root of the tongue. When the visarga is immediately followed by either *p* or *ph,* it is replaced by this ⨯ symbol which represents upadhmānīya. The place of articulation of the former is the root of the tongue, whereas the articulation of upadhmānīya takes place at the lips. 'अं अः' - here the dot above अ represents the segment *anusvāra* and is pronounced with the help of the nose. The two dots immediately following अ represent visarga and are pronounced in the throat. It deserves mention here that visarga, jihvāmūlīya, upadhmānīya and anusvāra are also called *ayogavāhas*. They share the characteristic of articulation with their attendant phonetic element.

Table 1 : Places of Pronunciation

kaṇṭha	tālu	oṣṭha	mūrdhā	danta	nāsikā	kaṇṭha-tālu	kaṇṭho-ṣṭha	danto-ṣṭha	jihvā-mūlīya
a	i	u	ṛ	ḷ	ñ	e	o	v	⨯k
k	c	p	ṭ	t	m	ai	au		⨯kh
kh	ch	ph	ṭh	th	ṅ				
g	j	b	ḍ	d	ṇ				
gh	jh	bh	ḍh	dh	n				
ṅ	ñ	m	ṇ	n					
h	y	⨯p	r	l					
visarga	ś	⨯ph	ṣ	s					

Table 2 : Internal effort

spṛṣṭa	īṣatspṛṣṭa	vivṛta	īṣadvivṛta	saṁvṛta
k kh g gh ṅ	y v r l	a i u ṛ ḷ e o	ś ṣ s h	a
c ch j jh ñ		ai au		(excepting
ṭ ṭh ḍ ḍh ṇ				grammatical
t th d dh n				operations)
p ph b bh m				

Table 3 : External effort

vivāra śvāsa aghoṣa	saṁvāra nāda ghoṣa	alpaprāṇa	mahāprāṇa	udātta anudātta svarita
k kh	g gh ṅ	k g ṅ	kh gh	a i u
c ch	j jh ñ	c j ñ	ch jh	ṛ ḷ
ṭ ṭh	ḍ ḍh ṇ	ṭ ḍ ṇ	ṭh ḍh	e o
t th	d dh n	t d n	th dh	ai au
p ph	b bh m	p b m	ph bh	
ś ṣ s	y v r l	y v r l	ś ṣ s h	
	h ac	ac		

(11) अणुदित्सवर्णस्य चाऽप्रत्ययः। ***aṇuditsavarṇasya cāpratyayaḥ.* 1. 1. 69**

लघु० – प्रतीयते विधीयते इति प्रत्ययः। अविधीयमानोऽण् उदिच्च सवर्णस्य संज्ञा स्यात्। अत्रैवाण् परेण णकारेण। कु चु टु तु पु एत उदितः। तदेवं अ इत्यष्टादशानां संज्ञा। तथेकारोकारौ। ऋकारस्त्रिंशतः । एवम् ऌकारोऽपि। एचो द्वादशानाम्। अनुनासिका-ऽननुनासिकभेदेन यवला द्विधा; तेनाऽननुनासिकास्ते द्वयोर्द्वयोः संज्ञा। *pratīyate vidhīyate iti pratyayaḥ. avidhīyamāno 'ṇ udicca savarṇasya saṁjñā syāt. atraivāṇ pareṇa ṇakāreṇa. ku cu ṭu tu pu eta uditaḥ. tadevam a ityaṣṭādaśānāṁ saṁjñā tathekārokārau. ṛkārastriṁśataḥ evam ḷkāro 'pi. eco dvādaśānām. anunāsikā 'nanunāsikabhedena yavalā dvidhā; tenā 'nanunāsikās te dvayor dvayoḥ saṁjñā.*

Trans. : That which is enjoined is *pratyaya*. Let the denotata of the pratyāhāra *aṇ* which are not enjoined and of the ones which are marked with *u* as *it* denote their homogeneous counterparts. It is only here that the pratyāhāra *aṇ* is taken by the latter *ṇ*. *ku, cu, ṭu, tu* and *pu* - these are called *udit*. In this way *a* denotes its eighteen forms. Similarly *i* and *u* will denote their eighteen forms. The vowel *ṛ* will denote thirty forms. In the same manner *ḷ* (will also denote its thirty varieties). The denotata of *ec* will each denote its twelve forms. Being anunāsika and ananunāsika, *y, v* and *l* have two forms each. Thus the ananunāsika *y, v* and *l* will denote both anunāsika and ananunāsika *y, v* and *l*.

PP. *aṇ udit savarṇasya ca apratyayaḥ svasya.*

Eluc. : The word *svaṁ* is carried over from the sūtra *svaṁ rūpaṁ śabdasyāśabdasaṁjñā* Pā. 1. 1. 68 and is changed into the genitive in the present sūtra. The word *udit* is a bahuvrīhi compound which is analysed as follows : *ut it yasya sa udit*. This denotes *ku cu ṭu tu pu*. The meaning of the word *apratyayaḥ* in the sūtra is 'that which is not being enjoined grammatically' and it qualifies the pratyāhāra *aṇ* only and not that which is signified by *udit*. If any of the denotata of *aṇ* pratyāhāra is not grammatically enjoined, then it will denote itself and all its homogeneous counterparts. This comes to mean that if *a* is not being enjoined, it will denote all its eighteen forms, but if it is being enjoined, it will denote only its six forms of the duration of a single mora and not those forms having the duration of two or three morae. In the sūtra *iko yaṇaci, ik* is not enjoined; hence every element signified by it will denote itself and all its homogeneous forms. On the other hand *yaṇ* is being enjoined in place of *ik*. The denotata of *yaṇ* will not signify all their homogeneous forms. It means one of the denotata of *yaṇ* , that is, *y* will denote its own form and not its anunāsika form. This is the reason why *i*-substituend may be any of its eighteen forms but the *y*-substitute will confine to itself. It will not include anunāsika yakāra. Similarly in the sūtra *sanāśaṁsabhikṣa uḥ* (837), the affix *u* is being enjoined. Hence it will stand for itself only and not for its long and prolated forms. Pāṇini does not intend to qualify *udit* by *apratyayaḥ*. It is clear from the sūtra *coḥ kuḥ* (305). On the basis of this sūtra *c ch j jh ñ* which are denoted by *cu* will be substituted by *k kh g gh ṅ* respectively at the end of a pada or when *jhal* follows. Had Pāṇini intended to qualify *udit* by *apratyayaḥ*, the sūtra *coḥ kuḥ* would have meant : only *k* is substituted in place of any of c *ch j jh* and *ñ*, which obviously is not the case.

The marker *ṇ* comes twice in the pratyāhārasūtras. The present sūtra is the only place in the Aṣṭādhyāyī where the pratyāhāra *aṇ* is formed with the latter *ṇ*, i.e. the *ṇ* of *laṇ*. In all other occurrences of *aṇ*, it is formed with the *ṇ* of *a i uṇ*. This has been clarified by Patañjali in the Mahābhāṣya on the *laṇ* sūtra. The conclusion is given in the following verse :

pareṇaivengrahāḥ sarve pūrveṇaivāṇgrahā matāḥ,
ṛte 'ṇuditsavarṇasyetyetadekaṁ pareṇa tu. (Mahābhāṣya edited by Vedavrata, *laṇ* sūtra, p. 115, fn †)

The *iṇ*-pratyāhāra, at all places, is accepted to be constituted by the *ṇ* of *laṇ*-pratyāhārasūtra. The pratyāhāra *aṇ* is understood to be formed with the *ṇ* of pratyāhārasūtra *a i uṇ*. This excludes the sūtra, *aṇudit savarṇasya cāpratyayaḥ* in which *aṇ* is accepted as formed by the latter ṇakāra (of *laṇ*).

Thus *a i u* will signify all their eighteen forms in the manner already explained. The vowels *ṛ* and *ḷ* will each denote its thirty varieties (*ṛ*'s 18 and *ḷ*'s 12 = 30) since they have been declared to be homogeneous by Kātyāyana's vārttika (1) under *tulyāsyaprayatnaṁ savarṇam* (10).

The vowels denoted by *ec* will denote their twelve forms because they do not have short counterparts. The ananunāsika *y*, *v* and *l* will each signify its two forms.

(12) परः संनिकर्षः संहिता । *paraḥ sannikarṣaḥ saṁhitā*. 1. 4. 109

लघु० - वर्णानामतिशयितः संनिधिः संहिता-संज्ञः स्यात् । *varṇānām atiśayitaḥ sannidhiḥ saṁhitā-saṁjñaḥ syāt.*

Trans. : Let extreme proximity between phonemes have the designation *saṁhitā*.

PP. *paraḥ sannikarṣaḥ saṁhitā.*

Eluc. : When there is extreme proximity between two phonemes, there occurs natural phonetic coalescence of the preceding and the following sounds. This extreme juxtaposition between the preceding and the following phonemes is the condition for the euphonic combination (sandhi) to take place. This will be explained at (15).

(13) हलोऽनन्तराः संयोगः । *halo 'nantarāḥ saṁyogaḥ.* 1. 1. 7

लघु० – अज्भिरव्यवहिता हलः संयोगसंज्ञाः स्युः । *ajbhir avyavahitā halaḥ saṁyoga-saṁjñāḥ syuḥ.*

Trans. : Let the consonants which are not separated by the vowels have the designation *saṁyoga*.

PP. *halaḥ anantarāḥ saṁyogaḥ.*

Eluc. : When two or more consonants (*hal*) are not separated by any vowel (*ac*), they are termed *saṁyoga* (conjunct). In the word *indra, n, d* and *r* are not separated by any vowel. Hence *n, d* and *r* will be designated as *saṁyoga*. Similarly in the word *uṣṭra, ṣ, ṭ* and *r* will be named *saṁyoga*. The application of this term will be seen in sūtras like *saṁyogāntasya lopaḥ* (20), etc.

(14) सुप्तिङन्तं पदम् । *suptiṅantaṁ padam.* 1. 4. 14

लघु० – सुबन्तं तिङन्तं च पदसंज्ञं स्यात् । *subantaṁ tiṅantaṁ ca pada-saṁjñaṁ syāt.*

Trans. : Let a word that terminates in *sup* or *tiṅ* be designated as *pada*.

PP. *suptiṅantam padam.*

Eluc. : Yāska divides the padas into four categories : nāma, ākhyāta, upasarga and nipāta but Pāṇini has reduced the classification to two, that is, subanta and tiṅanta. The terms *sup* and *tiṅ* are pratyāhāras which are respectively formed with the help of Pā. 4. 1. 2 and 3. 4. 78. In the former sūtra the inflectional affixes are given. These affixes are as follows : su au jas, am auṭ śas, ṭā bhyām bhis, ṅe bhyām bhyas, ṅasi bhyām bhyas, ṅas os ām, ṅi os sup. The pratyāhāra *sup* is formed by taking the initial *su* (underlined) and adding to it the final marker *p* (underlined) of the last inflectional affix *sup*. Similarly, *tiṅ* pratyāhāra is formed. This denotes the conjugational affixes which are given in the latter sūtra. The conjugational affixes given in the sūtra are as follows : *tip tas jhi, sip thas tha, mip vas mas, ta ātām jha, thās āthām dhvam, iṭ vahi mahiṅ*. The beginning *ti* (underlined) of *tip* with the marker *ṅ* (underlined) of the last conugational affix *mahiṅ* forms the pratyāhāra *tiṅ*. These are two examples where the technique of forming a pratyāhāra which is laid down by the sūtra *ādirantyena sahetā* (4) is also applied. The sup-affixes are added to the nominal stems (*prātipadikas*) to form nāma-padas and the affixes denoted by *tiṅ* pratyāhāra are added to the verbal roots (*dhātus*) to form kriyāpadas. If these affixes are not added, a word is not a finished word and hence not fit to be used in a sentence according to the Pāṇinian sytem of grammar. Thus, according to Pāṇini, the whole corpus of Sanskrit language is exhausted by these two categories.

One point is relevant in the present context. There is a metarule which says that where an affix is mentioned, it means the word ending with that affix : *pratyagrahaṇe yasmāt sa vihitas tadādes tadantasya grahaṇam* (Abhyankar, 23). In the sūtra under discussion, *sup* and *tiṅ* affixes have been mentioned. Why then has the word *anta* been used in the sūtra? It seems to be redundant when the above paribhāṣā is available. Thus the word *anta*, being redundant, implies another paribhāṣā : *saṁjñāvidhau pratyayagrahaṇe tadantagrahaṇaṁ nāsti* (Abhyankar, 27). When an affix is mentioned in the context of defining technical terms, it is not to be understood in the sense of the word ending with that affix. In this sūtra the pada is being defined, that is, the pada-designation (pada-saṁjñā) is being prescribed. Therefore the paribhāṣā, *pratyagrahaṇe yasmāt sa vihitas tadādes tadantasya grahaṇam* does not hold good here.

लघु० – इति संज्ञाप्रकरणं समाप्तम् । *iti saṁjñāprakaraṇaṁ samāptam.*

Trans. : Thus ends the chapter on technical terms.

सन्धिप्रकरणम्
Sandhi

अच्-सन्धिः
Vowel-Sandhi

(15) इको यणचि । *iko yaṇaci.* 6. 1. 77

लघु० – इकः स्थाने यण् स्याद् अचि संहितायां विषये। सुधी + उपास्य इति स्थिते –

ikaḥ sthāne yaṇ syād aci saṁhitāyāṁ viṣaye. sudhī + upāsya iti sthite –

Trans. : The condition of maximum proximity between two phonemes being available, let *yaṇ* be substituted in place of *ik*, when the latter is followed by *ac* (a vowel). In the context of the example *sudhī + upāsya,* (the next sūtra ensues) :

PP. *ikaḥ yaṇ aci saṁhitāyām.*

Eluc. : We know that saṁhitā means extreme proximity between two phonemes. The condition for the substitution of *yaṇ* (*y v r l*) in place of *ik* (*i u ṛ ḷ*) is saṁhitā. The domain of the governing rule *saṁhitāyām* Pā. 6. 1. 72 extends up to Pā. 6. 1. 158. The locative case in the word *saṁhitā* means *viṣaya* (domain). As a consequence, the grammatical operation in the form of replacement cannot take place unless the condition of maximum proximity between two phonemes is obtained. This condition is available in the present illustration since, according to *kartṛkaraṇe kṛtā bahulam* (922), this is a tṛtīyā tatpuruṣa compound : *sudhībhiḥ upāsyaḥ.* The nominal endings (*bhis* and *su*) have been elided (*luked*) by *supo dhātuprātipadikayoḥ* (718). The resultant form is *sudhī + upāsya* which means 'He who deserves to be worshipped by the intelligent'.

The grounds, which occasion maximum proximity (*saṁhitā*) between two phonemes, are enumerated in the following verse :

saṁhitaikapade nityā, nityā dhātūpasargayoḥ,
nityā samāse vākye tu, sā vivakṣāmapekṣate.

"saṁhitā is compulsory in a single finished word, between a preverb (*upsarga*) and a verbal root and in a compound, but in a sentence it depends upon the intention of the speaker." Since the present illustration is a compound, saṁhitā 'closest proximity' is necessarily available here. Thus in *sudhī + upāsya,* which is a compound, the present sūtra *iko yaṇ aci* is applicable.

The sūtra contains three terms : *ikaḥ, yaṇ* and *aci*. The first term *ikaḥ* is in the genitive, *yaṇ* in the nominative and *aci* in the locative. In pursuance of the sūtra *ṣaṣṭhī sthāneyogā* Pā. 1. 1. 49, *ikaḥ* means 'in place of *ik* (*i u ṛ ḷ*)'. The term *yaṇ* is in the nominative and as such it means that the elements denoted by this abbreviatory term will replace the elements denoted by the abbreviatory term *ik,* that is, *y v r* and *l* will replace *i u ṛ* and *ḷ*. The word *aci* which is in the locative case provides the condition when this replacement should take place. This means that when *ac* follows, *ik* will be substituted by *yaṇ*.

Bhimasena Shastri, following Bālamanoramā, says that the seventh case-ending in *aci* is sati-saptamī or bhāva-saptamī in accordance with *yasya ca bhāvena bhāvalakṣaṇam* Pā. 2. 3. 37. This rule enjoins saptamī vibhakti (locative case-ending) after a nominal stem when the action denoted by it indicates another action. This is so because a varṇa cannot be a locus of another varṇa. Cf. *varṇānāṁ varṇāntarādhikaraṇatvāsambhavād acīti satisaptamī* (BM, I, p. 55). Consequently the present sūtra would mean : the existence of *ac* indicates the act of substitution of *ik* by *yaṇ* (*aci sati ikaḥ sthāne yaṇ syāt*). However, this is not sufficient in that it would allow the replacement to apply to any vowel denoted by *ik* under unspecified circumstances, merely because there is another vowel. There is no specification of when or where this vowel should occur. In the illustration given in the Laghukaumudī the phoneme *u* of *upāsya,* may become the condition for the replacement of either *u* or *ī* of *sudhī.* As interpreted by Nāgeśa, the term *aci* contains the seventh case-ending in the sense of aupaśleṣika adhikaraṇa. He interprets the statement of Patañjali on Pā. 6. 1. 72 *acy upaśliṣṭasya* as *ac-samīpasthasya,* which virtually means that a speech element is an adhikaraṇa relative to another by virtue of occurring in its proximity[1] (*tasya samīpe*). This relation can hold whether a vowel follows or precedes a vowel denoted by *ik*. It is in such a context that the following sūtra presents itself :

1. Cf. *śabdasya tu śabdena ko 'nyo 'bhisambandho bhavitum arhati anyadata upaśleṣāt. iko yaṇaci acyupliṣṭasya iti saṁhitāyām ityatra bhāṣyaṁ saṅgacchate. acyupaśliṣṭasya acsamīpoccāritasyetyarthaḥ iti kaiyaṭaḥ.* BM, I, p. 695.

(16) तस्मिन्निति निर्दिष्टे पूर्वस्य । *tasminniti nirdiṣṭe pūrvasya.* 1. 1. 66

लघु० – सप्तमीनिर्देशेन विधीयमानं कार्यं वर्णान्तरेणाव्यवहितस्य पूर्वस्य बोध्यम् । *saptamīnirdeśena vidhīyamānaṁ kāryaṁ varṇāntareṇāvyavahitasya pūrvasya bodhyam.*

Trans. : When a term is stated in the locative case, let the grammatical operation directed by it be performed on that which precedes the term without being separated even by a single phoneme.

PP. *tasmin iti nirdiṣṭe pūrvasya.*

Eluc. : Interpreted with the help of this paribhāṣāsūtra, the seventh case-ending behaves as parasaptamī. In this light the interpretation of this sūtra given by Varadarāja in his vṛtti becomes cogent. In the flow of speech units, temporal precedence may be construed as *pūrva,* whereas the temporally consequent speech unit may be understood as *para.* In this case the following vowel beomes the condition for transformation in the immediately preceding *ik* by virtue of this sūtra. This does away with the ambiguity about whether the substitution should take place for *u* following *s* or *ī* following *dh* since immediate precedence means that no other phoneme should come between the following *ac* and the preceding *ik.*

As we have discussed under (2), the use of the term *iti* in śabdānuśāsana shifts the emphasis from the word itself to its meaning. Consequently the term *iti* after *tasmin* shifts the emphasis from the word *tasmin* to the meaning conveyed by it, that is, *tasmin* means 'the meaning conveyed by the term used in the locative nominal ending'. The term *aci* which ends in the locative denotes a vowel. In the illustration *sudhī* + *upāsya,* when a vowel (*ac,* in this case *u*) immediately follows *ik,* the immediately preceding *ik* (in this case *ī*) is replaced by the semi-vowel *y.* (See TB, I, p. 49 where Jñānendra Sarasvatī interprets *nirdiṣṭe* as *avyavahitoccārite sati*). The present aphorism also ensures that the substitution takes place only in place of what immediately precedes and not in place of that which immediately follows (*pūrvasyaiva bhavati na parasya ity etadartham idam ārabhyate* TB, I, p. 49). This does away with the instance of the intervention of a speech unit. The temporal intervention is taken care of by the adhikāra-sūtra *saṁhitāyām* Pā. 6. 1. 72. The contingency of replacement coming in place of *u* following *s* is also dispensed with in the light of this interpretation.

At this stage it is clear that an element denoted by *yaṇ* is to be substituted in place of the phoneme *ī* which is denoted by the abbreviatory term *ik* and which follows the consonant *dh*. There are four elements denoted by *yaṇ*. Which of the four is going to replace *ī*? The next sūtra, in the scheme of Varadarāja, helps remove this confusion with regard to the substitute which is to be used in place of the vowel *ī* in the present illustration.

(17) स्थानेऽन्तरतमः । *sthāne 'ntaratamaḥ*. 1. 1. 50

लघु० - प्रसङ्गे सति सदृशतम आदेशः स्यात् । *prasaṅge sati sadṛśatama ādeśaḥ syāt.*

Trans. : When (common) substitutes are available, let the most similar substitute replace the substituendum.

PP. *sthāne antaratamaḥ*.

Eluc. : This is also a metarule (*paribhāṣā sūtra*) and consequently it does away with the confusion which arises when several substitutes are possible in place of a single substituendum. In the present illustration, the substituendum is *ī*. The substitutes that are available are four in number. Now the question arises which substitute out of the four (*y v r l*) is to replace *ī* that follows *dh*. This has to be decided on the basis of similarity (*āntarya*) which is of four types : 1. similarity based on the place of articulation (*sthānakṛta*) 2. similarity based on signification (*arthakṛta*) 3. similarity based on sound quality (*guṇakṛta*) and 4. similarity based on duration (*pramāṇakṛta*). The term *sthāne* occurring in the sūtra could have been dispensed with when it was available by anuvṛtti from the preceding sūtra *ṣaṣṭhī sthāneyogā* Pā. 1. 1. 49. According to the Kāśikā, Pāṇini's use of *sthāne* in the present sūtra is simply to indicate that whenever there is a possibility of similarity based on more factors than one, similarity based on sthāna, place of articulation, should be considered decisive.

From this angle, the substitute *y* is the most similar to the substituendum *ī* since the place where both *y* and *ī* are produced or pronounced is the palate, although internal efforts made for producing them are different. The palate, being the place of pronunciation for both *y* and *ī*, determines their similarity. Consequently *y* replaces *ī*. After the process of substitution, *sudhī + upāsya* changes into *sudhy + upāsya*.

Scholars differ about invoking *sthāne 'ntaratamaḥ* in respect of *iko yaṇaci* (15). In such cases, where enumerated elements are equal, *yathāsaṅkhyamanudeśaḥ samānām* (23) should come into play. Of course, there is a problem that once *aṇudit savarṇasya cāpratyayaḥ* (11) is applied, the referents of *ik* and *yaṇ* are not equal. It is this problem that has been brought up by many Pāṇinīan scholars in such a context. They cite *syatāsī lṛluṭoḥ* (402) in this context. If we consider this sūtra at the first stage, both the substitutes and the substituenda are equal in number. Therefore, *yathāsaṅkhyamanudeśaḥ samānām* (23) can apply correctly. If, however, one interprets *lṛ* as both *lṛṭ* and *lṛṅ*, then the substitutes and the substituenda are unequal in number since, according to this interpretation, lakāras are three but the vikaraṇas remain two. How can then the sūtra *yathāsaṅkhyamanudeśaḥ samānām* (23) apply? The vikaraṇa *sya* occurs, as it should, in both the verbal forms *bhaviṣyati* and *abhaviṣyat*, in lṛṭ and lṛṅ respectively. The vikaraṇa *tāsi* occurs in *bhavitā* in luṭ. Accordingly, the convention should be that the sūtra *yathāsaṅkhyamanudeśaḥ samānām* (23) should apply at the first stage of the equally enumerated elements, before any of these is possibly further interpreted as an abbreviatory term denoting a group of elements. By the same reasoning, *ik* (*i u ṛ ḷ*) and *yaṇ* (*y v r l*) refer to an equal number of referents at the first stage so that *yathāsaṅkhyamanudeśaḥ samānām* (23) applies as it does also for *eco 'yavāyāvaḥ* (22). However, it is obvious that Varadarāja prefers the former interpretation.

Following either interpretation, in *sudhī + upāsya*, *ī* is replaced by *y* and the illustration resultantly changes into *sudhy + upāsya*. At this stage, the following sūtra applies :

(18) अनचि च । *anaci ca*. 8. 4. 47

लघु॰ – अचः परस्य यरो द्वे वा स्तो न त्वचि। इति धकारस्य द्वित्वम्। *acaḥ parasya yaro dve vā sto na tvaci. iti dhakārasya dvitvam.*

Trans. : The elements denoted by *yar* optionally undergo reduplication but not when followed by *ac*. So *dh* is reduplicated.

PP. *acaḥ yaraḥ dve vā anaci ca* (*saṁhitāyām*).

Eluc. : In this sūtra *acaḥ* and *dve* are carried over from *aco rahābhyāṁ dve* Pā. 8. 4. 46 and *yar* and *vā* from *yaro 'nunāsike 'nunāsiko vā* Pā. 8. 4. 45. When these four terms are read into this sūtra, it becomes a complete sentence as given by Varadarāja in his vṛtti. Thus for reduplication, the consonant *dh*, which is one of the denotata of *yar*, should be preceded by *ac* but not followed by it. The phoneme *dh* is such an element denoted by *yar*. As a result, *dh* is iterated and we have : *su dh dh y + upāsya.*

The term *anaci* in the sūtra is a nañ-tatpuruṣa compound (*na + ac*) and ends in the locative. The term *nañ* is a particle that conveys negation. The negation is of two kinds : 1. paryudāsa (exclusion) and 2. prasajya (prohibition connected with an action). The author of the Kāśikā interprets the negative particle here in the sense of exclusion, that is, the negative compound *anac* means tadbhinna-tatsadṛśa 'that which is similar to and different from *ac*'. In other words, the negative compound in the present sūtra conveys the sense of *anac-parasya*. This is one of the six meanings attributed to *na*. This is the paryudāsa sense of *na*. Nonetheless, this is not free from fault as it creates applicational problems at the end of a term, especially before a pause (*avasāna*). To illustrate, we cannot get two *k*-phonemes in *vākk* since there is nothing similar to and different from a vowel here. It is for this reason that Varadarāja has interpreted *na* here in the sense of prasajya negation, which allows the doubling of *k* (*yar*) at the end also. There is one more reason why *na* should be construed in the sense of prasajya negation. Had Pāṇini intended *na* in the sense of paryudāsa, he would have used *hali* instead of *anaci* and then it would have been more economical by one mora. Cf. the paribhāṣā *ardhamātrālāghavena putrotsavaṁ manyante vaiyākaraṇāḥ* {(Abhyankar, 122) on saving half a mora the grammarians rejoice as if celebrating the birth of a son}, which signifies that not a single element of utterance in Pāṇini's grammar is superfluous. Consequently, the sūtra means that doubling will be negated only when *ac* follows and not when a consonant follows. In this sense, the reduplication of *k* in *vākk* is allowed since at the end there is no phoneme. Although in a compound *na* generally means exclusion, exceptionally it also means prasajya negation in some of the sūtras such as *suḍanapuṁsakasya* (162), *cādayo 'sattve* (53), etc.

Thus after the optional doubling in the present illustration, *sudhī* + *upāsya* has two forms : *su dh dh y* + *upāsya* and *sudhy* + *upāsya*. At this stage, the following sūtra presents itself for application :

(19) झलां जश् झशि । *jhalāṁ jaś jhaśi.* 8. 4. 53

लघु० – स्पष्टमिति पूर्वधकारस्य दकारः । *spaṣṭamiti pūrvadhakārasya dakāraḥ.*

Trans. : It is self-explanatory. (Let the elements denoted by *jhal* be replaced by the elements denoted by *jaś* when the elements denoted by *jhaś* follow.) Therefore the preceding *dh* is replaced by the phoneme *d*.

PP. *jhalāṁ jaś jhaśi* (*saṁhitāyām*).

Eluc. : The genitive nominal ending in *jhal* is the substitution-genitive (*sthānaṣaṣṭhī*) and thus it means in place of the phonemes denoted by *jhal*. The locative nominal ending, by virtue of the paribhāṣā-sūtra *tasminniti nirdiṣṭe pūrvasya* (16) determines that it is the preceding *dh* which is to be replaced by *d* when two *dh*'s exist. That *d* is the substitute for *dh* is determined by the sūtra *sthāne 'ntaratamaḥ* (17), since out of the phonemes denoted by *jaś d*, being dental, is most similar to *dh*. After the operation of this sūtra, the two forms of the illustration now are as follows : 1. *suddhy* + *upāsya* and 2. *sudhy* + *upāsya*. At this stage the following sūtra applies :

(20) संयोगान्तस्य लोपः । *saṁyogāntasya lopaḥ*. 8. 2. 23

लघु॰ – संयोगान्तं यत् पदं तस्य लोपः स्यात्। *saṁyogāntaṁ yat padaṁ tasya lopaḥ syāt.*

Trans. : Let lopa be substituted in place of the pada which ends in a conjunct (*saṁyoga*).

PP. *saṁyogāntasya padasya lopaḥ.*

Eluc. : The present sūtra occurs in the domain of the governing rule *padasya* Pā. 8. 1. 16. Hence the term *padasya* recurs in the present sūtra also. It is worth mentioning here that a specification with *saṁyogasya* with no *anta* as part of the sūtra could also mean *saṁyogāntasya* by virtue of the sūtra *yena vidhis tadantasya* Pā. 1. 1. 72. Therefore it is accepted here that the addition of *anta* to *saṁyoga* has been made for the purpose of clarity. In the above illustration both *suddhy* and *sudhy* are padas that end in a conjunct. The cluster *ddhy* in the former and *dhy* in the latter are not separated by any vowel and are saṁyoga by *halo 'nantarāḥ saṁyogaḥ* (13). Although the nominal endings of both the members of the compound have been elided by *supo dhātuprātipadikayoḥ* (718), they still enjoy the status of a pada in accordance with the rule *pratyayalope pratyayalakṣaṇam* (189) In this way, the elision of *suddhy* and *sudhy* is available by the present rule. To avoid this contingency of the deletion of the whole pada ending in a conjunct, the following sūtra restricts the deletion only to the last sound segment coming at the end of a pada.

(21) अलोऽन्त्यस्य । *alo 'ntyasya*. 1. 1. 52

लघु॰ – षष्ठीनिर्दिष्टस्यान्त्यस्याल आदेशः स्यात्। इति यलोपे प्राप्ते — *ṣaṣṭhīnirdiṣṭasyāntyasyāla ādeśaḥ syāt. iti yalope prāpte* —

Trans. : Let the substitute enjoined for an item in the genitive come in place of the final phoneme (*al*). Thus when the lopa-replacement is to come in place of *y* —

PP. *alaḥ antyasya ṣaṣṭhī sthāne.*

Eluc. : The terms *ṣaṣṭhī* and *sthāne* have been carried over here from *ṣaṣṭhī sthāneyogā* Pā. 1. 1. 49. The word *ṣaṣṭhī* will be changed into the instrumental, which will give the sense 'indicated by the genitive' (*ṣaṣṭhyā nirdiṣṭasya*). This coupled with the word *sthāne* will mean that the substitute, which has been enjoined to come in place of a substituendum indicated by the use of substitution-genitive, will replace only the final element of the term used in the genitive[1]. By the preceding rule, the whole pada ending in a conjunct has to undergo deletion but the present rule restricts the deletion only to the last element of that which has been specified in the genitive. Thus in the illustration under discussion, the final *y* of both the forms has got to be elided. Here Kātyāyana's vārttika presents itself and prohibits the elision of *y* which is one of the elements denoted by *yaṇ*.

2. वा० – यणः प्रतिषेधो वाच्यः । *yaṇaḥ pratiṣedho vācyaḥ.*

लघु० – सुद्ध्युपास्यः सुध्युपास्यः । मद्ध्वरिः मध्वरिः । धात्त्रंशः धात्रंशः । लाकृतिः ।

suddhyupāsyaḥ, suddhyupāsyaḥ. maddhvariḥ, madhvariḥ. dhāttraṁśaḥ, dhātraṁśaḥ. lākṛtiḥ.

Trans. : If the last phoneme belongs to the elements denoted by *yaṇ*, then its deletion should be prohibited.

Eluc. : If the elements denoted by *yaṇ* are at the end of a term ending in a conjunct, then by virtue of Kātyāyana's vārttika, the elision of such a phoneme is prohibited. In the illustration the last element belongs to *yaṇ*-pratyāhāra, hence it is not to be deleted. After adding the nominative singular affix, the resultant two forms are : 1. *suddhyupāsyaḥ* and 2. *sudhyupāsyaḥ*.

The grammatical procedure for sandhi in *maddhvariḥ* and *madhvariḥ* (*madhoḥ ariḥ* --> *madhu* + *ari*, the enemy of the demon named Madhu) is the same as it is in the above illustration. In the third illustraton *dhāttraṁśaḥ, dhātraṁśaḥ* (*dhātoḥ aṁśaḥ* --> *dhātṛ* + *aṁśa*, a portion belonging to Brahman), *ṛ* occurring at the end of the first member of the genitive tatpuruṣa compound is transformed into *r* by *iko yaṇaci* (15) and the optional doubling of *t* takes place by *anaci ca* (18). All the rules that are applied in the preceding two examples, except *jhalāṁ jhaś jhaśi*

1. Cf. *ṣaṣṭhī sthāneyogā ity ataḥ ṣaṣṭhī, sthāne ity anuvartate. tac ca ṣaṣṭhīti prathamāntaṁ tṛtīyāntatayā vipariṇamyate. nirdiṣṭasyeti śeṣaḥ. sthāne ityanantaraṁ vidhīyamāna iti śeṣaḥ. sthāne vidhīyamāna ādeśaḥ ṣaṣṭhīnirdiṣṭasya yaḥ antyaḥ al tasya syād ityarthaḥ.* BM, I, p. 50.

(19), which is not required in this case, are applicable here. We have already expressed our view that *yathāsaṅkhyamanudeśaḥ samānām* (23) is to be preferred to *sthāne 'ntaratamaḥ* (17).[1] The last illustration is *lākṛtiḥ* (*ul ākṛtir iva ākṛtir yasya ḷ + ākṛti*). Here *ul* is the genitive form of *ḷ*. This is a bahuvrīhi compound which means 'the one who has a curved posture like *ḷ*', that is Lord Kṛṣṇa while playing on the flute. In this illustration, *ḷ* is replaced by *l* in accordance with the sūtra *iko yaṇaci* (15).

(22) एचोऽयवायावः । *eco 'yavāyāvaḥ*. 6. 1. 78

लघु० – एचः क्रमाद् अय् अव् आय् आव् एते स्युरचि । *ecaḥ kramād ay av āy āv ete syur aci.*

Trans. : When followed by *ac*, let the elements (*e o ai au*) denoted by *ec* be replaced by *ay av āy āv* respectively.

PP. *ecaḥ ayavāyāvaḥ aci saṁhitāyām.*

Eluc. : This sūtra is in the domain of *saṁhitāyām* Pā. 6. 1. 72. The term *aci* is carried over into it from *iko yaṇaci* Pā. 6. 1. 77. The word *ayavāyāvaḥ* is an itaretaradvandva compound. The locative nominal ending in *aci* is in the sense of aupaśleṣika adhikaraṇa which acts like parasaptamī with the help of the sūtra *tasminniti nirdiṣṭe pūrvasya* (16). This has already been discussed under (15). The term *kramād* occurs in the vṛtti because of the following sūtra :

(23) यथासंख्यमनुदेशः समानाम् । *yathāsaṅkhyamanudeśaḥ samānām*. 1. 3. 10

लघु० – समसम्बन्धी विधिर्यथासंख्यं स्यात् । हरये । विष्णवे । नायकः । पावकः । *sama-sambandhī vidhir yathāsaṁkhyaṁ syāt. haraye, viṣṇave, nāyakaḥ, pāvakaḥ.*

Trans. : Let the assignment of equally enumerated elements follow the order of their enumeration.

PP. *samānām anudeśaḥ yathāsaṅkhyam.*

Eluc. : The illustrations are single padas. So the condition of extreme proximity is necessarily available. Under this condition, by virtue of the substitution-genitive (*sthāna-ṣaṣṭhī*), the four substitutes (*ādeśa*) *ay av āy āv* are enjoined to replace respectively the four substituenda (*sthānī*) *e o ai au* when *ac* follows. Both of them being four, they are

1. See for explanation supra pp. 26-27.

equally enumerated. It is the equal enumeration that determines the order of replacement of the substitutes. The first substitute *ay* will come in place of the first substituendum *e*; the second in place of the second, and so on.

In the first two illustrations *e* represents the singular fourth nominal case-ending, that is *ṅe*. After the elision of *ṅ*, *e* remains. Because the nominal affix is *ṅit*, guṇa comes in place of *i* and *u* at the end of *hari* and *viṣṇu* respectively in accordance with the sūtra *gherṅiti* (171). *i* changes into *e* and *u* into *o*. Resultantly the first two illustrations are : *hare* + *e* and *viṣṇo* + *e*. At this stage, the present rule becomes applicable and *e* and *o* are replaced by *ay* and *av* respectively by the present sūtra. Thus *haraye* and *viṣṇave* are obtained. The derivational procedure of the last two illustrations will be as follows : We introduce the primary affix *ṇvul* to *nī* and *pū* by *ṇvultṛcau* (781). The affix *ṇvul* remains as *vu* after the elision of the anubandhas. It is then replaced with *aka* by *yuvoranākau* (782) and we have *nī* + *ṇvul* --> *nī* + *aka* and *pū* + *ṇvul* --> *pū* + *aka*. Now vṛddhi takes place by *aco 'ñṇiti* (181). Then we have *nai* + *aka* and *pau* + *aka*. At this stage, the present sūtra applies and the *ai* of *nai* and *au* of *pau* are replaced by *āy* and *āv* respectively and we obtain *nāyaka* and *pāvaka*. Adding the singular nominative affix to these forms, we have *nāyakaḥ* and *pāvakaḥ*.

(24) वान्तो यि प्रत्यये । *vānto yi pratyaye.* 6. 1. 79

लघु० - यकारादौ प्रत्यये परे ओदौतोरवाव् एतौ स्तः । गव्यम् । नाव्यम् । *yakārādau pratyaye pare odautor av āv etau staḥ. gavyam, nāvyam.*

Trans. : When an affix beginning with *y* follows, *o* and *au* are respectively replaced by *av* and *āv*.

PP. *vāntaḥ yi pratyaye* (*saṁhitāyām*).

Eluc. : The term *yi* is in the locative and qualifies *pratyaye*. When the qualifier is a single phoneme ending in the locative, the sūtra *yena vidhistadantasya* Pā. 1. 1. 72 does not apply as Kātyāyana's vārttika *yasmin vidhis tadādāvalgrahaṇe* Mbh 1. 1. 72 vtk 29 blocks it. With the help of this vārttika, the sūtra means : When an affix beginning with *y* follows, the vowels *o* and *au* are respectively replaced by *av* and *āv*. Although the substituenda are not mentioned in the rule, they are made available by the statement of Patañjali on *vāntādeśe sthāninirdeśaḥ* Mbh 6. 1. 79 vtk 1. He says on this vārttika that the vowels *o* and *au* should be enunciated as the substituenda to be replaced by *av* and *āv* (*okāraukārayor iti vaktavyam*). These substitutes end in *v* and hence they are *vānta*. In the illustrations given by Varadarāja, *gavyam* is formed by adding *yat* affix after the syntactically connected nominal stem *go* by *gopayasoryat* (1111). After the phoneme *t* is elided, *ya* remains. This affix *ya* begins with *y* and the syntactically connected nominal stem to which this is added ends in *o*. The conditions laid down in the sūtra are fulfilled and as a consequence *o* is replaced by *av*. The resultant form is *gavyam*, which means 'cow product' since the affix has been added in the sense of modification. The other illustration is *nāvyam*, which is derived by adding *yat* after the syntactically connected nominal stem *nau* in the sense of 'navigable'. This affix is prescribed by (1129). The nominal stem *nau* ends in *au* and it is replaced by *āv* and the resultant form is *nāvyam*, which means the water in which boats can be navigated or which can be crossed by boats. The sūtra *eco 'yavāyāvaḥ* (22) could not apply here since *o* and *au* are not followed by *ac*.

3. वा० - अध्वपरिमाणे च । *adhvaparimāṇe ca* (Mbh 6. 1. 79 vtk 3)
लघु० - गव्यूतिः । *gavyūtiḥ.*

Trans. : Let *av* replace the *o* of *go* before *yūti* when a measure of road is signified.

PP. *goḥ yūtau vāntaḥ adhvaparimāṇe ca.*

Eluc. : The term *vāntaḥ* has been carried over from the sūtra *vānto yi pratyaye* and *yūtau* from the vārttika *goryūtau chandasi* (Mbh 6. 1. 79 vtk 2) which just precedes this vārttika in the Mahābhāṣya. Thus the elliptical vārttika becomes a complete sentence and means that the vowel *o* of *go* is substituted by *av* when the word *yūti* follows. The resultant derivative *gavyūtiḥ* means a measurement of road. Since *yūti* is not an affix, the substitute could not take place without the help of this vārttika. The word *gavyūtiḥ* means a distance of nearly four miles.

(25)अदेङ् गुणः । ***adeṅ guṇaḥ*. 1. 1. 2**
लघु० - अद् एङ् च गुणसंज्ञः स्यात् । *ad eṅ ca guṇasaṁjñaḥ syāt.*

Trans. : Let *at* (*a*) and *eṅ* (*e* and *o*) be designated as *guṇa*.

PP. *at eṅ guṇaḥ.*

Eluc. : The term *guṇa* is applied to each of these three vowels *a, e* and *o* whether they are derived or otherwise. For example, if any of these three is obtained by applying the term *guṇa*, it is derived. Under

(22) it has been explained that the guṇa vowel *e* comes in place of *i* at the end of the nominal stem *hari* by the sūtra *gherṅiti* (171) as the dative singular affix is *ṅit*. Consequently, the phoneme *i* changes into *e* in the illustration : *hare* + *e*. The vowel *e* at the end of *hare* has been substituted by the express mention of the technical term *guṇa*. Hence it is an illustration of tadbhāvita guṇa. On the other hand, the vowel *e* in *paca* + *e* is as an example of atadbhāvita *guṇa*. Why is this is an instance of atadbhāvita guṇa? The reason is that the vowel *e* in this case has not been brought about by applying the term *guṇa*. Instead, the vowel *e* has been substituted by *ṭita ātmanepadānāṁ ṭere* (507) by expressly mentioning the substitute *e*. It is true that the vowel *i* has been replaced with the vowel *e* but this process of substitution is not brought about by the express mention of the term *guṇa*.

In this sūtra taparakaraṇa is meant for all the items (*a* *e* and *o*). The following sūtra explains what *tapara* means :

(26) तपरस्तत्कालस्य । *taparastatkālasya.* 1. 1. 70

लघु० – तः परो यस्मात् स च तात् परश्चोच्चार्यमाणसमकालस्यैव संज्ञा स्यात् । *taḥ paro yasmāt sa ca tāt paraścoccāryamāṇasamakālasyaiva saṁjñā syāt.*

Trans. : Let the phoneme (vowel) which is followed by *t* and which is articulated after *t* denote the (homogeneous) phonemes of the same duration.

PP. *taparaḥ tatkālasya svasya rūpasya savarṇasya.*

Eluc. : The terms *svam rūpaṁ* are carried over from *svaṁ rūpaṁ śabdasyāśabdasaṁjñā* Pā. 1. 1. 68 into the present sūtra. The carried over terms *svam rūpam* are changed into the genitive by the process of vibhaktivipariṇāma. The term *savarṇasya* comes from *aṇudit savarṇasya cāpratyayaḥ* Pā. 1. 1. 69. The term *taparaḥ* in the sūtra is interpreted both as tatpuruṣa and bahuvrīhi compound. When it is understood as bahuvrīhi, it means a phoneme that has *t* after it. As tatpuruṣa compound it means a phoneme which follows *t*. Here taparakaraṇa is meant for both *a* and the elements denoted by *eṅ*. In the case of *a*, *t* follows it and in the latter case *eṅ* follows *t*. Both *a* and *eṅ* are tapara. The sūtra thus means : The phoneme (vowel), which is followed by *t* and which follows *t*, denotes itself and the homogeneous phonemes of the same duration (*samakālasya*).

The sūtra (11) lays down that the vowel which is not enjoined denotes itself and all other seventeen homogeneous counterparts irrespective of their duration. It means that the short vowel *a* which is not enjoined denotes itself, the long and the prolated counterparts. Each has six varieties. The six varieties of short *a* have one mora, the six varieties of long *ā* have two morae and the other six varieties of the prolated one, three morae. The first six varieties which have one-mora-duration are to be denoted by the short *a* followed by *t* or preceded by it by virtue of the present sūtra and not its eighteen varieties which would have been the case in the absence of this sūtra. Similarly *e* and *o* which have no homogeneous short counterparts denote only the homogeneous long counterparts of two-mora-duration when either they are preceded by *t* or followed by it. They do not denote the prolated counterparts which have more than two morae. The same holds true in respect of the other vowel sounds, *i, u, ṛ, ḷ,* etc.

According to this sūtra, the vowels *a, e* and *o* have been assigned the guṇa designation which has its application in the following sūtra.

(27) आद् गुणः । *ādguṇaḥ*. 6. 1. 87

लघु० – अवर्णादचि परे पूर्वपरयोरेको गुण आदेशः स्यात्। उपेन्द्रः। गङ्गोदकम्। *avarṇād aci pare pūrvaparayor eko guṇa ādeśaḥ syāt. upendraḥ. gaṅgodakam.*

Trans. : When *a* is followed by *ac,* let a single guṇa substitute replace both the preceding and the following (phonemes).

PP. *āt aci pūrvaparayoḥ ekaḥ guṇaḥ saṁhitāyām.*

Eluc. : The compound term *pūrvaparayoḥ,* occurring in the vṛtti of Varadarāja, is given because this sūtra falls in the domain of *ekaḥ pūrvaparayoḥ* Pā. 6. 1. 84. The domain extends upto Pā. 6. 1. 112. The term *aci* has been carried over from *iko yaṇaci* Pā. 6. 1. 77. The sūtra *saṁhitāyām* Pā. 6. 1. 72 is also a governing rule. So the word *saṁhitāyām* recurs here also. This word is to recur in all the sūtras ranging from Pā. 6. 1. 72 to Pā. 6. 1. 158 in a similar way. In this way the completed sūtra means that when extreme proximity is intended (*saṁhitāyām*), one guṇa element substitutes both the preceding and the following phonemes if the vowel *a* is followed by *ac.* When *a* follows *a,* this sūtra is blocked by *akaḥ savarṇe dīrghaḥ* (42) and when *a* is followed by *ec,* it is debarred by *vṛddhireci* (33). Effectively, the sutra means that when *a* is followed by *i u ṛ ḷ,* both the preceding and following vowels are replaced by a guṇa vowel.

In *upendraḥ* (*upa* + *indra*), which is a prādisamāsa, the condition of maximum proximity between two phonemes (*a* and *i*) is necessarily available. Hence the present sūtra has its scope. Since *a* at the end of *upa* is followed by the *i* of *indra,* a guṇa vowel replaces both *a* and *i.* The substituenda *a* and *i* have respectively the throat and the palate as the places of pronunciation. Therefore the substitute should have the same places of articulation in order to be the most similar substitute. With the help of the sūtra *sthāne 'ntaratamaḥ* (17), the substitute *e* having both the throat and the palate as the places of articulation replaces both *a* and *i*. Thus *upendraḥ* is obtained. Similarly in *gaṅgodakam* (*gaṅgā* + *udaka*), the substituenda *ā* and *u* have both the throat and the lips as the places of articulation. Therefore *o* which is articulated with the help of both the throat and the lips, becomes the most similar substitute in place of both *a* and *u*. Thus the resultant form *gaṅgodakam* is obtained. There is no problem so far as the first illustration is concerned since the combination of both *a* and *i* have two morae and the guṇa vowel *e* also has two morae. This is not the case with the second illustration. The *ā of gaṅgā* and *u* of *udaka* together have three morae, whereas the substitute has only two morae. Should the replacement also have three morae? Here the sūtra *taparastatkālasya* (26) solves the problem. Since *eṅ* is preceded by *t*, only *e* and *o* having two morae can have the designation *guṇa*. Thus the sūtra *ādguṇaḥ* enjoins the guṇa substitute of two morae in place of both the following and preceding vowels. This is the reason why the guṇa substitute of two morae will replace even the substituenda having three or more morae.

In the other two illustrations in which *a* is followed by *ṛ* and *ḷ*, the sūtra *uraṇ raparaḥ* (29) is applied. According to Varadarāja, the term *ra* in the bahuvrīhi compound *raparaḥ*, which occurs in the sūtra (29), is a pratyāhāra. With the help of the sūtra *ādirantyena sahetā* (4), this pratyāhāra is formed with the repha of the pratyāhārasūtra *ha ya va raṭ* as the initial member and akāra within the *laṇ* pratyāhārasūtra as the last member of the *ra*-pratyāhāra since the phoneme *a* being anunāsika has been designated as *it* in accordance with the following sūtra :

(28) उपदेशेऽजनुनासिक इत्। ***upadeśe 'janunāsika it.* 1. 3. 2**

लघु० - उपदेशेऽनुनासिकोऽज् इत्संज्ञः स्यात्। प्रतिज्ञाऽऽनुनासिक्याः पाणिनीयाः। 'लण्'-सूत्रस्थावर्णेन सहोच्चार्यमाणो रेफो रलयोः संज्ञा। *upadeśe 'nunāsiko 'j itsaṁjñaḥ syāt. pratijñā ''nunāsikyāḥ pāṇinīyāḥ. 'laṇ'-sūtrasthāvarṇena sahoccāryamāṇo repho ralayoḥ saṁjñā.*

Trans. : Let the speech unit denoted by *ac* (vowel) which is anunāsika in upadeśa get the designation *it*. That a phonetic sound is nasalized is known by the (teacher-student) convention in Pāṇini's grammatical tradition. (It is the tradition of the Pāṇinīyas that determines whether a vowel in upadeśa is nasalized or not). The repha combined with the (nasalized) akāra within the pratyāhārasūtra *laṇ* denotes both repha and lakāra.

PP. *upadeśe ac anunāsikaḥ it.*

Eluc. : This sūtra enjoins that the nasalized vowel occurring in upadeśa is to be designated as *it*. It is known in Pāṇini's grammatical tradition by pratijñā (*guruśiṣyaparamparā*) that a particular vowel in upadeśa is nasalized. Here in the pratyāhārasūtra *laṇ*, akāra is accepted as nasalized and hence it is termed *it*. Then the repha occurring in the pratyāhārasūtra *ha ya va raṭ* combined with *a* within *laṇ* becomes *ra* pratyāhāra which denotes both repha and lakāra leaving the intervening *ṭ* since it is *it* by *halantyam* (1). The application of this pratyāhāra is observed in the following sūtra :

(29) उरण् रपरः । *uraṇ raparaḥ*. 1. 1. 51

लघु० – ऋ इति त्रिंशतः संज्ञा इत्युक्तं तत्स्थाने योऽण् स रपरः सन्नेव प्रवर्तते । कृष्णर्द्धिः । तवल्कारः । *ṛ iti triṁśataḥ saṁjñā ityuktam tatsthāne yo 'ṇ sa raparaḥ sanneva pravartate. kṛṣṇarddhiḥ. tavalkāraḥ.*

Trans. : It has been said that the vowel *ṛ* denotes its thirty (homogeneous) forms. The elements denoted by *aṇ* substituting *ṛ* are always followed by *ra* pratyāhāra.

PP. *uḥ sthāne aṇ raparaḥ.*

Eluc. : The word *sthāne* comes from *sthāne 'ntaratamaḥ* Pā. 1. 1. 50. The term *uḥ* is the genitive form of *ṛ*. The word *raparaḥ* is a bahuvrīhi compound which means that (the *aṇ* in this case), which is substituted in place of *ṛ* is always followed by *ra* pratyāhāra, that is, the substituted *aṇ* is either followed by *r* or *l*, for example *ar, al, āl, ār, ir, il, ur, ul,* etc. In the illustrations given in the Laghu, the first exemplifies *aṇ* being followed by *r* and the second illustrates the one followed by *l*. The compound word *kṛṣṇarddhiḥ* (*kṛṣṇasya ṛddhiḥ --> kṛṣṇa + ṛddhi*) is a genitive tatpuruṣa. This being a compound, close proximity is necessarily available. By *ādguṇaḥ* (27) a guṇa substitute has to come in place of both *a* at the end of *kṛṣṇa* and *ṛ* at the beginning of *ṛddhi*. So far as the place of articulation is concerned, the throat is common to all the three. The cerebrum or teeth are not common. By the present rule, *ra* pratyāhāra is to necessarily follow *aṇ* which is going to be substituted in place of *ṛ*. Thus *a* is rendered *ar* by the present sūtra. Now being most similar, the substitute *ar* replaces both *a* and *ṛ* with the help of the sūtra *sthāne 'ntaratamaḥ* (17). The substituenda being *a* and *ṛ* have the throat and the cerebrum as the places of articulation and the substitute being *ar* has both these places of articulation. Similarly *al* will be substituted in place of *a* and *ḷ* in accordance with the same sūtra since places of articulation of both the substitutes and the substituenda are the same. In *tavalkāraḥ* (*tava ḷkāraḥ*), the substitute is *al*. It is *rapara* since *l* is included in *ra* pratyāhāra. Thus *al*, being denti-guttural, is most similar to the substituenda, which also are articulated with the help of the throat and the teeth. At this stage, the sūtra *sthāne 'ntaratamaḥ* (17) applies and the form *tavalkara* is obtained. The word *tavalkāraḥ* (*tava ḷkāraḥ*) is not a compound. Hence saṁhitā (close proximity) depends upon the intention of the speaker. When it is intended, guṇa sandhi takes place. Otherwise it remains as it is : *tava ḷkāraḥ*.

We referred to the formation of *ra* pratyāhāra while commenting on the pratyāhārasūtras. The Kāśikā and Bhaṭṭoji Dīkṣita, interpreting akāra in the pratyāhārasūtra *laṇ* as anunāsika, advocate the formation of *ra* pratyāhāra. Nāgeśa criticizes this view and says that neither Pāṇini nor Patañjali has mentioned anywhere or dropped any hint to this effect. Moreover, had Pāṇini intended to treat the *a* within *laṇ* pratyāhāra-sūtra as anunāsika and as a consequence had he intended to have the *ra* pratyāhāra, he would not have enunciated the sūtra *ato lrāntasya* Pā. 7. 2. 2 as we have it. Instead he would have had the sūtra as *ato rāntasya* since *ra* would have included *l* in it. Half a mora would have been saved in that way. At the most a vārttika such as *lapara iti vaktavyam* could have sufficed.

(30) लोपः शाकल्यस्य । *lopaḥ śākalyasya*. 8. 3. 19

लघु० – अवर्णपूर्वयोः पदान्तयोर्यवयोर्लोपो वाऽशि परे । *avarṇapūrvayoḥ padāntayor yavayor lopo vā 'śi pare.*

Trans. : Let (the consonantal sounds) *y* and *v* occurring at the end of a pada when preceded by *a* and followed by *aś* be optionally replaced by lopa.

PP. *apūrvayoḥ padāntayoḥ vyoḥ lopaḥ śākalyasya aśi* (*saṁhitāyām*).

Eluc. : Three terms are carried over into this sūtra. The compound *apūrvayoḥ* comes from the sūtra *bho-bhago-agho-a-pūrvasya yo 'śi* Pā. 8. 3. 17 (by changing the genitive singular into the genitive dual). The process of changing of genitive singular *a-pūrvasya* into *apūrvayoḥ* which is genitive dual is known as vacanavipariṇāma. The dvandva compound *vyoḥ* is carried over from *vyorlaghuprayatnataraḥ śākaṭāyanasya* Pā. 8. 3. 18. The present sūtra is in the domain of *padasya* Pā. 8. 1. 16. Since the word *padasya* qualifies *vyoḥ* which is genitive dual, it changes into genitive dual by the process of vacanavipariṇāma. Also being a qualifier, it has to take *anta* at its end by tadantavidhi (Pā. 1. 1. 72). Hence *padasya* is read here as *padāntayoḥ*. With these terms read into the present sūtra, the meaning will be as follows : When *v* or *y* comes at the end of a pada and when either is preceded by akāra and followed by an element denoted by *aś* pratyāhāra, *y* and *v* are replaced by lopa. This is the view of Śākalya. Pāṇini's view is different. Hence the lopa-replacement comes optionally in place of the pada-final semi-vowel *y* or *v*.

In the illustration *hare + iha, e* at the end of *hare* is replaced by *ay* by *eco 'yavāyāvaḥ* (22) and the form becomes *haray + iha*. Since *hare* being vocative singular is a pada by *suptiṅantaṁ padam* (14), *y* is at the end of a pada. Similarly in *viṣṇo + iha, o* is replaced by *av*, as a consequence *v* occurs at the end of a pada (*viṣṇav + iha*). Both *y* and *v* are preceded by *a* in the illustrations and are followed by *i* which is signified by the *aś*-pratyāhāra. The conditions laid down by Śākalya are fulfilled. Hence they are replaced by zero (*lopa*). After the elision of *y* and *v*, the illustrations obtained are : *hara iha* and *viṣṇa iha*. At this stage, the sūtra *ādguṇaḥ* (27) presents itself since *a* is followed by *ac* in the form of *i* in both the illustrations. In the illustrations single guṇa substitutes, in the form of *e* and *o* respectively, become available. To block this, the following sūtra comes into force :

(31) पूर्वत्रासिद्धम्। *pūrvatrāsiddham.* 8. 2. 1

लघु० - सपादसप्ताध्यायीं प्रति त्रिपाद्यसिद्धा त्रिपाद्यामपि पूर्वं प्रति परं शास्त्रमसिद्धम्। हर इह; हरयिह। विष्ण इह; विष्णविह। *sapādasaptādhyāyīṁ prati tripādyasiddhā, tripādyām api pūrvaṁ prati paraṁ śāstram asiddham. hara iha, harayiha. viṣṇa iha, viṣṇaviha.*

Trans. : The triad of the last three quarters of the Aṣṭādhyāyī is considered inoperative (*asiddha*) with respect to the seven chapters and a quarter, i. e. that which precedes (this sūtra) and in the triad also the following aphorism is considered inoperative with respect to the ones that precede.

PP. *pūrvatra asiddham.*

Eluc. : This is a governing (*adhikāra*) sūtra. Its scope extends up to the end of Aṣṭādhyāyī. Through this rule Pāṇini virtually divides his

Aṣṭādhyāyī into two parts : Seven chapters and a quarter (*sapāda-saptādhyāyī*) on the one side and three quarter-chapters (*tripādī*) on the other. The rule says that if an operation is ordered by a rule in the last three quarter-chapters (*tripādī*), it will be deemed not to have taken place in the view of the rule that belongs to the sapādasaptādhyāyī.

In the illustrations *hara iha* and *viṣṇa iha*, *y* and *v* have been elided by the preceding sūtra *lopaḥ śākalyasya* Pā. 8. 3. 19 which belongs to the tripādī. The single guṇa substitute is made available here by *ādguṇaḥ* Pā. 6. 1. 87 which belongs to sapādasaptādhyāyī. The operation of the sūtra *lopaḥ śākalyasya* is deemed not to have taken place in view of *ādguṇaḥ* (27). As a consequence, the rule *ādguṇaḥ* does not apply, as it does not recognize the elision (*lopa*) of *y* and *v* in these illustrations. There is no *ac* following *a* because of the suspension of the operation of *lopaḥ śākalyasya* (30) resulting in the zero-replacement of *y* and *v*. The consonants *y* and *v* virtually exist and as a result there is an intervention of either *y* or *v* between *a* and *i*. So *hara iha* and *viṣṇa iha* remain as they are. This is according to the view of Śākalya.

According to Pāṇini *y* and *v* are not elided. Hence the forms of both the illustrations would be *harayiha* and *viṣṇaviha*. As such, where there is elision, the forms are *hara iha* and *viṣṇa iha* and where there is no elision of *y* or *v*, the forms are *harayiha* and *viṣṇaviha*.

(32) वृद्धिरादैच्। *vṛddhirādaic.* 1. 1. 1

लघु० - आदैच वृद्धिसंज्ञः स्यात्। *ādaic ca vṛddhisaṁjñaḥ syāt.*

Trans. : Let (the vowels) *ā*, *ai* and *au* be denoted by (the technical term) *vṛddhi*.

PP. *vṛddhiḥ āt aic.*

Eluc. : The taparakaraṇa in the sūtra is purported only for *aic* and not for a long *ā*. Since the vowel *ā* is not included in the *aṇ*-pratyāhāra, it does not denote its other homogeneous counterparts by the sūtra *aṇudit savarṇasya cāpratyayaḥ* (11). Hence there is no need to attribute a purpose to *t* for the sake of *ā*. It has a purpose as far as *ai* and *au* are concerned. Prolated *ai* and *au* are not denoted by *aic* since it follows *t*. Moreover, for the same reason, the substitute will be of two morae only even if the substituenda have more than two morae. Take, for example, the case of *gaṅgaughaḥ* (*gaṅgā* + *ogha*). In this illustration the substituenda are *ā* and *o*. They have four morae but the substitute (vṛddhi, in this case *au*) in place of the substituenda *ā* and *o* having four morae will be of two morae only. The reason is that *aic* is enunciated after *t* and as such *ai* and *au* of two morae only are available for replacement. This is the purpose of taparakaraṇa of *aic* in the sūtra *vṛddhirādaic* (32).

Like the guṇa designation, the vṛddhi designation also is assigned to both tadbhāvita and atadbhāvita *ā, ai* and *au*. In *āśvalāyanaḥ* and *aupagavaḥ* both the vowels *ā* and *au* are tadbhāvita (derived by the specific mention of vṛddhi). In the first, the vṛddhi substitution has taken place by *kiti ca* (997) when the taddhita affix *phak* has been introduced by *naḍādibhyaḥ phak* Pā. 4. 1. 99. In the second, *taddhiteṣvacāmādeḥ* (934) has brought about *au* in place of the initial vowel *u* also by the specific mention of vṛddhi when the taddhita affiix *aṇ* has been added after *upagu* by *prāgdīvyato 'ṇ* Pā. 4. 1. 83. We come across atadbhāvita *ā* in *mālā* and *śālā* since the vowel *ā* in both these words is not brought about by any vṛddhi injunction by Pāṇini as in the two illustrations mentioned above. Still this *ā* is termed *vṛddhi* by the present sūtra and that is why the affix *cha* has been introduced to the stems *mālā* and *śālā* by *vṛddhācchaḥ* (1073) and we have *mālīyaḥ* and *śālīyaḥ*.

The application of the technical term *vṛddhi* is seen in the following sūtra :

(33) वृद्धिरेचि । *vṛddhireci*. 6. 1. 88

लघु० - आदेचि परे वृद्धिरेकादेशः स्यात्। गुणापवादः। कृष्णैकत्वम्। गङ्गौघः। देवैश्वर्यम्। कृष्णौत्कण्ठ्यम्। *ād eci pare vṛddhir ekādeśaḥ syāt. guṇāpavādaḥ. kṛṣṇaikatvam. gaṅgaughaḥ. devaiśvaryam. kṛṣṇautkaṇṭhyam.*

Trans. : If *ec* follows *a*, then let a single vṛddhi replacement come (in place of both the preceding *a* and the following vowel denoted by *ec*). This is an exception to *ādguṇaḥ* (27).

PP. *āt eci pūrvaparayoḥ ekaḥ vṛddhiḥ saṁhitāyām.*

Eluc. : The terms *pūrvaparayoḥ* and *ekaḥ*, are carried over into this sūtra from the governing rule *ekaḥ pūrvaparayoḥ* Pā. 6. 1. 81. The term *āt* is lent into this rule from *ādguṇaḥ* Pā. 6. 1. 87. After these padas have been read into this sūtra, its meaning will be as follows : In saṁhitā when *e, o, ai or au* follows *a*, either *ai* or *au* replaces both *a* and the following phoneme denoted by *ec* on the basis of the similarity of articulation, aided by *sthāne 'ntaratamaḥ* (17).

This sūtra is an exception to *ādguṇaḥ* (27) which prescribes a single guṇa substitute in place of *a* and the following vowel denoted by *ac*. The vowels denoted by *ec* are included in the vowels denoted by *ac*. In the illustration *gaṅgaughaḥ* (*gaṅgā* + *ogha*), *ādguṇaḥ* (27) is applicable since here *ā* is a homogeneous counterpart of *a* and is denoted by it according to the sūtra *aṇudit savarṇasya cāpratyayaḥ* (11). Even then Pāṇini has enunciated the present sūtra. This comes to mean that *ādguṇaḥ* is a general rule which is blocked by *vṛddhireci* for fear of redundancy of the latter which has less scope than the former. The vṛddhi sūtra will carve out *ec* from *ac*. Out of the remaining vowel sounds, the vowel *a* when followed by *a* is also carved out by *akaḥ savarṇe dīrghaḥ* (42). Thus after leaving aside the area where the exception rules have performed their function, the scope of *ādguṇaḥ* is confined to the following situation : The guṇa vowel replaces both the preceding *a* and the following vowel denoted by *ik* (*i, u, ṛ* and *ḷ*). There is a paribhāṣā to this effect : *prakalpya cāpavādaviṣayam utsargo 'bhiniviśate* (Abhyankar, 63) 'the general rule becomes applicable only after leaving aside the cases where the exception rule has already performed its function.' In the light of the foregoing explanation, it can be fairly held that the present sūtra is an exception to *ādguṇaḥ* (27).

There are four illustrations given in the Laghu : 1. *kṛṣṇaikatvam* (oneness with Kṛṣṇa), 2. *gaṅgaughaḥ* (torrent of the Ganges), 3. *devaiśvaryam* (supremacy of a god) and 4. *kṛṣṇautkaṇṭhyam* (longing for Kṛṣṇa). Take the first example *kṛṣṇaikatvam* : *kṛṣṇa* + *ekatva*. In this example *a* and *e*, which have the throat and the palate as the places of articulation, are replaced by the vṛddhi vowel *ai* which also has the throat and the palate as the places of pronunciation. The replacement is in accordance with the sūtra *sthāne 'ntaratamaḥ* (17). Similarly, in *gaṅgaughaḥ*, *ā* and *o* being gutturo-labial are replaced by *au* which is also gutturo-labial. The vṛddhi substitution takes place in the same manner in the other two illustrations, namely, *devaiśvaryam* (*deva* + *aiśvarya*) and *kṛṣṇautkaṇṭhyam* (*kṛṣṇa* + *autkaṇṭhya*).

(34) एत्येधत्यूठ्सु । *etyedhatyūṭhsu*. 6. 1. 89

लघु० - अवर्णादेजाद्योरेत्येधत्योरूठि च परे वृद्धिरेकादेशः स्यात्। पररूपगुणापवादः। उपैति। उपैधते। प्रष्ठौहः। एजाद्योः किम्? उपेतः। मा भवान् प्रेदिधत्। *avarṇād ejādyor etyedhatyor ūṭhi ca pare vṛddhirekādeśaḥ syāt. pararūpaguṇāpavādaḥ. upaiti. upaidhate. praṣṭhauhaḥ. ejādyoḥ kim ? upetaḥ. mā bhavān predidhat.*

Trans. : When *a* is followed by the verbal forms of the roots *iṇ* and *edh* beginning with *ec* and also when it is followed by (the substitute) *ūṭh*, let a single vṛddhi vowel replace both *a* and the following *ec* or *ū*. This is an exception to *eṅi pararūpam* (38) and *ādguṇaḥ* (27).

PP. *āt eci eti-edhati-ūṭhsu pūrvaparayoḥ ekaḥ vṛddhiḥ saṁhitāyām.*

Eluc. : The terms *āt* and *eci* are respectively carried over from the sūtras *ādguṇaḥ* Pā. 6. 1. 87 and *vṛddhireci* Pā. 6. 1. 88. The terms *ekaḥ pūrvaparayoḥ* are carried over from the governing rule *ekaḥ pūrvaparayoḥ* Pā. 6. 1. 81.The term *eci* can qualify only *eti* and *edhati* and not *ūṭh* since the latter does not begin with a vowel denoted by *ec*. This is the reason why the dual number has been used in *etyedhatyoḥ* in Varadarāja's vṛtti. The term *ūṭhi* has been used separately with a singular number. By the vārttika *yasmin vidhistadādāvalgrahaṇe, ec* becomes a qualifier at the beginning since it is included in *al*. The vārttika prescribes that when a grammatical operation is qualified by an *al* ending in the locative, it always becomes a qualifier at the beginning. Hence the expression *ejādyor etyedhatyoḥ* which means 'when the verbal forms of *iṇ* and *edh* which begin with *ec* follow'. As a result the completed sūtra means : If the phoneme *a* is followed by the verbal forms of *iṇ* and *edh* beginning with a phoneme denoted by the abbreviatory term *ec,* both the preceding *a* and the following vowel signified by *ec* are replaced with a single vṛddhi vowel when extreme proximity is intended. Similarly, when *a* is followed by the substitute *ūṭh,* both *a* and *ū* are replaced with a vṛddhi vowel *au.* In this case *ādguṇaḥ* (27) is available for application but it is blocked by the present aphorism. In this sense it is an exception to *ādguṇaḥ*. In the first two illustrations *eṅi pararūpam* (38) is available. The sūtra says that if a verbal form beginning with a vowel denoted by *eṅ* follows a preverb ending in *a,* then a single substitute in the form of a vowel denoted by *eṅ* comes in place of the preceding *a* and the beginning *eṅ*-vowel of the verb form. The same condition is available in *upaiti* (*upa* + *eti* 'he comes near') and *upaidhate* (*upa* + *edhate* 'it increases'). The preverb is *upa* in both the illustrations and it ends in *a*. The verb forms also begin with the vowel *e,* a denotatum of *eṅ*. Here pararūpa substitution is made available by *eṅi pararūpam* (38) but the present sūtra overrules this. In that sense the present sūtra is an exception to *eṅi pararūpam*. The third illustration is *praṣṭhauhaḥ*. The form is derived like this : *praṣṭha* + *vah* + *ṇvi* --> *praṣṭhavāh* + *śas* --> *praṣṭha* + *ūh* + *as* {samprasāraṇa by *vāha ūṭh* (256) in respect of *bha*-designated *vāh*} --> *praṣṭhauha* + *as* (by the present rule) --> *praṣṭhauhaḥ* (ablative, genitive singular or accusative plural). The nominal stem *praṣṭhavāh* means a young bull being trained for the plough.

Why has it been said that the verb forms of *iṇ* and *edh* should begin with *ec?* Had this not been said, the rule would have applied in respect of all the verbal forms of these two roots. Take for example *upetaḥ* (approached). In this *a* is available and also the verbal form *itaḥ* of *iṇ* but it does not begin with *ec*. Hence no single vṛddhi replacement comes in place of *a* and *i*. Instead the guṇa substitution takes place. That is why the insertion of the term *ec* in the sūtra is significant. Similarly in *predidhat* (*pra* + *ididhat*), *ididhat* is the aorist third person singular form of *edh* with a causative affix. This is the verbal form of *edh* but does not have *ec* at the beginning because the augment *āṭ* has not been inserted at the head of the verbal root *edh* in accordance with *na māṅyoge* (440). The penultimate vowel *e* of *edh* has already been shortened by *ṇau caṅyupadhāyā hrasvaḥ* (529). Thus the verbal form has a short *i* at the beginning and not a vowel denoted by *ec*. Hence there is no single vṛddhi substitution for *a* of *pra* and *i* of *ididhat*. If *ejādi* were not there in the sūtra, then a vṛddhi substitution for both *a* of *pra* and *i* of *ididhat* would take place. In that case it would have been *praididhat* which is unwarranted.

4. वा० – अक्षादूहिन्यामुपसंख्यानम्। *akṣādūhinyāmupasaṅkhyānam.*
लघु० – अक्षौहिणी सेना। *akṣauhiṇī senā.*

Trans. : It may be said additionally that when *ūhinī* follows *akṣa*, let a single vṛddhi substitution replace both *a* (at the end of *akṣa*) and *ū* (at the beginning of *ūhinī*).

Eluc. : Here the incidence of guṇa has been blocked by this vārttika. The *n* of *ūhinī* is replaced by *ṇ* in accordance with the sūtra *pūrvapadāt saṁjñāyāmagaḥ* (1262). Thus *akṣauhiṇī*, which means an army having a particular arrangement, is obtained.

5. वा० – प्राद् उहोढोढ्येषैष्येषु। *prādūhoḍhoḍhyeṣaiṣyeṣu.*
लघु० – प्रौहः। प्रौढः। प्रौढिः। प्रैषः। प्रैष्यः। *prauhaḥ, prauḍhaḥ, prauḍhiḥ, praiṣaḥ, praiṣyaḥ.*

Trans. : When *a* obtaining at the end of *pra* is followed by *ūha*, *ūḍha*, *ūḍhi*, *eṣa* and *eṣya*, let a (single) vṛddhi substitution replace the preceding *a* and the following *ac* (at the beginning of these terms).

Eluc. : From the governing sūtra *ekaḥ pūrvaparayoḥ*, the terms *ekaḥ* and *pūrvaparayoḥ* are read into this vārttika. As such the vārttika prescribes a single vṛddhi substitute in place of the preceding *a* at the end of the preverb *pra* and the *ac* which obtains at the beginning of the words *ūha*, *ūḍha*, *ūḍhi*, *eṣa* and *eṣya*. *pra* + *ūha* --> *pr au ha*--> *prauhaḥ* which means 'a good argument' or 'one who uses a good argument'.

A vṛddhi replacement will take place similarly in respect of the following compounds : *pra* + *ūḍha* --> *pr au ḍha*--> *prauḍhaḥ* 'full-grown', *pra* + *ūḍhi* --> *pr au ḍhi* --> *prauḍhiḥ* 'audacity'. In the illustrations : *pra* + *eṣa* and *pra* + *eṣya*, *a* occurring at the end of *pra* and *e* occurring at the beginning of *eṣa* and *eṣya* are replaced by a single vṛddhi vowel, which in these cases is *ai*. *pra* + *eṣa* --> *pr ai ṣa* --> *praiṣaḥ* 'order or command', *pra* + *eṣya* --> *pr ai ṣya* --> *praiṣyaḥ* 'a servant'.

6. वा० – ऋते च तृतीयासमासे । *ṛte ca tṛtīyāsamāse.*
लघु० – सुखेन ऋतः सुखार्तः । तृतीयेति किम्? परमर्तः । *sukhena ṛtaḥ sukhārtaḥ. tṛtīyeti kim? paramartaḥ.*

Trans. : In tṛtīyā tatpuruṣa compound let *a* (at the end of the first member) and the following *ṛ* (at the beginning of the second member), *ṛta*, be replaced by a vṛddhi vowel.

Eluc. : In the compound *sukhārtaḥ*, *sukha* ends in the instrumental case-ending. It is followed by *ṛta*. Both the members are compounded in accordance with the sūtra *kartṛkaraṇe kṛtā bahulam* Pā. 2. 1. 32 (cf. KN, IV, p. 557). Hence it is a tṛtīyātatpuruṣa, *sukhena ṛtaḥ* --> *sukha ṭā ṛta su* and we have *sukha ṛta* after the case-endings have been elided by *supo dhātu...* (718). At this stage, the present vārttika becomes applicable. Then *a* at the end of *sukha* and *ṛ* at the beginning of *ṛta* become the substituenda to be replaced by a single vṛddhi vowel. The vṛddhi vowel *ā* is followed by *r* (*rapara*) by *uraṇ raparaḥ* (29). Now the substitute and the substituenda both have the throat and the cerebrum as the places of articulation. They are similar and hence *ā*(*r*) can replace both *a* and *ṛ*. The resultant term is *sukhārtaḥ* 'happy' (lit. 'visited by happiness').

Why does the vārttika say that the vṛddhi substitution takes place only in tṛtīyāsamāsa? This single vṛddhi substitution does not take place when the same condition obtains except in a tṛtīyātatpuruṣa.The compound word *paramartaḥ* is the counter-example : *paramaś cāsau ṛtaś ca*. It is a karmadhāraya compound and not a tṛtīyāsamāsa. Hence no vṛddhi substitution will take place. Instead, guṇa substitution replaces both *a* at the end of *parama* and *ṛ* at the beginning of *ṛta*. The guṇa substitution here is *a* followed by *r*. The finished form will be *paramartaḥ* which means 'liberated'.

7. वा० – प्र-वत्सतर-कम्बल-वसनार्ण-दशानाम् ऋणे । *pra-vatsatara-kambala-vasanārṇa-daśānām ṛṇe.*

लघु० – प्रार्णम्। वत्सतरार्णम् इत्यादि। *prārṇam. vatsatarārṇam ityādi.*

Trans. : When *pra, vatsatara, kambala, vasana, ṛṇa* and *daśa* are followed by *ṛṇa,* let *a* (at the end of these preceding six words) and the *ṛ* (at the beginning of *ṛṇa*) be replaced by a single vṛddhi substitute.

Eluc. : The genitive plural here should be taken in the sense of ablative plural. The carried over terms from the governing sūtra *ekaḥ pūrvaparayoḥ* are also paraphrased in this vārttika. The vārttika, then, prescribes a single vṛddhi substitution in place of the ending *a* of the six words and the *ṛ* at the beginning of the word *ṛṇa*. The vṛddhi substitution *ā,* rendered *ār* by *uraṇ raparaḥ* (29) replaces the preceding and following vowels. The illustrations are as follows :

1. *pra* + *ṛṇa* = *prārṇam* = principal debt
2. *vatsatara* + *ṛṇa* = *vatsatarārṇam* = debt of a young bull
3. *kambala* + *ṛṇa* = *kambalārṇam* = debt of a blanket
4. *vasana* + *ṛṇa* = *vasanārṇam* = debt of a cloth
5. *ṛṇa* + *ṛṇa* = *ṛṇārṇam* = debt for a debt
6. *daśa* + *ṛṇa* = *daśārṇaḥ* = name of a country

(35) उपसर्गाः क्रियायोगे । *upasargāḥ kriyāyoge.* 1. 4. 59

लघु० – प्रादयः क्रियायोगे उपसर्ग-संज्ञाः स्युः। 1. प्र 2. परा 3. अप 4. सम् 5. अनु 6. अव 7. निस् 8. निर् 9. दुस् 10. दुर् 11. वि 12. आङ् 13. नि 14. अधि 15. अपि 16. अति 17. सु 18. उद् 19. अभि 20. प्रति 21. परि 22. उप – एते प्रादयः। *prādayaḥ kriyāyoge upasarga-saṁjñāḥ syuḥ.* 1. *pra* 2. *parā* 3. *apa* 4. *sam* 5. *anu* 6. *ava* 7. *nis* 8. *nir* 9. *dus* 10. *dur* 11. *vi* 12. *āṅ* 13. *ni* 14. *adhi* 15. *api* 16. *ati* 17. *su* 18. *ud* 19. *abhi* 20. *prati* 21. *pari* 22. *upa - ete prādayaḥ.*

Trans. : Let the items enumerated in the list headed by *pra* be designated as *upasarga* when they are used with a verb (*kriyā*).

PP. *prādayaḥ upasargāḥ kriyāyoge.*

Eluc. : According to Patañjali one sūtra *prādaya upasargāḥ kriyāyoge* has been split here into two by the technique of yogavibhāga. Thus *prādayaḥ* becomes an independent sūtra which means that the items *pra*, etc. are termed *nipāta* if they do not denote a thing (*sattva*). The compound word *prādayaḥ* is carried over into the present sūtra and lays down that the items included in the list of *prādi* are designated as *upasarga* when they are used with a verb. Consequently the items enumerated in the *cādi* class cannot be assigned the upasarga designation. The compound word *prādayaḥ* is a tadguṇasaṁvijñāna-bahuvrīhi which is analysed as : *pra ādir yeṣām te prādayaḥ*. As such, this includes *pra* also in the list headed by *pra*. The sūtra then means : The items headed by *pra* get the designation *upasarga* when they are prefixed to a verb.

When the upsargas *nir* and *dur* are prefixed to the verbal root *ay*, the phoneme *r* occurring at the end of these upasargas is replaced by the phoneme *l*. The other upasargas, *nis* and *dus*, also change into *nir* and *dur* by the sūtra *sasajuṣo ruḥ* Pā. 8. 2. 66. Still the repha of these two upasargas is not replaced by lakāra by *upasargasyāyatau* Pā. 8. 2. 19. The reason is that the repha replacing the phoneme *s* by vitue of the sūtra *sasajuṣo ruḥ* is deemed not to have taken place in respect of the sūtra *upasargasyāyatau* Pā. 8. 2. 19 in deference to the sūtra *pūrvatrāsiddham* Pā. 8. 2. 1 since the former sūtra is subsequent to the latter. This explains why '*nis* and *nir*' and '*dus* and *dur*' have been separately given in the list of the preverbs. One more point should be borne in mind here. The upsarga *ud* is generally read as *ut*. This is not correct. The correct reading is *ud* as is clear from the sūtras *udaścaraḥ sakarmakāt* Pā. 1. 3. 53, *udi kūle rujivahoḥ* Pā. 3. 2. 31, *udi grahaḥ* Pā. 3. 3.35, *udi śrayatiyautipūdruvaḥ* Pā. 3. 3. 49, *udaḥ sthāstambhoḥ pūrvasya* Pā. 8. 4. 60, etc.

---

1. The term *tadguṇa-saṁvijñāna bahuvrīhi* refers to a kind of bahuvrīhi compound where the object denoted by the compound includes also what is denoted by the constituent members of the compound. In the expression *citravāsasam ānaya*, the compound *citravāsas* denotes a person wearing clothes of several hues. The object denoted by the compound is a person who wears a variegated dress. Obviously the object denoted by compound includes what is denoted by the constituent members of the compound. This is tadguṇa-saṁvijñāna bahuvrīhi. In the same manner the term *prādayaḥ* is a tadguṇa-saṁvijñāna bahuvrīhi since it includes the preverb *pra* in the list denoted by the compound *prādayaḥ*. The other is atadguṇa-saṁvijñāna bahuvrīhi since the object denoted by this compound does not include what is denoted by the constituent members of the compound. In the expression *dṛṣṭasamudram ānaya*, the compound *dṛṣṭasamudra* is an atadguṇa-saṁvijñāna bahuvrīhi since the object (here a person who has seen the ocean) denoted by the compound does not include the ocean in the manner in which the object denoted by the compound *citravāsas* includes the variegated clothes denoted by the term *citravāsas*.

(36) भूवादयो धातवः । ***bhūvādayo dhātavaḥ*. 1. 3. 1**
लघु० - क्रियावाचिनो भ्वादयो धातु-संज्ञाः स्युः । *kriyāvācino bhvādayo dhātu-saṁjñāḥ syuḥ.*

Trans. : Let the items bhū, etc. expressing action be designated as *dhātu.*

PP. *bhūvādayaḥ dhātavaḥ.*

Eluc. : The word *bhūvādayaḥ* is a dvandva-seeded bahuvrīhi compound. The dvandva compound is analysed as follows : *bhūś ca vāś ca bhūvau,* in this way *bhū* and *vā* are combined to yield an itaretara-dvandva compound. The analysed form of the bahuvrīhi compound with its internal itaretaradvandva compound would be like this : *bhūvau ādī yeṣāṁ te = bhūvādayaḥ.* There are two *ādi*'s in the analysis. The first *ādi* is interpreted in the sense of 'and so on' and paraphrased with *bhū.* The second *ādi* means *prakāra* 'type' and is paraphrased with *vā.* Thus the compound *bhūvādayaḥ* means 'the words beginning with *bhū*, etc. which are similar to *vā'*. The term *vā* is a gatyarathaka root (signifying movement). So the similarity in this respect consists in 'expressing action'. Consequently the items which begin with *bhū*, etc. and which are similar to *vā*, that is, which express action are assigned the designation *dhātu* (root). The significance of the word *kriyāvācī,* which is given in the *vṛtti*, lies in the fact that if it had not been given here, then the word *yā*, for example, in *yāḥ paśyati* would have got the designation *dhātu*. As a consequence the *ā* of *yā* would have undergone lopa-substitution by virue of *āto dhātoḥ* (166) since *yā* is seen in the list of *bhvādi*. This eventuality is warded off by the inclusion of the word *kriyāvācino* in the vṛtti, since the word *yā* used in the above sentence is similar to the word *yā* given in the list of *bhvādi* but it is not kriyāvācī. The word used in the sentence above is an accusative plural form of the feminine pronominal stem *yad*, meaning 'who'.

(37) उपसर्गादृ ऋति धातौ । ***upasargād ṛti dhātau*. 6. 1. 91**
लघु० - अवर्णान्तादृ उपसर्गादृ ऋकारादौ धातौ परे वृद्धिरेकादेशः स्यात्। प्रार्च्छति। *avarṇāntād upasargād ṛkārādau dhātau pare vṛddhir ekādeśaḥ syāt. prārcchati.*

Trans. : If a verbal root beginning with *ṛ* follows an upasarga which ends in *a*, let a single vṛddhi-substitution take place.

PP. *āt upasargāt ṛti dhātau pūrvaparayoḥ ekaḥ vṛddhiḥ (saṁhitāyām).*

Eluc. : Into the present sūtra, *āt* has been carried over from *ādguṇaḥ* Pā. 6. 1. 87 and *vṛddhi* from *vṛddhireci* Pā. 6. 1. 88. The sūtra *ekaḥ pūrvaparayoḥ* is the governing rule. The term *āt*, which has been carried forward, qualifies the term *upasargāt* occurring in the present sūtra. With the help of *yena vidhistadantasya* Pā. 1. 1. 72, the expression *āt upasargāt*, given in the vṛtti, means 'an upasarga that ends in the phoneme *a*'. The term *ṛti*, which is in the locative singular, qualifies the term *dhātau*. According to the vārttika *yasmin vidhistadādāvalgrahaṇe*, *ṛ* will qualify the term *dhātau* by being its initial component. Thus the whole sūtra will mean : When a dhātu, which begins with a short *ṛ*, follows an upasarga ending in a short *a*, a single vṛddhi replacement comes in place of both, *a* at the end of a preverb and *ṛ* at the beginning of a verbal root. In the illustration given by Varadarāja, the vowel *a* at the end of *pra*, which is an upasarga and the vowel *ṛ* at the beginning of the verb form *ṛcchati*, which is a third person singular laṭ lakāra form of *ṛcch*, which is a dhātu by the sūtra *bhūvādayo dhātavaḥ* (36). Both coalesce and are replaced by a single vṛddhi vowel followed by *r* in accordance with the rule *uraṇ raparaḥ* (29). This sūtra is an exception to *ādguṇaḥ* (27).

The taparakaraṇa in *ṛti* is used to block vṛddhi in examples such as *upa + ṝkārīyati = uparkārīyati*. In this example *ṝ* is long whereas *ṛ* qualified with taparakaraṇa in the sūtra is short. Hence there is no vṛddhi substitution. Instead guṇa takes place here by *ādguṇaḥ* (27).

(38) एङि पररूपम्। *eṅi pararūpam.* 6. 1. 94

लघु० - आदुपसर्गाद् एङादौ धातौ परे पररूपमेकादेशः स्यात्। प्रेजते। उपोषति। *ād upasargād eṅādau dhātau pare pararūpam ekādeśaḥ syāt. prejate. upoṣati.*

Trans. : Let the form of the second be a single substitute for both the preceding and the following phonemes when the root beginning with a vowel denoted by the abbreviatory term *eṅ* follows a preverb ending in a short vowel *a*.

PP. *āt upasargāt eṅi dhātau pūrvaparayoḥ ekam pararūpam (saṁhitāyām).*

Eluc. : The present sūtra occurs in the domain of the governing rule *ekaḥ pūrvaparayoḥ*. So the whole sūtra is read here but the term *ekaḥ* is changed into the neuter to accord with the word *pararūpam* occurring in the present sūtra. The term *āt* has been carried over into this sūtra from *ādguṇaḥ* Pā. 6. 1. 87 and it qualifies the term *upasargāt*. The term *dhātau* is carried over from *upasargād ṛti dhātau* Pā. 6. 1. 91 and is qualified by *eṅ*. The former is tadantavidhi by *yena vidhistadantasya* and the latter is tadādividhi by virtue of the vārttika *yasmin vidhistadādāv algrahaṇe*. Thus the meaning of the sūtra will be as follows : When an upasarga ending in *a* is followed by a verb form beginning with a vowel denoted by the abbreviatory term *eṅ* (*e*, *o*), a single substitute in the form of the following vowel sound, denoted by *eṅ*, comes in place of the vowel sound *a* and the vowel sound denoted by *eṅ*, which occurs at the beginning of a verbal form. The two illustrations given in the Laghu are *prejate* and *upoṣati*. In the former example, the preverb *pra* is followed by the verbal form *ejate* and in the latter, *upa* is followed by *oṣati*. Both the preverbs end in *a* and both the verbal forms begin with a vowel denoted by the abbreviatory term *eṅ*. The conditions laid down by the sūtra are fulfilled. As such, a single replacement in the form of the following vowel comes in place of both the vowel *a* of the preverbs *pra* and *upa* and the initial vowel of the verbal forms. This initial vowel is a denotatum of the abbreviatory term *eṅ* and the single replacement consists of the initial vowel (a denotatum of *eṅ*) of the verbal forms. In the former case, this is *e* and in the latter, it is *o*. The illustrations can be demonstrated as follows : *pra + ejate --> pr a + e jate --> pr e jate --> prejate* (He shines brilliantly); *upa + oṣati --> up a + o ṣati --> up o ṣati --> upoṣati* (He burns).

This sūtra is an exception to *vṛddhireci* (33) but with respect to the verbal forms *eti* and *edhate*, this rule is blocked by *etyedhatyūṭhsu* (34).

(39) अचोऽन्त्यादि टि । *aco 'ntyādi ṭi*. 1. 1. 64

लघु० - अचां मध्ये योऽन्त्यः स आदिर्यस्य तट्टिसंज्ञं स्यात् । *acāṁ madhye yo 'ntyaḥ sa ādir yasya taṭ ṭisaṁjñaṁ syāt.*

Trans. : Let that part of an item which begins with its last vowel be designated as *ṭi*.

PP. *acaḥ antyādi ṭi*.

Eluc. : The use of singular instead of the plural genitive *acām* can be explained by taking the singular genitive *acaḥ* as signifying jāti 'class' (cf. *jatyākhyāyām ekasmin bahuvacanam anyatarasyām* Pā. 1. 2. 58). That is why Varadarāja interprets *acaḥ* as *acāṁ madhye* in the vṛtti. When it is construed in the sense of plural, it makes sense to say that the genitive in *acaḥ* is in the sense of nirdhāraṇa which means 'singling out one from among many'. The word *antyādi* is a bahuvrīhi compound. The compound is analysed as follows : *antya ādir yasya*. The term *antya* means that which occurs at the end. In a word having more than one vowel, i.e. *manas*, the second vowel, which is the last in this context, constitutes the syllable *as*. The syllable *as* is given the designation *ṭi* according to the present sūtra. A single vowel constituting the last syllable can also be called *ṭi*, for by virtue of the sūtra *ādyantavad ekasmin* (277), operations applicable to an initial or final element of an item may be performed on an item which consists only of a single phoneme. The sūtra *ādyantavad ekasmin* is purported to make a provision whereby a grammatical operation specific to an initial (*ādi*) or final (*anta*) may be performed on an item consisting of a single phoneme only. In other words, a single element can be treated as its own initial or final element. Thus in the term *śaka*, *a* at the end can be termed *ṭi*. In the following vārttika with the comments of Varadarāja, the application of the designation of *ṭi* can be observed :

8. वा० – शकन्ध्वादिषु पररूपं वाच्यम्। *śakandhvādiṣu pararūpaṁ vācyam.*
लघु० – तच्च टेः। शकन्धुः। कर्कन्धुः। कुलटा। मनीषा। आकृतिगणोऽयम्। मार्तण्डः।
tacca ṭeḥ. śakandhuḥ. karkandhuḥ. kulaṭā. manīṣā. ākṛtigaṇo 'yam. mārtaṇḍaḥ.

Trans. : In the list beginning with *śakandhu*, let a single substitute in the form the second (of the two contiguous sounds) replace both *ṭi* and the following vowel sound. An item belonging to this class of items, can only be known from its form, *a posteriori*.

Eluc. : *śaka + andhu --> śak a ndhu --> śakandhuḥ* 'the well belonging to the *śakas*'. In this illustration, *a* at the end of *śaka* is *ṭi* and it merges into the beginning *a* of *andhu* or to put it in other words *a* is substituted for both *ṭi* and itself. Similarly pararūpa takes place in *karka + andhu --> karkandhuḥ* 'the well belonging to the *karkas*' (according to some it also means 'the jujube tree or its fruit') and in *kula + aṭā --> kulaṭā* 'an unchaste woman'. In these illustrations pararūpa has blocked the dīrgha substitution by *akaḥ savarṇe dīrghaḥ* (42). In *manīṣā*, there is coalescence between *manas + īṣā --> man as ī ṣā --> man ī ṣā --> manīṣā* 'intellect'. In this illustration *as* at the end of *manas* is *ṭi*. This *ṭi* and and the beginning *ī* of *īṣā* are replaced by *ī*.

This list beginning with the word *śakandhu* is identified by the grammatical operation known as pararūpa. This means that the list is not exhaustive. If we come across words in which this kind of pararūpa is observed, we should include such words in this list and perform the grammatical operation prescribed by this vārttika. The word *mārtaṇḍa* is well-known and is derived from *mṛtaṇḍa* in which we observe the pararūpa grammatical operation. So, we should include it in this list and bring it into the scope of this vārttika. In the karmadhāraya compound *mṛtaṁ ca ado 'ṇḍam,* the form which emerges after the nominal endings have been elided by (718) is *mṛta* + *aṇḍa*. At this stage the phoneme *a* at the end of *mṛta* and the beginning *a* of *aṇḍa* are replaced by the beginning *a* of *aṇḍa* (*pararūpa*). The resultant form is *mṛtaṇḍa*. The taddhita affix *aṇ* is introduced after *mṛtaṇḍa* either in the sense of *tatra bhavaḥ* 'occurring there' (1088) or in the sense of *tasyāpatyam* 'the progeny of' (1000). In both the cases by *taddhiteṣvacām ādeḥ* (934), the initial vowel *ṛ,* in *mṛtaṇḍa* + *aṇ,* is replaced by the vṛddhi substitution *ā* followed by *r* by virtue of *uraṇ raparaḥ* (29). After the elision of *a* at the end of *mārtaṇḍa* by *yasyeti ca* (235) and by the addition of the nominative singular affix *su,* the resultant form *mārtaṇḍaḥ* 'the Sun' is obtained. The grammatical process described above may be demonstrated as follows: *mṛtaṇḍa* + *aṇ* --> *m ā taṇḍa* + *a* --> *m ār taṇḍa* + *a* --> *m ār taṇḍ* + *a* --> *mārtaṇḍa* + *su* --> *mārtaṇḍaḥ*.

(40) ओमाङोश्च । *omāṅoś ca.* 6. 1. 95

लघु० - ओमि चाङि चात् परे पररूपम् एकादेशः स्यात्। शिवायों नमः। शिव एहि इति स्थिते - *omi cāṅi cāt pare pararūpam ekādeśaḥ syāt. śivāyoṁ namaḥ. śiva ehi iti sthite -*

Trans. : If *om* or *āṅ* follows *a,* then let a single substitute in the form of the second (of two contiguous phonemes) replace both the preceding (*a* in this case) and the following vowels.

PP. *āt omāṅoḥ ca pūrvaparayoḥ ekaṁ pararūpam* (*saṁhitāyām*).

Eluc. : The term *āt* has been lent into this sūtra from *ādguṇaḥ* Pā. 6. 1. 87. The sūtra *ekaḥ pūrvaparayoḥ* also extends here, being the governing rule. The term *pararūpam* is carried over into this sūtra from *eṅi pararūpam* Pā. 6. 1. 94. It is because of the word *pararūpam* that the word *ekaḥ* has been changed into the neuter gender. The sūtra, after adding the carried over items, means : A single substitute in the form of the second, i. e. the following vowel comes in place of the two contiguous preceding and following vowels when the vowel *a* is followed by either *om* or *āṅ*. To put it in other words, the preceding vowel *a* merges into the following vowel, which in this case is either *o* of *om* or *ā* of *āṅ*. The term *om* is an indeclinable and the term *āṅ* is a preverb. The last consonantal sound of the term *āṅ* is *it* by *halantyam* (1). Therefore it is elided by *tasya lopaḥ* (3). In the first illustration *śivāyoṁ namaḥ* (Salutations to Lord Śiva), the term *śivāya* is followed by *om* (*śivāya* + *om*). The vowel *a* occurring at the end of *śivāya* is followed by the vowel sound *o* which is at the beginning of *om*. The condition laid down by the sūtra is fulfilled. The preceding *a* merges itself into the following vowel sound *o* or we can say that a single substitute in the form of the following vowel *o* replaces both the preceding *a* and the following *o* of *om*.

The second illustration given in the vṛtti needs some explanation. The stage which is shown in the vṛtti is an outcome of *śiva* + *ā* + *ihi*. At this stage, two sūtras become applicable simultaneously : *akaḥ savarṇe dīrghaḥ* (42) between *śiva* + *ā* and *ādguṇaḥ* (27) between *ā* + *ihi*. Here if we join first the vowel *a* at the end of *śiva* with *ā* of *āṅ* by *akaḥ savarṇe dīrghaḥ*, both are replaced by a single long *ā*. Then *ādguṇaḥ* applies and a guṇa substitute in form of *e* comes in place of *ā* and *i* of *ihi*. We obtain *śivehi*. As such, it is not necessary to include *āṅ* in the present sūtra. Nevertheless the necessity of including *āṅ* in the present sūtra is explained like this : There is a paribhāṣā *asiddhaṁ bahiraṅgamantaraṅge* (Abhyankar, 50). A great deal of discussion is available on the nature of antaraṅga and bahiraṅga in grammatical literature. Here it suffices to know that a grammatical operation in respect of dhātu and upasarga is considered to be antaraṅga (cf. *dhātūpasargayor yatkāryaṁ tadantaraṅgam. kuta etat? pūrvam upasargasya hi dhātunā yogo bhavati nādyaśabdena*). In the light of this statement of Patañjali in the Mahābhāṣya on Pā. 6. 1. 108 vtk 9, we first join dhātu and upasarga. The sūtra *ādguṇaḥ* (27) applies and the coalescence between the *ā* of *āṅ* and the *i* of *ihi* takes place, that is, the guṇa substitute *e* comes in place of *ā* and *i*. This is how *śiva ehi* given in the vṛtti is obtained. Now after the coalescence between the *ā* of *āṅ* and *i* of *ihi* has taken place, *āṅ* given in the sūtra is not available. In order to show that the characteristic of being *āṅ* exists in the single guṇa substitute *e*, the following sūtra ensues :

(41) अन्तादिवच्च । *antādivacca.* 6. 1. 85

लघु० – योऽयमेकादेशः स पूर्वस्यान्तवत् परस्यादिवत् स्यात् । शिवेहि । *yo 'yamekādeśaḥ sa pūrvasyāntavat parasyādivat syāt. śivehi.*

Trans. : Let the single substitute (that comes in place of the preceding and the following elements) be treated as the final of that which precedes and the initial of that which follows.

PP. *ekaḥ pūrvaparayoḥ antādivat ca.*

Eluc. : Since *ekaḥ pūrvaparayoḥ* is the governing sūtra, it extends here also. The word *antādivat* is an indeclinable derived by adding *vati* affix to the compound *antādī*. The analysis of the indeclinable *antādivat* is as follows : *antaś ca ādiś ca antādī antādibhyāṁ tulyam antādivat.* The affix *vati* has been introduced by the sūtra *tena tulyaṁ kriyā ced vatiḥ* (1145).

A replacement coming in place of two contiguous elements or sounds is treated as the final of that which precedes and the initial of that which follows in that replacement in the form of a single substitution (*ekādeśa*). The words *anta* and *ādi* denote avayava 'part'. Therefore it is natural that they are understood with respect to their avayavin 'whole' with reference to which they are parts. In this illustration, the single substitute *e* that has come in place of the *ā* of *āṅ* and the *i* of *ihi* is the whole. As a result of this substitution, *āṅ* is not available. It is to bring about *āṅtva* in this single substitute that the present sūtra has been brought into service. By virtue of this sūtra, the single substitute here is to be treated as the final of that which precedes in this *ekādeśa* 'single substitute'. The preceding item in this ekādeśa, that is in *e*, is *āṅ*. Now the preceding element *āṅ* is nothing but *ā*, after *ṅ*, being *it* by *halantyam* (1), has been elided by *tasya lopaḥ* (3). It is single. Hence it is to be treated as its own final (see for explanation supra p. 51). Consequent upon this, the single substitute *e* in this illustration is treated as *āṅ*, which is precisely the condition laid down by the present sūtra for pararūpa ekādeśa. Thus *āṅ* being available, the single substitute in the form of the consequent element, that is *e* in the present case, takes place. The vowel sound *e* replaces both *a* at the end of *śiva* and *e* of *ehi*. This is the procedure by which the finished form *śivehi* illustrated in the vṛtti is obtained.

It is worth noting here that the sūtra *omāṅośca* is an exception to both the sūtras *vṛddhireci* (33) and *akaḥ savarṇe dīrghaḥ* (42).

(42) अकः सवर्णे दीर्घः । *akaḥ savarṇe dīrghaḥ.* 6. 1. 101

लघु० – अकः सवर्णेऽचि परे पूर्वपरयोर्दीर्घ एकादेशः स्यात्। दैत्यारिः । श्रीशः । विष्णूदयः । होतॄकारः । *akaḥ savarṇe 'ci pare pūrvaparayor dīrgha ekādeśaḥ syāt. daityāriḥ. śrīśaḥ. viṣṇūdayaḥ. hotṝkāraḥ.*

Trans. : If *ak* is followed by a homogeneous *ac*, let a single replacement consisting of a long vowel come in place of the preceding and the following vowels.

PP. *akaḥ savarṇe aci pūrvaparayoḥ ekaḥ dīrghaḥ* (*saṁhitāyām*).

Eluc. : The term *aci* is carried over from *iko yaṇaci* Pā. 6. 1. 77 and the terms *ekaḥ* and *pūrvaparayoḥ* are also carried over, being the constituents of the governing rule Pā. 6. 1. 84. The abbreviatory term *ak* denotes *a i u ṛ ḷ*. If these are followed by a homogeneous vowel (*ac*), then a single long replacement, determined by *sthāne 'ntaratamaḥ* (17), comes in place of both the preceding vowel denoted by the abbreviatory term *ak* and the homogeneous (*savarṇa*) vowel that follows.

The four illustrations given by Varadarāja are as follows :

1. The compound word *daityāriḥ* is a ṣaṣṭhītatpuruṣa which is analysed as *daityānām ariḥ*. The form of the illustration is as follows : *daitya + ari,* after the nominal endings have been dropped by *supo dhātuprātipadikayoḥ* (718). In this, the vowel *a* at the end of *daitya* is denoted by *ak* and the vowel *a* at the beginning of *ari* is a homogeneous vowel. With the help of *sthāne 'ntaratamaḥ* (17), both these vowels are replaced with a long vowel *ā*, which is most similar to the substituenda. The place of articulation of both akāra and ākāra is the same. Although their internal efforts differ, the internal effort of *a* is intended to be the same as that of *ā* so far as the grammatical operation is concerned. This is implied by Pā. 8. 4. 68 which is the last sūtra of the Aṣṭādhyāyī. After the addition of the singular nominative inflectional ending to it, the final form of the illustration is *daityāriḥ*. It means 'the enemy of demons', that is, Lord Viṣṇu.

2. *śrīśaḥ* (the Lord of Śrī) : In *śrī + īśa*, the long vowel *ī* at the end of *śrī*, which is a denotatum of *ak* by virtue of *aṇudit savarṇasya cāpratyayaḥ* (11) and that at the beginning of *īśa*, which is a homogeneous vowel denoted by *ac*, are replaced by a long *ī* with the help of *sthāne 'ntaratamaḥ* (17).

3. *viṣṇūdayaḥ* (the rise of Viṣṇu or the Sun) : The short *u* vowels coming at the end of *viṣṇu* and at the beginning of *udaya* (*viṣṇu + udaya*) are replaced by a long *ū* as has been done in the last two illustrations.

4. *hotṝkāraḥ* (the *ṛkāra* of *hotṛ* priest) : This is a compound word which is analysed as *hotur ṛkāraḥ*. It changes into *hotṛ + ṛkāra* after the elision of the nominal endings. Both the *ṛ* vowels are replaced by a long *ṝ* on the basis of extreme similarity as prescribed by *sthāne 'ntaratamaḥ* (17).

This sūtra is an exception to *ādguṇaḥ* (27) in respect of *a* and in other respects to *iko yaṇaci* (15) and thus limits their area of application.

(43) एङः पदान्तादति । *eṅaḥ padāntādati.* 6. 1. 109

लघु॰ – पदान्ताद् एङोऽति परे पूर्वरूपम् एकादेशः स्यात्। हरेऽव। विष्णोऽव। *padāntād eṅo 'ti pare pūrvarūpam ekādeśaḥ syāt. hare 'va. viṣṇo 'va.*

Trans. : Let a single vowel substitute in the form of the first of the two contiguous vowels denoted by the abbreviatory term *eṅ* replace both the pada-final *eṅ* and the following short initial *a*.

PP. *padāntāt eṅaḥ ati pūravaparayoḥ ekaḥ pūrvaḥ* (*saṁhitāyām*).

Eluc. : The sūtra *ekaḥ pūrvaparayoḥ* has its jurisdiction here also and the term *pūrvaḥ* is carried over from *ami pūrvaḥ* Pā. 6. 1. 107. Thus the sūtra means : If a short *a* follows pada-final *eṅ*, then a single vowel substitute homologous to the preceding element denoted by the abbreviatory term *eṅ* replaces both the pada-final *eṅ* and the short *a* which follows. The pratyāhāra *eṅ* denotes two elements : *e* and *o*. If either of the two comes at the end of a pada and is followed by *at* (short *a*), then both these vowels merge into the pada-final *e* or *o*.

The vocative singular forms of *hari* and *viṣṇu* respectively are *hare* and *viṣṇo*. The verb *ava* is a loṭ-lakāra second person singular form of the verbal root *av* 'to protect'. The sentences *hare ava* and *viṣṇo ava* mean respectively ' O Hari! protect (me)' and 'O Viṣṇu! protect (me)'. Both the words *hare* and *viṣṇo* are padas by *suptiṅantaṁ padam* (14). The vowels *e* and *o* occur at the end of padas. These are followed by short *a* (*at*). So the short *a* which follows merges into either *e* or *o*. Or to put it in other words, a single replacement in the form of *e* or *o* comes in place of both the preceding *e* or *o* and the following short *a*. The resultant forms are *hare 'va* and *viṣṇo 'va*. The apostrophe in English represents the symbol 'ऽ' in Sanskrit which indicates that the short vowel *a* had been here before it merged into the single substitute *e* or *o*. It should be borne in mind that short *a*, which is represented by the symbol 'ऽ', is not articulated since it has been replaced by the single substitute in the form of the pada-final *e* or *o*.

The mention of pada-final (*padāntāt*) in the sūtra has a purpose. If *e* or *o* is not a pada-final vowel then this sūtra does not apply even if a short *a* follows. For example, when the primary affix *ac* is added to the verbal root *ji* 'to win' by the rule *erac* (852), the guṇa replacement comes in place of *i* of *ji* by the rule *sārvadhātukārdhadhātukayoḥ* (387). After the guṇa replacement has taken place, we have *je* + *a*. Here the vowel *e* is not pada-final. Hence pūrvarūpa sandhi does not take place. Instead, the rule *eco 'yavāyāvaḥ* (22) becomes applicable and the vowel *e* is replaced by the substitute *ay* and we get the resultant form *jaya*. When we introduce the nominative singular affix *su*, we have the form *jayaḥ* after rutva and visarga.

(44) सर्वत्र विभाषा गोः । *sarvatra vibhāṣā goḥ.* 6. 1. 122

लघु० - लोके वेदे चैङन्तस्य गोरति वा प्रकृतिभावः पदान्ते । गोअग्रम् । एङन्तस्य किम् ? चित्रग्वग्रम् । पदान्ते किम् ? गोः । *loke vede caiṅantasya gor ati vā prakṛtibhāvaḥ padānte. go agram. eṅantasya kim ? citragvagram. padānte kim ? goḥ.*

Trans. : Let both the pada-final *eṅ* (of the nominal stem) *go* and the following short vowel *a* retain their original form optionally in the Vedas as well as in the secular literature.

PP. *sarvatra padāntasya eṅaḥ goḥ ati vibhāṣā prakṛtyā* (*saṁhitāyām*).

Eluc. : The word *sarvatra* is an indeclinable. It means 'everywhere'. The terms *padāntāt* and *ati* are carried over from *eṅaḥ padāntādati* Pā. 6. 1. 109. The term *padāntāt* is changed into the genitive form *padāntasya* by the process of vibhaktivipariṇāma. That is why Varadarāja has used *eṅantasya* instead of *eṅantāt* in the vṛtti. This qualifies the word *go*. By *yena vidhistadantasya* Pā. 1. 1. 72, it is construed as *eṅantasya* (*goḥ*). The word *prakṛtyā* is carried over into the present sūtra from Pā. 6. 1. 115 *prakṛtyāntaḥpādamavyapare*. The completed sūtra means : Everywhere, whether it is a Vedic usage or classical, the pada-final *eṅ* of the nominal stem *go* retains its original form optionally when it is followed by *at* (short *a*). In the illustration *goagram* which is a ṣaṣṭhītatpuruṣa compound analysed as *gavām agram* (*go ām agra su*), after the elision of the nominal endings (*sup*), the form of the illustration, before the coalescence takes place, is : *go + agra*. Even after the elision of nominal endings, *go* retains the status of pada by virtue of the rule *prayayalope pratyayalakṣaṇam* (189). Hence *go* is a pada and it is *eṅanta*. The short *a* at the beginning of *agra* follows. The requirement prescribed by the present sūtra for prakṛtibhāva (retaining the original form) is fulfilled. After the nominal affix has been added, we obtain the form *goagram* (ahead of cows). In case this option is not exercised, we can have *go 'gram* by *eṅaḥ padāntādati* (43).

The purpose of the term *eṅanta* is that prakṛtibhāva is denied to the nominal stem *go* when this does not end in *eṅ*. In the bahuvrīhi compound *citraguḥ*, the nominal stem *go* does not end in *o* since the final *o* of *go* is shortened into *u* by *gostriyorupasarjanasya* (948) and becomes *citragu* (*citrā gāvo yasya*). This is compounded with another subanta *agram* in ṣaṣṭhītatpuruṣa (*citragor agram*). After the nominal endings are elided, the saṁhitā stage is : *citragu + agra*. Since the nominal stem *go* does not end in *eṅ*, prakṛtibhāva is not available here. Instead *iko yaṇaci* (15) applies and the resultant form after sandhi is *citragvagram*.

The term *padāntasya* in respect of *eṅanta go* is purported to preclude prakṛtibhāva when *go* does not have a pada-final vowel denoted by *eṅ*. In the ablative and genitive, the nominal stem *go* has respectively the sup-affixes *ṅasi* and *ṅas*. The sūtra *laśakvataddhite* (135) assigns the designation *it* to the beginning *ṅ* of both the affixes. The vowel *i* at the end of *ṅasi* is also *it* by *upadeśe 'janunāsika it* (28). These *its* are elided by *tasya lopaḥ*(3). The remaining form of both the affixes is *as*. Thus in both the cases the form is : *go* + *as*. Here the short *a* follows *go* which ends in *eṅ* but *eṅ* (*o*) is not at the end of a pada since *go* is still in the process of becoming a pada. The nominal affix *sup* (*as* in this case) is yet to be added. Consequently the present sūtra has no scope and so prakṛtibhāva is not available. Instead pūrvarūpa takes place by *ṅasiṅasośca* (172). This means that the single replacement, in the form of the preceding of the two contiguous elements (*o* in this case), comes in place of both the preceding *o* and the following short *a* to obtain the final pada-form *gos* --> *goḥ*.

As this rule applies optionally, in the alternative, when prakṛtibhāva is not available, the sūtra *avaṅ sphoṭāyanasya* (47) enjoins the substitute *avaṅ*. In order to determine the substituendum (*sthānin*) to be replaced by this substitute, Varadarāja introduces two paribhāṣā sūtras :

(45) अनेकाल्शित् सर्वस्य । *anekālśit sarvasya*. 1. 1. 55

लघु० – इति प्राप्ते । *iti prāpte* --

Trans. : Let the substitute which consists of more than one *al* and which has *ś* as *it* replace the whole (of that for which the replacement has been enjoined). When this paribhāṣā sūtra becomes available for application (another one presents itself) --

PP. *anekālśit sarvasya sthāne.*

Eluc. : The term *sthāne* is continued from Pā.1. 1. 50. The compound word *anekālśit* is a bahuvrīhi-seeded samāhāradvandva which is analysed as follows : *anekaḥ al yasya saḥ anekāl* and *śakāraḥ it yasya saḥ śit; anekāl ca śit ca anekālśit* (BM, I, p. 51). The abbreviatory term *al* denotes the whole repertory of phonemes (*akṣarasamāmnāya*). If the substitute contains more than one phoneme or has the palatal *ś* as *it*, then such a substitute replaces the whole of the substituendum for which the replacement has been prescribed by using the genitive nominal ending. This sūtra is an exception to *alo 'ntyasya* (21) which says that the substitute replaces the last phoneme (*al*) of the substituendum for which the replacement has been enjoined by using the genitive nominal ending. The sūtra *asterbhūḥ* (575) prescribes the replacement *bhū* for the root *as*. Since the replacement *bhū* contains more than one *al*, the whole of *as* is replaced by *bhū*. In the absence of the present sūtra, the replacement would have come in place of the last *al* of *as*, that is, *s* by virtue of *alo 'ntyasya*. Similarly in the case of the substitute which is *śit*, the whole of substituendum (*sthānin*) is replaced by this kind of substitute. Take the sūtra *idama iś* (1195). The substitute *iś* is *śit*. Therefore it will replace the whole *idam* and not merely the last *al*, that is *m* in this case. One point is to be borne in mind here. The substitute *iś* as it is given consists of more than one *al*. Being *anekāl*, it can replace the whole of substituendum (*sthānin*). What is, then, the purpose of making it *śit*. The answer lies in the fact that, by making it *śit*, Pāṇini intends to imply that only that substitute, which has more than one non-*it* phoneme, is to be considered *anekāl*. In other words, the state of being *anekāl* is not determined by an *al* which is termed *it*. We have to first drop *it*s and then see whether the substitute is *anekāl* or not. Cf. *nānubandhakṛtam anekāltvam* (Abhyankar, 6).

(46) ङिच्च । *ṅicca*. 1. 1. 53

लघु० – ङिदनेकालप्यन्त्यस्यैव स्यात् । *ṅid anekālapyantyasyaiva syāt.*

Trans. : If the substitute consisting of more than one *al* is *ṅit*, let it replace only the last *al* of the substituendum (*sthānin*).

PP. *ṅit ca antyasya*.

Eluc. : The word *sthāne* comes from the sūtra *sthāne 'ntaratamaḥ* Pā. 1. 1. 50. This rule is an exception to *anekāl śit sarvasya* (45). The term *ṅit* is a bahuvrīhi compound. Its analysis is as follows : *ṅakāra it yasya sa ṅit*. The term *alaḥ* and *antyasya* are carried over from *alo 'ntyasya* (21) which says that a substitute enjoined for an item in the genitive comes in place of the final phoneme denoted by the abbreviatory term *al*. The rule *anekāl śit sarvasya* (45) is an exception to *alo 'ntyasya* (21). Now the present rule *ṅicca* is an exception to *anekāl śit sarvasya* (45). The following sūtra exemplifies the substitute which consists of more than one *al* and has the phoneme *ṅ* as *it*.

(47) अवङ् स्फोटायनस्य । *avaṅ sphoṭāyanasya*. 6. 1. 123

लघु० – पदान्ते एङन्तस्य गोरवङ् वा स्याद् अचि । गवाग्रम् । गोऽग्रम् । पदान्ते किम् ? गवि ।
padānte eṅantasya goravaṅ vā syād aci. gavāgram. go 'gram. padānte kim ? gavi.

Trans. : Let the substitute *avaṅ* optionally replace the nominal stem *go* ending in *eṅ* (*o*) occurring at the end of a pada when *ac* follows.

PP. *eṅaḥ padāntasya goḥ avaṅ sphoṭāyanasya aci vibhāṣā* (*saṁhitāyām*).

Eluc. : We get *eṅaḥ* from *eṅaḥ padāntādati* Pā. 6. 1. 109. The term *eṅaḥ* is in the ablative in the sūtra from which it is carried over. It is changed into the genitive by the process of vibhaktivipariṇāma. It qualifies the stem *go*. By *yena vidhistadantasya* Pā. 1. 1. 72 it is paraphrased with *go* as *eṅantasya goḥ*. The anuvṛtti of *ati* is suspended. Instead *aci* is carried over from *iko yaṇaci* Pā. 6. 1. 77 in the manner of the leap of a frog (*maṇḍūkapluti*). The word *vibhāṣā* is carried over from *sarvatra vibhāṣā goḥ* Pā. 6. 1. 122. This word means 'option'. The optional substitution could be had by virtue of this word without mentioning the name of Sphoṭāyana. It is, therefore, held that the name of Sphoṭāyana has been used to express respect for him. Now the meaning of the sūtra is as follows : The pada-final *eṅ* coming at the end of the word *go* (which in the case of *go* is *o*) is replaced with the substitute *avaṅ* in the opinion of the grammarian Sphoṭāyana.

The illustration *gavāgram* is a ṣaṣṭhītatpuruṣa compound analysed as *gavām agram* (*go ām agra su*). After the elision of the nominal endings (*sup*), the form of the illustration, before sandhi takes place, is : *go* + *agra*. Now *avaṅ sphoṭāyanasya* enjoins *avaṅ* in place of *go*. At this stage, the rule *alo 'ntyaṣya* (21) becomes applicable but it is blocked by *anekāl śit sarvasya* (45). This rule itself is further blocked by *ṅicca* (46) which applies and the vowel *o* at the end of *go* is replaced by *avaṅ* since it is *ṅit*. The consonantal sound *ṅ* coming at the end of *avaṅ* is *it* by *halantyam* (1) and is elided by *tasya lopaḥ* (3). After *o* has been replaced with *avaṅ*, we obtain the following form : *g ava agra*. Now applying *akaḥ savarṇe...* (42) we replace the vowel *a* at the end of *ava* and the vowel *a* at the beginning of *agra* with a long vowel *ā*. Thus we get the resultant form *gavāgram* after affixing the nominal ending *su*.

In the alternative, where the substitute *avaṅ* is not available, a single pūrvarūpa replacement takes place by *eṅaḥ padāntādati* (43). In *go* + *agra* a single replacement in the form of the preceding *o*, which occurs at the end of the nominal stem *go*, comes in place of both the preceding *o* and the short *a* that follows. So we also have the form *go 'gram*. Thus we have three forms including the instance of prakṛtibhāva : 1. *goagram* (prakṛtibhāva) 2. *gavāgram* and 3. *go 'gram* (2 and 3 in the absence of prakṛtibhāva).

The purpose of enunciating *padāntād* (pada-final *eṅ*) in the sūtra is to preclude the substitution of *avaṅ* in place of the vowel *o* at the end of the nominal stem *go* when it is not a pada. Take, for example, *gavi* which has the locative nominal ending : *go* + *ṅi* --> *go* + *i*. At this stage, the present sūtra would have been applicable, had the expression pada-final not been included in the body of the sūtra. Hence the substitute *avaṅ* does not become available here but instead *eco 'yavāyāvaḥ* (22) applies and we have the desired form *gavi*.

There is one more point to be taken note of here. The term *vibhāṣā* which is carried over into this sūtra from *sarvatra vibhāṣā goḥ* Pā. 6. 1. 122 is interpreted as vyavasthitavibhāṣā which means an option that does not apply universally in all the instances of the sūtra in which it occurs. It applies necessarily in some cases and does not apply at all in the other cases. It is this interpretation of vyavasthitavibhāṣā that explains the compulsory substitution of *avaṅ* in *gavākṣa* (*gavām akṣi iva* --> *go akṣi a* --> *g avaṅ akṣa* --> *g ava akṣa* --> *gavākṣa*). The replacement of *avaṅ* is not optional here but obligatory. To achieve this end the carried over term *vibhāṣā* has been interpreted here as vyavasthitavibhāṣā.

(48) इन्द्रे च । *indre ca*. 6. 1. 124

लघु० – गोरवङ् स्याद् इन्द्रे । गवेन्द्रः । *goravaṅ syād indre. gavendraḥ.*

Trans. : When the nominal stem *indra* follows, let the pada-final (*eṅ*) of *go* be replaced by *avaṅ*.

PP. *eṅaḥ goḥ indre ca avaṅ* (*saṁhitāyām*).

Eluc. : The term *eṅaḥ* is carried over from *eṅaḥ padāntādati* Pā. 6. 1. 109. It is in the ablative in the sūtra from which it is carried over but it is changed into the genitive by the process of vibhaktivipariṇāma. It qualifies the stem *go*. By *yena vidhistadantasya* it is paraphrased with *go* as *eṅantasya goḥ*. The words *goḥ* and *avaṅ* come from *sarvatra vibhāṣā goḥ* Pā. 6. 1. 122 and *avaṅ sphoṭāyanasya* Pā. 6. 1. 123 respectively. The completed sūtra means : If the pada-final *o* (*eṅ*) of the nominal stem *go* is followed by *indra*, then *o* is replaced with *avaṅ*. This sūtra is an exception to *avaṅ sphoṭāyanasya* (47). The substitute *avaṅ* was optionally available there. Here it is necessarily available. The word *gavendraḥ* is a tatpuruṣa compound. Its analysis (*vigraha*) is as follows : *gavām goṣu vā indraḥ* = *śreṣṭhaḥ* --> *go ām* or *sup indra su* --> *go indra* --> *g avaṅ indra* --> *g ava indra* --> *gavendraḥ* (*ādguṇaḥ*).

The Kāśikā reads the word *nityam* in the body of this sūtra and carries it forward to the following sūtra *plutapragṛhyā aci* (*nityam*) Pā. 6.

1. 125. However, this is not necessary. The sūtra *avaṅ sphoṭāyanasya* (47) enjoins the substitute *avaṅ* optionally when *ac* follows. Had Pāṇini intended *avaṅ* to be an optional substitute in the present case, he would have not enunciated this sūtra as *i* at the beginning of *indra* is also denoted by the abbreviatory term *ac*. Even then he has enunciated this sūtra, which implies that Pāṇini intends *avaṅ* to be a necessary (*nitya*) replacement. Hence there is no need to read *nityam* in this sūtra as has been done in the Kāśikā (cf. TB, I, p. 103; Bhaimī, I, p. 81).

(49) दूराद्धूते च । *dūrāddhūte ca*. 8. 2. 84

लघु० - दूरात् सम्बोधने वाक्यस्य टेः प्लुतो वा स्यात् । *dūrāt sambodhane vākyasya ṭeḥ pluto vā syāt.*

Trans. : In calling (a person) from a distance, let the *ṭi* of an utterance be optionally replaced by a prolated vowel.

PP. *dūrāt hūte ca vākyasya ṭeḥ plutaḥ vā.*

Eluc. : The words *plutaḥ, vākyasya* and *ṭeḥ* are carried over from the governing sūtra *vākyasya ṭeḥ pluta udāttaḥ* Pā. 8. 2. 82. Although the word *udāttaḥ* is also carried over into this sūtra, Varadarāja does not include it in the vṛtti, considering it to be of little use for an elementay book like the Laghukaumudī. The word *dhūte* is actually *hūte,* the hakāra of which has been replaced by the fourth homogeneous stop of tavarga in accordance with the rule *jhayo ho 'nyatarasyām* (75). This word has been derived by the addition of the primary affix *kta* to the verbal root *hveñ* 'to challenge, to call'. The indeclinable *vā* has been used by Varadarāja in the vṛtti since Patañjali has made optional the whole section on pluta (see Mbh on 8. 2. 92 vtk 2, SK, I, p. 110 and Bhairavī, a commentary on Prauḍhamanoramā, p. 246).

The use of *dūrāt* is relative to the words used for calling someone. A word which can be heard from a distance must be produced with some effort. It is also heard with some effort. It is important to note here that if the name of the person who is being called is used at the end of an utterance, then only the *ṭi* of that utterance is optionally replaced by a prolated vowel. The *ṭi* of an utterance means the last syllable of the relevant word used at the end of that utterance. If this is not the case, then the replacement in place of *ṭi* does not take place even though the utterance is used to call somebody from a distance. To illustrate, in the sentence *devadatta! ehi*. Devadatta is being called from a distance but the word *devadatta* is not used at the end of the utterance. Hence the last syllable of *devadatta* is not replaced by a prolated one but in the utterance : *ehi devadatta!* Devadatta is being called from a distance and the word has been used at the end of the sentence. Hence the *ṭi* of *devadatta* is replaced by the prolated *a* : *ehi devadatta3!* If the word ends in a consonant, then the last vowel preceding that consonant is to be replaced by a prolated one, since the term *ṭi* has been used in the sūtra. As the substitution of pluta is optional, the illustration in the absence of pluta will be : *ehi devadatta!*

(50) प्लुतप्रगृह्या अचि नित्यम्। *plutapragṛhyā aci nityam.* 6. 1. 125

लघु॰ – एतेऽचि प्रकृत्या स्युः। आगच्छ कृष्ण३ अत्र गौश्चरति। *ete 'ci prakṛtyā syuḥ. āgaccha kṛṣṇa3 atra gauś carati.*

Trans. : Let the prolated and *pragṛhya* vowels necessarily retain their original form when followed by *ac* (vowels).

PP. *plutapragṛhyā aci nityam prakṛtyā* (*saṁhitāyām*).

Eluc. : The term *prakṛtyā* is carried over from *prakṛtyāntaḥpādam avyapare* Pā. 6. 1. 115. The word means 'staying in the original form'. The vowels which are prolated and the vowels which have been termed *pragṛhya* necessarily remain in their original form when a vowel follows. In the illustration given by Varadarāja, the last vowel of the word *kṛṣṇa* is prolated since it has been used to call Kṛṣṇa from a distance. Hence a prolated *a* optionally replaces the *ṭi*, that is the last vowel *a* of this word by the preceding sūtra (49). When it is prolated and followed by *ac*, this sūtra becomes applicable. Hence there will not be any long replacement in place of both the akāras, the last *a* of Kṛṣṇa and the *a* at the beginning of *atra* by *akaḥ savarṇe dīrghaḥ* (42). In the absence of prolation, *akaḥ...* (42) applies and a long *ā* will replace both the akāras. The illustration, then, will be like this : *āgacha kṛṣṇātra gauś carati.*

The use of the word *nityam* in the present sūtra has a purpose. In *vāyū + atra*, the long *ū* is pragṛhya by *īdūded dvivacanaṁ pragṛhyam* (51). In this illustration, because of the use of the word *nityam*, prakṛtibhāva is not optional with the shortening of *ik* as is prescribed by *iko 'savarṇe śākalyasya hravaśca* (59). So the use of the word *nityam* ensures prakṛtibhāva. In addition, it blocks the short vowel substitution in place of a long vowel denoted by *ik* as enjoined by (59).

(51) ईदूदेद् द्विवचनं प्रगृह्यम्। *īdūded dvivacanaṁ pragṛhyam.* 1. 1. 11

लघु॰ – ईदूदेदन्तं द्विवचनं प्रगृह्यं स्यात्। हरी एतौ। विष्णू इमौ। गङ्गे अमू। *īdūdedantam dvivacanaṁ pragṛhyaṁ syāt. harī etau. viṣṇū imau. gaṅge amū.*

Trans. : Let a dual ending which terminates in *ī, ū* or *e* be designated as *pragṛhya.*

PP. *īdūded dvivacanam pragṛhyam.*

Eluc. : The word *īdūdet* is a samāhāradvandva compound which is analysed as *īc ca ūc ca ec ca* --> *īdūdet*. The taparakaraṇa is purported to remove doubt, if there is any, about their being long. The compound *īdūdet* qualifies the word *dvivacanam.* Therefore by *yena vidhistadantasya* Pā. 1. 1. 72, tadanta-vidhi beomes applicable. Consequently the meaning of the sūtra is as follows : The dual inflectional ending which ends with long *ī*, long *ū* or *e* is termed *pragṛhya.* The words *harī, viṣṇū* and *gaṅge* end with dual inflectional endings. Therefore *ī, ū* and *e* get the designation *pragṛhya* and as such they remain in their original state by *plutapragṛhyā aci nityam* (50). Remaining in the original state is also called *prakṛtibhāva* which obtains in the illustrations given below:

1. *harī etau* = These two horses or monkeys. In this illustration, sandhi by *iko yaṇaci* (15) has been blocked. So, the long *ī* is not replaced by the phoneme *y*.

2. *viṣṇū imau* = These two Viṣṇūs. In this illustration also *iko yaṇaci* has been blocked. So *ū* is not replaced by the semi-vowel *v*.

3. *gaṅge amū* = Those two Gaṅgā rivers. Here the operation of *eṅaḥ padāntād ati* (43) is precluded by prakṛtibhāva. Hence no pūrvarūpa replacement comes in place of the preceding *e* and the following *a*.

(52) अदसो मात्। *adaso māt.* 1. 1. 12

लघु॰ - अस्मात् परावीदूतौ प्रगृह्यौ स्तः। अमी ईशाः। रामकृष्णावमू आसाते। मात् किम्? अमुकेऽत्र। *asmāt parāv īdūtau pragṛhyau staḥ. amī īśāḥ. rāmakṛṣṇāvamū āsāte. māt kim? amuke 'tra.*

Trans. : (The inflectional endings) *ī* and *ū* which follow the phoneme *m* of *adas* are designated as *pragṛhya*.

PP. *adasaḥ māt īdūt pragṛhyam.*

Eluc. : The sixth inflectional ending after the pronominal stem *adas*, which refers to a distant entity, is in the sense of a part (*avayavaṣaṣṭhī*) and as such the meaning obtained is 'the *m* of *adas*' (cf. BM, I, p.113). The term *māt* ends in fifth case-ending which means 'what follows'. The use of *a* in *māt* is to facilitate its articulation. The word *īdūt* is to be understood as a samāhāradvandva compound as in the preceding aphorism. Although, according to the Kāśikā, all the three words *īt, ūt* and *et* are to be carried over from the sūtra Pā. 1. 1. 11 into this one, Varadarāja does not mention *et* in the vṛtti since there is no inflectional form of *adas* in which *e* follows *m*. It is for this reason that the phoneme *m* has been enunciated in the present sūtra so that the vowel *e* is not carried over. This has been mentioned by Bhaṭṭoji Dīkṣita (SK. I, p. 114): *asati mādgrahaṇe ekāro 'pyanuvarteta.*

The first illustration is *amī īśāḥ*. The pronominal term *amī* is the masculine nominative plural form of the pronominal stem *adas*. The phoneme *ī* at the end of *amī* follows *m* and as such it is termed *pragṛhya* according to the present sūtra. The sūtra *plutapragṛhyā aci nityam* (50) steps in and prakṛtibhāva ensues, i.e. the preceding and the following vowels retain their original form without undergoing any change that was due by *akaḥ savarṇe dīrghaḥ* (42).

The second illustration is *rāmakṛṣṇāv amū āsāte*. It is like this : *rāmakṛṣṇau + amū + āsāte --> rāmakṛṣṇāvamū + āsāte*. After the application of *eco 'yavāyāvaḥ* (22) *āv* replaces the vowel *au* of *rāmakṛṣṇau* because of the vowel *a* of *amū* that follows and the form *rāmakṛṣṇāvamū* results. Now comes the turn of coalescence between *rāmakṛṣṇāvamū* and *āsāte*. Here *ū* follows the *m* of *amū* which is the nominative dual form of *adas*. By the present sūtra this *ū* is pragṛhya and therefore both *ū* and *ā* of *āsāte* remain in their original form by *plutapragṛhyā aci nityam* (50). The replacement of *ū* by *v* by *iko yaṇaci* (15) does not take place because the vowel *ū* is pragṛhya by the present rule.

The example for the present sūtra is *amū āsāte* only. The form *rāmakṛṣṇau* is used here only to show that *amū* is the masculine form. In other words, the present sūtra is purported only for *adas* in the masculine. This needs some elaboration. In the feminine form, the word *adas* in the nominative dual takes the inflectional affix *au*. By *tyadādīnāmaḥ* (192), the phoneme *s* of *adas* is replaced by *a*. By *ato guṇe* (273), pararūpa takes place and the form becomes *ada*. To render it feminine, the affix *ṭāp* (*ā*) comes by *ajādyataṣṭāp* (1243). Then the long replacement comes by *akaḥ savarṇe dīrghaḥ* (42). At this stage the form of *adas* is *adā* + *au*. By *auṅa āpaḥ* (215) the substitute *śī* replaces *au*; then *ādguṇaḥ* (27) applies and the form becomes *ade* after guṇa replacement. At this stage, the rule *adaso 'serdādu do maḥ* Pā. 8. 2. 80 applies and *ū* replaces *e* and *m* replaces *d*. The resultant form is *amū*. The last grammatical operation, that is, the replacement of *e* by *ū* and of *d* by *m* is prescribed by *adaso 'serdādu do maḥ* Pā. 8. 2. 80 and hence it is deemed not to have taken place with respect to *īdūded dvivacanaṁ pragṛhyam* Pā. 1. 1. 11 by virtue of *pūrvatrāsiddham* Pā. 8. 2. 1. So *amū* is virtually *ade* with respect to *īdūded...* (51). Almost similar is the case with *amū*, the nominative and accusative dual form of *adas* in the neuter gender. So the pragṛhya designation for feminine and neuter forms can be had by *īdūded dvivacanaṁ pragṛhyam* (51) itself. However, it is not the case with *amū* and *amī*, which are respectively the nominative dual and plural forms of *adas* in the masculine. The form *amū* passes through the stage of *adau* which becomes *amū* by virtue of the rule *adaso 'serdādu do maḥ* Pā. 8. 2. 80. The suspension of *ū* in this case would virtually make available the form *adau*, which was obtained prior to the grammatical operation of the sūtra *adaso 'serdādu do maḥ* Pā. 8. 2. 80 but the dual form ending in the vowel *au* does not get the pragṛhya designation by (51). This is the reason why Pāṇini has enunciated the sūtra *adaso māt* (52) so that the suspension of *ū* is overruled and the form *amū* gets the pragṛhya designation. If blocking the suspension of the sūtra *adaso 'serdādu do maḥ* Pā. 8. 2. 80 was not resorted to, then the present sūtra would be rendered redundant.

Although the form *amī* in the nominative plural also passes through the stage of *ade* where *e* is replaced by long *ī* by *adaso 'serdādu do maḥ* Pā. 8. 2. 80, it is plural and not dual as required by *īdūded dvivacanaṁ pragṛhyam* (51). On the basis of this grammatical necessity, it can be said that the present sūtra is meant for the masculine forms of *adas* ending in *ī* and *ū* preceded by *m*. The sum and substance of this elaboration is that in the feminine and neuter nominative and accusative dual forms of *adas*, the designation *pragṛhya* is available by (51), whereas the pragṛhya designation in the masculine forms of *adas* ending in *ī* and *ū* immediately following the *m* of *adas* is obtained only by *adaso māt* (52).

The counter-illustration given by Varadarāja also needs some explanation. Why has it been said that the long *ī* and *ū* which immediately follow the *m* of *adas* are to be designated as *pragṛhya* when there is not a single declension of *adas* in which *ī* or *ū* follows any other consonant? Even without mentioning the consonant *m* in the aphorism, the long vowels *ī* and *ū* immediately following *m* in *amū* and *amī* would have got the designation *pragṛhya*. By giving the counter-illustration *amuke 'tra*, Varadarāja intends to clarify that if the phoneme *m* had not been mentioned in the present sūtra, then the vowel *e* immediately following *k* in the form *amuke* would also have got the pragṛhya designation. In that case there would have been no pūrvarūpa sandhi in *amuke 'tra*. In the form *amuke*, the affix *akac* has been introduced to *adas* by *avyaya-sarvanāmnāmakac prāk ṭeḥ* (1227). The affix comes prior to the *ṭi* of *adas* in accordance with the same sūtra (1227). The form of *adas* with this affix accordingly would be *adakas*. Here the phoneme *d* is replaced by *m* and the vowel *a* by *u* by *adaso 'serdādu do maḥ* Pā. 8. 2. 80 and the form of *adas* with this affix would be *amukas*. In the nominative plural the word takes *jas* and by *tyadādīnāmaḥ*, the phoneme *s* of *amukas* is replaced by the substitute *a*. The rule *ato guṇe* (273) applies, pararūpa takes place and we have the form *amuka* which is still a pronoun by virtue of the paribhāṣā *tanmadhyapatitas tadgrahaṇena gṛhyate* (Abhyankar, 89). Hence the affix *jas* is replaced by *śi* in accordance with *jaśśasoḥ śiḥ* (236). The short *i* of *śi* remains after *ś*, which is *it* by *laśakvataddhite* (135), has been elided by *tasya lopaḥ* (3). Then the guṇa substitution takes place by *ādguṇaḥ* (27). Thus *amuke*, the form of *adas* with *akac* in nominative plural is obtained. Now in the counter-example, *amuke 'tra* given by Varadarāja, the grammatical operation of *eṅaḥ padāntādati* (43), that is, pūrvarūpa replacement coming in place of both the vowels *e* and *a* has been illustrated. In this situation, the vowel *e* in *amuke* could have received the designation *pragṛhya* and consequently, prakṛtibhāva could have become due. In that case, the pūrvarūpa substitution in place of *e* and *a*, which is available by *eṅaḥ padāntādati* (43), would not take place. Now with *m* having been specifically mentioned as the immediately preceding element, the phoneme *e* ceases to be designated as *pragṛhya* since *e* in *amuke* follows *k* and not *m* and as a result *eṅaḥ padāntādati* (43) applies and we have pūrvarūpa replacement.

The limitation that the form should be dual does not apply in the context of this sūtra.

(53) चादयोऽसत्त्वे । *cādayo 'sattve*. 1. 4. 57

लघु० – अद्रव्यार्थाश्चादयो निपाताः स्युः । *adravyārthāś cādayo nipātāḥ syuḥ.*

Trans. : Let the members of the list headed by *ca* be designated as *nipāta* when they do not denote a substance.

PP. *cādayaḥ asattve nipātāḥ.*

Eluc. : The word *nipātāḥ* is carried over into this sūtra from the governing rule *prāgrīśvarānnipātāḥ* Pā. 1. 4. 56. The word *cādayaḥ* is a tadguṇasaṁvijñāna bahuvrīhi (see supra p. 47 fn 1) which is analysed as follows : *ca ādir yeṣāṁ te = cādayaḥ*. The word *asattve* is a nañ-tatpuruṣa compound. Its analysis is : *na sattve asattve*. The negation denoted by the first member of this compound is prasajya.

There are two points to be considered in connection with this sūtra. First, what does the word *sattva* mean? Does it mean a substance or an action? According to the commentators the word means a substance (dravya) and not kriyā (action).

The other point, which needs to be considered, relates to the nature of negation in *asattve*. If this negation is interpreted as paryudāsa, the meaning of the sūtra will be as follows : the members enumerated in the group beginning with *ca* are designated as *nipāta* when they denote something other than sattva. According to this interpretation the word *paśu,* which is a member of the group headed by *ca,* is assigned the nipāta designation when the word means a substance qualified by the universal since something qualified by the universal is different from that which is not qualified by the universal, that is, from the bare substance. As a result, it is termed *avyaya* (indeclinable) by *svarādi-nipātamavyayam* Pā. 1.1. 37. The nominal endings, which are added after an avyaya, are elided by *avyayād āpsupaḥ* (371), so we will never have *paśu* in the declined form even when it denotes 'an animal'. On the other hand, if the negation is construed as prasajya, then the sūtra will be interpreted as follows : the elements enlisted in the group beginning with *ca* are not designated as *nipāta* when they denote sattva. This means that a word is not treated as nipāta, if it is related to the substance even remotely. The word *paśu* is such a word since this means an animal which is a dravya qualified by the universal paśutva. So we can have a declined form of the word *paśu* according to the prasajya interpretation of the sūtra. When this word means 'in the manner of an animal' (*paśuvat*), we can have its indeclinable form also. Cf. *lodhaṁ nayanti paśu manyamānāḥ* (Ṛgveda 3. 3. 23) in which the word *paśu* has been interpreted by Sāyaṇa as *paśuvat* (*paśuvat manyamānā iti*). So, according to the prasajya interpretation, we can have both the declined and non-declined forms of the word *paśu* (see also KN, I, pp. 589-90).

(54) प्रादयः । *prādayaḥ.* 1. 4. 58
लघु० – एतेऽपि तथा । *ete 'pi tathā.*

Trans. : Let the members of the group beginning with *pra* be also assigned the designation *nipāta* when they do not signify a substance.

PP. *asattve prādayaḥ nipātāḥ.*

Eluc. : The word *asattve* has been carried over from *cādayo 'sattve* Pā. 1. 4. 57. The term *nipātāḥ* has been lent into this sūtra from the governing sūtra *prāgrīśvarānnipātāḥ* Pā. 1. 4. 56. Thus the meaning of the sūtra is as follows : The words enlisted in the group headed by *pra* are termed *nipāta* when they do not signify a substance.

The governing rule *prāgrīśvarānnipātāḥ* Pā. 1. 4. 56 has its jurisdiction until *adhirīśvare* Pā. 1. 4. 56 and including it. Under this jurisdiction nipātas have been delineated. In this very adhikāra, Pāṇini has enunciated *prādayaḥ upasargāḥ kriyāyoge* as a single sūtra (cf. Kielhorn: 1985, p. 341). This reading is based on the statement of Patañjali in the Mahābhāṣya. He says that this sūtra should be divided (split) into two (*prādaya iti yogavibhāgaḥ kartavyaḥ*, Kielhorn : 1985, p. 341) so that both the designations, that is, *upsarga* and *nipāta* may be assigned to these twenty-two words enlisted in the group beginning with *pra*. If the splitting of the sūtra was not effected, the assignment of these two designations to these words separately would not be possible. According to the view that this is a single sūtra, its meaning will be as follows : These enlisted words are designated as *nipāta* as well as *upasarga* when they are used in connection with a verb. This means that when these words are not used in connection with a verb, they cannot be assigned the designation *nipāta*. Moreover, when they are used in connection with a verb, they will get both the designations *nipāta* and *upasarga*. When this sūtra is split into two, this problem is resolved. The sūtra read as *prādayaḥ* will mean that these enlisted words are designated as *nipāta* (even when they have no connection with a verb). The next split portion of the sūtra read as *upasargāḥ kriyāyoge* will mean that these words when used with a verb are designated as *upasarga*. In the sentence *mohano 'pi caturaḥ*, the term *api* is a nipāta and as a consequence avyaya also. The purpose, in this case, is to elide the inflectional endings, introduced after *api*, by virtue of *avyayādāpsupaḥ* (371). The designation *nipāta* in respect of these words when connected with a verb is purported to elide the *sup* termination after *pra*, etc. preceding a verb as in *prārcchati*. When any one of these enlisted words signifies a substantial entity, it is not designated as *nipāta*. Take, for example, the word *vi* among the enlisted words. When it means a bird, it is not an indeclinable and as such it will have inflectional endings after it as in *viḥ, vim, vinā*, etc.

(55) निपात एकाजनाङ्। *nipāta ekājanāṅ*. 1. 1. 14

लघु॰ – एकोऽच् निपात आङ्वर्जः प्रगृह्यः स्यात्। इ इन्द्रः। उ उमेशः। वाक्यस्मरणयोर् अङित्। आ एवं नु मन्यसे। आ एवं किल तत्। अन्यत्र ङित्, ईषदुष्णम् ओष्णम्।

eko 'c nipāta āṅvarjaḥ pragṛhyaḥ syāt. i indraḥ. u umeśaḥ. vākyasmaraṇayor aṅit. ā evaṁ nu manyase. ā evaṁ kila tat. anyatra ṅit - īṣaduṣṇam = oṣṇam.

Trans. : Excepting *āṅ*, let a nipāta consisting of a single *ac* (vowel) be designated as *pragṛhya*. Examples : *i indraḥ, u umeśaḥ*. (The nipāta *ā* is not *ṅit* when it signifies :) 1. emphasis of a sentence as an expletive and 2. reminiscence. Examples : 1. *ā evaṁ nu manyase* (Now indeed you think so). 2. *ā evaṁ kila tat* (Ah, such indeed that was). Elsewhere, it is *ṅit*. Example, *oṣṇam* (luke-warm).

PP. *anāṅ ekāc nipātaḥ pragṛhyaḥ.*

Eluc. : The word *pragṛhya* is carried over into this sūtra from *īdūded dvivacanaṁ pragṛhyam* Pā. 1. 1. 17. The term *ekāc* is a karmadhāraya compound which is analysed as : *ekaś cāsau ac* --> *ekāc* which means that a nipāta of the form of a bare vowel is to be designated as *pragṛhya.* The nipāta *āṅ* is an exception. After the elision of the marker *ṅ*, only *ā* remains which is of the form of a single vowel and as a consequence it fulfills the criterion of being termed *pragṛhya*. That is why Pāṇini has excluded it from the purview of the pragṛhya designation by inserting the nañ-tatpuruṣa *anāṅ* which means 'different from *āṅ*'.

The first two illustrations are : *i indraḥ* (O! Indra), *u umeśaḥ* (Could be Umeśa!). In these illustrations, *i* and *u*, which convey respectively surprise and conjecture, are single vowels and are nipātas, being included in the list headed by *ca* and hence they are pragṛhyas. They retain their original form. In the absence of this rule the single *i* and the *i* of *indra* in the first example and the single *u* and the *u* of *umeśa* in the second example would respectively be replaced by long *ī* and *ū* in accordance with *akaḥ savarṇe dīrghaḥ* (42). This grammatical operation of substituting a long vowel is precluded by this sūtra and prakṛtibhāva takes place by (50).

There are two particles having *ā* as their form. One is bare *ā* (*aṅit*) and the other is *āṅ* (*ṅit*). The particle (*nipāta*) *ā* with marker *ṅ* denotes the sense of (1) a little (*īṣad-artha*), (2) connection with activity (*kriyā-yoga*), (3) exclusive limit (*maryādā*), (4) inclusive limit (*abhividhi*); but without the marker it signifies (5) emphasis in a sentence {when used as an expletive in a sentence (*vākya*)} and (6) reminiscence (*smaraṇa*) :

1. in the sense of 'a little' (*īṣad-artha*) : *ā* + *uṣṇam* --> *oṣṇam* 'a little warm',
2. connection with activity (*kriyā-yoga*) : *ā* + *ihi* --> *ehi* 'come',
3. exclusive limit (*maryādā*) : *ā* + *āndhrād* --> *āndhrād vṛṣṭo devaḥ* 'it rained up to Andhra (but not including it)',
4. inclusive limit (*abhividhi*) : *ā* + *āndhrād* --> *āndhrād vṛṣṭo devaḥ* 'it rained up to Andhra (including it)',
5. emphasis in a sentence : *ā evaṁ nu manyase* 'now you indeed think so',
6. reminiscence (*smaraṇa*) : *ā evaṁ kila tat* 'ah, such indeed that was'.

In the last two sentences the particle *ā* is aṅit. Consisting of a bare vowel, it gets the pragṛhya designation. As such prakṛtibhāva ensues and there is no vṛddhi-substitution in place of *ā* and *e* in both the sentences. In other senses, this particle *ā* is ṅit. Being ṅit, it does not get the pragṛhya designation. Hence there is no prakṛtibhāva. This is the reason why there is guṇa-sandhi in the first two illustrations and dīrgha-sandhi in the third and the fourth. Patañjali has explained the guidelines in the following verse to determine whether this particle is *ā* or *āṅ* :

īṣadarthe kriyāyoge maryādā 'bhividhau ca yaḥ,
etamātaṁ ṅitaṁ vidyād vākyasmaraṇayor aṅit. Mbh on Pā. 1. 1. 14.

When the particle *ā* means 'a little', 'connection with activity', 'exclusive limit' and 'inclusive limit', it is ṅit but when it means 'emphasis in a sentence' and 'reminiscence', it should be taken as aṅit.

(56) ओत्। *ot.* 1. 1. 15

लघु॰ – ओदन्तो निपातः प्रगृह्यः स्यात्। अहो ईशाः। *odanto nipātaḥ pragṛhyaḥ syāt. aho īśāḥ.*

Trans. : Let the nipāta which ends in *o* be designated as *pragṛhya.*

PP. *ot nipātaḥ pragṛhyaḥ.*

Eluc. : The word *nipāta* is carried over from the sūtra *nipāta ekājanāṅ* Pā. 1. 1. 14 and *pragṛhya* from *īdūded dvivacanaṁ pragṛhyam* Pā. 1. 1. 11. The term *ot* qualifies the word *nipāta*. By tadantavidhi, it gives the meaning *odantaḥ nipātaḥ*. Thus the completed sūtra means : The particle (*nipāta*) which ends in the vowel *o* is designated as *pragṛhya*. Take, for example, the expression *aho īśāḥ*. The word *aho* is read in the list headed by *ca*. It does not mean a substance. Therefore it is a nipāta. Since it ends in *o*, it is termed *pragṛhya* by the present rule. Consequently by *plutapragṛhyā aci nityam* (50), the vowel *o* at the end of *aho* retains its original form and is not replaced by *av* by the sūtra *eco 'yavāyāvaḥ* (22). This particle does not consist of a bare vowel as the particles *ā*, *i*, *u*, etc. do. Hence the necessity of the present sūtra.

(57) सम्बुद्धौ शाकल्यस्येतावनार्षे। *sambuddhau śākalyasyetāvanārṣe.* 1. 1. 16

लघु॰ – सम्बुद्धिनिमित्तक ओकारो वा प्रगृह्योऽवैदिक इतौ परे। विष्णो इति। विष्ण इति। विष्णविति। *sambuddhinimittaka okāro vā pragṛhyo 'vaidika itau pare. viṣṇo iti. viṣṇa iti. viṣṇaviti.*

Trans. : Let the vowel *o* (which is at the end) of the vocative singular followed by a non-Vedic *iti* get the designation *pragṛhya* in the opinion of Śākalya.

PP. *sambuddhau ot anārṣe itau pragṛhyaḥ śākalyasya.*

Eluc. : The terms *ot* and *pragṛhyam* are carried over into the present sūtra from *ot* Pā. 1. 1. 15 and *īdūded dvivacanaṁ pragṛhyam* Pā. 1. 1. 11 respectively. The seventh case-ending in the word *sambuddhau* is in the sense of a 'cause' (*nimittasaptamī*). This means that the final vowel *o*, which is brought about by its being in the vocative singular, is termed *pragṛhya* according to Śākalya, provided it is followed by an *iti* which is not a part of the Vedic text. Since the name of grammarian Śākalya has been quoted in the rule, it is considered to be optional. Pāṇini uses this kind of device in two ways : 1. either as a mark of respect (*pūjārthe*) or 2. to indicate the optional nature of the rule (*vibhāṣārthe*). The three illustrations, which are given by Varadarāja, demonstrate the application of this sūtra : *viṣṇo iti, viṣṇa iti* and *viṣṇaviti.* The term *viṣṇo* is the vocative singular of the nominal stem *viṣṇu*. The word *sambuddhi* is a technical term which means 'vocative singular' [*ekavacanaṁ sambuddhiḥ* (131)]. In this case, the nominal affix *su* in the vocative singular brings about the guṇa-substitution *o* in place of *u* at the end of *viṣṇu* by *hrasvasya guṇaḥ* (168). At this stage, the sūtra *eṅhrasvāt sambuddheḥ* (133) applies and the inflectional affix *su* is replaced by lopa. Thus we obtain the word *viṣṇo.* When it is followed by a non-Vedic *iti*, the rule *eco 'yavāyāvaḥ* (22) becomes available for application but, since *o* is pragṛhya according to Śākalya by virtue of the present sūtra, the sūtra *eco 'yavāyāvaḥ* (22) is blocked. Instead prakṛtibhāva takes place : *viṣṇo iti.* According to the view of the other grammarians, it is not pragṛhya. Then the sūtra *eco 'yavāyāvaḥ* (22) applies and *o* is replaced by *av* and we have *viṣṇaviti*. At this stage again, the sūtra *lopaḥ śākalyasya* (30) optionally prescribes the elision of the pada-final *v* : *viṣṇa iti*. When the elision of *v* takes place, the sūtra *ādguṇaḥ* (27) does not apply since *lopaḥ śākalyasya* Pā. 8. 3. 19 is deemed to have effected nothing so far as *ādguṇaḥ* Pā. 6. 1. 87 is concerned {see supra (31)}.

In the Kāśikā two counter-examples are given : 1. *vāyo 'tra* and 2. *etā gā brahmabandha ityabravīt*. In the first counter-example the ending *o* of the vocative singular form *vāyo* is followed by the *a* of *atra* and not by *iti.* The pragṛhya designation is not available, so *eṅaḥ padāntādati* (43) applies and a single vowel substitute, consisting of the first of the two contiguous vowels denoted by the abbreviatory term *eṅ*, replaces both the pada-final *eṅ* and the following initial short *a*. The second counter-example *brahmabandha iti* (*etā gā brahmabandha ityabravīt*) is relevant in the present context. We arrive at this stage in the following manner : *brahmabandho iti*. This *iti* is Vedic and as such pragṛhya designation is not available. In the absence of the pragṛhya designation, the sūtra *eco 'yavāyāvaḥ* (22) applies and the pada-final *o* is replaced by *av* : *brahmabandhav iti*. Then by virtue of *lopaḥ śākalyasya* (30) pada-final *v* is optionally elided and we obtain the form as quoted in the Kāśikā : *brahmabandha iti*.

(58) मय उञो वो वा । *maya uño vo vā*. 8. 3. 33

लघु० – मयः परस्य उञो वो वा स्यादचि । किम्वुक्तम् । किमु उक्तम् । *mayaḥ parasya uño vo vā syād aci. kimvuktam. kimu uktam.*

Trans. : Let the particle *uñ* following the elements denoted by *may*-pratyāhāra be optionally replaced by *v*, if *ac* follows.

PP. *mayaḥ uñaḥ vaḥ vā aci saṁhitāyām.*

Eluc. : The term *aci* is carried over into this sūtra from *ṅamo hrasvādaci ṅamuṇ nityam* Pā. 8. 3. 32. The term *saṁhitāyām* comes from the governing rule *tayoryvāvaci saṁhitāyām* Pā. 8. 2. 108. Its domain extends up to the end of the Aṣṭādhyāyī (Pā. 8. 4. 68). Thus the meaning of the sūtra will be as follows : When extreme proximity is intended, the particle *uñ* following the elements denoted by *may*-pratyāhāra is optionally replaced by *v*, if *ac* follows. In *va* the vowel *a* is for the sake of articulation. The particle *uñ* has been read in the list headed by *ca* and it consists of a bare *ac*, that is, *u* after the elision of *ñ* by *tasya lopaḥ* (3). Thus the pragṛhya designation is available by *nipāta ekājanāṅ* (55). The present sūtra blocks this rule and optionally prescribes *v*-replacement in place of *u*. We get the usage : *kimvuktam* from *kim u uktam*. In the absence of *v*-replacement, the pragṛhya designation will be available and *u* will retain its original form : *kimu uktam*. One point is worth noting here : In the first illustration, the *m* of *kim* is followed by *v* and as a consequence, the anusvāra-replacement for *m* is available by *mo 'nusvāraḥ* Pā. 8. 3. 23. Since the sūtra under discussion is subsequent to *mo 'nusvāraḥ* Pā. 8. 3. 23, the *v*-replacement is deemed to be suspended with respect to the sūtra *mo 'nusvāraḥ* in accordance with *pūrvatrāsiddham* (31). That is why *m* is not replaced by anusvāra.

(59) इकोऽसवर्णेऽचि शाकल्यस्य ह्रस्वश्च । *iko 'savarṇe 'ci śākalyasya hrasvaśca*. 6. 1. 127

लघु० – पदान्ता इको ह्रस्वा वा स्युरसवर्णेऽचि । ह्रस्वविधानसामर्थ्यान्न स्वरसन्धिः । चक्रि अत्र । चक्रयत्र । पदान्ता किम् ? गौर्यौ । *padāntā iko hrasvā vā syur asavarṇe 'ci. hrasvavidhānasāmarthyān na svarasandhiḥ. cakri atra. cakryatra. padāntā kim ? gauryau.*

Trans. : Let the pada-final vowel denoted by *ik* be optionally replaced by a corresponding short vowel when a non-homogeneous vowel (*ac*) follows. There is no svara-sandhi by the force of a short vowel-replacement being prescribed (by this sūtra).

PP. *padāntasya ikaḥ asarvarṇe aci hrasvaḥ śākalyasya ca* (*saṁhitāyām*).

Eluc. : The word *padāntād* has been carried over into this sūtra from *eṅaḥ padāntādati* Pā. 6. 1. 109 and has been changed into the genitive nominal ending by the process of vibhaktivipariṇāma. The term *aci* is carried over from the sūtra *iko yaṇaci* Pā. 6. 1. 77. The meaning of the sūtra according to Varadarāja is as follows : the pada-final vowel denoted by *ik* is shortened before a non-homogeneous vowel. Actually this means that the pada-final *ik* vowel is replaced by a corresponding short vowel. This is the reason why we say that *padāntāt* has been transformed into *padāntasya* (*ikaḥ*) by vibhaktivipariṇāma. The mention of the name of Śākalya in the sūtra means in effect that the rule is optional. The short vowel replacement takes place according to Śākalya. This does not take place according to other grammarians. The conclusion is that it takes place optionally.

The first illustration is *cakrī + atra*. Here *ik*-vowel exists at the end of *cakrī* and according to Śākalya it is replaced by a short *i*. The resultant form is *cakri atra*. The sūtra *iko yaṇaci* (15) does not apply here because of the shortening of the *ik*-vowel. If it applies, then the prescription of the shortening of pada-final *ik*-vowel would become redundant. If *y*-replacement takes place in both the cases, the shortening of *ik*-vowel becomes an exercise in futility. So *iko yaṇaci* (15) applies only where the *ik*-vowel does not shorten and the *ī* at the end of *cakrī* is replaced by the semi-vowel *y*.

The significance of the *ik*-vowel being pada-final lies in the fact that if the *ik*-vowel is not pada-final, then the shortening of the *ik*-vowel does not take place. Instead *iko yaṇaci* (15) applies : *gaurī + au --> gauryau*. Moreover, the significance of saying 'followed by non-homogeneous' lies in the fact that the pada-final vowel denoted by *ik* is not replaced by a corresponding short vowel if the following vowel is homogeneous. In the expression *yogī icchati*, the *ī* at the end of *yogī* is followed by the homogeneous *i* of *icchati*. The pada-final long *ī* is not substituted by a short *i* according to this sūtra.

It has already been pointed out at (50) that because of the use of the word *nitya* in that sūtra, this aphorism does not apply where prakṛti-bhāva has scope on account of an incidence of pragṛhya designation.

Consequently, by the present sūtra the pada-final long *ī* in *harī etau* is not replaced by a corresponding short *i* .

(60) अचो रहाभ्यां द्वे । *aco rahābhyāṁ dve.* 8. 4. 46

लघु० – अचः पराभ्यां रेफहकाराभ्यां परस्य यरो द्वे वा स्तः । गौर्य्यौ । *acaḥ parābhyāṁ rephahakārābhyāṁ parasya yaro dve vā staḥ. gauryyau.*

Trans. : A consonant denoted by the abbreviatory term *yar*, immediately occurring after *r* or *h* which again are preceded by a vowel (*ac*), is optionally reduplicated.

PP. *acaḥ rahābhyām dve yaraḥ vā (saṁhitāyām).*

Eluc. : The terms *yar* and *vā* are carried over into this sūtra from *yaro 'nunāsike 'nunāsiko vā* Pā. 8. 4. 45. The abbreviatory term *yar* denotes all consonants except *h*. The conditions for *yar* to be replaced by its double (gemination) are as follows : 1. The *yar*-consonant must follow either *r* or *h* and 2. The phoneme *r* or *h* should immediately be preceded by a vowel (*ac*). In the illustration given by Varadarāja *r* follows the vowel *au* and the *yar* consonant immediately follows *r* (*gaurī au* --> *gaury au*). The conditions are fulfilled and *y* is replaced by two *y*'s and thus we obtain the word *gauryyau*. Since the operation of this rule is optional, we have the alternative form : *gauryau*.

9. वा० – न समासे । वाप्यश्वः । *na samāse.*[1] *vāpyaśvaḥ.*

Trans. : In samāsa the pada-final vowel denoted by *ik* is not replaced by a corresponding short vowel when followed by a non-homogeneous vowel.

Eluc. : The illustration *vāpyaśvaḥ* 'a horse in a water-reservoir' is a saptamī-tatpuruṣa compound which is analysed as *vāpyam aśvaḥ*. After the elision of the sup-affixes by *supo dhātuprātipadikayoḥ* (718), we get *vāpī + aśva*. Although the locative nominal ending has been elided, the operation conditioned by it still takes place by virtue of the rule *pratyayalope pratyayalakṣaṇam* (189). Hence it is a pada and the shortening of *ī* is available by (59) since it is followed by a non-homogeneous vowel.

---

1. The vārttika, given here, is not available in the Mahābhāṣya and the Kāśikā in this form. Nevertheless, it conveys, in a simple way, the sense of *sinnityasamāsayoḥ śākalapratiṣedhaḥ* (Mbh 6. 1. 127 vtk 1). Since only this sense is relevant to spoken language (*bhāṣā*), Bhaṭṭoji Dīkṣita has partially paraphrased the original vārttika and Varadarāja follows him.

This vārttika blocks it and the semi-vowel *y* replaces the vowel *ī* by *iko yaṇaci* (15) and we obtain the form *vāpyaśvaḥ*.

(61) ऋत्यकः । *ṛtyakaḥ*. 6. 1. 128

लघु० - ऋति परे पदान्ता अकः प्राग्वद् वा । ब्रह्म ऋषिः । ब्रह्मर्षिः । पदान्ताः किम् ? आर्च्छत् । *ṛti pare padāntā akaḥ prāgvad vā. brahma ṛṣiḥ. brahmarṣiḥ. padāntāḥ kim ? ārcchat.*

Trans. : If a short *ṛ* immediately follows, then let the pada-final vowel denoted by *ak* be optionally replaced by a corresponding short vowel as stated earlier {under (59)}.

PP. *ṛti padāntasya akaḥ hrasvaḥ śākalyasya (saṁhitāyām).*

Eluc. : The term *padāntāt* is carried over from *eṅaḥ padāntādati* Pā. 6. 1. 109 and has been changed into the genitive nominal ending (*padāntasya*) by vibhakti-vipariṇāma so that it may accord with *akaḥ*, which is the intended meaning. The words *śākalyasya* and *hrasvaḥ* have also been carried over from *iko 'savarṇe 'ci śākalyasya hrasvaśca* Pā. 6. 1. 127. Thus the elliptical sūtra made into a complete sentence means : When a short *ṛ* immediately follows a pada-final vowel signified by the abbreviatory term *ak*, a vowel denoted by *ak* is replaced by a corresponding short *ak*-vowel. In the illustration *brahmā ṛṣiḥ*, *ā* is a pada-final vowel denoted by *ak* and is immediately followed by the short vowel *ṛ*. According to the present sūtra the long *ā* coming at the end of *brahmā*, which is a pada, is replaced by a corresponding short vowel. In this case it is a short *a*. Thus the sandhi form of the usage *brahma ṛṣi*, as given in the vṛtti, is obtained. When there is a short *ak*-vowel substitution, no other sandhi takes place because of the very fact that this sūtra has been enunciated by Pāṇini. In other words prakṛtibhāva takes place. In view of this interpretation, the mention of Śākalya in the sūtra is to show respect to him. In the absence of a short *ak*-vowel substitution, a guṇa substitution in place of both *ā* at the end of *brahmā* and *ṛ* at the beginning of *ṛṣi* takes place in accordance with the sūtra *ādguṇaḥ* (27). In this case the guṇa substitution *a* is followed by the phoneme *r* in accordance with *uraṇ raparaḥ* (29) and the alternative form of sandhi *brahmarṣiḥ* is obtained.

There are two grounds given in the Mahābhāṣya why Pāṇini has enunciated this sūtra :

1. *ṛtyakaḥ savarṇārthaḥ*. This sūtra is enunciated for a condition in which a homogeneous vowel follows. The sūtra *iko 'savarṇe 'ci śākalyasya*

hrasvaśca (59) does not apply in a situation in which a homogeneous vowel follows. Take, for example, the illustration : *hotṛ ṛkāraḥ*. The usage *hotṛ ṛkāraḥ* is a ṣaṣṭhītatpuruṣa compound analysed as *hotuḥ ṛkāraḥ*. After sup-affixes have been deleted in accordance with the rule *supo dhātu...* (718), the stage reached is *hotṛ ṛkāra*. At this stage, the sūtra *ṛtyakaḥ* (61) applies and the short *ṛ* which is denoted by *ak* is replaced by a short *ṛ* in pursuance of the paribhāṣā *parjanyaval lakṣaṇapravṛttiḥ*[1] (Abhyankar, 119). After introducing the nominative singular affix *su*, we get the form *hotṛ ṛkāraḥ*. Where the short vowel replacement takes place, prakṛtibhāva is optionally available. The prakṛtibhāva could not have been explained in the absence of this sūtra since in the illustration, given here, short *ṛ* is followed by a homogneous short *ṛ* whereas according to (59) prakṛtibhāva is available only when a non-homogeneous vowel follows.

2. *anigantārthaṁ ca*. This sūtra is enunciated for cases where the pada does not end in *ik*. The sūtra *iko 'savarṇe 'ci...* (59) is available for application in the case of vowels denoted by *ik*. In the illustration given in the vṛtti, it is the long *ā* at the end of *brahmā* which is different from the vowels denoted by *ik*, whereas the sūtra (59) applies in the context of vowels signified by *ik*. It should be borne in mind that, when there is a short vowel replacement, prakṛtibhāva does take place.

The significance of the inclusion of the word *padāntāḥ* is to preclude a short vowel replacement where *ak* does not occur at the end of a pada. Take, for example, the verbal usage *ārcchat*. This is the third person singular form of the verbal root *ṛcch* in laṅ lakāra. The augment *āṭ*, which is introduced by *āḍajādīnām* (443), remains as *ā* after the consonant *ṭ* has been elided by *tasya lopaḥ* (3) since it is *it* by *halantyam* (1). Here *ā* is followed by the non-homogeneous (*asavarṇa*) vowel *ṛ* of the verb *ṛcch*. The conditions for the substitution by a short vowel denoted by the abbreviatory term *ak* are available except that the vowel *ā* is not pada-final. Being an augment, it is a part of the verb *ṛcch* {*yadāgamās tadguṇībhūtās tadgrahaṇena gṛhyante* (Abhyankar, 11)}. Consequently, it is neither a pada nor pada-final. Thus the inclusion of the word pada-final precludes the short vowel substitution in place of *ā* in this situation. Now the grammatical situation for the application of the rule *āṭaśca* (196) becomes available and as a consequence a vṛddhi-vowel substitution takes place. Thus a vṛddhi vowel *ā* replaces both the *ā* of *āṭ* and the *ṛ* of

1. When it rains, it rains on dry land as well as on the sea surface. In the same manner, a grammatical rule applies whether its application is needed to bring about a visible grammatical change or not. In the present illustration, a short *ṛ* is replaced by a short *ṛ* without any visible change.

the verbal root *ṛcch*. Then by *uraṇ raparaḥ* (29), the long *ā* is accompanied by the phoneme *r* and the verbal form *ārcchat* is obtained.

Another point which needs to be borne in mind is that the sūtra *iko 'savarṇe 'ci śākalyasya hrasvaśca* (59) does not apply in the context of a compound since the vārttika *na samāse* is given at the sūtra (59) and its application is confined to it. The vārttika does not apply in the context of the present sūtra (*na samāse iti niṣedhavārttikam hi iko 'savarṇe 'ci śākalyasya hrasvaś ca iti sūtra eva na tu ṛtyakaḥ ityatreti siddhāntaḥ* TB, I, p. 107). This also explains the incidence of prakṛtibhāva in *sapta ṛṣīṇām* which is a karmadhāraya samāsa in accordance with the sūtra *diksaṁkhye saṁjñāyām* (931) in the sense of an appellation. In the absence of prakṛtibhāva, the guṇa substitution takes place and we have the alternative form *saptarṣīṇām* of this karmadhāraya samāsa.

लघु० – इत्यच्-सन्धिः । *ityac-sandhiḥ.*

Trans. : The chapter on *ac*-sandhi ends.

अथ हल्-सन्धिः
Consonant-Sandhi

(62) **स्तोः श्चुना श्चुः ।** ***stoḥ ścunā ścuḥ*. 8. 4. 40**

लघु० – सकारतकारयोः शकारचवर्गाभ्यां योगे शकारचवर्गौ स्तः । रामश्शेते । रामश्चिनोति । सच्चित् । शार्ङ्गिञ्जय । *sakāratakārayoḥ śakāracavargābhyāṁ yoge śakāracavargau staḥ. rāmaś śete. rāmaś cinoti. saccit. śārṅgiñjaya.*

Trans. : The dental sibilant *s* and the dental stops (*tu*) in close proximity with the palatal *ś* and the palatal stops (*cu*) are replaced by the palatal sibilant *ś* and the palatal stops.

PP. *stoḥ ścunā scuḥ* (*saṁhitāyām*).

Eluc. : The word *saṁhitāyām* in *tayoryvāvaci saṁhitāyām* Pā. 8. 2. 108 forms a governing rule which extends up to Pā. 8. 4. 68 (Katre : 1989, p. 1015). Since the present rule occurs in its governing domain, the word *saṁhitāyām* recurs here also. We have put it in the parenthesis only to show that it is carried over here and in the relevant rules of sandhi that follow. This word means 'when extreme proximity is intended' and this meaning should be taken as understood wherever this word occurs in the parentheses.

All the three constituents of the sūtra are samāhāradvandva compounds.The first is *stuḥ* which is analysed as *s ca tuś ca stuḥ*. In a samāhāra-dvandva, singular number and neuter gender are grammatically required. In the present sūtra the dvandva samāsa is in the singular number but the gender is masculine which has been interpreted as sautra by commentators, that is, it is peculiar to the sūtra only. The term *stoḥ* is the genitive form of *stu*. In a similar way, *ścunā* and *ścuḥ* may be interpreted and understood. The singular sup-affix of the third triplet in *ścunā* is by *sahayukte 'pradhāne* Pā. 2. 3. 19. Although the term *saha* is not used, the singular sup-affix of the third triplet in *ścunā* conveys its sense as it does in *vṛddho yūnā tallakṣaścedeva viśeṣaḥ* Pā. 1. 2. 65. Thus the meaning of the sūtra will be as follows : The dental sibilant s and the dental stops (*tu*), which are in close proximity with the palatal *ś* and the palatal stops (*cu*), are replaced by the palatal sibilant *ś* and the palatal stops.

The dental sibilant *s* and the dental stops are the subtituenda (*sthānin*) and the palatal *ś* and the palatal stops are the substitutes (*ādeśa*). When these consonantal sounds come in contact with each other, irrespective of their preceding or consequent position, and when there is no intervention of any other phoneme between them, the dental s and the dental stops are replaced by the palatal *ś* and palatal stops. A particular order is not intended. They may follow each other. What is required is the contact between them. This should be without any intervention; otherwise in the word *cit*, the dental stop *t* would become liable to be substituted by the palatal *c*. Since there is a vowel (*i*) between the two, the dental stop *t* will not be replaced by *c*.

The substituenda (*sthānin*) and the substitutes (*ādeśa*) are equally enumerated. It therefore invites the application of *yathāsaṁkhyam anudeśaḥ samānām* (23) but the one-to-one correspondence in order of enumeration applies to the subtituenda (*sthānin*) and the substitutes (*ādeśa*). It does not apply to yoga 'contact or proximity connection'. This is implied by the negative provision prescribed by Pāṇini in the sūtra *śāt* (63). This means that it should not be understood here that the dental *s* is replaced by the palatal *ś* only when it comes in contact with the palatal *ś*. Similarly it is not the case that the dental stop *t* is substituted by the palatal *c* only when it comes in contact with the palatal *c*, the dental *th* by the palatal *ch* only when the former comes in contact with the latter and so on and so forth. Had this been the case, Pāṇini would not have enunciated the sūtra *śāt* (63), which makes a negative provision. The sūtra *śāt* (63) says that the substitute palatal stops do not replace the dental stops when they occur after the palatal sibilant *ś*. If one-to-one correspondence were intended in this case, then the palatal sibilant *ś* would not be followed by the dental stops since one-to-one correspondence would have restricted the contact of the dental s to the palatal *ś*. This means that the contact between the dental s and the palatal *ś* and that between the dental stops and the palatal stops is not on the basis of one-to-one correspondence. The dental sibilant and the dental stops on the one hand and the palatal sibilant and the palatal stops on the other may come in contact with each other in any sequence. Still the dental sibilant *s* and the dental stops will be replaced by the palatal sibilant *ś* and the palatal stops. This is the reason why it is said that one-to-one correspondence is only with reference to the replacements and not with reference to the contact (*yoga*). The illustrations given by Varadarāja also endorse this interpretation. This will be clear in the sequel also.

The first illustration is : *rāmas* + *śete* (Rāma sleeps). In this illustration the dental s is followed by the palatal *ś* or it may be said that the dental sibilant comes in contact with the palatal sibilant. Consequently the dental s is replaced by the palatal *ś*. The resultant form obtained is : *rāmaś śete*. In this illustration it may also be noted that the phoneme s of the nominative inflectional ending *su* is replaced by *ru* in accordance with the sūtra *sasajuṣo ruḥ* (104). The remaining *r* of *ru* is replaced by visarga by virtue of the sūtra *kharavasānayorvisarjanīyaḥ* (93). Visarjanīya is replaced by s before *khar* but this replacement is optional before *śar* in accordance with the sūtra *vā śari* (103). The illustration relates to the stage when visarjanīya has been replaced by the dental sibilant s. In the event of this replacement not taking place, we have another form as *rāmaḥ śete*.

The second illustration : *rāmas* + *cinoti* proves the interpretation that one-to-one correspondence is only with respect to the replacements and not with respect to the contact for, in the second illustration, the dental sibilant s is followed by the palatal stop *c*. Still the dental s is replaced by the palatal *ś*. Had one-to-one correspondence been intended with respect to the contacts, the dental sibilant s would not have been required to come in contact with a palatal stop for this replacement. Instead it would only have sufficed to come in contact with the palatal *ś*. After s has been replaced by *ś* we get the usage : *rāmaś cinoti* (Rāma plucks or chooses). Here s is replaced by the palatal *ś* when the visarga substituted for the repha of *ru* has been replaced by s by virtue of the sūtra *visarjanīyasya saḥ* (96).

In the third illustration the dental stop *t* is in contact with the palatal stop *c* and is replaced by the palatal *c* : *sat* + *cit* --> *sac cit* (existence and consciousness). In this illustration it is worth noting that the present sūtra remains suspended vis-a-vis the sūtra *jhalāṁ jaśo 'nte* Pā. 8. 2. 39. Therefore, first *jhalāṁ jaśo 'nte* Pā. 8. 2. 39 applies and the *t* at the end gets replaced by *d*. The rule *khari ca* Pā. 8. 4. 55 is asiddha with respect to the present sūtra. As a consequence, the present rule applies first and *d* is replaced by *j*. Now *khari ca* (74) steps in and *j* is substituted by *c*. We get the usage *saccit*.

In the fourth illustration the fifth dental nasal stop is in contact with the third palatal stop. The nasal dental stop is replaced by the palatal nasal stop : *śārṅgin* + *jaya* --> *śārṅgiñ jaya* (O Viṣṇu ! Be thou victorious). This also endorses the view that one-to-one correspondence does not hold good in respect of the contact (*yoga*).

It has already been pointed out that a particular order for the contact between the dental sibilant and the dental stops on the one hand and the palatal sibilant and the palatal stops on the other is not intended. The author of the Kāśikā says in this regard that had Pāṇini intended order among the two kinds of consonants, he would have used the singular locative inflectional ending after *ścu* and the sūtra would have been in this form : *stoḥ ścau ścuḥ*. The locative inflectional ending could have determined the order between the two. Hence only contact is intended and not the order. Both can follow or precede each other but, according to this interpretation, the usages like *acsandhi, actva, jaśtva* etc. need explanation and justification. To account for these usages, it may, however, be said that Pāṇini has dropped a hint in this regard in the sūtra *alpāctaram* (985). In this sūtra *c* is in contact with *t* but *t* is not replaced by *c* in accordance with the present sūtra. The implication is that at some places this replacement is not effected in order that these consonants may stand clearly distinguished (*spaṣṭapratipattyartham*).

(63) शात्। *śāt*. 8. 4. 44

लघु० - शात् परस्य तवर्गस्य चुत्वं न स्यात्। विश्नः। प्रश्नः। *śāt parasya tavargasya cutvaṁ na syāt. viśnaḥ. praśnaḥ.*

Trans. : Let not the dental stops following the palatal sibilant *ś* be replaced by the palatal stops.

PP. *śāt toḥ na (saṁhitāyām)*.

Eluc. : The words *toḥ* and *na* are respectively carried over from the sūtras *toḥ ṣi* Pā. 8. 4. 43 and *na padāntāṭṭoranām* Pā. 8. 4. 42. Together with these words the sūtra makes a complete sentence. The particle *na* in the sūtra requires something to be negated. What is available after *ś* is negated by this sūtra. After *ś* the substitution of the palatal stops in place of the dental stops is available by the sūtra *stoḥ ścunā ścuḥ* (62). That is being negated by the present sūtra. Thus the sūtra means : The items denoted by *tu* are not replaced by those denoted by *cu* if they follow the palatal sibilant *ś*. The first illustration is *viśnaḥ*. When the affix *naṅ* is introduced after the verbal root *vicch* 'to go' by *yajayācayatavicchapraccharakṣo naṅ* (857), the consonant *ch* is replaced by *ś* by *cchvoḥ śūḍanunāsike ca* (840). At this stage (*viś* + *na*) the palatal *ñ* is to be substituted for the dental *n* by *stoḥ ścunā ścuḥ* (62) but this is blocked by the present rule *śāt* and we have the form *viśnaḥ*. In a similar way we have the form *praśnaḥ* from the verbal root *pracch* 'to enquire' with the addition of the same affix *naṅ*.

There are three points to be borne in mind : 1. The present sūtra is posterior to *stoḥ ścunā ścuḥ* Pā. 8. 4. 40. Therefore it is treated as suspended with respect to *stoḥ ścunā ścuḥ* (62). Nevertheless, if Pāṇini has enunciated this sūtra, this means that this sūtra would be treated as an exception to (62); otherwise finding no scope, it would be rendered redundant. 2. The grammatical operation of samprasāraṇa is available by *grahijyāvayivyadhivaṣṭivicativṛścatipṛcchatibhṛjjatīnāṁ ṅiti ca* (633) but the sūtra *praśne cāsannakāle* Pā. 3. 2. 117 blocks this by implication. 3. This very sūtra also additionally implies that, if dental stops follow the palatal *ś*, they will not be replaced by the palatal stops since Pāṇini himself has used it. This implication does away with the need of this sūtra. Jinendrabuddhi in his commentary[1] on the Kāśikā on this sūtra (*śāt*) says that, although it is possible to do away with this sūtra, it has been enunciated so that the less intelligent may not find it difficult to understand the implication of the sūtra *praśne cāsannakāle* Pā. 3. 2. 117.

(64) ष्टुना ष्टुः । *ṣṭunā ṣṭuḥ*. 8. 4. 41

लघु॰ – स्तोः ष्टुना योगे ष्टुः स्यात्। रामष्षष्ठः। रामष्टीकते। पेष्टा। तट्टीका। चक्रिण्ढौकसे।

stoḥ ṣṭunā yoge ṣṭuḥ syāt. rāmaṣṣaṣṭhaḥ. rāmaṣṭīkate. peṣṭā. taṭṭīkā. cakriṇḍhaukase.

Trans. : Let the dental sibilant s and the dental stops (*tu*) when in contact with the retroflex sibilant ṣ and retroflex stops (*ṭu*) be replaced by the latter.

PP. *stoḥ ṣṭunā ṣṭuḥ* (*saṁhitāyām*).

Eluc. : The term *stoḥ* is carried over from the sūtra *stoḥ ścunā*... Pā. 8. 4. 40. The word *ṣṭuḥ* is a samāhāradvandva like *stuḥ* in (62). The same argument, as was given in respect of *stoḥ*... (62), can be adduced here to explain the use of samāhāradvandva in the masculine in the present sūtra. The one-to-one correspondence is effective in respect of the replacements only. There is no such equivalence with regard to the contact between them as explained in the sūtra (62). This view is derived from the fact that the sūtra *toḥ ṣi* Pā. 8. 4. 43 says that the retroflex stops do not replace the dental stops before retroflex ṣ. This condition would not be available, were the one-to-one correspondence intended in the case of the contact between the substituenda and the substitutes.

In the first illustration *rāmaṣ ṣaṣṭhaḥ* (Rāma is the sixth), there is coalescence between *rāmas* and *ṣaṣṭhaḥ*. The nominative inflectional

---

1. *yadyapi praśne cāsannakāle iti nipātanād eva śāt parasya tavargasya cutvaṁ na bhavatītyeṣo 'rtho labhyate tathāpi mandadhiyāṁ pratipattigauravaparīhārārtham idam ārabhyate.* KN, VI, 651.

ending *su* comes after the nominal stem *rāma,* the s of *su* remains after the elision of *u* which is *it* according to *upadeśe 'janunāsika it* (28). Now *ru* replaces s (104) and then *r*(*u*) (repha) is replaced by visarjanīya (93). At this stage, the sūtra *vā śari* (103) applies and enjoins s-replacement for visarjanīya optionally. The illustration relates to the optional stage in which the dental s has replaced visarjanīya. The s of *rāmas* in contact with the ṣ of *ṣaṣṭhaḥ* is replaced by the retroflex ṣ and we have the usage *rāmaṣ ṣaṣṭhaḥ*.

In the second illustration at the similar stage, the s of *rāmas* in contact with the *ṭ* of *ṭīkate* is replaced by the retroflex ṣ and the usage *rāmaṣ ṭīkate* (Rāma goes) is obtained.

In the third illustration (*piṣ* + *tṛc* + *ḍā* --> *piṣ* + *tā* --> *guṇa* by *pugantalaghūpadhasya ca* (450) --> *peṣ* + *tā* --> *peṣṭā* => one who grinds) the retroflex ṣ is followed by *t* which is replaced by *ṭ* being in contact with the preceding retroflex ṣ.

The fourth illustration is *taṭ ṭīkā*. The stage from where we obtain this form is : *tad* + *ṭīkā*. Since here *d* is followed by the cerebral *ṭ*, the dental *d* of *tad* is replaced by the retroflex *ḍ*. With the help of the sūtra *khari ca* Pā. 8. 4. 55, the retroflex *ḍ* is replaced by *ṭ*. The sūtra *khari ca* being viewed as suspended (*asiddha*) does not apply until and unless *ṣṭunā ṣṭuḥ* Pā. 8. 4. 40 has done its job. This is the reason why the resultant usage *taṭ ṭīkā* is from *tad* + *ṭīkā* and not from *tat* + *ṭīkā* as is generally understood.

In the fifth illustration the dental nasal stop at the end of *cakrin* in *cakrin* + *ḍhaukase* is followed by the fourth retroflex stop. This dental nasal stop is replaced by the nasal retroflex stop by the present rule because of the close proximity of the dental nasal stop and the fourth retroflex stop. Thus we obtain the form *cakriṇ ḍhaukase* (O discus-bearer, thou goest).

In this sūtra also the third inflectional ending is in the sense of *saha* as we have already discussed under sūtra (62). The significance of not using *ṣṭu* in the locative is that in *peṣṭā* the *t* of *tā* is replaced by *ṭ* even when the retroflex ṣ precedes it.

(65) न पदान्ताट्टोरनाम्। *na padāntāṭṭoranām*. 8. 4. 42

लघु० – पदान्तात् टवर्गात् परस्यानामः स्तोः ष्टुर्न स्यात्। षट् सन्तः। षट् ते। पदान्तात् किम्? सर्पिष्टमम्। *padāntāt ṭavargāt parasyānāmaḥ stoḥ ṣṭur na syāt. ṣaṭ santaḥ. ṣaṭ te. padāntāt kim? sarpiṣṭamam.*

Trans. : With the exception of *nām* (the plural sixth inflectional ending), let not the dental *s* and stops following the pada-final cerebral stops be replaced by the cerebral *ṣ* and stops.

PP. *na padāntāt ṭoḥ anām stoḥ ṣṭuḥ (saṁhitāyām).*

Eluc. : The terms *stoḥ* and *ṣṭu* are carried over from *stoḥ ścunā ścuḥ* Pā. 8. 4. 40 and *ṣṭunā ṣṭuḥ* Pā. 8. 4. 41 respectively. The singular genitive sup-affix *ṅas* after *anām* is taken as elided (*anām iti luptaṣaṣṭhīkaṁ padam* SK, I, p. 124). The particle *na* is an indeclinable which negates what is already available by *ṣṭunā ṣṭuḥ* (64). Taking into account the carried over terms, the meaning of the sūtra is as follows : Leaving aside the dental *n* of *nām*, if the dental *s* and the dental stops (*tu*) follow the pada-final retroflex stops (*ṭu*), they are not substituted by the retroflex *ṣ* and retroflex stops.

The first illustration *ṣaṭ santaḥ* (six gentlemen) is had from *ṣaḍ* + *santaḥ*. The inflected form *ṣaḍ* is the nominative plural of *ṣaṣ* when the affix *jas* is substituted by luk-elision in accordance with *ṣaḍbhyo luk* (187) and the sibilant *ṣ* coming at the end of *ṣaṣ* is substituted by the retroflex *ḍ* according to *jhalāṁ jaśo 'nte* (67). We obtain the usage *ṣaṭ santaḥ* through the following grammatical process : At the stage *ṣaḍ* + *santaḥ*, the rule *ḍaḥ si dhuṭ* (86) is applicable which optionally prescribes the augment *dhuṭ* to be inserted before the dental sibilant *s* of *santaḥ*. The stage at which the augment *dhuṭ* is not available is relevant in the context of the present sūtra. At first, the sūtra *khari ca* Pā. 8. 4. 55 becomes available for application but, being suspended (*asiddha*) with respect to *ṣṭunā ṣṭuḥ* Pā. 8. 4. 41, it allows the latter to function. The present rule blocks *ṣṭunā ṣṭuḥ* but, still being available, the rule *khari ca* applies and the pada-final *ḍ* is replaced by *ṭ* and we get *ṣaṭ santaḥ*.

The second illustration is *ṣaṭ te* (six of them). In this illustration the dental stop *t* of *te* follows the pada-final retroflex *ḍ* in *ṣaḍ* + *te*. At this stage the sūtra *khari ca* Pā. 8. 4. 55 is available. Being asiddha, it allows *ṣṭunā ṣṭuḥ* Pā. 8. 4. 41 to apply which is blocked by the present sūtra. Then being available, *khari ca* applies. The retroflex *ḍ* is replaced by *ṭ* and we have the usage *ṣaṭ te*.

Varadarāja has explained the necessity of the terms *padāntāt* and *ṭoḥ* by giving two counter-examples : *īṭṭe* and *sarpiṣṭamam*. The first counter-example is the third person singular form of the verbal root *īḍa stutau* in laṭ lakāra : *īḍ* + *te*. The retroflex *ḍ* is followed by the dental *t* but since *ḍ* is not pada-final, the present sūtra does not negate what is available by the rule *ṣṭunā ṣṭuḥ*. The dental *t* of *te* is replaced by the retroflex *ṭ*. Then *khari ca* applies and *ḍ* is replaced by *ṭ* and we have the form *īṭṭe*.

The second counter-example explains the significance of the term *ṭoḥ* in the present sūtra. Had Pāṇini not used the term *ṭoḥ* in the sūtra, then the form of the sūtra would have been like this : *na padāntād anām* which would mean that the dental sibilant s and the dental stops preceded by both the pada-final cerebral ṣ and the cerebral stops would not be replaced by the retroflex consonants, of course, with the exception of the dental nasal stop of the affix *nām*. As a consequence, it would not be possible to explain the forms such as *sarpiṣṭamam* from *sarpis + tamam* --> *sarpiṣ + tamam*. The s of *sarpis* has been replaced by ṣ according to the rule *hrasvāttādau taddhite* Pā. 8. 3. 99. In this usage the dental stop *t* of *tamam* follows the retroflex sibilant ṣ, which is pada-final, by virtue of the sūtra *svādiṣvasarvanāmasthāne* (163). As such, the dental stop *t*, following the pada-final retroflex ṣ, cannot be replaced by the retroflex *ṭ*. This kind of eventuality could not have been avoided, if Pāṇini had not used the term *ṭoḥ* in the sūtra. By marking out *ṭoḥ* out of *ṣṭoḥ* Pāṇini used only *ṭoḥ* in the sūtra in order that if there is pada-final cerebral ṣ, then the negation conveyed by the present sūtra does not apply and the dental s and the dental stops following pada-final cerebral sibilant ṣ are replaced by the cerebral ṣ and cerebral stops by *ṣṭunā ṣṭuḥ* (64).

The problem relating to ṣ being replaced by *ḍ* by *jhalāṁ jaśo 'nte* Pā. 8. 2. 39 does not arise as the replacement of retroflex ṣ in place of the dental s of *sarpis* by *hrasvāttādau taddhite* Pā. 8. 3. 99 is deemed not to have taken place with respect to *jhalāṁ jaśo 'nte* Pā. 8. 2. 39.

10. वा० – अनाम्नवतिनगरीणामिति वाच्यम्। षण्णाम्। षण्णवतिः। षण्णगर्यः।
anāmnavatinagarīṇām iti vācyam. ṣaṇṇām, ṣaṇṇavatiḥ, ṣaṇṇagaryaḥ.

Trans.: The exception of *nām*, *navati* and *nagarī* should be stated in the sūtra *na padāntāṭṭoranām* (65).

Eluc. : The sūtra *na padāntāṭṭoranām* (65) negates the cerebral substitution in place of the dental s and the dental stops when they follow the pada-final cerebral stops except the dental nasal stop of the inflectional affix *nām*. Originally the affix is *ām* to which *nuṭ* has been introduced by the sūtra *ṣaṭcaturbhyaśca* (265). Kātyāyana adds two more words, *navati* and *nagarī*, to the list of exceptions. This means that the sūtra (65) denies the cerebral substitution, except the dental nasal stop at the beginning of *nām*, *navati* and *nagarī*. The first illustration is *ṣaṇṇām* which is obtained from *ṣaṣ + ām*. The nominal stem *ṣaṣ* is technically termed *ṣaṭ* by *ṣṇāntā ṣaṭ* (296). In accordance with the sūtra *ṣaṭcaturbhyaśca* the augment *nuṭ* is added to the beginning of *ām* and it becomes *nām* :

ṣaṣ + *ām* --> *ṣaṣ* + *nuṭ ām* --> *ṣaṣ* + *nām* (after the elision of the *its u* and *ṭ*). The nominal stem *ṣaṣ* gets the pada designation by *svādiṣvasarvanāmasthāne* (163) and the last cerebral sibilant is replaced by *ḍ* in accordance with the sūtra *jhalāṁ jaśo 'nte* (67) and the stage of the illustration which is relevant to the sūtra *na padāntāṭṭoranām* (65) is thus obtained : *ṣaḍ* + *nām*. The sūtra *na padāntāṭ...* (65) does not prohibit the cerebral replacement in place of the nasal dental stop *n* of *nām* available by *ṣṭunā ṣṭuḥ* (64) and we get *ṣaḍṇām*. The cerebral stop *ḍ* is necessarily substituted by the cerebral nasal stop according to *pratyaye bhāṣāyāṁ nityam* (Pā. 8. 4. 45 vtk 1). Thus we get *ṣaṇṇām*. The other two nasal dental stops undergo such a change optionally. The word *ṣaṇṇavatiḥ* is a compound which may be analysed in two ways : 1. *ṣaḍadhikā navatiḥ* 2. *ṣaṭ ca navatiś ca*. The first is a tatpuruṣa compound and the second is dvandva. In both the cases, the sup-endings are elided and the form relevant to the cerebral replacement is : *ṣaḍ navati*. Although the sūtra *na padāntāṭṭoranām* (65) does not permit cerebral substitution for the dental *s* and stops except the dental nasal stop of the genitive plural affix *nām*, the vārttika widens the scope of exception to include *navati* and *nagarī* and as a result the rule *ṣṭunā ṣṭuḥ* (64) applies and the dental nasal stop following the cerebral *ḍ* is replaced by the cerebral nasal stop. The cerebral *ḍ* is optionally replaced by the cerebral nasal stop in accordance with the sūtra *yaro 'nunāsike 'nunāsiko vā* (68). In the illustration *ṣaṇṇavatiḥ* this cerebral replacement has optionally taken place. The other optional form is *ṣaḍṇavatiḥ*. The usage *ṣaṇṇagaryaḥ* is obtained in a similar way : *ṣaṣ* + *jas* *nagarī* + *jas* --> *ṣaṣ* + 0 *nagarī jas* {*ṣaḍbhyo luk* (187)} --> *ṣaḍ nagaryaḥ* {*ḍ* in place of *ṣ* by *jhalāṁ jaśo 'nte* (67)} --> *ṣaḍ ṇagaryaḥ* with the help of the present vārttika and *ṣṭunā ṣṭuḥ* (64). The cerebral stop *ḍ* is optionally replaced by cerebral nasal stop by virtue of the sūtra *yaro 'nunāsike...* (68) and we have *ṣaṇṇagaryaḥ*.

(66) तोः षि । *toḥ ṣi*. 8. 4. 43

लघु॰ – न ष्टुत्वम् । सन्षष्ठः । *na ṣṭutvam. sanṣaṣṭhaḥ.*

Trans.: Let not the dental stops followed by the cerebral sibilant *ṣ* be replaced by the cerebral stops.

PP. *toḥ ṣi na ṣṭutvam* (*saṁhitāyām*).

Eluc. : The particle *na* is carried over from the sūtra *na padāntāṭṭor anām* Pā. 8. 4. 42. The word *padāntāt* is also carried over into this sūtra (Katre : 1989, p. 1061). This term is skipped in the sūtra *śāt* Pā. 8. 4. 44 and is again made to recur in the sūtra *yaro 'nunāsike 'nunāsiko vā* Pā. 8.

4. 45. If we take into account the carried over words, then the meaning of the sūtra will be a little different from the one given in the translation: When the cerebral sibilant ṣ follows, the pada-final dental stops are not replaced by the cerebral stops. Although the whole of *ṣṭuḥ* is carried over into the present sūtra, the cerebral ṣ is left out while translating the sūtra since the cerebral sibilant ṣ never replaces the dental stops. In the illustration *san ṣaṣṭhaḥ*, the substitute cerebral nasal *ṇ* is available in place of the dental nasal *n* occurring at the end of *san* in accordance with the sūtra *ṣṭunā ṣṭuḥ* Pā. 8. 4. 41 but this is negated by the present sūtra. The present sūtra is subsequent to *ṣṭunā ṣṭuḥ* Pā. 8. 4. 41 in the tripādī and hence is construed as not to have performed any grammatical function so far as *ṣṭunā ṣṭuḥ* (64) is concerned. Despite this, Pāṇini has enunciated the present sūtra. Therefore by implication, the present sūtra is construed as an exception to *ṣṭunā ṣṭuḥ* (64).

(67) झलां जशोऽन्ते । *jhalāṁ jaśo 'nte*. 8. 2. 39

लघु० – पदान्ते झलां जशः स्युः । वागीशः । *padānte jhalāṁ jaśaḥ syuḥ. vāgīśaḥ.*

Trans.: Let the pada-final non-nasal consonants (*jhal*) be replaced by the consonants denoted by the abbreviatory term *jaś*.

PP. *padasya ante jhalām jaśaḥ.*

Eluc. : The governing rule *padasya* Pā. 8. 1. 16 recurs in each subsequent sūtra up to and inclusive of Pā. 8. 3. 54. Taking into account the anuvṛtti of *padasya*, the meaning of the sūtra is as follows : The consonants signified by the abbreviatory term *jhal* occurring at the end of a pada are replaced by the consonants denoted by the abbreviatory term *jaś*. In other words, the voiced unaspirated stops denoted by *jaś* replace the non-nasal consonants denoted by *jhal*. The illustration given by Varadarāja is *vāgīśaḥ*, which is a ṣaṣṭhītatpuruṣa compound. It is analysed as *vācām īśaḥ* (*vāc ām īśa su*). The sup-endings are elided by *supo dhātuprātipadikayoḥ* (718). The stage reached is : *vāc* + *īśa*, the sūtra *coḥ kuḥ* (305) applies and the palatal *c* is substituted by the guttural *k*. At this stage, the present sūtra applies and the consonant *k* denoted by *jhal* is replaced by *g* denoted by *jaś*. The *jhal*-consonants which are to be substituted are twenty-six, whereas the substitute consonants signified by *jaś* are five. The metarule *sthāne 'ntaratamaḥ* (17) helps in selecting the most similar substitute for the substituendum. In consonance with this metarule the substituendum *k* is replaced by the most similar substitute *g*. The resultant form is *vāgīśa* which becomes *vāgīśaḥ* in the nominative singular.

(68) यरोऽनुनासिकेऽनुनासिको वा । *yaro 'nunāsike 'nunāsiko vā*. 8. 4. 45

लघु० – यरः पदान्तस्यानुनासिके परेऽनुनासिको वा । एतद्मुरारिः, एतन्मुरारिः । *yaraḥ padāntasyānunāsike pare 'nunāsiko vā. etadmurāriḥ, etanmurāriḥ.*

Trans. : Let a nasal stop optionally substitute a pada-final consonant denoted by the abbreviatory term *yar* before (an initial) nasal stop (of the following pada).

PP. *padāntasya yaraḥ anunāsike anunāsikaḥ vā* (*saṁhitāyām*).

Eluc. : The word *padāntāt* from *na padāntāṭṭoranām* Pā. 8. 4. 42 recurs in this sūtra and is changed into the genitive so that it may agree with *yaraḥ* which also ends in the genitive. The *yar* (consonants except *h*) should be pada-final and should be followed immediately by the initial nasal stop (*anunāsika*) of the following pada to be optionally replaced by the most similar nasal stop in consonance with the rule *sthāne 'ntaratamaḥ* (17). In this context only *hal*-anunāsikas are relevant as no vowel-anunāsika is seen to follow pada-final *yar*. A phoneme which is articulated with both the mouth and the nose at the same time is termed *anunāsika*. The *hal*-anunāsikas are five : *ṅ ñ ṇ n* and *m*. When any of these five *hal*-anunāsikas immediately follows a pada-final consonant denoted by the abbreviatory term *yar*, then the *yar*-consonant is optionally replaced by the most similar anunāsika. The illustrations *etadmurāriḥ* and *etanmurāriḥ* may be taken as either a ṣaṣṭhī-tatapuruṣa compound or a karmadhāraya. The compounds may be analysed as : *etasya murāriḥ --> etad ṅas murāri su* or *eṣa murāriḥ --> etad su murāri su.* In both the cases after the elision of sup-endings, the remaining common form is *etad murāri*. The pronoun *etad* is a pada by virtue of the sūtra *pratyayalope pratyayalakṣaṇam* (189). At this stage, the present sūtra finds its scope and the pada-final dental *d* is optionally replaced by the most similar dental anunāsika *n*. After adding the nominative singular affix *su*, the resultant two forms are : *etanmurāriḥ* and *etadmurāriḥ*. In this context one point is worth noticing. The injunction of the replacement of the most similar nasal stop in place of *yar* before a nasal stop from the points of view of articulation and internal effort has found its scope in the stops. Hence this injunction does not apply where repha is followed by a nasal stop as in the case of *caturmukhaḥ*.[1] According to Nāgeśa repha also indicates other semivowels (LS, p. 208).

---

1. *sthānaprayatnābhyām antaratame sparśe caritārthe vidhir ayaṁ rephe na pravartate*, SK, I, p. 126.

The significance of the term *padāntasya* in the sūtra is that if the consonant denoted by the abbreviatory term *yar* does not occur at the end of a pada, then, because of the following nasal stop, the *yar*-consonant is not replaced by the most similar nasal stop. Take, for example, *vedmi*, the first person singular verbal form of the root *vid* 'to know' : *vid + mip* --> *vid + mi* {after the elision of *p* which is *it* by *halantyam* (1)} --> *ved + mi* {guṇa-substitution in place of the penultimate *i* of *vid* by *pugantalaghūpadhasya ca* (450)}. At this stage of the verbal form : *ved mi*, *d* is not pada-final and therefore it is not replaced by the most similar nasal stop *n* and we have the verbal form *vedmi*.

11. वा० – प्रत्यये भाषायां नित्यम्। *pratyaye bhāṣāyāṁ nityam.*
लघु० – तन्मात्रम्। चिन्मयम्। *tanmātram, cinmayam.*

Trans. : In the domain of spoken language, if an affix beginning with a nasal stop follows, then the pada-final *yar* is to be necessarily replaced by a nasal stop.

Eluc. : This vārttika has been enunciated in respect of the sūtra *yaro 'nunāsike 'nunāsiko vā* (68). So, the vārttika addresses itself to what this sūtra prescribes. The sūtra prescribes optional replacement by a nasal stop in place of a pada-final *yar* before a nasal stop but this vārttika obligatorily prescribes the replacement of pada-final *yar* by a nasal stop, which is most similar to the the pada-final *yar*, if the following nasal stop is at the beginning of an affix which immediately follows the pada-final *yar*. The vārttika is applicable only in an example of spoken Sanskrit (*bhāṣā*). The optional replacement by a nasal stop in place of a pada-final *yar* before a nasal stop occurring at the beginning of an affix that immediately follows a phoneme denoted by the abbreviatory term *yar*, has been made compulsory by this vārttika.

The first illustration is *tanmātram*. The sūtra *pramāṇe dvayasaj-daghnañmātracaḥ* (1162) introduces affixes *dvayasac*, *daghnac* and *mātrac* after a syntactically related nominal stem ending in the nominative sup-triplet to signify 'it is the measure of this'. After adding the affix we have this form : *tad su mātrac*, which is a prātipadika according to the sūtra *kṛttaddhitasamāsāśca* (116). The affix *su* after *tad* is elided by *supo dhātuprātipadikayoḥ* (718). The pronoun *tad* is now a pada in accordance with the sūtra *pratyayalope pratyayalakṣaṇam* (189). At this stage (*tad + mātrac*), the vārttika applies and the pada-final *d* which is denoted by *yar* is necessarily replaced by the most similar nasal stop *n* before a labial nasal stop *m* which occurs at the beginning of the secondary affix *mātrac*. The final form that we obtain is *tanmātram* after the addition of the singular nominative inflectional ending *su*.

The second illustration is *cinmayam*. The splitting of the sūtra *nityaṁ vṛddhaśarādibhyaḥ* (1109) makes provision for the taddhita affix *mayaṭ* after the nominal stem *cit* : *cit su mayaṭ* (cf. *ārambhasāmarthyād eva siddhe nityaṁ vṛddha...* (1109) *iti nityagrahaṇaṁ yogavibhāgenānyatrāpi kvacid vidhānārtham* TB, I, p. 446; also see *ekāco nityam* vtk 5052, SK, I, p. 446). This (*cit su mayaṭ*) being a prātipadika by the sūtra *kṛttaddhita...* (116), the nominal ending *su* is elided by *supo...* (718). After the elision of *su* we have the stage : *cit mayaṭ*. Now *jhalāṁ jaśo 'nte* (67) applies and the dental stop *t* is replaced by *d*. At this stage, the present vārttika applies and the *d* of *cid* is necessarily replaced by the most similar nasal stop *n* since the labial nasal *m* occurring at the beginning of the affix *mayaṭ* follows the pada-final *d* which is a *yar*-consonant.

It should be borne in mind that the present sūtra Pā. 8. 4. 45 is construed as suspended with respect to *jhalāṁ jaśo 'nte* Pā. 8. 2. 39. Hence, when both the sūtras are available simultaneouly, the sūtra *jhalāṁ jaśo 'nte* Pā. 8. 2. 39 applies first and as a consequence the dental stop *t* is substituted by *d*. The vārttika related to the sūtra Pā. 8. 4. 45 proceeds after *jhalāṁ jaśo 'nte* Pā. 8. 2. 39 has performed its grammatical function.

(69) तोर्लि । *torli*. 8. 4. 60

लघु॰ – तवर्गस्य लकारे परे परसवर्णः। तल्लयः। विद्वाल्ँ लिखति। नस्यानुनासिको लः।
tavargasya lakāre pare parasavarṇaḥ. tallayaḥ. vidvālṁ̐ likhati. nasyānunāsiko laḥ.

Trans. : Let a dental stop immediately preceding the semi-vowel *l* be replaced by a phoneme homogeneous with the following (in this case *l*).

PP. *toḥ li parasavarṇaḥ* (*saṁhitāyām*).

Eluc. : The word *parasavarṇaḥ* is carried over into this sūtra from *anusvārasya yayi parasavarṇaḥ* Pā. 8. 4. 58. It is a ṣaṣṭhī-tatpuruṣa compound analysed as : *parasya savarṇaḥ*. The replacement is to be homogeneous with what follows. In this case the semi-vowel *l* follows and the dental stops are replaced by the semi-vowel *l*. This means that the sūtra allows a dental stop to be replaced by *l* when *l* follows. The first illustration is *tallayaḥ* which may be analysed as either ṣaṣṭhī tatpuruṣa or saptamī tatpuruṣa : *tasya layaḥ tasmin layo vā*. In both the cases the common form, which remains after the elision of sup-endings, is : *tad laya*. At this stage, the dental *d* coming at the end of *tad* is replaced by *l* since lakāra immediately follows it. The semi-vowel *l* is of two kinds: anunāsika and ananunāsika. When it is substituted for the nasal dental stop, it is the anunāsika lakāra that will be substituted in accordance with the sūtra *sthāne 'ntaratamaḥ* (17). In the second illustration : *vidvān likhati* the nasal dental stop *n* is followed by the semi-vowel *l*. This will be replaced by the anunāsika lakāra (*l̐*) and the usage after sandhi will be as follows : *vidvāl̐likhati*.

(70) उदः स्थास्तम्भोः पूर्वस्य । *udaḥ sthāstambhoḥ pūrvasya*. 8. 4. 61
लघु० - उदः परयोः स्थास्तम्भोः पूर्वसवर्णः । *udaḥ parayoḥ sthāstambhoḥ pūrva-savarṇaḥ*.

Trans. : Let the verbal roots *sthā* and *stambh* which follow the preverb *ud* be replaced by (a phoneme) homogeneous with the preceding one.

PP. *udaḥ sthāstambhoḥ pūrvasya savarṇaḥ* (*saṁhitāyām*).

Eluc. : The vṛtti of the sūtra contains the word *parayoḥ* in it by virtue of the paribhāṣā sūtra *tasmādityuttarasya* (71). The sūtra says : Whatever is enjoined, by using the ablative inflectional ending, is to be performed on the item which follows that which is expressed with an ablative inflectional ending. The preverb *ud* ends in the ablative. Therefore the grammatical operation has to be performed on an element which follows the preverb *ud*. The present sūtra enjoins that when the verbal roots, *sthā* 'to stay' and *stambh* 'to support' follow the preverb *ud*, they should be substituted by that which is homogeneous with the preceding phoneme *d* which occurs at the end of the preverb *ud*.

One point is worth noting with regard to the anuvṛtti of the word *savarṇa* into the present sūtra. This comes from the sūtra *anusvārasya yayi parasavarṇaḥ* Pā. 8. 4. 58. The word *parasavarṇaḥ*, that occurs in this sūtra, is a compound word. Only a part of the compound *parasavarṇa*, that is *savarṇa* is carried over into the sūtra although generally the whole compound word should have been carried over. Jñānendra Sarasvatī explains (TB, I, p. 127) why only a part of the compound word has been carried over. He says that the carrying over of a particular word into the following sūtra or sūtras is based on the marking of a particular word with a svarita accent {cf. *svaritenādhikāraḥ* (Pā. 1. 3. 11)}. Although there is no marking of accents available nowadays, it is to be determined or understood on the basis of the convention that is followed in the Pāṇinian Śāstra (*pratijñāsvaritāḥ pāṇinīyāḥ*, see Kāśikā on Pā. 1. 3. 11). This is known from the tradition that the word *savarṇa* which is a member of the compound word *parasavarṇaḥ* is understood to have been marked with a svarita accent. Hence only the word *savarṇa* from Pā. 8. 4. 58 is carried over into the present sūtra.

In order to arrive at a cogent and complete meaning of the present sūtra, it is necessary to take into account what the following two paribhāṣā sūtras have to say :

(71) तस्मादित्युत्तरस्य । *tasmādityuttarasya.* 1. 1. 67

लघु० - पञ्चमीनिर्देशेन क्रियमाणं कार्यं वर्णान्तरेणाव्यवहितस्य परस्य ज्ञेयम् ।

pañcamīnirdeśena kriyamāṇaṁ kāryaṁ varṇāntareṇāvyavahitasya parasya jñeyam.

Trans. : When a term is stated in the ablative case (*tasmāt*), the grammatical operation directed by it should be performed on that which follows the term without the intervention of a single phoneme.

PP. *tasmād iti nirdiṣṭe uttarasya.*

Eluc. : The terms ending in the ablative case in the Aṣṭādhyāyī are indicated by the term *tasmāt* used in the present sūtra just as the terms expressed in the locative case in the Aṣṭādhyāyī are indicated by the term *tasmin* used in the sūtra *tasminniti nirdiṣṭe pūrvasya* Pā. 1. 1. 66, which precedes the present sūtra in the Aṣṭādhyāyī. The meaning 'without the intervention of a single phoneme' is arrived at by virtue of the word *nirdiṣṭa* used in the sūtra. The word *nirdiṣṭe* is carried over into the present rule. Taking this into account, we are now in a position to interpret the sūtra in the following way : If some grammatical operation is directed by a term expressed in the ablative case, that grammatical operation is to be performed on that element which immediately follows the term stated in the ablative case. In the sūtra *udaḥ sthāstambhoḥ pūrvasya* (70), the preverb *ud* is stated in the ablative case. This means that the grammatical operation of substituting a homogeneous phoneme directed by the term *ud* should be performed on an item which immediately follows the term *ud*. In other words, the verbal roots *sthā* and *stambh* are the loci where this grammatical operation is to be performed. Now the last phoneme of either of these verbal roots is to be replaced by a homogeneous phoneme in accordance with the sūtra *alo 'ntyasya* (21) but the following sūtra, which is an exception to (21), makes provision for the substitution to come in place of the initial phoneme of these verbal roots.

(72) आदेः परस्य । *ādeḥ parasya.* 1. 1. 54

लघु॰ – परस्य यद् विहितं तत् तस्यादेर्बोध्यम् । *parasya yad vihitaṁ tat tasyāder bodhyam.*

Trans. : A substitute that has been enjoined to replace that which follows, should replace the initial phoneme of the following.

PP. *parasya ādeḥ alaḥ sthāne.*

Eluc. : The terms *sthāne* and *alaḥ* are respectively carried over from *sthāne 'ntaratamaḥ* Pā. 1. 1. 50 and *alo 'ntyasya* Pā. 1. 1. 52. The term *ādeḥ* qualifies *alaḥ*. The sūtra thus means that a grammatical operation, which is directed to be performed with respect to the following, will be performed on the initial phoneme of that which immediately follows the term stated in the ablative case.

With the help of these two paribhāṣā sūtras, the meaning of the injunctive rule (*vidhi-sūtra*) *udaḥ sthāstambhoḥ pūrvasya* (70) becomes clear. It helps in identifying the locus where the grammatical operation prescribed by this rule is to be performed. That locus is the initial phoneme of the term which follows the term expressed in the ablative case. In this vidhi-sūtra, the term which is stated in the ablative is *ud* and the following term is either *sthā* or *stambh.* The initial phoneme which is common to both these verbal roots is the dental sibilant s. This dental s has to be replaced by a phoneme which is homogeneous with the dental stop *d*, occurring at the end of the preverb *ud*. The sūtra *sthāne 'ntaratamaḥ* (17) becomes applicable and ensures that the most similar substitute will replace the dental sibilant s of either of the verbal roots *sthā* and *stambh.* This paribhāṣā sūtrā is an essential determining factor since there are five phonemes homogeneous with the preceding *d* : *t, th, d, dh, n.* In order to find out which is the most similar to s, we have to look at the table 3 on page 18. The consonantal sounds *th* and s are most similar since both of them have four external efforts : vivāra, śvāsa, aghoṣa and mahāprāṇa. In this way, taking into account the external efforts, we come to the conclusion that it is the dental *th*, which will replace the dental sibilant s of the verbal roots *sthā* or *stambh.* The grammatical procedure of the substitution of *th* for s may be demonstrated as follows : 1. *ud* + *sthānam* and 2. *ud* + *stambhanam.* Here with the help of the paribhāṣā sūtrās *tasmādityuttarasya* (71) and *ādeḥ parasya* (72), the initial *s* of both the words *sthānam* and *stambhanam* is replaced by *th*. Then we arrive at the following stage : 1. *ud +ththānam* 2. *ud + thtambhanam*. At this stage, the following sūtra ensues :

(73) झरो झरि सवर्णे । *jharo jhari savarṇe*. 8. 4. 65

लघु० – हलः परस्य झरो वा लोपः सवर्णे झरि । *halaḥ parasya jharo vā lopaḥ savarṇe jhari.*

Trans. : Let lopa optionally replace a consonant denoted by *jhar* following a consonant (*hal*), provided the consonant denoted by *jhar* is followed by a homogeneous *jhar* consonant.

PP. *halaḥ jharaḥ lopaḥ anyatarasyām savarṇe jhari* (*saṁhitāyām*).

Eluc. : The words *halaḥ* and *anyatarasyām* are carried over respectively from the sūtras *halo yamāṁ yami lopaḥ* Pā. 8. 4. 64 and *jhayo ho 'nyatarasyām* Pā. 8. 4. 62. After these words have been supplied, the sūtra means : If the consonants signified by the abbreviatory term *jhar* follow any of the consonants (denoted by *hal*), then a consonant denoted by *jhar* is optionally replaced by lopa if the *jhar*-consonant is followed by a homogeneous *jhar*-consonant. In the illustrations given above : 1. *ud +ththāna* 2. *ud + thtambhana*, the dental stop *d* occurring at the end of the preverb *ud* is a consonant denoted by *hal*. It is followed by *th* in both the cases. This *th* is followed by another *th* in the first illustration and *t* in the other illustration. The consonant *th* is obviously homogeneous with the following *th* and *t*. Therefore the conditions laid down by the present sūtra for the optional lopa-substitution are fulfilled. In both the illustrations the thakāras following the dental *d* are optionally replaced by lopa : 1. *ud +thāna* 2. *ud + tambhana*. In the alternative, where lopa has not taken place, both the thakāras are retained : 1. *ud +ththāna* 2. *ud + thtambhana*. At this stage, the following rule applies :

(74) खरि च । *khari ca*. 8. 4. 55

लघु० – खरि झलां चरः स्युः । इत्युदो दस्य तः । उत्थानम् । उत्तम्भनम् । *khari jhalāṁ caraḥ syuḥ. ityudo dasya taḥ. utthānam. uttambhanam.*

Trans. : Let the consonants denoted by the abbreviatory term *car* replace the consonants denoted by the abbreviatory term *jhal* before the consonants signified by the abbreviatory term *khar*.

PP. *khari ca jhalām caraḥ* (*saṁhitāyām*).

Eluc. : The term *jhalām* is carried over from Pā. 8. 4. 53 and the term *car* from *abhyāse carca* Pā. 8. 4. 54. The term *car* is changed into the plural by the process of vacanavipariṇāma. In the illustrations under discussion, the dental stop *d* at the end of *ud* is a consonant denoted by *jhal* and it is followed by *th* in the first illustration and by *t* in the second. Both are denoted by *khar*. Therefore *d* is replaced by *t* which is denoted by *car*-pratyāhāra. The paribhāṣā sūtra *sthāne 'ntaratamaḥ* (17) helps determine the most similar *car*-substitute on the basis of the place of articulation. This replaces a similar *jhal*-consonant and we get *t* in place of *d*. Thus the two forms of each illustration that are finally obtained are as follows :

1. *uththānam* and 2. *utthtambhanam* (with no lopa-substitution)
1. *utthānam* and 2. *uttambhanam* (with lopa-substitution).

(75) झयो होऽन्यतरस्याम्। *jhayo ho 'nyatarasyām.* 8. 4. 62

लघु० - झयः परस्य हस्य वा पूर्वसवर्णः। नादस्य घोषस्य संवारस्य महाप्राणस्य हस्य तादृशो वर्गचतुर्थः। वाग्घरिः। वाग्हरिः। *jhayaḥ parasya hasya vā pūrvasavarṇaḥ. nādasya ghoṣasya saṁvārasya mahāprāṇasya hasya tādṛśo vargacaturthaḥ. vāggharīḥ, vāg-harīḥ.*

Trans. : Let a phoneme homogeneous with the preceding one optionally replace the phoneme *h* which follows the consonants denoted by *jhay*-pratyāhāra.

PP. *jhayaḥ haḥ anyatarasyām pūrvasya savarṇaḥ* (*saṁhitāyām*).

Eluc. : The terms *pūrvasya* and *savarṇaḥ* are carried over respectively from *udaḥ sthāstambhoḥ pūrvasya* Pā. 8. 4. 61 and *anusvārasya yayi parasavarṇaḥ* Pā. 8. 4. 58. After these terms have been taken from the preceding sūtras, the meaning of the sūtra is as follows : If the phoneme *h* immediately follows a consonant signified by the term *jhay*, then that *h* is optionally replaced by a phoneme which is homogeneous with the preceding consonant which is denoted by the abbreviatory term *jhay*. The consonantal phoneme *h* has these external efforts : nāda, ghoṣa, saṁvāra and mahāprāṇa. The most similar substitute phoneme among the consonants denoted by *jhay* is the fourth class-consonant since the fourth class-consonant also has the same properties (external efforts). This comes to mean that the homogeneous fourth class-consonant optionally replaces the phoneme *h* which follows the *jhay*-consonant without the intervention of any other phoneme.

The illustration given in the Laghu is a compound which may be analysed either as ṣaṣṭhītatpuruṣa or as saptamītatpuruṣa : *vācaḥ hariḥ* or *vāci hariḥ* --> *vāc ṅas hari su* or *vāc ṅi hari su*. After these forms have been designated as *prātipadika* by *kṛttaddhitasamāsāśca* (116), the sup-endings are elided by *supo dhātuprātipadikayoḥ* (718). After the elision of the sup-endings, the remaining common form is : *vāc hari*. The sūtra *coḥ kuḥ* Pā. 8. 2. 30 (305) applies and the palatal *c* of *vāc* is replaced by *k*. At this stage, by *jhalāṁ jaśo 'nte* Pā. 8. 2 39 (67) *k* is replaced by *g*, a denotatum of *jaś*. We get *vāg hariḥ*. At this stage, the present sūtra applies. The phoneme *g* which is denoted by *jhay* is immediately followed by *h*. A phoneme, which is homogeneous with *g*, is to replace the consonant *h* optionally. The consonant *g* has five homogeneous class consonants : *k kh g gh* and *ṅ*. Which of these five class consonants is to replace the consonant *h*? At this stage, the paribhāṣā sūtra *sthāne 'ntaratamaḥ* (17) steps in and helps decide the most similar consonant to replace the consonant *h*. If we take into account similarity on the basis of the place of articulation, then all the five guttural class consonants are similar to *h* since kavarga and *h* are articulated with the help of the throat (*akuhavisarjanīyānāṁ kaṇṭhaḥ*). The similarity based on signification (*arthakṛta*) and duration (*pramāṇakṛta*) is not relevant here. What remains is the similarity on the basis of the properties of the phoneme (*guṇakṛta*). Now similarity on the basis of internal or external effort is to be determined. The internal effort cannot become the basis since the internal effort of *h* is īṣadvivṛta, whereas that of the five guttural class consonants is spṛṣṭa. When we take into account the external effort, we find that the consonant *h* has four external efforts : saṁvāra, nāda, ghoṣa and mahāprāṇa. The fourth, that is *gh*, among the guttural class-consonants also has the same four external efforts : saṁvāra, nāda, ghoṣa and mahāprāṇa. Being similar on this basis, *gh* optionally replaces *h* in this case. When the replacement takes place, the form is *vāgghariḥ* and when the consonant *h* is not replaced by the phoneme *gh*, the form of the usage is *vāg-hariḥ*.

(76) शश्छोऽटि । *śaścho 'ṭi*. 8. 4. 63

लघु० - झयः परस्य शस्य छो वाऽटि । 'तद् + शिव' इत्यत्र दस्य श्चुत्वेन जकारे कृते खरि च इति जकारस्य चकारः । तच्छिवः, तच्शिवः । *jhayaḥ parasya śasya cho vā 'ṭi. 'tad + śiva' ityatra dasya ścutvena jakāre kṛte khari ca iti jakārasya cakāraḥ. tacchivaḥ, tacśivaḥ.*

Trans. : Let the palatal stop *ch* optionally replace the palatal sibilant *ś* which follows a consonant denoted by the abbreviatory term *jhay* and which is followed by a phoneme signified by the abbreviatory term *aṭ*.

PP. *jhayaḥ śaḥ chaḥ anyatarasyām aṭi* (*saṁhitāyām*).

Eluc. : The vowel *a* occurring in *cha* is to facilitate its articulation. The words *jhay* and *anyatarasyām* are carried over from the preceding sūtra *jhayo ho 'nyatarasyām* Pā. 8. 4. 62. The word *padāntasya* is carried over from the sūtra *vā padāntasya* Pā. 8. 4. 59 and changed to have an ablative inflectional ending (*iha padāntād ityanuvartya padāntāj jhaya iti vyākhyeyam* TB, I, p. 129). It agrees with *jhay* which is also in the ablative case. There are two conditions laid down by this sūtra for the palatal sibilant *ś* to be optionally replaced by the palatal *ch*. The first condition is that it should follow a phoneme which is a denotatum of *jhay*-pratyāhāra. The second condition is that it should precede a phoneme denoted by the abbreviatory term *aṭ*. In the illustration given in the Laghu, both these conditions are met. In '*tad* + *śiva*', the dental stop *d* is a denotatum of *jhay*, even before it is replaced by the palatal *c*, and *ś* follows it. The vowel *i* that follows *ś* is signified by *aṭ*. The conditions are fulfilled and the sibilant *ś* is eligible to be optionally replaced by *ch*. At this stage, there are three sūtras which are applicable. In order to determine the sequence of their application, let us take into consideration their order in the Aṣṭādhyāyī. The three sūtras are : 1. *stoḥ ścunā scuḥ* Pā. 8. 4. 40, 2. *khari ca* Pā. 8. 4. 55 and 3. *śaścho 'ṭi* Pā. 8. 4. 63. The present sūtra is subsequent to the other two sūtras. Hence it is asiddha with respect to them. In other words, if the present rule applies first, it is deemed not to have performed any grammatical function with respect to *stoḥ ścunā ścuḥ* and *khari ca*. The sūtra *khari ca* is asiddha so far as *stoḥ ścunā ścuḥ* is concerned. Since *stoḥ ścunā scuḥ* is not deemed to be suspended in respect of the other two sūtras, it applies first of all. By *stoḥ ścunā scuḥ*, the dental *d* of *tad* is replaced by the palatal *j*. Then *khari ca* applies and *j* is substituted by *c*. Now the present sūtra applies. The palatal stop *c* is denoted by *jhay*-pratyāhāra. The phoneme that follows *ś* is also a denotatum of the abbreviatory term *aṭ*. Consequently, the palatal *ś* is to be optionally replaced by *ch*. The form thus obtained is *tacchivaḥ*. When *ś* is not replaced by *ch*, the form will be *tacśivaḥ*.

The carrying over of the word *padāntasya* is significant in the sense that the consonant denoted by *jhay*-pratyāhāra should occur at the end of a pada. Then only the palatal sibilant *ś* is optionally replaced by the palatal stop *ch*, the other condition remaining the same. In the liṭ-lakāra third person singular form *cakśau* of the verbal root *cakṣiṅ*, the palatal sibilant *ś* follows *k*, which is denoted by *jhay*-pratyāhāra and the phoneme *au*, which follows *ś*, is a denotatum of *aṭ*-pratyāhāra. Although the other conditions are fulfilled, the palatal sibilant *ś* is not replaced by *ch*. The reason is that the preceding phoneme *k* is not pada-final.

12. वा० – छत्वममीति वाच्यम् । *chatvam amīti vācyam.*
लघु० – तच्छ्लोकेन । *tacchlokena.*

Trans. : It should be stated that the substitute *ch* should optionally replace the palatal sibilant *ś* (even when) followed by *am*.

Eluc. : The sūtra *śaścho 'ṭi* (76) does not cover the usage given in the Laghu under this vārttika. This is the reason why Kātyāyana emends the term *aṭi* of the rule (76) to *ami*. It extends the scope by including the phoneme *l* and the nasal stops. Before coalescence, the form of the usage is *tad* + *ślokena*. Here also the sūtra *stoḥ ścunā ścuḥ* (62) applies first. The dental consonant *d* is replaced by *j*. Then the palatal *j* is substituted by *c* in accordance with the sūtra *khari ca* (74). Here the palatal *ś* is preceded by *c*, which is a *jhay*-consonant, but followed by the semi-vowel *l*, which is not the dentotatum of *aṭ*-pratyāhāra. At this stage, the present vārttika comes up and prescribes that the palatal *ś* should optionally be replaced by *ch* even when it is followed by a phoneme denoted by the abbreviatory term *am*. The semi-vowel *l* is signified by *am*-pratyāhāra. As such, the palatal *ś* is optionally replaced by *ch*. When the replacement takes place, the form of the usage is *tacchlokena*. When the replacement does not take place, the form will be *tacślokena*.

(77) मोऽनुस्वारः । ***mo 'nusvāraḥ*. 8. 3. 23**
लघु० – मान्तस्य पदस्यानुस्वारो हलि । हरिं वन्दे । *māntasya padasyānusvāro hali. hariṁ vande.*

Trans. : The substitute *ṁ* (*anusvāraḥ*) replaces the pada-final phoneme *m* before a consonant (*hal*).

PP. *maḥ padasya anusvāraḥ hali* (*saṁhitāyām*).

Eluc. : The word *maḥ* has the sixth case-ending. The term *padasya* is lent into this sūtra from the governing sūtra *padasya* Pā. 8. 1. 16. It is qualified by the term *maḥ*. In accordance with the sūtra *yen vidhis* *tadantasya* Pā. 1. 1. 72, the phrase obtained is *māntasya padasya*. In this way the completed sūtra means : The pada-final *m* is substituted by anusvāra (*ṁ*) provided the immediately following phoneme is a consonant denoted by *hal*-pratyāhāra. In the illustration *harim* + *vande* the phoneme *m* is at the end of *harim* which, having the accusative case-ending (*am*), is a pada by *suptiṅantaṁ padam* (14). The semi-vowel *v* is a denotatum of the *hal*-pratyāhāra. Thus the pada-final phoneme is replaced by *ṁ* (*anusvāra*) : *harim vande* --> *hariṁ vande.*

It is worth mentioning here that the pada-final *m* is replaced by *ṁ* (*anusvāra*) only when a consonant (*hal)* follows. If it is followed by a vowel, it is not replaced by *ṁ*. In the sentence *rāmaḥ vidyālayam āgacchati*, the phoneme *m* at the end of *vidyālayam* is followed by a vowel and not by a consonant. Hence *m* is not replaced by *ṁ* (*anusvāra*). It remains as it is.

(78) नश्चापदान्तस्य झलि । *naścāpadāntasya jhali.* 8. 3. 24

लघु० – नस्य मस्य चापदान्तस्य झल्यनुस्वारः । यशांसि । आक्रंस्यते । झलि किम् ? मन्यसे । *nasya masya cāpadāntasya jhalyanusvāraḥ. yaśāṁsi. ākraṁsyate. jhali kim ? manyase.*

Trans. : The substitute *ṁ* (*anusvāra*) replaces a non-pada-final phoneme *n* as well as *m* before a consonant denoted by the abbreviatory term *jhal*.

PP. *maḥ naḥ ca apadāntasya jhali anusvāraḥ* (*saṁhitāyām*).

Eluc. : Both the terms *maḥ* and *anusvāraḥ* are carried over from *mo 'nusvāraḥ* Pā. 8. 3. 23 into this sūtra. The word *apadāntasya* qualifies both *naḥ* and *maḥ*. Both of them have a sixth case-ending. The sūtra means : If *n* and *m* do not occur at the end of a pada and if they are followed by a consonant denoted by the abbreviatory term *jhal*, then they are replaced by *ṁ* (*anusvāra*). Let us take the illustrations one by one in order to see how and at what stage the present sūtra performs its grammatical function. The first illustration is *yaśāṁsi* (a lot of fame or glories). The form is either nominative or accusative plural of the nominal stem *yaśas*. The grammatical procedure to arrive at the stage where this rule becomes aplicable is as follows : *yaśas* + *jas* --> *yaśas* + *śi* {*jaśśasoḥ śi* (236)} --> *yaśa num s* + *i* {*num* by *napuṁsakasya jhalacaḥ* (238)} --> *yaśa n s* + *i* --> *yaśā n s* + *i* --> {upadhādīrgha by *sānta mahataḥ saṁyogasya* (341)}. It is at this stage that the present sūtra applies and the phoneme *n* which is non-pada final is replaced by *ṁ* (*anusvāra*). Thus we obtain the usage *yaśāṁsi.*

The second illustration is *ākraṁsyate* which means 'will rise'. This is the lṛṭ-lakāra third person singular form of *kramu pādavikṣepe* 'to place the footstep' preceded by the preverb *āṅ*. It takes ātmanepada substitutes by the rule *āṅa udgamane* Pā. 1. 3. 40. The grammatical process is like this : *āṅ kramu sya te* --> *ā kram sya te*. At this stage, the present sūtra applies since the phoneme *m* at the end of the verbal root *kram* is not pada-final. It is a non-pada-final *m* and it is followed by *s* which is a denotatum of the abbreviatory term *jhal*. Consequently, the phoneme *m* is replaced by *ṁ* and the form that we obtain is *ākraṁsyate* (will be overcome).

The reason why the abbreviatory term *jhal* has been stated in the sūtra is that the non-pada-final phonemes *n* and *m* should not be replaced by *ṁ* when the phoneme which follows either *n* or *m* is not a denotatum of the abbreviatory term *jhal*. In the counter-example *manyase*, although the phoneme *n* at the end of the verbal root *man* 'to think' is non-pada-final, it is not replaced by *ṁ* since the semi-vowel *y* which follows is not denoted by the abbreviatory term *jhal*.

(79) अनुस्वारस्य ययि परसवर्णः । *anusvārasya yayi parasavarṇaḥ*. 8. 4. 58

लघु॰ – स्पष्टम् । शान्तः । *spaṣṭam. śāntaḥ.*

Trans. : A nasal stop substitute homogeneous with the following phoneme denoted by the abbreviatory term *yay* replaces an *anusvāra* (*ṁ*).

PP. *anusvārasya yayi parasavarṇaḥ* (*saṁhitāyām*).

Eluc. : The sūtra is complete in itself as it does not require any other word to be carried over from the preceding sūtra or sūtras to complete its sense. This is the reason why Varadarāja says that the sūtra is self-explanatory. The word *parasavarṇa* that occurs in this sūtra is a compound word. The whole compound word is normally carried over into the following sūtra or sūtras but this is not the case here. Only a part of the compound *parasavarṇa*, that is, *savarṇa* is carried over into the sūtra Pā. 8. 4. 61. (See explanation under the sūtra (70) to make out why only a part of the compound *parasavarṇa* has been lent into the sūtra *udaḥ sthāstambhoḥ pūrvasya* Pā. 8. 4. 61).

The illustration given by Varadarāja is *śānta*. This is the past participle form of the verbal root *śamu upaśame* 'to be calm'. The primary affix *kta* has been added to it. The relevant form is arrived at when the augment *iṭ* is not inserted at the head of the affix *kta* on the basis of the sūtra *vā dāntaśāntapūrṇadastaspaṣṭacchannajñaptāḥ* Pā. 7. 2. 27. In the absence of *iṭ* we have : *śam* + *kta* --> *śam* + *ta*. At this stage, we have a dīrgha replacement in place of the penultimate (*upadhā*) vowel of the verbal root *śam* by the sūtra *anunāsikasya kvijhaloḥ kṅiti* (724). Then the rule *naścāpadāntasya jhali* (78) applies and the non-pada final phoneme *m* is substituted by *ṁ* (*anusvāra*). The form at this stage is *śāṁ ta* and now the present sūtra becomes applicable since *ṁ* (*anusvāra*) is here followed by a consonant denoted by *yay*-pratyāhāra. Consequently *ṁ* (*anusvāra*) is replaced by a nasal stop homogeneous with the following consonant *t* denoted by the abbreviatory term *yay*. Thus we obtain the form *śāntaḥ*.

Jñānendra Sarasvatī and Nāgeśa say that the term *yayi* in the present sūtra is only for the sake of clarity. Even if it had not been used in the sūtra, it would have not made any difference. Let us see how the sūtra would have done even without the word *yayi*. There is no anusvāra before *ac*. When the phonemes denoted by *śal*-pratyāhāra follow the anusvāra, no replacement homogeneous with the *śal*-consonants is possible (TB, I, p. 130) as these do not have any homogeneous counterparts . This can be said in the light of the sūtra *nājjhalau* Pā. 1. 1. 10 and on the basis of the statement : *rephoṣmaṇāṁ savarṇā na santi* (Mbh. U. p. 202). Thus even without the term *yayi*, the present sūtra could have served the purpose very well (also cf. Nageśa, LS, I, p. 211).

In the context of this sūtra, one important point should be remembered. Whenever we have a non-pada-final anusvāra before a group class consonant, it has to be necessarily replaced by a nasal stop homogeneous with the following class consonant. The words *aṅkitaḥ, añcitaḥ, kuṇṭhitaḥ, dāntaḥ* and *gumphitaḥ* illustrate this point. The non-pada-final anusvāra should not be left as it is; it has to be replaced necessarily by a nasal stop which is homogeneous with the following class-consonant.

(80) वा पदान्तस्य । *vā padāntasya*. 8. 4. 59

लघु॰ – त्वङ्करोषि, त्वं करोषि । *tvaṅ karoṣi, tvaṁ karoṣi.*

Trans. : A substitute nasal stop homogeneous with the following consonant which is denoted by the abbreviatory term *yay* optionally replaces a pada-final anusvāra.

PP. *vā padāntasya anusvārasya yayi parasavarṇaḥ* (*saṁhitāyām*).

Eluc. : All the words comprising the previous sūtra are lent into the present sūtra and then the completed sūtra means that the anusvāra which occurs at the end of a pada is optionally replaced by a nasal stop or by any of the anunāsika semi-vowels, *ym̐*, *vm̐* and *lm̐*, homogeneous with the following consonant denoted by the abbreviatory term *yay*. In the two illustrations given in the Laghu, the pada-final *m* is first to be replaced by anusvāra and then the pada-final anusvāra is optionally replaced by the nasal stop which is homogeneous with a class-consonant denoted by the abbreviatory term *yay*. In *tvaṅ karoṣi* and *tvaṁ karoṣi*, the first example demonstrates that the pada-final anusvāra is replaced by the guttural nasal stop which is homogeneous with the guttural *yay*-consonant *k* which follows the pada-final *ṁ*. This holds good in all such cases where the pada-final anusvāra is followed by a class consonant. If the pada-final anusvāra is followed by any of the three semi-vowels, the pada-final anusvāra is optionally replaced by one of these anunāsika semi-vowels. The anunāsika semi-vowels are *ym̐*, *vm̐* and *lm̐*. If the pada-final anusvāra is followed by *y*, then the anusvāra is replaced by anunāsika *ym̐*. If the anusvāra is before either *v* or *l*, then the anusvāra is replaced by either *vm̐* or *lm̐* in the respective order. The three respective examples are : *dānaym̐ yacchati*, *savm̐vatsaraḥ* and *ahalm̐ likhāmi*. The other optional forms will be *dānaṁ yacchati*, *saṁvatsaraḥ* and *ahaṁ likhāmi*. The paribhāṣā sūtra *sthāne 'ntaratamaḥ* is the determining factor in the process of replacing the anusvāra with a phoneme which is homogeneous with a class consonant or with an anunāsika *ym̐* or *vm̐* or *lm̐* (यँ् or वँ् or लँ्).

(81) मो राजि समः क्वौ । *mo rāji samaḥ kvau*. 8. 3. 25

लघु० – क्विबन्ते राजतौ परे समो मस्य म एव स्यात्। सम्राट् । *kvibante rājatau pare samo masya ma eva syāt. samrāṭ.*

Trans. : Let the substitute phoneme *m* replace the pada-final phoneme *m* of the preverb *sam* when the verbal root *rāj* with the affix *kvip* follows.

PP. *samaḥ maḥ maḥ kvau rāji* (*saṁhitāyām*).

Eluc. : The term *maḥ* is carried over into this sūtra from *mo 'nusvāraḥ* Pā. 8. 3. 23. It is in the genitive but the word *maḥ* in the present sūtra is in the nominative and the akāra in it is for the sake of articulaltion. The word *kvau* is the locative form of the *kvi* which stands for the affix *kvip*. When an affix has been stated in a sūtra it should be taken in the sense of a word which ends with that affix in accordance with the paribhāṣā *pratyayagrahaṇe... tadantagrahaṇam* (Abhyankar, 23). In this way, the term *kvip*, indicated by the word *kvi*, should be taken as *kvibanta* which qualifies the term *rāji* in the sūtra. All these points having been taken into account, the meaning of the sūtra is : If the verbal root *rājṛ* 'to rule or govern' ending with the affix *kvip* follows the preverb *sam*, then the phoneme *m* occurring at the end of *sam* remains as it is. The phoneme *m* at the end of *sam* is pada-final since *sam*, being a preverb, is an indeclinable and as such the sup-ending has been elided by *avyayād āpsupaḥ* (371). Thus being pada-final, the phoneme *m* is to be replaced by anusvāra according to the rule *mo 'nusvāraḥ* (77). The present sūtra is an exception to *mo 'nusvāraḥ* and blocks the replacement of *m* by anusvāra. The pada-final phoneme *m* in this particular case remains *m* and the form thus obtained at this stage is *samrāj*. When we add *su* in the nominative singular we get the form *samrāṭ*. The pada-final phoneme *j* of *rāj* is replaced with the retroflex *ṣ* by *vraścabhrasjasṛjamṛja-yajarājabhrājacchaśāṁ ṣaḥ* (306). Then by *jhalāṁ jaśo 'nte* (67) the pada-final *ṣ* is substituted by *ḍ*. Now the rule *vā 'vasāne* (145) applies and the phoneme *ḍ* is optionally replaced by *ṭ*. Thus we obtain the form *samrāṭ*.

The significance of stating *kvibanta* as follows : If the verbal root ends in a conjugational affix, then the pada-final phoneme *m* of the preverb *sam* does not remain as it is. Instead, it will be replaced by the anusvāra as we have it in the verbal form *saṁrājate*.

(82) हे मपरे वा । ***he mapare vā*. 8. 3. 26**

लघु० – मपरे हकारे मस्य मो वा । किम्ह्मलयति, किं ह्मलयति । *mapare hakāre masya mo vā. kimhmalayati, kiṁ hmalayati.*

Trans. : A pada-final *m* optionally remains as *m* , if it is followed by *h* which itself precedes *m*.

PP. *mapare he maḥ maḥ vā (saṁhitāyām).*

Eluc. : There are two *m*-phonemes which are carried over into this sūtra. The first *m* is from *mo 'nusvāraḥ* Pā. 8. 3. 23 and it is in the genitive. The other is carried over from the sūtra *mo rāji samaḥ kvau* Pā. 8. 3. 25. It is in the nominative case. The present sūtra makes optional that which has been prescribed by the sūtra *mo 'nusvāraḥ* (77). The word *mapare* in the sūtra is a bahuvrīhi compound which is analysed as : that which has the phoneme *m* after it. The compound *mapare* qualifies the phoneme *h*. This means that the phoneme *h* should have the phoneme *m* after it. The phoneme *h* itself should follow the pada-final *m*. This comes to mean that the phoneme *h* should be between two makāras. The preceding *m* of the two should be pada-final. At this stage, the pada-final phoneme *m* of *kim* in the illustration is optionally replaced by *m*. In these illustrations, the first form is (*kimhmalayati*) in which the phoneme *m* remains as it is. In other words, the phoneme *m* is replaced by the phoneme *m*. In the alternative form (*kiṁ hmalayati*), the phoneme *m* of *kim* is replaced by anusvāra (*ṁ*).

13. वा॰ – यवलपरे यवला वा । *yavalapare yavalā vā.*

लघु॰ – कियँ ह्यः, किं ह्यः । किवँ ह्वलयति, किं ह्वलयति । किलँ ह्लादयति, किम् ह्लादयति ।
kiyṁ hyaḥ, kiṁ hyaḥ. kivṁ hvalayati, kiṁ hvalayati. kilṁ hlādayati, kim hlādayati.

Trans. : If the phoneme *h* has *y* or *v* or *l* after it, then the pada-final *m* is optionally replaced by *y* or *v* or *l* in a respective order.

PP. *yavalapare he maḥ yavalāḥ vā* (*saṁhitāyām*).

Eluc. : The terms *he* and *maḥ* are to be carried over from the sūtras *he mapare vā* Pā. 8. 3. 26 and *mo 'nusvāraḥ* Pā. 8. 3. 23 respectively to make the sense of the vārttika complete. The word *yavalapare* in the vārttika is a dvandva-seeded bahuvrīhi compound which is analysed as : *yaś ca vaś ca laś ca yavalāḥ. yavalāḥ parāḥ yasmād asau yavalaparaḥ tasmin = yavalapare.* This word qualifies the phoneme *h* which should be between the phoneme *m* on the one side and any one of the semi-vowels *y*, *v* and *l* on the other in order that the phoneme *m* may optionally be replaced by any of these three semi-vowels. That is the sense conveyed by the vārttika. This means that the phoneme *m* is replaced optionally by either *y* or *v* or *l* when the phoneme *m* is followed by *h* which itself is followed by any of the three semi-vowels *y*, *v* and *l*. The paribhāṣā sūtra *yathāsaṅkhyam anudeśaḥ samānām* (23) helps decide which substitute will replace which substituendum since there are three substituenda to be replaced by the three substitutes. They are equally enumerated. Hence this paribhāṣā sūtra helps.

The first illustration is *kim* + *hyaḥ* 'what was it yesterday?' In this illustration the phoneme *y* follows the phoneme *h* which follows the pada-final *m* occurring at the end of the interrogative pronoun *kim*. According to the present vārttika, the phoneme *m* is optionally replaced by *y* but in accordance with the sūtra *sthāne 'ntaratamaḥ* (17) this *y* should be anunāsika since the substituendum *m* is anunāsika. As the semi-vowels are both anunāsika and ananunāsika, the anunāsika *yṁ* should replace the anunāsika *m*. The other optional form is *kiṁ hyaḥ* in which the phoneme *m* is not replaced by the anunāsika *yṁ* but by anusvāra (*ṁ*) in accordance with the sūtra *mo 'nusvāraḥ* (77). The same grammatical process is followed in the other two illustrations which are : *kivm̐ hvalayati, kiṁ hvalayati. kilm̐ hlādayati, kiṁ hlādayati.* The first illustration means 'what moves?' and the second means 'what gladdens?' In the former the phoneme *m* is replaced by the anunāsika *vm̐* since the phoneme *h* is followed by *v*. In the latter the phoneme *m* occurring at the end of *kim* is replaced by anunāsika *lm̐* since the phoneme *h* is followed by *l*. The other two optional forms are those where the anusvāra segment (*ṁ*) has replaced the phoneme *m*.

Nāgeśa has a different point of view with regard to the nature of the replacement prescribed by the vārttika. He says that since the semi-vowels are enjoined to be substituted in place of the phoneme *m* at the end of a pada, they do not denote their homogeneous counter-parts. In other words, ananunāsika *y, v* and *l* do not denote the anunāsika *ym̐, vm̐* and *lm̐* since they have been enjoined for replacement. This is the meaning conveyed by the word *apratyayaḥ* in the sūtra *aṇudit savarṇasya cāpratyayaḥ* (11) (*ete yavalā niranunāsikā eva vidhīyamānatvena savarṇāgrāhakatvāt*, LS, I, p. 213). According to Nāgeśa, Pāṇini meant this since he himself did not replace the anunāsika *m* by the anunāsika *v* in the sūtra *tadvānāsāmupadhāno mantra itīṣṭakāsu luk ca matoḥ* Pā. 4. 4. 125 which has the word *tadvān*. The word *tadvān* has the semi-vowel *v* which has replaced the consonant *m* of the affix *matup* by virtue of the sūtra *mādupadhāyāśca matorvo 'yavādibhyaḥ* Pā. 8. 2. 9. This is how Nāgeśa proves his point that the homogeneous anunāsika counterparts are not denoted by the niranunāsika *y, v* and *l* in this context. Therefore the niranunāsika *y, v* and *l* replace the anunāsika *m*.

The thinkers belonging to the camp of Bhaṭṭoji Dīkṣita differ with Nāgeśa. They say that the taparakaraṇa of the substitute *u* in the sūtra *ṛta ut* Pā. 6. 1. 111 implies that Pāṇini himself accepts that a phoneme, denoted by *aṇ*, sometimes does denote its homogeneous counterparts, even when it is being enjoined (*vidhīyamāna*). It is for this reason that Pāṇini has used *ut* as tapara in order to preclude the vowel *u* from denoting its homogeneous counterparts which it could have denoted in this case even when it is being enjoined. Hence the view that it is the anunāsika *ym̐, vm̐* and *lm̐*, which should be substituted for the anunāsika phoneme *m*, does not remain without support.

(83) नपरे नः । *napare naḥ*. 8. 3. 27

लघु० – नपरे हकारे मस्य नो वा । किन्ह्नुते, किं ह्नुते । *napare hakāre masya no vā. kinhnute, kiṁ hnute.*

Trans. : If the phoneme *m* is followed by *h* preceding *n*, then *m* is optionally replaced by the phoneme *n*.

PP. *napare he maḥ naḥ vā* (*saṁhitāyām*).

Eluc. : The words *he* and *maḥ* are respectively carried over from the sūtras *he mapare vā* Pā. 8. 3. 26 and *mo 'nusvāraḥ* Pā. 8. 3. 23. The word *napare* is a bahuvrīhi compound analysed as : *naḥ paro yasmāt sa naparaḥ, tasmin = napare*. If the phoneme *h*, itself followed by *n*, follows the phoneme *m*, then the phoneme *m* is optionally replaced by the phoneme *n*. In the illustration *kim hnute* (what does he hide?), the phoneme *m* is followed by *h* which itself is followed by the phoneme *n*. The phoneme *m* is optionally replaced by *n*. Thus we have the usage as *kinhnute*. When it is not replaced by *n*, the rule *mo 'nusvāraḥ* (77) applies and the phoneme *m* is replaced by the anusvāra (*ṁ*). The resultant optional form is *kiṁ hnute*.

(84) आद्यन्तौ टकितौ । *ādyantau ṭakitau*. 1. 1. 46

लघु॰ – टित्कितौ यस्योक्तौ तस्य क्रमादाद्यन्तावयवौ स्तः । *ṭitkitau yasyoktau tasya kramād ādyantāvayavau staḥ.*

Trans. : An augment marked with *ṭ* as *it* becomes the initial segment of the item to which it is introduced, and the one marked with *k* as *it* becomes the final segment.

PP. *ādyantau ṭakitau*.

Eluc. : Both the words constituting the present sūtra are compounds. The first is an itaretaradvandva and the second is a dvandva-seeded bahuvrīhi. The first is analysed as : *ādiś ca antaś ca ādyantau*. The analysis of the second is as follows : *ṭaś ca k ca ṭakau ṭakau itau yayos tau = ṭakitau*. This means that if the augment is marked with *ṭ* as *it*, it becomes the initial segment of that item to which it is introduced and if the augment is marked with *k* as *it*, it becomes the final segment of that element to which it has been prescribed. The item to which the augment is introduced is expressed with a sixth case-ending. In such cases there is no confusion but there are places where an augment has been introduced by using two case-endings as in *ḍaḥ si dhuṭ* (86). Here both the ablative and locative case-endings have been used and as such there is confusion as to which should be given preference. If preference is given to the seventh case-ending, then the grammatical function has to be performed on the preceding item. If preference is given to the fifth case-ending, then the grammatical function has to be performed on the following item. At such places, the paribhāṣā : *ubhayanirdeśe pañcamīnirdeśo balīyān* (Abhyankar, 70) is invoked and the locative case-ending is transformed into the sixth case-ending. As a consequence, the augment is added to the item which has been transformed into the genitive.

There is also a third kind of augment which is marked with the phoneme *m* as *it*. The sūtra *midaco 'nyātparaḥ* (239) clearly indicates the place where the augment marked with *m* as *it* should be inserted. According to this sūtra, the *mit* augment is added after the last vowel of the item to which this augment has been introduced.

(85) ङ्णोः कुक्टुक् शरि । *ṅṇoḥ kukṭuk śari.* 8. 3. 28
लघु० – वा स्तः । *vā staḥ.*

Trans. : The augments *kuk* and *ṭuk* are optionally inserted at the end of the padas which respectively end with the phonemes *ṅ* and *ṇ* followed by the sibilants denoted by the abbreviatory term *śar*.

PP. *ṅṇoḥ kukṭuk śari vā (saṁhitāyām).*

Eluc. : The indeclinable *vā* is carried over into this sūtra from *he mapare vā* Pā. 8. 3. 26. The term *ṅṇoḥ* is an itaretaradvandva while *kukṭuk* is a samāhāradvandva. The first is analysed as : *ṅ ca ṇ ca ṅṇau, tayoḥ.* The analysis of the second is : *kuk ca ṭuk ca kukṭuk.* Both the augments are *kit*. Consequently, both are inserted at the end of the padas ending respectively with *ṅ* and *ṇ*. The illustrations are : 1. *prāṅ ṣaṣṭhaḥ* (sixth in the east) and 2. *sugaṇ ṣaṣṭhaḥ* (sixth good mathematician). In the first illustration the word *prāṅ* ends with *ṅ* and as such *kuk* will be inserted at the end in accordance with the sūtra *ādyantau ṭakitau* (84). Similarly *ṭuk* will be inserted at the end of the word *sugaṇ* since the word ends with *ṇ*. Both these words are followed by the sibilant *ṣ* denoted by the abbreviatory term *śar*. The grammatical procedure of the illustrations given in the Laghu is as follows : 1. *prāṅ kuk ṣaṣṭhaḥ* 2. *sugaṇ ṭuk ṣaṣṭhaḥ* -->1. *prāṅ k ṣaṣṭhaḥ* 2. *sugaṇ ṭ ṣaṣṭhaḥ* (after the elision of *k*, *ṭ* and *u* out of which *k* and *ṭ* are *its* according to *halantyam* (1); *u* being a vowel is *it* by *upadeśe 'janunāsika it* (28). Since they are *its*, their elision takes place by *tasya lopaḥ* (3). At this stage, the following vārttika ensues :

14. वा० – चयो द्वितीयाः शरि पौष्करसादेरिति वाच्यम् । प्राङ्ख् षष्ठः, प्राङ्क्षष्ठः, प्राङ् षष्ठः । सुगण्ठ् षष्ठः, सुगण्ट् षष्ठः, सुगण् षष्ठः । *cayo dvitīyāḥ śari pauṣkarasāderiti* *vācyam. prāṅkh ṣaṣṭhaḥ, prāṅk ṣaṣṭhaḥ, prāṅ ṣaṣṭhaḥ. sugaṇṭh ṣaṣṭhaḥ sugaṇṭ sugaṇ, sugaṇ ṣaṣṭhaḥ*

Trans. : It should be stated that the consonants signified by *cay*-pratyāhāra are replaced by the second of their class, in the opinion of Pauṣkarasādi, when the sibilants denoted by *śar* follow.

Eluc. : The illustrations 1. *prāṅ k ṣaṣṭhaḥ* 2. *sugaṇ ṭ ṣaṣṭhaḥ* have two *cay*-consonants *k* and *ṭ* after the insertion of the augments has taken place. They are respectively and optionally replaced by *ch* and *ṭh* in accordance with the present vārttika : 1. *prāṅkh ṣaṣṭhaḥ* 2. *sugaṇṭh ṣaṣṭhaḥ*. It may be borne in mind that on the basis of the sūtra *sthāne 'ntaratamaḥ* (17) the second class-consonant will replace the first class-consonant of the same class. When the second class-consonants do not replace the *cay*-consonants, the forms of the illustrations are : 3. *prāṅkṣaṣṭhaḥ* 4. *sugaṇṭ ṣaṣṭhaḥ*. Again, when the augments *kuk* and *ṭuk* are not inserted, being optional, the forms obtained are : 5. *prāṅ ṣaṣṭhaḥ* 6. *sugaṇ ṣaṣṭhaḥ*.

One point is worth noting here. In the tripādī, the sūtra *khari ca* Pā. 8. 4. 55 is subsequent to the sūtra *nādinyākrośe putrasya* Pā. 8. 4. 48 where this vārttika is read. So *khari ca* is available even after the vārttika has performed its function. Nonetheless it does not apply in the sphere of this vārttika. For in that case the vārttika would become purposeless.

(86) डः सि धुट् । *ḍaḥ si dhuṭ*. 8. 3. 29

लघु० – डात् परस्य सस्य धुड् वा । षट्त्सन्तः, षट्सन्तः । *ḍāt parasya sasya dhuḍ vā. ṣaṭtsantaḥ, ṣaṭsantaḥ.*

Trans. : The augment *dhuṭ* is optionally inserted at the head of a pada beginning with the phoneme *s* after a pada which ends in the phoneme *ḍ*.

PP. *ḍaḥ si dhuṭ vā (saṁhitāyām).*

Eluc. : The indeclinable *vā* is carried forward from the sūtra *he mapare vā* Pā. 8. 3. 26 and with this the sūtra is rendered a complete sentence which means : The augment *dhuṭ* is optionally added to the dental sibilant *s* which exists at the beginning of a pada that immediately follows the retroflex *ḍ* occurring at the end of a preceding pada.

The word *ḍaḥ* is in the ablative case. This invites the application of the rule *tasmādityuttarasya* (71) which prescribes that the grammatical operation directed by the term ending in the ablative case will be performed on the element which immediately follows. It is also worth noting that the locative case-ending in the term *si* indicates that the grammatical operation should be performed on the preceding element (16). Both situations are available at the same time. As a result it is not clear to which element the augment *dhuṭ* should be added. In this kind of a situation, the paribhāṣā *ubhayanirdeśe pañcamīnirdeśo balīyān* (Abhyankar, 70) helps in doing away with the confusion and establishes order ensuring that the direction given by the word ending in the ablative case is to be preferred to that given by the word ending in the locative case. Since the term *ḍaḥ* has a fifth case-ending, the grammatical operation is to be performed on the following element and not on the preceding one. In this case the dental sibilant *s* follows the retroflex *ḍ*. By virtue of this interpretation the locative case-ending of the term *si* is transformed into the sixth case-ending. As such, the augment *dhuṭ* becomes a part of the phoneme *s* which occurs at the beginning of the pada that follows.

The augment *dhuṭ* prescribed by the present sūtra is marked with *ṭ* as *it*. According to the rule *ādyantau ṭakitau* (84), the augment *dhuṭ* being *ṭit* is inserted at the head of the item *s* to which it has been introduced. Here the phoneme *s* should be construed as a part of a pada since *padasya* is lent into the present sūtra from the govering rule *padasya* Pā. 8. 1. 16. The genitive case-ending here is construed as avayavaṣaṣṭhī. Thus we obtain the form *ṣaṭ tsantaḥ* through the following grammatical process : *ṣaḍ dhuṭ santaḥ* --> *ṣaḍ dh santaḥ* {after the elision of *u* and *ṭ* which are *its* according to *upadeśe 'janunāsika it* (28) and *halantyam* (1) respectively and their elision takes place by *tasya lopaḥ* (3)} --> *ṣaṭ t santaḥ* --> *ṣaṭ tsantaḥ*. Here *dh* is replaced by *t* and then *ḍ* by *ṭ* in accordance with the sūtra *khari ca* (74). In the alternative form we have *ṣaṭ santaḥ*, when *dhuṭ*, being optional, is not inserted.

It should be kept in mind that, when both the present rule and *khari ca* are simultaneously available for application in *ṣaḍ santaḥ*, it is the present rule which applies first since *khari ca* Pā. 8. 4. 55 is deemed to be suspended (*asiddha*) with respect to the present sūtra as *khari ca* is subsequent. This means that when the insertion of the augment *dhuṭ* has taken place, the rule *khari ca* performs its grammatical function.

Although the use of *saḥ* with a genitive case-ending could have done away with the confusion that has arisen due to the use of two case-endings in *ḍaḥ si dhuṭ* (86), Jñānendra Sarasvatī says that the use of the term *si* in place of *saḥ* is for the sake of economy. The term *si* (*s*=half and *i*=one mora=> one and a half) contains one and a half mora, whereas the term *saḥ* (*s*=half, *a*=1 and visarga=half=> two) has two morae (cf. *sīti saptamīnirdeśas tu lāghavārthaḥ*, TB, I, p. 134).

(87) नश्च । *naśca*. 8. 3. 30

लघु॰ – नान्तात् परस्य सस्य धुड् वा । सन्त्सः, सन्सः । *nāntāt parasya sasya dhuḍ vā. san tsaḥ, san saḥ.*

Trans.: After a pada which ends in the phoneme *n*, the augment *dhuṭ* is optionally inserted at the head of a pada beginning with the phoneme *s*.

PP. *naḥ ca si dhuṭ vā (saṁhitāyām).*

Eluc. : The terms *si* and *dhuṭ* are carried over into the present sūtra from the sūtra *ḍaḥ si dhuṭ* Pā. 8. 3. 29. The indeclinable *vā* is carried over from *he mapare vā* Pā. 8. 3. 26. As such the sūtra means : If a pada beginning with the phoneme s follows a pada which ends in the phoneme *n*, then the augment *dhuṭ* optionally becomes an initial segment of a pada beginning with the phoneme *s*. In the illustration *san saḥ* (he is a good man), the word *san* ends in the phoneme *n* and it is followed by the word *saḥ* which begins with the phoneme s. The condition required by the present sūtra is fulfilled for the insertion of the augment *dhuṭ* which becomes the initial segment of the pada which begins with the phoneme s. The grammatical process is as follows : *san dhuṭ saḥ* --> *san dh saḥ* (after the elision of *u* and *ṭ* by *tasya lopaḥ* (3) since they are *its* according to *upadeśe 'janunāsika it* (28) and *halantyam* (1) respectively). The sūtra *khari ca* (74) applies and the phoneme *dh* is replaced by *t* and we have the form, *san tsaḥ*. In the absence of the augment *dhuṭ* the form simply is *san saḥ*.

(88) शि तुक् । *śi tuk*. 8. 3. 31

लघु॰ – पदान्तस्य नस्य शे परे तुग्वा । सञ्छम्भुः, सञ्च्छम्भुः, सञ्च्शम्भुः, सञ्शम्भुः । *padāntasya nasya śe pare tug vā. sañchambhuḥ, sañcchambhuḥ, sañcśambhuḥ, sañśambhuḥ.*

Trans. : The augment *tuk* is optionally inserted at the end of a pada ending in the phoneme *n* if the palatal sibilant *ś* follows.

PP. *śi naḥ padasya vā tuk (saṁhitāyām).*

Eluc. : The words *naḥ, vā,* and *padasya* are respectively carried over into this sūtra from *naśca* Pā. 8. 3. 30, *he mapare vā* Pā. 8. 3. 26 and *padasya* Pā. 8. 1. 16. The last one is a governing rule. Hence the word *padasya* recurs here and is qualified by the word *naḥ* which is the genitive form of *n*. Thus the sūtra comes to mean as follows : For the pada-final *n* to qualify for the insertion of the augment *tuk* in a manner that it becomes the final segment of the pada ending in *n*, it should be immediately followed by the palatal sibilant *ś*. This virtually means that the following pada should begin with the palatal sibilant *ś*. When these two conditions are fulfilled, the augment *tuk* is inserted at the end of the preceding pada that ends in the phoneme *n*.

The illustration is *san* + *śambhuḥ* (Śambhu is Existence). Here the palatal sibilant *ś*, occurring at the beginning of the word *śambhuḥ*, follows the phoneme *n* which is at the end of the pada *san*. The augment *tuk* optionally becomes the final segment of the word *san*, that is, of *n*, by virtue of the sūtra *ādyantau ṭakitau* (84). After the elision of *u* and *k* of the augment *tuk*, the stage of the usage is *san t śambhuḥ*. By *stoḥ ścunā ścuḥ* (62), the phoneme *t* is first replaced by *c* and then in contact with *c*, the phoneme *n* is substituted by *ñ*. Now *śaścho 'ṭi* (76) applies and *ś* is optionally replaced by *ch* and the form becomes *sañc chambhuḥ*. When *c* is optionally elided by *jharo jhari savarṇe* (73), we have the form *sañ chambhuḥ*. This is the first illustration given in the Laghu. The second illustration is *sañc chambhuḥ* in which the palatal consonant *c*, which has replaced the phoneme *t* of *tuk*, is not replaced by lopa in accordance with the option available in (73). The third illustration is *sañc śambhuḥ* in which the palatal sibilant *ś* is not replaced by *ch*. The fourth illustration *sañ śambhuḥ* exemplifies the absence of the augment *tuk*.

(89) ङमो ह्रस्वादचि ङमुण् नित्यम् । *ṅamo hrasvādaci ṅamuṇ nityam.* 8. 3. 32

लघु० – ह्रस्वात् परो यो ङम् तदन्तं यत् पदं तस्मात्परस्याचो नित्यं ङमुट् । प्रत्यङ्ङात्मा । सुगण्णीशः । सन्नच्युतः । *hrasvāt paro yo ṅam tadantaṁ yat padaṁ tasmāt parasyāco nityaṁ ṅamuṭ. pratyaṅṅātmā, sugaṇṇīśaḥ, sannacyutaḥ.*

Trans. : The augment denoted by the abbreviatory term *ṅam* is necessarily inserted at the head of a pada beginning with a vowel and following a pada ending in the phonemes denoted by the pratyāhāra *ṅam* occurring after a short vowel.

PP. *ṅamaḥ hrasvāt aci ṅamuṭ nityam* (*saṁhitāyām*).

Eluc. : The word *padasya* is lent into the present sūtra from the governing rule *padasya* Pā. 8. 1. 16 and changed into one having the fifth case-ending so that it may accord with *ṅamaḥ* which is in the ablative case. By virtue of the sūtra *yena vidhistadantasya* Pā. 1. 1. 72 it yields the phrase *ṅamantāt padāt*. With the help of the paribhāṣā *ubhayanirdeśe* *pañcamīnirdeśo balīyān* (Abhyankar, 70), which rules that the fifth case-ending is preferable to the locative case-ending, the sūtra gives the following meaning : If the pada-final nasal stops denoted by the abbreviatory term *ṅam* (*ṅ*, *ṇ* and *n*) come after a short vowel and are followed by a vowel, then the augment *ṅamuṭ* necessarily becomes the initial segment of the following pada beginning with a vowel.

The word *ṅamuṭ* needs explanation. The word has two parts. One is the pratyāhāra *ṅam* which denotes *ṅ*, *ṇ* and *n*. The other is the indicatory *uṭ* which is to be used with each of these three. Thus three augments result : *ṅuṭ*, *ṇuṭ* and *nuṭ*. By invoking the rule *yathāsaṅkhyam anudeśaḥ samānām* (23), we come to understand that if the pada ends in *ṅ*, then *ṅuṭ* becomes the initial part of the following vowel. If the pada ends in *ṇ*, then *ṇuṭ* becomes the initial part of the following vowel and if the pada ends in *n*, then *nuṭ* becomes the initial segment of the following vowel. The three illustrations given in the Laghu are as follows :

1. *pratyaṅṅātmā* 'individual soul' 2. *sugaṇṇīśaḥ* 'head of good mathematicians' 3. *sannacyutaḥ* 'the Almighty Being or existing Viṣṇu'. In the first illustration, the pada *pratyaṅ* ends in guttural nasal phoneme *ṅ* preceded by the short vowel *a* which follows the semi-vowel *y*. The pada *pratyaṅ* is followed by the word *ātmā* which has the vowel *ā* at the beginning. The augment *ṅuṭ* becomes the initial part of the word *ātmā* which begins with the vowel *ā*. In other words the augment is inserted before *ā* according to the rule *ādyantau ṭakitau* (84) because it is *ṭit*. The phonemes *u* and *ṭ* are *its* respectively by the sūtras *upadeśe 'janunāsika it* (28) and *halantyam* (1). They are elided by *tasya lopaḥ* (3). A bare phoneme *ṅ* is inserted. This virtually means that the guttural nasal stop *ṅ* that comes at the end of a pada followed by *ac* is reduplicated. We have the form *pratyaṅṅātmā*.

The second and third illustrations can be explained similarly. In the second illustration *sugaṇṇīśaḥ*, the word *sugaṇ* is followed by the word *īśaḥ* and in the third, the word *san* is followed by the word *acyutaḥ*. The words that follow begin respectively with the vowels *ī* and *a*. The pada-final nasal stops *ṇ* and *n* occasion the insertion of the respective augments *ṇut* and *nut* before the initial vowels *ī* of the word *īśaḥ* and *a* of the word *acyutaḥ*. After the elision of the markers, the nasal stops *ṇ* and *n* become the initial segments of the vowels *ī* and *a*. The resultant forms of the illustrations are : *sugaṇṇīśaḥ* and *sannacyutaḥ*.

Although we have translated the word *nityam* as 'necessarily', this should be construed as meaning 'often' so that such Pāṇinian usages as *iko yaṇaci, suptiṅantaṁ padam, sanādyantā dhātavaḥ*, etc. that we come across in the Aṣṭādhyāyī can be accommodated.

(90) **समः सुटि ।** ***samaḥ suṭi*. 8. 3. 5**
लघु० – समो रुः स्यात् सुटि । *samo ruḥ syāt suṭi.*

Trans. : When followed by *suṭ*, let the phoneme *m* of the preverb *sam* be replaced by *ru*.

PP. *samaḥ suṭi ru* (*saṁhitāyām*).

Eluc. : The term *ru* is used without any nominal ending (*ru ityavibhaktiko nirdeśaḥ,* KP, VI, p. 479). It is carried over from *matuvaso ru sambuddhau chandasi* Pā. 8. 3. 1. The sūtra enjoins the substitute *ru* to replace the preverb *sam* but in deference to the sense conveyed by the sūtra *alo 'ntyasya* (21), the substitute *ru* will replace the last phoneme *m* of the preverb *sam*. This is the reason why it has been stated in the translation that the last phoneme *m* of the preverb *sam* is to be replaced by *ru*. The stage at which the substitute *ru* replaces the last phoneme of the preverb *sam* is as follows : *sam* + *skartā*. Here the verbal root *kṛ* 'to do' with the primary affix *tṛc*, that is *kartā*, follows the preverb *sam*. The augment *suṭ* is introduced to the verbal root *kṛ* in accordance with the rule *samparyupebhyaḥ karotau bhūṣaṇe* Pā. 6. 1. 137. The augment *suṭ*, being *ṭit*, becomes the initial part of *kṛ*. The *uṭ*-portion of *suṭ* is elided. Only the phoneme *s* remains and the stage where the present sūtra applies is thus obtained : *sam* + *skartā*. The augment *suṭ* follows the preverb *sam*. As such, *ru* replaces the final phoneme *m* of the preverb *sam* : *sa ru* + *skartā* --> *sa r* + *skartā* (after the elision of *u* of *ru*). The vowel *u* is *it* by *upadeśe 'janunāsika it* (28). Its elision takes place by *tasya lopaḥ* (3). This is the stage where the next sūtra applies :

(91) **अत्रानुनासिकः पूर्वस्य तु वा ।** ***atrānunāsikaḥ pūrvasya tu vā*. 8. 3. 2**
लघु० – अत्र रुप्रकरणे रोः पूर्वस्यानुनासिको वा स्यात् । *atra ruprakaraṇe roḥ pūrvasyānunāsiko vā syāt.*

Trans. : However, in this section dealing with *ru*, let a nasalized vowel (*anunāsika*) optionally replace the phoneme preceding *ru*.

PP. *atra anunāsikaḥ pūrvasya tu vā* (*saṁhitāyām*).

Eluc. : The section which begins with the rule *matuvaso ru sambuddhau chandasi* Pā. 8. 3. 1 extending up to *kānāmreḍite* Pā. 8. 3. 12 is called ru-prakaraṇa. The use of the word *atra* in the present sutra, which is a governing rule, restricts its application to this section. Consequently, the present sūtra does not apply where *ru* has been enjoined by the sūtra *sasajuṣo ruḥ* Pā. 8. 2. 66. The anunāsika vowel optionally replaces the vowel which precedes *ru*. In one case, the form is : *s aṁ r + skartā* and to have the other form, where the nasalized vowel does not replace the phoneme preceding *ru*, the following sūtra presents itself for application :

(92) **अनुनासिकात् परोऽनुस्वारः । *anunāsikāt paro 'nusvāraḥ*. 8. 3. 4**
लघु॰ – अनुनासिकं विहाय रोः पूर्वस्मात् परोऽनुस्वारः । *anunāsikaṁ vihāya roḥ pūrvasmāt paro 'nusvāraḥ.*

Trans. : Let the anusvāra (*ṁ*) be inserted after the vowel preceding *ru* when the nasalized vowel does not optionally replace the vowel before *ru*.

PP. *atra anunāsikaḥ pūrvasya tu vā* (*saṁhitāyām*).

Eluc. : The terms *ru* and *pūrvasya* are respectively carried over into the present sūtra from *matuvaso ru sambuddhau chandasi* Pā. 8. 3. 1 and *atrānunāsikaḥ pūrvasya tu vā* (91). Both the terms have undergone a change in case-endings. The former term, that is, *ru* is transformed into one having a fifth case-ending. The latter, that is *pūrvasya*, is changed into *pūrvasmāt* which is also in the ablative case. The ablative case-ending in *anunāsikāt* in this sūtra is interpreted in the light of the vārttika *pañcamīvidhāne lyablope karmaṇyupasaṅkhyānam* Mbh 2. 3. 28 vtk 1. Thus this word means 'leaving aside the case where a nasalized vowel has replaced the vowel preceding *ru*'. In other words, this means that 'in the absence of nasalized vowel substitution', the anusvāra (*ṁ*) augment is inserted after the vowel before *ru*. As such, we have two forms at this stage : 1. *s aṁ r + skartā* and 2. *saṁ r + skartā*. The first illustration exemplifies the nasalized vowel substitution and the second illustrates the augment of anusvāra (*ṁ*). In both the cases at this stage, the following sūtra applies :

(93) **खरवसानयोर्विसर्जनीयः । *kharavasānayorvisarjanīyaḥ*. 8. 3. 15**
लघु॰ – खरि अवसाने च पदान्तस्य रेफस्य विसर्गः स्यात् । *khari avasāne ca padāntasya rephasya visargaḥ syāt.*

Trans. : Let visarjanīya replace the pada-final repha when the unvoiced consonants denoted by *khar* follow or when there is a cessation (*avasāna*).

PP. *kharavasānayoḥ padasya raḥ visarjanīyaḥ* (*saṁhitāyām*).

Eluc. : The words *padasya* and *raḥ* are carried over from the governing rule *padasya* Pā. 8. 1. 16 and *ro ri* Pā. 8. 3. 14 respectively. The term *raḥ* qualifies the word *padasya* and in consonance with the sūtra *yena vidhistadantasya* Pā. 1. 1. 72, it yields the sense *rephāntasya padasya*. In this way, the meaning of the sūtra is as follows : When the consonants denoted by the abbreviatory term *khar* follow or when there is a cessation, the pada ending in repha is replaced by visarjanīya. With the help of the sūtra *alo 'ntyasya* (21), this actually means that the repha which comes at the end of a pada is replaced by visarjanīya. Thus after the application of this sūtra, we have these forms in both the cases : 1. *s aṁ ḥ+ skartā* and 2. *saṁ ḥ + skartā*. At this stage, *vā śari* Pā. 8. 3. 36, which is an exception to the sūtra *visarjanīyasya saḥ* Pā. 8. 3. 34, applies and the optional replacement by visarjanīya becomes available. In order to introduce the obligatory substitute *s* in place of visarjanīya, Kātyāyana enunciates the following vārttika :

15. वा० – सम्पुङ्कानां सो वक्तव्यः । *sampuṅkānāṁ so vaktavyaḥ.*
लघु० – संस्स्कर्ता, सँस्स्कर्ता । *saṁsskartā, saṁsskartā.*

Trans. : It should be stated that the final visarga of *sam*, *pum* and *kān* is to be replaced by the dental sibilant *s*.

Eluc. : The word *sampuṅkānāṁ* is an itaretaradvandva compound which is analysed as : *sam ca pum ca kān ca sampuṅkānaḥ, teṣām = sampuṅkānāṁ*. It means that the visarga which is understood here from the context is to be replaced by the phoneme *s* and not by jihvāmūlīya before *kān* or by upadhmānīya before *pum*. In the present two illustrations, the visarga obtained in place of *ru* occurs at the end of the preverb *sam*. By virtue of this vārttika, the visarga is to be necessarily replaced by *s*. Both the forms thus obtained are : *saṁsskartā, saṁsskartā*. The first with the augment of anusvāra and the second where a nasalized vowel has substituted the vowel preceding *ru*.

Some grammarians desire the optional deletion of the final phoneme *m* of *sam* (*samo vā lopameka icchanti*, Mbh 8. 3. 12). Since this has been mentioned in the Mahābhāṣya in the section on *ru*, both the substitution of anunāsika and the insertion of anusvāra are available here (see for explanation SK, I, p. 139 and BM, I, p. 139). Thus after the elision of the final *m* of *sam* and as a consequence even in the absence of substitution of *ru* in place of the final *m* of the preverb *sam*, we have two forms with a single *s* : *saṁskartā, saṁskartā*.

(94) पुमः खय्यम्परे । *pumaḥ khayyampare*. **8. 3. 6**

लघु० – अम्परे खयि पुमो रुः स्यात् । पुँस्कोकिलः, पुंस्कोकिलः । *ampare khayi pumo ruḥ syāt. pum̐skokilaḥ, puṁskokilaḥ.*

Trans. : Let the substitute *ru* replace the final phoneme of the word *pum* if it is followed by the consonants denoted by the abbreviatory term *khay* followed by the elements signified by *am*-pratyāhāra.

PP. *pumaḥ ru khayi ampare (saṁhitāyām).*

Eluc. : The term *ru* is lent into this sūtra from *matuvaso ru sambuddhau chandasi* Pā. 8. 3. 1. The word *ampare* is a bahuvrīhi compound which is analysed as : *am paro yasmād asau amparas tasmin = ampare*, qualifying *khayi*. The meaning of the sūtra is : The final *m* of *pum* is replaced by *ru* when it is followed by a consonant denoted by *khay*-pratyāhāra which itself is followed by the elements signified by *am*-pratyāhāra. The illustration is a karmadhāraya compound analysed as *pumāṁś cāsau kokilaś ca* : *puṁs su + kokila su*. The sup-endings are replaced by luk-elision in accordance with the rule *supo dhātuprātipadikayoḥ* (718). The last phoneme of *puṁs*, that is *s*, is elided by the sūtra *saṁyogāntasya lopaḥ* (20). The anusvāra is restored to *m* in the place of which it was substituted by the sūtra *naścāpadāntasya jhali* (78) since the phoneme *m* was followed by the dental sibilant *s* denoted by *jhal*-pratyāhāra. When the dental *s* is elided, the cause of the anusvāra substitution no longer exists. Hence, the anusvāra reverts to its original status, that is *m*. (Cf. *nimittāpāye naimittikasyāpyapāyaḥ* stated by Nāgeśa on paribhāṣā 56, see Abhyankar, p. 129). Now we have the form *pum + kokila*. At this stage, the present sūtra applies since we have the word *pum* followed by the guttural stop *k* which is denoted by *khay*-pratyāhāra. The vowel *o* that follows the guttural stop *k* is signified by *am*-pratyāhāra. Thus the condition for the *ru*-substitution that the stem *pum* should be followed by *am*-paraka *khay* is fulfilled. So, with the help of the rule *alo 'ntyasya* (21), the last phoneme *m* of *pum* is replaced by *ru* : *pu ru kokila*. The sūtra *atrānunāsikaḥ pūrvasya tu vā* (91) optionally brings about the nasal vowel substitution in place of the vowel preceding *ru*. In the alternative, the anusvāra (*ṁ*) is inserted after the vowel preceding *ru* by *anunāsikāt paro 'nusvāraḥ* (92). The latter grammatical operation takes place when the nasal vowel is not substituted for the vowel just preceding *ru*. In this way, we have two forms : 1. *pum̐ ru kokila* and 2. *puṁ ru kokila* --> 1. *pum̐ r kokila* and 2. *puṁ r kokila* after the vowel *u* of *ru* is elided. By the sūtra *kharavasānayorvisarjanīyaḥ* (93), the visarga is substituted for the phoneme *r* since it is followed by the abbreviatory term *khar*. The vārttika *sampuṅkānāṁ so vaktavyaḥ* steps in and the visarga is necessarily replaced by the dental sibilant *s*. The vārttika of Kātyāyana ensures that the sūtra *kupvoḥ...* (98) does not apply and the optional substitution by jihvāmūlīya in place of the visarga because of the following phoneme *k* of *kokila* does not take place. Thus we have two forms in the nominative singular : *puṁskokilaḥ* and *puṁskokilaḥ*.

The significance of saying *khay* as *am*-paraka lies in the fact that *ru* is not substituted for the last phoneme *m* of *pum* when it is not followed by such *khay*-consonants as are not followed by the phonemes denoted by *am*. In *puṅkṣīram*, the stem *pum* is followed by the phoneme *k*, which is denoted by *khay*-pratyāhāra but the phoneme *k* is followed by retroflex sibilant (*ṣ*) which is not denoted by *am*-pratyāhāra. Hence there is no *ru*-substitution in place of the last phoneme of *pum*. Instead *m* is replaced by anusvāra in accordance with *mo 'nusvāraḥ* (77) and then optional parasavarṇa takes place by *vā padāntasya* (80).

(95) नश्छव्यप्रशान् । *naśchavyapraśān*. 8. 3. 7

लघु० - अम्परे छवि नान्तस्य पदस्य रुः, न तु प्रशान्शब्दस्य । *ampare chavi nāntasya padasya ruḥ, na tu praśānśabdasya.*

Trans. : The substitute *ru* replaces the pada-final *n* before the phonemes denoted by the abbreviatory term *chav* followed by the phonemes signified by the abbreviatory term *am* but not in case of the word *praśān*.

PP. *naḥ padasya ru ampare chavi apraśān* (*saṁhitāyām*).

Eluc. : The words *padasya, ru* and *ampare* are respectively carried over from *padasya* Pā. 8. 1. 16, *matuvaso ru sambuddhau chandasi* Pā. 8. 3. 1 and *pumaḥ khayyampare* Pā. 8. 3. 6. The nominative singular term *apraśān*, which is a nañ-tatpuruṣa compound, is analysed as *na praśān apraśān*. Here the singular nominative nominal ending is in the sense of the genitive (*apraśān iti ṣaṣṭhyarthe prathamā* BM, I, pp. 141-42).The compound *ampare* has already been explained under *pumaḥ khayyampare* (94). The inflected word *naḥ* qualifies the word *padasya*. In accordance with the sūtra *yena vidhistadantasya* Pā. 1. 1. 72, the sense yielded is *nāntasya padasya*. Taking into account all these points, the sūtra gives the following meaning : The consonants signified by the abbreviatory term *chav* should be followed by the phonemes denoted by the abbreviatory term *am*. If any of such consonants denoted by *chav*-

pratyāhāra follows the pada-final phoneme *n*, then the substitute *ru* replaces that pada-final *n*, excluding that of the word *praśān*. By virtue of the sūtra *alo 'ntyasya* (21), the substitute *ru* replaces the pada-final *n* and not the whole word ending in the phoneme *n*.

The illustration of this sūtra is : *cakrin* + *trāyasva*. The word *cakrin* in the vocative case is a pada by *suptiṅantaṁ padam* (14). It is followed by the verbal form *trāyasva* which begins with the phoneme *t*, a denotatum of *chav*-pratyāhāra. It is followed by repha which is signified by *am*-pratyāhāra. As a consequence, the pada-final *n* is replaced by *ru*. The incidence of the *ru*-substitution in place of the pada-final *n* brings about both the nasal vowel substitution in place of the vowel preceding *ru* and the augment of anusvāra after the vowel preceding *ru*. These two grammatical functions are performed respectively by the rules *atrānunāsikaḥ pūrvasya tu vā* (91) and *anunāsikāt paro 'nusvāraḥ* (92). Besides, the visarga is substituted for the repha of *ru* by *kharavasānayor* ... (93). Then we have two forms : 1. *cakrim̐ḥ trāyasva* and 2. *cakriṁḥ trāyasva*. At this stage, the following rule applies :

(96) विसर्जनीयस्य सः । *visarjanīyasya saḥ*. 8. 3. 34

लघु० – खरि विसर्जनीयस्य सः स्यात्। चक्रिँस्त्रायस्व, चक्रिंस्त्रायस्व । अप्रशान् किम् ? प्रशान् तनोति । पदान्तस्येति किम् ? हन्ति । *khari visarjanīyasya saḥ syāt. cakrim̐strāyasva, cakriṁstrāyasva. apraśān kim ? praśān tanoti. padāntasyeti kim? hanti.*

Trans. : The visarga is replaced by the sibilant *s* when followed by the phonemes denoted by the abbreviatory term *khar*.

PP. *khari visarjanīyasya saḥ (saṁhitāyām).*

Eluc. : The term *khari*, which is traditionally understood to have been marked with a svarita accent, is carried over from the sūtra *kharavasānayorvisarjanīyaḥ* Pā. 8. 3. 15 in the manner of a frog's jump (*kharavasānayor... ityato maṇḍūkaplutyā kharītyanuvartate ekadeśe svaritatvapratijñānāt*, BM, I, p. 138). The vowel *a* after the phoneme *s* is for the sake of articulaion. Thus the meaning of the sūtra is : The visarga before the consonants denoted by the abbreviatory term *khar* is replaced by the phoneme *s*. In both the forms of the illustration *cakrin* + *trāyasva* the visarga is replaced by the dental *s*. 1. *cakrim̐ḥ trāyasva* and 2. *cakriṁḥ trāyasva* --> 1. *cakrim̐strāyasva* and 2. *cakriṁstrāyasva*.

The expression *praśān tanoti* is an exception. In this expression the phoneme *n* of *praśān* is pada-final. It is also followed by the consonants denoted by *chav*-pratyāhāra which themselves are followed by the phonemes denoted by *am*-pratyāhāra. The condition for *ru*-substitution laid down by the sūtra is fulfilled but still there is no *ru*-substitution in place of the pada-final *n* of *praśān*. The reason is that the word *praśān* has been specifically excluded from the sphere of the grammatical operation of *ru*-substitution in place of the pada-final *n*. Hence the pada-final *n* in *praśān tanoti* remains as it is.

The phoneme *n* which is not pada-final is not replaced by *ru* even if other conditions are met. In *hanti* the phoneme *n* is not pada-final. Hence it is not replaced by *ru*.

The phoneme *n* in the expression *san tsaruḥ* is not replaced by *ru* since the phoneme *t* is followed by the phoneme *s* which is not a denotatum of *am*-pratyāhāra.

(97) नॄन् पे । *nṝn pe.* 8. 3. 10

लघु० - नॄन् इत्यस्य रुर्वा पे । *nṝn ityasya rur vā pe.*

Trans. : The final phoneme *n* of *nṝn* is optionally replaced by *ru*, if it is followed by the labial stop *p*.

PP. *nṝn naḥ ru pe ubhayathā (saṁhitāyām).*

Eluc. : The word *nṝn* given in the sūtra represents the accusative plural form of the nominal stem *nṛ*. The singular sixth case-ending after *nṝn* is elided. Vāsudeva Dīkṣita remarks here that the elision of the sixth case-ending after *nṝn* is peculiar to the sūtra and the absence of the elision of the pada-final consonant *n* is also construed in the same manner (*nṝn iti dvitīyāntaśabdasvarūpaparaṁ ṣaṣṭhyantam. ṣaṣṭhyāḥ sautro luk. nalopābhāvo 'pi sautra eva*, BM, I, p. 142). This is the reason why we translate *nṝn* as 'the final phoneme *n* of *nṝn*'. The vowel *a* after the phoneme *p* is for the sake of pronunciation. The terms *naḥ* and *ru* are respectively carried over from the sūtras *matuvaso ru sambuddhau chandasi* Pā. 8. 3. 1 and *naśchavyapraśān* Pā. 8. 3. 7. The indeclinable *ubhayathā* is lent into the sūtra from *ubhayatharkṣu* Pā. 8. 3. 8. The word *ubhayathā* conveys the sense of being 'optional'. The sūtra *alo 'ntyasya* (21) explains that the *ru*-replacement is to come in place of the final *n* of the word *nṝn*. The illustration is *nṝn pāhi* (Protect the people!). The final *n* is to be optionally replaced by *ru* since the phoneme *p* follows. As in the preceding cases, the substitution by the nasalized vowel and the insertion of anusvāra are respectively obtained by *atrānunāsikaḥ pūrvasya...* (91) and *anunāsikāt...* (92). The forms thus obtained are : 1. *nṝm̐ ru pāhi* and 2. *nṝṁ ru pāhi* --> 1. *nṝm̐ r pāhi* and 2. *nṝṁ r pāhi*. After replacing the repha by visarjanīya, we have : 1. *nṝm̐ ḥ pāhi* and

2. *nṝṁ ḥ pāhi*. At this stage, the rule *visarjanīyasya saḥ* (96) becomes applicable but the following sūtra blocks it :

(98) कुप्वोः ×क×पौ च । *kupvoḥ× ka× pau ca*. 8. 3. 37

लघु॰ – कवर्गे पवर्गे च परे विसर्गस्य ×क × पौ स्तः । चाद् विसर्गः । नॄँ×पाहि । नॄँः पाहि । नॄं × पाहि । नॄंः पाहि । नॄन् पाहि । *kavarge pavarge ca pare visargasya × ka × pau staḥ. cād visargaḥ. nṝm̐ × pāhi, nṝm̐ḥ pāhi, nṝṁ × pāhi, nṝṁḥ pāhi, nṝn pāhi.*

Tıans. : The visarga is replaced by jihvāmūlīya or upadhmānīya if it is respectively followed by the kavarga or pavarga consonants. The use of *ca* in the sūtra means that the visarga is optionally retained as it is.

PP. *kupvoḥ visarjanīyasya ×ka × pau ca* (*saṁhitāyām*).

Eluc. : The term *visarjanīyasya* is carried over from *visarjanīyasya saḥ* Pā. 8. 3. 34. The word *× ka × pau* is an itaretaradvandva compound. It is analysed as : *× kaś ca × paś ca × k × pau*. The word *kupvoḥ* is also a compound. Its analysis is *kuś ca puś ca kupū tayoḥ = kupvoḥ*. The visarga is not available before every phoneme denoted by *ku* and *pu* but only before *k, kh* and *p, ph*. When *k* and *kh* follow, the visarga is optionally replaced by jihvāmūlīya and when *p* and *ph* follow, it is optionally replaced by upadhmānīya. Taking into consideration the optional replacement by upadhmānīya, anunāsika-substitution and the insertion of the anusvāra in the context of *ru*, we obtain four forms. When the nasalized vowel is substituted for the vowel preceding *ru*, we have two forms : One with visarjanīya : *nṝm̐ḥ pāhi* and the other with upadhmānīya *nṝm̐ × pāhi*. When the anusvāra is inserted just after the vowel preceding *ru*, we have two forms : One with upadhmānīya *nṝṁ × pāhi* and the other with visarjanīya *nṝṁḥ pāhi*. The fifth form is obtained when no *ru*-substitution takes place : *nṝn pāhi*.

(99) तस्य परमाम्रेडितम् । *tasya paramāmreḍitam*. 8. 1. 2

लघु॰ – द्विरुक्तस्य परम् आम्रेडितं स्यात् । *dviruktasya param āmreḍitaṁ syāt.*

Trans. : Of that which is iterated, let the second element be designated as *āmreḍita*.

PP. *tasya dviruktasya (dve) param āmreḍitam.*

Eluc. : The term *dve* is lent into this sūtra from *sarvasya dve* Pā. 8. 1. 1. It conveys the sense of dvitva. The second element of that which has been iterated is the denotatum of the technical term *āmreḍita*. The application of this term is seen in the following sūtra.

(100) कानाम्रेडिते । *kānāmreḍite*. 8. 3. 12

लघु० - कान्नकारस्य रुः स्याद् आम्रेडिते । काँस्कान्, कांस्कान् । *kānnakārasya ruḥ syād āmreḍite. kām̐skān, kāṁskān.*

Trans. : If an *āmreḍita* term follows, then the phoneme *n* of *kān* is replaced by *ru*.

PP. *kān āmreḍite naḥ ru (saṁhitāyām).*

Eluc. : The word *kān* in the sūtra represents the accusative plural of the masculine pronoun *kim*. Its sixth case-ending is taken as elided. By virtue of the elided sixth case-ending of *kān* and the carried over term *naḥ*, the expression comes to mean 'in place of the final phoneme *n* of *kān*'. The terms *naḥ* and *ru* respectively come from the sūtras *naśchavyapraśān* Pā. 8. 3. 7 and *matuvaso ru sambuddhau chandasi* Pā. 8. 3. 1. If the term *naḥ* is not carried over, even then we can arrive at the meaning 'in place of the final phoneme *n* of *kān*' with the help of the rule *alo'ntyasya* (21). In the doublet *kān kān* the word has been stated twice to denote either repetition or pervasion. The second *kān* has got the designation *āmreḍita* by the sūtra *tasya paramāmreḍitam* (99). Since āmreḍita in the form of *kān* follows, the final nakāra of the first *kān* is replaced by *ru*. When the *ru*-substitution has taken place, the sūtras *atrānunāsikaḥ pūrvasya...* (91) *anunāsikāt...* (92) bring about the nasalization of the vowel preceding *ru* and the augment *anusvāra* after the vowel preceding *ru*. The latter grammatical operation takes place when the nasal vowel is not substituted for the vowel just preceding *ru*. Thus after the following grammatical process : *kām̐ ru kān, kāṁ ru kān* --> *kām̐ r kān, kāṁ r kān*, we have these forms : *kām̐ḥ kān, kāṁḥ kān*. The repha has been replaced by visarjanīya in accordance with the sūtra *kharavasānayorvisarjanīyaḥ* (93). Now to necessarily replace the visarga by the dental sibilant *s*, the vārttika of Kātyāyana *sampuṅkānāṁ so vaktavyaḥ* becomes applicable. It blocks the replacement of the visarga by jihvāmūlīya before the phoneme *k* in this case and also overrules the optional retaining of the visarga before the consonants denoted by the abbreviatory term *khar*. Thus we have the resultant two forms : *kām̐skān* and *kāṁskān* meaning 'which of them'.

(101) छे च । *che ca.* 6. 1. 73

लघु० – ह्रस्वस्य छे तुक् । शिवच्छाया । *hrasvasya che tuk. śivacchāyā.*

Trans. : The augment *tuk* is inserted at the end of a short vowel before the phoneme *ch*.

PP. *hrasvasya tuk che ca* (*saṁhitāyām*).

Eluc. : The words *hrasvasya* and *tuk* are carried over from the sūtra *hrasvasya piti kṛti tuk* Pā. 6. 1. 71. The augment *tuk* has the phoneme *k* as *it* by *halantyam* (1). By *ādyantau ṭakitau* (84), the augment, being *kit*, becomes the last segment of the short vowel to which it has been introduced, when the short vowel is followed by the phoneme *ch*. The illustration given in the Laghu is a ṣaṣṭhī tatpuruṣa compound : *śivasya chāyā* --> *śiva ṅas chāyā su* --> *śiva chāyā* {after the luk-elision of the sup-endings by *supo dhātuprātipadikayoḥ* (718)}. At this stage, the present rule applies since both the conditions, a short vowel and the following phoneme *ch*, are available here. The augment *tuk* is inserted at the end of the short vowel : *śiva tuk chāyā*. The phonemes *u* and *k* are *its* respectively by *upadeśe 'janunāsika it* (28) and *halantyam* (1). Hence they are elided by *tasya lopaḥ* (3). The form at this stage is *śiva t chāyā*. Now the phoneme *t* is replaced by *d* in accordance with *jhalāṁ jaśo 'nte* (67) since the sūtra *stoḥ ścunā ścuḥ* (62) is subsequent to the former and hence asiddha. After the phoneme *d* has been substituted in place of *t*, *khari ca* Pā. 8. 4. 55 becomes applicable but being subsequent to *stoḥ ścunā ścuḥ* Pā. 8. 4. 40, it is treated as suspended. Hence the rule *stoḥ ścunā ścuḥ* (62) applies and the phoneme *d* is replaced by the phoneme *j*. Now *khari ca* (74) applies and *j* is replaced by *c* and we have the form *śivacchāyā*.

(102) पदान्ताद्वा । *padāntādvā.* 6. 1. 76

लघु० – दीर्घात् पदान्ताच्छे तुग्वा । लक्ष्मीच्छाया । लक्ष्मीछाया । *dīrghāt padāntāc che tug vā. lakṣmīcchāyā, lakṣmīchāyā.*

Trans. : The augment *tuk* is optionally inserted after the long vowel occurring at end of a pada before the phoneme *ch*.

PP. *dīrghāt padāntāt che tuk vā* (*saṁhitāyām*).

Eluc. : The word *dīrghāt* is carried over from the sūtra *dīrghāt* Pā. 6. 1. 75 which precedes the present sūtra in the Aṣṭādhyāyī. The word *che* is lent into it from *che ca* Pā. 6. 1. 73 and *tuk* comes from the sūtra *hrasvasya piti kṛti tuk* Pā. 6. 1. 71. Thus the completed sūtra means : If the pada-final vowel is long and if it is followed by the phoneme *ch*, then the augment *tuk* is optionally inserted after the long vowel at the end of a pada.

In the present sūtra the word *padāntāt* ends in the fifth case-ending. In the context of the augment, the use of the fifth case-ending invokes the paribhāṣā *ubhayanirdeśe pañcamīnirdeśo balīyān* (Abhyankar, 70) and as a result of it, the augment is introduced to the phoneme *ch*. Being *kit* it should be inserted at the end of the phoneme *ch* but Pāṇini's usage does not support such a position. In the rule *vibhāṣā senā-surācchāyā-śālā-niśānām* Pā. 2. 4. 25, it is obvious that the augment *tuk* is visible before the phoneme *ch* and not at the end of it. This Pāṇinian usage overrules the provision of the above-mentioned paribhāṣā and the augment *tuk* is inserted after the long vowel at the end of a pada. The insertion is optional. In the illustrations *lakṣmīcchāyā* and *lakṣmīchāyā*, the optional insertion is exemplified. The word is a ṣaṣṭhī-tatpuruṣa compound. The same grammatical process as in *śivacchāyā* is followed in this context except that this insertion is optional, whereas the insertion in the illustration *śivacchāyā* is obligatory. The second illustration here is to exemplify the absence of the augment *tuk*.

लघु० - इति हल्सन्धिः । *iti hal-sandhiḥ.*

Trans. : The chapter on *hal*-sandhi ends.

विसर्ग-सन्धिः
visarga-sandhi

*** विसर्जनीयस्य सः । *visarjanīyasya saḥ.* 8. 3. 34**

लघु॰ – खरि विसर्जनीयस्य सः स्यात् । विष्णुस्त्राता । *khari visarjanīyasya saḥ syāt. viṣṇus trātā.*

Trans. : Let the visarga followed by the consonants denoted by the abbreviatory term *khar* be replaced by the dental sibilant *s*.

PP. *khari visarjanīyasya saḥ* (*saṁhitāyām*).

Eluc. : The term *khari* is carried over from the sūtra *kharavasānayor visarjanīyaḥ* Pā. 8. 3. 15 in the manner of a frog's jump (*maṇḍūkapluti*). The vowel *a* in *sa* is for the sake of pronunciation. The visarga after the word *viṣṇu* in the illustration is immediately followed by *t* which is denoted by *khar*-pratyāhāra. As a consequence, the visarga is replaced by the dental sibilant s.

It should be kept in mind that the pada-final s is replaced by *ru*. Then after the elision of *u*, which is *it* by *upadeśe 'janunāsika it* (28), the remaining repha at the end of a pada is replaced by the visarga which is further replaced by the phoneme s in accordance with the present sūtra. The reason why this sakāra is not again replaced by *ru* is that the present sūtra is deemed to have performed nothing so far as the sūtra *sasajuṣo ruḥ* Pā. 8. 2. 66 is concerned. In other words, in the scheme of Pāṇini, the preceding sūtra *sasajuṣo ruḥ* Pā. 8. 2. 66 does not recognize the grammatical operation performed by the subsequent sūtra of tripādī, namely, *visarjanīyasya saḥ* 8. 3. 34 in view of the governing rule *pūrvatrāsiddham* Pā. 8. 2. 1. This is the reason why the pada-final s brought about by the present sūtra is not replaced by *ru*.

(103) वा शरि । *vā śari.* 8. 3. 36

लघु॰ – शरि विसर्गस्य विसर्गो वा स्यात् । हरिः शेते, हरिश्शेते । *śari visargasya visargo vā syāt. hariḥ śete, hariś śete.*

Trans. : If visarjanīya is followed by the phonemes denoted by *śar*-pratyāhāra, let visarjanīya optionally remain as it is.

PP. *śari visarjanīyasya visarjanīyaḥ vā* (*saṁhitāyām*).

Eluc. : The words *visarjanīyasya* and *visarjanīyaḥ* are respectively carried over from *visarjanīyasya saḥ* Pā. 8. 3. 34 and *śarpare visarjanīyaḥ* Pā. 8. 3. 35. With the genitive and the nominative forms of the word *visarjanīya*, the sūtra means : The visarga is optionally replaced by the visarga if it is followed by the phonemes denoted by the abbreviatory term *śar*. When the visarga is followed by the consonants signified by *śar*-pratyāhāra, it can also be said to be followed by the phonemes denoted by *khar*-pratyāhāra at the same time since the consonants denoted by *śar*-pratyāhāra are included among the consonants denoted by *khar*-pratyāhāra. This means that the present sūtra blocks the necessary replacement of the visarga by the phoneme s before *śar*-consonants and makes it optional. In other words, if the elements denoted by the abbreviatory term *śar* follow the visarga, then the visarga is replaced by the visarga optionally. When the visarga is not replaced by the visarga, it is replaced by sakāra by *visarjanīyasya saḥ* Pā. 8. 3. 34. Thus we have two forms given as illustrations in the Laghu. The first is when the visarga is replaced by the visarga (*hariḥ śete*) and the second is when, in the absence of the replacement of the visarga by the visarga, it is replaced by sakāra by *visarjanīyasya saḥ* Pā. 8. 3. 34 and then by the palatal sibilant *ś* (*hariś śete*) by virtue of the sūtra *stoḥ ścunā ścuḥ* (62).

(104) ससजुषो रुः । *sasajuṣo ruḥ*. 8. 2. 66

लघु० – पदान्तस्य सस्य सजुषश्च रुः स्यात्‌। *padāntasya sasya sajuṣaś ca ruḥ syāt.*

Trans. : Let the pada-final *s* and the word *sajuṣ* (friend) be replaced by *ru*.

PP. *sasajuṣoḥ ruḥ padasya.*

Eluc. : In this sūtra the itaretaradvandva compound *sasajuṣoḥ* is genitive dual and its analysis is as follows : *saś ca sajūś ca sasajuṣau tayoḥ = sasajuṣoḥ*. The repha at the end of *sasajuṣor* in the sūtra has been elided by *ro ri* Pā. 8. 3. 14. The word *padasya* recurs in this sūtra because of its being in the domain of the governing rule *padasya* Pā. 8. 1. 16. The term *padasya* is qualified by the compound word *sasajuṣoḥ*. By virtue of the sūtra *yena vidhistadantasya* Pā. 1. 1. 72, tadantavidhi comes into force. In the light of tadantavidhi the sūtra means : The pada which ends either in the phoneme s or in the word *sajuṣ* is prescribed to be replaced by *ru*. By *alo 'ntyasya* (21) *ru* will replace the pada-final s and also the retroflex ṣ occurring at the end of the pada ending in *sajuṣ*. There is no problem when we say that the pada which ends in s is replaced by *ru* since the sūtra *alo 'ntyasya* (21) helps but an explanation is due when we say that the pada which ends in *sajuṣ* is replaced by *ru*. According to this interpretation, this sūtra does not cover the word *sajuṣ* since it cannot be said to be at its own end. Vāsudeva Dīkṣita draws our attention to this fact (BM, I, p. 156). He says that by interpreting the sūtra as 'the pada having the word *sajuṣ* at the end is replaced by *ru*', there is no underpervasion in respect of the word *sajuṣ*. The word *sajuṣ* itself can be covered by invoking vyapadeśivadbhāva {see infra (277)}. So, both the compound word ending in the word *sajuṣ* and the word *sajuṣ* itself can be covered by this sūtra. Hence there is no underpervasion (*avyāpti*). This sūtra precludes the pada-final ṣ from being replaced by *ḍ* according to *jhalāṁ jaśo 'nte* (67). In this respect it is an exception to (67). After *ru* has replaced the pada-final s in *śivas arcyaḥ* --> *śivaru arcyaḥ* --> *śivar arcyaḥ*, the following sūtra applies :

(105) अतो रोरप्लुतादप्लुते । *ato roraplutādaplute*. 6. 1. 113
लघु॰ - अप्लुतादतः परस्य रोरुः स्यादप्लुतेऽति । शिवोऽर्च्यः । *aplutād ataḥ parasya ror uḥ syād aplute 'ti. śivo 'rcyaḥ.*

Trans. : Let the substitute short vowel *u* replace *ru* when it is preceded and followed by a non-prolated short vowel *a*.

PP. *aplutāt ataḥ roḥ ut aplute ati* (*saṁhitāyām*).

Eluc. : The terms *ut* and *ati* are respectively carried over from *ṛta ut* Pā. 6. 1. 111 and *eṅaḥ padāntādati* Pā. 6. 1. 109. The taparakaraṇa in both *ut* and *at* indicates a short *u* and a short *a* respectively. With these words, the sūtra means : The short *u* replaces the substitute *ru* when it (*ru*) is both preceded and followed by a non-prolated short vowel *a*. In *śiva r* + *arcyaḥ*, the repha representing *ru* is preceded by a non-prolated short *a*. It is also followed by a non-prolated vowel *a*. The conditions laid down by the sūtra are fulfilled and *ru* is replaced by the short vowel *u*. At this stage, *ādguṇaḥ* (27) applies and both the vowels *a* and *u* are replaced by one guṇa vowel *o* in consonance with the sūtra *sthāne 'ntaratamaḥ* (17). After the replacement by *o*, the sūtra *eṅaḥ padāntādati* (43) prescribes a single *eṅ*-vowel replacement for both the pada-final *eṅ* and the following short initial *a*. As a consequence we have the usage : *śivo 'rcyaḥ*.

The substitute *ru* that comes in place of the pada-final *s* should be deemed not to have taken place so far as the present sūtra is concerned. Nonetheless, this is not so since, if the replacement by *ru* were considered to be asiddha, the present sūtra would be rendered redundant. To avoid this eventuality, the function of *sasajuṣo ruḥ* Pā. 8. 2. 66 is taken to be as good as existent, even though it belongs to the tripādī. It should be borne in mind that the substitution of the short vowel *u* actually comes in place of the *r* of *ru* since being *it*, the *u* of *ru* is elided. Only the phoneme *r* remains and it is this repha which is replaced by the short vowel *u* and not any other repha. This is the reason why the repha of *prātar* before *atra* is not replaced by the short vowel *u* even when other conditions are available. Consequently, the usage remains *prātaratra*. This argument can be extended to other such cases.

The insertion of the word *aplutād* is significant in that it blocks the *u*-replacement in place of *ru* in the following expression[1] : *susrota3 atra snāhi* (SK, I, p. 158). (O Susrota! take bath here). The qualifying term *aplutād* seems redundant since the prolation brought about by the sūtra *dūrāddhūte ca* Pā. 8. 2. 84 is deemed not to have taken place with respect to the sūtra under discussion. The impending redundancy of the qualifying term *aplutād* implies that the prolation by virtue of the sūtra *dūrāddhūte ca* Pā. 8. 2. 84 should be considered to be effective even though this sūtra belongs to the tripādī. The *u*-replacement cannot be avoided by the taparakaraṇa of *at* in the present sūtra since its purpose has been served in blocking the *u*-replacement after a long vowel (cf. *plutasyāsiddhātvād ataḥ paro 'yam. aplutād iti viśeṣaṇe tu tatsāmarthyān nāsiddhatvam. taparakaraṇasya tu na sāmarthyam dīrghanivṛttyā caritārthatvāt*, SK, I, pp. 158-9). It is for this reason that we can say that the qualifying term *aplutāt* in the sūtra has a purpose to serve.

The purpose of the term *aplute* is to stop the *u*-replacement in the usages like *tiṣṭhatu paya a3gnidatta*. Because of the following prolated *a*3, the *u*-replacement in *payas* does not take place. The consonant *s* of *payas* is replaced by *ru* {*sasajuṣo*... (104)} and the substitute *ru* is not replaced by *u* because *a3* follows. When the *u*-replacement has not taken

1. The word *susrotas* is the name of some person. In the vocative singular, the single consonant affix *s* (*su*) is elided by the rule *halṅyābbhyo dīrghāt sutisyapṛktaṁ hal* (178). The *ṭi* of *susrotas* is prolated by the rule *dūrāddhūte ca* (49). When the rule *sasajuṣo ruḥ* (104) prescribes *ru* in place of the pada-final phoneme *s*, the form is as follows : *susrotar atra*. At this stage, the rule *bho-bhago-agho-a-pūrvasya yo 'śi* Pā. 8. 3. 17 applies and the *y*-replacement comes in place of *ru*. Now this substituted phoneme *y* is preceded by *a* and followed by *a* in the illustration *susrota y atra*. So, the rule *lopaḥ śākalyasya* Pā. 8. 3. 19 applies and the elision of the phoneme *y* takes place. This explains the form of the illustration quoted here from the Siddhāntakaumudī.

place, *ru* is replaced by *y* {*bho-bhago*... (107)} which is optionally elided {*lopa*... (30)}. This is how we have the usage *tiṣṭhatu paya a3gnidatta.*

(106) हशि च । *haśi ca*. 6. 1. 114

लघु० – तथा । शिवो वन्द्यः । *tathā. śivo vandyaḥ.*

Trans. : That also happens when the elements denoted by the abbreviatory term *haś* follow.

PP. *aplutāt ataḥ roḥ ut haśi ca (saṁhitāyām).*

Eluc. : Commenting on this sūtra Varadarāja only says : *tathā*. The word *tathā* refers to what he says about the preceding sūtra. This means that the *ru* coming after a non-prolated *a* is replaced by the short vowel *u* (*ut*) when followed by the consonants denoted by the abbreviatory term *haś*. We arrive at this meaning by carrying over the terms *aplutāt, ataḥ* and *roḥ* from the sūtra *ato roraplutādaplute* Pā. 6. 1. 113 and *ut* from the sūtra *ṛta ut* Pā. 6. 1. 111. The illustration given in the Laghu is *śivo vandyaḥ* which can be explained in the light of the present sūtra as follows : *śivas + vandyaḥ --> śiva ru + vandyaḥ --> śiva r + vandyaḥ --> śiva u + vandyaḥ --> śivo vandyaḥ*. The nominative singular nominal ending *su* has been replaced by *ru* by virtue of the sūtra *sasajuṣo ruḥ* (104). After the elision of the *u* of *ru*, the remaining repha is replaced by the short vowel *u* by the present sūtra. Then *ādguṇaḥ* (27) applies and the guṇa substitute *o* in place of *a* and *u* takes place and we have the usage *śivo vandyaḥ*.

(107) भो-भगो-अघो-अ-पूर्वस्य योऽशि । *bho-bhago-agho-a-pūrvasya yo 'śi*. 8. 3. 17

लघु० – एतत्पूर्वस्य रोयादिशोऽशि । देवा इह, देवायिह । भोस् भगोस् अघोस् इति सान्ता निपाताः । तेषां रोर्यत्वे कृते — *etatpūrvasya ror yādeśo 'śi. devā iha, devāyiha. bhos bhagos aghos iti sāntā nipātāḥ. teṣāṁ ror yatve kṛte —*

Trans. : The substitute *y* replaces *ru* when preceded by *bho, bhago, agho* and the phoneme *a* and followed by the elements denoted by the abbreviatory term *aś*.

PP. *bho-bhago-agho-a-pūrvasya roḥ yaḥ aśi (saṁhitāyām).*

Eluc. : The term *roḥ* is lent into this sūtra from *roḥ supi* Pā. 8. 3. 16. The word *bho-bhago-agho-a-pūrvasya* is a dvandva-seeded bahuvrīhi compound which is analysed as *bhoś ca bhagoś ca aghoś ca aś ca bho-*

bhago-agho-āḥ (itaretaradvandva), *bho-bhago-agho-āḥ pūrve yasmāt sa bho-bhago-agho-a-pūrvaḥ* (bahuvrīhi), *tasya*. The absence of sandhi between *bhago* and *agho* on the one hand and *agho* and *a* on the other is confined to the sūtra only, that is, it is sautra. Now the substitute *ru*, which replaces the phoneme *s* by virtue of the sūtra *sasajuṣo ruḥ* (104), is enjoined by the present sūtra to be further replaced by the phoneme *y*, if it is preceded by *bho*, *bhago*, *agho* and the class phoneme *a*. The illustration *devā iha* relates to the substitute *ru* preceded by the class phoneme *a*. In *devās* + *iha*, the phoneme *s* of *devās* is replaced by *ru*. After the elision of *u*, only repha remains. The repha is replaced by the consonant *y* by virtue of the present sūtra. At this stage, the sūtra *lopaḥ śākalyasya* (30) becomes applicable and the semi-vowel *y* is optionally elided and we have two forms : *devā iha* when *y* is substituted by lopa and *devāyiha* when *y* is not elided. It should be kept in mind that the sūtra *ādguṇaḥ* (27) does not have any scope here since the elision of *y* by *lopaḥ śākalyasya* (30) is deemed not to have taken place as the sūtra *lopaḥ śākalyasya* Pā. 8. 3. 19 belongs to the tripādī, whereas the sūtra *ādguṇaḥ* Pā. 6. 1. 87 belongs to the sapāda-saptādhyāyī.

The words *bhos* (an interjection), *bhagos* (illustrious) and *aghos* (sinner) are read in the *cādi* group. Hence they are called *nipātas*. Being nipātas, they get the designation *avyaya* (indeclinable) by virtue of the sūtra *svarādinipātamavyayam* Pā. 1. 1. 37. These indeclinables end in the phoneme *s*. When the last phoneme *s* of these indeclinables is substituted by *ru* in accordance with the sūtra *sasajuṣo ruḥ* (104) and the repha of *ru* is replaced by the semi-vowel *y*, the following sūtra presents itself for application :

(108) हलि सर्वेषाम् । *hali sarveṣām.* 8. 3. 22

लघु० – भो-भगो-अघो-अ-पूर्वस्य यस्य लोपः स्याद्धलि । भो देवाः । भगो नमस्ते । अघो याहि । *bho-bhago-agho-a-pūrvasya yasya lopaḥ syāddhali. bho devāḥ. bhago namaste. agho yāhi.*

Trans. : The phoneme *y* preceded by *bho, bhago, agho* and the phoneme *a* and followed by a consonant should be replaced by lopa (according to all grammarians).

PP. *bho-bhago-agho-a-pūrvasya yasya lopaḥ hali sarveṣām* (*saṁhitāyām*).

Eluc. : The whole compound word *bho-bhago-agho-apūrvasya* is carried over into this sūtra from Pā. 8. 3. 17. The semi-vowel *y* is carved out from the dvandva compound *vyoḥ* occurring in the sūtra *vyorlaghu-prayatnataraḥ śākaṭāyanasya* Pā. 8. 3. 18 and is carried over with a singular genitive case-ending by the process of vacanavipariṇāma. Thus only *yaḥ* (genitive singular) from Pā. 8. 3. 18 is lent into the present sūtra and not vakāra (*vakāras tu nānuvartate*, TB, I, p. 165).

The lopa-replacement prescribed by this rule is accepted by all grammarians. Hence it is obligatory. So, after the obligatory elision of the *y*-phoneme, we have the usage, *bho devāḥ* in the following manner : *bhos + devāḥ --> bho ru + devāḥ--> bho r + devāḥ--> bho y + devāḥ--> bho devāḥ*. Here the final phoneme *s* of *bhos* is replaced by *ru* in accordance with *sasajuṣo ruḥ* (104). Then the repha of *ru* is replaced with *y* by *bho-bhago-agho-a-pūrvasya yo 'śi* (107). At this stage, the present sūtra enjoins the lopa-substitution in place of the pada-final phoneme *y* as this sutra occurs in the domain of the governing rule *padasya* Pā. 8. 1. 16. The same grammatical process can be extended to other illustrations given in the Laghu, viz., *bhago namaste* and *agho yāhi*.

(109) रोऽसुपि । *ro 'supi*. 8. 2. 69.

लघु० – अह्नो रेफादेशो न तु सुपि । अहरहः । अहर्गणः । *ro 'supi ahno rephādeśo na tu supi. aharahaḥ. aharganaḥ.*

Trans. : Let the substitute repha replace the word *ahan* but not when followed by sup-affixes.

PP. *ahan raḥ asupi.*

Eluc. : The word *ahan* is carried over into this sūtra from the sūtra *ahan* Pā. 8. 2. 68. The word *ahan* is understood as having a genitive nominal ending which has been elided (*tac ca luptaṣaṣṭhīkaṁ padam*, BM, I, pp. 164-5). This is the reason why Varadarāja has used the term *ahnaḥ* in the vṛtti. By virtue of this genitive nominal ending, the last phoneme of the word *ahan* is to be replaced by the phoneme repha in accordance with the sūtra *alo 'ntyasya* (21). So, the meaning of the sūtra comes to this : The last phoneme of the word *ahan*, that is, the phoneme *n* is replaced by repha but this replacement does not take place when the affixes denoted by the abbreviatory term *sup* follow. The term *asupi* in the sūtra ends in the locative and is a nañ-tatpuruṣa compound (*na + sup = asup*). The negative particle here is used in the sense of prohibition connected with a verbal activity (*prasajya-pratiṣedha*) and not in the sense of exclusion (*paryudāsa*). If the negative particle in the compound were taken in the sense of exclusion, then the sūtra would become applicable only when an affix, similar to and different from, sup follows. It would not cover such cases as *aharahaḥ*, *aharganaḥ*, etc. The words *ahan*, *gaṇa* are different from sup but they are not similar to sup. To do away with such an eventuality, the negative particle is interpreted here in the sense of prasajya pratiṣedha. This comes to mean that the repha-replacement does not take place when the sup-affix follows. In this way, when the word *ahan* is followed by the sup-affixes such as *bhis, bhyām, bhyas* etc., the final phoneme *n* of *ahan* is not replaced by repha. Instead, it is replaced by *ru* in accordance with the sūtra *ahan* Pā. 8. 2. 68, which then changes to *u* by *haśi ca* (106). Then by *ādguṇaḥ* (27) we get the forms like *ahobhyām, ahobhiḥ,* etc. Had the phoneme repha replaced the last phoneme *n* of *ahan,* the sūtra *haśi ca* (106) would not have applied. The reason is that the sūtra *haśi ca* (106) applies where the substitute *ru* has come as a replacement and not the phoneme repha. These are the problems that can be avoided if the negative particle is construed in the sense of prasajya-pratiṣedha.

The present sūtra is an exception to *ahan* Pā. 8. 2. 68 which prescribes *ru*-replacement in place of the pada-final phoneme *n* of *ahan*. The present sūtra blocks it and enjoins repha-replacement in place of the phoneme *n*. Varadarāja gives two usages to illustrate this sūtra.

The first illustration is *aharahaḥ* (everyday) which is analysed as follows : The term *ahan* + *su* is reduplicated by virtue of the sūtra *nitya-vīpsayoḥ* Pā. 8. 1. 4 when a repetition of an action (*nitya*) or pervasion of a thing by property or action (*vīpsā*) is intended to be denoted. Two expressions are used in place of one expression : *ahan* + *su, ahan* + *su*. Both the sup-affixes are replaced by luk-substitution in accordance with the sūtra *svamornapuṁsakāt* (243). In other words, both the nominative nominal endings are elided. After the elision of the nominal endings, the form of the usage obtained is : *ahan ahan*. The nominal endings, which are elided, are not to be construed as existent by virtue of the sūtra *prayayalope pratyayalakṣaṇam* (189) since the zero-substitution which has taken place here is a luk-substitution and it is not understood as existent in accordance with the sūtra *na lumatāṅgasya* (190). Consequently, the affix *sup* is construed as non-existent. In other words, it can be said that the affix *sup* does not follow. Accordingly, the final *n*-phoneme of *ahan* is replaced by the phoneme *r* by the present sūtra and we have the usage *aharahaḥ* after the final repha is substituted by visarjanīya in accordance with the sūtra *kharavasānayor...* (93).

The second illustration is *aharganaḥ* which is a ṣaṣṭhī-tatpuruṣa compound analysed as *ahnāṁ gaṇaḥ* --> *ahan ām gaṇa su* --> *ahan gaṇa* {sup-affixes are replaced by luk-elision by *supo dhātuprātipadikayoḥ* (718)}. As in the case of *aharahaḥ,* here also the elided nominal endings *ām* and *su* are not understood as existent in accordance with the sūtra *na lumatāṅgasya* (190). So, a sup-affix does not follow *ahan* and consequently by the present sūtra *ro 'supi*, the phoneme *n* is substituted by repha and we have the usage *aharganaḥ* after introducing the nominal ending *su* after *ahargaṇa*.

(110) रो रि । *ro ri*. **8. 3. 14**
लघु० – रेफस्य रेफे परे लोपः । *rephasya rephe pare lopaḥ.*

Trans. : Let the repha followed by (another) repha be replaced by lopa.

PP. *raḥ ri lopaḥ (saṁhitāyām).*

Eluc. : The word *lopaḥ* is carried over into this sūtra from *ḍho ḍhe lopaḥ* Pā. 8. 3. 13. The word *raḥ* has the sixth case-ending. With the help of the sūtra *ṣaṣṭhī sthāneyogā* Pā. 1. 1. 49, this means that the substitute lopa is to come in place of the phoneme *r*. For this grammatical operation the repha has to be immediately followed by another repha. The meaning 'immediately followed' is conveyed by the seventh case-ending in the word *ri* in accordance with the sūtra *tasminniti nirdiṣṭe pūrvasya* (16).

The application of this sūtra and the preceding one, from which the term *lopa* has been carried over, is seen in the following sūtra.

(111) ढ्रलोपे पूर्वस्य दीर्घोऽणः । *ḍhralope pūrvasya dīrgho 'ṇaḥ*. **6. 3. 111**
लघु० – ढरेफयोर्लोपनिमित्तयोः पूर्वस्याणो दीर्घः स्यात्। पुना रमते। हरी रम्यः। शम्भू राजते। अणः किम् ? तृढः। वृढः। *ḍharephayor lopanimittayoḥ pūrvasyāṇo dīrghaḥ syāt. punā ramate. harī ramyaḥ. śambhū rājate. aṇaḥ kim ? tṛḍhaḥ, vṛḍhaḥ.*

Trans. : Let a substitute long vowel replace a vowel denoted by the abbreviatory term *aṇ* immediately preceding a lopa-replacement of the phoneme *ḍh* or *r* which has become the cause of the elision of the phoneme *ḍh* or *r*.

PP. *ḍhralope pūrvasya aṇaḥ dīrghaḥ.*

Eluc. : The word *ḍhralope* is an upapada tatpuruṣa compound with an internal dvandva. It is analysed as : *ḍh ca raś ca ḍhrau, ḍhrau lopayatīti ḍhralopaḥ, tasmin*. The phoneme *a* following the phoneme *r* is to facilitate its articulation. When either the phoneme *ḍh* or the phoneme *r*, which becomes the cause of the elision of either *ḍh* or *r* in a respective manner, follows a phoneme denoted by the abbreviatory term *aṇ*, the element denoted by *aṇ* is replaced by its long counterpart. Take, for example, the usage *punā ramate*. The basic form before sandhi is *punar ramate*. The phoneme *r* at the end of *punar* is elided by the rule *ro ri* (110). The cause of the lopa-replacement in place of the repha of *punar* is the phoneme *r* at the beginning of *ramate*. This repha of *ramate* immediately follows the vowel *a* which is a denotatum of the abbreviatory term *aṇ*. Consequently, the phoneme *a* is replaced by its long counterpart *ā* and we have the usage *punā ramate*.

The other two illustrations *haris ramyaḥ--> harir ramyaḥ --> hari ramyaḥ --> harī ramyaḥ* and *śambhus rājate--> śambhur rājate --> śambhu rājate --> śambhū rājate* can be explained in the same manner. The sūtras that apply in both the illustrations are in this order : *sasajuṣo ruḥ* (104), *ro ri* (110) and *ḍhralope pūrvasya dīrgho 'ṇaḥ* (111). The usage illustrating the long substitute replacing the element denoted by *aṇ*-pratyāhāra before *ḍh-lopa* is not given in the Laghu. The verbal form *līḍhaḥ* exemplifies the instance of *ḍh-lopa*. In this illustration the verbal root is *lih āsvādane* 'to lick'. The primary affix *kta* is introduced after it : *lih + kta* {the phoneme *k* is elided by *tasya lopaḥ* (3) since it is *it* by *laśakvataddhite* (135)} --> *lih + ta --> liḍh + ta* {*ho ḍhaḥ* (250) : *h* is replaced by *ḍh*} --> *liḍh + dha* {*jhaṣastathordho 'dhaḥ* (548) : the phoneme *t* of *ta* is replaced by *dh*} --> *liḍh + ḍha* {the dental *dh* is replaced by *ḍha* by virtue of the sūtra *ṣṭunā ṣṭuḥ* (64)}. At this stage, the sūtra *ḍho ḍhe lopaḥ* (549) applies and the phoneme *ḍh* of *liḍh* is replaced by lopa (zero-substitution) since it is followed by the phoneme *ḍh*. This prepares the ground for the application of the present sūtra. The long substitute in place of *i* preceding the cause of lopa-substitution (*ḍh*) takes place and we get the form *līḍhaḥ*.

The inclusion of the term *aṇ* in the sūtra is significant. If the lopa-substitution in place of the phonemes repha and *ḍh* takes place, the long susbstitute would replace none other than the vowels denoted by the abbreviatory term *aṇ*. The usages *tṛḍhaḥ* (destroyed) and *vṛḍhaḥ* (raised or ready) are given to illustrate this point. The verbal roots are respectively *tṛhū hiṁsāyām* 'to kill, to hurt' and *vṛhū udyamane* 'to raise, to get ready'. The long *ū* of both the roots is *it* by *upadeśe 'janunāsika it* (28) and is elided by *tasya lopaḥ* (3). The primary affix *kta* (*ta*) is added. Let us first take the root *tṛh*. The grammatical process can be shown as follows : *tṛh + ta --> tṛḍh + ta* {*ho ḍhaḥ* (250) : *h* is replaced by *ḍh*} --> *tṛḍh + dha* {*jhaṣastathordho 'dhaḥ* (548) : the phoneme *t* of *ta* is replaced by *dh*} --> *tṛḍh + ḍha* {the dental *dh* is replaced by *ḍha* by virtue of the sūtra *ṣṭunā ṣṭuḥ* (64)}. Now by virtue of the sūtra *ḍho ḍhe lopaḥ* (549), the phoneme *ḍh* of *tṛḍh* is elided and the condition for the long substitute 'before the cause of lopa-substitution (*ḍh*)' could be available. Since the substituendum vowel is *ṛ*, which is not denoted by the abbreviatoty term *aṇ*, the long substitute does not replace it. The same is the case with the usage *vṛḍhaḥ*.

लघु० – मनस् रथ इत्यत्र रुत्वे कृते हशि च इत्युत्वे रो रि इति लोपे प्राप्ते — *manas ratha ityatra rutve kṛte haśi ca* (106) *ityutve ro ri* (110) *iti lope prāpte* —

Trans. : In the expression *manas + ratha,* the phoneme *s* having been replaced by *ru,* the replacement of *ru* by *u* according to *haśi ca* (106) and the lopa-replacement (in place of the repha of *ru*) by *ro ri* (110) become available (simultaneously). (At this stage the following sūtra ensues) :

(112) **विप्रतिषेधे परं कार्यम्। *vipratiṣedhe paraṁ kāryam.* 1. 4. 2**

लघु० – तुल्यबलविरोधे परं कार्यं स्यात्। इति लोपे प्राप्ते — पूर्वत्रासिद्धमिति रो रि इत्यस्यासिद्धत्वादुत्त्वमेव। मनोरथः। *tulyabalavirodhe paraṁ kāryaṁ syāt. iti lope prāpte* — *pūrvatrāsiddham* (31) *iti ro ri* (110) *ityasyāsiddhatvād uttvameva. manorathaḥ.*

Trans. : When there is a conflict caused by two rules of equal strength, let the one which is subsequent in order (in the Aṣṭādhyāyī) apply.

PP. *vipratiṣedhe param kāryam.*

Eluc. : In the background of the sūtras *ro ri* (110) and *ḍhralope pūrvasya dīrgho 'ṇaḥ* (111), the compound *manorathaḥ* (a wish) is an illustration which gives rise to the situation that occasions the simultaneous availability of the sūtras *ro ri* (110) and *haśi ca* (106). These sūtras have already performed their grammatical functions separately : *haśi ca* (106) in the illustration *śivo vandyaḥ* and *ro ri* (110) in *harī ramayaḥ*. Therefore, when they are simultaneously available at one place, they are considered to be possessing equal strength (cf. *dvayoḥ śāstrayoḥ kvacil labdhāvakāśayor ekatra lakṣye yugapat sambhavas tulyabalavirodhaḥ,* BM, I, p. 169). Let us consider the usage *manorathaḥ* which is a ṣaṣṭhī tatpuruṣa. It is analysed as *manasaḥ rathaḥ* --> *manas ṅas ratha su* --> *manas ratha* (after the nominal endings have been elided in accordance with the sūtra *supo dhātuprātipadikayoḥ* (718). Now the sūtra *sasajuṣo ruḥ* (104) applies and we have *mana ru ratha* --> *manar ratha.* At this stage both the sūtras *ro ri* (110) and *haśi ca* (106) are available. When such a situation arises, there is confusion as to which rule should be preferred for application. The present paribhāṣā sūtra does away with this confusion by prescribing that in such a situation the rule which is subsequent in the Aṣṭādhyāyī should be allowed to operate. The sūtra *ro ri* (110), which prescribes the lopa-substitution in place of the repha of *manar*, is subsequent to *haśi ca* (106) which enjoins *ru* to be replaced by the vowel *u*. Being subsequent in the Aṣṭādhyāyī, *ro ri* should apply first and as a consequence the lopa-substitution in place of the repha of *manar* becomes available but the sūtra *ro ri* Pā. 8. 3. 14 belonging to the tripādī is deemed not to have performed any grammatical function with respect to the sūtra *haśi ca* Pā. 6. 1. 114 in consonance with the sūtra *pūrvatrāsiddham* Pā. 8. 2. 1. As a consequence, the sūtra *haśi ca*, which belongs to the sapādasaptādhyāyī, applies and *ru* is replaced by the vowel *u*. Now in *mana u ratha* both the vowel *a* following the consonant *n* and the vowel *u* which has replaced the substituendum *ru* are replaced by a single guṇa substitute *o* by virtue of the sūtra *ādguṇaḥ* (27) and thus we obtain the form *manorathaḥ* in the nominative singular. Let us take the declined form *rāmebhyaḥ* to illustrate this point further. When we introduce the sup-affix *bhyas* to the nominal stem *rāma*, both the sūtras *supi ca* Pā. 7. 3. 102 and *bahuvacane jhalyet* Pā. 7. 3. 103 apply simultaneously but in accordance with the present sūtra, the latter rule applies and we have the form *rāmebhyaḥ*.

(113) एतत्तदोः सुलोपोऽकोरनञ्समासे हलि । *etattadoḥ sulopo 'kor-anañsamāse hali.* 6. 1. 132

लघु० – अककारयोरेतत्तदोर्यः सुस्तस्य लोपः स्याद्धलि, न तु नञ्समासे । एष विष्णुः । स शम्भुः । अकोः किम् ? एषको रुद्रः । अनञ्समासे किम् ? असः शिवः । हलि किम् ? एषोऽत्र । *akakārayor etattador yaḥ sus tasya lopaḥ syāddhali, na tu nañsamāse. eṣa viṣṇuḥ, sa śambhuḥ. akoḥ kim? eṣako rudraḥ. anañsamāse kim? asaḥ śivaḥ. hali kim? eṣo 'tra.*

Trans. : Let lopa replace the affix *su* introduced after the pronominal stems *etad* (this) and *tad* (that) not having the consonant *k* and not being used as members of a nañ-samāsa, provided a consonant (*hal*) follows.

PP. *etattadoḥ sulopaḥ akoḥ anañsamāse hali* (*saṁhitāyām*).

Eluc. : The compound *etattadoḥ* is a genitive dual itaretaradvandva compound analysed as *etac ca tac ca etattadau, tayoḥ = etattadoḥ*. The word *sulopaḥ* is a ṣaṣṭhī-tatpuruṣa (*sor lopaḥ sulopaḥ*). The other word *akoḥ* is a bahuvrīhi compound which can be analysed as : *avidyamānaḥ k yayoḥ tau akau, tayoḥ = akoḥ*. The last compound word is *anañsamāse*. This is nañ-tatpuruṣa, *na nañsamāsaḥ anañsamāsaḥ, tasmin*. The word *akoḥ* means that the pronominal stems *etad* and *tad* should be without the phoneme *k*. The counter-example containing a form with the phoneme *k* is available when *akac* is inserted in the pronominal stems in accordance with the sūtra *avyayasarvanāmnāmakac prāk ṭeḥ* (1227). The affix *akac* is inserted before the *ṭi* of the pronominal stems and the indeclinables. When the affix *akac* is introduced, the pronominal stems *etad* and *tad* come to have the phoneme *k*. The forms of these pronominal stems with *akac*-insertion should not be construed as different from their forms without *akac* in view of the metarule (*paribhāṣā*) *tanmadhyapatitas tadgrahaṇena gṛhyate* (Abhyankar, 89) which means that any term used in grammar denotes not merely what is actually denoted by it but that it also denotes whatever word-form may result after something has been inserted in that which is directly denoted by it. Thus in the present example the form of *etad* with the affix *akac* added to it is *eṣakas* followed by *rudraḥ*. This form is taken on a par with *eṣas* which is the nominative singular of the pronominal stem *etad*. So, although a consonant follows the form *eṣakas*, the lopa-substitution does not come in place of the *su*-affix since it has the consonant *k* in it. Consequently the final phoneme s of the form *eṣakas* is replaced by *ru* by the rule *sasajuṣo ruḥ* (104). Then the sūtra *haśi ca* (106) applies and *ru* is substituted by the vowel *u*. With the help of the sūtra *ādguṇaḥ* (27), we have the form *eṣako rudraḥ*.

When the forms of these pronominal stems do not have the phoneme *k*, then before a consonant, the substitute lopa does replace the affix *su* added to these pronominal stems. The expressions *eṣa viṣṇuḥ* and *sa śambhuḥ* illustrate this aphorism. Before the nominative singular affix *su* is replaced by *ru*, the forms of *etad* and *tad* are *eṣas* and *sas*. The former is followed by the consonant *v* of *viṣṇuḥ* and the latter by the consonant *ś*. As such, the affix *su* introduced after these pronominal stems is elided and we have the usages *eṣa viṣṇuḥ* and *sa śambhuḥ*.

The negative particle in the compound *anañsamāsa* denotes prasajya (prohibition connected with a verbal activity). Had this negative particle meant exclusion (*paryudāsa*), it would have meant 'that which is similar to, and different from, nañsamāsa'. This is the paryudāsa sense of *na* which is interpreted as *tadbhinnatatsadṛśa*. This is one of the six meanings attributed to *na*. In this sense, the usages such as *eṣa viṣṇuḥ* and *sa śambhuḥ* would not be covered since there is no compound involved in these expressions. It is for this reason that the particle *na* is construed here in the sense of prasajya negation. This is exemplified in the illustration *asaḥ śivaḥ*. The nañ-tatpuruṣa *asaḥ* is analysed as : *na saḥ*

--> *asaḥ* {after the consonant *n* of the negative particle *nañ* has been elided by the rule *nalopo nañaḥ* (943)}. Since this is a nañsamāsa, the *su*-affix introduced in *asas* is not replaced by the lopa-substitution. In other words, it is not elided and we have the usage *asaḥ śivaḥ*. Here the sup-affix *su* has been replaced by *ru* and the repha of *ru* which remains after the elision of the *it* vowel *u* is in turn replaced by the visarga. The respective sūtras which apply here are *sasajuṣo ruḥ* (104) and *kharavasānayor visarjanīyaḥ* (93). At this stage, the replacement of the visarga by s in accordance with the rule *visarjanīyasya saḥ* (96) is made optional by the sūtra *vā śari* (103). The optional substitute dental s is replaced by the palatal *ś* in accordance with the sūtra *stoḥ ścunā ścuḥ* (62). The resultant form would be *asaś śivaḥ*.

According to this sūtra, the affix *su* is replaced by lopa when it is followed by a consonant (*hal*). This means that this replacement will not take place when a vowel follows. The usage *eṣo 'tra* explains this point. In this example, the affix *su* has not been replaced by lopa. We arrive at this form through the following grammatical process : *eṣas atra* --> *eṣa ru atra* by *sasajuṣo ruḥ* (104) --> *eṣa u atra* by *atororaplutādaplute* (105) --> *eṣo atra* by *ādguṇaḥ* (27) and --> *eṣo 'tra* : pūrvarūpa by *eṅaḥ padāntādati* (43).

(114) सोऽचि लोपे चेत्पादपूरणम्। *so 'ci lope cetpādapūraṇam.* 6. 1. 134

लघु० – सस् इत्यस्य सोर्लोपः स्यादचि पादश्चेल्लोपे सत्येव पूर्येत। सेमामविड्ढि प्रभृतिम् (ऋ० 2. 24. 1) सैष दाशरथी रामः। *sas ityasya sorlopaḥ syādaci pādaścel lope satyeva pūryeta. semāmaviḍḍhi prabhṛtim* (Ṛgveda, 2. 24. 1) *saiṣa dāśarathī rāmaḥ.*

Trans. : Let the affix *su* of *sas* be replaced by lopa (even) when followed by a vowel, provided that by the lopa-replacement (zero-substitution) only the quarter-verse becomes complete.

PP. *saḥ sulopaḥ aci lope cet pādapūraṇam* (*saṁhitāyām*).

Eluc. : The term *saḥ* in the sūtra stands for the nominative singular form of the pronominal stem *tad*, that is, for *sas* (*tad* + *su*). This term is construed as one ending in the genitive nominal ending, in place of which the *luk*-substitution has already occurred. The sūtras of Pāṇini are treated like the chandas and as a consequence, the zero-substitution in place of the singular sixth nominal ending occurs in accordance with the rule *supāṁ sulukpūrvasavarṇāccheyāḍāḍyāyājālaḥ* Pā. 7. 1. 39. As such, the sense of *sas* is 'in place of the affix *su* of the nominative singular form of the pronominal stem *tad*'. The word *sulopaḥ* is carried over from the sūtra Pā. 6. 1. 132. The sense of restriction, which is conveyed by the term *eva* in the vṛtti, is derived from the word *bahulam* which is carried over from the sūtra *syaśchandasi bahulam* Pā. 6. 1. 133. All these points having been taken into consideration, the meaning of the sūtra is as follows : If a vowel follows, the lopa-substitution in place of the affix *su* of the nominative singular form of the pronominal stem *tad* occurs provided a verse quarter becomes complete only by virtue of that lopa-substitution.

The first illustration which is given in the Laghu is a quarter of a mantra of the Ṛgveda. The metre of the mantra is jagatī. The first quarter of the mantra is : *semāmaviḍḍhi prabhṛtiṁ ya īśiṣe*. Every quarter of this metre has twelve syllables. In the absence of the lopa-substitution in place of the affix *su* introduced after the pronominal stem *tad*, there would be thirteen syllables. On the other hand, when the lopa-substitution comes in place of the affix *su* of *sas*, the quarter of the jagatī metre comes to have twelve syllables and becomes complete. This is the condition laid down by the sūtra for the lopa-substitution coming in place of the affix *su* of *sas* even when a vowel follows. To explain, *sas imām* are the two terms used in the first quarter of the mantra. If this sūtra did not apply, then the phoneme *s* of *sas* would be replaced by *ru* in accordance with the rule *sasajuṣo ruḥ* (104). In place of this *ru* the phoneme *y* is substituted in accordance with the rule *bho-bhago-agho-a-pūrvasya yo 'śi* (107). The aphorism *lopaḥ śākalyasya* Pā. 8. 3. 19 prescribes the optional lopa-replacement for the phoneme *y*. With the phoneme *y* remaining in the quarter, the syllables remain thirteen. This is a defect in the metre. Even when the lopa-substitution comes in place of *y*, the situation does not improve as both the vowels *a* and *i* cannot coalesce since the lopa in place of *y* by *lopaḥ śākalyasya* (30) is deemed not to have taken place in consonance with the sūtra *pūrvatrāsiddham* Pā. 8. 2. 1 so far as the sūtra *ādguṇaḥ* (27) is concerned. The problem of the completion of the quarter of a mantra gets resolved only when the lopa-substitution comes in place of affix *su* of *sas* by virtue of the present rule. The reason is that the present rule prescribing the lopa-substitution in place of the affix *su* does not belong to the tripādī and the lopa is considered to be existent (*siddha*). As such, there is no restriction with respect to the application of the sūtra *ādguṇaḥ* (27). When the sūtra *ād guṇaḥ* (27) applies and the guṇa substitute *e* replaces both the vowels *a* and *i*, the quarter of the metre comes to have twelve syllables and as a result becomes complete.

Some commentators hold that the word *pāda* not only refers to a quarter of a Vedic mantra but also to a quarter of a śloka. This is exemplified in the second illustration : *saiṣa dāśarathī rāmaḥ.* This is the quarter of an anuṣṭubh metre which has eight syllables. Here the substitute lopa replaces the affix *su* of *sas* in *sas + eṣa* before a vowel. At this stage, the sūtra *vṛddhireci* (33) applies and the substitute vṛddhi vowel *ai* replaces both *a* and *e* and we have a complete quarter of the anuṣṭubh metre having eight syllables.

लघु० - इति विसर्ग-सन्धिः । *iti visarga-sandhiḥ.* **इति पञ्चसन्धि-प्रकरणम् ।** *iti pañca-sandhi-prakaraṇam.*[1]

Trans. : The chapter on visarga-sandhi ends. The chapter on five sandhis ends here.

---

1. The word *pañca-sandhi-prakaraṇa* occurs in some editions of the Laghusiddhānta-kaumudī. It requires explanation. The Laghu has obviously three chapters on sandhi, whereas in the Siddhāntakaumudī sandhi is treated in five chapters. There is no controversy so far as the following four chapters are concerned : 1. ac-sandhi 2. hal-sandhi 3. visarga-sandhi and 4. svādi-sandhi. About the fifth, opinion is divided. Some consider prakṛtibhāva as the fifth kind of sandhi which is here included in the ac-sandhi. If this is so, then a prakaraṇa can be allotted to it and the mention of five sandhi prakaraṇas makes sense. The Gītā Press edition lays more emphasis on anusvāra as the fifth kind of sandhi. The argument runs like this : In prakṛtibhāva there is absence of sandhi. As such, it should not be construed as sandhi, whereas there is parasavarṇa of anusvāra by *anusvārasya yayi parasavarṇaḥ* (79) and *vā padāntasya* (80) and these rules occur in the context of hal-sandhi. So, anusvāra-sandhi should be considered as the fifth kind of sandhi. The portion assigned to it can be treated as the fifth chapter.

सुबन्त-प्रकरणम्
Declension

अजन्तपुँल्लिङ्गप्रकरणम्
Masculine words ending in a vowel

(115) अर्थवदधातुरप्रत्ययः प्रातिपदिकम् । ***arthavadadhāturapratyayaḥ prātipadikam*. 1. 2. 45**

लघु० – धातुं प्रत्ययं प्रत्ययान्तञ्च वर्जयित्वा अर्थवच्छब्दस्वरूपं प्रातिपदिकसंज्ञं स्यात् ।

dhātuṁ pratyayaṁ pratyayāntañca varjayitvā arthavacchabdasvarūpaṁ prātipadikasaṁjñaṁ syāt.

Trans. : Let any meaningful form of a word which is neither a verbal root, nor an affix, nor that which ends with an affix get the designation *prātipadika*.

PP. *arthavad adhātuḥ apratyayaḥ prātipadikam.*

Eluc. : The sūtra is a complete sentence in itself. The word *arthavat* is derived by introducing the taddhita affix *matup* after the word *artha* in the sense *artho 'syāstīti arthavat* by the sūtra *tadasyāstyasminniti matup* (1179). The phoneme *m* of the affix *matup* is substituted by the phoneme *v* in accordance with the sūtra *mādupadhāyāśca matorvo 'yavādibhyaḥ* (1061). Thus the word *arthavat* means 'meaningful'. The words *adhātuḥ* and *apratyayaḥ* are nañ-tatpuruṣa compounds which respectively mean 'other than a verbal root' and 'excepting an affix and that which ends in an affix'. The negation in these compounds means exclusion (*paryudāsa*). The latter meaning is arrived at by construing the word *pratyayaḥ* in the compound *apratyayaḥ* as both *pratyaya* and *pratyayānta*.[1] The word *arthavat* is an adjective. It is in the neuter gender. It requires the presence of a substantive to be qualified by it. Since the present work is related to śabdānuśāsana (grammar), the word *śabdasvarūpam* is made available.

1. Cf. *pratyayaṁ pratyayāntaṁ ceti. sūtre tantrādinā ubhayaṁ vivakṣitamiti bhāvaḥ.* Prauḍhamanoramā, p. 325.

The whole expression *arthavat śabdasvarūpam* means 'meaningful form of a word'. The negative compounds *adhātuḥ* and *apratyayaḥ* in the sūtra also qualify the supplied word *śabdasvarūpam*. Still, they end in the masculine since, in the tatpuruṣa samāsa, the gender of the last member of the compound is retained in accordance with the sūtra *paravalliṅgaṁ dvandvatatpuruṣayoḥ* (958). The word *prātipadika* is a technical term. Thus the whole sūtra comes to mean that any meaningful form of a word, leaving aside verbal roots, affixes and that which ends with an affix, is to be termed *prātipadika* (nominal stem).

Every word constituting the sūtra is significant. The use of the qualifying word *arthavat* in the sūtra dispenses with the contingency of every phoneme being called *prātipadika* as a result of which the introduction of nominal affixes would become available after every phoneme. By use of the word *arthavat* this undesirable situation is taken care of since every phoneme is not necessarily meaningful. The second constituent word is *adhātuḥ* which means that the word which is to be designated as *prātipadika* should be other than a verbal stem. By virtue of the word *adhātuḥ*, the application of the rule *na lopaḥ prātipadikāntasya* (179) would be stopped in respect of the elision of dental nakāra at the end of the verbal form *ahan* which is a third or second person singular laṅ-lakāra form of the verbal root *han*. This nakāra will not be elided since it belongs to a verb.

The word *apratyayaḥ* has also a purpose to serve. If it was not used in the sūtra, then the addition of nominal ending *su* after affixes would become applicable. In the words *gacchasi* and *rāmeṣu*, the affixes *si* and *su* are meaningful and at the same time they do not end with another affix. So these affixes would get the designation *prātipadika* in the absence of the expression *apratyayaḥ* in the sūtra. Consequently the introduction of the affix *su* after these affixes to denote in general a singular number would become applicable. The use of the compound word *apratyayaḥ* does away with this contingency.

The words which are given as illustrations above are meaningful combinations of base and affix. Being combinations, they are different from a bare affix. They are liable to be termed *prātipadika*, which is not desirable. In order to do away with this contingency, the word *apratyayaḥ* has been interpreted as including a form of a word which ends with an affix. So, the meaningful form of a word should be different from that which ends with an affix in order to be designated as *prātipadika*. Since both the words used as illustrations end with a conjugational affix and a nominal affix respectively, they would not be termed *prātipadika*. Not being termed *prātipadika*, they would not require any nominal affix to be introduced after them.

The grammatical term *prātipadika* can be explained as that form of a word which includes every (declined) pada as the following analysis shows : *pratipadaṁ gṛhṇāti tat prātipadikam* in accordance with the rule *padottarapadaṁ gṛhṇāti* Pā. 4. 4. 39. Although this term originally included verbal roots also, Pāṇini has defined it as a meaningful form of word which is neither a verbal root nor an affix.

There are two views which the grammarians hold in this context. Śākaṭāyana and his followers believed that all nominal stems were derivable from verbal roots, while others held that this was not always true. Pāṇini's view appears to postulate two sets of nominal stems : (1) underived (*avyutpanna*) nominal stems and (2) derived (*vyutpanna*) nominal stems. The present sūtra assigns the designation to the former kind of nominal stems. The following sūtra confers the prātipadika designation on the second kind of nominal stems.

(116) कृत्तद्धितसमासाश्च । *kṛttaddhitasamāsāśca.* 1. 2. 46

लघु० - कृत्तद्धितान्तौ समासाश्च तथा स्युः । *kṛttaddhitāntau samāsāśca tathā syuḥ.*

Trans. : Let (the derived forms of a word) ending in *kṛt* (primary affixes) and in *taddhita* (secondary affixes) and the compounds also be assigned the same (*prātipadika*) designation.

PP. *kṛttaddhitasamāsāḥ ca prātipadikāni.*

Eluc. : The word *prātipadikam* is carried over from the sūtra *arthavad-adhāturapratyayaḥ prātipadikam* Pā. 1. 2. 45 and is changed into the plural by the process of vacanavipariṇāma so that it may agree with the word *kṛttaddhitasamāsāḥ* which is in the plural. This word is an itaretara-dvandva samāsa which is analysed as *kṛc ca taddhitaś ca samāsaś ca kṛttaddhitasamāsāḥ*. The word *arthavat* is also carried over into this sūtra from the same sūtra (Bhaimī, I, p. 161). It is because of the word *arthavat* that the *kṛt* and *taddhita* used in the present sūtra denote those word forms which end in these affixes. This is the first argument based on the recurrence of the word *arthavat* in the present aphorism. The second argument is : The *kṛt* and *taddhita* affixes alone are not to be taken as meaningful units since Pāṇini intends to assign the term *prātipadika* to the combination of the base and the affix. It is implied by his usage of the negative compound *apratyayaḥ* in the preceding sūtra to preclude a word form ending in an affix[1] from being designated as *prātipadika* (cf. BM, I, p. 176). These two arguments ensure that the metarule *saṁjñāvidhau pratyayagrahaṇe tadantagrahaṇaṁ nāsti* (Abhyankar, 27) does not apply in respect of the present sūtra. To explain, although the terms *kṛt* and *taddhita* denoting respectively primary and secondary affixes have been used in the sūtra which is a saṁjñā-sūtra since it assigns prātipadika designation, still the kṛt and taddhita affixes stand for those word forms which end in these affixes. Resultantly, the terms *kṛt* and *taddhita* mean kṛdanta and taddhitānta word forms and not merely kṛt and taddhita affixes.

The term *kṛt* is defined by the sūtra *kṛdatiṅ* (301) which says that the affixes, other than the tiṅ affixes, introduced in the governing domain of *dhātoḥ* (Pā. 3. 1. 91) are termed *kṛt*. The taddhita affixes are introduced in the section beginning with the governing rule *taddhitāḥ* (Pā. 4. 1. 76) and continue up to the end of the fifth chapter. They are to be termed *taddhita* since the term *taddhita*, designating the affixes introduced in this section, recurs in each of the subsequent sūtras up to the end of the fifth chapter. The preceding sūtra (115) excludes the word forms ending in affixes from the purview of the prātipadika designation. The present sūtra assigns prātipadika designation to such forms of word as end in an affix. Thus the word forms which end in kṛt affixes are termed *prātipadika*. The word forms which end in taddhita affixes also get the same designation.

A compound, too, is to be designated as a *prātipadika*. The compound is other than a verbal root, an affix and that which ends in an affix but is a meaningful form of word. Therefore, it gets the prātipadika designation by the preceding sūtra. Then why has Pāṇini again assigned the prātipadika designation to it? The commentators view that the inclusion of samāsa in the present sūtra is for the sake of restriction (*niyama*). To explain, a form consisting of more than one meaningful unit can be designated as a *prātipadika* only when it is a samāsa (compound). Consequently, the compounds *rājapuruṣa*, *rāmalakṣmaṇa*, *citragu*, etc. get the prātipadika designation but a sentence like *rāmaḥ pibati* cannot qualify to be termed a *prātipadika* on the ground of being meaningful.

(117) स्वौजसमौट्छष्टाभ्याम्भिस्ङेभ्याम्भ्यस्ङसिभ्याम्भ्यस्ङसोसांङ्योस्सुप्।

***svaujasamauṭchaṣṭābhyāmbhisṅebhyāmbhyasṅasibhyāmbhyasṅasosāṁṅyossup*. 4. 1. 2**

1. *evaṁ tarhi ācāryapravṛttir jñāpayati - bhavati hi prakṛtipratyayasamudāyasya prātipadikasaṁjñeti yadayam apratyaya iti pratyayāntasya pratiṣedhaṁ śāsti.* KN, I, p. 345.

लघु॰ – सु औ जस् इति प्रथमा। अम् औट् शस् इति द्वितीया। टा भ्याम् भिस् इति तृतीया। ङे भ्याम् भ्यस् इति चतुर्थी। ङसि भ्याम् भ्यस् इति पञ्चमी। ङस् ओस् आम् इति षष्ठी। ङि ओस् सुप् इति सप्तमी। *su au jas iti prathamā. am auṭ śas iti dvitīyā. ṭā bhyām bhis iti tṛtīyā. ṅe bhyām bhyas iti caturthī. ṅasi bhyām bhyas iti pañcamī. ṅas os ām iti ṣaṣṭhī. ñi os sup iti saptamī.*

Trans. : *su au jas* is the first triplet (nominative). *am auṭ śas* is second (accusative). *ṭā bhyām bhis* is the third (instrumental). *ṅe bhyām bhyas* is the fourth (dative). *ṅasi bhyām bhyas* is the fifth (ablative). *ṅas os ām* is the sixth (genitive). *ṅi os sup* is the seventh (locative).

PP. *svaujasamauṭchaṣṭābhyāmbhisṅebhyāmbhyasṅasibhyāmbhyas-ṅasosāṁṅyossup* (*ṅyāpprātipadikāt*).

Eluc. : The sūtra is a *samāhāra* dvandva samāsa the analysis of which is as follows : *suś ca auś ca jaś ca am ca auṭ ca śaś ca ṭāś ca bhyāñ ca bhiś ca ṅeś ca bhyāñ ca bhyaś ca ṅasiś ca bhyāñ ca bhyaś ca ṅaś ca oś ca ām ca ṅiś ca oś ca sup ca eṣāṁ samāhāraḥ*. Twenty one sup-affixes have been enlisted in this sūtra. The term *sup* is an abbreviatory term. The initial *su* accompanied by the last pakāra of the affix *sup*, which is *it*, forms this pratyāhāra in accordance with the sūtra *ādirantyena sahetā* (4).

These twenty-one affixes constitute the nominal (declensional) endings, divided into seven triplets. The vowels *u* and *i* coming respectively at the end of *su* and *ṅasi* are *its* by the sūtra *upadeśe 'janunāsika it* (28). The consonants jakāra and śakāra coming at the beginning of the affixes *jas* and *śas* are *its* in the respective order by the sūtras *cuṭū* (128) and *laśakvataddhite* (135). The affixes *auṭ* and *ṭā* have ṭakāra as *it* by the sūtras *halantyam* (1) and *cuṭū* (128) respectively. The guttural nasal phoneme *ṅ* occurring at the beginning of the affixes *ṅe, ṅasi ṅas* and *ṅi* is *it* by the sūtra *laśakvataddhite* (135). The pakāra of *sup* is *it* by *halantyam* (1). After the elision of all the *its*, the forms of the declensional affixes will be as follows : *s au as* (prathamā), *am au as* (dvitīyā), *ā bhyām bhis* (tṛtīyā), *e bhyām bhyas* (caturthī), *as bhyām bhyas* (pañcamī), *as os ām* (ṣaṣṭhī) and *i os su* (saptamī). The vocative (*sambodhana*) is treated as a sub-class of the nominative (*prathamā*). Why *m* and *s* at the end of the affixes are not elided will be clear from *na vibhaktau tusmāḥ* (130)

To arrive at a complete sense of the present sūtra, it is essential to know which are the governing rules and in which domain this sūtra occurs. The following three sūtras provide the requisite details with the help of which we can interpret this sūtra in the right perspective.

(118) ङ्याप्प्रातिपदिकात् । *ṅyāpprātipadikāt.* **4. 1. 1**

(119) प्रत्ययः । *pratyayaḥ.* **3. 1. 1**

(120) परश्च । *paraśca.* **3. 1. 2**

लघु० – इत्यधिकृत्य । ङ्यन्तादाबन्तात् प्रातिपदिकाच्च परे स्वादयः प्रत्ययाः स्युः ।

Trans. : In view of these governing rules, (the present sūtra means) : Let the affixes *su*, etc. be introduced after a form of word, which ends in either feminine affix *ṅī* or *āp* or after a nominal stem (*prātipadika*).

PP. *svaujasamauṭchaṣṭābhyāmbhisṅebhyāmbhyasṅasibhyāmbhyasṅasosāṁṅyossup pratyayaḥ ṅyāpprātipadikāt paraḥ ca.*

Eluc. : It would have been better firstly, if these sūtras had been given in the Laghu before sūtra (117) and secondly, if the order of these sūtras had been like this : *pratyayaḥ, paraśca, ṅyāpprātipadikāt* (cf. Bhaimī, p. 163). It would also have been better if the governing rules had been given before the sūtra which occurs in their domain. The sūtra *ṅyāpprātipadikāt* occurs in the domain of the sūtras : *pratyayaḥ* (119) and *paraśca* (120). For this reason the sūtra *ṅyāpprātipadikāt* (118) should have been placed after these two sūtras. Consequently, it is appropriate that these sūtras are explained in the order in which they find their place in the Aṣṭādhyāyī.

The first governing sūtra is *pratyayaḥ* (119). The domain of this adhikāra sūtra extends up to the end of the fifth chapter of the Aṣṭādhyāyī. This is the largest section (covering three chapters) to be governed by a single sūtra in the Aṣṭādhyāyī. The word *pratyayaḥ* will thus recur in every subsequent rule up to the end of the fifth chapter.Therefore the items which are introduced after a verbal root (*dhātu*) or a nominal stem (*prātipadika*) in this section are to be designated by this technical term (*pratyaya*).

The second governing sūtra is *paraśca* (120). It also has the same range of operation as the preceding rule. It means that the affix is to follow that form of word to which it has been prescribed. As a consequence of this, the paribhāṣā sūtra *tasmādityuttarasya* (71) is not relevant with reference to the sūtra *ṅyāpprātipadikāt* (118) in which ablative case-ending has been used.

The sūtra *ṅyāpprātipadikāt* (118) occurs in the domain of these two governing sūtras. The word *ṅyāpprātipadikāt* is a samāhāradvandva compound. Had it been an itaretaradvandva, it would have been in the plural. The compound is analysed as *ṅī ca āp ca prātipadikaṁ ca eṣāṁ samāhāraḥ, ṅyāpprātipadikam, tasmāt = ṅyāpprātipadikāt*. The first two members of the compound, i.e. *ṅī* and *āp* have been used in the sūtra without the differentiating anubandhas. By doing this, Pāṇini intends to include all the feminine affixes in which *ṅī* and *āp* are common. As such, the element *ṅī* denotes the feminine affixes *ṅīp, ṅīṣ* and *ṅīn* and the element *āp* is a cover term for the feminine affixes *ṭāp, ḍāp* and *cāp*. The sūtra *svauja...* (117) occurs in the domain of the governing rule *ṅyāpprātipadikāt* (118). Taking into account this fact, the sūtra *svauja...* (117) means : The declensional affixes *su, au*, etc. are to be introduced after the word forms which end in *ṅīp, ṅīṣ, ṅīn, ṭāp, ḍāp* and *cāp* and also after nominal stems (*prātipadika*). The latter (nominal stems) are covered by the saṁjñā sūtras *arthavadadhāturapratyayaḥ prātipadikam* (115) and *kṛttaddhitasamāsāśca* (116).

According to the paribhāṣā *prātipadikagrahaṇe liṅgaviśiṣṭasyāpi grahaṇam* (Abhyankar, 71), a prātipadika also carries a reference to its counterparts in other genders. This means that the use of prātipadika in the sūtra can account for the basic forms ending in feminine affixes, *ṅī* and *āp*. So, there is no need to include *ṅyāp* in the sūtra for that purpose. Nonetheless, the commentators explain the purpose of the inclusion of *ṅyāp* in the sūtra. They say that this inclusion is made to ensure that a taddhita affix can also be introduced after a syntactically related nominal stem ending in these feminine affixes. If we do not interpret the inclusion of *ṅyāp* in this way, then we will not be able to get the optional forms *āryakā* and *āryikā*. If the taddhita affix was added first and was followed by the feminine affix *ṭāp*, we would not be able to get the form *āryakā*. The affix *kan* added to denote the sense of the nominal stem itself (*svārtha*) being most immediate (*antaraṅga*) is introduced after the word *ārya* prior to the feminine affix *ṭāp*. The result will be *āryakā*. At this stage, the rule *pratyayasthāt kāt pūrvasyāta idāpyasupaḥ* Pā. 7. 3. 44 applies in respect of the word *āryakā* to replace its *a*, which precedes *k*, by *i* and the result will be only one form *āryikā*. In this grammatical situation, the *i*-replacement for *a* is obligatory. If *ṭāp* is introduced prior to the introduction of the affix *kan*, then, given *āryā* + *ka*, the final *ā* of *āryā* is replaced by short *a* by the sūtra *ke 'ṇaḥ* Pā. 7. 4. 13. Thus *āryaka* is obtained. Now we can derive *āryikā* from *āryaka* + *ṭāp* where the short *a* before *k* will be treated as the *ā* it replaced. In this way the sūtra *udīcāmātaḥ sthāne yakapūrvāyāḥ* Pā. 7. 3. 46 becomes due and we have two optional forms, for the short *a* before *k* is optionally replaced by *i* and we have both *āryikā* and *āryakā*. This is the reason why Pāṇini has used the expression *ṅyāp* before *prātipadika* in the sūtra.

(121) सुपः । *supaḥ*. 1. 4. 103

लघु० – सुपस्त्रीणि त्रीणि वचनान्येकश एकवचनद्विवचनबहुवचनसंज्ञानि स्युः । *supastrīṇi trīṇi vacanānyekaśa ekavacanadvivacanabahuvacanasaṁjñāni syuḥ.*

Trans. : Let the triplets of the affixes denoted by the abbreviatory term *sup* taken one by one get the designations *ekavacana, dvivacana* and *bahuvacana* respectively.

PP. *supaḥ trīṇi trīṇi ekaśaḥ ekavacanadvivacanabahuvacanāni.*

Eluc. : The iterated term *trīṇi* has been carried over from the sūtra *tiṅastrīṇi trīṇi prathamamadhyamottamāḥ* Pā. 1. 4. 101 and the words *ekaśaḥ* and *ekavacanadvivacanabahuvacanāni* from Pā. 1. 4. 102. With these insertions carried over into the present sūtra, it becomes a complete sentence that assigns designations *ekavacana, dvivacana* and *bahuvacana* to the individual members of each triplet of sup-affixes in the order of their enumeration (23) in the same manner as the preceding sūtra in the Aṣṭādhyāyī assigns these very designations to the individual members of each triplet of tiṅ-affixes in the respective order. Thus the first triplet of sup-affixes, that is, *su, au* and *jas* will respectively be termed as *ekavacana, dvivacana* and *bahavacana.* The remaining triplets will receive these numerical designations in a similar manner.

The following sūtra prescribes where singular (*ekavacana*) or dual (*dvivacana*) is to be used :

(122) द्व्येकयोर्द्विवचनैकवचने । *dvyekayordvivacanaikavacane*. 1. 4. 22

लघु० – द्वित्वैकत्वयोरेते स्तः । *dvitvaikatvayor ete staḥ.*

Trans. : Let a dual or singular affix be used to respectively denote duality or singularity.

PP. *dvyekayoḥ dvivacanaikavacane.*

Eluc. : The word *dvivacanaikavacane* is an itaretaradvandva compound which is analysed as : *dvivacanaṁ ca ekavacanaṁ ca dvivacanaikavacane.* The other word *dvyekayoḥ* is also an itaretara-dvandva but the members used in the compound are purported to denote the numbers. This is the reason why dual number is used in the compound. The compound can be analysed as *dvi ca ekaṁ ca dvyeke tayoḥ = dvyekayoḥ.* Had they stood for the enumerated units, the compound would have ended in a plural affix. This is the reason why Varadarāja has interpreted these words in the sense of numbers : *dvitva* and *ekatva* (cf. *ayam api bhāvapradhāno nirdeśaḥ, anyathā hi bahutvād bahuvacanaṁ syāt,* KN, I, p. 530). These points having been taken into consideration, the sūtra prescribes a dual sup-affix to denote duality and a singular sup-affix to denote singularity.

(123) विरामोऽवसानम् । *virāmo 'vasānam.* 1. 4. 110

लघु० – वर्णानामभावोऽवसानसंज्ञः स्यात् । रुत्वविसर्गौ । रामः । *varṇānām abhāvo-'vasānasaṁjñaḥ syāt. rutvavisargau. rāmaḥ.*

Trans. : Let absence or termination of speech be designated as *avasāna* or cessation.

PP. *virāmaḥ avasānam.*

Eluc. : The Bālamanoramā derives the word *virāma* in two ways : 1. *virāma* is that in the vicinity of which the speech is being terminated. In this case the primary affix *ghañ* is introduced after *vi* + *ram* in the sense of locus of vicinity (*sāmīpika-adhikaraṇa*). In this sense a phoneme, which having been articulated is followed by the absence of the articulation of other succeeding phonemes, is assigned the technical term *avasāna* (*viramyate asminniti virāmaḥ sāmīpike 'dhikaraṇe ghañ,* BM, I, p. 38). 2. In the second derivation, the primary affix *ghañ* is introduced after the verbal root *ram* in the sense of the verbal root itself (*bhāva*). The derived word *virāma*, in this sense, means the absence of the articulation of any following speech-units, a situation which can emerge when the articulation of some phoneme is followed by the absence or cessation of the articulation of other succeeding phonemes. In the Kāśikā on this very sūtra, the term *virāma* is also derived in the sense of instrumentality (*viramyate 'neneti vā virāmaḥ*). In the first and third senses, the last phoneme is assigned the technical term *avasāna* and in the second sense, the absence of the articulation of succeeding speech units or phonemes is assigned the designation *avasāna*.

To illustrate, declensional affixes are added to the word *rāma*, which is a prātipadika either by *arthavadadhāturapratyayaḥ prātipadikam* (115) or by *kṛttaddhitasamāsāśca* (116) so that it may become usable in a sentence. In the domains of the governing rules (118), (119) and (120) the aphorism (117) makes available 21 affixes. To denote the singular number of the first triplet, the first sup-affix *su* becomes available. We have : *rāma* + *su*. The vowel *u* of the affix *su*, being anunāsika, is *it* by (28) and is elided by (3). At this stage, *rāmas* gets the designation *pada* by *suptiṅantaṁ padam* (14). Since it is a pada, the sūtra *sasajuṣo ruḥ* (104) applies and the pada-final *s* is replaced by *ru*. The vowel *u* in *ru* is anunāsika and hence *it*. After its elision we have the form *rāmar*. Here the sūtra *kharavasānayorvisarjanīyaḥ* (93) becomes applicable. The term *avasāna* occurring in the sūtra can be taken in all the senses and applied. In the first and the third senses, the last phoneme repha is designated as *avasāna*. Since the consonant repha itself constitutes avasāna, it will be replaced by visarjanīya when the scope of substitution in place of the substituendum beomes available. In this case, the sense of the affix *ghañ* may be either the locus of vicinity (*sāmīpika-adhikaraṇa*) or instrumentality. The last phoneme constitutes avasāna. The seventh case-ending in respect of the avasāna in the sūtra *kharavasānayor visarjanīyaḥ* (93) is construed as viṣaya-saptamī, whereas with reference to *khar* it is parasaptamī. The seventh inflectional ending is construed differently on account of difference in scope in both the cases (*asmiṁstu pakṣe kharavasānayoḥ ityekāpi saptamī viṣayabhedād bhidyate - khari pare rephasya visargaḥ, avasāne ca rephe sthānin̄īti*, TB, I, p. 39).

When the affix *ghañ* is introduced in the sense of bhāva, the absence of the articulation that follows the articulation of the last speech-unit is assigned the designation *avasāna*. In this sense the last phoneme repha is followed by avasāna consisting in the absence of the articulation of any succeeding speech-units. The pada-final repha of the word *rāmar* is followed by the absence of the articulation of any succeeding speech sounds and hence is replaced by visarjanīya. So the pada-final repha is either itself avasāna or is followed by avasāna, in both the cases it is replaced by visarjanīya in accordance with the sūtra *kharavasānayor visarjanīyaḥ* (93). In the latter case the locative case-ending used in the sūtra *kharavasānayorvisarjanīyaḥ* (93) is interpreted as parasaptamī. It is easier to follow.

(124) सरूपाणामेकशेष एकविभक्तौ । *sarūpāṇāmekaśeṣa ekavibhaktau.* 1. 2. 64

लघु० – एकविभक्तौ यानि सरूपाण्येव दृष्टानि तेषामेक एव शिष्यते । *ekavibhaktau yāni sarūpāṇyeva dṛṣṭāni teṣāmeka eva śiṣyate.*

Trans. : Only one of the available similar forms of a nominal base remains before the same nominal ending.

PP. *sarūpāṇām ekaśeṣaḥ eva ekavibhaktau.*

Eluc. : In this sūtra the genitive plural inflectional ending in the bahuvrīhi compound *sarūpāṇām* carries the sense of selection (*nirdhāraṇa*). The analysis of the compound can be shown in the following manner : *samānaṁ rūpaṁ yeṣāṁ te sarūpāḥ, teṣām*. The word *ekaśeṣa* is a karmadhāraya compound. Its analysis is as follows : *ekaś cāsau śeṣaś ca ekaśeṣaḥ*. The compound *ekavibhaktau* is also a karmadhāraya compound and is analysed as *ekā cāsau vibhaktiś ca ekavibhaktiḥ* which means *samānavibhaktiḥ*. The indeclinable *eva* has been brought here from the following sūtra *vṛddho yūnā tallakṣaṇaścedeva viśeṣaḥ* Pā. 1. 2. 65 through a process called *anukarṣaṇa* or *upakarṣa* (*etacca uttarasūtrasthasyaivakārasyehānukarṣaṇāl labhyate*, TB, I, p. 186; also cf. *vṛddho yūnā... ityuttarasūtrād evetyapakṛṣyate* BM, I, p. 184). With these insertions having been taken into account, this sūtra prescribes the retention of only one from among several similar forms when they occur before a single inflectional ending (*samāna-vibhakti*). Thus given the string *rāma* + *su*, *rāma* + *su*, where two similar forms of *rāma* are occurring before *su*, the rule enjoins that only one form remains; the other is dropped. As a result, we have *rāma* + *au*. It should be borne in mind that the singular inflectional ending would be replaced by the nominative dual ending *au* since here the duality residing in the nominal stem *rāma* is intended to be denoted. The same process operates in the retention of one in deriving *rāmāḥ*, nominative plural, from *rāma* + *su*, *rāma* + *su*, *rāma* + *su* = *rāma* + *jas*. The same inflectional ending, to wit *su* in the above illustration, is intended. It is not actually available as will be made clear in the sequel.

The idea behind the formation of this sūtra is that each unit of meaning requires a separate word for its denotation in deference to the principle that a single word can express only one single unit of meaning (*pratyarthaṁ śabdaniveśād naikenānekasyābhidhānaṁ tatrānekārthābhidhāne 'nekaśabdatvaṁ prāptaṁ tasmādekaśeṣaḥ*, Kāśikā, p. 43). In pursuance of this principle, more than one unit of meaning requires more than one word for its denotation. The purpose of the present sūtra is to facilitate the denotation of more than one unit of meaning by the use of a single word. For that the device of ekaśeṣa has been invoked and employed. The invocation of this device makes it possible to express two units of meaning of *rāma* to be expressed by *rāma* + *au* where the nominal stem is one. In a similar manner, more than two units of meaning can be expressed by *rāmāḥ* by introducing the sup-affix *jas* after a single nominal stem *rāma* which signifies the meanings of the forms of the word which have been dropped by this sūtra.

Although the compound word *sarūpa* pertains to the similarity of form, a single form before a single sup-affix could differ from otherwise similar forms of a word having similarity of form at the prātipadika stage. In such a situation ekaśeṣa does not take place. Take, for example, the word *mātṛ*. The word having the same form at the prātipadika level is derived in two ways : 1. The irregularly derived word *mātṛ* in accordance with the sūtra *naptṛneṣṭṛtvaṣṭṛhotṛpotṛbhrātṛjāmātṛmātṛpitṛduhitṛ* (Uṇādi Sūtra, 252). The root is *mān* 'to venerate', the nakāra of which is irregularly elided. It means 'mother'. The other word *mātṛ* has been derived from the verbal root *māṅ* 'to measure' by introducing *tṛc* in accordance with *ṇvultṛcau* (781). The word means 'one who measures'. If these two kinds of words enter into a dvandva compound, retention of one is not prescribed since they do not keep the same form before a similar sup-affix. Before the second singular case-ending *am*, the word *mātṛ* meaning 'mother' is declined as *mātaram*, whereas the word *mātṛ* meaning 'one who measures' is declined as *mātāram*. Although these words are of the same form at the prātipadika level and before other sup-affixes, they differ in their declined form before the same sup-affixes as in the case of the *am* affix. Because of this dissimilarity, even in the case of a single sup-affix, only one form is not retained. This is the significance of the attraction of the indeclinable *eva* from the following sūtra *vṛddho yūnā tallakṣaṇaścedeva viśeṣaḥ* Pā. 1. 2. 65. In other words, ekaśeṣa in the case of such words does not become operational.

The use of the word *ekavibhakti* in the sūtra is of an indicatory nature (*upalakṣaṇa*) and does not constitute the causal condition for the retention of one out of several similar forms (*vibhaktiḥ sārūpye upalakṣaṇam na tu ekaśeṣe nimittam*, TB, I, p. 185). Consequent upon this, the retention of one of the similar forms does not require any occasioning condition. Hence it becomes anaimittika (*antaraṅga*) and becomes applicable even before the sup-affixes become operational. Had this not been the case, then every form of the word would have sup-vibhakti after it and it would have occasioned the instance of dvandva compounding. In the case of ekaśeṣa taking precedence over the introduction of sup-affixes, the instance of dvandva would not be available in the absence of sup-affixes. It may be objected that the availability of the retention of one similar form before the application of sup-affixes makes the retained prātipadika denote only one unit of meaning and we cannot have the forms *rāmau* and *rāmāḥ* when the duality and the plurality are not denoted in the absence of sup-affixes. Jñānendra Sarasvatī dismisses this objection and avers that the retained prātipadika would denote the meanings of the dropped ones. This is the ground why ekaśeṣa has been accepted as a vṛtti since it expresses a sense different from the exact literal sense of a single nominal stem (cf. *śiṣyamāṇasya lupyamānārthābhidhāyitvāt. ata eva kṛttaddhitasamāsaikaśeṣa... ityekaśeṣo vṛttiṣu gaṇyate. parārthābhidhānaṁ hi vṛttiḥ*, TB, I, p. 185). However, there are others who do not subscribe to the view that ekaśeṣa is a vṛtti (see for details, Chaturvedi 2001, pp. 19-20).

So, when there is a case for two similar forms '*rāma rāma*', one is retained by virtue of the present sūtra even before the sup-affixes are added. When the duality of the nominative inflectional ending is intended, the sup-affix *au* after *rāma* becomes available by *dvyekayordvivacanaikavacane* (122). At this stage, *rāma* + *au*, the sandhi rule *vṛddhireci* (33) presents itself for application but it is blocked by the following sūtra :

(125) प्रथमयोः पूर्वसवर्णः । *prathamayoḥ pūrvasavarṇaḥ*. 6. 1. 102

लघु॰ - अकः प्रथमाद्वितीययोरचि पूर्वसवर्णदीर्घ एकादेशः स्यात्। इति प्राप्ते *akaḥ prathamādvitīyayor aci pūrvasavarṇadīrgha ekādeśaḥ syāt. iti prāpte* —

Trans. : If an element denoted by the abbreviatory term *ak* is followed by the vowel (*ac*) belonging to the first and second triplets of nominal endings, both (the preceding and the following vowels) should be replaced by a single long vowel homogeneous with the preceding one. When this condition is available —

PP. *akaḥ prathamayoḥ aci pūrvaparayoḥ ekaḥ pūrvasavarṇaḥ dīrghaḥ (saṁhitāyām)*.

Eluc. : The terms *akaḥ* and *dīrghaḥ* are carried over into this sūtra from *akaḥ savarṇe...* Pā. 6. 1. 101. The term *aci* comes from *iko yaṇaci* Pā. 6. 1. 77. The sūtra *ekaḥ pūrvaparayoḥ* Pā. 6. 1. 84 is the governing rule in the domain of which the present sūtra occurs. The word *prathamayoḥ* is construed as ekaśeṣa dvandva in the following way : *prathamā ca prathamā ca prathame* where only one *prathamā* is retained. The first word *prathamā* refers to the first triplet of inflectional endings *su au jas*. The second *prathamā* is interpreted as referring to the first among the remaining triplets of inflectional endings. In this way, the word *prathamayoḥ* refers to both prathamā and dvitīyā inflectional endings, i.e., *su au jas* and *am auṭ śas*. According to Haradatta, it is the dual number used in the word *prathamayoḥ* which brings *dvitīyā* within the denotatum of prathamā by association (KP, IV, p. 573). The compound *pūrvasavarṇaḥ* is a ṣaṣṭhītatpuruṣa analysed as *pūrvasya savarṇaḥ*.

Thus analysed, the sūtra gives the following meaning : If the elements denoted by the abbreviatory term *ak* are followed by the vowels (*ac*) belonging to either prathamā or dvitīyā, then the preceding and the following vowels are replaced by one long vowel homogeneous with the preceding vowel. In the illustration *rāma* + *au*, the vowel *a* occurring at the end of the nominal stem *rāma* is a denotatum of *ak*-pratyāhāra and is followed by the vowel *au* which belongs to the first triplet being its second member. Thus the conditions for the substitution of a long vowel homogeneous with the vowel *a* of *rāma* are available but the replacement by a long vowel-substitution is negated by the following sūtra :

(126) नादिचि । ***nādici*. 6. 1. 104**

लघु० – आद् इचि न पूर्वसवर्णदीर्घः । वृद्धिरेचि (33) । रामौ । *ād ici na pūrvasavarṇa-dīrghaḥ. vṛddhireci* (33). *rāmau.*

Trans. : If the vowel *a* is followed by an element denoted by the abbreviatory term *ic*, then a long vowel replacement homogeneous with that which precedes does not come in place of the preceding and the following vowels.

PP. *āt ici pūrvaparayoḥ ekaḥ pūrvasavarṇaḥ dīrghaḥ na* (*saṁhitāyām*).

Eluc. : The expression *nād* is split as *na āt*. The word *āt* is in the ablative. The words *pūrvasavarṇaḥ* and *dīrghaḥ* are respectively carried over from the sūtras *prathamayoḥ pūrvasarvarṇaḥ* Pā. 6. 1. 104 and *akaḥ savarṇe dīrghaḥ* Pā. 6. 1. 101. The sūtra *ekaḥ pūrvaparayoḥ* Pā. 6. 1. 84 is a governing rule which recurs in this sūtra also. With these carried over insertions, the sūtra means : If the vowel *a* is followed by an element denoted by *ic*-pratyāhāra, then a long vowel-replacement does not come in place of the preceding and the following elements. The vowel *a* occurring at the end of the nominal stem *rāma* is followed by the vowel *au* which constitutes the second member of the first triplet and which at the same time is a denotatum of the abbreviatory term *ic*. Consequently, a long vowel-replacement homogeneous with that which precedes does not take place. When the long replacement by *prathamayoḥ*... (125) is blocked by the present sūtra, the sūtra *vṛddhireci* (33) again becomes available for application and a vṛddhi vowel-replacement comes in place of both the preceding and following vowels (for a similar discussion see BM, I, p. 158 and TB, I, p.159). In this case the vowel *a* occurring at the end of the word *rāma* and the vowel *au* of the first triplet are both replaced by a vṛddhi-vowel *au* and we have the form *rāmau*.

(127) बहुषु बहुवचनम् । ***bahuṣu bahuvacanam*. 1. 4. 21**

लघु० – बहुत्वविवक्षायां बहुवचनं स्यात् । *bahutvavivakṣāyāṁ bahuvacanaṁ syāt.*

Trans. : Let a plural affix be used to denote plurality.

PP. *bahuṣu bahuvacanam.*

Eluc. : In this sūtra, the word *bahu* has been used in the sense of *bahutva* which stands for a number that expresses more than two objects. To express plurality of a nominal stem, the plural affix is used. In case we use more than two nominal stems *rāma rāma rāma* after each of which the first inflectional ending *su* is intended, only one out of these similar forms is retained, that is, *rāma*. In order to convey the sense of plurality existing in *rāma*, the plural sup-affix *jas* is used : *rāma* + *jas*. At this stage, the following sūtra ensues :

(128) **चुटू । *cuṭū*. 1. 3. 7**
लघु० – प्रत्ययाद्यौ चुटू इतौ स्तः । *pratyayādyau cuṭū itau staḥ.*

Trans. : The palatal and cerebral stops occurring at the beginning of the affixes are designated as *it*.

PP. *pratyuyasya ādī cuṭū itau.*

Eluc. : The term *it* is carried from *upadeśe 'janunāsika it* Pā. 1. 3. 2. The word *ādi* is carried over from the sūtra *ādirñiṭuḍavaḥ* Pā. 1. 3. 5. Both the words *it* and *ādi* are to be taken as ending in dual number through the process known as vacanavipariṇāma. They are to be read as *ādī* and *itau* in the present sūtra. The word *pratyayasya* is carried over from the sūtra *ṣaḥ pratyayasya* Pā. 1. 3. 6. Thus the whole sūtra means : The palatal and cerebral stops occurring at the beginning of an affix are to be designated as *it*. In the illustration *rāma* + *jas*, the palatal jakāra occurring at the beginning is *it* and hence it is elided by the sūtra *tasya lopaḥ* (3). The affix remains as *as*. The dental sibilant coming at the end of *jas* has also got to be termed *it* by *halantyam* (1) but this is debarred by the following two sūtras :

(129) **विभक्तिश्च । *vibhaktiśca*. 1. 4. 104**
लघु० – सुप्तिङौ विभक्तिसंज्ञौ स्तः । *suptiṅau vibhaktisaṁjñau staḥ.*

Trans. : The elements denoted by the abbreviatory terms *sup* and *tiṅ* are to be designated as *vibhakti*.

PP. *sup tiṅ vibhaktiḥ ca.*

Eluc. : The words *sup* and *tiṅ* are respectively carried over from the sūtras *supaḥ* Pā. 1. 4. 103 and *tiṅastrīṇi trīṇi prathamamadhyamottamāḥ* Pā. 1. 4. 101. Both the words are changed into nominative singular by the process of vibhaktivipariṇāma to be appositionally paraphrased with the word *vibhaktiḥ*. The word *sup* is an abbreviatory term denoting all the inflectional affixes. The word *tiṅ* is also an abbreviatory term which denotes all the conjugational affixes. The present sūtra assigns the technical term *vibhakti* to both these kinds of affixes. One point is to be taken note of here. It is a metarule that the affixes mentioned in the Aṣṭādhyāyī are taken in the sense of the words that end in those affixes (*pratyayagrahaṇe*... Abhyankar, 23). There is an exception to this metarule. If the affixes are mentioned in the context of assigning a designation, then they are to be taken as they are and not in the sense of the words ending in them (*saṁjñāvidhau pratyayagrahaṇe tadantagrahaṇaṁ nāsti*, Abhyankar, 27). Since the present sūtra also assigns the technical term *vibhakti*, the affixes *sup* and *tiṅ* are to be taken as denoting affixes alone and consequently the affixes themselves will be designated as *vibhakti*.

(130) न विभक्तौ तुस्माः । *na vibhaktau tusmāḥ*. 1. 3. 4

लघु॰ – विभक्तिस्थास्तवर्गसमा नेतः। इति सस्य नेत्त्वम्। रामाः। *vibhaktisthās tavargasamā netaḥ. iti sasya nettvam. rāmāḥ.*

Trans. : The dental stops, the phonemes *s* and *m* occurring in the vibhakti-affixes are not designated as *it*.

PP. *na vibhaktau tusmāḥ itaḥ*.

Eluc. : The word *it* has been carried over from *uapadeśe 'janunāsika it* Pā. 1. 3. 2 and it is read as *itaḥ* by using the technique known as vacanavipariṇāma. The word *tusmāḥ* is an itaretaradvandva compound which is analysed as *tuś ca s ca maś ca tusmāḥ*. The vowel *a* following *m* is for the sake of articulation. Thus the complete sūtra comes to mean : The dental stops (tavarga), *s* and *m* occurring in the affixes which have been designated as *vibhakti* are not to be assigned the technical term *it*. By virtue of this sūtra, the phonemes that occur at the end of the affixes *jas, śas, bhis, bhyas, ṅas, os, am, bhyām, ām*, etc. do not get the designation *it* in accordance with the sūtra *halantyam* (1) and as a consequence they are not elided by *tasya lopaḥ* (3). Some illustrations which exemplify the non-*it* nature of dental stops occurring in vibhakti-affixes are : *rāmāt, tasmāt, tasmin, labheran*, etc.

The initial stage of the formation is : *rāma* + *as*. Here the sūtra *akaḥ savarṇe dīrghaḥ* (42) is available for application but is blocked by its exception *ato guṇe* (273) which prescribes a single vowel-replacement homogeneous with the following in place of a non-pada final short *a* and the following guṇa vowel (*a, e, o*). The vowel *a* coming at the end of the stem *rāma* is a non-pada final short vowel denoted by *at* and the following *a* occurring at the beginning of the sup-affix *as* constitutes a guṇa vowel. The conditions for a single substitution laid down by this sūtra are fulfilled. Hence the sūtra *ato guṇe* Pā. 6. 1. 97 blocks *akaḥ savarṇe dīrghaḥ* (42) and presents itself for application. At this stage, the sūtra *prathamayoḥ pūrvasavarṇaḥ* Pā. 6. 1. 102 being subsequent in order applies and a single long vowel homogeneous with the preceding one replaces both the short vowel coming at the end of *rāma* and the short vowel *a* occurring at the beginning of the sup-affix *as* since the preceding vowel *a* is an element denoted by the abbreviatory term *ak* and is followed by the vowel (*ac*) belonging to the first and second triplets of nominal endings. In this case both (the preceding and the following vowels) are replaced by a single long vowel homogeneous with the preceding one.

The aphorism *ato guṇe* Pā. 6. 1. 97 is an exception to *akaḥ savarṇe dīrghaḥ* Pā. 6. 1. 101 and precedes it. The sūtra *prathamayoḥ pūrvasavarṇaḥ* Pā. 6. 1. 102 obviously follows the latter. Now by virtue of the metarule *purastādapavādā anantarān vidhīn bādhante nottarān* (Abhyankar, 59), the sūtra *ato guṇe* Pā. 6. 1. 97 can play the role of an exception only to *akaḥ savarṇe dīrghaḥ* Pā. 6. 1. 101 and not to the sūtra *prathamayoḥ pūrvasavarṇaḥ* Pā. 6. 1. 102 which is subsequent to the former. That is why the sūtra *prathamayoḥ pūrvasavarṇaḥ* Pā. 6. 1. 102 applies and we have the form *rāmās*, the pada-final s of which is replaced by *ru* in accordance with the rule *sasajuṣo ruḥ* (104). The remaining repha of *ru* is replaced by visarjanīya by the sūtra *kharavasānayorvisarjanīyaḥ* (93) and we have the form *rāmāḥ*.

(131) एकवचनं सम्बुद्धिः । *ekavacanaṁ sambuddhiḥ*. 2. 3. 49

लघु॰ – सम्बोधने प्रथमाया एकवचनं सम्बुद्धिसंज्ञं स्यात् । *sambodhane prathamāyā ekavacanaṁ sambuddhisaṁjñaṁ syāt*.

Trans. : In the sense of vocative, let the singular affix of the first triplet be termed *sambuddhi*.

PP. *sambodhane prathamāyāḥ ekavacanam sambuddhiḥ*.

Eluc. : The word *sambodhane* is carried over from the sūtra *sambodhane ca* Pā. 2. 3. 47. The word *prathamā* is carried over from the sūtra *prātipadikārthaliṅgaparimāṇavacanamātre prathamā* Pā. 2. 3. 46 and has been changed into one ending in the sixth case-ending by the process of vibhaktivipariṇāma. The preceding sūtra *sā 'mantritam* Pā. 2. 3. 46 assigns the designation *āmantrita* to the first triplet of the sup-affixes when the affixes of the first triplet are used in the sense of abhimukhī-karaṇa, that is, to attract the attention of someone. Taking all this into account, we can interpret the sūtra as follows : The singular sup-affix of āmantrita, that is, of the first triplet, when used in the sense of vocative, should be designated as *sambuddhi*.

This sūtra assigns sambuddhi-designation to the singular affix *su* when used in the sense of vocative.

(132) यस्मात्प्रत्ययविधिस्तदादि प्रत्ययेऽङ्गम्। *yasmātpratyayavidhis tadādi pratyaye 'ṅgam.* 1. 4. 13

लघु० – यः प्रत्ययो यस्मात् क्रियते तदादि शब्दस्वरूपं तस्मिन्नङ्गं स्यात्। *yaḥ pratyayo yasmāt kriyate tadādi śabdasvarūpaṁ tasminnaṅgaṁ syāt.*

Trans. : Let the word-form beginning with that after which an affix has been introduced be designated as *aṅga* when the affix follows.

PP. *yasmāt pratyayavidhiḥ tadādi pratyaye aṅgam.*

Eluc. : There are two compound words in the sūtra : 1. *pratyaya-vidhiḥ* 2. *tadādi*. The first is a ṣaṣṭhītatpuruṣa compound analysed as *pratyayasya vidhiḥ* which means 'the prescription of an affix'. The second is a bahuvrīhi compound and that too, a tadguṇasaṁvijñāna bahuvrīhi: *tat ādir yasya, tadādi*. The compound means a word-form at the beginning of which is the base, whether verbal or nominal, after which an affix has been introduced. It is that word-form which is to be designated as *aṅga*. The word-form includes that after which an affix has been prescribed. It may extend right up to the affix and include constituents coming between the initial form and the affix. This is the reason why the word *tadādi* is interpreted as tadguṇasaṁvijñāna bahuvrīhi.

The rule is formulated by using the variable *yat* (*yasmāt*) 'that which' with its correlative *tat* 'that'. With parts of the sūtra literally translated, it will read as follows : *yasmāt pratyayavidhiḥ* 'that (form) after which an affix has been prescribed; *tadādi* 'that (form) which begins with that (word-form after which an affix has been introduced)'; *pratyaye 'ṅgam,* (that form) is designated as *aṅga* when (that) affix follows.

The word *tadādi* needs explanation. The word *ādi* used in the compound is significant and that the compound is a tadguṇasaṁvijñāna bahuvrīhi is also significant. Had the word *ādi* not been used in the sūtra, then only the base would have got the *aṅga*-designation. Being a tadguṇasaṁvijñāna bahuvrīhi compound, it refers to a form which begins with a base after which an affix has been prescribed. A form beginning with a base along with other constituents before the affix in consonance with the sense of *tadādi* as a tadguṇasaṁvijñāna bahuvrīhi compound can be designated as *aṅga*. If no constituent is there, then a form constituted by the base itself can also be designated as *aṅga* in view of the sūtra *ādyantavad ekasmin* (277).

To illustrate this point, two verbal forms *bhavāmi* and *bhaviṣyāmi* have been given in the Siddhāntakaumudī under this sūtra (SK, I, p. 194). Let us take *bhavāmi* to explain this point : This is a first person singular laṭ-lakāra form of the verbal root *bhū* 'to be'. The derivational process may be demonstrated as follows : *bhū* + *śap* + *mip* --> (*kartari śap*) *bhū* + *a* + *mi* (after the elision of anubandhas) --> *bho* + *a* + *mi* {(guṇa by *sārvadhātukārdhadhātukayoḥ* (387)} --> *bhava* + *mi* {*eco 'yavāyāvaḥ* (22)}. So far as the affix *śap* is concerned the verbal base *bhū* is treated as aṅga in accordance with the sūtra *ādyantavad ekasmin* (277) but with regard to the affix *mip* the word-form *bhava*, which is constituted by *bhū* + *śap*, gets the designation *aṅga* in consonance with the interpretation of *tadādi* as a tadguṇasaṁvijñāna bahuvrīhi compound. Had this not been the case, only the verbal base *bhū* could have got the designation *aṅga*. Now with the expression *tadādi* interpreted as a tadguṇasaṁvijñāna bahuvrīhi, the verbal base *bhū* along with the infix *śap* is duly assigned the aṅga designation. Consequently the sūtra *ato dīrgho yañi* (389) becomes available for application. It prescribes that a long vowel replaces an aṅga-final short *a* when followed by a sārvadhātuka affix beginning with a consonant denoted by the abbreviatory term *yañ*. The affix *mip* is such an affix. Had the combination of the verbal root *bhū* and the vikaraṇa (infix) not got the designation *aṅga*, the sūtra *ato dīrgho yañi* (389) would not have become available for application in the present case and we would not be able to get the verbal form *bhavāmi*.

It is to be borne in mind that the aṅga-designation is contingent upon the presence of the affix that follows. A word-form cannot be designated as *aṅga* simply because an affix has been prescribed after it. For the aṅga-designation to become operational the affix has to be present after the base after which it has been prescribed. The scope of aṅga-designation is observed in the following sūtra :

(133) एङ्ह्रस्वात्सम्बुद्धेः । ***eṅhrasvātsambuddheḥ*. 6. 1. 69**

लघु० - एङन्ताद्ध्रस्वान्ताच्चाङ्गाद्धल्लुप्यते सम्बुद्धेश्चेत्। हे राम! हे रामौ! हे रामाः!

eṅantāddhrasvāntāc cāṅgāddhal lupyate sambuddheś cet. he rāma! he rāmau! he rāmāḥ!

Trans. : A consonantal phoneme of the vocative singular introduced after a nominal stem (*aṅga*) ending in a vowel denoted by the abbreviatory term *eṅ* or ending in a short vowel is replaced by lopa (zero).

PP. *eṅhrasvāt sambuddheḥ hal lopaḥ.*

Eluc. : The terms *hal* and *lopaḥ* are respectively carried over into this sūtra from *halṅyābbhyo dīrghāt sutisyapṛktaṁ hal* Pā. 6. 1. 68 and *lopo vyorvali* Pā. 6. 1. 66. The word *lopa* is derived by introducing *ghañ* after the verbal root *lup* 'to be elided' in the sense of karman (object) and consequently it means *lupyate* 'is elided'. Varadarāja has brought in the term *aṅga* and has qualified it by the terms *eṅ* and *hrasva* in accordance with the sūtra *yena vidhistadantasya* Pā. 1. 1. 72. He does not explain why he brings in the term *aṅga* even when the rule does not occur in the governing domain of aṅga. Bhaṭṭoji Dīkṣita (SK, I, p. 189) adduces an argument to this effect saying that the use of the technical term *sambuddhi* in the sūtra implies the term *aṅga* since the term *sambuddhi* denotes the singular vocative affix and the base before an affix is to be called *aṅga* by virtue of the sūtra *yasmātpratyayavidhistadādi pratyaye 'ṅgam* (132).

It is not without purpose that the term *aṅga* has been brought in by implication and that it has been qualified by the words *eṅ* and *hrasva.* Bhaṭṭoji Dīkṣita gives the expression *he katarat kula*! (SK, I, p. 189) to explain the significance of bringing in the word *aṅga*. The word *katara,* meaning 'which of the two', is derived from *kim* by introducing the affix *ḍatara* after it. In the vocative singular of the word *katara* we have *katara* + *su*. At this stage the sambuddhi-affix *su* is replaced by अड्ड् (*aḍḍ*) by the sūtra *aḍḍ ḍatarādibhyaḥ pañcabhyaḥ* (240). Since *aḍḍ* has *ḍ* as *it,* the last vowel (*ṭi*) of *katara,* which is a short *a* is elided and the form which we obtain is *katarad*. With the help of *vā 'vasāne* (145) we have *katarat*. If the term *aṅga* were not brought in here, then being a part of the sambuddhi-affix, the consonant *t* following the short vowel *a* would be elided. Now since the term *aṅga* has been supplied and made the qualificand of the terms *eṅ* and *hrasva,* no such problem crops up. After the elision of the short vowel *a* coming at the end of *katara* before the affix *aḍḍ,* the form *katar* which ends in repha becomes an aṅga which ends neither in a short vowel nor in the vowels denoted by *eṅ*. As such, the elision of the consonant *t* is not available and we have the desired form *katarat*.

The significance of the use of the term *eṅ* in the sūtra has been discussed in the Bālamanoramā. After the nominal stem *hari,* we introduce the sambuddhi affix *su* : *he hari* + *su*. The vowel *i* coming at the end of stem *hari* is replaced by a guṇa vowel *e* before sambuddhi by the rule *hrasvasya guṇaḥ* Pā. 7. 3. 108. We have *he hare* s. Had the term *eṅ* not been included in the rule, the consonant s of the vocative singular would not have been replaced by lopa since *hare* (aṅga) does not end in a short vowel. Hence the term *eṅ* has been included so that the elision of the consonant belonging to sambuddhi in such cases may be accounted for. Vāsudeva Dīkṣita continues the discussion saying that the elision of sakāra of sambuddhi could have taken place before the vowel *i* is replaced by a guṇa vowel *e* since *i* is a short vowel occurring at the end of *hari*. It is in this context that he suggests that there is no use including the term *eṅ* in the rule since the consonant of sambuddhi follows a short vowel *i* and therefore can be replaced by lopa. In order to buttress the inclusion of *eṅ* in the sūtra, he says that the prescription of guṇa vowel replacement is subsequent to the rule prescribing the lopa-substitution in place of the consonant belonging to the sambuddhi. The guṇa vowel replacement is also nitya since it remains applicable even after the consonant belonging to the vocative singular (*sambuddhi*) is elided since the sambuddhi-affix is construed as existent by virtue of the sūtra *pratyayalope pratyayalakṣaṇam* (189). The conclusion is that the guṇa replacement for the *i* of *hari* comes first since the rule prescribing guṇa-substitution is both subsequent and nitya with respect to the sūtra which enjoins the lopa-replacement for the consonant of the vocative singular affix and as such the phoneme s of sambuddhi does not follow a short vowel. As a consequence the lopa-substitution for the consonant s of sambuddhi cannot take place if the provision of *eṅ* is not made. It is for this reason that the term *eṅ* is included in the sūtra and the consonant s belonging to sambuddhi is properly replaced by lopa in accordance with the present rule.

The vocative singular of the nominal stem *rāma* is derived in the same manner : *rāma su* --> *rāma* s {the vowel *u* is termed *it* by the sūtra *upadeśe 'janunāsika it* (28) and hence elided by the rule *tasya lopaḥ* (3)}. The consonant s belonging to sambuddhi follows the aṅga *rāma* which ends in the short vowel *a*. The consonant, therefore, is replaced by lopa in accordance with the present sūtra. Thus the expression *he rāma!* is arrived at. The dual and plural forms of *rāma* (*he rāmau!* and *he rāmāḥ!*) in the vocative do not differ from those in the nominative. Hence their derivational process would be the same.

The derivation of *rāma* in the accusative singular is as follows : *rāma* + *am*. The consonant *m* at the end of *am* is not to be designated *it* by *halantyam* (1) since it is negated by the rule *na vibhaktau tusmāḥ* (130). First of all, the sūtra *akaḥ savarṇe dīrghaḥ* (42) becomes available for application to effect a homogeneous long vowel substitution in place of both the preceding and the following vowels denoted by the abbreviatory term *ak*. This is blocked by *ato guṇe* (273) which prescribes a single substitute in the form of the following guṇa vowel. This is also debarred by the rule *prathamayoḥ pūrvasavarṇaḥ* (125) which enjoins a single long vowel substitute homogeneous with the preceding of the two. This, too, is blocked by the following sūtra :

(134) अमि पूर्वः । ***ami pūrvaḥ*. 6. 1. 107**
लघु० – अकोऽम्यचि पूर्वरूपमेकादेशः । *ako 'myaci pūrvarūpam ekādeśaḥ.*

Trans. : When the vowel (*ac*) of *am* (the singular affix of the second triplet of sup) follows, the single replacement homogeneous with the preceding vowel (*ak*) comes in place of both the preceding and the following vowels.

PP. *akaḥ ami aci pūrvaparayoḥ ekaḥ pūrvaḥ* (*saṁhitāyām*).

Eluc. : The words *akaḥ* and *aci* are carried over here from the sūtras *akaḥ savarṇe dīrghaḥ* Pā. 6. 1. 101 and *iko yaṇaci* Pā. 6. 1. 77 respectively. The sūtra *ekaḥ pūrvaparayoḥ* Pā. 6. 1. 84 is the governing rule in the domain of which the present sūtra occurs. Taking into account all this, the sūtra comes to mean : If the vowel (*ac*) of *am* (the singular sup-affix of the second triplet) follows *ak*, then a single replacement homogeneous with the preceding element (denoted by *ak*) comes in place of both the preceding vowel (denoted by *ak*) and the following vowel (of the sup-affix *am*). In the present illustration *rāma* + *am*, the short vowel *a* at the end of *rāma* is denoted by the abbreviatory term *ak*. The vowel that follows belongs to the singular sup-affix of the second triplet. The conditions for the single replacement in the form of the preceding vowel denoted by the abbreviatory term *ak* in place of both the preceding and following vowels are fulfilled and the preceding short vowel *a* replaces both the preceding short vowel *a* at the end of *rāma* and the following vowel (*ac*) of the affix *am*. The form thus obtained is *rāmam*.

There is one point to be taken note of with regard to the carrying of *ac* from the sūtra *iko yaṇaci* (15) into this sūtra. Had this not been carried over into this sūtra, the single replacement homogeneous with the preceding vowel would have come also in place of the whole *am* affix. To avoid this undesirable contingency, the term *ac* has been carried over into this rule. It confines the single replacement to the vowel of *am*-affix, which otherwise would not have been possible (cf. *acītyanuvṛttau akaḥ ami pare pūrvaparayoḥ pūrvarūpam ekādeśaḥ syād iti labhyeta. tathā sati amo makārasahitasya pūrvarūpaṁ syāt. tan mā bhūd ityajanuvṛttiḥ*, BM, I, p. 190).

When the dual affix *auṭ* of the second triplet is introduced after *rāma*, we have the declensional stage of the word *rāma* as *rāma* + *auṭ*. At this stage the last cerebral consonant at the end of *auṭ* is *it* according to the rule *halantyam* (1) and as such it is replaced by lopa by the sūtra *tasya lopaḥ* (3). We have *rāma* + *au*. The declensional process does not differ from that of the nominative dual form *rāmau*. So the dual form of the second triplet is also *rāmau*.

For the declension of the plural form of *rāma* of the second triplet we have *rāma* + *śas*. The dental *s* at the end of *śas* is not *it* by *halantyam* (1) since it has been negated by the sūtra *na vibhaktau tusmāḥ* (130). To designate the initial *ś* of *śas* as *it* we have the following sūtra :

(135) **लशक्वतद्धिते । *laśakvataddhite*. 1. 3. 8**

लघु० – तद्धितवर्जप्रत्ययाद्या लशकवर्गा इतः स्युः । *taddhitavarjapratyayādyā laśakavargā itaḥ syuḥ.*

Trans. : Let the consonants lakāra, śakāra and kavarga (velar stops) occurring initially in the affixes except the taddhita ones be designated as *it*.

PP. *pratyayasya ādi laśaku it ataddhite* (*upadeśe*).

Eluc. : The words *pratyayasya, ādi* and *it* are carried over into the present sūtra respectively from *ṣaḥ pratyayasya* Pā. 1. 3. 6, *ādirñiṭuḍavaḥ* Pā. 1. 3. 5 and *upadeśe 'janunāsika it* Pā. 1. 3. 2. The word *laśaku* is a samāhāradvandva compound which is analysed as *laś ca śaś ca kuś ca eṣāṁ samāhāraḥ laśaku*. The compound word *ataddhite* is a negative compound (*nañ-tatpuruṣa*). In this way the sūtra means : The phonemes *l, ś, k, kh, g, gh* and *ṅ* occurring at the beginning of an affix are to be designated as *it* but not when they are at the beginning of taddhita affixes.

In *rāma* + *śas*, the affix *śas* is not a taddhita affix, therefore the initial *ś* of *śas* is designated as *it*. So, this is replaced by lopa by the rule *tasya lopaḥ* (3). After the elision of *ś*, we have *rāma* + *as*. The vowel *a* at the end of the stem *rāma* and the vowel *a* at the beginning of the remaining affix *as* are both replaced by a long vowel homogeneous with the preceding vowel *a* in accordance with the sūtra *prathamayoḥ pūrvasavarṇaḥ* (125). We now have *rāmās*. At this stage, the following sūtra ensues :

(136) तस्माच्छसो नः पुंसि । **tasmācchaso naḥ puṁsi. 6. 1. 103**
लघु० – पूर्वसवर्णदीर्घात् परो यः शसः सस्तस्य नः स्यात् पुंसि । *pūrvasavarṇadīrghāt paro yaḥ śasaḥ sas tasya naḥ syāt puṁsi.*

Trans. : The phoneme *s* of *śas* which occurs after a long vowel replacement homogeneous with that which precedes is replaced by *n* in the masculine.

PP. *tasmāt śasaḥ naḥ puṁsi (saṁhitāyām).*

Eluc. : The pronoun *tasmāt* in the sūtra refers to the long vowel replacement prescribed in a state of extreme proximity (*saṁhitā*) by the preceding sūtra *prathamayoḥ pūrvasavarṇaḥ* Pā. 6. 1. 102. When the phoneme s of affix *śas* occurs after the prescribed long vowel replacement homogeneous with the preceding nominal stem-final element denoted by the abbreviatory term *ak*, then the present sūtra prescribes that the dental nasal replaces the phoneme s of the affix *śas* in accordance with the rule *alo 'ntyasya* (21), provided the nominal stem which is being declined is in the masculine. In *rāmās*, the long vowel *ā* following the labial nasal *m* is pūrvasavarṇadīrgha (long vowel replacement homogeneous with the preceding *ak*), therefore the s of *śas* is replaced by nakāra and we have the form *rāmān*.

At this stage, the following sūtra becomes available for application and the contingency of nakāra coming at the end of *rāmān* to be replaced by ṇakāra arises. In order to show how this replacement is due, the author of the Laghu presents the following sūtra :

(137) अट्कुप्वाङ्नुम्व्यवायेऽपि । **aṭkupvāṅnumvyavāye 'pi. 8. 4. 2**
लघु० – अट्–कवर्ग–पवर्ग–आङ्–नुम्–एतैर्व्यस्तैर्यथासम्भवं मिलितैश्च व्यवधानेऽपि रषाभ्यां परस्य नस्य णः समानपदे । इति प्राप्ते — *aṭ-kavarga-pavarga-āṅ-num-etairvyastair-yathāsambhavaṁ militaiś ca vyavadhāne 'pi raṣābhyāṁ parasya nasya ṇaḥ samānapade. iti prāpte* —

Trans. : Even when separated by the intervention of the elements denoted by the abbreviatory term *aṭ*, velar stops, labial stops, (the particle) *āṅ* and (the infixed augment) *num* singly or combined in any possible way, let the cerebral ṇakāra replace the dental nakāra following repha and ṣakāra in the same pada.

PP. *aṭkupvāṅnumvyavāye api samānapade raṣābhyām naḥ ṇaḥ* (*saṁhitāyām*).

Eluc. : The preceding sūtra in the Aṣṭādhyāyī is *raṣābhyāṁ no ṇaḥ samānapade* Pā. 8. 4. 1 which prescribes the substitution of the cerebral for the dental nakāra when it follows the phonemes repha and ṣ without the separation caused by the intervention of any other phoneme. It is so because of the use of the ablative in the word *raṣābhyām*. The fifth case-ending, by virtue of the paribhāṣā sūtra *tasmādityuttarasya* (71), enjoins the grammatical operation on the element which immediately follows the one that ends in the ablative (KN, VI, p. 604). Thus when there is an intervention between the phonemes *r* or *ṣ* and the dental *n*, the substitution of the cerebral *ṇ* for the latter is not available by Pā. 8. 4. 1. Hence the need of the present sūtra. With the four words of the sūtra Pā. 8. 4. 1 having been lent into the present sūtra, it comes to mean that the cerebral ṇakāra shall replace the dental nakāra when the latter follows the phonemes repha and ṣ even when separated by the intervention of the elements denoted by *aṭ*-pratyāhāra, guttural and labial stops, the particle *āṅ* and the infixed augment *num*.

Let us first discuss the significance of the particle *āṅ* used in the sūtra. Why does Pāṇini specifically mention it when it can be denoted by the abbreviatory term *aṭ*. Jinendrabuddhi clarifies this point by saying that had it not been included in the sūtra, then the substitution of the cerebral for the dental *n* would not have taken place because of the prohibition by *padavyavāye 'pi* Pā. 8. 4. 38. Being a nipāta, *āṅ* is a pada. The sup-affix introduced after it has been elided by *avyayādāpsupaḥ* (371). The substitution of the cerebral is prohibited when there is an intervention of a pada (*asatyāṅgrahaṇe padavyavāye 'pi ityāṅvyavāye pratiṣedhaḥ syāt. atas tadbādhanārtham āṅgrahaṇam*, KN, VI, p. 604).

The use of the infixed augment *num* in the sūtra is to indicate the anusvāra. The anusvāra may either be a substitute in place of *num* or it may be a part of the original word itself.

Taking into consideration the present sūtra, we visualize three possible ways as to how the intervention of the elements mentioned in the sūtra could take place : 1. Intervention of one of the elements mentioned in the sūtra 2. When more elements than one intervene 3. When all the elements taken together simultaneously intervene between *r* or ṣ and the dental *n* which is going to be replaced by the cerebral ṇakāra. The third alternative is not possible[1] as there is no such word in Sanskrit language which has a cerebral ṇakāra preceded by *r* or *ṣ*

1. Bhaimīvyākhyā, I, p. 178.

separated by the intervention of all the elements taken together. The sūtra *karaṇe hanaḥ* Pā. 3. 4. 37 shows that the cerebral replacement takes place when there is an intervention of one of the elements. Another sūtra *sarūpāṇām ekaśeṣa ekavibhaktau* (124) indicates that the cerebral substitution for the dental *n* takes place when there is an intervention of more than one element. Taking these two and other such Pāṇinian sūtras into consideration, Varadarāja has said in his commentary 'by the intervention of the elements singly or combined in any possible way'.

The declined word *rāmān* is a pada by *suptiṅantaṁ padam* (14) and the dental nakāra is at its end. It follows the consonant repha. Both the consonant repha and the dental nakāra are separated by the intervention of *ā*, *m* and *ā*. The long *ā*'s are denoted by *aṭ* and *m* is included among the labials (*pavarga*). Thus in the light of Varadarāja's interpretation, the condition laid down by the present sūtra for the substitution of the cerebral for the dental nakāra is available. Consequently, the pada-final nakāra would be available for replacement by the cerebral nakāra but the following sūtra blocks it :

(138) पदान्तस्य । *padāntasya.* 8. 4. 37
लघु० - नस्य णो न । *nasya ṇo na.*

Trans. : Let the substitute cerebral nasal stop *ṇ* not replace a pada-final dental nasal stop *n*.

PP. *aṭkupvāṅnumvyavāye 'pi raṣābhyāṁ samānapade padāntasya naḥ ṇaḥ na.*

Eluc. : All the words of the sūtras *raṣābhyāṁ no ṇaḥ samānapade* Pā. 8. 4. 1 and *aṭkupvāṅnumvyavāye 'pi* Pā. 8. 4. 2 are carried over into the present rule. The first word *naḥ* is in the genitive while the second one (*ṇaḥ)* is in the nominative. The indeclinable *na* has been carried over from *na bhābhūpūkamigamipyāyīvepām* Pā. 8. 4. 34. With these words supplied from the preceding sūtras, the present sūtra means : If the dental nasal stop *n* occurs at the end of a pada, then it is not replaced by the cerebral stop *ṇ*, even if repha or cerebral sibilant (ṣ) happens to precede it in the same pada with the intervention of the elements allowed by *aṭkupvāṅnumvyavāye 'pi*. The word *rāmān* is a pada by *suptiṅantaṁ padam* (14) since it ends in *śas* which is denoted by the abbreviatory term *sup*. Here repha is the initial consonant in *rāmān* and the dental *n* follows it with the separation caused by intervention of two *ā*'s and *m*. So, the substitution of the cerebral *ṇ* for the dental nasal stop *n* is available by virtue of the preceding rule *aṭkupvāṅ...* (137) but the present sūtra prohibits it and the dental nakāra occurring at the end of a pada remains intact and we finally have the form *rāmān*.

Now we have *rāma* + *ṭā* with the singular third case-ending. In this context the following sūtra presents itself :

(139) टाङसिङसामिनात्स्याः । *ṭāṅasiṅasāminātsyāḥ*. 7. 1. 12
लघु० – अदन्तात् टादीनामिनादयः स्युः । णत्वम् – रामेण । *adantāt ṭādīnām ināḍayaḥ syuḥ. ṇatvam - rāmeṇa.*

Trans. : Let the substitute elements *ina, āt* and *sya* respectively replace *ṭā, ṅasi* and *ṅas* introduced after a nominal stem ending in a short vowel *a*. The cerebral *ṇ*-replacement takes place and we have *rāmeṇa*.

PP. *ataḥ aṅgāt ṭāṅasiṅasām ināṭsyāḥ.*

Eluc. : The word *ataḥ* is carried over from *ato bhisa ais* Pā. 7. 1. 9. The sūtra *aṅgasya* Pā. 6. 4. 1 is a governing rule in the domain of which the present sūtra occurs. The word *aṅgasya* is carried over into the present sūtra and is changed into the ablative by the process of vibhaktivipariṇāma. This word *aṅgāt* is qualified by the carried over word *ataḥ*. With the help of *yena vidhistadantasya* Pā. 1. 1. 72, the expression thus obtained results in *adantāt aṅgāt*. Although Varadarāja has not mentioned the term *aṅgāt* in his commentary, it should be understood as such. Now taking into consideration the sūtra *yathāsaṅkhyam anudeśaḥ samānām* (23), we can translate the present rule in the following manner : The three substitutes *ina, āt* and *sya* are to respectively replace the three substituenda *ṭā, ṅasi* and *ṅas* provided the latter are introduced after an aṅga that ends in a short vowel *a*.

The nominal stem *rāma* ends in a short vowel *a* and it is an aṅga by *yasmātpratyaya...* (132) since a sup-affix *ṭā* has been introduced after it. The causal condition for the *ina*-replacement is available and as such *ṭā* is replaced by *ina* and we have *rāma* + *ina* from *rāma* + *ṭā*. At this stage, *ādguṇaḥ* (27) applies and a single guṇa-substitute replaces both *a* and *i* and we have the form *rāmena*. The dental nakara is replaced by the cerebral ṇakara by *aṭkupvāṅnumvyavāye 'pi* (137) and the resultant form is *rāmeṇa*. Of course, the preceding rule *padāntasya* (138) does not apply since the dental *n* is not at the end of a pada.

(140) सुपि च । *supi ca.* 7. 3. 102

लघु० - यञादौ सुपि अतोऽङ्गस्य दीर्घः । रामाभ्याम् । *yañādau supi ato 'ṅgasya dīrghaḥ. rāmābhyām.*

Trans. : Let a substitute long vowel replace the aṅga-final short vowel *a* of a nominal stem before sup-affixes beginning with a consonant denoted by the abbreviatory term *yañ*.

PP. *supi ca aṅgasya ataḥ dīrghaḥ yañi.*

Eluc. : The term *aṅgasya* is carried over from the governing rule *aṅgasya* Pā. 6. 4. 1. All the constituent words of the sūtra *ato dīrgho yañi* Pā. 7. 3. 101 are also made to recur in the present sūtra. The word *yañ* is a pratyāhāra. It denotes semi-vowels, nasals, *jh* and *bh* and qualifies the term *supi*. In accordance with *yasmin vidhis tadādāvalgrahaṇe*, Mbh 1. 1. 72 vtk 29, the phrase thus obtained will be : *yañādau supi*. The word *ataḥ* qualifies the term *aṅgasya* and with the help of *yena vidhistadantasya* Pā. 1. 1. 72, it will give the expression : *adantasya aṅgasya*. With all these points having been taken into consideration, the meaning of the present sūtra will be as follows : If the sup-affixes, which begin with an element denoted by the abbreviatory term *yañ*, follow, then the short *a* occurring at the end of an aṅga is replaced by a long *ā* with the help of the rule *alo 'ntyasya* (21).

In the illustration *rāma* + *bhyām*, the condition for the long vowel replacement is available. The nominal stem *rāma* is an aṅga by *yasmāt pratyayavidhistadādi...* (132) since the dual sup-affix *bhyām* of the third triplet is introduced after it. It ends in a short *a*. The sup-affix that follows begins with the phoneme *bh* which is denoted by the abbreviatory term *yañ*. With the help of the sūtra *alo 'ntyasya* (21), the final short vowel *a* is replaced by a long vowel *ā* and we have the form *rāmābhyām*.

The significance of carrying over *yañi* into the sūtra lies in the fact that it stops the undesirable substitution of long *ā* for the aṅga-final short *a* of *rāma* before the singular sup-affix *su* of the first triplet. The dental sibilant *s* is not denoted by *yañ*-pratyāhāra.

The purpose of carrying over the term *ataḥ* into the present sūtra is to preclude the long substitution for the aṅga-final *i* of *agni* before *bhyām*, etc. Had the term *ataḥ* not been included in the sūtra, then the undesirable form *agnībhyām* would have been obtained instead of the grammatically correct form *agnibhyām*.

With the plural sup-affix *bhis* of the third triplet introduced after *rāma*, we have *rāma* + *bhis*.

(141) अतो भिस ऐस्। *ato bhisa ais.* 7. 1. 9

लघु० - अदन्ताद् अङ्गात् परस्य भिस ऐस् स्यात्। अनेकाल् शित् सर्वस्य — रामैः।

adantād aṅgāt parasya bhisa ais syāt. anekāl śit sarvasya — rāmaiḥ.

Trans. : Let the substitute *ais* replace the sup-affix *bhis* introduced after a pre-affixal base ending in the short vowel *a*. By the rule *anekāl śit sarvasya* (45), (the substitute *ais* replaces the whole of *bhis* and we have the form) *rāmaiḥ*.

PP. *ataḥ aṅgāt bhisa ais.*

Eluc. : The sūtra *aṅgasya* Pā. 6. 4. 1 is a governing rule. The present sūtra recurs in its domain. Hence the word *aṅgasya* is carried over into it. The genitive case-ending is changed into the ablative through the process known as vibhaktivipariṇāma. The word *ataḥ* qualifies the word *aṅgāt*. By tadantavidhi (Pā. 1. 1. 72), it will be interpreted as *adantād aṅgāt*. The sūtra thus means : If the plural sup-affix *bhis* comes after an aṅga ending in a short vowel *a*, then the whole of sup-affix *bhis* will be replaced by *ais*.[1]

Varadarāja has mentioned the sūtra *anekāl śit sarvasya* (45) in his commentary in order to drive home the following point : The *ais*-replacement is prescribed by using the sixth case-ending in the word *bhisa*. The replacement enjoined in this manner comes in place of the last phoneme of the substituendum ending in the genitive according to the sūtra *alo 'ntyasya* (21). The undesirable contingency of replacing the last phoneme *s* of *bhis* would be incurred. He reminds the reader by quoting the rule *anekāl śit sarvasya* (45), which is an exception to the rule *alo 'ntyasya* (21), that since the substitute contains more than one phoneme (*al*), it would replace the whole of *bhis* and not merely its last phoneme. Similarly, the rule *anekāl śit sarvasya* (45) can also be considered

---

1. In the illustration *rāma + bhis*, two rules are simultaneously applicable : 1. *bahuvacane jhalyet* Pā. 7. 3. 103 and 2. *ato bhisa ais* Pā. 7. 1. 9. Which of the two is to be applied in this context? On the basis of subsequent order in the Aṣṭādhyāyī, the former rule becomes applicable. If this was followed, then the substitute *ais* would not find any scope for application since with the replacement of *e* in place of *a* at the end of nominal stems, the short vowel *a* will not be available. As a consequence, this sūtra would be rendered redundant. To avoid this contingency, the sūtra *ato bhisa ais* (141) is construed as nitya in the light of the discussion on this sūtra in the Mahābhāṣya and KN, V, p. 540. Since Pāṇini has enunciated this sūtra, the substitution of *e* for the short vowel *a* by *bahuvacane...* (144) is to be treated as what it previously was (*vacanaprāmāṇyāt kṛte 'pyettve bhūtapūrvam akārāntatvam*, KN, V, p. 540). This means that it is to be considered as short vowel *a*.This makes possible the application of *ato bhisa...* (141) even if *bahuvacane...* (144) has already applied. In case *bahuvacane...* (144) does not apply, the rule *ato bhisa...* (141) is still applicable. Thus the rule *ato bhisa...* (141) becomes kṛtākṛtaprasaṅgi and hence nitya. In deference to the paribhāṣā *pūrvaparanityāntaraṅgāpavādānām uttarottaraṁ balīyaḥ*, the rule *ato bhisa ais* (141) will obligatorily block the rule *bahuvacane jhalyet* (144).

to be an exception to the rule *ādeḥ parasya* (72) which prescribes the replacement by using the fifth case-ending to come in place of the initial phoneme of the substituendum which follows the term used in the ablative. After the substitute *ais* has replaced the whole of *bhis*, a vṛddhi-vowel substitute replaces both the vowel *a* at the end of *rāma* and the initial vowel *ai* of *ais* by the sūtra *vṛddhireci* (33) and we have the form *rāmaiḥ*.

(142) ङेर्यः । *ṅeryaḥ*. 7. 1. 13

लघु॰ – अतोऽङ्गात् परस्य ङेर्यादेशः । *ato 'ṅgāt parasya ṅer yādeśaḥ*.

Trans. : Let the substitute *ya* replace the sup-affix *ṅe* introduced after a pre-affixal base (*aṅga*) ending in a short vowel *a*.

PP. *ataḥ aṅgāt ṅeḥ yaḥ*.

Eluc. : The term *ataḥ* is carried over from the sūtra *ato bhisa ais* Pā. 7. 1. 9. The sūtra *aṅgasya* Pā. 6. 4. 1 is a governing rule. The present sūtra occurs in its domain. So the word *aṅgasya* recurs here and is changed into the ablative by the process of vibhaktivipariṇāma. The word *ṅeḥ* has the substitution-genitive case-ending by virtue of which it means 'in place of *ṅe*' in accordance with the rule *ṣaṣṭhī sthāneyogā* Pā. 1. 1. 49. Taking all this into consideration, the sūtra means : The singular sup-affix *ṅe* (of the fourth triplet) introduced after a nominal stem ending in a short vowel *a* is replaced by *ya*.

Now, in the illustration *rāma + ya*, the rule *supi ca* (140) has to apply but the condition laid down in the sūtra is not available. This can be explained as follows : The nominal stem *rāma* ends in a short vowel *a* and it also has the designation *aṅga* since the affix *ṅe* is introduced after it to obtain the inflected form of *rāma* in dative singular. The rule *supi ca* (140) can apply in this case only when the substitute *ya* in place of the sup-affix *ṅe* is made to have the characteristic of being a sup-affix but the replacement *ya* coming in place of the sup-affix *ṅe* is not a denotatum of the abbreviatory term *sup*. This necessitates the following sūtra which prescribes the extension of the properties of a substituendum to the substitute. Consequent upon this, the grammatical operations which are dependent on the affix *ṅe* can also be performed on the basis of the substitute *ya*.

(143) स्थानिवदादेशोऽनल्विधौ । *sthānivadādeśo 'nalvidhau*. 1. 1. 56

लघु॰ – आदेशः स्थानिवत् स्यात्, न तु स्थान्यलाश्रयविधौ । इति स्थानिवत्त्वात् सुपि

चेति दीर्घः। रामाय, रामाभ्याम्। *ādeśaḥ sthānivat syāt na tu sthānyalāśraya-vidhau. iti sthānivattvāt supi ceti dīrghaḥ. rāmāya, rāmābhyām.*

Trans. : A substitute (*ādeśa*) is treated like a substituendum (*sthānin*) except with regard to an operation dependent on the phoneme (*al*) of the substituendum. By this, the substitute *ya* is treated as the substituendum *ṅe* which is a sup-affix. Consequently, the sutra *supi ca* applies and with a long-vowel replacement we have *rāmāya*.

PP. *sthānivat ādeśaḥ analvidhau.*

Eluc. : This sūtra is an extension (*atideśa*) rule which is purported to extend the properties of a substituendum (*sthānin*) to the substitute to allow a substitute (*ādeśa*) to be treated as if it were a substituendum. Consequently, the grammatical operations which are to be performed owing to a substituendum can also be performed on the basis of the substitute. There are eight kinds of substituenda as described in the Kāśikā on this sūtra. They are : 1. dhātu 2. aṅga 3. kṛt 4. taddhita 5. avyaya 6. sup 7. tiṅ and 8. pada. By virtue of this rule, the substitutes replacing these eight substituenda will be treated like dhātu, aṅga, etc. The illustrations of all these substituenda and substitutes can be looked up in the Kāśikā on this sūtra.

The word *analvidhau* needs explanation. This is a nañ-tatpuruṣa compound which can be analysed as *na alvidhiḥ, tasmin = analvidhau*. The word *alvidhi* which is a member of this compound is also a tatpuruṣa compound which is analysed in four ways :

1. *alā vidhiḥ*, tṛtīyā tatpuruṣa. Being an instrumental tatpuruṣa, it means 'operations which take place because of *al*'.[1]

---

1. In the bahuvrīhi compound *mahoraskena* (*mahat+su+uras+su+kap*)+*ṭā* --> (*maha+ā +uraḥ+kap*)+*ṭā* --> (*mahoraḥ+ka*)+*ṭā*, the visarga has replaced the phoneme *s* of *uras* by *sasajuṣo ruḥ* (104) and *kharavasānayorvisarjanīyaḥ* (93). The visarga is now replaced by *s* by *so 'padādau* Pā. 8. 3. 38. After *ṭā* has been replaced by *ina* by (139), the rule *aṭkupvāṅnumvyavāye 'pi* (137) becomes available for application, if the substitute *s* in place of the visarga is treated as the substituendum since the visarga is included among the elements denoted by *aṭ*-pratyāhāra. Thus we would have the grammatically incorrect form *mahoraskeṇa*. Now by the first interpretation of *alvidhi*, we can avoid this undesirable contingency. The substitution of the cerebral for the dental *n* of *ina* is dependent upon visarga which, being included among the elements denoted by *aṭ*-pratyāhāra, is construed as *al*. Therefore, the substitute is not to be treated like the substituendum in this case. Then the separation caused by the intervention of *s*, which is other than the elements included in the rule *aṭkupvāṅnumvyavāye 'pi* (137), will prevent the *ṇ*-replacement and we will have the correct form *mahoraskena*.

2. *alaḥ* (*parasya*) *vidhiḥ*, pañcamī tatpuruṣa. Here the compound *alvidhiḥ* is interpreted as an ablative tatpuruṣa which means 'operations which take place in an item occurring after *al*'.[1]

3. *alaḥ* (*sthāne*) *vidhiḥ*, ṣaṣṭhī tatpuruṣa. The compound is interpreted as a genitive tatpuruṣa which means 'operations which are performed in place of *al*'.[2]

4. *ali* (*pare*) *vidhiḥ*, saptamī tatpuruṣa. It is interpreted as a locative tatpuruṣa which means 'operations which take place when *al* follows'.[3]

Taking into account all that has been said above, the sūtra means : A replacement is treated like the substituendum except with regard to any of the following operations, dependent on the phoneme (*al*) of the substituendum : 1. when an operation is to be performed by a phoneme or because of a phoneme 2. when an operation is to be performed on an element occurring after a phoneme 3. when an operation is to be

---

1. The grammatical process of the derivation of the nominative singular form *dyauḥ* illustrates the second interpretation. In *div + su* --> *div + s*, the *v* of *div* is replaced by *au* in accordance with the rule *diva aut* Pā. 7. 1. 84. If *au* is treated like *v*, then the nominative affix *s* should be elided by *halṅyābbhyo dīrghātsutisyapṛktaṁ hal* Pā. 6. 1. 68, which is not desirable. Since the operation of elision is to be effected after *v* which is *al*, the substitute *au* is not to be treated like *v* according to the second interpretation. Consequently, the single consonant sup-affix (*apṛkta*) is not available after *hal* to be elided by Pā. 6. 1. 68. In that case, the following nominative singular affix *s*(*u*) will not be replaced by lopa and we have the correct nominative singular form *dyauḥ*.

2. The grammatical process of deriving the word *dyukāmaḥ* exemplifies the third interpretation of *alvidhi*. In *div+kāma*, the consonant *v* is replaced by *u* by the rule *diva ut* Pā. 6. 1. 131. In case the replacement *u* is treated like the substituendum *v*, then the elision of *u* is available by the sūtra *lopo vyorvali* Pā. 6. 1. 66 since the following *k* of *kāma* is a denotatum of *val*-pratyāhāra. This is not desirable. Now in consonance with the third interpretation of *al-vidhi*, the replacement, which has come in place of *v*, which is *al* is not to be treated like the substituendum. As a consequence, the *u*-replacement is not treated like *v*. So the elision of *u* would not be available.

3. The expression *ka iṣṭaḥ* illustrates the fourth interpretation of the compound *al-vidhi*. The word *iṣṭaḥ* in the illustration is derived by introducing *kta*-affix after the verbal root *yaj*. By the sūtra *vacisvapiyajādīnāṁ kiti* Pā. 6. 1.15, the initial *y* of *yaj* is replaced by samprasāraṇa, that is, *y* is replaced by *i*. The expression *ka iṣṭaḥ* is derived from *kas iṣṭaḥ*. The consonant *s* of the singular sup-affix *su* is replaced by *ru* in accordance with the rule *sasajuṣo ruḥ* (104). After the elision of *u* of *ru*, *r* remains. At this stage, we have *kar iṣṭaḥ*. Now if the initial *i* of *iṣṭaḥ* is to be treated like the substituendum *y* which is denoted by the abbreviatory term *haś*, it will cause *haśi ca* (106) to apply thereby causing the replacement of *r* by *u*, which is not desirable. Here the substituendum *al* is *y*. When it follows, the operation of replacing *r*(*u*) by *u* takes place. According to the fourth interpretation, the replacement is not to be treated like the substituendum. In other words, the samprasāraṇa vowel *i* is not treated like *y*. As such there is no element denoted by *haś*-pratyāhāra to follow. There is no occasion of *u*-replacement and we have the correct expression *ka iṣṭaḥ* after the application of *bhobhago...* (107) and *lopaḥ śākalyasya* (30).

performed in place of a phoneme and 4. when an operation is to be performed depending on the following phoneme.

In the illustration *rāma* + *ṅe*, the sup-affix *ṅe* has been replaced by *ya* by the sūtra *ṅeryaḥ* (142). Here *ṅe* is a substituendum (*sthānin*) and *ya* is a substitute (*ādeśa*) which is to replace it. The nominal affix *ṅe* is a sup-affix, whereas *ya* is not. This is the reason why *supi ca* (140) cannot apply when the replacement *ya* follows although it begins with a phoneme denoted by *yañ*-pratyāhāra. As such, the correct form *rāmāya* cannot be obtained. This necessitates the present sūtra. By virtue of this rule the substitute *ya* is treated like a sup-affix. Therefore the rule *supi ca* (140) becomes applicable since a sup-affix beginning with a phoneme denoted by the abbreviatory term *yañ* follows a pre-suffixal nominal stem ending in a short vowel *a*. A long vowel replacement in place of short vowel *a* takes place and we have the desired form *rāmāya*.

The sūtra *supi ca* (140) prescribes a long vowel substitution when a phoneme denoted by *yañ*-pratyāhāra follows and it appears to be a grammatical operation dependent on a phoneme indicated by the fourth interpretation of the compound *al-vidhi*. However, this is not so. For it is not the *yañ*-phoneme only that causes the long vowel replacement to take place, there should also be a sup-affix beginning with the *yañ*-phoneme. The characteristic of being a sup-affix resides in both the phonemes *y* and *a* together and not merely in *y*. The combination of both the phonemes does not consist in being *al*. Hence it is not an *al-vidhi*. As such, there is no occasion to invoke the fourth interpretation of *al-vidhi* to stop treating the replacement as the substituendum.

The form *rāmābhyām* is with a dual sup-affix of the fourth triplet and is derived with the help of *supi ca* (140) in the same manner as that with a dual sup-affix of the third triplet.

When the plural sup-affix is introduced after the nominal stem *rāma* we have *rāma* + *bhyas*. At this stage, the following sūtra applies :

(144) बहुवचने झल्येत्। *bahuvacane jhalyet*. 7. 3. 103

लघु० - झलादौ बहुवचने सुपि अतोऽङ्गस्यैकारः। रामेभ्यः। सुपि किम् ? पचध्वम्।

jhalādau bahuvacane supi ato 'ṅgasyaikāraḥ. rāmebhyaḥ. supi kim? pacadhvam.

Trans. : Let the substitute phoneme *e* replace the aṅga-final vowel of a nominal stem ending in a short vowel *a* when followed by a plural sup-affix beginning with a consonant denoted by the abbreviatory term *jhal*. Why (is it said) when a sup-affix follows? (The counter example is) *pacadhvam*.

PP. *ataḥ aṅgasya bahuvacane jhali supi et.*

Eluc. : The sūtra is in the domain of the governing rule *aṅgasya* Pā. 6. 4. 1. The term *aṅgasya,* therefore, recurs here. The words *ataḥ* and *supi* are respectively carried over from *ato dīrgho yañi* Pā. 7. 3. 101 and *supi ca* Pā. 7. 3. 102. The word *ataḥ* qualifies *aṅgasya*. By *yena vidhistadantasya* Pā. 1. 1. 72, the word *ataḥ* is interpreted as *adantasya* (*aṅgasya*). The term *jhali,* being in the locative singular, qualifies the carried over term *supi* which is also in the locative singular. In accordance with *yasmin vidhis tadādāvalgrahaṇe* Mbh 1. 1. 72 vtk 29, the term *jhali* is interpreted as *jhalādau* (*supi*). Thus the present sūtra comes to mean : If the pre-affixal nominal stem is followed by a sup-affix which begins with a consonant denoted by the abbreviatory term *jhal,* then the pre-affixal nominal stem is replaced by the vowel *e.* By virtue of the paribhāṣā sūtra *alo 'ntyasya* (21), the substitute vowel *e* replaces the aṅga-final short vowel *a.* In the illustration *rāma* + *bhyas,* the sup-affix *bhyas* is plural and begins with a *jhal*-consonant. The pre-affixal nominal stem *rāma* ends in the short vowel *a.* The condition for replacing the aṅga-final short vowel *a* by the vowel *e* is available. Hence the short vowel *a* is replaced by *e* and we have the form *rāmebhyaḥ.*

In order to explain the significance of the term *supi* being carried over into this sūtra, Varadarāja gives *pacadhvam* as the counter-example. If *supi* had not been carried over into this sūtra, then the aṅga-final short vowel *a* in *paca* would have been replaced by *e* since the following conjugational affix *dhvam* begins with a *jhal*-consonant. In that case we would have the form *pacedhvam* which is not correct. By including *supi,* this undesirable contingency is avoided. The reason is not far to seek. The affix *dhvam* beginning with a *jhal*-consonant follows the pre-affixal base *paca* that ends in the short vowel *a* but it is a tiṅ-affix. Since *dhvam* is not a sup-affix, the *e*-replacement would not come in place of the aṅga-final short vowel *a* of *paca* and we will get the correct form *pacadhvam.*

With the singular sup-affix of the fifth triplet having been introduced after *rāma,* we have *rāma* + *ṅasi.* The nominal ending *ṅasi* is replaced by *āt* in accordance with the rule *ṭāṅasiṅasāminātsyāḥ* (139). Then *akaḥ savarṇe dīrghaḥ* (42) applies and the aṅga-final short vowel *a* and *ā* of *āt,* are both replaced by a long vowel *ā* and we have the inflected form *rāmāt.* At this stage, being nitya, the sūtra *jhalāṁ jaśo 'nte* (67) becomes available for application but blocking it the following rule ensues[1] :

---

1. *jhalāṁ jaśo 'nte iti nityatayā jaśtvaṁ prāptam. tadapavādaś cartvavikalpa ārabhyata ityarthaḥ.* BM, I, pp. 199-200. Also cf. TB, I, p. 200.

(145) वाऽवसाने । *vā 'vasāne*. 8. 4. 56

लघु० - अवसाने झलां चरो वा। रामात्, रामाद्। रामाभ्याम्, रामेभ्यः, रामस्य।

avasāne jhalāṁ caro vā. rāmāt, rāmād. rāmābhyām, rāmebhyaḥ, rāmasya.

Trans. : An element denoted by the abbreviatory term *car* optionally comes in place of the element denoted by the abbreviatory term *jhal*, when an element denoted by *jhal* occurs in avasāna.

PP. *avasāne jhalāṁ caro vā* (*saṁhitāyām*).

Eluc. : The words *jhalāṁ* and *car* are respectively carried over from the sūtras *jhalāṁ jaś jhaśi* Pā. 8. 4. 53 *abhyāse carca* Pā. 8. 4. 54. The word *jhalāṁ* has substitution-genitive (*sthānaṣaṣṭhī*). The term *car* is changed into the plural by the process of vacanavipariṇāma. Taking into consideration the insertions, which are carried over and the sense of the genitive, the meaning of the sūtra is as follows : In avasāna, (whether the last phoneme is interpreted as avasāna or whether the last phoneme is followed by the cessation of speech units) the elements denoted by *car* optionally come in place of the elements denoted by the abbreviatory term *jhal* (for explanation see supra pp. 149-150). At this stage, the pada-final *t* is replaced by *t* {*parjanyaval lakṣaṇapravṛttiḥ* (Abhyankar, 111)}. In the alternative situation when the *car*-replacement does not take place, *jhalāṁ jaśo 'nte* (67) applies and we have the phoneme *d* substituted for the final phoneme *t*. Thus we have two forms of *rāma* with a singular nominal ending of the fifth triplet : *rāmāt* and *rāmād*.

The grammatical procedure adopted above is in consonance with Jñānendra Sarasvatī's view which in the context of this rule is worth noticing. He says that the application of the sūtra *jhalāṁ jaśo 'nte* (67) should not precede that of the present sūtra. Instead, by virtue of the paribhāṣā *yena nāprāpte yo vidhir ārbhyate sa tasya bādhako bhavati* (Abhyankar, on 57, p. 134), the present sūtra is considered to be an exception to *jhalāṁ jaśo 'nte* (67) in the avasāna instance. So, being an exception, the present sūtra first applies and the pada-final phoneme *t* is replaced by *t*. Since the sūtra *vā 'vasāne* (145) is optional, the rule *jhalāṁ jaśo 'nte* (67) applies in the alternative and the pada-final *t* is replaced by *d*. This is the manner in which we obtain two forms in consonance with this interpretation.[1]

---

1. TB, I, p. 200. For the other point of view that *jhalāṁ jaśo 'nte* should apply first and then the present rule, see Bhaimī, I, p. 184.

Jinendrabuddhi and Haradatta also endorse the apavāda view (see KN, VI and KP, VI, p. 658).

The process of the formation of dual and plural forms of *rāma* in the ablative does not differ from that of the dual and plural forms in the dative.

With the singular sup-affix of the sixth triplet, we have *rāma* + *ṅas*. The inflectional affix *ṅas* is replaced by *sya* in accordance with the rule *ṭāṅasiṅasāminātsyāḥ* (139). Although the affix *sya* begins with a *jhal*-consonant, it is not plural. This is the reason why the substitute *e* has not replaced the short vowel *a* coming at the end of *rāma*.

To form the genitive dual form of the word *rāma*, we introduce the sup-affix *os* after the nominal stem *rāma* : *rāma* + *os*. The sūtra *vṛddhireci* Pā. 6. 1. 88 is available but is blocked by *ato guṇe* Pā. 6. 1. 97. In case the latter rule applied here, the following sūtra *osi ca* (146) would be left with no scope for application. The incurrence of this redundancy occasions the blocking of *ato guṇe* Pā. 6. 1. 97 by the following rule. The paribhāṣā *vārṇād āṅgaṁ balīyaḥ* (Abhyankar, 55) may also be taken into consideration in the present context.

(146) ओसि च । *osi ca*. 7. 3. 104

लघु० – अतोऽङ्गस्यैकारः । रामयोः । *ato 'ṅgasyaikāraḥ. rāmayoḥ.*

Trans. : Let the aṅga-final short vowel *a* be replaced by the substitute *e*, when the sup-affix *os* follows.

PP. *osi ca ataḥ aṅgasya et.*

Eluc. : *aṅgasya* Pā. 6. 4. 1 is a governing rule. Hence the word *aṅgasya* recurs in the present sūtra. The words *ataḥ* and *et* respectively come from *ato dīrgho yañi* Pā. 7. 3. 101 and *bahuvacane jhalyet* Pā. 7. 3. 103. The consonant *t* at the end of *et* is *it* by *halantyam* (1) and is therefore elided by *tasya lopaḥ* (3). The term *ataḥ* qualifies the word *aṅgasya*. Accordingly, we will have the phrase *adantasya aṅgasya*. In this way the sūtra means : If the pre-affixal base ends in a short *a* and the sup-affix *os* follows, then the aṅga-final short *a* is replaced by the vowel *e*. Thus we have *rāme* + *os*. At this stage, the rule *eco 'ya...* (22) applies and the vowel *e* of *rāme* is replaced by *ay* and we have *rāmayos*. After replacing *s* with *ru* by *sasajuṣo ruḥ* (104) and *r* with visarjanīya by *kharavasānayo...* (93) we obtain the fully inflected form *rāmayoḥ*.

To inflect *rāma* with the plural sup-affix of the sixth triplet, we introduce *ām* after the nominal stem *rāma* and we have *rāma* + *ām*. Now the rule *akaḥ savarṇe dīrghaḥ* (42) becomes available for application but the following sūtra blocks it and applies :

(147) ह्रस्वनद्यापो नुट् । *hrasvanadyāpo nuṭ*. 7. 1. 54

लघु० – ह्रस्वान्ताद् नद्यन्ताद् आबन्ताच्चाङ्गात् परस्य नुडागमः । *hrasvāntād nadyantād ābantāc cāṅgāt parasya nuḍāgamaḥ.*

Trans. : Let the augment *nuṭ* be introduced to sup-affix *ām* when it occurs after an aṅga which ends in a short vowel or which is denoted by the technical term *nadī* or which ends in the feminine affix *āp* (*ābanta*).

PP. *hrasvanadyāpaḥ aṅgāt āmaḥ nuṭ.*

Eluc. : The word *aṅgasya* is carried over from the governing rule *aṅgasya* Pā. 6. 4. 1. This word is changed into ablative singular. The word *āmi* is lent into the sūtra from *āmi sarvanāmnaḥ suṭ* Pā. 7. 1. 52. The word *āmi* is also changed into one having the singular nominal ending of the sixth triplet. Both these endings have been changed by the process of vibhaktivipariṇāma. The compound *hrasvanadyāpaḥ* is a samāhāradvandva which is analysed as *hrasvaś ca nadī ca āp ca teṣāṁ samāhāraḥ hrasvanadyāp, tasmāt = hrasvanadyāpaḥ*. This word qualifies the word *aṅgāt*. Therefore tadanta-vidhi comes into play. The word *nadī* is a technical term which will be defined in the sūtra *yūstryākhyau nadī* (193). This rule assigns the designation *nadī* to the words which are always feminine and which at the same time end in either long *ī* or long *ū*. The word *āp* covers the following three feminine affixes : *ṭāp, ḍāp* and *cāp*. All these points having been taken into consideration, the sūtra means : If the pre-affixal base ends in a short vowel or in nadī or in *āp*, then the augment *nuṭ* is inserted at the head of the nominal ending *ām*. Since the augment has the phoneme *ṭ* as *it*, it is inserted at the beginning of the sup-affix *ām* in accordance with the rule *ādyantau ṭakitau* (84).

In the illustration *rāma + ām*, the nominal ending *ām* follows the pre-affixal base *rāma* which ends in the short vowel *a*. Therefore by the present sūtra, the augment *nuṭ* becomes the initial constituent of the inflectional ending *ām*. The cerebral consonant *ṭ* is *it* by *halantyam* (1) and the vowel *u* is for the sake of articulation. In this way what remains is the consonant *n* which is inserted prior to the vowel *ā* of the affix *ām* and the nominal affix becomes *nām*. Thus we have : *rāma + nām*. At this stage, the following sūtra applies :

(148) नामि । *nāmi*. 6. 4. 3

लघु० – अजन्ताङ्गस्य दीर्घः । रामाणाम् । रामे । रामयोः । एत्त्वे कृते — *ajantāṅgasya dīrghaḥ. rāmāṇām. rāme, rāmayoḥ. ettve kṛte* —

Trans. : Let the pre-affixal base ending in a vowel be replaced by a long vowel before *nām*.

(The following sūtra applies) after replacing the aṅga-final short *a* by the substitute *e*(*t*) in the case where the plural nominal affix (*sup*) of the seventh triplet follows.

PP. *nāmi aṅgasya dīrghaḥ*.

Eluc. : The present sūtra occurs in the domain of the governing rule *aṅgasya*. The word *dīrghaḥ* is carried over from the sūtra *ḍhralope pūrvasya dīrgho 'ṇaḥ* (111). The word *dīrghaḥ* by virtue of the paribhāṣā sūtra *acaśca* Pā. 1. 2. 28 causes the term *acaḥ* to present itself in the present rule. This term qualifies the carried over word *aṅgasya* which by tadantavidhi is interpreted as *ajantasya aṅgasya*. Thus the completed sūtra gives the following meaning : The aṅga that ends in a vowel is replaced by a long vowel when the plural sup-affix *nām* of the sixth triplet follows. With the help of the paribhāṣā sūtra *alo 'ntyasya* (21), this substitute long vowel comes in place of the last vowel of the pre-affixal base. In the illustration *rāma* + *nām*, the last vowel *a* occurring at the end of the pre-affixal base *rāma* is replaced by a long vowel *ā* and we have *rāmā* + *nām*. At this stage, the sūtra *aṭkupvāṅnumvyavāye 'pi* (137) becomes available for application and the dental *n* is replaced by the cerebral *ṇ* and we have the resultant form *rāmāṇām*.

One important point remains to be discussed here. The lengthening of the aṅga-final vowel could have been obtained by the rule *supi ca* Pā. 7. 3. 102 which is subsequent to the present sūtra but the rule *supi ca* (140) does not apply because of the meta-rule *sannipātalakṣaṇo vidhir animittaṁ tadvighātasya* (Abhyankar, 85). The augment *nuṭ* is inserted at the head of the affix *ām*, when it is introduced after an aṅga which ends in a short vowel. This very *nuṭ* now occasions the lengthening of the aṅga-final vowel by *supi ca* (140) and the present sūtra. In this way it leads to the destruction of its own cause in that the short vowel occasions the insertion of the augment *nuṭ* which becomes the cause of the lengthening of that very short vowel. In the context of the present rule, the meta-rule (Abhyankar, 85) is blocked by the very fact that the present sūtra has been enunciated by Pāṇini. Otherwise the present rule would be rendered vacuous[1] (cf. SK, I, pp. 203-04), which is not the case with the rule *supi ca* (140).

---

1. *yadyatra nāmīti dīrgho na syāt tarhi tadārambho vyarthaḥ syāt. tataśca niravakāśatvād rāmāṇām ityādau nāmi iti dīrghaḥ sannipātaparibhāṣāṁ bādhitvā pravartate*. BM, I, p. 204.

To decline *rāma* with the singular sup-affix *ṅi* of the seventh triplet we have *rāma* + *ṅi*. The initial phoneme *ṅ* of *ṅi* is *it* by the sūtra *laśakvataddhite* (135). Hence it is elided by *tasya lopaḥ* (3). The vowel that remains after the elision of *ṅ* is *i* and we have *rāma* + *i*. At this stage by *ādguṇaḥ* (27) a guṇa vowel *e* replaces both the aṅga-final *a* and the nominal ending *i* in consonance with the rule *sthāne 'ntaratamaḥ* (17). The resultant form is *rāme*.

The form of *rāma* with a dual nominal ending of the seventh triplet is derived in the same manner as the one with a dual sup-affix of the sixth triplet. The form is *rāmayoḥ*.

To inflect *rāma* with the plural sup-affix of the seventh triplet we have *rāma* + *sup*. The phoneme *p* being *it* is elided. Since the affix begins with a *jhal* consonant, the aṅga-final *a* of *rāma* is replaced by the vowel *e* by *bahuvacane jhalyet* (144) and we have *rāme* + *su*. At this stage, the following sūtra beomes available for application :

(149) आदेशप्रत्यययोः । *ādeśapratyayayoḥ*. 8. 3. 59

लघु० – इण्कुभ्यां परस्यापदान्तस्यादेशः प्रत्ययावयवश्च यः सस्तस्य मूर्धन्यादेशः । ईषद्विवृतस्य सस्य तादृश एव षः । रामेषु । एवं कृष्णादयोऽप्यदन्ताः । *iṇkubhyāṁ parasyāpadāntasyādeśaḥ pratyayāvayavaś ca yaḥ sas tasya mūrdhanyādeśaḥ. īṣadvivṛtasya sasya tādṛśa eva ṣaḥ. rāmeṣu. evaṁ kṛṣṇādayo 'pyadantāḥ.*

Trans. : Let the substitute cerebral ṣ replace a non-pada-final dental *s* of a replacement element or of an affix if it (*s*) follows the elements denoted by *iṇ*-pratyāhāra and ku. The īṣadvivṛta ṣ resembles most the dental *s* and is therefore the proper replacement.

PP. *numvisarjanīyaśarvyavāye'pi iṇkoḥ ādeśapratyayayoḥ apadāntasya saḥ mūrdhanyaḥ (saṁhitāyām).*

Eluc. : The sūtra *apadāntasya mūrdhanyaḥ* Pā. 8. 3 55 is the governing rule in the domain of which this sūtra occurs. Hence both the words *apadāntasya* and *mūrdhanyaḥ* are carried over into the present sūtra. The phoneme *saḥ*, which is in the genitive, is carried over from the sūtra *saheḥ sāḍaḥ saḥ* Pā. 8. 3. 56. This term is changed into the genitive dual so that it may syntactically agree with *ādeśapratyayayoḥ* which is also in the genitive dual. According to the Bālamanoramā, this will mean : the replacement *s* and the *s* which is a part of an affix.[1] The sūtra *iṇkoḥ*

1. *tacceha dvivacanāntatayā vipariṇamya ādeśapratyayayoḥ ityatra sambadhyate. tataśca iṇkavargābhyāṁ parayor apadāntayor ādeśātmakapratyayāvayavātmakayoḥ sakārayor mūrdhanyaḥ.* BM, I, p. 206.

Pā. 8. 3. 57 is also a governing rule. As such it also recurs in the present sūtra. The word *iṇkoḥ* is a samāhāradvandva compound. Its being in the masculine is peculiar to the sūtra (*samāhāradvandve sautraṁ puṁstvam,* TB, I, p. 205). After these points have been taken into consideration, the sūtra comes to mean : A non-pada-final dental s which is either a substitute (*ādeśa*) or a part of an affix is replaced by a cerebral ṣ. One more point is also to be taken note of in the context of this rule. The immediately preceding sūtra in the Aṣṭādhyāyī is *numvisarjanīya-śarvyavāye 'pi* Pā. 8. 3. 58. It is also read into the present sūtra. Then the sūtra will mean that the replacement cerebral ṣ does come in place of the dental s, even if there is an intervention of *num,* visarga and an element denoted by the abbreviatory term *śar* between *iṇku* and the dental s in the same pada. The *iṇ*-pratyāhāra is formed with the ṇakāra occurring subsequently in the *laṇ*-pratyāhārasūtra (see supra for explanation, sūtra (11) p. 20).

In the illustration *rāme + su,* the condition laid down by this sūtra is fufilled as the substitute *e* is denoted by *iṇ*-pratyāhāra and the dental sakāra which follows it is a part of the plural affix *sup* of the seventh triplet. The sakāra of *sup*-affix is replaced by the cerebral ṣ and we have the fully inflected form *rāmeṣu.*

The declensional paradigm of the nominal stem *rāma* will run as follows :

	Singular	Dual	Plural
prathamā	*rāmaḥ*	*rāmau*	*rāmāḥ*
dvitīyā	*rāmam*	*ramau*	*rāmān*
tṛtīyā	*rāmeṇa*	*rāmābhyām*	*rāmaiḥ*
caturthī	*rāmāya*	*rāmābhyām*	*rāmebhyaḥ*
pañcamī	*rāmāt, d*	*rāmābhyām*	*rāmebhyaḥ*
ṣaṣṭhī	*rāmasya*	*rāmayoḥ*	*rāmāṇām*
saptamī	*rāme*	*rāmayoḥ*	*rāmeṣu*
sambodhana	*he rāma!*	*he rāmau!*	*he rāmāḥ!*

This is how the word *rāma* is declined. The words like *kṛṣṇa,* etc. will be declined in the same manner. Some such words are : *aśva* 'a horse', *uṣṭra* 'a camel', *kāka* 'a crow', *kapota* 'a pigeon', *kukkuṭa* 'a cock', *kūrma* 'a tortoise', *khaga* 'a bird', *śuka* 'a parrot', *nakula* 'a mongoose', *sarpa* 'a snake', *maṇḍūka* 'a frog', *gaja* 'an elephant', *gardabha* 'a donkey', *janaka* 'father', *khala* 'rogue', *dhanika* 'a rich man', *pāvaka* 'fire', *jaya* 'victory', *kūpa* 'a well', *vidyālaya* 'school', *keśava* 'Śrī Kṛṣṇa', *pācaka* 'cook', *mātula* 'maternal uncle', *pika* 'cuckoo', *vānara* 'a monkey', *govinda* 'Śrī Kṛṣṇa' and *deva* 'god'.

(150) सर्वादीनि सर्वनामानि । *sarvādīni sarvanāmāni.* 1. 1. 27

लघु० - सर्वादीनि शब्दस्वरूपाणि सर्वनामसञ्ज्ञानि स्युः । सर्व । विश्व । उभ । उभय । डतर । डतम । अन्य । अन्यतर । इतर । त्वत् । त्व । नेम । सम । सिम । पूर्वपराऽवर-दक्षिणोत्तराऽपराऽधराणि व्यवस्थायामसञ्ज्ञायाम् । स्वमज्ञातिधनाख्यायाम् । अन्तरं बहिर्योगोपसंव्यानयोः । त्यद् । तद् । यद् । एतद् । इदम् । अदस् । एक । द्वि । युष्मद् । अस्मद् । भवतु । किम् । *sarvādīni śabdasvarūpāṇi sarvanāmasañjñāni syuḥ. sarva, viśva, ubha, ubhaya, ḍatara, ḍatama, anya, anyatara, itara, tvat, tva, nema, sama, sima. pūrvaparā 'varadakṣiṇottarā 'parā 'dharāṇi vyavasthāyāmasañjñāyām. svamajñātidhanākhyāyām. antaraṁ bahiryogopasaṁvyānayoḥ. tyad, tad, yad, etad, idam, adas, eka, dvi, yuṣmad, asmad, bhavatu, kim.*

Trans. : Let the members listed in the set headed by *sarva* 'all' be designated as *sarvanāman*. (The set consists of the following members): *sarva* 'all', *viśva*, 'all' *ubha* 'both', *ubhaya* 'both', *ḍatara ḍatama* (words which are formed with these affixes such as *katara* 'which of the two' and *katama* 'which of many'), *anya* 'other', *anyatara* 'either', *itara* 'other', *tvat* 'other', *tva* 'other', *nema* 'half', *sama* 'all', *sima* 'all'. *pūrva* 'front, east, prior', *para* 'subsequent, latter', *avara* 'lower, preceding, prior', *dakṣiṇa* 'south, right-hand side', *uttara* 'north, upper', *apara* 'western, posterior, other', *adhara* 'lower' - these seven words are called *sarvanāman* when the denotatum is 'relative difference or location in time and space' and not 'name'. So also the word *sva* 'own' when it does not denote 'relative' or 'wealth'. The word *antara* is also termed *sarvanāman* when either 'connection with the exterior location' or 'an undergarment' is signified. *tyad* 'he, she, it, that', *tad* ''he, she, it, that', *yad* 'who, which, what', *etad* 'this', *idam* 'this', *adas* 'that', *eka* 'one' *dvi* 'two', *yuṣmad* 'you', *asmad* 'I, we', *bhavatu* 'you (a respectful form of address)', *kim* 'who, what'.

PP. *sarvādīni (śabdasvarūpāṇi) sarvanāmāni.*

Eluc. The word *sarvādīni* is a tadguṇasaṁvijñāna bahuvrīhi compound which is analysed as follows : *sarvaḥ (śabdaḥ) ādir yeṣām* *śabdasvarūpāṇām tāni = sarvādīni*. Since the word *sarvādīni* being a tadguṇasaṁvijñāna bahuvrīhi is a qualifying term, it is expectant of *śabdasvarūpāṇi* in the form of a substantive to complete the sense in the present context. Thus the sūtra means as follows : The word-forms given in the list of *sarvādi* group are to be designated as *sarvanāman*.

(151) जसः शी । *jasaḥ śī*. 7. 1. 17

लघु० – अदन्तात् सर्वनाम्नो जसः शी स्यात्। अनेकाल्त्वात् सर्वादेशः। सर्वे। *adantāt sarvanāmno jasaḥ śī syāt. anekāltvāt sarvādeśaḥ. sarve.*

Trans. : After a pronominal stem ending in the short vowel *a*, let the substitute *śī* replace the sup-affix *jas*. As the substitute consists of more than one phoneme, it replaces the whole (of *jas*).

PP. *ataḥ sarvanāmnaḥ aṅgāt jasaḥ śī.*

Eluc. : The words *ataḥ* and *sarvanāmnaḥ* are respectively carried over from the sūtras *ato bhisa ais* Pā. 7. 1. 9 and *sarvanāmnaḥ smai* Pā. 7. 1. 14. The word *ataḥ* qualifies *sarvanāmnaḥ* and *aṅgāt*. The latter term comes from the governing rule *aṅgasya* Pā. 6. 4. 1 after having been changed into the ablative so that it may accord with *ataḥ* and *sarvanāmnaḥ*. With the help of tadantavidhi (Pā. 1. 1. 72), the completed sūtra means : If the affix *jas* follows a pronominal pre-affixal stem ending in the short vowel *a*, it is to be replaced by the substitute *śī*.

The rule *jasaḥ śī* is not in the governing domain of *pratyayaḥ* Pā. 3. 1. 1. Therefore, the substitute *śī* does not get the pratyaya-designation and as a consequence the initial palatal *ś* of *śī* does not become *it* by *laśakvataddhite* (135). As such, being *anekāl*, the substitute *śī* replaces the whole of *jas*. After replacement, the substitute *śī* gets the pratyaya-designation by virtue of the rule *sthānivad ādeśo 'nalvidhau* (143). Now being an initial phoneme of a non-taddhita affix, it gets the *it*-designation and is consequently replaced by lopa in accordance with *tasya lopah* (3). Only *ī* remains. After the application of *ādguṇaḥ* (27), both the vowel *a* at the end of *sarva* and the affix *ī* in *sarva* + *ī* are replaced by a guṇa substitute *e* with the help of *sthāne 'ntaratamaḥ* (17) and we have the form *sarve*.

The declined forms of the pronominal stem of *sarva* with the sup-affixes of the second and third triplets are : *sarvam, sarvau, sarvān. sarveṇa, sarvābhyām, sarvaiḥ*. The grammatical process of their declension does not differ from that which is followed in declining the corresponding forms of the nominal stem *rāma* with the affixes of the second and third triplets. When we introduce the singular sup-affix ṅe of the fourth triplet, we have *sarva* + *ṅe*. At this stage, the following rule becomes available for application, since the word *sarva* is sarvanāman by *sarvādīni sarvanāmāni* (150) :

(152) सर्वनाम्नः स्मै । *sarvanāmnaḥ smai*. 7. 1. 14

लघु० – अतः सर्वनाम्नो ङेः स्मै । सर्वस्मै । *ataḥ sarvanāmno ṅeḥ smai. sarvasmai.*

Trans. : Let the substitute *smai* replace the substituendum *ṅe*, if it follows the pronominal stem ending in a short vowel *a*.

PP. *ataḥ sarvanāmnaḥ ṅeḥ smai* (*aṅgasya*).

Eluc. : The words *ataḥ* and *ṅe* are lent into the present sūtra from *ato bhisa ais* (141) and *ṅeryaḥ* (142) respectively. The elision of the *su*-affix after *smai* is an ārṣa (belonging to the sages) usage. The completed sūtra means : The substituendum *ṅe* which follows a pronominal stem ending in *a* is to be replaced by the substitute *smai*. In *sarva* + *ṅe*, *ṅe* is replaced by *smai* and the inflected form *sarvasmai* is obtained. The dual and plural forms of *sarva* with the dual and plural affixes of the fourth triplet are *sarvābhyām* and *sarvebhyaḥ* which are derived in the same manner as the forms of *rāma* with the corresponding affixes.

When we introduce the singular affix of the fifth triplet after *sarva*, we have *sarva* + *ṅasi*. At this stage, the following sūtra presents itself for application :

(153) ङसिङ्योः स्मात्स्मिनौ । *ṅasiṅyoḥ smātsminau*. 7. 1. 15

लघु० – अतः सर्वनाम्न एतयोरेतौ स्तः । सर्वस्मात् । *ataḥ sarvanāmna etayor etau staḥ. sarvasmāt.*

Trans. : The affixes *ṅasi* and *ṅi* which follow a pronominal stem ending in the short vowel *a* are replaced respectively by the substitutes *smāt* and *smin*.

PP. *ataḥ sarvanāmnaḥ ṅasiṅyoḥ smātsminau* (*aṅgasya*).

Eluc. : The words *ataḥ* and *sarvanāmnaḥ* are carried over into this sūtra respectively from *ato bhisa ais* (141) and *sarvanāmnaḥ smai* (152). The word *ataḥ* qualifies *sarvanāmnaḥ*. Hence tadantavidhi comes into play. Thus the completed sūtra means : When the sup-affixes *ṅasi* and *ṅi* are introduced after a pronominal stem ending in a short *a*, they are respectively replaced by the substitutes *smāt* and *smin* with the help of the rule *yathāsaṁkhyamanudeśaḥ samānām* (23) since the substituenda and the substitutes are of equal enumeration. It is to be borne in mind that the last phonemes of these affixes are not to be designated as *it* by *halantyam* (1) as this rule is blocked by *na vibhaktau tusmāḥ* (130). As a consequence, the final consonantal phonemes *t* and *n* are not elided by *tasya lopaḥ* (3). Thus with the singular affix of the fifth triplet after *sarva* we have the form *sarvasmāt* (<-- *sarva* + *ṅasi*).

The genitive singular and dual forms of *sarva* (*sarvasya* and *sarvayoḥ*) are derived in the same manner as those of *rāma*.

With the plural affix of the sixth triplet we have *sarva* + *ām*. At this stage the following sūtra ensues :

(154) आमि सर्वनाम्नः सुट् । *āmi sarvanāmnaḥ suṭ*. 7. 1. 52

लघु० - अवर्णान्तात् परस्य सर्वनाम्नो विहितस्यामः सुडागमः । एत्वषत्वे — सर्वेषाम् । सर्वस्मिन् । *avarṇāntāt parasya sarvanāmno vihitasyāmaḥ suḍāgamaḥ. etvaṣatve. sarveṣām. sarvasmin.*

Trans. : The augment *suṭ* is added to the affix *ām* which is introduced after a pronominal stem ending in *a*.

PP. *āt aṅgāt sarvanāmnaḥ āmi suṭ*.

Eluc. : The word *āt* is carried over into the present sūtra from *ājjaserasuk* Pā. 7. 1. 50. The governing sūtra *aṅgasya* Pā. 6. 4. 1 extends here also since the present rule is in its domain and the word *aṅgasya* is changed into the ablative by the process of vibhakti-vipariṇāma. The word *āt* qualifies the word *aṅgāt*. By Pā. 1. 1. 72 tadanta-vidhi becomes applicable. Both the terms are syntactically connected and give rise to the phrase : *adantāt aṅgāt*. With these points, sūtra means as follows : The augment *suṭ* is added to *ām* which has been enjoined after a pronominal stem ending in *a*. Although the term *āmi* used in the sūtra is in the locative singular, it is to be taken as ending in the genitive singular because of the ablative singular used in the term *sarvanāmnaḥ* in consonance with the paribhāṣā *ubhayanirdeśe pañcamīnirdeśo balīyān* (Abhyankar, 70).[1] So the augment *suṭ* is inserted at the head of the sup-affix *ām* by virtue of the rule *ādyantau ṭakitau* (84) since the augment has

1. The locative ending used in *āmi* in the present sūtra directs the grammatical operation to be performed on the item which precedes it without the intervention of even a single phoneme by the paribhāṣā sūtra *tasminniti nirdiṣṭe pūrvasya* (16). Since the word *sarvanāmnaḥ* ends in the ablative, *tasmādityuttarasya* (71) directs the grammatical operation on the item which immediately follows the term used in the ablative. By the former rule, the augment *suṭ* should become the initial part of the *aṅga* preceding the affix *ām*, whereas by the latter

ṭ as *it* and we have *sarva* + *suṭ ām*--> *sarva* + *sām* (after the elision of the anubandhas). The combined affix *sām* (with the augment *suṭ*) is not to be taken as different from the affix *ām* in view of the paribhāṣā *yadāgamās tadguṇībhūtās tadgrahaṇena gṛhyante* (Abhyankar, 11) which means : That to which an augment is added denotes whatever results from its combination with that augment since the augment forms a part of it. Now since the sup-affix begins with a *jhal*-consonant, the rule *bahuvacane jhalyet* (144) applies and the aṅga-final *a* is replaced by the substitute *e*. At this stage, we have *sarve* + *sām*. The cerebral ṣ replaces the dental s of the affix *sām* by the rule *ādeśapratyayayoḥ* (149) and we have the fully inflected form *sarveṣām* (<-- *sarve* + *sām*).

In the locative singular we have *sarva* + *ṅi*. Here by the rule *ṅasiṅyoḥ smātsminau* (153), the singular affix *ṅi* of the seventh triplet is replaced by *smin* and we have *sarvasmin* (<-- *sarva* + *smin*). The declensional paradigm of the pronominal stem *sarva* will be as follows :

	Singular	Dual	Plural
prathamā	*sarvaḥ*	*sarvau*	*sarve*
dvitīyā	*sarvam*	*sarvau*	*sarvān*
tṛtīyā	*sarveṇa*	*sarvābhyām*	*sarvaiḥ*
caturthī	*sarvasmai*	*sarvābhyām*	*sarvebhyaḥ*
pañcamī	*sarvasmāt, d*	*sarvābhyām*	*sarvebhyaḥ*
ṣaṣṭhī	*sarvasya*	*sarvayoḥ*	*sarveṣām*
saptamī	*sarvasmin*	*sarvayoḥ*	*sarveṣu*
sambodhana	*he sarva!*	*he sarvau!*	*he sarve!*

The declension of the pronominal stems *viśva*, etc. which end in the short vowel *a* will be like that of the pronominal stem *sarva*.

लघु० – उभशब्दो नित्यं द्विवचनान्तः। उभौ 2। उभाभ्याम् 3। उभयोः 2। तस्येह पाठोऽकजर्थः। *ubhaśabdo nityaṁ dvivacanāntaḥ. ubhau 2, ubhābhyām 3, ubhayoḥ 2. tasyeha pāṭho 'kajarthaḥ*

---

it is to be inserted at the head of the affix *ām* which immediately follows the pre-affixal pronominal base. In order to put an end to this ambiguity, the paribhāṣā *ubhayanirdeśe pañcamīnirdeśo balīyān* (when both the ablative and the locative endings are given in a rule, the ablative possesses greater force) is invoked. By virtue of this metarule, the augment will become the initial part of the affix *ām*.

Trans. : The word *ubha* invariably takes a dual affix. The object of enlisting it here is to introduce the affix *akac* in respect of this word.

Eluc. : The word *ubha* which means 'both' always takes the dual nominal ending. This has been enlisted in the set beginning with the pronominal stem *sarva* so that the affix *akac* may be introduced before the *ṭi* of *ubha* by the rule *avyayasarvanāmnāmakac prāk ṭeḥ* (1227). After the addition of *akac*, the form of *ubha* becomes *ubh* + *akac* + *a* --> *ubhaka*. Had the word *ubha* not got the sarvanāman-designation, it would not have taken the affix *akac*. That the word *ubha* is invariably dual is not affected by the introduction of the affix *akac* since this affix is added before the last vowel; it is within the word and it will be considered to be the same as *ubha* by the meta-rule *tanmadhyapatitas tadgrahaṇena gṛhyate* (Abhyankar, 89). The affix *ka* would not have served the purpose since with the addition of *ka* the word *ubhaka* could have been obtained but the invariable nature of its being dual would have been compromised since in that case it would have been construed as a different word. (*akaci tu sati tanmadhyapatitas tadgrahaṇena gṛhyate iti nyāyena ubha-śabdena ubhakaśabdo 'pi gṛhyate*, BM, I, p. 212). It is for this reason that the word *ubha* has been enlisted in the set of sarva, etc. Both the pronominal stems, *ubha* and *ubhaka*, are declined invariably with the dual nominal ending:

	Dual	Dual
prathamā	*ubhau*	*ubhakau*
dvitīyā	*ubhau*	*ubhakau*
tṛtīyā	*ubhābhyām*	*ubhakābhyām*
caturthī	*ubhābhyām*	*ubhakābhyām*
pañcamī	*ubhābhyām*	*ubhakābhyām*
ṣaṣṭhī	*ubhayoḥ*	*ubhakayoḥ*
saptamī	*ubhayoḥ*	*ubhakayoḥ*
sambodhana	*he ubhau!*	*he ubhakau!*

लघु० – उभयशब्दस्य द्विवचनं नास्ति। डतर-डतमौ प्रत्ययौ। प्रत्ययग्रहणे तदन्तग्रहणम् इति तदन्ता ग्राह्याः। नेम इत्यर्धे। समः सर्वपर्यायः। तुल्यपर्यायस्तु न। यथासंख्यमनुदेशः समानाम् (23) इति ज्ञापकात्। *ubhayaśabdasya dvivacanaṁ nāsti. ḍatara-ḍatamau pratyayau. pratyayagrahaṇe tadantagrahaṇam iti tadantā grāhyāḥ.*

nema ityardhe. samaḥ sarvaparyāyaḥ. tulyaparyāyas tu na. yathāsaṁkhyam anudeśaḥ samānām iti jñāpakāt.

Trans. : The pronominal stem *ubhaya* does not have a form in the dual. The terms *datara* and *datama* are affixes. The words which end with these affixes are to be construed as pronominal stems by virtue of the paribhāṣā *pratyayagrahaṇe... tadantasya grahaṇam* (Abhyankar, 23). The word *nema* (is a pronominal stem when it) means 'half'. The pronominal stem *sama* is a synonym of *sarva* and not that of *tulya* 'equal'. It is implied by the use of the word *samānām* in the sūtra *yathāsaṁkhyamanudeśaḥ samānām* (23).

Eluc. : The word *ubhaya* follows the word *ubha* in the list of sarvādi. The word *ubhaya* is derived by adding *ayac* which invariably replaces the affix *tayap* introduced after *ubha* in the sense of 'this is the number of its parts'. As such, it means 'consisting of two parts'. There is no dual form of the pronominal stem *ubhaya*. The declension of this pronominal stem is as follows :

	Singular	Plural
prathamā	*ubhayaḥ*	*ubhaye*
dvitīyā	*ubhayam*	*ubhayān*
tṛtīyā	*ubhayena*	*ubhayaiḥ*
caturthī	*ubhayasmai*	*ubhayebhyaḥ*
pañcamī	*ubhayasmāt*	*ubhayebhyaḥ*
ṣaṣṭhī	*ubhayasya*	*ubhayeṣām*
saptamī	*ubhayasmin*	*ubhayeṣu*
sambodhana	*he ubhaya!*	*he ubhaye!*

The terms *ḍatara* and *ḍatama* which come after the pronominal stem *ubhaya* in the set consisting of sarva, etc. are affixes. By virtue of the paribhāṣā *pratyayagrahaṇe...tadantasya grahaṇam* (Abhyankar, 23), these affixes signify the words which end with these affixes even though these affixes have been enunciated in the context of saṁjñāvidhi. The reason is that in accordance with the maxim *na kevalā prakṛtiḥ prayoktavyā, nāpi kevalaḥ pratyayaḥ* (BM, I, p. 216), the bare affixes are not worth using in a sentence. Moreover, they do not serve any purpose so far as their sarvanāman-designation is concerned. It is for this reason that in order to impart meaningfulness to the terms *ḍatara* and *ḍatama*, these terms are taken to signify the words that end with these affixes. The sūtras which enjoin these affixes are : *kiṁyattadornirdhāraṇe dvyorekasya ḍatarac, vā bahūnāṁ jātiparipraśne ḍatamac* and *ekācca prācām* Pā. 5. 3. 92-94. By introducing these affixes after the pronominal stems, *kim, yad, tad* and *eka*, we obtain eight words which are to be designated as *sarvanāman*. These are : (1) *katara* 'which of two' (2) *katama* 'which of many' (3) *yatara* 'which of two' (4) *yatama* 'which of many' (5) *tatara* 'that of two' (6) *tatama* 'that of many' (7) *ekatara* 'one of two' and (8) *ekatama* 'one of many'. Since these words are assigned the sarvanāman-designation, their declension will be like that of the pronominal stem *sarva*.

Next come the words *anya* 'other', *anyatara* 'either', *itara* 'other', *tvat* 'other' and *tva* 'other'. They are also sarvanāman. Therefore they will also be declined like *sarva*.

The word *nema* is the next in order. This word is to be designated *sarvanāman* when it means 'half'. It does not get sarvanāman-designation when it is used in other senses (for other senses than 'half' see Apte's dictionary, s. v. *nema* and also cf. Bhaimī, I, p. 210). Its declension will be discussed under sūtra (159).

The next word is *sama*. It is used in two senses : (1) all and (2) equal. This word is a pronominal stem when it is synonymous with *sarva* 'all'. It is not so when it is synoymous with *tulya* 'equal'. We come to know this by Pāṇini's use of *samānām* in *yathāsaṁkhyamanudeśaḥ samānām* (23). This would have been *sameṣām* if the word, in that sense, had been a pronominal stem.

The next pronominal word is *sima* 'all'. This is also declined like *sarva*.

(155) पूर्वपरावरदक्षिणोत्तरापराधराणि व्यवस्थायामसंज्ञायाम्। *pūrva-parāvaradakṣiṇottarāparādharāṇi vyavasthāyāmasaṁjñāyām.* 1. 1. 34

लघु० – एतेषां व्यवस्थायामसंज्ञायां च सर्वनामसंज्ञा गणसूत्रात् सर्वत्र या प्राप्ता सा जसि वा स्यात्। पूर्वे, पूर्वाः। असंज्ञायां किम्? उत्तराः कुरवः। स्वाभिधेयापेक्षावधिनियमो व्यवस्था। व्यवस्थायां किम् ? दक्षिणा गाथकाः। कुशला इत्यर्थः। *eteṣāṁ vyavasthāyām asaṁjñāyāṁ ca sarvanāmasaṁjñā gaṇasūtrāt sarvatra yā prāptā sā jasi vā syāt. pūrve, pūrvāḥ. asaṁjñāyāṁ kim? uttarāḥ kuravaḥ. svābhidheyā-pekṣāvadhiniyamo vyavasthā. vyavasthāyāṁ kim? dakṣiṇā gāthakāḥ. kuśalā ityarthaḥ.*

Trans. : The seven words (*pūrva, para, avara, dakṣiṇa, uttara, apara* and *adhara*) which are assigned the sarvanāman-designation in every case by the gaṇasūtra are optionally designated so before *jas*-affix, provided they are employed in the sense of relative position (*vyavasthā*) and not used as proper names (*asaṁjñāyām*). Ex. *pūrve, pūrvāḥ*. Why do we say, 'not when they are names'? Ex. *uttarāḥ kuravaḥ*. (When the word is used as an appellation for the Kuru country, it is not a pronominal stem). The relative situation (*vyavasthā*) consists in the specification of a determinate point with reference to which something is described by the word itself. Why do we say,'when employed in the sense of a relative situation?' Ex. *dakṣiṇā gāthakāḥ, kuśalā ityarthaḥ*. (Here the word *dakṣiṇa* means 'expert' and does not signify any relation in space).

PP. *pūrvaparāvaradakṣiṇottarāparādharāṇi vyavasthāyām asaṁjñāyām vibhāṣā jasi sarvanāmāni.*

Eluc. : The words *vibhāṣā* and *jasi* are carried over from the sūtra *vibhāṣā jasi* Pā. 1. 1. 32. The term *sarvanāmāni* is lent into this sūtra from *sarvādīni sarvanāmāni* Pā. 1. 1. 27. The compound *pūrvaparāvara-dakṣiṇottarāparādharāṇi* occurring in the sūtra is an itaretaradvandva, which is analysed like this : *pūrvañca parañca avarañca dakṣiṇañca uttarañca aparañca adharañca pūrvaparāvaradakṣiṇottarāparādharāṇi*. The word *asaṁjñā* is a nañ-tatpuruṣa, the analysis of which is : *na saṁjñā asaṁjñā, tasyām*. The completed sūtra means : If these seven words are employed to convey the sense of relation in time and space (*vyavasthā*) and not as proper names, then their sarvanāman-designation is optional before the sup-affix *jas*.

The term *vyavasthā* requires some clarification. When we specify some determinate point (*avadhi*) in space or time and relate it to what is signified by one of the seven words used in the sūtra, vyavasthā is implied. To illustrate, let us take the example of Delhi. When we say 'Delhi is south (*dakṣiṇa*)', we require a point in space to which Delhi is in the south. We can mention the Himalayas in this context since Delhi is to the south of the Himalayas. This is with reference to space. Similarly some determinate point can be cited in respect of time. When we use an expression '*pūrve pāṇḍavādayaḥ*', we desire to know 'earlier than whom'. In reply we say 'earlier than us'. This is in relation to a determinate point of time about which we are speaking. Such usages imply vyavasthā. When these seven words are employed in this sense, they are optionally designated as *sarvanāman* before *jas*. The counter-illustration given in the Laghu makes the point clear. When the word *dakṣiṇa* is used in the sense other than that of vyavasthā, it is not to be designated as *sarvanāman*. As such, the affix *jas* is not optionally replaced by *śī* by the present sūtra and hence the nominative plural form of the word *dakṣiṇa* will be *dakṣiṇāḥ* only, as in the illustration *dakṣiṇā gāthakāḥ* since here the meaning of the word *dakṣiṇa* is 'adept'. Besides this, none of the seven words are pronominal stems when they are used as appellations as shown in the counter-example *uttarāḥ kuravaḥ*. Although the word *uttara* conveys the sense of vyavasthā in this example with reference to Sumeru mountain as a determinate point, it is also a name of the Kuru country. Being a name, it ceases to be a pronominal stem. Consequently, it would have only one form *uttarāḥ* in the nominative plural since the plural affix *jas* of the first triplet will not be optionally replaced by *śī*. So these seven words employed in the sense of relative situation (*vyavasthā*) will have two forms when declined with the plural affix of the first triplet. The forms of these words in the nominative plural are : *pūrve, pūrvāḥ; pare, parāḥ; avare, avarāḥ; dakṣiṇe, dakṣiṇāḥ; uttare, uttarāḥ; apare, aparāḥ; adhare, adharāḥ.*

(156) स्वमज्ञातिधनाख्यायाम् । ***svamajñātidhanākhyāyām.* 1. 1. 35**

लघु० – ज्ञातिधनान्यवाचिनः स्वशब्दस्य प्राप्ता संज्ञा जसि वा । स्वे, स्वाः । आत्मीया, आत्मान इति वा । ज्ञातिधनवाचिनस्तु स्वाः । ज्ञातयोऽर्था वा । *jñātidhanānyavācinaḥ svaśabdasya prāptā saṁjñā jasi vā. sve, svāḥ. ātmīyā ātmāna iti vā. jñātidhanavācinas tu svāḥ. jñātayo 'rthā vā.*

Trans. : The word *sva* signifying other than a kinsman or wealth optionally obtains the sarvanāman-designation before *jas*. Ex. *sve, svāḥ* in the sense of 'own' or 'selves'. In the sense of kinsmen or wealth, the form of *sva* in the nominative plural is *svāḥ* (only).

PP. *svam ajñātidhanākhyāyām vibhāṣā jasi sarvanāma.*

Eluc. : The words *vibhāṣā* and *jasi* are carried over into the present sūtra from *vibhāṣā jasi* Pā. 1. 1. 32. The word *sarvanāmāni* is carried over from *sarvādīni sarvanāmāni* Pā. 1. 1. 26 and has been changed into singular by the process of vacanavipariṇāma to make it syntactically agree with the word *svam*. The compound *ajñātidhanākhyāyām* is nañ-tatpuruṣa which contains in it dvandva-seeded ṣaṣṭhītatpuruṣa which is analysed as : *jñātiś ca dhanañ ca jñātidhane tayor ākhyā jñātidhanākhyā tasyām = jñātidhanākhyāyām. na jñātidhanākhyāyām ajñātidhanākhyāyām* (*nañ-tatpuruṣa*). Taking into account the carried over insertions and the analysis of the compound, we interpret the sūtra as follows : If the word *sva* is used in the senses other than that of kinsmen or property, then it is optionally designated as *sarvanāman* when followed by the plural affix of the first triplet of the inflectional endings. The word has four denotata : 1. self 2. own 3. kinsmen and 4. wealth. When the word *sva* is used in the first two senses, it obtains the sarvanāman-designation. This obtained designation is optional before *jas*. When *sva* is used to convey the sense of either 'kinsmen' or 'wealth', it is not designated as *sarvanāman* and its declension will be like that of *rāma*.

(157) अन्तरं बहिर्योगोपसंव्यानयोः । *antaraṁ bahiryogopasaṁvyānayoḥ*. 1. 1. 36

लघु० – बाह्ये परिधानीये चार्थेऽन्तरशब्दस्य प्राप्ता संज्ञा जसि वा । अन्तरे, अन्तरा वा गृहाः, बाह्या इत्यर्थः । अन्तरे, अन्तरा वा शाटकाः, परिधानीया इत्यर्थः । *bāhye paridhānīye cārthe 'ntaraśabdasya prāptā saṁjñā jasi vā. antare, antarā vā gṛhāḥ, bāhyā ityarthaḥ. antare, antarā vā śāṭakāḥ, paridhānīyā ityarthaḥ.*

Trans. : When the word *antara* is used to convey the sense of either 'outside' or 'clothing', it optionally obtains the sarvanāman-designation before *jas*. (In the illustration) *antare, antarā vā gṛhāḥ*, it has the sense of 'outside' (and in the illustration) *antare, antarā vā śāṭakāḥ*, it has the sense of undergarment.

PP. *antaram bahiryogopasaṁvyānayoḥ jasi vibhāṣā sarvanāma.*

Eluc. : The words *vibhāṣā* and *jasi* are carried over from the sūtra *vibhāṣā jasi* Pā. 1. 1. 32. The word *sarvanāmāni* is carried over from *sarvādīni sarvanāmāni* Pā. 1. 1. 26 and is changed into the singular by the process of vacanavipariṇāma to make it syntactically agree with the word *antaram*. The word *bahiryogopasaṁvyānayoḥ* is a dvandva compound, which is in the genitive dual. It is analysed as *bahiryogaś ca upasaṁvyānaṁ ca bahiryogopasaṁvyāne, tayoḥ*. The word *bahiryoga* itself is a tṛtīyā-tatpuruṣa. The Nyāsa analyses it as : *bahir ityanenānāvṛtadeśa ucyate. tena yogo bahiryogaḥ* (KN, I, p. 144). Thus the sūtra comes to mean : The sarvanāman-designation, which is already available if the word *antara* is used to convey the sense of 'the things connected with the exterior location' or 'undergarment', is assigned to it optionally when the plural affix of the first triplet follows. When it is a sarvanāman, the nominative plural form of *antara* is *antare* and when it is not, its form would be *antarāḥ*.

If the word *antara* carries a sense different from those mentioned above, then it is not designated as *sarvanāman* and consequently its declension would be like that of *rāma*. The counter-example given in the Kāśikā is : *anayor grāmayor antare tāpasaḥ prativasati*. In this illustration it is used in the sense of 'between' and as such it is not a pronominal stem. The locative singular form of *antara* in this case is *antare* and not *antarasmin*. The reason is that it is not a pronominal stem and as a consequence the singular affix *ṅi* of the seventh triplet is not replaced by *smin* by the rule *ṅasiṅyoḥ smātsminau* (153).

(158) पूर्वादिभ्यो नवभ्यो वा । ***pūrvādibhyo navabhyo vā*. 7. 1. 16**
लघु० - एभ्यो ङसिङ्योः स्मात्स्मिनौ वा स्तः । पूर्वस्मात्, पूर्वात्। पूर्वस्मिन्, पूर्वे। एवम् परादीनाम्। शेषं सर्ववत्। *ebhyo ṅasiṅyoḥ smātsminau vā staḥ. pūrvasmāt, pūrvāt. pūrvasmin, pūrve. evam parādīnām. śeṣaṁ sarvavat.*

Trans. : The sup-affixes *ṅasi* and *ṅi* are optionally replaced by *smāt* and *smin*, in this order, when they are introduced after the nine pronominal stems beginning with *pūrva*. Similar is the case with the pronominal stems beginning with *para*. The rest is like *sarva*.

PP. *pūrvādibhyaḥ navabhyaḥ ṅasiṅyoḥ smātsminau vā* (*ataḥ sarvanāmnaḥ aṅgasya*).

Eluc. : The compound words *ṅasiṅyoḥ* and *smātsminau* are carried over into the present sūtra from *ṅasiṅyoḥ smātsminau* (153). With these words, the completed sūtra means : The substitute elements *smāt* and *smin* optionally and respectively replace *ṅasi* and *ṅi* introduced after the nine pronominal stems beginning with *pūrva*. The nine stems occurring in the sūtras (155, 156 and 157) are : 1. *pūrva* 'prior, first' 2. *para* 'subsequent, other' 3. *avara* 'less, lower', 4. *dakṣiṇa* 'right' 5. *uttara* 'higher, upper, ahead' 6. *apara* 'other' 7. *adhara* 'lower' 8. *sva* 'own, one's own' and *antara* 'outer, clothing'. The preceding three sūtras assign optionally sarvanāman-designation to these nine words before *jas* when they are employed to convey the specific meanings. The present rule prescribes the optional substitute elements *smāt* and *smin* in place of *ṅasi* and *ṅi*. In conclusion, we can say that the three affixes *jas*, *ṅasi* and *ṅi* introduced after these nine words are optionally and respectively replaced by *śī*, *smāt* and *smin*. To illustrate this grammatical operation, the declension of the word *pūrva* is given below :

	Singular	Dual	Plural
prathamā	*pūrvaḥ*	*pūrvau*	*pūrve, pūrvāḥ*
dvitīyā	*pūrvam*	*pūrvau*	*pūrvān*

tṛtīyā	*pūrveṇa*	*pūrvābhyām*	*pūrvaiḥ*
caturthī	*pūrvasmai*	*pūrvābhyām*	*pūrvebhyaḥ*
pañcamī	*pūrvasmāt, d,* *purvāt, d*	*pūrvābhyām*	*pūrvebhyaḥ*
ṣaṣṭhī	*pūrvasya*	*pūrvayoḥ*	*pūrveṣām*
saptamī	*pūrvasmin,* *purve*	*pūrvayoḥ*	*pūrveṣu*
sambodhana	*he pūrva!*	*he pūrvau!*	*he pūrve! he pūrvāḥ!*

The declension of the remaining eight pronominal stems will be like that of the pronominal stem *pūrva*.

(159) प्रथमचरमतयाल्पार्धकतिपयनेमाश्च । *prathamacaramatayālpārdhakatipayanemāśca.* 1. 1. 33

लघु० – एते जसि उक्तसंज्ञा वा स्युः । प्रथमे, प्रथमाः । तयः प्रत्ययः । द्वितये, द्वितयाः । शेषं रामवत् । नेमे, नेमाः । शेषं सर्ववत् । *ete jasi uktasaṁjñā vā syuḥ. prathame, prathamāḥ. tayaḥ pratyayaḥ. dvitaye, dvitayāḥ. śeṣaṁ rāmavat. neme, nemāḥ. śeṣaṁ sarvavat.*

Trans. : The words *prathama* 'first', *carama* 'last', those which end in the affix *tayap, alpa* 'little, less', *ardha* 'half', *katipaya* 'some' and *nema* 'half' are optionally designated as *sarvanāman* before the sup-affix *jas*. Ex. *prathame, prathamāḥ. taya* is an affix. *dvitaye, dvitayāḥ.* The rest will be like *rāma. neme, nemāḥ.* The rest will be like *sarva.*

PP. *prathamacaramatayālpārdhakatipayanemāḥ ca jasi vibhāṣā sarvanāmāni.*

Eluc. : The words *jasi* and *vibhāṣā* are carried over from *vibhāṣā jasi* Pā. 1. 1. 32. The term *sarvanāmāni* is lent into the present sūtra from *sarvādīni sarvanāmāni* Pā. 1. 1. 27. With these insertions, the sūtra means: The words *prathama, carama,* those ending in the affix *tayap, alpa, ardha, katipaya* and *nema* are optionally termed *sarvanāman* when followed by *jas,* the plural affix of the first triplet. Leaving aside the word *nema,* no other word enunciated in the present sūtra is enlisted in the set beginning with *sarva.* So, the declension of these words will be like that of *rāma* except before *jas.* When the affix *jas* follows, it will be optionally replaced by *śī* in the case of these words. As such, we have two forms of these words in the nominative plural : *prathame, prathamāḥ; carame,* *caramāḥ; dvitaye, dvitayāḥ; alpe, alpāḥ; ardhe, ardhāḥ; katipaye, katipayāḥ.* The word *nema* will also have two forms with the plural affix of the first triplet : *neme* and *nemāḥ*. The rest of the declension of this word will be like that of *sarva*.

16. वा० – तीयस्य ङित्सु वा । *tīyasya ṅitsu vā.*

लघु० – द्वितीयस्मै, द्वितीयाय इत्यादि । एवं तृतीयः । *dvitīyasmai, dvitīyāya ityādi. evaṁ tṛtīyaḥ.*

Trans. : The words ending in *tīya*-affix are to be optionally designated as *sarvanāman* before sup-affixes having the guttural nasal *ṅ* as *it*.

Eluc. : The element *tīya* is an affix. It stands for a word which ends in this affix since no purpose is served in assigning a sarvanāman-designation to an affix. This is precisely the reason why in the present case, the paribhāṣā *saṁjñāvidhau pratyayagrahaṇe tadantagrahaṇaṁ nāsti* (Abhyankar, 27) does not block the paribhāṣā *pratyayagrahaṇe yasmāt sa vihitastadādestadantasya grahaṇam* (Abhyankar, 23).

The *tīya*-affix is introduced after *dvi* and *tri* by *dvestīyaḥ* (1173) and *treḥ samprasāraṇaṁ ca* (1174) and thus the words *dvitīya* and *tṛtīya* are derived. It is these two words which are optionally designated as *sarvanāman* before those sup-affixes which have the phoneme *ṅ* as *it*. Only four of the sup-affixes are *ṅit*. These are: *ṅe, ṅasi, ṅas* and *ṅi*.

The words which end in *tīya*-affix are not enumerated in the list consisting of *sarva*, etc. Hence they are not designated as *sarvanāman*. By the present vārttika, the words *dvitīya* and *tṛtīya* are optionally assigned the sarvanāman-designation before *ṅit* sup-affixes. When they are sarvanāman, the rules *sarvanāmnaḥ smai* (152) and *ṅasiṅyoḥ smātsminau* (153) will apply and as a consequence the singular affix of the fourth triplet (*ṅe*) will be replaced by *smai* and the ablative and the locative singular sup-affixes *ṅasi* and *ṅi* will respectively be replaced by *smāt* and *smin*. As far as the singular affix *ṅas* is concerned, there is no distinguishing characteristic brought about by the sarvanāman-designation in the neuter and masculine forms of these words but in declining the feminine form *dvitīyā* in the genitive singular the sarvanāman-designation has its role. In this case the rule *sarvanāmnaḥ syāḍḍhrasvaśca* (219) applies. The augment *syāṭ* is inserted at the head of the *ṅas* and the short vowel replaces the aṅga-final long vowel of *āp*. Thus the resultant form in the genitive singular will be *dvitīyasyāḥ*. The declension of the word *dvitīya* will be as follows :

	Singular	Dual	Plural
prathamā	*dvitīyaḥ*	*dvitīyau*	*dvitīyāḥ*
dvitīyā	*dvitīyam*	*dvitīyau*	*dvitīyān*
tṛtīyā	*dvitīyena*	*dvitīyābhyām*	*dvitīyaiḥ*
caturthī	*dvitīyasmai, dvitīyāya*	*dvitīyābhyām*	*dvitīyebhyaḥ*
pañcamī	*dvitīyasmāt, dvitīyāt*	*dvitīyābhyām*	*dvitīyebhyaḥ*
ṣaṣṭhī	*dvitīyasya*	*dvitīyayoḥ*	*dvitīyānām*
saptamī	*dvitīyasmin, dvitīye*	*dvitīyayoḥ*	*dvitīyeṣu*
sambodhana	*he dvitīya!*	*he dvitīyau!*	*he dvitīyāḥ*

The declension of the word *tṛtīya* will be like that of the word *dvitīya*.

(160) जराया जरसन्यतरस्याम्। *jarāyā jarasanyatarasyām.* 7. 2. 101
लघु० – अजादौ विभक्तौ। *ajādau vibhaktau.*

Trans. : The substitute *jaras* optionally replaces the aṅga *jarā* when a vowel-initial affix designated as *vibhakti* follows.

PP. *aci vibhaktau jarāyāḥ jaras anyatarasyām* (*aṅgasya*).

Eluc. : The *aci* and *vibhaktau* respectively come from *aci ra ṛtaḥ* Pā. 7. 2. 100 and *aṣṭana ā vibhaktau* Pā. 7. 2. 84. Since *aci* qualifies *vibhaktau*, it assumes the adjectival form as *ajādau* (tadādividhi) by virtue of the vārttika *yasmin vidhis tadādāvalgrahaṇe* Mbh 1. 1. 72 vtk 29. Thus the sūtra comes to mean : When a sup-affix (vibhakti) beginning with a vowel follows, the aṅga *jarā* is optionally replaced by *jaras*.

This sūtra has been presented here in the context of the declension of the word *nirjara*. It is a compound word. Its analysis is : *nirgato jarāyāḥ*. This compound is formed by the vārttika *nirādayaḥ krāntādyarthe pañcamyā* (Mbh 2. 2. 18 saunāga vtk 18). The long vowel *ā* occurring at the end of the stem *jarā* is shortened by *gostriyorupasarjanasya* (948). In the nominative singular we introduce the affix *su* after it and obtain the word *nirjaraḥ* after rutva and visarga.

In the nominative dual, we have the sup-affix *au* introduced after *nirjara*. The sup-affix is also designated as *vibhakti*. The affix *au* is a vowel-initial. It is in such a context that the present sūtra prescribes the replacement *jaras* optionally in place of the word *jarā*. What is the rationale for the present rule in the context of the word *nirjara*, which is different from *jarā*? The answer to this problem lies in the following paribhāṣās :

लघु० - पदाङ्गाधिकारे तस्य च तदन्तस्य च (प०) । *padāṅgādhikāre tasya ca tadantasya ca* (Abhyankar, 29).

Trans. : A grammatical operation prescribed for a word in the governing domain of pada or aṅga is performed on that word as well as on that which ends with that word.

Eluc. : The sūtra *padasya* Pā. 8. 1. 16 is a governing rule. Its domain extends up to 8. 3. 54. The other sūtra *aṅgasya* Pā. 6. 4. 1 is also a governing rule extending up to the end of the seventh chapter. In both the governing domains, the replacement that has been enjoined with respect to a particular word comes in place of that word or in place of that which ends with that word. In this particular context the *jaras*-replacement is prescribed to come in place of the word *jarā*. According to this paribhāṣā, this replacement is to come in place of the word *jarā* as well as in place of that which ends with the word *jarā* since the grammatical operation in the form of this replacement has been prescribed in the governing domain of *aṅgasya* Pā. 6. 4. 1.

Now since the substitute consists of more than one *al* (phoneme), it will replace the whole substituendum by *anekāl śit sarvasya* (45). In this case the substitute *jaras* is *anekāl*. Therefore, the whole word *nirjara* which ends with the word *jarā* is likely to be replaced by *jaras*. This undesirable contingency is warded off by the following paribhāṣā :

लघु० - निर्दिश्यमानस्य आदेशा भवन्ति (प०) । *nirdiśyamānasya ādeśā bhavanti* (Abhyankar, 12).

Trans. : Substitutes take the place of that which is actually enunciated (in a rule).

Eluc. : Whatever is actually enunciated as a substituendum in a rule is to be replaced by the substitute. In the sūtra *jarāyā jarasanyatarasyām* (160), the word *jarā*, being in the genitive singular, has actually been mentioned as a substituendum. So, only the *jarā*-portion will be replaced by *jaras*. Now the problem arises with regard to the nature or form of the substituendum. The word *nirjara* ends with *jara*, and not with *jarā*. This problem is addressed by the next meta-rule :

लघु० – एकदेशविकृतमनन्यवद् (प०)। इति जरशब्दस्य जरस्। निर्जरसौ। निर्जरसः। इत्यादि। पक्षे हलादौ च रामवत्। *ekadeśavikṛtam ananyavad* (Abhyankar, 37). *iti jaraśabdasya jaras. nirjarasau, nirjarasaḥ. ityādi. pakṣe halādau ca rāmavat.*

Trans. : That which has undergone a change in regard to one of its parts, is by no means something else (than what it was before the change had taken place). So *jaras* replaces *jara*. Hence (the forms will be) *nirjarasau, nirjarasaḥ*, etc. In the other alternative, before a consonant-initial sup-affix, the declension will be like that of *rāma*.

Eluc. : In the Mahābhāṣya, this paribhāṣā (Abhyankar, 37) is illustrated by the case of a dog. It, having lost its ears or tail, does not thereby lose its identity.[1] In the same manner the word *jarā*, altered by the shortening of a long *ā* at the end by *gostriyorupasarjanasya* (948) is construed as the same as it was before the shortening of the long *ā*. Hence the substitute *jaras* will optionally replace the substituendum *jara* before *au* which is a vowel-initial sup-affix and the dual form of *nirjara* will be *nirjarasau*. In the other alternative, the form of *nirjara* will be declined like *rāma* : *nirjarau*. When the plural sup-affix *bhis* is replaced with *ais* by *ato bhisa ais* (141) in the instrumental plural, the rule *jarāyā jarasanyatarasyām* (160) does not apply because of the paribhāṣā *sannipātalakṣaṇo vidhiranimittaṁ tadvighātasya* (Abhyankar, 85). The cause of replacement by *ais* can't be undone by *ais* itself.

The declension of *nirjara* in all its forms is as follows:

	Singular	Dual	Plural
prathamā	*nirjaraḥ*	*nirjarasau, nirjarau*	*nirjarasaḥ, nirjarāḥ*
dvitīyā	*nirjarasam, nirjaram*	*nirjarasau, nirjarau*	*nirjarasaḥ, nirjarān*
tṛtīyā	*nirjarasā nirjareṇa*	*nirjarābhyām*	*nirjaraiḥ*

1. *tad yathā śvā karṇe vā pucche vā chinne śvaiva bhavati nāśvo na gardabha iti.* Mahābhāṣya on Pā. 1. 1. 56, vtk 9.

caturthī	*nirjarase, nirjarāya*	*nirjarābhyām*	*nirjarebhyaḥ*
pañcamī	*nirjarasaḥ, nirjarāt*	*nirjarābhyām*	*nirjarebhyaḥ*
ṣaṣṭhī	*nirjarasaḥ, nirjarasya*	*nirjarasoḥ, nirjarayoḥ*	*nirjarasām, nirjarāṇām*
saptamī	*nirjarasi, nirjare*	*nirjarasoḥ, nirjarayoḥ*	*nirjareṣu*
sambodhana	*he nirjara!*	*he nirjarasau! nirjarau!*	*he nirjarasaḥ! nirjarāḥ!*

Here comes to an end the declension of the masculine stems ending in a short *a*. Now begins the declension of the masculine nominal stems ending in a long *ā*.

लघु० – विश्वपाः । *viśvapāḥ.*

Eluc. : The word *viśvapā* is an upapada compound which is analysed as : *viśvaṁ pāti. viśva + ṅas* (<-- *am*) *pā + vic*. The affix *vic* is introduced after the root *pā* by the rule *anyebhyo 'pi dṛśyante* Pā. 3. 2. 75. Nothing of it remains as all the elements constituting it are elided by different rules. In the nominative singular we have *viśvapā + su*. After the vowel *u* of *su*, which is *it* by *upadeśe 'janunāsika it* (28), has been elided by *tasya lopaḥ* (3), we have *viśvapā* + s. After the application of *sasajuṣo ruḥ* (104) and *kharavasānayorvisarjanīyaḥ* (93) we obtain *viśvapāḥ* in the nominative singular.

When we introduce the dual sup-affix of the first triplet, we have *viśvapā + au*. At this stage, the rule *vṛddhireci* (33) becomes available for application. When it is blocked by the sūtra *prathamayoḥ pūrvasavarṇaḥ* (125), the following negative rule ensues :

(161) दीर्घाज्जसि च । *dīrghājjasi ca.* **6. 1. 105**

लघु० – दीर्घाज् जसि इचि च परे न पूर्वसवर्णदीर्घः । वृद्धिः – विश्वपौ । विश्वपाः । हे विश्वपाः! विश्वपाम् । विश्वपौ । *dīrghāj jasi ici ca pare na pūrvasavarṇadīrghaḥ. vṛddhiḥ -- viśvapau. viśvapāḥ. he viśvapāḥ! viśvapām, viśvapau.*

Trans. : When a vowel of *jas* or *ic*-pratyāhāra follows an aṅga-final long vowel, the replacement by a single long vowel, homogeneous with the preceding, does not take place (in place of both).

PP. *dīrghāt jasi ici ca pūrvaparayoḥ ekaḥ pūrvasavarṇaḥ dīrghaḥ na* (*saṁhitāyām*).

Eluc. : The sūtra *ekaḥ pūrvaparayoḥ* Pā. 6. 1. 84 is a governing rule. All the words of this sūtra recur here also. The words *pūrvasavarṇaḥ* and *dīrghaḥ* are respectively carried over into this sūtra from *prathamayoḥ pūrvasavarṇaḥ* Pā. 6. 1. 102 and *akaḥ savarṇe dīrghaḥ* Pā. 6. 1. 101. The words *ici* and *na* come from *nādici* Pā. 6. 1. 104. The carried over insertions having been taken into account, the present sūtra means : When the sup-affix *jas* and the elements denoted by the abbreviatory term *ic* follow an aṅga-final long vowel, the long vowel homogeneous with the preceding vowel of the aṅga does not replace both the aṅga-final long vowel and the initial vowel of the sup-affix *jas* or any of the elements signified by *ic*-pratyāhāra.

In the illustration *viśvapā + au --> viśvapau*, the vowel *ā* following the phoneme *p* is a long vowel and the dual affix of the first triplet is *au* which is one of elements denoted by the abbreviatory term *ic*. The condition, which is laid down by the present rule, to negate the long vowel substitution homogeneous with the first of two contiguous vowels, is available. Hence the homogeneous long vowel replacement, due by *prathamayoḥ...* (125), is blocked by the present rule. As a consequence, the rule *vṛddhireci* (33) applies. After the vṛddhi-vowel *au* has replaced both the aṅga-final long vowel and the sup-affix *au*, which is denoted by *ic*-pratyāhāra, we obtain the resultant form : *viśvapau.*

When we introduce the plural sup-affix of the first triplet, we have *viśvapā + jas --> viśvapā + as.* At this stage, the long vowel substitution homogeneous with the preceding (*pūrvasavarṇadīrgha*) is blocked by the present sūtra. Then *akaḥ savarṇe dīrghaḥ* (42) applies and the homogeneous long vowel substitution takes place. Thus the desired form *viśvapāḥ* is obtained.

These two forms of *viśvapā* could have been obtained otherwise also. In the dual nominative, the sūtra *nādici* (126) could have served the purpose by blocking *prathamayoḥ...* (125) thus allowing *vṛddhireci* (33) to operate. In the nominative plural, no undesirable contingency would be incurred, even if the sūtra *prathamayoḥ...* (125) were applied to bring about the long vowel substitution homogeneous with the preceding (*pūrvasavarṇadīrgha*) to obtain *viśvapāḥ*. Even then *dīrghājjasi ca* (161), which is a prerequisite with regard to such forms as *gauryau, gauryaḥ*, etc., has been given here because of its logical viability,[1] for this rule also becomes available in the present context.

---

1. Cf. *yadyapīha auṅi nādici ityeva siddham. jasi tu satyapi pūrvasavarṇadīrghe kṣatir nāsti. tathāpi gauryau gauryaḥ ityādyarthaṁ sūtram ihāpi nyāyyatvād upanyastam.* SK, I, p. 241.

In declining the form of *viśvapā* with a singular sup-affix of the second triplet, we apply *ami pūrvaḥ* (134) which blocks *prathamayoḥ pūrvasavarṇaḥ* (125) and we have *viśvapām*. The declension of *viśvapā* with a dual affix of the second triplet is like that of the nominative dual. When we decline *viśvapā* with the plural affix *śas* of the second triplet, the rule *prathamayoḥ pūrvasavarṇaḥ* (125) becomes available for application but it is blocked by the coming sūtra *āto dhātoḥ* (166) in the following way :

(162) सुडनपुंसकस्य । *suḍanapuṁsakasya*. 1. 1. 43

लघु० – स्वादिपञ्चवचनानि सर्वनामस्थानसंज्ञानि स्युरक्लीबस्य । *svādipañcavacanāni sarvanāmasthānasaṁjñāni syur aklībasya.*

Trans. : Let the five sup-affixes denoted by the abbreviatory term *suṭ* be called *sarvanāmasthāna* when introduced after a stem other than a neuter one.

PP. *suṭ anapuṁsakasya sarvanāmasthānam.*

Eluc. : The word *sarvanāmasthānam* is carried over into the present sūtra from *śi sarvanāmasthānam* Pā. 1. 1. 42. The word *anapuṁsakasya* is a nañ-tatpuruṣa compound which can be analysed as : *na napuṁsakasya* --> *anapuṁsakasya*. The negative particle used in the compound carries the sense of exclusion (*paryudāsa*). Thus the meaning of the sūtra is as follows : The elements denoted by *suṭ*-pratyāhāra are termed *sarvanāmasthāna* when introduced after a stem which is either masculine or feminine. The *suṭ*-pratyāhāra is formed with the singular sup-affix (*su*) of the first triplet with the last consonantal phoneme of the dual sup-affix (*auṭ*) of the second triplet. It signifies the first five sup-affixes. If these five affixes are introduced after a stem other than a neuter one, then these affixes are termed *sarvanāmasthāna*. The purpose of this designation is served in the following aphorism.

(163) स्वादिष्वसर्वनामस्थाने । *svādiṣvasarvanāmasthāne*. 1. 4. 17

लघु० – कप्प्रत्ययावधिषु स्वादिष्वसर्वनामस्थानेषु पूर्वं पदं स्यात् । *kappratyayāvadhiṣu svādiṣvasarvanāmasthāneṣu pūrvaṁ padaṁ syāt.*

Trans. : When the affixes beginning with *su* and ending with *kap*, not being sarvanāmasthāna, follow, let a (preceding) stem be designated as *pada*.

PP. *svādiṣu asarvanāmasthāne padam.*

Eluc. : The word *padam* is carried over from *suptiṅantaṁ pādam* Pā. 1. 4. 14. The word *svādiṣu* is a bahuvrīhi compound which is analysed as *su ādir yeṣāṁ te svādayaḥ teṣu = svādiṣu.* The word *asarvanāmasthāne* is a nañ-tatpuruṣa samāsa the analysis of which is : *na sarvanāmasthāne asarvanāmasthāne.* The negative particle here also signifies 'exclusion'. According to Vāsudeva Dīkṣita the singular affix used in *asarvanāma-sthāne* is archaic (*ārṣa*) and it should be construed as conveying the sense of plurality so that it may accord with *svādiṣu* (BM, I, p. 232).

The word *svādi* denotes the class of affixes beginning with the *su* of the sūtra *svaujasamauṭchaṣṭābhyāmbhisṅebhyāmbhyasṅasibhyāmbhyas-ṅasosāṁṅyossup* Pā. 4. 1. 2 and ending with the affix *ka*(*p*) of the sūtra *uraḥprabhṛtibhyaḥ kap* Pā. 5. 4. 151. This is the last affix prescribed in the fifth chapter of the Aṣṭādhyāyī. Thus all the affixes prescribed in the fourth and fifth chapters of the Aṣṭādhyāyī are denoted by *svādi.* The five affixes, namely, *su, au, jas, am* and *auṭ* are called *sarvanāmasthāna.* Leaving aside these affixes, if any of the remaining affixes denoted by *svādi,* follows a stem, then that stem should be assigned the pada-designation.

With the plural affix of the second triplet, we have *viśvapā* + *śas* --> *viśvapā* + *as.* The phoneme *ś* being *it* by *laśakvataddhite* (135) is elided by *tasya lopaḥ* (3). The sup-affix *śas* is a denotatum of *svādi* and is not a sarvanāmasthāna. Hence the pada-designation is available for the nominal stem *viśvapā* before (*ś*)*as.* At this stage, the following sūtra ensues :

(164) यचि भम् । *yaci bham.* 1. 4. 18

लघु० - यकारादिषु अजादिषु च कप्प्रत्ययावधिषु स्वादिष्वसर्वनामस्थानेषु पूर्वं भसंज्ञं स्यात् । *yakārādiṣu ajādiṣu ca kappratyayāvadhiṣu svādiṣv asarvanāma-sthāneṣu pūrvaṁ bhasaṁjñaṁ syāt.*

Trans. : Let a stem followed by a non-sarvanāmasthāna *svādi* affix beginning with either the phoneme *y* or a vowel (*ac*) be designated as *bha.*

PP. *asarvanāmasthāne svādiṣu yaci bham.*

Eluc. : The words *asarvanāmasthāne* and *svādiṣu* are lent into this sūtra from *svādiṣvasarvanāmasthāne* (163). The word *yaci* is the locative singular form of *yac* which is a samāhāradvandva compound. Its analysis is : *y ca ac ca yac, tasmin yaci.* In accordance with *yasmin vidhis tadādāvalgrahaṇe* Mbh 1. 1. 72 vtk 29, tadādividhi becomes operational and accordingly the term *yaci* means : *yajādiṣu (svādiṣu)*. Taking all these points into account, the sūtra yields the following meaning : If any of the affixes, beginning with the term *su* of the sūtra Pā. 4. 1. 2 and ending with the affix *kap* of the sūtra Pā. 5. 4. 151, which are not sarvanāmasthāna and which begin with either the phoneme *y* or a vowel, follows a stem, then that stem is to be designated as *bha*. In the illustration *viśvapā + as*, the sup-affix that follows the stem *viśvapā* begins with a vowel. Therefore the stem gets the bha-designation.

As a consequence two designations *pada* and *bha* are available with regard to *viśvapā* before *as* (<-- *śas*) respectively by the sūtras *svādiṣvasarvanāmasthāne* (163) and *yaci bham* (164). The following rule decides that only one of the two designations is to be assigned to the stem *viśvapā* before the sup-affix *śas*.

(165) आ कडारादेका संज्ञा । *ā kaḍārādekā saṁjñā*. 1. 4. 1

लघु० – इत ऊर्ध्वं कडाराः कर्मधारये इत्यतः प्राग् एकस्यैकैव संज्ञा ज्ञेया या पराऽनवकाशा च । *ita ūrdhvaṁ 'kaḍārāḥ karmadhāraye' ityataḥ prāg ekasyaikaiva saṁjñā jñeyā yā parā 'navakāśā ca.*

Trans. : From this sūtra up to the rule *kaḍārāḥ karmadhāraye* Pā. 2. 2. 38, only one technical designation, which is the latter and liable to become vacuous, should be assigned to an element.

PP. *ā kaḍārād ekā saṁjñā.*

Eluc. : This is a governing rule. Its domain extends up to the rule *kaḍārāḥ karmadhāraye* Pā. 2. 2. 38. The purpose of the sūtra is to make it clear that wherever more than one technical designation is prescribed in this domain only one of the two becomes applicable. Which of the two designations is to become applicable is decided according to the rule *vipratiṣedhe paraṁ kāryam* (112). When more designations than one are applicable to a single element and the two simultaneously applicable designations appear in equal strength, a situation of conflict (*vipratiṣedha*) is created. In such instances, in accordance with the rule *vipratiṣedhe paraṁ kāryam* (112), the conflict should be resolved by accepting the latter rule and therefore the latter designation as valid. It is also to be borne in mind that the designation which is to be accepted as valid should be such as would be rendered vacuous, if not applied.

In the present illustration *viśvapā + as*, both the bha and pada designations are available. The prescription of bha-designation is subsequent in relation to pada-designation. Moreover, if the pada-designation is accepted applicable and valid, then the bha-designation will not find any opportunity for its application. In other words it will be rendered anavakāśa and hence vacuous. So, in this particular case, the bha-designation, being the latter and otherwise liable to be rendered anavakāśa, will prevail. Thus the stem *viśvapā* gets the bha-designation and the following sūtra presents itself for application :

(166) आतो धातोः । *āto dhātoḥ*. 6. 4. 140

लघु० - आकारान्तो यो धातुस्तदन्तस्य भस्याङ्गस्य लोपः। अलोऽन्त्यस्य। विश्वपः। विश्वपा। विश्वपाभ्याम् इत्यादि। *ākārānto yo dhātus tadantasya bhasyāṅgasya lopaḥ. alo 'ntyasya. viśvapaḥ. viśvapā, viśvapābhyām ityādi.*

Trans. : Let lopa replace the pre-affixal base (*aṅga*) which is also entitled to the bha-designation, if it ends in a verbal root having a long vowel *ā* as its last phoneme. By the rule *alo 'ntyasya* (21), (the long vowel *ā* of the verbal root is replaced by lopa). (The resultant form is) *viśvapaḥ. viśvapā, viśvapābhyām*, etc.

PP. *ātaḥ dhātoḥ bhasya aṅgasya lopaḥ.*

Eluc. : The sūtras *aṅgasya* Pā. 6. 4. 1 and *bhasya* Pā. 6. 4. 129 are governing rules in whose domain the present sūtra occurs. Therefore they recur in this sūtra. The word *lopaḥ* is carried over from *allopo 'naḥ* Pā. 6. 4. 134. The word *ātaḥ* qualifies the word *dhātoḥ*. By tadantavidhi it gives the sense of *ākārāntasya dhātoḥ*. The completed sūtra means : The bha-designated aṅga which ends with a verbal root ending in a long *ā* is to be replaced by lopa. With the help of the paribhāṣā sūtra *alo 'ntyasya* (21), the long *ā* which occurs at the end of the verbal root will be replaced by lopa since *viśvapā* is both aṅga and bha by the sūtras *yasmāt...* (132) and *yaci bham* (164) respectively. After the elision of the long vowel *ā* of the verbal root *pā* we have the form *viśvap + as* --> *viśvapas* --> *viśvapaḥ* (after rutva and visarga).

Similarly to decline the form of *viśvapā* with a singular affix of the third triplet we have *viśvapā + ṭā* --> *viśvapā + ā* --> *viśvap + ā* --> *viśvapā*. Here the same grammatical operation is to be followed as has been done in the case of *viśvapaḥ*. So leaving aside the sarvanāmasthāna sup-affixes, if vowel-initial affixes follow, then the same grammatical process is to be followed. So far as the consonant-initial affixes are concerned, no distinctive grammatical change is brought about.

In this way the nominal stem *viśvapā* will be declined in the following manner :

	Singular	Dual	Plural
prathamā	*viśvapāḥ*	*viśvapau*	*viśvapāḥ*
dvitīyā	*viśvapām*	*viśvapau*	*viśvapaḥ*
tṛtīyā	*viśvapā*	*viśvapābhyām*	*viśvapābhiḥ*
caturthī	*viśvape*	*viśvapābhyām*	*viśvapābhyaḥ*
pañcamī	*viśvapaḥ*	*viśvapābhyām*	*viśvapābhyaḥ*
ṣaṣṭhī	*viśvapaḥ*	*viśvapoḥ*	*viśvapām*
saptamī	*viśvapi*	*viśvapoḥ*	*viśvapāsu*
sambodhana	*he viśvapāḥ!*	*he viśvapau!*	*he viśvapāḥ!*

लघु० – एवं शङ्खध्मादयः । *evaṁ śaṅkhadhmādayaḥ.*

Eluc. : The words such as *śaṅkhadhmā*, etc. will be declined in the same manner. The word *śaṅkhadhmā* 'one who blows a conch' is an upapada compound like *viśvapā*. The verbal root at its end also ends in a long vowel *ā*. In this way, this word does not differ from *viśvapā* from the point of view of grammatical structure. The words *somapā, madhupā*, etc. also fall in the same category.

लघु० – धातोः किम्? हाहान्। *dhātoḥ kim? hāhān.*

Eluc. : The purpose of enunciating the word *dhātoḥ* in the rule is to preclude the elision of the vowel *ā* occurring at the end of a nominal stem if it does not end in a verbal root ending in *ā*. Take, for example, the word *hāhā* which is the name of a specific gandharva and which is a non-derivative word that ends in a long *ā*. Had the word *dhātoḥ* not been enunciated in the sūtra, the long *ā* at the end of the word *hāhā* would have been replaced by lopa, which is not desirable. The word *dhātoḥ* in the sūtra ensures that the long vowel *ā* will be replaced by lopa only when it is at the end of a verbal root. In the illustration *hāhān*, there is no elision of *ā* since it does not belong to a verbal root. Here, after the application of *prathamayoḥ pūrvasavarṇaḥ* (125), the phoneme s of *śas* is replaced by the dental nasal *n* by *tasmācchaso naḥ puṁsi* (136) and we have the form *hāhān* (<-- *hāhās* <-- *hāhā* + *as* <-- *hāhā* + *śas*). In *hāhai* (*hāhā* + *ṅe* --> *hāhā* + *e*), instead of the elision of *ā*, the rule *vṛddhireci* (33) applies and we have *hāhai*. In the ablative and genitive singular, we have *hāhā* + *ṅasi* or *ṅas*. After the elision of the anubandhas of the affixes in both the cases, we have *hāhā* + *as*. The rule *akaḥ savarṇe dīrghaḥ* (42) applies and we obtain the form *hāhāḥ*. Similarly, in respect of *hāhā* + *ām*, we have *hāhām* by the same rule (42). In the case of the locative singular form of *hāhā*, we have *hāhā* + *ṅi*--> *hāhā* + *i*. Here *ādguṇaḥ* (27) applies and we obtain the desired form as *hāhe*. The declension of the word *hāhā* is given below so that a comparison may be made with that of the word *viśvapā* :

	Singular	Dual	Plural
prathamā	*hāhāḥ*	*hāhau*	*hāhāḥ*
dvitīyā	*hāhām*	*hāhau*	*hāhān*
tṛtīyā	*hāhā*	*hāhābhyām*	*hāhābhiḥ*
caturthī	*hāhai*	*hāhābhyām*	*hāhābhyaḥ*
pañcamī	*hāhāḥ*	*hāhābhyām*	*hāhābhyaḥ*
ṣaṣṭhī	*hāhāḥ*	*hāhauḥ*	*hāhām*
saptamī	*hāhe*	*hāhauḥ*	*hāhāsu*
sambodhana	*he hāhāḥ!*	*he hāhau!*	*he hāhāḥ!*

Here comes to an end the declension of the masculine stems that end in a long *ā*.

Now begins the process of declining the nominal stems in the masculine that end in a short *i*.

लघु० – हरिः । हरी । *hariḥ, harī.*

Eluc. : In the nominative singular we have *hari* + *su*--> *haris*--> *hariḥ* (rutva and visarga). With the dual affix of the first triplet, we have *hari* + *au*. At this stage, the sūtra *prathamayoḥ pūrvasavarṇaḥ* (125) applies and a long vowel substitute homogeneous with the preceding vowel, which in this case is *i*, replaces both the preceding *i* and following *au* and we have *harī*. In declining the word *hari* with the plural sup-affix of the first triplet, the following sūtra presents itself for application :

(167) जसि च । ***jasi ca*. 7. 3. 109**

लघु० – ह्रस्वान्तस्याङ्गस्य गुणः । हरयः । *hrasvāntasyāṅgasya guṇaḥ. harayaḥ.*

Trans. : A substitute guṇa vowel replaces the aṅga-final element of a nominal stem ending in a short vowel when the plural sup-affix *jas* follows.

PP. *jasi ca hrasvasya aṅgasya guṇaḥ.*

Eluc. : The words *hrasvasya* and *guṇaḥ* are carried over from the sūtra *hrasvasya guṇaḥ* Pā. 7. 3. 108. This rule occurs in the domain of the sūtra *aṅgasya* Pā. 6. 4. 1, so this word also recurs in the present sūtra and it is qualified by the term *hrasvasya*. Therefore the expression in consonance with tadantavidhi becomes *hrasvāntasya aṅgasya*. Thus the sūtra means : If the plural sup-affix *jas* follows a stem ending in a short vowel, then a guṇa vowel replaces it. In accordance with the rule *alo 'ntyasya* (21) this guṇa vowel replaces the aṅga-final short vowel. In the present illustration *hari* + *jas*, the stem *hari* ends in a short *i* and the affix *jas* follows. The condition for guṇa-replacement is available. So the short *i* at the end of *hari* is replaced by a guṇa vowel *e* with the help of the rule *alo 'ntyasya* (21). With this guṇa vowel substitution we have *hare* + *jas* --> *hare* + *as*. Now with the help of the sūtra *eco 'yavāyāvaḥ* (22) the aṅga-final *e* is replaced by *ay* and after the grammatical functions of rutva and visarga-replacement have taken place, we have *haray* + *as* --> *harayas*--> *harayaḥ*.

In the vocative singular we introduce the singular affix *su* after the word *hari*. The singular affix of the vocative is designated as *sambuddhi* by the rule *ekavacanaṁ sambuddhiḥ* (131). As such, the sūtra *eṅhrasvāt sambuddheḥ* (133) becomes available for application for the elision of the consonant *s* of the vocative singular sup-affix. However, the following rule ensues :

(168) ह्रस्वस्य गुणः । *hrasvasya guṇaḥ*. 7. 3. 108
लघु० - सम्बुद्धौ । हे हरे ! हरीन् । *he hare! harīn.*

Trans. : When a singular affix designated as *sambuddhi* follows, the pre-suffixal base ending in a short vowel is replaced by a guṇa vowel.

PP. *sambuddau hrasvasya aṅgasya guṇaḥ.*

Eluc. : The word *sambuddhau* is carried over from *sambuddhau ca* Pā. 7. 3. 106. The sūtra *aṅgasya* Pā. 6. 4. 1 is a governing rule and hence the word *aṅgasya* is also carried over into the present sūtra. It is qualified by the word *hrasvasya* occurring in this sūtra. So the sūtra means : When the sambuddhi-designated affix follows an aṅga ending in a short vowel, the aṅga is replaced by a guṇa vowel. The sense that the aṅga-final short vowel is replaced by a guṇa vowel is arrived at by the rule *alo 'ntyasya* (21) which ensures that the whole of the pre-affixal base is not replaced but only its final phoneme. In the present illustration the stage at which this rule presents itself for application is : *hari* + *su* --> *hari* + *s*. Here the sambuddhi-designated affix *s* follows the stem *hari* which ends in a short vowel *i*. The aṅga-final *i* is replaced by the guṇa vowel *e* with the help of *sthāne 'ntara...* (17) and we get the declined vocative singular of *hari* : *hare!* after the elision of the affix *s* by (133).

In declining the form of *hari* with a singular affix of the second triplet, we apply *ami pūrvaḥ* (134). After a single substitution in the form of pūrvarūpa we obtain *harim* (<-- *hari* + *am*). The form of *hari* with a dual affix of the second triplet does not differ from that of the first triplet. With a plural sup-affix of the second triplet, we have *hari* + *śas* (--> *as*). First, the sūtra *prathamayoḥ pūrvasavarṇaḥ* (125) applies and a long vowel substitute homogeneous with the preceding, which in this case is *i*, replaces both the preceding *i* and the following *a* of the affix *as* (<-- *śas*) and we have *harīs*. Then by *tasmācchaso naḥ puṁsi* (136) the phoneme *s* of *śas* is replaced by the dental nasal *n* since the stem is masculine and we have the form *harīn*.

When we decline *hari* with a singular affix of the third triplet, we invoke the following sūtra :

(169) शेषो घ्यसखि । *śeṣo ghyasakhi*. 1. 4. 7

लघु० – शेष इति स्पष्टार्थम्। ह्रस्वौ याविदुतौ तदन्तं सखिवर्जं घिसंज्ञम्। *śeṣa iti spaṣṭārtham. hrasvau yāv idutau tadantaṁ sakhivarjaṁ ghisaṁjñam.*

Trans. : With the exception of *sakhi* 'friend', the rest of the nominal stems that end in a short *i* or *u* are designated as *ghi*. The enunciation of the word *śeṣa* (in the sūtra) is for the sake of clarity.

PP. *śeṣaḥ hrasvaḥ yū ghi asakhi.*

Eluc. : The word *hrasvaḥ* is carried over from *ṅiti hrasvaśca* Pā. 1. 4. 6. The compound word *yū* is lent into the present sūtra from *yū stryākhyau nadī* Pā. 1. 4. 3. Thus there are two compound words in the completed sūtra : *asakhi* and *yū*. The former is a nañ-tatpuruṣa and the latter is an itaretaradvandva. Their analysis is as follows : 1. *na sakhi asakhi* 2. *iś ca uś ca yū*. The word *yū* has been used without any inflectional ending in the sūtra (*avibhaktikanirdeśaḥ*, Kāśikā). The word *śeṣa* in the sūtra signifies those words which end in short *i* or *u* and which are not designated as *nadī*. The words which are not assigned the nadī-designation are : 1. The nominal stems in the masculine or neuter gender which end in a short *i* or *u*. 2. The feminine nominal stems ending in a short *i* or *u*, before *ṅit* sup-affixes when alternatively they are not to be designated as *nadī*. The purpose of the use of the word *śeṣa* in the rule is to ensure that the ghi-designation should be assigned only to those words which end in a short *i* or *u* and which have not been designated as *nadī*.

The statement *śeṣa iti spaṣṭārtham* given in the Laghu means that the purpose of the enunciation of the term *śeṣa* could have been served otherwise also. This means that there would be no harm if the sūtra did not have the word *śeṣa* in it. To explain, let us consider two sūtras: *ṅiti hrasvaśca* Pā. 1. 4. 6 and the present one without the term *śeṣa*, that is, *ghyasakhi* into which *yū* and *hrasvaḥ* are carried over. With these carried over insertions, the aphorism would read : *hrasvaḥ yū ghyasakhi*. It would mean : With the exception of *sakhi*, the nominal stems ending in a short *i* or *u* are to be assigned ghi-designation. It would then behave like a general rule covering all nominal stems ending in a short *i* or *u* except the word *sakhi*. The other sūtra prescribes optionally the nadī-designation to the words which are feminine and end in a short *i* or *u*. Before the application of the aphorism *ṅiti hrasvaśca*, the present rule is invariably available for application. Hence by virtue of the paribhāṣā *yena nāprāpte yo vidhir ārabhyate sa tasya bādhako bhavati* (Kielhorn, 57), the former rule becomes an exception to the present aphorism. There is another paribhāṣā *prakalpya cāpavādaviṣayaṁ tata utsargo 'bhiniviśate* (Abhyankar, 63) which means : Leaving aside the target area of the exception rule, the general performs its grammatical function. In this context, it would mean : Leaving aside the feminine words ending in a short *i* or *u* before *ṅit* sup-affixes, all other nominal stems ending in a short *i* or *u* are to be termed *ghi* with the exception of *sakhi*. Thus even wihout the term *śeṣa* in the sūtra, the intended meaning could very well have been arrived at. This is the reason why Varadarāja says that the word *śeṣa* has been used for the sake of the distinct comprehension of those words which are going to be designated as *ghi*.

So the word *hari* is assigned the ghi-designation, the significance of which is observed in the declensional form of *hari* with a singular sup-affix of the third triplet : *hari* + *ṭā* when the following sūtra applies :

(170) आङो नाऽस्त्रियाम्। *āṅo nā 'striyām.* 7. 3. 120

लघु० – घेः परस्याङो ना स्याद् अस्त्रियाम्। आङ् इति टासंज्ञा। हरिणा। हरिभ्याम्। हरिभिः। *gheḥ parasyāṅo nā syād astriyām. āṅ iti ṭāsaṁjñā. hariṇā, haribhyām, haribhiḥ.*

Trans. : Let *nā* be the substitute of the sup-affix *āṅ* coming after ghi but not in the feminine. *āṅ* is another name for *ṭā*.

PP. *gheḥ (aṅgasya) āṅaḥ nā astriyām.*

Eluc. : The term *gheḥ* is read into the present sūtra from *acca gheḥ* Pā. 7. 3. 119. The elision of the singular nominal ending after *nā* is archaic {*vibhaktilopa ārṣaḥ* (Bhaimī, I, p. 224)}. The word *astriyām* is a nañ-tatpuruṣa analysed as *na striyām* meaning 'in other than the feminine gender'. Thus the sūtra means : If the ghi-designated word is in a gender other than the feminine and if it is followed by *āṅ*, which is another term for the sup-affix *ṭā*, then the affix *āṅ* is to be replaced by *nā*. In the present illustration, *hari* is ghi-designated. As such the sup-affix *āṅ* (*ṭā*) is replaced by *nā* and we have *hari* + *ṭā* --> *hari* + *ā* --> *hari* + *nā*. At this stage, by the rule *aṭkupvāṅnumvyavāye 'pi* (137), the dental *n* is replaced by the cerebral *ṇ* and we have the form *hariṇā*.

The other form with the dual and plural nominal endings of the third triplet do not undergo any distinct grammatical operation.

With the singular nominal ending of the fourth triplet after *hari* we have *hari* + *ṅe*. Since *hari* is ghi, the following sūtra applies :

(171) घेर्ङिति । *gherṅiti*. 7. 3. 111

लघु० – घिसंज्ञकस्य ङिति सुपि गुणः । हरये । *ghisaṁjñakasya ṅiti supi guṇaḥ. haraye.*

Trans. : A guṇa vowel substitute comes in place of a ghi-designated nominal stem if a *ṅit* sup-affix follows.

PP. *gheḥ (aṅgasya) guṇaḥ ṅiti supi.*

Eluc. : The words *guṇaḥ* and *supi* are carried over respectively from the sūtras *hrasvasya guṇaḥ* Pā. 7. 3. 102 and *supi ca* Pā. 7. 3. 108. On completing the insertions, the aphorism means : When a sup-affix having the nasal guttural phoneme as *it* follows a ghi-designated nominal stem, the substitute guṇa vowel replaces the ghi-designated aṅga. With the help of the paribhāṣā-sūtra *alo 'ntyasya* (21), here the substitute guṇa vowel *e* replaces the aṅga-final phoneme *i*. In the illustration *hari* + *ṅe* --> *hari* + *e*, the aṅga-final vowel *i* is replaced by the guṇa-vowel *e*. We have *hare* + *e*. At this stage, we apply the aphorism *eco 'yavāyāvaḥ* (22) and the declensional form *haraye* is obtained.

In the ablative singular the sup-affix *ṅasi* is introduced after *hari* : *hari* + *ṅasi* --> *hari* + *as* --> *hare* + *as* {*gherṅiti* (171)}. Here *ay* substitute in place of the stem-final vowel *e* is available by *eco 'yavāyāvaḥ* (22) but the following sūtra blocks it.

(172) ङसिङसोश्च । *ṅasiṅasośca*. 6. 1. 110

लघु० – एङो ङसिङसोरति पूर्वरूपमेकादेशः । हरेः । हर्योः । हरीणाम् । *eṅo ṅasiṅasor ati pūrvarūpam ekādeśaḥ. hareḥ. haryoḥ, harīṇām.*

Trans. : A single substitute vowel denoted by the abbreviatory term *eṅ* replaces both itself and the following short initial vowel *a* of the affixes *ṅasi* and *ṅas*.

PP. *eṅaḥ ṅasiṅasoḥ ca ati pūrvaparayoḥ ekaḥ pūrvaḥ (saṁhitāyām).*

Eluc. : The term *eṅaḥ* is carried over from *eṅaḥ padāntādati* Pā. 6. 1. 109. The whole of the governing sūtra *ekaḥ pūrvaparayoḥ* Pā. 6. 1. 84 is also read into the present sūtra which occurs in its domain. The word *pūrvaḥ* is carried over from *ami pūrvaḥ* Pā. 6. 1. 107. Thus the completed sūtra means : When the short vowel *a* of the sup-affixes *ṅasi* and *ṅas* comes after a vowel denoted by the abbreviatory term *eṅ*, the form of the preceding should be a single substitute for both. After the elision of the anubandhas, what remains of both the affixes is *as*. In the illustrations, with both ablative and genitive singular affixes, we have one common form *hari* + *as* --> *hare* + *as* {*gherṅiti* (171)}. Here we have the short vowel *a* of *as* coming after *e* of *hare*. Therefore by the present rule the vowel *e* will replace both itself and the short vowel *a*. We obtain the form *hareḥ* which is common to both ablative and genitive singular.

In genitive dual *hari* + *os*, the sandhi rule *iko yaṇaci* (15) applies and we have *haryoḥ*.

In genitive plural we have *hari* + *ām*. Here the pre-affixal base ends in a short vowel. Hence by *hrasvanadyāpo nuṭ* (147), the augment *nuṭ* is inserted at the head of the sup-affix *ām*. With the augment *nuṭ*, *ām* becomes *nām*. Then by the rule *nāmi* (148), the *aṅga*-final short *i* is replaced by a long vowel *ī*. After the application of the sūtra *aṭkupvāṅnum-vyavāye 'pi* (137), we have *harīṇām*.

In locative singular we have *hari* + *ṅi*. Since the locative singular affix is *ṅit*, the rule *gherṅiti* (171) becomes available for application but it is blocked by the following sūtra :

(173) अच्च घेः । *acca gheḥ*. 7. 3. 119

लघु० – इदुद्भ्यामुत्तरस्य ङेरौत् घेरच्च । हरौ । हर्योः । हरिषु । एवं कव्यादयः । *idudbhyām uttarasya ṅer aut gher acca. harau. haryoḥ. hariṣu. evaṁ kavyādayaḥ.*

Trans. : When *ṅi* comes after a short *i* or *u*, it is replaced by *aut* and ghi is replaced by a short *a*.

PP. *idudbhyām ṅeḥ aut gheḥ (aṅgsya) at ca.*

Eluc. : The words *idudbhyām, ṅeḥ* and *aut* are respectively carried over from *idudbhyām* Pā. 7. 3. 117, *ṅerāmnadyāmnībhyaḥ* Pā. 7. 3. 116 and *aut* Pā. 7. 3. 118. The substitute *au* comes in place of the sup-affix *ṅi* when it comes after the vowel *i* or *u* of an aṅga designated as *ghi* and a short *a* comes in place of the final phoneme of the aṅga designated as *ghi*. Although the rule says that a short vowel replaces the stem which is termed *ghi*, the final phoneme of that stem will be replaced by *at* by virtue of the rule *alo 'ntyasya* (21). In the illustration *hari* + *ṅi*, we find this grammatical instance, in that the affix *ṅi* follows the short *i* of *hari* which is a ghi stem. So, the short *i* of *hari* is replaced by a short *a* and the following affix *ṅi* is replaced by *au*. After these grammatical operations, we have *hara* + *au*. At this stage, by *vṛddhireci* (33) a single long vowel replacement comes in place of both the aṅga-final short *a* and the affix *au*. Thus we obtain the form *harau*. With a locative dual affix *os*, we again have *haryoḥ* in the same manner as with a genitive dual affix. In the locative plural, when we introduce the affix *sup*, we have the following grammatical situation *hari* + *sup* --> *hari* + *su* in which the dental s of the affix *sup* is replaced by a cerebral ṣ by *ādeśapratyayayoḥ* (149). Thus we obtain the form *hariṣu*. The nominal stem *hari* will be declined as follows :

	Singular	Dual	Plural
prathamā	*hariḥ*	*harī*	*harayaḥ*
dvitīyā	*harim*	*harī*	*harīn*
tṛtīyā	*hariṇā*	*haribhyām*	*haribhiḥ*
caturthī	*haraye*	*haribhyām*	*haribhyaḥ*
pañcamī	*hareḥ*	*haribhyām*	*haribhyaḥ*
ṣaṣṭhī	*hareḥ*	*haryoḥ*	*harīṇām*
saptamī	*harau*	*haryoḥ*	*hariṣu*
sambodhana	*he hare!*	*he harī!*	*he harayaḥ!*

Some of the nominal stems which are declined like *hari* are : *kavi* 'poet', *agni* 'fire', *atithi* 'guest', *ahi* 'snake', *asi* 'sword', *kapi* 'monkey', *dhvani* 'sound', *giri* 'mountain', *ravi* 'sun', *udadhi* 'ocean', *payodhi* 'ocean', *nidhi* 'treasure', *granthi* 'knot', *paridhi* 'circumference', *pāṇi* 'hand', *śakuni* 'a bird' and *nṛpati* 'king'.

The nominal stem *sakhi* is not designated as *ghi*. Therefore its declension is different from that of *hari*. With a singular sup-affix of the first triplet introduced after *sakhi*, we have *sakhi* + *su* --> *sakhi* + s. At this stage, the following sūtra ensues :

(174) अनङ् सौ । ***anaṅ sau*. 7. 1. 93**

लघु० – सख्युरङ्गस्यानङादेशोऽसम्बुद्धौ सौ । *sakhyur aṅgasyānaṅ ādeśo 'sambuddhau sau.*

Trans. : Let the substitute *anaṅ* replace the pre-affixal base *sakhi* when the affix *su*, other than that of the vocative singular, follows.

PP. *sakhyuḥ aṅgasya anaṅ asambuddhau sau.*

Eluc. : The words *sakhyuḥ* and *asambuddhau* are carried over from *sakhyurasambuddhau* Pā. 7. 1. 92. The present sūtra occurs in the domain of the governing rule *aṅgasya* Pā. 6. 4. 1. So the word *aṅgasya* also recurs in this sūtra. Here the term *sau* is the locative singular form of the singular affix of the first triplet and not that of the *sup* (locative plural) since the particle nañ in asambuddhau is in the sense of exclusion (*paryudāsa*). The affix *su* is similar to, and different from, the *su* of the vocative singular. Thus the sūtra means : When the affix *su* of the first triplet, which is not of the vocative singular, comes after the nominal stem *sakhi*, the substitute *anaṅ* replaces the pre-affixal base *sakhi*. Since the substitute *anaṅ* is *ṅit*, it replaces the aṅga-final vowel *i* of *sakhi* in accordance with the rule *ṅicca* (46). The vowel *a* following the phoneme *n* in the substitute *anaṅ* is for the sake of articulation. Only *an*-portion of the substitute *anaṅ* remains. Thus we have *sakhi* + *su* --> *sakh an s* --> *sakhan s*. At this stage, the following sūtra presents itself in order to designate what upadhā is :

(175) अलोऽन्त्यात् पूर्व उपधा । ***alo 'ntyāt pūrva upadhā*. 1. 1. 65**

लघु० – अन्त्यादलः पूर्वो वर्ण उपधासंज्ञः । *antyād alaḥ pūrvo varṇa upadhā-saṁjñaḥ.*

Trans. : A phoneme that precedes the final phoneme of an item, (i.e. penultimate phoneme), is designated as *upadhā*.

PP. *antyāt alaḥ pūrva upadhā.*

Eluc. : The term *al* is an abbreviation which signifies all the phonemes in the alphabet of Pāṇini. In the verbal roots *pac* 'to cook' and *bhid* 'to split', the phonemes *a* and *i* are called *upadhā*. These are the examples of where the technical term *upadhā* is assigned to a given form (*rūpa*). The function of the assignment of the designation *upadhā* is seen in *pācaka* and *bhedaka* where the rules *ata upadhāyāḥ* Pā. 7. 2. 116 and *pugantalaghūpadhasya ca* Pā. 7. 3. 86 respectively prescribe vṛddhi and guṇa replacements in place of the upadhā-designated phonemes *a* and *i*. These constitute functional examples (*kāryodāharaṇa*).[1] The present illustration is also a functional example. In *sakhan* + *s*, the short vowel *a* that precedes the last phoneme *n* is assigned the upadhā designation. Now the following sūtra becomes applicable :

(176) सर्वनामस्थाने चासम्बुद्धौ । *sarvanāmasthāne cāsambuddhau.* 6. 4. 8

लघु० – नान्तस्योपधाया दीर्घोऽसम्बुद्धौ सर्वनामस्थाने । *nāntasyopadhāyā dīrgho-'sambuddhau sarvanāmasthāne.*

Trans. : A substitute long vowel replaces the penultimate vowel of an aṅga ending in the phoneme *n* before the sup-affixes called *sarvanāmasthāna* excluding the vocative singular.

PP. *na aṅgasya upadhāyāḥ dīrghaḥ asambuddhau sarvanāmasthāne ca.*

Eluc. : The word *na* is carried over from *nopadhāyāḥ* Pā. 6. 4. 7. The genitive case-ending after *na* has been elided by *supāṁ suluk...* Pā. 7. 1. 39 (cf. *na iti luptaṣaṣṭhīkaṁ padam.* BM, I, p. 247). It qualifies the word *aṅgasya* which is being read into the present sūtra from governing rule *aṅgasya* Pā. 6. 4. 1. Hence by tadantavidhi the expression becomes *nāntasya* (*aṅgasya*). The words *upadhāyāḥ* and *dīrghaḥ* are respectively carried over from *nopadhāyāḥ* Pā. 6. 4. 7 and *ḍhralope pūrvasya dīrgho-'ṇaḥ* Pā. 6. 3. 111. The compound word *asambuddhau* is a nañ-tatpuruṣa analysed as *na sambuddhau, asambuddhau*. With these points having been taken into consideration, the sūtra means : With the exception of the vocative singular sup-affix, if the affixes designated as *sarvanāmasthāna* {*suḍanapuṁsakasya* (162)} follow an aṅga ending in the phoneme *n*, then its penultimate phoneme is replaced by a long vowel. In the illustration *sakhan* + *s*, *sakhan* is an aṅga by *yasmāt pratyaya...* (132) and it ends in the phoneme *n*. The short vowel *a* which precedes this final *n* is upadhā

1. Rama Nath Sharma, *The Aṣṭādhyāyī of Pāṇini*, vol. 2, pp. 66-7.

by *alo 'ntyātpūrva upadhā* (175). The sup-affix *s* that follows *sakhan* is also other than the vocative singular. The conditions for a long vowel substitution in place of the penultimate short vowel *a* are available. After this replacement, we have *sakhān* + *s*. With respect to the status of the affix *s*, the following sūtra presents itself :

(177) अपृक्त एकाल् प्रत्ययः । *apṛkta ekāl pratyayaḥ*. 1. 2. 41

लघु० – एकाल् प्रत्ययो यः सोऽपृक्तसंज्ञः स्यात् । *ekāl pratyayo yaḥ so 'pṛktasaṁjñaḥ syāt.*

Trans. : Let an affix, which consists of a single phoneme (*al*), be designated as *apṛkta*.

PP. *apṛktaḥ ekāl pratyayaḥ.*

Eluc. : The word *ekāl* is a karmadhāraya compound which is analysed as : *ekaś cāsāv al ekāl*, which means 'an affix which consists of a single phoneme'. According to the wording of the rule, the designation *apṛkta* is to be assigned to that affix which consists of a single phoneme without taking into account the *its*. This means that the status of an affix, being *ekāl*, is determined after the elision of the anubandhas. Thus in the present illustration when the affix *s*(*u*) has been reduced to the status of *ekāl*, the following sūtra ensues :

(178) हल्ङ्याब्भ्यो दीर्घात् सुतिस्यपृक्तं हल् । *halṅyābbhyo dīrghāt sutisyapṛktaṁ hal*. 6. 1. 68

लघु० –हलन्तात् परं दीर्घौ यौ ङ्यापौ तदन्ताच्च परं सुतिसीत्येतदपृक्तं हल् लुप्यते । *halantāt paraṁ dīrghau yau ṅyāpau tadantāc ca paraṁ sutisītyetad apṛktaṁ hal lupyate.*

Trans. : The apṛkta-designated affixes *su*, *ti* and *si*, following a pre-affixal base (*aṅga*) ending in a consonant or a long vowel of the feminine affixes *ṅī* or *āp*, are replaced by lopa.

PP. *halṅyābbhyaḥ dīrghāt sutisi apṛktam hal lopaḥ.*

Eluc. : The word *lopaḥ* is carried over into this sūtra from *lopo vyorvali* Pā. 6. 1. 66. The word *halṅyābbhyaḥ* is an itaretaradvandva. Its analysis is as follows : *hal ca ṅī ca āp ca, halṅyāpaḥ, tebhyaḥ.* All three members of the compound are to qualify a pre-affixal base since by them the provision of lopa has been enjoined. By *yena vidhistadantasya* Pā. 1. 1. 72 tadantavidhi comes into force and all the words will yield the expressions : *halantāt, ṅyantāt* and *ābantāt*. The other compound word is *sutisi* which is a samāhāra-dvandva and is analysed as : *suś ca tiś ca siś ca, sutisi*. The word *dīrghāt* can be related to the affixes *ṅī* and *āp* and not to *hal* since it is only vowels that can be described as dīrgha. So all three yielded expressions given above can be presented like this : *halantāt, dīrghaṅyantāt* and *dīrghābantāt*. The expression *sutisi apṛktaṁ hal* requires some explanation. These affixes, as they are given, are not apṛkta since they consist of more than one *al*. However, when the vowels of these affixes being *it*s are elided, the consonantal phonemes *s*, *t* and *s* are left. They are then single consonants and as such can be assigned the technical term *apṛkta*. In the context of the present sūtra, this comes to mean that when these affixes are reduced to the status of apṛkta, they will be elided when they occur after a pre-affixal base ending in a consonant or a long vowel of the feminine affix *ṅī* or *āp*.

The significance of the term *dīrgha* in the sūtra lies in the fact that if the long vowel is replaced by a short one by some grammatical provision, then the apṛkta-designated affix is not replaced by lopa. Bhaṭṭoji Dīkṣita has given two examples to illustrate this point : *niṣkauśāmbiḥ* and *atikhaṭvaḥ* (SK, I, p. 249). The first prādi-tatpuruṣa compound is by *nirādayaḥ krāntādyarthe pañcamyā* Mbh 2. 2. 18 saunāga vtk 9 and the second is by *atyādayaḥ krāntyādyarthe dvitīyayā* Mbh 2. 2. 18 saunāga vtk 6. The shortening of the vowels long *ī* and *ā* takes place by *gostriyor-upasarjanasya* Pā. 1. 2. 48. The short vowels *i* and *a* represent the feminine affixes *ṅī* and *āp* but the elision of apṛkta-designated *su* does not take place since *s* (*su*) does not come after the long vowels *ī* and *ā* of *ṅī* and *āp*.

If an apṛkta affix follows a long *ī* which is not of *ṅī*, then also the apṛkta-designated affix is not elided just as in the word *grāmaṇīḥ*. The long *ī* in this word is of the verbal root *ṇīñ* 'to carry, to lead' and not of the feminine affix *ṅī*. This is the reason why the affix s, even being apṛkta, is not elided.

One point is worth noticing in this context. The affix designated as *apṛkta* coming after a consonant can be elided by the aphorism *saṁyogā*... (20). Then why has the term *hal* been enunciated in the sūtra? This is because, if *hal* had not been included in the sūtra, it would have given rise to the following grammatical problem. In declining the nominal stem *rājan*, in the nominative singular we have *rājān + su*, after the grammatical operation of replacing the penultimate vowel by a long one by the rule *sarvanāmasthāne cāsambuddhau* (176) has taken place. At this stage, if the apṛkta affix *s*(*u*) is elided by *saṁyogāntasya lopaḥ* Pā. 8. 2. 23, the elision would be deemed not to have taken place with respect to the sūtra *na lopaḥ prātipadikāntasya* Pā. 8. 2. 7 as *saṁyogāntasya lopaḥ* Pā. 8. 2. 23 is subsequent to *na lopaḥ*... Pā. 8. 2. 7 in the tripādī {see (31)}. As a result the phoneme *n*, not being pada-final, would not be elided by Pā. 8. 2. 7 and we cannot obtain the desired form *rājā*. Hence, the term *hal* has to form a part of the present sūtra.

In the present illustration, we have *sakhān* + *s*. The affix *s* is apṛkta. Hence it is elided by the present sūtra. After the elision of the apṛkta affix, we have *sakhān* which has the pada-final phoneme *n*. At this stage, the following sūtra becomes available for application :

(179) न लोपः प्रातिपदिकान्तस्य । *na lopaḥ prātipadikāntasya.* 8. 2. 7

लघु० – प्रातिपदिकसंज्ञकं यत्पदम् तदन्तस्य नस्य लोपः स्यात्। सखा। *prātipadika-saṁjñakaṁ yatpadam tadantasya nasya lopaḥ syāt. sakhā.*

Trans. : The substitute lopa replaces the final phoneme *n* of a nominal stem which is termed a *pada* (at the same time).

PP. *prātipadika padasya antasya na lopaḥ.*

Eluc. : The words *na* and *prātipadika* are both considered to be the padas which end in a singular affix of the sixth triplet (*neti prātipadiketi ca luptaṣaṣṭhīke pade*, SK, I, p. 238). Jñānendra Sarasvatī construes this elision as peculiar to the sūtra (*sautratvāt*, TB, I, p. 238). This rule occurs in the domain of the governing sūtra *padasya* Pā. 8. 1. 16. The word *padasya*, therefore, recurs in the present sūtra. Thus the sūtra means : The final phoneme *n* of a nominal stem which is also termed *pada* is replaced by lopa.

Both the words *prātipadika* and *pada* are read into the present rule with a purpose. If the term *prātipadika* along with the word *pada* had not been enunciated in the sūtra, then the pada-final *n* occurring at the end of *ahan*, which is a third or second person singular form of the verbal root *han* in laṅ-lakāra would have been elided since it is also a pada. If only prātipadika had been enunciated in the rule, then the elision of the stem-final *n* in *rājān* + *au* would be incurred since here *rājān* is prātipadika by virtue of the paribhāṣā *ekadeśavikṛtamananyavat* (Abhyankar, 37). This is the reason why it is necessary to include both the words in the present sūtra. As a consequence, the pada-final *n* of *ahan* would not be elided since, being a verbal form, it is not a prātipadika. In *rājān* + *au*, the elision of the final *n* would not take place since, even though *rājān* is a prātipadika, it is not a pada before the sup-affix *au*.

In the present illustration, *sakhān* + *s*, the word *sakhān* is a prātipadika by virtue of *ekadeśavikṛtamananyavat* (Abhyankar, 37) since it is a changed form of the word *sakhi* which is a prātipadika by *arthavadadhātu...* (115). When the affix *su* has been reduced to the status of apṛkta after the elision of the vowel *u*, it still retains the pada-designation by the aphorism *suptiṅantaṁ padam* (14) since the affix *su* which has been elided is considered to be effective for the grammatical operations dependent on it by virtue of the rule *pratyayalope pratyayalakṣaṇam* (189). Consequently, the expression *sakhān* is both a pada and a prātipadika. As a result, the final phoneme *n* is elided by the present aphorism.

With a dual affix of the first triplet introduced after the nominal stem *sakhi*, we have *sakhi* + *au*. Here the rule *prathamayoḥ pūrvasavarṇaḥ* (125) is available for application but the rule *aco ñṇiti* (181) blocks it in view of the following sūtra :

(180) सख्युरसम्बुद्धौ । *sakhyurasambuddhau.* 7. 1. 92

लघु० – सख्युरङ्गात् परं सम्बुद्धिवर्जं सर्वनामस्थानं णिद्वत् स्यात् । *sakhyur aṅgāt paraṁ sambuddhivarjaṁ sarvanāmasthānaṁ ṇidvat syāt.*

Trans. : With the exception of vocative singular, let a sup-affix designated as *sarvanāmasthāna* occurring after an aṅga, namely *sakhi*, be treated as if containing the phoneme *ṇ* as *it*.

PP. *sakhyuḥ aṅgāt asambuddhau sarvanāmasthānam ṇit.*

Eluc. : The sūtra *aṅgasya* Pā. 6. 4. 1 is a governing rule. The present sūtra occurs in its domain. So the word *aṅgasya* recurs here and this is changed into one ending in the ablative singular by the process of vibhaktipariṇāma so that it may accord with the word *sakhyuḥ* which is in the ablative singular. The word *sarvanāmasthāne* is carried from the sūtra *ito 't sarvanāmasthāne* Pā. 7. 1. 86 and is qualified by the word *asambuddhau* (*asambuddhāv ityanena viśeṣyate*, TB, I, p. 252). The term *ṇit* is carried over from the sūtra *goto ṇit* Pā. 7. 1. 90. Since the term *ṇit* is nominative singular, both the words *asambuddhau* and *sarvanāmasthāne* will be construed as ending in the nominative singular.[1] The word *asambuddhau* is a nañ-tatpuruṣa which is analysed as *na sambuddhiḥ asambuddhiḥ, tasyām*. So the completed sūtra means : With the exception of sambuddhi (vocative singular) if the sup-affixes designated as

1. *goto ṇit ityato ṇid iti prathamāntam anuvṛttam. tatsāmānādhikaraṇyād asambuddhāv iti sarvanāmasthāne iti ca saptamī prathamā kalpyate.* BM, I, p. 251.

sarvanāmasthāna follow an aṅga, namely *sakhi*, they should be treated as having the cerebral nasal *ṇ* as *it*. This is an extension rule (*atideśa sūtra*) since it transfers the characteristic of being *ṇit* to *su* (other than the vocative singular), *au, jas, am* and *auṭ* when they follow the pre-affixal base *sakhi*. This means that the grammatical operations, which are performed before a *ṇit* affix, would now be performed on *sakhi* before these five sup-affixes. In the illustration *sakhi + au*, the affix *au* is to be treated as *ṇit*. The consequence of its attaining the status of being *ṇit* is seen in the following aphorism :

(181) अचो ञ्णिति । *aco ñṇiti*. 7. 2. 115

लघु० - अजन्ताङ्गस्य वृद्धिः ञिति णिति च परे । सखायौ । सखायः । हे सखे ! सखायम् । सखायौ । सखीन् । सख्या । सख्ये । *ajantāṅgasya vṛddhiḥ ñiti ṇiti ca pare. sakhāyau, sakhāyaḥ, he sakhe! sakhāyam, sakhāyau, sakhīn, sakhyā, sakhye.*

Trans. : Let the substitute *vṛddhi* vowel replace an aṅga that ends in a vowel before an affix having either *ñ* or *ṇ* as *it*.

PP. *acaḥ aṅgasya ñṇiti vṛddhiḥ*.

Eluc. : The present sūtra occurs in the domain of the governing rule *aṅgasya* Pā. 6. 4. 1. Hence the word *aṅgasya* recurs in the present sūtra. The word *vṛddhiḥ* is carried over from *mṛjervṛddhiḥ* Pā. 7. 2. 114. The compound *ñṇiti* is a dvandva-seeded bahuvrīhi. Its analysis is as follows: *ñ ca ṇ ca ñṇau, tau itau yasya tat ñṇit, tasmin = ñṇiti*. In this way the sūtra means : When an affix, either *ñit* or *ṇit*, follows, the pre-affixal base ending in a vowel is replaced by a vṛddhi vowel. With the help of the paribhāṣā sūtra *alo 'ntyasya* (21), the substitute vṛddhi vowel replaces the aṅga-final vowel. In the illustration *sakhi + au*, the affix *au* is treated as *ṇit* by (180) and consequently the vṛddhi vowel *ai* will replace the vowel *i* occurring at the end of the aṅga, namely *sakhi* and we have *sakhai + au*. At this stage, the rule *eco 'yavāyāvaḥ* (22) applies. The vowel *ai* is replaced by *āy* and the inflected form *sakhāyau* is obtained.

With the plural affix *jas* introduced, we have *sakhi + jas* --> *sakhi + as*. The sup-affix *as* is treated as *ṇit*. Then vṛddhi and *āy* replacements take place and we obtain the form *sakhāyaḥ*.

The vocative singular of *sakhi* is declined in the same manner as *hari*. *he sakhi + su* --> *he sakhi + s* --> *he sakhe + s* {guṇa substitution in place of the of *i* of by *hrasvasya guṇaḥ* (168)} --> *he sakhe* {the phoneme s of sambuddhi (vocative singular) is elided by *eṅhrasvāt sambuddheḥ* (133)}. Because of the word *asambuddhau* in the rule (180), the affix *su* of sambuddhi is not treated as *ṇit*.

In *sakhi* + *am*, the affix *am* is treated as *ṇit*. As a result we have vṛddhi and *āy* replacements and the form *sakhāyam* is obtained. With the dual affix of the second triplet, the stem *sakhi* is declined like that of the nominative dual.

With the plural sup-affix *śas* of the second triplet introduced, we have *sakhi* + *śas*, which is not a sarvanāmasthāna. In place of the stem-final *i* of *sakhi* a long vowel replacement homogeneous with the preceding takes place by *prathamayoḥ pūrvasavarṇaḥ* (125). After this *tasmācchaso naḥ puṁsi* (136) applies and the phoneme *s* of the affix *śas* --> *as* is replaced by the phoneme *n* since the nominal stem *sakhi* is masculine. The process by which we arrive at the inflected form of *sakhi* in the accusative plural is as follows : *sakhi* + *śas* --> *sakhi* + *as* --> *sakhīs* --> *sakhīn*.

With a singular sup-affix of the third triplet, we have *sakhi* + *ā* (*ṭā*). Since the nominal stem *sakhi* is not a ghi-stem, the sūtra *āṅo nāstriyām* (170) does not apply and the affix *ṭā* after *sakhi* is not replaced by *nā*. At this stage, the rule *iko yaṇaci* (15) applies. As a consequence, the vowel *i* is replaced by *y* and we have *sakhyā*. With the dual and plural affixes of the third triplet the forms are *sakhibhyām* and *sakhibhiḥ*.

In the dative singular of *sakhi* before *ṅe*, the phoneme *y* replaces the final *i* of *sakhi* by *iko yaṇaci* (15) and we obtain *sakhye*. Here the rule *gherṅiti* (171) does not apply since *sakhi* is excluded from the class of nominal stems which have been assigned the ghi-designation. The dual and plural common forms with the affixes of the fourth and fifth triplets are *sakhibhyām* and *sakhibhyaḥ*

In the ablative singular, the affix *ṅasi* is introduced after *sakhi*. In *sakhi* +*as* (<--*ṅasi*), the vowel *i* of *sakhi* is replaced with *y* by *iko yaṇaci* (15) and we have *sakhy* + *as*. At this stage, the following sūtra ensues :

(182) ख्यत्यात्परस्य । *khyatyātparasya*. 6. 1. 112

लघु० – खि-ति शब्दाभ्यां खी-ती शब्दाभ्यां कृतयणादेशाभ्यां परस्य ङसि-ङसोरत उः । सख्युः । *khi-ti śabdābhyāṁ khī-tī śabdābhyāṁ kṛtayaṇādeśābhyāṁ parasya ṅasi-ṅasor ata uḥ. sakhyuḥ.*

Trans. : A short vowel *u* replaces the short vowel *a* of *ṅasi* and *ṅas* following the words *khi-ti* or *khī-tī* after the vowel *i* or *ī* of these words has been replaced by *yaṇ*.

PP. *khyatyāt parasya ṅasiṅasoḥ ataḥ ut* (*saṁhitāyām*).

Eluc. : The words *ṅasi* and *ṅas* are carried over from *ṅasiṅasośca* Pā. 6. 1. 110. The term *ataḥ* is read into the present rule from *eṅaḥ* *padāntādati* Pā. 6. 1. 109 with *ati* changed into the genitive singular by the process of vibhaktivipariṇāma. The word *ut* is lent into this sūtra from *ṛta ut* Pā. 6. 1. 111. The word *khyatyāt* is a samāhāradvandva which is analysed as *khyañ ca tyañ ca khyatyam, tasmāt = khyatyāt*. The purpose of the vowel *a* after the phoneme *y* in both the words is to facilitate the articulation (*yakārād akāra uccāraṇārthaḥ*, BM, I, p. 252).[1] The words *khya* and *tya* are enunciated in the sūtra to show that the words *khi-ti* or *khī-tī* are to be taken here when the vowel *i* or *ī* has already been replaced by *yaṇ*. The use of the fifth singular nominal ending in the word *khyatyāt* is enough to invoke the paribhāṣā sūtra *tasmādityuttarasya* (71) which yields the sense of *para* 'after'. Why has then Pāṇini used the word *parasya* in the rule? Jñānendra Sarasvatī says that Pāṇini has used it to suggest that the governing sūtra *ekaḥ pūrvaparayoḥ* Pā. 6. 1. 84 does not extend here.[2] With these points having been taken into consideration, the meaning of the sūtra is as follows : The short vowel *u* replaces the short *a* of the sup-affixes *ṅasi* and *ṅas*, when these affixes follow the words *khi/ti* or *khī/tī* after the *i* or *ī* has been replaced by *yaṇ*.

In the illustration *sakhy + as*, we have the word *khy* after the vowel *i* of *sakhi* has been replaced by *yaṇ*. Consequently the vowel *a* of the affix *ṅasi* is replaced by the vowel *u* in accordance with the present rule and we have the form as *sakhyus*. After the application of the rules *sasajuṣo ruḥ* (104) and *kharavasānayorvisarjanīyaḥ* (93), we obtain the declined form *sakhyuḥ*.

The genitive singular form will also be *sakhyuḥ*. In the genitive dual we have *sakhi + os*. Here the rule *iko yaṇaci* (15) applies. The form *sakhyoḥ* is obtained after the application of the sūtras *sasajuṣo ruḥ* (104) and *kharavasānayorvisarjanīyaḥ* (93). In the genitive plural with the introduction of the affix *ām*, we have *sakhi + ām*. Since the pre-affixal base ends in a short vowel, the rule *hrasvanadyāpo nuṭ* (147) applies and the augment *nuṭ* is inserted at the head of the affix *ām*. After the deletion of the anubandhas of *nuṭ* we have *sakhi + nām*. At this stage the sūtra *nāmi* (148) applies and after replacing the short vowel *i* of *sakhi* by a long one, we obtain *sakhīnām* in the genitive plural.

In the locative singular after the introducton of the singular affix *ṅi*, we have *sakhi + ṅi* --> *sakhi + i*. The sūtra *acca gheḥ* (173) does not apply since the word *sakhi* is not designated as *ghi*. At this stage, the following sūtra applies :

---

1. Cf. TB, I, p. 253.

2. *pañcamīnirdeśād eva parasyeti labdhe parasyeti grahaṇam ekaḥ pūrvaparayoḥ iti nivṛttam iha tu nādhikriyate iti dhvananārtham*. Ibid., p. 253.

(183) औत्। *aut.* 7. 3. 118

लघु॰ – इदुद्भ्यां परस्य ङेरौत्। सख्यौ। शेषं हरिवत्। *idudbhyāṁ parasya ṅer aut. sakhyau. śeṣaṁ harivat.*

Trans. : The sup-affix *ṅi* which follows a short vowel *i* or *u* is replaced by *au*. The rest (of the declension of *sakhi*) is like *hari*.

PP. *idudbhyām ṅeḥ aut (aṅgasya).*

Eluc. : The expression *idudbhyām*[1] is carried over from the sūtra *idudbhyām* Pā. 7. 3. 117. The word *ṅeḥ* is read into the present sūtra from *ṅerāmnadyāmnībhyaḥ* Pā. 7. 3. 116. Thus the sūtra means : If the affix *ṅi* comes after either *i* or *u*, then it is replaced by *au*. Incidentally, *t* in *aut* is not *it*. It is here used for taparakaraṇa {*taparastatakālasya* (26)}.

In the illustration *sakhi + i,* the affix *i* is replaced by *au* and we have *sakhi + au*. At this stage, the rule *iko yaṇaci* (15) enjoins *y* in place of the *i* of *sakhi* and the form *sakhyau* is obtained. In locative dual the declension does not differ from that of the genitive dual.

In the locative plural the *s* of the *sup* after *sakhi* is replaced by the cerebral *ṣ* by the rule *ādeśapratyayayoḥ* (149). Thus *sakhi + sup--> sakhi + su--> sakhi + ṣu --> sakhiṣu* is obtained. The declension of *sakhi* is as follows :

	Singular	Dual	Plural
prathamā	*sakhā*	*sakhāyau*	*sakhāyaḥ*
dvitīyā	*sakhāyam*	*sakhāyau*	*sakhīn*
tṛtīyā	*sakhyā*	*sakhibhyām*	*sakhibhiḥ*
caturthī	*sakhye*	*sakhibhyām*	*sakhibhyaḥ*
pañcamī	*sakhyuḥ*	*sakhibhyām*	*sakhibhyaḥ*
ṣaṣṭhī	*sakhyuḥ*	*sakhyoḥ*	*sakhīnām*
saptamī	*sakhyau*	*sakhyoḥ*	*sakhiṣu*
sambodhana	*he sakhe!*	*he sakhāyau!*	*he sakhāyaḥ!*

1. We have adopted the reading given by Bhimsena Shastri, which differs from that given in the Gita Press Gorakhpur and Balllantyne editions. The reason given in the Gita Press edition is that there is no purpose of carrying over the word *ud* and secondly, the word *id* is traditionally recognized as marked with a svarita accent. Hence only *id* is carried over into the present sūtra. However, Bhaṭṭoji Dīkṣita also says that reading *ud* into this aphorism is for the sake of the following sūtra (SK, I, p. 253). I think that, although carrying over of *ud* is not required in the present sūtra, it is still required for the rule *acca gheḥ* Pā. 7. 3. 119.

Whether the nominal stem *pati* occurs as the constituent of a compound or not, it could be designated as *ghi* by the sūtra *śeṣo ghyasakhi* (169) but the following sūtra restricts the scope of the assignment of the designation *ghi* in respect of this nominal stem.

(184) पतिः समास एव । ***patiḥ samāsa eva*. 1. 4. 8**
लघु० - (पतिः समास एव) घि-संज्ञः । पत्या । पत्ये । पत्युः । पत्यौ । शेषं हरिवत् । समासे तु - भूपतये । *(patiḥ samāsa eva) ghi-saṁjñaḥ. patyā, patye, patyuḥ, patyau. śeṣaṁ harivat. samāse tu, bhūpataye.*

Trans. : Let the nominal stem *pati* be designated as *ghi* only when it occurs in a compound. The rest is like *hari* but in the compound (it is ghi), e. g. *bhūpataye.*

PP. *patiḥ samāse eva ghi.*

Eluc. : The term *ghi* is carried over into this sūtra from *śeṣo ghyasakhi* (Pā. 1. 4. 7). This sūtra rules that the nominal stem *pati* can be assigned this technical term only when it occurs as a member of a compound. Actually this rule is not meant to designate the word *pati* as *ghi* but it is purported to restrict the assignment of the technical term *ghi* in respect of *pati.* The provision already made by *śeṣo ghyasakhi* (170) is restricted by the present aphorism.

Since the ghi-designation with reference to the nominal stem *pati* was already available by *śeṣo ghyasakhi* (169), the present sūtra, even without the use of the indeclinable *eva,* could have functioned as a niyama-sūtra by virtue of the statement in the Mahābhāṣya[1] on *naḥ kye* Pā. 1. 4. 15, which means that when some grammatical function has already been defined, Pāṇini's enunciation to define the same function again is purported to restrict that function. Vāsudeva Dīkṣita[2] states that the purpose of the word *eva* in the aphorism is to do away with the ambiguity that could have arisen if this indeclinable had not been used. In the absence of the distinct placement of the word *eva* in the sūtra, it could have been taken as paraphrased with the word *pati* (*patir eva samāse*) rather than with the word *samāsa* as is given in the present form. In this sense, it would not be possible to obtain the declined form *mahākavinā* of the compound word *mahākavi* with a singular sup-affix of the third triplet, for, according to this hypothetically possible placement of the word *eva* in the sūtra, only *pati* would be assigned the

1. *kimartham idam ucyate na subantaṁ padam ityeva siddham. niyamārtho 'yam ārambhaḥ.*
2. BM, I, p. 256.

designation *ghi* as a constituent of the compound, and not any other nominal stem. The use of the indeclinable *eva* in the present form is necessary to dispense with any such ambiguity.

The declension of the nominal stem *pati* will be like that of *sakhi* when it does not occur as a constituent of a compound since in this case it is not assigned the ghi-designation. When the word *pati* is a constituent of a compound, it is designated as *ghi* and as such its declension will be like that of *hari*.

In this context it may be mentioned that there are three grammatical operations that take place owing to ghi-designation. The three sūtras that enjoin ghi-related grammatical operations are *āṅo nā 'striyām* (170) *gherṅiti* (171) and *acca gheḥ* (173). According to the sūtra (170), the singular affix *ṭā* of the third triplet is replaced by *nā*. The rule (171) enjoins guṇa-substitution and the sūtra (173) prescribes the substitutes *aut* and *at* to respectively replace the locative singular affix *ṅi* and the last phoneme of the ghi-designated nominal stem. These grammatical operations do not take place in respect of the nominal stem *pati* when it is not a member of a compound. Its declension will be like that of *sakhi*. For the sake of comparison, the declension of the nominal stem *pati* in both the forms (1. uncompounded and 2. in a compound) are given below :

pati

	Singular	Dual	Plural
prathamā	*patiḥ*	*patī*	*patayaḥ*
dvitīyā	*patim*	*patī*	*patīn*
tṛtīyā	*patyā*	*patibhyām*	*patibhiḥ*
caturthī	*patye*	*patibhyām*	*patibhyaḥ*
pañcamī	*patyuḥ*	*patibhyām*	*patibhyaḥ*
ṣaṣṭhī	*patyuḥ*	*patyoḥ*	*patīnām*
saptamī	*patyau*	*patyoḥ*	*patiṣu*
sambodhana	*he pate!*	*he patī!*	*he patayaḥ!*

bhūpati

prathamā	*bhūpatiḥ*	*bhūpatī*	*bhūpatayaḥ*
dvitīyā	*bhūpatim*	*bhūpatī*	*bhūpatīn*

tṛtīyā	*bhūpatinā*	*bhūpatibhyām*	*bhūpatibhiḥ*
caturthī	*bhūpataye*	*bhūpatibhyām*	*bhūpatibhyaḥ*
pañcamī	*bhūpateḥ*	*bhūpatibhyām*	*bhūpatibhyaḥ*
ṣaṣṭhī	*bhūpateḥ*	*bhūpatyoḥ*	*bhūpatīnām*
saptamī	*bhūpatau*	*bhūpatyoḥ*	*bhūpatiṣu*
sambodhana	*he bhūpate!*	*he bhūpatī!*	*he bhūpatayaḥ!*

The declension of the words in which the nominal stem *pati* occurs as a constituent of a compound will be like that of *bhūpati*. Some of the words of this class are : *narapati, gaṇapati, paśupati* and *senāpati*. In the expression *sītāyāḥ pataye namaḥ*, the dative singular form *pataye* of the stem *pati* is archaic according to Vāsudeva Dīkṣita (BM, I, p. 256).

लघु० - कतिशब्दो नित्यं बहुवचनान्तः । *katiśabdo nityaṁ bahuvacanāntaḥ.*

Trans. : The word *kati* 'how many' takes only the plural sup-affixes.

(185) बहुगणवतुडति संख्या । ***bahugaṇavatuḍati saṅkhyā.* 1. 1. 23**

Trans. : Let the words *bahu, gaṇa* and those which end in *vatu* and *ḍati* affixes be designated as *saṅkhyā*.

PP. *bahugaṇavatuḍati saṅkhyā.*

Eluc. : The word *bahugaṇavatuḍati* is a samāhāradvandva which is analysed as *bahuś ca gaṇaś ca vatuś ca ḍatiś ca bahugaṇavatuḍati*. When the words *bahu* and *gaṇa* mean *vaipulya* 'multitude' and *saṁgha* 'group', they are not to be designated as *saṅkhyā* (cf. Kāśikā on this sūtra). Only when they denote number, they are to be assigned the term *saṅkhyā*. The terms *vati* and *ḍati* are affixes. Hence they will denote the words that end in these affixes. Although tadantavidhi is not applicable in case of the affixes when a rule prescribes a designation (*saṁjñā*) {cf. *saṁjñāvidhau pratyayagrahaṇe tadantagrahaṇaṁ nāsti* (Abhyankar, 27)}, these terms will still denote the words ending in these affixes since no purpose is served by assigning the designation *saṅkhyā* to the bare terms, *vati* and *ḍati* (*vatuḍatyoḥ kevalayoḥ saṁjñāvidhau phalābhāvāt*, TB, I, p. 257).

The word *kati* ends in *ḍati* affix. Therefore it gets the designation *saṅkhyā*. Since always a plural affix is introduced after it, we have *kati* +

jas in the nominative plural. At this stage, the following sūtra presents itself to prescribe the designation *ṣaṭ* for the nominal stem *kati* :

(186) डति च । *ḍati ca.* 1. 1. 25

लघु० – डत्यन्ता संख्या षट्संज्ञा स्यात् । *ḍatyantā saṅkhyā ṣaṭsaṁjñā syāt.*

Trans. : Let a saṅkhyā which ends in the affix *ḍati* be designated as *ṣaṭ*.

PP. *ḍati ca saṅkhyā ṣaṭ.*

Eluc. : The words *saṅkhyā* and *ṣaṭ* are respectively carried over from *bahugaṇavatuḍati saṅkhyā* Pā. 1. 1. 23 and *ṣṇāntā ṣaṭ* Pā. 1. 1. 24. The meaning of the sūtra will be : The saṅkhyā-designated nominal stem ending in the affix *ḍati* should be assigned the technical term *ṣaṭ*. Since the rule does not occur in the governing domain of the sūtra *ākaḍārādekā saṁjñā* (165), the stem *kati* has both the designations : 1. *saṅkhyā* 2. *ṣaṭ*.

The ṣaṭ-designation has been assigned to the nominal stem *kati*. So, when we decline it in the nominative plural with the sup-affix *jas*, the following aphorism applies :

(187) षड्भ्यो लुक् । *ṣaḍbhyo luk.* 7. 1. 22

लघु० – जश्शसोः । *jaśśasoḥ.*

Trans. : Let there be luk-elision of *jaś* and *śas* introduced after the nominal stems designated as *ṣaṭ*.

PP. *ṣaḍbhyaḥ jaśśasoḥ luk.*

Eluc. : The compound word *jaśśasoḥ* is read into the present sūtra from *jaśśasoḥ śiḥ* Pā. 7. 1. 20. With this carried over insertion, this sūtra means : If the sup-affixes *jaś* and *śas* are introduced after the words, which are assigned the designation *ṣaṭ*, then they are replaced by luk-elision. Now in order to identify what the term *luk* signifies, the following sūtra ensues :

(188) प्रत्ययस्य लुक्श्लुलुपः । *pratyayasya lukślulupaḥ.* 1. 1. 61

लघु० – लुक्-श्लु-लुप्-शब्दैः कृतं प्रत्ययादर्शनं क्रमात् तत्तत्संज्ञं स्यात् । *luk-ślu-lup-śabdaiḥ kṛtaṁ pratyayādarśanaṁ kramāt tattatsaṁjñaṁ syāt.*

Trans. : Let the non-perception of an affix brought about by the terms *luk*, *ślu* and *lup* be designated respectively by these terms.

PP. *pratyayasya adarśanam lukślulupaḥ.*

Eluc. : The word *adarśanam* is carried over from *adarśanaṁ lopaḥ* Pā. 1. 1. 60. The sūtra, as it is given, apparently means that the non-cognition of an affix is assigned three designations, namely, *luk, ślu* and *lup*. However, if all the three designations are assigned to the non-cognition of an affix, then there arises confusion in respect of these designations. When there is elision of an affix by the term *luk*, this elision could also be called *ślu* or *lup*. While conjugating the verbal root *han* of adādi class in the third person singular in laṭ lakāra, *han + śap + tip -->* *han + luk +ti*, if we take the elision called *luk* as *ślu*, then the reduplication of the verbal root becomes applicable by the aphorism *ślau* (604). Similarly while conjugating the verbal root *hu* of the juhotyādi class, if the elision of *śap* by the term *ślu* were construed as *luk*, then a vṛddhi vowel replacement would come in place of the vowel *u* of *hu* by *uto vṛddhirluki hali* (565). To dispense with this kind of confusion, the expression *lukślulupaḥ* is iterated. Consequent upon this, the elision of an affix brought about by the express mention of any of these terms, will be assigned one of these three designations in accordance with the order of enumeration by virtue of the paribhāṣā sūtra *yathāsaṅkhyam anudeśaḥ samānām* (23).[1]

In the illustration *kati + jas*, the plural sup-affix *jas* is introduced after the nominal stem *kati*, which is designated as *saṅkhyā* and *ṣaṭ* at the same time. Since the nominal stem *kati* is designated as *ṣaṭ*, the affix *jas* is replaced by luk-elision. In other words, there is zero-substitution in place of the affix *jas*. We obtain the form *kati* in the nominative plural. Although the affix *jas* has been elided, the guṇa-replacement is still available by *jasi ca* (167) since the following sūtra allows an operation dependent on the affix which has been elided :

(189) प्रत्ययलोपे प्रत्ययलक्षणम्। *pratyayalope pratyayalakṣaṇam.* 1. 1. 62

लघु० - प्रत्यये लुप्ते तदाश्रितं कार्यं स्यात्। इति जसि च इति गुणे प्राप्ते — *pratyaye lupte tadāśritaṁ kāryaṁ syāt. iti jasi ca iti guṇe prāpte* —

1. *evaṁ sati ekasyaiva pratyayādarśanasya tisro 'pi saṁjñāḥ syuḥ. tataśca hantītyatra śabluki ślau iti dvitvaṁ syāt juhotītyatra ślau sati uto vṛddhir luki hali iti vṛddhiḥ syāt. ato naivam arthaḥ. kiṁ tu lukślulupa ityāvartate. tataś ca luk ślu lup ityuccārya vihitaṁ pratyayādarśanaṁ yathāsaṅkhya-paribhāṣayā kramād lugādisaṁjñaṁ syād iti labhyate. ato noktasaṅkaraḥ.* BM, I, p. 257.

Trans. : When an affix is replaced by zero (*lopa*), operations conditioned by it still apply (as if the affix were still present). As a result the guṇa-substitution beomes available by the aphorism *jasi ca* (167).

PP. *pratyayalope pratyayalakṣaṇam.*

Eluc. : The word *pratyayalope* is a ṣaṣṭhī-tatpuruṣa compound, the analysis of which is : *pratyayasya lopaḥ, tasmin.* The other word *pratyayalakṣaṇam* is a bahuvrīhi compound which is analysed as : *pratyayo lakṣaṇaṁ (nimittam) yasya tat = pratyayalakṣaṇam.* This comes to mean that a grammatical function, dependent on an affix that has been elided, does take place.

In the illustration *kati + jas,* the affix *jas* has been elided by *ṣaḍbhyo luk* (187) but by virtue of the present sūtra its presence is recognized and consequently the grammatical operation, namely, the guṇa-replacement by *jasi ca* (167), dependent on it, is still available. The following sūtra debars it.

(190) न लुमताऽङ्गस्य । *na lumatā 'ṅgasya.* 1. 1. 63

लघु० – लुमता शब्देन लुप्ते तन्निमित्तमङ्गकार्यं न स्यात्। कति। कतिभिः। कतिभ्यः। कतीनाम्। कतिषु। *lumatā śabdena lupte tannimittam aṅgakāryaṁ na syāt. kati, katibhiḥ, katibhyaḥ, katīnām, katiṣu.*

Trans. : When an affix is replaced by zero by the use of the word that contains *lu* in it, let the operation dependent on this affix not take place on a pre-affixal base (*aṅga*).

PP. *lumatā pratyayalope aṅgasya pratyayalakṣaṇam na.*

Eluc. : The word *pratyayalope* is carried from the sūtra *pratyayalope pratyayalakṣaṇam* Pā. 1. 1. 62. The word *lumatā* is formed by adding a singular sup-affix of the third triplet after *lumān*. The word *lumān* itself is derived by introducing *matup* affix after *lu* by *tadasyāstyasminniti...* (1179). Thus the sūtra means : If an affix is replaced by zero by using a word which contains *lu* in it (*luk, ślu* or *lup*), then the grammatical operation to be performed on a pre-affixal base (*aṅga*) because of it (the elided affix) does not take place.

In the illustration *kati + jas,* the affix *jas* has been elided by the word *luk* {*ṣaḍbhyo luk* (187)} which contains the word segment *lu* in it. Hence the guṇa-replacement by *jasi ca* (167), which depends on *jas* which has been elided by *luk,* does not take place, for guṇa-substitution is a pre-affixal operation (*aṅga-kārya*). We thus obtain the form *kati*. The plural form *kati* with the plural affix *śas* of the second triplet is obtained in the same manner since the affix *śas* is also replaced by luk-elision.

With the plural affixes of the third, fourth and fifth triplets, there is no distinct grammatical operation worth mentioning. With the plural affix of the sixth triplet, the form *katīnām* can be obtained in two ways : 1. *kati* + *ām*. Here the augment *nuṭ* is inserted at the head of the affix *ām* by *hrasvanadyāpo nuṭ* (147) and then by the rule *nāmi* (148) a long vowel replacement in place of the aṅga-final vowel *i* takes place. Thus the form *katīnām* is obtained. 2. The nominal stem *kati* is designated as *ṣaṭ* by *ḍati ca* (186). So by the rule *ṣaṭcaturbhyaśca* (265), the augment *nuṭ* is added at the beginning of *ām* and we have *kati* + *ām* --> *kati* + *nām*. At this stage *nāmi* (148) applies and a long vowel substitution takes place. Thus we obtain the form *katīnām*.

Which of the two grammatical procedures is to be preferred in the context of the genitive plural form *katīnām*? Jñānendra Sarasvatī says that the augment *nuṭ* on the basis of the ṣaṭ-designation is bahiraṅga, whereas the same augment on the basis of the aṅga ending in a short vowel is antaraṅga. So the antaraṅga grammatical operation is to be preferred.[1]

With plural sup-affix of the seventh triplet , we have *kati* + *sup* --> *kati* + *su*. At this stage, the rule *ādeśapratyayayoḥ* (149) applies and the dental s of the affix *sup* is replaced by the cerebral ṣ. Thus the form *katiṣu* is obtained.

The nominal stem *kati* is declined in the plural only. Its declension is as follows :

	Plural		Plural
prathamā	*kati*	pañcamī	*katibhyaḥ*
dvitīyā	*kati*	ṣaṣṭhī	*katīnām*
tṛtīyā	*katibhiḥ*	saptamī	*katiṣu*
caturthī	*katibhyaḥ*	sambodhana	*he kati!*

लघु० – युष्मदस्मत्षट्संज्ञकास्त्रिषु सरूपाः । *yuṣmadasmatṣaṭsañjñakās triṣu sarūpāḥ.*

---

1. *bahiraṅgaḥ ṣaṭsaṁjñāśrayo nuṭ. tathā cāntaraṅgatvāt katīnām ityatra hrasvāśraya eva nuḍ iti nāmīti dīrghaḥ sannipātaparibhāṣāṁ bādhitvaiva pravartate.* TB, I, p. 204.

Trans. : The pronominal stems *yuṣmad, asmad* and the words which have been assigned the designation *ṣaṭ* retain the same form in all the three genders.

Eluc. : The word *kati* is designated as *ṣaṭ*. It will retain the same form in all the three genders. For exmple, *kati bālakāḥ, kati nadyaḥ* and *kati pustakāni*. In the same way the pronominal stems *yuṣmad* and *asmad* retain their form : *ahaṁ kṛṣṇaḥ, ahaṁ rādhā, ahaṁ mitram, tvaṁ rāmaḥ, tvaṁ sītā, tvaṁ mitram,* etc.

लघु० – त्रिशब्दो नित्यं बहुवचनान्तः। त्रयः। त्रीन्। त्रिभिः। त्रिभ्यः 2। *triśabdo nityaṁ bahuvacanāntaḥ. trayaḥ, trīn, tribhiḥ, tribhyaḥ* 2.

Trans. : The word *tri* 'three' is always plural.

Eluc. : The word *tri* means 'three'. Since the stem *tri* primarily denotes a plural number, it always takes a plural nominal ending. When it is used in a secondary sense as in a compound, it does not necessarily take a plural ending.

In the first illustration, with a nominative plural ending we have *tri + jas*. At this stage, the aphorism *jasi ca* (167) applies and a *guṇa*-replacement (*e*) comes in place of the aṅga-final *i* and then after the application of *eco 'yavāyāvaḥ* (22), the form *trayaḥ* (<-- *tre + as* <--*tri + as* <-- *tri + jas*) is obtained.

In the second illustration, we have *tri + śas*. Here, firstly in place of the stem-final *i* of *tri* a long vowel replacement homogeneous with the preceding takes place by *prathamayoḥ pūrvasavarṇaḥ* (125) --> *trīs*. After this *tasmācchaso naḥ puṁsi* (136) applies and the phoneme s of the affix *śas* --> *as* is replaced by the phoneme *n*. Thus we obtain the form *trīn*.

In the third and fourth illustrations *tri + bhis* and *tri + bhyas* (dative and ablative plural, after the application of *sasajuṣo ruḥ* (104) and *kharavasānayorvisarjanīyaḥ* (93), we have *tribhiḥ* and *tribhyaḥ*.

In the genitive plural with the plural sup-affix *ām*, we have *tri + ām*. At this stage, the following sūtra applies :

(191) **त्रेस्त्रयः। *trestrayaḥ*. 7. 1. 53**

लघु० – त्रिशब्दस्य त्रयादेशः स्यादामि। त्रयाणाम्। त्रिषु। गौणत्वेऽपि — प्रियत्रयाणाम्।
triśabdasya trayādeśaḥ syādāmi. trayāṇām, triṣu. gauṇatve 'pi — priya-trayāṇām.

Trans. : When the sup-affix *ām* follows, the pre-affixal base *tri* is replaced by the substitute *traya*, e. g. *trayāṇām* (genitive plural). (The example of *tri* in seventh case-affix is) *triṣu*. Even when its use is secondary (as in a compound), this rule applies -- *priyatrayāṇām*.

PP. *treḥ trayaḥ āmi (aṅgasya)*.

Eluc. : The term *āmi* is carried over from *āmi sarvanāmnaḥ suṭ* Pā. 7. 1. 52. Then the sūtra means : When the affix *ām* follows, the word *tri* is replaced by the substitute *traya*.

In the aphorism, the word *tri* does not denote number. Instead it denotes its own form *tri*. Hence it has been declined in the genitive singular (*treḥ*) in the sūtra like *hari*.

In the genitive plural we have *tri* + *ām*. At this stage, the present rule applies and the pre-affixal base *tri* is wholly replaced by *traya* in accordance with *anekāl śit sarvasya* (45) since the substitute *traya* contains more than one phoneme (*al*) --> *traya* + *ām*. As the aṅga ends in a short vowel, the augment *nuṭ* is inserted at the head of *ām* --> *traya* + *nām* by *hrasvanadyāpo nuṭ* (147). At this stage, the rules *nāmi* (149) and *aṭkupvāṅnumvyavāye 'pi* (137) apply in sequence and the substitutes long vowel and cerebral *ṇ* respectively replace the aṅga-final short vowel *a* and the dental *n* of *nām*. Thus we obtain the form *trayāṇām*.

In the locative plural we have *tri* + *sup* --> *tri* + *su*. Now by the rule *ādeśapratyayayoḥ* (149) the dental *s* of the affix *sup* is replaced by the cerebral *ṣ* and thus the form *triṣu* is obtained. The declension of *tri* is as follows :

	Plural		Plural
prathamā	*trayaḥ*	pañcamī	*tribhyaḥ*
dvitīyā	*trīn*	ṣaṣṭhī	*trayāṇām*
tṛtīyā	*tribhiḥ*	saptamī	*triṣu*
caturthī	*tribhyaḥ*	sambodhana	No form

The word *tri* in a bahuvrīhi compound is a subordinate (*upasarjana*) member since the compound primarily denotes the meaning of something other than that of its own constituents. The word *priyatri* 'one who has three friends' is a bahuvrīhi compound. It is analysed as : *priyāḥ trayaḥ yasya saḥ* = *priyatriḥ*. Even though the use of *tri* is in a secondary sense in a bahuvrīhi compound, the substitute *traya* still replaces the word *tri* before *ām*. This is so because of the use of *treḥ* in the singular in the sūtra. Otherwise Pāṇini would have used the plural form *trayāṇām* here as he did in the sūtra *aṣṭābhya auś* Pā. 7. 1. 21 to convey the primacy of the meaning.[1] The genitive plural form of *priyatri* will be *priyatrayāṇām*. The declension of *priyatri* will be as given below :

	Singular	Dual	Plural
prathamā	*priyatriḥ*	*priyatrī*	*priyatrayaḥ*
dvitīyā	*priyatrim*	*priyatrī*	*priyatrīn*
tṛtīyā	*priyatriṇā*	*priyatribhyām*	*priyatribhiḥ*
caturthī	*priyatraye*	*priyatribhyām*	*priyatribhyaḥ*
pañcamī	*priyatreḥ*	*priyatribhyām*	*priyatribhyaḥ*
ṣaṣṭhī	*priyatreḥ*	*priyatryoḥ*	*priyatrayāṇām*
saptamī	*priyatrau*	*priyatryoḥ*	*priyatriṣu*
sambodhana	*he priyatre!*	*he priyatrī!*	*he priyatrayaḥ!*

The word *dvi* denoting a number always takes the dual inflectional endings. In the process of declining *dvi*, the following sūtra presents itself for application :

(192) त्यदादीनामः । *tyadādīnāmaḥ*. 7. 2. 102

लघु० – एषामकारो विभक्तौ । द्विपर्यन्तानामेवेष्टिः । द्वौ 2 । द्वाभ्याम् 3 । द्वयोः 2 । *eṣām akāro vibhaktau. dviparyantānām eveṣṭiḥ. dvau 2, dvābhyām 3, dvayoḥ 2.*

Trans. : Let the vowel *a* replace the stems enumerated in the list headed by *tyad* 'that' when an affix termed *vibhakti* follows. (This replacement) is intended only for the items (beginning with *tyad* and) up to (and including) *dvi*.

PP. *tyadādīnām aḥ vibhaktau (aṅgasya).*

Eluc. : The word *vibhaktau* is carried over from *aṣṭana ā vibhaktau* Pā. 7. 2. 84. The word *tyadādīnām* is a bahuvrīhi compound. Its analysis is as follows : *tyad ādīr yeṣām te tyadādayaḥ, teṣām*. It is a tadguṇa-saṁvijñāna bahuvrīhi. The tyadādi group is a sub-set of the group beginning with *sarva*. It consists of *tyad* 'that', *tad* 'that', *yad* 'which, what, who (relative), *etad* 'this (very near)', *idam* 'this', *adas* 'that (very far)', *eka* 'one' and *dvi* 'two'. The substitute vowel *a* which is to replace

1. *arthaprādhānyabodhakasya bahuvacanasyābhāvād gauṇatve 'pi trayādeśo nyāyyaḥ*. TB, I, p. 261.

the words enlisted in the tyadādi group will actually replace the final phoneme of the constituents of this group in accordance with the paribhāṣā sūtra *alo 'ntyasya* (21). The word *dvi* denotes duality. Consequently it will always take dual sup-affixes. When a dual sup-affix which is also designated as *vibhakti* comes after it, the *i* of *dvi* is replaced by the short vowel *a*, e.g. *dvi + au --> dva + au*. The rule *vṛddhireci* (33) applies. Thus the form *dvau* is obtained. After changing into *dva*, the word *dvi* is declined like the nominal stem *rāma*. The declension of *dvi* is as follows :

	Dual		Dual
prathamā	*dvau*	pañcamī	*dvābhyām*
dvitīyā	*dvau*	ṣaṣṭhī	*dvayoḥ*
tṛtīyā	*dvābhyām*	saptamī	*dvayoḥ*
caturthī	*dvābhyām*	Generally there is no vocative form of the words of *tyadādi* group.	

Here comes to an end the declension of the masculine stems that end in a short *i*.

Now begins the process of declining the masculine nominal stems that end in a long *ī*.

लघु॰ – पाति लोकमिति पपीः सूर्यः। दीर्घाज्जसि च (161)। पप्यौ 2। पप्यः। हे पपीः! पपीम्। पपीन्। पप्या। पपीभ्याम् 3। पपीभिः। पप्ये। पपीभ्यः 2। पप्यः 2। पप्योः 2। दीर्घत्वान्न नुट् पप्याम्। ङौ तु सवर्णदीर्घः पपी। पप्योः। पपीषु। एवं वातप्रम्यादयः। ***pāti lokam iti papīḥ sūryaḥ. dīrghājjasi ca — papyau 2. papyaḥ. he papīḥ! papīm. papīn. papyā. papībhyām 3. papībhiḥ. papye. papībhyaḥ 2. papyaḥ 2. papyoḥ 2. dīrghatvān na nuṭ — papyām. ṅau tu savarṇadīrghaḥ — papī. papyoḥ. papīṣu. evaṁ vātapramyādayaḥ.***

Eluc. : One that protects the world is *papī* 'the sun'. Its nominative singular form is *papīḥ*. Here the affix *su* is not elided. We obtain this form after the application of *sasajuṣo ruḥ* (104) and *kharavasānayor-visarjanīyaḥ* (93).

In *papī + au*, after the rule *prathamayoḥ pūrvasavarṇaḥ* (125) has been blocked by *dīrghājjasi ca* (161), the sūtra *iko yaṇaci* (15) applies and we have *papyau* after *yaṇ*-replacement in place of *ī*. In a similar way after the blocking of pūrvasavarṇadīrgha, *yaṇ*-replacement takes place and the nominative plural form *papyaḥ* is obtained.

In *papī* + *am*, pūrvasavarṇadīrgha is debarred. The aphorism *ami pūrvaḥ* prescribes the single vowel substitution homogeneous with the preceding and we have *papīm*. With the plural affix of the second triplet, we have *papī* + *śas* --> *papī* + *as*. At this stage the rule *prathamayoḥ pūrvasavarṇaḥ* (125) applies and then the dental s of *śas* is replaced by the phoneme *n* by virtue of the sūtra *tasmācchaso naḥ puṁsi* (136). Thus the form *papīn* is obtained.

With sup-affix *ṭā*, we have *papī* + *ṭā* --> *papī* + *ā*, *iko yaṇaci* (15) applies and we obtain the form *papyā*. With the affix *bhyām* of the third, fourth and fifth triplets, we have *papībhyām*. After the application of the rules *sasajuṣo ruḥ* (104) and *kharavasānayor...* (93) with the plural affix *bhis* of the third triplet, we have *papībhiḥ*. In dative singular after the application of *iko yaṇaci* (15), we obtain *papye*.

With the introduction of the affixes *ṅasi* and *ṅas*, we have in both the cases *papī* + *as* after the elision of the anubandhas. The rule *iko yaṇaci* (15) prescribes *yaṇ*-substitution and we obtain *papyaḥ* in both ablative and genitive singular. In the genitive and locative dual when we introduce the sup-affix *os*, the rule *iko...* (15) operates, *yaṇ*-replacement takes place and we have *papyoḥ* in both the cases. After the introduction of the genitive plural affix *ām*, *yaṇ*-substitution takes place by the aphorism *iko...* (15) and the form *papyām* is obtained.

In the locative singular, the rule *akaḥ savarṇe dīrghaḥ* (42) applies and after the homogeneous long vowel substitution, we have the form *papī*. After the introduction of the locative plural affix *sup*, the aphorism *ādeśapratyayayoḥ* (149) becomes operational, the dental s of *sup* is replaced by the cerebral ṣ and we obtain the locative plural form *papīṣu*. The complete declension of the word *papī* is as follows :

	Singular	Dual	Plural
prathamā	*papīḥ*	*papyau*	*papyaḥ*
dvitīyā	*papīm*	*papyau*	*papīn*
tṛtīyā	*papyā*	*papībhyām*	*papībhiḥ*
caturthī	*papye*	*papībhyām*	*papībhyaḥ*
pañcamī	*papyaḥ*	*papībhyām*	*papībhyaḥ*
ṣaṣṭhī	*papyaḥ*	*papyoḥ*	*papyām*
saptamī	*papī*	*papyoḥ*	*papīṣu*
sambodhana	*he papīḥ!*	*he papyau!*	*he papyaḥ!*

The declension of *vātapramī* 'an antelope' and the like will be like that of *papī*.

लघु० – बह्व्यः श्रेयस्यो यस्य स बहुश्रेयसी । ***bahvyaḥ śreyasyo yasya sa bahuśreyasī.***

Eluc. : The word *bahuśreyasī* is a bahuvrīhi compound. Its analysis is as follows : *bahvyaḥ śreyasyo yasya* 'one who has many excellent women'. The word *śreyasī* is a comparative feminine form of *praśasya* with the affix *īyasun*. The adjectival stem *praśasya* is replaced by *śra* by *praśasyasya śraḥ* (1217). The affix remains as *īyas* after the elision of the *its* --> *śra* + *īyas* --> *śreyas* {guṇa-replacement by *ādguṇaḥ* (27)}. To derive its feminine form, we introduce *ṅīp* after *śreyas* by *ugitaśca* (1244). The grammatical analysis other than the syntactical one is : *bahvī jas śreyasī jas*. The feminine affix *ṅīp* after *bahvī* is dropped when the aphorism *striyāḥ puṁvad bhāṣitapuṁskādanūṅ samānādhikaraṇe...* (965) prescribes a change of the feminine form into that of masculine. The form then becomes *bahuśreyasī*. The shortening of the last vowel of *bahuśreyasī* by *gostriyorupasarjanasya* (948) is prohibited by the vārttika *īyaso bahuvrīher neti vācyam*.[1] The affix *kap* prescribed by *nadyṛtaśca* Pā. 5. 4. 153 is debarred by *īyasaśca* Pā. 5. 4. 156 and we have the form *bahuśreyasī*. Being a compound, it is a prātipadika. To render it a pada, the nominative singular affix *su* is introduced. Since the word *śreyasī* ends in *ṅīp*, the affix *s*(*u*) is elided by the rule *halṅyābbhyo...* (178) and we obtain the nominative singular form *bahuśreyasī*.

The forms of *bahuśreyasī* in the nominative dual and plural are *bahuśreyasyau* and *bahuśreyasyaḥ* since the *yaṇ*-replacement takes place by *iko yaṇaci* (15) after pūrvasavarṇadīrgha by *prathamayoḥ...* (125) has been blocked by *dīrghājjasi ca* (161).

In the vocative singular, we have *bahuśreyasī* + *su* --> *bahuśreyasī* + *s*. At this stage, the following sūtra presents itself :

(193) यू स्त्र्याख्यौ नदी । *yū stryākhyau nadī.* 1. 4. 3

लघु० – ईदूदन्तौ नित्यस्त्रीलिङ्गौ नदीसंज्ञकौ स्तः । *īdūdantau nityastrīliṅgau nadīsaṁjñakau staḥ.*

Trans. : The words which are always feminine and end in *ī* or *ū* are designated as *nadī*.

---

1. This vārttika in the Mahābhāṣya on Pā. 1. 2. 48 is available in the following form : *īyaso bahuvrīhau puṁvadvacanam*, whereas in the Kāśikā it is given on the same sūtra as *īyaso bahuvrīheḥ pratiṣedho vācyaḥ*.

PP. *yū stryākhyau nadī.*

Eluc.: The word *yū* is an itaretaradvandva. Its analysis is : *īś ca ūś ca yū + au*. The sup-affix *au* is elided by *supāṁ suluk* ... Pā. 7. 1.39 and as such *yū* is without any sup-affix (*vibhakti*) in the sūtra (*avibhaktiko nirdeśaḥ*, Kāśikā on the present sūtra). The term *stryākhyau* is an upapada compound which is analysed as : *striyam ācakṣāte stryākhyau* '(the two) which denote a feminine object'. The significance of the use of the word *stryākhyau* instead of using the word *striyām* in the sūtra is explained in the Padamañjarī. Haradatta[1] says that by using the word *stryākhyau*, Pāṇini intends to convey that only those words are meant here which have an inherent capacity to denote feminine so that the words *grāmaṇī*, *khalapū*, etc. are not termed *nadī* even when they are used in the feminine. In this way the, sūtra means : The words which, on their own, have an inherent capacity to denote feminine and which end in either *ī* or *ū* are designated as *nadī*. The words *nadī*, *gaurī*, *vadhū* are such words as can be assigned the nadī-designation.

In the present illustration, the word *śreyasī* ends in *ṅī* and hence it is inherently a feminine word but in a bahuvrīhi compound it becomes a subordinate member. As a consequence, the word *śreyasī* cannot be assigned the nadī-designation. In this situation, the following vārttika ensues and assigns the nadī-designation to it :

17. वा० – प्रथमलिङ्गग्रहणञ्च । *prathamaliṅgagrahaṇañca.*

लघु० – पूर्वं स्त्र्याख्यस्योपसर्जनत्वेऽपि नदीत्वं वक्तव्यमित्यर्थः । *pūrvaṁ stryākhyasyopasarjanatve 'pi nadītvaṁ vaktavyam ityarthaḥ.*

Trans. The status of nadī should be accorded to the original inherent feminine word even if it is a secondary member (in a compound).

Eluc. : By virtue of this vārttika (Mbh 1. 4. 3. vtk 2.) the inherent feminine word *śreyasī* retains its nadī-designation even in a bahuvrīhi compound. As a consequence, the following aphorism becomes operational in the context of *bahuśreyasī* :

(194) **अम्बार्थनद्योर्ह्रस्वः** । ***ambārthanadyorhrasvaḥ*. 7. 3. 107**

लघु० – सम्बुद्धौ । **हे बहुश्रेयसि!** *sambuddhau. he bahuśreyasi!*

---

1. *ākhyāgrahaṇasāmarthyāt padāntaram anapekṣya yau svayameva striyam ācakṣāte ityāśrīyate.* KP, I, pp. 504-05.

Trans. : When the affix of the vocative singular follows, the pre-affixal bases signifying 'mother' and those ending in the words designated as *nadī* are to be replaced by a short vowel.

PP. *ambārthanadyoḥ aṅgayoḥ hrasvaḥ sambuddhau.*

Eluc. : The sūtra *aṅgasya* Pā. 6. 4. 1 is a governing rule. The present rule occurs in its domain. So the word *aṅgasya* is carried over into the present sūtra and it is changed into the genitive dual so that it may agree with *ambārthanadyoḥ* by which it is qualified. As a result tadantavidhi by *yena vidhis...* Pā. 1. 1. 72 becomes operational. This will give : *ambārthasya aṅgasya nadyantasya ca aṅgasya.* The word *ambārthanadyoḥ* is a bahuvrīhi-seeded itaretaradvandva compound : *ambā artho yasya ambārthaḥ, ambārthaś ca nadī ca ambārthanadyau, tayoḥ = ambārthanadyoḥ.* With all these points having been taken into account, the sūtra means : The pre-affixal bases which signify 'mother' and those which end in the words designated as *nadī* are replaced by a short vowel. This short vowel will actually replace the aṅga-final phoneme by virtue of the rule *alo 'ntyasya* (21). In the illustration, the pre-affixal base is a bahuvrīhi compound which ends in a nadī stem. After it there is an affix of the vocative singular (*sambuddhi*). As a consequence, the aṅga-final phoneme is replaced by a short vowel and we obtain the vocative singular form *bahuśreyasi!*

In this situation, the rule *hrasvasya guṇaḥ* (168) does not apply since this short vowel replacement is brought about by the present rule. Otherwise Pāṇini could have enunciated this aphorism in the following form : *ambārthanadyorguṇaḥ,*[1] which would have served the purpose and would have been more economical.

With a singular affix of the second triplet, we have *bahuśreyasī* + *am*. Here pūrvasavarṇadīrgha is debarred by *ami pūrvaḥ* (135) and a single vowel replacement homogeneous with the preceding vowel takes place. Thus the form *bahuśreyasīm* is obtained. With the plural affix of the second triplet, we apply the rule *tasmācchaso naḥ puṁsi* (137) after a long vowel replacement homogeneous with the preceding vowel and obtain the form *bahuśreyasīn*.

With the singular affix of the third triplet, we have *bahuśreyasyā* after applying *iko yaṇaci* (15). With the dual affix of the third, fourth and fifth triplets, we have *bahuśreyasībhyām*. With plural affix of the third triplet we have *bahuśreyasībhiḥ* after rutva and visarga. With the dative singular affix, we have *bahuśreyasī* + *ṅe* --> *bahuśreyasī* + *e*. At this stage, the following sūtra ensues :

---

1. *atra hrasvavidhānasāmarthyād guṇo na pravartate. anyathā ambārthanadyorguṇaḥ ityeva brūyāt.* TB, I, p. 265.

(195) आण्‌ नद्याः । āṇ nadyāḥ. 7. 3. 112

लघु० – नद्यन्तात्‌ परेषां ङिताम्‌ आडागमः । *nadyantāt pareṣāṁ ṅitām āḍāgamaḥ.*

Trans. : The augment *āṭ* is introduced to the affixes which have *ṅ* as *it*, when they follow a pre-affixal base ending with a word designated as *nadī*.

PP. *āṭ nadyāḥ ṅitaḥ aṅgāt.*

Eluc. : The present sūtra occurs in the domain of *aṅgasya* Pā. 6. 4. 1, which is a governing rule. The word *aṅgasya* is changed into one having a singular affix of the fifth triplet by the process of vibhaktivipariṇāma. In a similar way, the word *ṅiti* which is carried over from *gherṅiti* (171) into the present sūtra is changed into the genitive. As given in the sūtra, the phoneme *ṭ* of *āṭ* has been replaced by the cerebral nasal phoneme *ṇ* by *yaro 'nunāsike 'nunāsiko vā* (68).

The meaning of this sūtra is : The augment *āṭ* is added at the beginning of an affix which is marked with *ṅ* as *it* when this affix occurs after an aṅga terminating with a word designated as *nadī*. The insertion of the augment *āṭ* at the head of a *ṅit* affix is effected with the help of the rule *ādyantau ṭakitau* (84).

In *bahuśreyasī + e*, the affix *e* is *ṅit*. Therefore the augment *āṭ* is introduced to the beginning of *e* and we have *bahuśreyasī + āṭ e* --> *bahuśreyasī + ā e*. At this stage, the following sūtra presents itself :

(196) आटश्च । āṭaśca. 6. 1. 90

लघु० – आटोऽचि परे वृद्धिरेकादेशः । बहुश्रेयस्यै । बहुश्रेयस्याः 2 । नद्यन्तत्वान्‌ नुट्‌ — बहुश्रेयसीनाम्‌ । *āṭo 'ci pare vṛddhir ekādeśaḥ. bahuśreyasyai. bahuśreyasyāḥ 2. nadyantatvān nuṭ — bahuśreyasīnām.*

Trans. : If *ac* follows *āṭ*, then a single vṛddhi vowel substitute replaces both *āṭ* and the following vowel.

PP. *āṭaḥ ca aci pūrvaparayoḥ ekaḥ vṛddhiḥ (saṁhitāyām).*

Eluc. : The term *aci* is lent into the sūtra from *iko yaṇaci* Pā. 6. 1. 77. The words *pūrvaparayoḥ* and *ekaḥ* are carried over from the governing rule *ekaḥ pūrvaparayoḥ* Pā. 6. 1. 84. The word *vṛddhi* comes from *vṛddhireci* Pā. 6. 1. 88. With the insertions which have been carried over, the sūtra means : When a vowel (*ac*) follows the augment *āṭ*, a single vṛddhi substitute comes in place of both the preceding augment *āṭ* and the following vowel (*ac*). Thus in *bahuśreyasī +ā e*, *ā* and *e* are replaced by the vṛddhi vowel *ai* and we have *bahuśreyasī + ai.* At this stage, the rule *iko yaṇaci* (15) applies, the vowel *ī* is replaced by *y* and the form *bahuśreyasyai* is obtained. Although the purpose could have been served by *vṛddhireci* (33), this sūtra is necessarily required for the forms like *aikṣata.* Here it has been used because of its logical viability (*yadyapi vṛddhireci ityeva siddham, tathāpi aikṣata ityādyartham āṭaśca iti sūtram ihāpi nyāyyatvād upanyastam,* BM, I, p. 266).

The sup-affix *bhyas* is common to both dative and ablative plural. After the application of *sasajuṣo ruḥ* (104) and *kharavasānayorvisarjanīyaḥ* (93), we have the form *bahuśreyasībhyaḥ.* With the singular affix of the ablative and genitive, we have *bahuśreyasī + as* (after the elision of the anubandhas). At this stage, since the word *śreyasī* is assigned nadī designation, the rule *āṇ nadyāḥ* (195) prescribes the insertion of *āṭ.* After that the aphorisms *āṭaśca* (196) and *iko yaṇaci* (15) apply and we have *bahuśreyasyāḥ.* In genitive dual we have *bahuśrcyasyoḥ* by the application of *iko...* (15). With the plural affix of the sixth triplet, we have *bahuśreyasī + ām.* At this stage, we have *nuṭ* inserted at the head of *ām* by *hrasvanadyāpo nuṭ* (147) and thus the genitive plural form *bahuśreyasīnām* (<-- *bahuśreyasī + nām*) is obtained. With the singular affix of the seventh triplet, we have *bahuśreyasī + ṅi.* At this stage, the following sūtra applies:

(197) ङेराम्नद्याम्नीभ्यः। *ṅerāmnadyāmnībhyaḥ.* 7. 3. 116

लघु॰ – नद्यन्तादाबन्तान्नीशब्दाच्च परस्य ङेराम्। बहुश्रेयस्याम्। शेषं पपीवत्। *nadyantād ābantān nīśabdācca parasya ṅer ām. bahuśreyasyām. śeṣaṁ papīvat.*

Trans. : When the affix *ṅi* follows the words ending in nadī and *āp,* and the word *nī* 'leader', it is replaced by *ām.*

PP. *ṅeḥ ām nadyāmnībhyaḥ aṅgebhyaḥ.*

Eluc. : Because of the governing sūtra *aṅgasya* Pā. 6. 4. 1, the word *aṅgasya* recurs in the present rule and its nominal ending and number are changed in consonance with those of its qualifier. The itaretara-dvandva compound *nadyāmnībhyaḥ* is analysed as *nadī ca āp ca nīś ca nadyāmnyaḥ, tebhyaḥ = nadyāmnībhyaḥ.* The phoneme *p* of *āp* is replaced by the nasal labial *m* in the sūtra by *yaro 'nunāsike 'nunāsiko vā* (68). According to Varadarāja, the terms *nadī* and *āp* qualify the term *aṅga.* So by tadantavidhi, they will come to mean *nadyantād aṅgād* and *ābantād aṅgād.* The word *nī* has been placed separately in the commentary but this could also have been clubbed together with the other two. As such the affix *ṅi* following *grāmaṇī,* which ends in *nī,* can be replaced by *ām* to obtain the form *grāmaṇyām.* So far as the term *āp* is concerned, tadantavidhi can take place with reference to it even by virtue of the paribhāṣā *pratyayagrahaṇe... tadantasya grahaṇam* (Abhyankar, 23). Thus the sūtra comes to mean : If the affix *ṅi* follows the pre-affixal bases ending in the words designated as *nadī* or in the affix *āp* (which is a cover term for *cāp, ḍāp* and *ṭāp*) and the word *nī*, then the affix *ṅi* is replaced by *ām*. In the illustration, *bahuśreyasī + ṅi*, the augment *āṭ* is available by *āṇnadyāḥ* Pā. 7. 3. 112, while the augment *nuṭ*, by *hrasvanadyāpo nuṭ* Pā. 7. 1. 54. Being subsequent in the Aṣṭādhyāyī *āṇnadyāḥ* (195) applies and we have *bahuśreyasī + āṭ ṅi*. Then the present rule prescribes the substitute *ām* in place of *ṅi* and we have *bahuśreyasī + āṭ ām; āṭaśca* (196) applies --> *bahuśreyasī + ām*. Thus the form *bahuśreyasyām* is obtained by *iko yaṇaci* (15).

In the locative plural form *bahuśreyasī + sup --> bahuśreyasī + su*, the dental s of the affix *sup* is replaced by the retroflex ṣ by *ādeśapratyayayoḥ* (149) and we obtain the form *bahuśreyasīṣu*. The complete declension of *bahuśreyasī* is as follows :

	Singular	Dual	Plural
prathamā	*bahuśreyasī*	*bahuśreyasyau*	*bahuśreyasyaḥ*
dvitīyā	*bahuśreyasīm*	*bahuśreyasyau*	*bahuśreyasīn*
tṛtīyā	*bahuśreyasyā*	*bahuśreyasībhyām*	*bahuśreyasībhiḥ*
caturthī	*bahuśreyasyai*	*bahuśreyasībhyām*	*bahuśreyasībhyaḥ*
pañcamī	*bahuśreyasyāḥ*	*bahuśreyasībhyām*	*bahuśreyasībhyaḥ*
ṣaṣṭhī	*bahuśreyasyāḥ*	*bahuśreyasyoḥ*	*bahuśreyasīnām*
saptamī	*bahuśreyasyām*	*bahuśreyasyoḥ*	*bahuśreyasīṣu*
sambodh.	*he bahuśreyasi!*	*he bahuśreyasyau!*	*he bahuśreyasyaḥ!*

लघु॰ – अङ्यन्तत्वान्न सुलोपः। अतिलक्ष्मीः। शेषं बहुश्रेयसीवत्। *aṅyantatvān na sulopaḥ. atilakṣmīḥ. śeṣaṁ bahuśreyasīvat.*

Eluc. : The word *lakṣmī* is derived from the verbal root *lakṣa*, when the affix *ī* with the augment *muṭ* is introduced after it by *lakṣermuṭ ca* (SK, IV, Uṇādi Sūtra, 440). Although the word *lakṣmī* does not end in feminine affix *ṅī* it is inherently a feminine word. It is assigned the nadī-designation since it ends in *ī* . The word *atilakṣmī* is a *prādi* compound by *atyādayaḥ krāntādyarthe dvitīyayā*, Mbh 2. 2. 18 saunāga vtk 2. It is analysed as *lakṣmīm atikrāntaḥ* 'one who has surpassed Lakṣmī'. The word which is designated as *nadī* retains its designation even in a compound by *prathamaliṅgagrahaṇaṁ ca* (vtk 17). So the word *lakṣmī* is nadī but since it does not end in a feminine affix, the nominative singular affix *su* is not elided. Hence we have the form *atilakṣmīḥ*. The rest of the declension is like that of *bahuśreyasī*.

	Singular	Dual	Plural
prathamā	*atilakṣmīḥ*	*atilakṣmyau*	*atilakṣmyaḥ*
dvitīyā	*atilakṣmīm*	*atilakṣmyau*	*atilakṣmīn*
tṛtīyā	*atilakṣmyā*	*atilakṣmībhyām*	*atilakṣmībhiḥ*
caturthī	*atilakṣmyai*	*atilakṣmībhyām*	*atilakṣmībhyaḥ*
pañcamī	*atilakṣmyāḥ*	*atilakṣmībhyām*	*atilakṣmībhyaḥ*
ṣaṣṭhī	*atilakṣmyāḥ*	*atilakṣmyoḥ*	*atilakṣmīṇām*
saptamī	*atilakṣmyām*	*atilakṣmyoḥ*	*atilakṣmīṣu*
sambodh.	*he atilakṣmi!*	*he atilakṣmyau !*	*he atilakṣmyaḥ!*

लघु० – प्रधीः । *pradhīḥ.*

Eluc. : The word *pradhī* (*pradhyāyatīti pradhīḥ* 'one who meditates properly') is formed with the affix *kvip* added after the verbal root *dhyai* by *dhyāyateḥ samprasāraṇaṁ ca* Mbh 3. 2. 178 vtk 4, which prescribes *kvip* as well as samprasāraṇa. *pra + dhyai + kvip --> pra+ dhyai +* 0 *--> pradhī*. The primary affix *kvip* is completely elided. The phonemes *k, i* and *p* are *its* by *laśakvataddhite* (135), *upadeśe'janunāsika* (28) and *halantyam* (1) respectively and they are elided by *tasya lopaḥ* (3). The consonant *v* is elided by *verapṛktasya* (302). In *pradhyai* (*dh y ai*), the semi-vowel *y* is replaced by *i* (*samprasāraṇa*) *--> pradh i ai*. Then by *samprasāraṇāc ca* (257), a single vowel replacement in the form of the preceding one comes in place of both the vowels (*i* and *ai*) and we have *dhi*. At this stage, the rule *halaḥ* (816) applies and the lengthening of short *i* takes place. In this way we get *pradhī*. The vowel *ī*, at the end of the word *pradhī*, which is brought about by the process of samprasāraṇa, is obviously not a feminine affix. This is the reason why in *pradhī + su*, there is no elision of *su* and we have the form *pradhīḥ* in the nominative singular after rutva and visarga.

With the nominative dual affix of the first triplet, we have *pradhī + au*. In this situation, first of all the rule *prathamayoḥ pūrvasavarṇaḥ* (125) applies. This is blocked by the aphorism *dīrghājjasi ca* (161). Then the sūtra *iko yaṇaci* (15) becomes applicable but it is also blocked by the following sūtra :

(198) अचि श्नुधातुभ्रुवां य्वोरियङुवङौ । *aci śnudhātubhruvāṁ yvor iyaṅuvaṅau.* 6. 4. 77

लघु० – श्नुप्रत्ययान्तस्य इवर्णोवर्णान्तस्य धातोः भ्रू इत्यस्य च अङ्गस्य इयङुवङौ स्तोऽजादौ प्रत्यये परे । इति प्राप्ते — *śnupratyayāntasya ivarṇovarṇāntasya dhātoḥ bhrū ityasya ca aṅgasya iyaṅuvaṅau sto 'jādau pratyaye pare. iti prāpte —*

Trans. : The substitutes *iyaṅ* and *uvaṅ* respectively replace the vowels *i* and *u* when an affix beginning with a vowel follows an aṅga which ends in the affix *śnu*, or which is a verbal root which ends in *i* or *u* or which is constituted by the stem *bhrū*.

PP. *aci śnudhātubhruvām aṅgānām yvoḥ iyaṅuvaṅau.*

Eluc. : The present sūtra occurs in the domain of *aṅgasya* Pā. 6. 4. 1 which is a governing rule. Hence the word *aṅgasya* recurs here and is changed into the genitive plural to accord with the three qualifiers in the form of that which ends in *śnu*, that which is a verbal root ending in *i* or *u* and the nominal stem *bhrū*. The designation *aṅga* depends on the affix that follows. So the term *aci* which is in the locative singular qualifies in a manner that it beomes the initial qualifier of the affix that follows in accordance with the vārttika *yasmin vidhis tadādāvalgrahaṇe* (Mbh 1. 4. 72 vtk 29). The term *śnu* is an affix. So by the metarule *pratyayagrahaṇe... tadantasya grahaṇam* (Abhyankar, 23), it will give the meaning : That which ends in the affix *śnu*. The nominal stem *bhrū* ends in *ū*. The word *yvoḥ* is an itaretaradvandva : *iś ca uś ca yū, tayoḥ = yvoḥ*. This qualifies only *dhātu* which is one of the three members of the itaretaradvandva compound word *śnudhātubhruvām* since it can have no connection with the words *śnu* and *bhrū*, which always end in *u*. Being a qualifier of the word *dhātu*, by tadantavidhi (Pā. 1. 1. 72), it will yield the sense : The verbal root which ends in either *i* or *u*. Thus the whole sūtra comes to mean : If the following three types of pre-affixal bases - 1. that which ends in the affix *śnu* (*śnupratyayānta*) 2. that which is a verbal root which ends in either *i* or *u* (*ivarṇovarṇāntadhātu*) 3. that which is constituted by the word *bhrū* - are followed by an affix that begins with a vowel, then the substitutes *iyaṅ* and *uvaṅ* will replace these pre-affixal bases (*aṅgas*). Since these substitutes are *ṅit*, they will come in place of the aṅga-final *i* and *u* respectively with the help of sūtras *ṅicca* (46) and *sthāne 'ntaratamaḥ* (17). The segments *iy* and *uv* remain respectively of *iyaṅ* and *uvaṅ* after the *its* (*a* and *ṅ*) are elided. In the illustration *pradhī* + *au*, the verb *dhī* ends in *ī* and is followed by an affix that begins with a vowel. The original verbal root is *dhyai* and it is still construed as such in accordance with the paribhāṣā *ekadeśavikṛtam ananyavat* (Abhyankar, 37). Moreover, it does not give up its status as a verbal root (*dhātu*) even though it ends in the primary affix *kvip*. This is so by virtue of the paribhāṣā *kvibantā dhātutvaṁ na jahati*... (Paribhāṣāsaṅgraha, p. 43) 'the words ending in *kvip* do not give up their status as a dhatu'. All the conditions laid down by the present rule are fulfilled. Hence the *iyaṅ*-replacement in place of the aṅga-final *ī* is available. The following sūtra, however, presents itself to block the *iyaṅ*-replacement and prescribes *yaṇ*-replacement :

(199) एरनेकाचोऽसंयोगपूर्वस्य । ***eranekāco 'saṁyogapūrvasya*. 6. 4. 82**

लघु० – धात्ववयवसंयोगपूर्वो न भवति य इवर्णस्तदन्तो यो धातुस्तदन्तस्यानेकाचोऽङ्गस्य यणजादौ प्रत्यये । प्रध्यौ २ । प्रध्यम् । प्रध्यः । प्रध्यि । शेषं पपीवत् । *dhātvavayava-saṁyogapūrvo na bhavati ya ivarṇas tadanto yo dhātus tadantasyānekāco-'ṅgasya yaṇ ajādau pratyaye. pradhyau 2. pradhyam. pradhyaḥ. pradhyi. śeṣaṁ papīvat.*

Trans. : A polysyllabic aṅga, which ends in a verbal root that ends in *i*, where *i* is not preceded by a conjunct of the verbal root, is replaced by *yaṇ*, if an affix, beginning with a vowel, follows.

PP. *eḥ anekācaḥ asaṁyogapūrvasya dhātoḥ aṅgasya yaṇ aci.*

Eluc. : All the three words *eḥ*, *anekācaḥ* and *asaṁyogapūrvasya* comprising the present sūtra are the genitive singular forms of *i*, *anekāc* and *asaṁyogapūrva* respectively. The terms *śnu* and *bhrū* end in *u* and as such they are incompatible with the vowel *i* in respect of anuvṛtti since it cannot qualify them. Consequently, the term *dhātu* is segregated from the itaretaradvandva compound *śnudhātubhruvām* in Pā. 6. 4. 77 and is carried over into the present sūtra. The term *dhātoḥ*, which is carried over, is iterated. One of them is qualified by the term *eḥ*. By tadantavidhi it gives the sense : The verbal root which ends in the vowel *i*. The other is paraphrased with the word *saṁyoga*, which is a part of the nañ-bahuvrīhi samāsa *asaṁyogapūrvasya*. The present rule occurs in the domain of the governing sūtra *aṅgasya* Pā. 6. 4. 1. So the word *aṅgasya* recurs here and is qualified by the expression *ivarṇāntasya dhātoḥ* and *anekācaḥ*. The word *anekācaḥ* is a bahuvrīhi compound. Its analysis is : *aneke aco yasya yasmin vā so 'nekāc, tasya = anekācaḥ*. The term *eḥ* is in apposition with the word *asaṁyogapūrvasya*, which is a bahuvrīhi samāsa analysed as : *nāsti saṁyogaḥ pūrvo yasya so 'saṁyogapūrvaḥ*. The word *yaṇ* is carried over from the rule *iṇo yaṇ* Pā. 6. 4. 81. The breakup of the complete meaning, which the present sūtra offers in this way, is given below for an easy comprehension. 1. An aṅga will be replaced by *yaṇ* (*aṅgasya yaṇ*), provided : (i) The aṅga possesses more than one vowel; (ii) It ends in a verbal root ending in the vowel *i* (*ivarṇāntasya dhātoḥ*); (iii) This vowel *i* should not be preceded by a conjunct consonant which is a part of the same verbal root; (iv) It is followed by an affix which begins with a vowel. 2. With the help of paribhāṣā sūtra *alo 'ntyasya*, the *yaṇ*-replacement will come in place of the aṅga-final vowel *i*.

In the present illustration *pradhī + au*, the verbal root ends in *ī* . It does not have any conjunct consonant which precedes *ī*. Although *pr* in *pra* is a conjunct consonant, it is a part of the preverb *pra* and not that of the verbal root. Moreover, it is separated by the intervention of two phonemes *a* and *dh*. This verbal root occurs at the end of *pradhī* which is a polysyllabic pre-affixal base (*anekāc aṅga*). This aṅga is followed by an affix *au*, which can be said to begin with a vowel by virtue of the maxim according to which a secondary thing is treated as the principal one (*vyapadeśivad-bhāva*). Here, by the paribhāṣā sūtra *alo 'ntyasya*, the aṅga-final vowel *i* is replaced by *y* (*yaṇ*). Thus we obtain the form *pradhyau*.

With nominative plural affix *jas*, we have *pradhī + jas --> pradhī + as*. Here first of all, the rule *iko yaṇaci* (15) becomes available for application. It is blocked by *prathamayoḥ pūrvasavarṇaḥ* (125), which is debarred by *dīrghājjasi ca* (161). After this, again the *yaṇ*-substitution by (15) becomes available. The rule *aci śnudhātubhruvāṁ yvoriyaṅuvaṅau* (198) prescribes *iyaṅ*-substitution but the present sūtra blocks it and instead prescribes *yaṇ*-replacement. As a result, the aṅga-final vowel *i* is replaced by *yaṇ*. Thus the form *pradhyaḥ* is obtained.

In *pradhī + am* also *iko yaṇaci* (15) first applies. It is blocked by *ami pūrvaḥ* (134). Being subsequent, the sūtra *aciśnudhātu...* (198) becomes available for application. Then the rule *eranekāco 'saṁyogapūrvasya* (199), which is an exception to (198), applies and the aṅga-final vowel *i* is replaced by *yaṇ*. Thus we obtain the form *pradhyam*.

With the plural sup-affix of the second triplet, we have *pradhī + śas*. At this stage, both the sūtras *prathamayoḥ pūrvasavarṇaḥ* (125) and *aciśnudhātubhruvāṁ yvoriyaṅuvaṅau* (198) apply simultaneously and being subsequent, the latter becomes available. It is blocked by the exception rule *eranekāco 'saṁyogapūrvasya* (199), which prescribes *yaṇ*-

substitution in place of the aṅga-final vowel *i*. After rutva and visarga, the form *pradhyaḥ* is obtained. In the absence of pūrvasavarṇadīrgha, the rule *tasmācchaso naḥ puṁsi* (136) does not apply and as a result the dental *s* of the plural affix *śas* is not replaced by the phoneme *n*.

In the cases of the sup-affixes *ṭā, ṅe, ṅasi, ṅas* and *os*, the *iyaṅ*-replacement by *aci śnudhātu...* (198) is blocked by *yaṇ*-replacement in accordance with the rule *eranekāco...* (199) and we respectively have *pradhyā, pradhye, pradhyaḥ, pradhyaḥ* and *pradhyoḥ*. With the affixes *bhyām, bhis* and *bhyas*, no change takes place.

In the genitive plural, the augment *nuṭ* by *hrasva...* (147) is not available since the nominal stem *pradhī* does not qualify for being designated as *nadī*. The rule *eranekāco...* (199) applies and we have *pradhyām*.

In the locative singular *pradhī + ṅi --> pradhī+ i*, a homogeneous long substitution is available but is blocked by *eranekāco...* (199) by which *yaṇ*-replacement takes place and the form *pradhyi* is obtained.

In the locative plural form, the rule *ādeśapratyayayoḥ* (149) applies and the dental *s* of *sup* is replaced by *ṣ*. Thus the form *pradhīṣu* is obtained. The declension of *pradhī* is as follows :

	Singular	Dual	Plural
prathamā	*pradhīḥ*	*pradhyau*	*pradhyaḥ*
dvitīyā	*pradhyam*	*pradhyau*	*pradhyaḥ*
tṛtīyā	*pradhyā*	*pradhībhyām*	*pradhībhiḥ*
caturthī	*pradhye*	*pradhībhyām*	*pradhībhyaḥ*
pañcamī	*pradhyaḥ*	*pradhībhyām*	*pradhībhyaḥ*
ṣaṣṭhī	*pradhyaḥ*	*pradhyoḥ*	*pradhyām*
saptamī	*pradhyi*	*pradhyoḥ*	*pradhīṣu*
sambodhana	*he pradhīḥ!*	*he pradhyau!*	*he pradhyaḥ!*

लघु० – एवं ग्रामणीः। ङौ तु ग्रामण्याम्। *evaṁ grāmaṇīḥ. ṅau tu grāmaṇyām.*

Eluc. : The word *grāmaṇī* 'a village leader' is an upapada compound, which is analysed as : *grāmaṁ nayatīti --> grāma ṅas nī kvip--> grāmanī --> grāmaṇī*. The retroflex *ṇ* replaces the dental *n* by *agragrāmābhyāṁ nayaterṇo vācyaḥ* (SK, IV, vtk 5064). This word is not inherently a feminine word as Ballantyne has understood it to be when he says that the word means 'a female head of a village' (see his *Laghukaumudī of*

Varadarāja, p. 70). It is common to all the three genders. As a result it is not assigned the designation *nadī*.

The verbal root *nī* ends in long *ī*. There is also no conjunct consonant of the verbal root which precedes it. The pre-affixal base is polysyllabic. Hence the *yaṇ*-replacement will take place before an affix which begins with a vowel in accordance with the rule *eranekāco...* (199). It will be declined like *pradhī* except when the locative singular affix *ṅi* follows. The affix *ṅi* will be replaced by *ām* by the rule *ṅerāmnadyāmnībhyaḥ* (197) since this rule contains the root *nī* in it. As such the locative singular form will be *grāmaṇyām*. The declension of *grāmaṇī* will be as follows :

	Singular	Dual	Plural
prathamā	*grāmaṇīḥ*	*grāmaṇyau*	*grāmaṇyaḥ*
dvitīyā	*grāmaṇyam*	*grāmaṇyau*	*grāmaṇyaḥ*
tṛtīyā	*grāmaṇyā*	*grāmaṇībhyām*	*grāmaṇībhiḥ*
caturthī	*grāmaṇye*	*grāmaṇībhyām*	*grāmaṇībhyaḥ*
pañcamī	*grāmaṇyaḥ*	*grāmaṇībhyām*	*grāmaṇībhyaḥ*
ṣaṣṭhī	*grāmaṇyaḥ*	*grāmaṇyoḥ*	*grāmaṇyām*
saptamī	*grāmaṇyām*	*grāmaṇyoḥ*	*grāmaṇīṣu*
sambodhana	*he grāmaṇīḥ!*	*he grāmaṇyau!*	*he grāmaṇyaḥ!*

Varadarāja now presents the counter-examples in order to make the meaning of the sūtra clear and easy to comprehend :

लघु० – अनेकाचः किम्? नीः, नियौ, नियः। अमि शसि च परत्वाद् इयङ् - नियम्, नियः। ङेरामि - नियाम्। *anekācaḥ kim? nīḥ, niyau, niyaḥ. ami śasi ca paratvād iyaṅ - niyam, niyaḥ. ṅer āmi - niyām.*

Eluc. : What is the significance of saying that the aṅga should be polysyllabic; that is to say, it should possess more than one vowel? To answer this question, Varadarāja gives the illustration of the relevant inflectional forms of the word *nī*. Since it is not polysyllabic (*anekāc*), the aṅga-final *ī* will not be replaced by *yaṇ* before the affix which begins with a vowel. So, the *yaṇ*-replacement does not take place in the dual and plural nominative forms of *nī* when the vowel-initial affixes *au* and *as* (*jas*) follow since the aṅga is monosyllabic (*ekāc*). Instead the aṅga-final *ī* will be replaced by *iyaṅ* by *aci śnudhātu...* (198). With the singular and plural affixes of the second triplet, *ami pūrvaḥ* (134) and *prathamayoḥ pūrvasavarṇaḥ* (125) are blocked by *aci śnudhātu...* (198). The forms respectively will be *niyam* and *niyaḥ*. In the locative singular, the affix *ṅi* is replaced by *ām* by *ṅerāmnadyāmnībhyaḥ* (197). The complete declension of the nominal stem *nī* is as follows :

	Singular	Dual	Plural
prathamā	*nīḥ*	*niyau*	*niyaḥ*
dvitīyā	*niyam*	*niyau*	*niyaḥ*
tṛtīyā	*niyā*	*nībhyām*	*nībhiḥ*
caturthī	*niye*	*nībhyām*	*nībhyaḥ*
pañcamī	*niyaḥ*	*nībhyām*	*nībhyaḥ*
ṣaṣṭhī	*niyaḥ*	*niyoḥ*	*niyām*
saptamī	*niyām*	*niyoḥ*	*nīṣu*
sambodhana	*he nīḥ!*	*he niyau!*	*he niyaḥ!*

लघु० – असंयोगपूर्वस्य किम् ? सुश्रियौ, यवक्रियौ । *asaṁyogapūrvasya kim? suśriyau, yavakriyau.*

Eluc. : It has been given in the sūtra *eranekāco 'saṁyogapūrvasya* (199) that the phoneme *i* occurring at the end of a verbal root should not be preceded by a conjunct consonant which forms a part of the verbal root itself. Its consequence is observed in the illustrations *suśriyau, yavakriyau* given by Varadarāja.

The compound words in prātipadika form are *suśrī* and *yavakrī*. The word *suśrī* is derived in the following two ways : *suṣṭhu śrayatīti suśrīḥ = su śri + kvip*. The affix *kvip* is introduced by the vārttika *kvibvaci-pracchyāyatastukaṭaprujuśrīṇāṁ dīrgho 'samprasāraṇaṁ ca* (Kāśikā on Pā. 3. 2. 178).[1] The primary affix *kvip* is wholly elided (see supra p. 240). The final vowel of the root *śri* is elongated by this vārttika. As per this derivation, the word *suśrī* means 'one who takes shelter properly'. When it is derived in the sense *śrayati harim*, the word *śrī* means 'Goddess of wealth'. It is inherently feminine. Then the word *suśrī* will be analysed as *śobhanā śrīḥ yasya sa suśrīḥ*. This word will be declined alike in both the senses. Since in the second sense, the word *śrī* ends in long *ī* and

1. This vārttika is given in the Mahābhāṣya as 3. 2. 178 vtk 2, which does not contain the initial affix *kvip* and the expression *dīrgho 'samprasāraṇaṁ ca*.

retains its inherent feminine status by the vārttika *prathamaliṅga-grahaṇaṁ ca* {see supra (193) vtk 17}, it is designated as *nadī* by *yūstryākhyau nadī* (193) but the function of assigning nadī-designation is debarred by *neyaṅuvaṅsthānāvastrī* (228). As a result, the substitute *iyaṅ* will replace the aṅga-final *ī* since the word is not nadī and secondly the root-final *i* is preceded by a conjunct consonant *śr*.

The second compound word is *yavakrī* 'one who purchases barley'. It is analysed as *yavān krīṇātīti yavakrīḥ*. The grammatical analysis is : *yava ām krī kvip*. The *kvip* is enjoined here by *kvip ca* Pā. 3. 2. 76 and the form *yavakrī* is obtained.

Both the pre-affixal bases end in a long *ī* which is preceded by the conjunct consonant *śr* in *suśrī* and by *kr* in the compound word *yavakrī*. In both the cases the verbal roots retain their status as dhātu by virtue of the paribhāṣā *kvibantā dhātutvaṁ na jahati* (Paribhāṣā-saṅgraha, p. 43) even after the primary affix *kvip* has been introduced after them. These conjunct consonants form a part of the verbal roots themselves and precede the aṅga-final *ī*. This is the reason why *yaṇ*-replacement has not taken place by the rule *eranekāco 'saṁyogapūrvasya* (199). Instead the substitute *iyaṅ* has replaced the aṅga-final *ī* by the rule *aci śnudhātu-bhruvāṁ yvoriyaṅuvaṅau* (198).

The declension of the word *suśrī* does not differ from that of the word *yavakrī*. The declension of *suśrī* is given below :

	Singular	Dual	Plural
prathamā	*suśrīḥ*	*suśriyau*	*suśriyaḥ*
dvitīyā	*suśriyam*	*suśriyau*	*suśriyaḥ*
tṛtīyā	*suśriyā*	*suśrībhyām*	*suśrībhiḥ*
caturthī	*suśriye*	*suśrībhyām*	*suśrībhyaḥ*
pañcamī	*suśriyaḥ*	*suśrībhyām*	*suśrībhyaḥ*
ṣaṣṭhī	*suśriyaḥ*	*suśriyoḥ*	*suśriyām*
saptamī	*suśriyi*	*suśriyoḥ*	*suśrīṣu*
sambodhana	*he suśrīḥ!*	*he suśriyau!*	*he suśriyaḥ!*

(200) गतिश्च । *gatiśca.* **1. 4. 60**
लघु॰ – प्रादयः क्रियायोगे गतिसंज्ञाः स्युः । *prādayaḥ kriyāyoge gatisaṁjñāḥ syuḥ.*

Trans. : Let the items enumerated in the list headed by *pra* be also designated as *gati* when they are used with a verb (*kriyā*).

PP. *prādayaḥ kriyāyoge gatiḥ ca.*

Eluc. : The words *prādayaḥ* and *kriyāyoge* are respectively carried over from the sūtras *prādayaḥ* Pā. 1. 4. 58 and *upasargāḥ kriyāyoge* Pā. 1. 4. 59. Thus the meaning of the sūtra is : The particles, which are enlisted in the group headed by the word *pra,* are also designated as *gati* when they are used in combination with a verb.

The significance of the particle *ca* enunciated in the sūtra can be explained in the following way : The present sūtra occurs in the domain of *ākaḍārādekā saṁjñā* (165). The particles included in the list headed by *pra* have already been designated as *upasarga.* The second designation cannot be assigned to these particles. To do away with this restriction, the author of the Aṣṭādhyāyī has used the particle *ca* in the sūtra (*gatyupasargasaṁjñayos tu gatiś ceti cakārād eva samāveśaḥ siddhyati.* BM, I, p. 34). Thus the enumerated particles beginning with *pra* will have two designations : *upasarga* and *gati.*

The word *gati* used in the present sūtra is in the masculine as attested by the sūtra *gatiranantaraḥ* Pā. 6. 2. 49. The masculine word *gati* is derived by introducing the affix *ktic* after the verbal root *gam* by the rule *kticktau ca saṁjñāyām* Pā. 3. 3. 174 but the application of the rule *na ktici dīrghaśca* Pā. 6. 4. 39 in respect of this word is blocked by nipātana.[1]

18. वा॰ – गतिकारकेतरपूर्वपदस्य यण् नेष्यते ।[2] *gatikārakaketarapūrvapadasya yaṇ neṣyate.*
लघु॰ – शुद्धधियौ । *śuddhadhiyau.*

Trans. : The *yaṇ*-replacement is not desirable in respect of an aṅga where the preceding member is other than a gati or a kāraka.

---

1. *gatiranantaraḥ iti puṁliṅganirdeśād gamyata iti gatiḥ kticktau ca saṁjñāyām iti ktic nipātanāc ca na ktici dīrghaśca iti na bhavati.* KP, I, p. 596.

2. This vārttika is given in the Mahābhāṣya on Pā. 6. 4. 82 in the form of an iṣṭi as *gatikārakapūrvasyaiveṣyate.* Cf. *iṣṭir evaiṣā.* KP, V, p. 436.

Eluc. : This vārttika is purported to block the *yaṇ*-replacement coming in place of an aṅga-final vowel *i* if the preceding member is other than a gati or a kāraka word. This is what the author of the Mahābhāṣya wishes in this context. This is why Varadarāja explains the technical term *gati* and cites the rule *gatiśca* (200) in the present context. What a kāraka is will be explained in the chapter on the meaning of case-endings (*vibhaktyarthaprakaraṇa*).

The illustration given in the Laghu is *śuddhadhiyau*. This is the nominative dual form of *śuddhadhī*, which is a bahuvrīhi compound analysed as : *śuddhā dhīr yasya saḥ*. The word *śuddhā*, which qlualifies the word *dhī*, is neither a gati nor a kāraka word. It is in the context of such instances that the *yaṇ*-replacement is proposed to be blocked by the vārttika, although all the conditions laid down by the rule *eranekāco...* (199) for *yaṇ*-replacement are available. Instead, the substitute *iyaṅ* will replace the aṅga-final vowel *ī*. Thus the form *śuddhadhiyau* is obtained (*śuddhadhiy* + *au* <-- *śuddhadhī* + *au*).

The nominal stem *dhī* is inherently feminine before it becomes a member of the bahuvrīhi compound. It retains its feminine status by *prathamaliṅgagrahaṇañca* (vārttika, 17) even when it has become a subordinate member in the compound. The nadī-designation, which was thus available, is prohibited by the rule *neyaṅuvaṅsthānāvastrī* Pā. 1. 4. 4. Then the present vārttika becomes operational.

The declension of the word *śuddhadhī* is as follows :

	Singular	Dual	Plural
prathamā	*śuddhadhīḥ*	*śuddhadhiyau*	*śuddhadhiyaḥ*
dvitīyā	*śuddhadhiyam*	*śuddhadhiyau*	*śuddhadhiyaḥ*
tṛtīyā	*śuddhadhiyā*	*śuddhadhībhyām*	*śuddhadhībhiḥ*
caturthī	*śuddhadhiye*	*śuddhadhībhyām*	*śuddhadhībhyaḥ*
pañcamī	*śuddhadhiyaḥ*	*śuddhadhībhyām*	*śuddhadhībhyaḥ*
ṣaṣṭhī	*śuddhadhiyaḥ*	*śuddhadhiyoḥ*	*śuddhadhiyām*
saptamī	*śuddhadhiyi*	*śuddhadhiyoḥ*	*śuddhadhīṣu*
sambodh.	*he śuddhadhiḥ!*	*he śuddhadhiyau!*	*he śuddhadhiyaḥ!*

(201) न भूसुधियोः । *na bhūsudhiyoḥ*. 6. 4. 85

लघु० –एतयोरचि सुपि यण् न । सुधियौ । सुधियः । इत्यादि । *etayor aci supi yaṇ na. sudhiyau, sudhiyaḥ. ityādi.*

Trans. : The substitute *yaṇ* does not replace (the aṅga-final phoneme of) the nominal stems *bhū* and *sudhī* when followed by the sup-affixes which begin with a vowel.

PP. *aci supi yaṇ na bhūsudhiyoḥ* (*aṅgasya*).

Eluc. : The words *aci, supi* and *yaṇ* are respectively carried over from the sūtras *aci śnudhātubhruvāṁ yvoriyaṅuvaṅau* Pā. 6. 4. 77, *oḥ supi* Pā. 6. 4. 83 and *iṇo yaṇ* Pā. 6. 4. 81. The word *aci*, which is in the locative singular, qualifies the term *supi*. Hence tadādividhi becomes operational by virtue of the vārttika *yasmin vidhis tadādāvalgrahaṇe* Mbh 1. 1. 72 vtk 29. Thus the meaning of *aci supi* will be : 'a sup-affix which begins with a vowel' (*ajādau supi*). The compound word *bhūsudhiyoḥ* is an itaretara-dvandva. It is analysed as follows : *bhūś ca sudhīś ca bhūsudhiyau tayoḥ = bhūsudhiyoḥ*. Thus the sūtra means : If a sup-affix, which begins with a vowel, follows, then the nominal stems *bhū* and *sudhī* will not be replaced by *yaṇ*. With the help of the paribhāṣā-sūtra *alo 'ntyasya* (21), the *yaṇ*-replacement which is being blocked by the present rule was to come in place of the final vowel of *bhū* and *sudhī*.

The word *sudhī* is derived from *su* + *dhyai* + *kvip* (*sudhyāyatīti sudhīḥ*) by *dhyāyateḥ samprasāraṇaṁ ca* Mbh 3. 2. 178 vtk 4. The particle *su* in *sudhī* is designated as *gati* by *gatiśca* (200). Since the particle *su* is gati, the *yaṇ*-replacement available by (199) is not blocked by the vārttika *gatikāraketarapūrvapadasya yaṇ neṣyate* (vtk 18). The present sūtra blocks it and instead the *iyaṅ*-replacement comes in place of the aṅga-final vowel *ī* of *sudhī* by *aci śnudhātubhruvāṁ yvoriyaṅuvaṅau* (198) since the vowel *ī* of *dhī*, which ends in the affix *kvip*, is construed as the final vowel of a verbal root by virtue of the paribhāṣā *kvibantā dhātutvaṁ na jahati...* (Paribhāṣāsaṅgraha, p. 43).

The declension of the nominal stem *sudhī* is as follows :

	Singular	Dual	Plural
prathamā	*sudhīḥ*	*sudhiyau*	*sudhiyaḥ*
dvitīyā	*sudhiyam*	*sudhiyau*	*sudhiyaḥ*
tṛtīyā	*sudhiyā*	*sudhībhyām*	*sudhībhiḥ*
caturthī	*sudhiye*	*sudhībhyām*	*sudhībhyaḥ*
pañcamī	*sudhiyaḥ*	*sudhībhyām*	*sudhībhyaḥ*
ṣaṣṭhī	*sudhiyaḥ*	*sudhiyoḥ*	*sudhiyām*

saptamī	*sudhiyi*	*sudhiyoḥ*	*sudhīṣu*
sambodhana	*he sudhīḥ!*	*he sudhiyau!*	*he sudhiyaḥ!*

लघु० – सुखमिच्छतीति सुखीः। सुतमिच्छतीति सुतीः। सुख्यौ। सुत्यौ। सुख्युः। सुत्युः। शेषं प्रधीवत्। *sukham icchatīti sukhīḥ. sutam icchatīti sutīḥ. sukhyau. sutyau. sukhyuḥ. sutyuḥ. śeṣaṁ pradhīvat.*

Eluc. : The word *sukhī* 'one who wishes pleasure for oneself' is derived in the following way : The affix *kyac* is introduced after the word *sukham* (*sukha + am*) in the sense of '*sukham ātmana icchati*' by the sūtra *supa ātmanaḥ kyac* (717). The grammatical analysis is as follows : *sukh am + kyac*. The group of these grammatical items is called a verbal root (*dhātu*) by the rule *sanādyantā dhātavaḥ* (467). The sup-affix is replaced by luk-elision by the rule *supo dhātuprātipadikayoḥ* (718) and we have *sukha + kyac --> sukha + ya* (after the anubandhas have been elided). At this stage, the *ī*-replacement comes in place of the final *a* of *sukha* by *kyaci ca* (719) and we have the derived verbal root *sukhīya*. Now the affix *kvip* in the sense of 'agent' is introduced after it by *kvip ca* (799). The phoneme *v* remains of *kvip* after the elision of the *its*. At this stage of the formation, *sukhīya + v*, the phonemes *a* and *y* are elided respectively by the sūtras *ato lopaḥ* (469) and *lopo vyorvali* (428). When the phoneme *v* is also elided by *verapṛktasya* (302), we have the form *sukhī*, which retains its status as dhātu by virtue of the paribhāṣā *kvibantā dhātutvaṁ na jahati...* (Paribhāṣā-saṅgraha, p. 43). In the same way the word *sutī* is derived. The following are the distinguishing characteristics of the declension of the words *sukhī* and *sutī* : 1. There is no elision of the nominative singular affix *su* since these words do not end in the feminine affix *ṅī*. 2. The *yaṇ*-replacement by *eranekāco...* (199) will take place where an affix, which begins with a vowel, follows. 3. In respect of the singular sup-affixes of the fifth and sixth triplets, namely, *ṅasi* and *ṅas*, which begin with a vowel, the rule *khyatyāt parasya* (182) prescribes the vowel *u* to be substituted in place of the vowel *a* of these affixes after the *yaṇ*-replacement has taken place. With these charateristics, the declension of *sukhī* is given below :

	Singular	Dual	Plural
prathamā	*sukhīḥ*	*sukhyau*	*sukhyaḥ*
dvitīyā	*sukhyam*	*sukhyau*	*sukhyaḥ*
tṛtīyā	*sukhyā*	*sukhībhyām*	*sukhībhiḥ*

caturthī	*sukhye*	*sukhībhyām*	*sukhībhyaḥ*
pañcamī	*sukhyuḥ*	*sukhībhyām*	*sukhībhyaḥ*
ṣaṣṭhī	*sukhyuḥ*	*sukhyoḥ*	*sukhyām*
saptamī	*sukhyi*	*sukhyoḥ*	*sukhīṣu*
sambodhana	*he sukhīḥ!*	*he sukhyau!*	*he sukhyaḥ!*

The declension of the word *sutī* will be exactly like that of *sukhī*.

Here comes to an end the declension of the masculine nominal stems ending in the vowel *ī*. Now begins the declension of the masculine nominal stems ending in *u*.

लघु० – शम्भुर्हरिवत्। एवम् भान्वादयः। *śambhur harivat. evam bhānvādayaḥ.*

Eluc. : The declension of the nominal stem *śambhu* is like that of the word *hari*. The words *bhānu* and so on will be declined in the same manner.

The word *śambhu* is a ghi-stem by *śeṣo ghyasakhi* (169). As such, in declining *śambhu* the ghi-specific grammatical operations will take place. These grammatical operations along with others are as follows : The guṇa-replacement *o* comes in place of the vowel *u* occurring at the end of *śambhu* by *jasi ca* (167), *gherṅiti* (171) and *hrasvasya guṇaḥ* (168). The singular affix *ṭā* of the third triplet is replaced by *nā* by *āṅo nāstriyām* (170). In the ablative and genitive singular declensional forms, after the guṇa-substitution has taken place, a single substitute homogeneous with the preceding (*pūrvarūpa*) replaces both the vowel *o* of the stem and the vowel *a* of the affixes *ṅasi* and *ṅas* by the rule *ṅasiṅasośca* (172). In the locative singular form, the affix *ṅi* is replaced by the substitute *au*, and the stem-final *u* is replaced by a short *a*. Taking all these points into account, the declension of the word *śambhu* is as follows :

	Singular	Dual	Plural
prathamā	*śambhuḥ*	*śambhū*	*śambhavaḥ*
dvitīyā	*śambhum*	*śambhū*	*śambhūn*
tṛtīyā	*śambhunā*	*śambhubhyām*	*śambhubhiḥ*
caturthī	*śambhave*	*śambhubhyām*	*śambhubhyaḥ*
pañcamī	*śambhoḥ*	*śambhubhyām*	*śambhubhyaḥ*

ṣaṣṭhī	*śambhoḥ*	*śambhvoḥ*	*śambhūnām*
saptamī	*śambhau*	*śambhvoḥ*	*śambhuṣu*
sambodhana	*he śambho!*	*he śambhū!*	*he śambhavaḥ!*

Some of the words that are declined like *śambhu* are *aṁśu* 'ray', *ākhu* 'mouse', *indu* 'the moon', *iṣu* 'arrow', *guru* 'teacher', *tantu* 'thread', *bāhu* 'arm', *dayālu* 'kind-hearted person', *paśu* 'animal', *pipāsu* 'thirsty', *bhānu* 'the sun', *mṛtyu* 'death', *manyu* 'anger', *ripu* 'enemy', *vāyu* 'wind', *vidhu* 'the moon', *śatru* 'enemy', *śiśu* 'child', *sādhu* 'gentleman', *sānu* 'mountain-peak', *sudhāṁśu* 'the moon', *setu* 'bridge' and *hetu* 'cause'.

The nominal stem *kroṣṭu* ends in the vowel *u* but its declension differs from that of *śambhu*. Therefore Varadarāja now presents the sūtras relevant to its declension :

(202) तृज्वत्क्रोष्टुः । *tṛjvatkroṣṭuḥ*. 7. 1. 95

लघु० – असम्बुद्धौ सर्वनामस्थाने परे। क्रोष्टुशब्दस्य स्थाने क्रोष्टृशब्दः प्रयोक्तव्य इत्यर्थः।

asambuddhau sarvanāmasthāne pare. kroṣṭuśabdasya sthāne kroṣṭṛśabdaḥ prayoktavya ityarthaḥ.

Trans. : With the exception of the vocative singular affix *su*, when the affixes, designated as *sarvanāmasthāna*, follow [the nominal, the pre-affixal base *kroṣṭu* 'jackal' is treated like one ending in the affix *tṛc*]. That is to say, the word *kroṣṭṛ* should be employed in place of the word *kroṣṭu*.

PP. *tṛjvat kroṣṭuḥ asambuddhau sarvanāmasthāne* (*aṅgasya*).

Eluc. : The words *asambuddhau* and *sarvanāmasthāne* are respectively carried over from *sakhyurasambuddhau* Pā. 7. 1. 92 and *ito 'tsarvanāmasthāne* Pā. 7. 1. 86. The commentary given by Varadarāja requires some explanation. The Gita Press Gorakhpur edition (footnote 6 on page 44) inserts a full stop (*pūrṇavirāma*) after the word *pare* and adds a footnote to complete the sense: *aṅgasaṁjñakaḥ kroṣṭuśabdas tṛjantavad rūpaṁ labhate iti vṛttau vākyaśeṣaḥ*. Then the next sentence given in the vṛtti makes sense. It means : That is to say, the substitute *kroṣṭṛ* should be employed in place of the word *kroṣṭu*. It looks as if Varadarāja has kept the wording of the sūtra in mind while giving his comments. If we add the sūtra, then the vṛtti would read as follows : *asambuddhau sarvanamasthāne pare kroṣṭu tṛjvat*. The translation provided here is on this basis. The translation of the supplied portion is kept in parentheses.

From this point of view, the vṛtti, as presented in the Bhaimīvyākhyā on page 262, appears to have missed what Varadarāja actually wants to convey in his commentary.

The word *tṛjvat* in the sūtra does not mean 'like the affix *tṛc*' but 'like a word ending in the affix *tṛc*'. This is an extension rule. It offers an extension of form (*rūpātideśa*). The meaning of the sūtra is : Before the first five sup-affixes, excluding the vocative singular affix *su*, the word *kroṣṭu* is to be replaced by one ending in the affix *tṛc*, that is *kroṣṭṛ*.

With the nominative singular affix, we have *kroṣṭu* + *su*. This affix is sarvanāmasthāna. Therefore, the pre-affixal base *kroṣṭu* is replaced by *kroṣṭṛ* and we have *kroṣṭṛ* + *s*. At this stage, the following sūtra beomes available for application :

(203) ऋतो ङिसर्वनामस्थानयोः । *ṛto ṅisarvanāmasthānayoḥ*. 7. 3. 110

लघु० - ऋतोऽङ्गस्य गुणो ङौ सर्वनामस्थाने च । इति प्राप्ते — *ṛto 'ṅgasya guṇo ṅau sarvanāmasthāne ca. iti prāpte* —

Trans. : The guṇa-substitute replaces the pre-affixal base which ends in *ṛ* when followed by the affixes *ṅi* and sarvanāmasthāna. When this sūtra is available for guṇa-substitution —

PP. *ṛtaḥ aṅgasya guṇaḥ ṅisarvanāmasthānayoḥ*.

Eluc. : The words *guṇaḥ* and *aṅgasya* are carried over from the sūtras *hrasvasya guṇaḥ* Pā. 7. 3. 108 and *aṅgasya* Pā. 6. 4. 1. The latter is a governing rule and the present sūtra occurs in its domain. Hence the word *aṅgasya* recurs here. The word *ṅisarvanāmasthānayoḥ* is an itaretaradvandva compound, which is analysed as : *ṅiś ca sarvanāmasthānaṁ ca tayoḥ* = *ṅisarvanāmasthānayoḥ*. The word *ṛtaḥ* qualifies the word *aṅgasya*. Hence tadantavidhi operates and both the words yield the meaning : *ṛdantasya aṅgasya*. Thus the meaning of the sūtra will be: When the first five sup-affixes and the singular affix of the seventh triplet follow, the pre-affixal base, which ends in the phoneme *ṛ*, is to be replaced by a guṇa vowel. With the help of the paribhāṣā sūtras *alo-'ntyasya* (21) and *iko guṇavṛddhī* Pā. 1. 1. 3, the guṇa vowel replacement will come in place of the last phoneme of the pre-affixal base *kroṣṭṛ*, that is *ṛ*. The guṇa vowel *a* will replace it and by *uraṇ raparaḥ* (29), it will be followed by repha. In conclusion, the substitute *ar* is available to replace the vowel *ṛ* but this is blocked by the ensuing sūtra :

(204) ऋदुशनस्पुरुदंसोऽनेहसां च । *ṛduśanaspurudaṁso 'nehasāṁ ca.*
7. 1. 94
लघु॰ – ऋदन्तानाम् उशनसादीनां चानङ् स्याद् असम्बुद्धौ सौ । *ṛdantānām uśanasādīnāṁ cānaṅ syād asambuddhau sau.*

Trans. : When a non-vocative singular affix *su* follows, the substitute *anaṅ* replaces the pre-affixal bases, which end in the vowel *ṛ* and which are (constituted by) *uśanas* 'the planet Venus, the preceptor of the asuras', *purudaṁsas* 'an epithet of Indra' and *anehas* 'time'.

PP. *asambuddhau sau ṛduśanaspurudaṁso 'nehasām ca aṅgānām anaṅ.*

Eluc. : The term *asambuddhau* is carried over from the sūtra *sakhyurasambuddhau* Pā. 7. 1. 92. The words *anaṅ* and *sau* are from the rule *anaṅ sau* Pā. 7. 1. 93. The word *aṅgasya* from the governing rule *aṅgasya* Pā. 6. 4. 1 is changed into the genitive plural to accord with the qualificand compound word *ṛduśanaspurudaṁso 'nehasām*. The word *ṛduśanaspurudaṁso 'nehasām* is an itaretaradvandva which is analysed as : *ṛc ca uśanā ca purudaṁsā ca anehā ca ṛduśanaspurudaṁso 'nehasaḥ, teṣām = ṛduśanaspurudaṁso 'nehasām*. The meaning of the sūtra is as follows : Before the non-vocative singular affix *su* of the first triplet, the aṅgas (pre-affixal bases), which end in the short vowel *ṛ* and which are constituted by the words *uśanas, purudaṁsas* and *anehas* are replaced by the substitute *anaṅ*.

Only the *an*-segment of the substitute *anaṅ* remains. Since the substitute *anaṅ* has the guttural nasal *ṅ* as *it*, it will replace the last phoneme of these pre-affixal bases by *ṅicca* (46). After this grammatical operation, *kroṣṭṛ* + s changes into *kroṣṭan* + s. At this stage, the following sūtra applies :

(205) अप्-तृन्-तृच्-स्वसृ-नप्तृ-नेष्टृ-त्वष्टृ-क्षतृ-होतृ-पोतृ-प्रशास्तॄणाम् । ***ap-tṛn-tṛc-svasṛ-naptṛ-neṣṭṛ-tvaṣṭṛ-kṣatṛ-hotṛ-potṛ-praśāstṝṇām.***
6. 4. 11
लघु॰ – अबादीनामुपधाया दीर्घोऽसम्बुद्धौ सर्वनामस्थाने । क्रोष्टा, क्रोष्टारौ, क्रोष्टारः, क्रोष्टारम्, क्रोष्टून् । *abādīnāmupadhāyā dīrgho 'sambuddhau sarvanāmasthāne. kroṣṭā, kroṣṭārau, kroṣṭāraḥ, kroṣṭāram, kroṣṭūn.*

Trans. : A substitute long vowel replaces the penultimate vowel (*upadhā*) of (pre-affixal stems) *ap* 'water', (those ending in the affixes) *tṛn* and *tṛc, svasṛ* 'sister', *naptṛ* 'grandson', *neṣṭṛ* 'an official priest at a soma sacrifice', *tvaṣṭṛ* 'carpenter', *kṣatṛ* 'charioteer, an attendant', *hotṛ* 'a priest who recites the Ṛgveda at a sacrifice', *potṛ* 'an assistant of the priest called brahman' and *praśāstṛ* 'a ruler' when they are followed by the affixes designated as *sarvanāmasthāna* with the exception of the vocative singular affix *su*.

PP. *ap-tṛn-tṛc-svasṛ-naptṛ-neṣṭṛ-tvaṣṭṛ-kṣatṛ-hotṛ-potṛ-praśāstṝṇām aṅgānām upadhāyāḥ dīrghaḥ asambuddhau sarvanāmasthāne.*

Eluc. : The word *upadhāyāḥ* is carried over from the sūtra *nopadhāyāḥ* Pā. 6. 4. 7. The word *dīrghaḥ* is lent from *ḍhralope pūrvasya dīrgho 'ṇaḥ* Pā. 6. 3. 111. The words *asambuddhau* and *sarvanāmasthāne* are carried over from *sarvanāmasthāne cāsambuddhau* Pā. 6. 4. 9. The present sūtra occurs in the domain of the governing rule *aṅgsya* Pā. 6. 4. 1. So the term *aṅgsya* is carried over here and changed into the genitive plural to accord with the compound word *ap-tṛn-tṛc-... praśāstṝṇām*.

The terms *tṛn* and *tṛc* are affixes. Therefore in accordance with the paribhāṣā *pratyayagrahaṇe... tadantasya grahaṇam* (Abhyankar, 23), these terms denote the stems which end in these affixes. In this way, the sūtra means : When a sarvanāmasthāna affix, which is other than the vocative singular affix *su*, follows, the penultimate vowel of the pre-affixal stems *ap* 'water', those ending in the affixes *tṛn* and *tṛc*, *svasṛ*, *naptṛ*, *neṣṭṛ*, *tvaṣṭṛ*, *kṣatṛ*, *hotṛ*, *potṛ* and *praśāstṛ* is replaced by its long counter-part.

In the illustration *kroṣṭan + s*, the stem *kroṣṭan* is construed as one ending in the affix *tṛc* according to the paribhāṣā *ekadeśavikṛtam ananyavat* (Abhyankar, 37). As such, the penultimate vowel *a* of the pre-affixal stem *kroṣṭan* is replaced by a long *ā* since the affix *su*, which follows, is a non-vocative sarvanāmasthāna affix. Now we have *kroṣṭān + s*. At this stage, the apṛkta affix *s* is elided by *halṅyābbhyo dīrghāt sutisyapṛktaṁ hal* (178). After that the final phoneme *n* is replaced by lopa according to *na lopaḥ prātipadikāntasya* (179). Thus the form *kroṣṭā* is obtained.

With the dual sup-affix *au* introduced after the stem *kroṣṭu*, a guṇa-replacement comes in place of the final phoneme *ṛ* by the rule *ṛto ṅisarvanāmasthānayoḥ* (203). The substituted guṇa-vowel *a* is followed by the phoneme repha with the help of the rule *uraṇ raparaḥ* (29) and we have *kroṣṭar + au*. At this stage, the present rule applies and the penultimate vowel is replaced by a long *ā* and we obtain the form *kroṣṭār + au --> kroṣṭārau*.

With the nominative plural affix *jas*, the same grammatical process operates and we have the form as *kroṣṭār + jas --> kroṣṭār + as --> kroṣṭāras*.

After the application of the sūtras *sasajuṣo ruḥ* (104) and *kharavasānayor visarjanīyaḥ* (93), we obtain the fully inflected form *kroṣṭāraḥ*.

With the singular affix *am* of the second triplet, we have *kroṣṭāram* after the guṇa-replacement and the elongation of the penultimate vowel respectively by *ṛto ṅisarvanāmasthānayoḥ* (203) and the present rule. The form *kroṣṭārau* with the dual affix of the second triplet does not differ from the one with the dual affix of the first triplet.

In the plural form of the word *kroṣṭu*, the sūtra *tṛjvatkroṣṭuḥ* (202) does not apply since no sarvanāmasthāna affix follows it. Hence, after the application of the rules *prathamayoḥ pūrvasavarṇaḥ* (125) and *tasmācchaso naḥ puṁsi* (136), we have the form *kroṣṭūn* (<-- *kroṣṭūs* <-- *kroṣṭu + as* <-- *kroṣṭu + śas*).

With the singular affix of the third triplet, we have *kroṣṭu + ṭā* --> *kroṣṭu + ā*. At this stage, the following sūtra becomes available for application since the affix begins with a vowel (*ac*) —

(206) विभाषा तृतीयादिष्वचि । *vibhāṣā tṛtīyādiṣvaci.* 7. 1. 97

लघु० – अजादिषु तृतीयादिषु क्रोष्टुर्वा तृज्वत् । *ajādiṣu tṛtīyādiṣu kroṣṭur vā tṛjvat.*

Trans. : The pre-affixal stem *kroṣṭu* is optionally treated as if ending in the affix *tṛc* when the sup-triplets with initial vowels beginning with the third follow.

PP. *tṛtīyādiṣu aci kroṣṭuḥ tṛjvat vibhāṣā* (*aṅgasya*).

Eluc. : The words *kroṣṭu* and *tṛjvat* are carried over from the sūtra *tṛjvat kroṣṭuḥ* Pā. 7. 1. 95. The word *aci* qualifies the word *tṛtīyādiṣu*. By tadādividhi it will yield the sense *ajādiṣu*. The meaning of the sūtra is now as follows : If the vowel-initial sup-triplets beginning with the third follow, then the pre-affixal stem *kroṣṭu* is optionally treated like one ending in the affix *tṛc*. The sup-affixes, which belong to the triplets beginning with the third one and which begin with a vowel, are eight in number : 1. *ṭā* (*ā*) 2. *ṅe* (*e*) 3. *ṅasi* (*as*) 4. *ṅas* (*as*) 5. *os* 6. *ām* 7. *ṅi* (*i*) 8. *os*. When these affixes follow, there will be two forms of the word *kroṣṭu*. One form will be as if the word *kroṣṭu* ended in the affix *tṛc*. Alternatively, the word *kroṣṭu* will be declined like *śambhu*.

With the singular affix of the third triplet, we have *kroṣṭu + ṭā* --> *kroṣṭu + ā* --> *kroṣṭṛ + ā* (*tṛjvadbhāva*). The rule *iko yaṇaci* (15) applies and we obtain the form *kroṣṭrā*. In the absence of tṛjvadbhāva, the word *kroṣṭu* is ghi. Therefore, the affix *ṭā* is replaced by *nā* in accordance with the rule *āṅo nā 'striyām* (170). The inflected form will be *kroṣṭunā*.

The dual and plural sup-affixes of the third, fourth and fifth triplets do not begin with a vowel. Hence the word *kroṣṭu* is not treated as though ending in the affix *tṛc*. So, the stem *kroṣṭu* remains as it is before these affixes : *kroṣṭubhyām, kroṣṭubhiḥ, kroṣṭubhyām, kroṣṭubhyaḥ, kroṣṭubhyām* and *kroṣṭubhyaḥ*.

In tṛjvadbhāva when we introduce the singular affix of the fourth triplet, we have the form *kroṣṭre* after the application of *iko yaṇaci* (15). In the absence of tṛjvadbhāva, the word *kroṣṭu* is treated as ghi and by virtue of the rule *gherṅiti* (171), the guṇa-substitute *o* replaces the aṅga-final vowel *u* of *kroṣṭu*. The rule *eco...* (22) applies and we have the form *kroṣṭave* (<-- *kroṣṭav + e* <-- *kroṣṭo + e* <-- *kroṣṭu + e* <-- *kroṣṭu + ṅe*).

When we introduce the singular affix of the fifth triplet, we have *kroṣṭṛ + ṅasi* --> *kroṣṭṛ + as* (after the anubandhas are elided). At this stage, the following rule becomes available for application :

(207) ऋत उत् । *ṛta ut.* **6. 1. 111**

लघु० – ऋतो ङसिङसोरति उदेकादेशः । रपरः । *ṛto ṅasiṅasor ati ud ekādeśaḥ. raparaḥ.*

Trans. : If the short vowel *a* of the affixes *ṅasi* and *ṅas* follows the short vowel *ṛ*, then a single substitute, namely, the short vowel *u* replaces both (the vowels *ṛ* and *a*).

PP. *ṛtaḥ ṅasiṅasoḥ ati pūrvaparayoḥ ekaḥ ut (saṁhitāyām).*

Eluc. : The terms *ṅasi* and *ṅas* are carried over from the sūtra *ṅasiṅasośca* Pā. 6. 1. 110. The word *ati* comes from *eṅaḥ padāntādati* Pā. 6.1. 109. The sūtra *ekaḥ pūrvaparayoḥ* Pā. 6. 1. 84 is a governing rule. The present rule occurs in its domain. Hence all the three words recur in this sūtra also. With this, the present sūtra means : If a short vowel *ṛ* is followed by the short vowel *a* of the affixes *ṅasi* and *ṅas*, then both the vowels are replaced by a single substitute *u(t)*. In the illustration *kroṣṭṛ + as*, the final vowel, short *ṛ*, is followed by the short vowel *a* of the sup-affix *ṅasi*. Therefore the substitute *ut* replaces both *ṛ* and *a* and we have the form : *kroṣṭu s*. Now the rule *uraṇ raparaḥ* (29) applies. The substituted *u* becomes *ur* with the help of the rule *sthāne 'ntaratamaḥ* (17) and resultantly the form becomes : *kroṣṭur s*. At this stage, the following rule ensues :

(208) रात् सस्य । *rāt sasya.* **8. 2. 24**

लघु० – रेफात् संयोगान्तस्य सस्यैव लोपो नान्यस्य । रेफस्य विसर्गः । क्रोष्टुः । क्रोष्ट्रोः ।

rephāt saṁyogāntasya sasyaiva lopo nānyasya. rephasya visargaḥ. kroṣṭuḥ, kroṣṭroḥ.

Trans. : If the substitute *lopa* is to replace the conjunct-final phoneme after repha, then it replaces only *s* and not any other phoneme.

PP. *rāt samyogāntasya sasya lopaḥ (padasya).*

Eluc. : Both the words of *saṁyogāntasya lopaḥ* Pā. 8. 2. 23 are carried over into this sūtra. This is a niyama sūtra which restricts the lopa substitution for the pada-final phoneme to s which occurs at the end of a conjunct and which also occurs after the phoneme repha in that conjunct. The elision of *s* is already available by the rule *saṁyogāntasya lopaḥ* (20) but even so Pāṇini has enunciated this sūtra. This means that it has something more to convey. That something more consists in the incidence of restriction (*siddhe sati niyamārthaḥ*). The form of restriction is as follows : If a pada ends in a conjunct whose final phoneme comes after *r*, then the lopa-substitute replaces only *s* in such a grammatical situation and not any other conjunct-final phoneme. Thus the meaning of this sūtra is : If a phoneme follows repha in a conjunct in which a pada ends, then only the conjunct-final *s* is to be elided and not any other phoneme. The significance of this restriction is observed in the word *ūrk* in which the guttural phoneme is to be elided by *saṁyogāntasya lopaḥ* (20) but it is not elided since the phoneme *k* follows repha and is at the end of a saṁyoga in which the pada *ūrk* ends. Being other than the phoneme s, it is not elided.

In the illustration *kroṣṭur s*, the phoneme *s* follows repha and is at the end of a conjunct. As such, it is replaced by lopa by the present rule and we have *kroṣṭur*. At this stage, the rule *kharavasānayorvisarjanīyaḥ* (93) applies and the form *kroṣṭuḥ* is obtained. In the same way, we get the genitive singular form of the nominal stem *kroṣṭu*.

In the absence of tṛjvadbhāva, the word *kroṣṭu*, which is assigned the designation *ghi*, will be declined like the nominal stem *śambhu*. The rule *gherṅiti* (171) prescribes the guṇa-substitution. After the guṇa-substitution, the rule *ṅasiṅasośca* (172) applies and a single substitute homogeneous with the preceding vowel replaces both the vowel *o* and the short *a* of the affix *ṅasi* and we obtain the form *kroṣṭoḥ* after rutva and visarga. The form of *kroṣṭu* in the genitive singular will be similarly derived.

In the genitive dual, the affix *os* is employed. It begins with a vowel. Hence tṛjvadbhāva is optionally available. When there is tṛjvadbhāva, the rule *iko yaṇaci* (15) applies and the form *kroṣṭroḥ* (<-- *kroṣṭr* + *os* <-- *kroṣṭṛ* + *os*) is obtained. We have the locative dual form in the same way. In the absence of tṛjvadbhāva, again the rule *iko yaṇaci* (15) applies and the phoneme *v* replaces the vowel *u* of *kroṣṭu* and we obtain the form *kroṣṭvoḥ* (<-- *kroṣṭv* + *os* <-- *kroṣṭu* + *os*) after rutva and visarga.

With the plural affix of the sixth triplet, we have *kroṣṭu* + *ām*. At this stage, the sūtras *hrasvanadyāpo nuṭ* (147) and *tṛjvat kroṣṭuḥ* (202) become applicable simultaneously. The former has its scope in the formation of *harīṇām* and the latter in *kroṣṭā*. Thus both the rules have performed their grammatical functions as shown in the illustrations above. In such a grammatical situation, the paribhāṣā sūtra *vipratiṣedhe paraṁ kāryam* (112) becomes applicable and decides that the subsequent of the two conflicting rules would apply. In this case, the sūtra *tṛjvat kroṣṭuḥ* Pā. 7. 1. 95 is subsequent to *hrasvanadyāpo nuṭ* Pā. 7. 1. 54. Hence, the rule which prescribes tṛjvadbhāva becomes available for application. However, the following vārttika presents itself and blocks the application of tṛjvadbhāva :

19. वा० – नुम्-अचि र-तृज्वद्भावेभ्यो नुट् पूर्वविप्रतिषेधेन । *num-aci ra-tṛjvadbhāvebhyo nuṭ pūrvavipratiṣedhena.*

Trans. : As a prior exception, the augment *nuṭ* blocks these grammatical operations : 1. insertion of the augment *num*, 2. repha-substitution before *ac* and 3. tṛjvadbhāva.

लघु० – क्रोष्टूनाम् । क्रोष्टरि । पक्षे हलादौ शम्भुवत् । *kroṣṭūnām. kroṣṭari. pakṣe halādau śambhuvat.*

Eluc. : The grammatical operation of inserting the augment *num* is brought about by *iko 'ci vibhaktau* (244). The other grammatical function of replacing the final vowel *ṛ* of the words *tisṛ* and *catasṛ* by repha before the vowel-initial sup-affixes takes place by *aci ra ṛtaḥ* (224). The third grammatical operation is tṛjvadbhāva by *tṛjvat kroṣṭuḥ* (202). When these functions are in conflict with that of inserting the augment *nuṭ* as is available in the present case, the rule, which prescribes the augment *nuṭ*, blocks the other rule that enjoins any of these three grammatical operations. The present vārttika proposes that the paribhāṣā sūtra *vipratiṣedhe paraṁ kāryam* (112), which determines which of the two simultaneouly available grammatical operations is to be performed, should not apply. A general interpretation of the rule (112) allows the grammatical operation, which is subsequent in the Aṣṭādhyāyī, to take effect. In the present illustration, when the plural affix of the sixth triplet is introduced after the nominal stem *kroṣṭu,* we have *kroṣṭu + ām.* Here the grammatical operation of inserting the augment *nuṭ* by *hrasvanadyāpo nuṭ* Pā. 7. 1. 54 and that of treating the nominal stem *kroṣṭu* as ending in the affix *tṛc* by *tṛjvat kroṣṭuḥ* Pā. 7. 1. 95 simultaneously become applicable. The latter rule, being subsequent, blocks the former and presents itself for application. It is in this context that the vārttika (18) ensues and proposes that the sūtra *hrasvanadyāpo nuṭ* (147), though prior, should block *tṛjvat kroṣṭuḥ* (202) and be applied. As a result, we have only one form of *kroṣṭu* in the genitive plural, that is, *kroṣṭūnām.* The grammatical process deriving this form is as follows : *kroṣṭu + ām --> kroṣṭu + nuṭ ām --> kroṣṭu + nām --> kroṣṭūnām* {a long vowel-replacement takes place by *nāmi* (148)} --> *kroṣṭūnām.* In this context, Vāsudeva Dīkṣita and Jñānendra Sarasvatī observe that the augment *nuṭ* cannot be construed as nitya since, if tṛjvadbhāva is introduced, the augment *nuṭ* will be blocked by the metarule *sannipātalakṣaṇo vidhir...* (Abhyankar, 85). The reason is that, if *nuṭ* is inserted, the affix *ām* will lose its vowel-initial status which actually caused tṛjvadbhāva (BM, I and TB, I, p.281).

When we introduce the singular affix *ṅi* after *kroṣṭu,* the optional tṛjvadbhāva is available. With tṛjvadbhāva, the rule *ṛto ṅisarvanāmasthānayoḥ* (203) applies and the aṅga-final vowel *ṛ* is replaced by a guṇa-vowel *a* and it is followed by repha by *uraṇ raparaḥ* (29). We obtain the locative singular form through this process : *kroṣṭu + ṅi --> kroṣṭṛ + i --> kroṣṭar + i --> kroṣṭari.* In the absence of tṛjvadbhāva, the rule *acca gheḥ* (173) applies. The affix *ṅi* is replaced by *au* and the vowel *u* of *kroṣṭu,* by a short vowel *a.* After the application of *vṛddhireci* (33), we obtain the form *kroṣṭau* (<-- *kroṣṭa + au* <-- *kroṣṭu + ṅi*).

The sūtra *tṛjvat kroṣṭuḥ* (202) does not prescribe tṛjvadbhāva for the nominal stem *kroṣṭu* when the vocative singular affix *su* (*sambuddhi*) follows. In the absence of tṛjvadbhāva the stem *kroṣṭu* is declined like the nominal stem *śambhu.* So, by the rule *hrasvasya guṇaḥ* (168), the aṅga-final vowel *u* of *kroṣṭu* is replaced by the guṇa vowel *o.* After the guṇa-vowel replacement, the phoneme *s* of the vocative singular affix *su* is elided by the sūtra *eṅhrasvāt sambuddheḥ* (133). Thus the form *kroṣṭo* is obtained. The declension of *kroṣṭu* with all the affixes of the seven triplets is as follows :

	Singular	Dual	Plural
prathamā	*kroṣṭā*	*kroṣṭārau*	*kroṣṭāraḥ*
dvitīyā	*kroṣṭāram*	*kroṣṭārau*	*kroṣṭūn*

tṛtīyā	*kroṣṭrā, kroṣṭunā*	*kroṣṭubhyām*	*kroṣṭubhiḥ*
caturthī	*kroṣṭre, kroṣṭave*	*kroṣṭubhyām*	*kroṣṭubhyaḥ*
pañcamī	*kroṣṭuḥ, kroṣṭoḥ*	*kroṣṭubhyām*	*kroṣṭubhyaḥ*
ṣaṣṭhī	*kroṣṭuḥ, kroṣṭoḥ*	*kroṣṭroḥ kroṣṭvoḥ*	*kroṣṭūnām*
saptamī	*kroṣṭari, kroṣṭau*	*kroṣṭroḥ kroṣṭvoḥ*	*kroṣṭuṣu*
sambodhana	*he kroṣṭo!*	*he kroṣṭārau!*	*he kroṣṭāraḥ!*

Here comes to an end the declension of the masculine stems that end in a short *u*. Now begins the process of declining the masculine nominal stems that end in a long *ū*.

लघु० – हूहूः, हूह्वौ, हूह्वः । हूहून् । *hūhūḥ, hūhvau, hūhvaḥ, hūhūn.*

Eluc. : The nominal stem *hūhū* 'the name of a gandharva' is an underived nominal stem. Its declension is as follows :

	Singular	Dual	Plural
prathamā	*hūhūḥ*	*hūhvau*	*hūhvaḥ*
dvitīyā	*hūhūm*	*hūhvau*	*hūhūn*
tṛtīyā	*hūhvā*	*hūhūbhyām*	*hūhūbhiḥ*
caturthī	*hūhve*	*hūhūbhyām*	*hūhūbhyaḥ*
pañcamī	*hūhvaḥ*	*hūhūbhyām*	*hūhūbhyaḥ*
ṣaṣṭhī	*hūhvaḥ*	*hūhvoḥ*	*hūhvām*
saptamī	*hūhvi*	*hūhvoḥ*	*hūhūṣu*
sambodhana	*he hūhūḥ!*	*he hūhvau!*	*he hūhvaḥ!*

In the declension of the nominal stem *hūhū*, the grammatical operations that deserve mention are as follows : 1. With the dual affixes *au* and *auṭ* of the first and second triplets, we have the form *hūhvau* in both the cases by applying the rule *iko yaṇaci* (15) after *prathamayoḥ pūrvasavarṇaḥ* (125) has been blocked by the sūtra *dīrghājjasi ca* (161). 2. In the singular form of the second triplet, the rule *ami pūrvaḥ* (134) applies. 3. In the plural form of the second triplet, the *n*-replacement by the rule *tasmācchaso naḥ puṁsi* (136) takes place after a long vowel-substitution has taken effect by *prathamayoḥ*... (125). In the rest of the declension, the sūtra *iko yaṇaci* (15) applies when a vowel-initial affix follows. At other places also, no new rules apply.

लघु० - 'अतिचमू' शब्दे तु नदीकार्यविशेषः। हे अतिचमु ! अतिचम्वै। अतिचम्वाः। अतिचमूनाम्। अतिचम्वाम्। *aticamū-śabde tu nadīkāryaviśeṣaḥ. he aticamu! aticamvai. aticamvāḥ. aticamūnām. aticamvām.*

Eluc. : The word *aticamū* 'one who has won the army' is a prāditatpuruṣa compound which is analysed as : *camūm atikrāntaḥ*. The compound is formed with the help of the vārttika *atyādayaḥ krāntādyarthe dvitīyayā*, Mbh 2. 2. 18 saunāga vtk 2. The last member of the compound is *camū* 'army', which is feminine. Although it has attained a subordinate status in the compound, it is still treated as feminine by virtue of the vārttika (17) *prathamaliṅgagrahaṇañca*. As such, it is designated as *nadī*. Hence it will have nadī-specific grammatical features in its declension :

	Singular	Dual	Plural
prathamā	*aticamūḥ*	*aticamvau*	*aticamvaḥ*
dvitīyā	*aticamūm*	*aticamvau*	*aticamūn*
tṛtīyā	*aticamvā*	*aticamūbhyām*	*aticamūbhiḥ*
caturthī	*aticamvai*	*aticamūbhyām*	*aticamūbhyaḥ*
pañcamī	*aticamvāḥ*	*aticamūbhyām*	*aticamūbhyaḥ*
ṣaṣṭhī	*aticamvāḥ*	*aticamvoḥ*	*aticamūnām*
saptamī	*aticamvām*	*aticamvoḥ*	*aticamūṣu*
sambodhana	*he aticamu!*	*he aticamvau!*	*he aticamvaḥ!*

The elision of the apṛkta affix *s*(*u*) of the nominative singular form does not take effect by *halṅyābbhyo dīrghāt sutisyapṛktaṁ hal* (178) since the stem does not end in the feminine affix *ṅī*. With the singular affixes of the fourth, fifth and sixth triplets, the sūtras *āṇnadyāḥ* (195), *āṭaśca* (196) and *iko yaṇaci* (15) respectively prescribe the augment *āṭ*, *vṛddhi* and *yaṇ*-replacements in *aticamvai*, *aticamvāḥ* and *aticamvāḥ*. The rule *hrasvanadyāpo nuṭ* (147) applies in the genitive plural form *aticamūnām*. In the locative singular form *aticamvām*, the substitute *ām* replaces the singular sup-affix *ṅi* of the seventh triplet by *ṅerāmnadyāmnībhyaḥ* (197). After the application of the sūtras *āṇnadyāḥ* (195), *āṭaśca* (196) and *iko yaṇaci* (15), we have the form *aticamvām*. In the vocative singular, the sūtra *ambārthanadyorhrasvaḥ* (194) applies and prescribes the short vowel replacement in place of the last phoneme of the pre-affixal stem *aticamū*. After the short vowel replacement, the rule *eṅhrasvāt sambuddheḥ* (133) enjoins the lopa-substitution in place of the phoneme *s* of the vocative singular affix *su* and we obtain the form *aticamu*.

लघु० – खलपूः । *khalapūḥ*.

Eluc. : The word *khalapūḥ* 'one who cleans a threshing floor' is an upapada compound. Its analysis is : *khalaṁ punātīti*. The verbal root is *pūñ* 'to clean, to purify' and the affix *kvip* is introduced after it. The affix *kvip* is wholly replaced by lopa. Thus the word *khalapū* is obtained. Since the word does not end in the feminine *ṅī*, the single-consonant affix (*apṛkta*) *s*(*u*) is not elided by the rule *halṅyābbhyo dīrghāt sutisyapṛktaṁ hal* (178). In the form with the dual affix of the second triplet *au*, the pūrvasavarṇadīrgha is debarred by *dīrghājjasi ca* (161). Then the sūtra *iko yaṇaci* (15) becomes applicable. It is blocked by virtue of the paribhāṣā *kvibantā dhātutvaṁ na jahati* (Paribhāṣāsaṅgraha, p. 43) which occasions the availability of *uvaṅ*-substitute by the sūtra *aci śnudhātubhruvāṁ yvoriyaṅuvaṅau* (198). At this stage, the following sūtra ensues :

(209) ओः सुपि । *oḥ supi*. 6. 4. 83

लघु० – धात्ववयवसंयोगपूर्वो न भवति य उवर्णः, तदन्तो यो धातुः, तदन्तस्यानेकाचोऽङ्गस्य यण् स्याद् अचि सुपि । खल्प्वौ, खलप्वः । *dhātvavayavasaṁyogapūrvo na bhavati ya uvarṇaḥ tadanto yo dhātuḥ tadantasyānekāco 'ṅgasya yaṇ syād aci supi. khalpvau, khalapvaḥ.*

Trans. : A polysyllabic pre-affixal base (*aṅga*) which ends in a verbal root that ends in *u*, where *u* is not preceded by a conjunct of the verbal root, is replaced by *yaṇ*, if a sup-affix, which begins with a vowel, follows.

PP. *oḥ supi anekācaḥ asaṁyogapūrvasya aṅgasya aci yaṇ dhātoḥ.*

Eluc. : The words *anekācaḥ* and *asaṁyogapūrvasya* are carried over from *eranekāco 'saṁyogapūrvasya* Pā. 6. 4. 82. The terms *dhātoḥ* and *aci* come from *aci śnudhātubhruvāṁ yvoriyaṅuvaṅau* Pā. 6. 4. 77 but the former comes in the manner of a frog's leap. The word *yaṇ* is read into this sūtra from *iṇo yaṇ* Pā. 6. 4. 81. The term *dhātoḥ* is iterated. The term *oḥ,* which is a genitive singular form of the vowel *u,* qualifies the term *dhātoḥ.* By tadantavidhi (Pā. 1. 1. 72) it yields the expression : *uvarṇāntasya dhātoḥ* 'a verbal root that ends in the vowel *u*'. The second term *dhātoḥ* gets connected with the word *saṁyoga,* which forms a part of the compound word *asaṁyogapūrvasya.* The sūtra *aṅgasya* 6. 4. 1 is a governing rule in the domain of which the present sūtra occurs. The terms *oḥ* and *dhātoḥ* together qualify the word *aṅgasya.* Again by tadantavidhi (Pā. 1. 1. 72) the meaning they yield is : the aṅga, which ends in a verbal root that ends in the vowel *u.* The word *anekācaḥ* also qualifies the word *aṅgasya.* The words *asaṁyogapūrvasya* and *oḥ* are in appositional relationship. With these points taken into account, the meaning of the sūtra is : A polysyllabic (*anekāc*) pre-affixal base, which ends in a verbal root (*dhātoḥ*) that ends in the vowel *u,* where the vowel *u* is not preceded by a conjunct contained in the verbal root (*dhātoḥ*), is replaced by the phoneme *v* (a denotatum of *yaṇ*-pratyāhāra), provided that a sup-affix, which begins with a vowel, follows. With the help of the rule *alo 'ntyasya* (21), the *v*-replacement comes in place of the aṅga-final vowel *u.*

The present sūtra prescribes the *yaṇ*-replacement in place of the vowel *u,* whereas the sūtra *eranekāco 'saṁyogapūrvasya* (199) enjoins the *yaṇ*-replacement in place of the vowel *i,* other conditions remaining the same. Both these rules are exceptions to the rule *aci śnudhātubhruvāṁ yvoriyaṅuvaṅau* (198).

When we introduce the dual affix of the first triplet, we have *khalapū* + *au.* The verbal root ends in a long *ū.* This is not preceded by a conjunct of the verbal root. The word *khalapū* is a polysyllabic pre-affixal base. The sup-affix, which follows it, begins with a vowel. Therefore, the final vowel *ū* is replaced by the phoneme *v* (*yaṇ*) with the help of the rule *alo 'ntyasya* (21). Thus we obtain the form *khalapvau.*

This nominal stem is not inherently feminine. Hence this is not assigned the nadī designation and the grammatical operations, which take place in the declension of the stems designated as *nadī,* do not take place in the case of the word *khalapū.* Before all the vowel-initial sup-affixes, the *yaṇ*-replacement takes place. The declension of the stem *khalapū* is as follows :

	Singular	Dual	Plural
prathamā	*khalapūḥ*	*khalapvau*	*khalapvaḥ*
dvitīyā	*khalapvam*	*khalapvau*	*khalapvaḥ*

tṛtīyā	*khalapvā*	*khalapūbhyām*	*khalapūbhiḥ*
caturthī	*khalapve*	*khalapūbhyām*	*khalapūbhyaḥ*
pañcamī	*khalapvaḥ*	*khalapūbhyām*	*khalapūbhyaḥ*
ṣaṣṭhī	*khalapvaḥ*	*khalapvoḥ*	*khalapvām*
saptamī	*khalapvi*	*khalapvoḥ*	*khalapūṣu*
sambodhana	*he khalapūḥ!*	*he khalapvau!*	*he khalapvaḥ!*

लघु० – एवं सुल्वादयः । सुलूः । *evaṁ sulvādayaḥ. sulūḥ.*

Eluc. : The declension of the words *sulū* 'one who reaps well', etc. will be like that of *khalapū*. The word *sulū* is derived as follows : *suṣṭhu lunātīti sulūḥ. su + lūñ* 'to reap, to cut' + *kvip* --> *su + lū + v* --> *sulū* --> *sulūḥ* (in the nominative singular after the introduction of the singular affix *su* of the first triplet).

लघु० – स्वभूः । स्वभुवौ । स्वभुवः । *svabhūḥ, svabhuvau, svabhuvaḥ.*

Eluc. : The grammatical explanation of this word is : *svasmāt bhavatīti svabhūḥ* (*sva + bhū + kvip* --> *sva + bhū + v* --> *svabhū* --> *svabhūḥ*). The elision of the affix *su* does not take place since the stem does not end in feminine affix *ṅī.*

With the nominative dual affix of the first triplet, we have *svabhū + au*. In this situation, the rule *iko yaṇaci* (15) becomes available for application but instead *prathamayoḥ pūrvasavarṇaḥ* (125) prescribes pūrvasavarṇa-dīrgha. The rule *dīrghājjasi ca* (161) debars it. Again the rule (15) becomes available for application. The sūtra *aci śnudhātu-bhruvāṁ yvoriyaṅuvaṅau* (198) blocks it and prescribes the *uvaṅ*-substitution. This is also blocked by the rule *oḥ supi* (209) which enjoins the *yaṇ*-replacement which is prohibited by the rule *na bhūsudhiyoḥ* (201). Thus we have *svabhuvau* by the application of the sūtra *aci śnudhātu...* (198). In the same way we will have *uvaṅ*-substitution before the other vowel-initial sup-affixes. Keeping these points in view, we will decline the word *svabhū* in the following manner :

	Singular	Dual	Plural
prathamā	*svabhūḥ*	*svabhuvau*	*svabhuvaḥ*
dvitīyā	*svabhuvam*	*svabhuvau*	*svabhuvaḥ*
tṛtīyā	*svabhuvā*	*svabhūbhyām*	*svabhūbhiḥ*

caturthī	*svabhuve*	*svabhūbhyām*	*svabhūbhyaḥ*
pañcamī	*svabhuvaḥ*	*svabhūbhyām*	*svabhūbhyaḥ*
ṣaṣṭhī	*svabhuvaḥ*	*svabhuvoḥ*	*svabhuvām*
saptamī	*svabhuvi*	*svabhuvoḥ*	*svabhūṣu*
sambodhana	*he svabhūḥ!*	*he svabhuvau!*	*he svabhuvaḥ!*

लघु० – वर्षाभूः । *varṣābhūḥ.*

Eluc. : The word *varṣābhū* (*varṣāsu bhavatīti varṣābhūḥ*) is derived by introducing the affix *kvip* after the verbal root *bhū*. The *yaṇ*-replacement, which is available by *oḥ supi* (209) is debarred by *na bhūsudhiyoḥ* (201) but the following sūtra prescribes the *yaṇ*-replacement :

(210) वर्षाभ्वश्च । ***varṣābhvaśca*. 6. 4. 84**
लघु० – अस्य यण् स्याद् अचि सुपि । वर्षाभ्वौ इत्यादि । *asya yaṇ syād aci supi. varṣābhvau ityādi.*

Trans. : Let *yaṇ* be the substitute for the nominal stem *varṣābhū* 'a frog' when a sup-affix, which begins with a vowel (*ac*), follows.

PP. *aci supi varṣābhvaḥ yaṇ ca* (*aṅgasya*).

Eluc. : The terms *aci* and *supi* are respectively carried over from the sūtras *aci śnudhātubhruvāṁ yvoriyaṅuvaṅau* 6. 4. 77 and *oḥ supi* 6. 4. 83. The term *yaṇ* is lent into the present sūtra from *iṇo yaṇ* 6. 4. 81. Thus the meaning of the sūtra will be : When a sup-affix, which begins with a vowel, follows, the nominal stem *varṣābhū* is replaced by *yaṇ*. With the help of the paribhāṣā sūtra *alo 'ntyasya* (21), the *yaṇ*-replacement will come in place of the final vowel *ū* occurring at the end of the stem *varṣābhū*. This sūtra is an exception to *na bhūsudhiyoḥ* (201) which prohibits the *yaṇ*-replacement available by *oḥ supi* (209). Thus we get the nominative dual form *varṣābhvau* and so on.
The declension of the nominal stem *varṣābhū* is as follows :

	Singular	Dual	Plural
prathamā	*varṣābhūḥ*	*varṣābhvau*	*varṣābhvaḥ*
dvitīyā	*varṣābhvam*	*varṣābhvau*	*varṣābhvaḥ*
tṛtīyā	*varṣābhvā*	*varṣābhūbhyām*	*varṣābhūbhiḥ*

caturthī	*varṣābhve*	*varṣābhūbhyām*	*varṣābhūbhyaḥ*
pañcamī	*varṣābhvaḥ*	*varṣābhūbhyām*	*varṣābhūbhyaḥ*
ṣaṣṭhī	*varṣābhvaḥ*	*varṣābhvoḥ*	*varṣābhvām*
saptamī	*varṣābhvi*	*varṣābhvoḥ*	*varṣābhūṣu*
sambodhana	*he varṣābhūḥ!*	*he varṣābhvau!*	*he varṣābhvaḥ!*

लघु० – दृन्भूः । *dṛnbhūḥ.*

Eluc. : The nominal stem *dṛnbhū* is derived by introducing the affix *kvip* after *bhū* with *dṛn* as an upapada. Jñānendra Sarasvatī says that according to some, this stem means 'a kind of snake' while others say that it denotes 'a monkey' (*sarpajātibheda ityeke. kapir ityanye,* TB, I, p. 284). The grammatical operation, which is specific to this nominal stem, is that the following vārttika enjoins the *yaṇ*-substitution before the sup-affixes which begin with a vowel (*ac*), whereas the same, prescribed by *oḥ supi* (209), has been prohibited by the rule *na bhūsudhiyoḥ* (201) :

20. वा० – दृन्करपुनःपूर्वस्य भुवो यण् वक्तव्यः । *dṛnkarapunaḥpūrvasya bhuvo yaṇ vaktavyaḥ.*

Trans. : The substitute *yaṇ* should be enunciated in place of *bhū* when preceded by *dṛn, kara* and *punar.*

Eluc. : This vārttika is purported to replace the aṅga-final *ū* of *bhū* by the phoneme *v* of *yaṇ* when it is preceded by *dṛn* or *kara* or *punar* and followed by a sup-affix that begins with a vowel. The nominal stem *dṛnbhū* is declined in the same way as the nominal stem *khalapū* :

	Singular	Dual	Plural
prathamā	*dṛnbhūḥ*	*dṛnbhvau*	*dṛnbhvaḥ*
dvitīyā	*dṛnbhvam*	*dṛnbhvau*	*dṛnbhvaḥ*
tṛtīyā	*dṛnbhvā*	*dṛnbhūbhyām*	*dṛnbhūbhiḥ*
caturthī	*dṛnbhve*	*dṛnbhūbhyām*	*dṛnbhūbhyaḥ*
pañcamī	*dṛnbhvaḥ*	*dṛnbhūbhyām*	*dṛnbhūbhyaḥ*
ṣaṣṭhī	*dṛnbhvaḥ*	*dṛnbhvoḥ*	*dṛnbhvām*

saptamī	*dṛnbhvi*	*dṛnbhvoḥ*	*dṛnbhūṣu*
sambodhana	*he dṛnbhūḥ!*	*he dṛnbhvau!*	*he dṛnbhvaḥ!*

The declension of the nominal stems *karabhū* 'finger-nail' and *punarbhū* 'which is born again' is like that of *dṛnbhū*. The stem *punarbhū* in the sense of 'a woman who has married again' is always in the feminine. Its declension may be looked up in the Siddhāntakaumudī and its commentary Bālamanoramā (SK and BM, I, pp. 320-21).

Here comes to an end the declension of the maculine stems that end in a long *ū*.

Now begins the declension of the masculine nominal stems that end in the vowel *ṛ*.

लघु० – धाता । हे धातः! धातारौ । धातारः । *dhātā, he dhātaḥ! dhātārau. dhātāraḥ.*

Eluc. : The nominal stem *dhātṛ* 'God, Brahman' is derived by introducing either *tṛn* or *tṛc* after the verbal root *ḍudhāñ* 'to hold, to sustain, to bear up'. Its declension will be almost like that of *kroṣṭṛ*.

In the nominative singular form of *dhātṛ*, the rule *ṛduśanaspurudaṁso 'nehasāṁ ca* (204) prescribes *anaṅ*-substitute in place of the vowel *ṛ*. After this, the sūtra *ap-tṛn-tṛc-svasṛ-naptṛ-neṣṭṛ-tvaṣṭṛ-kṣatṛ-hotṛ-potṛ-praśāstṝṇām* (205) enjoins the elongation of the penultimate vowel *a* (*upadhā*). The single-consonant affix (*apṛkta*) is elided by the rule *halṅyābbhyo dīrghāt sutisyapṛktaṁ hal* (178). Then the pada-final phoneme *n* is elided by the rule *na lopaḥ prātipadikāntasya* (179) and the inflected form *dhātā* is obtained.

In the vocative singular, there is no *anaṅ*-substitution. Instead the guṇa vowel *a* replaces *ṛ* by *ṛto ṅisarvanāmasthānayoḥ* (203). This is followed by repha by virtue of the rule *uraṇ raparaḥ* (29). We have *he dhātar s*(*u*). Now the affix *s*(*u*) is elided by *halṅyābbhyo...* (178) and we have the form *he dhātaḥ!* after repha has been replaced by the visarga according to the rule *kharavasānayorvisarjanīyaḥ* (93).

With the dual affix of the first triplet, we have *dhātṛ* + *au*. Here the rule *ṛto ṅisarvanāmasthānayoḥ* (203) prescribes guṇa-replacement and the rule *ap-tṛn-tṛc...* (205) prescribes a long vowel substitute in place of the penultimate vowel (*upadhā*) and we have *dhātārau*. In the same manner, we will have the forms *dhātāraḥ, dhātāram* and *dhātārau* after the sup-affixes *jas, am* and *auṭ* respectively are added after the nominal stem *dhātṛ*.

The affix *śas* is not sarvanāmasthāna. Hence the rule *ṛto ṅisarva...* (203) does not apply. After the application of *prathamayoḥ...* (125) and *tasmācchaso...* (136), we have the inflected form *dhātṝn*.

In the third and fourth singular forms, the sandhi rule *iko yaṇaci* (15) applies and we obtain the forms *dhātrā* and *dhātre*. In the dual and plural forms with the affixes of the third, fourth and fifth triplets, there is nothing worth mentioning. With the singular affixes of the fifth and sixth triplets, we have *dhātṛ + as*. Here the sūtras *ṛta ut* (207), *rāt sasya* (208) and *kharavasānayorvisarjanīyaḥ* (93) respectively prescribe single substitution *ur* with the help of *uraṇ raparaḥ* (29), the elision of the conjunct-final phoneme *s* and visarga-replacement. We obtain the common form *dhātuḥ* in the ablative and genitive singular.

In the genitive dual form, the rule *iko yaṇaci* (15) applies and we have *dhātroḥ*. In the genitive plural form, the rules *hrasvanadyāpo nuṭ* (147) and *nāmi* (148) respectively enjoin the augment *nuṭ* and dīrgha-replacement. The rule *raṣābhyāṁ no ṇaḥ samānapade* (266) does not apply since there is neither repha nor cerebral *ṣ* to occasion the *ṇ*-replacement. Hence for the substitute cerebral *ṇ* to come in place of the dental *n*, the following vārttika ensues :

21. वा० – ऋवर्णान्नस्य णत्वं वाच्यम्। *ṛvarṇān nasya ṇatvaṁ vācyam.*[1]
लघु० – धातृणाम्। *dhātṝṇām.*

Trans. : The cerebral *ṇ*-replacement should be enunciated after the phoneme *ṛ*.

Eluc. : For *ṇ*-replacement the conditions, which are prescribed by *raṣābhyāṁ no ṇaḥ.....* (266) and *aṭkupvāṅnumvyavāye 'pi*, should be understood in the context of the present vārttika too. In the present illustration, the dental *n* immediately follows the vowel *ṝ*. As such, it is replaced by the cerebral *ṇ* and we obtain the form *dhātṝṇām*. The intervention instance is exemplified in the form *gṛhāṇām*.

In the locative singular form, the rule *ṛto ṅisarva...* (203) prescribes guṇa-replacement and we have *dhātari*. In the plural form, we have *dhātṛṣu* with the help of *ādeśapratyayayoḥ* (149).

Keeping in view all the rules *ṛto ṅisarva...* (203), *ṛduśanas* (204), *aptṛntṛc...* (205), *halṅyābbhyo...* (178), etc. which are applicable in declining a nominal stem that ends in the vowel *ṛ*, we will decline the word *dhātṛ* in the following way :

---

1. This vārttika appears to be a paraphrase of *raṣābhyāṁ ṇatve ṛkāragrahaṇam*, Mbh 8. 4. 1, vtk 1.

	Singular	Dual	Plural
prathamā	*dhātā*	*dhātārau*	*dhātāraḥ*
dvitīyā	*dhātāram*	*dhātārau*	*dhātṝn*
tṛtīyā	*dhātrā*	*dhātṛbhyām*	*dhātṛbhiḥ*
caturthī	*dhātre*	*dhātṛbhyām*	*dhātṛbhyaḥ*
pañcamī	*dhātuḥ*	*dhātṛbhyām*	*dhātṛbhyaḥ*
ṣaṣṭhī	*dhātuḥ*	*dhātroḥ*	*dhātṝṇām*
saptamī	*dhātari*	*dhātroḥ*	*dhātṛṣu*
sambodhana	*he dhātaḥ!*	*he dhātārau !*	*he dhātāraḥ!*

लघु० – एवं नप्त्रादयः । *evaṁ naptrādayaḥ.*

Trans. : In the same way, *naptṛ*, etc.

Eluc. : The declension of the nominal stems *naptṛ, neṣṭṛ, tvaṣṭṛ, kṣatṛ, hotṛ, potṛ and praśāstṛ,* which are cited in the sūtra *aptṛntṛc-svasṛnaptṛ...* (205) will be like that of the stem *dhātṛ*. Consequently, when a non-vocative sarvanāmasthāna follows, the penultimate vowel will be replaced by a long counterpart, e. g. *naptā, naptārau, naptāraḥ, naptāram, naptārau*, etc.

लघु० – नप्त्रादीनां ग्रहणं व्युत्पत्तिपक्षे नियमार्थम्। तेनेह न — पिता, पितरौ, पितरः। पितरम्। शेषं धातृवत्। एवं जामात्रादयः। ना, नरौ। *naptrādīnāṁ grahaṇaṁ vyutpattipakṣe niyamārtham. teneha na — pitā, pitarau, pitaraḥ. pitaram. śeṣaṁ dhātṛvat. evaṁ jāmātrādayaḥ. nā, narau.*

Trans. : According to the view that the uṇādi-stems are derivatives, the citation of the nominal stems beginning with *naptṛ* is for the sake of restriction. Hence there is no long vowel replacement in these cases, e. g. *pitā, pitarau, pitaraḥ. pitaram.* The rest of the declension will be like that of *dhātṛ*. In the same way, *jāmātṛ* and so on.

Eluc. : There is a difference of opinion among grammarians with regard to the status of uṇādi-stems. Some regard them as irregular derivatives without any reference to bases and affixes and others accept them as derived with reference to bases and affixes. Those who regard the uṇādi-stems as irregularly derived (*avyutpanna prātipadikas*) aver that the citation of the stems, *naptṛ, neṣṭṛ,* etc. in the sūtra *aptṛntṛc-svasṛnaptṛ...* (205), is essential for a long vowel substitution in place of the penultimate vowel (*upadhā*) of these stems before non-vocative sarvanāmasthāna sup-affixes. According to the view that the uṇādi-stems are regular derivatives (*vyutpanna prātipadikas*), the citation of the affixes *tṛn* or *tṛc* would have sufficed to effect a long replacement in place of the penultimate vowel of the stems beginning with *naptṛ* cited in (205). To avoid their being redundant, their citation in the rule is construed to restrict the long replacement only with reference to these cited seven stems (cf. *siddhe sati niyamārthaḥ*) out of the tṛjanta and tṛnnanta derivatives. This means that the penultimate vowel of the uṇādi nominal stems other than those cited in the rule (205) is not replaced by a long counter-part. As a consequence, the penultimate vowel (*upadhā*) of the uṇādi-stems, *jāmātṛ, pitṛ, bhrātṛ,* etc. is not replaced by a long counterpart before non-vocative sarvanāmasthāna sup-affixes (205). The words, which are derived with either *tṛn* or *tṛc* occurring in the Aṣṭādhyāyī, do get the penultimate elongated by *aptṛntṛc...* (205). For a comparison, the declension of *pitṛ* is given below :

	Singular	Dual	Plural
prathamā	*pitā*	*pitarau*	*pitaraḥ*
dvitīyā	*pitaram*	*pitarau*	*pitṝn*
tṛtīyā	*pitrā*	*pitṛbhyām*	*pitṛbhiḥ*
caturthī	*pitre*	*pitṛbhyām*	*pitṛbhyaḥ*
pañcamī	*pituḥ*	*pitṛbhyām*	*pitṛbhyaḥ*
ṣaṣṭhī	*pituḥ*	*pitroḥ*	*pitṝṇām*
saptamī	*pitari*	*pitroḥ*	*pitṛṣu*
sambodhana	*he pitaḥ!*	*he pitarau !*	*he pitaraḥ!*

Now Varadarāja declines the nominal stem *nṛ*. There is no long vowel substitution in place of the penultimate vowel (*upadhā*) of the stem *nṛ* which is derived with the addition of the uṇādi affix *ṛ* by *nayaterḍicca* (US, 257). The declension of the stem *nṛ* is like that of *pitṛ*. Only the genitive plural form differs. The grammatical operation of effecting an obligatory long vowel replacement in place of the aṅga-final short vowel by *nāmi* (148) in *nṛ + nām* (<-- *nṛ + ām*) is made optional by the following sūtra :

(211) नृ च । *nṛ ca.* 6. 4. 6

लघु॰ – अस्य नामि वा दीर्घः। नॄणाम्। नृणाम्। *asya nāmi vā dīrghaḥ. nṝṇām, nṛṇām.*

Trans. : [The aṅga-final vowel *ṛ* of] the stem *nṛ* is optionally replaced by a long one, when *nām* follows.

PP. *nṛ ca nāmi ubhayathā dīrghaḥ (aṅgasya).*

Eluc. : The term *nṛ* in the sūtra should be taken as genitive singular since its genitive nominal ending has been elided (*nṛ iti luptaṣaṣṭhīkaṁ*, BM, I, p. 286). The word *ubhayathā* is carried over from the preceding sūtra *chandasyubhayathā* Pā. 6. 4. 5. In this context, it means 'option'. The words *dīrghaḥ* and *nāmi* are respectively carried over from the sūtras *ḍhralope pūrvasya dīrgho 'ṇaḥ* Pā. 6. 3. 111 and *nāmi* Pā. 6. 4. 3. The term *dīrghaḥ* becomes a constituent of the sūtra. So, with the help of the paribhāṣā sūtra *acaśca* Pā. 1. 2. 28, the present sūtra comes to mean : The long vowel replacement will come in place of the aṅga-final vowel *ṛ* of *nṛ* when the affix *nām* follows.

In the illustration *nṛ* + *nām*, the aṅga-final vowel *ṛ* is replaced optionally by a long *ṝ*. We have two grammatical situations : *nṝ nām* and *nṛ nām*. In both the cases, we replace the dental *n* of *nām* by a cerebral *ṇ* in accordance with the vārttika (21) *ṛvarṇānnasya ṇatvaṁ vācyam* and we obtain two forms in the genitive plural : *nṝṇām* and *nṛṇām*.

The nominal stem *nṛ* is declined as follows :

	Singular	Dual	Plural
prathamā	*nā*	*narau*	*naraḥ*
dvitīyā	*naram*	*narau*	*nṝn*
tṛtīyā	*nrā*	*nṛbhyām*	*nṛbhiḥ*
caturthī	*nre*	*nṛbhyām*	*nṛbhyaḥ*
pañcamī	*nuḥ*	*nṛbhyām*	*nṛbhyaḥ*
ṣaṣṭhī	*nuḥ*	*nroḥ*	*nṝṇām, nṛṇām*
saptamī	*nari*	*nroḥ*	*nṛṣu*
sambodhana	*he naḥ!*	*he narau!*	*he naraḥ!*

Here comes to an end the declension of the maculine stems that end in *ṛ*.

Now Varadaraja begins describing the declension of the masculine nominal stems that end in *o* since there is no nominal stem, which ends in *ṝ*, *ḷ* or *e* and which also requires an explanation in an elementary book like the Laghusiddhāntakaumudī.

(212) गोतो णित्। *goto ṇit.* 7. 1. 90

लघु॰ - ओकाराद् विहितं सर्वनामस्थानं णिद्वत्। गौः, गावौ, गावः। *okārād vihitaṁ sarvanāmasthānaṁ ṇidvat. gauḥ, gāvau, gāvaḥ.*

Trans. : The sarvanāmasthāna sup-affixes introduced after a nominal stem that ends in the vowel *o* (such as *go*) is treated as if having the phoneme *ṇ* as *it*.

PP. *gotaḥ sarvanāmasthānam ṇit (aṅgasya).*

Eluc. : The word *sarvanāmasthāne* is carried over from *ito 't sarvanāmasthāne* Pā. 7. 1. 86. By the process of vibhaktivipariṇāma, it is changed into one having a singular nominal ending of the first triplet so that it may agree with the term *ṇit* appositionally. This is an extension rule. It means that the grammatical operations, which are available before an affix having *ṇ* as *it*, also become available with regard to the sarvanāmasthāna sup-affixes, if they follow the nominal stem *go*.The Kāśikā on this sūtra says that some read this sūtra as *oto ṇit* so that the sarvanāmasthāna sup-affixes introduced after such nominal stems as *dyo* may also be treated as *ṇit*. In the Siddhāntakaumudī, two vārttikas are given on this sūtra : 1. *oto ṇiditi vācyam* 2. *vihitaviśeṣaṇaṁ ca* (SK, I, p. 292). The sense conveyed by these two vārttikas appears to have been taken care of in the vṛtti by Varadarāja. He says that the sarvanāmasthāna sup-affixes, when enjoined after a nominal stem that ends in *o*, are to be treated as if they were *ṇit*. The first vārttika is in consonance with the variant reading suggested in the Kāśikā and takes care of the nominal stems such as *dyo*. The purpose of the second vārttika is to avoid the problem in the usages like *vāyo s* where the sarvanāmasthāna affix *su* happens to be after a stem that ends in *o*. In the absence of the second vārttika, the affix *su* after the stem *vāyo* would have been treated as if having *ṇ* as *it*, which is not desirable. The second vārttika says that the sarvanāmasthāna affix, which is to be treated as *ṇit*, should have been enjoined after a nominal stem which originally ends in *o*. The nominal stem *vāyu* ends in *u*, which has been replaced by a guṇa vowel *o* before the vocative singular affix. As such, the vocative singular affix *su* is not treated as having the cerebral *ṇ* as *it*. Moreover, the taparakaraṇa in the term *goto* in the present sūtra is purported to convey the sense of *okārānta* (*taparakaraṇam okārāntopalakṣaṇārtham*, Udyota on Mbh 7. 1. 90). In this way the meaning of the sūtra will be : The sarvanāmasthāna affixes, which are enjoined after a nominal stem that ends in o, are to be treated as if having *ṇ* as *it*.

The nominal stem *go* ends in *o*. Therefore, the affix *su*, introduced after it, is treated as *ṇit* by the present rule. By virtue of the rule *aco ñṇiti* (181), the vowel *o* is replaced by a vṛddhi vowel *au*. After rutva and visarga, we obtain *gauḥ* through the following grammatical process : *go + su --> go + s --> gaus --> gaur --> gauḥ*. With the dual affixes of the first and second triplets, we have the form *gāvau* after the application of *eco 'yavāyāvaḥ* (22) : *go + au --> gau+ au --> gāv + au --> gāvau*. With the plural affix *jas*, ṇidvadbhāva takes place and we have likewise the form *gāvaḥ* after the application of *eco 'yavāyāvaḥ* (22).

With the singular affix of the second triplet, we have *go + am*. At this stage, the present sūtra becomes available for application but the following sūtra blocks the anticipated vṛddhi consequent upon ṇidvadbhāva :

(213) औतोऽम्शसोः । ***auto 'mśasoḥ*. 6. 1. 93**

लघु० - ओतोऽम्शसोरचि आकार एकादेशः । गाम्, गावौ, गाः । गवा, गवे, गोः 2 इत्यादि । *oto 'mśasor aci ākāra ekādeśaḥ. gām, gāvau, gāḥ. gavā, gave, goḥ* 2 *ityādi.*

Trans. : If the vowel of sup-affixes *am* and *śas* follows the vowel *o*, then the substitute *ā* replaces both the preceding and following substituenda.

PP. *otaḥ aci amśasoḥ pūrvaparayoḥ ekaḥ ā* (*saṁhitāyām*).

Eluc. : *autaḥ* is a combination of the two terms *ā + otaḥ*. The nominal ending after *ā* should be understood as elided (Bhaimī, I, p. 282). The word *aci* is carried over from *iko yaṇaci* Pā. 6. 1. 77. The present sūtra occurs in the domain of the governing rule *ekaḥ pūrvaparayoḥ* Pā. 6. 1. 84. Therefore all the terms of the governing rule recur in the present sūtra. Thus the sūtra means : If the vowel (*ac*) of either *am* or *śas* follows the aṅga-final *o*, then a single substitute *ā* replaces both the preceding vowel *o* and the following vowel *a*. In the illustration *go + am*, the vowel *ā* replaces *o* and *a*. We obtain the form *gām* (<-- *g ā m*). Similarly with the plural affix *śas* (*as*), the substitute *ā* replaces *o* and *a* of *śas* and we have *gās*. Here the substituted vowel *ā* is not pūrvasavarṇadīrgha by *prathamayoḥ pūrvasavarṇaḥ* (125). That is the reason why *tasmācchaso naḥ puṁsi* (136) does not apply and the phoneme *s* is not replaced by *n*. After rutva and visarga, we have the form *gāḥ*.

With the singular affixes of the third and fourth triplets, we have {*go* + (*ṭ*)*ā*} and {*go* + (*ṅ*)*e*}. After the application of *eco 'yavāyāvaḥ* (22) we respectively obtain the declined forms *gavā* and *gave*.

When we introduce the singular affixes of the fifth and sixth triplets, we have *go* + *ṅasi* --> *go* + *as* and *go* + *ṅas* --> *go* +*as* . At this stage in both the cases, the substitute in the form of the preceding vowel replaces both the preceding *o* and the following *a* by *ṅasiṅasośca* (172).

The declension of the nominal stem *go* is as follows :

	Singular	Dual	Plural
prathamā	*gauḥ*	*gāvau*	*gāvaḥ*
dvitīyā	*gām*	*gāvau*	*gāḥ*
tṛtīyā	*gavā*	*gobhyām*	*gobhiḥ*
caturthī	*gave*	*gobhyām*	*gobhyaḥ*
pañcamī	*goḥ*	*gobhyām*	*gobhyaḥ*
ṣaṣṭhī	*goḥ*	*gavoḥ*	*gavām*
saptamī	*gavi*	*gavoḥ*	*goṣu*
sambodhana	*he gauḥ!*	*he gāvau!*	*he gāvaḥ!*

Here comes to an end the declension of the masculine stems ending in *o*.

Now begins the declension of the masculine stem *rai* ending in *ai* :

(214) रायो हलि । *rāyo hali*. 7. 2. 85

लघु० – अस्याकारादेशो हलि विभक्तौ । राः, रायौ, रायः, राभ्याम् इत्यादि । *asyākārādeśo hali vibhaktau. rāḥ, rāyau, rāyaḥ, rābhyām ityādi.*

Trans. : When a sup-affix beginning with a consonant (*hal*) follows, the (aṅga-final) vowel *ai* is replaced by *ā*.

PP. *rāyaḥ ā hali vibhaktau* (*aṅgasya*).

Eluc. : The words *ā* and *vibhaktau* are carried over into the present sūtra from Pā. 7. 2. 84. With these insertions, the sūtra means : The (aṅga-final) vowel *ai* of *rai* is replaced by *ā* when a sup-affix beginning with a consonant (*hal*) follows.

The nominal stem *rai* 'wealth, gold' is derived by introducing the uṇādi affix *ḍai* after *rā* 'to give' by *rāterḍaiḥ* (Uṇādi Sūtra, 224). Because the affix is *ḍit*, the *ṭi* of *rā* (*ā*) is elided and the nominal stem *rai* is obtained. There are eight sup-affixes which begin with a consonant. Before these affixes, the vowel *ai* of *rai* is replaced by *ā*. In the case of the sup-affixes, which begin with a vowel, the rule *eco 'yavāyāvaḥ* (22) will apply. Thus the declension of *rai* will be as follows :

	Singular	Dual	Plural
prathamā	*rāḥ*	*rāyau*	*rāyaḥ*
dvitīyā	*rāyam*	*rāyau*	*rāyaḥ*
tṛtīyā	*rāyā*	*rābhyām*	*rābhiḥ*
caturthī	*rāye*	*rābhyām*	*rābhyaḥ*
pañcamī	*rāyaḥ*	*rābhyām*	*rābhyaḥ*
ṣaṣṭhī	*rāyaḥ*	*rāyoḥ*	*rāyām*
saptamī	*rāyi*	*rāyoḥ*	*rāsu*
sambodhana	*he rāḥ!*	*he rāyau!*	*he rāyaḥ!*

Now begins the declension of the nominal stem *glau* :

लघु० – ग्लौः, ग्लावौ, ग्लावः, ग्लौभ्याम् इत्यादि । *glauḥ, glāvau, glāvaḥ, glaubhyām ityādi.*

Eluc. : The word *glau* 'the moon' is derived by adding the uṇādi affix *ḍau* after the verbal root *glai* 'to feel depressed' by *glānudibhyāṁ ḍauḥ* (Uṇādi Sūtra, 222). Since the affix is *ḍit*, the *ṭi* of *glai* is elided and we have nominal stem *glau*.

In declining the nominal stem *glau*, there are two points to be kept in mind : 1. The rule *eco 'yavāyāvaḥ* (22) will apply where a sup-affix beginning with a vowel follows. 2. There will be no change before a sup-affix beginning with a consonant.

With these points taken into consideration, the declension of the nominal stem *glau* will be as follows:

	Singular	Dual	Plural
prathamā	*glauḥ*	*glāvau*	*glāvaḥ*
dvitīyā	*glāvam*	*glāvau*	*glāvaḥ*
tṛtīyā	*glāvā*	*glaubhyām*	*glaubhiḥ*
caturthī	*glāve*	*glaubhyām*	*glaubhyaḥ*
pañcamī	*glāvaḥ*	*glaubhyām*	*glaubhyaḥ*
ṣaṣṭhī	*glāvaḥ*	*glāvoḥ*	*glāvām*
saptamī	*glāvi*	*glāvoḥ*	*glauṣu*
sambodhana	*he glauḥ!*	*he glāvau!*	*he glāvaḥ!*

Here comes to an end the declension of the stem ending in *au*.

लघु० – इत्यजन्तपुंलिङ्गाः । *ityajantapuṁliṅgāḥ.*

Trans. : Here comes to an end (the process of declining) the masculine nominal stems ending in a vowel (*ac*).

अजन्तस्त्रीलिङ्गप्रकरणम्

Feminine Words Ending in a Vowel

The declension of nominal stems in the feminine starts with that of a nominal stem that ends in a long vowel *ā* since no feminine nominal stem ends in a short vowel *a*. The first stem that is given in the Laghu is *ramā*. The word is derived by introducing the primary affix *ac* after the verbal root *ram* 'to play, to take delight in' in accordance with the rule *nandigrahipacādibhyo lyuṇinyacaḥ* (783). In order to express it in the feminine, the affix *ṭāp* is added by the sūtra *ajādyataṣṭāp* (1242) and we obtain the word *ramā*. Although the word *ramā*, ending in an affix, cannot be designated as *prātipadika*, the sup-affixes are made available either by the separate citation of *ṅī* and *āp* in the sūtra *ṅyāpprātipadikāt* (118) or by virtue of the paribhāṣā *prātipadikagrahaṇe liṅgaviśiṣṭasyāpi grahaṇam* (BM, I, p. 294; for more details, see also TB, I, p. 295).

With the singular affix *su* of the first triplet, we have *ramā* + *su*. The word *ramā* ends in the feminine affix *ṭāp*. The nominative singular affix *su* is reduced to the status of an apṛkta (a single-phoneme affix) after the elision of the vowel *u* by *tasya lopaḥ* (3). Then the apṛkta *s* is elided by the rule *halṅyābbhyo dīrghāt sutisyapṛktaṁ hal* (178). After the elision of the affix *su*, we obtain the form *ramā* but the elision of the nominative singular affix leads to its non-cognition. Still the word *ramā* can be designated as *pada* according to *pratyayalope pratyayalakṣaṇam* which means that the grammatical operation, which depends on an affix, still takes place even when the affix has been replaced by lopa. So the affix is still effective and the term *ramā* is a pada by *suptiṅantaṁ padam* (14).

When we introduce the dual affix of the first triplet, we have the form *ramā* + *au*. At this stage, the rule *prathamayoḥ pūrvasavarṇaḥ* (125) applies but is blocked by the sūtra *dīrghājjasi ca* (161). Then the sūtra *vṛddhireci* (33) becomes available for application. In this situation the following sūtra presents itself :

(215) औङ आपः । *auṅa āpaḥ*. 7. 1. 18

लघु० – आबन्ताद् अङ्गात् परस्य औङः शी स्यात् । औङ् इत्यौकारविभक्तेः संज्ञा । रमे । रमाः । *ābantād aṅgāt parasya auṅaḥ śī syāt. auṅ ityaukāravibhakteḥ saṁjñā. rame. ramāḥ.*

Trans. : When the affix *auṅ* follows a nominal stem that ends in *āp*, let it be replaced by the substitute *śī*. The term *auṅ* is the designation of the sup-ending *au*.

PP. *āpaḥ aṅgāt auṅaḥ śī.*

Eluc. : The present sūtra occurs in the governing domain of the rule *aṅgasya* Pā. 6. 4. 1. This has been changed into one ending in the ablative case-ending by the process of vibhaktivipariṇāma. This word is qualified by the term *āpaḥ*. By tadantavidhi, it yields the sense : after the pre-affixal base that ends in *āp* (a cover term for the feminine affixes *ṭāp, ḍāp, cāp*). The term *śī* is carried over from the sūtra *jasaḥ śī* Pā. 7. 1. 17. Thus the meaning of the sūtra is : If a pre-affixal base ends in the affix *āp* and if it is followed by the dual sup-affix of the first triplet, namely, *auṅ*, then this affix is replaced by the substitute *śī*.

The predecessors of Pāṇini used the term *auṅ* for the dual affixes (*au* and *auṭ*) of the first and second triplets. To show respect to them, Pāṇini has retained the same term to convey that meaning.

In the illustration *ramā* + *śī*, the substitute *śī* is treated as a sup-affix by virtue of the rule *sthānivadādeśo 'nalvidhau* (143). After that the rule *laśakvataddhite* (135) applies and the palatal *ś*, being *it*, is elided by *tasya lopaḥ* (3). At this stage, we have the form *ramā* + *ī*. Now the sūtra *ād guṇaḥ* (27) applies and we obtain the form *rame*.

With the plural sup-affix of the first triplet, we have *ramā* + *jas*. In this case, the application of the rule *prathamayoḥ pūrvasavarṇaḥ* (125) is blocked by *dīrghājjasi ca* (161) since the sup-affix *jas* follows a long vowel here. Then the sūtra *akaḥ savarṇe dīrghaḥ* (42) applies and after rutva and visarga, we obtain the form *ramāḥ*.

When a vocative singular sup-affix is introduced after *ramā*, the following sūtra becomes available for application :

(216) सम्बुद्धौ च । *sambuddhau ca*. 7. 3. 106

लघु० – आप एकारः स्यात् सम्बुद्धौ । एङ्ह्रस्वात्सम्बुद्धेः इति सम्बुद्धिलोपः । हे रमे । हे रमे । हे रमाः । रमाम् । रमे । रमाः । *āpa ekāraḥ syāt sambuddhau. eṅhrasvātsambuddheḥ iti sambuddhilopaḥ. he rame! he rame! he ramāḥ! ramām. rame. ramāḥ.*

Trans. : When a vocative singular sup-affix follows, let the affix *āp* be replaced by the substitute vowel *e*. (Then) the vocative singular sup-affix is replaced by lopa in accordance with the rule *eṅhrasvāt sambuddheḥ* (133).

PP. *sambuddhau ca āpaḥ aṅgasya et.*

Eluc. : The term *āpaḥ* is carried over from the sūtra *āṅi cāpaḥ* Pā. 7. 3. 105. The sūtra *aṅgasya* Pā. 6. 4. 1 is a governing rule in the domain of which the present sūtra occurs. The term *et* is carried over from *bahuvacane jhalyet* Pā. 7. 3. 103. The word *āpaḥ* qualifies the word *aṅgasya*. As such, by tadantavidhi, the sense yielded is *ābantasya aṅgasya*. With all these points the sūtra means : When a vocative singular sup-affix follows, the pre-affixal base, which ends in the affix *āp*, is replaced by the substitute *e* (*et*). With the help of the paribhāṣā sūtra *alo 'ntyasya* (21), this substitute will replace the aṅga-final *ā*. We obtain the form *rame* through the following grammatical process : *ramā* + s --> *rame* + s by the present rule and then --> *rame* when the phoneme s of the vocative singular affix is elided by *eṅhrasvāt sambuddheḥ* (133).

The dual and the plural forms of the vocative do not differ from those of the nominative. Although the form of the vocative singular does not differ from that of the vocative dual, their grammatical process differs a great deal.

In declining the word *ramā* with a singular sup-affix *am* of the second triplet, we invoke the rule *ami pūrvaḥ* (134) and the form *ramām* (<-- *ramā* + *m* <-- *ramā* + *am*) is obtained. The dual form with the dual affix of the second triplet is obtained in the same manner as the dual form of the nominative. With the plural sup-affix of the second triplet, we have *ramā* + *śas*. The initial phoneme *ś* is elided by *laśakvataddhite* (135) and *tasya lopaḥ* (3). Then we have the form *ramā* + *as*. The sūtra *dīrghājjasi ca* (161) does not block *prathamayoḥ pūrvasavarṇaḥ* (125), which therefore applies and we get the form *ramāḥ* after rutva and visarga. Since the word *ramā* is feminine, the sūtra *tasmācchaso naḥ puṁsi* (136) is not applicable after pūrvasavarṇadīrgha.

When the singular affix *ṭā* of the third triplet is introduced after the word *ramā*, the following rule applies :

(217) आङि चापः । *āṅi cāpaḥ*. 7. 3. 105

लघु० – आङि ओसि चाप एकारः । रमया । रमाभ्याम् । रमाभिः । *āṅi osi cāpa ekāraḥ. ramayā. ramābhyām. ramābhiḥ.*

Trans. : The substitute vowel *e*(*t*) also replaces the aṅga-final *ā*(*p*) when either *os* or *āṅ* follows.

PP. *āṅi osi ca āpa aṅgasya et.*

Eluc. : The term *osi* is carried over from *osi ca* Pā. 7. 3. 104. The sūtra *aṅgasya* Pā. 6. 4. 1 is a governing rule. Accordingly, the term *aṅgasya* recurs here. It is qualified by the term *āpaḥ*. The expression thus obtained is *ābantasya aṅgasya*. The meaning of the sūtra is : When either *āṅ* or *os* follows, the pre-affixal base that ends in the feminine affix *āp* is replaced by the substitute vowel *e*. The term *āṅ* has been used by earlier ācāryas for *ṭā*. By virtue of the paribhāṣā sūtra *alo 'ntyasya* (21), the vowel *e* will replace the aṅga-final *ā*. Thus we have *ramā* + *ṭā* --> *ramā* + *ā* {after *ṭ* which is *it* by *cuṭū* (128) has been elided by *tasya lopaḥ* (3)}. After the aṅga-final *ā* is replaced by *e*, we have *rame* + *ā*. At this stage, the rule *eco 'yavāyāvaḥ* (22) applies and we obtain the form *ramayā*. The dual and plural forms of *ramā* respectively are *ramābhyām* and *ramābhiḥ*. One point is to be noted here. The word *ramā* does not end in a short *a*. That is why the sup-affix *bhis* is not replaced by *ais*.

To get the dative singular form of the word *ramā*, we introduce the sup-affix *ṅe* after it : *ramā* + *ṅe* --> *ramā* + *e*. At this stage, the following sūtra ensues :

(218) याडापः । *yāḍāpaḥ*. 7. 3. 113

लघु० – आपो ङितो याट् । वृद्धिः – रमायै । रमाभ्याम् 2 । रमाभ्यः 2 । रमायाः 2 । रमयोः 2 । रमाणाम् । रमायाम् । रमासु । *āpo ṅito yāṭ. vṛddhiḥ – ramāyai. ramābhyām* 2. *ramābhyaḥ* 2. *ramāyāḥ* 2. *ramayoḥ* 2. *ramāṇām. ramāyām, ramāsu.*

Trans. : The augment *yāṭ* is added to the sup-affixes which have *ṅ* as *it* and occur after an aṅga that terminates in *āp*.

PP. *āpaḥ aṅgāt yāṭ ṅiti.*

Eluc. : The term *aṅgasya* carried over from the governing rule Pā. 6. 4. 1 is changed into the ablative singular by the process of vibhakti-vipariṇāma. The term *āpaḥ* qualifies it. By tadantavidhi, the sense yielded is : *ābantād aṅgāt*. The word *ṅiti* is carried over from the sūtra *gherṅiti* Pā. 7. 3. 111 and is changed to have a genitive singular ending. With all this, the sūtra means : If the sup-affixes, which have *ṅ* as *it*, follow a word that terminates in the affix *āp* (*cāp*, *ṭāp* and *ḍāp*), the augment *yāṭ* is inserted at the head of such affixes.

In the illustration *ramā* + *e*, the sup-affix *e* is *ṅit*. Therefore the augment *yāṭ*, being *ṭit*, becomes an initial part of the affix *e* and we have *ramā* + *yāṭ e* --> *ramā* + *yā e*. The phoneme *ṭ* is *it* by *halantyam* (1) and it is elided by *tasya lopaḥ* (3). Then *vṛddhireci* (33) applies and we obtain the form *ramāyai*.

In both the ablative and genitive singular forms of *ramā*, we have *ramā* + *as*. Of both the affixes *ṅasi* and *ṅas* only *as* remains after the elision of the *its* by *tasya lopaḥ* (3). The phoneme *ṅ* is *it* by *laśakvataddhite* (135) and the vowel *i* in *ṅasi* is *it* by *upadeśe 'janunāsika it* (28). The rule *akaḥ savarṇe dīrghaḥ* (42) applies and we obtain the form *ramāyāḥ*, which is common to both the ablative and genitive singular.

The sup-affix *os* is common to both the forms of genitive and locative dual. When we introduce the affix *os* to the nominal stem *ramā*, we have *ramā* + *os*. At this stage, the rule *āṅi cāpaḥ* (217) applies and the aṅga-final *ā* of *ramā* is replaced by the substitute *e* and we arrive at the following form: *rame* + *os*. The rule *eco 'yavāyāvaḥ* (22) applies and we get the form *ramayoḥ*.

In the genitive plural of *ramā*, we invoke the rule *hrasvanadyāpo nuṭ* (147) and insert the augment *nuṭ* at the head of the sup-affix *ām* in *ramā* + *ām* --> *ramā* + *nuṭ ām* --> *ramā* + *nām* with the help of the rule *ādyantau ṭakitau* (84). Now by *aṭkupvāṅnumvyavāye 'pi* (137), the dental *n* of the *nām* is replaced by *ṇ*. Thus we obtain the form *ramāṇām* in the genitive plural.

With the singular affix of the seventh triplet, we have *ramā* + *ṅi*. At this stage, the sup-affix *ṅi* is replaced by *ām* according to the sūtra *ṅerāmnadyāmnībhyaḥ* (197). The characteristic of being *ṅit*, is extended to the substitute *ām* by *sthānivadādeśo 'nalvidhau* (143). Then we obtain the ground to insert the augment *yāṭ* by the present rule. We have *ramā* + *ām* --> *ramā* + *yāṭ ām* --> *ramā* + *yām* --> *ramāyām*.

The word *ramā* is declined as follows :

	Singular	Dual	Plural
prathamā	*ramā*	*rame*	*ramāḥ*
dvitīyā	*ramām*	*rame*	*ramāḥ*
tṛtīyā	*ramayā*	*ramābhyām*	*ramābhiḥ*
caturthī	*ramāyai*	*ramābhyām*	*ramābhyaḥ*
pañcamī	*ramāyāḥ*	*ramābhyām*	*ramābhyaḥ*
ṣaṣṭhī	*ramāyāḥ*	*ramayoḥ*	*ramāṇām*
saptamī	*ramāyām*	*ramayoḥ*	*ramāsu*
sambodhana	*he rame!*	*he rame!*	*he ramāḥ!*

लघु० – एवं दुर्गाम्बिकादयः । *evaṁ durgāmbikādayaḥ.*

Trans. : The words *durgā, ambikā* and so on will be declined in the same manner.

Eluc. : Some of the words, which fall under this category, are : *acalā* 'the earth', *arcā* 'worship', *avidyā* 'ignorance', *āpagā* 'river', *kathā* 'story', *umā* 'pārvatī', *kanyā* 'unmarried girl', *guhā* 'cave' and *dayā* 'kindness'.

The declension of the pronominal stems ending in the feminine affix *āp* (*cāp, ṭāp* and *ḍāp*) differs slightly from that of the nominal stems that end in the affix *āp* such as *ramā*. The author of the Laghu now takes up the declension of the pronominal stems that end in *ṭāp*. When we introduce the feminine affix *ṭāp* after the pronominal stem *sarva*, we have the word *sarvā*. This word is also assigned the designation *sarvanāman* in accordance with the metarule *prātipadikagrahaṇe liṅgaviśiṣṭasyāpi grahaṇam* (Abhyankar, 71). This means that whenever a word denoting a particular prātipadika is employed, it must be understood to denote also that which is derived from it by the addition of an affix denoting gender. The word *sarvā*, therefore, should be taken as a pronominal stem. The declensional forms of the pronominal stem *sarvā* differ from those of the word *ramā* only before the four sup-affixes, which have *ṅ* as *it*. These affixes are : *ṅe ṅasi ṅas* and *ṅi*.

When we introduce the affix *ṅe* after *sarvā*, the rule *yāḍāpaḥ* (218) becomes available for application but the following rule, which is an exception, blocks it and applies :

(219) सर्वनाम्नः स्याड्ढ्रस्वश्च । *sarvanāmnaḥ syāḍḍhrasvaśca*. 7. 3. 114

लघु० – आबन्तात् सर्वनाम्नो ङितः स्याट् स्याद् आपश्च ह्रस्वः । सर्वस्यै । सर्वस्याः 2 । सर्वासाम् । सर्वस्याम् । शेषं रमावत् । *ābantāt sarvanāmno ṅitaḥ syāṭ syād āpaś ca hrasvaḥ. sarvasyai. sarvasyāḥ 2. sarvāsām. sarvasyām. śeṣaṁ ramāvat.*

Trans. : If a sup-affix, which has *ṅ* as *it*, follows a pronominal stem ending in the affix *āp*, then the augment *syāṭ* should be inserted at its beginning and the aṅga-final long *ā* should also be shortened.

PP. *āpaḥ sarvanāmnaḥ aṅgāt syāṭ ṅiti* (*āpaḥ*) *hrasvaḥ ca.*

Eluc. : The term *āpaḥ* is carried over from the rule *yāḍāpaḥ* Pā. 7. 3. 113 and the term *ṅitaḥ*, from *gherṅiti* Pā. 7. 3. 111 by the process of vibhaktivipariṇāma. The term *āpaḥ* qualifies the word *sarvanāmnaḥ* and by tadantavidhi it yields the meaning *ābantāt sarvanāmnaḥ*. The expression *syāḍḍhrasvaśca* is disjoined as *syāṭ + hrasvaḥ + ca*. The cerebral *ṭ* of the augment *syāṭ* changes into *ḍ* by the rule *jhalāṁ jaśo 'nte* (67) and the *h* of the term *hrasvaḥ* is optionally substituted by *ḍh*, which is homogeneous with the preceding phoneme *ḍ* (pūrvasavarṇa) by the rule *jhayo ho 'nyatarasyām* (75). The dental s is replaced by the palatal ś by the rule *stoḥ ścunā ścuḥ* (62). This explains the expression *syāḍḍhrasvaśca* used in the sūtra. The term *āpaḥ* is iterated here (*āpaḥ ityanuvṛttam āvartate*, BM, I, p. 297). The first term (*āpaḥ*) accords with the word *sarvanāmnaḥ*. This is the first sentence. The second term, after having been changed into the genitive singular, enters into relation with the word *hrasvaḥ*. This is the second sentence (*hrasvaśceti vākyāntaram*). In this way the sūtra yields the following meaning : The augment *syāṭ* is to be inserted at the head of the sup-affix having *ṅ* as *it*, if this follows a pronominal stem that ends in the affix *āp* (*cāp*, *ṭāp* and *ḍāp*). Simultaneously the aṅga-final long vowel *ā* of the feminine affix is shortened.

In the illustration *sarvā + ṅe*, the augment *syāṭ*, being *ṭit*, is inserted at the beginning of the affix *e* (*ṅe*) and the aṅga-final long vowel *ā* is shortened by the present rule. We now have *sarva + syā e*. At this stage, the rule *vṛddhireci* (33) applies and we obtain the fully inflected pronominal form *sarvasyai*.

In the ablative and genitive singular form, we have *sarvā + as* (*ṅasi or ṅas*). The augment *syāṭ* is inserted at the head of the affix *as* and the aṅga-final long vowel *ā* is shortened in the same manner as above. Now we have *sarva + syā as --> sarvasyā as*. At this stage, the rule *akaḥ savarṇe dīrghaḥ* (42) applies and we get the form *sarvasyāḥ* after rutva and visarga.

In the genitive plural form of the pronominal stem *sarvā*, we have *sarvā + ām*. In this grammatical situation, the rule *āmi sarvanāmnaḥ suṭ* (154) applies and we insert the augment *suṭ* at the head of the sup-affix *ām*. After dropping the anubandhas, we obtain the form *sarvāsām* (<-- *sarvā + sām* <-- *sarvā + suṭ ām*).

The locative singular affix *ṅi* is replaced by *ām* according to the rule *ṅerāmnadyāmnībhyaḥ* (197) in the following grammatical situation *sarvā + ṅi --> sarvā + ām*. At this stage, the augment *syāṭ* is also added at the beginning of the *ṅit* affix *ām* and the aṅga-final long vowel *ā* is shortened. We have *sarvā + syāṭ ām --> sarva + syā ām --> sarva + syām* {*akaḥ savarṇe dīrghaḥ* (42)} and get the locative singular form *sarvasyām*.

The feminine pronominal stem *sarvā* is declined in the following manner :

	Singular	Dual	Plural
prathamā	*sarvā*	*sarve*	*sarvāḥ*
dvitīyā	*sarvām*	*sarve*	*sarvāḥ*
tṛtīyā	*sarvayā*	*sarvābhyām*	*sarvābhiḥ*

caturthī	*sarvasyai*	*sarvābhyām*	*sarvābhyaḥ*
pañcamī	*sarvasyāḥ*	*sarvābhyām*	*sarvābhyaḥ*
ṣaṣṭhī	*sarvsyāḥ*	*sarvayoḥ*	*sarvāsām*
saptamī	*sarvasyām*	*sarvayoḥ*	*sarvāsu*
sambodhana	*he sarve!*	*he sarve!*	*he sarvāḥ!*

लघु० – एवं विश्वादय आबन्ताः । *evaṁ viśvādaya ābantāḥ.*

Trans. : The pronominal stems *viśvā* and so on, which end in the feminine affix *āp*, will be declined in the same manner.

Eluc. : The pronominal stems ending in the feminine affix *āp* are declined like the nominal stem *ramā* except in the case of *ṅit* sup-affixes. This means that the grammatical operations, which effect distinctive declensional characteristics with respect to the pronominal stems ending in the feminine affix *āp* (*cāp*, *ṭāp* and *ḍāp*) relate only to the *ṅit* sup-affixes. We have specifically dealt with this aspect while discussing the declension of the pronominal stem *sarvā*. Some other feminine pronominal stems, which are declined like *sarvā*, are : *viśvā* 'all, whole', *pūrvā* 'front, east, prior', *parā* 'subsequent, latter', *svā* 'self, one's own', *ekā* 'one, some' *dakṣiṇā* 'south, right-hand side', *uttarā* 'upper, north', *anyā* and *itarā* 'other'.

(220) विभाषा दिक्समासे बहुव्रीहौ । ***vibhāṣā diksamāse bahuvrīhau.* 1. 1. 28**

लघु० – सर्वनामता वा । उत्तरपूर्वस्यै, उत्तरपूर्वायै । *sarvanāmatā vā. uttarapūrvasyai, uttarapūrvāyai.*

Trans. : Let the members listed in the set headed by *sarva* 'all' be optionally designated as *sarvanāman* if they occur in a bahuvrīhi compound composed of members denoting *diś* 'direction'.

PP. *diksamāse bahuvrīhau sarvādīni vibhāṣā sarvanāmāni.*

Eluc. : The words *sarvādīni* and *sarvanāmāni* are carried over from the sūtra *sarvādīni sarvanāmāni* Pā. 1. 1. 27. The compound *diksamāse* is a ṣaṣṭhītatpuruṣa. Its analysis is : *diśām samāsaḥ, diksamāsaḥ, tasmin = diksamāse.* The meaning of the sūtra is as follows : In a bahuvrīhi samāsa of words denoting direction, the members of the set beginning with the word *sarva* are to be optionally designated as *sarvanāman*.

The word *uttarapūrvā* is a bahuvrīhi compound formed in accordance with the sūtra *diṅnāmānyantarāle* Pā. 2. 2. 26, which prescribes the combining of the words that denote the names of directions to form a bahuvrīhi compound denoting the intermediate direction. Its analysis is as follows: *uttarasyāś ca pūrvasyāś ca diśor yad antarālaṁ sā dik uttarapūrvā*. Thus the compound *uttarapūrvā* means 'the northeast'. When this word is treated as a pronominal base (*sarvanāman*), its declension will be like that of *sarvā*. In the absence of the sarvanāman-designation, it will be declined like *ramā*. Thus when *ṅit* affixes follow, the word will have two forms.

The declension of *uttarapūrvā* is as follows :

	Singular	Dual	Plural
prathamā	*uttarapūrvā*	*uttarapūrve*	*uttarapūrvāḥ*
dvitīyā	*uttarapūrvām*	*uttarapūrve*	*uttarapūrvāḥ*
tṛtīyā	*uttarapūrvayā*	*uttarapūrvābhyām*	*uttarapūrvābhiḥ*
caturthī	*uttarapūrvasyai, uttarapūrvāyai*	*uttarapūrvābhyām*	*uttarapūrvābhyaḥ*
pañcamī	*uttarapūrvasyāḥ, uttarapūrvāyāḥ*	*uttarapūrvābhyām*	*uttarapūrvābhyaḥ*
ṣaṣṭhī	*uttarapūrvasyāḥ uttarapūrvāyāḥ*	*uttarapūrvayoḥ*	*uttarapūrvāsām uttarapūrvāṇām*
saptamī	*uttarapūrvasyām, uttarapūrvāyām*	*uttarapūrvayoḥ*	*uttarapūrvāsu*
sambodh.	*he uttarapūrve!*	*he uttarapūrve!*	*he uttarapūrvāḥ!*

The other compound words such as *uttarapaścimā* 'the northwest', *dakṣiṇapūrvā* 'the southeast', which have been formed by the sūtra *diṅnāmānyantarāle* Pā. 2. 2. 26, are declined like *uttarapūrvā*.

लघु॰ – तीयस्येति वा संज्ञा । द्वितीयस्यै, द्वितीयायै । एवं तृतीया । *tīyasyeti vā saṁjñā. dvitīyasyai, dvitīyāyai. evaṁ tṛtīyā.*

Eluc. : According to *tīyasya ṅitsu vā* (vtk 16), the words ending in *tīya*-affix are to be optionally designated as *sarvanāman* before sup-affixes having guttural nasal *ṅ* as *it*. When the the affix *ṭāp* is introduced after these words, we get the words *dvitīyā* and *tṛtīyā*. These feminine words will also be optionally designated as *sarvanāman* before *ṅit* affixes by virtue of the liṅgaviśiṣṭa-paribhāṣā. In declining these feminine forms before these affixes, the rule *sarvanāmnaḥ syāḍḍhrasvaśca* (219) applies. The augment *syāṭ* is inserted at the head of these affixes and the aṅga-final long vowel *ā* is replaced by a short vowel *a*. In the absence of sarvanāman-designation, the rule *yāḍāpaḥ* (218) applies. Thus we have two forms of these words before *ṅit* sup-affixes. The declension of the word *dvitīyā* is as follows :

	Singular	Dual	Plural
prathamā	*dvitīyā*	*dvitīye*	*dvitīyāḥ*
dvitīyā	*dvitīyām*	*dvitīye*	*dvitīyāḥ*
tṛtīyā	*dvitīyayā*	*dvitīyābhyām*	*dvitīyābhiḥ*
caturthī	*dvitīyasyai, dvitīyāyai*	*dvitīyābhyām*	*dvitīyebhyaḥ*
pañcamī	*dvitīyasyāḥ, dvitīyāyāḥ*	*dvitīyābhyām*	*dvitīyābhyaḥ*
ṣaṣṭhī	*dvitīyasyāḥ, dvitīyāyāḥ*	*dvitīyayoḥ*	*dvitīyānām*
saptamī	*dvitīyasyām, dvitīyāyām*	*dvitīyayoḥ*	*dvitīyāsu*
sambodhana	*he dvitīye!*	*he dvitīye!*	*he dvitīyāḥ!*

The declension of the word *tṛtīyā* will be like that of *dvitīyā*.

लघु० - अम्बार्थेति ह्रस्वः । हे अम्ब ! हे अक्क ! हे अल्ल ! *ambārtheti hrasvaḥ. he amba! he akka! he alla!*

Eluc.. : The words *ambā, akkā, allā,* etc. denote 'mother or Goddess Pārvatī'. Their declension is like that of the word *ramā*. The only difference that exists in the declensional process of these two words is in respect of the form with the vocative singular affix. In this case the rule *ambārthanadyorhrasvaḥ* (194) prescribes a short vowel substitution in place of the long aṅga-final vowel *ā*. When the aṅga-final vowel *ā* is shortened, the vocative singular affix *s(u)* is elided by *eṅhrasvāt sambuddheḥ* (133). The vocative singular forms *he amba! he akka! he alla!*, given in the vṛtti, are respectively of the words *ambā, akkā* and *allā* which have two vowels. The rule *ambārthanadyorhrasvaḥ* (194) does not apply in the case of the words which denote 'mother' and have more than two syllables (cf. *ambārthaṁ dvyakṣaraṁ yadi* Mbh 7. 3. 107 vtk 3). This is the reason why the aṅga-final vowel *ā* of the words such as *ambikā* is not shortened in the vocative singular. The vocative singular form of *ambikā* is : *he ambike!* The rest of the declension of the words *ambā, akkā, allā,* etc. will be like that of *ramā.*

लघु० – जरा, जरसौ इत्यादि । पक्षे हलादौ च रमावत् । *jarā, jarasau ityādi. pakṣe haladau ca ramāvat.*

Eluc. : The word *jarā* 'old age' is optionally replaced by *jaras* when a sup-affix beginning with a vowel follows. In the absence of *jaras*-replacement this is declined like the word *ramā* when the affixes which begin with a consonant follow. One point is worth noticing in this context. When the sup-affix *au* or *auṭ* follows, the *jaras*-replacement, being subsequent, takes place first because the rule Pā. 7. 2. 101 which prescribes the *jaras*-replacement, is subsequent to the rule Pā. 7. 1. 18, which enjoins the substitute *śī* in place of the dual sup-affix *au* or *auṭ.*[1]

The word *jarā* is declined in the following manner :

	Singular	Dual	Plural
prathamā	*jarā*	*jarasau,* *jare*	*jarasaḥ,* *jarāḥ*
dvitīyā	*jarasam,* *jarām*	*jarasau,* *jare*	*jarasaḥ,* *jarāḥ*
tṛtīyā	*jarasā* *jarayā*	*jarābhyām*	*jarābhiḥ*
caturthī	*jarase,* *jarāyai*	*jarābhyām*	*jarābhyaḥ*
pañcamī	*jarasaḥ,* *jarāyāḥ*	*jarābhyām*	*jarābhyaḥ*
ṣaṣṭhī	*jarasaḥ,* *jarāyāḥ*	*jarasoḥ,* *jarayoḥ*	*jarasām,* *jarāṇām*

1. *śībhāvāt paratvāt jaras,* SK, I, p. 300.

saptamī	*jarasi,* *jarāyām*	*jarasoḥ,* *jarayoḥ*	*jarāsu*
sambodhana	*he jare!*	*he jarasau!* *he jare!*	*he jarasaḥ!* *he jarāḥ!*

लघु० - गोपा विश्वपावत्। *gopā viśvapāvat.*

Eluc. : The feminine word *gopā* will be declined like *viśvapā*. It is an upapada samāsa; its analysis is : *gāṁ pātīti gopā* {<-- *go pā* <-- *go ṅas pā vic* or *kvip* (Pā. 3. 2. 75 or 76)}. Since the word *gopā* does not end in the affix *ṭāp*, the nominative singular ending *su* is not elided by *halṅyābbhyo...* (178). We obtain the inflected form *gopāḥ* after rutva and visarga.

With the dual sup-affix of the second triplet, we have *gopā* + *au*. In this situation, the *śī*-replacement does not take place because the word does not end in the feminine affix *ṭāp*. The application of the rule *prathamayoḥ...* (125) is blocked by *dīrghājjasi ca...* (161). Then by *vṛddhireci* (33), we obtain the form *gopau*.

In *gopā* + *as* (*jas*) also the rule *prathamayoḥ pūrvasavarṇaḥ* (125) is blocked and then by *akaḥ savarṇe dīrghaḥ* (42), we get the form *gopāḥ*. When we introduce the singular affix of the second triplet, we apply the rule *ami pūrvaḥ* (134) and get the form *gopām*. When the plural affix *śas* is added after the word *gopā*, it gets the designation *bha* by *yaci bham* (164). As a consequence, the long vowel *ā* of *gopā* is replaced by lopa according to the rule *āto dhātoḥ* (166). Thus the inflected form *gopaḥ* is obtained.

The declension of the word *gopā* is as follows :

	Singular	Dual	Plural
prathamā	*gopāḥ*	*gopau*	*gopāḥ*
dvitīyā	*gopām*	*gopau*	*gopaḥ*
tṛtīyā	*gopā*	*gopābhyām*	*gopābhiḥ*
caturthī	*gope*	*gopābhyām*	*gopābhyaḥ*
pañcamī	*gopaḥ*	*gopābhyām*	*gopābhyaḥ*
ṣaṣṭhī	*gopaḥ*	*gopoḥ*	*gopām*
saptamī	*gopi*	*gopoḥ*	*gopāsu*
sambodhana	*he gopāḥ!*	*he gopau!*	*he gopāḥ!*

The feminine form of the word *gopa*, which is derived in accordance with the sūtra *āto 'nupasarge kaḥ* (788), is *gopī* when the feminine affix *ṅīṣ* is introduced after it by the rule *jāterastrīviṣayādayopadhāt* (1263). Its declension will then be like that of the word *gaurī*, which is going to be discussed after the sūtra *na tisṛcatasṛ* (225).

Here comes to an end the declension of the feminine words that end in a long *ā*. Now begins the process of declining the feminine words that end in a short *i*.

लघु० – मतीः। मत्या। *matīḥ. matyā.*

Eluc. : The word *mati* 'intellect, knowledge' is derived by adding the affix *ktin* after the verbal root *man* 'to know'. It is declined like the word *hari* when sup-affixes other than the *ṅit* ones follow. When *ṅit* sup-affixes follow, the word *mati* is optionally designated as *nadī*.

The nominative singular form *matiḥ* is obtained after rutva and visarga.

When the dual affix of the first triplet is introduced after the word *mati*, the sūtra *prathamayoḥ pūrvasavarṇaḥ* (125) applies and a long vowel homogeneous with the preceding one replaces both the vowel *i* of *mati* and *au*. The form *matī* (<-- *mat ī* <-- *mati* + *au*) is thus obtained.

With the plural affix *jas* we have *mati* + *as*. At this stage, the rule *jasi ca* (167) enjoins a guṇa replacement for the aṅga-final vowel *i* and we get the form *matayaḥ* after the application of the rule *eco 'ya...* (22).

When the plural affix *śas* of the second triplet is introduced, the rule *prathamayoḥ pūrva...* (125) applies and we have *matīḥ*. The final phoneme of *śas* is not replaced by *n* as *mati* is a feminine nominal stem.

With the singular affix *ṭā* of the third triplet added after *mati* (*mati* + *ṭā*), the rule *iko yaṇaci* (15) applies and we get the form *matyā*. Although *mati* is a ghi-stem here, the affix *ṭā* is not replaced by *nā* by the sūtra *āṅo nā...* (170) as the word *mati* is feminine.

When we add a singular sup-affix of the fourth triplet after *mati*, the rule *gherṅiti* (171) prescribes a guṇa substitution for the anga-final vowel *i*. Now the following sūtra optionally designates *mati* as *nadi* :

(221) ङिति ह्रस्वश्च । *ṅiti hrasvaśca.* 1. 4. 6

लघु० – इयङुवङ्स्थानौ स्त्रीशब्दभिन्नौ नित्यस्त्रीलिङ्गावीदूतौ ह्रस्वौ च इवर्णोवर्णौ स्त्रियां वा नदीसंज्ञौ स्तो ङिति। मत्यै, मतये। मत्याः 2। मतेः 2। *iyaṅuvaṅsthānau strīśabdabhinnau nityastrīliṅgāv īdūtau hrasvau ca ivarṇovarṇau striyāṁ vā nadīsaṁjñau sto ṅiti. matyai, mataye. matyāḥ 2. mateḥ 2.*

Trans. : With the exception of the word *strī*, (i) the word-forms which invariably denote feminine, which end in *ī* and *ū* and which are subject to replacement by *iyaṅ* and *uvaṅ* and also (ii) the feminine words, ending in short *i* and *u*, are optionally designated as *nadī* if a sup-affix, marked with *ṅ* as *it*, follows.

PP. *iyaṅuvaṅsthānau astrī stryākhyau yū ṅiti hrasvaḥ vā nadī.*

Eluc. : The words *astrī* and *iyaṅuvaṅsthānau* are carried over from the sūtra *neyaṅuvaṅsthānāvastrī* Pā. 1. 4. 4. The terms *stryākhyau* and *yū* are read into this sūtra from *yū stryākhyau nadī* Pā. 1. 4. 3. The indeclinable *vā* is carried over from *vā "mi* Pā. 1. 4. 5. The compound *astrī* is a nañ-tatpuruṣa. This means 'leaving the word *strī*'. The word *iyaṅuvaṅsthānau* is a dvandva-seeded bahuvrīhi samāsa, which is analysed as *iyaṅ ca uvaṅ ca iyaṅuvaṅau* (itaretaradvandva), *iyaṅuvaṅoḥ sthānaṁ yayos tau = iyaṅuvaṅsthānau.* The word *stryākhyau*, which comes from *yū stryākhyau nadī* Pā. 1. 4. 3, means 'the two which express the feminine'. The term *yū* is also an itaretaradvandva analysed as *īś ca ūś ca yū*. Here we give the meaning of the sūtra into two parts for clear comprehension. In the first part the terms *iyaṅ* and *uvaṅ* are carried over but not in the second part : 1. With the exception of the word *strī*, the words, which denote feminine and which end in *ī* or *ū* and are subject to replacement by *iyaṅ* and *uvaṅ* respectively are designated as *nadī* optionally provided a *ṅit* sup-affix follows. 2. The feminine words which end in short *i* or *u* are to be designated as *nadī* optionally if a *ṅit* sup-affix follows.

This rule is an exception to *neyaṅuvaṅsthānāvastrī* Pā. 1. 4. 4 and *vā "mi* Pā. 1. 4. 5, which deny nadī-designation obligatorily, whereas this sūtra optionally prescribes nadī-designation in respect of the words, which invariably denote feminine and which end in *ī* or *ū* and are subject to replacement by *iyaṅ* and *uvaṅ*. The present rule also includes those feminine words which end in a short *i* or *u* to be covered by the optional nadī-designation when a *ṅit* sup-affix follows.

The sum and substance of this sūtra is as follows : The words which end in a long *ī* or *ū* but which undergo the *iyaṅ* and *uvaṅ* replacement were denied the nadi-designation by *neyaṅuvaṅsthānāvastrī* (228). Now by the present rule they are to be optionally designated as *nadī* before *ṅit* sup-affixes. The word *strī* is an exception. Secondly, feminine words which end in a short *i* or *u* are also optionally designated as *nadī* before *ṅit* sup-affixes. It is to be borne in mind that the words ending in a short *i* or *u* need not denote the feminine gender obligatorily. Only their use in the feminine is needed for the assignment of the optional nadī-designation. If this interpretation is not resorted to, then the nadī-designation cannot be assigned to such words as are used both in feminine and masculine genders and to those which are used in all the genders. As such, the words *iṣu, aśani*, etc. would not be assigned the nadī-designation since they are used in both masculine and feminine genders and also the qualifying words *paṭu, mṛdu*, etc. would be kept out of the ambit of nadī-designation, even when they are used in the feminine since they are also used in all the three genders (cf. *hrasvayos tu striyām ityeva viśeṣaṇam, na tu nityastrītvaparyantam. anyathā iṣvaśaniprabhṛtīnām ubhayaliṅgānāṁ paṭumṛduprabhṛtīnāṁ sarvaliṅgānāṁ ca strītve 'pi nadītvaṁ na syāt.* TB, I, p. 306).

The word *mati* is optionally assigned nadī-designation before *ṅit* sup-affixes. The dative singular affix *ṅe* has *ṅ* as *it*. With this affix, we have *mati* + *e* (*ṅe*). In this situation, when it is assigned nadī-designation, the rules *āṇnadyāḥ* (195) and *āṭaśca* (196) apply and we get the form *matyai* (<-- *mati* + *āi* <-- *mati* + *āṭ e*). In the absence of nadī-designation, it is assigned ghi-designation. As a consequence, the rule *gherṅiti* (171) applies and the aṅga-final *i* is replaced by a guṇa-vowel *e*. The rule *eco-'yavāyāvaḥ* (22) applies and we have the form *mataye*.

With the ablative and genitive singular affixes *ṅasi* and *ṅas*, we get a common form of the word *mati*. In the case of nadī-designation, we get the form *matyāḥ* through the following grammatical operations : 1. the augment *āṭ* by *āṇnadyāḥ* (195), 2. vṛddhi substitution by *āṭaśca* (196), 3. *yaṇ* by *iko...* (15), 4. rutva by *sasajuṣo...* (104) and 5. visarga by *kharava...* (93). In the absence of nadī-designation, we obtain the form *mateḥ* through the following grammatical process : 1. ghi-designation 2. guṇa-replacement by *gherṅiti* (171) and 3. pūrvarūpa ekādeśa by *ṅasi...* (172).

With the locative singular affix *ṅi*, we have *mati* + *ṅi*. When the word *mati* gets the nadī-designation, the rule *ṅerāmnadyāmnībhyaḥ* (197), which enjoins *ām*-replacement in place of the affix *ṅi* and the rule *aut* (183), which prescribes the *aut*-substitution for the affix *ṅi*, simultaneously become applicable. With the help of the rule *vipratiṣedhe paraṁ kāryam* (112), the rule *aut* (183) supersedes *ṅerām...* (197) and applies. As a consequence, the form of *mati* in the locative singular thus obtained would be *matyau* like *sakhyau*, which is not desirable. The following sūtra does away with this undesirable contingency and makes provision for *ṅi* to be replaced by *ām* in the context of *mati*, when it is designated as *nadī*.

(222) इदुद्भ्याम्। *idudbhyām.* 7. 3. 117

लघु० - इदुद्भ्यां नदीसंज्ञकाभ्यां परस्य ङेराम्। मत्याम्। मतौ। शेषं हरिवत्। एवं बुद्ध्यादयः। *idudbhyāṁ nadīsaṁjñakābhyāṁ parasya ṅer ām. matyām. matau. śeṣaṁ harivat. evaṁ buddhyādayaḥ.*

Trans. : Let the sup-affix *ṅi,* which follows the words designated as *nadī* that end in a short *i* or *u,* be replaced by *ām.* [The optional locative singular form will be] : *matyām, matau.* The rest of the declension will be like that of *hari.* The words *buddhi,* etc. will be declined in the same way.

PP. *idudbhyām nadībhyām ṅeḥ ām* (*aṅgasya*).

Eluc. : The terms *āp* and *nī* from *ṅerāmnadyāmnībhyaḥ* Pā. 7. 3. 116 are not made to recur in the present sūtra since a short *i* and a short *u* have been enunciated in it. There is no possibility of short *i* and *u* being present in these two terms. So, only the word *nadībhyām* is carried over into this sūtra by the process of vacanavipariṇāma. The segregated term *nadībhyaḥ* has been changed into dual number to accord with *idudbhyām.* The terms *ṅeḥ* and *ām* have been carried over from *ṅerām...* Pā. 7. 3. 116. The compound word *idudbhyām* is an itaretaradvandva, which is analysed as *ic ca uc ca idutau, tābhyām = idudbhyām.* Thus the meaning of the sūtra is : If the singular affix *ṅi* of the seventh triplet follows the words ending in a short *i* or *u,* which are designated as *nadī,* then the affix *ṅi* is replaced by *ām.* This is an exception to the sūtra *aut* (183).

The illustration *matyām* is arrived at in the following way : *mati + ṅi* --> *mati + i* --> *mati + ām* (by the present rule) --> *mati + āṭ ām* {*āṇnadyāḥ* (195)} --> *mati + ām* {vṛddhi by *āṭaśca* (196)}. Then the rule *iko yaṇaci* (15) applies and we get the form *matyām.* This illustration exemplifies *mati* as a nadī word. In the absence of nadī-designation, the word *mati* gets the ghi-designation. The sūtra *acca gheḥ* (173) applies. The affix *ṅi* is replaced by *au* and the aṅga-final *i* of *mati* is substituted by a short *a.* We obtain the form *matau* after the application of *vṛddhireci* (33).

In the vocative singular form of *mati,* the rule *hrasvasya guṇaḥ* (168) enjoins guṇa-replacement in place of the aṅga-final *i.* Then the affix *su* of *sambuddhi* is elided by *eṅhrasvāt sambuddheḥ* (133). Thus the vocative singular form *mate* is obtained. The nominal stem *mati* is declined in the following manner :

	Singular	Dual	Plural
prathamā	*matiḥ*	*matī*	*matayaḥ*
dvitīyā	*matim*	*matī*	*matīḥ*
tṛtīyā	*matyā*	*matibhyām*	*matibhiḥ*
caturthī	*matyai, matayе*	*matibhyām*	*matibhyaḥ*

pañcamī	*matyāḥ, mateḥ*	*matibhyām*	*matibhyaḥ*
ṣaṣṭhī	*matyāḥ, mateḥ*	*matyoḥ*	*matīnām*
saptamī	*matyām, matau*	*matyoḥ*	*matiṣu*
sambodhana	*he mate!*	*he matī!*	*he matayaḥ!*

The words such as *buddhi*, etc. will be declined like *mati*. Some of the words, which are declined like *mati* are : *avani* 'earth', *ākṛti* 'form', *iṣṭi* 'sacrifice', *kṛti* 'work', *kṣati* 'loss', *gati* 'gait', *tithi* 'date', *niyati* 'fate', *nīti* 'policy', *bhakti* 'devotion', *bhūmi* 'earth', *mukti* 'liberation', *śakti* 'power, strength', *yuvati* 'young woman', *śānti* 'peace', *sampatti* 'wealth', *smṛti* 'remembrance, memory', *stuti* 'eulogy' and *hāni* 'loss'.

The word *tri* in the masculine has already been declined (see supra pp. 229-30). It is always used in the plural. In the feminine when we introduce the plural affix of the first triplet, we have *tri* + *jas*. At this stage, the following sūtra ensues :

(223) त्रिचतुरोः स्त्रियां तिसृचतसृ । *tricaturoḥ striyāṁ tisṛcatasṛ*. 7. 2. 99

लघु० – स्त्रीलिङ्गयोरेतयोरेतौ स्तो विभक्तौ । *strīliṅgayor etayor etau sto vibhaktau.*

Trans. : When a sup-affix follows, the words *tri* and *catur* in the feminine are respectively replaced by *tisṛ* and *catasṛ*.

PP. *tricaturoḥ striyāṁ tisṛcatasṛ vibhaktau* (*aṅgasya*).

Eluc. : The word *vibhaktau* is carried over from *aṣṭana ā vibhaktau* Pā. 7. 2. 84. The compound word *tricaturoḥ* is an itaretaradvandva. Its analysis is : *triś ca catuś ca tricaturau tayoḥ* = *tricaturoḥ*. The other compound word is a samāhāradvandva : *tisṛ ca catasṛ ca tayoḥ samāhāraḥ*.

In the illustration *tri* + *jas*, the sup-affix (vibhakti) *jas* follows the stem *tri*. As a consequence, the morpheme *tisṛ* replaces the word *tri* by the present sūtra. Then we have *tisṛ* + *as* after the elision of the anubandha *j* by *tasya lopaḥ* (3) since it is *it* by *cuṭū* (128). At this stage, the guṇa-subtitution becomes available by the rule *ṛto ṅisarvanāmasthānayoḥ* (203), which has blocked the application of the sūtra *prathamayoḥ pūrvasavarṇaḥ* (125). In this situation, the following sūtra becomes available for application :

(224) अचि र ऋतः । *aci ra ṛtaḥ*. 7. 2. 100

लघु० – तिसृचतसृ एतयोर्ऋकारस्य रेफादेशः स्यादचि । गुणदीर्घोत्त्वानामपवादः । तिस्रः 2 । तिसृभिः । तिसृभ्यः 2 । आमि नुट् । *tisṛcatasṛ etayor ṛkārasya rephādeśaḥ syād aci. guṇadīrghottvānām apavādaḥ. tisraḥ 2. tisṛbhiḥ. tisṛbhyaḥ 2. āmi nuṭ.*

Trans. : When a vowel follows, the repha will replace the vowel *ṛ* of *tisṛ* and *catasṛ*. This is an exception to other grammatical operations, viz., guṇa, dīrgha and *ut* replacements. [The plural form of *tri* in the feminine will be] : *tisraḥ* 2. (Other illustrations are) *tisṛbhiḥ*. *tisṛbhyaḥ* 2. Before the affix *ām, nuṭ* comes.

PP. *aci ra ṛtaḥ tisṛcatasṛ (vibhaktau, aṅgasya)*.

Eluc. : The compound word *tisṛcatasṛ* is carried over from *tricaturoḥ striyāṁ tisṛcatasṛ* 7. 2. 99 and is changed into the genitive dual by the process of vibhaktivipariṇāma. The meaning of the sūtra is : The vowel *ṛ* of the morphemes *tisṛ* and *catasṛ* is replaced by repha, when they are followed by a vowel (*ac*).

The expression *guṇadīrghottvānām apavādaḥ* in Laghu needs elaboration. Although the vowel *ṛ* can be replaced with repha by the rule *iko yaṇaci* (15), the present sūtra is needed to block the following grammatical operations : 1. the guṇa-replacement in *tisṛ + as* by *ṛto ṅisarvanāma-sthānayoḥ* (203) 2. the pūrvasavarṇadīrgha in the above illustraion by *prathamayoḥ pūrvasavarṇaḥ* (125) and 3. the *ut*-replacement in place of the vowel *ṛ* in the illustration *priyatisṛ + as (ṅas)* by *ṛta ut* (207).[1] Thus the present rule is an exception to these three grammatical operations.

In the illustration *tisṛ + as (jas)*, the phoneme *r* will replace the vowel *ṛ*, by the present rule, when the guṇa-substitution by *ṛto ṅi...* (203) has been blocked by it. We have the form *tisraḥ* after rutva and visarga.

In the formation *tisṛ + as*, the rule *prathamayoḥ pūrvasavarṇaḥ* (125) becomes available for application but the present rule blocks it and prescribes *r*-substitution in place of the vowel *ṛ* and we obtain the form *tisraḥ* after rutva and visarga.

With the plural sup-affix *ām*, we have *tri + ām*. At this stage, the rule *trestrayaḥ* (191) enjoins that *tri* be replaced by *traya* before *ām* but this is debarred by *tricaturoḥ striyāṁ tisṛcatasṛ* (223) which instead

---

1. *tisras tiṣṭhantītyatra ṛto ṅi sarvanāmasthānayoḥ iti guṇasya ratvam apavādaḥ tisraḥ paśyetyatra tu prathamayoḥ pūrvasavarṇaḥ iti pūrvasavarṇadīrghasyāpavādaḥ priyatisra āgataḥ priyatisraḥ svam ityatra ṛta ut ityutvasyeti vivekaḥ.* TB, I, p. 308. Also compare BM, I, p. 308.

prescribes the substitute *tisṛ* to come in place of *tri*. Now from *tri* + *ām*, we have : *tisṛ* + *ām*. At this stage, both the insertion of the augment *nuṭ* by *hrasvanadyāpo nuṭ* (147) and the *r*-replacement by *aci ra ṛtaḥ* (224) simultaneously become available. In this grammatical situation, according to the sūtra *vipratiṣedhe paraṁ kāryam* (112), the *r*-substitution is applicable but *num-aci ra-tṛjvadbhāvebhyo nuṭ pūrvavipratiṣedhena* (vtk 19)[1] rules that that which is prior will prevail. As a consequence, by pūrvavipratiṣedha the insertion of the augment *nuṭ* is effected. Then we have *tisṛ* + *nuṭ ām* --> *tisṛ* + *nām* (after the elision of *its*). Now by virtue of the rule *nāmi* (148), the aṅga-final long vowel substitution is due but the following sūtra prohibits this :

(225) न तिसृचतसृ । *na tisṛcatasṛ*. 6. 4. 4

लघु० – एतयोर्नामि दीर्घो न । तिसृणाम् । तिसृषु । द्वे 2 । द्वाभ्याम् 3 । द्वयोः 2 । *etayor nāmi dīrgho na. tisṛṇām, tisṛṣu. dve* 2. *dvābhyām* 3. *dvayoḥ* 2.

Trans. : A long vowel substitution does not replace (the aṅga-final vowel of) the words *tisṛ* and *catasṛ* when *nām* follows.

PP. *tisṛcatasṛ nāmi na dīrghaḥ (aṅgasya)*.

Eluc. : The genitive nominal ending after the compound word *tisṛcatasṛ* should be considered to have been elided (*luptaṣaṣṭhīkaṁ padam*, BM, I, p. 308). The words *nāmi* and *dīrghaḥ* are respectively carried over from *nāmi* Pā. 6. 4. 3 and *ḍhralope pūrvasya dīrgho 'ṇaḥ* Pā. 6. 3. 111. With these insertions, the sūtra means : When *nām* follows, there is no long vowel replacement in place of *tisṛ* and *catasṛ*. With the help of the paribhāṣā sūtra *alo 'ntyasya* (21), this long vowel substitute is to come in place of the aṅga-final vowel *ṛ* instead of the words *tisṛ* and *catasṛ*. This comes to mean that the aṅga-final vowel *ṛ* is not replaced by a long counter-part when *nām* follows. Then the phoneme *n* of *nām* is replaced by the cerebral *ṇ* by *ṛvarṇānnasya ṇatvaṁ vācyam* (vtk 21) and we get the form *tisṛṇām* (*tisṛ* + *ṇām* <-- *tisṛ* + *nām*).

The dental *s* of the locative plural affix *sup* is replaced by the cerebral *ṣ* in accordance with the rule *ādeśapratyayayoḥ* (149) and thus the form *tisṛṣu* is obtained. The word *tri* in the feminine is declined as follows :

	Plural		Plural
prathamā	*tisraḥ*	tṛtīyā	*tisṛbhiḥ*
dvitīyā	*tisraḥ*	caturthī	*tisṛbhyaḥ*

1. For explanation, see supra p. 260 .

pañcamī	*tisṛbhyaḥ*	saptamī	*tisṛṣu*
ṣaṣṭhī	*tisṛṇām*	sambodhana	no form

The word *catur* in the feminine will be declined in the same manner. This will be explained in the chapter on halanta strīliṅga.

The word *dvi* denotes duality. As such, it will always be declined in the dual. The process of declining the word *dvi* in the feminine is as follows : When we introduce the dual affix of the first triplet, we have : *dvi + au*. In this situation, the rule *tyadādīnāmaḥ* (192) applies and the short *i* of *dvi* is replaced by a short *a*. This will be the case before every sup-affix. Then, to express it in the feminine, we add the affix *ṭāp* by *ajādyataṣṭāp* (1243). Now we have *dva + ṭāp + au --> dva + ā + au --> dvā + au* {savarṇadīrgha by *akaḥ savarṇe dīrghaḥ* (42)}. The dual sup-affix *au* is replaced with *śī* by *auṅa āpaḥ* (215). So *dvā + śī --> dvā + ī* (the palatal *ś* is dropped). Then by *ādguṇaḥ* (27), we get the form *dve*. With the dual affix *auṭ* of the second triplet, the form of *dvi* in the feminine will also be *dve*. There is no significant change in the dual form with the affixes of the third, fourth and fifth triplets. This will be *dvābhyām*, after the short *i* has been replaced with a short *a* by *tyadādīnāmaḥ* (192) and the affix *ṭāp* has been added by *ajādyataṣṭāp* (1243). In the dual forms of the genitive and locative, the rule *āṅi cāpaḥ* (217) applies, we have the substitute *e* in place of the vowel *ā* of *dvā*. We have *dve + os*. After the application of *eco 'yavāyāvaḥ* (22), we get *dvayoḥ*. The declension of the word *dvi* in the feminine is as follows :

	Dual		Dual
prathamā	*dve*	pañcamī	*dvābhyām*
dvitīyā	*dve*	ṣaṣṭhī	*dvayoḥ*
tṛtīyā	*dvābhyām*	saptamī	*dvayoḥ*
caturthī	*dvābhyām*	sambodhana	no form

Here comes to an end the declension of the feminine words ending in a short *i*.

Now begins the declension of the feminine words that end in a long *ī*.

लघु० – गौरी । गौर्यौ । गौर्यः । हे गौरि ! गौर्यै इत्यादि । एवं नद्यादयः । *gaurī. gauryau. gauryaḥ. he gauri! gauryai ityādi. evaṁ nadyādayaḥ.*

Eluc. : The word *gaurī* is derived by introducing the feminine affix *ṅīṣ* after the word *gaura* by *ṣidgaurādibhyaśca* (1249). The affix *ṅīṣ* remains as *ī* after the *its* have been dropped. After eliding by *yasyeti ca* (235) the short *a* of *gaura*, which is *bha* by *yaci bham* (164), we get *gaurī* after the addition of *ī*. The word *gaurī*, which is in the feminine, means 'the daughter of the Himālaya, the consort of Śiva'. It gets the nadī designation by *yū stryākhyau nadī* (193) since it is always in the feminine and ends in a long *ī*.

The singular affix *su* of the first triplet is elided by *halṅyābbhyo dīrghāt sutisyapṛktaṁ hal* (178) because the affix *su* is reduced to the status of apṛkta after the elision of the vowel *u* and because it follows the word *gaurī* which ends in *ṅī*. We get the form *gaurī* in the nominative singular.

With the dual affix of the first triplet, we have *gaurī + au*. Here pūrvasavarṇadīrgha is available by *prathamayoḥ pūrvasavarṇaḥ* (125), which is prohibited by *dīrghājjasi ca* (161). Then the rule *iko yaṇaci* (15) applies and we obtain the form *gauryau*. By virtue of the rule *aco rahābhyāṁ dve* (60), we also get the form *gauryyau* with two yakāras (reduplication of *yar*). With the affix *jas* also, pūrvasavarṇadīrgha is blocked. The rule *iko yaṇaci* (15) applies and we have *gauryaḥ*.

In *gaurī + am*, the rule *ami pūrvaḥ* (134) applies and we have *gaurīm*. With the plural affix *śas*, pūrvasavarṇadīrgha takes place by *prathamayoḥ pūrvasavarṇaḥ* (125) and we have the form *gaurīḥ* after rutva and visarga.

With the singular affix of the third triplet, we have *gauryā* after the application of *iko yaṇaci* (15).

With the singular affix *ṅe* of the fourth triplet, we have *gaurī + ṅe* --> *gaurī + e* after the elision of the anubandha *ṅ*. Since the word is nadī by *yū stryākhyau nadī* (193), the rule *āṇnadyāḥ* (195) prescribes the augment *āṭ* to be inserted at the head of the affix *e* {*ādyantau ṭakitau* (84)}. In *gaurī + āṭ e*, the rule *āṭaśca* (196) enjoins a vṛddhi replacement and we have *gaurī + ai*. We obtain the form *gauryai* by *iko yaṇaci* (15).

With the same grammatical process, we get the common singular form *gauryāḥ* in the ablative and genitive singular.

In the genitive and locative dual form we apply the rule *iko yaṇaci* (15) and have the common form *gauryoḥ*. In the plural form of the genitive, we first assign nadī-designation, as a result of which the augment *nuṭ* is added by *hrasvanadyāpo nuṭ* (147) and then the dental *n* of *nām* is replaced by cerebral *ṇ* {*aṭkupvāṅ...* (137)}. We obtain the form *gaurīṇām* through the following process : *gaurī + ām* --> *gaurī + nuṭ ām* --> *gaurī + nām* --> *gaurī + ṇām* --> *gaurīṇām*.

In the locative singular form *gauryām*, we apply the rule *ṅerām nadyāmnībhyaḥ* (197) and replace the affix *ṅi* by *ām*. Then the augment *āṭ* comes by *āṇnadyāḥ* (195) and the vṛddhi substitution takes place by *āṭaśca* (196). After the application of the rule *iko yaṇaci* (15) we get the form *gauryām* through these grammatical stages : *gaurī* + *ṅi* --> *gaurī* + *ām* --> *gaurī* + *āṭ ām* --> *gaurī* + *ā ām* --> *gaurī* + *ām* --> *gauryām*.

In the vocative singular form of the word *gaurī*, the aṅga-final long *ī* is shortened by *ambārthanadyorhrasvaḥ* (194) and then the affix *su* of the vocative singular is elided by *eṅhrasvāt sambuddheḥ* (133) and we get the form *he gauri!* The declension of the word *gaurī* is as follows :

	Singular	Dual	Plural
prathamā	*gaurī*	*gauryau*	*gauryaḥ*
dvitīyā	*gaurīm*	*gauryau*	*gaurīḥ*
tṛtīyā	*gauryā*	*gaurībhyām*	*gaurībhiḥ*
caturthī	*gauryai*	*gaurībhyām*	*gaurībhyaḥ*
pañcamī	*gauryāḥ*	*gaurībhyām*	*gaurībhyaḥ*
ṣaṣṭhī	*gauryāḥ*	*gauryoḥ*	*gaurīṇām*
saptamī	*gauryām,*	*gauryoḥ*	*gaurīṣu*
sambodhana	*he gauri!*	*he gauryau!*	*he gauryaḥ!*

The words *nadī* and so on will be declined in the same manner. Some of the words of this class are as follows : *nadī* 'river', *aṭavī* 'forest', *anīkinī* 'army', *urvī* 'the earth', *kādambarī* 'wine', *kumārī* 'unmarried girl' *taṭinī* 'river', *dāsī* 'maid', *nārī* 'woman', *patnī* 'wife', *bhāratī* 'speech, language', *mahī* 'the earth', *mātulī* 'maternal aunt', *muralī* 'flute', *maitrī* 'friendship' and *lekhanī* 'pen'.

लघु० – लक्ष्मीः। शेषं गौरीवत्। एवं तरीतन्त्र्यादयः। *lakṣmīḥ. śeṣaṁ gaurīvat. evaṁ tarītantryādayaḥ.*

Eluc. : The nominative singular affix *su* after the word *lakṣmī* is not elided since it does not end in *ṅī*. As such, *lakṣmīḥ* is the nominative singular form. The rest of the declension is like that of *gaurī*. The words *tarī* 'boat', *tantrī* 'a kind of musical instrument', etc., which are derived by introducing the affix *ī* by *avitṝstṝtatribhya īḥ* (Uṇādi Sūtra, 438) will be declined like the word *lakṣmī*. Since they do not end in *ṅī*, there is no elision of the affix *su* after these words.

लघु० – स्त्री। हे स्त्रि! *strī. he stri!*

Eluc. : Now Varadarāja takes up the declension of the word *strī* 'a woman', which is derived from the verbal root *styai* 'to be collected into a heap, to sound' by introducing the uṇādi affix *ḍraṭ* by *styāyaterḍraṭ* (Uṇādi Sūtra, 605) and *ṅīp* by *ṭiḍḍhāṇañ*... (1245). Since the derived word *strī* ends in *ṅī*, the singular nominative affix *su* is elided by the rule *halṅyābbhyo*... (178) and we have the form *strī* in the nominative singular.

In the vocative singular form, the aṅga-final long *ī* is shortened by *ambārthanadyorhrasvaḥ* (194) since the word *strī* is assigned nadī-designation by *yū stryākhyau nadī* (193). Then by *eṅhrasvāt*... (133) the *s* of the vocative singular affix *su* is elided and the form (*he*) *stri* is obtained.

With the dual affix *au* of the first triplet, we have *strī* + *au*. Since the aṅga-final long *ī* does not belong to a verbal root, the rule *aci śnu*... (198) is not available to prescribe it to be substituted by *iyaṅ* (cf. *strī au iti sthite adhātvikāratvāt aci śnudhātu iti iyaṅyaprāpte*, BM, I, p. 312). The rule *prathamayoḥ pūrvasavarṇaḥ* (125) is also debarred by *dīrghājjasi ca* (161). In this situation, the rule *iko yaṇaci* (15) becomes available for application but the following sūtra blocks it and applies :

(226) स्त्रियाः । *striyāḥ*. **6. 4. 79**

लघु० – अस्येयङ् स्याद् अजादौ प्रत्यये परे । स्त्रियौ । स्त्रियः । *asyeyaṅ syād ajādau pratyaye pare. striyau, striyaḥ.*

Trans. : The (aṅga-final) *ī* of the word *strī* is replaced by *iyaṅ* when an affix, which begins with a vowel (*ac*), follows.

PP. *striyāḥ iyaṅ aci* (*aṅgasya*).

Eluc. : The words *iyaṅ* and *aci* are carried over from *aci śnudhātu-bhruvāṁ yvoriyaṅuvaṅau* Pā. 6. 4. 77. Since the present rule occurs in the governing domain of *aṅgasya* Pā. 6. 4. 1, the necessary element *pratyaye* is supplied here and the term *aci* becomes its qualifier. By tadādividhi, it gives the sense 'the affix, which begins with a vowel, follows'. The whole sūtra thus means : When an affix, which begins with a vowel, follows, the word *strī* is replaced by *iyaṅ*. With the help of the paribhāṣā sūtra *alo 'ntyasya* (21), the final phoneme *ī* of *strī* is replaced by *iyaṅ*. In the illustration *strī* + *au*, we have *str iy*(*aṅ*) + *au* --> *striyau*.

In the same manner we have *strī* +*jas* --> *str iy* + *as* --> *striyaḥ* in the nominative plural.

In *strī* + *am*, the rule *ami pūrvaḥ* (134) beomes available for application but the present sūtra blocks it and prescribes the *iyaṅ*-substitute in place of the aṅga-final long *ī*. At this stage, the obligatory *iyaṅ*-substitute is rendered optional by the following sūtra.

(227) वाऽम्शसोः । *vā 'mśasoḥ.* 6. 4. 80

लघु० – अमि शसि च स्त्रिया इयङ् वा स्यात् । स्त्रियम्, स्त्रीम् । स्त्रियः, स्त्रीः । स्त्रिया । स्त्रियै । स्त्रियाः 2 । परत्वान्नुट्- स्त्रीणाम् । स्त्रीषु । *ami śasi ca striyā iyaṅ vā syāt. striyam, strīm. striyaḥ, strīḥ. striyā. striyai. striyāḥ 2. paratvān nuṭ - strīṇām. strīṣu.*

Trans. : Let the substitute *iyaṅ* optionally replace the aṅga-final *ī* of the word *strī* when either *am* or *śas* follows. Being subsequent, the augment *nuṭ* will come instead of *iyaṅ* in *strīṇām.*

PP. *vā amśasoḥ striyā iyaṅ (aṅgasya).*

Eluc. : The words *striyāḥ* and *iyaṅ* are respectively carried over from *striyāḥ* Pā. 6. 4. 79 and *aci śnu...* Pā. 6. 4. 77. Thus the meaning of the sūtra is : When either *am* or *śas* follows, the aṅga-final long *ī* of the word *strī* should optionally be replaced by *iyaṅ.*

In the illustration *strī + am*, there will be two situations. 1. When the present rule enjoins *iyaṅ*-substitute, we have *str iy + am--> striyam.* 2. In the absence of *iyaṅ*-substitute, the rule *ami pūrvaḥ* (134) applies and we have the form *strīm.* In this way, with the singular affix of the second triplet, we have two forms : *striyam* and *strīm.*

In the same way, when the plural affix *śas* of the second triplet follows, we have two forms : With *iyaṅ*-substitute, we have *striyaḥ.* In the absence of *iyaṅ*-substitute, there is pūrvasavarṇadīrgha by *prathamayoḥ pūrvasavarṇaḥ* (125) and we have the form *strīḥ.*

With the singular affix of the third triplet, we have *strī + ā (ṭā).* Now the rule *striyāḥ* (226) prescribes *iyaṅ*-substitute and we have *striyā.*

When we introduce the singular dative affix *ṅe*, we have *strī + e (ṅe).* The word *strī*, being always in the feminine, ends in a long *ī*. As such it is obligatorily assigned nadī-designation by *yū stryākhyau nadī* (193). Although the word *strī* is subject to replacement by *iyaṅ*, the rule *ṅiti hrasvaśca* (221) does not make the nadī-designation to this word optional since it has been excluded from the purview of the optional nadī-designation by virtue of carrying over the term *astrī* into *ṅiti hrasvaśca* Pā. 1. 4. 6 from *neyaṅuvaṅsthānāvastrī* Pā. 1. 4. 4 . Now since it is a nadī word, the sūtra *āṇnadyāḥ* (195) enjoins the augment *āṭ*. In *strī + ā (ṭ) e,* the rule *āṭaśca* (196) prescribes a single vṛddhi-replacement in place of both *ā* and *e*. Then we have *strī + ai.* At this stage, the rule *striyāḥ* (226) applies and after the *iyaṅ*-substitution we get the form *striyai.*

The singular affixes of the fifth and the sixth triplets, that is, *ṅasi* and *ṅas* remain as *as* after the elision of the *its*. Here also because the word *strī* is nadī, the grammatical operations of augmenting the word *strī* with *āṭ*, effecting a single vṛddhi-replacement and bringing about the *iyaṅ*-substitution take place and we have the common form *striyāḥ* in the ablative and genitive singular.

With the sup-affix *os*, we apply the rule *striyāḥ* (226) and after the *iyaṅ*-replacement, we have the form *striyoḥ* (<-- *striyos*), which is common to both the genitive and the locative dual.

In the genitive plural form of the word *strī*, both the augment *nuṭ* and the *iyaṅ*-substitution simultaneously become available for application but being subsequent in the order of enumeration in the Aṣṭādhyāyī, the rule *hrasvanadyāpo nuṭ* (147) applies and the augment *nuṭ* is inserted at the head of the affix *ām*. The form at this stage is *strī + n ām* --> *strīnām*. Now by *aṭkupvāṅ*... (137), the phoneme *n* is replaced by *ṇ* and we obtain the form *strīṇām*.

With the singular affix *ṅi*, we have *strī + ṅi*. The affix *ṅi* is replaced by *ām* according to the rule *ṅerām*... (197). After this substitution, the augment *āṭ* comes. A single vṛddhi-replacement takes place. Then by *striyāḥ* (226), *iyaṅ* is substituted and we get the form *striyām*.

In the locative plural form of *strī*, the dental phoneme s of the affix *sup* is substituted by the cerebral ṣ by the sūtra *adeśapratyayayoḥ* (149) and we obtain the form *strīṣu*.

The complete declension of the word *strī* will be as follows :

	Singular	Dual	Plural
prathamā	*strī*	*striyau*	*striyaḥ*
dvitīyā	*striyam, strīm*	*striyau*	*striyaḥ, strīḥ*
tṛtīyā	*striyā*	*strībhyām*	*strībhiḥ*
caturthī	*striyai*	*strībhyām*	*strībhyaḥ*
pañcamī	*striyāḥ*	*strībhyām*	*strībhyaḥ*
ṣaṣṭhī	*striyāḥ*	*striyoḥ*	*strīṇām*
saptamī	*striyām*	*striyoḥ*	*strīṣu*
sambodhana	*he stri!*	*he striyau!*	*he striyaḥ!*

लघु० – श्रीः । श्रियौ । श्रियः । *śrīḥ, śriyau, śriyaḥ.*

Eluc. : The word *śrī* is derived from the verbal root *śriñ* 'to serve' by adding the affix *kvip* by applying *kvibvacipracchiśrisrudruprujvāṁ dīrgho 'samprasāraṇañca* (Uṇādi Sūtra 215) which also prescribes the lengthening of the last vowel of the verbal base. Thus the nominal stem *śrī* is obtained which does not end in the affix *ṅī*. Consequently, the nominative singular affix *su* is not elided by *halṅyābbhyaḥ...* (178) and the nominative singular form *śrīḥ* is obtained.

In *śrī + au,* the last vowel of the base is a constituent of the verbal root and it is preceded by a conjunct *śr* which is also contained in the verbal root. The pre-affixal base also does not contain more than one vowel so the rule *eranekācaḥ...* (199) has no scope to apply. Now the rule *aciśnu...* (198) applies and after the *iyaṅ*-substitution, the form *śriyau* in the nominative dual is obtained. In the nominative plural after the application of *aciśnu...* (198), we have the form *śriyaḥ.*

In the vocative singular *śrī* + *s*, the shortening of the aṅga-final vowel *ī* is available by the sūtra *ambārthanadyorhrasvaḥ* (194) since it has got the obligatory nadī designation by *yū stryākhyau nadī* (193) but this is not desirable. To dispense with this problem, the following sūtra denies nadī designation to this word :

(228) नेयङुवङ्स्थानावस्त्री । *neyaṅuvaṅsthānāvastrī.* 1. 4. 4

लघु० – इयङुवङोः स्थितिर्ययोस्तावीदूतौ नदीसंज्ञौ न स्तः, न तु स्त्री। हे श्रीः। श्रियै, श्रिये। श्रियाः 2, श्रियः 2 । *iyaṅuvaṅoḥ sthitir yayos tāvīdūtau nadīsaṁjñau na staḥ, na tu strī. he śrīḥ! śriyai, śriye. śriyāḥ 2, śriyaḥ 2.*

Trans. : With the exception of the word *strī*, the long *ī* and *ū*, which are subject to replacement by *iyaṅ* and *uvaṅ* (in a respective manner), are not designated as *nadī*.

PP. *na iyaṅuvaṅsthānau yū nadī astrī.*

Eluc. : The terms *yū* and *nadī* are carried over from *yū stryākhyau nadī* Pā. 1. 4. 3. The compound word *iyaṅuvaṅsthānau* is a dvandva-seeded bahuvrīhi : *iyaṅ ca uvaṅ ca iyaṅuvaṅau* (itaretaradvandva), *iyaṅuvaṅoḥ sthānaṁ yayos tav iyaṅuvaṅsthānau*. Jñānendra Sarasvatī explains this compound in a different way. According to him, it is a dvandva-seeded ṣaṣṭhītatpuruṣa. He derives the word *sthāna* by adding the primary affix *lyuṭ* in the sense of locus (*adhikaraṇa*). Then he explains the compound in the following way : *iyaṅuvaṅoḥ sthānau,* which means that the vowels *ī* and *ū,* which become the loci of the substitutes *iyaṅ* and *uvaṅ* are *iyaṅuvaṅsthānau.* According to him, the interpretation given by Bhaṭṭoji Dīkṣita in the Siddhāntakaumudī is the intended meaning of the dvandva-seeded ṣaṣṭhītatpuruṣa (cf. *adhikaraṇe lyuṭ iyaṅuvaṅoḥ sthānāv iti ṣaṣṭhīsamāsaḥ. tathā ca phalitārtham āha iyaṅuvaṅoḥ sthitir* *yayor iti*, TB, I, p. 316). The word *astrī* is a nañ-tatpuruṣa : *na strī, astrī*. The particle *na* here carries the sense of exclusion. As a consequence, the negative compound means 'excluding the word *strī*'. Thus the sūtra gives the following meaning : The long *ī* and *ū*, which become the substituenda for the substitutes *iyaṅ* and *uvaṅ* respectively are not designated as *nadī*. The word *strī* is an exception to this negation. In conclusion, if the words are feminine and end in a long *ī* or *ū*, which become the places for replacement by *iyaṅ* or *uvaṅ* in a respective manner, they are not to be designated as *nadī*, with the exception of the word *strī*.

In the vocative singular form *śrī* + s, the shortening of the aṅga-final vowel *ī* by *ambārthanadyorhrasvaḥ* (194) is blocked since the nadī-designation is denied to the word *śrī* by the present rule. As a result, the vocative singular of the word *śrī* is *he śrīḥ!*

With singular affix *am* of the second triplet, we get *śriyam* and with the singular affix *ṭā* of the third triplet we obtain *śriyā* by applying the rule *aci śnu*... (198) which prescribes *iyaṅ*-replacement.

When we introduce the singular affix *ṅe* of the fourth triplet, we have *śrī* + *ṅe* --> *śrī* + *e*. Here the nadī-designation, which is available by *yū stryākhyau nadī* (193), is debarred by the present rule. Then the rule *ṅiti hrasvaśca* (221) assigns nadī-designation optionally to word-forms which denote feminine and which end in *i, u, ī* or *ū*, provided they are subject to replacement by *iyaṅ* and *uvaṅ* (in a respective manner) and are followed by the affixes marked with *ṅ*. In the illustration under discussion, both the grammatical situations are available : 1. availability of nadī-designation and 2. absence of nadī-designation. When we assign nadī-designation to the word *śrī*, the grammatical operations of augmenting the word *śrī* with *āṭ*, effecting a single vṛddhi-replacement and bringing about the *iyaṅ*-substitution, take place and we have the form *śriyai* (*śrī +āṭ e--> śrī +ai--> śr iy +ai*). In the absence of nadī-designation, only *iyaṅ*-substitution takes place in *śrī + e --> śr iy +e --> śriye*.

The singular affixes of the fifth and sixth triplets are *ṅasi* and *ṅas*, which remain as *as* after the elision of the anubandhas. The common remaining form of both the affixes begins with a vowel. As such, the same grammatical process as we had in the formation of *śriye* will take place and we have two forms in each case : ablative and genitive singular in the case of nadī-designation : *śrī + as --> śrī + āṭ as --> śrī + ās --> śr iy ās --> śriyās --> śriyāḥ* (after rutva and visarga); in the absence of nadī-designation, when only *iyaṅ*-substitution takes place : *śrī + as --> śr iy + as --> śriyas --> śriyaḥ*.

To get the form in the genitive plural, we add the sup-affix *ām* to have *śrī* + *ām*. In this situation, the nadī-designation, which is available by *yū stryākhyau...* (193), is denied to the word *śrī* by *neyaṅuvaṅ...* (228). The following rule optionally assigns it nadī-designation before *ām*.

(229) वाऽऽमि । *vā "mi.* 1. 4. 5

लघु० - इयङुवङ्स्थानौ स्त्र्याख्यौ यू आमि वा नदीसंज्ञौ स्तः, न तु स्त्री । श्रीणाम्, श्रियाम् । श्रियाम्, श्रियि । *iyaṅuvaṅsthānau stryākhyau yū āmi vā nadīsaṁjñau staḥ, na tu strī. śrīṇām, śriyām. śriyām, śriyi.*

Trans. : With the exception of the word *strī*, the long *ī* and *ū*, which express the feminine obligatorily but which are subject to replacement by *iyaṅ* and *uvaṅ* (in a respective manner), are optionally designated as *nadī* when the sup-affix *ām* follows.

PP. *iyaṅuvaṅsthānau stryākhyau yū āmi vā nadīsaṁjñau.*

Eluc. : The compound word *iyaṅuvaṅsthānau* is carried over from *neyaṅuvaṅ...* Pā. 1. 4. 4. The words *yū* and *nadī* come from Pā. 1. 4. 3. With this, the meaning of the sūtra is : The long *ī* and *ū*, which denote feminine obligatorily and which are to be replaced by *iyaṅ* and *uvaṅ* respectively, are optionally assigned nadī-designation. The word *strī* is an exception to this rule.

In the illustration *śrī* + *ām*, the word *śrī* receives optionally nadī-designation by the present rule. When it is a nadī word, *ām* is augmented by *nuṭ* according to *hrasvanadyāpo nuṭ* (147) and subsequently the dental *n* is replaced by *ṇ* by *aṭkupvāṅ...* (137) and we get the form *śrīṇām* through the following grammatical procedure : *śrī* + *ām* --> *śrī* + *nuṭ ām* --> *śrī* + *n ām* --> *śrīṇām*. In the absence of nadī-designation, only *iyaṅ*-substitution takes place by *aci śnu...* (198) and the form *śriyām* is obtained.

With the locative singular affix *ṅi*, we have *śrī* + *ṅi*. At this stage also, the nadī-designation with respect to the word *śrī* is optional by *ṅiti hrasvaśca* (221). When it is nadī, we have the form *śriyām* by replacing the affix *ṅi* with *ām* by *ṅerām...* (197), inserting *āṭ* by *āṇna...* (195), effecting vṛddhi substitution by *āṭaśca* (196) and then replacing the *ī* of *śrī* with *iyaṅ* by *aci śnu...* (198). In the absence of nadī-designation, only *iyaṅ* replaces *ī* and we have the form *śriyi*. The declension of *śrī* is as follows:

	Singular	Dual	Plural
prathamā	*śrīḥ*	*śriyau*	*śriyaḥ*
dvitīyā	*śriyam*	*śriyau*	*śriyaḥ*

tṛtīyā	*śriyā*	*śrībhyām*	*śrībhiḥ*
caturthī	*śriyai, śriye*	*śrībhyām*	*śrībhyaḥ*
pañcamī	*śriyāḥ, śriyaḥ*	*śrībhyām*	*śrībhyaḥ*
ṣaṣṭhī	*śriyāḥ, śriyaḥ*	*śriyoḥ*	*śrīṇām, śriyām*
saptamī	*śriyām, śriyi*	*śriyoḥ*	*śrīṣu*
sambodhana	*he śrīḥ!*	*he śriyau!*	*he śriyaḥ!*

Here comes to an end the process of declining the words that end in a long *ī*.

Now begins the declension of the feminine words ending in a short *u*.

लघु० – धेनुर्मतिवत्। *dhenur mativat.*

Eluc. : The word *dhenu* is declined like *mati*. Although the word *dhenu* is ghi, the rule *āṅo nā'striyām* (170) does not become applicable to replace *ṭā* by *nā* because the word *dhenu* is feminine. When the sup-affix *ṅe* follows, it is optionally designated as *nadī*. When it is nadī, the *ṅit* affix is augmented by *āṭ* {*āṇnadyāḥ* (195)}, vṛddhi substitution takes place by *āṭaśca* (196) and the *yaṇ*-replacement comes by *iko yaṇaci* (15). The same process repeats when the sup-affixes *ṅasi* and *ṅas* follow but when the affix *ṅi* follows, it is replaced by *ām* by *idudbhyām* (222). Then the augment *āṭ* is inserted by *āṇnadyāḥ* (195), the vṛddhi substitution takes place by *āṭaśca* (196), the rule *iko yaṇaci* (15) prescribes *yaṇ*-replacement and the form *dhenvām* is obtained. This is how the word *dhenu* is declined when the *ṅit* affixes follow. In the absence of nadī-designation, the word will be declined like *śambhu* before *ṅit* affixes.

The word *dhenu* is declined as follows :

	Singular	Dual	Plural
prathamā	*dhenuḥ*	*dhenū*	*dhenavaḥ*
dvitīyā	*dhenum*	*dhenū*	*dhenūḥ*
tṛtīyā	*dhenvā*	*dhenubhyām*	*dhenubhiḥ*
caturthī	*dhenvai, dhenave*	*dhenubhyām*	*dhenubhyaḥ*
pañcamī	*dhenvāḥ, dhenoḥ*	*dhenubhyām*	*dhenubhyaḥ*

ṣaṣṭhī	*dhenvāḥ, dhenoḥ*	*dhenvoḥ*	*dhenūnām*
saptamī	*dhenvām, dhenau*	*dhenvoḥ*	*dhenuṣu*
sambodhana	*he dheno!*	*he dhenū!*	*he dhenavaḥ!*

Some of the words, which end in a short *u* and are declined like the word *dhenu*, are as follows : *hanu* 'chin', *tanu* 'body', *sindhu* 'river', *reṇu* 'dust', *cañcu* 'beak', *uḍu* 'star, constellation', *kuhu* 'note of a cuckoo', *sarayu* 'a river', *danu* 'mother of the demons', *rajju* 'rope' and *kareṇu* 'female elephant'.

Now Varadaraja takes up the process of declining the word *kroṣṭu* 'a female jackal'.

(230) स्त्रियाञ्च । *striyāñca*. 7. 1. 96

लघु० – स्त्रीवाची क्रोष्टुशब्दस्तृजन्तवद् रूपं लभते । *strīvācī kroṣṭuśabdas tṛjantavad rūpaṁ labhate.*

Trans. : The word *kroṣṭu* is also treated like one ending in the affix *tṛc* when its denotation is feminine.

PP. *striyām ca kroṣṭuḥ tṛjvad (aṅgasya).*

Eluc. : The words *kroṣṭu* and *tṛjvat* are carried over from *tṛjvatkroṣṭuḥ* Pā. 7. 1. 95. The sūtra thus means : When the word *kroṣṭu* is to denote feminine, that is, when it is followed by a feminine affix, it is also treated like the word that ends in the affix *tṛc*. By virtue of the similarity based on signification (*arthakṛta*), the substitute *kroṣṭṛ* will replace the word *kroṣṭu* in the feminine. When the word *kroṣṭu* has been replaced by the word *kroṣṭṛ*, the following sūtra ensues :

(231) ऋन्नेभ्यो ङीप् । *ṛnnebhyo ṅīp*. 4. 1. 5

लघु० – ऋदन्तेभ्यो नान्तेभ्यश्च स्त्रियां ङीप् ।क्रोष्ट्री गौरीवत् । *ṛdantebhyo nāntebhyaś ca striyāṁ ṅīp. kroṣṭrī gaurīvat.*

Trans. : After the words ending in *ṛ* and after the words ending in *n*, the affix *ṅīp* is introduced to denote the feminine gender. Thus the word *kroṣṭrī* is formed. It will be declined like *gaurī*.

PP. *ṛnnebhyaḥ prātipadikebhyaḥ ṅīp striyām.*

Eluc. : The word *ṛnnebhyaḥ* is an itaretaradvandva. Its analysis is : *ṛtaś ca nāś ceti ṛnnās tebhyaḥ ṛnnebhyaḥ*. The word *prātipadikāt* is carried over from *ṅyāpprātipadikāt* Pā. 4. 1. 1 and it is changed to *prātipadikebhyaḥ* by the process of vacanavipariṇāma. This word is qualified by the word *ṛnnebhyaḥ*. By tadantavidhi it gives the following meaning : *ṛdantebhyaḥ nāntebhyaḥ prātipadikebhyaḥ*. The present sūtra occurs in the domain of the governing rule *striyām* Pā. 4. 1. 3. Thus the sūtra means : After the words, which end in a short *ṛ* or in the phoneme *n*, the affix *ṅīp* is added to denote the feminine.

The word *kroṣṭṛ* ends in a short *ṛ*. Therefore, the affix *ṅīp* is introduced after it to have its feminine form. After the elision of the anubandhas the affix *ṅīp* remains as *ī*. In *kroṣṭṛ + ṅīp --> kroṣṭṛ + ī, iko...* (15) applies and we have the feminine form *kroṣṭrī*. This will be declined like *gaurī*.

	Singular	Dual	Plural
prathamā	*kroṣṭrī*	*kroṣṭryau*	*kroṣṭryaḥ*
dvitīyā	*kroṣṭrīm*	*kroṣṭryau*	*kroṣṭrīḥ*
tṛtīyā	*kroṣṭryā*	*kroṣṭrībhyām*	*kroṣṭrībhiḥ*
caturthī	*kroṣṭryai,*	*kroṣṭrībhyām*	*kroṣṭrībhyaḥ*
pañcamī	*kroṣṭryāḥ*	*kroṣṭrībhyām*	*kroṣṭrībhyaḥ*
ṣaṣṭhī	*kroṣṭryāḥ*	*kroṣṭryoḥ*	*kroṣṭrīṇām*
saptamī	*kroṣṭryām*	*kroṣṭryoḥ*	*kroṣṭrīṣu*
sambodhana	*he kroṣṭri!*	*he kroṣṭryau!*	*he kroṣṭryaḥ!*

Here comes to an end the declension of the words that end in a short *u*.

Now begins the process of declining the words that end in a long *ū*.

लघु० – भ्रूः श्रीवत्। स्वयम्भूः पुंवत्। *bhrūḥ śrīvat. svayambhūḥ puṁvat.*

Eluc. : The word *bhrū* 'eyebrow' is declined like the word *śrī* and the word *svayambhū* 'Self-existent' in the feminine will be declined like its counterpart in the masculine.

In declining the word *bhrū*, we have to take note of the fact that the word has been specifically enunciated for *uvaṅ* substitution in the rule *aci śnudhātubhruvām...* (198). So, the word *bhrū* is denied the nadī-designation by the rule *neyaṅuvaṅ...* (228) because of the *uvaṅ*-substitution.

Then by the rules *ṅiti hrasvaśca* (221) and *vā ''mi* (229), the nadī-designation is optionally assigned to the word *bhrū* before *ṅit* affixes and *ām*. That is why the word *bhrū* is declined like *śrī* in the following manner :

	Singular	Dual	Plural
prathamā	*bhrūḥ*	*bhruvau*	*bhruvaḥ*
dvitīyā	*bhruvam*	*bhruvau*	*bhruvaḥ*
tṛtīyā	*bhruvā*	*bhrūbhyām*	*bhrūbhiḥ*
caturthī	*bhruvai, bhruve*	*bhrūbhyām*	*bhrūbhyaḥ*
pañcamī	*bhruvāḥ, bhruvaḥ*	*bhrūbhyām*	*bhrūbhyaḥ*
ṣaṣṭhī	*bhruvāḥ, bhruvaḥ*	*bhruvoḥ*	*bhrūṇām, bhruvām*
saptamī	*bhruvām, bhruvi*	*bhruvoḥ*	*bhrūṣu*
sambodhana	*he bhrūḥ!*	*he bhruvau!*	*he bhruvaḥ!*

The word *svayambhū* is not obligatorily feminine. Its gender depends on that of the substantive it qualifies. The rule *yū stryākhyau nadī* (193) therefore does not assign nadī-designation to it. The *yaṇ*-substitution available by *oḥ supi* (209) is prohibited by *na bhūsudhiyoḥ* (201). Then the rule *aciśnudhātubhruvāṁ yvoriyaṅuvaṅau* (198) prescribes the *uvaṅ*-substitute.

The word *svayambhū* in the feminine will be declined in the following manner :

	Singular	Dual	Plural
prathamā	*svayambhūḥ*	*svayambhuvau*	*svayambhuvaḥ*
dvitīyā	*svayambhuvam*	*svayambhuvau*	*svayambhuvaḥ*
tṛtīyā	*svayambhuvā*	*svayambhūbhyām*	*svayambhūbhiḥ*
caturthī	*svayambhuve*	*svayambhūbhyām*	*svayambhūbhyaḥ*
pañcamī	*svayambhuvaḥ*	*svayambhūbhyām*	*svayambhūbhyaḥ*
ṣaṣṭhī	*svayambhuvaḥ*	*svayambhuvoḥ*	*svayambhuvām*

saptamī	*svayambhuvi*	*svayambhuvoḥ*	*svayambhūṣu*
sambodh.	*he svayambhūḥ!*	*he svayambhuvau!*	*he svayambhuvaḥ!*

The word *vadhū* 'bride' is inherently feminine. The singular affix of the first triplet is not elided since the word does not end in the feminine affix *ṅī*. The rest of the declension will be like that of the word *gaurī*.

	Singular	Dual	Plural
prathamā	*vadhūḥ*	*vadhvau*	*vadhvaḥ*
dvitīyā	*vadhūm*	*vadhvau*	*vadhūḥ*
tṛtīyā	*vadhvā*	*vadhūbhyām*	*vadhūbhiḥ*
caturthī	*vadhvai*	*vadhūbhyām*	*vadhūbhyaḥ*
pañcamī	*vadhvāḥ*	*vadhūbhyām*	*vadhūbhyaḥ*
ṣaṣṭhī	*vadhvāḥ*	*vadhvoḥ*	*vadhūnām*
saptamī	*vadhvām*	*vadhvoḥ*	*vadhūṣu*
sambodhana	*he vadhu!*	*he vadhvau !*	*he vadhvaḥ!*

Some of the words which are declined like *vadhū* are : *camū* 'army', *śvaśrū* 'mother-in-law', *tanū* 'body', *karkandhū* 'jujube tree and its fruit', *cañcū* 'beak' and *jambū* 'the rose apple tree and its fruit'.

Here comes to an end the declension of the feminine words that end in a long *ū*.

Now begins the process of declining the feminine words that end in a short *ṛ*.

After the feminine words ending in a short *ṛ*, the affix *ṅīp* becomes due to be introduced by the sūtra *ṛnnebhyo ṅīp*. The word *svasṛ* 'sister', for example, is a feminine word. So the affix *ṅīp* is to be added after it by *ṛnnebhyo ṅīp* (231) but it is negated by the following sūtra :

(232) न षट्स्वस्रादिभ्यः । *na ṣaṭsvasrādibhyaḥ*. 4. 1. 10

लघु० – ङीप्टापौ न स्तः। *ṅīpṭāpau na staḥ.*

स्वसा तिस्रश्चतस्रश्च ननान्दा दुहिता तथा।
याता मातेति सप्तैते स्वस्रादय उदाहृताः॥
svasā tisraś catasraś ca nanāndā duhitā tathā,
yātā māteti saptaite svasrādaya udāhṛtāḥ.

स्वसा। स्वसारौ। *svasā. svasārau.*

Trans. : The feminine affixes *ṅīp* and *ṭāp* are not introduced after the words that are designated as *ṣaṭ* and after those beginning with *svasṛ* (which are enlisted in the verse) : 1. *svasṛ* 'sister', 2. *tisṛ* 'three', 3. *catasṛ* 'four', 4. *nanāndṛ* 'husband's sister', 5. *duhitṛ* 'daughter', 6. *yātṛ* 'husband's brother's wife' and 7. *mātṛ* 'mother'.

PP. *ṣaṭsvasrādibhyaḥ (prātipadikebhyaḥ) ṅīp ṭāp na.*

Eluc. : The terms *ṅīp* and *ṭāp* are respectively carried over from *ṛnnebhyo ṅīp* Pā. 4. 1. 5 and *ajādyataṣṭāp* Pā. 4. 1. 4. The compound word *ṣaṭsvasrādibhyaḥ* is an itaretaradvandva : *ṣaṭ ca svasrādayaś ca ṣaṭsvasrādayaḥ, tebhyaḥ*. Thus the meaning of the sūtra is : The feminine affixes *ṅīp* and *ṭāp* are not introduced after the words, which are designated as *ṣaṭ* and the words of the *svasrādi* set which contains the following seven words : *svasṛ, tisṛ, catasṛ, nanāndṛ, duhitṛ, yātṛ* and *mātṛ*. The *ṣaṭ* designation is assigned to *ṣaṣ, pañcan, saptan*, etc. by the sūtra *ṣṇāntā ṣaṭ* (296).

The word *svasṛ* is declined like the stem *dhātṛ* with the only difference being in the form with the plural affix of the second triplet. The s of the affix *śas* is not replaced by *n* by *tasmācchaso...* (136). In the nominative singular, there is *anaṅ* by *ṛduśanas...* (204), lengthening of the penultimate (*upadhā*) by *aptṛntṛc...* (205), the elision of *s* by *halṅyābbhyo...* (178) and the elision of *n* by *na lopaḥ...* (179). The form is *svasā*. In the form of the nominative dual, there is guṇa-replacement by *ṛto ṅi...* (203) and the lengthening of the penultimate vowel by *aptṛntṛc...* (205) and we have the form *svasārau.*

In the common form of the ablative and genitive singular, we apply *ṛta ut* (207) to replace the vowel *ṛ* by a short *u* and *rātsasya* (208) to elide the phoneme s. The form *svasuḥ* is thus obtained. In the locative singular, there is guṇa-replacement by *ṛto ṅi...* (203) to have the form *svasari*. In the form of the vocative singular, we again apply *ṛto ṅi...* (203) and then we elide the s of the vocative singular affix by *halṅyābbhyo...* (178). The feminine nominal stem *svasṛ* is declined in the following way :

	Singular	Dual	Plural
prathamā	*svasā*	*svasārau*	*svasāraḥ*
dvitīyā	*svasāram*	*svasārau*	*svasṝḥ*
tṛtīyā	*svasrā*	*svasṛbhyām*	*svasṛbhiḥ*
caturthī	*svasre*	*svasṛbhyām*	*svasṛbhyaḥ*

pañcamī	*svasuḥ*	*svasṛbhyām*	*svasṛbhyaḥ*
ṣaṣṭhī	*svasuḥ*	*svasroḥ*	*svasṝṇām*
saptamī	*svasari*	*svasroḥ*	*svasṛṣu*
sambodhana	*he svasaḥ!*	*he svasārau !*	*he svasāraḥ!*

लघु० – माता पितृवत्। शसि मातॄः। *mātā pitṛvat. śasi mātṝḥ.*

Eluc. : The nominal stem *mātṛ* is declined like *pitṛ* except in the case of the form with the plural affix of the second triplet. The form with that affix is *mātṝḥ* as *tasmācchaso naḥ puṁsi* (136) does not apply here. The nominal stem *mātṛ* is declined in the following way :

	Singular	Dual	Plural
prathamā	*mātā*	*mātarau*	*mātaraḥ*
dvitīyā	*mātaram*	*mātarau*	*mātṝḥ*
tṛtīyā	*mātrā*	*mātṛbhyām*	*mātṛbhiḥ*
caturthī	*mātre*	*mātṛbhyām*	*mātṛbhyaḥ*
pañcamī	*mātuḥ*	*mātṛbhyām*	*mātṛbhyaḥ*
ṣaṣṭhī	*mātuḥ*	*mātroḥ*	*mātṝṇām*
saptamī	*mātari*	*mātroḥ*	*mātṛṣu*
sambodhana	*he mātaḥ!*	*he mātarau !*	*he mātaraḥ!*

Here comes to an end the declension of the nominal stems in the feminine which end in a short *ṛ*.

Now begins the declension of the feminine stems that end in *o, ai* and *au* in a sequential way.

लघु० – द्यौर्गोवत्। राः पुंवत्। नौर्ग्लौवत्। *dyaur govat. rāḥ puṁvat. naur glauvat.*

Eluc. : The (feminine) nominal stem *dyo* 'sky or heaven' is declined like *go*. The word *rai* 'wealth' is declined like its counterpart in the masculine and the word *nau* 'boat', in the feminine, like *glau* .

In declining the nominal stem *dyo*, the rule *goto ṇit* (212) confers the characteristic of being *ṇit* upon the sarvanāmasthāna sup-affixes and the rule *aco ñṇiti* (181) brings about the vṛddhi-replacement in the stem-final *o* before *su*, etc. Thus in the nominative singular, we have the form *dyauḥ* (<-- *dyau* + *s*(*u*) <-- *dyo* + *su*) after rutva and visarga. The rule *auto 'mśasoḥ* (213) prescribes a single ākāra-substitution when the singular and plural affixes of the second triplet are introduced after *dyo* and we have *dyām* and *dyāḥ* respectively. In the ablative and genitive singular, a single replacement in the form of the preceding vowel takes place by *ṅasiṅsośca* (172) and we have the common form *dyoḥ*. The declension of the nominal stem *dyo* is as follows :

	Singular	Dual	Plural
prathamā	*dyauḥ*	*dyāvau*	*dyāvaḥ*
dvitīyā	*dyām*	*dyāvau*	*dyāḥ*
tṛtīyā	*dyavā*	*dyobhyām*	*dyobhiḥ*
caturthī	*dyave*	*dyobhyām*	*dyobhyaḥ*
pañcamī	*dyoḥ*	*dyobhyām*	*dyobhyaḥ*
ṣaṣṭhī	*dyoḥ*	*dyavoḥ*	*dyavām*
saptamī	*dyavi*	*dyavoḥ*	*dyoṣu*
sambodhana	*he dyauḥ!*	*he dyāvau!*	*he dyāvaḥ!*

In the process of declining the nominal stem *rai*, *ā* replaces the final vowel *ai* by *rāyo hali* (214) before the affixes that begin with a consonant. When the affixes, which begin with a vowel, follow, the rule *eco-'yavāyāvaḥ* (22) prescribes *ayādi*-replacement. The nominal stem *rai* is declined in the same manner as its counterpart in the masculine :

	Singular	Dual	Plural
prathamā	*rāḥ*	*rāyau*	*rāyaḥ*
dvitīyā	*rāyam*	*rāyau*	*rāyaḥ*
tṛtīyā	*rāyā*	*rābhyām*	*rābhiḥ*
caturthī	*rāye*	*rābhyām*	*rābhyaḥ*
pañcamī	*rāyaḥ*	*rābhyām*	*rābhyaḥ*
ṣaṣṭhī	*rāyaḥ*	*rāyoḥ*	*rāyām*
saptamī	*rāyi*	*rāyoḥ*	*rāsu*
sambodhana	*he rāḥ!*	*he rāyau!*	*he rāyaḥ!*

The declension of the nominal stem *nau* in the feminine is like that of the nominal stem *glau* :

	Singular	Dual	Plural
prathamā	*nauḥ*	*nāvau*	*nāvaḥ*
dvitīyā	*nāvam*	*nāvau*	*nāvaḥ*
tṛtīyā	*nāvā*	*naubhyām*	*naubhiḥ*
caturthī	*nāve*	*naubhyām*	*naubhyaḥ*
pañcamī	*nāvaḥ*	*naubhyām*	*naubhyaḥ*
ṣaṣṭhī	*nāvaḥ*	*nāvoḥ*	*nāvām*
saptamī	*nāvi*	*nāvoḥ*	*nauṣu*
sambodhana	*he nauḥ!*	*he nāvau!*	*he nāvaḥ!*

लघु० - इति अजन्ताः स्त्रीलिङ्गाः । *iti ajantāḥ strīliṅgāḥ.*

Trans. : Thus ends the chapter on the feminine stems that end in a vowel .

अजन्तनपुंसकलिङ्गप्रकरणम्

Neuter Words Ending in a Vowel

The nominal stem *jñāna* is derived from the verbal root *jñā* 'to know' after the introduction of the primary affix *lyuṭ* after it. After the anubandhas *l* and *ṭ* have been elided, the remaining affix *yu* is replaced by *ana* according to *yuvoranakau* (782). In *jñā + ana*, the rule *akaḥ savarṇe...* (42) prescribes savarṇadīrgha and thus the primary derivative *jñāna* is obtained. It is in the neuter gender since the stems, which are derived with the introduction of the affix *lyuṭ*, are generally in the neuter gender. Being a primary derivative, it is assigned the prātipadika-designation by the rule *kṛttaddhitasamāsāśca* (116). When we introduce the singular affix of the first triplet, we have *jñāna + su* --> *jñāna + s*. At this stage, the following sūtra applies :

(233) अतोऽम् । *ato 'm*. **7. 1. 24**

लघु० – अतोऽङ्गात् क्लीबात् स्वमोरम् । अमि पूर्वः – ज्ञानम् । एङ्ह्रस्वात् सम्बुद्धेः इति हल्लोपः । हे ज्ञान ! *ato 'ṅgāt klībāt svamor am. ami pūrvaḥ – jñānam. eṅhrasvāt sambuddheḥ iti hallopaḥ. he jñāna!*

Trans. : The affixes *su* and *am*, which are introduced after a neuter pre-affixal base that ends in a short *a*, are replaced by *am*.

PP. *ataḥ aṅgāt napuṁsakāt svamoḥ am.*

Eluc. : This sūtra occurs in the governing domain of the rule *aṅgasya* Pā. 6. 4. 1. The term *aṅgasya* is changed to have a singular ablative ending by the process of vibhaktivipariṇāma in order that it may accord with the qualifying term *ataḥ*. The sense yielded will be *adantād aṅgāt*. The whole sūtra *svamornapuṁsakāt* Pā. 7. 1. 23 recurs in the present rule. The compound word *svamoḥ* is an itaretaradvandva. Its analysis is *suś ca am ca svamau, tayoḥ = svamoḥ*. Thus the sūtra means : If the pre-affixal base is in the neuter gender and ends in a short *a*, then the affixes *su* and *am* are replaced by *am*. Since the substitute *am* contains more than one phoneme (*al*), it will replace the whole substituendum by *anekāl śit sarvasya* (45). The morpheme *am*, which has replaced both *su* and *am*, is understood to possess the characteristic of being a vibhakti by virtue of the rule *sthānivadādeśo 'nalvidhau* (143). This is the reason why the consonant *m* occurring at the end of *am* is not *it* according to the rule *na vibhaktau tusmāḥ* (130). Therefore it is not elided.

Vāsudeva Dīkṣita says that the substitution of *am* by *am* is to block the recurrence of the term *luk* coming from *svamornapuṁsakāt* Pā. 7. 1. 23 (*amo 'mvidhānaṁ tu svamornapuṁsakāt iti luṅnivṛttyartham*, BM, I, p. 323). In the illustration *jñāna + su --> jñāna + s*, the affix *s*(*u*) is replaced by *am* according to the present rule and we have *jñāna + am*. At this stage, the rule *ami pūrvaḥ* (134) applies and we have the form *jñānam* in the nominative singular.

In the vocative singular, the affix *su* is replaced by *am* by the present rule as it has been done in the nominative singular. After it has been replaced, the consonant *m* of the vocative singular affix is elided by the rule *eṅhrasvāt sambuddheḥ* (133) when the rule *ami pūrvaḥ* (134) has already brought about a single replacement in the form of the preceding vowel and we obtain the form *he jñāna!*

Two points are worth noticing in this context. The first is about the wording of the sūtra. Some read the sūtra as : *ato 'm*. According to this reading, the sūtra would mean : The affixes *su* and *am*, introduced after a neuter stem ending in a short *a*, are replaced by *m* (and not by *am*). On this reading, the form *jñānam*, which is common to both nominative and accusative singular, can be explained in the following way : In the nominative singular, the affix *su* is replaced by *m* and the form *jñānam* is obtained. When the singular affix of the second triplet is introduced, the substitute *m* will replace the initial *a* of *am* by the rule *ādeḥ parasya* (72) and we have the form *jñāna mm*. The last phoneme *m* is elided by *saṁyogāntasya lopaḥ* (20). Thus the form *jñānam*, with a singular affix of the second triplet, is obtained. The declension of the form in the vocative singular also becomes easier in that after replacing the vocative singular affix *su* by *m*, it is elided by the rule *eṅhrasvāt sambuddheḥ* (133) and the form *he jñāna!* is obtained.

Vāsudeva Dīkṣita does not subscribe to this view. He says that this reading leads to a problem. In the nominative singular form, when the affix *su* has been replaced by *m* (*jñāna m*), the rule *supi ca* (140) becomes applicable and the lengthening of the aṅga-final short *a* in *jñānam* becomes contingent. The proposal to invoke the sannipātaparibhāṣā to dispense with this undesirable contingency is controverted by Vāsudeva Dīkṣita. He avers that this paribhāṣā (metarule) does not hold good in the case of the rule *supi ca* (140).[1] Moreover, the Mahābhāṣya on this sūtra also endorses the view that the original reading is correct (*ato 'm ityambhāvena*

1. SK, I, p. 198.

bhavitavyam). This is the reason why the original reading, that is, *ato 'm* should be preferred.[1]

The second point relates to the expression Bhaṭṭoji Dīkṣita uses in the Siddhāntakaumudī on this sūtra. The expression is : *halmātralopaḥ*, which means that only the consonant belonging to the singular vocative affix is elided (*halmātralopaḥ*). Varadarāja instead says that the consonant of the vocative singular affix is elided (*hallopaḥ*). The significance of what Bhaṭṭoji Dīkṣita says can properly be appreciated when we consider what Vāsudeva Dīkṣita says in this regard. Interpreting Bhaṭṭoji Dīkṣita's expression *halmātralopaḥ*, he says that after effecting a single substitution homogeneous with the preceding one by *ami pūrvaḥ* (134), the only remaining consonant *m* of the vocative singular affix is elided by *eṅhrasvāt sambuddheḥ* (133). According to him, this is what Bhaṭṭoji Dīkṣita means by the statement *halmātralopaḥ*. It is because of the mention of the term *sambuddhi* in the rule (133) that the pre-affixal base (*aṅga*) is taken as understood. Consequently, the aṅga should syntactically accord with the singular vocative affix (*sambuddhi*) but this is not the case. Keeping in view the target (*śiṣṭaprayoga*), he further says, the pre-affixal base is required to syntactically accord with the consonant of the vocative singular affix in this context. Then it would mean that if the consonant of the singular vocative affix follows a pre-affixal base which ends in *eṅ* or a short vowel, then that consonant is also elided. In the present illustration, even after the single substitution has been brought about by *ami pūrvaḥ* (134), the single consonant of the vocative singular affix does become available in the form of the phoneme *m* after the pre-affixal base *jñāna*. So, the elision of the only consonant that follows the aṅga takes place[2] and we obtain the form *he jñāna!*.

When we introduce the dual affix of the first triplet, we have *jñāna* + *au*. At this stage, the following rule applies :

(234) नपुंसकाच्च । *napuṁsakācca*. 7. 1. 19

1. *nanu 'ataḥ' 'm' ityeva chedo 'stu, sor makārādeśe jñānam iti siddheḥ. ami ca 'ādeḥ parasya' iti akārasya makāre antyasya makārasya saṁyogāntalopenaiva jñānam iti siddher iti cet, maivam. evaṁ sati jñānam ityatra 'supi ca' iti dīrghāpatteḥ. na ca adantasannipātam āśritya pravṛttasya mādeśasya tadvighātakadīrghanimittatvaṁ na sambhavati, sannipātaparibhāṣāvirodhād iti vācyam, 'supi ca' iti dīrghe kartavye sannipātaparibhāṣāyā apravṛtter ityuktatvād ityalam*. BM, I, p. 323.

2. *pūrvarūpe kṛte sambuddher makāramātraṁ yat pariśiṣṭaṁ tasya 'eṅhrasvāt...' iti lopa ityarthaḥ. lakṣyānurodhāt sambuddhyākṣiptam aṅgaṁ sambuddhau nānveti, kiṁ tu sambuddhyavayavahalyevānveti. tataś ca eṅantād hrasvāntāc cāṅgāt paro yaḥ sambuddhyavayavahal tasya lopa iti labhyate. prakṛte ca pūrvarūpe kṛte 'pi hrasvād aṅgāt paratvaṁ sambuddhyavayavasya makāramātrasya astyeveti tasya 'eṅhrasvāt....'iti lopo nirbādha ityanyatra vistaraḥ*. BM, I, pp. 323-24.

लघु० - क्लीबाद् औङः शी स्यात्। भसंज्ञायाम् — *klībād auṅaḥ śī syāt. bha-saṁjñāyām* —

Trans. : If the dual affix *auṅ* (*au* or *auṭ*) follows a pre-affixal base, which is neuter, then this is replaced by *śī*. As that which precedes this affix is termed *bha* (the following rule becomes applicable) :

PP. *napuṁsakāt aṅgāt auṅaḥ śī*.

Eluc. : The governing term *aṅgasya* (Pā. 6. 4. 1) is changed to *aṅgāt* by the process of vibhaktivipariṇāma. The terms *śī* and *auṅ* are respectively carried over from *jasaḥ śī* Pā. 7. 1. 17 and *auṅa āpaḥ* Pā. 7. 1. 18. Thus the sūtra gives the following meaning : Let the affix *auṅ* (*au* or *auṭ*) introduced after a neuter pre-affixal base be replaced by *śī*. The term *auṅ* denotes both the dual affixes of the first and second triplets (see supra p. 280 for explanation). *śī* is an affix (*pratyaya*) by *sthānivadbhāva*. So the initial consonant *ś* of *śī* is *it* by the rule *laśakvataddhite* (135). Hence it is elided by *tasya lopaḥ* (3). In the illustration, *jñāna* + *au*, the affix *au* is replaced by *śī*. After the elision of the anubandha *ś*, we have *jñāna* + *ī*. The substitute *ī* has replaced the sup-affix *au*. By sthānivadbhāva, it is also treated as a sup-affix. This is not a sarvanāmasthāna affix, since the stem after which it is introduced is neuter {*suḍanapuṁsakasya* (162)}. It begins with a vowel and as such the stem *jñāna* gets the bha-designation by *yaci bham* (164). Consequently the following sūtra presents itself :

(235) यस्येति च । *yasyeti ca.* 6. 4. 148

लघु० - ईकारे तद्धिते च परे भस्येवर्णावर्णयोर्लोपः। इत्यल्लोपे प्राप्ते – *īkāre taddhite ca pare bhasyevarṇāvarṇayor lopaḥ. ityallope prāpte* –

Trans. : The final *i* or *a* of a bha is elided when a long *ī* or a taddhita affix follows. Thus when the elision of a short *a* is available (the following vārttika ensues) :

PP. *bhasya yasya taddhite īti ca lopaḥ* (*aṅgasya*).

Eluc. : The term *bhasya* is carried over from the governing rule Pā. 6. 4. 129. The words *taddhite* and *lopaḥ* are respectively carried over from *nastaddhite* Pā. 6. 4. 144 and *allopo 'naḥ* Pā. 6. 4. 134. The term *yasya* is a samāhāradvandva. It is analysed as : *iś ca aś ca yam tasya = yasya*. The meaning of the sūtra is : In case a long *ī* or a taddhita affix follows, then the final *i* or *a* of a bha is elided. This condition is available in the present illustration *jñāna* + *ī*. So, the elision of the short *a* occurring at the end of *jñāna* is due. In this situation, the following vārttika blocks it :

22. वा० – औङः श्यां प्रतिषेधो वाच्यः । *auṅaḥ śyāṁ pratiṣedho vācyaḥ.*[1]

Trans. : It should be enunciated that the application of the present sūtra is prohibited when *śī*, replacing the affix *auṅ*, follows.

Eluc. : The present vārttika prohibits the application of the sūtra *yasyeti ca* in this case since the substitute *śī* has replaced the affix *auṅ*. So, in the absence of the elision of the final vowel *a* of *jñāna*, the rule *ādguṇaḥ* (27) applies in *jñāna* + *ī* and we get the form *jñāne*.

With the plural affix of the first triplet, we have *jñāna* + *jas*. In this situation, the following sūtra applies :

(236) जश्शसोः शिः । *jaśśasoḥ śiḥ*. 7. 1. 20
लघु० – क्लीबाद् अनयोः शिः स्यात् । *klībād anayoḥ śiḥ syāt.*

Trans. : The affixes *jaś* and *śas*, which are introduced after a neuter stem, are replaced by *śi*.

PP. *napuṁsakāt jaśśasoḥ śiḥ* (*aṅgasya*).

Eluc. : The word *napuṁsakāt* is carried over from *svamornapuṁsakāt* Pā. 7. 1. 23. The compound *jaśśasoḥ* is an itaretaradvandva, which is analysed as : *jas ca śas ca, tayoḥ= jaśśasoḥ*. The sūtra means : If the sup-affixes *jas* and *śas* follow a stem which is neuter, then these are replaced by *śi*. The substitute *śi*, which has replaced the sup-affixes, is treated as a sup-affix by sthānivadbhāva. When the initial *ś*, which is *it* by *laśakvataddhite* (135), is elided by *tasya lopaḥ* (3), only the vowel *i* remains. Now we have *jñāna* + *jas* --> *jñāna* + *śi* --> *jñāna* + *i*. At this stage, the following sūtra applies :

(237) शि सर्वनामस्थानम् । *śi sarvanāmasthānam*. 1. 1. 42
लघु० – शि इत्येतद् उक्तसंज्ञं स्यात् । *śi ityetad uktasaṁjñaṁ syāt.*

Trans. : Let *śi* be designated as *sarvanāmasthāna*.

---

1. This vārttika is read as *yasyetyādau śyāṁ pratiṣedhaḥ* as the first vārttika in the Mahābhāṣya on *yasyeti ca* Pā. 6. 4. 148.

PP. *śi sarvanāmasthānam.*

Eluc. : The rule *suḍanapuṁsakasya* (162) denies sarvanāmasthāna designation to the sup-affix *jas* when it is introduced after a stem in the neuter gender but the plural affix of the second triplet, that is *śas*, being other than the sup-affixes denoted by the abbreviatory term *suṭ*, does not get the sarvanāmasthāna designation in any gender. Thus both the affixes *jas* and *śas* are not sarvanāmasthāna when they are introduced after a stem in the neuter gender. Consequently, the substitute *śi* also does not get the sarvanāmasthāna designation by sthānivadbhāva. However, it is desirable that the sarvanāmasthāna designation be assigned to the substitute *śi*. This is the reason why Pāṇini assigns the sarvanāmasthāna designation to the substitute *śi* by the present rule. In the illustration *jñāna + i*, after *śi* has been designated as *sarvanāmasthāna*, the following sūtra ensues :

(238) नपुंसकस्य झलचः । *napuṁsakasya jhalacaḥ*. 7. 1. 72

लघु० – झलन्तस्याजन्तस्य च क्लीबस्य नुम् स्यात् सर्वनामस्थाने । *jhalantasyājantasya ca klībasya num syāt sarvanāmasthāne.*

Trans. : Let the augment *num* be introduced to a neuter pre-affixal base that ends either in a consonant denoted by the abbreviatory term *jhal* or in a vowel (*ac*), if an affix designated as *sarvanāmasthāna* follows.

PP. *napuṁsakasya jhalacaḥ aṅgasya num sarvanāmasthāne.*

Eluc. : The term *num* is carried over from *idito num dhātoḥ* Pā. 7. 1. 58 and the word *sarvanāmasthāne* from *ugidacāṁ sarvanāmasthāne 'dhātoḥ* Pā. 7. 1. 70. The word *jhalacaḥ* is a samāhāradvandva, which is analysed as *jhal ca ac ca jhalac tasya = jhalacaḥ*. The samāhāradvandva compound ends in the palatal phoneme *c*. Therefore the rule *dvandvāccudaṣahāntātsamāhāre* (988) prescribes the samāsānta affix *ṭac*, but, since the samāsāntavidhi is not obligatory, the samāsānta affix *ṭac* is not added after the compound *jhalac* in the sūtra. The compound *jhalacaḥ* is in the genitive and it will qualify the governing term *aṅgasya* which is carried over from the sūtra Pā. 6. 4. 1 (*aṅgasya ityadhikṛtaṁ viśeṣyate, tadantavidhiḥ*). The expression, by tadantavidhi, would be : *jhalantasya ajantasya ca aṅgasya*. It would be of advantage to note here that when the augment *num* is to be introduced to a neuter pre-affixal base which ends in a *jhal*-consonant, the consonant denoted by *jhal*-pratyāhāra should follow a vowel since the augment *num* is to be inserted after the last of the vowels in the stem to which *num* has been introduced. With these points having been taken into account, the sūtra will mean : The augment *num* is introduced to the neuter pre-affixal base which ends either in a *jhal*-consonant or in a vowel (*ac*) when a sarvanāmasthāna affix follows. The augment *num* has the phoneme *m* as *it*. Accordingly, the following sūtra applies to determine the place where *num* is to be inserted :

(239) मिदचोऽन्त्यात्परः । *midaco 'ntyātparaḥ*. 1. 1. 47

लघु० - अचां मध्ये योऽन्त्यः, तस्मात् परस्तस्यैवान्तावयवो मित् स्यात्। उपधादीर्घः - ज्ञानानि। पुनस्तद्वत्। शेषं पुंवत्। एवं धनवनफलादयः। *acāṁ madhye yo 'ntyaḥ, tasmāt paras tasyaivāntāvayavo mit syāt. upadhādīrghaḥ – jñānāni. punas tadvat. śeṣaṁ puṁvat. evaṁ dhanavanaphalādayaḥ*

Trans. : Let the augment marked with *m* as *it* be inserted after the last of the vowels and become the final constituent of that (which it augments). The lengthening of the penultimate vowel (*upadhā*) takes place and we have *jñānāni*. Again, with the affixes of the second triplet, it is the same. The rest is like the masculine. The nominal stems, *dhana* 'wealth', *vana* 'forest', *phala* 'fruit' and so on are declined in the same manner.

PP. *mit antyāt acaḥ paraḥ antaḥ*.

Eluc. : The term *antaḥ* is carried over from *ādyantau ṭakitau* Pā. 1. 1. 46 (cf. *pūrvasūtrād anta ityanuvartate, ekadeśe svaritatvapratijñānāt*, TB, I, p. 43). The word *mit* is a bahuvrīhi compound which is analysed as *m it yasya sa mit*. The genitive nominal ending used in the word *acaḥ* is in the sense of selection (*nirdhāraṇa*) and as such the singular number is intended to convey the sense of universal. Thus the meaning of the sūtra is : The augment which has *m* as *it* is inserted after the last of the vowels of the stem to which it has been introduced and it becomes the last portion of that stem. In the illustration *jñāna + i*, the augment is placed after the last vowel of *jñāna* in *jñāna num + i* since it is the nominal stem *jñāna* which ends in *a* and to which the augment has been introduced before the sarvanāmasthāna affix *śi*. Now we have *jñānan + i* after the elision of the anubandhas. It is important to note that the augment *num* becomes the final constituent of *jñānan*. As such, the pre-affixal base is construed as ending in *n*. This is the reason why the vṛtti says that the augment *num* becomes the last portion of the stem to which this has been introduced. Otherwise, if the augment *num* did not become the last portion, the rule *sarvanāmasthāne cāsambuddhau* (176) would not apply.

Therefore, according to the vṛtti, the stem is understood to end in *n* and the sūtra *sarvanāmasthāne...* (176) applies and the penultimate vowel is lengthened -- *jñānān + i* -- and we obtain the form *jñānāni*.

With the introduction of the singular affix of the second triplet, we have *jñāna + am*, the sup-affix is replaced by *am* by *ato 'm* (233). The rule *ami pūrvaḥ* (134) applies and the form *jñānam* is obtained.

The form with the dual affix of the second triplet is derived in the same manner as that of the nominative dual. Similarly the form of *jñāna* with the plural affix of the second triplet is declined like that of the nominative plural. The rest of the declension is like that of a masculine word ending in a short *a*.

The complete declension of the nominal stem *jñāna* is as follows :

	Singular	Dual	Plural
prathamā	*jñānam*	*jñāne*	*jñānāni*
dvitīyā	*jñānam*	*jñāne*	*jñānāni*
tṛtīyā	*jñānena*	*jñānābhyām*	*jñānaiḥ*
caturthī	*jñānāya*	*jñānābhyām*	*jñānebhyaḥ*
pañcamī	*jñānāt, d*	*jñānābhyām*	*jñānebhyaḥ*
ṣaṣṭhī	*jñānasya*	*jñānayoḥ*	*jñānānām*
saptamī	*jñāne*	*jñānayoḥ*	*jñāneṣu*
sambodhana	*he jñāna!*	*he jñāne!*	*he jñānāni!*

Some of the nominal stems that are neuter and also end in a short *a* are listed below :

agāra 'a house', *agha* 'sin', *araṇya* 'forest', *ānana* 'face', *indriya* 'sense-organ', *udaka* 'water', *upavana* 'a garden', *kamala* 'a lotus', *jala* 'water', *tattva* 'truth, reality, an element', *cibuka* 'chin', *nayana* 'an eye', *dhana* 'wealth', *netra* 'an eye', *navanīta* 'butter', *paṅkaja* 'a lotus', *puṣpa* 'a flower', *pānīya* 'water', *phala* 'fruit', *bīja* 'seed', *bhaya* 'fear', *mukha* 'mouth', *mūlya* 'price', *rajata* 'silver', *ratna* 'jewel', *rahasya* 'secret', *lalāṭa* 'forehead', *vacana* 'a statement', *vākya* 'a sentence', *vāsara* 'a day', *vīrya* 'strength' *vṛtta* 'conduct, character', *vetana* 'salary', *vyasana* 'a bad habit, calamity', *śastra* 'a weapon', *śāstra* 'a scripture, a treatise', *satya* 'truth', *sadana* 'a house, a palace', *sarasija* 'a lotus', *sādhana* 'a means, an instrument', *sādhvasa* 'fear', *sukha* 'pleasure', *sopāna* 'steps, a ladder', *sthāna* 'place', *syandana* 'a chariot', *hala* 'a plough', *hima* 'snow' and *hṛdaya* 'heart'.

The word *katara* 'which of the two' is a sarvanāman and it has already been said that in the masculine it is declined like *sarva* (see supra p. 188). Since the gender of this pronominal stem depends on the substantive it qualifies, it is used in all the three genders. Now we are going to discuss its declensional process, when it is used in the neuter. When we introduce the singular affix of the first triplet after this stem, we have *katara* + *su* --> *katara* + s. In this grammatical situation, the rule *ato 'm* (233) prescribes *am* substitute to come in place of the affix *su* but the following sūtra applies in the neuter :

(240) अद्ड् डतरादिभ्यः पञ्चभ्यः । ***adḍ ḍatarādibhyaḥ pañcabhyaḥ.***
7. 1. 25
लघु० – एभ्यः क्लीबेभ्यः स्वमोरद्ड् आदेशः स्यात् । *ebhyaḥ klībebhyaḥ svamor adḍ ādeśaḥ syāt.*

Trans. : Let the substitute *adḍ* replace the sup-affixes *su* and *am* introduced after the five (members of the *sarvādi* class) beginning with *ḍatara*, when they are neuter.

PP. *ḍatarādibhyaḥ pañcabhyaḥ napuṁsakebhyaḥ svamoḥ adḍ.*

Eluc. : The term *napuṁsakāt* is carried over from *svamornapuṁsakāt* Pā. 7. 1. 23 and is changed into *napuṁsakebhyaḥ*, which is synonymous with *klībebhyaḥ* given in the vṛtti by Varadarāja.This process of change of number is known as vacanavipariṇāma. The word *ḍatarādibhyaḥ* is a bahuvrīhi compound which is analysed as *ḍatara ādir yeṣām te ḍatarādayaḥ, tebhyaḥ* = *ḍatarādibhyaḥ*. The five stems beginning with *ḍatara* are enlisted in the *sarvādi* class. The first two members, *ḍatara* and *ḍatama*, are affixes. Therefore by virtue of the paribhāṣā *pratyaya-grahaṇe... tadantasya grahaṇam* (Abhyankar, 23), they will denote the words that end in these affixes. The interrogative pronominal stems *katara* and *katama* exemplify these two affixes. The remaining three members, namely, *anya*, *anyatara* and *itara* are the pronominal stems. Thus the sūtra comes to mean : When the stems that end in the affixes *ḍatara* and *ḍatama* as well as the stems *anya*, *anyatara* and *itara* are used in the neuter gender, the sup-affixes *su* and *am*, introduced after these five stems, are replaced by *adḍ*. This rule is an exception to *ato 'm* (233), which prescribes the substitute *am* to come in place of *su* and *am* introduced after the neuter stems ending in a short *a*.

When we introduce the nominative singular affix *su* after the pronominal stem *katara*, we have *katara* + *su* --> *katara* + *s*. In this illustration, the affix *s* is replaced by the substitute *aḍḍ*. The consonant *ḍ* is *it* by *halantyam* (1) and as such it is elided by *tasya lopaḥ* (3). Now the stage of the declension is : *katara + ad*. At this stage, the rule *prathamayoḥ pūrvasavarṇaḥ* (125) prescribes a single long substitute homogeneous with the preceding vowel but this is not in consonance with the usage of the cultured. To have a form used by the cultured, the elision of *ṭi* is a pre-requisite. The following sūtra enjoins the elision of the *ṭi* of *katara* to obtain the desired form.

(241) टेः । *ṭeḥ*. 6. 4. 143

लघु० – डिति भस्य टेर्लोपः । कतरत्, कतरद् । कतरे । कतराणि । हे कतरत् । शेषं पुंवत् । एवं कतमत् इतरत् अन्यत् अन्यतरत् । अन्यतमस्य तु अन्यतममित्येव । *ḍiti bhasya ṭer lopaḥ. katarat, katarad. katare. katarāṇi. he katarat. śeṣaṁ puṁvat. evaṁ katamat, itarat, anyat, anyatarat. anyatamasya tu anyatamam ityeva.*

Trans. : The *ṭi* of a *bha* is elided when an affix, having the phoneme *ḍ* as *it*, follows. Examples : *katarat, d* (nominative and accusative singular), *katare* (nominative and accusative dual) and *katarāṇi* (nominative and accusative plural), *he katarat!* (vocative singular). The declensional process of the rest will be like that of the masculine (pronominal stem, *katara*). The pronominal stems *katamat, itarat, anyat* and *anyatarat* will be declined in the same manner but the nominative singular of the pronominal stem *anyatama* will be *anyatamam*.

PP. *ḍiti bhasya ṭer lopaḥ* (*aṅgasya*).

Eluc. : The word *ḍiti* is carried over from *ti viṁśaterḍiti* Pā. 6. 4. 142. The present sūtra occurs in the domain of the governing rule *bhasya* Pā. 6. 4. 129. So the term *bhasya* recurs here. The word *lopaḥ* is carried over from *allopo 'naḥ* Pā. 6. 4. 134. Thus the whole sūtra means : When a *ḍit* affix follows, the *ṭi* of a bha is elided. In the illustration *katara + ad,* the substitute *ad* is treated as a sup-affix by sthānivadbhāva (143). It begins with a vowel and is other than a sarvanāmasthāna affix. So the pre-affixal base *katara* is designated as *bha* before *ad* in accordance with *yaci bham* (164). As a consequence, the present sūtra becomes applicable. The affix *ad*, being *ḍit*, effects the elision of the *ṭi* of *katara,* that is, of the final vowel *a* following repha and we have *katar + ad* --> *katarad*. By virtue of the rule *vā 'vasāne* (145), the pada-final *d* is optionally replaced by *t* (*car*) and we have two forms in the nominative singular : *katarat* and *katarad*.

With the dual nominative affix, we have *katara* + *au*. The sup-affix *au*, which is introduced after a neuter stem, is replaced by *śī* according to the rule *napuṁsakācca* (234). The substitute *śī* remains as *ī* after the elision of the anubandha *ś* {*laśakvataddhite* (135)} by *tasya lopaḥ* (3). In *katara* + *ī*, the rule *ādguṇaḥ* (27) applies and we have *katare*.

When the plural affix *jas* of the first triplet is introduced after the neuter pronominal stem *katara*, we have *katara* + *jas*. The affix *jas* is replaced by *śi* according to the rule *jaśśasoḥ śiḥ* (236). The substitute *śi* is designated as *sarvanāmasthāna* by *śi sarvanāmasthānam* (237). Then the augment *num* is introduced to *katara* by *napuṁsakasya jhalacaḥ* (238). By the rule *midaco 'nyātparaḥ* (239), the augment *num* is inserted after the last vowel *a* that follows repha. Then we have *katara num śi* ---> *kataran i*. The penultimate vowel (*upadhā*) is lengthened by the sūtra *sarvanāmasthāne cāsambuddhau* (176) and the dental *n* is replaced by the cerebral *ṇ* {*aṭkupvāṅ*... (137)}. Thus the nominative plural form *katarāṇi* is obtained.

In the vocative singular also, the singular affix *su* is replaced by *adḍ* according to *adḍḍatarādibhyaḥ*... (240). Then the *ṭi* of *katara*, which is bha by *yaci bham* (164), is elided in accordance with the present rule. By applying the rule *vā 'vasāne* (145), we have two forms, namely, *katarat* and *katarad*. During the declensional process, we have *katara* + *ad* --> *katar* + *ad*. At this stage of the formation, the pre-affixal base ends in repha and the short vowel *a*, after which the phoneme *t* occurs, is a part of the sup-affix *ad* {*sthānivadādeśo*.... (143)}. As such the phoneme *t* in *katar at* is not elided by the rule *eṅhrasvātsambuddheḥ* (133) and we obtain the form *katarat*. The alternative form will be *katarad* (see supra p. 160 for more explanation).

Vāsudeva Dīkṣita[1] discusses in detail the significance of the substitute *adḍ* having the consonant *ḍ* as *it*. He says that the form *katarat* may be obtained even by taking recourse to pararūpa in *katara* + *ad* by *ato guṇe* (273) but in this case, the grammatical operation of pūrvasavarṇadīrgha blocks it and effects a long vowel substitute homogeneous with the preceding one. Then we would have the undesirable form *he katarād!* or

1. *nanu pararūpeṇa katarad iti siddheḥ adḍo ḍitkaraṇasya kiṁ prayojanam ityata āha ṭer luptatvād iti. ṭer luptatvāt pūrvasavarṇadīrgho na bhavatītyanvayaḥ. ḍittvābhāve ṭeḥ iti lopasyāprāptyā pararūpaṁ bādhitvā pūrvasavarṇadīrghaḥ prasajyeta iti bhāvaḥ. nanu pūrvasavarṇadīrghābhāvāya dakāra evādeśaḥ kriyatām ityata āha eṅhrasvādityādi. sor dakārādeśe sati tasya sthānivattvena sambuddhitvād hrasvāntād aṅgāt paratvāc ca lopaḥ prasajyeta. adḍādeśe tu ṭilope sati katar ityaṅgam, na tad hrasvāntam. yat tu hrasvāntaṁ katara iti, na tadaṅgam, rephād akārasya pratyayāvayavatvena tadantasya pratyayaparakatvābhāvena aṅgatvābhāvāt. ataṣṭilopapravṛttaye adḍādeśavidhir iti bhāvaḥ*. BM, I, p. 326.

he katarāt!. When we have the substitute which has *ḍ* as *it*, the *ṭi* of *katara* is elided and there would arise no contingency of applying a rule prescribing either pararūpa or pūrvasavarṇadīrgha.

He makes another proposal on behalf of the opponent that the substitute may be conceived to consist of a single phoneme *d* only. This would not allow the grammatical situation to arise in which a rule prescribing either pararūpa or pūrvasavarṇadīrgha would become applicable. In that case, replies Vāsudeva Dīkṣita, the elision of the phoneme *d* by *eṅhrasvāt...* (133) would become inevitable, which will lead to the undesirable form *he katara!* If the substitute is *ḍit*, the *ṭi* of *katara* is elided and the pre-affixal base then ends in repha. This means that the pre-affixal base does not end in a short vowel and the consonant *t* that was likely to be elided comes after a short *a*, which is a part of the affix and not of the pre-affixal base *katar*. In conclusion, it may be averred that the purpose of having the substitute *adḍ* in place of *ad* is for the sake of the elision of *ṭi*, which removes all impediments such as pararūpa or pūrvasavarṇadīrgha in arriving at the form *he katarad!* or *he katarat!*

The stem *katara* in the neuter, with the affixes of the second triplet, is declined in the same way as it has been declined with those of the first triplet. The rest of the declension of *katara* is like that of the masculine. The Bālamanoramā clarifies 'like masculine' implies 'like *sarva*' (BM, I, p. 326). The complete declension of the interrogative pronominal stem *katara* is as follows :

	Singular	Dual	Plural
prathamā	*katarat, d*	*katare*	*katarāṇi*
dvitīyā	*katarat, d*	*katare*	*katarāṇi*
tṛtīyā	*katareṇa*	*katarābhyām*	*kataraiḥ*
caturthī	*katarasmai*	*katarābhyām*	*katarebhyaḥ*
pañcamī	*katarasmāt, d*	*katarābhyām*	*katarebhyaḥ*
ṣaṣṭhī	*katarasya*	*katarayoḥ*	*katareṣām*
saptamī	*katarasmin*	*katarayoḥ*	*katareṣu*
sambodhana	*he katarat, d!*	*he katare!*	*he katarāṇi!*

The substitutes *smai* in place of *ṅe* of the dative singular, *smāt* in place of *ṅasi* of the ablative singular and *smin* in place of *ṅi* of the locative singular are respectively prescribed by *sarvanāmnaḥ smai* (152) and *ṅasiṅyoḥ smātsminau* (153). The augment *suṭ* is added to the plural affix *ām* by *āmi sarvanāmnaḥ suṭ* (154). According to *ādyantau...* (84), the augment *suṭ* is inserted at the head of the affix *ām*. Then the final short *a* of *katara* before *sām* is replaced by *e* in accordance with the rule *bahuvacane...* (144). The dental *s* changes into *ṣ* by *ādeśa...* (149).

The pronominal stems *katama, itara, anya* and *anyatara* in the neuter will be declined in the same way as *katara* in the neuter gender but the case of the stem *anyatama* is different. It is not declined in that manner since it is not listed in the *sarvādi* class, whereas the term *anyatara* finds place in the *sarvādi* class. Its declension is like that of the nominal stem *jñāna*.

The word *ekatara* ends in the affix *ḍatara* but it is not declined like the interrogative pronominal stem *katara* in accordance with the following vārttika :

23. वा० – एकतरात् प्रतिषेधो वक्तव्यः । एकतरम् । *ekatarāt pratiṣedho vaktavyaḥ. ekataram.*

Trans. : The prohibition of the substitution by *adḍ* for *su* and *am* after *ekatara* should be stated.

Eluc. : This vārttika appears to be a paraphrase of *itarācchandasi pratiṣedha ekatarāt sarvatra* Mbh 7. 1. 26 vtk 1, with some variation. Hence it is meant for the prohibition of the substitution of *su* and *am* by *adḍ* when they are introduced after the word *ekatara* in the neuter gender. When the affixes of the first and second triplets as well as the vocative singular are introduced after *ekatara*, it is declined in the same way as the nominal stem *jñāna*. The rest of the declension is like that of the pronominal stem *sarva*.

	Singular	Dual	Plural
prathamā	*ekataram*	*ekatare*	*ekatarāṇi*
dvitīyā	*ekataram*	*ekatare*	*ekatarāṇi*
tṛtīyā	*ekatareṇa*	*ekatarābhyām*	*ekataraiḥ*
caturthī	*ekatarasmai*	*ekatarābhyām*	*ekatarebhyaḥ*
pañcamī	*ekatarasmāt, d*	*ekatarābhyām*	*ekatarebhyaḥ*
ṣaṣṭhī	*ekatarasya*	*ekatarayoḥ*	*ekatareṣām*
saptamī	*ekatarasmin*	*ekatarayoḥ*	*ekatareṣu*
sambodhana	*he ekatara!*	*he ekatare!*	*he ekatarāṇi!*

Here comes to an end the declension of the neuter words that end in a short *a*.

Now begins the declension of the neuter stems that end in a long *ā*.

The word *śrīpā* 'protector of wealth' is an upapada compound which is analysed as *śriyam pāti* : *śrī* + *ṅas* (<-- *am*) *pā* + *vic*. The affix *vic* is introduced after the root *pā* by *anyebhyo 'pi dṛśyante* Pā. 3. 2. 75. The whole of the affix *vic* is elided. The gender of the word *śrīpā* depends upon the substantive it qualifies. This way it is used in all the genders. In the masculine and the feminine gender it is declined like the word *viśvapā*. When the word *śrīpā* qualifies words like *kula* (family) or *mitra* (friend), which are in the neuter gender, it is to be used in the neuter. As such, it is to be declined in the neuter. In this context, the following sūtra becomes available for application :

(242) ह्रस्वो नपुंसके प्रातिपदिकस्य । *hrasvo napuṁsake prātipadikasya.* 1. 2. 47

लघु० - अजन्तस्येत्येव । श्रीपम् । ज्ञानवत् । *ajantasyetyeva. śrīpam. jñānavat.*

Trans. : The nominal stem which ends in a vowel is replaced by a short vowel in the neuter gender.

PP. *hrasvaḥ napuṁsake prātipadikasya.*

Eluc. : The paribhāṣā sūtra *acaśca* Pā. 1. 2. 28 says that a replacement which is specified by *hrasva, dīrgha* or *pluta* should come in place of a vowel (*ac*). The present sūtra also prescribes a replacement which is specified by *hrasva* (short); so the paribhāṣā sūtra *acaśca* will apply in the present context. This will qualify the term *prātipadikasya* and by tadantavidhi, it will give the meaning : *ajantasya prātipadikasya*. Now with the help of another paribhāṣā sūtra *alo 'ntyasya* (21), a short vowel will replace the final long vowel of the nominal stem in the neuter gender.

Since the word *śrīpā* is being declined in the neuter, the final long *ā* is replaced by a short *a* by the present rule and we have *śrīpa,* which ends in a short *a*. Accordingly, its declension will be like that of the nominal stem *jñāna* in the following manner :

	Singular	Dual	Plural
prathamā	*śrīpam*	*śrīpe*	*śrīpāṇi*
dvitīyā	*śrīpam*	*śrīpe*	*śrīpāṇi*
tṛtīyā	*śrīpeṇa*	*śrīpābhyām*	*śrīpaiḥ*

caturthī	*śrīpāya*	*śrīpābhyām*	*śrīpebhyaḥ*
pañcamī	*śrīpāt, d*	*śrīpābhyām*	*śrīpebhyaḥ*
ṣaṣṭhī	*śrīpasya*	*śrīpayoḥ*	*śrīpāṇām*
saptamī	*śrīpe*	*śrīpayoḥ*	*śrīpeṣu*
sambodhana	*he śrīpa!*	*he śrīpe!*	*he śrīpāṇi!*

One point is to be kept in mind in the context of the declensional process of *śrīpā*. In the forms *śrīpāṇi, śrīpeṇa* and *śrīpāṇām*, the dental *n* is replaced by a cerebral *ṇ* by the sūtra *ekājuttarapade ṇaḥ* (285) and not by *aṭkupvāṅ...* (137) since the dental *n*, which has been replaced by a cerebral *ṇ*, occurs in a different pada. The rule *aṭkupvāṅ...* (137) prescribes the substitution of *n* by *ṇ* in the same pada.

Here comes to an end the declension of the neuter words that end in a long *ā*.

Now begins the declension of the nominal stems that end in a short *i*.

The nominal stem *vāri* 'water' is neuter. When we introduce *su* after it, we have *vāri* + *su*. Here we do not apply the rule *ato 'm* (233) since the stem does not end in a short *a*. Instead, the following sūtra presents itself for application :

(243) स्वमोर्नपुंसकात्। *svamornapuṁsakāt*. 7. 1. 23
लघु० - लुक् स्यात्। वारि। *luk syāt. vāri.*

Trans. : Let there be the elision called *luk* of the affixes *su* and *am*, introduced after a neuter nominal stem.

PP. *svamoḥ napuṁsakāt luk* (*aṅgasya*).

Eluc. : The term *luk* is carried over from *ṣaḍbhyo luk* (187). The compound word *svamoḥ* is an itaretaradvandva : *suś ca am ca svamau, tayoḥ*. Thus the sūtra means : If the affixes *su* and *am* are introduced after a neuter stem, then the zero-replacement (*luk*) should come in their place. This is a general (*utsarga*) rule.

The Bālamanoramā[1] discusses an important point with regard to this sūtra. It says that there could be a contingency to invoke the paribhāṣā sūtra *ādeḥ parasya* (72) to elide only the initial vowel *a* of the

1. *na ca ādeḥ parasya iti amaḥ akārasyaiva luk syāt na tu makārasyāpīti śaṅkyam. pratyayasya lopa eva hi lug ityucyate. am iti samudāya eveha pratyayaḥ na tu tadekadeśabhūtam akāramātram. ato lug amaḥ sarvādeśa eva bhavati.* BM, I, p. 332.

sup-affix *am* because the term *napuṁsakāt* is in the ablative singular. As such the remaining portion *m* would remain intact. This would lead to an undesirable consequence. The commentary draws our attention to the fact that the luk-elision is enjoined in place of the affix by *pratyayasya lukślulupaḥ* (42). Neither the initial *a* nor the final *m* of *am* constitutes an affix. Consequently, the luk-elision will come in place of the whole affix and not in place of the initial *a* as contested by the opponent.

After the luk-elision of *su* and *am* has taken place, we obtain the form *vāri* both in the nominative and accusative singular.

Introducing the dual affix of the first triplet, we have *vāri* + *au*. The affix *au* is replaced by *śī* by *napuṁskācca* (234). After the elision of the anubandha *ś*, the grammatical situation is : *vāri* + *ī*. At this stage, the following sūtra becomes available for application :

(244) इकोऽचि विभक्तौ । *iko 'ci vibhaktau*. 7. 1. 73

लघु० – इगन्तस्य क्लीबस्य नुम् अचि विभक्तौ । वारिणी । वारीणि । *igantasya klībasya num aci vibhaktau. vāriṇī. vārīṇi.*

Trans. : If a sup-affix which begins with a vowel follows, then the augment *num* is introduced to the neuter pre-affixal base that ends in a vowel denoted by the abbreviatory term *ik*.

PP. *ikaḥ napuṁsakasya* (*aṅgasya*) *num aci vibhaktau*.

Eluc. : The terms *napuṁsakasya* and *num* are respectively carried over from *napuṁsakasya jhalacaḥ* Pā. 7. 1. 72 and *idito num dhātoḥ* Pā. 7. 1. 58. The term *ikaḥ* qualifies the term *napuṁsakasya*. By tadantavidhi, it gives the sense : *igantasya napuṁsakasya*. The term *aci*, which in the locative singular, qualifies the term *vibhaktau* and this by tadādividhi means : *ajādau vibhaktau*, that is, 'when a vowel-initial sup-affix follows'. Thus the whole sūtra means : The augment *num* is introduced to a neuter pre-affixal base, which ends in a vowel denoted by *ik*-pratyāhāra, when a vowel-initial sup-affix follows. Since the augment is *mit*, it is inserted after the last vowel, that is, after *i* in this illustration and it becomes a part of the *iganta* neuter pre-affixal base : *vāri num* + *ī* --> *vārin* + *ī*. After the application of the rule *aṭkupvāṅ...* (137), we have *vāriṇī* in the nominative dual.

With plural sup-affix *jas* introduced after *vāri*, we have *vāri* + *as* (*jas*). In this situation, the affix *jas* is replaced by *śi* according to the rule *jaśśasoḥ śiḥ* (236). The substitute *śi* is treated as a sup-affix by sthānivad-bhāva (143). Then it gets the sarvanāmasthāna designation by *śi sarvanāmasthānam* (237). The augment *num* is introduced by the present rule. The lengthening of the penultimate vowel (*upadhā*) takes place by *sarvanāmasthāne...* (176). The dental *n* is replaced by *ṇ* by *aṭkupvāṅnum...* (137). Thus the form *vārīṇi* is obtained through the following grammatical process : *vāri + as --> vāri + śi --> vāri num + i --> vārin + i --> vārīn + i --> vārīṇ + i --> vārīṇi.*

In the vocative singular form of *vāri,* the elision of the affix *su* takes place by *svamornapuṁsakāt* (243) and we have the form *he vāri!* The elided affix *su* is to be treated as if existent by virtue of the rule *pratyayalope pratyayalakṣaṇam* (189) but it is negated by *na lumatāṅgasya* (190). This is the reason why the elided affix *su* cannot be treated as existent. Nonetheless, Varadarāja says that the negation by *na lumatā...* (190) is not obligatory :

लघु० – न लुमता... (190) इत्यस्यानित्यत्वात् पक्षे सम्बुद्धिनिमित्तो गुणः - हे वारे! हे वारि! आङो ना... (170) - वारिणा। घेर्ङिति (171) इति गुणे प्राप्ते -- *na lumatā...* (190) *ityasyānityatvāt pakṣe sambuddhinimitto guṇaḥ - he vāre! he vāri! āṅo nā...* (170) -- *vāriṇā. gherṅiti* (171) *iti guṇe prāpte --*

Trans. : The rule *na lumatā...*(190) is not universally applicable. So, when it is not applicable, the vocative singular affix *su,* which has been elided by *svamornapuṁsakāt* (243), is treated as effective and there is a guṇa-vowel replacement because of the singular vocative affix. Then we have the form *he vāre!* (the alternative form is) *he vāri!*

Eluc. : The statement that the rule *na lumatā...* (190) is not universal needs explanation. How do we come to know that this rule is not universally applicable? The commentators generally agree that the use of the term *aci* in the sūtra *iko 'ci vibhaktau* (244) implies that the sūtra *na lumatā...* (190) is non-universal. In order to justify this implication, we have to show that the term *aci* has no purpose to serve in the sūtra *iko 'ci...* (244). This can be done in the following way. With respect to the declension of *vāri,* for example, it can be accepted that there is no need of the term *aci* to block the introduction of the augment *num* before the sup-affixes which begin with a consonant. In *vāribhyām,* it will receive pada-designation by *svādiṣvasarva...* (163). Even if *num* is inserted, the phoneme *n* will be elided by the sūtra *na lopaḥ prātipadikāntasya* (179). So, we can dispense with the dental *n* of *num* even without the inclusion of *aci* in *iko 'ci...* (244).

It may be argued that the purpose of the term *aci* in the sūtra *iko...* (244) is to dispense with the presence of the phoneme *n* in the vocative singular form since the elision of *n*, in this context, is denied by the sūtra *na ṅisambuddhyoḥ* (280). However, sambuddhi is not present since the elision of the singular vocative affix *su* has been brought about by *svamornapuṁsakāt* (243), which means that the elision of *su* in this case has taken place by the term *luk*. Hence, it is not to be treated as effective with respect to the pre-affixal grammatical operation by virtue of *na lumatāṅgasya* (190). So, there is no need to include the term *aci* in the rule *iko 'ci...* (244) to block the introduction of the augment *num* even when the vocative singular affix follows. Consequently, the term *aci* does not serve any purpose in the rule *iko 'ci...* (244). Still the author of the Aṣṭādhyāyī has enunciated this term in the sūtra *iko 'ci...* (244). It, therefore, leads to the implication that the sūtra *na lumatā...* (190) is not universally applicable. When this is not applicable, the introduction of *num* in the vocative singular form can be blocked only by the use of the term *aci* in *iko 'ci...* (244). The vocative singular affix *su* is not a vowel-initial affix and hence there will be no scope for the introduction of *num* in the vocative singular form. Thus because of the non-universal nature of the sūtra *na lumatā...* (190) we obtain two forms of *vāri* in the vocative singular : 1. *he vāri!* In this illustration, the rule *na lumatā...* (190) is applicable and hence the affix *su*, elided by *svamor...* (243), is not treated as effective, so we have this form. 2. *he vāre!* Here the rule *na lumatā...* (190) is not applicable and as such the elided affix *su* is considered to be effective by *pratyalope...* (189). As a consequence, the guṇa-vowel replacement by *hrasvasya guṇaḥ* (168) comes in place of the final *i* of *vāri + su --> vāre* + s. Then by *eṅhrasvāt...* (133), the s of sambuddhi is elided and we obtain the alternative form *he vāre!* This helps us understand why Patañjali uses two forms of the neuter nominal stem *trapu* : 1. *he trapo!* on *iko 'ci...* (244) and 2. *he trapu!* on *eṅhrasvāt...* (133).[1]

With the sup-affixes of the second triplet, the nominal stem *vāri* will be declined the same way as with those of the first triplet.

Introducing the singular affix of the third triplet, we have *vāri + ṭā*. The nominal stem *vāri* is assigned the term *ghi* by *śeṣo ghyasakhi* (169). The rule *āṅo nāstriyām* Pā. 7. 3. 120, being subsequent to *iko 'ci...* Pā. 7. 1. 73, applies and the affix *ṭā* is replaced by *nā*. We have the form *vāriṇā* after the application of *aṭkupvāṅ...* (137).

---

1. Cf. *atra ca iko 'ci vibhaktau ityatrājgrahaṇaṁ jñāpakam. halādiṣu bhyāmādiṣu satyapi numi na lopaḥ prātipadikāntasya iti tasya lopasambhavād acīti vyartham. na ca sambuddhivyāvṛttyartham ajgrahaṇam tatra numi sati na ṅisambuddhyoḥ iti niṣedhe sati nakāraśravaṇaprasaṅgād iti vācyam sambuddher lukā luptatayā pratyayalakṣaṇābhāvena tatra numaḥ prapter evābhāvāt na lumatā...iti niṣedhasyānityatve tu sambuddhau pratyayalakṣaṇena prāptaṁ numaṁ vārayitum ajgrahaṇam arthavad iti bhavatyajgrahaṇaṁ na lumatā...ityasyānityatve liṅgam ityāhuḥ. ata eva iko 'ci iti sūtre he trapo iti eṅhrasvāt iti sūtre he trapu iti ca bhāṣyaṁ saṅgacchate.* BM, I, p. 332.

When we introduce the singular affix of the fourth triplet, we have *vāri + ṅe*. The rule *iko 'ci...* Pā. 7. 1. 73, which prescribes the introduction of *num*, is blocked by the subsequent rule *gherṅiti* Pā. 7. 3. 111 which prescribes a guṇa-substitution in place of the final *i* of *vāri*. However, the following vārttika prescribes the introduction of *num* by pūrvavipratiṣedha (giving preference to the rule which is prior in sequence) :

24. वा० – वृद्ध्यौत्वतृज्वद्भावगुणेभ्यो नुम् पूर्वविप्रतिषेधेन । *vṛddhyautvatṛjvadbhāvaguṇebhyo num pūrvavipratiṣedhena.*

लघु० – वारिणे । वारिणः 2 । वारिणोः 2 । नुमचिर... वा० 19 इति नुट् -- वारीणाम् । वारिणि । हलादौ हरिवत् । *vāriṇe, vāriṇaḥ* 2. *vāriṇoḥ* 2. *numacira...* (*vtk* 19) *iti nuṭ – vārīṇām. vāriṇi. halādau harivat.*

Trans. : When the grammatical operations effecting vṛddhi, autva, tṛjvadbhāva and guṇa are in conflict with that introducing the augment *num*, the latter takes precedence even though it is prior in sequence in the Aṣṭādhyāyī. Similarly by the vārttika 19, the grammatical operation of inserting the augment *nuṭ* takes precedence over the grammatical operation of introducing the augment *num* in the case of the plural genitive form *vārīṇām*. The declension of *vāri* before the sup-affixes which begin with a consonant will be like that of *hari*.

Eluc. : When the grammatical operations of enjoining vṛddhi by *aco 'ñṇiti* Pā. 7. 2. 115, *autva* by *acca gheḥ* Pā. 7. 3. 119, *tṛjvadbhāva* by *tṛjvatkroṣṭuḥ* Pā. 7. 1. 95 and *vibhāṣā tṛtīyādiṣvaci* Pā. 7. 1. 97 and guṇa-substitution by *gherṅiti* Pā. 7. 3. 111 are in conflict with the grammatical operation of introducing the augment *num* by *iko 'ci...* Pā. 7. 1. 73, the latter takes precedence over the former (grammatical operations) according to the present vārttika, even though by virtue of the rule *vipratiṣedhe paraṁ kāryam* (112), the former grammatical operations should take precedence over the latter. So, in the illustration *vāri + ṅe*, the guṇa-substitution by *gherṅiti* Pā. 7. 3. 111 does not take place when the augment *num* is being introduced by the rule *iko 'ci...* (244). Then we have *vāri num + ṅe* --> *vārin + e* --> *vāriṇ + e* {after the application of *aṭkupvāṅ...*(137)} --> *vāriṇe*.

Similarly, in the ablative and genitive singular forms, the guṇa-substitution by *gherṅiti* is blocked by the introduction of *num* and we obtain the form *vāriṇaḥ* (<-- *vāri ṇ + as* <-- *vāri n + as* <-- *vāri num + ṅasi* or *ṅas*) after the rule *aṭkupvāṅ...* (137) has applied.

With the dual affix *os* of the sixth triplet, we have *vāri + os*. Here the rule *iko yaṇaci* Pā. 6. 1. 77 is available for application but the rule *iko 'ci vibhaktau...* Pā. 7. 1. 73, being subsequent to *iko yaṇaci* (15), applies and prescribes the insertion of *num*. Thus we obtain the form : *vāri n + os* --> *vāri ṇ + os* --> *vāriṇos* --> *vāriṇoḥ* (after rutva and visarga).

When we introduce the plural affix of the sixth triplet, there is a conflict between the augments *num* by *iko 'ci...* Pā. 7. 1. 73 and *nuṭ* by *hrasvanadyāpo nuṭ* Pā. 7. 1. 54 but by virtue of *numacira...* (vārttika, 19), the latter takes precedence over the former, even though the former is subsequent to the latter. We get the form *vārīṇām* after the application of *nāmi* (148) and *aṭkupvāṅ...* (137).

Vāsudeva Dīkṣita[1] draws our attention to the distinction between *num* and *nuṭ*. The augment *num* becomes a part of the pre-affixal base, whereas the augment *nuṭ* forms a part of the affix *ām* in the present illustration. Had the augment *num* instead of *nuṭ* been introduced, then the lengthening by the rule *nāmi* (148) could not have taken place.

The present vārttika *vṛddhyautvatṛjvadbhāva...* blocks *autva* by *acca...* (173) and introduces *num* by *iko 'ci...* (244) and we obtain the form *vāriṇi* after the application of the rule *aṭkupvāṅ...* (137). The declension of the neuter nominal stem *vāri* is given below :

	Singular	Dual	Plural
prathamā	*vāri*	*vāriṇī*	*vārīṇi*
dvitīyā	*vāri*	*vāriṇī*	*vārīṇi*
tṛtīyā	*vāriṇā*	*vāribhyām*	*vāribhiḥ*
caturthī	*vāriṇe*	*vāribhyām*	*vāribhyaḥ*
pañcamī	*vāriṇaḥ*	*vāribhyām*	*vāribhyaḥ*
ṣaṣṭhī	*vāriṇaḥ*	*vāriṇoḥ*	*vārīṇām*
saptamī	*vāriṇi*	*vāriṇoḥ*	*vāriṣu*
sambodhana	*he vāri!*, *he vāre!*	*he vāriṇī!*	*he vārīṇi!*

The nominal stem *dadhi* is neuter and ends in a short *i* like *vāri* but its declension slightly differs from that of *vāri*. With the affixes of the first and second triplets, the nominal stem *dadhi* is declined like *vāri*.

---

1. *numnuṭoḥ ko viśeṣa ityata āha nāmīti dīrgha iti. numi tu sati tasyāṅgabhaktatvād nāmi iti dīrgho na syād iti bhāvaḥ*. BM, I, p. 333.

There is some difference in the declensional process of *dadhi* when the vowel-initial sup-affixes of the rest of the triplets follow. When we introduce the singular affix of the third triplet, we have *dadhi* + *ṭā*. The initial *ṭ* of *ṭā* is *it* by *cuṭū* (128) and it is elided by *tasya lopaḥ* (3). Thus the affix is *ā*, which can be said to begin with a vowel in accordance with the sūtra *ādyantavadekasmin* (277). Since the nominal stem *dadhi* is ghi, the affix *ā* has got to be replaced by *nā* by the rule *āṅo nāstriyām* (170). In this situation, the following sūtra presents itself :

(245) अस्थिदधिसक्थ्यक्ष्णामनङुदात्तः । *asthidadhisakthyakṣṇām-anaṅudāttaḥ*. 7. 1. 75

लघु॰ - एषामनङ् स्याट् टादौ अचि । *eṣām anaṅ syāṭ ṭādau aci.*

Trans. : Let the substitute *anaṅ*, with a high pitch accent, replace the nominal stems *asthi* 'a bone', *dadhi* 'curd', *sakthi* 'thigh' and *akṣi* 'eye' when the vowel-initial sup-affixes, beginning with the instrumental case onward, follow.

PP. *asthidadhisakthyakṣṇām anaṅ udāttaḥ tṛtīyādiṣu akṣu vibhaktiṣu.*

Eluc. : The words *aci* and *vibhaktau* are carried over from the sūtra *iko 'ci vibhaktau* Pā. 7. 1. 73 but by the process of vacanvipariṇāma they are changed to have a plural number : *akṣu vibhaktiṣu*. The word *ṭādau* in the vṛtti is meant by the term *tṛtīyādiṣu*, which has been carried over from *tṛtīyādiṣu bhāṣitapuṁskaṁ puṁvad gālavasya* Pā. 7. 1. 74. The compound word *asthidadhisakthyakṣṇām* is an itaretaradvandva. Its analysis is as follows : *asthi ca dadhi ca sakthi ca akṣi ca asthidadhi-sakthyakṣīṇi, teṣām* = *asthidadhisakthyakṣṇām*. The expression *akṣu vibhaktiṣu* gives the meaning 'the sup-affixes which begin with a vowel' with the help of *yasmin vidhis tadādāvalgrahaṇe* Mbh 1. 1. 72 vtk 29. Thus the whole sūtra means : When vowel-initial sup-affixes beginning with the instrumental case onwards follow, the substitute *anaṅ*, with a high pitch accent, shall replace the nominal stems *asthi* 'a bone', *dadhi* 'curd', *sakthi* 'thigh' and *akṣi* 'eye'. Since the substitute is *ṅit*, it will replace the last phoneme *i* of these nominal stems according to the rule *ṅicca* (46). The substitute contains the phoneme *ṅ* as *it* and the vowel *a* after the phoneme *n* is purported to facilitate the pronunciation. So, *anaṅ* remains as *an*.

In the illustration *dadhi* + *ā*, *an*(*aṅ*) replaces the final *i* of *dadhi* and we have *dadhan* + *ā*. At this stage the following sūtra ensues :

(246) अल्लोपोऽनः । *allopo 'naḥ*. 6. 4. 134h

लघु० – अङ्गावयवोऽसर्वनामस्थान-यजादि-स्वादिपरो योऽन्, तस्याकारस्य लोपः । दध्ना । दध्ने । दध्नः 2 । दध्नोः 2 । *aṅgāvayavo 'sarvanāmasthāna-yajādi-svādiparo yo 'n tasyākārasya lopaḥ. dadhnā. dadhne. dadhnaḥ* 2, *dadhnoḥ* 2.

Trans. : The short *a* (*at*) of *an*, which forms part of a pre-affixal base (*aṅga*), is elided when it is followed by sup-affixes beginning with *y* or *ac*, with the exception of those which are denoted by the technical term *sarvanāmasthāna*.

PP. *at lopaḥ anaḥ bhasya aṅgasya.*

Eluc. : The term *at* (*al*), which is a different pada, is construed as ending in the genitive singular (*at iti luptaṣaṣṭhīkaṁ bhinnaṁ padam*, BM, I, p. 234). The genitive ending in the term *anaḥ* is in the sense of part (*avayavaṣaṣṭhī*). As a consequence there exists a part-and-whole relationship between *at* and *an*. Accordingly, we arrive at the meaning 'the short *a* of *an*'. The present sūtra occurs in the governing domain of both *aṅgasya* Pā. 6.4.1 and *bhasya* Pā. 6.4.129. The term *bhasya* is construed to yield the sense that the word-segment *an* should be followed by sup-affixes beginning with *y* or *ac* but these affixes should be other than sarvanāmasthāna..This is exactly how the term *bha* has been defined by the rule *yaci bham* (164). The word *aṅgasya* goes with *an*. It gives the sense 'the syllable *an* which forms part of a pre-affixal base (*aṅga*)'. If this procedure of syntactic relations is not followed, some grammatical problems crop up (see BM, I, p. 235). Thus from both these syntactic relations, the meaning arrived at is : the short *a* of *an* which is a part of an aṅga. In this light the present sūtra means : The word-segment *an* should be a part of an aṅga and it should be followed by non-sarvanāmasthāna sup-affixes beginning with *y* or *ac*. Then the short *a* of *an* is replaced by lopa.

In the illustration *dadhan* + *ā*, the word-segment *an* forms a part of *dadhan*, which is an aṅga by *yasmāt pratyaya*... (132). The affix *ā* is a sup-affix and it is other than sarvanāmasthāna. Consequently, the short *a* of *an* is elided and we obtain the form *dadhnā*.

In the same way the short *a* of *an* in the following forms will be elided before the vowel-initial sup-affixes : *dadhan* + (*ṅ*)e, *dadhan* + (*ṅ*)*as*(*i*), *dadhan* + (*ṅ*)*as* and *dadhan* + *os*. We will respectively have the forms *dadhne, dadhnaḥ* 2, *dadhnoḥ* 2. In the locative singular, we have *dadhan* + (*ṅ*)*i*. At this stage also, the *a* of *an* has got to be elided but the following sūtra makes the provision optional :

(247) विभाषा ङिश्योः । *vibhāṣā ṅiśyoḥ*. **6. 4. 136**

लघु० – अङ्गावयवोऽसर्वनामस्थान-यजादि-स्वादिपरो योऽन् तस्याकारस्य लोपो वा स्याद् ङिश्योः परयोः । दध्नि दधनि । शेषं वारिवत् । एवम् अस्थि-सक्थ्यक्षि । *aṅgāvayavo 'sarvanāmasthāna-yajādi-svādiparo yo 'n tasyākārasya lopo vā syād ṅiśyoḥ parayoḥ. dadhni, dadhani. śeṣaṁ vārivat. evam asthisakthyakṣi.*

Trans. : The short *a* (*at*) of *an* which forms part of a pre-affixal base (*aṅga*) is optionally elided when it is followed by *ṅi* or *śī*, with the exception of those affixes which are denoted by the technical term *sarvanāmasthāna*.

PP. *vibhāṣā ṅiśyoḥ at lopaḥ anaḥ bhasya aṅgasya.*

Eluc. : Both the terms *bhasya* and *aṅgasya* also recur here because they constitute the governing rules. The terms *at*, *lopaḥ* and *anaḥ* are carried over from *allopo 'naḥ* Pā. 6. 4. 134. The compound *ṅiśyoḥ* is an itaretaradvandva, which is analysed as follows : *ṅiś ca śīś ca ṅiśyau tayoḥ* = *ṅiśyoḥ*. Thus the sūtra means : If the word-segment *an* is part of a pre-affixal base and is followed by *ṅi* or *śī* with the exception of sarvanāmasthāna sup-affixes beginning with either *y* or *ac*, then the short *a* of *an* is optionally elided.

In the illustration *dadhan* + *ṅi*, the affix *ṅi* follows. Hence the *a* of *an* is optionally elided. When it is elided we have the form *dadhni* and when it is not elided we have the form *dadhani*. The rest of the declension of *dadhi* is like that of *vāri*. The neuter nominal stem *dadhi* is declined in the following way :

	Singular	Dual	Plural
prathamā	*dadhi*	*dadhinī*	*dadhīni*
dvitīyā	*dadhi*	*dadhinī*	*dadhīni*
tṛtīyā	*dadhnā*	*dadhibhyām*	*dadhibhiḥ*
caturthī	*dadhne*	*dadhibhyām*	*dadhibhyaḥ*
pañcamī	*dadhnaḥ*	*dadhibhyām*	*dadhibhyaḥ*
ṣaṣṭhī	*dadhnaḥ*	*dadhnoḥ*	*dadhnām*
saptamī	*dadhni*, *dadhani*	*dadhnoḥ*	*dadhiṣu*
sambodhana	*he dadhi! he dadhe!*	*he dadhinī!*	*he dadhīni!*

The neuter words *asthi*, *sakthi* and *akṣi* will be declined in the same manner.

Here comes to an end the declension of the neuter nominal stems ending in a short *i*.

Now begins the declension of the neuter stems that end in a long *ī*.

The word *sudhī* ends in a long *ī*. It is used in all the three genders since its gender depends on that of the substantive it qualifies. When it qualifies neuter words like *kula*, *mitra*, etc., it is used in the neuter gender. In the neuter, the long *ī* at the end of *sudhī* is shortened by the rule *hrasvo napuṁsake prātipadikasya* (242). With the sup-affixes of the first and second triplets, the word *sudhi* is declined like *vāri*. There is some distinction in respect of its declensional forms before the vowel-initial sup-affixes from the third triplet onward. When we introduce the singular affix *ṭā* of the third triplet, we have *sudhi* + *ṭā*. At this stage, the following sūtra becomes available for application :

(248) तृतीयादिषु भाषितपुंस्कं पुंवद् गालवस्य । *tṛtīyādiṣu bhāṣita-puṁskaṁ puṁvad gālavasya*. 7. 1. 74
लघु० – प्रवृत्तिनिमित्तैक्ये भाषितपुंस्कम् इगन्तं क्लीबं पुंवद्वा टादावचि । सुधिया, सुधिना इत्यादि । *pravṛttinimittaikye bhāṣitapuṁskam igantaṁ klībaṁ puṁvad vā ṭādāvaci. sudhiyā, sudhinā ityādi.*

Trans. : If the cause of the application of a word is the same, then the neuter nominal stem, which has a masculine counter-part and which ends in a vowel denoted by the abbreviatory term *ik*, is optionally treated like a masculine stem before vowel-initial sup-affixes from the third case (*ṭā*) onward.

PP. *tṛtīyādiṣu akṣu vibhaktiṣu bhāṣitapuṁskaṁ napuṁskam puṁvad gālavasya (aṅgasya)*.

Eluc. : The words *aci* and *vibhaktau* are carried over from the sūtra *iko 'ci vibhaktau* Pā. 7. 1. 73 but by the process of vacanvipariṇāma they are changed into the plural number : *akṣu vibhaktiṣu*. By virtue of *yasmin vidhis tadādāvalgrahaṇe*, Mbh 1. 1. 72 vtk 29, the expression *akṣu vibhaktiṣu* means 'the sup-affixes which begin with a vowel'. The term *napuṁskam* is carried over from *napuṁskasya jhalacaḥ* Pā. 7. 1. 72. The term *ik* is carried over from *iko 'ci vibhaktau* Pā. 7. 1. 73. It qualifies the neuter stem. Hence by tadantavidhi, it means *igantasya napuṁskasya*. The word *bhāṣitapuṁskam* is a bahuvrīhi compound. It is analysed as : *bhāṣitaḥ pumān yena pravṛttinimittena tat* = *bhāṣitapuṁskam*. The affix *ac* {*arśa ādibhyo 'c* (1189)}, which conveys the sense 'belonging to' or 'being in this', is introduced after the word *bhāṣitapuṁska*. This compound stands for a word which has a masculine counterpart having the same cause for its application in usage. Thus the sūtra comes to mean : If a neuter nominal stem ends in a vowel denoted by the abbreviatory term *ik* and if it has a masculine counterpart with the same cause for its use (*pravṛttinimittaikye*), then, according to the grammarian Gālava, it is optionally treated like a masculine nominal stem before the vowel-initial sup-affixes starting with the third triplet onward. The word *sudhi* is used in the sense of 'one who meditates well'. When it is used to qualify a masculine nominal stem, the cause of its usage is the same, i.e. it has the same meaning. Hence the word *sudhi* is bhāṣitapuṁska. So, it is optionally treated like a masculine. When it is thus treated, it remains with a long *ī* and will be declined like *sudhī* in the masculine. The rule *na bhūsudhiyoḥ* (201) precludes *yaṇ*-substitution. Then by applying the rule *aciśnu*... (198), we obtain the form *sudhiyā* after the substitute *iyaṅ* has replaced the long *ī* of *sudhī* before the singular affix of the third triplet. When it is in the neuter, it will be declined like the nominal stem *vāri* and we have the form *sudhinā* like *vāriṇā*. The complete declension of this neuter bhāṣitapuṁska nominal stem *sudhi* is given below :

	Singular	Dual	Plural
prathamā	*sudhi*	*sudhinī*	*sudhīni*
dvitīyā	*sudhi*	*sudhinī*	*sudhīni*
tṛtīyā	*sudhiyā, sudhinā*	*sudhibhyām*	*sudhibhiḥ*
caturthī	*sudhiye, sudhine*	*sudhibhyām*	*sudhibhyaḥ*
pañcamī	*sudhiyaḥ, sudhinaḥ*	*sudhibhyām*	*sudhibhyaḥ*
ṣaṣṭhī	*sudhiyaḥ, sudhinaḥ*	*sudhiyoḥ sudhinoḥ*	*sudhiyām sudhīnām*
saptamī	*sudhiyi, sudhini*	*sudhiyoḥ ṣudhinoḥ*	*sudhiṣu*
sambodhana	*he sudhe! he sudhi!*	*he sudhinī!*	*he sudhīni!*

Here comes to an end the declension of the neuter nominal stems ending in a long *ī*. Now begins the declension of the neuter nominal stems that end in a short *u*.

लघु० – मधु । मधुनी । मधूनि । हे मधो! हे मधु! *madhu. madhunī. madhūni. he madho! he madhu!*

Eluc. : The nominal stem *madhu* is both masculine and neuter. The masculine stem means 'spring season', 'the month of Caitra' 'a demon', etc. In the neuter gender, it means 'honey', 'wine', etc. Its declension is like that of *vāri*. Since the cause of its usage in both the genders is not the same, it is not a bhāṣitapuṁska.

	Singular	Dual	Plural
prathamā	*madhu*	*madhunī*	*madhūni*
dvitīyā	*madhu*	*madhunī*	*madhūni*
tṛtīyā	*madhunā*	*madhubhyām*	*madhubhiḥ*
caturthī	*madhune*	*madhubhyām*	*madhubhyaḥ*
pañcamī	*madhunaḥ*	*madhubhyām*	*madhubhyaḥ*
ṣaṣṭhī	*madhunaḥ*	*madhunoḥ*	*madhūnām*
saptamī	*madhuni*	*madhunoḥ*	*madhuṣu*
sambodhana	*he madho!, he madhu!*	*he madhunī!*	*he madhūni!*

Here comes to an end the declension of the neuter nominal stems ending in *u*. Now begins the declension of the neuter stems ending in *ū*.

लघु० – सुलु । सुलुनी । सुलूनि । सुलुनेत्यादि । *sulu, sulunī, sulūni, sulunetyādi.*

Eluc. : The word *sulū* 'that which cuts well' is derived with the introduction of the affix *kvip* after *su* + *lū* (*suṣṭhu lunātīti kvip* BM, I, p. 337). The gender of *sulū* depends on the substantive it qualifies. The cause of its application in the neuter is the same as in the masculine. Hence it is a bhāṣitapuṁska stem. When *sulū* is used in the neuter, its long *ū* is shortened by *hrasvo napuṁsake...* (242). It will be declined almost like *sudhī* --> *sudhi* in the neuter gender. In the optional masculine form of *sulū*, the *yaṇ*-replacement takes place by *oḥ supi* (209) before vowel-initial sup-affixes (from the third triplet onward).

	Singular	Dual	Plural
prathamā	*sulu*	*sulunī*	*sulūni*
dvitīyā	*sulu*	*sulunī*	*sulūni*
tṛtīyā	*sulvā, sulunā*	*sulubhyām*	*sulubhiḥ*
caturthī	*sulve, sulune*	*sulubhyām*	*sulubhyaḥ*
pañcamī	*sulvaḥ, sulunaḥ*	*sulubhyām*	*sulubhyaḥ*
ṣaṣṭhī	*sulvaḥ, sulunaḥ*	*sulvoḥ, sulunoḥ*	*sulvām, sulūnām*
saptamī	*sulvi, suluni*	*sulvoḥ, sulunoḥ*	*suluṣu*
sambodhana	*he sulo!, he sulu!*	*he sulunī!*	*he sulūni!*

Here comes to an end the declension of the neuter nominal stems ending in *ū*. Now begins the declension of the neuter stems ending in *ṛ*.

लघु० – धातृ । धातृणी । धातॄणि । हे धातः ! हे धातृ ! धातॄणाम् । एवं ज्ञात्रादयः । *dhātṛ. dhātṛṇī. dhātṝṇi. he dhataḥ! he dhātṛ! dhātṝṇām. evaṁ jñātrādayaḥ.*

Eluc. : The nominal stem *dhātṛ* 'one who nourishes, supports' is also dependent on the gender of the substantive it qualifies. The cause of its application remains the same in all the three genders. As such, it is bhāṣitapuṁska. So, it will be optionally treated like a masculine before the vowel-initial sup-affixes of the third and the following triplets. In the declensional process of this word, the following points are to be kept in mind : 1. In the nominative and accusative singular, the affixes *su* and *am* respectively, will be elided by *svamornapuṁsakāt* (243) and the form will be *dhātṛ*. The rule *ṛduśanas...* (204) prescribing *anaṅ* in the nominative singular will not apply because the elided affix *su* is not effective because of *na lumatā...* (190). The case with the singular affix of the second triplet is similar. 2. In the dual and plural forms, *iko 'ci...* (244) introduces the augment *num* to *dhātṛ*. The dental *n* is replaced by the cerebral *ṇ* by *ṛvarṇānnasya ṇatvaṁ vācyam* (vtk 21). We obtain the form *dhātṛṇī* with the dual nominative affix *śī*, which has come in place of *au*. In the plural form, *śi* replaces *jas*. This is sarvanāmasthāna by *śi sarvanāmasthānam* (237). By *sarvanāmasthāne...* (176), the lengthening of the vowel *ṛ* takes place and we get the form *dhātṝṇi*. 3. When the vowel-initial sup-affixes follow, *num* is inserted after the last vowel of the pre-affixal stem. When the vowel-initial sup-affixes beginning with the third triplet follow, the nominal stem is optionally treated like the masculine according to *tṛtīyādiṣu bhāṣitapuṁskaṁ puṁvadgālavasya* (248) and is declined like the masculine *dhātṛ*. 4. In the genitive plural form, the augment *nuṭ* takes precedence over *num*. 5. Because of the non-universal nature of the *na lumatā...* (190), we have two forms of the vocative singular. When the rule *na lumatā...* (190) is not effective, the guṇa-substitution takes place by *hrasvasya guṇaḥ* (168) and not by *ṛto ṅisarvanāmasthānayoḥ* (203) since the vocative singular affix *su* is not sarvanāmasthāna in the neuter. The declension of the bhāṣitapuṁska *dhātṛ* will be as follows :

	Singular	Dual	Plural
prathamā	*dhātṛ*	*dhātṛṇī*	*dhātṝṇi*
dvitīyā	*dhātṛ*	*dhātṛṇī*	*dhātṝṇi*
tṛtīyā	*dhātrā, dhātṛṇā*	*dhātṛbhyām*	*dhātṛbhiḥ*
caturthī	*dhātre, dhātṛṇe*	*dnātṛbhyām*	*dhātṛbhyaḥ*
pañcamī	*dhātuḥ, dhātṛṇaḥ*	*dhātṛbhyām*	*dhātṛbhyaḥ*
ṣaṣṭhī	*dhātuḥ, dhātṛṇaḥ*	*dhātroḥ, dhātṛṇoḥ*	*dhātṝṇām*
saptamī	*dhātari, dhātṛṇi*	*dhātroḥ, dhātṛṇoḥ*	*dhātṛṣu*
sambodhana	*he dhātṛ!* *he dhātaḥ!*	*he dhātṛṇī!*	*he dhātṝṇi!*

The neuter nominal stems *jñātṛ* and so on will be declined in the same manner as *dhātṛ*.

Here ends the declension of the neuter stems ending in *ṛ*. Now begins the declension of the neuter nominal stems ending in *o*.

The nominal stem *pradyo* is a bahuvrīhi compound. Its analysis is : *prakṛṣṭā dyauḥ yasya yasmin vā tat = pradyu* (dinam)'(the day) when the sky is clear'. Since the compound word qualifies the neuter word *dina*, it is used in the neuter also. As such, the rule *hrasvo napuṁsake prātipadikasya* (242) prescribes the shortening of the last vowel of *pradyo*. The two short vowels *a* and *u* are available to come in place of the vowel *o* of *pradyo* on the basis of the similarity of the place of articulation. In order to decide which of the two subtitutes should come in place of *o*, the following sūtra ensues :

(249) **एच इग्घ्रस्वादेशे । *eca igghrasvādeśe.* 1. 1. 48**
लघु० – आदिश्यमानेषु ह्रस्वेषु मध्ये एच इगेव स्यात् । प्रद्यु । प्रद्युनी । प्रद्यूनि । प्रद्युना इत्यादि । *ādiśyamāneṣu hrasveṣu madhye eca ig eva syāt. pradyu. pradyunī. pradyūni. pradyunā ityādi.*

Trans. : When the short vowels are enjoined to replace the vowels denoted by *ec*-pratyāhāra, let only the vowels denoted by *ik*-pratyāhāra replace them.

PP. *eca ik hrasvādeśe.*

Eluc. : The word *hrasvādeśe* is a ṣaṣṭhītatpuruṣa which is analysed as *hravasya ādeśaḥ hrasvādeśaḥ, tasmin = hrasvādeśe.* When a short vowel is being prescribed to replace a vowel denoted by *ec*-pratyāhāra, it is only the vowel denoted by *ik*-pratyāhāra which should replace that substituend vowel. Take, for example, the word *pradyo.* When it is to be used in the neuter, the present rule applies and the final vowel *o* is replaced by a short vowel. In this case, out of the two substitutes, namely short *a* and short *u,* only *u,* a denotatum of *ik,* will replace *o.*

The declension of the word *pradyu* will be like that of the neuter stem *madhu.* As a bhāṣitapuṁska stem, it is also declined in a different way before the vowel initial sup-affixes beginning with the singular affix of the third triplet onward. The alternative declensional forms are explained in the sequel.

	Singular	Dual	Plural
prathamā	*pradyu*	*pradyunī*	*pradyūni*
dvitīyā	*pradyu*	*pradyunī*	*pradyūni*
tṛtīyā	*pradyunā*	*pradyubhyām*	*pradyubhiḥ*
caturthī	*pradyune*	*pradyubhyām*	*pradyubhyaḥ*
pañcamī	*pradyunaḥ*	*pradyubhyām*	*pradyubhyaḥ*
ṣaṣṭhī	*pradyunaḥ*	*pradyunoḥ*	*pradyūnām*
saptamī	*pradyuni*	*pradyunoḥ*	*pradyuṣu*
sambodhana	*he pradyo!, he pradyu!*	*he pradyunī!*	*he pradyūni!*

With the vowel-initial affixes *ā* (*ṭā*), *e* (*ṅe*), *as* (*ṅasi, ṅas*), *os, ām* and *i* (*ṅi*), we respectively have the alternative forms : *pradyavā, pradyave, pradyoḥ* 2 , *pradyavoḥ* 2 , *pradyavām* and *pradyavi.*

Both the words, *pradyo* and *pradyu* have the same denotation. Still, according to some, the term *pradyu* is not considered a bhāṣitapuṁska stem since in the masculine it ends in *o*, whereas in the neuter it ends in a short *u*. As such, it is not treated like a masculine stem before the vowel-initial sup-affixes from the third triplet onward. Others have a different view. According to them, it is actually *pradyo* which is changed into *pradyu*. So, by the metarule *ekadeśavikṛtam*... (Abhyankar, 37), *pradyu* is not considered different from *pradyo*. This comes to mean that the same word *pradyo* is now *pradyu* in the neuter. So, it can optionally be treated as masculine.[1] When this word is treated like a masculine, it will be restored to the form *pradyo* and will be declined like *go* before the vowel-initial affixes starting with the singular affix of the third triplet.

Here comes to an end the declension of the neuter nominal stems ending in *o*. Now begins the declension of the neuter stems ending in *ai*.

लघु० – प्ररि । प्ररिणी । एकदेशविकृतमनन्यवत् – प्रराभ्याम् । प्ररीणाम् । *prari, prariṇī. ekadeśavikṛtam ananyavat - prarābhyām. prarīṇām.*

Eluc. : The word *prarai* 'one who possesses great wealth' is a bahuvrīhi compound analysed as : *prakṛṣṭā rāḥ* (*dhanaṁ*) *yasya tat* = *prari* (*kulam*) 'a very rich (family)'. In this case also, the last vowel *ai* is replaced by *i* according to *eca igghrasvādeśe* (249). By invoking the paribhāṣā *ekadeśavikṛtam*... (Abhyankar, 37), the stem *prari* will be treated as *prarai*. As a consequence, the rule *rāyo*... (214) applies, when a consonant-initial sup-affix follows. The neuter stem *prari* will be declined as follows :

	Singular	Dual	Plural
prathamā	*prari*	*prariṇī*	*prarīṇi*
dvitīyā	*prari*	*prariṇī*	*prarīṇi*
tṛtīyā	*prariṇā*	*prarābhyām*	*prarābhiḥ*
caturthī	*prariṇe*	*prarābhyām*	*prarābhyaḥ*
pañcamī	*prariṇaḥ*	*prarābhyām*	*prarābhyaḥ*

1. *pradyośabda odantaḥ puṁsi. pradyuśabdas tu udanto napuṁsake. tathā ca puṁsi pradyośabdasya bhāṣitapuṁskatve 'pi napuṁsake pradyuśabdasya tadapekṣayā bhinnatvena bhāṣitapuṁskatvābhāvān na puṁvattvam ityarthaḥ. kecittu puṁsi yaḥ pradyośabda odantaḥ sa evedānīṁ napuṁsakaḥ tasya hrasvāntatve 'pi ekadeśavikṛtasyānanyatvāt. ataḥ puṁvattvavikalpo-'styevetyāhuḥ.* BM, I, pp. 338-9.

ṣaṣṭhī	*prariṇaḥ*	*prariṇoḥ*	*prarīṇām*
saptamī	*prariṇi*	*prariṇoḥ*	*prarāsu*
sambodhana	*he prari!*, *he prare!*	*he prariṇī!*	*he prarīṇi!*

According to the optional puṁvadbhāva view, with the vowel-initial affixes *ā* (*ṭā*), *e* (*ṅe*), *as* (*ṅasi, ṅas*), *os*, *ām* and *i* (*ṅi*), we respectively have the alternative forms : *prarāyā, prarāye, prarāyaḥ* 2, *prarāyoḥ* 2, *prarāyām* and *prarāyi*.

Here comes to an end the declension of the neuter stems ending in *ai*. Now begins the declension of the neuter stems ending in *au*.

The word *sunau* 'one that possesses good boats' is changed into *sunu* in the neuter by virtue of *eca igghrasvādeśe* (249). This will be declined like *madhu*.

	Singular	Dual	Plural
prathamā	*sunu*	*sununī*	*sunūni*
dvitīyā	*sunu*	*sununī*	*sunūni*
tṛtīyā	*sununā*	*sunubhyām*	*sunubhiḥ*
caturthī	*sunune*	*sunubhyām*	*sunubhyaḥ*
pañcamī	*sununaḥ*	*sunubhyām*	*sunubhyaḥ*
ṣaṣṭhī	*sununaḥ*	*sununoḥ*	*sunūnām*
saptamī	*sununi*	*sununoḥ*	*sunuṣu*
sambodhana	*he suno!*, *he sunu!*	*he sununī!*	*he sunūni!*

Here also, we have the alternative forms before the vowel-initial affixes : *sunāvā, sunāve, sunāvaḥ* 2, *sunāvoḥ* 2, *sunāvām, sunāvi* according to the optional puṁvadbhāva view.

लघु० – इत्यजन्तनपुंसकलिङ्गाः । *ityajantanapuṁsakaliṅgāḥ.*

Trans. : Thus ends the chapter on the neuter nominal stems that end in a vowel.

हलन्तपुंलिङ्गप्रकरणम्

Masculine Words Ending in a Consonant

In this chapter we will discuss the declensional process of the nominal stems in the masculine gender that end in a consonant. The stems are given here in the alphabetical order which is followed in the repertory of phonemes (*pratyāhārasūtras*). The first consonantal phoneme in the pratyāhārasūtra is *h*. So, the first nominal stem that is taken up is *lih* 'one who licks', which ends in *h*. When we introduce the singular affix of the first triplet, we have the following grammatical situation : *lih* + *su*. In this situation, the following sūtra applies :

(250) **हो ढः । *ho ḍhaḥ*. 8. 2. 31**
लघु० – हस्य ढः स्याज् झलि पदान्ते च। लिट्, लिड्। लिहौ। लिहः। लिड्भ्याम्। लिट्त्सु, लिट्सु। *hasya ḍhaḥ syāj jhali padānte ca. liṭ, liḍ. lihau. lihaḥ. liḍbhyām. liṭtsu, liṭsu.*

Trans. : If the consonantal phoneme *h* is followed by *jhal*-pratyāhāra or if it occurs at the end of a pada, it is replaced by *ḍh*.

PP. *haḥ ḍhaḥ jhali padasya ante ca.*

Eluc. : The term *jhali* in the locative singular is carried over from *jhalo jhali* Pā. 8. 2. 26. The present sūtra occurs in the domain of the governing rule *padasya* Pā. 8. 1. 16. Hence *padasya* recurs here. The words *ante* and *ca* are carried over from *skoḥ saṁyogādyorante ca* Pā. 8. 2. 29. Thus the sūtra means : The phoneme *h*, followed by a consonant denoted by the abbreviatory term *jhal* or occurring at the end of a pada, is replaced by *ḍh*.

The stem *lih* is derived by introducing the affix *kvip* after the verbal root *lih* 'to lick' by *kvip ca* (799). The whole of *kvip* is elided (see supra p. 240). The word *lih* gets the prātipadika designation by *kṛttaddhita-samāsāśca* (116). In the illustration *lih* + *su*, the consonantal phoneme *h* is followed by apṛkta (one-consonantal affix) *s*. It is elided by *halṅyābbhyo dīrghāt sutisyapṛktaṁ hal* (178). The elided affix *su* is considered effective by *pratyayalope pratyayalakṣaṇam* (189). Hence *lih* is designated as *pada*. Since the phoneme *h* occurs at the end of a pada, it is replaced by *ḍh* by the present rule. Now the rule *jhalāṁ jaśo 'nte* (67) applies and *ḍha* is replaced by *ḍ*. According to the rule *vā 'vasāne* (145), *ḍ* is optionally replaced by *ṭ* and we have two forms *liṭ* and *liḍ* in the nominative singular.

With the sup-affixes *au, jas* (*as*), *am, auṭ* (*au*), *śas* (*as*) and *ṭā* (*ā*), we respectively have *lihau, lihaḥ, liham, lihau, lihaḥ* and *lihā*. Similarly in the case of other vowel-initial affixes, there is no specific grammatical operation worth mentioning but when we add *bhyām*, the primary derivative *lih* in the illustration *lih + bhyām* gets pada-designation by *svādiṣvasarvanāmasthāne* (163). The consonant *h* occurs at the end of a pada. In this grammatical situation the rule *ho ḍhaḥ* (250) applies changing *h* into *ḍh*. Then by *jhalāṁ jaśo 'nte* (67), we have *liḍbhyām*. Similarly, with *bhis* and *bhyas* we respectively have *liḍbhiḥ* and *liḍbhyaḥ*. With the plural affix of the seventh triplet, we have *lih + sup* --> *lih + su*. In this illustration, the pada-final consonant *h* is replaced by *ḍh* according to the rule *ho ḍhaḥ* (250). Then by *jhalāṁ*.... (67), *ḍh* is replaced by *ḍ* and we have *liḍ + su*. At this stage, the rule *khari ca* Pā. 8. 4. 55 becomes applicable but, being asiddha with respect to *ḍaḥ si dhuṭ* Pā. 8. 3. 29, it allows the latter to apply. The augment *dhuṭ* is optionally inserted and thus we obtain two forms : 1. *liḍ + dhuṭ su* --> *liḍ + dh su* and 2. *liḍ + su*. According to the rule *ṣṭunā ṣṭuḥ* Pā. 8. 4. 41, the consonant *dh* in form 1 should have been replaced by *ḍh* and the consonant *s*, by *ṣ* but both these replacements are negated by *na padāntāṭṭoranām* (65). Then again by *khari ca* (74), the phoneme *dh* in the first form is replaced by *t* which is a *khar*-consonant. As a consequence, the preceding *ḍ* is replaced by *ṭ* and we obtain the form *liṭtsu*. In the second form the phoneme *ḍ* is replaced by *ṭ* and we have the form *liṭsu*. The substituted cerebal phoneme *ṭ* is not replaced by its second class consonant *ṭh* since it is understood not to have taken place with respect to the vārttika *cayo dvitīyāḥ śari pauṣkarasāderiti vācyam* (vtk 14), which is read at the sūtra Pā. 8. 4. 48 (cf. *ḍhasya jaśtvena ḍaḥ, tasya khari ca iti cartvena ṭaḥ, tasyāsiddhatvāt cayo dvitīyāḥ iti pakṣe ṭho na*, TB, I, p. 340).

The declension of the nominal stem *lih* is given below :

	Singular	Dual	Plural
prathamā	*liṭ, liḍ*	*lihau*	*lihaḥ*
dvitīyā	*liham*	*lihau*	*lihaḥ*
tṛtīyā	*lihā*	*liḍbhyām*	*liḍbhiḥ*
caturthī	*lihe*	*liḍbhyām*	*liḍbhyaḥ*

pañcamī	*lihaḥ*	*liḍbhyām*	*liḍbhyaḥ*
ṣaṣṭhī	*lihaḥ*	*lihoḥ*	*lihām*
saptamī	*lihi*	*lihoḥ*	*liṭtsu, liṭsu*
sambodhana	*he liṭ, ḍ!*	*he lihau!*	*he lihaḥ!*

The words *madhulih* 'a bee', *puṣpalih* 'a bee', *bhūruh* 'a tree', *saroruh* 'a lotus', etc. will be declined in a similar way.

The primary derivative *duh* is derived by introducing the affix *kvip* after the verbal root *duh* 'to milk' by *kvip ca* (799). The whole of *kvip* is elided. The word *duh* gets the prātipadika designation by *kṛttaddhita...* (116) and then sup-affixes are introduced after it to make it a pada. When we add the singular affix *su* of the first triplet after it, the rule *halṅyābbhyo dīrghāt sutisyapṛktaṁ hal* (178) applies and the affix *s*(*u*) is elided. Although at this stage, the rule *ho ḍhaḥ* (250) becomes available for application but in this case the following sūtra blocks it :

(251) दादेर्धातोर्घः । ***dāderdhātorghaḥ*. 8. 2. 32**

लघु० – झलि पदान्ते चोपदेशे दादेर्धातोर्हस्य घः स्यात्। *jhali padānte copadeśe dāder dhātor hasya ghaḥ syāt.*

Trans. : The consonant *h* of a verbal-root, which begins with *d* in the original enunciation, is replaced by *gh* when it is followed by a phoneme denoted by the abbreviatory term *jhal* or when it occurs at the end of a pada.

PP. *dādeḥ dhātoḥ ghaḥ jhali padasya ca ante.*

Eluc. : The term *haḥ* is carried over from *ho ḍhaḥ* Pā. 8. 2. 31. The word *jhali* comes from *jhalo jhali* Pā. 8. 2. 26. The sūtra occurs in the domain of the governing rule *padasya* Pā. 8. 1. 16. Hence the term *padasya* recurs here. The word *ante* and the particle *ca* are carried over from *skoḥ saṁyogādyorante ca* Pā. 8. 2. 29. The word *dādeḥ* is a bahuvrīhi, which is analysed as *daḥ ādau yasya sa dādiḥ, tasya* = *dādeḥ*. Thus the meaning of the sūtra is as follows : When followed by a phoneme denoted by *jhal*-pratyāhāra or occurring at the end of a pada, the consonant *h* of a verbal root, which begins with *d* in the original enunciation, is replaced by *gh*. In the sūtra, the term *ghaḥ* has the vowel *a* for the sake of pronunciation. Although the present sūtra is subsequent and thus asiddha, it is still considered to be an exception to the rule *ho ḍhaḥ* Pā. 8. 2. 31 since Pāṇini has enunciated this (cf. *apavādo vacanaprāmāṇyāt*, Mbh on the present sūtra). Had this sūtra been treated as not to have performed any grammatical function with respect to *ho ḍhaḥ* , then finding no scope, it would have been rendered purposeless.

Varadarāja has followed Bhaṭṭoji Dīkṣita in giving the term *upadeśe* in the vṛtti. Bhaṭṭoji explains the significance of this term in the Siddhāntakaumudī on this sūtra. According to him, the term has been used to do away with the defects of underpervasion (*avyāpti*) in *adhok* and overpervasion (*ativyāpti*) in *dāmaliṭ*, which otherwise would have been incurred. Let us first take up the case where the defect of overpervasion could be incurred. In this context the illustration given by Bhaṭṭoji is *dāmaliṭ*, which is derived by introducing the affix *kvip* after *dāmalihya*. The term *dāmalihya* is a derived verb. The word *dāma* means 'a rope' which is tied around the neck of animals. The animal that licks the rope is called *dāmaliṭ* (*dāma lihyatīti*). The derivative process is as follows : The affix *kyac* is added after the word *dāmalih* in the sense *dāmaliham ātmana icchati* by the rule *supa ātmanaḥ kyac* (717) and we have *dāmalihya*, which is also a verbal root by *sanādyantā dhātavaḥ* (467). Its singular laṭ-lakāra verbal form is *dāmalihyati*. We can now have the affix *kvip* introduced after it in the sense of agent by *kvip ca* (799). In *dāmalihya* + *kvip*, the whole of the affix *kvip* is elided. Then by treating the elided *kvip* as grammatically effective, the phonemes *y* and *a* are elided respectively by *yasya halaḥ* (712) and *ato lopaḥ* (469). Thus we obtain the primary derivative *dāmalih* which, at the same time, does not lose its status as a verbal root by *kvibantā dhātutvaṁ na jahati* (Paribhāṣāsaṅgraha, p. 43). As a consequence, the defect of overpervasion is incurred since the verbal root begins with the phoneme *d* and the present rule would become applicable in the absence of the expression *upadeśe dādeḥ* in the vṛtti. The defect is called overpervasion since the rule applies in the context of those words which should not have been covered by it. This defect is done away with by the inclusion of *upadeśe* in the vṛtti since the derived verbal root *dāmalih* does not exist in the original enunciation, that is, in the dhātupāṭha.

The defect of underpervasion is exemplified by the verbal form *adhok* which is the second or third person singular laṅ-lakāra form of the verbal root *duh*. The verbal root begins with *d* in the dhātupāṭha, that is, in the original enunciation. When it is augmented by *aṭ*, the augment *aṭ* becomes a part of the verbal root itself according to the paribhāṣā *yadāgamās tadguṇībhūtās tadgrahaṇena gṛhyante* (Abhyankar, 11). The grammatical situation that emerges is as follows : *aṭ duh* + *tip* or *sip* --> *a duh* + 0 --> *adoh.* {the augment *aṭ* is inserted at the beginning of the verbal root *duh* by *luṅlaṅlṛṅkṣvaḍudāttaḥ* (422). The single consonant-affix (*apṛkta*) *t* or *s* of *tip* or *sip* respectively is elided by *halṅyābbhyo...* (178). Then by *pratyayalope*... (190) the elided affix is treated as effective. Hence the penultimate short vowel *u* of *duh* is replaced by guṇa vowel *o* by *pugantalaghū*... (450) and we have the present form of the illustration}. In *adoh*, the verbal root now has the vowel *a* at the beginning. Had the expression *upadeśe dādeḥ* not been included in the vṛtti, the consonant *h* would not have been replaced by *gh*, which is required for the desired form *adhok*. This is the defect of underpervasion since the desired form would remain uncovered by the present rule. This defect of underpervasion has been removed by using the term *upadeśe* since the verbal root begins with *d* in the original enunciation (*upadeśa*). Hence the consonant *h* is replaced by *gh*. At this stage, the following sūtra applies :

(252) एकाचो बशो भष् झषन्तस्य स्ध्वोः । *ekāco baśo bhaṣ jhaṣantasya sdhvoḥ*. 8. 2. 37

लघु० – धात्ववयवस्यैकाचो झषन्तस्य बशो भष् से ध्वे पदान्ते च । धुक्, धुग् । दुहौ । दुहः । धुग्भ्याम् । धुक्षु । *dhātvavayavasyaikāco jhaṣantasya baśo bhaṣ se dhve padānte ca. dhuk, dhug. duhau. duhaḥ. dhugbhyām. dhukṣu.*

Trans. : A phoneme denoted by the abbreviatory term *baś*, which forms part of a monosyllabic part of a verbal root ending in a phoneme denoted by the abbreviatory term *jhaṣ*, is replaced by a phoneme denoted by the abbreviatory term *bhaṣ*, before *s* and *dhva* and also at the end of a pada.

PP. *dhātoḥ ekācaḥ baśaḥ bhaṣ jhaṣantasya sdhvoḥ jhali padasya ante ca.*

Eluc. : This sūtra occurs in the governing domain of the rule *padasya* Pā. 8. 1. 16. So the term *padasya* recurs in the present sūtra. The term *dhātoḥ* is carried over from *dāderdhātorghaḥ* Pā. 8. 2. 32. The words *ante* and *ca* are carried over from *skoḥ saṁyogādyorante ca* Pā. 8. 2. 29. The word *jhaṣantasya* is a qualifier and is in syntactic coordination with *ekācaḥ*. However, there is no such coordination between *dhātoḥ* and *ekācaḥ jhaṣantasya*. The translation, given above, follows this syntactic arrangement. If this is not done, then the *bhaṣ*-replacement will not take place in respect of the verbal roots which are not monosyllabic. Take, for example, *gardabha* + *ṇic* (where *ṇic* is introduced by *tatkaroti tadācaṣṭe*, gaṇasūtra in *curādi* class). From this we derive the verbal root *gardabhi* {*sanādyantā dhātavaḥ* (467)}. From the derived verbal root *gardabhi* the primary derivative *gardabh* is obtained by introducing the affix *kvip* after it in the sense of agent. The affix *kvip* is wholly deleted since the phonemes *k*, *i* and *p* are *its* and the phoneme *v* is elided by *verapṛktasya* (302). The vowel *i* is elided by *ṇeraniṭi* (528). The word *gardhabh* enjoys the status of a verbal root {*kvibantā dhātutvaṁ na jahati* (Paribhāṣā-saṅgraha, p. 43)} but it is not monosyllabic. Consequently, the phoneme *d* could not be replaced by *dh* in the nominative singular. Nonetheless, the desirable form is *gardhap*. This is the reason why no syntactic coordination has been accepted between *dhātoḥ* and *ekācaḥ jhaṣantasya*. Therefore, in deference to the incidence of the usage of the cultured, a part-and-whole relationship is intended to exist between *dhātoḥ* and *ekācaḥ jhaṣantasya*. Then the meaning arrived at would be : The *baś*-phoneme of a *jhaṣanta* monosyllabic part of a verbal root is replaced by a *bhaṣ*-phoneme. By resorting to this interpretation, we do not encounter any problem in obtaining the desired form *gardhap* since according to this interpretation, the monosyllabic part *dabh* of the derived verbal root *gardabh* ends in a *jhaṣ*-consonant, which occurs at the end of a pada and as such the phoneme *d* of *dabh* is replaced by *dh*, a denotatum of *bhaṣ*-prayāhāra and we obtain the desired form *gardhap* after the nominative singular affix *su* has been introduced after it.

The sum and substance of the present sūtra is as follows : If a *jhaṣanta* monosyllabic part of a verbal root contains a *baś*-phoneme in it and if this part is followed by *s* or *dhva* or if there is a padānta-instance, then the *baś*-phoneme of such a monosyllabic verbal part is replaced by a denotatum of *bhaṣ*-pratyāhāra. The abbreviatory term *jhaṣ* denotes *jh, bh, gh, ḍh* and *dh*. The denotata of *baś* are *b, g, ḍ* and *d* and those of *bhaṣ* are *bh, gh, ḍh* and *dh*. The phonemes *b, g* and *d* of the monosyllabic part of a verbal root are respectively replaced by *bh, gh* and *dh* in accordance with similarity based on the place of articulation. The rule *yathā...* (23) does not apply here since no equivalence exists between the substitutes and the substituenda as there is no instance in which *ḍ* is found to be at the beginning of such a monosyllabic part of a verbal root (Cf. Kāśikā on the present sūtra and also KP, VI, p. 402).

The illustration *dugh* is monosyllabic and can also be treated as its own part by vyapadeśivadbhāva as Patañjali has suggested in *vyapadeśivadekasmin*, a revised form of the sūtra *ādyantavad ekasmin* (277). So, the phoneme *d* (*baś*) of *dugh* is replaced by *dh* (*bhaṣ*) since it ends in *jhaṣ* which happens to be pada-final after the elision of the one-consonant affix *s*(*u*) has taken place by *halṅyābbhyo...* (178). Thus we have *dhugh*. At this stage, the final phoneme *gh* is replaced by *g* by *jhalāṁ jaśo 'nte* (67). We have two optional forms *dhuk* and *dhug* by *vā 'vasāne* (145).

With the introduction of the affixes *bhis, bhyām* and *bhyas* after *duh*, the pada-final *h* is replaced by *gh* by *dāderdhātorghaḥ* (251). Then by the present sūtra, the consonant *d* is replaced by *dh* since *gh* is pada-final. It is replaced with *g* by *jhalām...* (67) and we obtain the forms : *dhugbhiḥ, dhugbhyām* and *dhugbhyaḥ*.

In *duh* + *sup*, the pada-final *h* is substituted by *gh* by *dāderdhātorghaḥ* (251). According to the present sūtra, the *baś*-phoneme *d* is replaced with *dh* and the pada-final *gh* is replaced with *g* by *jhalām...* (67). Then by *khari ca* (74) the phoneme *g* is substituted by *k* and we obtain the form *dhukṣu* after the dental *s* of the affix *sup* has been substituted by the cerebral *ṣ* by *ādeśapratyayayoḥ* (149).

The declension of the primary derivative *duh*, which is a prātipadika by *kṛttaddhitasamāsāśca* (116), is given below :

	Singular	Dual	Plural
prathamā	*dhuk*, g	*duhau*	*duhaḥ*
dvitīyā	*duham*	*duhau*	*duhaḥ*
tṛtīyā	*duhā*	*dhugbhyām*	*dhugbhiḥ*
caturthī	*duhe*	*dhugbhyām*	*dhugbhyaḥ*
pañcamī	*duhaḥ*	*dhugbhyām*	*dhugbhyaḥ*
ṣaṣṭhī	*duhaḥ*	*duhoḥ*	*duhām*
saptamī	*duhi*	*duhoḥ*	*dhukṣu*
sambodhana	*he dhuk, g!*	*he duhau!*	*he duhaḥ!*

(253) वा द्रुह-मुह-ष्णुह-ष्णिहाम् । *vā druha-muha-ṣṇuha-ṣṇihām.* 8. 2. 33

लघु० - ध्रुक्, ध्रुग्, ध्रुट्, ध्रुड् । द्रुहौ । द्रुहः । ध्रुग्भ्याम्, ध्रुड्भ्याम् । ध्रुक्षु, ध्रुट्त्सु, ध्रुट्सु । एवम् - मुक्, मुग्, मुट्, मुड् इत्यादि । *dhruk, dhrug, dhruṭ, dhruḍ. druhau, druhaḥ. dhrugbhyām, dhruḍbhyām. dhrukṣu, dhruṭtsu, dhruṭsu. evam -- muk, mug, muṭ, muḍ ityādi.*

Trans. : The phoneme *h* of the verbal roots *druh, muh, ṣṇuh* and *ṣṇih* is optionally replaced by *gh,* when it is followed by a *jhal*-phoneme or occurs at the end of a pada.

PP. *druha-muha-ṣṇuha-ṣṇihām vā haḥ ghaḥ jhali padasya ante ca.*

Eluc. : The terms *haḥ* and *ghaḥ* are respectively carried over from *ho ḍhaḥ* Pā. 8. 2. 31 and *dāderdhātorghaḥ* Pā. 8. 2. 32. The word *padasya* is made to recur in the present sūtra since it occurs in the domain of the governing rule *padasya* Pā. 8. 1. 16. The term *jhali* is carried from *jhalo jhali* Pā. 8. 2. 26 and the expression *ante ca* comes from *skoḥ saṁyogādyor ante ca* Pā. 8. 2. 29. The word *druha-muha-ṣṇuha-ṣṇihām* is an itaretaradvandva which is analysed as follows : *druhaś ca muhaś ca ṣṇuhaś ca ṣṇiṭ ca druha-muha-ṣṇuha-ṣṇihaḥ, teṣām = druha-muha-ṣṇuha-ṣṇihām*. The vowel *a* in the first three members of the dvandva compound is for the sake of articulation. Thus the meaning of the sūtra is : The phoneme *h* of the verbal roots *druh, muh, ṣṇuh* and *ṣṇih* is optionally substituted by *gh* when it is followed by a phoneme denoted by the abbreviatory term *jhal* or when it occurs at the end of a pada.

The word *druh* 'one who bears hatred or one who desires to injure' is derived from the verbal root *druh* 'to bear hatred, to seek to hurt' by introducing the affix *kvip* after it in the sense of agent. This verbal root begins with the phoneme *d*, so the replacement of *h* by *gh* was obligatory by *dāderdhātorghaḥ* (251). When it is made optional, the option is called prāptavibhāṣā. The other three verbal roots do not begin with the phoneme *d* and as such the substitution of the phoneme *h* of these verbal roots by *gh* was not available. In this case, the replacement, which was not available, is made optional by the present rule. It is aprāptavibhāṣā. Consequently, the option enjoined by the present sūtra is a prāptāprāpta-vibhāṣā.

When we add the singular affix of the first triplet, we have *druh* + s (*su*). The one-consonant (*apṛkta*) affix s is elided by *halṅyābbhyo*... (178). Then the pada-final *h* is substituted optionally by *gh* by the present rule. In the absence of *gh*-replacement, the rule *ho ḍhaḥ* (250) applies and the pada-final *h* is substituted by *ḍh*. In both the cases, the rule *ekāco baśo bhaṣ*... (252) enjoins the phoneme *d* of *druh* to be replaced by *dh* (*bhaṣ*). Thus we have *dhrugh* and *dhruḍh*. At this stage, the phoneme *gh* of *dhrugh* is replaced by *g* and the phoneme *ḍh* of *dhruḍh* by *ḍ* by the sūtra *jhalāṁ*... (67). Now the rule *vā 'vasāne* (145) applies. The phonemes *g* and *ḍ* are replaced by *k* and *ṭ* optionally. Thus we have four forms of *druh* in the nominative singular : *dhruk, dhrug, dhruṭ* and *dhruḍ*.

With the dual affix *bhyām* introduced after *druh*, we have *druh* + *bhyām*. In this situation, the pada-final phoneme *h* is replaced optionally by *gh*. In the alternative case, the phoneme *h* is replaced by *ḍh*. In both the cases, the initial *d* is substituted by *dh* by *ekāco baśo bhaṣ*... (252). Then the rule *jhalāṁ*... (67) applies. We obtain two forms *dhrugbhyām* and *dhruḍbhyām*. The same grammatical procedure will take place when we add the affixes *bhis* and *bhyas*.

In the locative plural, we add the affix *sup* after *druh*. Here also the pada-final *ha* is optionally replaced by *gh* which is a denotatum of the abbreviatory term *jhaṣ*. By *ekāco baśo bhaṣ*... (252), the phoneme *d* of *drugh* is replaced by *dh*. The sūtra *jhalāṁ*... (67) prescribes the substitution of *gh* by *g*. Since the rule *khari ca* (74) is asiddha with respect to *ādeśapratyayayoḥ* (149), the latter applies and the dental *s* of the affix *sup* is replaced by *ṣ*. Then by *khari ca* (74), the phoneme *g* is replaced by *k* and we obtain the form *dhrukṣu*. In the absence of *gh*-substitution, the phoneme *h* is replaced by *ḍh* according to *ho ḍhaḥ* (250). Then again by *ekāco baśo bhaṣ...* (252), the phoneme *d* of *druḍh* is replaced by *dh*. The final phoneme *ḍh* is substituted by *ḍ* by *jhalāṁ...* (67). By *ḍaḥ si dhuṭ* (86), the augment *dhuṭ* is inserted optionally. The augment *dhuṭ* remains as *dh* after the elision of the anubandhas. *khari ca* (74) applies and the phoneme *dh* is replaced by *t*. We have two forms : 1. *dhruṭtsu* (with *dhuṭ* augment) and 2. *dhruṭsu* (in the absence of *dhuṭ*). Thus in the locative plural, we have three forms : 1. *dhrukṣu* 2. *dhruṭtsu* 3. *dhruṭsu*. The prāptavibhāṣā is exemplified by the declensional process of *druh*. The complete declension of the nominal stem *druh* is as follows :

	Singular	Dual	Plural
prathamā	*dhruk, g* *dhruṭ, ḍ*	*druhau*	*druhaḥ*
dvitīyā	*druham*	*druhau*	*druhaḥ*
tṛtīyā	*druhā*	*dhrugbhyām* *dhruḍhyām*	*dhrugbhiḥ* *dhruḍbhiḥ*
caturthī	*druhe*	*dhrugbhyām* *dhruḍbhyām*	*dhrugbhyaḥ* *dhruḍbhyaḥ*
pañcamī	*druhaḥ*	*dhrugbhyām* *dhruḍbhyām*	*dhrugbhyaḥ* *dhruḍbhyaḥ*
ṣaṣṭhī	*druhaḥ*	*druhoḥ*	*druhām*
saptamī	*druhi*	*druhoḥ*	*dhrukṣu, dhruṭtsu* *dhruṭsu*
sambodhana	*he dhruk, g!* *dhruṭ, ḍ!*	*he druhau!*	*he druhaḥ!*

The word *muh* is derived in the same way as the primary derivative *druh*. The declension of *muh* is like that of the nominal stem *druh* except that the rule *ekāco baśo bhaṣ jhaṣantasya sdhvoḥ* (252) does not apply here. This is an illustration of aprāptavibhāṣā. Thus the nominal stem *muh* will be declined as follows :

	Singular	Dual	Plural
prathamā	*muk, g* *muṭ, ḍ*	*muhau*	*muhaḥ*
dvitīyā	*muham*	*muhau*	*muhaḥ*
tṛtīyā	*muhā*	*mugbhyām* *muḍhyām*	*mugbhiḥ* *muḍbhiḥ*
caturthī	*muhe*	*mugbhyām* *muḍbhyām*	*mugbhyaḥ* *muḍbhyaḥ*
pañcamī	*muhaḥ*	*mugbhyām* *muḍbhyām*	*mugbhyaḥ* *muḍbhyaḥ*
ṣaṣṭhī	*muhaḥ*	*muhoḥ*	*muhām*
saptamī	*muhi*	*muhoḥ*	*mukṣu, muṭtsu* *muṭsu*
sambodhana	*he muk, g!* *muṭ, ḍ!*	*he muhau!*	*he muhaḥ!*

(254) धात्वादेः षः सः । *dhātvādeḥ ṣaḥ saḥ*. 6. 1. 64

लघु० – स्नुक्, स्नुग्, स्नुट्, स्नुड् । एवं स्निक्, स्निग्, स्निट्, स्निड् । विश्ववाट्, विश्ववाड् । विश्ववाहौ विश्ववाहः । विश्ववाहम्, विश्ववाहौ । *snuk, snug, snuṭ, snuḍ. evaṁ snik, snig, sniṭ, sniḍ. viśvavāṭ, viśvavāḍ. viśvavāhau, viśvavāhaḥ. viśvavāham, viśvavāhau.*

Trans. : The initial cerebral *ṣ* of a verbal root is replaced by the dental *s*.

PP. *dhātvādeḥ ṣaḥ saḥ*.

Eluc. : The sūtra is a complete sentence. The word *dhātvādeḥ* is a ṣaṣṭhītatpuruṣa. Its analysis is : *dhātor ādiḥ dhātvādiḥ, tasya = dhātvādeḥ*. The term *saḥ* is in the nominative singular and the vowel *a* in it is for the sake of pronunciation. The term *ṣaḥ* is a genitive singular of *ṣ*. Thus the sūtra means : The initial cerebral *ṣ* of a verbal root is substituted by *s*. Accordingly, the cerebral *ṣ* of the verbal roots *ṣṇuh* and *ṣṇih* is replaced by the dental *s*. When this is done, the cerebral *ṇ* is restored to *n* according to the principle : *nimittāpāye naimittikasyāpyapāyaḥ* (PS, p. 306) 'When the cause has been destroyed, the modification brought about by it is also destroyed'. The 'destruction' in this context means 'restoration to its original form'. Here the dental *n* was replaced by *ṇ* because of the cerebral *ṣ* by *raṣābhyāṁ no ṇaḥ samānapade* (266). The phoneme *ṣ*, which is the cause of cerebralization, has been replaced by the dental *s* in accordance with the present sūtra. So, the cerebral *ṇ* is replaced by *n*; in other words the cerebral *ṇ* has been restored to its original form, that is the dental nasal stop *n*.

The affix *kvip* in the sense of agent is added after the verbal roots *snuh* and *snih* and we obtain the primary derivatives *snuh* 'one who vomits' and *snih* 'one who feels affection for' after the whole of the affix *kvip* has been elided. Except the grammatical operation prescribed by *ekāco baśo bhaṣ...* (252), the rest of the declension of *snuh* and *snih* will be like that of *druh*.

	Singular	Dual	Plural
prathamā	*snuk, g* *snuṭ, ḍ*	*snuhau*	*snuhaḥ*
dvitīyā	*snuham*	*snuhau*	*snuhaḥ*
tṛtīyā	*snuhā*	*snugbhyām* *snuḍhyām*	*snugbhiḥ* *snuḍbhiḥ*
caturthī	*snuhe*	*snugbhyām* *snuḍbhyām*	*snugbhyaḥ* *snuḍbhyaḥ*
pañcamī	*snuhaḥ*	*snugbhyām* *snuḍbhyām*	*snugbhyaḥ* *snuḍbhyaḥ*
ṣaṣṭhī	*snuhaḥ*	*snuhoḥ*	*snuhām*
saptamī	*snuhi*	*snuhoḥ*	*snukṣu, snuṭtsu* *snuṭsu*
sambodhana	*he snuk, g!* *he snuṭ, ḍ!*	*he snuhau!*	*he snuhaḥ!*

The declension of the nominal stem *snih* will be exactly like that of *snuh*.

The word *viśvavāh* (the sustainer of the world) is an upapada-samāsa which is analysed as follows : *viśvaṁ vahatīti viśvavāṭ --> viśva am vahati --> viśva ṅas vah ṇvi* (the affix *ṇvi* is added by *vahaśca* Pā. 3. 2. 64 and the second case-affix *am* is changed to *ṅas* by *kartṛkarmaṇoḥ kṛti*) --> *viśvavāh* {the penultimate *a* of *vah* is lengthened by *ata upadhāyāḥ* (454) after the whole of *ṇvi* has been elided.The phonemes *ṇ* and *i* are *its* respectively by *cuṭū* (128) and *upadeśe 'janunāsika it* (28). Hence they are elided by *tasya lopaḥ* (3). The semi-vowel *v* is deleted by *verapṛktasya* (302). Nevertheless, it is still treated as effective by *pratyayalope...* (189)}. Thus the word *viśvavāh* is obtained and is designated as *prātipadika* by *kṛttaddhitasamāsāśca* (116). The word *viśvavāh* is declined like *lih* before the sarvanāmasthāna sup-affixes. When it is assigned the bha-designation by *yaci bham* (164), some specific grammatical functions take place. These are explained in the next three sūtras :

(255) इग्यणः सम्प्रसारणम् । *igyaṇaḥ samprasāraṇam.* 1. 1. 45

लघु० – यणः स्थाने प्रयुज्यमानो य इक्, स सम्प्रसारणसंज्ञः स्यात् । *yaṇaḥ sthāne prayujyamāno ya ik, sa samprasāraṇasaṁjñaḥ syāt.*

Trans. : Let *ik* which comes in the place of *yaṇ* be designated as *samprasāraṇa*.

PP. *ik yaṇaḥ samprasāraṇam.*

Eluc. : Pāṇini assigns the samprasāraṇa designation to the phonemes denoted by the abbreviatory term *ik* when they are substituted in place of the phonemes denoted by the abbreviatory term *yaṇ*. This means that the denotata of *ik* cannot be designated as *samprasāraṇa* unless they have replaced the phonemes denoted by *yaṇ*. Pāṇini uses this term in two ways : 1. The use of the term *samprasāraṇa* in respect of the sūtras which enjoin it as a vidheya, i.e. when it is yet to take place. The sūtras *vacisvapi.....* (546), *vāha ūṭh* (256), etc. illustrate the use of the term *samprasāraṇa* in this sense. 2. The use of the term *samprasāraṇa* for the sake of other grammatical operations which are dependent on it. The sūtras *samprasāraṇācca* (257), *halaḥ* (816), *samprasāraṇasya* Pā. 6. 3. 139, etc. prescribe the grammatical operations which take place on the basis of samprasāraṇa itself. Hence they exemplify the second way of using this term.

When the term *samprasāraṇa* is used for the sake of other grammatical operations dependent on it, this means that the process of replacing the semi-vowel by the denotata of *ik*-pratyahāra has already taken place. It is this reason that the usage of the term *samprasāraṇa* in the sūtras relating to the second sense is called repetition (anuvāda). When the term *samprasāraṇa* is used in the first sense, this means that it is yet to be brought about (*bhāvī*). We are confronted with a problem here. When we assign a designation, the elements to which a designation is being assigned should already be present. In the first sense, the phonemes denoted by the abbreviatory term *ik* are first to replace the phonemes denoted by *yaṇ* through the process known as *samprasāraṇa*. Then they are available to be designated. This problem is known as reciprocal dependence (*anyo 'nyāśraya*). The Kāśikā resolves this problem by interpreting the term *samprasāraṇa* as a name for both *bhūta* and *bhāvī* *ik*-replacements in place of *yaṇ*. The third vārttika in the Mahābhāṣya on this sūtra *vibhaktiviśeṣanirdeśas tu jñāpaka ubhayasaṁjñātvasya* offers another explanation : The use of different nominal endings after the word *samprasāraṇa* in the sūtras of both kinds shows that the vowels that replace the semi-vowels and the process of replacing the semi-vowels by the *ik*-vowels may both be termed *samprasāraṇa*.[1]

The application of the samprasāraṇa-designation in the first sense is illustrated in the following sūtra :

(256) वाह ऊठ् । *vāha ūṭh*. 6. 4. 132

लघु० – भस्य वाहः संप्रसारणम् ऊठ् । *bhasya vāhaḥ samprasāraṇam ūṭh.*

Trans. : The bha-designated *vāh* is to be replaced by the samprasāraṇa *ūṭh*.

PP. *bhasya vāhaḥ samprasāraṇam ūṭh* (*aṅgasya*).

Eluc. : The sūtra *bhasya* Pā. 6. 4. 129 is a governing rule. The present rule occurs in its domain. So, the term *bhasya* recurs here. The term *samprasāraṇam* is carried over from the sūtra *vasoḥ samprasāraṇam* Pā. 6. 4. 31. Thus the meaning of the sūtra is : The term *vāh* which has been designated as *bha* is to be replaced by the samprasāraṇa substitute element *ūṭh*. According to the preceding rule, this will replace the semi-vowel *v* of *vāh*.

In *viśvavāh* + (*ś*)*as*, the last member *vāh* of the upapada-samāsa is *bha* by *yaci bham* (164). Therefore, by virtue of the present sūtra, the semi-vowel *v* is replaced by *ūṭh*. The phoneme *ṭh* is *it* by *halantyam* (1). It is elided by *tasya lopaḥ* (3). Thus we arrive at the following stage of the declensional form : *viśva ū āh* + *as*. At this stage, the following sūtra ensues, which illustrates the second way of using the term *samprasāraṇa*:

(257) सम्प्रसारणाच्च । *samprasāraṇācca*. 6. 1. 108

लघु० – सम्प्रसारणादचि पूर्वरूपमेकादेशः । वृद्धिः । विश्वौहः, इत्यादि । *samprasāraṇād aci pūrvarūpam ekādeśaḥ. vṛddhiḥ. viśvauhaḥ ityādi.*

---

1. *yattāvad āha samprasāraṇāt paraḥ pūrvo bhavati samprasāraṇasya dīrgho bhavatīti. tena jñāyate varṇasya bhavatīti. yadapyāha ṣyaṅaḥ samprasāraṇam iti. tena jñāyate vākyasya sañjñā bhavatīti.* Mbh on Pā. 1. 1. 45 vtk 3.

Trans. : If a vowel follows a samprasāraṇa element, then a single substitute in the form of the preceding vowel comes in place of both the vowels (preceding as well as the following).

PP. *samprasāraṇāt ca aci pūrvaparayoḥ ekaḥ pūrvaḥ (saṁhitāyām).*

Eluc. : The sūtra *ekaḥ pūrvaparayoḥ* Pā. 6. 1. 84 is the governing rule. All the words of this rule recur in the present sūtra. The term *aci* and *pūrvaḥ* are respectively carried over from *iko yaṇaci* Pā. 6. 1. 77 and *ami pūrvaḥ* Pā. 6. 1. 107. In this way the sūtra means : When a vowel (*ac*) follows a samprasāraṇa phoneme, a single substitute in the form of the preceding vowel replaces both the preceding and the following vowels. In *viśva ū āh + as*, the vowel *ā* follows the samprasāraṇa *ū*. Therefore, according to the present rule, the vowel *ū* will replace both itself and *ā* and we have *viśva ū h + as*. In this grammatical situation, the rule *etyedhatyūṭhsu* (34) applies and a single vṛddhi replacement *au* comes in place of both *ū* and the *a* of *viśva* and we obtain the form *viśvauhaḥ* after rutva and visarga. The same grammatical operation will be followed in all the instances of bha-designation (i.e. when a vowel-initial affix follows) with respect to the inflectional forms of the word *viśvavāh*. When a sup-affix, which begins with a consonant is introduced, the sūtras *ho ḍhaḥ* (250) and *jhalāṁ jaśo 'nte* (67) apply and we have the pada-final phoneme *ḍ* in an inflected form of *viśvavāh*, e.g. *viśvavāḍbhiḥ*. With the optional insertion of the augment *dhuṭ* by *ḍaḥ si dhuṭ* (86) before the nominal ending *sup*, we have two forms in the locative plural. The complete declension of the nominal stem *viśvavāh* is as follows :

	Singular	Dual	Plural
prathamā	*viśvavāṭ, ḍ*	*viśvavāhau*	*viśvavāhaḥ*
dvitīyā	*viśvavāham*	*viśvavāhau*	*viśvauhaḥ*
tṛtīyā	*viśvauhā*	*viśvavāḍbhyām*	*viśvavāḍbhiḥ*
caturthī	*viśvauhe*	*viśvavāḍbhyām*	*viśvavāḍbhyaḥ*
pañcamī	*viśvauhaḥ*	*viśvavāḍbhyām*	*viśvavāḍbhyaḥ*
ṣaṣṭhī	*viśvauhaḥ*	*viśvauhoḥ*	*viśvauhām*
saptamī	*viśvauhi*	*viśvauhoḥ*	*viśvavāṭtsu* *viśvavāṭsu*
sambodhana	*he viśvavāṭ, ḍ!*	*he viśvavāhau!*	*he viśvavāhaḥ!*

The word *anaḍuh* 'an ox' is derived as follows : *anaḥ śakaṭaṁ vahatīti anaḍvān*. Bhoja's Sarasvatīkaṇṭhābharaṇa[1] explains this word by formulating the rule *anasi vaheḥ kvip ḍaścānasaḥ* (2. 1. 349) by which the affix *kvip* is added after the verbal root *vah* and the phoneme *s* is replaced by *ḍ* when the word *anas* is an upapada. The whole of the affix *kvip* is elided as in the system of Pāṇini. In the same way, the affix is still effective even though it has been elided. Then the sūtras *vacisvapi...* (546) and *samprasāraṇācca* (257) apply. By the former, the semi-vowel *v* is replaced by *u* in *anaḍ vah* + 0 --> *anaḍ u ah*. According to the latter, both the vowels *u* and *a* are replaced by *u* and we have the stem *anaḍuh*.

To decline the stem *anaḍuh*, we introduce the singular nominal ending after it : *anaḍuh* + *su*. At this stage, the following sūtra applies :

(258) चतुरनडुहोरामुदात्तः । *caturanaḍuhorāmudāttaḥ*. 7. 1. 98

लघु० – अनयोराम् स्यात् सर्वनामस्थाने परे । *anayor ām syāt sarvanāmasthāne pare.*

Trans. : The augment *ām* marked with udātta is introduced to the words *catur* and *anaḍuh* when a sarvanāmasthāna affix follows.

PP. *caturanaḍuhoḥ aṅgayoḥ ām udāttaḥ sarvanāmasthāne.*

Eluc. : The term *sarvanāmasthāne* comes from *ito 'tsarvanāmasthāne* Pā. 7. 1. 86. The present sūtra occurs in the domain of the governing rule *aṅgasya* Pā. 6. 4. 1. So, the term *aṅgasya* recurs here and is changed into dual by vacanavipariṇāma. Then the meaning of the sūtra is : When a sarvanāmasthāna affix follows, the augment *ām* marked with udātta is inserted after the last vowel of the pre-affixal bases *catur* and *anaḍuh* with the help of the rule *midaco 'ntyātparaḥ* (239) since the phoneme *m* of the augment *ām* is *it*. In *anaḍuh* + *s*, the affix *su* is a sarvanāmasthāna by *suḍana...* (162). Therefore, the augment *ām* is inserted after the vowel *u* in *anaḍu ām h* + *s*. The consonant *m*, being *it*, is elided. Thus we have *anaḍu ā h* + *s*. By the application of the rule *iko yaṇaci* (15), we arrive at the declensional stage *anaḍvāh* + *s*. At this point, the following sūtra presents itself :

(259) सावनडुहः । *sāvanaḍuhaḥ*. 7. 1. 82

लघु० – अस्य नुम् स्यात् सौ परे । अनड्वान् । *asya num syāt sau pare. anaḍvān.*

Trans. : If the singular affix *su* follows, then the augment *num* is inserted in *anaḍuh* (after the last vowel of *anaḍuh* in *anaḍvāh* + *s*).

1. Bhaimī, p. 358.

PP. *sāu aṅgasya anaḍuhaḥ num.*

Eluc. : The term *num* is carried over from *ācchīnadyornum* Pā. 7. 1. 80. The term *aṅgasya* recurs here from the governing rule Pā. 6. 4. 1. The meaning of the sūtra is : If the singular affix *su* follows, then the augment *num* becomes a part of the pre-affixal base *anaḍuh*. In other words, the augment *num* is inserted after the last vowel of *anaḍuh*. Both the augments *ām* and *num* are *mit*. Consequently, both of them are to be inserted after the last vowel of *anaḍuh*. The augment *ām* is available before the sarvanāmasthāna affixes. It may be construed as a general augment, whereas the augment *num* becomes available only before *su*. So, it is *su*-specific. Hence it may be construed as an exception. As a consequence, only *num* is to be inserted before *su* and not *ām*. However, if the augment *num*, being considered as an exception to *ām*, blocks the latter, then the form of *anaḍuh* in the nominative singular would be *anaḍun* and not *anaḍvān*. The process to arrive at the form *anaḍun* is as follows : *anaḍuh + su --> anaḍu num h + su --> anaḍu n h + s* {*sāvanaḍuhaḥ*(209)}--> *anaḍu n h* {*halṅyābbhyo...* (178)} --> *anaḍun* {*saṁyogāntasya...* (20)}. This is the pūrvapakṣa view as presented by Vāsudeva Dikṣita, the author of the Bālamanoramā.[1] Bhaṭṭoji Dīkṣita[2] resolves this problem by carrying over the term *āt* from *ācchīnadyornum* Pā. 7. 1. 80 into the present sūtra. Then the meaning of the sūtra will be as follows : The augment *num* will be inserted after the vowel *a* in *anaḍuh*. This kind of situation becomes available only when the augment *ām* has already been inserted before *su*, which is a sarvanāmasthāna affix. After the insertion of *ām*, we have *anaḍvāh* + *s*. Now we have the vowel *ā*, after which the augment *num* can be inserted : *anaḍvā num h + s* --> *anaḍvā n h + s* --> *anaḍvān h* {the affix s is elided by *halṅyābbhyo*....(178)} --> *anaḍvān* {the consonant *h* is elided by *saṁyogāntasya lopaḥ* (Pā. 8. 2. 23)}. The elision of *h* is treated as not to have taken place with respect to *na lopaḥ*... Pā. 8. 2. 7. Therefore, the elision of the consonant *n* will not take place by the latter and thus we obtain the form *anaḍvān*.

In the vocative, the singular affix *su* is introduced after the stem *anaḍuh* and we have *anaḍuh* + *s* (*su*). Here the augment *ām* is available by *caturanaḍuhorām*... (258) but the following sūtra , which is an exception to it, applies and the augment *am* is inserted :

---

1. *nanu āmnumau etau mittvād antyād acaḥ ukārāt parau prāptau tatra caturanaḍuhoḥ ityām sarvanāmasthānanimittakaḥ sāmānyavihitaḥ sāvanaḍuhaḥ iti num tu sarvanāmasthānaviśeṣe sau vihitatvād viśeṣavihitaḥ sa ca niravakāśatvāt sāmānyavihitam āmaṁ bādheta. sor anyatrāmvidheś caritārthatvāt. tathā ca anaḍun iti syāt anaḍvān iti na syāt.* BM, I, p. 346.

2. *āt ityadhikārād avarṇāt paro 'yaṁ num. ato viśeṣavihitenāpi numā ām na bādhyate. āmā ca num na bādhyate.* SK, I, pp. 346-7.

(260) अम् सम्बुद्धौ । *am sambuddhau.* 7. 1. 99

लघु० – हे अनड्वन् ! अनड्वाहौ । अनड्वाहः । अनडुहः । अनडुहा । *he anaḍvan! anaḍvāhau, anaḍvāhaḥ, anaḍuhaḥ, anaḍuhā.*

Trans. : If the vocative singular affix *su* follows, then the augment *am* is introduced to *catur* and *anaḍuh.*

PP. *caturanaḍuhoḥ* (*aṅgayoḥ*) *am sambuddhau.*

Eluc. : The word *caturanaḍuhoḥ* is carried over from *caturanaḍuhor āmudāttaḥ* Pā. 7. 1. 98. The meaning of the sūtra will be : If the vocative singular affix *su* follows, then the augment *am* (marked with udātta) is inserted after the last vowel of the stems *catur* and *anaḍuh.* This sūtra is an exception to the sūtra *caturanaḍuhorāmudāttaḥ* (258). When this rule has performed its grammatical function of inserting *am,* the sūtra *sāvanaḍuhaḥ* (259) applies and we arrive at the declensional stage of the form (*he anaḍvan!*) in the following way : *he anaḍuh + s --> he anaḍu a*(*m*) *h + s* {*am sambuddhau* (260)} --> *he anaḍ vah + s* {*iko...* (15)} --> *he anaḍ va n*(*um*) *h + s* {*sāvanaḍuhaḥ* (259)} --> *he anaḍ va n h + s --> he anaḍ va n h* {*halṅyābbhyo dīrghāt...* (178)} --> *he anaḍvan!* {*saṁyogā...* (20)}.

Before the plural affix *śas* of the second triplet, the augment *ām* is not inserted since it is not sarvanāmasthāna. Simply by adding *as* (*śas*) to *anaḍuh,* we obtain the form *anaḍuhaḥ* after rutva and visarga.

With the dual affix of the third triplet, we have *anaḍuh + bhyām.* This affix begins with a consonant. The rule *svādiṣva...* (163) applies and *anaḍuh* gets the pada-designation. At this stage, the following sūtra becomes applicable :

(261) वसुस्रंसुध्वंस्वनडुहां दः । *vasusraṁsudhvaṁsvanaḍuhāṁ daḥ.* 8. 2. 72

लघु० – सान्तवस्वन्तस्य स्रंसादेश्च दः स्यात् पदान्ते । अनडुद्भ्याम् इत्यादि । सान्तेति किम् ? विद्वान् । पदान्तेति किम् ? स्रस्तम् , ध्वस्तम् । *sāntavasvantasya sraṁsādeś ca daḥ syāt padānte. anaḍudbhyām ityādi. sānteti kim ? vidvān. padānteti kim ? srastam, dhvastam.*

Trans. : At the end of a pada, let the phoneme *d* be the substitute of that which, formed by the affix *vasu,* ends in *s,* and of *sraṁsu,* etc. The illustrations are *anaḍudbhyām,* etc. Why has it been said 'ending in the phoneme *s*'? Witness *vidvān.* Why has it been said 'at the end of a pada'? Witness *srastam, dhvastam.*

PP. *vasusraṁsudhvaṁsvanaḍuhāṁ padānām saḥ daḥ.*

Eluc. : The sūtra *padasya* Pā. 8. 1. 16 is a governing rule. Hence the term *padasya* recurs in the present sūtra but it is changed to the genitive plural by the process of vacanavipariṇāma. The term *sa* is a part of *ṣasajuṣo ruḥ* Pā. 8. 2. 66 and is carried over into this sūtra. The genitive nominal ending after it is understood as having been elided (*sasajuṣo ruḥ ityataḥ sa iti luptaṣaṣṭhīkam anuvṛttam,* BM, I, p. 349). The term *saḥ* qualifies the word *vasu* only since *sraṁsu* and *dhvaṁsu* invariably end in s and the word *anaḍuh* never ends in s (*tena ca vasur viśeṣyate. tadantavidhi. sāntatvaṁ sraṁsudhvaṁsor na viśeṣaṇam avyabhicārāt. nāpyanaḍuhaḥ asambhavāt,* BM, I, p. 349). The word *vasu* is an affix by sthānivadbhāva since it replaces the primary affix *śatṛ* after the verbal root *vid* 'to know' by the sūtra *videḥ śaturvasuḥ* (830). Since this is an affix, tadantavidhi comes into force and accordingly the affix *vasu* means the word which ends in it, according to the paribhāṣā *pratyayagrahaṇe... tadantasya grahaṇam* (Abhyankar, 23). The compound word *vasusraṁsudhvaṁsvanaḍuhām* is an itaretaradvandva. Its analysis is as follows : *vasuś ca sraṁsuś ca dhvaṁsuś ca anaḍvān ca vasusraṁsudhvaṁsvanaḍuhaḥ, teṣām = vasusraṁsudhvaṁsvanaḍuhām.* The word which ends in the affix *vasu* and which ends in s and the words *sraṁsu, dhvaṁsu* and *anaḍuh* are to be replaced by the phoneme *d.* According to the paribhāṣā sūtra *alo 'ntyasya* (21), the phoneme *d* will replace the pada-final phonemes of these stems.

In *anaḍuh + bhyām,* the pada-final *h* {*svādiṣva...* (163)} is replaced by the phoneme *d* and we obtain the form *anaḍudbhyām.* In the locative plural the phoneme *d* is replaced by the phoneme *t* in accordance with the rule *khari ca* (74). The declension of the word *anaḍuh* is given below:

	Singular	Dual	Plural
prathamā	*anaḍvān*	*anaḍvāhau*	*anaḍvāhaḥ*
dvitīyā	*anaḍvāham*	*anaḍvāhau*	*anaḍuhaḥ*
tṛtīyā	*anaḍuhā*	*anaḍudbhyām*	*anaḍudbhiḥ*
caturthī	*anaḍuhe*	*anaḍudbhyām*	*anaḍudbhyaḥ*
pañcamī	*anaḍuhaḥ*	*anaḍudbhyām*	*anaḍudbhyaḥ*
ṣaṣṭhī	*anaḍuhaḥ*	*anaḍuhoḥ*	*anaḍuhām*
saptamī	*anaḍuhi*	*anaḍuhoḥ*	*anaḍutsu*
sambodhana	*he anaḍvan!*	*he anaḍvāhau!*	*he anaḍvāhaḥ!*

Why has it been said 'the word which ends in the affix *vasu* should also end in the phoneme *s*'? The reason is that if it had not been said, there would have been a defect of overpervasion. The word *vidvas* ends in *vasu* but in the nominative singular the form of this stem is *vidvān*, which would have resulted in the replacement of *n* by *d* in the absence of the above-mentioned qualification. With the phoneme s qualifying a word ending in the affix *vasu*, the defect of overpervasion is dispensed with.

The second counter-question is with respect to the pada-final replacement. Had it not been said, then the s of *sras* and *dhvas* would have been replaced by the phoneme *d* even in *srasta* and *dhvasta*. The phoneme s is not replaced by *d* since the phoneme s is not pada-final before the affix *ta*.

The word *turāsāh* 'Indra' is derived in the Siddhāntakaumudī in the following way : *loke tu sāhayateḥ kvip. anyeṣāmapi dṛśyate iti pūrvapadasya dīrghaḥ* (SK, I, p. 350). In spoken language, the affix *kvip* is introduced after the causal verbal root *sāhi* (with *ṇic*). Thus we have *tura* + *sāhi* + *kvip* --> *tura* + *sāh* + *kvip*. The affix *ṇic* is elided by *ṇeraniṭi* (528) --> *turā* + *sāh* + *kvip*. The vowel *a* of the upapada *tura* is lengthened by *anyeṣāmapi dṛśyate* Pā. 6. 3. 137. *turā* + *sāh* + 0. The affix *kvip* is elided completely as usual and we obtain the upapada compound word *turāsāh*. After the introduction of the nominative singular affix *su*, we have *turāsāh* + *s*(*u*). The one-consonant affix s is elided by *halṅyābbhyo...* (178). The rule *ho ḍhaḥ* (250) applies and the phoneme *h* is replaced by *ḍh*. We have *turāsāḍh*. The phoneme *ḍh* is substituted by *ḍ* in accordance with the rule *jhalāṁ...* (67). We arrive at the form *turāsāḍ*. At this stage, the following sūtra ensues :

(262) सहेः साडः सः । *saheḥ sāḍaḥ saḥ*. 8. 3. 56

लघु० – साड्-रूपस्य सहेः सस्य मूर्धन्यादेशः स्यात्। तुराषाट्, तुराषाड्। तुरासाहौ। तुरासाहः। तुराषाड्भ्याम् इत्यादि। *sāḍ-rūpasya saheḥ sasya mūrdhanyādeśaḥ syāt. turāṣāṭ, turāṣāḍ. turāsāhau. turāsāhaḥ. turāṣāḍbhyām ityādi.*

Trans. : Let the phoneme *s* of the word *sāḍ* derived from the verbal stem *sah* be replaced by the cerebral sibilant.

PP. *saheḥ sāḍaḥ saḥ mūrdhanyaḥ* (*saṁhitāyām*).

Eluc. : The term *mūrdhanyaḥ* is carried over from *apadāntasya mūrdhanyaḥ* Pā. 8. 3. 55. Then the sūtra yields the following meaning : The dental s of the word segment *sāḍ* which is derived from the verbal root *sah* as explained above is replaced by a cerebral phoneme. In this case, the substitute will be the cerebral sibilant ṣ since, being a voiceless spirant and having the same internal effort (*īṣadvivṛta*), it is most similar to the substituendum s. The form *sāḍ* is brought about in the pada-final state. It comes to mean that the cerebral replacement takes place when there is a pada-final state (cf. *sūtre sāḍa iti kṛtajaśtvanirdeśasya padāntopa-lakṣaṇatvād iti bhāvaḥ*, BM, I, p. 349). In *turāsāḍ*, the dental s of *sāḍ* is replaced by the phoneme ṣ and we have *turāṣāḍ*. By *vā 'vasāne* (145), we have two optional forms : *turāṣāṭ, turāṣāḍ*. The complete declension of the stem *turāsāh* is as follows :

	Singular	Dual	Plural
prathamā	*turāṣāṭ,* *turāṣāḍ*	*turāsāhau*	*turāsāhaḥ*
dvitīyā	*turāsāham*	*turāsāhau*	*turāsāhaḥ*
tṛtīyā	*turāsāhā*	*turāṣāḍbhyām*	*turāṣāḍbhiḥ*
caturthī	*turāsāhe*	*turāṣāḍbhyām*	*turāṣāḍbhyaḥ*
pañcamī	*turāsāhaḥ*	*turāṣāḍbhyām*	*turāṣāḍbhyaḥ*
ṣaṣṭhī	*turāsāhaḥ*	*turāsāhoḥ*	*turāsāhām*
saptamī	*turāsāhi*	*turāsāhoḥ*	*turāṣāṭtsu* *turāṣāṭsu*
sambodhana	*he turāṣāṭ, ḍ!*	*he turāsāhau!*	*he turāsāhaḥ!*

Here comes to an end the declension of the stems, which end in the phoneme *h*.

Now begins the declension of the words that end in the phoneme *v* since the words, which end in the phoneme *y*, are rare.

The word *sudiv* 'a bright day', 'a person who has a good heaven to his credit', etc is a bahuvrīhi compound. It is in the masculine, although the word *div* is always feminine. After the introduction of the nominative singular affix *su*, we have *sudiv* + *su*. In this grammatical situation, the rule *halṅyābbhyo...* (178) becomes available for application but the following sūtra also presents itself :

(263) दिव औत्। *diva aut*. 7. 1. 84

लघु० – दिव् इति प्रातिपदिकस्य औत् स्यात् सौ। सुद्यौः। सुदिवौ। *div iti prātipadikasya aut syāt sau. sudyauḥ, sudivau.*

Trans. : Let the substitute *aut* replace the nominal stem *div*, when the affix *su* follows.

PP. *divaḥ aut sau* (*aṅgasya*).

Eluc. : The term *sau* is carried over from *sāvanaḍuhaḥ* Pā. 7. 1. 82. The phoneme *t* in *aut* is for the sake of articulation. Had this been not so, then the substitute *aut* would have replaced the whole of *div* according to *anekālśit sarvasya* (45). The meaning of the sūtra is : The nominal stem *div* is replaced by *au*(*t*) when the affix *su* follows. This sūtra occurs in the domain of the governing rule *aṅgasya* Pā. 6. 4. 1. Hence by virtue of the paribhāṣā *padāṅgādhikāre tasya ca tadantasya ca* (Abhyankar, 29), the sūtra applies to both the nominal stem *div* and the word which ends in *div*. With the help of the metarule *alo 'ntyasya* (21), the substitute *au* will replace the last phoneme of *div*, that is, the phoneme *v* is replaced by *au* and we have *sudi au + su*. At this stage, the rule *iko yaṇaci* (15) applies and we obtain *sudyaus* and then *sudyauḥ* after rutva and visarga.

In the illustration *sudiv + s*, both *halṅyābbhyo...* (178) and *diva aut* (263) are simultaneously available for application but the latter, being nitya, blocks the former and applies. This can be explained in the following way : If we first apply the present rule, then the semi-vowel *v* is replaced by *au* and as a consequence, the condition for the elision of the affix *s*(*u*) ceases to be available. On the other hand, if we apply *halṅyābbhyo...* (178), the rule *diva aut* (263) remains available for application, for the elided affix is still effective by virtue of the sūtra *pratyayalope pratyalakṣaṇam* (189). Thus the sūtra *diva aut* is nitya in comparison with *halṅyābbhyo dīrghāt...* (178) {cf. *kṛtākṛtaprasaṅgī yo vidhiḥ sa nityaḥ* (Paribhāṣāsaṅgrahaḥ, p. 42)}. Being nitya, it applies and we obtain the form *sudyauḥ*.

When the dual affix *bhyām* of the third triplet is introduced, the word *sudiv* gets the pada-designation by *svādiṣva...* (163) and the following sūtra presents itself for application :

(264) दिव उत् । *diva ut*. **6. 1. 131**

लघु॰ – दिवोऽन्तादेश उकारः स्यात् पदान्ते । सुद्युभ्याम् इत्यादि । *divo 'ntādeśa ukāraḥ syāt padānte. sudyubhyām ityādi.*

Trans. : At the end of a pada, let the substitute vowel short *u* replace the final phoneme of *div*.

PP. *diva ut padānte.*

Eluc. : The word *padāntāt* comes from *eṅaḥ padāntādati* Pā. 6. 1. 109 and is changed into *padānte* by the process of vibhaktivipariṇāma. The word *antādeśa* which is given in the vṛtti is obtained by virtue of the paribhāṣā sūtra *alo 'ntyasya* (21) as pointed out by Vāsudeva Dīkṣita (*antādeśa iti alo 'ntyasūtralabhyam,* BM, I, p. 351). Thus the meaning of the sūtra is as follows : The pada-final *v* of the nominal stem *div* is replaced by a short vowel *u*. In *sudiv + bhyām,* the stem *sudiv* is a pada by *svādiṣva...* (163). Therefore, the final *v* is replaced by *u* and we obtain the form *sudyubhyām* after the application of the rule *iko...* (15). The similar grammatical operation is performed before *bhis, bhyas* and *sup* also. The complete declension of the word *sudiv* is as follows :

	Singular	Dual	Plural
prathamā	*sudyauḥ*	*sudivau*	*sudivaḥ*
dvitīyā	*sudivam*	*sudivau*	*sudivaḥ*
tṛtīyā	*sudivā*	*sudyubhyām*	*sudyubhiḥ*
caturthī	*sudive*	*sudyubhyām*	*sudyubhyaḥ*
pañcamī	*sudivaḥ*	*sudyubhyām*	*sudyubhyaḥ*
ṣaṣṭhī	*sudivaḥ*	*sudivoḥ*	*sudivām*
saptamī	*sudivi*	*sudivoḥ*	*sudyuṣu*
sambodhana	*he sudyauḥ!*	*he sudivau!*	*he sudivaḥ!*

One point is to be taken note of in this context. There is a difference of opinion on the taparakaraṇa in *ut*. Vāsudeva Dīkṣita says that the taparakaraṇa in *ut* is to imply the metarule that the vowel *u* denotes its homogeneous counterparts even when it is enjoined (*utas taparatvaṁ tu bhāvyamāna ukāraḥ savarṇagrāhakaḥ iti jñāpanārtham iti titsvaritam iti sūtre bhāṣye spaṣṭam,* BM, I, p. 351). On the other hand Jñānendra Sarasvatī[1] says the taparakaraṇa in *ut* is to block the lengthening of *u*, which is available by the sūtra *halaḥ* (816). This is based on what Bhaṭṭoji says in the Prauḍhamanoramā but the use of the verbal form *āhuḥ* by Jñānendra Sarasvatī indicates that he does not agree with Bhaṭṭoji's explanation since the purpose mentioned in the Prauḍhamanoramā for

1. *taparakaraṇam iha dyubhyām ityādāvukārasya samprasāraṇatvād halaḥ iti dīrghe prāpte tannivāraṇāyetyāhuḥ,* TB, I, p. 351. Also compare, *ukārasya samprasāraṇatvāt halaḥ iti dīrghaḥ prāpta ut iti taparatvasāmarthyān na bhavati,* Prauḍhamanoramā, pp. 581-2.

the justification of taparakaraṇa in *ut* is not in consonance with that which the author of the Mahābhāṣya says on *titsvaritam* Pā. 6. 1. 185. In other words the view of Vāsudeva Dīkṣita finds endorsement in the Mahābhāṣya.

Here comes to an end the declension of masculine words that end in the semi-vowel *v*.

Varadarāja now takes up the word *catur*, which ends in repha and is always used in the plural. After the introduction of the plural affix of the first triplet, we have *catur* + *jas*. The affix *jas* is a sarvanāmasthāna affix. Therefore the sūtra *caturanaḍuhorāmudāttaḥ* (258) applies and the augment *ām* is inserted after the last vowel *u* in *catur* : *catu ā(m) r + as (jas)* --> *catu ā r + as*. By *iko yaṇaci* (15), the vowel *u* is replaced by *v* and we obtain the form *catvāraḥ* after the application of *sasajuṣo...* (104) and *kharava...* (93). Since the plural affix *śas* of the second triplet is not sarvanāmasthāna, the augment *ām* is not available. We will simply add *as* (*śas*) after the stem *catur* + *as* and obtain the form *caturaḥ* after rutva and visarga. Similarly, we will have *caturbhiḥ*, *caturbhyaḥ*, etc. In the genitive plural when we introduce the affix *ām*, we have *catur* + *ām*. At this stage, the following sūtra becomes applicable :

(265) षट्चतुर्भ्यश्च । *ṣaṭcaturbhyaśca*. 7. 1. 55
लघु० – एभ्य आमो नुडागमः । *ebhya āmo nuḍāgamaḥ*.

Trans. : The augment *nuṭ* is inserted at the head of the affix *ām* which is introduced after stems designated as *ṣaṭ* and after the word *catur*.

PP. *ṣaṭcaturbhyaḥ ca āmaḥ nuṭ* (*aṅgasya*).

Eluc. : The words *āmi* and *nuṭ* are respectively carried over from *āmi sarvanāmnaḥ suṭ* Pā. 7. 1. 52 and *hrasvanadyāpo nuṭ* Pā. 7. 1. 54. The word *āmi* has been changed to have the genitive nominal ending in consonance with the paribhāṣā *ubhayanirdeśe pañcamīnirdeśo balīyān* (Abhyankar, 70). Thus the sūtra with the help of *ādyantau...* (84) means: If the affix *ām* is introduced after stems designated as *ṣaṭ* and after the word *catur*, then the augment *nuṭ* becomes an initial part of affix *ām*. The technical term *ṣaṭ* will be discussed at *ṣṇāntā ṣaṭ* (296). In the present context, the word *catur* is relevant. Now we have *catur* + *ām* --> *catur* + *nuṭ ām* --> *catur* + *nām*. At this stage, the following sūtra applies :

(266) **रषाभ्यां नो णः समानपदे । *raṣābhyāṁ no ṇaḥ samānapade.* 8. 4. 1**
लघु० - अचो रहाभ्यां द्वे (60) **। चतुर्ण्णाम् , चतुर्णाम् ।** *aco rahābhyāṁ dve* (60) *caturṇṇām, caturṇām.*

Trans. : Let the phoneme *ṇ* replace the dental *n* coming after *r* or *ṣ* in the same pada.

PP. *raṣābhyāṁ naḥ ṇaḥ samānapade (saṁhitāyām).*
Eluc. : The sūtra is almost complete in itself. The compound word *raṣābhyām* is an itaretaradvandva which is analysed as : *raś ca ṣaś ca raṣau tābhyām = raṣābhyām.* The word *samānapade* is a karmadhāraya compound. Its analysis is : *samānaṁ cādaḥ padam samānapadam tasmin = samānapade.* The vowel *a* in repha, *ṣa* and *ṇa* is to facilitate their articulation. The meaning of the sūtra is : If the dental *n* follows either repha or *ṣ* in the same pada, then it is replaced by the cerebral *ṇ*. In the illustration *catur + nām,* the dental *n* is substituted by the cerebral *ṇ* and we obtain the form *caturṇām.* At this stage, the rule *aco rahābhyāṁ dve* (60) applies and the cerebral *ṇ* is optionally reduplicated. As a consequence, we have the alternative form *caturṇṇām* also.
When we introduce the plural affix *sup* of the seventh triplet after *catur,* we have *catur + sup --> catur + su.* In this grammatical situation, the rule *kharava...* (93) becomes available for application, but the following restrictive rule presents itself for application :

(267) **रोः सुपि । *roḥ supi.* 8. 3. 16**
लघु० - रोरेव विसर्गः सुपि । षत्वम् । षस्य द्वित्वे प्राप्ते - *ror eva visargaḥ supi. ṣatvam. ṣasya dvitve prāpte -*

Trans. : When the sup-affix *sup* (locative plural) follows let the visarga replace *ru* (only).

PP. *roḥ supi visarjanīyaḥ (saṁhitāyām).*
Eluc. : The word *visarjanīyaḥ* is carried over from *kharavasānayor visarjanīyaḥ* Pā. 8. 3. 15. The term *supi* is the locative singular form of the plural affix *sup* of the seventh triplet. Thus the meaning of the sūtra will be as follows : When the plural affix *sup* of the locative follows, only the repha of *ru* is replaced by visarjanīya. The visarga-replacement in place of the repha of *ru* is already available by *kharava...* (93). Still Pāṇini has enunciated this sūtra. If the grammatical operation, which is already

available, is enunciated again, then it is meant for the sake of restriction (*siddhe sati niyamārthaḥ*). Before *sup*, only the repha of *ru* is replaced by visarga, not any other repha. In the illustration *catur + su*, the phoneme *r* is not of *ru*. Hence it will not be replaced by visarga and we have *caturṣu* after the dental *s* of *su* has been replaced by *ṣ* according to *ādeśapratyayayoḥ* (149). At this stage, the rule *aco rahābhyām...* (60) prescribes optional reduplication of the cerebral ṣ but the following sūtra debars it.

(268) शरोऽचि । *śaro 'āci*. 8. 4. 49
लघु० – अचि परे शरो न द्वे स्तः । चतुर्षु । *aci pare śaro na dve staḥ. caturṣu.*

Trans. : When an element denoted by *ac* follows, an element denoted by *śar* is not reduplicated.

PP. *aci śaraḥ dve na* (*saṁhitāyām*).

Eluc. : The words *dve* and *na* are respectively carried over from *aco rahābhyāṁ dve* Pā. 8. 4. 46 and *nādinyākrośe putrasya* Pā. 8. 4. 48. Then the meaning of the sūtra will be as follows : Before *ac* (a vowel), a consonant denoted by the abbreviatory term *śar* is not reduplicated. In the illustration *caturṣu*, the phoneme *ṣ* is followed by *u*. Hence it does not undergo reduplication. Thus we obtain the form *caturṣu*. The declension of the stem *catur* is as follows :

	Plural		Plural
prathamā	*catvāraḥ*	pañcamī	*caturbhyaḥ*
dvitīyā	*caturaḥ*	ṣaṣṭhī	*caturṇām, caturṇṇām*
tṛtīyā	*caturbhiḥ*	saptamī	*caturṣu*
caturthī	*caturbhyaḥ*	sambodhana	No form

Here comes to an end the declension of the stems that end in repha.

The next word is *praśām*, which is derived from the verbal stem (*pra*) *śamu* 'to be quiet, to come to an end' after the primary affix *kvip* has been added to it. The penultimate vowel of *śam* is lengthened according to *anunāsikasya kvijhaloḥ...* (724) and we have the primary derivative *praśām*. When we introduce the singular affix of the first triplet, we have *praśām + su*. At this stage, after the elision of the affix *s*(*u*) by *halṅyābbhyo...* (178), the following sūtra beomes applicable :

(269) **मो नो धातोः । *mo no dhātoḥ*. 8. 2. 64**

लघु० – धातोर्मस्य नः पदान्ते । प्रशान् । प्रशान्भ्याम् इत्यादि । *dhātor masya naḥ padānte. praśān. praśānbhyām ityādi.*

Trans. : At the end of a pada, the phoneme *m* of a verbal root is replaced by *n*.

PP. *dhātoḥ maḥ naḥ padasya ante.*

Eluc. : The present sūtra occurs in the domain of the governing rule *padasya* Pā. 8. 1. 16. Hence the term *padasya* recurs in this sūtra also. The term *ante* comes from *skoḥ saṁyogādyor ante ca* Pā. 8. 2. 29 (cf. BM, I, p. 354) The word *maḥ* qualifies the word *dhātoḥ*. By tadantavidhi, it comes to mean 'a verbal root which ends in *m*'. Thus the sūtra means : If the phoneme *m* of a verbal root occurs at the end of a pada, then it is replaced by *n*. In the illustration *praśām + su*, the phoneme *m* is understood to be that of the verbal root *śam* according to the paribhāṣā *ekadeśavikṛtam ananyavat* (Abhyankar, 37). When the pada-final *m* has been replaced by *n* after the elision of the singular one-consonant affix *s* (*su*), we have the form *praśān* in the nominative singular. The rule *na lopaḥ prātipadikāntasya* Pā. 8. 2. 7 prescribing the elision of the phoneme *n* does not apply since the replacement of *m* by *n* is considered not to have taken place as the present sūtra is subsequent to the *nalopa*-sūtra. In the locative plural form, the rule *naśca* (87) optionally prescribes *dhuṭ* to be inserted at the head of the phoneme *n*. Then by *khari ca* (74), the phoneme *dh* is replaced by *t* and we obtain two forms : *praśāntsu* and *praśānsu*. The declension of the stem *praśām* is as follows :

	Singular	Dual	Plural
prathamā	*praśān*	*praśāmau*	*praśāmaḥ*
dvitīyā	*praśāmam*	*praśāmau*	*praśāmaḥ*
tṛtīyā	*praśāmā*	*praśānbhyām*	*praśānbhiḥ*
caturthī	*praśāme*	*praśānbhyām*	*praśānbhyaḥ*
pañcamī	*praśāmaḥ*	*praśānbhyām*	*praśānbhyaḥ*
ṣaṣṭhī	*praśāmaḥ*	*praśāmoḥ*	*praśāmām*
saptamī	*praśāmi*	*praśāmoḥ*	*praśāntsu, praśānsu*
sambodhana	*he praśān!*	*he praśāmau!*	*he praśāmaḥ!*

The pronominal stem *kim* is the next to be declined. It is used in all the genders. Since the chapter deals with the masculine stems, its declension in the masculine will be explained here. In the singular nominative form of *kim*, we have *kim* + *su*. When the elision of the nominative singular affix *su* becomes available by *halṅyābbhyo...* (178), the following sūtra applies :

(270) किमः कः। *kimaḥ kaḥ*. **7. 2. 103**
लघु० – किमः कः स्याद्विभक्तौ। कः। कौ। के इत्यादि। शेषं सर्ववत्। *kimaḥ kaḥ syād vibhaktau. kaḥ. kau. ke ityādi. śeṣaṁ sarvavat.*

Trans. : The pronominal stem *kim* is replaced by *ka* when a vibhakti (nominal ending) follows.

PP. *kimaḥ kaḥ vibhaktau* (*aṅgasya*).

Eluc. : The word *vibhaktau* is carried over from *aṣṭana ā vibhaktau* Pā. 7. 2. 84. The substitute *ka* contains more than one phoneme. Hence this will replace the whole of *kim* according to *anekālśit sarvasya* (45). Thus the meaning of the sūtra is as follows : The interrogative pronominal stem *kim* is wholly replaced by *ka* when a sup-affix follows. The replaced *ka* retains the sarvanāman-designation by sthānivadbhāva. As such, this will be declined like *sarva*.

According to *jasaḥ śī* (151), the plural affix *jas* of the first triplet is replaced by *śī*, which remains as *ī* after the elision of the anubandha *ś*. The affixes *ṅe, ṅasi* and *ṅi* are respectively replaced by *smai, smāt* and *smin* by *sarvanāmnaḥ smai* (152) *ṅasiṅyoḥ smātsminau* (153). Instead of *nuṭ*, the augment *suṭ* is inserted at the head of *ām* by *āmi sarvanāmnaḥ suṭ* (154). There is no vocative form of this word. In this way the pronominal stem *kim* will be declined as follows :

	Singular	Dual	Plural
prathamā	*kaḥ*	*kau*	*ke*
dvitīyā	*kam*	*kau*	*kān*
tṛtīyā	*kena*	*kābhyām*	*kaiḥ*
caturthī	*kasmai*	*kābhyām*	*kebhyaḥ*
pañcamī	*kasmāt, d*	*kābhyām*	*kebhyaḥ*
ṣaṣṭhī	*kasya*	*kayoḥ*	*keṣām*
saptamī	*kasmin*	*kayoḥ*	*keṣu*

The next word is *idam* 'this (near the speaker)', which is a member of the sarvādi group. Hence this is a sarvanāman. The declension of *idam* in the masculine is described below :

With the singular affix of the first triplet, we have *idam* + *su*. In this situation, the rule *tyadādīnāmaḥ* (192) prescribes the replacement of the final phoneme *m* by *a* but the following sūtra blocks it.

(271) इदमो मः । *idamo maḥ*. 7. 2. 108

लघु० - इदमो मस्य मः स्यात् सौ परे । त्यदाद्यत्वापवादः । *idamo masya maḥ syāt sau pare. tyadādyatvāpavādaḥ.*

Trans. : When the affix *su* follows, the phoneme *m* of *idam* is replaced by *m*. This sūtra is an exception to *tyadādīnāmaḥ* (192).

PP. *idamo maḥ sau (aṅgasya).*

Eluc. : The term *sau* is carried over from *tadoḥ saḥ sāvanantyayoḥ* Pā. 7. 2. 106. The vowel *a* in *ma* is for the sake of pronunciation. The meaning of the sūtra is : The word *idam* is to be replaced by the phoneme *m* when the singular affix *su* of the first triplet follows. With the help of *alo 'ntyasya* (21), only the last phoneme of *idam*, that is, *m* is to be replaced by *m*. The purpose of the sūtra is to block the grammatical operation prescribed by *tyadādīnāmaḥ* (192). With respect to the illustration *idam* + *s*, the following sūtra presents itself for application :

(272) इदोऽय् पुंसि । *ido 'y puṁsi*. 7. 2. 111

लघु० - इदम इदोऽय् स्यात् सौ पुंसि । सोर्लोपः । अयम् । त्यदाद्यत्वे - *idama ido 'y syāt sau puṁsi. sor lopaḥ. ayam. tyadādyatve —*

Trans. : Let the segment *id* of the word *idam* be replaced by *ay* in the masculine, when the affix *su* follows. The elision of *su* takes place.

PP. *idamaḥ idaḥ ay sau puṁsi (aṅgasya).*

Eluc. : The word *idamaḥ* and *sau* are carried over from *idamo maḥ* Pā. 7. 2. 106 and *yaḥ sau* Pā. 7. 2. 110 in the respective order. Then the meaning of the sūtra will be : When the affix *su* follows the word *idam* in the masculine, the whole segment *id* of *idam* is replaced by *ay* according to *anekāl śit sarvasya* (45). The genitive nominal ending in *idaḥ* is sthānaṣaṣṭhī, whereas in *idamaḥ* it is avayavaṣaṣṭhī (*ida iti sthānaṣaṣṭhī. idama ityanuvartate 'vayavaṣaṣṭhī eṣā*, BM, I, p. 355). In the illustration *idam* + s --> *ay am* + s, the one-consonant affix s is elided by *halṅyābbhyo...* (178) and we obtain the form *ayam*.

When we add the dual affix *au* of the first triplet after *idam*, we have *idam* + *au*. Here the rule *idamo...* (271) does not apply since the affix *su* does not follow. Instead the rule *tyadādīnāmaḥ* (192) becomes applicable and the phoneme *m* of *idam* is replaced by *a* and we have *ida a au*. At this stage, the following sūtra presents itself for application :

(273) अतो गुणे । *ato guṇe*. 6. 1. 97

लघु० – अपदान्तादतो गुणे पररूपमेकादेशः । *apadāntād ato guṇe pararūpam ekādeśaḥ*.

Trans. : If a guṇa (*a, e, o*) vowel follows a non-pada-final short *a*, then a single substitute in the form of the subsequent comes in place of both the preceding and the following vowels.

PP. *apadāntāt ataḥ guṇe pūrvaparayoḥ pararūpam ekaḥ* (*saṁhitāyām*).

Eluc. : The word *apadāntāt* is carried over from *usyapadāntāt* Pā. 6. 1. 96. All the constituent terms of the governing rule *ekaḥ pūrvaparayoḥ* Pā. 6. 1. 84 recur in the present rule also.The word *pararūpam* is carried over from *eṅi pararūpam* Pā. 6. 1. 94. The technical term *guṇa* has been defined by the rule *adeṅ guṇaḥ* (25) which designates *a, e* and *o* as *guṇa*. Thus the meaning of the sūtra is : If any one of the guṇa vowels follows a short *a*, which is not pada-final, then a single substitute in the form of the subsequent comes in place of both the preceding and following vowels. In the illustration *ida a au*, the short vowel *a* following the phoneme *d* is a non-pada-final short *a* and the following *a* is a guṇa vowel. By the present rule both the akāras are replaced by a single *a*, which is subsequent in the present case and we have *ida* + *au*. Now the following sūtra ensues :

(274) दश्च । *daśca*. 7. 2. 109

लघु० – इदमो दस्य मः स्याद् विभक्तौ । इमौ । इमे । त्यदादेः सम्बोधनं नास्तीत्युत्सर्गः । *idamo dasya maḥ syād vibhaktau. imau. ime. tyadādeḥ sambodhanaṁ nāstītyutsargaḥ*.

Trans. : The *d* of *idam* is replaced by *m* when a sup-affix (*vibhakti*) follows. (The illustrations of this substitution are) *imau, ime*. A general feature of the pronominal stems *tyad*, etc. is that they are not used in the vocative.

PP. *idamaḥ daḥ ca maḥ vibhaktau* (*aṅgasya*).

Eluc. : The word *vibhaktau* is carried over from *aṣṭana ā vibhaktau* Pā. 7. 2. 84 and the words *idamaḥ* and *maḥ* from *idamo maḥ* Pā. 7. 2. 108. The vowel *a* used in *ma* is to facilitate its articulation. The meaning of the sūtra is : The phoneme *d* of the pronominal stem *idam* is replaced by *m* when a sup-affix (*vibhakti*) follows.

In the illustration *ida* + *au*, the sup-affix (*vibhakti*) *au* follows. Hence by virtue of the present rule, the *d* of *idam* is replaced by *m* and we have *ima* + *au*. In this situation, the rule *prathama*... (125) becomes applicable but is debarred by *nādici* (126) since the vowel *a* is followed by *au* which is a denotatum of *ic*-pratyāhāra. Then according to the rule *vṛddhireci* (33), we obtain the form *imau*.

With the introduction of the plural affix *jas* of the first triplet, we have *idam* + *jas*. Here the rule *tyadādīnāmaḥ* (192) enjoins *a* in place of *m* of *idam* --> *ida a* + *as*. After this, the rule *ato guṇe* (273) prescribes pararūpa --> *ida as*. Then according to the rule *daśca* (274) the *d* of *idam* is replaced by *m* --> *ima* + *as*. The transformed stem *ima* still retains the sarvanāman designation by virtue of the ekadeśavikṛta paribhāṣā (Abhyankar, 37). This leads to the replacement of *jas* by *śī* according to *jasaḥ śī* (151), which remains as *ī* after the elision of *ś*, which is *it* by *laśakvataddhite* (135). Then *ādguṇaḥ* (27) applies and we have the form *ime*.

The pronominal stems *tyad, tad, yad, etad, idam, adas, eka, dvi, yuṣmad, asmad, bhavatu* and *kim* are not generally used in the vocative.

When the affix *am* is introduced after *idam*, the same grammatical process is followed up to *ima* + *am* as is followed in the preceding paragraph up to *ima* + *as*. Then *ami pūrvaḥ* (134) applies and we obtain the form *imam*.

With the sup-affix *śas*, we have *imān*, when the rules *prathama*... (125) and *tasmācchaso naḥ puṁsi* (136) have performed their grammatical functions.

With the introduction of *ṭā*, we have *idam* + *ṭā*. We reach the stage *ida* + (*ṭ*)*ā* through the following grammatical process : *idam* + *ṭā* --> *ida a* + *ā* {*tyadādīnāmaḥ* (192)} --> *ida* + *ā* {*ato guṇe* (273)}. At this stage, the following sūtra applies :

(275) अनाप्यकः । *anāpyakaḥ*. 7. 2. 112

लघु० – अककारस्येदम इदोऽन् आपि विभक्तौ । आब् इति प्रत्याहारः । अनेन । *akakārasyedama ido 'n āpi vibhaktau. āb iti pratyāhāraḥ. anena.*

Trans. : The substitute *an* replaces the segment *id* of *idam* before sup-affixes (*vibhakti*) denoted by the abbreviatory term *āp*, provided the pronominal stem *idam* does not co-occur with (the infixed affix) *k*. The term *āp* is a pratyāhāra.

PP. *akaḥ idamaḥ idaḥ an āpi vibhaktau* (*aṅgasya*).

Eluc. : The words *idamaḥ* and *idaḥ* are respectively carried over from *idamo maḥ* Pā. 7. 2. 108 and *ido 'y puṁsi* Pā. 7. 2. 111. The word *vibhaktau* comes from *aṣṭana ā vibhaktau* Pā. 7. 2. 84. The term *āp* is a pratyāhāra which is formed with the *ā* of the singular affix *ṭā* of the third triplet ending with the phoneme *p* of plural sup-affix of the seventh triplet. In this way the abbreviatory term *āp* denotes the affixes of the third, fourth, fifth, sixth and seventh triplets. The word *akaḥ* is a bahuvrīhi compound which is analysed as : *nāsti kakāraḥ yasmin saḥ ak, tasya = akaḥ*. Thus the meaning of the sūtra is as follows : If the pronominal stem *idam* is without the addition of kakāra, then the *id* portion of *idam* is replaced by *an* when the sup-affixes, denoted by *āp*-pratyāhāra, follow. The stem *idam* is said to possess *ka* when the rule *avyayasarvanāmnāmakac prāk ṭeḥ* (1227) enjoins the affix *akac* to be introduced before the *ṭi* of an indeclinable or a sarvanāman. The substitute *an* contains more than one phoneme. Being anekāl, it will replace the whole of *id*. In the illustration *ida + ā*, the *id*-portion is replaced by *an* and we have *an a + ā --> ana + ā*. Then by the rule *ṭāṅasiṅasāminātsyāḥ* (139), the affix *ṭā* is replaced by *ina --> ana + ina*. At this stage, the rule *ādguṇaḥ* (27) applies and we obtain the form *anena*.

With the introduction of the dual affix of the third triplet, we have *idam + bhyām*. At this stage, the rule *anāpyakaḥ* (275) makes available the substitute *an* in place of the *id*-portion of *idam* but the following sūtra blocks it :

(276) हलि लोपः । *hali lopaḥ*. 7. 2. 113

लघु० – अककारस्येदम इदो लोपः स्यादापि हलादौ । नानर्थकेऽलोऽन्त्यविधिरनभ्यासविकारे ।
akakārasyedama ido lopaḥ syād āpi halādau. nānarthake 'lo 'ntyavidhir anabhyāsavikāre (Abhyankar, 96).

Trans. : The *id*-portion of the pronominal stem *idam* is replaced by lopa if a consonant-initial sup-affix, denoted by *āp*-pratyāhāra, follows and if *idam* does not co-occur with the phoneme *k*. The rule *alo 'ntyasya* (21) does not apply to a meaningless element except in the case of modifications connected with a reduplicative syllable (*abhyāsa*).

PP. *akaḥ idamaḥ idaḥ lopaḥ āpi hali vibhaktau (aṅgasya).*

Eluc. : The words *akaḥ, idamaḥ, idaḥ* and *vibhaktau* are respectively carried over from *anāpyakaḥ* Pā. 7. 2. 112, *idamo maḥ* Pā. 7. 2. 108, *ido 'y puṁsi* Pā. 7. 2. 111 and *aṣṭana ā vibhaktau* Pā. 7. 2. 84. The word *hali* qualifies the word *vibhaktau*. So, it gives the meaning 'an *āp*-affix which begins with a consonant' in accordance with the paribhāṣā *yasmin vidhistadādāval...* (Abhyankar, 33). Thus the meaning of the sūtra is as follows : If the pronominal stem *idam* is without kakāra and is followed by a consonant-initial sup-affix denoted by *āp*-pratyāhāra, then the *id*-portion of *idam* is replaced by lopa. The present rule is an exception to *anāpyakaḥ* (275).

In the illustration *idam + bhyām --> ida + bhyām* {*tyadādīnāmaḥ* (192) and *ato guṇe* (273)}, the sup-affix *bhyām* follows, which begins with a consonant and which is also denoted by the abbreviatory term *āp*. Consequently, the *id*-portion of *idam* is elided. Varadarāja brings here an important point to our notice. The paribhāṣā sūtra *alo 'ntyasya* (21) becomes available and prescribes the lopa-replacement in place of the final phoneme *d* of *id* but the paribhāṣā *nānarthake 'lo 'ntyavidhir anabhyāsavikāre* (Abhyankar, 96) rules that the sūtra *alo 'ntyasya* (21) does not apply to an element which does not bear any meaning. The whole of *idam* is meaningful but a part of it does not bear any meaning. The *id*-portion of *idam* is meaningless and hence the rule *alo 'ntyasya* does not apply in this context. Therefore instead of the final *d* of *id*, the whole of *id* will be elided. Then we have *a + bhyām*. In this situation the rule *supi ca* (140) would have applied to lengthen the short vowel *a* had it been at the end of a pre-affixal base, which is a requisite for the lengthening of *a*. At this stage, the following sūtra presents itself for application :

(277) आद्यन्तवदेकस्मिन्। *ādyantavadekasmin.* 1. 1. 21

लघु० - एकस्मिन् क्रियमाणं कार्यमादाविव अन्त इव च स्यात्। सुपि च इति दीर्घः। आभ्याम्। *ekasmin kriyamāṇaṁ kāryam ādāviva anta iva ca syāt. supi ca iti dīrghaḥ. ābhyām.*

Trans. : When a grammatical operation is to be applied to a single phoneme unit, it is treated as though it were the initial or the final element.

PP. *ādyantavat ekasmin.*

Eluc. : The word *ādyantavat* is an indeclinable. The word *ādyantau* is an itaretaradvandva. The affix *vati* is introduced after it by *tatra tasyeva*

(1146). Its analysis is as follows : *ādiś ca antaś ca ādyantau, tayor iva ādyantavat*. Thus the sūtra means : The grammatical operation specific to the initial or the final element of a given unit is performed even on a single element treating it as if it were an initial or a final element.

In the illustration *a + bhyām*, the pre-affixal base consists of a single phoneme *a* after the *id*-portion of *idam* has been elided. The present rule makes a provision by which operations to be performed on an initial or a final element of a unit may be performed on a unit which consists of a single phoneme. According to this rule, a single element is treated as its own initial or final element. Interpreted in this way the sūtra does not cover the instances of the rules like *ekāco dve prathamasya, ādeśapratyayayoḥ*, etc. The word *ekācaḥ* is construed as a bahuvrīhi compound which means 'that which has one vowel'. In other words, it is more than one vowel. The verbal root *pac* is such an item and as such it is iterated but the verbal root *i* is a bare vowel. How can this be covered by the term *ekāc*, construed as a bahuvrīhi? To cover such cases, Patañjali has proposed that the sūtra be reformulated as *vyapadeśivadekasmin* (Mahābhāṣya on the present sūtra, vtk 2; also cf. supra, p. 352 for another illustration).

By virtue of this reformulation, even the verbal root consisting of a bare vowel will be treated like one consisting of a vowel along with consonants. Patañjali specifically mentions the verbal roots *pac* and *paṭh* on this sūtra and says that a verbal root in the form of a single vowel will also be treated like *pac*. By this revision the scope of the rule has increased. In the same way, a pre-affixal base consisting of a single phoneme can be treated as its own initial and its own final. In the case of *a + bhyām*, the substitute pre-affixal base for *idam* consists of a single phoneme *a*, which by the present rule is regarded as aṅga-final. Consequently, the aṅga-final short *a* is lengthened by *supi ca* (140) and we obtain the form *ābhyām* after the application of the sūtras *tydādīnāmaḥ* (192), *ato guṇe* (273) and *hali lopaḥ* (276)

When we introduce the plural affix *bhis* after *idam*, we have *idam + bhis*. After the application of the sūtras *tydādīnāmaḥ* (192), *ato guṇe* (273) and *hali lopaḥ* (276), we have *a + bhis* through the following grammatical process : *idam + bhis* --> *ida a + bhis* --> *ida + bhis* --> *a + bhis*. At this stage, the rule *ato bhisa ais* (141) becomes available for application by virtue of vyapadeśivadbhāva to prescribe the replacement of *bhis* by *ais* since a pre-affixal base consisting of a bare vowel *a* is treated as though it ends in *a*. The following sūtra negates this replacement —

(278) नेदमदसोरकोः । *nedamadasorakoḥ*. **7. 1. 11**
लघु० - अककारयोरिदमदसोर्भिस ऐस् न। एभिः। अस्मै। एभ्यः। अस्मात्। अस्य। अनयोः। एषाम्। अस्मिन्। एषु। *akakārayor idamadasor bhisa ais na. ebhiḥ. asmai. ebhyaḥ. asmāt. asya. anayoḥ. eṣām. asmin. eṣu.*

Trans. : The affix *bhis*, introduced after the pronominal stems *idam* and *adas* without *k*, is not replaced by *ais*.

PP. *akoḥ idamadasoḥ bhisaḥ ais na (aṅgasya)*.

Eluc. : The terms *bhisaḥ* and *ais* are carried over from *ato bhisa ais* Pā. 7. 1. 9. The word *akoḥ* is a bahuvrīhi compound which is analysed as : *na asti k yayos tau akau, tayoḥ = akoḥ*. Now the meaning of the sūtra is as follows : If the pronominal stems *idam* and *adas* are without the phoneme *k* and if they are followed by the affix *bhis*, then the affix *bhis* is not replaced with *ais* by *ato bhisa ais* (141) even though the pre-affixal base is construed as ending in the vowel *a* by vyapadeśivadbhāva. In the illustration *a* + *bhis* then, the rule *bahuvacane jhalyet* (144) applies and the vowel *a* is replaced by *e*. After rutva and visarga we obtain the form *ebhiḥ*.

In the dative singular form of *idam* we have *idam* + *ṅe* --> *ida* + *e* {*tydādīnāmaḥ* (192), *ato guṇe* (273)}. In this grammatical situation, both the rules *sarvanāmnaḥ smai* Pā. 7. 1. 14 and *anāpyakaḥ* Pā. 7. 2. 112 are simultaneously available for application. With the help of the rule *vipratiṣedhe paraṁ kāryam* (112), the latter becomes applicable but, being nitya, the former applies in accordance with the paribhāṣā *pūrvapara-nityāntaraṅgāpavādānām uttarottaraṁ balīyaḥ* (Abhyankar, 38). The rule *sarvanāmnaḥ smai* is considered to be nitya since it could apply even if the rule *anāpyakaḥ* has performed its grammatical function. In this way after the application of *sarvanāmnaḥ smai* (152), we have *ida* + *smai*. Now the rule *hali lopaḥ* prescribes the elision of the *id*-portion of *idam* and we obtain the form *asmai*.

In the same manner in *ida* + *ṅasi* --> *ida* + *as*, the rule *ṅasiṅyoḥ smātsminau* (153), being nitya, applies and we have *ida* + *smāt* --> *asmāt* after the application of *hali lopaḥ* (276).

In the genitive singular, the affix *ṅas* is replaced by the substitute *sya* according to the rule *ṭāṅasi...* (139) and we obtain the form *asya* after the rules *tydādīnāmaḥ* (192), *ato guṇe* (273) and *hali lopaḥ* (276) have performed their grammatical operations.

In the genitive dual form of *idam*, we have *idam* + *os* --> *ida* + *os*. The *id*-portion is replaced by *an* in accordance with *anāpyakaḥ* (275) and we have *ana* + *os*. At this stage, the substitute vowel *e* replaces the aṅga-final *a* by *osi ca* (146). After replacing *e* by *ay* according to *eco 'ya...* (22), we obtain the form *anayoḥ*.

When we add *ām* after *idam*, we have *idam* + *ām* --> *ida a ām* {*tydādīnāmaḥ* (192)} --> *ida* + *ām* {*ato guṇe* (273)}. At this stage, the rule *āmi sarvanāmnaḥ suṭ* (154) introduces the augment *suṭ* at the head of *ām*. The *id*-portion of *idam* is then elided by *hali lopaḥ* (276). After that the aṅga-final *a* is replaced by *e* according to *bahuvacane jhalyet* (144) and we get *esām*. Now the rule *ādeśapratyayayoḥ* (149) prescribes the replacement of *s* by *ṣ* and we obtain the form *eṣām* in the genitive plural.

In the locative singular we introduce the affix *ṅi* after *idam*. In *ida* + *ṅi*, the affix *ṅi* is replaced by *smin* in accordance with the rule *ṅasiṅyoḥ smātsminau* (153). Then in *ida* + *smin*, the *id*-portion of *idam* is elided by *hali lopaḥ* (276) and we get the form *asmin*.

In the locative plural form of *idam*, we have *idam* + *sup* --> *ida* + *su* by *tydādīnāmaḥ* (192) and *ato guṇe* (273) --> *a* + *su* {*hali lopaḥ* (276)} --> *e* + *su* by *bahuvacame jhalyet* (144) --> *eṣu* {*ādeśapratyayayoḥ* (149)}.

Thus the declension of the pronominal stem *idam* in the masculine will run as follows :

	Singular	Dual	Plural
prathamā	*ayam*	*imau*	*ime*
dvitīyā	*imam*	*imau*	*imān*
tṛtīyā	*anena*	*ābhyām*	*ebhiḥ*
caturthī	*asmai*	*ābhyām*	*ebhyaḥ*
pañcamī	*asmāt, d*	*ābhyām*	*ebhyaḥ*
ṣaṣṭhī	*asya*	*anayoḥ*	*eṣām*
saptamī	*asmin*	*anayoḥ*	*eṣu*
sambodhana	No form in the vocative		

The following sūtra prescribes that the whole of *idam* and *etad* are to be replaced by the substitute *ena* when they are used anaphorically (*anvādeśe*) :

(279) द्वितीयाटौस्स्वेनः । *dvitīyāṭaussvenaḥ*. 2. 4. 34

लघु० – इदमेतदोरन्वादेशे । किञ्चित् कार्यं विधातुमुपात्तस्य कार्यान्तरं विधातुं पुनरुपादानम् अन्वादेशः । यथा अनेन व्याकरणमधीतमेनं छन्दोऽध्यापयेति । अनयोः पवित्रं कुलम् एनयोः प्रभूतं स्वम् इति । एनम् । एनौ । एनान् । एनेन । एनयोः 2 । *idametador anvādeśe*.

kiñcit kāryaṁ vidhātum upāttasya kāryāntaraṁ vidhātuṁ punar upādānam anvādeśaḥ. yathā — anena vyākaraṇam adhītam enaṁ chando 'dhyāpayeti. anayoḥ pavitraṁ kulam enayoḥ prabhūtaṁ svam iti. enam. enau. enān. enena. enayoḥ 2.

Trans. : When the pronominal stems *idam* and *etad* are used anaphorically, let the substitute *ena* replace them when they are followed by the sup-affixes of the second triplet, *ṭā* and *os*. The anaphoric use (*anvādeśa*) consists in again employing an element, to direct an operation other than the one for which that element has already been employed. Examples : The grammar has been studied by him; (now) teach him prosody. The family of these two is illustrious; their wealth (too) is great.

PP. *idamaḥ etadaḥ anvādeśe dvitīyāṭaussu enaḥ* (*anudāttaḥ*).

Eluc. : The words *idamaḥ* and *anvādeśe* are carried from the sūtra *idamo 'nvādeśe 'śanudāttastṛtīyādau* Pā. 2. 4. 32 and the term *etadaḥ*, from *etadastratasostratasau cānudāttau* Pā. 2. 4. 33. The word *dvitīyāṭaussu* is an itaretaradvandva compound, which is analysed as : *dvitīyā ca ṭāś ca os ca dvitīyāṭausaḥ teṣu = dvitīyāṭaussu*. Thus the sūtra yields the following meaning : In anaphoric usage, the pronominal stems *idam* and *etad* are to be replaced by the substitute *ena* when they are followed by the affixes of the second triplet, *ṭā* and *os*.

In the words of Jinendrabuddhi the term *anvādeśa* means a second reference to one and the same item already referred to by an earlier word (*ekasyaivābhidheyasya pūrvaṁ śabdena pratipāditasya dvitīyaṁ pratipādanam*, KN, II, p. 280). This corresponds to what is known as anaphora in classical Western grammar, namely, the use of a word to refer back to an element previously used. The pronominal stems are the most familiar instances of anaphora as has been demonstrated in the illustrations given in the Laghu.

In the first illustration, the pronoun *anena*, to refer to a particular person, has been used in the context of the act of finishing the study of grammar. Now the act of teaching prosody has been directed for the same person. The use of the same pronoun to refer to the same person is an anaphora (*anvādeśa*). It is in this sense that the pronominal stems *idam* and *etad* are replaced by *ena* when the affixes of the second triplet, *ṭā* and *os* follow.

In the second illustration, the pronoun *anayoḥ* refers to the two persons whose family is good. Now the greatness of wealth has been attributed to the same two persons by using the same pronoun. It is *anvādeśa*. Hence the substitute *ena* has replaced the pronominal stem *idam*.

In the sense of anvādeśa, the substitution of the pronominal stems *idam* and *etad* by *ena* takes place when the following five affixes are added after these two pronouns : *am, auṭ, śas, ṭā* and *os*. The forms respectively are : 1. *idam* + *am* --> *ena* + *am* --> *enam* {*ami pūrvaḥ* (134)}. 2. *idam* + *auṭ* --> *ena* + *au*--> *enau* {*vṛddhireci* (33)}. 3. *idam* + *śas* --> *ena* + *as* --> *enān* {*prathamayoḥ pūrvasavarṇaḥ* (125) and *tasmācchaso naḥ puṁsi* (136)}. 4. *idam* + *ṭā* --> *ena* + *ā* --> *ena* + *ina* --> *enena* {*ṭāṅasiṅasām inātsyāḥ* (139) and *ādguṇaḥ* (27)}. 5. *idam* + *os* --> *ena* + *os* --> *ene* + *os* --> *enayos* {*osi ca* (146) and *eco 'yavāyāvaḥ* (22)} --> *enayoḥ* (after rutva and visarga).

One point is worth noticing. It is not necessary that *anvādeśa* means the second reference of the same pronoun. The first reference may be made by any one of the pronominal stems *yad, tad* etc. If the same person is again referred to by either *idam* or *etad*, then this is the incidence of anvādeśa. As a consequence, the substitute *ena* replaces *idam* and *etad*, when these are followed by the five sup-affixes mentioned above.

Here comes to an end the words, which end in the phoneme *m* and now begins the declension of the words that end in the phoneme *n*.

The word *rājan* is derived from the verbal root *rājṛ dīptau* with the addition of the affix *kanin* by *kanin yuvṛṣitakṣirājidhanvidyupratidivaḥ* US, 154. When we start declining the word *rājan*, we first introduce the affix *su* : *rājan* + *su*. In this grammatical situation, the sūtra *sarvanāmasthāne cāsambuddhau* (176) prescribes the lengthening of the penultimate vowel *a* (*upadhā*) and we have *rājān* + *s*(*u*). Then by *halṅyābbhyo dīrghāt sutisyapṛktaṁ hal* (178), the one-consonant affix *s* is elided {see SK, I, and BM, I, p. 360 for the sequence of the application of the sūtras *sarvanāmasthāne...* (176) and *halṅyābbhyo...* (178)}. After this, the pada-final *n* is elided by *na lopaḥ prātipadikāntasya* (179) and we obtain the fully declined form *rājā* in the nominative singular.

With the dual affix *au*, the rule *sarvanāmasthāne cāsambuddhau* (176) applies. The penultimate vowel *a* is lengthened and we have the form *rājānau*. In a similar way, this rule prescribes the lengthening of the penultimate vowel up to the affix *auṭ*. Thus we obtain the forms *rājānaḥ* (*jas*), *rājānam* (*am*) and *rājānau* (*auṭ*).

In the vocative singular we have *rājan* + *su*. The singular affix *su* in the vocative is designated as *sambuddhi*. Because of the exclusion of sambuddhi in *sarvanāmasthāne cāsambuddhau* (176), the penultimate vowel does not get lengthened in the vocative singular. Only the single-consonant affix *s* is elided by *halṅyābbhyo...* (178). The form thus obtained is *he rājan!*. Here the elision of the phoneme *n* is available by *na lopaḥ...* (179) but the following sūtra negates it —

(280) न ङिसम्बुद्ध्योः । *na ṅisambuddhyoḥ*. 8. 2. 8

लघु० - नस्य लोपो न ङौ सम्बुद्धौ च । हे राजन्! *nasya lopo na ṅau sambuddhau ca. he rājan!*

Trans. : The elision of the phoneme *n* does not take place when either *ṅi* or a vocative singular affix (*sambuddhi*) follows.

PP. *na lopaḥ ṅisambuddhyoḥ na* (*prātipadikāntasya, padasya*).

Eluc. : The two words *na* and *lopaḥ* are carried over from *na lopaḥ prātipadikāntasya* Pā. 8. 2. 7. The word *na* is understood to end in a singular genitive nominal ending (*tatra neti luptaṣaṣṭhīkam*, BM, I, p. 361). The word *ṅisambuddhyoḥ* is an itaretaradvandva. Its analysis is : *ṅiś ca sambuddhiś ca ṅisambuddhī, tayoḥ = ṅisambuddhyoḥ*. The meaning of the sūtra is : When the affixes *ṅi* and *sambuddhi* follow, the elision of the phoneme *n* does not take place. The illustration of the non-elision of *n* before *ṅi* is found in the Veda : *parame vyoman* (*ṅau tu chandasyudāharaṇam* SK, I, p. 361). Although the affix *ṅi* is deleted by *luk* [*supāṁ suluk...* (Pā. 7. 1. 39)], it is still considered to be effective by the force of the negation (*niṣedhasāmarthyāt pratyayalakṣaṇam*, SK, I, p. 361). In the illustration *he rājan!* the vocative singular affix *s*(*u*) is elided by *halṅyābbhyo...* (178). It is considered to be grammatically effective by virtue of the rule *pratyayalope...* (189).

25. वा० - ङावुत्तरपदे प्रतिषेधो वक्तव्यः । *ṅāvuttarapade pratiṣedho vaktavyaḥ*.

लघु० - ब्रह्मनिष्ठः । राजानौ । राजानः । राज्ञः । *brahmaniṣṭhaḥ. rājānau. rājānaḥ. rājñaḥ.*

Trans. : When the locative singular affix *ṅi*, followed by a final member (in a compound), follows, the rule *na ṅisambuddhyoḥ* (280) prescribing non-elision of *n* does not apply.

Eluc. : The vārttika by Kātyāyana only enunciates the negation. It does not specifically mention 'what should be negated' before the affix *ṅi*, which is followed by the final member of a compound. Since the vārttika has been enunciated in the context of the sūtra *na ṅisambuddhyoḥ* (280), the non-elision of the phoneme *n* by this rule is being negated by the present vārttika.

The illustration given in this context is *brahmaniṣṭhaḥ*. This is a bahuvrīhi compound which is analysed as : *brahmaṇi niṣṭhā yasya brahmaniṣṭhaḥ*. The grammatical analysis is : *brahman ṅi + niṣṭhā su*. By *supo dhātu...* (718), the affixes *ṅi* and *su* are replaced by luk-elision. By the force of negation, the elided affixes are to be considered to be grammatically effective as has been shown in the case of the Vedic illustration *parame vyoman* given above. This is being negated by the present vārttika when the locative singular affix *ṅi* is followed by the final member of a compound as in the case of the illustration *brahmaniṣṭhaḥ*, for the affix *ṅi* is here followed by *niṣṭhā*, the final member (*uttarapada*) of the bahuvrīhi compound *brahmaniṣṭhaḥ*. So, the negation prescribed by *na ṅisambuddhyoḥ* (280) is negated by the present vārttika. The negation of negation here means that the elision of the phoneme *n* does take place and we obtain the compound form *brahmaniṣṭhaḥ* after the long *ā* has been shortened by the rule *gostriyorupasarjanasya* (948).

With the introduction of the plural affix *śas* after *rājan*, we have *rājan* + *śas*. Here the pre-affixal base *rājan* is bha by the rule *yaci bham* (164). The rule *allopo 'naḥ* (246) prescribes the elision of the vowel *a* of the *an*-portion of the bha-designated pre-affixal base *rājan* in *rājan + as --> rājn + as*. The rule *stoḥ ścunā ścuḥ* (62) applies and the dental *n* is replaced by the palatal *ñ* and we get the form *rājñaḥ* after rutva and visarga.

In the same way when we introduce the singular affix of the third triplet (*ṭ*)*ā*, the vowel *a* of the *an*-portion of bha is elided by *allopo 'naḥ* (246) and we have *rājñā* after the dental *n* has been replaced by the palatal *ñ* by *stoḥ ścunā ścuḥ* (62).

With the dual affix of the third triplet, we have *rājan + bhyām*. The pre-affixal base has got the pada-designation by *svādiṣvasarvanāmasthāne* (163). Then the rule *na lopaḥ prātipadikāntasya* (179) applies and the phoneme *n* of *rājan* is elided. In *rāja + bhyām*, the sūtra *supi ca* (140) is applicable and as such the lengthening of the pada-final *a* becomes available but the following sūtra ensues :

(281) नलोपः सुप्स्वरसंज्ञातुग्विधिषु कृति । *nalopaḥ supsvarasaṁjñā-tugvidhiṣu kṛti.* 8. 2. 2

लघु० – सुब्विधौ स्वरविधौ संज्ञाविधौ कृति तुग्विधौ च नलोपोऽसिद्धो नान्यत्र – राजाश्व इत्यादौ । इत्यसिद्धत्वाद् आत्वमेत्वमैस्त्वम् च न । राजभ्याम् । राजभिः । राजभ्यः 2 । राज्ञि, राजनि । राजसु । *subvidhau svaravidhau saṁjñāvidhau kṛti tugvidhau ca nalopo 'siddho nānyatra – rājāśva ityādau. ityasiddhatvād ātvam etvam aistvam ca na. rājabhyām. rājabhiḥ. rājabhyaḥ 2. rājñi, rājani. rājasu.*

Trans. : The elision of *n* is treated as if it had not taken effect when a grammatical operation relating to sup, accent, naming (*saṁjñā*) and the introduction of the augment *tuk* before a kṛt affix is to be performed but the elision of *n* will not be regarded so elsewhere such as in *rājāśva*, etc. So, the elision of *n* being suspended, there is no lengthening of the vowel *a*, nor the replacement of *a* by *e*, nor the substitution of *bhis* by *ais*.

PP. *nalopaḥ supsvarasaṁjñātugvidhiṣu kṛti asiddhaḥ.*

Eluc. : Only the word, *asiddham*, is being carried over from *pūrvatrāsiddham* Pā. 8. 2. 1 to complete the sense of the present sūtra and by the process of liṅgavipariṇāma it is changed to the masculine so that it may accord with the word *nalopaḥ* in the sūtra. The word *nalopaḥ* is a ṣaṣṭhītatpuruṣa - *nasya lopaḥ nalopaḥ*. The other word is *supsvarasaṁjñātugvidhiṣu*, which is an itaretaradvandva-seeded ṣaṣṭhītatpuruṣa. Its analysis is as follows : *sup ca svaraś ca saṁjñā ca tuk ca supsvarasaṁjñātukaḥ, teṣāṁ vidhayaḥ, sup-svara-saṁjñā-tug-vidhayaḥ, teṣu = sup-svara-saṁjñā-tug-vidhiṣu.* The sup-vidhi means the operation relating to sup-affixes. It can be of two kinds : 1. The operation of replacing a sup-affix by a substitute as in the case of *rājabhiḥ* {*ato bhisa ais* (141)}. 2. The grammatical operation, which takes place when a sup-affix follows as in the illustration *rājabhyām*, where the lengthening of the pada-final vowel *a* is to take place when a particular sup-affix follows {*supi ca* (140)}. Similar is the case with grammatical operations relating to accent, naming and the insertion of the *tuk*-augment. The last grammatical operation occurs only when a particular kṛt affix follows. So, the term *kṛti* relates only to *tug*-vidhi since it can have no possible relation with any other term used in the sūtra. In this way the meaning of the sūtra is as follows : The elision of the phoneme *n* is considered not to have taken place in respect of the grammatical operations relating to sup-affixes, accent, naming and the insertion of the augment *tuk* before a kṛt affix.

The grammatical operations mentioned in the sūtra belong to the seven-and-a-quarter Aṣṭādhyāyī (*sapādasaptādhyāyī*). So the elision of *n* belonging to the tripādī is considered not to have taken place with respect to these grammatical operations by *pūrvatrāsiddham* Pā. 8. 2. 1. The fact that Pāṇini has enunciated this again in this sūtra means that the elision of *n* is considered to be suspended (*asiddha*) only in the context of these grammatical operations. This is the reason why the elision of the phoneme *n* in the illustration *rājāśva* is treated as effective in spite of Pā. 8. 2. 1. To explain, the compound *rājāśva* is a ṣaṣṭhītatpuruṣa. Its analysis is : *rājñaḥ aśvaḥ = rājan ṅas aśva su*. The sup-affixes *ṅas* and *su* are deleted by *supo...* (718). Then the phoneme *n* is elided by *na lopaḥ...* Pā. 8. 2. 7, which belongs to the tripādī. Its operation of eliding *n* should naturally be deemed as not to have taken place but by virtue of the present restrictive rule (*niyama sūtra*), it is not considered to be so. Hence the sandhi rule *akaḥ savarṇe dīrghaḥ* (42) applies and we obtain the desirable form *rājāśvaḥ*. In the absence of the present restrictive rule, *akaḥ savarṇe dīrghaḥ* (42) would not become applicable because the elision of the phoneme *n* by *na lopaḥ...* Pā. 8. 2. 7 was to be construed as not to have taken place in respect of the rule *akaḥ savarṇe...* (42) in accordance with *pūrvatrāsiddham* Pā. 8. 2. 1.

In *rājan + bhyām*, the pre-affixal base *rājan* is a pada by the *svādiṣva...* (163). Therefore by *na lopaḥ...* Pā. 8. 2. 7, the pada-final phoneme *n* is elided. Now we have a short vowel *a* at the end of an aṅga in *rāja + bhyām*. So, the rule *supi ca* (140) becomes applicable to prescribe the lengthening of *a* but because of the present rule, the elision of *n* is considered not to have taken place when some grammatical operation relating to sup-affixes is to be performed. It is so in the context of the present illustration. Hence there is no lengthening of the aṅga-final vowel *a* by *supi ca* (140) and we obtain the correct form *rājabhyām*.

In the same manner, in *rājan + bhis --> rāja + bhis*, there is no replacement of *bhis* by *ais* after the pada-final short vowel *a*. Also in *rājan + bhyas --> rāja + bhyas*, the rule *bahuvacane jhalyet* (144) does not apply for the same reason. Thus we get the forms *rājabhiḥ* and *rājabhyaḥ* after rutva and visarga.

In the locative singular when we introduce the affix *ṅi*, the rule *vibhāṣā ṅiśyoḥ* (247) prescribes optional elision of the short *a* of bha-designated *an* and we get two forms in the following manner : 1. *rājan + ṅi*. The rule *vibhāṣā ṅiśyoḥ* (247) applies : *rājn + ṅi --> rājñ + i* {*stoḥ ścunā ścuḥ* (62)} --> *rājñi*. 2. *rājan + ṅi --> rājan + i --> rājani*. The complete declension of the nominal stem *rājan* is given below :

	Singular	Dual	Plural
prathamā	*rājā*	*rājānau*	*rājānaḥ*
dvitīyā	*rājānam*	*rājānau*	*rājñaḥ*
tṛtīyā	*rājñā*	*rājabhyām*	*rājabhiḥ*
caturthī	*rājñe*	*rājabhyām*	*rājabhyaḥ*
pañcamī	*rājñaḥ*	*rājabhyām*	*rājabhyaḥ*
ṣaṣṭhī	*rājñaḥ*	*rājñoḥ*	*rājñām*

saptamī	*rājñi, rājani*	*rājñoḥ*	*rājasu*
sambodhana	*he rājan!*	*he rājānau!*	*he rājānaḥ!*

लघु० – यज्वा । यज्वानौ । यज्वानः । *yajvā. yajvānau. yajvānaḥ.*

Eluc. : The nominal stem *yajvan* means 'one who has performed the sacrifice in accordance with Vedic precepts'. This is derived from the verbal root *yaj* with the introduction of the affix *ṅvanip* by *suyajorṅvanip* Pā. 3. 2. 103. The declension of *yajvan* is like that of *rājan* except that the elision of *a* of bha-designated *an* is debarred by the following sūtra :

(282) **न संयोगाद्वमन्तात् ।** ***na saṁyogādvamantāt.* 6. 4. 137**
लघु० – वमन्तसंयोगादनोऽकारस्य लोपो न । यज्वनः । यज्वना । यज्वभ्याम् । ब्रह्मणः । ब्रह्मणा । *vamantasaṁyogād ano 'kārasya lopo na. yajvanaḥ. yajvanā, yajvabhyām. brahmaṇaḥ, brahmaṇā.*

Trans. : The phoneme *n* of *an*, which follows a conjunct consonant ending in *v* or *m*, is not elided.

PP. *vamantāt saṁyogāt anaḥ allopaḥ na (bhasya, aṅgasya).*
Eluc. : The words *anaḥ* and *allopaḥ* are carried over from *allopo 'naḥ* Pā. 6. 4. 134. The word *vamantāt* is an itaretaredvandva-seeded bahuvrīhi compound, which is analysed as follows : *vaś ca maś ca vamau* (itaretara-dvandva). *vamau antau yasya sa vamantaḥ, tasmāt = vamantāt*. Thus the meaning of the sūtra is : If bha-designated *an* follows a conjunct that ends in either *v* or *m*, then the vowel *a* of such *an* is not elided.

In *yajvan + śas --> yajvan + as*, the pre-affixal *yajvan* gets bha-designation by *yaci bham* (164). The segment *jv* is a conjunct that ends in *v*. This is followed by *an*. By the present rule, the vowel *a* of *an* is not elided and we obtain the form *yajvanaḥ*. This grammatical operation takes place where *yajvan* gets bha-designation before vowel-initial sup-affixes. The same grammatical operation will be performed in the case of the nominal stem *brahman* since the conjunct consonant *hm* ends in *m*. So, in the declensional process of the word *brahman* also, the *a* of *an* will not be elided. Thus the stem *yajvan* will be declined as follows :

	Singular	Dual	Plural
prathamā	*yajvā*	*yajvānau*	*yajvānaḥ*
dvitīyā	*yajvānam*	*yajvānau*	*yajvanaḥ*

tṛtīyā	*yajvanā*	*yajvabhyām*	*yajvabhiḥ*
caturthī	*yajvane*	*yajvabhyām*	*yajvabhyaḥ*
pañcamī	*yajvanaḥ*	*yajvabhyām*	*yajvabhyaḥ*
ṣaṣṭhī	*yajvanaḥ*	*yajvanoḥ*	*yajvanām*
saptamī	*yajvani*	*yajvanoḥ*	*yajvasu*
sambodhana	*he yajvan!*	*he yajvānau!*	*he yajvānaḥ!*

The nominal stem *brahman* illustrates the conjunct that ends in *m*. The phoneme *n* of *brahman* changes to *ṇ* by *aṭkupvāṅnumvyavāye 'pi* (137). The word *brahman* will be declined as follows :

	Singular	Dual	Plural
prathamā	*brahmā*	*brahmāṇau*	*brahmāṇaḥ*
dvitīyā	*brahmāṇam*	*brahmāṇau*	*brahmaṇaḥ*
tṛtīyā	*brahmaṇā*	*brahmabhyām*	*brahmabhiḥ*
caturthī	*brahmaṇe*	*brahmabhyām*	*brahmabhyaḥ*
pañcamī	*brahmaṇaḥ*	*brahmabhyām*	*brahmabhyaḥ*
ṣaṣṭhī	*brahmaṇaḥ*	*brahmaṇoḥ*	*brahmaṇām*
saptamī	*brahmaṇi*	*brahmaṇoḥ*	*brahmasu*
sambodhana	*he brahman!*	*he brahmāṇau!*	*he brahmāṇaḥ!*

Varadarāja next takes up the word *vṛtrahan* 'Indra'. Indra is so called because he killed the demon Vṛtra. The word is an upapada compound. Its analysis is : *vṛtraṁ hatavān --> vṛtra + han kvip*. According to the rule *brahmabhrūṇavṛtreṣu kvip* Pā. 3. 2. 87, the affix *kvip* has been added after the verbal root *han* to denote 'agent and the action accomplished by him in the past' and we get the word *vṛtrahan*. In declining this word, we first introduce the affix *su*. In *vṛtrahan + su*, the rule *sarvanāmasthāne...* (176) becomes available to lengthen the penultimate vowel *a* since the pre-affixal base ends in *n* and the affix that follows is sarvanāmasthāna. At this stage the following sūtra ensues :

(283) इन्हन्पूषार्यम्णां शौ । *inhanpūṣāryamṇāṁ śau.* 6. 4. 12

लघु० - एषां शावेवोपधाया दीर्घो नान्यत्र । इति निषेधे प्राप्ते — *eṣāṁ śāvevopadhāyā dīrgho nānyatra. iti niṣedhe prāpte* —

Trans. : A long vowel replaces the penultimate vowel of a pre-affixal base that ends in *in, han, pūṣan* and *aryaman* only when the affix *śi* follows and not in any other situation.

PP. *inhanpūṣāryamṇām aṅgānām śau upadhāyāḥ dīrghaḥ.*

Eluc. : The word *aṅgasya* is carried over from the governing rule *aṅgasya* Pā. 6. 4. 1 and is changed to *aṅgānām* in the genitive plural by the process of vacanavipariṇāma so that it may agree with the word *inhanpūṣāryamṇām*. The words *upadhāyāḥ* and *dīrghaḥ* respectively come from *nopadhāyāḥ* Pā. 6. 4. 7 and *ḍhralope pūrvasya dīrgho 'ṇaḥ*. Since the word *inhanpūṣāryamṇām* qualifies the word *aṅgānām*, tadantavidhi comes into play and it gives the sense 'a pre-affixal base that ends in these words'. Thus the meaning of the sūtra will be : A long vowel substitute replaces the penultimate vowel of a pre-affixal base that ends in *in, han, pūṣan* and *aryaman* only when the affix *śi* follows and not when any other element follows.

In the declension of neuter nominal stems, the rule *jaśśasoḥ śiḥ* (236) prescribes the replacement of the affixes *jas* and *śas* by *śi*, which is designated as *sarvanāmasthāna* by *śi sarvanāmasthānam* (237). Therefore the words given in the present rule can get their penultimate vowel lengthened by *sarvanāmasthāne...* (176). Hence the lengthening of the penultimate vowel by the present rule is a repetition which renders it a restrictive rule. The penultimate vowel of these aṅga-final words is lengthened only when *śi* follows.

In *vṛtrahan + su*, the sup-affix *su* is present which is other than *śi*. As a consequence, the lengthening of the penultimate vowel of this word is not available. In this situation, the following sūtra presents itself :

(284) सौ च । *sau ca.* 6. 4. 13

लघु० – इन्नादीनामुपधाया दीर्घोऽसम्बुद्धौ सौ । वृत्रहा । हे वृत्रहन्! *innādīnām upadhāyā dīrgho 'sambuddhau sau. vṛtrahā. he vṛtrahan!*

Trans. : The penultimate vowel of a pre-affixal base that ends in *in, han, pūṣan* and *aryaman* is lengthened when *su*, other than sambuddhi (vocative singular), follows.

PP. *inhanpūṣāryamṇām aṅgānām upadhāyāḥ dīrghaḥ asambuddhau sau ca.*

Eluc. : The sūtra *aṅgasya* Pā. 6. 4. 1 is a governing rule. Hence the term *aṅgasya* recurs in the present sūtra but it is changed to have a genitive plural affix, that is, *aṅgānām* by the process of vacanavipariṇāma so that it may agree with the word *inhanpūṣāryamṇām*. The words *upadhāyāḥ, dīrghaḥ* and *asambuddhau* are carried over respectively from *nopadhāyāḥ* Pā. 6. 4. 7, *ḍhralope pūrvasya dīrgho 'ṇaḥ* Pā. 6. 3. 111 and *sarvanāmasthāne cāsambuddhau* Pā. 6. 4. 8. Since the word *inhanpūṣāryamṇām* qualifies the word *aṅgānām*, tadantavidhi comes into play and it gives the sense 'a pre-affixal base that ends in these words'. So, the present sūtra yields the sense : If the affix *su*, other than the vocative one, follows, the penultimate vowel of a pre-affixal base that ends in *in*, *han*, *pūṣan* and *aryaman* is replaced by a long one. Since the lengthening of the penultimate vowel is not available by the preceding restrictive sutra, the present rule makes it available before *su*, which is other than the vocative singular. So we reach the stage of the illustration as *vṛtrahān* + *su*. The single consonant affix *s*(*u*) is elided by rule *halṅyābbhyo*... (178) and the pada-final *n*, by *na lopaḥ*... (179). Then we obtain the form *vṛtrahā*.

In *vṛtrahan* + *au*, the lengthening of the penultimate is negated by *inhanpūṣāryamṇāṁ śau* (283) and the *ṇ*-replacement for *n* by *aṭkupvāṅ*... (137) is also not available because it does not occur in the same pada. In this grammatical situation, the following sūtra presents itself :

(285) एकाजुत्तरपदे णः । ***ekājuttarapade ṇaḥ*. 8. 4. 12**

लघु० – एकाजुत्तरपदं यस्य तस्मिन् समासे पूर्वपदस्थान्निमित्तात् परस्य प्रातिपदिकान्तनुम्विभक्तिस्थस्य नस्य णः स्यात्। वृत्रहणौ । *ekāj uttarapadaṁ yasya tasmin samāse pūrvapadasthān nimittāt parasya prātipadikāntanumvibhaktisthasya nasya ṇaḥ syāt. vṛtrahaṇau.*

Trans. : The cerebral *ṇ* replaces the dental *n* of the posterior monosyllabic member of a compound if it occurs as nominal stem-final or in the augment *num* or in a vibhakti (sup-affix) when it follows (the condition for replacement in the form of) the phoneme *r* or *ṣ* of a prior member.

PP. *pūrvapadābhyām raṣābhyām prātipadikāntanumvibhaktiṣu ekāj-uttarapade naḥ ṇaḥ* (*aṭkupvāṅnumvyavāye 'pi saṁhitāyām*).

Eluc. : The word *pūrvapadāt* is carried over from *pūrvapadāt saṁjñāyāmagaḥ* Pā. 8. 4. 3. The words *raṣābhyām* and *naḥ* are carried over from *raṣābhyāṁ no ṇaḥ samānapade* Pā. 8. 4. 1. The compound word *prātipadikāntanumvibhaktiṣu* comes from *prātipadikāntanumvibhaktiṣu ca* Pā. 8. 4. 11. The word *ekājuttarapade* is a bahuvrīhi-seeded bahuvrīhi, which is analysed as *eko 'c yasmin tad ekāc* (bahuvrīhi) *ekāc uttarapadaṁ yasya sa ekājuttarapadaḥ* (bahuvrīhi), *tasmin* = *ekājuttarapade*. The word *pūrvapadāt* needs explanation in the context of the present sūtra. According to the Bālamanoramā, the word *pūrvapada* is a bahuvrīhi compound : *pūrvaṁ padaṁ yasya tat pūrvapadam*. Its singular number is not intended. It is to be changed to have a dual number to accord with *raṣābhyām*. Both the repha and the cerebral *ṣ* bring about the cerebral substitution in the monosyllabic posterior member of a compound even when there is an intervention of *aṭ*, kavarga, *num* and *āṅ* provided the dental *n* occurs as nominal stem-final or is in the augment *num* or in a vibhakti. Thus the meaning of the sūtra is as follows : If either repha or the cerebral *ṣ* or both occur in the prior member of a compound and the posterior member is monosyllabic, then the dental *n* occurring as stem-final or in the augment *num* or in a sup-affix is replaced by the cerebral *ṇ* (cf. BM, I, p. 320).

In the illustration *vṛtrahan + au*, the stem *vṛtrahan* is an upapada compound, the posterior member of which is monosyllabic. The repha occurs in the prior member *vṛtra* and the dental *n* occurs as nominal stem-final. The posterior member *han* is monosyllabic. Consequently, the dental *n* is replaced by *ṇ* and we obtain the form *vṛtrahaṇau*. We have the same declensional process in the forms *vṛtrahaṇaḥ*, *vṛtrahaṇam*, *vṛtrahaṇau*.

When we introduce the plural affix of the second triplet, we have *vṛtrahan + śas*. Here the sūtra *ekājuttarapade ṇaḥ* Pā. 8. 4. 12 is deemed not to be effective (asiddha) so far as the rule *allopo 'naḥ* Pā. 6. 4. 134 is concerned. This is the reason why the latter rule applies and the vowel *a* of *an* is elided and we have *vṛtrahn + as*. At this stage, the following sūtra becomes applicable :

(286) हो हन्तेर्ञ्णिन्नेषु । *ho hanterñṇinneṣu*. 7. 3. 54

लघु० – ञिति णिति प्रत्यये नकारे च परे हन्तेर्हकारस्य कुत्वम् । वृत्रघ्नः इत्यादि । एवं शार्ङ्गिन् , यशस्विन् , अर्यमन् , पूषन् । *ñiti ṇiti pratyaye nakāre ca pare hanter hakārasya kutvam. vṛtraghnaḥ ityādi. evaṁ śārṅgin, yaśasvin, aryaman, pūṣan.*

Trans. : Let the phoneme *h* of *han* be replaced by a guttural when an affix that has *ñ* or *ṇ* as *it* or the phoneme *n* follows.

PP. *hanteḥ aṅgasya haḥ ku ñṇinneṣu.*

Eluc. : The present sūtra occurs in the domain of the governing rule *aṅgasya* Pā. 6. 4. 1. Therefore the word *aṅgasya* recurs here. The word *ku* is carried over from *cajoḥ ku ghiṇṇyatoḥ* Pā. 7. 3. 52. The compound word *ñṇinneṣu* is analysed as follows : *ñ ca ṇ ca ñṇau* (itaretaradvandva) *ñṇau itau yayos tau* = *ñṇitau* (bahuvrīhi). *ñṇitau ca naś ca ñṇinnās teṣu* = *ñṇinneṣu*. Then the meaning of the sūtra will be as follows : The phoneme *h* of the pre-affixal base *han* is to be replaced by a guttural when an affix that ends in either *ñ* or *ṇ* or the phoneme *n* follows. In *vṛtrahn + as*, since the phoneme *n* immediately follows the phoneme *h* of *han* after the elision of *a* of *an*, the *h* of *han* is replaced by *gh* which is similar to *h* on the basis of the external efforts, viz., saṁvāra, nāda, ghoṣa and mahāprāṇa. The dental *n* of the posterior member is not to be replaced by *ṇ*, since the posterior member ceases to be monosyllabic after the elision of *a* of *han*. We obtain the form *vṛtraghnaḥ*. In the same way, the vowel *a* of *an* of *vṛtrahan* is elided by *allopo 'naḥ* (246) before vowel-initial affixes. The *h* is replaced by *gh* and we have *vṛtraghnā*, *vṛtraghne*, etc. In the locative singular, we have two forms because of the optional elision of the vowel *a* of *an* in accordance with the rule *vibhāṣā ṅiśyoḥ* (247). In this way the complete declension of *vṛtrahan* will be as follows :

	Singular	Dual	Plural
prathamā	*vṛtrahā*	*vṛtrahaṇau*	*vṛtrahaṇaḥ*
dvitīyā	*vṛtrahaṇam*	*vṛtrahaṇau*	*vṛtraghnaḥ*
tṛtīyā	*vṛtraghnā*	*vṛtrahabhyām*	*vṛtrahabhiḥ*
caturthī	*vṛtraghne*	*vṛtrahabhyām*	*vṛtrahabhyaḥ*
pañcamī	*vṛtraghnaḥ*	*vṛtrahabhyām*	*vṛtrahabhyaḥ*
ṣaṣṭhī	*vṛtraghnaḥ*	*vṛtraghnoḥ*	*vṛtraghnām*
saptamī	*vṛtraghni, vṛtrahaṇi*	*vṛtraghnoḥ*	*vṛtrahasu*
sambodhana	*he vṛtrahan!*	*he vṛtrahaṇau!*	*he vṛtrahaṇaḥ!*

The nominal stems *śārṅgin* (Viṣṇu), *yaśasvin* (famous), *aryaman* (the sun) and *pūṣan* (the sun) are declined in the same way but the declensional forms of the nominal stems that have a short penultimate *i* have some declensional charateristics distinct from those of the nominal stems that have a short penultimate *a*. This needs to be explained. The word *śārṅgin* is derived after the introduction of *ini* affix after *śārṅga*. Since this does not have a short penultimate *a*, the rule *allopo 'naḥ* (246) does not apply. In the nominative singular, the lengthening of the penultimate vowel takes effect by *sau ca* (284) after it has been debarred by the restrictive rule *inhan...* (283). The cerebral substitution in the following declensional forms takes place according to the rule *aṭkupvāṅ...* (137). In the locative plural, there is no grammatical operation which relates to sup-affixes. Therefore the elision of *n* will be construed as effective {cf. *nalopaḥ sup...* (281)}. The declension of *śārṅgin* is as follows :

	Singular	Dual	Plural
prathamā	*śārṅgī*	*śārṅgiṇau*	*śārṅgiṇaḥ*
dvitīyā	*śārṅgiṇam*	*śārṅgiṇau*	*śārṅgiṇaḥ*
tṛtīyā	*śārṅgiṇā*	*śārṅgibhyām*	*śārṅgibhiḥ*
caturthī	*śārṅgiṇe*	*śārṅgibhyām*	*śārṅgibhyaḥ*
pañcamī	*śārṅgiṇaḥ*	*śārṅgibhyām*	*śārṅgibhyaḥ*
ṣaṣṭhī	*śārṅgiṇaḥ*	*śārṅgiṇoḥ*	*śārṅgiṇām*
saptamī	*śārṅgiṇi*	*śārṅgiṇoḥ*	*śārṅgiṣu*
sambodhana	*he śārṅgin!*	*he śārṅgiṇau!*	*he śārṅgiṇaḥ!*

Some of the words that end in *in* and are declined like *śārṅgin* are as follows : *ajñānin* 'ignorant', *adhītin* 'scholar', *antevāsin* 'disciple', *karin* 'elephant', *guṇin* 'a person possessed of qualities', *tapasvin* 'ascetic', *dehin* 'soul', *dvīpin* 'leopard', *dhanin* 'wealthy', *nivāsin* 'resident', *paripanthin* 'enemy', *pinākin* 'Lord Śiva', *balin* 'strong', *lobhin* 'greedy', *śarīrin* 'soul', *sahakārin* 'associate', *sākṣin* 'witness', *svāmin* 'master', *hastin* 'elephant' and *yogin* 'yogi'.

In declining the word *pūṣan*, the lengthening of the penultimate vowel takes effect by *sau ca* (284). In the other four forms before sarvanāmasthāna affixes, the lengthening of the penultimate is blocked by the restrictive rule *inhan...* (283). The rule *allopo 'naḥ* (246) applies before vowel-initial affixes but in the locative singular the elision of *a* of *an* is optional by *vibhāṣā ṅiśyoḥ* (247). Hence we have two forms in the locative singular. The cerebral *ṇ*-substitution is in accordance with *aṭkupvāṅ...* (137). The word *pūṣan* is declined as follows :

	Singular	Dual	Plural
prathamā	*pūṣā*	*pūṣaṇau*	*pūṣaṇaḥ*
dvitīyā	*pūṣaṇam*	*pūṣaṇau*	*pūṣṇaḥ*
tṛtīyā	*pūṣṇā*	*pūṣabhyām*	*pūṣabhiḥ*
caturthī	*pūṣṇe*	*pūṣabhyām*	*pūṣabhyaḥ*

pañcamī	*pūṣṇaḥ*	*pūṣabhyām*	*pūṣabhyaḥ*
ṣaṣṭhī	*pūṣṇaḥ*	*pūṣṇoḥ*	*pūṣṇām*
saptamī	*pūṣṇi, pūṣaṇi*	*pūṣṇoḥ*	*pūṣasu*
sambodhana	*he pūṣan!*	*he pūṣaṇau!*	*he pūṣaṇaḥ!*

The declension of the word *aryaman* is like that of *pūṣan*; *yaśasvin* is declined like *śārṅgin*. The significance of giving two separate words that end in *in* (*yaśasvin* and *śārṅgin*) lies in the fact that Varadarāja intends to draw our attention to the paribhāṣā *aninasmangrahaṇānyarthavatā cānarthakena ca tadantavidhiṁ prayojayanti* (Abhyankar, 16) which says that the qualifying word segments *an, in, as, man*, which are employed in grammar are to be taken to be the ending segments of the nominal stems, which are qualified by these word segments whether they possess meaning or not. This can be explained by taking an example. In the word *śārṅgin*, the word segment *in*, in which *śārṅgin* ends, is an affix and therefore it is meaningful. This is not the case with the nominal stem *yaśasvin*. Here the affix *vin* is meaningful but a part of *vin*, that is, *in* is not meaningful. So, in such cases (where these word segments are meaningless) the rules *inhan...* (283) and *sau ca* (284) should not apply in accordance with the paribhāṣā *arthavadgrahaṇe nānarthakasya* (Abhyankar, 14). The present paribhāṣā makes provision that these word segments, whether they are meaningful or not, are to be treated on a par. This is the reason why the rule *inhan...* (283) and *sau ca* (284) apply in the case of both *śārṅgin* and *yaśasvin*. This is also precisely the reason why they have been mentioned separately by Varadarāja.

Varadarāja now takes up the nominal stem *maghavan* 'Indra' to explain its declensional process. The following sūtra prescribes that the stem-final phoneme be replaced by *tṛ* optionally :

(287) मघवा बहुलम्। *maghavā bahulam*. 6. 4. 128

लघु० – 'मघवन्' शब्दस्य वा तृ इत्यन्तादेशः स्यात्। ऋ इत्। *maghavan śabdasya vā tṛ ityantādeśaḥ syāt. ṛ it.*

Trans. : Let the substitute *tṛ* optionally replace the nominal stem-final phoneme of *maghavan*. The vowel *ṛ* is *it*.

PP. *maghavā bahulam tṛ* (*aṅgasya*).

Eluc. : The nominative singular ending in *maghavā* is in the sense of genitive (*maghaveti tu ṣaṣṭhyarthe prathamā*, BM, I, p. 371). The term *tṛ* is carried over from *arvaṇastrasāvanañaḥ* Pā. 6. 4. 127. The vowel *ṛ* is *it* and is given without a nominal ending in the vṛtti by Varadarāja. Thus the meaning of the sūtra will be as follows : The nominal stem *maghavan* is optionally replaced by the substitute *tṛ*. The substitute *tṛ* has more than one *al* (phoneme). So, it should replace the whole of *maghavan* by *anekāl...* (45). However, a grammatical element is not considered to have more than one *al* on the basis of an anubandha {cf. *nānubandhakṛtam anekāltvam* (Abhyankar, 6)}. When the vowel *ṛ* in *tṛ* is elided by *tasya lopaḥ* (3), the substitute consists of *t* only. Hence the substitute, consisting of one *al* only, will replace the final phoneme of the substituendum by *alo 'ntyasya* (21), that is, the phoneme *n* of *maghavan* and thus we have *maghvat*.

In *maghavat* + *su*, the following rule applies :

(288) उगिदचां सर्वनामस्थानेऽधातोः । *ugidacāṁ sarvanāmasthāne-'dhātoḥ*. 7. 1. 70

लघु० - अधातोरुगितो नलोपिनोऽञ्चतेश्च नुमागमः स्यात् सर्वनामस्थाने परे । मघवान् । मघवन्तौ । मघवन्तः । हे मघवन्! मघवद्भ्याम् । तृत्वाभावे मघवा । सुटि राजवत् । *adhātor ugito nalopino 'ñcateś ca numāgamaḥ syāt sarvanāmasthāne pare. maghavān. maghavantau. maghavantaḥ. he maghavan! maghavadbhyām. tṛtvābhāve – maghavā. suṭi rājavat.*

Trans. : When a sarvanāmasthāna affix follows, let *num* be inserted in that which, not being a verbal root, has an *it* denoted by *uk*, and in the verbal root *añcu*, the *n* of which has been elided.

PP. *ugidacām sarvanāmasthāne adhātoḥ num* (*aṅgasya*).

Eluc. : The term *num* is carried over from *idito num dhātoḥ* Pā. 7. 1. 58. The compound *ugidacām* is a bahuvrīhi-seeded itaretaradvandva. Its analysis is as follows : *uk it yeṣām te ugitaḥ* (bahuvrīhi compound). *ugitaś ca ac ca ugidacaḥ* (itaretaradvandva), *teṣām* = *ugidacām*. The word *ac* occurring in the compound represents the verbal root *añcu* 'to go, to worship', the phoneme *n* of which has been elided. The word *adhātoḥ* is a nañ-tatpuruṣa which is analysed as follows : *na dhātuḥ adhātuḥ, tasya* = *adhātoḥ*. This word *adhātoḥ* qualifies the word *ugid* since this cannot qualify *añcateḥ* which is a verbal root (*dhātu*). Thus the meaning of the sūtra is as follows : The augment *num* is inserted after the last vowel of the words which, with the exception of verbal roots, have an *it* denoted by *uk* and after that of the verbal root *añcu* with its *n* having been elided, when a sarvanāmasthāna affix follows. This means that the words which are other than verbal roots and which have *uk* (*u* or *ṛ* or *ḷ*) as *it* and also the verbal root *añcu*, the phoneme *n* of which has been elided, have *num* as their part when followed by a sarvanāmasthāna affix.

In *maghavat + su*, the phoneme *ṛ* in *tṛ*, being *it*, has been elided. So, the nominal stem *maghavat* is *ugit*. According to the present rule, the augment *num* is inserted after the last vowel of *maghavat* {*midaco 'ntyāt paraḥ* (239)} and we have *maghava num t + su --> maghava n t + su*. The rule *halṅyābbhyo...* (178) applies and the affix *s(u)* is elided. Then *saṁyogāntasya lopaḥ* (20) prescribes the elision of the phoneme *t* and we get the form *maghavan*. Then by taking the elided *su* as effective by *pratyayalope...* (189), we apply the rule *sarvanāmasthāne...* (176) and the penultimate vowel *a* is lengthened and we obtain the form *maghavān*. The elision of the phoneme *t* by *saṁyogāntasya lopaḥ* Pā. 8. 2. 33 is not considered to be ineffective (asiddha) vis-a-vis *sarvanāmasthāne...* Pā. 6. 4. 8 because of the use of the term *bahulam* in the sūtra *maghavā bahulam*. The use of *bahulam* not only makes provision for an optional substitution of *tṛ* but it also removes any obstruction in obtaining the desired declensional form. In the declensional process of the forms *maghavantau*, *maghavantaḥ* and *maghavantam*, the phoneme *n* of the augment *num* is replaced by anusvāra in accordance with *naścāpadāntasya jhali* (78) and the anusvāra is replaced by a phoneme which is homogeneous with the following class consonant by *anusvārasya yayi parasavarṇaḥ* (79). In the present context it will obviously be the dental nasal *n*. Before *bhyām*, *bhis* and *bhyas* the pada-final *t* is replaced by *d* according to the rule *jhalāṁ jaśo 'nte* (67). In the vocative singular form of *maghavan*, the lengthening of the penultimate vowel does not take place in accordance with *sarvanāmasthāne cāsambuddhau* (176) and the pada-final *n* is not elided since its elision is blocked by *na ṅisambuddhyoḥ* (280). When there is a *tṛ*-replacement with respect to the word *maghavan*, it will be declined in the following manner :

	Singular	Dual	Plural
prathamā	*maghavān*	*maghavantau*	*maghavantaḥ*
dvitīyā	*maghavantam*	*maghavantau*	*maghavataḥ*
tṛtīyā	*maghavatā*	*maghavadbhyām*	*maghavadbhiḥ*
caturthī	*maghavate*	*maghavadbhyām*	*maghavadbhyaḥ*
pañcamī	*maghavataḥ*	*maghavadbhyām*	*maghavadbhyaḥ*
ṣaṣṭhī	*maghavataḥ*	*maghavatoḥ*	*maghavatām*

saptamī	*maghavati*	*maghavatoḥ*	*maghavatsu*
sambodhana	*he maghavan!*	*he maghavantau!*	*he maghavantaḥ!*

In the absence of *tṛ*-replacement, the declension of *maghavan* before sup-affixes denoted by the abbreviatory term *suṭ* (*su, au, jas, am, auṭ*) is like that of the nominal stem *rājan* : *maghavā, maghavānau, maghavānaḥ, maghavānam, maghavānau.*

In *maghavan* + *śas* --> *maghavan* + *as,* the following sūtra becomes applicable :

(289) श्वयुवमघोनामतद्धिते । *śvayuvamaghonāmataddhite.* 6. 4. 133

लघु० - अन्नन्तानां भसंज्ञकानाम् एषाम् अतद्धिते परे सम्प्रसारणं स्यात्। मघोनः। मघवभ्याम्। एवं श्वन्, युवन्। *annantānāṁ bhasaṁjñakānām eṣām ataddhite pare samprasāraṇaṁ syāt. maghonaḥ. maghavabhyām. evaṁ śvan, yuvan.*

Trans. : Let the nominal stems *śvan, yuvan* and *maghavan* which end in *an* and are designated as *bha* go through samprasāraṇa when a non-taddhita affix follows.

PP. *anām bhānām śvayuvamaghonām samprasāraṇam ataddhite* (*aṅgasya*).

Eluc. : The term *anaḥ* is carried over from *allopo 'naḥ* Pā. 6. 4. 134 and changed to *anām* to accord with the compound word *śvayuvamaghonām* by the process of vacanavipariṇāma. In the same way, the term *bhasya* coming from the governing rule *bhasya* Pā. 6. 4. 129 is also changed to have the genitive plural sup-affix. The term *samprasāraṇam* is carried over from *vasoḥ samprasāraṇam*. By tadantavidhi the word *anām,* being a qualifying term, yields the sense 'the nominal stems that end in *an*'. The compound word *śvayuvamaghonām* is an itaretara-dvandva which is analysed as follows : *śvā ca yuvā ca maghavā ca śvayuvamaghavānaḥ, teṣām* = *śvayuvamaghonām*. The word *ataddhite* is a nañ-tatpuruṣa : *na taddhite ataddhite* which means an affix that is other than a taddhita affix. As such, the meaning of the sūtra is as follows : When a non-taddhita affix follows, the bha-designated nominal stems *śvan, yuvan* and *maghavan* which end in *an* undergo the process of samprasāraṇa.

In the illustration *maghavan* + *as,* the nominal stem *maghavan* ends in *an*. This is designated as *bha* by *yaci bham* (164). The sup-affix that follows is not a taddhita affix and the conditions that bring about samprasāraṇa are available. The phoneme *v* is changed to *u* with the help of *igyaṇaḥ samprasāraṇam* (255) and the vowels *u* and *a* are replaced by *u* in accordance with the rule *samprasāraṇācca* (257). Thus we have *maghavan + as --> magha u an + as --> magha un + as --> maghonas* {guṇa by *ādguṇaḥ* (27)}. After rutva and visarga, we obtain the form *maghonaḥ*.

In all the forms in which the stem gets the pada-designation, the elision of *n* will take place by *na lopaḥ...* (179). Thus in the absence of *tṛ*-replacement, the declension of *maghavan* will be as follows :

	Singular	Dual	Plural
prathamā	*maghavā*	*maghavānau*	*maghavānaḥ*
dvitīyā	*maghavānam*	*maghavānau*	*maghonaḥ*
tṛtīyā	*maghonā*	*maghavabhyām*	*maghavabhiḥ*
caturthī	*maghone*	*maghavabhyām*	*maghavabhyaḥ*
pañcamī	*maghonaḥ*	*maghavabhyām*	*maghavabhyaḥ*
ṣaṣṭhī	*maghonaḥ*	*maghonoḥ*	*maghonām*
saptamī	*maghoni*	*maghonoḥ*	*maghavasu*
sambodhana	*he maghavan!*	*he maghavānau!*	*he maghavānaḥ!*

Both Jñānendra Sarasvatī and Vāsudeva Dīkṣita discuss the significance of carrying over the term *anām* (*annantānām*) into the present sūtra. In the grammatical situation where the *tṛ*-replacement comes in place of the stem-final *n* of *maghavan*, the transformed stem *maghavat* can still be treated like *maghavan* by the paribhāṣā *ekadeśavikṛtam ananyavat* (Abhyankar, 37). Thus the stem *maghavat* can be looked upon as ending in *an*. Now the question arises : Why should *anām* be carried over into the present rule when the transformed stem can still be treated as ending in *an* without its being carried over into the present sūtra. Vāsudeva Dīkṣita[1] answers this question by saying that the anuvṛtti of *anām* is to block the process of samprasāraṇa in *maghavan* when its stem-final *n* is replaced by *t* (*tṛ*). Although, by virtue of the paribhāṣā mentioned above, the word *maghavat*, even after *tṛ*-replacement, can be treated as ending in *an*, the term *anām*, being present because of the anuvṛtti, qualifies the stems mentioned in the sūtra. Since the term *anām*

---

1. *śvayuvamaghonām annantatvāvyabhicārāt kimartham annantatvaviśeṣaṇam, maghavanśabde nakārasya trādeśapakṣe 'pi ekadeśavikṛtasyānanyatayā annantatvasattvād iti praśnaḥ. trādeśapakṣe maghavanśabde samprasāraṇanivṛtyartham annantatvaviśeṣaṇam. yadyapy ekadeśavikṛtasyānanyatayā annantatvam astyeva, tathāpi viśeṣaṇasāmarthyāt śrūyamāṇanakārāntasyaiva samprasāraṇam ityāhuḥ*. BM, I, pp. 374-5. Cf. also TB, I, p. 375.

directly qualifies the words mentioned in the rule, the process of samprasāraṇa will take place only when the phoneme *n* is present. In the case of *tṛ*-replacement, the phoneme *n* is not present.

The nominal stem *śvan* 'a dog' is declined in the same way except that in cases where samprasāraṇa takes place, the operation of guṇa sandhi is absent in the declensional process of *śvan*.

	Singular	Dual	Plural
prathamā	*śvā*	*śvānau*	*śvānaḥ*
dvitīyā	*śvānam*	*śvānau*	*śunaḥ*
tṛtīyā	*śunā*	*śvabhyām*	*śvabhiḥ*
caturthī	*śune*	*śvabhyām*	*śvabhyaḥ*
pañcamī	*śunaḥ*	*śvabhyām*	*śvabhyaḥ*
ṣaṣṭhī	*śunaḥ*	*śunoḥ*	*śunām*
saptamī	*śuni*	*śunoḥ*	*śvasu*
sambodhana	*he śvan!*	*he śvānau!*	*he śvānaḥ!*

The nominal stem *yuvan* 'young' is declined like the word *rājan*, when sarvanāmasthāna affixes follow. In *yuvan* + *śas* --> *yuvan* + *as*, the stem goes through the process of samprasāraṇa by *śvayuvamaghonām-ataddhite* (289) and we have *yu u an* + *as*. At this stage, the rule *samprasāraṇācca* (257) applies and a single replacement in the form of the preceding phoneme, that is, *u* comes in place of *u* and *a*. After the application of *akaḥ savarṇe dīrghaḥ* (42), the form reaches the following stage : *yūn* + *as*. In this situation, the rule *śvayuvamaghonāmataddhite* (289) again becomes applicable to prescribe samprasāraṇa in place of *y* but the following sūtra prohibits this :

(290) न सम्प्रसारणे सम्प्रसारणम् । *na samprasāraṇe samprasāraṇam.* 6. 1. 37

लघु० – सम्प्रसारणे परतः पूर्वस्य यणः सम्प्रसारणं न स्यात् । इति यकारस्य नेत्वम् । अत एव ज्ञापकादन्त्यस्य यणः पूर्वं सम्प्रसारणम् । यूनः । यूना । युवभ्याम् इत्यादि ।

samprasāraṇe parataḥ pūrvasya yaṇaḥ samprasāraṇaṁ na syāt. iti yakārasya netvam. ata eva jñāpakād antyasya yaṇaḥ pūrvaṁ samprasāraṇam. yūnaḥ. yūnā. yuvabhyām ityādi.

Trans. : Let the process of samprasāraṇa not apply in the case of a prior *yaṇ* when samprasāraṇa follows. Therefore the (prior) phoneme *y* is not replaced by *i*. In this way, the rule implies that the final *yaṇ* undergoes the process of samprasāraṇa first.

PP. *na samprasāraṇe samprasāraṇam.*

Eluc. : A phoneme denoted by the abbreviatory term *yaṇ* is not replaced by a corresponding phoneme denoted by the abbreviatory term *ik* when it is followed by samprasāraṇa. This sūtra blocks the process of samprasāraṇa when samprasāraṇa has already taken place. As such, the rule implies that the samprasāraṇa replacement of a semi-vowel takes place from right to left if there are more phonemes than one to undergo the process of samprasāraṇa.

In the illustration *yūn + as*, the semi-vowel *y* preceding the vowel *ū* does not undergo the process of samprasāraṇa since the semi-vowel *v* has already undergone the process of samprasāraṇa, which follows the semi-vowel *y*. Thus we obtain the form *yūnaḥ* after rutva and visarga. The complete declension of *yuvan* runs as follows :

	Singular	Dual	Plural
prathamā	*yuvā*	*yuvānau*	*yuvānaḥ*
dvitīyā	*yuvānam*	*yuvānau*	*yūnaḥ*
tṛtīyā	*yūnā*	*yuvabhyām*	*yuvabhiḥ*
caturthī	*yūne*	*yuvabhyām*	*yuvabhyaḥ*
pañcamī	*yūnaḥ*	*yuvabhyām*	*yuvabhyaḥ*
ṣaṣṭhī	*yūnaḥ*	*yūnoḥ*	*yūnām*
saptamī	*yūni*	*yūnoḥ*	*yuvasu*
sambodhana	*he yuvan!*	*he yuvānau!*	*he yuvānaḥ!*

The nominal stem *arvan* 'a horse' is derived with the addition of the affix *vanip* after the verbal root *ṛ* 'to go' in accordance with the rule *anyebhyo 'pi dṛśyante* (796). The declensional forms of the word *arvan* in the nominative and vocative singular respectively are *arvā* and *he arvan!* like those of the nominal stem *rājan*.

When we introduce the dual affix of the first triplet, we have *arvan + au*. At this stage, the following sūtra ensues :

(291) अर्वणस्त्रसावनञः । *arvaṇastrasāvanañaḥ.* **6. 4. 127**
लघु० – नञा रहितस्य अर्वन् इत्यस्याङ्गस्य तृ इत्यन्तादेशो न तु सौ । अर्वन्तौ । अर्वन्तः । अर्वद्भ्याम् इत्यादि । *nañā rahitasya arvan ityasyāṅgasya tṛ ityantādeśo na tu sau. arvantau. arvantaḥ. arvadbhyām ityādi.*

Trans. : The substitute *tṛ* replaces the final phoneme of the pre-affixal base *arvan* if it is without the negative particle *nañ*, but not when it is followed by the affix *su*.

PP. *anañaḥ arvaṇaḥ aṅgasya tṛ asau.*

Eluc. : The term *anañaḥ* is a bahuvrīhi compound and is in the genitive singular. It is analysed as : *na vidyate nañ yasya saḥ anañ, tasya = anañaḥ.* The compound *asau* is a nañ-tatpuruṣa which is analysed as : *na suḥ asuḥ, tasmin = asau.* Thus the sūtra yields the following meaning : If the pre-affixal base *arvan* is without the particle *nañ* and if it is followed by a sup-affix other than *su*, then the substitute *tṛ* replaces its final phoneme. After the elision of the vowel *ṛ* in *tṛ*, the substitute remains as *t*. Therefore it will replace the final phoneme of the pre-affixal base *arvan* according to the sūtra *alo 'ntyasya* (21). This comes to mean that the final *n* of *arvan* is replaced by *t*. Thus we have *arvat + au*. At this stage, the rule *ugidacāṁ sarvanāmasthāne 'dhātoḥ* (288) prescribes the insertion of *num* after the last vowel in *arvat* : *arva num t + au --> arva n t + au* and we have *arvantau* after *naścāpadāntasya jhali* (78) and *anusvārasya yayi parasavarṇaḥ* (79) have performed their grammatical operations. Thus in the declensional process of the nominal stem *arvan*, the insertion of *num* takes place when a sarvanāmasthāna affix other than *su*, follows. The rule *jhalāṁ jaśo'nte* (67) applies and the *jaś*-substitution takes place when the affixes *bhyām, bhis,* etc. follow. The complete declension of the nominal stem *arvan* is as follows :

	Singular	Dual	Plural
prathamā	*arvā*	*arvantau*	*arvantaḥ*
dvitīyā	*arvantam*	*arvantau*	*arvataḥ*
tṛtīyā	*arvatā*	*arvadbhyām*	*arvadbhiḥ*
caturthī	*arvate*	*arvadbhyām*	*arvadbhyaḥ*
pañcamī	*arvataḥ*	*arvadbhyām*	*arvadbhyaḥ*
ṣaṣṭhī	*arvataḥ*	*arvatoḥ*	*arvatām*

saptamī	*arvati*	*arvatoḥ*	*arvatsu*
sambodhana	*he arvan!*	*he arvantau!*	*he arvantaḥ!*

The nominal stem *pathin* ends in *n*. When the singular affix of the first triplet is introduced after *pathin*, the following sūtra ensues :

(292) पथिमथ्यृभुक्षामात्। *pathimathyṛbhukṣāmāt*. 7. 1. 85
लघु० – एषामाकारोऽन्तादेशः सौ परे। *eṣām ākāro 'ntādeśaḥ sau pare.*

Trans. : Let the stem-final phoneme of the nominal stems *pathin* 'a road, a path', *mathin* 'a churning stick' and *ṛbhukṣin* 'Indra' be replaced by a long *ā* when the affix *su* follows.

PP. *pathimathyṛbhukṣām āt sau* (*aṅgasya*).
Eluc. : The term *sau* is carried over from *sāvanaḍuhaḥ* Pā. 7. 1. 82. The compound word *pathimathyṛbhukṣām* is an itaretaradvandva which is analysed as follows : *panthāś ca manthāś ca ṛbhukṣāś ca pathimathyṛbhukṣāṇaḥ, teṣām = pathimathyṛbhukṣām*. With the help of *alo 'ntyasya* (21), the sūtra means as follows : When the affix *su* follows, the final phoneme of *pathin, mathin* and *ṛbhukṣin* is replaced by a long *ā*.

In *pathin + su*, the phoneme *n* is replaced by *ā* and we have *pathi ā + su --> pathi ā + s*. At this stage the following sūtra applies :

(293) इतोऽत् सर्वनामस्थाने। *ito 't sarvanāmasthāne*. 7. 1. 86
लघु० – पथ्यादेरिकारस्य अकारः स्यात् सर्वनामस्थाने परे। *pathyāder ikārasya akāraḥ syāt sarvanāmasthāne pare.*

Trans. : When a sarvanāmasthāna affix follows, the vowel *i* occurring in the nominal stems *pathin*, etc. is replaced by a short *a*.

PP. *pathimathyṛbhukṣām itaḥ at sarvanāmasthāne* (*aṅgasya*).
Eluc. : The compound word *pathimathyṛbhukṣām* comes from *pathimathyṛbhukṣāmāt* Pā. 7. 1. 85. The sūtra means : The vowel *i* of *pathin, mathin* and *ṛbhukṣin* is replaced by a short *a* when a sarvanāmasthāna affix follows. In the illustration *pathi ā + s*, the vowel *i* following the consonant *th* is replaced by a short *a* : *patha ā + s*. At this stage, the following sūtra presents itself for application :

(294) थोऽन्थः। *tho 'nthaḥ*. 7. 1. 87
लघु० – पथिमथोस् थस्य न्थादेशः स्यात्, सर्वनामस्थाने परे। पन्थाः। पन्थानौ। पन्थानः।

pathimathos thasya nthādeśaḥ syāt sarvanāmasthāne pare. panthāḥ, panthānau, panthānaḥ.

Trans. : When a sarvanāmasthāna affix follows, let the phoneme *th* of *pathin* and *mathin* be replaced by *nth*.

PP. *pathimathoḥ thaḥ nthaḥ sarvanāmasthāne (aṅgasya).*

Eluc. : Because of the mention of *thaḥ*, the compound *pathimathoḥ* is marked out from *pathimathyṛbhukṣām* and is carried over into the present sūtra. The vowel *a* in *nthaḥ* occurring in the sūtra is for the sake of articulation. The word *sarvanāmasthāne* is carried over from *ito 't sarvanāmasthāne* Pā. 7. 1. 86. Thus the sūtra yields the following meaning: The consonant *th* occurring in the words *pathin* and *mathin* is replaced by *nth* provided a sarvanāmasthāna affix follows. The nominal stem *ṛbhukṣin* is not made to recur in the present rule since the stem *ṛbhukṣin* does not have the consonant *th* in it.

In the illustration *patha ā* + s, the phoneme *th* is replaced by *nth* and we have *pantha ā* + s. After the application of the rule *akaḥ savarṇe...* (42), we get the form *panthāḥ* after rutva and visarga. In the same way, by applying this rule and the preceding one, we obtain the other four forms : *panthānau, panthānaḥ, panthānam* and *panthānau*. In these four forms the penultimate vowel is lengthened by *sarvanāmasthāne...* (176).

When we introduce the plural affix of the second triplet, we have *pathin* + *śas* --> *pathin* + *as*. In this illustration, the rules *ito 't...* (293) and *sarvanāmasthāne...* (176) have no scope since the affix *śas* is other than sarvanāmasthāna. In this situation, the following sūtra presents itself :

(295) भस्य टेर्लोपः । **bhasya ṭerlopaḥ. 7. 1. 88**

लघु० - भसंज्ञकस्य पथ्यादेष्टेर्लोपः स्यात्। पथः। पथा। पथिभ्याम्। एवम् मथिन्, ऋभुक्षिन्। *bhasaṁjñakasya pathyādeṣ ṭer lopaḥ syāt. pathaḥ. pathā. pathibhyām. evam mathin, ṛbhukṣin.*

Trans. : The *ṭi* of the nominal stems *pathin*, etc. is elided when they are designated as *bha*.

PP. *pathimathyṛbhukṣām bhānām ṭer lopaḥ (aṅgasya).*

Eluc. : By the process of vacanavipariṇāma the word *bhasya* is changed to *bhānām* so that it may agree with the compound word *pathimathyṛbhukṣām* carried over from the sūtra *pathimathyṛbhukṣāmāt* 7. 1. 85. Now the sūtra gives the following meaning : When *pathin, mathin* and *ṛbhukṣin* receive bha-designation, their *ṭi* is elided. In the illustration *pathin* + *as*, the stem *pathin* is bha according to *yaci bham* (164). Therefore the segment *in* in *pathin*, which is *ṭi* according to *aco 'ntyādi ṭi* (39), is elided and we get the form *pathaḥ* after *s* has been replaced by *ru* {*sasajuṣo...* (104)}, which is further substituted by visarga according to *kharavasāna...* (93). When *pathin* gets the pada-designation before *bhyām*, etc., the phoneme *n* is elided by *na lopaḥ...* (179). Thus the nominal stem *pathin* will be declined as follows:

	Singular	Dual	Plural
prathamā	*panthāḥ*	*panthānau*	*panthānaḥ*
dvitīyā	*panthānam*	*panthānau*	*pathaḥ*
tṛtīyā	*pathā*	*pathibhyām*	*pathibhiḥ*
caturthī	*pathe*	*pathibhyām*	*pathibhyaḥ*
pañcamī	*pathaḥ*	*pathibhyām*	*pathibhyaḥ*
ṣaṣṭhī	*pathaḥ*	*pathoḥ*	*pathām*
saptamī	*pathi*	*pathoḥ*	*pathiṣu*
sambodhana	*he panthāḥ!*	*he panthānau!*	*he panthānaḥ!*

The nominal stem *mathin* will be declined exactly like *pathin* but the nominal stem *ṛbhukṣin* is declined slightly differently. In the nominative singular, there is no *nth*-replacement since there is no *th* in *ṛbhukṣin*. So, the form of *ṛbhukṣin* in the nominative singular is *ṛbhukṣāḥ* through the following grammatical process : *ṛbhukṣin* + *su* --> *ṛbhukṣi ā* + *s* {*pathimathy...* (292)} --> *ṛbhukṣa ā* + *s* by *ito...* (293) --> *ṛbhukṣās* {*akaḥ...* (42)} --> *ṛbhukṣāḥ* (after rutva and visarga). The *ṇ*-replacement in the declensional forms of *ṛbhukṣin* is according to the rule *aṭkupvāṅ...* (137). In this way, the nominal stem *ṛbhukṣin* is declined as follows :

	Singular	Dual	Plural
prathamā	*ṛbhukṣāḥ*	*ṛbhukṣāṇau*	*ṛbhukṣāṇaḥ*
dvitīyā	*ṛbhukṣāṇam*	*ṛbhukṣāṇau*	*ṛbhukṣaḥ*
tṛtīyā	*ṛbhukṣā*	*ṛbhukṣibhyām*	*ṛbhukṣibhiḥ*
caturthī	*ṛbhukṣe*	*ṛbhukṣibhyām*	*ṛbhukṣibhyaḥ*
pañcamī	*ṛbhukṣaḥ*	*ṛbhukṣibhyām*	*ṛbhukṣibhyaḥ*

ṣaṣṭhī	*ṛbhukṣaḥ*	*ṛbhukṣoḥ*	*ṛbhukṣām*
saptamī	*ṛbhukṣi*	*ṛbhukṣoḥ*	*ṛbhukṣiṣu*
sambodhana	*he ṛbhukṣāḥ!*	*he ṛbhukṣāṇau!*	*he ṛbhukṣāṇaḥ!*

The word *pañcan* 'five' that ends in the consonant *n* is technically designated as *ṣaṭ* by the following sūtra :

(296) ष्णान्ता षट् । *ṣṇāntā ṣaṭ.* 1. 1. 24

लघु० – षान्ता नान्ता च संख्या षट्संज्ञा स्यात् । पञ्चन्-शब्दो नित्यं बहुवचनान्तः । पञ्च । पञ्च । पञ्चभिः । पञ्चभ्यः । पञ्चभ्यः । नुट् – *ṣāntā nāntā ca saṁkhyā ṣaṭsaṁjñā syāt. 'pañcan' śabdo nityaṁ bahuvacanāntaḥ. pañca. pañca. pañcabhiḥ. pañcabhyaḥ. pañcabhyaḥ. nuṭ –*

Trans. : Let a numeral which ends in *ṣ* or *n* be designated as *ṣaṭ*. The word *pañcan* is always plural.

PP. *ṣṇāntā saṁkhyā ṣaṭ.*

Eluc. : The word *saṁkhyā* is carried over from *bahuganavatuḍati saṅkhyā* Pā. 1. 1. 23. The word *ṣṇāntā* is a dvandva-seeded bahuvrīhi compound. Its analysis is as follows : *ṣ ca naś ca ṣṇau* (dvandva). *ṣṇau antau yasyāḥ sā = ṣṇāntā* (bahuvrīhi : qualifying *saṁkhyā*). The vowel *a* after *n* is for the sake of pronunciation. The dental *n* is replaced by cerebral *ṇ* occurring after *ṣ* in accordance with the sūtra *raṣābhyāṁ no ṇaḥ...* (266). Thus the meaning of the sūtra is : A numeral which ends either in *ṣ* or in *n* is to be designated as *ṣaṭ*. The word *pañcan* ends in *n*. So, this gets the designation *ṣaṭ*. Consequently, both the plural affixes *jas* and *śas*, introduced after the stem *pañcan*, are deleted by *ṣaḍbhyo luk* (187) and we obtain a common form *pañca* both in nominative and accusative plural after the elision of the pada-final *n* by *na lopaḥ...* (179). With the plural affixes of the third, fourth and fifth triplets, the word *pañcan* gets the pada-designation and the elision of *n* takes place by *na lopaḥ prātipadikāntasya* (179) and we have *pañcabhiḥ, pañcabhyaḥ* and *pañcabhyaḥ* in a respective order.

In *pañcan + ām,* the augment *nuṭ* is prescribed to be inserted at the head of the affix *ām* by *ṣaṭcaturbhyaśca* (265) with the help of *ādyantau ṭakitau* (84) and we have *pañcan + nuṭ ām --> pañcan + nām*. At this stage, the following sūtra presents itself for application :

(297) नोपधायाः । *nopadhāyāḥ*. 6. 4. 7

लघु० – नान्तस्य उपधाया दीर्घः स्यान्नामि परे । पञ्चानाम् । पञ्चसु । *nāntasya upadhāyā dīrghaḥ syān nāmi pare. pañcānām. pañcasu.*

Trans. : Let the penultimate (*upadhā*) of the pre-affixal base, which ends in the consonant *n*, be replaced by a long vowel.

PP. *na aṅgasya upadhāyāḥ dīrghaḥ nāmi.*

Eluc. : The term *aṅgasya* recurs here since the present sūtra occurs in the domain of the governing rule *aṅgasya* Pā. 6. 4. 1. The genitive case-ending of the word *na* is taken as elided. This word qualifies the term *aṅgasya* (*luptaṣaṣṭhīkam aṅgasyetyadhikṛtasya viśeṣaṇam*, BM, I, p. 383). By tadantavidhi it gives the sense *nāntasya aṅgasya*. The words *dīrghaḥ* and *nāmi* respectively come from *ḍhralope pūrvasya dīrgho 'ṇaḥ* Pā. 6. 3. 111 and *nāmi* Pā. 6. 4. 3. Thus the meaning of the sūtra will be as follows : When *nām* follows, the penultimate vowel of the pre-affixal base that ends in *n* is replaced by a long vowel.

In the illustration *pañcan* + *nām*, the word *pañcan* is technically a pada by *svādiṣvasarvanāmasthāne* (163). Therefore the rule *na lopaḥ...* Pā. 8. 2. 2 applies and the elision of *n* takes place but the elision of *n* is deemed as not to have taken effect with respect to *nopadhāyāḥ* 6. 4. 7, which therefore applies and the penultimate *a* of *pañcan* gets replaced by a long *ā*. We obtain the form *pañcānām*.

If this sūtra had not been enunciated by Pāṇini, the pada-final *a* of *pañca* would not have been replaced by a long vowel since the elision of *n* is deemed not to have taken effect with respect to *nāmi* Pā. 6. 4. 3. The problem has been sorted out by the present rule.

The word *pañcan* which is always used in the plural is declined as follows :

	Plural		Plural
prathamā	*pañca*	pañcamī	*pañcabhyaḥ*
dvitīyā	*pañca*	ṣaṣṭhī	*pañcānām*
tṛtīyā	*pañcabhiḥ*	saptamī	*pañcasu*
caturthī	*pañcabhyaḥ*	sambodhana	No form

The declension of the word *saptan* which is designated as *ṣaṭ* by *ṣṇāntā ṣaṭ* (296) will be exactly like that of the word *pañcan*. The numerical word *aṣṭan* which ends in the phoneme *n* is also *ṣaṭ* and is always used in the plural. To decline it, when we introduce the plural sup-affixes of the first and second triplets, we have *aṣṭan* + *as* (*jas* or *śas*). In this situation, the following sūtra ensues :

(298) अष्टन आ विभक्तौ । *aṣṭana ā vibhaktau*. 7. 2. 84

लघु० – अष्टन आत्वं वा स्याद् हलादौ विभक्तौ । *aṣṭana ātvaṁ vā syād halādau vibhaktau.*

Trans. : When a sup-affix which begins with a consonant (*hal*) follows, the pre-affixal base-final phoneme of *aṣṭan* is optionally replaced by a long *ā*.

PP. *aṣṭana āḥ hali vibhaktau* (*aṅgasya*).

Eluc. : The term *hali* is drawn back from the succeeding sūtra *rāyo hali* Pā. 7. 2. 85 (cf. *halītyasyānapakarṣaṇe tvaṣṭānāmiti na sidhyet*, TB, I, p. 385). This is the process of apakarṣa, which is also known as *siṁhāvalokitanyāya*. It is named on the analogy of the backward look peculiar to a lion who always looks back at the ground covered as he advances. This term is used in grammar with reference to a word taken back from a subsequent rule to the preceding one. The technical name of this process is apakarṣa (Dictionary, pp. 32 and 428). The term *hali* qualifies the word *vibhaktau*. By tadādividhi, it gives the sense *halādau vibhaktau* by virtue of the paribhāṣā *yasmin vidhis tadādāv algrahaṇe* (Abhyankar, 33). Thus the meaning of the sūtra is as follows : The aṅga-final phoneme of *aṣṭana* is optionally replaced by a long *ā* when a consonant-initial sup-affix follows. The consonant *n* of *aṣṭan* is optionally replaced by *ā* with the help of *alo 'ntyasya* (21).

The term *dīrghāt* in the sūtra *aṣṭano dīrghāt* Pā. 6. 1. 172 implies that the *ā*-replacement is optional (SK, I, p, 384). Had this *ā*-replacement been universally available, the use of the term *dīrghāt* would have been meaningless. Hence it implies that the replacement of a long *ā* is optional.

The present sūtra becomes available for application before the sup-affixes which begin with a consonant. So, this rule has no scope before *jas* and *śas* which remain as *as* after the elision of *j* and *ś* which are *its*. The following sūtra makes provision for the replacement of the stem-final phoneme of *aṣṭan* by a long *ā* even before a vowel-initial affix :

(299) अष्टाभ्य औश् । *aṣṭābhya auś*. 7. 1. 21

लघु० – कृताकाराद् अष्टनः परयोर्जश्शसोर् औश् स्यात् । अष्टभ्य इति वक्तव्ये कृतात्वनिर्देशो जश्शसोर्विषय आत्वं ज्ञापयति । अष्टौ । अष्टौ । अष्टाभिः । अष्टाभ्यः 2 । अष्टानाम् । अष्टासु ।

आत्वाभावे -- अष्ट 2 इत्यादि पञ्चवत्। *kṛtākārād aṣṭanaḥ parayor jaśśasor auś syāt. aṣṭabhya iti vaktavye kṛtātvanirdeśo jaśśsor viṣaya ātvaṁ jñāpayati. aṣṭau. aṣṭau. aṣṭābhiḥ. aṣṭābhyaḥ* 2. *aṣṭānām. aṣṭāsu. ātvābhāve -- aṣṭa* 2 *ityādi pañcavat.*

Trans. : Let the substitute *auś* replace the affixes *jas* and *śas* when they follow the pre-affixal base *aṣṭan*, the final phoneme of which has been replaced by a long *ā* (298). Although it would be proper to use the term *aṣṭabhyaḥ*, the enunciation of the term with a long *ā* instead, implies that the replacement by a long *ā* does take place in the case of *jas* and *śas* (even though they do not begin with a consonant).

PP. *aṣṭābhyaḥ jaśśasoḥ auś* (*aṅgasya*).

Eluc. : The compound word *jaśśasoḥ* is carried over from *jaśśasoḥ śiḥ* Pā. 7. 1. 20. The word *aṣṭābhyaḥ* used in the sūtra is a declensional form of the stem *aṣṭā* which is an imitation of the word *aṣṭan* with its final phoneme having been replaced by a long *ā*. The use of the plural affix *bhyas* is to refer to the primary word *aṣṭan*. The meaning of the sūtra is as follows : The affixes *jas* and *śas* are to be replaced by *auś* when they follow the pre-affixal base *aṣṭan*, the final phoneme of which has been replaced by a long *ā* according to *aṣṭana ā...* (298). Since *auś* is *śit*, it replaces the whole substituendum by *anekāl śit sarvasya* (45).

Explaining the sūtra *aṣṭana ā vibhaktau* (298), Varadarāja uses the term *halādau* in his vṛtti. This means that, according to him, the term *hali* is to be drawn back from the succeeding sūtra *rayo hali* Pā. 7. 2. 85 to qualify the term *vibhaktau*. Accordingly, a long *ā* will replace the phoneme *n* when the stem *aṣṭan* is followed by a sup-affix which begins with a consonant {cf. *yasmin vidhis...* (Abhyankar, 33)}. Since the affixes (*j*)*as* and (*ś*)*as* begin with a vowel, the final *n* is not to be replaced by a long *ā*. Then how can there be a replacement of *jas* and *śas* by *auś* when the final *n* of *aṣṭan* has not been replaced by *ā* before vowel-initial affixes. Had Pāṇini intended to only replace the affixes *jas* and *śas* by *auś*, he would have enunciated *aṣṭabhyaḥ* instead of *aṣṭābhyaḥ* in the present sūtra. That would have saved one mora. In spite of this, Pāṇini has used the term *aṣṭābhyaḥ* in order to imply that the pre-affixal base-final phoneme *n* is to be replaced by a long *ā* even when *jas* and *śas* follow.

So, by virtue of this implication, the pre-affixal base-final *n* is replaced by *ā*. As a consequence of this, the substitute *auś* replaces the affixes *jas* and *śas* in the illustration *aṣṭan* + *as* (*jas* or *śas*) and we have *aṣṭa ā* + *auś* in both the cases. After the application of the rules *akaḥ savarṇe dīrghaḥ* (42) and *vṛddhireci* (33), we obtain the declined form *aṣṭau*.

With the affixes *bhis, bhyas*, etc., the *n* of *aṣṭan* is optionally replaced by *ā* and we get the forms *aṣṭābhiḥ, aṣṭabhiḥ, aṣṭābhyaḥ, aṣṭabhyaḥ*, etc.

With the introduction of the affix *ām* after *aṣṭan*, the augment *nuṭ* is inserted at the head of the affix *ām* by *ṣaṭcaturbhyaśca* (265) with the help of *ādyantau ṭakitau* (84). Now since *nām* begins with a consonant, the pre-affixal base final *n* is replaced by a long *ā* and we obtain the form *aṣṭānām* after the application of *akaḥ savarṇe...* (42) through the following grammatical process : *aṣṭan + ām --> aṣṭan + nuṭ ām --> aṣṭan + nām --> aṣṭa ā + nām --> aṣṭānām*.

In *aṣṭan + sup*, we obtain *aṣṭa ā + su --> aṣṭāsu* after the application of *aṣṭana ā vibhaktau* (298).

In the absence of the replacement of *n* by *ā*, the declension of *aṣṭan* will be like that of *pañcan*. Although the form of *aṣṭan* with a genitive plural affix *ām* is the same in both the cases, there is a difference in the grammatical process. In the absence of *ā*-substitution, the augment *nuṭ* is inserted at the head of the affix *ām* and then the elision of *n* takes place by *na lopaḥ*... Pā. 8. 2. 7, which is deemed not to have taken place with respect to *nopadhāyāḥ* Pā. 6. 4. 7. Hence the rule *nopadhāyāḥ* brings about the lengthening of the penultimate vowel of *aṣṭan* and we obtain the form *aṣṭānām*. How we obtain the same form in the alternative of *ā*-substitution has been explained above.

1. When replacement by *ā* takes place, the declension is as follows :

	Plural		Plural
prathamā	*aṣṭau*	pañcamī	*aṣṭābhyaḥ*
dvitīyā	*aṣṭau*	ṣaṣṭhī	*aṣṭānām*
tṛtīyā	*aṣṭābhiḥ*	saptamī	*aṣṭāsu*
caturthī	*aṣṭābhyaḥ*	sambodhana	No form

2. In the absence of the replacement of *n* by *ā*, the declension of *aṣṭan* will be as follows :

	Plural		Plural
prathamā	*aṣṭa*	pañcamī	*aṣṭabhyaḥ*
dvitīyā	*aṣṭa*	ṣaṣṭhī	*aṣṭānām*
tṛtīyā	*aṣṭabhiḥ*	saptamī	*aṣṭasu*
caturthī	*aṣṭabhyaḥ*	sambodhana	No form

The declension of the numerals ranging from *navan* to *navadaśan* will be like that of the numerical stem *pañcan*.

Here comes to an end the declension of the masculine nominal stems that end in the phoneme *n*.

Now begins the declension of the masculine nominal stems that end in the phoneme *j*. The first word that is taken up in the Laghu in this context is *ṛtvij*, the derivation of which is explained in the following sūtra :

(300) ऋत्विग्दधृक्स्रग्दिगुष्णिगञ्चुयुजिक्रुञ्चां च । *ṛtvigdadhṛgsragdiguṣṇig añcuyujikruñcāṁ ca*. 3. 2. 59

लघु० – एभ्यः क्विन्, अञ्चेः सुप्युपपदे, युजिक्रुञ्चोः केवलयोः, क्रुञ्चेर्नलोपाभावश्च निपात्यते । कनावितौ । *ebhyaḥ kvin añceḥ supyupapade yujikruñcoḥ kevalayoḥ kruñcer nalopābhāvaś ca nipātyate. kanāv itau.*

Trans. : The affix *kvin* occurs by nipātana in the derivation of *ṛtvij 'ṛtau yajatīti*, a priest who performs ritual sacrifices regularly', *dadhṛṣ* 'audacious', *sraj* 'a garland', *diś* 'direction', *uṣṇih* 'a Vedic metre with seven syllables in a quarter' and after the verbal roots *añcu* 'to go, to worship' *yuji* 'to join' and *kruñc* 'to be crooked'. The affix is introduced after *añcu* when a word ending with a nominal ending precedes it as an upapada. It comes after *yuj* and *kruñc* when they are without upapada. The absence of the elision of *n* of *kruñc* is also by nipātana.

PP. *ṛtvigdadhṛgsragdiguṣṇig añcuyujikruñcāṁ ca kvin* (*supi dhātoḥ*).

Eluc. : The affix *kvin* is carried over from *spṛśo 'nudake kvin* Pā. 3. 2. 58. According to the Kāśikā, this sūtra can be divided into two parts : 1. The five words *ṛtvik, dadhṛk, srak, dik* and *uṣṇik* are shown as derived irregularly with the introduction of the primary affix *kvin*. 2. The other three verbal roots are given separately (*ṛtvigādayaḥ pañca śabdāḥ kvinpratyayāntā nipātyante. apare trayo dhātavo nirdiśyante*). This comes to mean that the rule has two sentences : 1. *ṛtvigdadhṛgsragdiguṣṇig* 2. *añcuyujikruñcāṁ ca*. Pāṇini has first enumerated the five nominal stems which have been derived with the addition of the primary affix *kvin* in an irregular way (*nipātana*). Then he has given three verbal roots after which the affix *kvin* has been prescribed. The first compound word constituting the first sentence is a samāhāradvandva. Its analysis is as follows : *ṛtvik ca dadhṛk ca srak ca dik ca uṣṇik ca, ṛtvigdadhṛgsragdiguṣṇig*.

The compound word *añcuyujikruñcāṁ* is an itaretaradvandva which is analysed as follows : *añcuś ca yujiś ca kruṅ ca = añcuyujikruñcaḥ, teṣām = añcuyujikruñcāṁ.*

The process of nipātana consists in grammatical operations, which are seen to have been carried out in a finished word but which are not prescribed directly by the rules. How this process takes place will be clear from the following details :

1. *ṛtvij* - The word is derived from *ṛtau, ṛtuṁ, ṛtuprayukto vā yajati* (cf. *ṛtuśabde upapade yajer dhātoḥ kvinpratyayo nipātyate -- ṛtau yajati ṛtuṁ vā yajati ṛtuprayukto vā yajatīti ṛtvik,* Kāśikā on this rule; for more details see KN, II, pp. 582-3). In the third explanatory sentence *ṛtuprayukto yajati,* the elision of the posterior member *prayuktaḥ* takes effect by nipātana. The affix *kvin* is not enjoined by any rule to be added after the verbal root *yaj* when the word *ṛtu* precedes it as upapada. Hence its introduction after *yaj* is also by nipātana. As a consequence, the verbal root *yaj* undergoes the process of samprasāraṇa by *vacisvapi...* (546) and we obtain the word *ṛtvij* after the application of the rules *samprasāraṇācca* (257) and *iko yaṇaci* (15).

2. The derivation of *dadhṛṣ* entails the reduplication of *dhṛṣ* before *kvin* through nipātana. In other words it may be said that both the introduction of *kvin* and the reduplication of *dhṛṣ* are irregular.

3. In the derivation of *sraj* from the verbal root *sṛj,* both the introduction of the affix *kvin* and the augment of *am* are through nipātana.

4. The introduction of *kvin* after the verbal root *diś* in the sense of an object (*karma*) is irregular.

5. The addition of *kvin*, the elision of the final phoneme of the prefix *ud* in *ud + snih + kvin* and the replacement of the dental s by the cerebral ṣ have taken effect by nipātana. In this way the nominal stem *uṣṇih* is obtained.

The three verbal roots *añcu, yuji* and *kruñca* are enunciated along with the five irregularly formed words discussed just now. Therefore, there also has to be some irregular grammatical operation with regard to these verbal roots. This is explained as follows :

1. The introduction of the affix *kvin* after *añcu* when an inflected term precedes it as upapada is through nipātana.

2. Although occurring in the governing domain of *sup* and *karma*, the introduction of the affix *kvin* after the verbal root *yuj* and *kruñc* which are not preceded by upapada is because of nipātana (cf. KN, II, p. 583).

3. The absence of the elision of the nasal consonant *n* of *kruñc,* which is available by *aniditāṁ hala upadhāyāḥ...* (333) is due to the grammatical technique of nipātana.

The nominal stem *ṛtvij* as has been explained is derived by adding the affix *kvin* after *yaj* when it is preceded by *ṛtu* as upapada. The whole affix *kvin* is elided in the following way : The initial consonant *k* is *it* by *laśakvataddhite* (135) and the final *n* is *it* by *halantyam* (1); both are elided by *tasya lopaḥ* (3). The vowel *i* is for the sake of articulation. In this way we reach this stage of the derivational form : *ṛtvij* + *v*. Now the following sūtra presents itself :

(301) कृदतिङ् । *kṛdatiṅ*. 3. 1. 93

लघु० – अत्र धात्वधिकारे तिङ्-भिन्नः प्रत्ययः कृत्संज्ञः स्यात्। *atra dhātvadhikāre tiṅ-bhinnaḥ pratyayaḥ kṛtsaṁjñaḥ syāt.*

Trans. : In this governing domain of *dhātoḥ* Pā. 3. 1. 91, let the affix other than the one denoted by the abbreviatory term *tiṅ* be designated as *kṛt*.

PP. *tatra atiṅ kṛt (dhātoḥ, pratyayaḥ).*

Eluc. : This sūtra occurs in the domain of the governing rule *dhātoḥ* Pā. 3. 1. 91. This means that the affixes enjoined in this domain, which extends up to the end of the third chapter of the Aṣṭādhyāyī, are to be introduced after a verbal root. The indeclinable *tatra* is carried over from *tatropapadaṁ saptamīstham* Pā. 3. 1. 92. The word *tatra* means in the governing domain of *dhātoḥ* {*tatraitasmin dhātvadhikāre* (Mbh on 3. 1. 92 vtk 1)}. The word *atra* given by Varadarāja carries this sense. Thus the meaning of the sūtra is : The affix which is enjoined after a verbal root in the domain of *dhātoḥ* Pā. 3. 1. 91 is to be designated as *kṛt* provided that it is different from the affix that is denoted by the abbreviatory term *tiṅ*. The affix *kvin* is a *kṛt* affix since it is prescribed in this domain and is different from *tiṅ*.

In the illustration *ṛtvij* + *v* (*kvin*), the remaining part of the affix is also deemed as a *kṛt* affix by virtue of the paribhāṣā *ekadeśavikṛtam...* (Abhyankar, 37). At this stage, the following sūtra ensues :

(302) वेरपृक्तस्य । *verapṛktasya*. 6. 1. 67

लघु० – अपृक्तस्य वस्य लोपः। *apṛktasya vasya lopaḥ.*

Trans. : The single consonant affix *v* of *vi* (which is designated as *apṛkta*) is elided.

PP. *veḥ apṛktasya lopaḥ.*

Eluc. : The term *lopaḥ* is carried over from *lopo vyorvali* Pā. 6. 1. 66. The vowel *i* in *vi* is for the sake of articulation since *vi*, consisting of two phonemes, cannot be designated as *apṛkta*. This is the reason why the vowel *i* has been purported to facilitate the articulation. The meaning of the sūtra is : The single consonant affix *v* of *vi* is to be elided.

In the illustration *ṛtvij* + *v*, the affix *v* is elided according to the present rule and we obtain the primary nominal stem *ṛtvij*. Being a primary derivative (*kṛdanta*), the word *ṛtvij* gets the prātipadika designation by *kṛttaddhitasamāsāśca* (116). In the nominative singular, we have *ṛtvij* + *su*. At this stage, the following sūtra becomes available for application :

(303) क्विन्प्रत्ययस्य कुः । ***kvinpratyayasya kuḥ*. 8. 2. 62**

लघु० – क्विन्प्रत्ययो यस्मात् तस्य कवर्गोऽन्तादेशः स्यात् पदान्ते । अस्यासिद्धत्वाच् चोः कुः इति कुत्वम् । ऋत्विक्, ऋत्विग् । ऋत्विजौ । ऋत्विग्भ्याम् । ***kvinpratyayo yasmāt tasya kavargo 'ntādeśaḥ syāt padānte. asyāsiddhatvāc coḥ kuḥ iti kutvam. ṛtvik ṛtvig. ṛtvijau. ṛtvigbhyām.***

Trans. : The final phoneme of a pada, which ends in the affix *kvin*, is replaced by a consonant denoted by *ku* (kavarga). The rule is deemed as suspended in respect of the rule *coḥ kuḥ* Pā. 8. 2. 30 which, therefore, prescribes the substitute *ku* in place of *cu* (cavarga).

PP. *kvinpratyayasya kuḥ padasya ante.*

Eluc. : The present sūtra occurs in the domain of the governing rule *padasya* Pā. 8. 1. 16. Hence the term *padasya* recurs in the present sūtra. The word *ante* is carried over from *jhalāṁ jaśo 'nte* Pā. 8. 2. 39 (BM, I, p. 390. According to Bhaimī, I, p. 408, the term *ante* is carried over from *skoḥ saṁyogādyorante ca* Pā. 8. 2. 29; also cf. Pradīpa on Mbh 8. 2. 62). The word *kvinpratyayasya* is interpreted as a bahuvrīhi compound. It is analysed as follows : *kvin pratyayo yasmāt sa kvinpratyayaḥ, tasya = kvinpratyayasya*. Thus the sūtra means : A consonant denoted by *ku* replaces the pada-final phoneme of a nominal stem ending in the affix *kvin*. The nominal stem *ṛtvij* ends in the affix *kvin*. So by virtue of this rule, the pada-final phoneme, that is, *j* in the present case is to be replaced by a consonant of the *k*-series but by *pūrvatrāsiddham* Pā. 8. 2. 1, this is construed as suspended with respect to the rule *coḥ kuḥ* Pā. 8. 2. 30 which also prescribes the replacement of the pada-final cavarga by kavarga. In the illustration *ṛtvij* + *su*, the affix *s*(*u*) is elided by *halṅyābbhyo...* (178). Then the word *ṛtvij* gets the pada-designation by *suptiṅantaṁ padam* (14). According to Varadarāja both *coḥ kuḥ* (303) and the present rule simultaneously become available for application but the present rule, construed as suspended (asiddha) with respect to *coḥ kuḥ* Pā. 8. 2. 30, does not apply. As a consequence, the latter (*coḥ kuḥ*) applies and the pada-final *j* is replaced by *g*. Thus we obtain the form *ṛtvig*. In accordance with the rule *vā 'vasāne* (145), we can also have *ṛtvik*.[1] The present rule has its application in *yuṅ, prāṅ*, etc.

When the affixes *bhyām, bhis, bhyas* and *sup* follow, the nominal stem *ṛtvij* gets the pada-designation by *svādiṣvasarvanāmasthāne* (163). The pada-final phoneme *j* is substituted by *g* according to the rule *coḥ kuḥ* (305). In the locative plural, after the replacement of *j* by *g*, the dental *s* of *sup* is replaced by the cerebral *ṣ* in accordance with the sūtra *ādeśapratyayayoḥ* (149). After *ṣ*-replacement, the rule *khari ca* (74) applies and the phoneme *g* is replaced by *k*. Then the locative plural form of *ṛtvij* will be *ṛtvikṣu*. The complete declension of *ṛtvij* is given below :

	Singular	Dual	Plural
prathamā	*ṛtvik, g*	*ṛtvijau*	*ṛtvijaḥ*
dvitīyā	*ṛtvijam*	*ṛtvijau*	*ṛtvijaḥ*
tṛtīyā	*ṛtvijā*	*ṛtvigbhyām*	*ṛtvigbhiḥ*
caturthī	*ṛtvije*	*ṛtvigbhyām*	*ṛtvigbhyaḥ*
pañcamī	*ṛtvijaḥ*	*ṛtvigbhyām*	*ṛtvigbhyaḥ*
ṣaṣṭhī	*ṛtvijaḥ*	*ṛtvijoḥ*	*ṛtvijām*
saptamī	*ṛtviji*	*ṛtvijoḥ*	*ṛtvikṣu*
sambodhana	*he ṛtvik, g!*	*he ṛtvijau !*	*he ṛtvijaḥ!*

The nominal stem *yuj* 'yogin' is derived from the verbal root *yujir* after the introduction of the affix *kvin* via nipātana in accordance with the sūtra *ṛtvigdadhṛgsragdiguṣṇigañcuyujikruñcāṁ ca* (300). Thus the

1. According to Bhaṭṭoji Dīkṣita, the replacement of the pada-final phoneme of *ṛtvij* by a consonant denoted by *ku* (*kavarga*) takes place in accordance with the rule *kvinpratyayasya kuḥ* (304) only. Vāsudeva Dīkṣita explains that the substitution by a guttural consonant by *coḥ kuḥ* Pā. 8. 2. 30 is blocked by *vraścabhrasja*... Pā. 8. 2. 36 but it is not the case with the present rule since the very use of the expression *kvinpratyayasya* in the present sūtra ensures that the replacement by a guttural consonant by the present rule cannot be blocked by *vraścabhrasja*... Pā. 8. 2. 36. For this very purpose, the present rule enjoins the affix *kvin*. Cf. *etadartham eva kvinvidhānam iti bhāvaḥ. na ca kvipi coḥ kuḥ iti kutvenaivaitat sidhyatīti vācyam coḥ kuḥ iti kutvaṁ hi vraśca... iti ṣatvena apavādatvād bādhyeta kvinpratyayasya iti kutvaṁ tu kvinvidhisāmarthyād eva na bādhyate. yaṣṭetyādau ṣavidheś caritārthatvād iti bhāvaḥ.* BM, I, p. 394.

word *yuj* is a primary derivative (*kṛdanta*) and as such receives the prātipadika designation by *kṛttaddhitasamāsāśca* (116). In the nominative singular we introduce the affix *su* : *yuj* + *su*. At this stage, the following sūtra applies :

(304) **युजेरसमासे । *yujerasamāse*. 7. 1. 71**

लघु० - युजेः सर्वनामस्थाने नुम् स्यादसमासे । सुलोपः । संयोगान्तलोपः । कुत्वेन नस्य ङः । युङ् । अनुस्वारपरसवर्णौ - युञ्जौ, युञ्जः । युग्भ्याम् । *yujeḥ sarvanāmasthāne num syād asamāse. sulopaḥ. saṁyogāntalopaḥ. kutvena nasya ṅaḥ. yuṅ. anusvāraparasavarṇau - yuñjau, yuñjaḥ. yugbhyām.*

Trans. : When a sarvanāmasthāna affix follows, the augment *num* is inserted (after the last vowel) in *yuj*, but not in a compound. The elision of *su* takes place {by *halṅyābbhyo....* (178)} and the conjunct-final *j* is elided {by *saṁyogāntasya lopaḥ* (20)}. Then the nasal consonant *n* is replaced by the fifth guttural *ṅ* {*kvinpratyayasya kuḥ* (303)}. In the nominative dual and plural, the consonant *n* is replaced by anusvāra by *naścāpadāntasya...* (78) and the anusvāra by a nasal stop homogeneous with the following phoneme by *anusvārasya yayi parasavarṇaḥ* (79).

PP. *yujeḥ num sarvanāmasthāne asamāse* (*aṅgasya*).

Eluc. : The word *sarvanāmasthāne* is carried over from *ugidacāṁ sarvanāmasthāne...* Pā. 7. 1. 70. The term *num* is carried from *idito num...* Pā. 7. 1. 58. Thus the sūtra means as follows : Before a sarvanāmasthāna affix, the augment *num* becomes a part of the pre-affixal base *yuj* if it is not in a compound. The word *yuji* in the present rule represents the verbal root *yujir* 'to join', not *yuja* 'to meditate' (BM, I, p. 391).

In the illustration *yuj* + *s*(*u*), the affix *su* is sarvanāmasthāna. Hence by the present rule, the augment *num* is inserted after the last vowel - *yu n*(*um*) *j* + *s* --> *yu n j* + *s* --> *yu n j* {*halṅyābbhyo...* (178)} --> *yu n* {*saṁyogāntasya lopaḥ* (20)} --> *yuṅ* {*kvinpratyayasya kuḥ* (303)}. Elsewhere in the declensional forms of *yuj*, the replacement of the phoneme *j* by a guttural consonant before a consonant-initial affix takes place by the rule *coḥ kuḥ* Pā. 8. 2. 30 since the rule *kvinpratyayasya kuḥ* 8. 2. 62 is deemed not to have taken place with respect to *coḥ kuḥ*.

In the nominative dual form of the nominal stem *yuj*, we have *yuj* + *au*. The affix *au* is also sarvanāmasthāna. In the same way the augment *num* is inserted after the last vowel : *yu n j* + *au* by the present rule. According to the rule *naścāpadāntasya jhali* (78), the nasal stop *n* is replaced by anusvāra and the anusvāra is replaced by a consonant homogeneous with the following class consonant in accordance with the rule *anusvārasya yayi parasavarṇaḥ* (79) and we obtain the form *yuñjau* through the following grammatical process : *yu n j + au* --> {*yujerasamāse* (304)} --> *yu ṁ j + au* {*naścāpadāntasya*... (78)} --> *yu ñ j + au* {*anusvārasya*... (79)} --> *yuñjau*. One point is to be taken note of here. The replacement of the anusvāra by a nasal stop homogeneous with the following phoneme is treated as not to have taken place (asiddha). This is the reason why the palatal *ñ* is not replaced by guttural nasal stop by *coḥ kuḥ* (305). The locative plural form of *yuj* is declined like that of the nominal stem *ṛtvij*. The complete declension of the nominal stem *yuj* will be as follows :

	Singular	Dual	Plural
prathamā	*yuṅ*	*yuñjau*	*yuñjaḥ*
dvitīyā	*yuñjam*	*yuñjau*	*yujaḥ*
tṛtīyā	*yujā*	*yugbhyām*	*yugbhiḥ*
caturthī	*yuje*	*yugbhyām*	*yugbhyaḥ*
pañcamī	*yujaḥ*	*yugbhyām*	*yugbhyaḥ*
ṣaṣṭhī	*yujaḥ*	*yujoḥ*	*yujām*
saptamī	*yuji*	*yujoḥ*	*yukṣu*
sambodhana	*he yuṅ!*	*he yuñjau !*	*he yuñjaḥ!*

The word *suyuj* 'an excellent yogin' is a compound. Therefore the augment *num* will not be introduced to *suyuj* because of the expression *asamāse* in *yujerasamāse* (304). In *suyuj + su*, the single-consonant affix (*apṛkta*) s is elided by *halṅyābbhyo*... (178). Then we have *suyuj*. At this stage, the following sūtra becomes applicable :

(305) चोः कुः । *coḥ kuḥ.* 8. 2. 30
लघु० – चवर्गस्य कवर्गः स्याज् झलि पदान्ते च । सुयुक्, सुयुग् । सुयुजौ । सुयुग्भ्याम् । खन् । खञ्जौ । खन्भ्याम् । *cavargasya kavargaḥ syāj jhali padānte ca. suyuk, suyug. suyujau. suyugbhyām. khan. khañjau. khanbhyām.*

Trans. : Let the palatal stops be replaced by the guttural stops when a consonant denoted by *jhal* follows or at the end of a pada.

PP. *coḥ kuḥ jhali padasya ante ca.*

Eluc. : The term *jhali* is carried over from *jhalo jhali* Pā. 8. 2. 26. The present sūtra occurs in the domain of the governing rule *padasya* Pā. 8. 1. 16. Therefore the word *padasya* recurs here. The words *ante* and *ca* are carried over from *skoḥ saṁyogādyorante ca* Pā. 8. 2. 29. Thus the sūtra comes to mean : When a *jhal*-consonant follows or at the end of a pada, the palatal stops are replaced by the velar stops.

In the illustration *suyuj*, the pada-final *j* is replaced by *g* and then according to *vā 'vasāne* (145) the phoneme *g* is optionally replaced by *k*. Thus we get two forms in the nominative singular : *suyuk* and *suyug*. In the rest of the declensional forms of *suyuj*, the phoneme *j* is replaced by *g* when followed by an affix that begins with a phoneme denoted by the abbreviatory term *jhal*. In the locative plural, the same grammatical process is followed as in that of the nominal stem *ṛtvij*. The complete declension of *suyuj* is given below :

	Singular	Dual	Plural
prathamā	*suyuk, g*	*suyujau*	*suyujaḥ*
dvitīyā	*suyujam*	*suyujau*	*suyujaḥ*
tṛtīyā	*suyujā*	*suyugbhyām*	*suyugbhiḥ*
caturthī	*suyuje*	*suyugbhyām*	*suyugbhyaḥ*
pañcamī	*suyujaḥ*	*suyugbhyām*	*suyugbhyaḥ*
ṣaṣṭhī	*suyujaḥ*	*suyujoḥ*	*suyujām*
saptamī	*suyuji*	*suyujoḥ*	*suyukṣu*
sambodhana	*he suyuk, g!*	*he suyujau !*	*he suyujaḥ!*

The primary derivative *khañj* 'a lame person is derived from the verbal root *khaji* 'to limp, to walk lame' with the introduction of the affix *kvip*. The augment *num* is inserted after the last vowel (*kha num j*) by *idito num dhātoḥ* (462). The nasal consonant *n* of *num* is first replaced by anusvāra according to *naścāpadāntasya jhali* (78). The anusvāra is replaced by the nasal consonant homogeneous with the following class consonant by *anusvārasya yayi...* (79), in this case by *ñ*, and we obtain the nominal stem *khañj*. In the nominative case when we introduce the singular affix, we have *khañj* + *su*. The single-consonant-affix *s*(*u*) is elided by *halṅyābbhyo...* (178). Then the rule *saṁyogāntasya...* (20) applies and the phoneme *j* is elided. Now, in accordance with the maxim *nimittāpāye naimittikasyāpyapāyaḥ* (Dictionary, p. 221; PS, pp. 40, 45, etc.), the palatal nasal consonant *ñ* is restored to the status of the dental nasal stop since the palatal *j*, because of which it was replaced by the palatal nasal stop, ceases to exist. Since the elision of the phoneme *j* is deemed not to have taken place, the pada-final *n* is not elided and we obtain the form *khan* in the nominative singular. Before *bhyām*, *bhis*, *bhyas* and *sup*, pada-designation comes into force and the conjunct-final phoneme *j* is elided by *saṁyogāntasya*... (20).

In the locative plural, the rule *naśca* (87) optionally introduces the augment *dhuṭ* at the head of the affix *sup*. The consonant *dh* is replaced by *t* by *khari ca* (74) and we get the form *khantsu*. In the absence of the augment *dhuṭ*, we have the alternative form *khansu*. The phoneme *n* in *khansu* is not changed to anusvāra by *naścāpadā*... (78) since *khan* gets the pada-designation before *sup* by *svādiṣvasarvanāmasthāne* (163). Thus the complete declension of the nominal stem *khañj* will be as follows :

	Singular	Dual	Plural
prathamā	*khan*	*khañjau*	*khañjaḥ*
dvitīyā	*khañjam*	*khañjau*	*khañjaḥ*
tṛtīyā	*khañjā*	*khanbhyām*	*khanbhiḥ*
caturthī	*khañje*	*khanbhyām*	*khanbhyaḥ*
pañcamī	*khañjaḥ*	*khanbhyām*	*khanbhyaḥ*
ṣaṣṭhī	*khañjaḥ*	*khañjoḥ*	*khañjām*
saptamī	*khañji*	*khañjoḥ*	*khantsu, khansu*
sambodhana	*he khanj!*	*he khañjau!*	*he khañjaḥ!*

The next nominal stem to be declined is *rāj* 'a king' which is derived from the verbal root *rājṛ* 'to shine' with the introduction of the affix *kvip*. The whole of the affix *kvip* is elided and we obtain the primary derivative *rāj* which receives the prātipadika designation by *kṛttaddhita*... (116). In the nominative singular, we introduce the affix *su* and we have *rāj* + *su*. The affix *s*(*u*) is elided by *halṅyābbhyo*... (178). Then we get the declensional stage : *rāj*, which is a pada by *suptiṅatam*... (14) since the elided affix *su* is taken as effective by *pratyayalope*... (189). In this grammatical situation the following sūtra is applied :

(306) व्रश्च-भ्रस्ज-सृज-मृज-यज-राज-भ्राजच्छशां षः । *vraśca-bhrasja-sṛja-mṛja-yaja-rāja-bhrājacchaśāṁ ṣaḥ*. 8. 2. 36

लघु० - व्रश्चादीनां सप्तानां छशान्तयोश्च षकारोऽन्तादेशः स्याज् झलि पदान्ते च। जश्त्व-चर्त्वे। राट्, राड्। राजौ। राजः। राड्भ्याम्। एवं विभ्राट्। देवेट्। विश्वसृट्। *vraścādīnāṁ saptānāṁ chaśāntayoś ca ṣakāro 'ntādeśaḥ syāj jhali padānte ca. jaśtva-cartve. rāṭ, rāḍ. rājau. rājaḥ. rāḍbhyām. evaṁ vibhrāṭ. deveṭ. viśvasṛṭ.*

Trans. : When a consonant denoted by the abbreviatory term *jhal* follows or at the end of a pada, the final phoneme of these seven verbal roots : *vraśca-bhrasja-sṛja-mṛja-yaja-rāja-bhrāja* and of the words, which end in *ch* or *ś*, is replaced by *ṣ*.

PP. *vraśca-bhrasja-sṛja-mṛja-yaja-rāja-bhrājacchaśāṁ ṣaḥ jhali padsya ante ca.*

Eluc. : The terms *jhali* and *ante* are respectively carried over from *jhalo jhali* Pā. 8. 2. 26 and *skoḥ saṁyogādyorante ca* Pā. 8. 2. 29. The present sūtra occurs in the domain of the governing rule *padasya* Pā. 8. 1. 16. The word *padasya*, therefore, recurs in the present rule. The compound word *vraśca-bhrasja-sṛja-mṛja-yaja-rāja-bhrājacchaśām* is an itaretara-dvandva and is analysed as : *vraścaś ca bhrasjaś ca sṛjaś ca mṛjaś ca yajaś ca rājaś ca bhrājaś ca chaś ca ś ca vraśca-bhrasja-sṛja-mṛja-yaja-rāja-bhrājacchaśaḥ, teṣām = vraśca..... bhrājacchaśām.* The vowel *a* occurring in these verbal roots and *cha* is to facilitate the articulation. The two consonants *ch* and *ś* qualify the qualificand word-form and as such, by tadantavidhi, this means the word-form which ends in *ch* or *ś* (*chaśau varṇau tābhyāṁ śabdasvarūpa-viśeṣyam ādāya tadantavidhiḥ*, BM, I, p. 304). The meaning of the whole sūtra will be as follows : Let the final phoneme of the seven verbal roots, *vraśca*, etc. and of the words that end in *ch* or *ś* be replaced by the cerebral ṣ when a consonant denoted by *jhal*-pratyāhāra follows or at the end of a pada.

In the illustration *rāj*, which is a pada, the consonant *j* is at the end of a pada. The word *rāj* is treated as a verbal root as well as a nominal stem according to the paribhāṣā of Vyāḍi *kvibantā dhātutvaṁ na jahati prātipadikatvaṁ ca* (PS, p. 43). So by virtue of the present sūtra, the final phoneme *j* is replaced by ṣ. Then by *jhalāṁ jaśo 'nte* (67), the cerebral ṣ is replaced by *ḍ*. According to *vā 'vasāne* (145), *ḍ* is optionally replaced by *ṭ*. Thus we obtain two forms of *rāj* in the nominative singular : *rāṭ* and *rāḍ*. When followed by *bhyām, bhis* and *bhyas*, the stem *rāj* gets the pada-designation by *svādiṣvasarvanāmasthāne* (163). Consequently, the phoneme *j* changes to ṣ by the present rule. It is further replaced by *ḍ* in accordance with the rule *jhalāṁ jaśo 'nte* (67). We get the forms *rāḍbhyām, rāḍbhiḥ* and *rāḍbhyaḥ*.

In the locative plural, when we introduce the affix *sup*, we have *rāj*+ *su*. The rule *svādiṣva*... (163) designates the stem *rāj* as *pada* and, as a result of that, the final *j* is substituted by *ṣ* by the present rule and then the cerebral *ṣ* is replaced by the cerebral stop *ḍ* by *jhalām*... (67). At this stage, the rule *ḍaḥ si dhuṭ* (84) applies and optionally introduces the augment *dhuṭ*. When the augment *dhuṭ* is inserted at the head of the affix *sup*, the consonant *dh* is replaced by *t* according to the rule *khari ca* (74). In the absence of the augment *dhuṭ*, *khari ca* (74) substitutes the *ḍ* of *rāḍ* by *ṭ*. Thus we obtain two forms in the locative plural : *rāṭtsu* and *rāṭsu*. The declension of the nominal stem *rāj* runs as follows :

	Singular	Dual	Plural
prathamā	*rāṭ, ḍ*	*rājau*	*rājaḥ*
dvitīyā	*rājam*	*rājau*	*rājaḥ*
tṛtīyā	*rājā*	*rāḍbhyām*	*rāḍbhiḥ*
caturthī	*rāje*	*rāḍbhyām*	*rāḍbhyaḥ*
pañcamī	*rājaḥ*	*rāḍbhyām*	*rāḍbhyaḥ*
ṣaṣṭhī	*rājaḥ*	*rājoḥ*	*rājām*
saptamī	*rāji*	*rājoḥ*	*rāṭtsu, rāṭsu*
sambodhana	*he rāṭ, ḍ!*	*he rājau!*	*he rājaḥ!*

The declension of the nominal stems *vibhrāj* 'one who shines brightly', *devej* 'one who performs sacrifice for the gods' and *viśvasṛj* 'the creator of the world' will be like that of *rāj*.

Varadarāja now quotes the Uṇādisūtra to explain the derivation of the nominal stem *parivrāj* 'a wandering mendicant' :

लघु० – परौ व्रजेः षः पदान्ते । (उणादिसूत्र 218). परावुपपदे व्रजेः क्विप् स्याद् दीर्घश्च पदान्ते षत्वमपि । परिव्राट्, परिव्राड् । परिव्राजौ । *parau vrajeḥ ṣaḥ padānte.* (US, 218). *parāv upapade vrajeḥ kvip syād dīrghaś ca padānte ṣatvam api. parivrāṭ, parivrāḍ. parivrājau.*

Trans. : When the verbal root *vraj* is preceded by the preverb *pari* as upapada, the affix *kvip* is introduced after it. The vowel *a* of the verbal root *vraj* is lengthened and the pada-final phoneme *j* is substituted by the cerebral *ṣ*.

Eluc. : The derivational process of the nominal stem *parivrāj* is as follows : *pari + vraj + kvip --> pari + vrāj + kvip --> parivrāj*. When the singular affix *su* of the first triplet is introduced after the nominal stem *parivrāj*, we have *parivrāj + su*. The affix *s*(*u*) is elided by *halṅyābbhyo...* (178) and then the cerebral sibilant *ṣ* replaces the pada-final *j* by virtue of the present Uṇādi Sūtra. The cerebral *ṣ* is replaced by a phoneme denoted by *jaś*-pratyāhāra, that is, by *ḍ* in the present context, in accordance with *jhalāṁ jaśo 'nte* (67). The rule *vā 'vasāne* (145) applies and the phoneme *ḍ* at the end of a pada is optionally replaced by a *car*-consonant. Thus we obtain two forms in the nominative singular : *parivrāṭ* and *parivrāḍ*. When followed by the affixes *bhyām, bhis* and *bhyas*, the cerebral *ṣ* is replaced by *ḍ* according to *jhalāṁ jaśo 'nte* (67) and we get the forms : *parivrāḍbhyām, parivrāḍbhiḥ* and *parivrāḍbhyaḥ*. In the locative plural too, the nominal stem gets the pada designation by *svādiṣva...* (163) and the pada-final *ṣ* is replaced by *ḍ* in accordance with *jhalāṁ jaśo 'nte* (67). At this stage, the augment *dhuṭ* is introduced optionally by *ḍaḥ si dhuṭ* (86). The phoneme *t* replaces *dh* by *khari ca* (74). Thus we get two forms : one, when the augment *dhuṭ* is inserted and the other when it is not : *parivrāṭtsu* and *parivrāṭsu*. The nominal stem *parivrāj* is declined as follows :

	Singular	Dual	Plural
prathamā	*parivrāṭ, ḍ*	*parivrājau*	*parivrājaḥ*
dvitīyā	*parivrājam*	*parivrājau*	*parivrājaḥ*
tṛtīyā	*parivrājā*	*parivrāḍbhyām*	*parivrāḍbhiḥ*
caturthī	*parivrāje*	*parivrāḍbhyām*	*parivrāḍbhyaḥ*
pañcamī	*parivrājaḥ*	*parivrāḍbhyām*	*parivrāḍbhyaḥ*
ṣaṣṭhī	*parivrājaḥ*	*parivrājoḥ*	*parivrājām*
saptamī	*parivrāji*	*parivrājoḥ*	*parivrāṭtsu, parivrāṭsu*
sambodhana	*he parivrāṭ, ḍ!*	*he parivrājau!*	*he parivrājaḥ!*

The word *viśvarāj* 'God, the Lord of the universe' is an upapada compound. Its analysis is : *viśvasmin rājate iti viśvārāṭ. viśva ṅi + rāj kvip* (*satsūdviṣa...* Pā. 3. 2. 61) --> *viśva + rāj kvip* --> (*supo...* 718). After the elision of the anubandhas and of *v* (by *vera...* 302), we have *viśvarāj*. In the nominative singular, we introduce the affix *su* : *viśvarāj + su*. Here the affix *s*(*u*) is elided by *halṅyābbhyo...* (178). The pada-final *j* is substituted by the cerebral sibilant *ṣ* by *vraśca-bhrasja...* (306). The cerebral *ṣ* is replaced by *ḍ* according to *jhalāṁ jaśo 'nte* (67). Then by *vā-'vasāne* (145), the phoneme *ḍ* is optionally replaced by *ṭ* and we have two forms *viśvarāṭ, viśvarāḍ*. At this stage, the following sūtra ensues :

(307) विश्वस्य वसुराटोः । *viśvasya vasurāṭoḥ.* 6. 3. 128

लघु० – विश्वशब्दस्य दीर्घोऽन्तादेशः स्याद् वसौ राट्शब्दे च परे। विश्वाराट्, विश्वाराड्। विश्वराजौ। विश्वाराड्भ्याम्। *viśvaśabdasya dīrgho 'ntādeśaḥ syād vasau rāṭśabde ca pare. viśvārāṭ, viśvārāḍ. viśvarājau. viśvārāḍbhyām.*

Trans. : Let the final vowel of the word *viśva* be replaced by a long one when the words *vasu* and *rāṭ* follow.

PP. *viśvasya dīrghaḥ vasurāṭoḥ (pūrvasya, aṇaḥ, uttarapade, saṁhitāyām).*

Eluc. : The term *dīrghaḥ* comes from *ḍhralope pūrvasya dīrgho 'ṇaḥ* Pā. 6. 3. 111. The meaning of the sūtra is as follows : When the words *vasu* and *rāṭ* follow, the word *viśva* should be replaced by a long vowel. By virtue of the rule *alo 'ntyasya* (21), the vowel that is going to be replaced by a long one is the last vowel of the word *viśva*. The word *rāṭ* has been mentioned with a *car*-consonant in the sūtra, that is, with *ṭ*. This has been enunciated to indicate the pada-final position of the nominal stem *rāj*. As such, both the pada-final consonants *ṭ* and *ḍ* of the word *rāṭ* are to be construed as conditions for replacing the final vowel of *viśva* with a long one (*cartvanirdeśasya padāntopalakṣaṇatvād jaśtvapakṣe 'pi dīrghaḥ*, BM, I, p. 393; cf. also *cartvam avivakṣitam*, SK, I, p. 393). This means the final vowel of *viśva* is lengthened when either *rāṭ* or *rāḍ* follows and also when the word *vasu* follows. The word *viśvāvasu* 'a demi-god' is declined like *śambhu*.

When we decline the word *viśvarāj* with the affixes *bhyām, bhis* and *bhyas*, the pada-final *j* is replaced by *ḍ* according to *jhalāṁ jaśo 'nte* (67). In the locative plural, the augment *dhuṭ* is inserted optionally by *ḍaḥ si...* (86). By *khari ca* (74), the consonant *dh* is replaced by *t* and *ḍ* by *ṭ*. Thus we get two forms : one with the augment *dhuṭ* and the other without it. The complete declension of the word *viśvarāj* will be as follows :

	Singular	Dual	Plural
prathamā	*viśvārāṭ, ḍ*	*viśvarājau*	*viśvarājaḥ*
dvitīyā	*viśvarājam*	*viśvarājau*	*viśvarājaḥ*
tṛtīyā	*viśvarājā*	*viśvārāḍbhyām*	*viśvārāḍbhiḥ*

caturthī	*viśvarāje*	*viśvārāḍbhyām*	*viśvārāḍbhyaḥ*
pañcamī	*viśvarājaḥ*	*viśvārāḍbhyām*	*viśvārāḍbhyaḥ*
ṣaṣṭhī	*viśvarājaḥ*	*viśvarājoḥ*	*viśvarājām*
saptamī	*viśvarāji*	*viśvarājoḥ*	*viśvārāṭtsu, viśvārāṭsu*
sambodhana	*he viśvārāṭ, ḍ!*	*he viśvarājau!*	*he viśvarājaḥ!*

The next nominal stem is *bhṛsj* 'one who fries or roasts' *bhṛjjatīti bhṛṭ*. It is derived from the verbal root *bhrasj* 'to fry, to roast' with the introduction of the affix *kvip* by *kvip ca* (799). The rule *grahijyā...* (633) prescribes samprasāraṇa since the affix *kvip* follows. The repha is replaced by *ṛ* : *bhrasj + kvip --> bhṛasj + kvip --> bhṛasj*. By *samprasāraṇācca* (257), a single substitution homogeneous with the preceding (*pūrvarūpa*) takes place. In other words, the vowel *ṛ* replaces both *ṛ* and *a* and we get the primary derivative *bhṛsj*, which gets the prātipadika designation by *kṛttaddhita...* (116). Now with the introduction of the singular nominative affix, we have *bhṛsj + su*. The affix *s*(*u*) is elided by *halṅyābbhyo...* (178). Only *bhṛsj* remains. In this grammatical situation, the rule *saṁyogāntasya lopaḥ* (20) becomes available for application but the following sūtra blocks it and applies :

(308) स्कोः संयोगाद्योरन्ते च । *skoḥ saṁyogādyorante ca.* 8. 2. 29

लघु० – पदान्ते झलि च परे यः संयोगस्तदाद्योः सकारककारयोर्लोपः स्यात् । भृट् । सस्य श्चुत्वेन शः । झलां जश् झशि इति शस्य जः । भृज्जौ । भृड्भ्याम् । *padānte jhali ca pare yaḥ saṁyogas tadādyoḥ sakārakakārayor lopaḥ syāt. bhṛṭ. sasya ścutvena śaḥ. jhalāṁ jaś jhaśi iti śasya jaḥ. bhṛjjau. bhṛḍbhyām.*

Trans. : Let the phonemes *s* and *k* occurring at the beginning of a conjunct be elided, if the conjunct is at the end of a pada or followed by a consonant denoted by the abbreviatory term *jhal*.

PP. *skoḥ saṁyogādyoḥ lopaḥ jhali padasya ante ca.*

Eluc. : The present sūtra occurs in the domain of the governing rule *padasya* Pā. 8. 1. 16. So the word *padasya* also recurs here. The words *lopaḥ* and *jhali* are respectively carried over from *saṁyogāntasya lopaḥ* Pā. 8. 2. 23 and *jhalo jhali* 8. 2. 26. The word *skoḥ* is an itaretaradvandva. Its analysis is : *s ca k ca skau, tayoḥ = skoḥ*. The word *saṁyogādyoḥ* is a ṣaṣṭhītatpuruṣa : *saṁyogasya ādī = saṁyogādī, tayoḥ = saṁyogādyoḥ*. Thus the meaning of the sūtra is : If a conjunct occurs at the end of a pada or is followed by a *jhal*-consonant, the phonemes s and *k* occurring at the beginning of such a conjunct are to be elided. The present rule is considered to be suspended (*asiddha*) with respect to *saṁyogāntasya lopaḥ* Pā. 8. 2. 23. Still this rule is construed as an exception to *saṁyogāntasya lopaḥ* Pā. 8. 2. 23 by the force of its having been enunciated by Pāṇini. In the illustration *bhṛsj*, the conjunct *sj* occurs at the end of a pada (*bhṛsj*). So the phoneme *s*, which is at the beginning of the conjunct *sj*, is elided and we have *bhṛj*. Now the pada-final *j* is replaced by *ṣ* according to *vraścabhrasja*... (306) and the cerebral *ṣ* is replaced by *ḍ* in accordance with *jhalāṁ jaśo 'nte* (67). The rule *vā 'vasāne* (145) applies and the phoneme *ḍ* is optionally replaced by *ṭ* and we obtain two forms in the nominative singular : *bhṛṭ* and *bhṛḍ*.

In the dual form of the stem *bhṛsj*, we introduce the affix *au*, which does not begin with a *jhal*-consonant. Both the rules *jhalāṁ jaś jhaśi* Pā. 8. 4. 53 and *stoḥ ścunā ścuḥ* 8. 4. 40 are simultaneously available for application. The former, being subsequent in the tripādī, is treated as suspended with respect to the latter. So by the latter, the phoneme *s* is first replaced by *ś* (*bhṛśj*) and then by virtue of the former the palatal *ś* is substituted by *j* and we get the form *bhṛjjau*. Before the affixes *bhyām*, etc. the pre-affixal base *bhṛsj* gets the pada designation by *svādiṣva*... (163) and the pada-final *j* is first replaced by *ṣ* in accordance with *vraścabhrasja*... (306) and *ṣ* by *ḍ* according to *jhalāṁ jaśo 'nte* (67). The whole declension of the nominal stem *bhṛsj* runs as follows :

	Singular	Dual	Plural
prathamā	*bhṛṭ, ḍ*	*bhṛjjau*	*bhṛjjaḥ*
dvitīyā	*bhṛjjam*	*bhṛjjau*	*bhṛjjaḥ*
tṛtīyā	*bhṛjjā*	*bhṛḍbhyām*	*bhṛḍbhiḥ*
caturthī	*bhṛjje*	*bhṛḍbhyām*	*bhṛḍbhyaḥ*
pañcamī	*bhṛjjaḥ*	*bhṛḍbhyām*	*bhṛḍbhyaḥ*
ṣaṣṭhī	*bhṛjjaḥ*	*bhṛjjoḥ*	*bhṛjjām*
saptamī	*bhṛjji*	*bhṛjjoḥ*	*bhṛṭtsu, bhṛṭsu*
sambodhana	*he bhṛṭ, ḍ!*	*he bhṛjjau!*	*he bhṛjjaḥ!*

Here comes to an end the declension of the masculine nominal stems that end in the phoneme *j*.

Now begins the declensional process of the masculine nominal stems which end with the phoneme *d*.

लघु० - त्यदाद्यत्वं पररूपत्वं च । *tyadādyatvaṁ pararūpatvaṁ ca.*

Eluc. : The pronominal stem *tyad* 'he' belongs to the sarvādi class. As a consequence in *tyad + su*, the rule *tyadādīnāmaḥ* (192) applies and the phoneme *d* is replaced by *a*. This happens in every case when a sup-affix follows an item of the tyadādi class. By *ato guṇe* (273), a single replacement in the form of the following vowel comes in place of both the preceding and the following vowels : *tya a + su* --> *tya* + *s*. At this stage, the following sūtra becomes applicable :

(309) तदोः सः सावनन्त्ययोः । ***tadoḥ saḥ sāvanantyayoḥ*. 7. 2. 106**
लघु० - त्यदादीनां तकारदकारयोरनन्त्ययोः सः स्यात् सौ । स्यः । त्यौ । त्ये । सः । तौ । ते । यः । यौ । ये । एषः । एतौ । एते । अन्वादेशे एनम् । एनौ । एनान् । एनेन । एनयोः ।
tyadādīnāṁ takāradakārayor anantyayoḥ saḥ syāt sau. syaḥ. tyau. tye. saḥ. tau. te. yaḥ. yau. ye. eṣaḥ. etau. ete. anvādeśe – enam. enau. enān. enena. enayoḥ.

Trans. : Let the non-final phonemes *t* and *d* of the items enumerated in the list headed by *tyad* 'that', be replaced by the phoneme *s* when the affix *su* follows.

PP. *tyadādīnām anantyayoḥ tadoḥ saḥ sau (vibhaktau, aṅgasya).*

Eluc. : The word *tyadādīnām* comes from the rule *tyadādīnāmaḥ* Pā. 7. 2. 102 in the manner of the leap of a frog (*maṇḍūkaplutyā*). The word *anantyayoḥ* is a nañ-tatpuruṣa which is analysed as : *na antyayoḥ* = *anantyayoḥ*. The meaning of the sūtra is as follows : When the affix *su* follows, let the phoneme *s* replace the phonemes *t* and *d* which do not occur at the end of the items enumerated in the list beginning with *tyad*.

In the illustration *tya* + *s*, the initial phoneme *t*, not being final, is replaced by *s* in accordance with the present rule and we have *sya* + *s* --> *syaḥ* after rutva and visarga. The rest of *tyad* is now declined like the pronouns that end in a short *a*. The complete declension of the pronominal stem *tyad* is given below :

	Singular	Dual	Plural
prathamā	*syaḥ*	*tyau*	*tye*
dvitīyā	*tyam*	*tyau*	*tyān*

tṛtīyā	*tyena*	*tyābhyām*	*tyaiḥ*
caturthī	*tyasmai*	*tyābhyām*	*tyebhyaḥ*
pañcamī	*tyasmāt, d*	*tyābhyām*	*tyebhyaḥ*
ṣaṣṭhī	*tyasya*	*tyayoḥ*	*tyeṣām*
saptamī	*tyasmin*	*tyayoḥ*	*tyeṣu*
sambodhana		No form	

The declension of the pronominal stem *tad* 'he' will be like that of the word *tyad*. Its declension is as follows :

	Singular	Dual	Plural
prathamā	*saḥ*	*tau*	*te*
dvitīyā	*tam*	*tau*	*tān*
tṛtīyā	*tena*	*tābhyām*	*taiḥ*
caturthī	*tasmai*	*tābhyām*	*tebhyaḥ*
pañcamī	*tasmāt, d*	*tābhyām*	*tebhyaḥ*
ṣaṣṭhī	*tasya*	*tayoḥ*	*teṣām*
saptamī	*tasmin*	*tayoḥ*	*teṣu*
sambodhana		No form	

The present rule does not apply in declining *yad* 'who' since there is neither non-final *t* nor *d* in it. After the application of *tyadādīnāmaḥ* (192) and *ato guṇe* (273), it will be declined like *sarva*. The declension of *yad* runs as follows :

	Singular	Dual	Plural
prathamā	*yaḥ*	*yau*	*ye*
dvitīyā	*yam*	*yau*	*yān*
tṛtīyā	*yena*	*yābhyām*	*yaiḥ*
caturthī	*yasmai*	*yābhyām*	*yebhyaḥ*
pañcamī	*yasmāt, d*	*yābhyām*	*yebhyaḥ*
ṣaṣṭhī	*yasya*	*yayoḥ*	*yeṣām*

saptamī	*yasmin*	*yayoḥ*	*yeṣu*
sambodhana		No form	

The pronominal stem *etad* 'this' changes to *eta* by *tyadā...* (192) and *ato guṇe* (273). When the nominative singular affix *su* follows, the non-final *t* is replaced by *s* in accordance with the present rule. Then the rule *ādeśa...* (149) applies and the cerebral *ṣ* replaces this *s*, which is a substitute for *t*. In the locative plural (*eta + sup*), we get *ete su* by *bahuvacane...* (144). The phoneme *s* which is a part of the affix *sup* changes to *ṣ* by *ādeśa...* (149). So we obtain *eteṣu*. In the genitive plural also, the dental *s* is replaced by *ṣ* according to *ādeśa...* (149) since this *s*, being of the augment *suṭ*, belongs to the affix *ām*.

	Singular	Dual	Plural
prathamā	*eṣaḥ*	*etau*	*ete*
dvitīyā	*etam*	*etau*	*etān*
tṛtīyā	*etena*	*etābhyām*	*etaiḥ*
caturthī	*etasmai*	*etābhyām*	*etebhyaḥ*
pañcamī	*etasmāt, d*	*etābhyām*	*etebhyaḥ*
ṣaṣṭhī	*etasya*	*etayoḥ*	*eteṣām*
saptamī	*etasmin*	*etayoḥ*	*eteṣu*
sambodhana		No form	

When it is used in the sense of anaphora (*anvādeśa* : see supra pp. 381-83), the rule *dvitīyāṭaussvenaḥ* (280) becomes applicable, which prescribes the substitute *ena* in place of the pronominal stem *etad* when followed by the sup-affixes of the second triplet, *ṭā* and *os*. The pronominal stem *etad* in the anaphoric sense (*anvādeśa*) will be declined as follows :

	Singular	Dual	Plural
prathamā	*eṣaḥ*	*etau*	*ete*
dvitīyā	*enam*	*enau*	*enān*
tṛtīyā	*enena*	*etābhyām*	*etaiḥ*
caturthī	*etasmai*	*etābhyām*	*etebhyaḥ*
pañcamī	*etasmāt, d*	*etābhyām*	*etebhyaḥ*

ṣaṣṭhī	*etasya*	*enayoḥ*	*eteṣām*
saptamī	*etasmin*	*enayoḥ*	*eteṣu*
sambodhana		No form	

The pronominal stems *yuṣmad* and *asmad* are used in all the three genders. These two words have been expounded together by Pāṇini so far as their declensional process is concerned. We will also explain the declensional process of these pronominal stems together.

When we add the nominative singular affix *su* after these words, we have the following stage : *yuṣmad + su, asmad + su*. At this stage, the following sūtra applies :

(310) **ङे प्रथमयोरम्।** ***ṅe prathamayoram.*** **7. 1. 28**

लघु० – युष्मदस्मद्भ्यां परस्य ङे इत्येतस्य प्रथमाद्वितीययोश्चामादेशः। *yuṣmadasmad-bhyāṁ parasya ṅe ityetasya prathamādvitīyayoś cāmādeśaḥ.*

Trans. : The affix *ṅe* and those of the first and second triplets are replaced by *am*, when they follow the pronominal stems *yuṣmad* and *asmad*.

PP. *yuṣmadasmadbhyāṁ ṅe prathamayor am* (*aṅgasya*).

Eluc. : The compound word *yuṣmadasmadbhyām* is carried over from *yuṣmadasmadbhyāṁ ṅaso 'ś* Pā. 7. 1. 27. Its analysis is as follows : *yuṣmac ca asmac ca yuṣmadasmadī, tābhyām = yuṣmadasmadbhyām*. The genitive singular sup-affix after the term *ṅe* is taken as elided (*ṅe iti pṛthak padaṁ luptaṣaṣṭhīkam*, TB, I, p. 397). The dual affix of the sixth triplet used in word *prathamayoḥ* indicates that the affixes of both the first and second triplet are to be understood by this word (*prathamayor iti dvivacanabalena prathamāśabdaḥ prathamādvitīyobhayārthakaḥ*, TB, I, p. 397). Then the meaning of the sūtra will be as follows : If the affix *ṅe* and those of the first and second triplet follow the words *yuṣmad* and *asmad*, they are to be replaced by the substitute *am*.

In the illustrations *yuṣmad + su, asmad + su*, the affix *su* is replaced by *am* in both the cases by the present rule and we have *yuṣmad + am, asmad + am*. The final phoneme *m* of the substitute *am* is not designated as *it* by *halantyam* (1) because the phoneme *m* does not receive the *it*-designation according to *na vibhaktau tusmāḥ* (130). By virtue of the rule *sthānivadādeśo 'nalvidhau* (143), the substitute *am* is construed as a vibhakti since it has replaced the sup-affix *su* (*vibhakti*). In this situation, the following sūtra presents itself for application :

(311) त्वाहौ सौ । *tvāhau sau.* **7. 2. 94**

लघु० – अनयोर्मपर्यन्तस्य त्वाहावादेशौ स्तः । *anayor maparyantasya tvāhāv ādeśau staḥ.*

Trans. : The substitutes *tva* and *aha* replace the portion up to *m* of *yuṣmad* and *asmad* (in a respective manner), when the nominative singular affix *su* follows.

PP. *yuṣmadasmadoḥ maparyantasya tvāhau sau (vibhaktau, aṅgasya).*

Eluc. : The word *yuṣmadasmadoḥ* is carried over from *yuṣmadasmador-anādeśe* Pā. 7. 2. 86. The present sūtra occurs in the domain of the governing rule *maparyantasya* Pā. 7. 2. 91. The word *maparyantasya*, therefore, recurs in the present sūtra. The compound word *tvāhau* is an itaretaradvandva which is analysed as *tvaś ca ahaś ca tvāhau*. Thus the sūtra means as follows : The portion *yuṣm* of *yuṣmad* and the portion *asm* of *asmad* are respectively replaced by *tva* and *aha* when the singular affix of the first triplet, that is, *su* follows them. The replaced *am* is taken as *su* by sthānivadbhāva (143). After the replacement, we have the following grammatical situation : *tva ad + am, aha ad + am*. Now *ato guṇe* (273) applies and we have *tvad + am* and *ahad + am*. At this stage, the following sūtra presents itself for application :

(312) शेषे लोपः । *śeṣe lopaḥ.* **7. 2. 90**

लघु० – एतयोष्टिलोपः । त्वम् । अहम् । *etayoṣ ṭilopaḥ. tvam. aham.*

Trans. : The *ṭi* of *yuṣmad* and *asmad* is elided.

PP. *yuṣmadasmadoḥ maparyantāt śeṣe lopaḥ (vibhaktau, aṅgasya).*

Eluc. : The word *yuṣmadasmadoḥ* is carried over from *yuṣmadasmador-anādeśe* Pā. 7.2. 86. The word *maparyantasya* is drawn back from the following sūtra to this one by apakarṣa (*siṁhāvalokitanyāya*) and is changed into the ablative singular : *maparyantāt*. The locative case-ending in the term *śeṣe* is to be understood in the sense of sthānaṣaṣṭhī.[1] Thus the sūtra *śeṣe lopaḥ* means that the remaining portion of *yuṣmad* and *asmad* is elided. The remaining portion of *yuṣmad* and *asmad* beyond the phoneme *m* is *ad* in both the pronominal stems. The *ad*-portion can be termed as the *ṭi* of both *yuṣmad* and *asmad*. This is elided by the present sūtra and we get *tv am* --> *tvam* and *ah am* --> *aham*. This is in accordance with the vṛtti of Varadarāja.

---

1. *śeṣasya sthāne ityāśrayaṇenetyarthaḥ*. BM, I, p. 399. Also cf. SK, I, p. 399.

This sūtra has been interpreted in two ways in the Siddhāntakaumudī. J. R. Ballantyne,[1] unlike Varadarāja, has followed the other interpretation given by Bhaṭṭoji Dīkṣita in the Siddhāntakaumudī. The alternative interpretation, which is not adopted by Varadarāja, is as follows : *ātvayatvanimittetaravibhaktau parato yuṣmadasmador antyasya lopaḥ syāt*. According to this interpretation, the term *śeṣe* means 'when the remaining sup-affixes follow'. Accordingly, the sūtra means : The final phoneme of the pronominal stems, *yuṣmad* and *asmad*, is elided when followed by those sup-affixes which do not condition the replacement by *ā* and *y*. The affix *su* (*am*) conditions neither *ā* nor *y*. In the illustrations *tva ad* + *am*, *aha ad* + *am*, the rule *ato guṇe* (273), being internally conditioned (antaraṅga : having a smaller number of causes), applies earlier than the present rule and we have *tvad* + *am*, *ahad* + *am*. Now according to this alternative interpretation, when the present rule applies, the final phoneme *d* is elided with the help of the paribhāṣā sūtra *alo 'ntyasya* (21) and we obtain the forms *tvam* and *aham* in the nominative singular after the grammatical operation pūrvarūpa has been effected by the rule *ami pūrvaḥ* (134).

If this interpretation is adopted, then the locative ending in the term *śeṣe* need not be interpreted the way it has been done according to the vṛtti adopted by Varadarāja. This is appropriate in the light of the alternative interpretation in which the term *śeṣe* means 'when the remaining sup-affixes follow'. This accords well with the locative case-ending in the term *śeṣe*. By the remaining sup-affixes, those vibhaktis are meant which are not covered by earlier rules, i.e. which do not condition the *ā*-substitution in place of the final phoneme of the pronominal stems *yuṣmad* and *asmad* by Pā. 7. 2. 86-88 and *y*-substitution by Pā. 7. 2. 89.[2] The Kāśikā has enumerated those vibhaktis, meant by the term *śeṣe*, in the following verse.

pañcamyāś ca caturthyāś ca ṣaṣṭhīprathamayor api,
yāny advivacanāny atra śeṣe lopo vidhīyate.

The verse gives the following sense : The singular and plural sup-affixes of the fifth, fourth, sixth and first are meant by the term *śeṣe*. If any one of these sup-affixes follows, the final phoneme *d* is elided.

When we decline these pronominal stems in the nominative dual, we have *yuṣmad* + *au*, *asmad* + *au*. Here also the affix *au* is replaced by *am* according to *ṅe prathamayoram* (310) --> *yuṣmad* + *am*, *asmad* + *am*. At this stage, the following sūtra applies :

---

1. *The Laghukaumudī of Varadarāja*, p. 104.

2. Cf. Kāśikā 7. 2. 90 : *śeṣe vibhaktau yuṣmadasmador lopo bhavati. kaśca seṣaḥ? yatrākāro yakāraś ca na vihitaḥ.*

(313) युवावौ द्विवचने । *yuvāvau dvivacane.* **7. 2. 92**
लघु० - द्वयोरुक्तावनयोर्मपर्यन्तस्य युवावौ स्तो विभक्तौ । *dvayoruktāv anayor maparyantasya yuvāvau sto vibhaktau.*

Trans. : When duality is to be expressed, the portions of *yuṣmad* and *asmad* extending up to the phoneme *m* are respectively replaced by the substitutes *yuva* and *āva* before a sup-affix (*vibhakti*).

PP. *yuṣmadasmadoḥ maparyantasya dvivacane yuvāvau vibhaktau* (*aṅgasya*).

Eluc. : The present sūtra occurs in the domain of the governing rule *maparyantasya* Pā. 7. 2. 91. Therefore the term *maparyantasya* recurs in the present sūtra. The word *yuṣmadasmadoḥ* is carried over from *yuṣmadasmadoranādeśe* Pā. 7. 2. 86. The word *dvivacane* is a ṣaṣṭhī-tatpuruṣa which is analysed as : *dvayor vacanam dvivacanam, tasmin* = *dvivacane.* The significance of use of the term *dvivacane* lies in the fact that it does not mean a sup-affix that denotes a dual number. Rather it means any sup-affix. However, if duality is intended to be expressed, the portions up to the phoneme *m* of the pronominal stems *yuṣmad* and *asmad* will be replaced by *yuva* and *āva* in a respective manner. To illustrate this point, let us take the example of the compound word *atiyuvām* which is analysed as *atikrāntam yuvām* 'one who has surpassed both of you'. In the illustration {(*ati yuṣmad* + *au*)} + *su* --> {(*ati yuṣmad* + *au*)} + *am,* we introduce the affix *su* which is replaced by *am* according to *ṅeprathamayoram* (310) but the word *yuṣmad* as a member of the compound conveys the sense of duality. Therefore, the portion of *yuṣmad* up to the phoneme *m* is replaced by *yuva* and we get the compound word *atiyuvām*. This is the reason why Pāṇini has used the term *dvivacane* in the present sūtra instead of the term *dvitve,* which would have been appropriate, had Pāṇini intended to mean the dual sup-affix by the term *dvivacane.* The sūtra thus comes to mean : If the pronominal stems *yuṣmad* and *asmad* are used in the sense of duality and if they are followed by a sup-affix, then their portions up to the phoneme *m* are replaced by *yuva* and *āva* respectively. In the illustrations, *yuṣmad* + *am* and *asmad* + *am,* the pronominal stems are obviously intended to convey the sense of duality. Hence the portions up to the phoneme *m* are respectively replaced by *yuva* and *āva* ---> *yuva ad* + *am* and *āva ad* + *am*. Now, being antaraṅga, i.e. having a smaller number of causes, the rule *ato guṇe* (273) applies and we have *yuvad* + *am* and *āvad* + *am*. In this grammatical situation, the following sūtra ensues :

(314) प्रथमायाश्च द्विवचने भाषायाम्। ***prathamāyāśca dvivacane bhāṣāyām.* 7. 2. 88**

लघु० - औङ्येतयोरात्वं लोके। युवाम्। आवाम्। *auṅy etayor ātvaṁ loke. yuvām. āvām.*

Trans. : The final phoneme of these two stems is replaced by a long *ā* in classical Sanskrit (*bhāṣāyām*) when a sup-affix (*vibhakti*) of the first triplet, denoting duality, follows.

PP. *prathamāyāḥ ca dvivacane bhāṣāyām yuṣmadasmadoḥ āḥ* (*vibhaktau, aṅgasya*).

Eluc. : The word *yuṣmadasmadoḥ* is carried over from *yuṣmadasmador anādeśe* Pā. 7.2. 86. The term *āḥ* comes from *aṣṭana ā vibhaktau* Pā. 7. 2. 84. The meaning of the present sūtra is as follows : In classical language, when the sup-affix of the first triplet, denoting duality, follows, the pre-affixal base-final (aṅga-final) phoneme of *yuṣmad* and *asmad* is replaced by a long *ā*. In this context the final phoneme is *d*. In the illustrations, *yuvad + am* and *āvad + am*, the final *d* is replaced by *ā* in accordance with the present rule and we have *yuva ā + am* and *āva ā + am*. At this stage, the rule *akaḥ savarṇe dīrghaḥ* (42) applies and a long *ā* replaces both the vowels *a* and *ā* and we reach the following derivational stage : *yuvā am* and *āvā + am*. Now *ami pūrvaḥ* (134) applies and a single substitute in the form of the preceding vowel comes in place of the preceding and the following vowels and we obtain the forms : *yuvām* and *āvām*.

In the nominative plural we introduce the affix *jas* after both the pronominal stems : *yuṣmad + jas* and *asmad + jas*. The sup-affix *jas* is replaced by *am* according to the rule *ṅe prathamayoram* (310) and we have *yuṣmad + am* and *asmad + am*. At this stage, the following sūtra applies :

(315) यूयवयौ जसि। ***yūyavayau jasi.* 7. 2. 93**

लघु० - अनयोर्मपर्यन्तस्य यूयवयौ स्तो जसि। यूयम्। वयम्। *anayor maparyantasya yūyavayau sto jasi. yūyam. vayam.*

Trans. : When the affix *jas* follows, the portions of *yuṣmad* and *asmad*, extending up to the phoneme *m*, are replaced respectively by *yūya* and *vaya*.

PP. *yuṣmadasmadoḥ maparyantasya yūyavayau jasi (vibhaktau, aṅgasya).*

Eluc. : The present sūtra occurs in the domain of the governing rule *maparyantasya* Pā. 7. 2. 91, hence its recurrence in the present sūtra. The word *yuṣmadasmadoḥ* is carried over from *yuṣmadasmadoranādeśe* Pā. 7. 2. 86. The meaning of the sūtra is as follows : The portions of *yuṣmad* and *asmad* up to the phoneme *m* are respectively replaced by *yūya* and *vaya* if the affix *jas* follows.

In the illustrations *yuṣmad + am* and *asmad + am*, the substitute *am* is construed as *jas* by sthānivadbhāva (143). Therefore by virtue of the present rule, the portions of these words up to *m* are respectively replaced by *yūya* and *vaya* and we have the following grammatical situation : *yūya ad + am* and *vaya ad + am*. The rule *ato guṇe* (273) applies and we have *yūyad + am* and *vayad + am*. At this stage, the rule *śeṣe lopaḥ* (312) applies. When the *ad*-portion (*ṭi*) is elided, we have *yūy + am* --> *yūyam* and *vay + am* --> *vayam*. According to the alternative interpretation, the final phoneme *d* is elided and we get the forms *yūyam* and *vayam* after the grammatical operation of the rule *ami pūrvaḥ* (134) has taken effect.

In *yuṣmad + am* and *asmad + am*, the following sūtra presents itself for application :

(316) **त्वमावेकवचने ।** ***tvamāvekavacane.*** **7. 2. 97**
लघु॰ - एकस्योक्तावनयोर्मपर्यन्तस्य त्वमौ स्तो विभक्तौ । *ekasyoktāv anayor maparyantasya tvamau sto vibhaktau.*

Trans. : When singularity (with respect to these pronominal stems) is to be expressed, the portions of *yuṣmad* and *asmad*, extending up to the phoneme *m*, are respectively replaced by the substitutes *tva* and *ma* when a sup-affix (*vibhakti*) follows.

PP. *yuṣmadasmadoḥ maparyantasya tvamau vibhaktau ekavacane (aṅgasya).*

Eluc. : The present sūtra occurs in the domain of the governing rule *maparyantasya* Pā. 7. 2. 91. So, the word *maparyantasya* recurs in the present sūtra. The word *yuṣmadasmadoḥ* comes from *yuṣmadasmador anādeśe* Pā. 7.2. 86. The word *ekavacane* in the sūtra is a ṣaṣṭhītatpuruṣa which is analysed as follows : *ekasya vacanam ekavacanam, tasmin = ekavacane*. The significance of the use of the term *ekavacane* lies in the fact that it is to denote the singularity of the pronominal stems and not that of the sup-affix. The compound word *atitvām* may be analysed as *tvām atikrāntau* 'the two who have surpassed you'. Here the word *yuṣmad* as a member of the compound is used to convey the sense of singularity. Therefore, the portion of *yuṣmad* up to the phoneme *m* is replaced by *tva* and we get the compound word *atitvām*. It is in this sense that Pāṇini has used the term *ekavacane* in the present sūtra instead of the term *ekatve*. The meaning of the sūtra is as follows : When singularity of the pronominal stems *yuṣmad* and *asmad* is intended to be expressed, the portions of these words up to the phoneme *m* are respectively replaced by *tva* and *ma* before a sup-affix.

In the illustrations *yuṣmad* + *am* and *asmad* + *am*, the substitutes *tva* and *ma* replace the portions up to *m* and we have *tva ad* + *am* and *ma ad* + *am* --> *tvad* + *am* and *mad* + *am* {*ato guṇe* (273)}. At this stage, the following sūtra applies :

(317) द्वितीयायाञ्च । *dvitīyāyāñca*. 7. 2. 87

लघु० – अनयोरात् स्यात्। त्वाम्। माम्। *anayor āt syāt. tvām. mām.*

Trans. : When the affixes of the second triplet follow, the final phoneme of these pronominal stems is replaced by *āt*.

PP. *yuṣmadasmadoḥ āḥ dvitīyāyām ca vibhaktau (aṅgasya)*.

Eluc. : The word *yuṣmadasmadoḥ* is carried over from *yuṣmadasmador anādeśe* Pā. 7. 2. 86. The term *āḥ* comes from *aṣṭana ā vibhaktau* Pā. 7. 2. 84. It has been paraphrased as *āt* by Varadarāja in his vṛtti on the present sūtra. The meaning of the sūtra is as follows : The final phoneme, {*d*, with the help of *alo 'ntyasya* (21)}, of the pronominal stems *yuṣmad* and *asmad* is replaced by a long *ā*, when a sup-affix of the second triplet follows.

In the illustrations *tvad* + *am* and *mad* + *am*, the phoneme *d* is replaced by *ā* and we arrive at the following stage : *tva ā* + *am* and *ma ā* + *am*. Now with the help of the rule *akaḥ savarṇe dīrghaḥ* (42), a long *ā* replaces both the homogeneous akāras (*a* + *ā* = *ā*). Then we reach the following stage : *tvā* + *am* and *mā* + *am*. According to the rule *ami pūrvaḥ* (134), a single substitute in the form of the preceding vowel *ā* comes in place of both *ā* and *a*. We thus obtain the forms : *tvām* and *mām*.

With the introduction of the dual affix *auṭ* of the second triplet, we have : *yuṣmad* + *auṭ* and *asmad* + *auṭ*. Here also the rule *ṅe prathamayoram* (310) prescribes the replacement of the affix *auṭ* by *am*. We have : *yuṣmad* + *am* and *asmad* + *am*. Then by *yuvāvau dvivacane* (313), we replace the portions up to *m* by *yuva* and *āva* --> *yuva ad* + *am* and *āva ad* + *am*. The rule *ato guṇe* (273) applies and we have *yuvad* + *am* and *āvad* + *am*. At this stage, the present rule enjoins the replacement of the phoneme *d* by a long *ā* --> *yuva ā + am* and *āva ā + am*. The rule *akaḥ savarṇe dīrghaḥ* (42) applies and we have *yuvā + am* and *āvā + am*. Then by *ami pūrvaḥ* (134) after replacing both the preceding and the following vowels by a single substitution in the form of the preceding vowel, we obtain the desired forms : *yuvām* and *āvām*.

When we add the plural affix of the second triplet after *yuṣmad* and *asmad*, we have : *yuṣmad + śas* and *asmad + śas*. After the elision of the anubandha *ś* by *tasya lopaḥ* (3), we have : *yuṣmad + as* and *asmad + as*. At this stage, the rule *ṅe prathamayor am* (310) becomes available for application but the following sūtra blocks it :

(318) शसो न । *śaso na*. 7. 1. 29

लघु० – आभ्यां शसो नः स्यात्। अमोऽपवादः। आदेः परस्य। संयोगान्तलोपः। युष्मान्। अस्मान्। *ābhyāṁ śaso naḥ syāt. amo 'pavādaḥ. ādeḥ parasya. saṁyogānta-lopaḥ. yuṣmān. asmān.*

Trans. : The sup-affix *śas*, that follows the pronominal stems *yuṣmad* and *asmad*, is replaced by the phoneme *n*.This is an exception to *am* {prescribed by (310)}. The rule *ādeḥ parasya* (72) directs the replacement of the initial phoneme *a* of (*ś*)*as*. Then by *saṁyogāntasya lopaḥ* (20), the pada-final *s* occurring at the end of a conjunct is elided.

PP. *yuṣmadasmadbhyām śasaḥ nah*(*aṅgasya*).

Eluc. : The compound word *yuṣmadasmadbhyām* comes from *yuṣmad-asmadbhyāṁ ṅaso 'ś* Pā. 7. 1. 27. The term *na* has been used without a nominal ending (*netyavibhaktikaṁ padam*, SK, I, p. 403). The meaning of the sūtra is as follows : If the sup-affix *śas* comes after the words *yuṣmad* and *asmad*, then the affix *śas* is replaced by the phoneme *n*. The affix *śas* belongs to the second triplet. Hence the rule *ṅe prathamayoram* (310) is available to prescribe the substitute *am* to come in place of the affix *śas* but the present rule instead enjoins the substitute *n* to come in place of the affix *śas*. So, this is an exception to the rule *ṅe prathamayoram* (310). Although the substitute *n* was to replace the final phoneme of the affix *śas*, that is the phoneme *s* by *alo 'ntyasya* (21), the paribhāṣā sūtra *ādeḥ parasya* (72) blocks it and prescribes the substitution of the initial *a* of *as* (*śas*) by the phoneme *n*. So, we have the following grammatical situation: *yuṣmad +n s* and *asmad + n s*. Now accoding to the rule *dvitīyāyāñca* (317), the phoneme *d* is replaced by *ā* --> *yuṣma ā + n s* and *asma ā + n s*. By *akaḥ savarṇe dīrghaḥ* (42), we arrive at : *yuṣmāns* and *asmāns*. Now the rule *saṁyogāntasya lopaḥ* (20) applies and with the help of the rule *alo 'ntyasya* (21), the last phoneme s is elided and we have *yuṣmān* and *asmān*. The pada-final *n* will not be elided since the elision of the last phoneme s by *saṁyogāntasya lopaḥ* Pā. 8. 2. 23 is deemed not to have taken place with respect to the rule *na lopaḥ*... Pā. 8. 2. 7. The former, being subsequent to the latter, is considered to be suspended by *pūrvatrāsiddham* Pā. 8. 2. 1.

In the illustration, *yuṣmān*, the dental *n* is to be replaced by a cerebral *ṇ* in accordance with the rule *aṭkupvāṅnumvyavāye 'pi* (137) since the cerebral *ṣ* occurs in the same pada, but this grammatical operation of cerebralization is blocked by the rule *padāntasya* (138) and there is no change in the pada-final dental nasal stop.

With the introduction of the singular affix of the third triplet after the pronominal words *yuṣmad* and *asmad*, we have : *yuṣmad* + *ṭā* and *asmad* + *ṭā* --> *yuṣmad* + *ā* and *asmad* + *ā* (after the anubandha *ṭ* has been elided). Since the singularity of the pronominal stems is intended, the portions of these stems up to *m* are respectively replaced by the substitutes *tva* and *ma* according to the rule *tvamāvekavacane* (316) and we reach the following stage : *tva ad* + *ā* and *ma ad* + *ā*. By *ato guṇe* (273) we have : *tvad* + *ā* and *mad* + *ā*. In this situation, the following sūtra presents itself for application :

(319) योऽचि । *yo 'ci.* 7. 2. 89

लघु० – अनयोर्यकारादेशः स्यादनादेशेऽजादौ परतः । त्वया । मया । *anayor yakārādeśaḥ* syädanädeçe 'jädau parataù. *tvayā. mayā.*

Trans. : Let the substitute *y* replace these two (*yuṣmad* and *asmad*) if a vowel-initial vibhakti, which has not been subject to replacement, follows.

PP. *yuṣmadasmadoḥ yaḥ anādeśe aci vibhaktau (aṅgasya).*

Eluc. : The words *yuṣmadasmadoḥ* and *anādeśe* are carried over from *yuṣmadasmadoranādeśe* Pā. 7.2. 86. The term *vibhaktau* comes from *aṣṭana ā vibhaktau* Pā. 7. 2. 84. The vowel *a* in the substitute *ya* is for the sake of articulation. The word *aci* in the sūtra qualifies the term *vibhaktau*, which, by tadādividhi, comes to mean that the sup-affix, that follows, should begin with a vowel (*ac*). This is in accordance with *yasmin vidhis tadādāv algrahaṇe* (Mbh 1. 1. 72 vtk 29). In this way the sūtra means as follows : When a vowel-initial sup-affix, not having been subject to replacement, follows, the pronominal stems *yuṣmad* and *asmad* are to be replaced by the substitute *y*. In the illustrations, the affix *ā* (*ṭā*) has not undergone any replacement. Hence the sup-affix *ā* (*ṭā*) is anādeśa. Now according to the rule *alo 'ntyasya* (21), the substitute *y* replaces the last phoneme of the pronominal stems *yuṣmad* and *asmad*. In other words, the final phoneme *d* is replaced by *y*. In the illustrations, *tvad* + *ā* and *mad* + *ā*, we replace the phoneme *d* by *y* and get the forms : *tvayā* and *mayā*.

If a sup-affix is replaced by another substitute, then it ceases to be an anādeśa affix. By the rules *pañcamyā at* (324) and *ekavacanasya ca* (323), the affixes *bhyas* and *ṅasi* are replaced by the substitute *at*. Now *at*, which is an affix by sthānivadbhāva, is an ādeśa or a replaced affix. When such an affix follows, the present rule does not enjoin the replacement of the final phoneme of *yuṣmad* and *asmad* by the phoneme *y*. Consequently, there is no *y*-replacement in the forms *tvat*, *mat*, *yuṣmat* and *asmat*.

With the introduction of the dual affix of the third triplet, we have *yuṣmad* + *bhyām* and *asmad* + *bhyām*. In this grammatical situation, the portions of the pronominal stems *yuṣmad* and *asmad* up to the phoneme *m* are respectively replaced by *yuva* and *āva* --> *yuva ad* + *bhyām* and *āva ad* + *bhyām*. After the application of the rule *ato guṇe* (273), we have : *yuvad* + *bhyām* and *āvad* + *bhyām*. At this stage, the following sūtra ensues :

(320) युष्मदस्मदोरनादेशे । *yuṣmadasmadoranādeśe*. 7. 2. 86

लघु० - अनयोरात् स्याद् अनादेशे हलादौ विभक्तौ । युवाभ्याम् । आवाभ्याम् । युष्माभिः । अस्माभिः । *anayor āt syād anādeśe halādau vibhaktau. yuvābhyām. āvābhyām. yuṣmābhiḥ. asmābhiḥ.*

Trans. : Let the substitute *āt* replace the pronominal stems *yuṣmad* and *asmad* if a consonant-initial sup-affix (*vibhakti*) follows, which has not been subject to replacement.

PP. *yuṣmadasmadoḥ āḥ anādeśe vibhaktau* (*aṅgasya*).

Eluc. : The term *hali* is carried over from *rāyo hali* Pā. 7. 2. 85. The terms *āḥ* and *vibhaktau* come from *aṣṭana ā vibhaktau* Pā. 7. 2. 84. The meaning of the sūtra is as follows : If a sup-affix, beginning with a consonant and having not undergone any replacement, follows, then the final phoneme {*alo 'ntyasya* (21)} of the pronominal stems *yuṣmad* and *asmad* is replaced by a long *ā*. In the illustrations *yuvad* + *bhyām* and *āvad* + *bhyām*, the phoneme *d* is replaced by *ā* --> *yuva ā* + *bhyām* and *āva ā* + *bhyām*. The rule *akaḥ savarṇe dīrghaḥ* (42) applies and we obtain the forms *yuvābhyām* and *āvābhyām*.

We get the plural forms in the same manner when we introduce the plural sup-affix of the third triplet. In *yuṣmad + bhis* and *asmad + bhis*, the final phoneme is replaced by a long *ā* according to the present rule since the affix *bhis* has not been subject to any replacement and we reach the following stage : *yuṣma ā + bhis* and *asma ā + bhis*. The rule *akaḥ savarṇe dīrghaḥ* (42) applies and we get the forms : *yuṣmābhiḥ* and *asmābhiḥ* after rutva and visarga.

With the addition of the singular affix *ṅe*, we have *yuṣmad + ṅe* and *asmad + ṅe*. Here the rule *ṅe prathamayoram* (310) applies and the affix *ṅe* is replaced by *am* --> *yuṣmad + am* and *asmad + am*. At this stage, the following sūtra presents itself for application :

(321) तुभ्यमह्यौ ङयि । *tubhyamahyau ṅayi*. 7. 2. 95

लघु० - अनयोर्मपर्यन्तस्य । टिलोपः । तुभ्यम् । मह्यम् । *anayor maparyantasya. ṭilopaḥ. tubhyam. mahyam.*

Trans. : The substitutes *tubhya* and *mahya* replace the portions of these two pronominal stems up to the phoneme *m* in a respective manner when the affix *ṅe* follows.

PP. *yuṣmadasmadoḥ maparyantasya tubhyamahyau ṅayi (vibhaktau, aṅgasya).*

Eluc. : The present sūtra occurs in the domain of the governing rule *maparyantasya* Pā. 7. 2. 91. So, the term *maparyantasya* recurs here. The compound word *yuṣmadasmadoḥ* comes from *yuṣmadasmadoranādeśe* Pā. 7. 2. 86. Then the sūtra means as follows : When the affix *ṅe* follows, the portions up to the phoneme *m* of *yuṣmad* and *asmad* are respectively replaced by *tubhya* and *mahya*.

In the illustrations *yuṣmad + am* and *asmad + am*, the substitute *am* is construed as *ṅe* by sthānivadbhāva (143). Therefore, the portions up to the *m* of *yuṣmad* and *asmad* are respectively replaced by *tubhya* and *mahya* --> *tubhya ad + am* and *mahya ad + am*. Now by the rule *śeṣe lopaḥ* (312), the *ṭi*-portion is elided and we obtain *tubhyam* and *mahyam*. When the final phoneme *d* of both the stems is elided, we obtain the forms *tubhyam* and *mahyam* after the grammatical operation of the rule *ami pūrvaḥ* (134) in both the cases.

To decline these pronominal stems in dative plural, we introduce the affix *bhyas* : *yuṣmad + bhyas* and *asmad + bhyas*. In this grammatical situation, the following sūtra applies :

(322) **भ्यसो भ्यम्। *bhyaso bhyam.* 7. 1. 30**

लघु० – आभ्यां परस्य भ्यसो भ्यम् इत्यादेशः स्यात्। युष्मभ्यम्। अस्मभ्यम्। *ābhyāṁ parasya bhyaso bhyam ityādeśaḥ syāt. yuṣmabhyam. asmabhyam.*

Trans. : Let the sup-affix *bhyas*, which follows the words *yuṣmad* and *asmad*, be replaced by *bhyam*.

PP. *yuṣmadasmadbhyām bhyasaḥ bhyam (aṅgasya).*

Eluc. : The compound word *yuṣmadasmadbhyām* comes from *yuṣmadasmadbhyāṁ ṅaso 'ś* Pā. 7. 1. 27. The meaning of the sūtra is : The affix *bhyas* is to be replaced by *bhyam*, when it follows the pronominal stems *yuṣmad* and *asmad*.

The other reading of the present sūtra is *bhyaso 'bhyam*. According to this reading, the substitute is *abhyam*. In the illustrations *yuṣmad* + *bhyas* and *asmad* + *bhyas*, the affix *bhyas* in both the cases is replaced by *abhyam* --> *yuṣmad* + *abhyam* and *asmad* + *abhyam*. When the *ṭi*-protion *ad* is elided by *śeṣe lopaḥ* (312), we get *yuṣm* + *abhyam* --> *yuṣmabhyam* and *asm* + *abhyam* --> *asmabhyam*. When the final *d* is elided by *śeṣe lopaḥ* (312) in accordance with the alternative interpretation, we get the desired forms : *yuṣmabhyam* and *asmabhyam* after pararūpa has taken place by *ato guṇe* (273).

Taking into account the reading as given in the sūtra above, when we replace the substituendum *bhyas* by *bhyam*, we have : *yuṣmad* + *bhyam* and *asmad* + *bhyam*. After the final phoneme *d* is elided in accordance with the alternative interpretation of the rule *śeṣe lopaḥ* (312), the rule *bahuvacane jhalyet* Pā. 7. 3. 103 becomes available for application in *yuṣma* + *bhyam* and *asma* + *bhyam*. As a consequence, the aṅga-final *a* is to be replaced by the vowel *e* since the initial consonant in *bhyam* is a denotatum of *jhal*-pratyāhāra. We can ward off this undesirable contingency by invoking the paribhāṣā *aṅgavṛtte punarvṛttāv avidhiḥ* (Abhyankar, 92) : If an operation, enunciated in the governing domain of aṅga (from Pā. 6. 4. 1 up to 7. 4. 97), has taken place and if another operation of the same domain is subsequently applicable, then the latter operation is not allowed to operate. In the present case, the final *d* is elided by *śeṣe lopaḥ* Pā. 7. 2. 90. After the elision of the phoneme *d*, the aṅga-final *a* becomes due to be replaced by *e* according to *bahuvacane jhalyet* Pā. 7. 3. 103. Both the rules occur in the domain of aṅga. The rule *śeṣe lopaḥ* has already performed its function of eliding the final phoneme *d*. Consequently, the latter rule is not allowed to apply. Resultantly, the forms *yuṣmabhyam* and *asmabhyam* remain intact (cf. Kielhorn, pt. II, p. 437, fn. 1).

In the ablative singular we introduce the sup-affix *ṅasi* and we have the following situation : *yuṣmad* + *ṅasi* and *asmad* + *ṅasi*. In this situation the following sūtra ensues :

(323) एकवचनस्य च । *ekavacanasya ca*. 7. 1. 32

लघु० – आभ्यां ङसेरत्। त्वत्। मत्। *ābhyāṁ ṅaser at. tvat. mat.*

Trans. : The affix *ṅasi*, which follows *yuṣmad* and *asmad*, is replaced by the substitute *at*.

PP. *yuṣmadasmadbhyām pañcamyāḥ ekavacanasya ca at* (*aṅgasya*).

Eluc. : The compound word *yuṣmadasmadbhyām* is carried over from *yuṣmadasmadbhyāṁ ṅaso 'ś* Pā. 7. 1. 27. The term *pañcamyāḥ* comes from *pañcamyā at* Pā. 7. 1. 31. Then the sūtra means as follows : When the singular affix *ṅasi* of the fifth triplet follows the pronominal stems *yuṣmad* and *asmad*, it is replaced by *at*. This grammatical operation is exemplified in the following illustrations : *yuṣmad* + *ṅasi* and *asmad* + *ṅasi* --> *yuṣmad* + *at* and *asmad* + *at*. The substitute *at* has more than one phoneme (*al*) since the consonant *t* at the end of *at* is not *it* by *halantyam* (1) as it has been negated by *na vibhaktau tusmāḥ* (130). Therefore the substitute *at* replaces the whole substituendum as is shown in the illustrations above. In this situation, the pre-affixal bases *yuṣmad* and *asmad* are respectively replaced by *tva* and *ma* according to *tvamāvekavacane* (316) and we reach the following declensional stage : *tva ad* + *at* and *ma ad* + *at* --> *tvad* + *at* and *mad* + *at* { pararūpa by *ato guṇe* (273)}. At this stage, the *ad*-portion (*ṭi*) of both the pre-affixal bases is elided by *śeṣe lopaḥ* (312) and we obtain *tv* + *at* --> *tvat* and *m* + *at* --> *mat*. When the aṅga-final *d* is elided by the rule *śeṣe lopaḥ* (312), the rule *ato guṇe* (273) applies again to bring about pararūpa and we obtain the forms *tvat* and *mat*.

In the ablative plural we add the affix *bhyas* and have the following declensional stage : *yuṣmad* + *bhyas* and *asmad* + *bhyas*. In this situation, the following sūtra applies :

(324) पञ्चम्या अत्। *pañcamyā at*. 7. 1. 31

लघु० – आभ्यां पञ्चम्या भ्यसोऽत् स्यात्। युष्मत्। अस्मत्। *ābhyāṁ pañcamyā bhyaso 't syāt. yuṣmat. asmat.*

Trans. : Let the ablative affix *bhyas*, coming after *yuṣmad* and *asmad*, be replaced by *at*.

PP. *yuṣmadasmadbhyām pañcamyāḥ bhyasaḥ at (aṅgasya).*

Eluc. : The compound word *yuṣmadasmadbhyām* is carried over from *yuṣmadasmadbhyāṁ ṅaso 'ś* Pā. 7. 1. 27. The term *bhyasaḥ* comes from *bhyaso bhyam* Pā. 7. 1. 30. The meaning of the sūtra is as follows : The plural affix *bhyas* of the fifth triplet, which follows *yuṣmad* and *asmad*, is replaced by *at*. It has more than one phoneme (*al*) since the consonant *t* is not *it* because of *na vibhaktau tusmāḥ* (130). Therefore the substitute *at* replaces the whole of *bhyas*. After the replacement, we have : *yuṣmad* + *at* and *asmad* + *at*. At this stage, the *ad*-portion (*ṭi*) is elided by *śeṣe lopaḥ* (312) and we have *yuṣm* + *at* --> *yuṣmat* and *asm* + *at* --> *asmat*. According the alternative interpretation of the rule *śeṣe lopaḥ* (312), when the final phoneme *d* is elided, we obtain the forms : *yuṣmat* and *asmat* after the application of *ato guṇe* (273).

With the introduction of the singular affix of the sixth triplet, we have the following grammatical stage : *yuṣmad* + *ṅas* and *asmad* + *ṅas* --> *yuṣmad* + *as* and *asmad* + *as* (after the elision of the anubandha *ṅ*). In this situation, the rule *tvamāvekavacane* (316) becomes available for application, but the following sūtra blocks it and applies :

(325) तवममौ ङसि । *tavamamau ṅasi.* 7. 2. 96

लघु० – अनयोर्मपर्यन्तस्य तवममौ स्तो ङसि । *anayor maparyantasya tavamamau sto ṅasi.*

Trans. : The portions up to *m* of these two (*yuṣmad* and *asmad*) are respectively replaced by *tava* and *mama* when the affix *ṅas* follows.

PP. *yuṣmadasmadoḥ maparyantasya tavamamau ṅasi (vibhaktau, aṅgasya).*

Eluc. : The compound word *yuṣmadasmadoḥ* is carried over from *yuṣmadasmadoranādeśe*. 7. 2. 86. The present sūtra occurs in the domain of the governing rule *maparyantasya* Pā. 7. 2. 91. The word *maparyantasya* therefore recurs in this sūtra also. The meaning of the sūtra is : If the genitive singular affix *ṅas* follows the pronominal stems *yuṣmad* and *asmad*, then their portions up to the phoneme *m* are respectively replaced by *tava* and *mama*. After the replacement has taken place, we arrive at the following declensional stage : *tava ad* + *ṅas* and *mama ad* + *ṅas*. Now the rule *ato guṇe* (273) brings about a single replacement in the form of the following guṇa vowel *a* in place of both the preceding and the following vowels and we have *tavad* + *ṅas* and *mamad* + *ṅas*. At this stage, the following sūtra presents itself for application :

(326) युष्मदस्मद्भ्यां ङसोऽश्। *yuṣmadasmadbhyāṁ ṅaso 'ś.* 7. 1. 27
लघु॰ – तव। मम। युवयोः। आवयोः। *tava. mama. yuvayoḥ. āvayoḥ.*

Trans. : Let the affix *ṅas*, coming after *yuṣmad* and *asmad*, be replaced by *aś*.

PP. *yuṣmadasmadbhyām ṅasaḥ aś* (*aṅgasya*).

Eluc. : The substitute is *aś*. It has the phoneme *ś* as *it*. This is the reason why the rule *ādeḥ parasya* (72) is debarred by *anekāl śit sarvasya* (45) which allows the substitute *aś* to replace the whole of *ṅas*. This point having been taken into consideration, the sūtra gives the following meaning : If the sup-affix *ṅas* happens to follow the pronominal stems *yuṣmad* and *asmad*, then it is wholly substituted by *aś* in accordance with the rule *anekāl...* (45). After the replacement by *aś*, we have the following stage : *tavad + aś* and *mamad + aś*. In this grammatical situation, the *ad*-portion (*ṭi*) is elided by *śeṣe lopaḥ* (312) and we obtain *tava* and *mama*. When the final phoneme *d* of *tavad* and *mamad* is elided in accordance with the alternative interpretation of *śeṣe lopaḥ* (312), we get the forms *tava* and *mama* after pararūpa by *ato guṇe* (273).

When we add the affix *os* after these words, we have : *yuṣmad + os* and *asmad + os*. At this stage, the rule *yuvāvau dvivacane* (313) applies and the portions up to *m* of *yuṣmad* and *asmad* are replaced by *yuva* and *āva* respectively and we arrive at the following stage : *yuva ad + os* and *āva ad + os*. Now the rule *ato guṇe* (273) prescribes a single substitute in the form of the preceding vowel and we have the following situation : *yuvad + os* and *āvad + os*. Now the rule *yo 'ci* (319) becomes applicable since the vowel-initial affix *os* has not undergone any replacement. Thus we get the forms *yuvayoḥ* and *āvayoḥ* through the following grammatical process : *yuvad + os* and *āvad + os* --> *yuvay + os* and *āvay + os* --> *yuvayos* and *āvayos* --> *yuvayoḥ* and *āvayoḥ* (after rutva and visarga).

In genitive plural, we add the affix *ām* and we have : *yuṣmad + ām* and *asmad + ām*. At this stage, the following sūtra applies:

(327) साम आकम्। *sāma ākam.* 7. 1. 33
लघु॰ – आभ्यां परस्य साम आकम् स्यात्। युष्माकम्। अस्माकम्। त्वयि। मयि। युवयोः। आवयोः। युष्मासु। अस्मासु। *ābhyāṁ parasya sāma ākam syāt. yuṣmākam. asmākam. tvayi. mayi. yuvayoḥ. āvayoḥ. yuṣmāsu. asmāsu.*

Trans. : Let the substituendum *sām* coming after *yuṣmad* and *asmad* be replaced by *ākam*.

PP. *yuṣmadasmadbhyām sāmaḥ ākam (aṅgasya).*

Eluc. : The compound word *yuṣmadasmadbhyām* is carried over from *yuṣmadasmadbhyāṁ ṅaso 'ś* Pā. 7. 1. 27. The meaning of the sūtra will be as follows : If the genitive plural affix *sām* (*suṭ* + *ām*) follows the pronominal stems *yuṣmad* and *asmad*, then it will be replaced by the substitute *ākam*. In the illustrations *yuṣmad* + *ām* and *asmad* + *ām*, we could apply *āmi sarvanāmnaḥ suṭ* (154) after the elision of the phoneme *d* by *śeṣe lopaḥ* (312) since these words, being sarvanāman, would then be available ending in a short *a*. The augment *suṭ* would then be inserted at the head of the affix *ām* { *ādyantau ṭakitau* (84)} to have the grammatical stage required by the present rule : *yuṣma* + *suṭ ām* and *asma* +*suṭ ām* --> *yuṣma* + *sām* and *asma* + *sām* (after the elision of the anubandhas). At this stage, the present rule becomes applicable and the affix *sām* is replaced by *ākam* --> *yuṣma* + *ākam* and *asma* + *ākam*. Then we get the forms : *yuṣmākam* and *asmākam* after the rule *akaḥ savarṇe dīrghaḥ* (42) has performed its grammatical function.

We have tried to explain the grammatical process of declining the pronominal stems *yuṣmad* and *asmad* in the genitive plural in a manner which is easy to comprehend. Nonetheless, the grammatical process of declining the genitive plural forms of these words requires a little more elucidation in the light of what the commentators have said on this sūtra. Jñānendra Sarasvatī raises a query in order to situate the statement of Bhaṭṭoji in the Siddhāntakaumudī in the proper perspective : The enunciation of the affix *ām* with the augment *suṭ* is to dispense with the yet-to-be insertion of the augment *suṭ* (*bhāvino suṭo nivṛttyarthaṁ sasuṭkanirdeśaḥ*, SK, I, p. 407). The question he raises is : What is the need of indicating the substituendum with the augment *suṭ* when no such grammatical situation in the present context is available. In the illustrations *yuṣmad* + *ām* and *asmad* + *ām*, the augment *suṭ* by *āmi sarvanāmnaḥ suṭ* (154) is not available since the pre-affixal bases do not end in a short *a*. He clarifies it by saying that the augment *suṭ* would be available to be inserted at the head of *ākam* when the final phoneme *d* has been elided by *śeṣe lopaḥ* (312) after the affix *ām* has been replaced by *ākam*. The grammatical situation would be as follows : *yuṣmad* + *ām* and *asmad* + *ām* --> *yuṣma* + *ākam* and *asma* + *ākam* by the present rule. At this stage, the rule *āmi sarvanāmnaḥ suṭ* (154) becomes applicable since the pre-affixal base ends in a short *a* and the substitute *ākam* is treated like the substituendum *ām* by virtue of sthānivadbhāva (143). In this situation the augment *suṭ* is due and with the insertion of the augment *suṭ* the grammatical situation would be : *yuṣma* + *sākam* and *asma* + *sākam*. At this stage, the rule *bahuvacane jhalyet* (144) would apply and the pre-affixal final *a* would be replaced by *e*. In such a grammatical situation (*yuṣme* + *sākam* and *asme* + *sākam*), the dental *s* of *sākam* becomes liable to change into the cerebral *ṣ* by *ādeśapratyayayoḥ* (149). The resultant forms would be **yuṣmeṣākam* and **asmeṣākam*. Vāsudeva Dīkṣita says that the enunciation of the affix *ām* accompanied by the augment *suṭ* is to avoid such an undesirable contingency. In short, the indication of the substituendum accompanied by the augment *suṭ* is purported to block the insertion of the augment *suṭ* at the head of the substitute *ākam*.[1] Now in *yuṣma* + *ākam* and *asma* + *ākam*, the rule *akaḥ savarṇe...* (42) applies and we obtain the forms : *yuṣmākam* and *asmākam*. In the other alternative, when the *ṭi*-portion is elided, we have *yuṣm* + *ām* and *asm* + *ām*. In this grammatical situation, the reading *sāma* in the present sūtra appears to be redundant. This redundancy leads to the implication that it is the elision of the final phoneme of the pronominal stems *yuṣmad* and *asmad*, which is intended by Pāṇini by the sūtra *śeṣe lopaḥ* (312) and not the elision of *ṭi* as interpreted by Varadarāja even though both the interpretations are given in the Mahābhāṣya. In the other alternative, the affix *ām* would be replaced by *ākam* and we can have the desired forms *yuṣm* + *ākam* --> *yuṣmākam* and *asm* + *ākam* --> *asmākam* without applying the rule *akaḥ savarṇe dīrghaḥ* (42).

We get the locative singular forms *tvayi* and *mayi* by introducing the affix *ṅi* after *yuṣmad* and *asmad* in a respective manner. In *yuṣmad* + *ṅi* and *asmad* + *ṅi*, the portions up to *m* are replaced by *tva* and *ma* by *tvamāvekavacane* (316) and we have : *tva ad* + *ṅi* and *ma ad* + *ṅi* --> *tva ad* + *i* and *ma ad* + *i*. The rule *ato guṇe* (273) applies and we have : *tvad* + *i* and *mad* + *i*. At this stage, the rule *yo 'ci* (319) prescribes the replacement of *d* by *y* and the forms *tvayi* and *mayi* are obtained.

The forms *yuvayoḥ* and *āvayoḥ* have already been explained under the rule *yuṣmadasmadbhyām...* (326).

In the locative plural we introduce the affix *sup* after *yuṣmad* and *asmad* : *yuṣmad* + *sup* and *asmad* + *sup* --> *yuṣmad* + *su* and *asmad* + *su* (after the elision of the anubandha *p*). In this situation, the aṅga-final *d* is replaced by *ā* in both the cases by *yuṣmadasmadoranādeśe* (320) : *yuṣma ā* + *su* and *asma ā* + *su*. After the application the rule *akaḥ savarṇe dīrghaḥ* (42) we obtain the forms : *yuṣmāsu* and *asmāsu*. The declension of both the pronominal stems *yuṣmad* and *asmad* are given below :

---

1. *yadi tu āma ākam ityevocyeta tarhi āma ākamādeśe kṛte dakārasya śeṣalope sati sthānivattvena ākamādeśasya āmtvāt tasya ca avarṇāt paratvāt suḍāgamaḥ syāt. tata etvaṣatvayor yuṣmeṣākam asmeṣākam iti syāt. ataḥ sasuṭkanirdeśaḥ. yadyapi ākamādeśapravṛttikāle suṭo na prasaktiḥ. tathāpi ākamādeśottaraṁ dakāralope kṛte sthānivattvena yaḥ suḍ bhaviṣyati tasyāpi sthānaṣaṣṭhyāḥ svīkaraṇān nivṛttir bhavati. anyathā sasuṭkanirdeśavaiyarthyād iti bhāvaḥ.* BM, I, p. 407. Also cf. TB, I, p. 407.

yuṣmad

	Singular	Dual	Plural
prathamā	*tvam*	*yuvām*	*yūyam*
dvitīyā	*tvām*	*yuvām*	*yuṣmān*
tṛtīyā	*tvayā*	*yuvābhyām*	*yuṣmābhiḥ*
caturthī	*tubhyam*	*yuvābhyām*	*yuṣmabhyam*
pañcamī	*tvat*	*yuvābhyām*	*yuṣmat*
ṣaṣṭhī	*tava*	*yuvayoḥ*	*yuṣmākam*
saptamī	*tvayi*	*yuvayoḥ*	*yuṣmāsu*
sambodhana		No form	

asmad

	Singular	Dual	Plural
prathamā	*aham*	*āvām*	*vayam*
dvitīyā	*mām*	*āvām*	*asmān*
tṛtīyā	*mayā*	*āvābhyām*	*asmābhiḥ*
caturthī	*mahyam*	*āvābhyām*	*asmabhyam*
pañcamī	*mat*	*āvābhyām*	*asmat*
ṣaṣṭhī	*mama*	*āvayoḥ*	*asmākam*
saptamī	*mayi*	*āvayoḥ*	*asmāsu*
sambodhana		No form	

The alternative declensional forms of the pronominal stems *yuṣmad* and *asmad* with the sup-affixes of the second, fourth and sixth triplets are explained in the following sūtras :

(328) युष्मदस्मदोः षष्ठी-चतुर्थी-द्वितीयास्थयोर्वान्नावौ । *yuṣmadasmadoḥ ṣaṣṭhī-caturthī-dvitīyāsthayorvānnāvau.* 8. 1. 20

लघु० – पदात्परयोरपादादौ स्थितयोः षष्ठ्यादिविशिष्टयोर्युष्मदस्मदोर्वान्नावौ इत्यादेशौ स्तः ।

padāt parayor apādādau sthitayoḥ ṣaṣṭhyādiviśiṣṭayor yuṣmadasmador vānnāvau ityādeśau staḥ.

Trans. : The substitutes *vām* and *nau* respectively replace the inflected pronominal stems *yuṣmad* and *asmad* co-occurring with the affixes of second, fourth and sixth triplets, provided they occur after a pada, and not at the beginning of the quarter of a verse.

PP. *padāt ṣaṣṭhī-caturthī-dvitīyāsthayoḥ yuṣmadasmadoḥ padayoḥ vānnāvau apādādau.*

Eluc. : The words *padāt* and *apādādau* are carried over into the present sūtra from the governing rules *padāt* Pā. 8. 1. 17 and *anudāttaṁ sarvamapādādau* Pā. 8. 1. 18. The term *padasya* also recurs here since the present rule occurs in the domain of the governing rule *padasya* Pā. 8. 1. 16. It is changed into the genitive dual (*padayoḥ*) by the process of vacanavipariṇāma to accord with *yuṣmadasmadoḥ*. The compound *apādādau* is a ṣaṣṭhī-tatpuruṣa-seeded nañ-tatpuruṣa, the analysis of which is as follows : *pādasya ādiḥ pādādiḥ, tasmin = pādādau, na pādādau apādādau*. The negative particle in the compound conveys the sense of prasajya-pratiṣedha (negation connected with a verb). Thus the sūtra means as follows : After a pada, co-occurring with the sup-affixes of the second, fourth and sixth triplets, the inflected pronominal stems *yuṣmad* and *asmad* are respectively replaced by the substitutes *vāṁ* and *nau*, provided they do not occur at the beginning of the quarter of a verse. This is a general rule but it applies in the case of the dual affixes only since its application with respect to the other nominal endings is blocked by the rules that follow.

The other three sūtras, which prescribe other substitutes in place of *yuṣmad* and *asmad*, are as follows :

(329) बहुवचनस्य वस्नसौ । *bahuvacanasya vasnasau*. 8. 1. 21

लघु० – उक्तविधयोरनयोः षष्ठ्यादिबहुवचनान्तयोर्वस्नसौ स्तः । *uktavidhayor anayoḥ ṣaṣṭhyādibahuvacanāntayor vasnasau staḥ.*

Trans. : The substitutes *vas* and *nas* respectively replace the inflected pronominal stems *yuṣmad* and *asmad* co-occurring with the plural affixes of second, fourth and sixth triplets, provided they occur after a pada and not at the beginning of the quarter of a verse.

PP. *padāt ṣaṣṭhī-caturthī-dvitīyāsthayoḥ yuṣmadasmadoḥ padayoḥ bahuvacanasya vasnasau apādādau.*

Eluc. : The words *padāt* and *apādādau* come from the governing rules *padāt* Pā. 8. 1. 17 and *anudāttaṁ sarvamapādādau* Pā. 8. 1. 18. The word *bahuvacanasya* qualifies the words *yuṣmad* and *asmad*. Hence by tadantavidhi and by the process of vacanavipariṇāma it comes to mean 'the pronominal stems *yuṣmad* and *asmad* that end in the plural affixes'. Thus the meaning of the sūtra is as follows : When the pronominal stems *yuṣmad* and *asmad* are accompanied by the plural affixes and when they do not occur at the beginning of the quarter of a verse, they are respectively replaced by the substitutes *vas* and *nas*. The rule applies only in the case of plural case-endings. Therefore this is an exception to the preceding sūtra.

The following sūtra is also an exception to the rule *yuṣmadasmadoḥ ṣaṣṭhī-caturthī-dvitīyāsthayorvānnāvau* (328) :

(330) तेमयावेकवचनस्य । *temayāvekavacanasya*. 8. 1. 22

लघु० - उक्तविधयोरनयोः षष्ठीचतुर्थ्येकवचनान्तयोस्ते मे एतौ स्तः । *uktavidhayor anayoḥ ṣaṣṭhīcaturthyekavacanāntayos te me etau staḥ.*

Trans. : The substitutes *te* and *me* respectively replace the pronominal stems *yuṣmad* and *asmad* co-ocurring with the singular affixes of the sixth and fourth triplets, provided they occur after a pada and not at the beginning of the quarter of a verse.

PP. *padāt ṣaṣṭhī-caturthī-dvitīyāsthayoḥ yuṣmadasmadoḥ ekavacanasya temayau apādādau (padasya).*

Eluc. : The words *padāt* and *apādādau* are carried over from the governing rules *padāt* Pā. 8. 1. 17 and *anudāttaṁ sarvamapādādau* Pā. 8. 1. 18. The term *ekavacanasya* qualifies the words *yuṣmad* and *asmad*. By tadantavidhi and also by the process of vacanavipariṇāma, this gives the sense 'both the forms of *yuṣmad* and *asmad* that end in the singular'. The compound words *yuṣmadasmadoḥ* and *ṣaṣṭhī-caturthī-dvitīyāsthayoḥ* are carried over from *yuṣmadasmadoḥ ṣaṣṭhī-caturthī-dvitīyāsthayor vānnāvau* Pā. 8. 1. 20. The portion *ṣaṣṭhī-caturthī-sthayoḥ* is marked out from *ṣaṣṭhī-caturthī-dvitīyāsthayoḥ* and is explained by Varadarāja in his vṛtti since only this is relevant to the present sūtra. The reason is that the rule *tvāmau dvitīyāyāḥ* (331), which is an exception to the present sūtra, prescribes the substitutes to come in place of the accusative singular forms of *yuṣmad* and *asmad*. So, according to the paribhāṣā *prakalpya cāpavādaviṣayaṁ tata utsargo 'bhiniviśate* (Abhyankar, 63) 'the general rule beomes applicable leaving aside the area of operation of the exception rule'. It is for this reason that the present rule applies only with respect to the dative and genitive singular forms of *yuṣmad* and *asmad*. In this way the present sūtra means as follows : The pronominal stems *yuṣmad* and *asmad*, co-occurring with the singular affixes of the fourth and sixth triplets, are respectively replaced by *te* and *me* when they occur after a pada and not at the beginning of the quarter of a verse.

Now follows the sūtra which is an exception to the preceding rule :

(331) त्वामौ द्वितीयायाः । *tvāmau dvitīyāyāḥ*. 8. 1. 23

लघु॰ – द्वितीयैकवचनान्तयोस्त्वा मा इत्यादेशौ स्तः । *dvitīyaikavacanāntayos tvā mā ityādeśau staḥ.*

Trans. : The pronominal stems *yuṣmad* and *asmad* co-occurring with a singular affix of the second triplet are respectively replaced by *tvā* and *mā*, provided they occur after a pada and not at the beginning of the quarter of a verse.

PP. *padāt ṣaṣṭhī-caturthī-dvitīyāsthayoḥ yuṣmadasmadoḥ dvitīyāyāḥ ekavacanasya tvāmau apādādau* (*padasya*).

Eluc. : The words *padāt* and *apādādau*, being the constituents of a governing rule, recur in the present sūtra {see explanation under *temayāvekavacanasya* (330)}. The term *ekavacanasya*, which is carried over from *temayāveka*... Pā. 8. 1. 22, qualifies the words *yuṣmad* and *asmad*. As such, by tadantavidhi and by the process of vacanaviparināma, it gives the sense 'the words *yuṣmad* and *asmad* that end in the singular affix'. The sūtra means as follows : If the stems are accompanied by the singular affix of the second triplet and if they occur after a pada and not at the beginning of the quarter of a verse, then they are respectively replaced by *tvā* and *mā*.

All the four sūtras are being illustrated in the two verses which are given below :

लघु॰ – श्रीशस्त्वाऽवतु माऽपीह, दत्तात्ते मेऽपि शर्म सः ।
स्वामी ते मेऽपि स हरिः, पातु वामपि नौ विभुः ॥ 1 ॥
सुखं वां नौ ददात्वीशः, पतिर्वामपि नौ हरिः ।
सोऽव्याद्वो नः, शिवं वो नो दद्यात्, सेव्योऽत्र वः स नः ॥ 2 ॥

1. *śrīśas tvā 'vatu mā 'pīha, dattāt te me 'pi śarma saḥ,*
svāmī te me 'pi sa hariḥ, pātu vām api nau vibhuḥ.
2. *sukhaṁ vāṁ nau dadātvīśaḥ, patir vām api nau hariḥ.*
so 'vyād vo naḥ, śivaṁ vo no dadyāt, sevyo 'tra vaḥ sa naḥ.

Eluc. : May the Lord of the Goddess of Wealth (*śrīśaḥ*) protect (*avatu*) you (*tvā*) and me (*mā*) also (*api*) here (*iha*); may He (*saḥ*) bestow (*dattāt*) happiness (*śarma*) upon you (*te*) and me (*me*) too (*api*). That Hari (*sa hariḥ*) is your (*te*) Lord (*svāmī*) and mine (*me*) also (*api*). May the Omnipresent (*vibhuḥ*) protect (*pātu*) you two (*vām*) as well as (*api*) us two (*nau*). May God (*īśaḥ*) give (*dadātu*) happiness (*sukham*) to you two (*vām*) and to us two (*nau*); Hari (*hariḥ*) is the Lord (*patiḥ*) of you two (*vām*) and also (*api*) of us two (*nau*). May He (*saḥ*) protect (*avyād*) you all (*vaḥ*) and us all (*naḥ*); may He confer (*dadyāt*) welfare (*śivam*) upon you all (*vaḥ*) as well as upon us all (*naḥ*); He (*saḥ*) is the object of worship (*sevyaḥ*) here (*atra*) of you all (*vaḥ*) and of us all (*naḥ*).

The illustrations given in the two verses need elucidation : In the first quarter of the verse, the words *tvā* and *mā* illustrate the sūtra *tvāmau dvitīyāyāḥ* (331). These substitutes have replaced the accusative singular forms *tvām* and *mām*. The two pairs do not differ in meaning.

In the second and the third quarters of the first verse the terms *te* and *me* are used twice. The first pair of *te* and *me* stands for the singular dative forms of *yuṣmad* and *asmad*, that is, *tubhyam* and *mahyam*. In other words, the forms *te* and *me* have replaced *tubhyam* and *mahyam*. The second pair of *te* and *me* stands for the singular genitive forms of *yuṣmad* and *asmad*, that is, *tava* and *mama*. These two quarters illustrate the sūtra : *temayāvekavacanasya* (330).

The fourth quarter of the first verse and the first and second quarters of the second verse illustrate the sūtra : *yuṣmadasmadoḥ ṣaṣṭhī-caturthī-dvitīyāsthayorvānnāvau* (328). The alternative forms *vām* and *nau* are the substitutes of the forms of *yuṣmad* and *asmad* with the dual affixes of the second, fourth and sixth triplets. In other words, these alternative forms respectively replace the following forms of *yuṣmad* and *asmad* : *yuvām* and *āvām* (dual affix of the second triplet), *yuvābhyām* and *āvābhyām* (dual affix of the fourth triplet) and *yuvayoḥ* and *āvayoḥ* (dual affix of the sixth triplet).

The last two quarters illustrate the alternative forms of *yuṣmad* and *asmad* declined with the plural affixes of the second, fourth and sixth triplets, that is, *śas*, *bhyas* and *ām*. The form *vaḥ* replaces *yuṣmān*, *yuṣmabhyam* and *yuṣmākam*, whereas the altenative form *naḥ* replaces *asmān*, *asmabhyam* and *asmākam*.

One point is to be kept in mind with regard to these alternative forms. They are not used at the beginning of the quarter of a verse and secondly they should occur after a pada. For example, we can use the genitive dual form of *yuṣmad* at the beginning of a sentence but the alternative form cannot be so used. *yuvayor idam dhanam asti* is a correct sentence but not *vām idam dhanam asti* which instead should be *dhanam idam vām asti.* The statement that they should not be used at the beginning of the quarter of a verse is to ward off such a possibility. In the following verse, the genitive plural form of *yuṣmad,* that is *yuṣmākaṁ* is used at the beginning of the quarter :

rudro viśveśvaro devo yuṣmākaṁ kuladevatā,
sa eva nātho bhagavān asmākaṁ śatrumardanaḥ. Kāśikā, 8. 1. 18

The use of the term *apādādau* in the sūtra ensures that the word *yuṣmākaṁ* will not be replaced by the alternative form *vaḥ* since it has been used at the beginning of the quarter of a verse. The same rule can be extended to the term *asmākam* used at the beginning of the fourth quarter of the verse.

We are giving below a selected declension of the stems *yuṣmad* and *asmad* along with the alternative forms in the sequential order of their mention so that they may easily be comprehended in contrast :

	Singular	Dual	Plural
dvitīyā	*tvām (tvā)*	*yuvām (vām)*	*yuṣmān (vaḥ)*
caturthī	*tubhyam (te)*	*yuvābhyām(vām)*	*yuṣmabhyam (vaḥ)*
ṣaṣṭhī	*tava (te)*	*yuvayoḥ (vām)*	*yuṣmākam (vaḥ)*

	Singular	Dual	Plural
dvitīyā	*mām (mā)*	*āvām (nau)*	*asmān (naḥ)*
caturthī	*mahyam (me)*	*āvābhyām (nau)*	*asmabhyam (naḥ)*
ṣaṣṭhī	*mama (me)*	*āvayoḥ (nau)*	*asmākam (naḥ)*

26 वा० – समानवाक्ये युष्मदस्मदादेशा वक्तव्याः । *samānavākye yuṣmadasmadādeśā vaktavyāḥ.*[1]

लघु० - एकतिङ् वाक्यम् । तेनेह न - ओदनं पच तव भविष्यति । इह तु स्यादेव - शालीनान्ते ओदनं दास्यामि । *ekatiṅ vākyam. teneha na -- odanaṁ paca tava bhaviṣyati. iha tu syād eva - śālīnān te odanaṁ dāsyāmi.*

Trans. : It should be stated that the substitutes of *yuṣmad* and *asmad* should replace them in the same sentence. A sentence is that which contains one finite verb (*tiṅanta*). Therefore the replacement does not take place here - cook the rice, it will be yours (Here the substitute *te* has not replaced *tava*). Nonetheless, the replacement does take place here - I will give boiled rice to you.

1. Cf. *samānavākye nighātayuṣmadasmadādeśāḥ.* Mbh 2. 1. 1 vtk 11.

Eluc. : The substitutes *tvā, vām, vaḥ, mā, nau* and *naḥ* replace the corresponding forms of the pronominal stems *yuṣmad* and *asmad* when they occur after a pada but only in the same sentence. A sentence has been defined as 'that which contains a finite verb (*tiṅanta*)'.

The first illustration given by Varadarāja contains two sentences since there are two tiṅanta padas (finite verbs). The expression '*odanaṁ paca*' is a sentence and '*tava bhaviṣyati*' is another. The form *tava* occurs at the beginning of a sentence. Hence *tava* is not replaced by *te*. Although the term *tava* occurs after a pada, that is *paca* (as given in the illustration), but it belongs to the preceding sentence which is a different sentence. Therefore, it is not in the same sentence. The other illustration consists of a single sentence : *śālīnānte odanaṁ dāsyāmi*. The substitute *te* has replaced the dative singular form of *yuṣmad*, that is, *tubhyam* since it occurs after a pada *śālīnām* which occurs in the same sentence.

27. वा० - एते वान्नावादयोऽनन्वादेशे वा वक्तव्याः । *ete vānnāvādayo 'nanvādeśe vā vaktavyāḥ.*

लघु० - धाता ते भक्तोऽस्ति धाता तव भक्तोऽस्तीति वा । अन्वादेशे तु नित्यं स्युः - तस्मै ते नम इत्येव । *dhātā te bhakto 'sti dhātā tava bhakto 'stīti vā. anvādeśe tu nityaṁ syuḥ - tasmai te nama ityeva.*

Trans. : It should be stated that these substitutes, *vām, nau,* etc. optionally replace the inflected forms of *yuṣmad* and *asmad* when they are not used anaphorically. When they are used anaphorically, these substitutes replace the inflected forms of *yuṣmad* and *asmad* obligatorily.

Eluc. : The word *anvādeśa* means a second reference to one and the same item already referred to by an earlier word (*ekasyaivābhidheyasya pūrvaṁ śabdena pratipāditasya dvitīyaṁ pratipādanam*, KN, II, p. 280). This exactly corresponds to what is known as 'anaphora', namely, the use of a word to refer back to a word previously used.

In the illustration *dhātā te bhakto 'sti, dhātā tava bhakto 'stīti vā*, there is no subsequent reference; there is no anaphoric reference, therefore the substitute replaces the pronominal stem *tava* optionally but when there is subsequent reference, the replacement by these substitutes is obligatory as in the illustration - (*ya indro vajrabāhuḥ*) *tasmai te namaḥ* (BM, I, p. 417). Here Indra has been subsequently referred to. Hence the substitute *te* has replaced *tubhyam* obligatorily.

लघु० – सुपात्, सुपाद् । सुपादौ । *supāt, supād. supādau.*

Eluc. : The next masculine nominal stem, that ends in the phoneme *d*, is *supād* 'one who has handsome feet', which is a bahuvrīhi compound. Its analysis is as follows : *śobhanau pādau yasya saḥ supāt*. The final vowel *a* of the last member of the compound is elided by *saṅkhyāsupūrvasya* (971) and we get the compound form *supād*, which is designated as *prātipadika* by *kṛttaddhitasamāsāśca* (116).

To decline *supād* in the nominative singular, we introduce the singular affix of the first triplet and we have : *supād* + *su* --> *supād* + s. The single consonant affix s is elided by *halṅyābbhyo*... (178) and we get *supād*. At this stage, the rule *vā 'vasāne* (145) applies and we obtain two forms : *supāt* and *supād*.

When we introduce the affix *śas*, we have : *supād* + *śas* --> *supād* + *as* (after the elision of the anubandha *ś*). In this grammatical situation, the following sūtra becomes applicable :

(332) पादः पत् । ***pādaḥ pat*. 6. 4. 130**

लघु० – पाच्छब्दान्तं यदङ्गं भं तदवयवस्य पाच्छब्दस्य पदादेशः स्यात् । सुपदः । सुपदा । सुपाद्भ्याम् । *pācchabdāntaṁ yadaṅgaṁ bhaṁ tadavayavasya pācchabdasya padādeśaḥ syāt. supadaḥ. supadā. supādbhyām.*

Trans. : If a pre-affixal base (*aṅga*), termed *bha*, ends in *pād*, then let the word *pād*, which is a part of that bha, be replaced by the substitute *pad*.

PP. *bhasya aṅgasya pādaḥ pat*.

Eluc. : The word *pādaḥ* qualifies the term *aṅga*. So by tadantavidhi it gives the sense 'the aṅga that ends in the word *pād*'. The present sūtra occurs in the domain of the governing rules *aṅgasya* Pā. 6. 4. 1 and *bhasya* Pā. 6. 4. 129. Therefore the words *aṅgasya* and *bhasya* recur here. Then the meaning of the sūtra will be : If the word *pād* occurs at the end of a pre-affixal base (*aṅga*) which is also bha, then the word *pād* is to be replaced by *pat*. According to the paribhāṣā *nirdiśyamānasyādeśā bhavanti* (Abhyankar, 12), the word *pād* is replaced by *pat*. Pāṇini has enunciated the substitute *pad* as *pat* in consonance with the rule *vā 'vasāne* (145).

In the illustration *supād* + *as*, the word is a pre-affixal base (*aṅga*), which is also bha by *yaci bham* (164). Hence the word *pād* is replaced by *pad* and we get the form *supadaḥ* in the accusative plural. In all the instances of bha, that is, where a vowel-initial affix, not being a sarvanāmasthāna, follows, the substitute *pad* will replace the word *pād*. In the locative plural, the phoneme *d* before the affix *sup* is replaced by *t* according to the rule *khari ca* (74). The complete declension of the word *supād* will be as follows :

	Singular	Dual	Plural
prathamā	*supāt, d*	*supādau*	*supādaḥ*
dvitīyā	*supādam*	*supādau*	*supadaḥ*
tṛtīyā	*supadā*	*supādbhyām*	*supādbhiḥ*
caturthī	*supade*	*supādbhyām*	*supādbhyaḥ*
pañcamī	*supadaḥ*	*supādbhyām*	*supādbhyaḥ*
ṣaṣṭhī	*supadaḥ*	*supadoḥ*	*supadām*
saptamī	*supadi*	*supadoḥ*	*supātsu*
sambodhana	*he supāt, d!*	*he supādau!*	*he supādaḥ!*

Here comes to an end the declension of the masculine words ending in the phoneme *d*. Now begins the declension of the word that ends in the phoneme *th*.

The word is *agnimath* 'one who churns fire'. It is derived in the following manner : *agniṁ mathnātīti agnimat, agni + manth + kvip*. Here the elision of *n* takes place by *aniditāṁ hala upadhāyā kṅiti* (333). The affix *kvip* is wholly elided and we get the word *agnimath*. In the nominative singular, the affix *s*(*u*) is elided by *halṅyābbhyo...* (178) and we obtain the forms *agnimat* and *agnimad* after the application of the rules *jhalāṁ jaśo 'nte* (67) and *vā 'vasāne* (145). In the instances where the stem gets the pada-designation, the phoneme *th* is replaced by *d* as, for example, in the form *agnimadbhyām* by *jhalāṁ jaśo...* (67). In the locative plural, two rules, *jhalāṁ jaśo...* (67) and *khari ca* (74) apply and we get the form *agnimatsu*. The declension of the word *agnimath* will be as follows :

	Singular	Dual	Plural
prathamā	*agnimat, d*	*agnimathau*	*agnimathaḥ*
dvitīyā	*agnimatham*	*agnimathau*	*agnimathaḥ*
tṛtīyā	*agnimathā*	*agnimadbhyām*	*agnimadbhiḥ*

caturthī	*agnimathe*	*agnimadbhyām*	*agnimadbhyaḥ*
pañcamī	*agnimathaḥ*	*agnimadbhyām*	*agnimadbhyaḥ*
ṣaṣṭhī	*agnimathaḥ*	*agnimathoḥ*	*agnimathām*
saptamī	*agnimathi*	*agnimathoḥ*	*agnimatsu*
sambodhana	*he agnimat, d!*	*he agnimathau!*	*he agnimathaḥ!*

Here comes to an end the declension of the word that ends in the phoneme *th*.

Now begins the declension of the masculine nominal stems that end in the phoneme *c*. The first sūtra, that is taken up by Varadarāja in this context, is as follows :

(333) अनिदितां हल उपधाया क्ङिति । *aniditāṁ hala upadhāyā kṅiti.* 6. 4. 24

लघु० – हलन्तानामनिदितानामङ्गानामुपधाया नस्य लोपः किति ङिति । नुम् । संयोगान्तस्य लोपः । नस्य कुत्वेन ङः । प्राङ् । प्राञ्चौ । प्राञ्चः । *halantānām aniditānām aṅgānām upadhāyā nasya lopaḥ kiti ṅiti. num. saṁyogāntasya lopaḥ.. nasya kutvena ṅaḥ. prāṅ. prāñcau. prāñcaḥ.*

Trans. : The penultimate phoneme *n* of pre-affixal bases, which end in a consonant (*hal*) and do not have a short *i*(*t*) as *it*, is elided, provided an affix, having either *k* or *ṅ* as *it*, follows.

PP. *aniditāṁ hala aṅgasya upadhāyā na lopaḥ kṅiti.*

Eluc. : The present sūtra occurs in the domain of the governing rule *aṅgasya* Pā. 6. 4. 1. By the process of vacanavipariṇāma and being qualified by the term *halaḥ*, it means : *halantānām aṅgānām*. The words *na* and *lopaḥ* are carried over from *śnānna lopaḥ* Pā. 6. 4. 23. The word *na* is construed as ending in the singular genitive ending (*śnānna lopaḥ iti sūtrān neti luptaṣaṣṭhīkaṁ padam anuvartate* TB, I, p. 423). The word *aniditām* is a bahuvrīhi-seeded nañ-tatpuruṣa which is analysed as follows : *it it* (where the first *it* stands for a short *i*) *asti yeṣām te iditaḥ, na iditaḥ aniditaḥ, teṣām = aniditām*. The word *kṅiti* is a dvandva-seeded bahuvrīhi. The analysis of the compound is as follows : *k ca ṅ ca kṅau* (itaretaradvandva). *kṅau itau yasya, tasmin = kṅiti*. For an easy comprehension, the meaning of the sūtra is given in a break-up form as follows : 1. If pre-affixal bases do not have a short *i* (*it*) as *it* (*aniditām aṅgānām*), 2. if they end in a consonant (*halantānām*), 3. and if an affix having either *k* or *ṅ* as *it* follows (*kṅiti*), 4. then the penultimate *n* of such pre-affixal bases is elided.

The word *prāc* 'directed forwards, being in front' is derived when the affix *kvin* is introduced after the verbal root *añcu* 'to go, to worship' preceded by the preverb *pra* in accordance with *ṛtvigdadhṛgsragdiguṣṇig-añcuyujikruñcāṁ ca* (300). Since the affix *kvin* has the phoneme *k* as *it*, the penultimate palatal nasal stop is elided by the present rule. The reason is that the anusvāra and the fifth stops which are given in the dhātupāṭha are understood to be born of the dental nasal stop (*dhātupāṭhe nakārajau anusvārapañcamau ityabhiyuktavādāt*, BM, III, p. 108). Both the replacement by anusvāra according to Pā. 8. 3. 24 and the substitution by the fifth nasal stop homogeneous with the following (*parasavarṇa*) by Pā. 8. 4. 58 are deemed not to have taken place with respect to the present rule. Hence the elision of the penultimate *n* takes place in accordance with the present rule and we obtain *pra ac*.[1] To decline it in the nominative singular, we introduce the affix *su* : *pra ac + su*. In this grammatical situation, the augment *num*, is inserted after the final vowel by *ugidacāṁ sarvanāmasthāne 'dhātoḥ* (288) --> *pra a num c + su* --> *pra a n c + s* (after the elision of the anubandhas *u* and *m*). At this stage, the affix *s* is elided by *halṅyābbhyo....* (178) and the elision of the palatal stop *c* occurring at the end of the pada-final conjunct *nc* takes place by *saṁyogāntasya lopaḥ* (20) and we arrive at : *pra an*. Now the rule *kvinpratyayasya kuḥ* (303) applies and the dental *n* is replaced by the guttural nasal stop (*ṅ*) and we obtain the form : *prāṅ* after the rule *akaḥ savarṇe dīrghaḥ* (42) has performed its grammatical operation.

When we introduce the dual affix of the first triplet, we have the following stage : *pra ac + au* --> *pra a num c + au* by *ugidacām...* (288) --> *pra a n c + au* (after the elision of the anubandhas). We arrive at the following stage *pra a ñ c + au* = *pra añcau* after the application of *naścāpadā...* (78) and *anusvārasya...* (79). The rule *akaḥ savarṇe dīrghaḥ* (42) applies and we obtain the form *prāñcau*. This declensional process will continue up to the sarvanāmasthāna affix *auṭ* and we will have the forms : *prāñcaḥ*, *prāñcam* and *prāñcau*.

In declining the form of *pra ac* with the plural affix of the second triplet, we have the following situation : --> *pra ac + śas* --> *pra ac + as*. The affix (*ś*)*as* is not a sarvanāmasthāna affix. Hence the rule *ugidacām...* (288) is not available for application. The affix *śas* begins with a vowel after the elision of the anubandha *ś*. Hence it gets bha-designation by

1. The nominal stems *pra ac*, *prati ac*, *ud ac* etc. are shown in non-sandhi form to facilitate an easy and clear comprehension of the elision of the vowel *a* by *acaḥ* (334), the lengthening of the preceding denotatum of *aṇ* by *cau* (335), the replacement of the vowel *a* of the verbal root *añcu* by *uda īt* etc. during their declensional process.

yaci bham (164) and as a consequence the following sūtra becomes applicable:

(334) अचः । *acaḥ.* 6. 4. 138

लघु० -- लुप्तनकारस्याञ्चतेर्भस्याकारस्य लोपः स्यात्। *luptanakārasyāñcater bhasyākārasya lopaḥ syāt.*

Trans. : Let there be elision of the *a* of *ac* (*añcu*), of which the phoneme *n* has been elided, when it is entitled to bha-designation.

PP. *acaḥ bhasya at lopaḥ* (*aṅgasya*).

Eluc. : The present sūtra occurs in the domain of the governing rule *bhasya* Pā. 6. 4. 129. So the term *bhasya* recurs here also. The term *acaḥ* stands for the verbal root *āñcu* of which the phoneme *n* has been elided by (333). The term *allopaḥ* is carried over from *allopo 'naḥ* Pā. 6. 4. 134. Thus the meaning of the sūtra is as follows : If the phoneme *n* of the verbal root *āñcu* has been elided and it gets the bha-designation, the vowel *a* occurring in it is substituted by lopa.

In the illustration *pra ac + as*, we have *ac*, which stands for the verbal root *āñcu* of which the phoneme *n* has been elided. It also gets bha-designation by *yaci bham* (164). So, the *a* of *ac* is elided by the present rule : *pra c + as*. At this stage, the following sūtra presents itself for application :

(335) चौ । *cau.* 6. 3. 138

लघु० – लुप्ताऽकारनकारेऽञ्चतौ परे पूर्वस्याणो दीर्घः स्यात्। प्राचः। प्राचा। प्राग्भ्याम्। प्रत्यङ्। प्रत्यञ्चौ। प्रतीचः। प्रत्यग्भ्याम्। उदङ्। उदञ्चौ। *luptā 'kāranakāre 'ñcatau pare pūrvasyāṇo dīrghaḥ syāt. prācaḥ. prācā. prāgbhyām. pratyaṅ. pratyañcau. pratīcaḥ. pratyagbhyām. udaṅ. udañcau.*

Trans. : Let the preceding vowel denoted by the abbreviatory term *aṇ* be replaced by a long one, provided the verbal root *āñcu*, the *a* and *n* of which have been elided, follows.

PP. *cau pūrvasya aṇaḥ dīrghaḥ* (*uttarapade, saṁhitāyām*).

Eluc. : The term *cau* is the locative singular form of *cu* (the vowel *u* in it is for the sake of articulation) and stands for the verbal root *āñcu*, of which the phonemes *n* and *a* have already been elided. The terms *pūrvasya, dīrghaḥ* and *aṇaḥ* come from *ḍhralope pūrvasya dīrgho 'ṇaḥ* Pā. 6. 3. 111. The sūtra thus gives the following meaning : When the verbal root *añcu*, having its phonemes *n* and *a* elided (*cau*), follows, the preceding vowel denoted by *aṇ* is replaced by a long one.

In the illustration *pra c + as*, the consonant *c*, which stands for the verbal root *añcu* with its *a* and *n* having been elided, follows and as a consequence the preceding *aṇ* (the vowel following repha) is replaced by a long vowel. Then we obtain the desired form : *prācaḥ* after rutva and visarga. Even without applying the rules *acaḥ* (334) and *cau* (335), the form *prācaḥ* could have been obtained only by *akaḥ savarṇe dīrghaḥ* (42). Nonetheless, the rules *acaḥ* (334) and *cau* (335) are necessarily required in the derivation of such forms as *pratīcaḥ*. This is the reason why these rules have been applied in the declensional process of the form *prācaḥ* also.

When the stem *prāc* gets the pada-designation during the declensional process, the rule *coḥ kuḥ* Pā. 8. 2. 30 applies since the rule *kvinpratyayasya kuḥ* Pā. 8. 2. 62 is deemed to be suspended with respect to it. As a consequence, the phoneme *c* is replaced by *k*. After that *jhalāṁ jaśo 'nte* (67) applies and *k* is substituted by a *jaś*-consonant *g*. We get the form *prāgbhyām*, etc. In the locative plural, the rule *coḥ kuḥ* applies first and then by *ādeśapratyayayoḥ* (149), the dental *s* of the affix *sup* is replaced by the cerebral *ṣ* and we obtain the form *prākṣu*. The complete declension of the stem *prāc* is as follows :

	Singular	Dual	Plural
prathamā	*prāṅ*	*prāñcau*	*prāñcaḥ*
dvitīyā	*prāñcam*	*prāñcau*	*prācaḥ*
tṛtīyā	*prācā*	*prāgbhyām*	*prāgbhiḥ*
caturthī	*prāce*	*prāgbhyām*	*prāgbhyaḥ*
pañcamī	*prācaḥ*	*prāgbhyām*	*prāgbhyaḥ*
ṣaṣṭhī	*prācaḥ*	*prācoḥ*	*prācām*
saptamī	*prāci*	*prācoḥ*	*prākṣu*
sambodhana	*he prāṅ!*	*he prāñcau!*	*he prāñcaḥ!*

The word *pratyac* 'going in an opposite direction, westward' is derived in the following manner : *prati + añcu + kvin* by *ṛtvigdadhṛk...* (300) --> *prati + ac + kvin* after the phoneme *n* has been elided by *aniditām...* (333). It gets the prātipadika designation by *kṛttaddhitasamāsāśca* (116). Then the declensional affixes become available to be introduced after *pratyac*.

prati ac + su --> *prati ac* + s. The augment *num* is introduced by *ugidacām...* (288) : *prati a num c + s* --> *prati a n c + s*. The affix *s* is elided by *halṅyābbhyo...* (178) and the phoneme *c* occurring at the end of the conjunct *nc* is elided by *saṁyogāntasya lopaḥ* (20) and we arrive at the following grammatical stage : *prati an*. The rule *kvinpratyayasya kuḥ* (303) applies and we get the form *pratyaṅ* in the nominative singular after the application of the rule *iko yaṇaci* (15).

With the introduction of the affix *śas*, the stem *pratyac* gets the bha-designation and as such the elision of the *a* of *ac* takes place by *acaḥ* (334) and a long vowel replaces the preceding vowel denoted by the abbreviatory term *aṇ* by *cau* (335). We obtain the form *pratīcaḥ*. It is here that the rules *acaḥ* (334) and *cau* (335) are actually required; otherwise a wrong form *pratyañcaḥ* would have resulted. When the stem gets the pada-designation by *svādiṣvasarvanāmasthāne* (163), the phoneme *c* is replaced by *k* according to *coḥ kuḥ* (305) and *k* changes to *g* by *jhalāṁ jaśo 'nte* (67). Then we get *pratyagbhyām, pratyagbhiḥ*, etc. The locative plural will be declined in the same way as *prākṣu*. The declension of *pratyac* will be as follows :

	Singular	Dual	Plural
prathamā	*pratyaṅ*	*pratyañcau*	*pratyañcaḥ*
dvitīyā	*pratyañcam*	*pratyañcau*	*pratīcaḥ*
tṛtīyā	*pratīcā*	*pratyagbhyām*	*pratyagbhiḥ*
caturthī	*pratīce*	*pratyagbhyām*	*pratyagbhyaḥ*
pañcamī	*pratīcaḥ*	*pratyagbhyām*	*pratyagbhyaḥ*
ṣaṣṭhī	*pratīcaḥ*	*pratīcoḥ*	*pratīcām*
saptamī	*pratīci*	*pratīcoḥ*	*pratyakṣu*
sambodhana	*he pratyaṅ!*	*he pratyañcau!*	*he pratyañcaḥ!*

Like the word *prāc*, the word *udac* 'going upwards, northern' is derived from the verbal root *añcu* preceded by the preverb *ud* with the introduction of the primary affix *kvin* by *ṛtvigdadhṛksrag...* (300). The elision of the phoneme *n* takes place by *aniditām...* (333). The declension of this stem will be like that of *prāc*, except for the instances in which it gets the bha-designation. In such instances, the following sūtra presents itself for application :

(336) उद ईत्। *uda īt.* **6. 4. 139**

लघु॰ - उच्छब्दात् परस्य लुप्तनकारस्याञ्चतेर्भस्याकारस्य ईत्। उदीचः। उदीचा। उदग्भ्याम्। *ucchabdāt parasya luptanakārasyāñcater bhasyākārasya īt. udīcaḥ. udīcā. udagbhyām.*

Trans. : Let the *a* of *ac* (*añcu*), preceded by *ud* and having its *n* elided, be replaced by a long *ī*(*t*), when it beomes entitled to bha-designation.

PP. *udaḥ acaḥ bhasya at* (*ataḥ*) *īt* (*aṅgasya*).

Eluc. : The present sūtra occurs in the domain of the governing rule *bhasya* Pā. 6. 4. 129. As a consequence, the term *bhasya* recurs in this sūtra. The term *acaḥ* is carried over from *acaḥ* Pā. 6. 4. 138. It represents the verbal root *añcu* with its *n* having been elided by *aniditāṁ hala upadhāyāḥ kṅiti* (333). The term *at* comes from *allopo 'naḥ* Pā. 6. 4. 134. The sixth case-ending after *at* should be taken as elided as it has been interpreted in that sense in the vṛtti by Varadarāja. Thus the meaning of the sūtra will be as follows : The short *a* of the verbal root *ac* (*añcu*), preceded by *ud*, is to be replaced by a long *ī*, provided the verbal root *ac* (*añcu*) has its *n* elided and is designated as *bha* by *yaci bham* (164).

When the plural affix of the second triplet is added after *udac*, we have the following grammatical situation : *udac* + *śas* --> *udac* + *as*. In this illustration, the stem *udac* is bha and as such the condition for the replacement of the *a* of *ac* by a long *ī* becomes available and we get the form : *udīc* + *as* --> *udīcaḥ* after rutva and visarga. The stem *udac* will be declined as follows :

	Singular	Dual	Plural
prathamā	*udaṅ*	*udañcau*	*udañcaḥ*
dvitīyā	*udañcam*	*udañcau*	*udīcaḥ*
tṛtīyā	*udīcā*	*udagbhyām*	*udagbhiḥ*
caturthī	*udīce*	*udagbhyām*	*udagbhyaḥ*
pañcamī	*udīcaḥ*	*udagbhyām*	*udagbhyaḥ*
ṣaṣṭhī	*udīcaḥ*	*udīcoḥ*	*udīcām*
saptamī	*udīci*	*udīcoḥ*	*udakṣu*
sambodhana	*he udaṅ!*	*he udañcau!*	*he udañcaḥ!*

The word *samyac* 'going together or in one direction' is derived in the following manner : When the verbal root *añcu* is preceded by the preverb *sam* and followed by the affix *kvin* by *ṛtvigdadhṛksragdiguṣṇigañcuyujikruñcāṁ ca* (300), the substitute *sami* replaces the preverb *sam* in accordance with the following sūtra :

(337) **समः समि ।** ***samaḥ sami.* 6. 3. 93**

लघु० – वप्रत्ययान्तेऽञ्चतौ परे । सम्यङ् । सम्यञ्चौ । समीचः । सम्यग्भ्याम् । *vapratyayānte 'ñcatau pare. samyaṅ. samyañcau. samīcaḥ. samyagbhyām.*

Trans. : If the verbal root *añcu* ending in the affix *va* follows the preverb *sam*, then the preverb *sam* is replaced by *sami*.

PP. *samaḥ sami añcatau vapratyaye (uttarapade).*

Eluc. : The words *vapratyaye* and *añcatau* are carried over from *viṣvagdevayośca ṭeradryañcatau vapratyaye* Pā. 6. 3. 92. The term *sami*, used in the sūtra, is without any case-affix (*samītyavibhaktiko nirdeśaḥ*, TB, I, p. 428). The word *vapratyaye* is a bahuvrīhi compound : *vaḥ pratyayo yasmāt, vapratyayaḥ, tasmin = vapratyaye.* The phoneme *v* stands for the affixes which contain it, such as *kvin, kvip*, etc. In *sam añcu + kvin*, the phoneme *n* is elided by *aniditām...* (333). Here the verbal root has the affix *kvin* introduced after it by *ṛtvigdadhṛk...* (300). Thus the verbal root ends in the affix *v*. It also follows the preverb *sam*. Therefore the preverb *sam* is replaced by *sami* and we have the following derivational stage : *sami ac --> samyac* by *iko yaṇaci* (15). The derived word gets the prātipadika designation by *kṛttaddhitasamāsāśca* (116) and we introduce the sup-affix *su* after it to decline it in the nominative singular : *samyac + su*. In this situation, we introduce the augment *num* by *ugidacām...* (288). After the elision of the anubandhas we have : *samya n c + s (<-- samya num c + su)*. At this stage, after the elision of the affix *s* by *halṅyābbhyo...* (178), the rule *saṁyogāntasya lopaḥ* (20) applies and the conjunct-final *c* is elided and we have : *samyan*. Now by the rule *kvinpratyayasya kuḥ* (303) the dental *n* is replaced by the fifth guttural and we obtain the form *samyaṅ*. The forms *samyañcau, samyañcaḥ, samyañcam* and *samyañcau* are obtained in the same manner as the corresponding forms of *udac* or *prāc*.

The accusative plural form *samīcaḥ* is derived as follows : *sami ac + śas --> sami ac + as -->* the *a* of *ac* is elided by *acaḥ* (334) *--> sami c + as*. Now by the rule *cau* (335), the preceding vowel *i* of *sami* is replaced by a long *ī* and we get *samīcaḥ* after rutva and visarga. The complete declension of *samyac* is as follows :

	Singular	Dual	Plural
prathamā	*samyaṅ*	*samyañcau*	*samyañcaḥ*
dvitīyā	*samyañcam*	*samyañcau*	*samīcaḥ*
tṛtīyā	*samīcā*	*samyagbhyām*	*samyagbhiḥ*
caturthī	*samīce*	*samyagbhyām*	*samyagbhyaḥ*
pañcamī	*samīcaḥ*	*samyagbhyām*	*samyagbhyaḥ*
ṣaṣṭhī	*samīcaḥ*	*samīcoḥ*	*samīcām*
saptamī	*samīci*	*samīcoḥ*	*samyakṣu*
sambodhana	*he samyaṅ!*	*he samyañcau!*	*he samyañcaḥ!*

The word *sadhryac* 'friend, one who accompanies' is derived from *saha añcu + kvin* --> *saha añc + kvin*. In this illustration, the verbal root *añcu*, after which the affix *kvin* has been introduced, follows the indeclinable *saha*. At this stage, the following sūtra applies :

(338) सहस्य सध्रिः । ***sahasya sadhriḥ*. 6. 3. 95**
लघु० – वप्रत्ययान्तेऽञ्चतौ परे । सध्र्यङ् । *vapratyayānte 'ñcatau pare. sadhryaṅ.*

Trans. : If the verbal root *añcu*, accompanied by the affix *va*, follows, then the word *saha* is replaced by the substitute *sadhri*.

PP. *sahasya sadhriḥ vapratyaye añcatau* (*uttarapade*).

Eluc. : The words *vapratyaye* and *añcatau* are carried over from *viṣvagdevayośca ṭeradryañcatau vapratyaye* Pā. 6. 3. 92. Then the meaning of the sūtra will be as follows : The word *saha* is replaced by *sadhri* when followed by the verbal root *añcu* ending in the affix *va*. The substitute contains more than one phoneme. Therefore, the whole of *saha* is to be replaced by *sadhri*. The declension of the word *sadhryac* (*sadhri ac*) will be exactly like that of *samyac* :

	Singular	Dual	Plural
prathamā	*sadhrayaṅ*	*sadhryañcau*	*sadhryañcaḥ*
dvitīyā	*sadhryañcam*	*sadhryañcau*	*sadhrīcaḥ*
tṛtīyā	*sadhrīcā*	*sadhryagbhyām*	*sadhryagbhiḥ*
caturthī	*sadhrīce*	*sadhryagbhyām*	*sadhryagbhyaḥ*

pañcamī	*sadhrīcaḥ*	*sadhryagbhyām*	*sadhryagbhyaḥ*
ṣaṣṭhī	*sadhrīcaḥ*	*sadhrīcoḥ*	*sadhrīcām*
saptamī	*sadhrīci*	*sadhrīcoḥ*	*sadhryakṣu*
sambodhana	*he sadhryaṅ!*	*he sadhryañcau!*	*he sadhryañcaḥ!*

(339) तिरसस्तिर्यलोपे । *tirasastiryalope.* 6. 3. 94

लघु० – अलुप्ताकारेऽञ्चतौ वप्रत्ययान्ते परे तिरसस्तिर्यादेशः स्यात् । तिर्यङ् । तिर्यञ्चौ । तिरश्चः । तिर्यग्भ्याम् । *aluptākāre 'ñcatau vapratyayānte pare tirasas tiryādeśaḥ syāt. tiryaṅ. tiryañcau. tiraścaḥ. tiryagbhyām.*

Trans. : If the verbal root *añcu*, which ends in the affix *va* and of which the *a* has not been elided, follows, then let the substitute *tiri* replace *tiras*.

PP. *tirasaḥ tiri alope añcatau vapratyaye (uttarapade).*

Eluc. : The words *vapratyaye* and *añcatau* are carried over from *viṣvagdevayośca ṭeradryañcatau vapratyaye* Pā. 6. 3. 92. The word *alope* is a bahuvrīhi compound, which is analysed as follows : *nāsti lopo yasya alopaḥ, tasmin = alope.* The constituent member *lopa* in the bahuvrīhi compound *alopaḥ* stands for the elision of the vowel *a* by the aphorism *acaḥ* (334). The meaning of the sūtra is as follows : The indeclinable *tiras* is replaced by the substitute *tiri* when the verbal root *añcu* follows, provided it ends in the affix *va* and its *a* has not been elided.

The word *tiryac* (*tiras* + *ac*) means 'going transversely, a bird or an animal'. Here also the affix *kvin* is introduced after the verbal root *añcu* preceded by the indeclinable *tiras*. The elision of the nasal stop *n* takes place by *aniditām...* (333) and the word *tiras* is replaced by *tiri* since the verb ends in the affix *va* (*kvin*) and the phoneme *a* of the verbal root *añcu* has not been elided. When, in the instances of bha-designation, the *a* of the verbal root *añcu* is elided, the replacement of *tiras* by *tiri* does not take place. In the plural form, the affix (*ś*)*as* is added after the stem *tiras ac*, which gets the bha-designation by *yaci bham* (164). The rule *acaḥ* (334) applies and the vowel *a* of *añcu* is elided and we arrive at the following declensional stage : *tiras c + as*. Now the rule *stoḥ ścunā ścuḥ* (62) applies and the dental s is replaced by the palatal *ś* --> *tiraścas*. After rutva and visarga we obtain *tiraścaḥ*. Since the *a* of *ac* has been elided, the word *tiras* is not replaced by *tiri*. The complete declension of *tiras ac* (*tiryac*) is as follows :

	Singular	Dual	Plural
prathamā	*tiryaṅ*	*tiryañcau*	*tiryañcaḥ*
dvitīyā	*tiryañcam*	*tiryañcau*	*tiraścaḥ*
tṛtīyā	*tiraścā*	*tiryagbhyām*	*tiryagbhiḥ*
caturthī	*tiraśce*	*tiryagbhyām*	*tiryagbhyaḥ*
pañcamī	*tiraścaḥ*	*tiryagbhyām*	*tiryagbhyaḥ*
ṣaṣṭhī	*tiraścaḥ*	*tiraścoḥ*	*tiraścām*
saptamī	*tiraści*	*tiraścoḥ*	*tiryakṣu*
sambodhana	*he tiryaṅ!*	*he tiryañcau!*	*he tiryañcaḥ!*

(340) नाञ्चेः पूजायाम्। *nāñceḥ pūjāyām.* 6. 4. 30

लघु० – पूजार्थस्याञ्चतेरुपधाया नस्य लोपो न। प्राङ्। प्राञ्चौ। नलोपाभावाद् अलोपो न। प्राञ्चः। प्राङ्भ्याम्। प्राङ्क्षु। एवं पूजार्थे प्रत्यङ्ङादयः। *pūjārthasyāñcater upadhāyā nasya lopo na. prāṅ. prāñcau. nalopābhāvād alopo na. prāñcaḥ. prāṅbhyām. prāṅkṣu. evaṁ pūjārthe pratyaṅṅādayaḥ.*

Trans. : The penultimate *n* of the verbal root *añcu* is not elided if it signifies 'honour or worship'.

PP. *añceḥ upadhāyāḥ nalopaḥ na pūjāyām (aṅgasya).*

Eluc. : The word *upadhāyāḥ* comes from *aniditām...* Pā. 6. 4. 24 and the word *na* is carried over from *śnānna lopaḥ* Pā. 6. 4. 23. The sixth case-ending after *na* is taken as elided (*neti luptaṣaṣṭhīkam*, BM, III, p. 368). The meaning yielded by the sūtra is as follows : When the sense of 'worship' is signified by the verbal root *añcu*, the elision of its penultimate *n*, available by *aniditām...* (333), is debarred. The verbal root *añcu* has two distinct meanings : 'movement' and 'worship'. The present rule applies only when the second meaning is denoted. In the foregoing declensional process of the stems ranging from *prāc* up to *tiryac*, the verbal root has been used in the sense of movement. Hence in those declensional forms, the penultimate *n* of *añcu* has been elided by *aniditām...* (333). Now in the declensional process that follows, the verbal stem *añcu* is used in the sense of 'worship'. Therefore the penultimate *n* will not be elided.

The word *prāñc* 'one who performs worship in an excellent manner' is derived with the introduction of the affix *kvin* after *añcu* preceded by the preverb *pra*. In the illustration *pra añc + kvin*, the affix *kvin* is wholly elided. The elision of the penultimate *n* is negated by the present rule. Then the rule *akaḥ savarṇe dīrghaḥ* (42) applies and we get the word *prāñc*, which gets the prātipadika designation by *kṛttaddhitasamāsāśca* (116). In the nominative singular we add *su* after it : *prāñc + su*. Since the elision of the penultimate *n* has not taken place by virtue of the present rule, the augment *num* will not be inserted by *ugidacām*... (288). The affix *s*(*u*) is elided by *halṅyābbhyo*... (178). By *saṁyogāntasya lopaḥ* (20), the conjunct-final *c* is also elided and the palatal *ñ* is restored to its original status, that is *n*. At this stage, the dental *n* is replaced by the guttural fifth (*ṅ*) according to the rule *kvinpratyayasya kuḥ* (303) and we obtain the form *prāṅ* in the nominative singular. With the plural affix of the seventh triplet, we have the following grammatical situation : *prāñc + sup* --> *prāñc + su*. In this situation, the stem *prāñc* gets the pada-designation by *svādiṣvasarvanāma*... (163) and therefore the conjunct-final *c* is elided by *saṁyogāntasya lopaḥ* (20). The palatal *ñ* is restored to its original status, that is *n* by *nimittāpāye naimittikasyāpyapāyaḥ* (see PS, p. 158) and then the dental *n* is replaced by the fifth guttural --> *prāṅ + su* by *kvinpratyayasya*... (303). At this stage, the rule *ṅṇoḥ kukṭuk śari* (85) applies. The augment *kuk*, being *kit*, is optionally inserted at the end of the phoneme *ṅ*. We get the following declensional stage : *prāṅ kuk + su* --> *prāṅ k + su*. By virtue of *cayo dvitīyāḥ śari pauṣkarasāderiti vācyam* (vtk 14), the phoneme *k* is optionally replaced by the second guttural class consonant, *kh*. In this case, we have two derivational situations : *prāṅ k + su* and *prāṅ kh + su*. In the absence of the augment *kuk*, we have: *prāṅ + su*. In all the three instances, the dental *s* is replaced by the cerebral *ṣ* by *ādeśapratyatyayoḥ* (149) and we obtain the following three forms in the locative plural : *prāṅkṣu*, *prāṅkhṣu*, *prāṅṣu*. The complete declension of *prāñc* will be as follows :

	Singular	Dual	Plural
prathamā	*prāṅ*	*prāñcau*	*prāñcaḥ*
dvitīyā	*prāñcam*	*prāñcau*	*prāñcaḥ*
tṛtīyā	*prāñcā*	*prāṅbhyām*	*prāṅbhiḥ*
caturthī	*prāñce*	*prāṅbhyām*	*prāṅbhyaḥ*
pañcamī	*prāñcaḥ*	*prāṅbhyām*	*prāṅbhyaḥ*
ṣaṣṭhī	*prāñcaḥ*	*prāñcoḥ*	*prāñcām*

saptamī	*prāñci*	*prāñcoḥ*	*prāṅkṣu, prāṅkhṣu, prāṅṣu*
sambodhana	*he prāṅ!*	*he prāñcau!*	*he prāñcaḥ!*

The words *pratyañc* 'one who performs worship in an opposite manner', *udañc* 'one worships excellently', *samyañc* 'one who worships in a right way', *sadhryañc* 'one who performs worship along with others' and *tiryañc* 'one who worships in a crooked manner', will be similarly declined.

The word *kruñc* is derived with the addition of the affix *kvin* after the verbal root *kruñc* 'to go towards, to move crookedly, to shrink'. The affix *kvin* is wholly elided but the penultimate nasal stop is not elided by *aniditām...* (333) in an irregular way (by *nipātana*). We thus obtain the nominal stem *kruñc* 'curlew'. When we add the nominative singular affix *su*, we have the following declensional stage : *kruñc + su --> kruñc + s*. The single consonant affix (*apṛkta*) is elided by *halṅyābbhyo...* (178) and the conjunct-final *c* is elided by *saṁyogāntasya lopaḥ* (20). After the phoneme *c* has been elided, the palatal nasal stop reverts to its original status of being dental (see PS, p. 158). Then the guttural nasal stop replaces the dental *n* by *kvinpratyayasya kuḥ* (303) and we get the nominative singular form *kruṅ*.

With the affixes *bhyām, bhis, bhyas*, the rules *saṁyogāntasya lopaḥ* (20) and *kvinpratyayasya kuḥ* (303) will apply and we have the forms *kruṅbhyām, kruṅbhiḥ*, etc. In the locative plural we will have the three forms in the same manner as in the case of *prāñc*. The declension of the nominal stem *kruñc* will be as follows:

	Singular	Dual	Plural
prathamā	*kruṅ*	*kruñcau*	*kruñcaḥ*
dvitīyā	*kruñcam*	*kruñcau*	*kruñcaḥ*
tṛtīyā	*kruñcā*	*kruṅbhyām*	*kruṅbhiḥ*
caturthī	*kruñce*	*kruṅbhyām*	*kruṅbhyaḥ*
pañcamī	*kruñcaḥ*	*kruṅbhyām*	*kruṅbhyaḥ*
ṣaṣṭhī	*kruñcaḥ*	*kruñcoḥ*	*kruñcām*
saptamī	*kruñci*	*kruñcoḥ*	*kruṅkṣu, kruṅkhṣu, kruṅṣu*
sambodhana	*he kruṅ!*	*he kruñcau!*	*he kruñcaḥ!*

The word *payomuc* 'cloud' is derived with addition of *kvip* (not *kvin)* after the verbal root *muc* 'to give up' with *payas* as upapada. At the end of the pada, the rule *coḥ kuḥ* (305) will apply. In the nominative singular, the rules *halṅyābbhyo...* (178), *coḥ kuḥ* (305), *jhalāṁ jaśo 'nte* (67) and *vā 'vasāne* (145) become applicable and we have two forms : *payomuk, g*. The declension of the nominal stem *payomuc* will be as follows :

	Singular	Dual	Plural
prathamā	*payomuk, g*	*payomucau*	*payomucaḥ*
dvitīyā	*payomucam*	*payomucau*	*payomucaḥ*
tṛtīyā	*payomucā*	*payomugbhyām*	*payomugbhiḥ*
caturthī	*payomuce*	*payomugbhyām*	*payomugbhyaḥ*
pañcamī	*payomucaḥ*	*payomugbhyām*	*payomugbhyaḥ*
ṣaṣṭhī	*payomucaḥ*	*payomucoḥ*	*payomucām*
saptamī	*payomuci*	*payomucoḥ*	*payomukṣu,*
sambodhana	*he payomuk, g!*	*he payomucau!*	*he payomucaḥ!*

Here comes to an end the declension of the masculine nominal stems which end in the phoneme *c*.

Now begins the process of declining the nominal stems that end in the phoneme *t*.

The word *mahat* is an irregular derivative from the verbal root *maha* 'to honour, to value greatly' with the addition of the affix *ati* in accordance with *vartamāne pṛṣadbṛhanmahajjagat śatṛvacca* (Uṇādi Sūtra, 241), which also prescribes that the affix *ati* should be treated like *śatṛ*, which has *ṛ* as *it*. This means that the derived word *mahat* is *ugit* since the vowel *ṛ* is a denotatum of the abbreviatory term *uk*.

In the nominative singular, we add the affix *su* after it and have the following stage : *mahat + su*. Now *ugidacāṁ sarvanāmasthāne 'dhātoḥ* (288) applies and with the help of the paribhāṣā sūtra *midaco 'ntyātparaḥ* (239), the augment *num* is inserted after the last vowel in the nominal stem. Thus *mahat + su--> maha num t + s --> maha n t + s* (after the elision of the anubandhas). At this stage, the following sūtra ensues :

(341) सान्त महतः संयोगस्य । *sānta mahataḥ saṁyogasya*. 6. 4. 10

लघु० – सान्तसंयोगस्य महतश्च यो नकारस्तस्योपधाया दीर्घः स्यादसम्बुद्धौ सर्वनामस्थाने ।

महान्। महान्तौ। महान्तः। हे महन्! महद्भ्याम्। *sāntasaṁyogasya mahataś ca yo nakāras tasyopadhāyā dīrghaḥ syād asambuddhau sarvanāmasthāne. mahān. mahāntau. mahāntaḥ. he mahan! mahadbhyām.*

Trans. : When a sarvanāmasthāna affix, except the vocative, follows, let a counterpart long vowel replace the penultimate vowel which immediately precedes the consonant *n* of a conjunct consonant ending in *s* or that of the stem *mahat*.

PP. *sānta saṁyogasya mahataḥ na upadhāyā dīrghaḥ asambuddhau sarvanāmasthāne (aṅgasya).*

Eluc. : The word *na* is carried over from *nopadhāyāḥ* Pā. 6. 4.7. Its singular genitive nominal ending is taken as elided (*neti luptaṣaṣṭhīkaṁ padam*, BM, I, p. 327). The word *dīrghaḥ* is carried over from *ḍhralope pūrvasya dīrgho 'ṇaḥ* Pā. 6. 3. 111. The words *sarvanāmasthāne* and *asambuddhau* are carried over from *sarvanāmasthāne cāsambuddhau* Pā. 6. 4. 8. The genitive singular ending of the word *sānta* is also taken as elided and it qualifies the term *saṁyogasya* (*saṁyogāntasya*); cf. *sānteti luptaṣaṣṭhīkaṁ saṁyogāntasyetyanena samānādhikaraṇam iti*, TB, I, pp. 327-8. Thus the sūtra yields the following meaning : The penultimate vowel, i.e. the vowel preceding the phoneme *n* of a conjunct which ends in *s* or that of the word *mahat* is replaced by a long vowel if a sarvanāmasthāna affix, barring the vocative singular, follows.

In the illustration *maha n t* + s, the penultimate vowel *a*, preceding the consonant *n*, which is a constituent of the derivational form : *maha n t* + *s*, is substituted by a long *ā* and we arrive at the following declensional stage of the word *mahat* : *mahā n t* + *s*. Now the affix *s* is elided by *halṅyābbhyo...* (178) and the conjunct-final *t* is elided by *saṁyogāntasya lopaḥ* Pā. 8. 2. 23. Since the operation of eliding the conjunct-final *t* by Pā. 8. 2. 23 is deemed not to have taken place with respect to *na lopaḥ prātipadikāntasya* Pā. 8. 2. 7, the pada-final phoneme *n* remains intact and we obtain the form *mahān* in the nominative singular.

In the nominative dual form of the stem *mahat*, the augment *num* is inserted by *ugidacām...* (288). The lengthening of the penultimate vowel preceding the consonant *n* takes place by the present rule. Then the consonant *n* is replaced by the anusvāra (*ṁ*) by *naścāpadāntasya...* (78). The anusvāra is substituted by the fifth nasal stop homogeneous with the following by *anusvārasya...* (79). Thus the form *mahāntau* is obtained. The same grammatical operation is applied up to the affix *auṭ*. So far as the vocative singular form of the word *mahat* is concerned, the penultimate vowel is not replaced by a long counter-part as the vocative singular affix has been excluded by the present rule.

In the declensional form of the accusative plural, the affix *śas* is added to the word *mahat*. It is not a sarvanāmasthāna affix. So the augment *num* is not inserted, nor does the lengthening of the penultimate vowel take place. Thus from *mahat* + *as*, we get the form *mahataḥ* after rutva and visarga. In the forms in which the word *mahat* gets the pada-designation, the rule *jhalāṁ jaśo 'nte* (67) applies and the pada-final consonant *t* is replaced by *d*, which is a denotatum of *jaś*-pratyāhāra. The complete declension of the word *mahat* is as follows :

	Singular	Dual	Plural
prathamā	*mahān*	*mahāntau*	*mahāntaḥ*
dvitīyā	*mahāntam*	*mahāntau*	*mahataḥ*
tṛtīyā	*mahatā*	*mahadbhyām*	*mahadbhiḥ*
caturthī	*mahate*	*mahadbhyām*	*mahadbhyaḥ*
pañcamī	*mahataḥ*	*mahadbhyām*	*mahadbhyaḥ*
ṣaṣṭhī	*mahataḥ*	*mahatoḥ*	*mahatām*
saptamī	*mahati*	*mahatoḥ*	*mahatsu*
sambodhana	*he mahan!*	*he mahāntau!*	*he mahāntaḥ!*

The word *dhīmat* 'wise' is derived from the word *dhī* 'intellect' with the addition of the possessive affix *matup* by *tadasyāstyasminniti matup* (1179). The phonemes *u* and *p* in the affix *matup* are *its*. Hence they are elided by *tasya lopaḥ* (3). When we decline the stem *dhīmat* in the nominative singular, the following sūtra presents itself for application :

(342) अत्वसन्तस्य चाधातोः । *atvasantasya cādhātoḥ*. 6. 4. 14

लघु० – अत्वन्तस्योपधाया दीर्घो धातुभिन्नस्यासन्तस्य चासम्बुद्धौ सौ परे। धीमान्। धीमन्तौ। धीमन्तः। हे धीमन्! शसादौ महद्वत्। *atvantasyopadhāyā dīrgho dhātubhinnasyāsantasya cāsambuddhau sau pare. dhīmān. dhīmantau. dhīmantaḥ. he dhīman! śasādau mahadvat.*

Trans.: The penultimate vowel of that which ends in *atu* and of that which, not being a verbal root, ends in *as*, is replaced by a long counter-part when the nominative singular affix *su*, other than the vocative, follows.

PP. *atvasantasya ca adhātoḥ aṅgasya upadhāyāḥ dīrghaḥ asambuddhau sau.*

Eluc. : The genitive nominal ending of the word *atu* is taken as elided. This is a separate pada and qualifies the term *aṅga*, which is carried over here from the governing rule *aṅgasya* Pā. 6. 4. 1. By tadantavidhi, it means as follows : a pre-affixal base that ends in *atu* (*atu iti luptaṣaṣṭhīkaṁ pṛthak padam. aṅgaviśeṣaṇatvāt tadantavidhiḥ*, BM, I, p. 431). The word segment *atu* represents the affixes *matup, vatup, ḍavatu, ktavatu*, etc. The compound word *adhātoḥ* qualifies the pre-affixal base that ends in *as* (*adhātor ity asantasya viśeṣaṇam*, BM, I, p. 431). The word *upadhāyāḥ* comes from the sūtra *nopadhāyāḥ* Pā. 6. 4. 7. The word *upadhāyāḥ* is in syntactic relation with both *atvantasya* and *adhātoḥ asantasya*. The word *dīrghaḥ* is carried over from *ḍhralope pūrvasya dīrgho 'ṇaḥ* Pā. 6. 3. 111. The term *asambuddhau* is carried over from *sarvanāmasthāne cāsambuddhau* Pā. 6. 4. 8. All these points having been taken into consideration, the sūtra comes to mean as follows : If the penultimate vowel of a pre-affixal base ends in *atu* and also if such a vowel belongs to a pre-affixal base which, not being a verbal root, ends in *as*, then such a vowel is replaced by its long counter-part when the nominative singular affix *su*, other than the vocative, follows.

It is explained in two ways why the word *adhātoḥ* is construed as the qualification of only the pre-affixal base that ends in *as*. Nāgeśa says that it is because of the word *ca*, which is used here in the sense of *tu*, that the expression *adhātoḥ* syntactically accords with the pre-affixal base that ends in *as* (*adhātoḥ ityasantasyaiva viśeṣaṇaṁ tuśabdāt*, LS, p. 544). The second explanation is provided by Jñānendra Sarasvatī in the Tattvabodhinī. He invokes the technique of yogavibhāga to explain this point. Accordingly he divides the present sūtra into two: 1. *atvasantasya ca* 2. *adhātoḥ*. By virtue of the yogavibhāga, the second division, that is, the word *adhātoḥ*, which now behaves like a separate rule, will enter into syntactic relation with the word *asantasya* which immediately precedes it (*iha adhātor iti yogo vibhajyate tatsāmarthyād anantarasyaiva pratiṣedhaḥ na tu atvantasya*, TB, I, p. 432). It will not enter into syntactic relation with the word *atvantasya*, which is separated by the intervention of the word *asantasya* (cf. the paribhāṣā *anatarasya vidhir vā bhavati pratiṣedho vā*, Abhyankar, 61).

The other important point with respect to this sūtra is as follows : In the illustration *dhīmat + su* --> *dhīmat + s*, the replacement of the penultimate vowel by a long counter-part by the present rule and the augment *num* by *ugidacāṁ*... Pā. 7. 1. 70 become simultaneously available. The augment *num* by Pā. 7. 1. 70 is both nitya and subsequent in order of enumeration in the Aṣṭādhyāyī so far as the present sūtra is concerned. Still the operation of replacing the penultimate vowel of *dhīmat* gets precedence over the insertion of the augment *num*. The reason is that if the insertion of the augment of *num* takes place before the replacement, then the penultimate vowel would not be available for replacement as is shown in the following illustration : *dhīma n t + s* since that position would be occupied by the phoneme *n*. As such, the enunciation of this sūtra would be rendered infructuous. It is this undesirable contingency which leads to the view that by enunciating this sūtra Pāṇini intends that even the subsequent and nitya grammatical operation of inserting the augment of *num* be superseded by the present rule. Consequently, the replacement of the penultimate vowel by a long counterpart takes place first, according to the present rule, and then the insertion of the augment *num* is brought about by *ugidacāṁ*... (288). After these grammatical operations, we have the following grammatical situation : *dhīmā n t + s*. At this stage, the affix *s*(*u*) is elided by *halṅyābbhyo*... (178). The conjunct-final *t* is elided by *saṁyogāntasya lopaḥ* (20) and we obtain the form *dhīmān* in the nominative singular. The elision of the pada-final *n* does not take place because the elision of *t* by *saṁyogāntasya lopaḥ* Pā. 8. 2. 23 is deemed not to have taken place with respect to the rule *na lopaḥ*... Pā. 8. 2. 7.

This replacement of the penultimate vowel by a long counter-part does not take place in the vocative singular. As a consequence we get the form *he dhīman!* in the vocative singular. When *śas* and the remaining affixes follow, the declension of the word *dhīmat* will be like that of *mahat*. The complete declension of the stem *dhīmat* is as follows :

	Singular	Dual	Plural
prathamā	*dhīmān*	*dhīmantau*	*dhīmantaḥ*
dvitīyā	*dhīmantam*	*dhīmantau*	*dhīmataḥ*
tṛtīyā	*dhīmatā*	*dhīmadbhyām*	*dhīmadbhiḥ*
caturthī	*dhīmate*	*dhīmadbhyām*	*dhīmadbhyaḥ*
pañcamī	*dhīmataḥ*	*dhīmadbhyām*	*dhīmadbhyaḥ*
ṣaṣṭhī	*dhīmataḥ*	*dhīmatoḥ*	*dhīmatām*
saptamī	*dhīmati*	*dhīmatoḥ*	*dhīmatsu*
sambodhana	*he dhīman!*	*he dhīmantau!*	*he dhīmantaḥ!*

लघु० – भातेर्डवतु । डित्त्वसामर्थ्यादभस्यापि टेर्लोपः । भवान् । भवन्तौ । भवन्तः । शत्रन्तस्य – भवन् । *bhāter ḍavatu. ḍittvasāmarthyād abhasyāpi ṭer lopaḥ. bhavān. bhavantau. bhavantaḥ. śatrantasya – bhavan.*

Eluc. : The word *bhavatu* (*bhavat*) is a respectful pronominal stem meaning 'your honour'. It is derived from the verbal stem *bhā* 'to shine' with the addition of the affix *ḍavatu* by *bhāterḍavatuḥ* (Uṇādi Sūtra, 63). In *bhā* + *ḍavatu*, the consonant *ḍ* is *it* by *cuṭū* (128) and the vowel *u* by *upadeśe...* (28). After the elision of the anubandhas by *tasya lopaḥ* (3), the affix remains as *avat*. The *ṭi* of *bhā* is elided by *ṭeḥ* (241) since the affix following it has the phoneme *ḍ* as *it*. Thus the word *bhavat* is obtained through the following grammatical process : *bhā* + *ḍavatu* --> *bhā* + *avat* --> *bh* + *avat* --> *bhavat*. The declension of the word *bhavat* is like that of the word *dhīmat* :

	Singular	Dual	Plural
prathamā	*bhavān*	*bhavantau*	*bhavantaḥ*
dvitīyā	*bhavantam*	*bhavantau*	*bhavataḥ*
tṛtīyā	*bhavatā*	*bhavadbhyām*	*bhavadbhiḥ*
caturthī	*bhavate*	*bhavadbhyām*	*bhavadbhyaḥ*
pañcamī	*bhavataḥ*	*bhavadbhyām*	*bhavadbhyaḥ*
ṣaṣṭhī	*bhavataḥ*	*bhavatoḥ*	*bhavatām*
saptamī	*bhavati*	*bhavatoḥ*	*bhavatsu*
sambodhana	*he bhavan!*	*he bhavantau!*	*he bhavantaḥ!*

When the word *bhavat* 'being or becoming' is derived from the verbal root *bhū* 'to be' with the introduction of the primary affix *śatṛ* after it, its nominative singular form will be *bhavan* in the following way : The vowel *ṛ* in the affix *śatṛ* is *it* by *upadeśe...* (28). Hence it is *ugit* and the word formed with this affix is also treated as *ugit*. As a consequence, the rule *ugidacāṁ...* (288) adds *num* to it. The rule *atvasantasya...* (342) does not have any scope to apply as the stem *bhavat* does not end in *atu*. To decline it in the nominative singular, we have the following situation : *bhavat* + *su* --> *bhava num t* + *su* --> *bhavat n t* + s. At this stage, the affix s(*u*) is elided by *halṅyābbhyo...* (178) and the elision of *t* takes place by *saṁyogāntasya...* (20). Thus we obtain the form *bhavan* in the nominative singular. The rest of the declension is like that of *bhavat* 'your honour'.

(343) उभे अभ्यस्तम्। *ubhe abhyastam.* 6. 1. 5

लघु० – षाष्ठद्वित्वप्रकरणे ये द्वे विहिते ते उभे समुदिते अभ्यस्तसंज्ञे स्तः। *ṣāṣṭhadvitva-prakaraṇe ye dve vihite te ubhe samudite abhyastasaṁjñe staḥ.*

Trans. : The two, which are enjoined in the sixth chapter where reduplication is treated, are collectively designated as *abhyasta.*

PP. *ubhe dve abhyastam.*

Eluc. : The term *dve* is carried over from *ekāco dve prathamasya* Pā. 6. 1. 1. The carried over term *dve* in the present sūtra in which the word *ubhe* is already present, implies that the reduplicated syllables, taken together, are to be designated as *abhyasta* but not when they are separate (cf. *dve iti vartamāna ubhegrahaṇaṁ samudāyasaṁjñāpratipattyartham,* Kāśikā on Pā. 6. 1. 5). The absence of sandhi in the present sūtra and in *te ubhe samudite abhyastasaṁjñe* (Varadarāja's vṛtti) is by virtue of the rules *īdūded dvivacanaṁ pragṛhyam* (51) and *plutapragṛhyā aci...* (50).

There are two places in the Aṣṭādhyāyī where the reduplication is enjoined : 1. from Pā. 6. 1. 1 to Pā. 6. 1. 12 and 2. from Pā. 8. 1. 1 to Pā. 8. 1. 15. The present rule belongs to the former in deference to the paribhāṣā *anantarasya vidhir vā bhavati pratiṣedho vā* (Abhyankar, 61) as it has been enunciated in the first quarter of the sixth chapter of the Aṣṭādhyāyī where the present sūtra prescribes the abhyasta designation.

The present participle of the verbal root *dā* is *dadat* which is derived with the introduction of the affix *śatṛ* : *dā* + *śatṛ*. The affix *śatṛ* is sārva-dhātuka and threrfore *śap* is introduced after the verbal stem *dā* by *kartari śap* (386). The affix *śap* is replaced with *ślu* by *juhotyādibhyaḥ śluḥ* (603). The sūtra *ślau* (604) prescribes the reduplication of *dā* and we get *dadat* through the following grammatical process : *dā + laṭ --> dā + śatṛ --> dā śap + śatṛ --> dā ślu + at --> dā dā + at --> dadat*. Here the first of the reduplicated syllables *dā dā* is abhyāsa by *pūrvo 'bhyāsaḥ* (394). The shortening of the vowel of abhyāsa takes place by *hrasvaḥ* (396). The vowel *ā* of the second member of the reduplicated syllables is elided by *śnābhyastayorātaḥ* (618). Thus the present participle *dadat* is obtained and the segment *dad* in it is designated as *abhyasta* by the present sūtra since the reduplication has taken place here by *ślau* Pā. 6. 1. 10.

The following sūtra prohibits the introduction of *num* to *śatṛ* after a pre-affixal base, which has been designated as *abhyasta.*

(344) नाभ्यस्ताच्छतुः। *nābhyastācchatuḥ.* 7. 1. 78

लघु० – अभ्यस्तात् परस्य शतुर्नुम् न स्यात्। ददत्, ददद्। ददतौ। ददतः। *abhyastāt parasya śatur num na syāt. dadat, dadad. dadatau. dadataḥ.*

Trans. : The augment *num* is not introduced to the affix *śatṛ* occurring after abhyasta.

PP. *na abhyastāt (aṅgāt) śatuḥ num* .

Eluc. : The term *num* is carried over from *idito num dhātoḥ* Pā. 7. 1. 58. So, the meaning of the sūtra is as follows : If the affix *śatṛ* occurs after that which has been designated as *abhyasta,* then the augment *num* does not become a part of that *śatṛ.*

In the nominative singular form of *dadat,* that is, in *dadat + su, ugidacāṁ...* (288) does not apply since it is prohibited by the present rule. The affix *su* is elided by *halṅyābbhyo...* (178) and we get two forms: *dadat* and *dadad* by applying first the exception rule *vā 'vasāne* (145) by which the phoneme *t* remains as it is and then alternatively it is replaced by *jaś*-phoneme *d* according to *jhalāṁ jaśo 'nte* (67). In the declensional forms in which the stem *dadat* gets the pada-designation, as in *dadadbhyām,* etc. the pre-affix-final phoneme *t* is replaced by *d* by *jhalāṁ jaśo 'nte* (67). The complete declension of *dadat* is given below :

	Singular	Dual	Plural
prathamā	*dadat, d*	*dadatau*	*dadataḥ*
dvitīyā	*dadatam*	*dadatau*	*dadataḥ*
tṛtīyā	*dadatā*	*dadadbhyām*	*dadadbhiḥ*
caturthī	*dadate*	*dadadbhyām*	*dadadbhyaḥ*
pañcamī	*dadataḥ*	*dadadbhyām*	*dadadbhyaḥ*
ṣaṣṭhī	*dadataḥ*	*dadatoḥ*	*dadatām*
saptamī	*dadati*	*dadatoḥ*	*dadatsu*
sambodhana	*he dadat, d!*	*he dadatau!*	*he dadataḥ!*

(345) जक्षित्यादयः षट् । *jakṣityādayaḥ ṣaṭ.* 6. 1. 6

लघु० – षड् धातवोऽन्ये जक्षितिश्च सप्तम एतेऽभ्यस्तसंज्ञाः स्युः । जक्षत्, जक्षद् । जक्षतौ । जक्षतः । एवं जाग्रत्, दरिद्रत्, शासत्, चकासत् । *ṣaḍ dhātavo 'nye jakṣitiś ca saptama ete 'bhyastasaṁjñāḥ syuḥ. jakṣat, jakṣad. jakṣatau. jakṣataḥ. evaṁ jāgrat, daridrat, śāsat, cakāsat.*

Trans. : Let *jakṣ,* etc., i.e. six other verbal stems, with the verbal stem *jakṣ* itself as the seventh, be designated as *abhyasta.*

PP. *jakṣityādayaḥ ṣaṭ abhyastam.*

Eluc. : The term *abhyastam* is carried over from *ubhe abhyastam* Pā. 6. 1. 5. The word *iti* in *jakṣiti* (*jakṣ* + *iti*) is a separate pada and it refers to the verbal stem *jakṣ* (*sūtre jakṣ iti pṛthak padam. itinā jakṣiḥ parāmṛśyate,* BM, I, p. 435). The compound (*jakṣ*)*ityādayaḥ* is bahuvrīhi which is analysed as follows : *iti ādiḥ yeṣām ity atadguṇasaṁvijñānabahuvrīhiḥ.* That the compound in this context is atadguṇasaṁvijñānabahuvrīhi is determined on the basis of the term *ṣaṭ* used in the present sūtra. This is the reason why six verbal stems other than *jakṣ* are intended to be conveyed by *ityādayaḥ* (*tataś ca ity ādayaḥ ṣaṭ ityanena jakṣadhātoḥ anye jāgṛ ityārabhya ṣaḍ dhātavo vivakṣitāḥ,* BM, I, p. 435). According to Vāsudeva Dīkṣita, the term *ca* should be read into the sūtra. Thus the meaning of the sūtra will be as follows : The verbal stem *jakṣ* and the six other verbal stems, beginning with *jāgṛ* - these seven verbal stems - are to be designated as *abhyasta* (*caśabdaḥ adhyāhāryaḥ. evaṁ ca jakṣadhātuś ca jāgṛdhātum ārabhya ṣaḍ dhātavaś cetyevaṁ sapta dhātavaḥ abhyasta-sañjñakāḥ syur iti phalatītyarthaḥ,* BM, I, p. 435). This sūtra assigns the abhyasta designation to these seven verbal stems, which have not undergone reduplication or iteration by a rule in the sixth chapter of the Aṣṭādhyāyī. The seven verbal stems, which are designated as *abhyasta* by the present rule, are as follows : 1. *jakṣ* 'to eat, to laugh' 2. *jāgṛ* 'to remain awake' 3. *daridrā* 'to be poor' 4. *cakāsṛ* 'to shine' 5. *dīdhīṅ* 'to reflect' 6. *vevīṅ* 'to move 7. *śāsṛ* 'to instruct'.

Since these verbal roots have been designated as *abhyasta,* the insertion of *num* by *ugidacām...* (288) will not take place before sarvanāma-sthāna affixes. To illustrate how the participial forms of these seven verbal stems are declined, the declension of *jakṣat,* which is like that of *dadat,* is given below :

	Singular	Dual	Plural
prathamā	*jakṣat, d*	*jakṣatau*	*jakṣataḥ*
dvitīyā	*jakṣatam*	*jakṣatau*	*jakṣataḥ*
tṛtīyā	*jakṣatā*	*jakṣadbhyām*	*jakṣadbhiḥ*
caturthī	*jakṣate*	*jakṣadbhyām*	*jakṣadbhyaḥ*
pañcamī	*jakṣataḥ*	*jakṣadbhyām*	*jakṣadbhyaḥ*
ṣaṣṭhī	*jakṣataḥ*	*jakṣatoḥ*	*jakṣatām*
saptamī	*jakṣati*	*jakṣatoḥ*	*jakṣatsu*
sambodhana	*he jakṣat, d!*	*he jakṣatau!*	*he jakṣataḥ!*

Here comes to an end the declension of the masculine words ending in the phoneme *t*. Now begins the declension of the words ending in *p*.

The next masculine word is *gup* 'one who protects'. It is derived from the verbal stem *gup(ū)* 'to protect' with the introduction of the affix *kvip* by *kvip ca* (799). The affix *kvip* is an ārdhadhātuka affix by *ārdhadhātukaṁ śeṣaḥ* Pā. 3. 4. 114. The affix *āya*, etc. are optionally available by *āvādaya ārdhadhātuke vā* Pā. 3. 1. 31 when the affix *kvip* is intended to be introduced. In the absence of the affix *āya*, when the affix *kvip* is wholly elided, we get the word *gup* (*kvipi vivakṣite 'āyādaya ārdhadhātuke vā 'iti vaikalpikatvād ihāyapratyayābhāvaḥ*, TB, I, p. 435). There are three points worth mentioning with respect to the declensional process of the primary derivative *gup* which gets the prātipadika designation by *kṛttaddhitasamāsāśca* (116). 1. In the nominative singular form, the affix *su* is elided by *halṅyābbhyo*...(178) and we get : *gup + su* --> *gup + s* --> *gup*. Now by applying the rules *vā 'vasāne* (145) and *jhalāṁ jaśo 'nte* (67), we obtain two forms *gup* and *gub* in the nominative singular. 2. We apply *jhalāṁ jaśo 'nte* (67) before the affixes *bhyām, bhyas*, etc. where the stem gets the pada designation by *svādiṣva*... (163) and we get *gubbhyām, gubbhyaḥ*, etc. 3. In the locative plural *jhalāṁ jaśo 'nte* (67) and *khari ca* (74) apply and we obtain the form *gupsu*. The complete declension of the nominal stem *gup* is as follows :

	Singular	Dual	Plural
prathamā	*gup, b*	*gupau*	*gupaḥ*
dvitīyā	*gupam*	*gupau*	*gupaḥ*
tṛtīyā	*gupā*	*gubbhyām*	*gubbhiḥ*
caturthī	*gupe*	*gubbhyām*	*gubbhyaḥ*
pañcamī	*gupaḥ*	*gubbhyām*	*gubbhyaḥ*
ṣaṣṭhī	*gupaḥ*	*gupoḥ*	*gupām*
saptamī	*gupi*	*gupoḥ*	*gupsu*
sambodhana	*he gup, b!*	*he gupau!*	*he gupaḥ!*

Here ends the declension of the masculine stems that end in the phoneme *p*.

Now begins the declensional process of the masculine words that end in the palatal sibilant (*ś*).

(346) त्यदादिषु दृशोऽनालोचने कञ्च । *tyadādiṣu dṛśo 'nālocane kañca.* **3. 2. 60**

लघु॰ – त्यदादिषूपपदेष्वज्ञानार्थाद् दृशेः कञ् स्याच्चात् क्विन् । *tyadādiṣūpapadeṣvajñānārthād dṛśeḥ kañ syāc cāt kvin.*

Trans. : The affixes *kañ* and *kvin* are introduced after the verb *dṛś* 'to see' when it does not signify perception (by means of the eyes) and when it is preceded by the words *tyad*, etc. as upapadas.

PP. *tyadādiṣu dṛśaḥ anālocane kvin kañ ca (supi, dhātoḥ).*

Eluc. : The term *kvin* is carried over from *spṛśo 'nudake kvin* Pā. 3. 2. 58. The word *anālocane* is a nañ-tatpuruṣa : *na ālocanam, anālocanam, tasmin = anālocane.* With these points, the sūtra comes to mean : when the verb *dṛś* is not used in the sense of perceiving with the eyes (*ālocana*), the affixes *kañ* and *kvin* are added after it, provided the words *tyad*, etc. occur before it as upapadas. The words *tyad*, etc. are used in the locative plural. Hence they are assigned the upapada designation by *tatropapadaṁ saptamīstham* (949).

The verbal root *dṛś* does not mean 'seeing' in words like *tādṛś, yādṛś*, etc. The expression *anālocane* has been interpreted in this way in the context of the verbal root *dṛś*. Two explanations are given to justify this interpretation. 1. The words *tādṛś, yādṛś*, etc. are conventional (*rūḍha*) and as such they convey meaning as a whole. Hence the constituents of these words are not accepted to convey any meaning. In this sense the verbal root *dṛś* may be interpreted not to convey the meaning 'perception by means of the eyes' (*tādṛśādayas tu rūḍhiśabdatvād asatāpyavayavārthena vyutpādyante. ata evājñānārthād dṛśer iti saṅgacchate*, TB, I, p. 436). 2. Following the derivation of the word *tādṛś*, etc. given in the Mahābhāṣya, Jñānendra Sarasvatī presents this argument in a manner that it can be easily comprehended. He says that the primary affix *kvin*, etc. in deriving the words *tādṛś, yādṛś*, etc. are used in the sense of karmakartā. The derivation given by him is as follows : *sa ivāyaṁ paśyati* (This looks like him). In this derivation, the meaning of the verbal root *dṛś* is not 'perceiving with the eyes'. Rather the object (karma) of the verbal root *dṛś* is used in the sense of agent. The verbal root thus loses its property of being transitive. Hence it may be interpreted that the verbal root *dṛś* is not used in the sense of 'perceiving by means of the eyes' (*sa ivāyaṁ paśyati. jñānaviṣayo bhavatītyarthād ajñānārthād iti tu saṅgacchate*, TB, I, p. 436). In case the verbal root *dṛś* is used as a transitive verb as in the expression *taṁ paśyati*, then the affix *aṇ* would be introduced after it by *karmaṇyaṇ* (787) and the resultant form would be *taddarśaḥ* after the application of *pugantalaghūpadhasya ca* (450).

The grammatical situations with both the primary affixes *kañ* and *kvin* are as follows : 1. *tad + dṛś + kañ* 2. *tad + dṛś + kvin*. In both these grammatical situations, the following sūtra applies :

(347) आ सर्वनाम्नः । *ā sarvanāmnaḥ*. 6. 3. 91

लघु० – सर्वनाम्न आकारोऽन्तादेशः स्यात् दृग्दृशवतुषु । तादृक्, तादृग्। तादृशौ । तादृशः । तादृग्भ्याम्। *sarvanāmna ākāro 'ntādeśaḥ syāt dṛgdṛśavatuṣu. tādṛk, tādṛg. tādṛśau. tādṛśaḥ. tādṛgbhyām.*

Trans. : The final phoneme of a pronominal stem is replaced by a long *ā* when the word *dṛg* or *dṛśa* or the affix *vatu* follows.

PP. *ā sarvanāmnaḥ dṛgdṛśavatuṣu (uttarapade).*

Eluc. : The compound word *dṛgdṛśavatuṣu* comes from *dṛgdṛśavatuṣu* Pā. 6. 3. 89. Its analysis is as follows : *dṛk ca dṛśaś ca vatuś ca, dṛgdṛśavatavaḥ, teṣu = dṛgdṛśavatuṣu*. The term *ā* in the sūtra is used without any case-ending (*ā ityavibhaktikanirdeśaḥ*, BM, I, p. 435). The meaning of the sūtra is now as follows : When the word *dṛg* or *dṛśa* or the affix *vatu* follows, the pronominal stem is replaced by a long *ā*. According to the paribhāṣā sūtra *alo 'ntyasya* (21), the final phoneme of the pronominal stem gets replaced by *ā*. In both the illustrations : 1. *tad + dṛś + kañ*, 2. *tad + dṛś + kvin*, the final phoneme *d* is replaced by *ā* and we get : 1. *ta ā + dṛś + kañ --> ta ā + dṛś + a*, 2. *ta ā + dṛś + kvin --> ta ā + dṛś +* 0 (after the elision of the anubandhas and the phoneme *v*). The rule *akaḥ savarṇe dīrghaḥ* (42) applies and we obtain the forms : *tādṛśa* and *tādṛś*. The declension of the word *tādṛśa*, which ends in a short *a*, is like that of the nominal stem *rāma*. The declensional process of *tādṛś* differs. In the nominative singular *tādṛś + su*, the affix *s*(*u*) is elided by *halṅyābbhyo...* (178). Now the rule *kvinpratyayasya kuḥ* Pā. 8. 2. 62 becomes applicable but it is deemed to be asiddha with respect to the rule *vraścabhrasja...* Pā. 8. 2. 36 which, therefore, applies and the phoneme *ś* is replaced by *ṣ*. At this stage, the rule *jhalāṁ jaśo 'nte* (67) applies and the cerebral sibilant *ṣ* is replaced by *ḍ*, which is further replaced by the guttural stop *g* in accordance with *kvinpratyayasya kuḥ* Pā. 8. 2. 62. Now the rule *vā 'vasāne* (145) becomes applicable and we have two forms *tādṛk* and *tādṛg* in the nominative singular. In the declensional forms in which the stem *tādṛś* gets the pada designation, the same grammatical process is repeated except for the grammatical operation of *vā 'vasāne* (145). In the locative plural when the affix *sup* is introduced, we have the following grammatical situation *tādṛś + sup --> tādṛś + su --> tādṛṣ + su* (*vraścabhrasja...* Pā. 8. 2. 36) --> *tādṛḍ + su* {*jhalāṁ jaśo 'nte* (67)} --> *tādṛg + su*. At this stage, *khari ca* Pā. 8. 4. 55 is applicable but is asiddha with respect to *ādeśapratyayayoḥ* Pā. 8. 3. 59. This is the reason that the latter rule applies first and we have *tādṛg + ṣu*. Then *khari ca* applies and we obtain the form *tādṛkṣu* in the locative plural. The complete declension of the word *tādṛś* is given below :

	Singular	Dual	Plural
prathamā	*tādṛk, g*	*tādṛśau*	*tādṛśaḥ*
dvitīyā	*tādṛśam*	*tādṛśau*	*tādṛśaḥ*
tṛtīyā	*tādṛśā*	*tādṛgbhyām*	*tādṛgbhiḥ*
caturthī	*tādṛśe*	*tādṛgbhyām*	*tādṛgbhyaḥ*
pañcamī	*tādṛśaḥ*	*tādṛgbhyām*	*tādṛgbhyaḥ*
ṣaṣṭhī	*tādṛśaḥ*	*tādṛśoḥ*	*tādṛśām*
saptamī	*tādṛśi*	*tādṛśoḥ*	*tādṛkṣu*
sambodhana	*he tādṛk, g!*	*he tādṛśau!*	*he tādṛśaḥ!*

The word *viś* 'a vaiśya, people' is derived from the verbal root *viś* 'to enter' with the introduction of the affix *kvip*, which is wholly elided. Its declensional process is described in the Laghu as follows :

लघु० – व्रश्चभ्रस्ज० इति षः। जश्त्वचर्त्वे। विट्, विड्। विशौ। विशः। विड्भ्याम्।
vraścabhrasja... iti ṣaḥ. jaśtvacartve. viṭ, viḍ. viśau. viśaḥ. viḍbhyām.

Eluc. : In the nominative singular when the affix *su* is added after the word *viś*, it is elided by *halṅyābbhyo...* (178). By virtue of the rule *vraścabhrasja...* (306), the pada-final phoneme *ś* is replaced by *ṣ* which is further replaced by *ḍ* by *jhalāṁ jaśo 'nte* (67). Then *vā 'vasāne* (145) applies and we obtain two forms *viṭ* and *viḍ* in the nominative singular. In the declensional forms in which the stem gets the pada designation, the pada-final phoneme is replaced by *ḍ* by *jhalāṁ jaśo 'nte* (67) and we get *viḍbhyām, viḍbhiḥ*, etc. In the locative plural, the augment *dhuṭ* is optionally inserted by *ḍaḥ si dhuṭ* (86) after the rules *vraścabhrasja...* (306) and *jhalāṁ jaśo 'nte* (67) have performed their grammatical functions. With the application of *khari ca* (74), the *dh* of *dhuṭ*, changes to *t* and we obtain two forms : *viṭtsu* and *viṭsu*. The declension of the stem *viś* is as follows :

	Singular	Dual	Plural
prathamā	*viṭ, ḍ*	*viśau*	*viśaḥ*
dvitīyā	*viśam*	*viśau*	*viśaḥ*
tṛtīyā	*viśā*	*viḍbhyām*	*viḍbhiḥ*
caturthī	*viśe*	*viḍbhyām*	*viḍbhyaḥ*
pañcamī	*viśaḥ*	*viḍbhyām*	*viḍbhyaḥ*
ṣaṣṭhī	*viśaḥ*	*viśoḥ*	*viśām*
saptamī	*viśi*	*viśoḥ*	*viṭṭsu, viṭsu*
sambodhana	*he viṭ, ḍ!*	*he viśau!*	*he viśaḥ!*

The primary derivative *naś* 'that which disappears, that which is destroyed' is obtained with the addition of the affix *kvip* after the verbal root *ṇaśa* 'to disappear'. In the nominative singular *naś* + *su*, the affix *s*(*u*) is elided by *halṅyābbhyo...* (178). At this stage, the following sūtra becomes applicable :

(348) नशेर्वा । ***naśervā*. 8. 2. 63**

लघु० - नशेः कवर्गोऽन्तादेशो वा स्यात् पदान्ते । नक्, नग् , नट्, नड् । नशौ । नशः । नग्भ्याम् , नड्भ्याम् । *naśeḥ kavargo 'ntādeśo vā syāt padānte. nak, nag, naṭ, naḍ. naśau. naśaḥ. nagbhyām, naḍbhyām.*

Trans. : The final phoneme of *naś* is optionally replaced by a guttural stop at the end of a pada.

PP. *naśeḥ vā kuḥ padasya ante.*

Eluc. : The term *kuḥ* is carried over from *kvinpratyayasya kuḥ* Pā. 8. 2. 62. The present sūtra occurs in the governing domain of *padasya* Pā. 8. 1. 16. Hence the word *padasya* recurs here also. The word *ante* comes from *skoḥ saṁyogādyor ante ca* Pā. 8. 2. 29. Thus the sūtra means as follows : The phoneme at the end of *naś* as a pada is optionally replaced by a phoneme denoted by *ku* (by a consonant of *k*-series). Here Jñānendra Sarasvatī points out that some commentators carry over the word *jhali* from *jhalo jhali* Pā. 8. 2. 26 and say that the replacement in place of the final phoneme *ś* of *naś* by a guttural stop takes place also when it is followed by a *jhal*-consonant. He, however, does not subscribe to this view saying that it will lead to the defect of overpervasion in *naṣṭa*, etc. (*kecid iha jhalītyanuvartya jhali padānte ceti vyācakṣate. tan na naṣṭam* *ityādāv atiprasaṅgāt*, TB, I, p. 437). According to this interpretation, in *naṣṭa* the phoneme *ś* is to be optionally replaced by a guttural since a *jhal*-consonant *t* follows, which is not desirable.

After the elision of the nominative singular affix *su*, the rule *vraścabhrasja*... Pā. 8. 2. 36 becomes applicable with respect to which the present rule *naśervā* 8. 2. 63 is deemed to be asiddha. So, the former rule applies first and the pada-final *ś* is replaced by *ṣ*. Then *jhalāṁ*... (67) applies and the cerebral sibilant *ṣ* is replaced by *ḍ*. By *vā 'vasāne* (145), *ḍ* optionally changes to *ṭ* and we have two forms in the nominative singular : *naṭ, naḍ*. In the other alternative after the application of *vraścabhrasja*... (306) and *jhalāṁ*... (67), the present rule prescribes the replacement of the pada-final *ś* by a guttural stop and we get two forms *nak* and *nag* by *vā 'vasāne* (145). In all, we have four forms in the nominative singular : *nak, nag, naṭ, naḍ*. In the declensional forms in which the stem *naś* gets the pada-designation, we have two forms : *nagbhyām* and *naḍbhyām* by virtue of the present rule . In the locative plural, we will have three forms. The form *nakṣu* is obtained in the following way : First *vraścabhrasja*... (306) applies and *ś* changes into *ṣ* which then changes into *ḍ* by *jhalāṁ*... (67). Now *naśervā* (348) optionally prescribes *g* in place of *ḍ* which subsequently changes to *k* by *khari ca* (74). Then the phoneme *s* of the affix *sup* is replaced by *ṣ* according to *ādeśapratyayayoḥ* (149) and thus we have *nakṣu*. The other two forms are obtained as follows : By the rule *vraścabhrasja*... (306), the pada-final *ś* is replaced by *ṣ* which changes to *ḍ* according to *jhalāṁ*... (67). Then the rule *ḍaḥ si dhuṭ* (86) applies and prescribes the optional insertion of the augment *dhuṭ*. With the help of *khari ca* (74) we get two forms : One when the augment *dhuṭ* is inserted (*naṭtsu*) and the other in the absence of *dhuṭ* (*naṭsu*). The complete declension of *naś* runs as follows:

	Singular	Dual	Plural
prathamā	*nak, nag* *naṭ, naḍ*	*naśau*	*naśaḥ*
dvitīyā	*naśam*	*naśau*	*naśaḥ*
tṛtīyā	*naśā*	*nagbhyām,* *naḍbhyām*	*nagbhiḥ,* *naḍbhiḥ*
caturthī	*naśe*	*nagbhyām,* *naḍbhyām*	*nagbhyaḥ,* *naḍbhyaḥ*
pañcamī	*naśaḥ*	*nagbhyām,* *naḍbhyām*	*nagbhyaḥ,* *naḍbhyaḥ*

ṣaṣṭhī	*naśaḥ*	*naśoḥ*	*naśām*
saptamī	*naśi*	*naśoḥ*	*nakṣu, naṭtsu, naṭsu*
sambodhana	*he nak, nag! he naṭ, naḍ!*	*he naśau!*	*he naśaḥ!*

(349) स्पृशोऽनुदके क्विन्। ***spṛśo 'nudake kvin*. 3. 2. 58**
लघु० - अनुदके सुप्युपपदे स्पृशेः क्विन्। घृतस्पृक्, घृतस्पृग्। घृतस्पृशौ। घृतस्पृशः।
anudake supyupapade spṛśeḥ kvin. ghṛtaspṛk, ghṛtaspṛg. ghṛtaspṛśau. ghṛtaspṛśaḥ.

Trans. : The affix *kvin* is introduced after the verbal stem *spṛś* when it is preceded by an inflected word, other than *udaka*, as upapada.

PP. *anudake supi spṛśaḥ (dhātoḥ) kvin.*

Eluc. : The term *supi* is carried over from *supi sthaḥ* Pā. 3. 2. 4. The meaning of the present sūtra is as follows : When the preceding member of the upapada compound is other than *udaka*, the affix *kvin* is introduced after the verbal root *spṛś*. In the compound word *ghṛtaspṛś* 'one who touches ghee', the inflected word *ghṛta* is an upapada. Hence the affix *kvin* is added after the verbal root *spṛś*. The affix *kvin* is wholly elided, making *spṛś* a prātipadika by *kṛttaddhita*... (116). In the nominative singular, when the affix *su* is elided by *halṅyābbhyo*... (178), the rule *vraścabhrasja*... (306) applies and the palatal sibilant *ś* is replaced by *ṣ* which is then replaced by *ḍ* according to *jhalāṁ*... (67). The phoneme *ḍ* is replaced by *g* in accordance with *kvinpratyaya*... (303). The rule *vā 'va*... (145) applies and we obtain two forms *ghṛtaspṛk* and *ghṛtaspṛg*. Before the affixes *bhyām, bhis*, etc., the rules *vraścabhrasja*... (306), *jhalāṁ*... (67) and *kvinpratyaya*... (303) apply and we get the forms *ghṛtaspṛgbhyām, ghṛtaspṛgbhiḥ*, etc. In the locative plural before the affix *sup*, *vraścabhrasja*... (306), *jhalāṁ*... (67) and the *kvinpratyaya*... (303) apply. Besides, *khari ca* and *ādeśapratya*... (149) also apply and we have the form *ghṛtaspṛkṣu*. The complete declension of *ghṛtaspṛś* is given below :

	Singular	Dual	Plural
prathamā	*ghṛtaspṛk, g*	*ghṛtaspṛśau*	*ghṛtaspṛśaḥ*
dvitīyā	*ghṛtaspṛśam*	*ghṛtaspṛśau*	*ghṛtaspṛśaḥ*

tṛtīyā	*ghṛtaspṛśā*	*ghṛtaspṛgbhyām*	*ghṛtaspṛgbhiḥ*
caturthī	*ghṛtaspṛśe*	*ghṛtaspṛgbhyām*	*ghṛtaspṛgbhyaḥ*
pañcamī	*ghṛtaspṛśaḥ*	*ghṛtaspṛgbhyām*	*ghṛtaspṛgbhyaḥ*
ṣaṣṭhī	*ghṛtaspṛśaḥ*	*ghṛtaspṛśoḥ*	*ghṛtaspṛśām*
saptamī	*ghṛtaspṛśi*	*ghṛtaspṛśoḥ*	*ghṛtaspṛkṣu*
sambodhana	*he ghṛtaspṛk! he ghṛtaspṛg!*	*he ghṛtaspṛśau!*	*he ghṛtaspṛśaḥ!*

Here comes to an end the declension of the masculine nominal stems ending in the phoneme *ś*. Now begins the declensional process of the masculine nominal stems that end in *ṣ*.

लघु० – दधृक् , दधृग्। दधृषौ। दधृषः। दधृग्भ्याम्। *dadhṛk, dadhṛg. dadhṛṣau. dadhṛṣaḥ. dadhṛgbhyām.*

Eluc. : The word *dadhṛṣ* 'impudent' is irregularly derived by the rule *ṛtvig-dadhṛg...* (300) with the introduction of the affix *kvin* after the verbal root *dhṛṣ*. The reduplication is also irregular. In the declensional process of this word, mainly *jhalāṁ jaśo 'nte* (67) and *kvinpratyayasya kuḥ* (303) apply. With the application of these two rules, we have two forms in the nominative singular : *dadhṛk* and *dadhṛg* {*vā 'vasāne* (145)}. We also get *dadhṛgbhyām*, etc. before the affixes *bhyām*, etc. in the same manner. In the locative plural, when we introduce the affix *sup*, we have *dadhṛṣ + sup* --> *dadhṛṣ + su* --> *dadhṛk + su* --> {by *ṣaḍhoḥ kaḥ si* (547), the phoneme *ṣ* is replaced by *k*} --> *dadhṛk + ṣu* {the dental *s* of the affix *sup* is replaced by the cerebral *ṣ* by *ādeśapratyayayoḥ* (149)} and we get *dadhṛkṣu*. The complete declension of the word *dadhṛṣ* is as follows :

	Singular	Dual	Plural
prathamā	*dadhṛk, g*	*dadhṛṣau*	*dadhṛṣaḥ*
dvitīyā	*dadhṛṣam*	*dadhṛṣau*	*dadhṛṣaḥ*
tṛtīyā	*dadhṛṣā*	*dadhṛgbhyām*	*dadhṛgbhiḥ*
caturthī	*dadhṛṣe*	*dadhṛgbhyām*	*dadhṛgbhyaḥ*
pañcamī	*dadhṛṣaḥ*	*dadhṛgbhyām*	*dadhṛgbhyaḥ*
ṣaṣṭhī	*dadhṛṣaḥ*	*dadhṛṣoḥ*	*dadhṛṣām*

saptamī	*dadhṛṣi*	*dadhṛṣoḥ*	*dadhṛkṣu*
sambodhana	*he dadhṛk, g!*	*he dadhṛṣau!*	*he dadhṛṣaḥ!*

लघु० – रत्नमुट्, रत्नमुड् । रत्नमुषौ । रत्नमुड्भ्याम् । षट्, षड् । षड्भिः । षड्भ्यः 2 । षण्णाम् । षट्त्सु , षट्सु । *ratnamuṭ, ratnamuḍ. ratnamuṣau. ratnamuḍbhyām. ṣaṭ, ṣaḍ. ṣaḍbhiḥ. ṣaḍbhyaḥ* 2. *ṣaṇṇām. ṣaṭtsu, ṣaṭsu.*

Eluc. : The etymology of the word *ratnamuṣ* 'one who steals jewels' is *ratnāni muṣṇātīti*. It is derived with the introduction of the affix *kvip* after the verbal root *muṣ* preceded by the word *ratna* as upapada. Since it does not end in *kvin*, the rule *kvinpratyayasya kuḥ* (303) does not apply. This is how it differs from *dadhṛṣ* from the point of view of declension. By applying *jhalāṁ jaśo 'nte* (67) , the pada-final *ṣ* is first replaced by *ḍ* and then by *vā 'vasāne* (145) *ḍ* is optionally replaced by a *car*-consonant. Thus we obtain two forms in the nominative singular : *ratnamuṭ, ratnamuḍ*. When we decline it with the introduction of the affixes *bhyām, bhis*, etc., *jhalāṁ jaśo 'nte* (67) applies and we obtain *ratnamuḍbhyām, ratnamuḍbhiḥ*, etc. In the locative plural also we will have two forms. One, when the insertion of the augment *dhuṭ* takes place by the rule *ḍaḥ si dhuṭ* (86) and the other in its absence. The complete declension of *ratnamuṣ* is as follows :

	Singular	Dual	Plural
prathamā	*ratnamuṭ, ḍ*	*ratnamuṣau*	*ratnamuṣaḥ*
dvitīyā	*ratnamuṣam*	*ratnamuṣau*	*ratnamuṣaḥ*
tṛtīyā	*ratnamuṣā*	*ratnamuḍbhyām*	*ratnamuḍbhiḥ*
caturthī	*ratnamuṣe*	*ratnamuḍbhyām*	*ratnamuḍbhyaḥ*
pañcamī	*ratnamuṣaḥ*	*ratnamuḍbhyām*	*ratnamuḍbhyaḥ*
ṣaṣṭhī	*ratnamuṣaḥ*	*ratnamuṣoḥ*	*ratnamuṣām*
saptamī	*ratnamuṣi*	*ratnamuṣoḥ*	*ratnamuṭtsu* *ratnamuṭsu*
sambodhana	*he ratnamuṭ, ḍ!*	*he ratnamuṣau!*	*he ratnamuṣaḥ!*

The word *ṣaṣ* 'six' is a numeral. It is always declined in the plural and is alike in all the three genders : When we introduce either *jas* or *śas*, the luk-elision of the affix takes place by *ṣaḍbhyo luk* (187) since the stem is designated as *ṣaṭ* by *ṣṇāntāḥ ṣaṭ* (296). In *ṣaṣ* + 0, the rule *jhalāṁ jaśo 'nte* (67) prescribes the replacement of the pada-final *ṣ* by *ḍ*. Then the pada-final *ḍ* is optionally replaced by a *car*-consonant, in this case, by *ṭ* in accordance with *vā 'vasāne* (145). Thus two forms are obtained : *ṣaṭ* and *ṣaḍ* in the nominative and accusative plural. In the instrumental, dative and ablative plural, we respectively get the forms : *ṣaḍbhiḥ*, *ṣaḍbhyaḥ* and *ṣaḍbhyaḥ*.

In the genitive plural we have *ṣaṣ* + *ām*. At this stage, the augment *nuṭ* is inserted at the head of the genitive plural affix *ām* by *ṣaṭcaturbhyaśca* (265) and we have : *ṣaṣ* + *nuṭ ām* --> *ṣaṣ* + *nām*. In this situation, the pre-affixal base *ṣaṣ* gets the pada-designation by *svādiṣvasarvanāmasthāne* (163) and the pada-final *ṣ* is replaced by *ḍ* according to *jhalāṁ jaśo 'nte* (67). Now the rule *ṣṭunā ṣṭuḥ* (64) applies and the dental *n* of *nām* is replaced by the cerebral nasal stop *ṇ*. Although the phoneme *ḍ* (a denotatum of *ṭu*) is pada-final, it is replaced by *ṇ* since the prohibition prescribed by the sūtra *na padāntāṭṭoranām* (65) does not apply here as it excludes *nām* from its scope. The phoneme *ḍ* is substituted by *ṇ* obligatorily according to *pratyaye bhāṣāyāṁ nityam* (vtk 11). Thus we obtain the form *ṣaṇṇām*.

In *ṣaṣ* + *sup* --> *ṣaṣ* + *su*, the phoneme *ṣ* is replaced by *ḍ* in accordance with *jhalāṁ jaśo'nte* (67). Then by *ḍaḥ si dhuṭ* (86), the optional insertion of the augment *dhuṭ* takes place. In both the cases the rule *khari ca* (74) applies and we have two forms in the locative plural : *ṣaṭtsu* and *ṣaṭsu*. The declension of the numeral *ṣaṣ* is as follows :

	Plural		Plural
prathamā	*ṣaṭ, ḍ*	pañcamī	*ṣaḍbhyaḥ*
dvitīyā	*ṣaṭ, ḍ*	ṣaṣṭhī	*ṣaṇṇām*
tṛtīyā	*ṣaḍbhiḥ*	saptamī	*ṣaṭtsu, ṣaṭsu*
caturthī	*ṣaḍbhyaḥ*	sambodhana	no form

The word *pipaṭhiṣ* 'one who desires to read' is derived with the introduction of the affix *kvip* after the derivative verbal stem *pipaṭhiṣa* {its derivation will be explained under the sūtra *sanyaṅoḥ* (703)}. The affix *kvip* is wholly elided and the short *a*, occurring at the end of the derivative verbal root *pipaṭhiṣa*, is elided by the rule *ato lopaḥ* (469). The stem *pipaṭhiṣ* is taken as a verbal root by virtue of the paribhāṣā *kvibantā dhātutvaṁ na jahati...* (PS, p. 43). In *pipaṭhiṣ* + *su* --> *pipaṭhiṣ* + *s*, the affix *s* is elided by *halṅyābbhyo...* (178) and we get *pipaṭhiṣ*. In this grammatical situation, the rule *sasajuṣo ruḥ* Pā. 8. 2. 66 cannot apply since it is the cerebral *ṣ* that occurs at the pada-final position, and not the dental *s*. The solution to this problem has been given by Varadarāja in the Laghu as follows :

लघु॰ - रुत्वं प्रति षत्वस्यासिद्धत्वात् ससजुषो रुरिति रुत्वम्। *rutvaṁ prati ṣatvasyāsiddhatvāt sasajuṣo rur iti rutvam.*

Eluc. : The substitution of the cerebral *ṣ* in place of the dental *s* of the affix *san* has taken place by the rule *ādeśapratyayayoḥ* Pā. 8. 3. 59 which is deemed not to have taken place with respect to the sūtra *sasajuṣo ruḥ* Pā. 8. 2. 66 since the former is subsequent to the latter in the tripādī. So, the sūtra *sasajuṣo ruḥ* Pā. 8. 2. 66 applies and the pada-final *ṣ* is replaced by *ru*. After this we have *pipaṭhiru* --> *pipaṭhir* after the elision of the anubandha *u*. The word *pipaṭhir* is a pada which is constituted by a verbal root that ends in *r*. At this stage, the following sūtra applies :

(350) र्वोरुपधाया दीर्घ इकः। ***rvorupadhāyā dīrgha ikaḥ*. 8. 2. 76**
लघु॰ - रेफवान्तस्य धातोरुपधाया इको दीर्घः स्यात् पदान्ते। पिपठीः। पिपठिषौ। पिपठीर्भ्याम्। *rephavāntasya dhātor upadhāyā iko dīrghaḥ syāt padānte. pipaṭhīḥ. pipaṭhiṣau. pipaṭhīrbhyām.*

Trans. : The penultimate vowel, denoted by the abbreviatory term *ik*, of a verbal root ending in *r* or *v*, occurring at the end of a pada, is replaced by its long counterpart.

PP. *rvoḥ dhātoḥ upadhāyā dīrgha ikaḥ* (*padasya, ante*).

Eluc. : The word *dhātoḥ* is carried over from *sipi dhāto rurvā* Pā. 8. 2. 74 and it is qualified by *rvoḥ* which is an itaretaradvandva. Its analysis is as follows : *r ca v ca rvau, tayoḥ = rvoḥ*. By tadantavidhi, it comes to mean 'the verbal root that ends in *r* or *v*'. The present sūtra occurs in the domain of the governing rule *padasya* Pā. 8. 1. 16. Hence the term *padasya* recurs here. The term *ante* is carried over from *skoḥ saṁyogādyorante ca* Pā. 8. 2. 29 (BM, I, p. 439). Thus the meaning of the sūtra is as follows : In pada-final position, the penultimate vowel of a verbal root that ends in *r* or *v* is replaced by a long counterpart if this penultimate vowel is a denotatum of *ik*-pratyāhāra. The illustration *pipaṭhir* is a pada constituted by a verbal root that ends in *r*. Hence the penultimate vowel *i* is replaced by a long *ī* and we get the following derivational stage : *pipaṭhīr*. At this stage, the rule *kharava...* (93) applies and the phoneme *r* is replaced by visarga and we obtain the inflected form *pipaṭhīḥ* in the nominative singular.

When followed by the sup-affixes *bhyām, bhis, bhyas,* etc., the replacement of the pada-final *ṣ* by *ru* by the rule *sasajuṣo ruḥ* (104) and the substitution of *i* by a long *ī* by the present rule take place and we get *pipaṭhīrbhyām, pipaṭhīrbhiḥ, pipaṭhīrbhyaḥ,* etc.

When *pipaṭhiṣ* is followed by the plural affix of the seventh triplet, the following grammatical process takes place : *pipaṭhiṣ + sup --> pipaṭhiṣ + su*. Both the rules *sasajuṣo ruḥ* (104) and *rvorupadhāyā dīrgha ikaḥ* (350) apply and we arrive at the following derivational stage : *pipaṭhīr + su*. At this stage, the rules *ādeśapratyayayoḥ* Pā. 8. 3. 59 and *kharava...* Pā. 8. 3. 15 become simultaneously available. Since the former rule is subsequent to the latter and hence asiddha, the latter applies first and the phoneme *r* (*ru*) is replaced by visarga and we have *pipaṭhīḥ + su*. In this grammatical situation, the visarga optionally remains as it is by the rule *vā śari* (103). In the other alternative, it is replaced by the dental *s* according to *visarjanīyasya saḥ* (96). After this we get two forms : 1. *pipaṭhīḥsu* and 2. *pipaṭhīssu*. In these forms, there is an intervention by visarga in the first and by *s* in the second illustration between *iṇ* and the dental *s* of the affix *sup*. The rule *ādeśapratyayayoḥ* (149) causing the cerebralization of the dental *s* of the affix *sup* does not become operational because of the separation caused by this intervention. For the sake of the cerebralization of s, the following sūtra becomes applicable and takes care of the intervention in both the forms :

(351) नुम्विसर्जनीयशर्व्यवायेऽपि । *numvisarjanīyaśarvyavāye 'pi.* 8. 3. 58

लघु० - एतैः प्रत्येकं व्यवधानेऽपि इण्कुभ्यां परस्य सस्य मूर्धन्यादेशः स्यात्। ष्टुत्वेन पूर्वस्य षः। पिपठीष्षु। पिपठीःषु। चिकीः। चिकीर्षौ। चिकीर्भ्याम्। चिकीर्षु। *etaiḥ pratyekaṁ vyavadhāne 'pi iṇkubhyāṁ parasya sasya mūrdhanyādeśaḥ syāt. ṣṭutvena pūrvasya ṣaḥ. pipaṭhīṣṣu. pipaṭhīḥṣu. cikīḥ. cikīrṣau. cikīrbhyām. cikīrṣu.*

Trans. : Even when there is an intervention of anyone of these singly, namely, *num*, visarga and a sibilant , the dental *s*, occurring after the phonemes denoted by *iṇ*-pratyāhāra and *ku* (velar stops), is replaced by a cerebral substitute.

PP. *iṇkoḥ numvisarjanīyaśarvyavāye api saḥ mūrdhanyaḥ* (*apadāntasya, saṁhitāyām*).

Eluc. : The present sūtra occurs in the domain of the governing rule *iṇkoḥ* Pā. 8. 3. 57. So the compound word *iṇkoḥ*, which is in the ablative singular, recurs in this rule also. It is because of the ablative case-ending in the word *iṇkoḥ* that the cerebralization of the dental s cannot take place because of the intervention of either visarga or s. Hence the present rule is required to tide over this difficulty. The words *saḥ* and *mūrdhanyaḥ* are respectively carried over from the rules *saheḥ sāḍaḥ saḥ* Pā. 8. 3. 56 and *apadāntasya mūrdhanyaḥ* Pā. 8. 3. 55. The word *numvisarjanīyaśar-vyavāye* is an itaretaradvandva-seeded ṣaṣṭhītatpuruṣa. Its analysis is as follows : *num ca visarjanīyaś ca śar ca numvisarjanīyaśaraḥ, teṣāṁ vyavāyo numvisarjanīyaśarvyavāyaḥ, tasmin = numvisarjanīyaśarvyavāye.* The indeclinable *api* is paraphrased with every member of the dvandva compound (see Kāśikā on the present sūtra). The word *vyavāya* is also paraphrased with every member of the dvandva samāsa, since it occurs at its end. That the rule allows only a single intervention of any one of these three, *num,* visarga and a sibilant, is clear from the statement of the Mahābhāṣya : *pratyekaṁ vyavāyaśabdaḥ parisamāpyate* (Mbh on this sūtra). In this way, the meaning of the sūtra is as follows : The dental s coming after the phonemes denoted by the abbreviatory term *iṇ* and the velar stops (*ku*) is replaced by a cerebral ṣ even when there is an intervention of either *num* or visarga or a sibilant.

In the illustrations 1. *pipaṭhīḥsu* and 2. *pipaṭhīssu,* there is an intervention by visarga in the first and by a sibilant in the second. The condition prescribed by the rule is that if there is an intervention by a single element out of the three, namely, *num,* visarga and a sibilant, the process of cerebralization takes place. In the illustrations given above, the condition for the process of cerebralization is available. Thus we obtain the form *pipaṭhīḥṣu* in the first illustration. In the second illustration, the replacement of the dental s of *pipaṭhīs* by a cerebral ṣ takes place by *ṣṭunā ṣṭuḥ* (64) and we get *pipaṭhīs su* --> *pipaṭhīṣṣu.* The complete declension of *pipaṭhiṣ* is given below :

	Singular	Dual	Plural
prathamā	*pipaṭhīḥ*	*pipaṭhiṣau*	*pipaṭhiṣaḥ*
dvitīyā	*pipaṭhiṣam*	*pipaṭhiṣau*	*pipaṭhiṣaḥ*
tṛtīyā	*pipaṭhiṣā*	*pipaṭhīrbhyām*	*pipaṭhīrbhiḥ*
caturthī	*pipaṭhiṣe*	*pipaṭhīrbhyām*	*pipaṭhīrbhyaḥ*
pañcamī	*pipaṭhiṣaḥ*	*pipaṭhīrbhyām*	*pipaṭhīrbhyaḥ*
ṣaṣṭhī	*pipaṭhiṣaḥ*	*pipaṭhiṣoḥ*	*pipaṭhiṣām*
saptamī	*pipaṭhiṣi*	*pipaṭhiṣoḥ*	*pipaṭhīḥṣu* *pipaṭhīṣṣu*
sambodhana	*he pipaṭhīḥ!*	*he pipaṭhiṣau!*	*he pipaṭhiṣaḥ!*

The word *cikīrṣ* 'one who desires to do something' ends in the affix *kvip* introduced after the derivative verbal stem *cikīrṣa* {(*kṛ* + *san*) : its derivation will be explained under the sūtra *iko jhal* (706)}. The short *a* at the end of the derivative verbal stem is elided by *ato lopaḥ* (469) and thus we get the primary derivative *cikīrṣ* which gets the prātipadika designation by *kṛttaddhitasamāsāśca* (116). When we introduce the nominative singular affix *su*, we have : *cikīrṣ* + *su* --> *cikīrṣ* + *s*. After the elision of the affix *s*(*u*) by *halṅyābbhyo...* (178), the rule *saṁyogāntasya lopaḥ* (20) becomes applicable, but the restrictive rule *rātsasya* (208) prescribes that if a conjunct-final phoneme is to be elided after *r*, it is only the phoneme *s* that is elided. However, in the present case, the elision by *rātsasya* (208) takes place by treating the cerebral *ṣ* of *cikīrṣ* as the dental *s* since the cerebralizaion of the *s* of the affix *san* by *ādeśa-pratyayayoḥ* Pā. 8. 3. 59 is deemed not to have taken place with respect to *rātsasya* Pā. 8. 2. 24. The rule *kharava...* (93) prescribes visarga in place of the pada-final *r* and we obtain *cikīḥ* in the nominative singular. In the forms *cikīrbhyām*, *cikīrbhiḥ*, etc. the phoneme *ṣ* is elided by *rātsasya* as explained just now. In the locative plural, the repha is not replaced by visarga on account of restrictive rule *roḥ supi* (267) which prescribes visarga only in place of *ru* when the affix *sup* follows. The complete declension of *cikīrṣ* is as follows :

	Singular	Dual	Plural
prathamā	*cikīḥ*	*cikīrṣau*	*cikīrṣaḥ*
dvitīyā	*cikīrṣam*	*cikīrṣau*	*cikīrṣaḥ*
tṛtīyā	*cikīrṣā*	*cikīrbhyām*	*cikīrbhiḥ*
caturthī	*cikīrṣe*	*cikīrbhyām*	*cikīrbhyaḥ*
pañcamī	*cikīrṣaḥ*	*cikīrbhyām*	*cikīrbhyaḥ*
ṣaṣṭhī	*cikīrṣaḥ*	*cikīrṣoḥ*	*cikīrṣām*
saptamī	*cikīrṣi*	*cikīrṣoḥ*	*cikīrṣu*
sambodhana	*he cikīḥ!*	*he cikīrṣau!*	*he cikīrṣaḥ!*

Here comes to an end the declension of the masculine nominal stems that end in the cerebral phoneme *ṣ*.

Now begins the declensional process of the nominal stems that end in the dental phoneme *s*.

लघु० – विद्वान्। विद्वांसौ। हे विद्वन्! *vidvān. vidvāṁsau. he vidvan!*

Eluc. : The word *vidvas* 'wise' is formed with the introduction of the affix *śatṛ* after the verbal stem *vid* 'to know'. The affix *śatṛ* is optionally replaced by *vasu* according to the rule *videḥ śaturvasuḥ* (830) and we obtain the form *vidvas* which is ugit since the vowel *u*, in the affix *vasu*, is *it*. The alternative form is *vidan*. It is the former form *vidvas*, which is being declined in the masculine here.

In the nominative singular *vidvas* + s(*u*), the rule *ugidacām...* (288) prescribes the insertion of *num* and we have the following grammatical situation : *vidva n s* + *s* (<-- *vidva num s* + *s*). At this stage, the rule *sānta mahataḥ saṁyogasya* (341) applies and the penultimate vowel preceding the consonant *n* forming a conjunct ending in the phoneme *s* is replaced by a long counterpart and we obtain the form *vidvān* after the elision of the affix s(*u*) by *halṅyābbhyo dīrghāt...* (178) and the conjunct-final *s* by *saṁyogāntasya lopaḥ* (20). The pada-final *n* is not elided by *na lopaḥ prātipadikāntasya* Pā. 8. 2. 7 since the elision of the conjunct-final consonant by *saṁyogāntasya lopaḥ* Pā. 8. 2. 23 is deemed not to have taken place with respect to it. In the vocative singular, the rule *sānta mahataḥ saṁyogasya* (341) does not apply because of the condition *asambuddhau* and we get the form *he vidvan!*

With the nominative dual affix *au* added after *vidvas*, the augment *num* is inserted in the same manner. We have *vidva num s* + *au* --> *vidva n s* + *au*. At this stage, the rule *sānta mahataḥ...* (341) applies and the penultimate vowel preceding the consonant *n* is replaced by a long counterpart. We get the form *vidvāṁsau* after the consonant *n* is replaced with anusvāra (*ṁ*) by *naścāpadāntasya jhali* (78). The forms like *vidvāṁsaḥ*, etc. are declined in a similar manner.

With the plural affix of the second triplet, the word *vidvas* undergoes the following grammatical situation : *vidvas* + *śas* --> *vidvas* + *as* after the elision of the anubandha *ś*. In this situation, the pre-affixal base gets the bha-designation by *yaci bham* (164) and the following sūtra presents itself for application :

(352) वसोः सम्प्रसारणम्। ***vasoḥ samprasāraṇam*. 6. 4. 131**

लघु० – वस्वन्तस्य भस्य सम्प्रसारणं स्यात्। विदुषः। वसुस्रंसु... (261) इति दः। विद्वद्भ्याम्। *vasvantasya bhasya samprasāraṇaṁ syāt. viduṣaḥ. vasusraṁsu...* (261) *iti daḥ. vidvadbhyām.*

Trans. : Let the pre-affixal base (*aṅga*), ending in the affix *vasu* and designated as *bha*, undergo samprasāraṇa.

PP. *vasoḥ bhasya aṅgasya samprasāraṇam.*

Eluc. : The present sūtra occurs in the domain of two governing rules *bhasya* Pā. 6. 4. 120 and *aṅgasya* Pā. 6. 4. 1. So, both the words recur in the present sūtra which thus comes to mean as follows : If the pre-affixal base is designated as *bha* that ends in the affix *vasu* (by sthānivadbhāva), then it should undergo samprasāraṇa.

In the illustration *vidvas + as*, if we keep in mind the implication of the rule *na samprasāraṇe samprasāraṇam* (290), then the second vakāra undergoes samprasāraṇa and consequently the semi-vowel *v* is replaced by *u* denoted by *ik* and we have the following grammatical situation : *vid u a s + as*. By the rule *samprasāraṇācca* (257), a single replacement in the form of the preceding, that is *u* comes in place of the both *u* and *a* and we arrive at : *vidus + as*. At this stage, the rule *ādeśapratyayayoḥ* (149) applies and the dental *s* of the affix (or substitute) *vas* is replaced by *ṣ* and we obtain the form *viduṣaḥ* in the accusative plural after rutva and visarga.

When followed by the affixes *bhyām, bhis,* etc., the dental *s* of the stem *vidvas* is replaced by the phoneme *d* in accordance with the rule *vasusraṁsudhvaṁsvanuḍuhāṁ daḥ* (261) and we get the declensional forms *vidvadbhyām, vidvadbhiḥ*, etc. In the locative plural, the substituted phoneme *d* is replaced by *t* according to *khari ca* (93). The declension of the word *vidvas* is as follows :

	Singular	Dual	Plural
prathamā	*vidvān*	*vidvāṁsau*	*vidvāṁsaḥ*
dvitīyā	*vidvāṁsam*	*vidvāṁsau*	*viduṣaḥ*
tṛtīyā	*viduṣā*	*vidvadbhyām*	*vidvadbhiḥ*
caturthī	*viduṣe*	*vidvadbhyām*	*vidvadbhyaḥ*
pañcamī	*viduṣaḥ*	*vidvadbhyām*	*vidvadbhyaḥ*
ṣaṣṭhī	*viduṣaḥ*	*viduṣoḥ*	*viduṣām*
saptamī	*viduṣi*	*viduṣoḥ*	*vidvatsu*
sambodhana	*he vidvan!*	*he vidvāṁsau!*	*he vidvāṁsaḥ!*

(353) पुंसोऽसुङ् । *puṁso 'suṅ*. **7. 1. 89**

लघु० – सर्वनामस्थाने विवक्षिते पुंसोऽसुङ् स्यात्। पुमान्। हे पुमन्! पुमांसौ। पुंसः। पुंभ्याम्। पुंसु। *sarvanāmasthāne vivakṣite puṁso 'suṅ syāt. pumān. he puman! pumāṁsau. puṁsaḥ. puṁbhyām. puṁsu.*

Trans. : Let the word *puṁs* 'a man' be replaced by the substitute *asuṅ*, when a sarvanāmasthāna affix is to be introduced after it.

PP. *sarvanāmasthāne puṁsaḥ asuṅ* (*aṅgasya*).

Eluc. : The word *puṁs* is derived with the introduction of the affix *ḍumsun* by *pāterḍumsun* (Uṇādi Sūtra, 617) after the verbal stem *pūñ* 'to purify'. There are three anubandhas in the affix *ḍumsun* : the phoneme *ḍ* by *cuṭū* (128) (not the whole segment *ḍu* by *ādirñiṭuḍavaḥ* (461) because of the mention of *bahulam* in the rule *uṇādayo bahulam* Pā. 3. 3. 1), the vowel *u* following the consonant s and the final consonant *n*. The affix *ḍumsun*, being *ḍit*, occasions the elision of *ū* (*ṭi*) of *pū* and we have *puṁs* after the application of *naścāpadāntasya*... (78).

The term *sarvanāmasthāne* is carried over from *ito 'tsarvanāmasthāne* Pā. 7.1. 86. The seventh case-ending in *sarvanāmasthāne* denotes the domain (*viṣaya*). In other words, it is viṣayasaptamī which is contrasted with the parasaptamī that requires the thing mentioned with the locative case-ending to be present in front (cf. Dictionary, p. 363). That is why Varadarāja uses the expression *vivakṣite* in his vṛtti, which means 'when a sarvanāmasthāna affix is intended to be introduced after the stem *puṁs* (not actually added)', the final phoneme of the stem is replaced by *asuṅ*. Had the seventh case-ending been construed as parasaptamī, then the vowel *u* in the compound *paramapuṁs* would have got the acute accent by the rule *samāsasya* Pā. 6. 1. 223 before the replacement by *asuṅ*. The reason is that the rule *samāsasya* requires fewer conditions to be fulfilled than the present rule. On the other hand, if the locative case-ending is construed as viṣayasaptamī, then the replacement by *asuṅ* takes place as soon as a sarvanāmasthāna affix is intended to be introduced after the stem *puṁs*, not actually added. The rule *samāsasya* would become applicable afterwards thereby making the vowel *a* following the phoneme *m* have an acute accent, which is desirable.[1] Thus the meaning of the sūtra will be as follows : When a sarvanāmasthāna affix is intended to be added after the word *puṁs*, the final phoneme *s* of *puṁs* is replaced by *asuṅ*. Although the substitute consists of more than one phoneme, it still replaces the final consonant s of *puṁs* since the substitute has *ṅ* as *it* {cf. *ṅicca* (46)}. So we get the form *pumas* after the elision of anubandhas. Since the final consonant s has been

1. *nanu tatpuruṣāt paramapuṁsśabdāt suṭi asuṅādeśāt prāg eva samāsasya ityantodāttatvaṁ pakārād ukārasya syāt. sarvanāmasthānotpatteḥ prāg eva samāsasvarasya antaraṅgatvāt prāpteḥ. iṣyate tu asuṅi kṛte paramapumas ityatra makārād akārasya. ata āha vivakṣita iti. puṁso'suṅ ityatra sarvanāmasthāne iti na parasaptamī kiṁ tu vivakṣite ityadhyāhṛtya sarvanāmasthāne prayoktum iṣṭe sati tataḥ prāg eva asuṅ ityartha āśrīyate. evaṁ ca sarvanāmasthānotpatteḥ prāgeva asuṅi kṛte samāsasya ityantodāttatvaṁ paramapumas ityatra makārād akārasya bhavatīti na doṣaḥ.* BM, I, p. 446.

replaced by *as*, the anusvāra is restored to its original state, that is, to *m* in deference to the principle : *nimittāpāye naimittikasyāpyapāyaḥ* (PS, p. 158) 'When the cause has been destroyed, the modification brought about by that cause is also destroyed'. The 'destruction' in this context means 'restoration to its original form'. Here the consonant *s*, which caused the phoneme *m* to be replaced by anusvāra by *naścāpadāntasya jhali* (78), is no longer there. As such, the anusvāra is restored to its original state, that is *m*. Thus we have *pumas*. As we introduce the nominative singular affix after it, we have : *pumas* + *su* in the nominative singular. At this stage, the rule *ugidacām...* (288) applies and the augment *num* is inserted after the last vowel : *puma num s* + *su* --> *puma n s* + *s*. By *sānta mahataḥ...* (341), the penultimate vowel preceding the phoneme *n* is replaced by a long counterpart and we reach the following stage : *pumān s* + *s*. Now the affix *su* is elided by *halṅyābbhyo...* (178) and the conjunct-final *s* is elided by *saṁyogāntasya lopaḥ* (20). We obtain the form *pumān*. In the vocative singular, the rule *sānta mahataḥ...* (341) does not apply and we have the form *he puman!*

When the affix *śas*, etc. are introduced, the replacement by *asuṅ* does not take place and we get the forms like *puṁs* + *śas* --> *puṁs* + *as* --> *puṁsas* --> *puṁsaḥ*, *puṁs* + *ṭā* --> *puṁs* + *ā* --> *puṁsā*, etc. When followed by the affixes *bhyām*, *bhis*, etc., the rule *saṁyogānta...* (20) prescribes the elision of the conjunct-final *s* and in accordance with the principle : *nimittāpāye naimittikasyāpyapāyaḥ*, the anusvāra is restored to its original form, that is *m*. We reach the following stage : *puṁs* + *bhyām* --> *pum* + *bhyām*. Now the rules *mo 'nusvāraḥ* (77) and *vā padāntasya* (80) apply and we obtain two inflected forms : *puṁbhyām* and *pumbhyām*. In these illustrations, the stem *puṁs* gets the pada-designation by *svādiṣvasarva...* (163). This is the reason why *saṁyogānta...* (20) and *vā padāntasya* (80) apply. When the plural affix of the seventh triplet is introduced, the rule *saṁyogāntasya...* (20) applies. The anusvāra is restored to its original form : *puṁs* + *sup* --> *pum* + *sup* --> *pum* + *su*. Now the rule *mo 'nusvāraḥ* (77) applies but *vā padāntasya* (80) does not, since no *yay*-consonant follows. The other important point, to be taken note of in this regard, is that the dental *s* of the affix *sup* is not replaced by the cerebral *ṣ* by *numvisarjanīya...* (351). The reason is that the intervention by anusvāra, which has replaced the augment *num*, is exempted by *numvisarjanīya...* (351), while the one in *puṁs* does not belong to *num* but is derived from the phoneme *m* in *pums*.[1] Thus we get the form *puṁsu*. The complete declension of the nominal stem *puṁs* will be as follows :

---

1. *atra yayparatvābhāvān na parasavarṇaḥ. numsthānikānusvārasyaivopalakṣaṇād numvisarjanīya - iti ṣatvaṁ neti bhāvaḥ*, BM, I, p. 447.

	Singular	Dual	Plural
prathamā	*pumān*	*pumāṁsau*	*pumāṁsaḥ*
dvitīyā	*pumāṁsam*	*pumāṁsau*	*puṁsaḥ*
tṛtīyā	*puṁsā*	*pumbhyām,* *puṁbhyām*	*pumbhiḥ,* *puṁbhiḥ*
caturthī	*puṁse*	*pumbhyām,* *puṁbhyām*	*pumbhyaḥ,* *puṁbhyaḥ*
pañcamī	*puṁsaḥ*	*pumbhyām,* *puṁbhyām*	*pumbhyaḥ,* *puṁbhyaḥ*
ṣaṣṭhī	*puṁsaḥ*	*puṁsoḥ*	*puṁsām*
saptamī	*puṁsi*	*puṁsoḥ*	*puṁsu*
sambodhana	*he puman!*	*he pumāṁsau!*	*he pumāṁsaḥ!*

The next masculine word that is going to be discussed is *uśanas* 'Śukrācārya'.

लघु० – ऋदुशनस्० इत्यनङ् । उशना । उशनसौ । *ṛduśanas... ityanaṅ. uśanā. uśanasau.*

Eluc. : To decline the nominal stem *uśanas* with the singular affix of the first triplet, we add *su* after it : *uśanas + su*. The rule *ṛduśanas...* (204) prescribes the substitute *anaṅ* to come in place of the phoneme *s* and we have *uśana anaṅ + su* --> *uśana an* + s (after the elision of anubandhas). At this stage, the rule *ato guṇe* (273) applies and a single replacement in the form of the guṇa vowel *a* comes in place of both the akāras and we reach the following grammatical situation : *uśanan + s*. Now the penultimate vowel of the pre-affixal base that ends in *n* is replaced by a long counterpart --> *uśanān* + s. The affix s(*u*) is elided by *halṅyābbhyo...* (178), the elision of the pada-final *n* takes place by *na lopaḥ...* (179) and we obtain the form *uśanā*. We get *uśanasau* just by adding dual affix of the first triplet, that is, *au* after the nominal stem *uśanas*.

28. वा० – अस्य सम्बुद्धौ वाऽनङ् नलोपश्च वा वाच्यः ।[1] *asya sambuddhau vā 'naṅ nalopaśca vā vācyaḥ.*

1. The authenticity of the present vārttika is doubtful according to Vāsudeva Dīkṣita : *bhāṣyādṛṣṭatvād idam aprāmāṇikam eveti prāmāṇikāḥ.* BM, I, p. 448.

लघु० – हे उशन! हे उशनन्! हे उशनः! हे उशनसौ! उशनोभ्याम्। उशनःसु, उशनस्सु।
he uśana! he uśanan! he uśanaḥ! he uśanasau! uśanobhyām. uśanaḥsu, uśanassu.

Tran. : When the vocative singular affix *su* follows, it should be stated that *anaṅ* is optionally the substitute of this word (*uśanas*) and the consonant *n* is optionally elided.

Eluc. : In the context of the illustration : *he uśanas* + *s*(*u*), the present vārttika prescribes two optional grammatical operations : 1. the optional replacement of the stem-final consonant s by *anaṅ*, 2. the optional elision of the consonant *n*. When we optionally replace the consonant s by *anaṅ*, we obtain two forms in the following way : *uśana anaṅ* + s --> *uśanan* + s {*ato guṇe* (273)} --> *uśanan* (after elision of *su*). Now because of the optional elision of *n*, the two forms which we obtain are : *he uśanan!* and *he uśana!* In the absence of the replacement by *anaṅ* we get one form as follows : *he uśanas* + *s*(*u*). Here the affix *su* is elided by *halṅyābbhyo...* (178). Then the pada-final s is replaced by *ru* {*sasajuṣo ruḥ* (104)} and *ru* by visarga according to *kharava...* (93). Thus we obtain *he uśanaḥ!* In all we have three forms in the vocative singular by virtue of this vārttika : *he uśanan! he uśana!* and *he uśanaḥ!*

When *uśanas* is followed by the affixes *bhyām*, etc., the rules *sasajuṣo ruḥ* (104), *haśi ca* (106) and *ādguṇaḥ* (27) apply and we get the forms *uśanobhyām*, etc. In the locative plural *uśanas* + *su*, first by the rules *sasajuṣo ruḥ* (104) and *kharava...* (93) we have visarga in place of the consonant s. Then by *vā śari*, the visarga optionally remains as visarga. In the alternative, the visarga is replaced by s and we obtain two forms, *uśanaḥsu* and *uśanassu* in the locative plural. The complete declension of *uśanas* is as follows :

	Singular	Dual	Plural
prathamā	*uśanā*	*uśanasau*	*uśanasaḥ*
dvitīyā	*uśanasam*	*uśanasau*	*uśanasah*
tṛtīyā	*uśanasā*	*uśanobhyām,*	*uśanobhiḥ*
caturthī	*uśanase*	*uśanobhyām,*	*uśanobhyaḥ*
pañcamī	*uśanasaḥ*	*uśanobhyām,*	*uśanobhyaḥ*
ṣaṣṭhī	*uśanasaḥ*	*uśanasoḥ*	*uśanasām*

saptamī	*uśanasi*	*uśanasoḥ*	*uśanaḥsu* *uśanassu*
sambodhana	*he uśanan!* *uśana! uśanaḥ!*	*he uśanasau!*	*he uśanasaḥ!*

लघु० – अनेहा । अनेहसौ । हे अनेहः ! वेधाः । वेधसौ । हे वेधः ! *anehā. anehasau. he anehaḥ! vedhāḥ. vedhasau. he vedhaḥ!*

Eluc. : The word *anehas* 'time' is declined like *uśanas* except that in the vocative singular it has only one form *he anehaḥ!* because the vārttika prescribing *anaṅ* is not applicable in this case. In this illustration, the elision of *s*(*u*) takes place by *halṅyābbhyo dīrghāt sutisyapṛktaṁ hal* (178). The pada-final *s* is replaced by *ru* according to *sasajuṣo ruḥ* (104) and *r*(*u*) is replaced by visarga in accordance with *kharavasānayor visarjanīyaḥ* (93). As far as the declension of *vedhas* 'creator, brahmā' is concerned, it is like that of *anehas* except in the nominative singular. In the nominative singular, *vedhas* + *su*, the rule *atvasantasya...* (342) applies and the penultimate vowel is replaced by a long counterpart --> *vedhās* + *su*. After this, the single consonant-affix *s*(*u*) is elided by *halṅyābbhyo dīrghāt sutisyapṛktaṁ hal* (178). The pada-final *s* is replaced by *ru* and then visarga replaces *r*(*u*) by *kharavasānayorvisarjanīyaḥ* (93) and thus we obtain *vedhāḥ* in the nominative singular. The declension of both the words is given below :

anehas

	Singular	Dual	Plural
prathamā	*anehā*	*anehasau*	*anehasaḥ*
dvitīyā	*anehasam*	*anehasau*	*anehasaḥ*
tṛtīyā	*anehasā*	*anehobhyām,*	*anehobhiḥ*
caturthī	*anehase*	*anehobhyām,*	*anehobhyaḥ*
pañcamī	*anehasaḥ*	*anehobhyām,*	*anehobhyaḥ*
ṣaṣṭhī	*anehasaḥ*	*anehasoḥ*	*anehasām*
saptamī	*anehasi*	*anehasoḥ*	*anehaḥsu* *anehassu*
sambodhana	*he anehaḥ!*	*he anehasau!*	*he anehasaḥ!*

vedhas

	Singular	Dual	Plural
prathamā	*vedhāḥ*	*vedhasau*	*vedhasaḥ*
dvitīyā	*vedhasam*	*vedhasau*	*vedhasaḥ*
tṛtīyā	*vedhasā*	*vedhobhyām,*	*vedhobhiḥ*
caturthī	*vedhase*	*vedhobhyām,*	*vedhobhyaḥ*
pañcamī	*vedhasaḥ*	*vedhobhyām,*	*vedhobhyaḥ*
ṣaṣṭhī	*vedhasaḥ*	*vedhasoḥ*	*vedhasām*
saptamī	*vedhasi*	*vedhasoḥ*	*vedhaḥsu* *vedhassu*
sambodhana	*he vedhaḥ!*	*he vedhasau!*	*he vedhasaḥ!*

(354) अदस औ सुलोपश्च । *adasa au sulopaśca.* 7. 2. 107

लघु० - अदस औत् स्यात् सौ परे सुलोपश्च । तदोः० (309) इति सः । असौ । त्यदाद्यत्वम् । पररूपत्वम् । वृद्धिः । *adasa aut syāt sau pare sulopaś ca. tadoḥ...* (309) *iti saḥ. asau. tyadādyatvam. pararūpatvam. vṛddhiḥ.*

Trans. : When the affix *su* follows, let the consonant *s* at the end of the pronominal stem *adas* be replaced by *au*(*t*) and the affix *su* elided.

PP. *sau adasaḥ au sulopaḥ ca (vibhaktau, aṅgasya).*

Eluc. : The word *sau* is carried from *tadoḥ saḥ sāvanantyayoḥ* Pā. 7. 2. 106. The term *au* used in the sūtra is without any case-ending (*au ityavibhaktikanirdeśaḥ*, BM, I, p. 448). There are two versions of Varadarāja's vṛtti on this sūtra. The other version, which tallies with that of the Siddhāntakaumudī, is as follows : *adasa aukāro 'ntādeśaḥ syāt sau pare sulopaś ca* (GP edition, p. 68), which, I think, may be preferred to that given in NS edition, p. 39 which I have followed here. The use of the term *aut* in the vṛtti is enigmatic. That is why the consonant *t* has been put in the parentheses in the 'translation'. The compound word *sulopaḥ* is a ṣaṣṭhītatpuruṣa. Its analysis is *sor lopaḥ sulopaḥ*. The sūtra yields the following meaning : The final consonant *s* of the pronominal stem *adas* is to be replaced by *au* when the affix *su* follows. The replacement by *au*, in this case, precludes the *a*-replacement by *tyadādīnāmaḥ* (192). This means that when the rule *tyadādīnāmaḥ* (192) becomes available for application, the present rule applies. In the illustration *adas* + *su*, the rule *tyadādīnāmaḥ* (192) is debarred and the present rule prescribes the replacement of *s* by *au* and the elision of the affix *su*. Thus we have : *ada au*. Now the rule *vṛddhireci* (33) applies and we reach the derivational stage : *adau*. At this stage, the elided affix *su* is considered to be effective according to the rule *pratyayalope pratyayalakṣaṇam* (189). Consequently, the rule *tadoḥ saḥ sāvanantyayoḥ* (309) applies. The phoneme *d* is replaced by *s* and we obtain the form *asau* in the nominative singular. At the derivational stage : *adau*, the rule *adaso 'ser dādu do maḥ* Pā. 8. 2. 80 also becomes available for application, but it does not apply since it is deemed to be suspended (*asiddha*) with respect to the rule *tadoḥ saḥ sāvanantyayoḥ* Pā. 7. 2. 106.

To decline *adas* in nominative dual, we have *adas* + *au*. Now, the rule *tyadādīnāmaḥ* (192) applies. We get *ada a* + *au*. By the rule *ato guṇe* (273), we get *ada* + *au* and then by *vṛddhireci* (33), we have : *adau*. At this stage, the following sūtra applies :

(355) **अदसोऽसेर्दादु दो मः । *adaso 'serdādu do maḥ*. 8. 2. 80**
लघु० – अदसोऽसान्तस्य दात् परस्य उदूतौ स्तो दस्य मश्च । आन्तरतम्याद् ह्रस्वस्य – उः, दीर्घस्य – ऊः । अमू । जसः शी (152) । गुणः । *adaso 'sāntasya dāt parasya udūtau sto dasya maś ca. āntaratamyād hrasvasya – uḥ, dīrghasya – ūḥ. amū. jasaḥ śī* (152). *guṇaḥ.*

Trans. : The short *u* or the long *ū* replaces the vowel that follows the phoneme *d* of *adas*, which does not end in *s*, and the phoneme *d* is replaced by *m*. On the basis of similarity, the short vowel is to be replaced by *u* and the long one, by *ū*.

PP. *aseḥ adasaḥ dāt u daḥ maḥ* (*padasya*).

Eluc. : The word *aseḥ* is a bahuvrīhi compound which is analysed as : *na asti siḥ yasmin asiḥ, tasya = aseḥ*. The vowel *i* after the phoneme *s* is to facilitate the articulation. The vowel *u* means both the short *u* and long *ū* since it is a samāhāradvandva and is analysed as : *uś ca ūś ca u*. The word *aseḥ* qualifies *adasaḥ*, which means that these replacements in respect of *adas* take place when it ceases to end in *s*. The meaning of the sūtra is as follows : When the pronominal stem *adas* ceases to end in *s*, the short vowel following *d* is replaced by *u* and the long, by *ū* and the *d* of *adas* is replaced by *m*. That the short *u* will replace the short vowel that follows *d* and the long *ū* will be the replacement if the vowel that follows *d* is long, has been said on the basis of similarity based on duration (*pramāṇakṛta āntarya*, see supra, p. 26 for explanation)

In the illustration *adau*, the vowel following *d* is a long one. Hence it will be replaced by a long *ū* and the phoneme *d* is substituted by *m* and we obtain the form *amū*.

When we introduce the affix *jas* after *adas*, we apply the rules *tyadādīnāmaḥ* (192) and *ato guṇe* (273) in the same manner as above and we arrive at *ada* + *jas*. At this stage, the rule *jasaḥ śī* (151) applies. After the application of *ādguṇaḥ* (27), we reach the following derivational stage: *ade* (<-- *ada* + *ī* <-- *ada* + *śī* <-- *ada* + *jas*). Now the present rule (355) becomes available for application but the following sūtra, which is an exception to it, applies :

(356) एत ईद्‌ बहुवचने । *eta īd bahuvacane.* 8. 2. 81

लघु० – अदसो दात्‌ परस्य एत ईद्‌ दस्य च मो बह्वर्थोक्तौ । अमी । पूर्वत्रासिद्धम्‌ (31) इति विभक्तिकार्यं प्राक्‌, पश्चाद्‌ उत्वमत्वे । अमुम्‌। अमू। अमून्‌। मुत्वे कृते घिसंज्ञायां नाभावः । *adaso dāt parasya eta īd dasya ca mo bahvarthoktau. amī. pūrvatrāsiddham* (31) *iti vibhaktikāryaṁ prāk, paścād utvamatve. amum. amū. amūn. mutve kṛte ghisaṁjñāyāṁ nābhāvaḥ.*

Trans. : The vowel *et* occurring after the phoneme *d* of *adas* is to be replaced by *īd* and *d* by *m* when plurality of things is to be expressed.

PP. *adasaḥ dāt etu īd bahuvacane daḥ maḥ* (*padasya*).

Eluc. : The words *adasaḥ*, *dāt*, *daḥ* and *maḥ* are carried over from *adaso 'serdādu do maḥ* Pā. 8. 2. 80. The compound *bahuvacane* is a ṣaṣṭhītatpuruṣa which is analysed as *bahūnām vacanam, bahuvacanam, tasmin* = *bahuvacane*. Thus the sūtra means : When a plurality of things is to be expressed, the vowel *e* following the phoneme *d* of *adas* is to be substituted by a long *ī* and *d* is to be replaced by *m*, provided the pronominal stem *adas* ceases to end in the consonant *s*. In the illustration *ade*, the vowel *e* is replaced by *ī* and the phoneme *d* by *m* and we finally obtain the form *amī* in the nominative plural.

After the application of *tyadādīnāmaḥ* (192) and *ato guṇe* (273), the declensional stage *adas* + *am* changes to *ada* + *am*. At this stage, the rules *ami pūrvaḥ* Pā. 6. 1. 103 and *adaso 'serdādu do maḥ* Pā. 8. 2. 80 become simultaneously applicable. The latter rule belongs to the tripādī and hence is deemed to be suspended (*asiddha*) so far as the rules which occur in the seven chapters and a quarter are concerned. So, the rules that precede the tripādī and concern the declensional process in this context apply first according to the view that considers the rule to be suspended (*śāstrāsiddha*).[1] However, the view according to which the operation of the rule is to be considered as suspended (*kāryāsiddha*) is not followed in this context. So, first the rule *ami pūrvaḥ* Pā. 6. 1. 103 applies and we get *adam*. It is at this stage that the rule *adaso 'serdādu do maḥ* Pā. 8. 2. 80 applies and after the replacement of *a* and *d* by *u* and *m* respectively we obtain the form *amum*.

With the plural affix *śas* of the second triplet, we have *adas* + *śas*. After the application of *tyadādīnāmaḥ* (192) and *ato guṇe* (273), we reach the following stage : *ada* + *śas* --> *ada* + *as*. By virtue of *pūrvatrāsiddham* Pā. 8. 2. 1, the rule *adaso 'serdādu do maḥ* Pā. 8. 2. 80 is understood to be suspended with respect to *prathamayoḥ pūrvasavarṇaḥ* Pā. 6. 1. 102 and *tasmācchaso naḥ puṁsi* Pā. 6. 1. 103. So, the rules preceding the rule *pūrvatrāsiddham* Pā. 8. 2. 1 will apply first. As a consequence, a single long vowel substitution homogeneous with that which precedes and the replacement of *s* by *n* take place and we get the derivational form *adān*. This is the stage where the rule *adaso 'serdādu do maḥ* Pā. 8. 2. 80 applies and the replacement of *ā* by *ū* and of *d* by *m* takes place and we obtain the form *amūn* in the accusative plural.

In *adas* + *ṭā*, we have the following grammatical process : *ada a* + *ā* {s is replaced with *a* by *tyadādīnāmaḥ* (192)} --> *ada* + *ā* {pararūpa by *ato guṇe*(273)}. Since *adaso 'ser...* Pā. 8. 2. 80 is asiddha, the rule *ṭāṅasiṅasām inātsyāḥ* Pā. 7. 1. 12 prescribes *ina*-replacement in place of *ṭā*, but if the *ina*-replacement takes place by *ṭāṅasi...* (139) in this case, then the rule *na mu ne* (358) would be rendered redundant. It is to avoid this undesirable contingency that the rule *adaso 'ser...* (356) applies first and the vowel *a* following *d* is replaced by *u* and *d* itself is replaced by *m*. After this grammatical operation, we arrive at the following situation : *amu* + *ā*. It is at this stage that the following sūtra ensues :

(357) न मु ने । *na mu ne*. 8. 2. 3

लघु० - ना-भावे कर्तव्ये कृते च मुभावो नासिद्धः। अमुना। अमूभ्याम् 3। अमीभिः। अमुष्मै। अमीभ्यः 2। अमुष्मात्। अमुष्य। अमुयोः 2। अमीषाम्। अमुष्मिन्। अमीषु।
nā-bhāve kartavye kṛte ca mubhāvo nāsiddhaḥ. amunā, amūbhyām 3. *amībhiḥ. amuṣmai. amībhyaḥ* 2. *amuṣmāt. amuṣya. amuyoḥ* 2. *amīṣām. amuṣmin. amīṣu.*

Trans. : When the replacement (of *ṭā*) by *nā* has taken place or is to take place, the replacement by *mu* is not to be regarded as if it had not been effected.

1. For a detailed explanation of the śāstrāsiddha and kāryāsiddha views, see Rama Nath Sharma, VI, pp. 475-76. Also cf. TB, I, pp. 450-51 and KN, VI, pp. 329-30.

PP. *na mu ne asiddham.*

Eluc. : The word *asiddham* is carried over from *pūrvatrāsiddham* Pā. 8. 2. 1. The word *mu* is a samāhāra dvandva which is analysed as follows : *m ca uś ca, mu.* This term denotes both the replacements : *m* in place of *d* and *u* in place of *a*. The word *ne* is a locative form of the word *nā*. The seventh case-ending here is construed both as viṣayasaptamī and parasaptamī. This is reflected in the translation of the vṛtti. The meaning of the sūtra is as follows : When the replacement by *nā* has taken place (parasaptamī interpretation) or is to take place (viṣayasaptamī interpretation), the grammatical operation in the form of the replacement by *m* and *u* should not be considered as asiddha.

If *mu* is considered as siddha in *amu* + *ā*, only then the stem *amu* gets the ghi-designation according to the rule *śeṣo ghyasakhi* (169). As a consequence, the rule *āṅo nā 'striyām* (170) applies and *ṭā* gets replaced by *nā*. Thus we obtain the form *amunā*. If *mu* is construed as asiddha in the illustration *amu* + *ā*, then *amu* will be treated as *ada* and consequently does not get the ghi-designation. Moreover, the lengthening of the final vowel *a* would also become due by *supi ca* (140). In order to avoid this undesirable contingency, the locative case-ending has been interpreted in both the senses : viṣayasaptamī as well as parasaptamī. Now whether *nā* follows or whether it is to be effected, in either case the *mu*-replacement is considered to be siddha. Accordingly *amu* gets the ghi-designation and the nominal ending *ṭā* is replaced by *nā* according to *āṅo nā 'striyām* (170).

In *adas* + *bhyām* --> *ada a* + *bhyām*, the replacement of *s* by *a* takes place by *tyadādīnāmaḥ* (192) and a single substitution in the form of pararūpa in *ada* + *bhyām* is brought about by *ato guṇe* (273). At this stage, the rule *supi ca* (140) applies and we have *adābhyām*. Now the rule *adaso...* (355) applies and we get *amūbhyām*.

With the plural affix of the third triplet, we have *adas* + *bhis* --> *ada a bhis* by *tyad...* (192) --> *ada* + *bhis* by *ato...* (273). At this stage, the rule *ato bhisa ais* (141) becomes available for application but this is negated by *nedamadaso...* (278). Then *bahuvacane jhalyet* (144) prescribes *e* in place of *a*. It is this *e* which gets replaced by *ī* and *d* by *m* in accordance with the rule *eta īd bahuvacane* (356) and we obtain the form *amībhiḥ* in the instrumental plural.

In the dative singular the affix *ṅe* is replaced by *smai* by *sarvanāmnaḥ smai* (152) and the dental *s* is replaced by *ṣ* according to *ādeśapratyayayoḥ* (149) and we get the form *amuṣmai* through the following grammatical process : *ada* + *smai* --> *amu* + *smai* --> *amuṣmai*. In the ablative, genitive and locative singular forms, the affixes *ṅasi, ṅas* and *ṅi* get replaced by *smāt, sya* and *smin* respectively by the rules *ṅasiṅyoḥ smātsminau* (153), *ṭāṅasiṅasāmināātsyāḥ* (139) and *ṅasiṅyoḥ...* (153). Thus we respectivley get *amuṣmāt, amuṣya* and *amuṣmin* after the cerebral *ṣ* has replaced the dental *s* by *ādeśa...* (149).

In *adas + os --> ada a + os {tyad...* (192)} --> *ada + os {ato...* (273)}, the rule *osi ca* (146) prescribes *e* in place of *a* following *d* and we get *adayoḥ* by *eco...* (22). At this stage, by replacing *a* by *u* and *d* by *m* according to *adaso...* (355), we obtain the form *amuyoḥ*. In the genitive plural by applying the rules *āmi sarva...* (154), *bahuvacane...* (144), *eta īd...* (356) and *ādeśa...* (149), we obtain the form *amīṣām*.

In the locative plural, we get *amīṣu*, again by applying the rules *bahuvacane...* (144), *eta īd...* (356) and *ādeśa...* (149). The complete declension of *adas* in the masculine will be as follows :

	Singular	Dual	Plural
prathamā	*asau*	*amū*	*amīḥ*
dvitīyā	*amum*	*amū*	*amūn*
tṛtīyā	*amunā*	*amūbhyām,*	*amībhiḥ*
caturthī	*amuṣmai*	*amūbhyām,*	*amībhyaḥ*
pañcamī	*amuṣmāt*	*amūbhyām,*	*amībhyaḥ*
ṣaṣṭhī	*amuṣya*	*amuyoḥ*	*amīṣām*
saptamī	*amuṣmin*	*amuyoḥ*	*amīṣu*
sambodhana		No form	

Here comes to an end the declension of the masculine words that end in *s*.

लघु० – इति हलन्ताः पुंलिङ्गाः । *iti halantāḥ puṁliṅgāḥ.*

Trans. : Here comes to an end the declension of the masculine words that end in a consonant.

हलन्तस्त्रीलिङ्गप्रकरणम्

Feminine Words ending in a Consonant

In this chapter we will discuss the declensional process of the feminine nominal stems that end in a consonant. The alphabetical order that is followed here is exactly the same as is followed in the repertory of phonemes (*pratyāhāra-sūtras*). The first consonantal phoneme in the pratyāhārasūtra is *h*. So, the first nominal stem that is taken up here is *upānah* 'a shoe'. When we introduce the singular affix of the first triplet, we have the following grammatical situation : *upānah* + *su*. In this situation, the sūtra, which becomes applicable, is as follows :

(358) **नहो धः । *naho dhaḥ*. 8. 2. 34**

लघु॰ – नहो हस्य धः स्याज्झलि पदान्ते च । *naho hasya dhaḥ syāj jhali padānte ca*.

Trans. : The consonantal phoneme *h* of the verbal root *nah* is replaced by *dh* when followed by a consonant denoted by *jhal*-pratyāhāra or at the end of a pada.

PP. *nahaḥ dhatoḥ haḥ dhaḥ jhali padasya ante ca.*

Eluc. : The present sūtra occurs in the domain of the governing rule *padasya* Pā. 8. 1. 16. Hence the word *padasya* recurs in this sūtra. The term *jhali* is carried over from *jhalo jhali* Pā. 8. 2. 26 and the expression *ante ca* comes from *skoḥ saṁyogādyorante ca* Pā. 8. 2. 29. The terms *dhatoḥ* and *haḥ* are respectively carried over from *ho ḍhaḥ* Pā. 8. 2. 31 and *dāderdhātorghaḥ* Pā. 8. 2. 32. The vowel *a* after *dh* in the sūtra is to facilitate its articulation. In this way the sūtra comes to mean : The phoneme *h* of the root *nah* is replaced by *dh* when it is followed by a consonant denoted by the abbreviatory term *jhal or* when it occurs at the end of a pada. The present sūtra is an exception to the sūtra *ho ḍhaḥ* (250).

The derivation of the nominal stem *upānah,* for which the present rule has been taken up by Varadarāja, is explained in the following sūtra :

(359) नहि-वृति-वृषि-व्यधि-रुचि-सहि-तनिषु क्वौ ।[1] ***nahi-vṛti-vṛṣi-vyadhi-ruci-sahi-taniṣu kvau.*** **6. 3. 116**

लघु० – क्विबन्तेषु पूर्वपदस्य दीर्घः । उपानत्, उपानद् । उपानहौ । उपानत्सु । *kvibanteṣu pūrvapadasya dīrghaḥ. upānat, upānad. upānahau. upānatsu.*

Trans. : The lengthening of the preceding pada takes place when the verbal roots *nah* 'to bind', *vṛt* 'to be', *vṛṣ* 'to rain', *vyadh* 'to pierce', *ruc* 'to shine', *sah* 'to bear' and *tan* 'to extend' ending in the affix *kvip* follow.

PP. *nahi-vṛti... taniṣu kvau pūrvasya dīrghaḥ* (*uttarapade, saṁhitāyām*).

Eluc. : The words *pūrvasya* and *dīrghaḥ* are carried over into the present sūtra from *ḍhralope pūrvasya dīrgho 'ṇaḥ* Pā. 6. 3. 111. Since the present sūtra occurs in the governing domain of *uttarapade* Pā. 6. 3. 1, the word *uttarapade* recurs in the present rule. Accordingly, the word *pūrvasya* is construed as *pūrvapadasya* as there is nothing else in the sūtra to be qualified by the word *pūrvasya* as in the rule *ḍhralope pūrvasya dīrgho 'ṇaḥ* (111). There the word *aṇaḥ* exists to be qualified by the word *pūrvasya*. The compound word *nahi-vṛti-vṛṣi-vyadhi-ruci-sahi-taniṣu* is an itaretaradvandva which is analysed as follows : *nahiś ca vṛtiś ca vṛṣiś ca vyadhiś ca ruciś ca sahiś ca taniś ca nahivṛtivṛṣivyadhirucisahitanayaḥ, teṣu = nahi-vṛti-vṛṣi-vyadhi-ruci-sahi-taniṣu.* The affix *kvip* is introduced after the verbal root *nah* 'to bind' by the vārttika *sampadādibhyaḥ kvip* Mbh 3. 3. 108, vtk 9. The affix *kvip* is completely elided. Then the primary derivative *nah* enters into prādisamāsa with the preverb *upa*. With the help of the paribhāṣā sūtras *alo 'ntyasya* (21) and *acaśca* Pā. 1. 2. 28, the final vowel *a* of the preceding pada will be lengthened, that is to say, of the preverb *upa* (*upa + nah + kvip --> upā nah +* 0 --> *upānah* 'a sleeper, shoe'. The segment *kvi* is common to both *kvin* and *kvip* but in the present sūtra it stands for the affix *kvip* since there is no provision in the Aṣṭādhyāyī for the introduction of the affix *kvin* after these verbal roots. Both the constituent padas of the sūtra are in the locative. This comes to mean that the lengthening of the final vowel of the preceding pada takes place when these verbal roots, ending in the affix *kvip*, follow.

---

1. The rule (359) should have come before (358) as it deals with the formation of the nominal stem *upānah* which is sought to be declined with the help of *naho dhaḥ* (358).

The other illustrations of the sūtra are : *nīvṛt* 'an inhabited place', *prāvṛṣ* 'rainy season', *hṛdayāvidh* 'piercing the heart', *nīruc* 'shining incessantly', *ṛtīṣah* 'conquering enemies' and *parītat* 'encircling'.

In the illustration *upānah + su*, the affix *su* is elided by *halṅyābbhyo...* (178) and then the phoneme *h* is replaced by *dh* according to the preceding rule *naho dhaḥ* (358) and we have *upānadh*. At this stage, *jhalāṁ jaśo 'nte* (67) prescribes *dh* to be replaced by *d* and then by *vā 'vasāne* (145) the phoneme *d* is optionally replaced by *t* (*car*) and thus we obtain two forms *upānat* and *upānad* in the nominative singular.

In *upānah + bhyām*, the consonant *h* is pada-final in view of the rule *svādiṣvasarvanāmasthāne* (163). Therefore, the rule *naho dhaḥ* (358) applies and *dh* replaces *h*, which is further replaced by *d* in accordance with the rule *jhalāṁ jaśo 'nte* (67). Thus we obtain the form *upānadbhyām*. The forms *upānadbhiḥ, upānadbhyaḥ*, etc. will be declined in the same manner.

In *upānah + sup --> upānah + su*, the consonant *h* is substituted by *dh* according to *naho dhaḥ* (358). Then by *khari ca* (74) *t* replaces *dh* and we get the form *upānatsu* in the locative plural. The complete declension of the nominal stem *upānah* is as follows :

	Singular	Dual	Plural
prathamā	*upānat, d*	*upānahau*	*upānahaḥ*
dvitīyā	*upānaham*	*upānahau*	*upānahaḥ*
tṛtīyā	*upānahā*	*upānadbhyām*	*upānadbhiḥ*
caturthī	*upānahe*	*upānadbhyām*	*upānadbhyaḥ*
pañcamī	*upānahaḥ*	*upānadbhyām*	*upānadbhyaḥ*
ṣaṣṭhī	*upānahaḥ*	*upānahoḥ*	*upānahām*
saptamī	*upānahi*	*upānahoḥ*	*upānatsu*
sambodhana	*he upānat, d!*	*he upānahau!*	*he upānahaḥ!*

लघु० - क्विन्नन्तत्वात् कुत्वेन घः। उष्णिक्, उष्णिग्। उष्णिहौ। उष्णिग्भ्याम्।
kvinnantatvāt kutvena ghaḥ. uṣṇik, uṣṇig. uṣṇihau, uṣṇigbhyām.

Eluc. : The stem *uṣṇih* is irregularly derived with the addition of the affix *kvin* in accordance with the rule *ṛtvigdadhṛksragdiguṣṇigañcuyujikruñcāṁ ca* (300). Since the stem *uṣṇih* is derived with the affix *kvin*, the rule *kvinpratyayasya kuḥ* (303) applies and the pre-affixal final phoneme *h* is replaced by *gh* in *uṣṇih + su* and we have *uṣṇigh* + 0 after the elision of the affix s(*u*) by *halṅyābbhyo...* (178). Then by *jhalāṁ jaśo 'nte* (67) the phoneme *gh* is replaced by *g* which is further optionally substituted by *k* (*car*) according to *vā 'vasāne* (145). In this way we get two forms *uṣṇik* and *uṣṇig* in the nominative singular. The same grammatical process will be followed in declining the stem *uṣṇih* with affixes *bhyām, bhis*, etc. In the locative plural the rules *kvinpratyayasya kuḥ* (303), *jhalāṁ jaśo 'nte* (67), *ādeśapratyayayoḥ* (149) and *khari ca* (74) respectively prescribe the replacement of *h* by *gh*, of *gh* by *g*, of the phoneme s of *sup* by ṣ and of *g* by *k*. Thus we obtain the form *uṣṇikṣu* in the locative plural. The complete declension of *uṣṇih* is given below :

	Singular	Dual	Plural
prathamā	*uṣṇik, g*	*uṣṇihau*	*uṣṇihaḥ*
dvitīyā	*uṣṇiham*	*uṣṇihau*	*uṣṇihaḥ*
tṛtīyā	*uṣṇihā*	*uṣṇigbhyām*	*uṣṇigbhiḥ*
caturthī	*uṣṇihe*	*uṣṇigbhyām*	*uṣṇigbhyaḥ*
pañcamī	*uṣṇihaḥ*	*uṣṇigbhyām*	*uṣṇigbhyaḥ*
ṣaṣṭhī	*uṣṇihaḥ*	*uṣṇihoḥ*	*uṣṇihām*
saptamī	*uṣṇihi*	*uṣṇihoḥ*	*uṣṇikṣu*
sambodhana	*he uṣṇik, g!*	*he uṣṇihau!*	*he uṣṇihaḥ!*

Here comes to an end the declension of the feminine stems that end in the phoneme *h*.

Now begins the process of declining the feminine stems ending in the phoneme *v*.

लघु० – द्यौः । दिवौ । दिवः । द्युभ्याम् । *dyauḥ. divau. divaḥ. dyubhyām.*

Eluc. : The declension of the feminine nominal stem *div* is like that of the masculine compound word *sudiv* {see the rules *diva aut* (263) and *diva ut* (264), supra pp. 366-68. The former rule applies in the nominative singular and the latter in other declensional forms where it ges the pada-designation by virtue of the rule {*svādiṣvasarvanāmasthāne* (163)}.

The complete declension of the feminine nominal stem *div* is given below :

	Singular	Dual	Plural
prathamā	*dyauḥ*	*divau*	*divaḥ*
dvitīyā	*divam*	*divau*	*divaḥ*
tṛtīyā	*divā*	*dyubhyām*	*dyubhiḥ*
caturthī	*dive*	*dyubhyām*	*dyubhyaḥ*
pañcamī	*divaḥ*	*dyubhyām*	*dyubhyaḥ*
ṣaṣṭhī	*divaḥ*	*divoḥ*	*divām*
saptamī	*divi*	*divoḥ*	*dyuṣu*
sambodhana	*he dyauḥ!*	*he divau!*	*he divaḥ!*

Here comes to an end the declensional process of the feminine nominal stems that end in the phoneme *v*.

Now begins the declension of the feminine nominal stems that end in repha.

लघु० – गीः । गिरौ । गिरः । एवं पूः । चतस्रः । चतसृणाम् । *gīḥ. girau. giraḥ. evaṁ pūḥ. catasraḥ. catasṛṇām.*

Eluc. : The nominal stem *gir* 'speech' is derived from the verbal root *gṝ* 'to swallow' with the addition of the affix *kvip* which is completely elided. Then according to the rules *ṝta iddhātoḥ* (659) and *uraṇ raparaḥ* (29), the vowel *ṝ* is replaced by *ir* and we obtain the form *gir*.

In *gir + su,* the affix *su* is elided by *halṅyābbhyo...* (178). The nominal stem *gir* is treated as a verbal root in accordance with the paribhāṣā *kvibantā dhātutvaṁ na jahati...* (Paribhāṣāsaṅgraha, p. 43). As such, the penultimate vowel is lengthened by *rvorupadhāyāḥ dīrgha ikaḥ* (350) and we get *gīḥ* after rutva and visarga.

In the declensional forms with the affixes *bhyām, bhis* in which the stem assumes pada designation by *svādiṣvasarvanāmasthāne* (163), the rule *rvorupadhāyāḥ...* (350) prescribes the lengthening of the penultimate vowel *i* of *gir* in the same way as in the nominative singular and we obtain the forms *gīrbhyām, gīrbhiḥ,* etc.

In the locative plural *gir + sup* also, the penultimate vowel gets lengthened as above. Then the consonant *s* after the repha, which is a denotatum of *iṇ*-pratyāhāra, is replaced by *ṣ* in accordance with the rule *ādeśapratyayayoḥ* (149). In this case, the pada-final repha is not replaced by visarga according to *kharavasānayorvisarjanīyaḥ* (93) because of the restrictive rule *roḥ supi* (267) since the repha here is other than that of *ru*. In this way we get the form *gīrṣu*. The complete declension of *gir* is given below :

	Singular	Dual	Plural
prathamā	*gīḥ*	*girau*	*giraḥ*
dvitīyā	*giram*	*girau*	*giraḥ*
tṛtīyā	*girā*	*gīrbhyām*	*gīrbhiḥ*
caturthī	*gire*	*gīrbhyām*	*gīrbhyaḥ*
pañcamī	*giraḥ*	*gīrbhyām*	*gīrbhyaḥ*
ṣaṣṭhī	*giraḥ*	*giroḥ*	*girām*
saptamī	*giri*	*giroḥ*	*gīrṣu*
sambodhana	*he gīḥ!*	*he girau!*	*he giraḥ!*

The nominal stem *pur* 'a city' is derived from the verbal root *pṝ* 'to nourish, to complete, to fill' with the introduction of the affix *kvip*. We apply the rules *udoṣṭhyapūrvasya* (610) and *uraṇ raparaḥ* (29) and obtain the stem *pur*. The declension of the nominal stem *pur* will be like that of *gir* :

	Singular	Dual	Plural
prathamā	*pūḥ*	*purau*	*puraḥ*
dvitīyā	*puram*	*purau*	*puraḥ*
tṛtīyā	*purā*	*pūrbhyām*	*pūrbhiḥ*
caturthī	*pure*	*pūrbhyām*	*pūrbhyaḥ*
pañcamī	*puraḥ*	*pūrbhyām*	*pūrbhyaḥ*
ṣaṣṭhī	*puraḥ*	*puroḥ*	*purām*
saptamī	*puri*	*puroḥ*	*pūrṣu*
sambodhana	*he pūḥ!*	*he purau!*	*he puraḥ!*

In accordance with the rule *tricaturoḥ striyāṁ tisṛcatasṛ* (223), the numeral *catur* in the feminine is replaced by the substitute *catasṛ* when it is followed by sup-affixes (*vibhakti*). It will be declined in the plural only. In the nominative plural when we introduce the affix *jas*, we have *catasṛ + jas --> catasṛ + as*. At this stage, the rule *ṛto ṅisarvanāmasthānayoḥ* (203) becomes available to replace the aṅga-final *ṛ* of *catasṛ* by a guṇa vowel but the rule *aci ra ṛtaḥ* (224), being an exception to *ṛto ṅi...* (203), debars it and instead prescribes the replacement of *ṛ* by repha. Thus we obtain the form *catasraḥ* in the nominative plural.

With the affix *śas* after *catasṛ*, the rule *ṛto ṅisarvanāmasthānayoḥ* (203) is not applicable since the affix *śas* is not a sarvanāmasthāna. So, by the rule *aci ra ṛtaḥ* (224) the vowel *ṛ* is replaced by repha and we obtain the form *catasraḥ* in the accusative plural.

In the genitive plural, with the affix *ām*, we have *catasṛ + ām*. In this grammatical situation, the rule *aci ra ṛtaḥ* (224) becomes available for application but this is blocked by the vārttika *num-acira-tṛjvadbhāvebhyo nuṭ pūrvavipratiṣedhena* (see supra pp. 260-61 for explanation). So by *hrasvanadyāpo nuṭ* (147), the augment *nuṭ* is inserted at the head of the affix *ām* and we have *catasṛ + nuṭ ām --> catasṛ + nām*. Now the lengthening of the aṅga-final vowel *ṛ* by the rule *nāmi* (148) becomes available but this is negated by the rule *na tisṛcatasṛ* (225) and we get the form *catasṛṇām* after the dental *n* has been replaced by *ṇ* according to the vārttika *ṛvarṇānnasya ṇatvaṁ vācyam* (vtk 21).

In the locative plural the dental *s* of the plural affix *sup* of the seventh triplet is replaced by the cerebral *ṣ* by the rule *ādeśapratyayayoḥ* (149) and we get the form *catasṛṣu*. The complete declension of the numeral *catur* in the feminine is given below :

	Plural		Plural
prathamā	*catasraḥ*	pañcamī	*catasṛbhyaḥ*
dvitīyā	*catasraḥ*	ṣaṣṭhī	*catasṛṇām*
tṛtīyā	*catasṛbhiḥ*	saptamī	*catasṛṣu*
caturthī	*catasṛbhyaḥ*	sambodhana	No form

Here comes to an end the declensional process of the feminine stems ending in repha.

Now begins the declension of the feminine words that end in the phoneme *m*.

लघु० - का । के । काः । सर्वावत् । *kā. ke. kāḥ. sarvāvat.*

Eluc. : The masculine form of the pronominal stem *kim* has already been explained (see supra p. 373). Now the feminine form of *kim* is going to be explained. When the pronominal stem *kim* is followed by a sup-affix, it is wholly replaced by the substitute *ka* {see the rule *kimaḥ kaḥ* (270)} since it has more than one phoneme. Then to express it in the feminine, the feminine affix *ṭāp* is introduced after it by the rule *ajādyataṣṭāp* (1243). We get the word *kā* after the rule *akaḥ savarṇe dīrghaḥ* (42) has performed its grammatical function. Since it is designated as *sarvanāman*, its declension will be like that of *sarvā*. In declining the word *kā* in the instrumental singular, genitive dual and locative dual, we apply the rule *āṅi cāpaḥ* (217) and with the help of *eco 'yavāyāvaḥ* (22) have the forms *kayā, kayoḥ* and *kayoḥ* respectively. In dative, ablative, genitive and locative singular forms of *kā*, the rule *sarvanāmnaḥ syāḍḍhrasvaśca* (219) prescribes the insertion of the augment *syā*(*ṭ*) at the head of *ṅit* affixes and the shortening of the feminine affix *āp*. We respectively obtain the forms *kasyai, kasyāḥ, kasyāḥ* and *kasyām*. In the genitive plural declensional form of *kā*, the rule *āmi sarvanāmnaḥ suṭ* (154) prescribes the insertion of the augment *suṭ* at the head of *ām* and we obtain the form *kāsām*. The complete declension of *kā* is given below :

	Singular	Dual	Plural
prathamā	*kā*	*ke*	*kāḥ*
dvitīyā	*kām*	*ke*	*kāḥ*
tṛtīyā	*kayā*	*kābhyām*	*kābiḥ*
caturthī	*kasyai*	*kābhyām*	*kābhyaḥ*
pañcamī	*kasyāḥ*	*kābhyām*	*kābhyaḥ*
ṣaṣṭhī	*kasyāḥ*	*kayoḥ*	*kāsām*
saptamī	*kasyām*	*kayoḥ*	*kāsu*

(360) यः सौ । *yaḥ sau*. 7. 2. 110

लघु० – इदमो दस्य यः । इयम् । त्यदाद्यत्वम् । पररूपत्वम् । टाप् । दश्च (274) इति मः । इमे । इमाः । इमाम् । अनया । हलि लोपः (276) । आभ्याम् । आभिः । अस्यै । अस्याः । अनयोः । आसाम् । अस्याम् । आसु । *idamo dasya yaḥ. iyam. tyadādyatvam. pararūpatvam. ṭāp. daśca* (274) *iti maḥ. ime. imāḥ. imām. anayā. hali lopaḥ* (276). *ābhyām. ābhiḥ. asyai. asyāḥ. anayoḥ. āsām. asyām. āsu.*

Trans. : The phoneme *d* of *idam* is replaced by *y* when the affix *su* follows.

PP. *idamaḥ daḥ yaḥ sau (vibhaktau, aṅgasya)*

Eluc. : The words *idamaḥ* and *daḥ* are respectively carried over from *idamo maḥ* Pā. 7. 2. 108 and *daśca* Pā. 7. 2. 109. Thus the meaning of the sūtra is as follows : When the nominative singular affix *su* follows, the phoneme *d* of the pronominal stem *idam* is substituted by the semi-vowel *y*. In *idam + su*, the phoneme *d* is replaced by *y* and we have *iyam + su*. In this situation, the affix *su* is elided by the rule *halṅyābbhyo...* (178) and thus the form *iyam* is obtained. In this case, the rule *tyadādīnāmaḥ* (192) does not become applicable since it is debarred by *idamo maḥ* (271). The present rule applies only in case of the feminine form of *idam* since in the masculine the *id*-portion of *idam* is replaced by *ay* according to the rule *ido 'y puṁsi* (272), when the affix *su* follows. In the case of neuter forms the present rule is not applicable as the affix *su* is elided by luk-elision {*svamornapuṁsakāt* (243)}.

In *idam + au*, the rule *tyadādīnāmaḥ* (192) applies and the phoneme *m* is replaced by *a*. Then in *ida a + au*, by *ato guṇe* (273) a single substitute in the form of the following (*pararūpa*) comes in place of both the vowels --> *ida a + au*. Now *ajādyataṣṭāp* (1243) applies and after the elision of the anubandhas we arrive at the following derivational stage : *idā + au*. In this situation we have the phoneme *m* in place of *d* by *daśca* (274). The affix *au* is substituted by *śī* according to *auṅa āpaḥ* (215) and we have *imā + śī --> imā + ī* {after the elision of *ś*, which is *it* by *laśakvataddhite* (135)}. The rule *ādguṇaḥ* (27) applies and we get the form *ime*.

After the application of the rules *tyadādīnāmaḥ* (192), *ato guṇe* (273), *ajādyataṣṭāp* (1243), *akaḥ savarṇe dīrghaḥ* (42) and *daśca* (274) in *idam + jas*, we arrive at the following stage : *imā + as*. At this stage, the rule *dīrghājjasi ca* (161) blocks pūrvasavarṇadīrgha which was available by *prathamayoḥ...* (125). Then we obtain the form *imāḥ* by applying the rule *akaḥ savarṇe dīrghaḥ* (42).

In *idam + am*, we get *ida a + am* by *tyadādīnāmaḥ* (192), *ida + am* by *ato guṇe* (273), *ida + ṭāp + am* by *ajādyataṣṭāp* (1243) --> *ida + ā + am* (after the elision of anubandhas), *idā + am* by *akaḥ savarṇe dīrghaḥ* (42) and *imā + am* by *daśca* (274). At this stage, the rule *ami pūrvaḥ* (134) applies and we obtain the form *imām* in the accusative singular.

In the accusative plural, we have *idam + śas --> ida a + as* by *tyadā...* (192) --> *ida + as* by *ato...* (273) --> *ida ṭāp + as* by *ajādya...* (1243) and *idā + as* --> by *akaḥ...* (42). At this stage, the rule *dīrghājjasi ca* (161) does not block *prathamayoḥ pūrvasavarṇaḥ* (125) and by changing *idās* to *imās* by *daśca* (274) we get the form *imāḥ* after rutva and visarga.

In the declensional form of instrumental singular *idam + ṭā*, we reach the grammatical stage *idā + ā* as above. In this grammatical situation, the rule *anāpyakaḥ* (275) prescribes the *id*-portion to be replaced by *an*. The *ā* of the pre-affixal base is replaced by *e* by *āṅi cāpaḥ* (217). We have *an e + ā*. Then the rule *eco 'ya...* (22) applies and we get the form *anayā*.

The *id*-portion in *idā* before *bhyām* is elided by *hali lopaḥ* (276) and we get the form *ābhyām*. When a sup-affix beginning with a consonant follows, the declensional process will be similar, that is, in the forms such as *ābhiḥ, āsām, āsu,* etc.

In the dative singular declensional form of *idam*, the grammatical process is as follows : *idam + ṅe --> idā + ṅe --> idā + e*. Now the rule *sarvanāmnaḥ syāḍ ḍhrasvaśca* (219) prescribes the insertion of the augment *syāṭ* at the head of the affix *e* and also the shortening of the long vowel *ā* of *idā*. Then in *ida syā e*, the vṛddhi vowel *ai* replaces both *ā* and *e* by *vṛddhireci* (33). By *hali lopaḥ* (276), the *id*-portion of *ida* is elided and we obtain the form *asyai*.

With the introduction of the affixes *ṅasi* or *ṅas*, we have *idā + as*. The insertion of the augment *syāṭ* and the shortening of the vowel *ā* of *āp* take place by *sarvanāmnaḥ syāḍḍhrasvaśca* (219). Then the rule *akaḥ savarṇe dīrghaḥ* (42) applies and we have *asyāḥ* after the *id*-portion has been elided by *hali lopaḥ* (276) through the grammatical process that follows : *idā + as --> ida + syāṭ as --> ida + syā as --> ida + syās --> asyās --> asyāḥ* (after rutva and visarga).

In genitive and locative dual, we introduce the affix *os* after *idam*. The rule *anāpyakaḥ* (275) prescribes the replacement of *id* by *an* (*idā + os --> anā + os*) and the replacement of the vowel *ā* of *āp* by *e* (*an e + os*) according to the rule *āṅi cāpaḥ* (217). Then by *eco 'yavā...* (22), the vowel *e* is replaced by *ay* and we get the form *anayoḥ* (<-- *an ay os*).

In the genitive plural *idā + ām*, the rule *āmi sarvanāmnaḥ suṭ* (154) prescribes the insertion of *suṭ* at the head of the affix *ām* and we have *idā + suṭ ām --> idā + sām*. We obtain the form *āsām*, after the elision of *id* by the rule *hali lopaḥ* (276).

In *idam + ṅi --> idā + ṅi*, the affix *ṅi* is replaced by *ām* according to the rule *ṅerāmnadyāmnībhyaḥ* (197). After this, the rule *sarvanāmnaḥ syāḍ-ḍhrasvaśca* (219) prescribes the insertion of the augment *syāṭ* at the head of *ām* and also the shortening of the long vowel *ā* of *idā*. We have *idā + syāṭ ām --> ida + syā ām*. Then by the rule *hali lopaḥ* (276), the *id*-portion is elided --> *a + syā ām* and we obtain *asyām* after sarvarṇadīrgha by *akaḥ savarṇe dīrghaḥ* (42).

In the locative plural, with the introduction of the affix *sup*, we have *idā + sup*. The rule *hali lopaḥ* (276) prescribes the elision of the *id*-portion of *idā* and we get the form *āsu* The complete declension of the feminine form of *idam* is given below :

	Singular	Dual	Plural
prathamā	*iyam*	*ime*	*imāḥ*
dvitīyā	*imām*	*ime*	*imāḥ*
tṛtīyā	*anayā*	*ābhyām*	*ābhiḥ*
caturthī	*asyai*	*ābhyām*	*ābhyaḥ*
pañcamī	*asyāḥ*	*ābhyām*	*ābhyaḥ*
ṣaṣṭhī	*asyāḥ*	*anayoḥ*	*āsām*
saptamī	*asyām*	*anayoḥ*	*āsu*

Here comes to an end the declension of the feminine stems that end in the phoneme *m*.

Now begins the declensional process of the feminine words that end in the phoneme *d*.

लघु० – त्यदाद्यत्वम्। टाप्। स्या, त्ये, त्याः। एवं तद्, एतद्। *tyadādyatvam. ṭāp. syā, tye, tyāḥ. evaṁ tad, etad.*

Eluc. : The next word is *tyad* 'he, she, it, that'. The declensional forms of the masculine pronominal stem *tyad* have been explained. Now the declensional process of its feminine form is being explained. In the nominative singular, we have *tyad* + *su*. Now we get *tya a* + *su* by *tyadādīnāmaḥ* (192), *tya* + *su* by *ato guṇe* (273), *tya* + *ṭāp* + *su* by *ajādyataṣṭāp* (1243), *tya* + *ā* + *su* (after the elision of anubandhas) and *tyā* + *su* by *akaḥ savarṇe dīrghaḥ* (42). At this stage, the phoneme *t* of *tyā* is replaced by *s* in accordance with the rule *tadoḥ saḥ sāvanantyayoḥ* (309) and we get *syā* after the affix *su* has been elided by *halṅyābbhyo...* (178).

In the rest of the declension the pronominal stem becomes *tya* + *ṭāp* --> *tyā* after the addition of the feminine affix *ṭāp* by *ajādyataṣṭāp* (1243) when followed by the sup-affixes. As such, this will be declined like *sarvā*. The declension of the pronominal *tyā* is as follows :

	Singular	Dual	Plural
prathamā	*syā*	*tye*	*tyāḥ*
dvitīyā	*tyām*	*tye*	*tyāḥ*
tṛtīyā	*tyayā*	*tyābhyām*	*tyābhiḥ*
caturthī	*tyasyai*	*tyābhyām*	*tyābhyaḥ*

pañcamī	*tyasyāḥ*	*tyābhyām*	*tyābhyaḥ*
ṣaṣṭhī	*tyasyāḥ*	*tyayoḥ*	*tyāsām*
saptamī	*tyasyām*	*tyayoḥ*	*tyāsu*

The declensional process of the pronominal stem *tad* in the feminine is the same as is followed in declining the feminine form of *tyad*. After the addition of the feminine affix *ṭāp* before the singular affix of the first triplet, we obtain the declensional form *sā* through the following grammatical process (*tad + su --> ta a + su --> ta + su --> ta ṭāp + su --> tā + su --> sā + su --> sā*). The pronoun *tad* in the feminine will be declined in the same way before the remaining sup-affixes. Its declension is as follows :

	Singular	Dual	Plural
prathamā	*sā*	*te*	*tāḥ*
dvitīyā	*tām*	*te*	*tāḥ*
tṛtīyā	*tayā*	*tābhyām*	*tābhiḥ*
caturthī	*tasyai*	*tābhyām*	*tābhyaḥ*
pañcamī	*tasyāḥ*	*tābhyām*	*tābhyaḥ*
ṣaṣṭhī	*tasyāḥ*	*tayoḥ*	*tāsām*
saptamī	*tasyām*	*tayoḥ*	*tāsu*

The declension of the pronominal stem *etad* will also be like the pronominal stems *tyad* and *tad* except that in the nominative singular the dental s is replaced by cerebral ṣ by *ādeśapratyayayoḥ* (149).

	Singular	Dual	Plural
prathamā	*eṣā*	*ete*	*etāḥ*
dvitīyā	*etām*	*ete*	*etāḥ*
tṛtīyā	*etayā*	*etābhyām*	*etābhiḥ*
caturthī	*etasyai*	*etābhyām*	*etābhyaḥ*
pañcamī	*etasyāḥ*	*etābhyām*	*etābhyaḥ*
ṣaṣṭhī	*etasyāḥ*	*etayoḥ*	*etāsām*
saptamī	*etasyām*	*etayoḥ*	*etāsu*

Here comes to an end the declensional process of the feminine words that end in the phoneme *d*.

Now begins the process of declining the feminine stems that end in the phoneme *c*.

लघु० – वाक्, वाग्। वाचौ। वाग्भ्याम्। वाक्षु। *vāk, vāg. vācau. vāgbhyām. vākṣu.*

Eluc. : The nominal stem *vāc* is derived by introducing the affix *kvip* after the verbal root *vac* 'to speak' by the vārttika *kvibvacipracchyāyatastu-kaṭaprujuśrīṇāṁ dīrgho 'samprasāraṇañca.*[1] By virtue of this vārttika, the vowel *a* following the phoneme *v* gets lengthened and the semi-vowel *v* does not undergo samprasāraṇa which is due by *vacisvapiyajādīnāṁ kiti* (546) because the affix *kvip* is *kit*.

In the declensional process of this stem, the rule *coḥ kuḥ* (305) will prescribe the replacement of the palatal stops by the guttural ones in the pada-final stage. In the nominative singular when the affix *s*(*u*) is elided by *halṅyābbhyo...* (178), the palatal stop *c* is replaced by *k* according to *coḥ kuḥ* (305). Then the rules *vā 'vasāne* (145) and *jhalāṁ jaśo 'nte* (67) apply and we get two forms *vāk* and *vāg* in the nominative singular.

Before *bhyām, bhis,* etc. the stem gets the pada-designation by *svādiṣvasarvanāmasthāne* (163). As such, the pada-final *c* is substituted by *k* in accordance with *coḥ kuḥ* (305) and then by *jhalāṁ jaśo 'nte* (67), it is replaced by *g* and we have *vāgbhyām, vāgbhiḥ,* etc.

In the locative plural *vāc* + *sup* --> *vāc* + *su*, the stem *vāc* assumes pada-designation by *svādiṣva...* (163). By *coḥ kuḥ* (305), the pada-final *c* is replaced by *k*. By *jhalāṁ jaśo 'nte* (67), the phoneme *k* is substituted by *g*. According to the rule *ādeśapratyayayoḥ*(149), the dental *s* of the affix *sup* is replaced by *ṣ*. The rule *khari ca* (74) prescribes the replacement of *g* by *k* and we obtain the form *vākṣu*. The complete declension of the nominal stem *vāc* will be as follows :

	Singular	Dual	Plural
prathamā	*vāk, g*	*vācau*	*vācaḥ*
dvitīyā	*vācam*	*vācau*	*vācaḥ*
tṛtīyā	*vācā*	*vāgbhyām*	*vāgbhiḥ*
caturthī	*vāce*	*vāgbhyām*	*vāgbhyaḥ*

1. In the Mahābhāṣya this vārttika is given as *vacipracchyāyatastukaṭaprujuśrīṇāṁ dīrghaśca,* Mbh 3. 2. 178 vtk 2.

pañcamī	*vācaḥ*	*vāgbhyām*	*vāgbhyaḥ*
ṣaṣṭhī	*vācaḥ*	*vācoḥ*	*vācām*
saptamī	*vāci*	*vācoḥ*	*vākṣu*
sambodhana	*he vāk, g!*	*he vācau!*	*he vācaḥ!*

Here comes to an end the declensional process of the words that end in the phoneme *c*.

Now begins the declension of the words that end in the phoneme *p*.

लघु० – अप्शब्दो नित्यबहुवचनान्तः। अप्तृन्तृच् ० (205) इति दीर्घः। आपः। अपः। *apśabdo nityabahuvacanāntaḥ. aptṛntṛc...* (205) *iti dīrghaḥ. āpaḥ. apaḥ.*

Eluc. : The nominal stem *ap* is derived by adding the affix *kvip* after the verbal root *āp* 'to pervade' by *āpnoterhrasvaśca* (Uṇādi Sūtra, 216). The long *ā* of the root also gets shortened by this rule. This stem is obligatorily used in the plural.

In the nominative plural we add the affix *jas* after it. Since the affix *jas* is a sarvanāmasthāna, the penultimate vowel of the stem *ap* in *ap* + *jas* --> *ap* + *as* is lengthened by *aptṛntṛc...* (205) and we get the form *āpaḥ* after rutva and visarga.

In declining the stem *ap* in the accusative plural we introduce the affix *śas* after it. In *ap* + *śas* --> *ap* + *as*, the affix *śas* is not a sarvanāmasthāna. So, there is no lengthening of the penultimate vowel and we get *apaḥ* after rutva and visarga.

When we introduce the affix *bhis* after *ap*, we have *ap* + *bhis*. At this stage, the following sūtra applies :

(361) अपो भि। ***apo bhi.* 7. 4. 48**

लघु० – अपस्तकारो भादौ प्रत्यये। अद्भिः। अद्भ्यः 2। अपाम्। अप्सु। *apas takāro bhādau pratyaye. adbhiḥ. adbhyaḥ* 2. *apām. apsu.*

Trans. : When an affix, beginning with the phoneme *bh*, follows, the pre-affixal base *ap* is replaced by the phoneme *t*.

PP. *apaḥ aṅgasya taḥ bhi.*

Eluc. : The term *taḥ* is carried over from *aca upasargāttaḥ* Pā. 7. 4. 47. The present sūtra occurs in the domain of the governing rule *aṅgasya* Pā. 6. 4. 1. Accordingly, the term *pratyaye* is supplied here to complete the sense. By tadādividhi (*yasmin vidhistadādāval...* Mbh 1. 1. 72 vtk 29) the word *bhi*, qualifying the word *pratyaye*, means 'When an affix which begins with the phoneme *bh* follows'. Thus the sūtra means : The pre-affixal base *ap* is replaced by the phoneme *t* when the affix which begins with the phoneme *bh* follows it. By virtue of the paribhāṣāsūtra *alo-'ntyasya* (21), the phoneme *t* will replace the aṅga-final phoneme *p*.

In the illustration *ap* + *bhis*, the affix *bhis* begins with the phoneme *bh*. Accordingly, the aṅga-final phoneme *p* is replaced by *t* giving *at* + *bhis*. In accordance with the rule *svādiṣvasarvanāmasthāne* (163), the term *at* (*p*) is a pada and phoneme *t* is pada-final. As such, this will be replaced by *d* by *jhalāṁ jaśo 'nte* (67) and after rutva and visarga we get the form *adbhiḥ* in the instrumental plural. We will obtain the form *adbhyaḥ* in a similar way. The complete declension of *ap* is given below :

	Plural		Plural
prathamā	*āpaḥ*	pañcamī	*adbhyaḥ*
dvitīyā	*apaḥ*	ṣaṣṭhī	*apām*
tṛtīyā	*adbhiḥ*	saptamī	*apsu*
caturthī	*adbhyaḥ*	sambodhana	*he āpaḥ!*

Here comes to an end the declensional process of the feminine words that end in the phoneme *p*.

Now begins the process of declension of the words that end in the phoneme *ś*.

लघु० – दिक्, दिग्। दिशः। दिग्भ्याम्। *dik, dig. diśaḥ. digbhyām.*

Eluc. : The word *diś* 'direction' is irregularly derived with the affix *kvin* according to the rule *ṛtvigdadhṛk...* (300). That is why in the illustration *diś* + *su*, the rule *kvinprayayasya kuḥ* (303) applies after the sūtras *vraścabhrsja...* (306) and *jhalāṁ jaśo 'nte* (67) have performed their grammatical functions of replacing the phoneme *ś* by *ṣ* and then *ṣ* by *ḍ* respectively. We get *dig* (<-- *diḍ* + *su* <-- *diṣ* + *su* <-- *diś* + *su*) after *s*(*u*) has been elided by *halṅyābbhyo...* (178). Now by applying the rule *vā 'vasāne* (145), we obtain the alternative form *dik*. Thus we get *dik* and *dig* in the nominative singular.

When we decline this stem with the affix *bhyām*, the same rules will apply in the same sequence and we have the form *digbhyām*. The declension of *diś* is as follows :

	Singular	Dual	Plural
prathamā	*dik, g*	*diśau*	*diśaḥ*
dvitīyā	*diśam*	*diśau*	*diśaḥ*
tṛtīyā	*diśā*	*digbhyām*	*digbhiḥ*
caturthī	*diśe*	*digbhyām*	*digbhyaḥ*
pañcamī	*diśaḥ*	*digbhyām*	*digbhyaḥ*
ṣaṣṭhī	*diśaḥ*	*diśoḥ*	*diśām*
saptamī	*diśi*	*diśoḥ*	*dikṣu*
sambodhana	*he dik, g!*	*he diśau!*	*he diśa!*

लघु० – त्यदादिषु० (346) इति दृशेः क्विन्विधानादन्यत्रापि कुत्वम्। दृक्, दृग्। दृशौ। दृग्भ्याम्। *tyadādiṣu... (346) iti dṛśeḥ kvinvidhānād anyatrāpi kutvam. dṛk, dṛg. dṛśau. dṛgbhyām.*

Eluc. : By *tyadādiṣu dṛśo 'nālocane kañ ca* (346), the affixes *kañ* and *kvin* are introduced after the verb *dṛś* 'to see' when it is preceded by the words *tyad*, etc. as upapadas. If we construe the compound word *kvinprayayasya* as a bahuvrīhi, we can apply the rule *kvinprayayasya kuḥ* (303) in respect of the nominal stem *dṛś* which has been derived by adding the affix *kvip* after it. The compound word *kvinprayayasya* construed as a bahuvrīhi means 'the stem which has the affix *kvin* prescribed after it in any form'. Thus the rule *kvinprayayasya kuḥ* (303) can apply in case of *dṛś* even if it is not derived with the introduction of the affix *kvin* in a particular instance since the affix *kvin* has been prescribed after the verbal root *dṛś* in *tādṛś, etādṛś*, etc. This means that the nominal stem *dṛś* is a stem which is seen with the affix *kvin* added after it in the forms mentioned above. Therefore the final phoneme of the word *dṛś* can be replaced by a guttural one by the rule *kvinprayayasya kuḥ* (303) after the phoneme *ś* has been replaced by *ṣ* in accordance with the rule *vraścabhrsja...* (306) and then *ṣ* by *ḍ* according to *jhalāṁ jaśo 'nte* (67). The phoneme *ḍ* changes to *g* by *kvinprayayasya kuḥ* (303). By applying *vā 'vasāne* (145), we get two forms *dṛk* and *dṛg* in the same manner as we got *dik* and *dig* in the nominative singular.[1] The complete declension of the stem *dṛś* is given below :

---

1. *tyadādyupapadābhāve 'pītyarthaḥ. kvinpratyayaḥ yasmād vihita iti bahuvrīhyāśrayaṇād iti bhāvaḥ. dṛg iti. ṣaḍagakāḥ prāgvat.* BM, I, p. 457.

	Singular	Dual	Plural
prathamā	*dṛk, g*	*dṛśau*	*dṛśaḥ*
dvitīyā	*dṛśam*	*dṛśau*	*dṛśaḥ*
tṛtīyā	*dṛśā*	*dṛgbhyām*	*dṛgbhiḥ*
caturthī	*dṛśe*	*dṛgbhyām*	*dṛgbhyaḥ*
pañcamī	*dṛśaḥ*	*dṛgbhyām*	*dṛgbhyaḥ*
ṣaṣṭhī	*dṛśaḥ*	*dṛśoḥ*	*dṛśām*
saptamī	*dṛśi*	*dṛśoḥ*	*dṛkṣu*
sambodhana	*he dṛk, g!*	*he dṛśau!*	*he dṛśaḥ!*

Here comes to an end the declension of the words that end in the phoneme *ś*.

Now begins the process of declining the feminine words that end in the phoneme *ṣ*.

लघु० - त्विट्, त्विड्। त्विड्भ्याम्। ससजुषो रुः (104) इति रुत्वम्। सजूः। सजुषौ। सजूर्भ्याम्। आशीः। आशिषौ। आशीर्भ्याम्। *tviṭ, tviḍ. tviḍbhyām. sasajuṣo ruḥ* (104) *iti rutvam. sajūḥ. sajuṣau. sajūrbhyām. āśīḥ. āśiṣau. āśīrbhyām.*

Eluc. : The word *tviṣ* 'light' is derived with the introduction of the affix *kvip* after the verbal root *tviṣ* 'to shine'. The declension of the primary derivative *tviṣ* is like that of the masculine nominal stem *ratnamuṣ* (see supra, pp. 484). By applying *jhalāṁ jaśo 'nte* (67) and *vā-'vasāne* (145), we get *tviṭ* and *tviḍ* in the nominative singular. In the declensional forms of *tviṣ* in which it gets the pada-designation, the rule *jhalāṁ jaśo 'nte* (67) applies and we have *tviḍbhyām*, etc. When we decline *tviṣ* in the locative plural we first apply the rule *jhalāṁ jaśo 'nte.* After this, the process of optionally inserting the augment *dhuṭ* takes place and we obtain *tviṭtsu* and *tviṭsu* with the help of *khari ca* (74). The declension of *tviṣ* is given below :

	Singular	Dual	Plural
prathamā	*tviṭ, ḍ*	*tviṣau*	*tviṣaḥ*
dvitīyā	*tviṣam*	*tviṣau*	*tviṣaḥ*
tṛtīyā	*tviṣā*	*tviḍbhyām*	*tviḍbhiḥ*

caturthī	*tviṣe*	*tviḍbhyām*	*tviḍbhyaḥ*
pañcamī	*tviṣaḥ*	*tviḍbhyām*	*tviḍbhyaḥ*
ṣaṣṭhī	*tviṣaḥ*	*tviṣoḥ*	*tviṣām*
saptamī	*tviṣi*	*tviṣoḥ*	*tviṭtsu, tviṭsu*
sambodhana	*he tviṭ, ḍ!*	*he tviṣau!*	*he tviṣaḥ!*

The word *sajuṣ* 'companion' is derived from the verbal root *juṣ* 'to delight, to serve' with the addition of the affix *kvip* in the following manner : *saha juṣate* --> *saha* + *juṣ* + *kvip* --> *sa* + *juṣ* + *kvip* (after the indeclinable *saha* is replaced by *sa* by *sahasya saḥ saṁjñāyām* Pā. 6. 3. 78). We obtain the nominal stem *sajuṣ* after the elision of the whole of *kvip*.

In the nominative singular we add the affix *su* after it and have *sajuṣ* + *su*. At this stage, the affix *su* is elided by *halṅyābbhyo...* (178) and the final phoneme *ṣ* of *sajuṣ* is replaced by *ru* according to the rule *sasajuṣo ruḥ* (104) which specifically mentions this word. We have *saju ru* --> *sajur*. Now by the rule *rvorupadhāyā dīrgha ikaḥ* (350), the penultimate *ik*-vowel *u* is replaced by its long counterpart and we get *sajūr*. After replacing the repha by visarjanīya, we obtain the fully inflected form *sajūḥ*.

Before the affix *bhyām*, etc. the stem gets the pada-designation and the final phoneme *ṣ* is similarly replaced by *ru* according to *sasajuṣo ruḥ* (104) and the penultimate vowel *u* is similarly lengthened by (350) and we obtain *sajūrbhyām*.

In the locative plural with the affix *sup*, we have *sajuṣ* + *sup* --> *sajuṣ* + *su*. The replacement of *ṣ* by *ru* and the lengthening of the penultimate vowel *u* take place by *sasajuṣo ruḥ* (104) and *rvorupadhāyā dīrgha ikaḥ* (350) respectively and we have *sajūr su*. In this grammatical situation, the rule *ādeśapratyayayoḥ* Pā. 8. 3. 59 becomes available for application but it is subsequent to *kharavasānayorvisarjanīyaḥ* Pā. 8. 3. 15. Therefore, the rule *kharavasānayo...* Pā. 8. 3. 15 applies and the repha is replaced by visarjanīya. Now we have *sajūḥ su*. At this stage, the rule *vā śari* (103) applies and the visarga optionally remains as it is and alternatively it is replaced by s. Thus we get two forms : *sajūḥ su* and *sajūs su*. In both the cases, the dental s of the affix *sup* is replaced by *ṣ* according to the sūtra *numvisarjanīyaśarvyavāye 'pi* (351) and the forms we obtain are : 1. *sajūḥṣu* and 2. *sajūs ṣu*. In the second form the aṅga-final dental s is replaced by *ṣ* in accordance with the rule *ṣṭunā ṣṭuḥ* (64) since the final dental s is in contact with the cerebral *ṣ*. Thus we come to have forms *sajūṣṣu* and *sajūḥṣu* in the locative plural. The complete declension of the stem *sajuṣ* is as follows :

	Singular	Dual	Plural
prathamā	*sajūḥ*	*sajuṣau*	*sajuṣaḥ*
dvitīyā	*sajuṣam*	*sajuṣau*	*sajuṣaḥ*
tṛtīyā	*sajuṣā*	*sajūrbhyām*	*sajūrbhiḥ*
caturthī	*sajuṣe*	*sajūrbhyām*	*sajūrbhyaḥ*
pañcamī	*sajuṣaḥ*	*sajūrbhyām*	*sajūrbhyaḥ*
ṣaṣṭhī	*sajuṣaḥ*	*sajuṣoḥ*	*sajuṣām*
saptamī	*sajuṣi*	*sajuṣoḥ*	*sajūḥṣu, sajūṣṣu*
sambodhana	*he sajūḥ!*	*he sajuṣau!*	*he sajuṣaḥ!*

The word *āśiṣ* 'blessing' is derived from *ā* + *śās* with the addition of the affix *kvip*. The penultimate vowel *ā* of *śās* is replaced by *i* by the vārttika *āśāsaḥ kvāvupasaṅkhyānam* (In the Mahābhāṣya, this vārttika is given as *śāsa ittva āśāsa kvau*, Mbh 6. 4. 34 vtk 1). The dental *s* of *śās* is replaced by *ṣ* according to the rule *śāsivasighasīnāṁ ca* (553) and we obtain the stem *āśiṣ*. The cerebral *ṣ* of *āśiṣ* brought about by Pā. 8. 3. 60 is deemed not to have taken effect with respect to the rule *sasajuṣo ruḥ* Pā. 8. 2. 66. This is the reason why the rule *sasajuṣo ruḥ* applies in *āśiṣ* + *su* after the elision of the affix *s*(*u*) by *halṅyābbhyo*... (178) and the cerebral *ṣ* is replaced by *ru* and we get *āśir*. The rule *rvorupadhāyā dīrgha ikaḥ* (350) applies and the penultimate vowel *i* gets lengthened and we obtain *āśīḥ* after the phoneme *r* has been replaced by visarjanīya according to *kharavasāna*... (93). The rest of the declension is like that of *sajuṣ*.

	Singular	Dual	Plural
prathamā	*āśīḥ*	*āśiṣau*	*āśiṣaḥ*
dvitīyā	*āśiṣam*	*āśiṣau*	*āśiṣaḥ*
tṛtīyā	*āśiṣā*	*āśīrbhyām*	*āśīrbhiḥ*
caturthī	*āśiṣe*	*āśīrbhyām*	*āśīrbhyaḥ*
pañcamī	*āśiṣaḥ*	*āśīrbhyām*	*āśīrbhyaḥ*
ṣaṣṭhī	*āśiṣaḥ*	*āśiṣoḥ*	*āśiṣām*

saptamī	*āśiṣi*	*āśiṣoḥ*	*āśīḥṣu, āśīṣṣu*
sambodhana	*he āśīḥ!*	*he āśiṣau!*	*he āśiṣaḥ!*

Here comes to an end the declension of the feminine words that end in ṣ. Now begins the declensional process of the feminine words that end in s.

लघु० - असौ। उत्वमत्वे — अमू। अमूः। अमुया। अमूभिः। अमुष्यै। अमूभ्यः। अमुष्याः। अमुयोः। अमूषाम्। अमुष्याम्। अमूषु। *asau. utvamatve — amū. amūḥ. amuyā. amūbhiḥ. amuṣyai. amūbhyaḥ. amuṣyāḥ. amuyoḥ. amūṣām. amuṣyām. amūṣu.*

Eluc. : The declensional process of the masculine pronominal stem *adas* has been explained (see supra, pp. 497-502). The feminine form *adas* is being declined now.

In *adas* + *su*, the aṅga-final phoneme *s* is replaced by *au* and the affix *su* is elided by the rule *adasa au sulopaśca* (354). By *tadoḥ saḥ sāvanantyayoḥ* (309) the phoneme *d* is replaced by *s*. Then by *vṛddhireci* (33), the single vṛddhi-replacement takes place in *asa* + *au* and we get *asau* in the nominative singular.

In *adas* + *au*, the rules *tyadādīnāmaḥ* (192), *ato guṇe* (273), *ajādyataṣṭāp* (1243) and *akaḥ savarṇe...* (42) apply and we get *adā* + *au*. Now according to the rule *auṅa āpaḥ* (215), we replace *au* by *śī* and have *adā* + *śī* --> *adā* + *ī* . The rule *ādguṇaḥ* (27) applies and we get *ade*. At this stage, the vowel *e* is replaced by *ū* and *d* by *m* according to the rule *adaso 'serdādu do maḥ* (355). Thus the fully inflected form *amū* is obtained.

Similarly from *adas* + *jas* we reach *adā* + *as*, after which the rule *dīrghājjasi ca* (161) blocks the rule *prathamayoḥ pūrvasavarṇaḥ* (125). Then by *akaḥ savarṇe dīrghaḥ* (42) we have *adās*. At this stage by the rule *adaso-'ser...* (355), the vowel *ā* is replaced by *ū* and the phoneme *d* by *m* and we obtain the form *amūḥ* after rutva and visarga.

In *adas* + *am* --> *adā* + *am*, by *ami pūrvaḥ* (134), we get *adām*. Then we obtain *amūm* according to the rule *adaso 'serdādu do maḥ* (355).

In *adas* + *ṭā* --> *adā* + *ā*, the vowel *ā* of *āp* (*ṭāp*) is replaced with *e* by the rule *āṅi cāpaḥ* (217) and by applying *eco...* (22) we have *adayā*. Then we obtain *amuyā* after utva and matva by *adaso...* (355).

From *adas* + *bhyām* --> *adā* + *bhyām*, we obtain *amūbhyām* by *adaso...* (355).

In *adas* + *ṅe* --> *adā* + *e*, the rule *sarvanāmnaḥ syāḍḍhrasvaśca* (219) prescribes the insertion of the augment *syāṭ* and the shortening of the affix *āp* and we have *ada* + *syā e*. Now the rule *vṛddhireci* (33) applies and we get *adasyai*. At this stage, the rules *adaso 'serdādu do maḥ* (355) and *ādeśapratyayayoḥ* (149) apply and we obtain the form *amuṣyai*.

In *adas* + *as* (*ṅasi* or *ṅas*), we have *adā* + *as* and then by applying the rule *sarvanāmnaḥ syāḍḍhrasvaśca* (219) we get *adasyāḥ*. Now by applying *adaso'ser*... (355) and *ādeśa*... (149) we obtain the form *amuṣyāḥ*.

In *adas* + *os* --> *adā* + *os*, the rule *āṅi cāpaḥ* (217) prescribes the replacement of *ā* of *āp* by *e*. Then by applying the rule *eco 'yavā*... (22) we get *adayoḥ*. We obtain *amuyoḥ* after utva and matva by *adaso'ser*... (355).

In the genitive plural we introduce the affix *ām* after *adas* and have *adas* + *ām* --> *adā* + *ām*. By the rule *āmi sarvanāmnaḥ suṭ* (154) the augment *suṭ* is inserted at the head of *ām* and we have *adā* + *suṭ ām* --> *adā* + *sām*. At this stage, the rules *adaso'serdādu*... (355) and *ādeśapratyayayoḥ* (149) apply and we obtain the form *amūṣām*.

In *adas* + *ṅi* --> *adā* + *ṅi*, the affix *ṅi* is replaced with *ām* by the rule *ṅerāmnadyāmnībhyaḥ* (197). Then the augment *syāṭ* is inserted and the *ā* of *āp* shortened by *sarvanāmnaḥ syāḍḍhrasvaśca* (219) and we have *adasyām*. After utva and matva by *adaso'serdādu*... (355) and ṣatva by *ādeśapratyayayoḥ* (149) we obtain the form *amuṣyām*.

In *adas* + *sup* --> *adā* + *su*, the rules *adaso'ser*... (355) and *ādeśa*... (149) apply and we obtain the form *amūṣu*. The complete declension of the pronominal stem *adas* in the feminine is as follows :

	Singular	Dual	Plural
prathamā	*asau*	*amū*	*amūḥ*
dvitīyā	*amūm*	*amū*	*amūḥ*
tṛtīyā	*amuyā*	*amūbhym*,	*amūbhiḥ*
caturthī	*amuṣyai*	*amūbhyām*,	*amūbhyaḥ*
pañcamī	*amuṣyāḥ*	*amūbhyām*,	*amūbhyaḥ*
ṣaṣṭhī	*amuṣyāḥ*	*amuyoḥ*	*amūṣām*
saptamī	*amuṣyām*	*amuyoḥ*	*amūṣu*

Here comes to an end the declension of the feminine words that end in the phoneme *s*.

लघु० – इति हलन्ताः स्त्रीलिङ्गाः । *iti halantāḥ strīliṅgāḥ.*

Trans. : Here ends the chapter on the feminine stems that end in a consonant.

हलन्तनपुंसकलिङ्गप्रकरणम्

Neuter Words Ending in a Consonant

लघु० – स्वमोर्लुक्। दत्वम्। स्वनडुत्, स्वनडुद्। स्वनडुही। चतुरनडुहो० (258) इत्याम्। स्वनड्वांहि। पुनस्तद्वत्। शेषं पुंवत्। *svamor luk. datvam. svanaḍut, svanaḍud. svanaḍuhī. caturanaḍuhoḥ...* (258) *ityām. svanaḍvāṁhi. punas tadvat. śeṣaṁ puṁvat.*

Eluc. : In the declensional process of the neuter words that end in a consonant, the rule *svamornapuṁsakāt* (243), being an exception, blocks the rule *halṅyābbhyo dīrghāt sutisyapṛktaṁ hal* (178) and prescribes the luk-elision of the sup-affixes *su* and *am*. For example, in declining the word *svanaḍuh* (*kulam*) '(a family) having good oxen', we have *svanaḍuh* + *su*. In this illustration the affix *su* follows a consonant *h* and accordingly the rule *halṅyābbhyo...* (178) becomes available. Since the stem *svanaḍuh* is neuter, the rule *svamornapuṁsakāt* (243), which debars the rule *halṅyābbhyo...* (178), applies. The affix *su* is elided but it is taken as effective by *pratyayalope pratyayalakṣaṇam* (189) and as such *svanaḍuh* assumes the pada designation by *suptiṅantaṁ padam* (14). The pada-final *h* of *svanaḍuh* is replaced by *d* according to the sūtra *vasusraṁsu...* (261) which applies here by virtue of the paribhāṣā *padāṅgādhikāre tasya ca tadantasya ca* (Abhyankar, 29). Then the phoneme *d* is optionally replaced by *t* in accordance with *vā 'vasāne* (145) and we obtain two forms *svanaḍut, svanaḍud* in the nominative singular.

In *svanaḍuh* + *au*, the rule *napuṁsakācca* (234) prescribes the affix *au* to be replaced by *śī* which remains as *ī* after the elision of the anubandha *ś*. By joining the two we get the form *svanaḍuhī*.

In declining the stem *svanaḍuh* in the nominative plural, we add the affix *jas*. In *svanaḍuh* + *jas*, the affix *jas* is substituted by *śi* in accordance with the sūtra *jaśśasoḥ śi* (236). The substitute *śi* is sarvanāmasthāna by *śi sarvanāmasthānam* (237). Now the sūtras *caturanaḍuhorāmudāttaḥ* (258) and *napuṁsakasya jhalacaḥ* (238) respectively prescribe the augments *ām* and *num* and we have the following grammatical situation *svanaḍu ām num h + i* --> *svanaḍu ā n h + i* (after the elision of the anubandhas of the augments). In this situation, the vowel *u* is replaced by *v* according to *iko yaṇaci* (15) and the phoneme *n* is substituted by anusvāra in accordance with *naścāpadāntasya*... (78) and we obtain the fully declined form *svanaḍvāṁhi*.

In *svanaḍuh + am*, the affix *am* is elided according to the rule *svamornapuṁsakāt* (243). In the same way with the help of *pratyayalope*... (189) it assumes the pada-designation by *suptiṅantaṁ padam* (14) and the pada-final *h* is replaced by *ḍ* in accordance with *vasusraṁsu*... (261). Then by having optional *car*-replacement by *vā 'vasāne* (145) we get two forms *svanaḍut, svanaḍud* in the accusative singular.

The forms of *svanaḍuh* declined with the affixes *auṭ* and *śas* are respectively like those declined with the affixes *au* and *jas*. The pada-final *h* of *svanaḍuh* before *bhyām, bhis*, etc. is replaced by the phoneme *ḍ* according to *vasusraṁsu*... (261) since in these instances the stem *svanaḍuh* gets the pada-designation by *svādiṣvasarvanāmasthāne* (163). The rest of the declension will be like that of the masculine stem *anaḍuh*. In this way the declension of *svanaḍuh* will be as follows :

	Singular	Dual	Plural
prathamā	*svanaḍut, d*	*svanaḍuhī*	*svanaḍvāṁhi*
dvitīyā	*svanaḍut, d*	*svanaḍuhī*	*svanaḍvāṁhi*
tṛtīyā	*svanaḍuhā*	*svanaḍudbhyām*	*svanaḍudbhiḥ*
caturthī	*svanaḍuhe*	*svanaḍudbhyām*	*svanaḍudbhyaḥ*
pañcamī	*svanaḍuhaḥ*	*svanaḍudbhyām*	*svanaḍudbhyaḥ*
ṣaṣṭhī	*svanaḍuhaḥ*	*svanaḍuhoḥ*	*svanaḍuhām*
saptamī	*svanaḍuhi*	*svanaḍuhoḥ*	*svanaḍutsu*
sambodhana	*he svanaḍut, d!*	*he svanaḍuhī!*	*he svanaḍvāṁhi!*

Here comes to an end the declension of the neuter nominal stems that end in the phoneme *h*.

Now begins the declensional process of the neuter words that end in repha (*r*).

लघु० – वाः । वारी । वारि । वार्भ्याम् । चत्वारि । *vāḥ. vārī. vāri. vārbhyām. catvāri.*

Eluc. : The word *vār* 'water' is in the neuter gender. In *vār* + *su*, the affix *su* is elided by *svamornapuṁsakāt* (243). Then the repha is replaced by visarga in avasāna and thus we have *vāḥ* in the nominative singular.

In *vār* + *au*, the affix *au* is replaced by *śī* according to *napuṁsakācca* (234). We get the form *vārī* after the anubandha *ś* has been elided.

In *vār* + *jas*, the affix *jas* is replaced by *śi* by the rule *jaśśasoḥ śiḥ* (236). Since repha is not a denotatum of the abbreviatory term *jhal*, the rule prescribing insertion of the augment *num* does not apply and we obtain the form *vāri*.

In the locative plural when we introduce the affix *sup*, we have *vār* + *sup* --> *vār* + *su*. In this illustration the repha is not replaced by visarga because of the restrictive rule *roḥ supi* (267) which prescribes the replacement of the repha of *ru* only if the affix *sup* follows. In the present case the repha does not form a part of *ru*. The dental s of the affix *sup* is replaced by ṣ in accordance with the rule *ādeśapratyayayoḥ* (149). Thus we obtain the form *vārṣu*. The complete declension of the stem *vār* is as follows :

	Singular	Dual	Plural
prathamā	*vāḥ*	*vārī*	*vāri*
dvitīyā	*vāḥ*	*vārī*	*vāri*
tṛtīyā	*vārā*	*vārbhyām*	*vārbhiḥ*
caturthī	*vāre*	*vārbhyām*	*vārbhyaḥ*
pañcamī	*vāraḥ*	*vārbhyām*	*vārbhyaḥ*
ṣaṣṭhī	*vāraḥ*	*vāroḥ*	*vārām*
saptamī	*vāri*	*vāroḥ*	*vārṣu*
sambodhana	*he vāḥ!*	*he vārī!*	*he vāri!*

The declension of the numeral *catur* 'four' in the masculine and feminine has been explained (see supra, pp. 369-71 and pp. 508-09). Now it is being declined in the neuter. In the nominative plural *catur* + *jas*, the affix *jas* is replaced by *jaśśasoḥ śiḥ* (236) and we have *catur* + *śi*. Since *śi* is sarvanāmasthāna by *śi sarvanāmasthānam* (237), the rule *caturanaḍuhorāmudāttaḥ* (258) prescribes the insertion of the augment *ām*. We have the following grammatical stage : *catu ām r* + *i*. In this grammatical situation, the rule *iko yaṇaci* (15) applies and we obtain the form *catvāri*. The same process is repeated when *śas* follows the stem. The rest of the declension will be like that of the masculine stem :

	Plural		Plural
prathamā	*catvāri*	pañcamī	*caturbhyaḥ*
dvitīyā	*catvāri*	ṣaṣṭhī	*caturṇām,*
tṛtīyā	*caturbhiḥ*	saptamī	*caturṣu*
caturthī	*caturbhyaḥ*	sambodhana	No form

Here comes to an end the declensional process of the neuter words that end in repha.

Now begins the declension of the neuter words that end in the phoneme *m*.

लघु० – किम्। के। कानि। इदम्। इमे। इमानि। *kim. ke. kāni. idam. ime. imāni.*

Eluc. : The declension of the pronominal stem *kim* in the neuter gender is now being explained. In *kim + su,* the affix *su* is elided by *svamornapuṁsakāt* (243) and we have the form *kim* in the nominative singular. The stem *kim* is not replaced by the substitute *ka* since the sup-affix (*vibhakti*) *su* has already been elided and hence it does not follow the stem *kim*. The rule *pratyayalope pratyayalakṣaṇam* (189) does not apply here since the elision of the affix *su* is the luk-elision and the replacement that was available by *kimaḥ kaḥ* (270) is an aṅgakārya. Therefore by the rule *na lumatāṅgasya* (190) it will be taken as grammatically ineffective in so far as it concerns the pre-affixal base (*āṅga*) here. This is the reason why the stem *kim* is not replaced by *ka*.

In *kim + au,* the stem *kim* is replaced by *ka* according to the rule *kimaḥ kaḥ* (270) since the affix *au* follows and we have *ka + au*. Now the affix *au* is replaced by *śī* by the rule *napuṁsakācca* (234). In *ka + śī --> ka +ī,* the pre-affixal base *ka* gets the bha-designation by *yaci bham* (164) and as such the elision of the final vowel *a* of *ka* is due by the rule *yasyeti ca* (235). This is blocked by *auṅaḥ śyāṁ pratiṣedho vācyaḥ* (vārttika, 22). Then the rule *ādguṇaḥ* (27) applies and we obtain the form *ke* (<-- *ka + ī*).

In *kim + jas --> ka + jas,* the affix *jas* is replaced with *śi* by *jaśśasoḥ śiḥ* (236). The substitute *śi* is sarvanāmasthāna by *śi sarvanāmasthānam* (237) and accordingly by *napuṁsakasya jhalacaḥ* (238) the augment *num* is inserted after the last vowel *a* of *ka* with the help of *midaco...* (239). We have *ka num + śi --> ka n + i.* At this stage, the rule *sarvanāmasthāne cā...* (176) prescribes the lengthening of the penultimate vowel since it ends in the phoneme *n* and we obtain the form *kāni* in the nominative plural.

With the affixes of the second triplet, we will have the same forms as with the affixes of the first triplet : *kim, ke, kāni*. In other vibhaktis it is declined like a masculine pronominal stem ending in *a*. In the dative singular the rule *sarvanāmnaḥ smai* (152) applies. In the ablative and locative singular the rule *ṅasiṅyoḥ smātsminau* (153) becomes applicable and in the genitive plural, the rule *āmi sarvanāmnaḥ suṭ* (154) prescribes the insertion of the augment *suṭ*. After the insertion of the augment *suṭ*, the rule *bahuvacane jhalyet* (144) prescribes the replacement of the aṅga-final *a* by *e* and we get the form *keṣām* after the dental *s* of *suṭ*, inserted at the head of the affix *ām*, is replaced by *ṣ* in accordance with the rule *ādeśa...* (149). In the locative plural the dental *s* is replaced by *ṣ* by *ādeśa...* (149). The complete declension of *kim* is as follows :

	Singular	Dual	Plural
prathamā	*kim*	*ke*	*kāni*
dvitīyā	*kim*	*ke*	*kāni*
tṛtīyā	*kena*	*kābhyām*	*kaiḥ*
caturthī	*kasmai*	*kābhyām*	*kebhyaḥ*
pañcamī	*kasmāt, d*	*kābhyām*	*kebhyaḥ*
ṣaṣṭhī	*kasya*	*kayoḥ*	*keṣām*
saptamī	*kasmin*	*kayoḥ*	*keṣu*
sambodhana	No form		

Almost a similar declensional process will be followed in the declension of the pronominal stem *idam* in the neuter gender.

In *idam* + *su* or *am*, the affixes *su* and *am* are elided by *svamor napuṁsakāt* (243) and we get *idam* both in the nominative and accusative singular.

With the dual affixes of the first and second triplets we have *idam* + *au* or *auṭ*. In both the cases the aṅga-final *m* is replaced by *a* by the rule *tyadādīnāmaḥ* (192) and then pararūpa takes place by *ato guṇe* (273) and we have *ida* + *au*. At this stage the affix *au* is replaced by *śī* according to the rule *napuṁsakācca* (234). In *ida* + *ī*, a guṇa is substituted for both *a* and *ī* and we arrive at the following grammatical stage : *ide*. Now the rule *daśca* (274) prescribes the replacement of the phoneme *d* by *m* and we obtain the form *ime*.

When we introduce either *jas* or *śas*, we have *idam* + *as* (*jas* or *śas*). By *tyadādīnāmaḥ* (192) we replace the phoneme *m* by *a* and we have *ida a* + *as* --> *ida* + *as* by *ato guṇe* (273). The affix *as* is replaced by *śi* by *jaśśasoḥ śiḥ* (236). The substitute *śi* is sarvanāmasthāna by *śi sarvanāmasthānam* (237) and accordingly by *napuṁsakasya jhalacaḥ* (238) the augment *num* is inserted after the last vowel *a* of *ida* with the help of *midaco...* (239). We have *ida num* + *śi* --> *ida n* + *i*. At this stage, the rule *sarvanāmasthāne ca...* (176) prescribes the lengthening of the penultimate vowel since it ends in the phoneme *n* and after replacing the phoneme *d* with *m* by *daśca* (274), we obtain the form *imāni* both in the nominative and accusative plural. The rest of the declension is like that of the masculine pronominal stem *idam* :

	Singular	Dual	Plural
prathamā	*idam*	*ime*	*imāni*
dvitīyā	*idam*	*ime*	*imāni*
tṛtīyā	*anena*	*ābhyām*	*ebhiḥ*
caturthī	*asmai*	*ābhyām*	*ebhyaḥ*
pañcamī	*asmāt, d*	*ābhyām*	*ebhyaḥ*
ṣaṣṭhī	*asya*	*anayoḥ*	*eṣām*
saptamī	*asmin*	*anayoḥ*	*eṣu*
sambodhana		No form	

29. वा० – अन्वादेशे नपुंसक एनद्वक्तव्यः । *anvādeśe napuṁsaka enad vaktavyaḥ.* एनत्, एनद् । एने । एनानि । एनेन । एनयोः 2 । *enat, enad. ene. enāni. enena. enayoḥ* 2.

Trans. : It should be stated that the pronominal stems *idam* and *etad* in the neuter, when anaphorically used, are to be replaced by *enat* when the affixes of the second triplet, *ṭā* and *os* follow.

Eluc. : In the Mahābhāṣya this vārttika has been read as follows : *enaditi napuṁsakaikavacane*[1] Pā. 2. 4. 34 vtk 1. This replacement has been prescribed for the singular affix of the second triplet as is clear from the vārttika given in the Mahābhāṣya. So far as the other sup-affixes (*vibhaktis*) are concerned in the context of anaphora, they can be taken care of by the sūtra *dvitīyāṭaussvenaḥ* Pā. 2. 4. 34.

1. Cf. Bhaimī, I, p. 497. Also see the explanation of *dvitīyāṭaussvenaḥ* Pā. 2. 4. 34, supra pp. 382-83 to comprehend the context and the meaning of the present vārttika.

In *idam* + *am*, the sup-affix *am* is elided by *svamornapuṁsakāt* (243). Being a luk-elision it should not be considered as grammatically effective even by the rule *pratyayalope pratyalakṣaṇam* (189). However, in deference to the present vārttika, the sup-affix *am* should be taken as grammatically effective. Otherwise, the vārttika would be rendered infructuous. The pronominal stem *idam* is thus replaced by *enat*. By applying the rules *vā 'vasāne* (145) and *jhalāṁ jaśo 'nte* (67), we get two forms, *enat* and *enad*, in the accusative singular.

In *idam* + *auṭ*, we have *idam* + *śī* by *napuṁsakācca* (234). In anvādeśa, we have *enat* + *śī*. The rule *tyadādīnāmaḥ* (192) applies and we arrive at the following stage : *ena a* + *ī*. Then we have *ena* + *ī* by *ato guṇe* (273). Now the rule *ādguṇaḥ* (27) applies and we obtain the form *ene*.

In *idam* + *śas* --> *enat* + *śas*, by applying the rules *tyadādīnāmaḥ* (192), *ato guṇe* (273) and *jaśśasoḥ śiḥ* (236) we have *ena* + *i*. At this stage, applying the rules *napuṁsakasya jhalacaḥ* (238) and *sarvanāmasthāne cāsambuddhau* (176), we get the form *enāni*.

With the singular affix of the third triplet we have *idam* + *ṭā* --> *enat* + *ṭā* --> *ena a* + *ṭā* {*tyadā*... (192)} --> *ena* + *ṭā* {*ato*... (273)}. Then the affix *ṭā* is replaced by *ina* by *ṭāṅasiṅasāmināṭsyāḥ* (139) and we have *ena* + *ina*. By applying *ādguṇaḥ* (27), we obtain the form *enena*.

In *idam* + *os* --> *enat* + *os* --> *ena a* + *os* {*tyadādīnāmaḥ* (192)} --> *ena* + *os* {*ato*... (273)}. Then by *osi ca* (146), the *a* of *ena* is replaced by *e* we have *ene* + *os*. The rule *eco*... (22) applies and we obtain the form *enayoḥ*.

The declensional process above has been given in the context of the vārttika given in the Laghu. If we take into account the form of the vārttika as available in the Mahābhāṣya, then the substitute *enat* will replace the pronominal stem *idam* only before *am*. In other instances, the substitute *ena* will replace the stem *idam* by the sūtra *dvitīyāṭaussvenaḥ* Pā. 2. 4. 34 (cf. Bhaimī, I, pp. 496-97). The grammatical process in this case will not involve *tyadādīnāmaḥ* (192) and *ato guṇe* (273).

When the pronominal stem *idam* is anaphorically used, its declension will be as follows :

	Singular	Dual	Plural
prathamā	*idam*	*ime*	*imāni*
dvitīyā	*enat, d*	*ene*	*enāni*
tṛtīyā	*enena*	*ābhyām*	*ebhiḥ*
caturthī	*asmai*	*ābhyām*	*ebhyaḥ*
pañcamī	*asmāt, d*	*ābhyām*	*ebhyaḥ*

ṣaṣṭhī	*asya*	*enayoḥ*	*eṣām*
saptamī	*asmin*	*enayoḥ*	*eṣu*
sambodhana	No form		

Here comes to an end the declension of the neuter words that end in the phoneme *m*.

Now starts the declensional process of the neuter words that end in the phoneme *n*.

लघु० – अहः । विभाषा ङिश्योः (248) -- अह्नी, अहनी । अहानि । *ahaḥ. vibhāṣā ṅiśyoḥ* (248) -- *ahnī, ahanī. ahāni.*

Eluc. : The nominal stem *ahan* 'day' is in the neuter gender. To decline it in the nominative singular we introduce the affix *su* : *ahan* + *su*. The affix *su* is elided by *svamornapuṁsakāt* (243). Then by the rule *ro 'supi* (109), the phoneme *n* is replaced by repha which is substituted by visarga according to the rule *kharava...* (93). We obtain the form *ahaḥ*. The accusative singular form *ahaḥ* will be declined similarly.

In *ahan* + *au* or *auṭ*, we have *ahan* + *śī* --> *ahan* + *ī* by *napuṁsakācca* (234). In this situation, the stem *ahan* is bha according to the rule *yaci bham* (164). Accordingly, the vowel *a* of the segment *an* is optionally elided by the rule *vibhāṣā ṅiśyoḥ* (247) and we obtain two forms : *ahnī* and *ahanī*.

In *ahan* + *as* (*jas* or *śas*), the affix *jas* or *śas* is replaced by *śi* in accordance with the rule *jaśśasoḥ śiḥ* (236) and we have *ahan* + *śi*. The substitute *śi* is a sarvanāmasthāna affix by *śi sarvanāmasthānam* (237). At this stage, the rule *sarvanāmasthāne cāsambuddhau* (176) prescribes the lengthening of the penultimate vowel as it ends in the phoneme *n* and we get the form *ahāni*.

In *ahan* + *ṭā* --> *ahan* + *ā*, the stem *ahan* is bha by *yaci bham* (164) and therefore the vowel *a* of the segment *an* is elided by *allopo 'naḥ* (246). Thus we obtain the form *ahnā*.

In *ahan* + *bhyām*, the following sūtra applies :

(362) अहन् । *ahan*. 8. 2. 68

लघु० – अहन् इत्यस्य रुः पदान्ते । अहोभ्याम् । *ahan ityasya ruḥ padānte. ahobhyām.*

Trans. : The pada-final phoneme *n* of *ahan* is replaced by *ru*.

PP. *ahan ru padasya ante.*

Eluc. : The word *ahan* is in the genitive singular. Its genitive case-ending is taken as elided (*ahan iti luptaṣaṣṭhīkaṁ padam,* BM, I, p. 462). The term *ru* is carried over from *sasajuṣo ruḥ* Pā. 8. 2. 66. The word *ante* is carried over from *skoḥ saṁyogādyorante ca* Pā. 8. 2. 29 (cf. BM, I, p. 462). The present rule occurs in the domain of the governing rule *padasya* Pā. 8. 1. 16. Thus we have *padasya ante* which gives the sense 'at the end of a pada or pada-final'. With the help of the paribhāṣā sūtra *alo 'ntyasya* (21) we arrive at the following meaning : At the end of a pada the pada-final phoneme *n* of *ahan* is replaced by *ru.*

In *ahan + bhyām,* the stem gets the pada-designation by *svādiṣvasarva-nāmasthāne* (163). Accordingly, the phoneme *n* is pada-final and as such it is replaced by *ru* and we have *aha ru + bhyām.* The rule *haśi ca* (106) prescribes *ru* to be replaced by *u.* By *ādguṇaḥ* (27) we obtain the form *ahobhyām.*

In *ahan + ṅi,* the stem *ahan* gets the bha-designation. Accordingly by the rule *vibhāṣaṅiśyoḥ* (247), the *a* of *an* is optionally elided and we obtain two forms in the locative singular : *ahni* and *ahani.*

In the locative plural we have *ahan + sup --> ahan + su.* By the present rule, the substitute *ru* replaces the pada-final *n* and we have *aha ru + su.* The repha of *ru* is replaced by visarga by *kharava...* (93) and then by applying the rules *visarjanīyasya saḥ* (96) and *vā śari* (103) we get two forms : *ahaḥsu* and *ahassu.* The complete declension of the nominal stem *ahan* is as follows :

	Singular	Dual	Plural
prathamā	*ahaḥ*	*ahnī, ahanī*	*ahāni*
dvitīyā	*ahaḥ*	*ahnī, ahanī*	*ahāni*
tṛtīyā	*ahnā*	*ahobhyām*	*ahobhiḥ*
caturthī	*ahne*	*ahobhyām*	*ahobhyaḥ*
pañcamī	*ahnaḥ*	*ahobhyām*	*ahobhyaḥ*
ṣaṣṭhī	*ahnaḥ*	*ahnoḥ*	*ahnām*
saptamī	*ahni, ahani*	*ahnoḥ*	*ahaḥsu, ahassu*
sambodhana	*he ahaḥ!*	*he ahnī, ahanī!*	*he ahāni!*

लघु० – दण्डि। सुपथि। टेर्लोपः – सुपथी। सुपन्थानि। *daṇḍi. supathi. ṭer lopaḥ — supathī. supanthāni.*

Eluc. : The nominal stem *daṇḍin* is derived with the taddhita affix *ini* added after the word *daṇḍa* by *ata iniṭhanau* (1185). In this case it qualifies a neuter word like *kulam* 'family'; hence it will be declined in the neuter gender.

In the nominative singular, we have the following grammatical situation : *daṇḍin* + *su*. At this stage, the affix *s*(*u*) is elided by the rule *svamornapuṁsakāt* (243) and we have *daṇḍi* after the pada-final *n* has been elided by *na lopaḥ*... (179).

When we decline it in the vocative singular, after the elision of the affix *su*, the elision of *n* is due as in the nominative singular but the following vārttika renders it optional.

30. वा० – सम्बुद्धौ नपुंसकानां नलोपो वा वाच्यः ।[1] *sambuddhau napuṁsakānāṁ nalopo vā vācyaḥ.*

Trans. : The phoneme *n* of the neuter words is optionally elided when the vocative singular affix follows.

Eluc. : In *he daṇḍin* + *su*, the affix *su* has been elided by *svamor*... (243). Then by virtue of the rule *pratyayalope pratyayalakṣaṇam* (189), the elided *su* will be deemed to be effective. Accordingly, by the present vārttika, the phoneme *n* is optionally elided and we obtain two forms in the vocative singular : *he daṇḍi!* (when there is an elision of *n*) *he daṇḍin!* (in the absence of the elision of *n*).

In *daṇḍin* + *au*, the affix *au* is replaced by *śī* by *napuṁsakācca* (234) and we have *daṇḍin* + *śī* --> *daṇḍin* + *ī* --> *daṇḍinī*.

In *daṇḍin* + *jas*, the affix *jas* is replaced by *śi* {*jaśśasoḥ śiḥ* (236)} --> *daṇḍin* + *śi* --> *daṇḍin* + *i* . The substitute *śi* is sarvanāmasthāna by *śi sarvanāmasthānam* (237). Then by *sarvanāmasthāne cāsambuddhau* (176), the penultimate vowel gets lengthened and we obtain the form *daṇḍīni*. The complete declension of the neuter word *daṇḍin* will be as follows :

	Singular	Dual	Plural
prathamā	*daṇḍi*	*daṇḍinī*	*daṇḍīni*
dvitīyā	*daṇḍi*	*daṇḍinī*	*daṇḍīni*
tṛtīyā	*daṇḍinā*	*daṇḍibhyām*	*daṇḍibhiḥ*
caturthī	*daṇḍine*	*daṇḍibhyām*	*daṇḍibhyaḥ*

1. In the Mahābhāṣya this vārttika has been given as *vā napuṁsakānām* Mbh 8. 2. 8 vtk 2.

pañcamī	*daṇḍinaḥ*	*daṇḍibhyām*	*daṇḍibhyaḥ*
ṣaṣṭhī	*daṇḍinaḥ*	*daṇḍinoḥ*	*daṇḍinām*
saptamī	*daṇḍini*	*daṇḍinoḥ*	*daṇḍiṣu*
sambodhana	*he daṇḍi, n!*	*he daṇḍinī!*	*he daṇḍīni!*

The word *supathin* '(a city) that has good roads' is a bahuvrīhi compound which is analysed as follows : *sundarāḥ panthāno yasmin, tat* = *supathi* (*nagaram*).

In the nominative singular we have *supathin* + *su*. In this situation, the affix *su* is elided by *svamornapuṁsakāt* (243) and the pada-final *n* by *na lopaḥ*... (179). Thus we get the form *supathi*.

When we introduce the nominative dual affix *au*, the stem *supathin* gets the bha designation by *yaci bham* (164) after the affix *au* has been replaced by *śī* by *napuṁsakācca* (234). Now the rule *bhasya ṭerlopaḥ* (295) applies and the *ṭi*-portion of the *supathin*, that is, *in* is elided and we obtain the form *supathī*.

In the nominative plural we introduce the affix *jas* after *supathin*. The affix *jas* is replaced by *śi* in accordance with *jaśśasoḥ śiḥ* (236) and we have *supathin* + *śi*. The substitute *śi* is a sarvanāmasthāna affix by *śi sarvanāma*... (237). At this stage, the rule *ito 'tsarvanāma*... (293) applies and the vowel *i* is replaced by *a*. The phoneme *th* is substituted by *nth* according to *tho 'nthaḥ* (294) and we get *supanthan* + *i*. In this grammatical situation, the penultimate vowel *a* is lengthened by *sarvanāmasthāne cāsambuddhau* (176). Thus we obtain the form *supanthāni*. During the declensional process, the *ṭi*-portion of the *supathin* will be elided by *bhasya ṭerlopaḥ* (295) wherever it gets the bha-designation by *yaci bham* (164) and pada-final *n* is elided by *na lopaḥ*... (179) wherever it gets the pada-designation by *svādiṣvasarvanāmasthāne* (163). In this way the complete declension of the neuter word *supathin* is as follows :

	Singular	Dual	Plural
prathamā	*supathi*	*supathī*	*supanthāni*
dvitīyā	*supathi*	*supathī*	*supanthāni*
tṛtīyā	*supathā*	*supathibhyām*	*supathibhiḥ*
caturthī	*supathe*	*supathibhyām*	*supathibhyaḥ*
pañcamī	*supathaḥ*	*supathibhyām*	*supathibhyaḥ*
ṣaṣṭhī	*supathaḥ*	*supathoḥ*	*supathām*

saptamī	*supathi*	*supathoḥ*	*supathiṣu*
sambodhana	*he supathi, n!*	*he supathī!*	*he supanthāni!*

Here comes to an end the declension of the neuter stems that end in the phoneme *n*.

Now begins the declension of the neuter stems that end in *j*.

लघु० – ऊर्क्, ऊर्ग् । ऊर्जी । ऊन्र्जि । नरजानां संयोगः । *ūrk, ūrg. ūrjī. ūnrji. narajānāṁ saṁyogaḥ.*

Eluc. : The nominal stem *ūrj* 'strength' is derived from the verbal root *ūrj* 'to strengthen, to invigorate' with the introduction of the affix *kvip* which is wholly elided.

In *ūrj + su,* the affix *su* is elided by *halṅyābbhyo...* (178). The conjunct-final *j* is not elided because of the restrictive rule *rāt sasya* (208). By *coḥ kuḥ* (305) the pada-final *j* is replaced with *g*. Then *vā 'vasāne* (145) applies and we have two forms *ūrk* and *ūrg* in the nominative singular.

In *ūrj + au,* the affix *au* is replaced by *śī* and we get the form *ūrjī.*

In *ūrj + jas --> ūrj + śi,* the substitute affix *śi* is sarvanāmasthāna. As such, the augment *num* is inserted after the last vowel by the rule *napuṁsakasya jhalacaḥ* (238) and we have the following grammatical situation *ū num rj + śi --> ū n rj + i*. From this we obtain the form *ūnrji.* It has to be kept in mind that the conjunction of the consonants is in the order of *n, r* and *j*. Varadarāja specifically mentions this in the vṛtti.

In the locative plural, applying the rules *coḥ kuḥ* (305), *ādeśa...* (149) and *khari ca* (74), we get the form *ūrkṣu.* The complete declension of the nominal stem *ūrj* is given below :

	Singular	Dual	Plural
prathamā	*ūrk, ūrg*	*ūrjī*	*ūnrji*
dvitīyā	*ūrk, ūrg*	*ūrjī*	*ūnrji*
tṛtīyā	*ūrjā*	*ūrgbhyām*	*ūrgbhiḥ*
caturthī	*ūrje*	*ūrgbhyām*	*ūrgbhyaḥ*
pañcamī	*ūrjaḥ*	*ūrgbhyām*	*ūrgbhyaḥ*
ṣaṣṭhī	*ūrjaḥ*	*ūrjoḥ*	*ūrjām*
saptamī	*ūrji*	*ūrjoḥ*	*ūrkṣu*
sambodhana	*he ūrk, ūrg!*	*he ūrjī!*	*he ūnrji!*

Here comes to an end the declension of the neuter words ending in *j*.

Now begins the declension of the neuter stems ending in *d*.

लघु० – तत्। ते। तानि। यत्। ये। यानि। एतत्। एते। एतानि। *tat. te. tāni. yat. ye. yāni. etat. ete. etāni.*

Eluc. : The pronominal stems *tad, yad* and *etad* in the masculine and feminine have already been explained. Now their declension in the neuter is being explained.

In *tad + su,* the affix *su* is elided by *halṅyābbhyo...* (178) and we have two forms *tat* and *tad* by applying *vā 'vasāne* (145). In this case the rule *tadoḥ saḥ sāvanantyayoḥ* (309) does not apply since the affix *su* has been substituted by luk-elision. The elided *su* is not treated as effective by *pratyayalope pratyayalakṣaṇam* (189) since this has been prohibited by *na lumatā 'ṅgasya* (190) as the replacement of *t* by *s* in accordance with *tadoḥ saḥ sāvanantyayoḥ* (309) is an aṅga-function.

In *tad + au,* the rule *tyadādī...* (192) applies and the phoneme *d* of *tad* is replaced by *a* and we have *ta a + au --> ta + au* {*ato guṇe* (273)}. Now the affix *au* is replaced by *śī* in accordance with *napuṁsakācca* (234). By applying *ādguṇaḥ* (27) we get *te* in the nominative dual.

In *tad + jas,* we have *ta a + jas* {*tyadādī...* (192)} --> *ta + jas* {*ato...* (243)} --> *ta + śi* {*jaśśasoḥ śiḥ* (236)} --> *ta num + śi* {*napuṁsakasya jhalacaḥ* (238)} --> *ta n + i*. At this stage, the rule *sarvanāmasthāne...* (176) applies and the penultimate vowel of *ta n* gets lengthened and we obtain the form *tāni*. Exactly the same process applies in respect of the pronominal stems *yad* and *tad*.The declension of the pronominal stems *tad, yad* and *etad* in the neuter are given below :

	Singular	Dual	Plural
prathamā	*tat, tad*	*te*	*tāni*
dvitīyā	*tat, tad*	*te*	*tāni*
tṛtīyā	*tena*	*tābhyām*	*taiḥ*
caturthī	*tasmai*	*tābhyām*	*tebhyaḥ*
pañcamī	*tasmāt, d*	*tābhyām*	*tebhyaḥ*
ṣaṣṭhī	*tasya*	*tayoḥ*	*teṣām*
saptamī	*tasmin*	*tayoḥ*	*teṣu*
sambodhana		No form	

The declension of *yad* in the neuter is as follows :

prathamā	*yat, yad*	*ye*	*yāni*
dvitīyā	*yat, yad*	*ye*	*yāni*

The rest of the declension is like that of *yad* in the masculine.

The declension of *etad* in the neuter is as follows :

prathamā	*etat, etad*	*ete*	*etāni*
dvitīyā	*etat, etad*	*ete*	*etāni*

The rest of the declension is like that of the pronominal stem *etad* in the masculine.

Here comes to an end the declension of the neuter words that end in the phoneme *d*.

Now begins the declension of the neuter stems ending in *c*.

लघु० - गवाक्, गवाग्। गोची। गवाञ्चि। पुनस्तद्वत्। गोचा। गवाग्भ्याम्। *gavāk, gavāg. gocī. gavāñci. punas tadvat. gocā, gavāgbhyām.*

Eluc. : The word *go añc* '(a friend or a family) that follows or worships a cow' is derived with the addition of the affix *kvin* after the verbal root *añc* 'to go, to worship' according to the rule *ṛtvigdadhṛk*... (300) when it is preceded by the word *go* as an upapada in the form of an object. The affix *kvin* is wholly elided like *kvip*. Since the affix is *kit*, the penultimate nasal stop of the verbal root is elided by *aniditām*... (333) when the verbal root *añc* is used to convey the meaning 'to go'. Then we get the word *go ac* which gets the prātipadika designation by *kṛttaddhita*... (116). As the word *go ac* qualifies the neuter substantive (such as *kulam* or *mitram*), it will be declined in the neuter gender.

In the Laghu, only the word derived from the verbal root *añc* 'to go' has been explained and not the word in which the verbal root *añc* has the sense 'to worship'. The nominal stem *go ac* '(a friend or a family) that follows a cow' is being explained below.

In *go ac + su*, the affix *su* is elided by *svamor*... (243). In this situation, the rules *coḥ kuḥ* Pā. 8. 2. 30 and *kvinpratyayasya kuḥ* Pā. 8. 2. 62 become applicable simultaneously but the latter rule, being subsequent in the tripādī and hence being suspended, does not apply. So, *coḥ kuḥ* applies and we have *go ak* after the phoneme *c* has been replaced by *k*. After the application of the sūtras *vā 'vasāne* (145) and *jhalāṁ jaśo 'nte* (67), we get two forms : *go ak* and *go ag*. In this grammatical situation, three kinds of sandhi take place between the vowel *o* of *go* and the vowel *a* of *ak*. The substitute *avaṅ* optionally replaces the vowel *o* of *go* by *avaṅ sphoṭāyanasya* (47). Then the rule *akaḥ savarṇe dīrghaḥ* (42) prescribes a homogeneous long vowel substitution (*savarṇadīrgha*) in *gava + ak* (or *ag*) and we get 1. *gavāk* and 2. *gavāg* in the nominative singular. In the other alternative, i.e. when *avaṅ* does not come as a substitute, the rule *sarvatra vibhāṣā goḥ* (44) enjoins optional prakṛtibhāva. When there is prakṛtibhāva, we again have two forms 3. *go ak* and 4. *go ag*. In the absence of prakṛtibhāva, there is pūrvarūpa sandhi by *eṅaḥ padāntādati* (43) and we get two forms 5. *go 'k* and 6. *go 'g*. Thus we obtain six forms in all in the nominative singular : two with *avaṅ* and four without it.

In *go ac + au*, the substitute *śī* replaces the affix *au* by *napuṁsakācca* (234). Since the substitute affix *śī* begins with a vowel after the elision of the anubandha *ś*, the stem *go ac* gets the bha-designation by *yaci bham* (164). Then the rule *acaḥ* (334) prescribes the elision of vowel *a* of *ac* and we obtain the form *gocī* in the nominative dual. This grammatical function should be kept in mind wherever a vowel-initial sup-affix, other than a sarvanāmasthāna, follows.

In *go ac + jas*, the affix *jas* is replaced with *śi* by *jaśśasoḥ śiḥ* (236). The substitute affix *śi* is sarvanāmasthāna by *śi sarvanāmasthānam* (237). As such, the rule *ugidacāṁ sarvanāmasthāne 'dhātoḥ* (288) prescribes the insertion of the augment *num* after the last vowel in *go ac* and we have the following grammatical situation : *go a num c + śi --> go a n c + i*. At this stage, the rules *naścāpadāntasya jhali* (78) and *anusvārasya yayi parasavarṇaḥ* (79) respectively prescribe the replacement of *n* by anusvāra and parasavarṇa. By applying the sandhi rules *avaṅ*... (47), *sarvatra vibhāṣā*... (44) and *eṅaḥ*... (43), we obtain three forms : 1. *gavāñci* (with *avaṅ*) 2. *goañci* (without *avaṅ* and with prakṛtibhāva) and 3. *go 'ñci* (with pūrvarūpa) in a respective manner.

The same grammatical process is repeated when this stem is declined with the sup-affixes of the second triplet.

In *go ac + ṭā --> go ac + ā*, the stem *go ac* gets the bha-designation by *yaci bham* (164). Accordingly, the vowel *a* of *ac* is elided by *acaḥ* (334) and we get the form *gocā*.

In *go ac + bhyām*, the stem *go ac* gets the pada-designation by *svādiṣvasarvanāmasthāne* (163). As such, the rule *coḥ kuḥ* (305) prescribes the replacement of the phoneme *c* by *k* and then by *jhalāṁ jaśo 'nte* (67), the consonant *k* is substituted by *g*. Now the same three kinds of sandhi take place and we obtain three forms : 1. *gavāgbhyām* (*avaṅ*-substitution) 2. *goagbhyām* (in prakṛtibhāva) 3. *go 'gbhyām* (pūrvarūpa sandhi in the absence of prakṛtibhāva). The same grammatical process is repeated in the declensional process of *go ac* before *bhis* and *bhyas*. In *go ac + sup*, the same grammatical operation is again repeated and in addition, the rule *khari ca* (74) applies and the phoneme *g* is replaced by *k* after the dental s of the affix *sup* has been substituted by ṣ in accordance with *ādeśapratyayayoḥ* (149) and we have the forms *gavākṣu*, etc. The complete declension of this stem is given below :

	Singular	Dual	Plural
prathamā	*gavāk, g* *go ak, g* *go 'k, g*	*gocī*	*gavāñci* *goañci* *go 'ñci*
dvitīyā	*gavāk, g* *go ak, g* *go 'k, g*	*gocī*	*gavāñci* *goañci* *go 'ñci*
tṛtīyā	*gocā*	*gavāgbhyām* *goagbhyām* *go 'gbhyām*	*gavāgbhiḥ* *goagbhiḥ* *go 'gbhiḥ*
caturthī	*goce*	*gavāgbhyām* *goagbhyām* *go 'gbhyām*	*gavāgbhyaḥ* *goagbhyaḥ* *go 'gbhyaḥ*
pañcamī	*gocaḥ*	*gavāgbhyām* *goagbhyām* *go 'gbhyām*	*gavāgbhyaḥ* *goagbhyaḥ* *go 'gbhyaḥ*
ṣaṣṭhī	*gocaḥ*	*gocoḥ*	*gocām*
saptamī	*goci*	*gocoḥ*	*gavākṣu* *goakṣu* *go 'kṣu*
sambodhana	*he gavāk, g!* *he goak, g!* *he go 'k, g!*	*he gocī !*	*he gavāñci!* *he goañci!* *he go'ñci!*

Here comes to an end the declension of the neuter words that end in the phoneme *c*.

Now begins the declension of the neuter nominal stems that end in the phoneme *t*.

लघु० – शकृत्। शकृती। शकृन्ति। *śakṛt. śakṛtī. śakṛnti.*

Eluc. : The nominal stem *śakṛt* 'excrement' is in the neuter gender. When we decline it in the nominative singular we have *śakṛt + su*. The affix *su* is elided by *svamor...* (243) and then by applying *vā 'vasāne* (145) and *jhalāṁ jaśo 'nte* (67), we obtain two forms : *śakṛt* and *śakṛd*.

In *śakṛt + au*, the substitute *śī* replaces the affix *au* by *napuṁsakācca* (234) and we get the form *śakṛtī* after the elision of the anubandha *ś*.

In *śakṛt + jas*, *jaśśasoḥ śiḥ* (236) prescribes the affix *jas* to be replaced by *śi*. The substitute affix *śi* is sarvanāmasthāna by *śi sarvanāmasthānam* (237). Accordingly, the augment *num* is inserted after the last vowel by the rule *napuṁsakasya jhalacaḥ* (238) and we have *śakṛ num t + śi --> śakṛ n t + i*. In this situation, the rules *naścāpadāntasya jhali* (78) and *anusvārasya yayi parasavarṇaḥ* (79) respectively prescribe the replacement of *n* by anusvāra and that of anusvāra by the homogeneous fifth nasal stop, that is *n* in this particular case and the form *śakṛnti* is obtained. The declension of the nominal stem *śakṛt* is as follows :

	Singular	Dual	Plural
prathamā	*śakṛt, d*	*śakṛtī*	*śakṛnti*
dvitīyā	*śakṛt, d*	*śakṛtī*	*śakṛnti*
tṛtīyā	*śakṛtā*	*śakṛdbhyām*	*śakṛdbhiḥ*
caturthī	*śakṛte*	*śakṛdbhyām*	*śakṛdbhyaḥ*
pañcamī	*śakṛtaḥ*	*śakṛdbhyām*	*śakṛdbhyaḥ*
ṣaṣṭhī	*śakṛtaḥ*	*śakṛtoḥ*	*śakṛtām*
saptamī	*śakṛti*	*śakṛtoḥ*	*śakṛtsu*
sambodhana	*he śakṛt, d!*	*he śakṛtī!*	*he śakṛnti*

लघु० – ददत्। ददती। *dadat. dadatī.*

Eluc. : The word *dadat* is derived from the verbal root *ḍudāñ* 'to give' with the addition of the primary affix *śatṛ* by *laṭaḥ śatṛ...* (828). This verbal root belongs to the juhotyādi class. As such, in *ḍudāñ + śatṛ --> dā + at* (after the elision of the anubandhas), the infix (*vikaraṇa*) *śap* is introduced by *kartari śap* (386). The infix *śap* is replaced by *ślu* by *juhotyādibhyaḥ śluḥ* (603) and we have *dā śap + at --> dā ślu + at*. Now by the rule *ślau* (604), the verbal root is reduplicated --> *dā dā + at --> da dā*

+ *at* {*hrasvaḥ* (396)} --> *da d* + *at* --> {*śnābhyastayorātaḥ* (618)} --> *dadat*. When the participial form *dadat* qualifies a neuter substantive such as *mitra* (friend), it will be declined in the neuter.

In *dadat* + *su*, the affix *su* is elided by *svamor...* (243). Then the rules *vā 'vasāne* (145) and *jhalāṁ jaśo 'nte* (67) apply and we have two forms *dadat* and *dadad* in the nominative singular.

In *dadat* + *au*, the affix *au* is replaced by *śī* by *napuṁsakācca* (234). By joining them, we get *dadatī* in the nominative dual.

In *dadat* + *jas*, the affix *jas* is substituted by *śi* which is sarvanāmasthāna by *śi sarvanāmasthānam* (237). Accordingly, the augment *num*, which was due to be introduced by *napuṁsakasya jhalacaḥ* (238), is blocked by the rule *nābhyastācchatuḥ* (344). The rule says that if the affix *śatṛ* occurs after that which has been designated as *abhyasta*, then the augment *num* does not become a part of that which ends in the affix *śatṛ*. Here *śatṛ* occurs after the reduplicated segment *dā dā* which has been designated as *abhyasta* by *ubhe abhyastam* (343). In such a situation, the following sūtra optionally prescribes the insertion of the augment *num* :

(363) वा नपुंसकस्य । *vā napuṁsakasya.* 7. 1. 79

लघु० – अभ्यस्तात् परो यः शता तदन्तस्य क्लीबस्यस्य वा नुम् सर्वनामस्थाने । ददन्ति, ददति । *abhyastāt paro yaḥ śatā tadantasya klībasya vā num sarvanāmasthāne. dadanti, dadati.*

Trans. : The augment *num* is optionally introduced to the neuter stem that ends in the affix *śatṛ* occurring after an abhyasta, when a sarvanāmasthāna affix follows.

PP. *abhyastāt śatuḥ napuṁsakasya aṅgasya vā num sarvanāmasthāne.*

Eluc. : The words *abhyastāt* and *śatuḥ* are carried over from the sūtra *nābhyastācchatuḥ* Pā. 7. 1. 78. The term *num* is lent into the sūtra from *idito num dhātoḥ* Pā. 7. 1. 58 and the word *sarvanāmasthāne* comes from *ugidacāṁ sarvanāmasthāne 'dhātoḥ* Pā. 7. 1. 70. The present sūtra occurs in the domain of the governing rule *aṅgasya* Pā. 6. 4. 1. Hence the word *aṅgasya* recurs in the present sūtra (for the terms which are carried over into the present sūtra cf. BM, I, p. 475). The word *śatā* in the vṛtti is the nominative singular form of the affix *śatṛ*. The meaning of the sūtra is as follows : If the neuter pre-affixal base ends in the affix *śatṛ* which occurs after an abhyasta, then the augment *num* is optionally introduced to such a pre-affixal base when a sarvanāmasthāna affix follows.

In *dadat + i,* the substitute affix (*ś*)*i* is sarvanāmasthāna. Hence the augment *num* is inserted optionally : 1. *dada n*(*um*) *t + i* 2. *dada t + i.* From the second illustration we get the form *dadati*. In the first illustration, the rules *naścāpadāntasya jhali* (78) and *anusvārasya yayi parasavarṇaḥ* (79) respectively prescribe the replacement of *n* by anusvāra and that of anusvāra by the homogeneous fifth nasal stop, that is *n* in this case. Thus we obtain the form *dadanti*. In this way we can decline the neuter stem *dadat* in the following manner :

	Singular	Dual	Plural
prathamā	*dadat, d*	*dadatī*	*dadanti, dadati*
dvitīyā	*dadat, d*	*dadatī*	*dadanti, dadati*
tṛtīyā	*dadatā*	*dadadbhyām*	*dadadbhiḥ*
caturthī	*dadate*	*dadadbhyām*	*dadadbhyaḥ*
pañcamī	*dadataḥ*	*dadadbhyām*	*dadadbhyaḥ*
ṣaṣṭhī	*dadataḥ*	*dadatoḥ*	*dadatām*
saptamī	*dadati*	*dadatoḥ*	*dadatsu*
sambodhana	*he dadat, d!*	*he dadatī!*	*he dadanti, dadati!*

लघु० – तुदत्। *tudat.*

Eluc. : The word *tudat* is a participial form of the verbal root *tud* 'to give trouble, to pain'. Its grammatical derivation is as follows : *tud + śatṛ* {*laṭaḥ śatṛ...* (828)} --> *tud + śa + śatṛ* {*tudādi...* (650)} --> *tud +a + at* (after the elision of the anubandhas) --> *tudat* {by *ato guṇe* (273)}.

In *tudat + su,* the affix *su* is elided by *svamornapuṁsakāt* (243). Now by applying the rules *vā 'vasāne* (145) and *jhalāṁ jaśo 'nte* (67), we get two forms *tudat* and *tudad* in the nominative singular.

In *tudat + au,* the affix *au* is replaced by *śī* in accordance with *napuṁsakācca* (234) and we have *tudat + śī*. At this stage, the following sūtra presents itself for application :

(364) आच्छीनद्योर्नुम् । *ācchīnadyornum.* 7. 1. 80

लघु० – अवर्णान्तादङ्गात् परो यः शतुरवयवस्तदन्तस्य नुम् वा शीनद्योः। तुदन्ती, तुदती। तुदन्ति। *avarṇāntād aṅgāt paro yaḥ śatur avayavas tadantasya num vā śīnadyoḥ. tudantī, tudatī. tudanti.*

Trans. : The augment *num* is optionally introduced to the aṅga that ends with a portion (*t*) of the affix *śatṛ* occurring after the pre-affixal base (aṅga) that ends in the vowel *a*, when *śī* or a nadī affix follows.[1]

PP. *āt śatuḥ aṅgasya śīnadyoḥ vā num.*

Eluc. : The present sūtra occurs in the domain of the governing rule *aṅgasya* Pā. 6. 4. 1. Hence the word *aṅgasya* recurs in the present sūtra. It is changed into the ablative singular nominal ending by the process of vibhaktivipariṇāma. Thus the word *aṅgāt* will be qualified by *āt*. By tadantavidhi, this will give the meaning 'after the aṅga that ends in the vowel *a*' The term *śatuḥ* comes from the sūtra *nābhyastācchatuḥ* Pā. 7. 1. 78. The indeclinable *vā* is carried over from *vā napuṁsakasya* 7. 1. 79. The mention of the term *num* in the sūtra does not serve any purpose since it can normally be carried over from the sūtra *idito num dhātoḥ* Pā. 7. 1. 58. In this context Jñānendra Sarasvatī says that the purpose of the enunciation of the term *num* in the present sūtra is questionable (*numgrahaṇam iha cintyaprayojanam*, TB, I, pp. 475-76), whereas Vāsudeva Dīkṣita accepts 'clarity' as its purpose (*numgrahaṇaṁ spaṣṭārtham*, BM, I, p. 476). The meaning of the sūtra is as follows : When *śī* or a nadī affix follows, the augment *num* will optionally become a part of that aṅga which ends with a portion of the affix *śatṛ* occurring after a pre-affixal base that ends in the vowel *a*. The term *nadī* stands for the feminine words that end in long *ī* or *ū* but here by this term the feminine affixes *ṅīp*, etc. are intended.

---

1. In *tud a* + *śatṛ* + *au* --> *tuda* + *śatṛ* + *śī*, the affix *śatṛ* occurs after a pre-affixal base ending in the vowel *a* and the nominative dual affix *au* is replaced by *śī* according to *napuṁsakācca* (234). In this grammatical situation two grammatical operations are due : 1. the insertion of the augment *num* by the present rule and 2. a single vowel substitution by *ato guṇe* (274). The single vowel substitution, the pararūpa sandhi, being dependent on phonemes is considered to be antaraṅga (internally conditioned), whereas the insertion of the augment of *num* is bahiraṅga since it requires many conditions to be fulfilled. So, the rule *ato guṇe* (274) applies first and a single vowel substitution in the form of *a* comes in place of both the akāras. In *tudat* + *śī*, the affix *śatṛ* is not available after an aṅga which ends in *a* since the *a* of *śatṛ* has become one with the *a* of *tuda*. If we take the single substitute *a* as the final of the preceding then we have an aṅga ending in *a* but in this way also the affix *śatṛ* is not available. On the other hand, if we take this single substitute as the initial of what follows, then we have the affix *śatṛ* but the aṅga ceases to end in *a*. Such a practice is not allowed as is clear from the following statement : *ubhayata āśrayaṇe nāntādivat*, which means that the same single substitute, at one point of time, cannot be treated as the final of the preceding and the initial of the following.This is the reason why the affix *śatṛ* has been interpreted by Bhaṭṭoji Dīkṣita and following him by Varadarāja as if it were its own part (*śatur avayavaḥ*). In the above grammatical situation, the phoneme *t*, which is a part of the affix *śatṛ*, follows an aṅga which ends in *a*. So, the augment *num* will be duly introduced to this aṅga, which ends in *t*, a part of the affix *śatṛ*, by the present rule when *śī* follows. Cf. BM, I and TB, I, p. 476.

In *tudat* + *śī*, the segment *tuda* is a pre-affixal base that ends in the vowel *a* which is followed by *t* (a portion of the affix *śatṛ*). Thus the participial form *tudat* ending in that portion (*t*) becomes an aṅga followed by the substitute affix *śī*. Hence the optional insertion of the augment *num* takes place. When we insert *num*, the rules *naścāpadāntasya jhali* (78) and *anusvārasya yayi parasavarṇaḥ* (79) respectively prescribe the replacement of *n* by anusvāra and that of anusvāra by the homogeneous fifth nasal stop, that is, *n* in this case. In this way the form *tudantī* is obtained. In the absence of *num*, we have *tudatī*.

In *tudat* + *jas* or *tudat* + *śas*, the affix is replaced by *śi* which is a sarvanāma-sthāna affix by *śi sarvanāmasthānam* (237). Accordingly, the augment *num* is introduced by the rule *napuṁsakasya jhalacaḥ* (238). By applying the rules *naścāpadāntasya jhali* (78) and *anusvārasya yayi parasavarṇaḥ* (79), we obtain the form *tudanti*. The complete declension of *tudat* in the neuter is as follows :

	Singular	Dual	Plural
prathamā	*tudat, d*	*tudantī, tudatī*	*tudanti*
dvitīyā	*tudat, d*	*tudantī, tudatī*	*tudanti*
tṛtīyā	*tudatā*	*tudadbhyām*	*tudadbhiḥ*
caturthī	*tudate*	*tudadbhyām*	*tudadbhyaḥ*
pañcamī	*tudataḥ*	*tudadbhyām*	*tudadbhyaḥ*
ṣaṣṭhī	*tudataḥ*	*tudatoḥ*	*tudatām*
saptamī	*tudati*	*tudatoḥ*	*tudatsu*
sambodhana	*he tudat, d!*	*he tudantī,* *he tudatī!*	*he tudanti!*

The insertion of the augment *num* is made obligatory with respect to the participial forms of the verbal roots belonging to bhvādi, divādi and curādi classes by the following sūtra :

(365) शप्श्यनोर्नित्यम् । *śapśyanornityam.* 7. 1. 81

लघु० – शप्श्यनोरात् परो यः शतुरवयवस्तदन्तस्य नित्यं नुम् शीनद्योः। पचन्ती। पचन्ति। दीव्यत्। दीव्यन्ती। दीव्यन्ति। *śapśyanor āt paro yaḥ śatur avayavas tadantasya nityaṁ num śīnadyoḥ. pacantī. pacanti. dīvyat. dīvyantī. dīvyanti.*

Trans. : The augment *num* is invariably introduced to that which ends with a portion (*t*) of the affix *śatṛ* occurring after the vowel *a* of *śap* or *śyan* when *śī* or a nadī affix follows.

PP. *śapśyanoḥ āt śatuḥ aṅgasya nityam num śīnadyoḥ.*

Eluc. : The terms *āt* and *num* are carried over into the present sūtra from *ācchīnadyornum* (365) and the word *śatuḥ* comes from *nābhyastāc-chatuḥ* Pā. 7. 1. 78. Since the present sūtra occurs in the domain of the governing rule *aṅgasya* Pā. 6. 4. 1, the word *aṅgasya* recurs here. Thus the sūtra comes to mean : When *śī* or a nadī affix follows, the augment *num* obligatorily forms a part of that which ends with a portion (*t*) of the affix *śatṛ* that occurs after the vowel *a* of *śap* or *śyan.*

The infix (*vikaraṇa*) *śap* is introduced to the verbal roots of the bhvādi and curādi class, whereas the infix *śyan* is added after the verbal roots of the divādi class when a sārvadhātuka affix, denoting agent, follows.

In *pacat* 'cooking', the affix *śatṛ* is introduced after the verbal root *pac* 'to cook' and we have *pac + śatṛ* by *laṭaḥ śatṛśānacā...* (828). Since the affix *śatṛ* is sārvadhātuka by *tiṅśit sārvadhātukam* (385) and denotes agent, the infix is introduced by *kartari śap* (386). Thus we have *pac + śap+ śatṛ --> pac + a + at* (after the anubandhas have been elided). In *paca + at*, the word segment *paca* is an aṅga since the affix *at* (*śatṛ*) follows. Now being internally conditioned (*antaraṅga*), the pararūpa single substitution takes place by *ato guṇe* (273) and we have *pacat.*

In *pacat + su*, the affix *su* is elided by *svamornapuṁsakāt* (243). Then by applying the rules *vā 'vasāne* (145) and *jhalāṁ jaśo 'nte* (67), we get two forms *pacat* and *pacad* in the nominative singular.

In *pacat + au*, the affix *au* is replaced by *śī* by *napuṁsakācca* (234) and we have *pacat + śī*. In this grammatical situation, *paca* is an aṅga by virtue of the rule *antādivacca* (41) and the phoneme *t* which is a part of the affix *śatṛ* follows. With this phoneme *t*, the pre-affixal base *pacat* ends with a portion of *śatṛ* and is followed by the substitute affix *śī*. The conditions specified in the present sūtra are available. As such, the augment *num* is obligatorily inserted after the last vowel *a* in *pacat*. Thus we arrive at following stage : *paca num t + śī --> paca n t + ī*. Now the rules *naścāpadāntasya jhali* (78) and *anusvārasya yayi parasavarṇaḥ* (79) apply and we obtain the form *pacantī.*

In *pacat + jas*, the affix *jas* is replaced with *śi* by *jaśśasoḥ śiḥ* (236). The substitute *śi* is a sarvanāmasthāna affix. Accordingly, the rule *napuṁsakasya jhalacaḥ* (238) applies and the augment *num* is inserted after the last vowel *a* of *pacat* and we have the following stage : *paca num t + i --> paca n t + i*. We obtain the form *pacanti* by applying *naścāpadāntasya jhali* (78) and *anusvārasya yayi parasavarṇaḥ* (79). Thus, when the participial form *pacat* qualifies a neuter substantive like *mitra* 'friend', it is in the neuter gender and is declined as follows :

	Singular	Dual	Plural
prathamā	*pacat, d*	*pacantī*	*pacanti*
dvitīyā	*pacat, d*	*pacantī*	*pacanti*
tṛtīyā	*pacatā*	*pacadbhyām*	*pacadbhiḥ*
caturthī	*pacate*	*pacadbhyām*	*pacadbhyaḥ*
pañcamī	*pacataḥ*	*pacadbhyām*	*pacadbhyaḥ*
ṣaṣṭhī	*pacataḥ*	*pacatoḥ*	*pacatām*
saptamī	*pacati*	*pacatoḥ*	*pacatsu*
sambodhana	*he pacat, d!*	*he pacantī!*	*he pacanti!*

Eluc. : The participial form *dīvyat* is derived by adding the affix *śatṛ* after the verbal root *div* 'to play, to gamble or to shine'. Since the affix *śatṛ* is sārvadhātuka, the vikaraṇa *śyan* is introduced by *divādibhyaḥ śyan* (628). Thus we have *div + śyan + śatṛ --> div + ya + at* (after the anubandhas are elided). The rule *hali ca* (611) prescribes the lengthening of the penultimate vowel *ik* (*i, u, ṛ, ḷ*) of a verbal root ending in *r* or *v* when a consonant follows. Accordingly, the penultimate *i* of *div* is lengthened. Then the rule *ato guṇe* (273) applies and we get the form *dīvyat*. When the participial form *dīvyat* qualifies a substantive like *kula* or *mitra* (family or a friend), it is declined in the neuter like *pacat* :

	Singular	Dual	Plural
prathamā	*dīvyat, d*	*dīvyantī*	*dīvyanti*
dvitīyā	*dīvyat, d*	*dīvyantī*	*dīvyanti*
tṛtīyā	*dīvyatā*	*dīvyadbhyām*	*dīvyadbhiḥ*
caturthī	*dīvyate*	*dīvyadbhyām*	*dīvyadbhyaḥ*
pañcamī	*dīvyataḥ*	*dīvyadbhyām*	*dīvyadbhyaḥ*
ṣaṣṭhī	*dīvyataḥ*	*dīvyatoḥ*	*dīvyatām*
saptamī	*dīvyati*	*dīvyatoḥ*	*dīvyatsu*
sambodhana	*he dīvyat, d!*	*he dīvyantī!*	*he dīvyanti!*

Here comes to an end the declensional process of the neuter words that end in the phoneme *t*.

Now begins the declension of the nominal stems ending in *ṣ*.

लघु० – धनुः । धनुषी । सान्त० इति दीर्घः । नुम्विसर्जनीय० इति षः । धनूंषि । धनुषा । धनुर्भ्याम् । एवम् चक्षुर्हविरादयः । *dhanuḥ. dhanuṣī. sānta... iti dīrghaḥ. numvisarjanīya... iti ṣaḥ. dhanūṁṣi. dhanuṣā. dhanurbhyām. evam – cakṣur havir ādayaḥ.*

Eluc. : The neuter nominal stem *dhanuṣ* is derived from the verbal root *dhan* 'to bear fruit, to cause to move quickly' after the uṇādi affix *us* has been introduced after it by Uṇādi Sūtra, 274. By *ādeśapratyayayoḥ* (149), the dental *s* of the affix *us* is replaced by *ṣ*. We get the stem *dhanuṣ*.

In *dhanuṣ + su*, the affix *su* is elided by *svamornapuṁsakāt* (243). The replacement of *s* by the cerebral *ṣ* is deemed not to have taken place with respect to *sasajuṣo ruḥ* Pā. 8. 2 . 66 since the grammatical operation performed by *ādeśapratyayayoḥ* Pā. 8. 3. 59 is suspended (*asiddha*) by virtue of *pūrvatrāsiddham* Pā. 8. 2. 1. Accordingly, the rule *sasajuṣo ruḥ* applies and we have *dhanu ru --> dhanur*. The repha is replaced by visarga according to *kharava...* (93) and we obtain the form --> *dhanuḥ* in the nominative singular.

In *dhanuṣ + au*, the substitute *śī* replaces *au* according to *napuṁsakācca* (234) and we get the form *dhanuṣī* after the elision of the anubandha *ś*.

In *dhanuṣ + jas*, the affix *jas* is replaced by *śi* which is a sarvanāmasthāna affix by *śi sarva...* (237). Consequently, the rule *napuṁsakasya...* (238) prescribes the insertion of the augment of *num* before *śi*. Thus we arrive at the following stage : *dhanu num ṣ + śi --> dhanu n ṣ + i*. Then by *sānta mahataḥ...* (341), the penultimate vowel *u* gets lengthened and we have *dhanū n ṣ + i*. The cerebral *ṣ* also reverts to the dental status since the vowel *u*, which is the immediate cause of the replacement by *ṣ*, is now separated by the intervention of the phoneme *n* {*nimittāpāye naimittikasyāpyapāyaḥ* (Paribhāṣā-saṅgraha, p. 158)}. After the phoneme *n* has been replaced with anusvāra by *naścāpadāntasya...* (78), the dental *s* is again replaced by the cerebral *ṣ* in accordance with *numvisarjanīya...* (351). Thus we obtain the form *dhanūṁṣi* in the nominative plural. The procedure is the same when sup-affixes of the second triplet follow.

When the stem *dhanuṣ* is followed by *bhyām*, *bhis* or *bhyas*, the rule *sasajuṣo ruḥ* Pā. 8. 2 . 66 applies since the cerebral *ṣ* is treated as *s* by this rule as the cerebralization by *ādeśapratyayayoḥ* Pā. 8. 3. 59 is deemed not to have taken place with respect to *sasajuṣo ruḥ* Pā. 8. 2 . 66. Thus we get the forms *dhanurbhyām*, *dhanurbhiḥ* and *dhanurbhyaḥ*.

In *dhanuṣ* + *sup*, the phoneme ṣ is asiddha. Hence it is taken as s and the rule *sasajuṣo ruḥ* (104) prescribes its replacement by *ru*. The repha is substituted by visarga in accordance with *kharava*... (93). Now according to the rule *vā śari* (103), the visarga optionally remains as it is. Alternatively, it is replaced by s in accordance with *visarjanīyasya saḥ* (96). We reach the following stage : 1. *dhanuḥ* + *su* and 2. *dhanus* + *su*. In the first illustration, there is an intervention of the visarga between *u* and s and in the second, of the phoneme s. In both the cases, the rule *numvisarjanīyaśarvyavāye 'pi* (351) applies and the dental *s* of the affix *sup* is substituted by the cerebral ṣ. Thus we obtain two forms : *dhanuḥṣu* and *dhanuṣṣu* after the rule *ṣṭunā ṣṭuḥ* (64) has performed its grammatical function of replacing the s of *dhanus* by ṣ in the second illustration. The complete declension of the nominal stem *dhanuṣ* is given below :

	Singular	Dual	Plural
prathamā	*dhanuḥ*	*dhanuṣī*	*dhanūṁṣi*
dvitīyā	*dhanuḥ*	*dhanuṣī*	*dhanūṁṣi*
tṛtīyā	*dhanuṣā*	*dhanurbhyām*	*dhanurbhiḥ*
caturthī	*dhanuṣe*	*dhanurbhyām*	*dhanurhyaḥ*
pañcamī	*dhanuṣaḥ*	*dhanurbhyām*	*dhanurbhyaḥ*
ṣaṣṭhī	*dhanuṣaḥ*	*dhanuṣoḥ*	*dhanuṣām*
saptamī	*dhanuṣi*	*dhanuṣoḥ*	*dhanuḥṣu, dhanuṣṣu*
sambodhana	*he dhanuḥ*!	*he dhanuṣī*!	*he dhanūṁṣi*!

The neuter nominal stems *cakṣuṣ* 'an eye', *haviṣ* 'an oblation, clarified butter', etc. are declined in the same manner.

Here comes to an end the declension of the neuter nominal stems that end in the phoneme ṣ.

Now begins the declension of the stems ending in s.

लघु० – पयः । पयसी । पयांसि । पयसा । पयोभ्याम् । सुपुम् । सुपुंसी । सुपुमांसि । अदः । विभक्तिकार्यम् । उत्वमत्वे । अमू । अमूनि । शेषं पुंवत् । *payaḥ. payasī. payāṁsi. payasā. payobhyām. supum. supuṁsī. supumāṁsi. adaḥ. vibhaktikāryam. utvamatve. amū, amūni. śeṣaṁ puṁvat.*

Eluc. : The nominal stem *payas* 'water, milk' is neuter. In *payas + su*, the affix *su* is elided by *svamornapuṁsakāt* (243) and we get the form *payaḥ* after rutva and visarga.

In *payas + au*, the affix *au* is replaced by *śī* according to *napuṁsakācca* (243) and we have *payasī* after the elision of the anubandha *ś*.

In *payas + jas*, the affix *jas* is replaced by *śi* by *jaśśasoḥ śiḥ* (236). Then the augment *num* is inserted by *napuṁsakasya jhalacaḥ* (238). The rule *sānta mahataḥ saṁyogasya* (341) prescribes the lengthening of the penultimate vowel (*upadhā*). The nasal stop *n* is replaced by anusvāra according to *naścāpadāntasya jhali*. Thus we obtain the form *payāṁsi*.

In *payas + bhyām*, the consonant *s* is replaced by *ru* by *sasajuṣo ruḥ* (104). Then the substitute *u* replaces *ru* by *haśi ca* (106) and we obtain the form *payobhyām* after guṇa-sandhi by *ādguṇaḥ* (27).

In *payas + sup*, the visarga, which has replaced the consonant *s* (93), is optionally substituted by *s* by *vā śari* (103) and we get two forms : *payaḥsu* and *payassu*. The declension of *payas* is given below :

	Singular	Dual	Plural
prathamā	*payaḥ*	*payasī*	*payāṁsi*
dvitīyā	*payaḥ*	*payasī*	*payāṁsi*
tṛtīyā	*payasā*	*payobhyām*	*payobhiḥ*
caturthī	*payase*	*payobhyām*	*payobhyaḥ*
pañcamī	*payasaḥ*	*payobhyām*	*payobhyaḥ*
ṣaṣṭhī	*payasaḥ*	*payasoḥ*	*payasām*
saptamī	*payasi*	*payasoḥ*	*payaḥsu, payassu*
sambodhana	*he payaḥ!*	*he payasī!*	*he payāṁsi!*

The word *supuṁs* 'of which the men are good' is a bahuvrīhi compound. It may be analysed as follows : *śobhanāḥ pumāṁso yasya yasmin vā tat* (*kulam*). Here the qualificand is *kulam* 'a family' which is neuter. Hence it will be declined as a neuter stem.

In *supuṁs + su*, the affix *su* is elided by *svamornapuṁsakāt* (243) and then the elision of the conjunct-final *s* takes place by *saṁyogāntasya lopaḥ* (20). After the elision of the *s*, the anusvāra changes into *m* by virtue of the paribhāṣā *nimittāpāye naimittikasyāpyapāyaḥ* (Paribhāṣā-saṅgraha, p. 158) and we get the form *supum* in the nominative singular.

In *supuṁs + au*, the affix *au* is replaced by *śī* in accordance with *napuṁsakācca* (234) and we get the form *supuṁsī*.

In *supuṁs* + *jas*, when the replacement of *jas* by *śi* is intended, the rule *puṁso 'suṅ* (353) beomes applicable and prescribes the substitution of the final phoneme *s* by *asuṅ* {*ṅicca* (46)} and we have *supumas* + *jas*. Now the affix *jas* is replaced by *śi* in accordance with *jaśśasoḥ śiḥ* (236). The augment *num* is inserted by *napuṁsakasya jhalacaḥ* (238). Then the rule *sānta mahataḥ*... (341) prescribes the lengthening of the penultimate vowel (*upadhā*). The nasal stop *n* is replaced by anusvāra according to *naścāpadānta*... (78). Thus we obtain the form *supumāṁsi*.

The stem *supuṁs* gets the pada-designation before *bhyām*, *bhis* and *bhyas*. As such, the conjunct-final *s* is elided by *saṁyogāntasya*... (20). Then *vā padāntasya* (80) applies and we have two forms.

In *supuṁs* + *sup*, the phoneme *s* at the end of a conjunct is elided by *saṁyogā*... (20). As a result the anusvāra changes to *m*. It is then replaced with anusvāra by *mo 'nusvāraḥ* (77). Thus we obtain the form *supuṁsu*. The complete declension of the neuter stem *supuṁs* is as follows :

	Singular	Dual	Plural
prathamā	*supum*	*supuṁsī*	*supumāṁsi*
dvitīyā	*supum*	*supuṁsī*	*supumāṁsi*
tṛtīyā	*supuṁsā*	*supumbhyām*, *supuṁbhyām*	*supumbhiḥ*, *supuṁbhiḥ*
caturthī	*supuṁse*	*supumbhyām*, *supuṁbhyām*	*supumbhyaḥ*, *supuṁbhyaḥ*
pañcamī	*supuṁsaḥ*	*supumbhyām*, *supuṁbhyām*	*supumbhyaḥ*, *supuṁbhyaḥ*
ṣaṣṭhī	*supuṁsaḥ*	*supuṁsoḥ*	*supuṁsām*
saptamī	*supuṁsi*	*supuṁsoḥ*	*supuṁsu*
sambodhana	*he supum!*	*he supuṁsī!*	*he supumāṁsi!*

The declensional process of the pronominal stem *adas* 'that' in the neuter is now being explained.

In *adas* + *su*, the affix *su* is elided by *svamornapuṁsakāt* (243) and we obtain the form *adaḥ* after rutva and visarga.

In *adas* + *au*, the substitute *śī* replaces *au* by *napuṁsakācca* (234). Since *adaso 'ser*... Pā. 8. 2. 80 belongs to the tripādī, the rules *tyadādīnāmaḥ* Pā. 7. 2. 102 and *ato guṇe* Pā. 6. 1. 97 apply first and we have *ada* + (*ś*)*ī*. By *ād guṇaḥ* (27) it is *ade*. Now by *adaso 'ser*... Pā. 8. 2. 80, the phoneme *d* is replaced by *m* and the vowel *e*, by *ū* and we obtain the form *amū*.

In *adas* + *jas*, the substitute *śi* replaces the affix *jas* by *jaśśasoḥ śiḥ* (236) and we have *adas* + *śi*. At this stage, the rules *tyadādīnāmaḥ* (192) and *ato guṇe* (273) apply and we have *ada* + *śi*. In this grammatical situation, the insertion of the augment *num* is prescribed by the rule *napuṁsakasya jhalacaḥ* (238) and we arrive at the following grammatical stage : *ada num* + *śi* --> *ada n* + *i*. Now the penultimate vowel of the pre-affixal base, which ends in the phoneme *n*, gets lengthened by the rule *sarvanāmasthāne cāsambuddhau* (176) and thus we have *adāni*. At this stage, the rule *adaso 'serdādu do maḥ* (355) prescribes the substitution of the phoneme *d* by *m* and that of the vowel *ā* by *ū*. We obtain the form *amūni*. The same process is repeated before the affixes of the second triplet. The rest of the declension will be like that of the masculine :

	Singular	Dual	Plural
prathamā	*adaḥ*	*amū*	*amūni*
dvitīyā	*adaḥ*	*amū*	*amūni*
tṛtīyā	*amunā*	*amūbhyām,*	*amībhiḥ*
caturthī	*amuṣmai*	*amūbhyām,*	*amībhyaḥ*
pañcamī	*amuṣmāt*	*amūbhyām,*	*amībhyaḥ*
ṣaṣṭhī	*amuṣya*	*amuyoḥ*	*amīṣām*
saptamī	*amuṣmin*	*amuyoḥ*	*amīṣu*
sambodhana		No form	

Here comes to an end the declension of the neuter words that end in the phoneme s.

लघु० – इति हलन्तनपुंसकलिङ्गाः । *iti halantanapuṁsakaliṅgāḥ.*

Trans. : Here ends the chapter on the neuter words ending in consonants.

लघु० – इति षड्लिङ्गप्रकरणम् । *iti ṣaḍliṅgaprakaraṇam.*

Trans. : Here comes to an end the chapter on the six genders (three genders of those stems that end in a vowel and three of those that end in a consonant).

अव्ययप्रकरणम्

The Indeclinables

Indeclinables (*avyayas*) constitute a group of nominals which can be included in the category of declined words (*subanta*) but the declensional endings introduced after them are invariably elided by *avyayādāpsupaḥ* (371). However, an avyayībhāva compound which ends in a short *a* is an exception. Although an avyayībhāva compound is designated as an *avyaya* by *avyayībhāvaśca* (370), the instrumental, ablative and locative endings are treated variously. To illustrate, the compound *upakṛṣṇa* is an avyayībhāva. Since this compound ends in a short *a*, the sup-affixes introduced after it are not elided but instead, with the exception of the ablative case-endings, they are substituted by *am* in accordance with the rule *nāvyayībhāvādato 'm tvapañcamyāḥ* (908). Moreover, the rule *tṛtīyāsaptamyorbahulam* (909) optionally prescribes the replacement of instrumental and locative case-endings by *am*. Thus we have four forms of the avyayībhāva compound *upakṛṣṇa* ending in a short *a* : *upakṛṣṇam, upakṛṣṇena, upakṛṣṇāt* and *upakṛṣṇe*. As such, although we have given the word 'indeclinable' as its English equivalent, it does not mean that all the avyayas are indeclinable.

Commenting on the Vākyapadīya III. 14. 105, Helārāja says that avyayas do not express a meaning which is of the nature of sattva and have, therefore, no gender and number (*aliṅgasaṅkhyam avyayam ity asaṅkhyatvam avyayānāṁ svabhāvaḥ*, Helārāja on the above kārikā). In a like manner, Jinendrabuddhi says that the fact that the indeclinables (*avyayas*) do not have any gender, kāraka and number proves that they do not by nature undergo various grammatical modifications *liṅgakārakasaṅkhyāviśeṣānupādānān na vyeti = vividhatvaṁ na gacchatīty avyayam* (KN, I, p. 146).

One point may be noted in this context. The word *tatra* is an avyaya by virtue of the rule *taddhitaścāsarvavibhaktiḥ* (367). It is not always the case that an avyaya does not have a substantial referent (*sattva*). In the illustration *tatra śālāyām*, given by Varadarāja under the rule (371), *tatra* stands for *tasyām* but, being an avyaya, it does not retain the feminine affix *ṭāp* as well as the locative case-ending. However, this refers to an entity like *śālā* which does possess substancehood. This means that the word which is designated as an avyaya can also have a substantial entity as its referent. Charudev Shastri says that the class of words beginning with *svar* may denote a substantial entity as the case may be but the items included in the set beginning with *ca* never denotes a substantial entity (Vyā. cand., IV, p. 218). This is the reason why Pāṇini has mentioned them separately in the following sūtra which Varadarāja now presents to define what an avyaya is :

(366) स्वरादिनिपातमव्ययम् । ***svarādinipātamavyayam*. 1. 1. 37**
लघु० – स्वरादयो निपाताश्चाव्ययसंज्ञाः स्युः । *svarādayo nipātāś cāvyayasaṁjñāḥ syuḥ.*

Trans. : Let the members of the class headed by *svar* 'sun, heaven' and the particles be assigned the class name *avyaya*.

PP. *svarādinipātam avyayam.*

Eluc. : The compound *svarādinipātam* is a bahuvrīhi-seeded samāhāradvandva which can be analysed as follows : *svar ādir yeṣām te = svarādayaḥ (bahuvrīhi) svarādayaś ca nipātāś ca svarādinipātam (samāhāradvandva)*. Then the sūtra means : The items of the set which begins with *svar* as well as the particles (*nipātas*) are to be assigned the avyaya designation. In general, the purpose of assigning the avyaya designation is the elision of the feminine affix *ṭāp* and sup-affixes introduced after an avyaya.

The words, enlisted in the set of *svar*, etc., may or may not denote a substantial entity (*sattva*). They are given below with illustrations :

1. *svar* 'heaven, the other world or a kind of happiness'. Ex. **svar gamyāsam iti me āśīḥ.*[1] 'I wish I would go to heaven.'

2. *antar* 'in, inside, internally'. *apsv antar amṛtam apsu bheṣajam* (Ṛgveda, 1. 23. 19). 'Nectar resides in the water, medicinal properties are in it.' * *sa apamānād antar adahyata.* 'He burnt inside when insulted.'

3. *prātar* 'in the morning'. * *prātar udeti sūryaḥ.* 'The sun rises in the morning.'

4. *punar* 'again, for the second time'. *vighnaiḥ punaḥpunar api pratihanyamānāḥ prārabdham uttamajanā na parityajanti* (Nītiśataka, 72). 'Confronted by obstacles again and again, men of excellence do not give up what they have undertaken.'

---

1. The illustrations marked with an asterisk are coined by the author.

5. *sanutar* 'secretly, stealthily'. *sanutaś ca cauro gacchati* (Gaṇaratna). 'A thief goes away stealthily.'

6. *uccais* 'loudly, high'. *śuśrāva kuñjeṣu yaśaḥ svam uccair udgīyamānaṁ vanadevatābhiḥ* (Raghu, 2. 12). 'He heard his own glory sung loudly in the bowers of creepers by the sylvan deities.'

7. *nīcaiḥ* 'low'. *vapuḥprakarṣād ajayad guruṁ raghus tathāpi nīcair vinayād adṛśyata* (Raghu, 3. 34). 'Raghu excelled his father in bodily excellence. However he looked lowly on account of humility.'

8. *śanaiḥ* 'slowly'. (*adharmaḥ*) *śanair āvartamānas tu kartur mūlāni kṛntati* (Manusmṛti, 4. 172). 'Sin committed reverts slowly to the doer and exterminates him.'

9. *ṛdhak* 'truth'. *ṛdhag vadanti vidvāṁsaḥ* (Gaṇaratna quoted in Bhaimī, p. 517). 'Scholars speak the truth.'

10. *ṛte* 'without'. *ṛte raveḥ kṣālayituṁ kṣameta kaḥ kṣapātamaskāṇḍa-malīmasaṁ nabhaḥ* (Śiśu, 1. 38). 'Except the sun, who else can render clean the sky sullied by dense nocturnal darkness?'

11. *yugapat* 'simultaneously'. *yugapajjñānānutpattir manaso liṅgam* Nyāyasūtra, 1. 1. 16. 'That different kinds of cognition (visual, auditory, etc.) do not originate simultaneouly indicates the existence of the mind.'

12. *ārāt* 'distant or near'. * *ārād durjanāt sadā vaset*. 'Always keep away from a wicked person.' *tam arcyam ārād abhivartamānam avākiran bālalatāḥ prasūnaiḥ* (Raghu, 2. 10). 'The tender creepers showered their flowers on him, worthy of adoration, as he was passing by.'

13. *pṛthak* 'separately'. *śaṅkhān dadhmuḥ pṛthak pṛthak* (Bh. G. 1. 18). '(They) blew their conches separately.'

14. *hyas* 'yesterday'. * *hyo 'ham haridvāram agaccham*. 'Yesterday I went to Haridwar.'

15. *śvas* 'tomorrow'. * *śvo 'haṁ mumbaīnagarīṁ gantāsmi*. 'Tomorrow I will leave for Mumbai.'

16. *divā* 'during the day'. *nidrayā hriyate naktaṁ divā ca vyartha-karmabhiḥ* (Bhāg. Pu., 1. 16. 9). 'We pass the night sleeping and while away the day doing worthless deeds.'

17. *rātrau* 'at night'. *rātrau vṛttaṁ tu drakṣyasi* (Gaṇaratna quoted in Bhaimī, p. 518). 'You will definitely see what happens at night.'

18. *sāyam* 'in the evening'. *prayatā prātar anvetu sāyaṁ pratyudvrajed api* (Raghu, 1. 90). 'Let your self-disciplined wife follow her (the cow) in the morning and let her also go half way to receive her in the evening.'

19. *ciram* 'for long'. *ciraṁ jīvatu bhadre!* (Svapnavāsavadattam, Act I). 'May the noble lady live long!' *tataḥ prajānāṁ ciram ātmnā dhṛtāṁ nitāntagurvīṁ laghayiṣyatā dhuram* (Raghu, 3. 35). 'Then the king (became) desirous of lightening the very heavy yoke of governing his subjects, which he had borne so long!'

20. *manāk* 'a little, slightly'. *re pāntha vihvalamanā na manāgapi syāḥ* (Bhāminīvilāsa, 1. 37). 'O traveller! do not feel even slightly perturbed.'

21. *īṣat* 'slightly, easily' *īṣad īṣaccumbitāni bhramaraiḥ* (Śākuntala, 1. 3). '(Flowers) slightly kissed by the bees.' **īṣatkaraḥ kaṭo bhavatā* {for explanation see sūtra (873)}. 'It is easy for you to make a mat.'

22. *joṣam* 'quiet, silent or happily'. *joṣam āpa na viśiṣya babhāṣe* (Naiṣadha, 5. 78). 'He kept quiet (and) did not say anything specific.' *bhoḥ rājan kimiti joṣamāsyate* (Śākuntala, 5) . 'O King ! Why do you thus sit silent?'

23. *tūṣṇīm* 'quiet,silent'. *na yotsya iti govindam uktvā tūṣṇīṁ babhūva ha* (Bh. G., 2. 9). 'Telling Govinda 'I shall not fight', he (Arjuna) verily became silent.'

24. *bahis* 'outside'. *nivasannāvasathe purād bahiḥ* (Raghu, 8. 14). 'Living in a place outside the city.'

25. *avas* 'down, outside, etc.' *avo gacchati* (Gaṇaratna quoted in Bhaimī, p. 520). 'He goes out or he goes down.' This indeclinable (avyaya) can be obtained with the help of the sūtra *pūrvādharāvarāṇāmasi puradhavaścaiṣām* Pā. 5. 3. 39 and then it can be assigned the designation *avyaya* by *taddhitaścāsarvavibhaktiḥ* (367). Therefore the inclusion of this word in the list of *svarādi* is subject to careful examination.[1]

26. *adhas* 'below, down'. *adha āsane tiṣṭha* (Vyā. cand., IV, p. 274). 'Take the lower seat.'

27. *samayā* 'near, in the vicinity'. *guṇadoṣābhivyaktir vacasāṁ sañjāyate sataḥ samayā* (Vyā. cand., IV, p. 237). 'The qualities or defects of our speech become evident in the company of the wise.'

28. *nikaṣā* 'near'. *vilaṅghya laṅkāṁ nikaṣā haniṣyati* (Śiśu, 1. 68)? 'Do you remember that crossing the ocean you killed Rāvaṇa near Laṅkā?' The use of the lṛṭ lakāra here is in the sense of recollection of the action of the past which is other than the present day (*anadyatana*).

29. *svayam* 'oneself, in one's own person, personally'. *siktaṁ svayam iva snehād vandhyam āśramavṛkṣakam* (Raghu, 1. 70). '(you would surely be pained to see) a young plant of this hermitage, which, through affection, has been personally watered by you, failing to produce any fruit.'

30. *vṛthā* 'useless' *alaṁ mahīpāla tava śrameṇa prayuktam apy astram ito vṛthā syāt* (Raghu, 2. 34). 'There is no need, O ruler of the earth, of any effort on your part. Even if discharged, your shafts will be of no use here.'

31. *naktam* 'at night, by night'. *na naktaṁ dadhi bhuñjīta* (Caraka-sūtra, 7. 58). 'Don't take curd at night.' *kṛtvākhur vivaraṁ svayaṁ nipatito*

---

1. Bhaimī, p. 520.

naktaṁ mukhe bhoginaḥ (Nītiśataka, 82). 'The mouse, having dug a hole, himself fell into the mouth of the snake at night.'

32. *nañ* 'no, prohibition'. *ekaḥ svādu na bhuñjīta* (Subhāṣitasudhānidhi). 'One should not relish a tasty eatable alone.' This indeclinable has many meanings. A simple meaning of negation has been illustrated here.

33. *hetau* 'because of'. *hetau hṛṣyati* (Gaṇaratna). 'He feels happy with a purpose.'

34. *iddhā* 'manifest'. *samiddham iddheśa maho dadāsi* (Gaṇaratna) 'O God! (So) manifestly you bestow resplendent glory (upon me).' This avyaya is found in the Vācaspatyam, which ascribes the illustration, given here, to the Bhāgavata Purāṇa but it is not traced in it.[1]

35. *addhā* 'really, in reality'. *tasmān na baddhyate 'ddhā na mucyate nāpi saṁsarati kaścit*. (Sāṅkhya Kārikā, 62). 'Therefore, there is no one who is really bound, no one who is released and no one who transmigrates.'

36. *sāmi* 'half' (cf. 'semi' in English). *sāmikṛtam akalyāṇakāri bhavati* (Vyā. cand., IV, p. 292). 'An act half-done is not conducive to welfare.'

37. *vat* 'like'. *brāhmaṇavat, kṣatriyavat*. *vat* is a taddhita affix. The words *brāhmaṇavat, kṣatriyavat* are the illustrations of this affix. The Kāśikā presents these two illustrations prefacing them with the following expression : *vadantam avyayasaṁjñaṁ bhavati, brāhmaṇavat, kṣatriyavat*. 'The word which ends in the affix *vat* gets the avyaya designation.' However, it is not proper to include this affix in the list of svarādi when the avyaya designation can easily be assigned to a word that ends in the affix *vat* by the rule *taddhitaścāsarvavibhaktiḥ* (367).[2] The following popular sentence is another illustration of this affix : *rāmādivad vartitavyaṁ na rāvaṇādivat*. 'One should lead one's life like Rāma, not like Rāvaṇā.'

38. *sanā* 'always, for eternity'. *sanā bhūvan dyumnāni mota jāriṣuḥ* (Ṛgveda, 1. 139. 8). 'May wealth stay for eternity, may it never get lost !'

39. *sanat* 'always'. '*sanatkumāra*, a son of brahmā who is always celibate.'

40. *sanāt* 'always'. *aśatrur januṣā sanādasi* (Ṛgveda, 1. 102. 8). '(O Indra), from birth thou art always without enemy.'

41. *upadhā*. The Kāśikā does not include *upadhā* in the svarādigaṇa and in the form of an indeclinable it has not been found used anywhere.[3]

42. *tiras* 'obliquely, secretly, invisibly, bending'. *tiraḥ kṛtvā śākhāṁ nirgataḥ* and *tirobhūte śaśini* (Vyā. cand., IV, pp. 292-3). 'Bending the

1. Bhaimī, p. 521.
2. Ibid., p. 522.
3. Ibid., p. 523.

branch to one side, he went away' and 'when the moon set'. *striyas tira iva vai puṁso jighatsanti* (Śatapatha Brāhmaṇa, 3. 3. 4. 6). 'Women invisibly devour men, as it were.'

43. *antarā* 'in the middle, between, without'. *triśaṅkuriva antarā tiṣṭha* (Śākuntala, 2). 'Stay between the two like Triśaṅku.' *na ca prayojanam antarā cāṇakyaḥ svapne 'pi ceṣṭate* (Mudrārākṣasa, 3). 'Without motive Cāṇakya does not act even in a dream.'

44. *antareṇa* 'without, between, with regard to, about'. *pramāṇam antareṇa nārthapratipattiḥ* (NB, p. 1). 'There is no cognition of an object without the means of valid cognition.' * *tvāṁ māṁ cāntareṇa ayam agniḥ.* 'This fire is between you and me.' *kiṁ nu khalu mām antareṇa cintayati vaiśampāyanaḥ* (Kādambarī)? 'What, indeed, does Vaiśampāyana think about me?'

45. *jyok* 'in brightness'.[1] *sarvamāyureti jyog jīvati mahān prajayā paśubhir bhavati mahān kīrtyā* (Ch. U. 2. 11. 2). 'He lives full life in brightness; he becomes rich in children, in cattle and in fame.' According to Śaṅkara, the word *jyok* means 'in brightness' whereas According to Bhimasena Shastri it means 'for a long time' (Bhaimī, p. 524).

46. *kam* 'water, happiness'. *kaṁ jale jāyate kañjam kamalam* (Vyā. cand., IV, p. 268). 'That which is born in water is a lotus.' *kam sukham astyasyeti kaṁyuḥ* (Bhaimī, p. 524). The term *kaṁyuḥ* means 'happy'.

47. *śam* 'happiness, peace, welfare'. *śaṁ kalyāṇaṁ karotīti śaṅkaraḥ* (Bhaimī, p. 525). 'Śaṅkara is so called since he bestows happiness and peace (on us).'

48. *sahasā* 'suddenly, without giving a proper thought'. *sahasā vidadhīta na kriyām avivekaḥ param āpadāṁ padam* (Kirāta, 2. 30). 'Do not perform any act suddenly; indiscrimination is a great source of calamities.'

49. *vinā* 'without'. *nāsti ceṣṭā vinā hiṁsām* (Vyā. cand., IV, p. 232). 'There is no physical activity without violence.'

50. *nānā* 'without'. *nānā nārīṁ niṣphalā lokayātrā* (Gaṇaratna). 'Without a woman, life is purposeless.'

51. *svasti* 'propitious, welfare'. *svastyastu te* (Raghu, 5. 17). 'May it be propitious to you!'

52. *svadhā* 'an exclamation uttered on offering an oblation to the Manes.' *pitṛbhyaḥ svadhā*. 'Let the oblations be unto Manes.'

53. *alam* 'ornament, a match for, sufficient for, enough of'. *anutsekaḥ khalu vikramālaṅkāraḥ* (Vikramorvaśīya, 1). 'Humility is indeed the ornament of valour.' *alaṁ mallo mallāya* (Kāśikā, 2. 3. 16). 'The wrestler

---

1. *jyog ujjvalaṁ jīvati*, Śaṅkara's commentary on Ch. U., 2. 11. 2.

is a match for the other.' *tasyālameṣā kṣudhitasya tṛptyai* (Raghu, 2. 39). 'This (meal) is sufficient for the satisfaction of a hungry man.' *alaṁ mahīpāla tava śrameṇa* (Raghu, 2. 34). 'There is no need, O ruler of the earth, for any effort on your part.' * *alaṁ kolāhalena*. 'Do not make a noise.'

54. *vaṣaṭ* 55. *śrauṣaṭ* 56. *vauṣaṭ*. All the three indeclinables are used as exclamations in making an oblation to a deity. *indrāya vaṣaṭ* (Apte's dictionary). 'Oblation be unto Indra!' Similarly, *astu śrauṣaṭ puro agniṁ dhiya dadhe* (Ṛgveda, 1. 139. 1) and *somasyāgne vīhi vauṣaṭ* (Aitareya-brāhmaṇa, 3. 5. 4. 6 quoted in Bhaimī, p. 526) are illustrations of these fomulae to be used at the time of making an offering to the gods.

57. *anyat* 'besides'. *devadatta āyāto 'nyac ca yajñadattaḥ* (Gaṇaratna). 'Besides Yajñadatta, Devadatta has come.'

58. *asti* 'existent, present, possession'. Charudeva Shastri says that the word *asti* is an avyaya which is an imitation of the verbal form *asti* and it means 'wealth, possession'. According to him, the word *astimān* means 'a wealthy person' (Vyā. cand., IV, p. 220). The other meaning 'existent' is visible in the compound *astikṣīrā* (*gauḥ*) 'a cow having milk'. The word *āstika* 'one who believes in the existence of the other world' derived with the introduction of the taddhita affix *ṭhak* by *astināstidiṣṭaṁ matiḥ* Pā. 4. 4. 60 also illustrates this meaning.

59. *upāṁśu* 'solitude'. *paricetum upāṁśu dhāraṇāṁ kuśapūtaṁ pravayās tu viṣṭaram* (Raghu, 8. 18). 'However, the aged king sat in solitude, on a seat made holy by the kuśa grass, to practice meditation.' The word *upāṁśu* has been used adverbially in the Vākyapadīya in the sense of 'silently'. *avyaktaḥ kramavān śabda upāṁśv ayam adhīyate* (VP 2. 19). 'An indistict word uttered silently seems to have a sequence.'

60. *kṣamā* 'forgiveness'. *kṣamā karotu bhavān*. '(Please) forgive me' (Vyā. sudhā. quoted in Bhaimī, p. 527).

61. *vihāyasā* 'sky'. *vihāyasā paśya vihaṅgarājam* (Hemacandra). 'Look at Garuda in the sky.' *vihāyasā ramyam ito vibhāti* (Vyā. sudhā.). 'The sky looks charming from here.' (Quoted in Bhaimī, p. 527).

62. *doṣā* 'night'. *doṣā śivaḥ sahasaḥ sūno agne* (Ṛgveda, 4. 11. 6c). 'O Agni ! the progeny of strength, (You) be propitious at night.'

63. *mṛṣā* 'falsely, untruth' *mṛṣā na cakre 'lpitakalpapādapaḥ praṇīya dāridryadaridratāṁ nalaḥ*. (Naiṣadha, 1. 15). 'Even though Nala slighted or excelled the Kalpavṛkṣa, he did not falsify (the writ of Brahmā) by accomplishing the poverty of poverty.'

64. *mithyā* 'untruth, wrongly'.

maṇau mahānīla iti prabhāvād alpapramāṇe 'pi yathā na mithyā,
śabdo mahārāja iti pratītas tathaiva tasmin yuyuje 'rbhake 'pi. (Raghu, 18. 42). 'Even as the title *mahānīla* is not a false epithet to a sapphire of a

small dimension, on account of its bright splendour, so the well-known title of *mahārāja* was rightly applied to that prince even though he was then a mere child.' *mithyaiva vyasanaṁ vadanti mṛgayāmīdṛgvinodaḥ kutaḥ* (Śākuntala, 2. 5). 'They wrongly call hunting a bad habit. Where is such a pastime?'

65. *mudhā* 'uselessly'. *paribhramasi kiṁ mudhā kvacana citta viśrāmyatām* (Vairāgyaśataka, 62). 'O Mind! Why do you wander uselessly? Rest at some place.'

66. *purā* 'in the olden time'. *purā śakram upasthāpya tavorvīṁ prati yāsyataḥ* (Raghu, 1. 75). 'In the olden time, when you were returning to the earth after waiting upon Indra.'

67. *mitho* 'in private, reciprocally'. *mantrayante mitho.*[1] 'They are deliberating in private.'

68. *mithas* 'in private, mutually'. *tanmithaḥ savarṇasañjñaṁ syāt* (Laghu (10). 'Let them mutually be called homogeneous.' *ratnākaraṁ vīkṣya mithaḥ sa jāyāṁ rāmābhidhāno harir ityuvāca* (Raghu, 13. 1). 'Looking at the ocean, Hari, who was called by the name of Rāma, spoke to his wife in private.'

69. *prāyas* 'often, so many times'. *prāyo gacchati yatra daivahatakas tatraiva yāntyāpadaḥ* (Nītiśataka, 84). 'Calamities often throng the place where an unfortunate person goes.'

70. *muhus* 'again and again' *gurūṇāṁ sannidhāne 'pi kaḥ kūjati muhur muhuḥ* (Apte's Dictionary). 'Who is it that chirps again and again even when the elders are nearby?'

71. *pravāhukam* 72. *pravāhikā* 'at the same time, on high'. In the Kāśikā, these indeclinables have been read as *prabāhukam* and *prabāhikā*. Apte's Dictionary has these indeclinables as given in the Kāśikā. *pravāhukaṁ gṛhṇīyāt* (Gaṇaratna).[2] 'Take (it) at the same time.'

73. *āryahalam* 'forcibly'. *āryahalaṁ gṛhṇāti* (Gaṇaratna). 'He takes it forcibly.'

74. *abhīkṣṇam* 'continuously, again and again. *kṣate prahārā nipatanty abhīkṣṇam* (Vyā. cand., IV, p. 281). 'The injured part is likely to be struck again and again.'

75. *sākam* 'with, together with' *āssva sākaṁ mayā saudhe mādhiṣṭhā nirjanaṁ vanam* (Bhaṭṭikāvyam, 8. 79). 'Remain with me in the palace. Do not live in the desolate forest.'

76. *sārdham* 'with'. *nāśnīyāt bhāryayā sārdhaṁ naināṁ īkṣeta cāśnatīm* (Manusmṛti, 4. 43). 'Neither share food with your wife nor watch her taking her meal.'

---

1. Śabdakaustubhaḥ, p. 177.
2. Bhaimī, p. 529.

77. *namas* 'salutation, obeisance, adoration'. *namaste 'stu brahman svasti me 'stu* Kaṭhopaniṣad, 1. 1. 9. 'Salutation to you, O Brāhmaṇa ! May I be blessed!'

78. *hiruk* 'without, near'. *hiruk karma na mokṣaḥ syāt* (Vyā. cand., IV, p. 235). 'There is no salvation without karma.' *parvatasya hiruṅ nadī* (Ibid.). 'The river is near the mountain.'

79. *dhik* 'an interjection of censure or displeasure, fie'. *atha cāstamitā tvamātmnā dhigimāṁ dehabhṛtām asāratām* (Raghu, 8. 51). 'You yourself are dead. Oh fie upon the frailty of human beings !'

nairguṇyameva sādhīyo dhig astu guṇagauravam,
śākhino 'nye virājante khaṇḍyante candanadrumāḥ. Bhāmv. I. 88.

'Being devoid of qualities is preferable. Fie upon being laden with good properties. The ordinary trees stand intact, whereas the sandal trees are cut into pieces.'

80. *atha* 'beginning, afterwards, but, if, question, entirety, doubt, either...or'. *atha yogānuśāsanam.* 'Now begins the instruction of yoga.'

atha cet tvam imaṁ dharmyaṁ saṅgrāmaṁ na kariṣyasi,
tataḥ svadharmaṁ kīrtiṁ ca hitvā pāpam avāpsyasi. Bh. G. 2. 33.

'On the other hand, if you do not undertake this righteous battle, then, forsaking your own duty and fame, you will incur sin.'

atha dharmaṁ vyākhyāsyāmaḥ (Gaṇaratna). 'We shall explain the entire dharma.' *atha ko 'sya vyapadeśaḥ* (Śākuntala, 7). 'To which family does he belong?' *śabdo nityo 'thānityaḥ* (Gaṇaratna). 'Whether the word is eternal or non-enternal?'

81. *am* 'quickly, a little' (Bhaimī, p. 530). In the Kāśikā on *amu ca chandasi* Pā. 5. 4. 12, this has obviously been accepted as an item in svarādi list. It is also used to convey the sense 'excellence of a thing' (cf. *svarādiṣu am ām iti paṭhyate tasmāt tadantasyāvyayatvam*). The illustration *prataraṁ nayāmaḥ*, given in the Kāśikā, then means : we carry (a thing) relatively well. However, the word in this sense need not have been included in the list of svarādi as it would have been taken care of by *taddhitaścāsarvavibhaktiḥ* (367).

82. *ām* 'yes, acceptance, indeed'. *ām jñātam* (Śākuntala, 3) ! 'Yes, I have come to know (of it).' Like *am,* this has been accepted as a taddhita affix by some grammarians. Accordingly, they are of opinion that the words ending in this affix should be designated as *avyayas* according to the rule *taddhitaścāsarvavibhaktiḥ* (367).

83. *pratām* 'exhaustion, fatigue' (Bhaimī, p. 531). The word is derived with the introduction of the primary affix *kvip* and as such the penultimate vowel of the verbal root *tam* is lengthened by *anunāsikasya kvijhaloḥ kṅiti* (724). After the elision of the affix *su,* the final consonant

m is not replaced by *n* by *mo no dhātoḥ* (269). Had this not been the case, Pāṇini would not have enunciated the word *praśān* with the phoneme *n* at the end. The illustrations of this indeclinable are not traced in the extant Sanskrit literature. The word *pratān* has additionally been enlisted in the svarādi class in the Kāśikā.

84. *praśān* 'equal, similar'. *praśān devadatto yajñadattena* (Gaṇaratna). 'Devadatta is equal or similar to Yajñadatta.' The Gita Press and NS editions additionally read the word *pratān* here.

85. *mā* 'prohibition, do not'. *mā te saṅgo 'stvakarmaṇi* (Bh. G. 2. 47). 'Let there be no attachment in you to inaction.'

86. *māṅ* 'prohibition, do not'. *klaibyaṁ mā sma gamaḥ pārtha naitattvayyupapadyate* (Bh. G. 2. 3). 'O Pārtha, do not yield to unmanliness. This does not befit you.' We can easily distinguish the indeclinable *mā* from *māṅ* with the help of a verbal form used in the sentence in which either of the words has been used. If the luṅ or laṅ verbal form preceded by the term *sma* is used in the sentence, then the indeclinable *mā* used in the sentence represents *māṅ*. In other cases it may be accepted as *mā*. (Cf. *kecid āhuḥ aṅid aparo māśabdo vidyate tasyāyaṁ prayogaḥ*, Kāśikā on *māṅi luṅ* Pā. 3. 3. 175).

The words enumerated in the list beginning with *svar* can only be known from the form, *a posteriori* (*ākṛtigaṇa*). As such the list is not exhaustive. If we come across such words as undergo the grammatical operations like an avyaya, then we should also include such words in this list. Some important words, which can be included in the svarādi set, are illustrated as follows :

(i) *añjasā* 'rightly, soon'. *sākṣād dṛṣṭo 'si na punar vidmas tvām vayam añjasā* (Kumāra, 6. 22). 'Although you are perceived directly, we do not know you rightly.' *sa gacchatyañjasā vipro brahmaṇaḥ sadma śāśvatam.* (Manu. 2. 244). 'That brahmin goes to the eternal abode of Brahman very soon.'

(ii) *avaśyam* 'definitely'. *avaśyaṁ yātāraś ciratararam uṣitvāpi viṣayāḥ* (Vairāgyaśataka, 12). 'The objects of the senses will definitely vanish even if they stay for long.'

(iii) *āvis* 'before the eyes, evidently'. *āvirbabhūva kuśagarbhamukhaṁ mṛgāṇāṁ yūthaṁ tadagrasaragarvitakṛṣṇasāram* (Raghu, 9. 55). 'Led by a proud black antelope, a herd of deer with kuśa grass in their mouths came before the eyes.'

(iv) *om* 'acceptance, Brahman or God'. *om ityucyatām amātyaḥ* (Mālatīmādhava, 6). 'Tell the minister that we accept this.'

(v) *kāmam* 'granted that'. *kāmaṁ dhīrasvabhāveyaṁ strīsvabhāvas tu kātaraḥ* (Svapna, 4. 8). 'Granted that this lady is strong-minded but women are timid by nature.'

(vi) *cirāt* 'after a long time'. *upāntasammīlitalocano nṛpaś cirāt sutasparśarasajñatāṁ yayau* (Raghu, 3. 26). 'After a long time the king, with his eyes closed at their corners, experienced the state of enjoying the bliss derived from the touch of his own child.'

(vii) *jhaṭiti* 'quickly'. *jhaṭiti parāśayavedino hi vijñāḥ* (Naiṣadha). 'The learned do read others' mind quickly.'

(viii) *drāk* 'forthwith, quickly, immediately'. *drāg vidrutaṁ kātaraiḥ* (Gaṇaratna). 'The cowards ran away immediately.'

(ix) *na* 'negation'. *yogayukto munir brahma nacireṇādhigacchati.* (Bh. G. 5. 6). 'A person engaged in yoga, having become a meditator (muni), attains Brahman without delay.'

(x) *bhūyas* 'again'. *bhūyaḥ sa bhūteśvarapārśvavartī kiñcid vihasyārthapatiṁ babhāṣe* (Raghu, 2. 46). 'The servant of the Lord of all beings laughed a little and again spoke to the lord of wealth.'

(xi) *varam* 'better'. *varam adya kapotaḥ śvo mayūrāt* (proverb). 'A bird in hand is better than two in the bush.' Literally the illustration means 'A pigeon today is better than a peacock tomorrow.'

(xii) *sapadi* 'at once'. *(te) sārundhatīkāḥ sapadi prādurāsan puraḥ prabhoḥ* (Kumāra, 6. 4). '(The seven seers) along with Arundhatī at once appeared before the Lord (Śiva).'

(xiii) *samam* 'with'. *samunnayan bhūtimanāryasaṅgamād varaṁ virodho 'pi samaṁ mahātmabhiḥ* (Kirāta, 1. 8). 'Even enmity with the noble, which brings about prosperity, is to be preferred to the companionship with the wicked.'

(xiv) *samprati* 'now'. *sampratyavatīrṇā rajanīti netaḥ prastheyam.* (Vyā. cand., IV, p. 287). 'Now the night has fallen ; we should not set out from here.'

(xv) *sākṣād* 'directly'. *sākṣātpriyām upagatām apahāya pūrvaṁ citrārpitāṁ punar imāṁ bahu manyamānaḥ* (Śākuntala, 6. 16). ' Having first repudiated my beloved when she came to me in person, I now think highly of her drawn in this picture.'

(xvi) *sāmpratam* 'proper, now'. *viṣavṛkṣo 'pi saṁvardhya svayaṁ chettum asāmpratam.* 'It is not proper to cut down even a poisonous tree when (it has been) nurtured by oneself (Kumāra, 2. 55).' *yā sāmprataṁ coddhatadaityatāpitair asmābhir īśā ca surair namasyate* (Mā. Pu., 82. 39). 'The Goddess who is now being bowed to reverentially by us (gods) who have been tormented by the haughty demon.'

Other such words as are accepted in usage and grammatically behave like an avyaya can be enlisted in the svarādi set.

The present sūtra also provides that the words called *nipāta* are assigned the avyaya designation. These words are given in the rules that begin with *prāgrīśvarānnipātāḥ* Pā. 1. 4. 37 and end with *vibhāṣā kṛñi* Pā. 1. 4. 98 which optionally assigns the karmapravacanīya designation to *adhi* when it is linked with the verbal root *kṛ*. Since *adhi* is a part of the set that begins with *pra*, it is then optionally designated as *gati*. The nipāta class includes the subgroups of the words called upasarga, gati and karmapravacanīya. After nipātas, as after most of the avyayas, the sup-affixes are elided by *avyayādāpsupaḥ* (371). The following five particles from *ca* to *eva* are not used at the beginning of a sentence or a quarter (pāda). The words enlisted in the *cādi* class are being illustrated below :

1. *ca* 'conjunction, still, certainty, condition, joining a subordinate with a principal one (*anvācaya*), collective combination (*samāhāra*), mutual conjunction (*itaretarayoga*), aggregation (*samuccaya*). The illustrations are given here in the order of their mention. *tau gurur gurupatnī ca prītyā pratinanandatuḥ* (Raghu, 1. 57). 'The preceptor and his wife welcomed them with love.' *śāntam idam āśramapadaṁ sphurati ca bāhuḥ* (Śākuntala, 1.16). 'This hermitage is peaceful. Still my arm throbs.' *karmakṣayāc ca nirvāṇam* (Vyā. cand., IV, p. 252). 'The cessation of karmas certainly leads to liberation.' *jīvituṁ cecchase mūḍha hetuṁ me gadataḥ śṛṇu* (Mahābhārata, quoted under the particle *ca* in Apte's Dictionary). 'If you have a desire to live, O fool, then hear from me the cause.' *bhikṣām aṭa gāṁ cānaya* (Gaṇaratna). 'Beg alms and bring a cow (If you spot her on the way).' *pāṇī ca pādau ca pāṇipādam* (Gaṇaratna). 'An aggregation of hands and feet.' **rāmaśca lakṣmaṇaśca rāmalakṣmaṇau.* 'Rāma and Lakṣmaṇa.' *gārgyo vātsyāyanaś cāgatau* (Vyā. cand., IV, p. 252). 'Gārgya and Vātsyāyana have come.'

2. *vā* 'option, or, also, like'. *vā cittavirāge* Pā. 6. 4. 91. 'In the causal the *u* of *duṣ* is lengthened optionally when it means to pervert the mind.'

ubhe eva kṣame voḍhum ubhayor bījam āhitam,
sā vā śambhos tadīyā vā mūrtir jalamayī mama. (Kumāra, 2. 60)

'Two only are able to bear the seed of us two; either she (Pārvatī) of Śambhu or his watery form, mine.' *vāyur vā dahano vā* (Gaṇaratna). 'Air as well as fire.' *asti te mātā smarasi vā tātam* (Uttara, 4). 'Have you a mother and do you remember your father?' *jātāṁ manye śiśiramathitāṁ padminīṁ vānyarūpām* (Meghdūta, 2. 23). 'I think that (young lady) has become like a lotus struck down by the cold.'

3. *ha* 'to indicate a bygone event, as an expletive, obviously'. *dvayā ha prājāpatyā devāś cāsurāś ca* (Bṛh. Up., 1. 3. 1). 'The offspring of Prajāpati were of two kinds, the gods and the demons.' *iti ha smāhur ācāryāḥ* (Gaṇaratna). 'The preceptor used to say like this.' *guṇadoṣabhidādṛṣṭir nigamāt te na hi svataḥ, nigamenāpavādaś ca bhidāyā iti ha bhramaḥ*. (Bhāg. Pu. 11. 20. 5). 'My confusion is obviously due to the fact that the very difference between good and evil, not existing by itself, is made known by the Veda and it is also denied by the same.' (Please dispel my confusion, Uddhava implores Kṛṣṇa).

4. *aha* 'impropriety, praise, sending'. *svayam aha rathena yāti upādhyāyaṁ padātiṁ gamayati* (Kāśikā, 8. 2. 104). 'He himself goes by chariot but sends his teacher on foot. '*aha māṇavako bhuṅkte* (Gaṇaratna). 'A religious student is having his meal!' *tvam aha grāmaṁ gaccha ayam ahāraṇyaṁ gacchatu* (Gaṇaratna). '(You) go to the village and he will go to the forest.'

5. *eva* 'only, alone (implying exclusion), as soon as, like'. *satyam eva jayate nānṛtam* (Mu. Up., 1. 3. 1). 'Truth alone triumphs, not falsehood.' *upasthiteyaṁ kalyāṇī nāmni kīrtita eva yat* (Raghu, 1. 87). 'For as soon as her name is mentioned, this blessed cow has thus made her appearance.' *śrīs tavaiva me 'stu* (Gaṇaratna). 'May I possess wealth like you.'

6. *evam* 'like this'. *tasmād evaṁ viditvainaṁ nānuśocitum arhasi* (Bh. G. 2. 25). 'Therefore, having known the soul like this, you should not grieve.'

7. *nūnam* 'definitely, in all probability'. *kṣudre 'pi nūnaṁ śaraṇaṁ prapanne mamatvam uccaiḥśirasāṁ satīva* (Kumāra, 1. 12). 'The great definitely have the same regard for a petty person who has come to take refuge as they would have for a gentle man.' *pūrvaṁ mayā nūnam abhīpsitāni pāpāni karmāṇyasakṛt kṛtāni* (Vālmīkirāmāyaṇa, 3. 63. 4). 'In all probability, I could have intentionally committed sins many a time in my previous incarnations.'

8. *śaśvat* 'ever, eternal, repeatedly, together'. *jīvan punaḥ śaśvad upaplavebhyaḥ prajāḥ prajānātha piteva pāsi* (Raghu, 2. 48). 'But if you live, you will, O lord of people, ever protect your subjects, as their father, from all their troubles.' *kṣipraṁ bhavati dharmātmā śaśvacchāntiṁ nigacchati* (Bh. G., 9. 31). 'He soon becomes endowed with a virtuous mind; he attains eternal peace.' *upadā viviśuḥ śaśvannotsekāḥ kośaleśvaram* (Raghu, 4. 70). 'The presents repeatedly reached the king of Kosala but insolence did not.' *śaśvat te munayas tatra tam asevanta yoginam* (Vyā. cand., IV, p. 252). 'The hermits together attended upon that yogī.'

9. *yugapat* 'simultaneously'.

vṛddhā yuvānaḥ śiśavaḥ kapotāḥ khale yathāmī yugapat patanti,

tathaiva sarve yugpat padārthāḥ parasparenānvayino bhavanti.
(Nyāyasiddhāntamuktāvalī, Śabdakhaṇḍa)

'Just as those pigeons -- old, full-grown and young -- fall upon a barn-yarn simultaneously, similarly the meanings of all the words enter simultaneously into a relationship with one another.'

10. *bhūyas* 'Frequently, repeatedly'. *svayameva bhūyodarśanena yatra dhūmas tatrāgnir iti mahānasādau vyāptiṁ gṛhītvā parvatasamīpaṁ gataḥ* (Tarkasaṅgraha, anumāna). 'A man having himself ascertained by frequent observation the generalization (invariable concomitance), viz. wherever there is smoke there is fire as in a kitchen, approaches a mountain.'

11. *kūpat* 'praise'. *kūpad ayaṁ gāyati* (Gaṇaratna). 'He sings in a praiseworthy manner.'

12. *sūpat* 'praise'. Its usage is not traced.

13. *kuvit* 'in great quantity'. *kuvit somasyāpām* (Ṛgveda, 10. 119. 1). 'I drank a large quantity of soma.'

14. *net* 'lest'. *necchatruḥ prāśaṁ jayāti* (Atharvaveda, 2. 27. 1).[1] '... lest the enemy snatch away our food.'

15. *cet* 'if, in case'. *utsīdeyur ime lokā na kuryāṁ karma ced aham* (Bh. G. 3. 24). 'These worlds will be annihilated, if I do not perform action.'

atha cet tvam imaṁ dharmyaṁ saṅgrāmaṁ na kariṣyasi,
tataḥ svadharmaṁ kīrtiṁ ca hitvā pāpam avāpsyasi. (Bh. G. 2. 33)

'However in case you do not undertake this righteous battle, then forsaking your own duty and fame, you will incur sin.'

This indeclinable is never used at the beginning of a sentence.

16. *caṇ* 'if'. This particle has *ṇ* as *it* and occurs in Pā. 8. 1. 30. The Kāśikā illustrates this and explains its meaning as follows : *ayaṁ ca mariṣyati. ayaṁ ced mariṣyatītyarthaḥ.* "If he dies', this is the meaning."

17. *yatra* 'where, in which place'. *prāyo gacchati yatra daivahatakas tatraiva yāntyāpadaḥ* (Nītiśataka, 84). 'Calamities often throng the place where the unfortunate goes.' The word *yatra* has been repeated in the nipāta class in order to preclude a pada, which ends in *tiṅ*, from being marked with anudātta, if the tiṅanta pada is used with the particles *yatra*, etc. (cf. Pā. 8. 1. 30 and the Kāśikā thereon).

18. *kaccit* 'a particle of interrogation which is translated by 'I hope'. The NS edition reads this indeclinable as *kvacit*.

kriyānimitteṣvapi vatsalatvād abhagnakāmā munibhiḥ kuśeṣu,
tadaṅkaśayyācyutanābhinālā kaccinmṛgīṇām anaghā prasūtiḥ.
(Raghu, 5. 7)

---

1. Bhaimī, p. 539.

'I hope that the fawns are delivered safely by female-deer whom the sages through extreme affection, indulge in the desire of feeding even upon the Kuśa grass, required in their ceremonial rites, and who drop down the umbilical cords on their laps, which formed, as it were, their beds.'

19. *naha* 'not indeed'. *naha bhokṣyase. nahādhyeṣyase* (Kāśikā on Pā. 8. 1. 31). 'Indeed you would not eat! Indeed you would not study!' In this context Jinendrabuddhi says that this particle is a combination of *na* and *ha*.

20. *hanta* 'used to express joy or grief'. *hanta bhoḥ śakuntalāṁ patikulaṁ visṛjya labdham idānīṁ svāsthyam* (Śākuntala, 4). 'Ah! Calm of mind has now been attained by me after having sent Śakuntalā to her husband's house.' *kācamūlyena vikrīto hanta cintāmaṇir mayā* (cited as an exmaple of nidarśanā alaṅkāra in Sāhityadarpaṇa, chapter 10). 'Alas! A philosopher's stone has been sold by me for the price of a crystal.'

21. *mākir* 'do not'. *mākir devānāmapbhūriha syāḥ* (Ṛgveda, 10. 11. 19d). 'Do not go away. Stay here.'

22. *mākīm* 'not'. *mākīm saṁśāri kevaṭe* (Ṛgveda, 6. 54. 7b). 'Let no cow meet its end by falling into a well (Vyā. cand., IV, p. 268).' The reading in GP and NS editions is *mākim*, which is not correct.

23. *nakir* 'nobody'. *nakir asya pra minanti vratāni* (Ṛgveda, 10. 10. 5c). 'No one deviates from his principles.' *nakir vaktā na dād iti* (Ṛgveda, 8. 32. 15c). 'Let no one say that (Indra) does not give (Vyā. cand., IV, p. 268).'

24. *nakīm* 'none'. *nakīm indro nikartave* (Ṛgveda, 8. 78. 5a). 'None can disregard Indra (Vyā. cand., IV, p. 268).' Ballantyne reads *ākīm* whereas the GP and NS editions read *nakim.* Both the readings are wrong (cf. Bhaimī, p. 541 and Vyā. cand. IV, p. 268).

25. *māṅ* 'do not, prohibition'. *mā karmaphalahetur bhūr mā te saṅgo-'stv akarmaṇi* (Bh. G. 2. 47). 'Do not become the producer of the result of action. Let there be no attachment in you to inaction!' This particle remains *mā* after the elision of the anubandha *ṅ*. It has been included in the svarādi set. Its repetition in the set of nipātas is questionable. According to Nāgeśa, its inclusion in the svarādi class is an interpolation (*evaṁ māṅo 'pi svarādau prakṣiptaḥ pāṭhaḥ*, LS, p. 575). Jñānendra Sarasvatī is of the opinion that it should not have been included in both the sets. According to him, the view of those, who say that its inclusion in the nipātas has the purpose of marking the initial vowel with an udātta accent, is wrong since this purpose is very well served by the phiṭsūtras. He further says that the view that its inclusion in the svarādi set has the purpose that the words included in this class may be assigned

the avyaya designation even when they denote a substantial entity, is also wrong since in that case the word *mā* meaning the goddess of wealth would become liable to be designated as an *avyaya*. This is the reason why this word should not have been included in both the sets.

26. *nañ* 'no, not'. According to Nāgeśa its inclusion in the svarādi class is not proper (*nañaḥ svarādiṣvaprāmāṇikaḥ pāṭhaḥ*, LS, p. 574). *na hi jñānena sadṛśaṁ pavitramiha vidyate* (Bh. G. 4. 38). 'Indeed there is nothing as purifying as knowledge.' *tānyahaṁ veda sarvāṇi na tvaṁ vettha parantapa* (Bh. G. 4. 5). 'I know them all; you do not know, O scorcher of enemies!'

27. *yāvat* 'whole (when it is used with *tāvat*), till, so long as'. *yāvad dattaṁ tāvad bhuktam* (Gaṇaratna). 'All that has been given is eaten.' *tāvat pratipālaya māṁ yāvad etan mocayāmi* (Śākuntala, 1). 'Wait for me till I release it.' *dhriyate yāvad eko 'pi ripus tāvat kutaḥ sukham* (Śiśu, 2. 35). 'So long as there is a single enemy, there is no happiness.'

28. *tāvat* 'till then, before, indeed'. *tāvacca śobhate mūrkho yāvat kiñcinna bhāṣate* (Hitopadeśa, Prastāvikā, 40). 'A fool looks fine as long as he doesn't say anything.' *ārye itas tāvad āgamyatām* (Śākuntala, 1). 'O noble lady! first come this side.' *tvam eva tāvat prathamo rājadrohī* (Mudrārākṣasa, 1). 'You are indeed the first traitor.'

29. *tvai* 'specifically' *ayaṁ tvai prakṛṣyate* (Gaṇaratna). 'This is specifically enhanced.'

30. *nvai* 'guess'. *nvai*. 'Who could be going!'

31. *dvai* 'guess'. Its usage is not traced (Bhaimī, p. 542).

32. *rai* 'disregard'. *tvaṁ rai kiṁ kariṣyasi* (Gaṇaratna)? 'What can you do to me?' (You cannot do anything to me).

33. *śrauṣaṭ* 34. *vauṣaṭ* 35. *svāhā* 36. *svadhā* 37. *vaṣaṭ*. The indeclinable *svāhā* is pronounced at the time of offering oblations to the gods, e. g., *indrāya svāhā*. 'The oblation be unto Indra!' The other four indeclinables have been explained in the *svarādi* class. They have been included here so that their initial vowel may be marked with an udātta accent.

38. *tum* 'sound of defiance to show disrepect'.

guruṁ huṁkṛtya tuṁkṛtya vipraṁ nirjitya vādataḥ,
śmaśāne jāyate ghore kākagṛdhropasevite.[1]

'One who shows disrespect to the preceptor by making sounds of *hum* and *tum* and defeats a brāhmaṇa in a discussion is born in a crematorium frequented by the crows and vultures.'

39. *tathāhi* 'for, as for instance'.

taṁ vedhā vidadhe nūnaṁ mahābhūtasamādhinā,
tathāhi sarve tasyāsan parārthaikaphalā guṇāḥ. (Raghu, I. 29).

---

1. Bhaimī, p. 543.

'Brahmā surely made him with the substance of the great elements; for he inherited all virtues the sole effect of which was the good of others.' *pravṛttinivṛttiprayojanatvācchāstrasya. tathāhi śāstratātparyavida āhuḥ dṛṣṭo hi tasyārthaḥ karmāvabodhanam iti* (Brahmasūtraśāṅkara-bhāṣya, 1. 1. 4). 'The scriptures have in view either persuasion or dissuasion from activities, as for instance the knowers of the import of the scriptures say : The obvious purport of the Vedas is to generate knowledge about duties.'

40. *khalu* 'a particle that implies certainty, entreaty, prohibition, reason'. *mārge padāni khalu te viṣamībhavanti* (Śākuntala, 4). 'Your footsteps are indeed falling unevenly on the road.' *na khalu na khalu bāṇaḥ sannipātyo 'yam asmin mṛduni mṛgaśarīre puṣparāśāvivāgniḥ* (Śākuntala, 1). 'Please do not cause this arrow to descend on this tender body of the deer, which is like a heap of flowers.' **khāditvā khalu.* 'Don't eat.' *na vidīrye kaṭhināḥ khalu striyaḥ* (Kumāra, 4. 5). 'I am not torn (with grief), for women are hard-hearted.'

41. *kila* 'verily, report of an old event, a feigned action'. *arhati kila kitava upadravam* (Mālavikā, 4). ' The rogue verily deserves misfortune.' *jaghāna kaṁsaṁ kila vāsudevaḥ* (Mahābhāṣya, 3. 2. 111). 'They say that the son of Vasudeva killed Kaṁsa.' *prasahya siṁhaḥ kila tāṁ cakarṣa* (Raghu, 2. 27). 'A lion feigned to seize her forcibly.'

42. *atho* 'collection, immediately after'.

striyo ratnānyatho vidyā dharmaḥ śaucaṁ subhāṣitam,
vividhāni ca śilpāni samādeyāni sarvataḥ. Manusmṛti, 2. 240.

'Women, jewels and education, religion, cleanliness, good saying and also different kinds of arts should be procured from all sides.' *atho vayasyāṁ paripārśvavartinīṁ vivarttitā'nañjananetram aikṣata* (Kumāra, 5. 51). 'She with eyes devoid of collyrium immediately looked at her friend standing by her side.' Ballantyne's and NS editions do not have this word.

43. *atha* 'auspiciousness'. This particle is used at the beginning of works mostly as a sign of auspiciousness. Properly speaking, auspiciousness is not the denotation of *atha* but the very utterance or hearing of the word is considered to be indicative of auspiciousness as the word is supposed to have emanated from the throat of Brahmā. Śaṅkara says: *arthāntaraprayukta eva hyathaśabdaḥ śrutyā maṅgalaprayojano bhavati* (Śāṅkarabhāṣya on Brahmasūtra, 1. 1. 1). 'The word *atha* used even to convey another sense is purported to indicate auspiciousness as soon as it is heard.' For example, in *athāto brahmajijñāsā*, the word *atha* is used in the sense of afterwards but when it is heard it is said to lead to auspiciousness.

44. *suṣṭhu* 'well, excellently'. *suṣṭhu khalvidam ucyate* (Vyā. cand., IV, p. 287). 'Indeed it is well said.'*suṣṭhu śobhase āryaputra etena vinaya-māhātmyena* (Uttararāmacarita, 1). 'Honoured Sir, you look excellent with this magnanimous decency.'

45. *sma* 'to indicate the sense of the past tense, pleonastic use'. *bhāsurako nāma siṁhaḥ prativasati sma* (Pañcatantra, 1). 'A lion named Bhāsuraka used to live there.' *bhartur viprakṛtāpi roṣaṇatayā mā sma pratīpaṁ gamaḥ* (Śākuntala, 4). 'Though wronged, do not, in a fit of anger, act in a refractory way towards your husband.'

46. *ādaha* 'censure, violence'. *kurvādaha yadi kariṣyasi* (Gaṇaratna). 'If you (want) censure, then do it.'

47. Here we have a gaṇasūtra : *upasarga-vibhakti-svara-pratirūpakāśca*, 'Words which have the appearance of a preverb (*upasarga*), of either a nominal or conjugational ending and of a vowel should be added to the list of cādi class.'

The words which have the appearance of a preverb are *ava, vi, pra, su, anu* and *ni* which are given in the following verse. They look like a preverb but are actually nipātas :

avadattaṁ vidattaṁ ca pradattañcādikarmaṇi,
sudattam anudattañca nidattam iti ceṣyate. Mbh, 7. 4. 46

The illustration, given in the Laghu, is *avadattam*. The word *ava* has the appearance of a preverb (*upasarga*) but it is actually not a preverb. If this had been a preverb, then the substitute *ta* would have replaced the ghu-designated verbal root *dā* by *aca upasargāttaḥ* Pā. 7. 4. 47 and the form would have been *avattam* and not *avadattam*. So, *ava* in *avadattam* is a nipāta and not a preverb. In a similar manner, *vi, pra, su, anu* and *ni* illustrated in this verse are nipātas.

48. The word *aham* in *ahaṁyuḥ* 'egotistic' has the appearance of a word that ends in a sup-affix but it is not so. Had this been the nominative singular form of the pronominal stem *asmad*, then the form would have been *madyuḥ* in accordance with the rule *pratyayottarapadayośca* Pā. 7. 2. 98. So the word *aham* in this illustration is a nipāta and not an inflected nominative singular form of *asmad*. The other illustration is *śubhaṁyuḥ* in which *śubham* is a nipāta which has the appearance of an inflected word *śubham*.

49. The bahuvrīhi compound *astikṣīrā* 'that which has milk' illustrates the nipāta which has the appearance of a conjugated verbal form. The word *asti* in the compound looks like a laṭ lakāra third person singular form of the verbal root *as* but actually it is a nipāta. If it was a verbal form (*tiṅanta*), there would be no compounding of the word *kṣīra* with

asti since the term *sup* is carried over into *anekamanyapadārthe* (962) which prescribes bahuvrīhi.[1]

The nipātas, which have the appearance of a vowel, are *a, ā, i, ī, u, ū, e, ai, o,* and *au.*

50. *a* 'used in addressing, in reproach'. *a apehi* (Kāśikā, 1. 1. 14). O! get lost. *apacasi tvaṁ jālma* (SK, II, p. 89).[2] 'Rascal ! You cook in a bad manner.'

51. *ā* 'emphasis in a sentence, reminiscence'. *ā evaṁ nu manyase.* 'Now indeed you think so.' 2. *ā evaṁ kila tat.* 'Such indeed was then the case.'[3]

52. *i* 'address'. *i indraṁ paśya* (Kāśikā, 1. 1. 14). 'O ! Behold Indra.'

53. *ī* 'address' *ī īśa* ! (Gaṇaratna). 'O ! God.'

54. *u* 'guess' *u umeśa.* (SK, I, p. 116). 'It could be Umeśa!'

55. *ū* 'address'. *ū ūṣare bījaṁ vapati.* 'Aye ! You sow the seed in the infertile land.'

56. *e* 'address'. *e ito bhava.* 'Aye ! You be here.' 57. *ai* 'address'. *ai vācaṁ dehi.* 'Aye ! Speak out.' 58. *o* 'address'. *o ! śrāvaya.* 'Aye ! Inform (the deity that the offering is being given. Cf. Paddhati on VP, I. 17).' 59. *au* 'address'. *au mahātman.* 'O great soul!' (Bhaimī, p. 548).

60. *paśu* 'in a proper manner'. The illustration *lodhaṁ nayanti paśu manyamānāḥ,* which is generally given to explain its connotation, is from the Ṛgveda, 3. 53. 23. Sāyaṇa, in his bhāṣya on this mantra, says that it is a nipāta. However, he explains the word *paśu* as *paśuvat* 'like an animal' when he comments on it (*ete nayanti paśuvan manyamānāḥ*). The meaning, which is generally assigned to this word, is not illustrated.

61. *śukam* 'quickly'. *śukam gacchhati* (Gaṇaratna). 'He goes quickly.'

62. *yathākathāca* 'anyhow (in a disrespectful way)'. *yathākathāca dīyate* (Gaṇaratna). 'It is given anyhow.'

63. *pāṭ* 'hallo, ho'. 64. *pyāṭ* 'hallo'. *pāṭ pāntha* ! (Hemacandra). 'Hallo traveller!' *pyāṭ pāvaka* (Hemacandra). 'Ho agni!' (See Bhaimī, p. 549).

65. *aṅga* 'a vocative particle meaning 'well', 'indeed', 'yes', etc.' *aṅga kaccit kuśalī tātaḥ* (Kādambarī). 'Well, I hope father is doing well.' *aṅga adhīṣva, odanaṁ te dāsyāmi* (Kāśikā, 8. 2. 96). 'Yes, you study, I will feed you rice.'

66. *hai* 'a vocative particle'. **hai kṛṣṇa! pāhi mām.* 'Hey Kṛṣṇa! Save me.'

67. *he* 'address'. *sakheti matvā prasabhaṁ yaduktaṁ he kṛṣṇa he yādava he sakheti* (Bh. G., 11. 41). 'Thinking that you are a friend, whatever was said rashly, like O Kṛṣṇa, O Yādava, O friend, etc.'

---

1. Also cf. vtks 21 and 22 in the Mahābhāṣya on *anekamanyapadārthe* 2. 2. 24.

2. Vāsudeva Dīkṣita says that *a* is an avyaya which is not the remnant of *nañ* as is clear from the following statement : *nañsamānārthakena a ityavyayenāpi siddham iti.* BM, II, p. 89.

3. See supra pp. 70-1 for these illustrations and explanations.

68. *bhos* 'address'. *bhos tapodhanāḥ cintayannapi na khalu svīkaraṇam atrabhavatyāḥ smarāmi* (Śākuntala, 5). 'O hermits, though trying to recall, I do not really remember having espoused this lady.'

69. *aye* 'a gentle address, also indicating surprise'. *aye gaurīnātha tripurahara śambho trinayana* (Vairāgyaśataka, 123). 'O Lord of Gaurī, vanquisher of Tripura, Śambhu, Three-eyed!' *aye mātaliḥ* (Śākuntala, 6). 'Ah ! It is Mātali.'

70. *dya* 'expletive, violence'. *dya hinasti mṛgaṁ vyādhaḥ* (Prakriyākaumudī, quoted in Bhaimī, p. 550). 'The hunter kills a deer (in a violent way).'[1]

71. *viṣu* 'on all sides'. The derivation of the word *viṣvac* 'everywhere' illustrates this indeclinable : *viṣu añcatīti viṣvak* (*viṣu* + *añcu* + *kvin*). 'That which goes in all directions is *viṣvak*.'

72. *ekapade* 'instantly, at once'. *katham ekapade nirāgasaṁ janam ābhāṣyam imaṁ na manyase* (Raghu, 8. 48). 'Why don't you instantly consider this innocent person as one everyway worthy of being spoken to?'

73. *yut* 'blame'. **sabhāyāṁ yun na bhāṣitavyam*. 'One should not speak in an improper way in a meeting.'

74. *ātaḥ* 'hence'. *ātaś ca sūtrata eva* (Mbh, Paspaśāhnika). 'Hence (this all must be) from the sūtra itself.'

The words enumerated in the list beginning with *ca* are also known from the form, *a posteriori* (*ākṛtigaṇa*). As such, the list is considered to be illustrative and not exhaustive. Some of the words, which can be included in the cādi class, are illustrated as follows :

(i) *ayi* 'a gentle address'. *ayi kaṭhora yaśaḥ kila te priyam* (Uttara). 'O ruthless one, that fame is dear to you is a travesty of truth.'

(ii) *re* 'address'. *saṁsāre re manuṣyā vadata yadi sukhaṁ svalpamapyasti kiñcit* (Vairāgyaśataka, 37). 'O men! tell if there is an iota of happiness in the world.'

(iii) *are* 'addressing inferiors' *ātmā vā are draṣṭavyaḥ śrotavyo mantavyo nididhyāsitavyo maitreyi* (Bṛh. Up., 2. 4. 5). 'The soul alone, O Maitreyī, is to be seen, heard, thought and intently contemplated upon.'

(iv) *bhagos* 'a term of addressing gods and a respectable person'. *bhago namaste*. 'O adoration to you!'

(v) *agho* 'a term of addressing an ignoble person'. *agho yāhi*. 'O wretch! Go.'

(vi) *hā* 'alas'. *hā hā devi sphuṭati hṛdayam* (Uttara). 'Alas! Noble lady, my heart breaks.'

(vii) *aho* 'to express wonder or grief'. *aho ceṣṭāpratirūpikā kāmijanamanovṛttiḥ* (Śākuntala, 1). 'Ah, how similar to action is the working of a

1. The translation without parentheses illustrates its usage as an expletive.

lover's mind?' *aho bata mahatpāpaṁ kartuṁ vyavasitā vayam* (Bh. G. 1. 45). 'Alas! We have resolved to commit a great sin.'

(viii) *saha* 'with, along with'. *śaśinā saha yāti kaumudī saha meghena taḍit pralīyate* (Kumāra, 4. 33). 'Moonlight goes with the moon and lightning disappears along with the cloud.'

(ix) *jātu* 'at all, at any time'. *na jātu kāmaḥ kāmānām upabhogena śāmyati* (Manu, 2. 94). 'Desire is not at all satisfied by enjoying the pleasures of senses.' *na tvevāhaṁ jātu nāsaṁ na tvaṁ neme janādhipāḥ* (Bh. G. 2. 12). 'Never, at any time, have I not existed ; nor you nor these rulers of men.'

(x) *no cet* 'otherwise'. *parīkṣā te vārṣikī sannihitā anāratam adhītyāṁ vyāpriyasva no cet te sakāmatā tatra dūre* (Vyā. cand., IV, p. 248). 'The annual examination is at hand; be busy with your studies uninterruptedly; otherwise it is difficult to succeed in that.'

(xi) *na hi* 'not at all, definitely not'. *na hi praphullaṁ sahakāram etya vṛkṣāntaraṁ kāṅkṣati ṣaṭpadālī* (Raghu, 6. 69). 'A row of bees does not at all long for any other tree when it reaches a fully blossomed mango tree.'

(xii) *uta* 'a particle expressing uncertainty or guess'. *tat kim ayam ātapadoṣaḥ syād uta yathā me manasi vartate* (Śākuntala, 3). 'May it be the effect of the heat or is it as it is in my mind?'

(xiii) *kimuta* 'far less, not to speak of'. *api svadehāt kimutendriyārthād yaśodhanānāṁ hi yaśo garīyaḥ* (Raghu, 14. 35). 'Those who prize their fame above all, value their good name even above their own body not to speak of (valuing it more than) an object of sensuous enjoyment.'

(xiv) *kimapi* 'indescribably, very much'. *kimapi kamanīyaṁ vapur idam* (Śākuntala, 3). 'The body of my beloved is indescribably lovely.'

(xv) *pratyuta* 'on the contrary'. *viṣāde kartavye vidadhati jaḍāḥ pratyuta mudam* (Vairāgyaśataka, 58). 'When it is time to express sorrow, the foolish, on the contrary, express happiness.'

(xvi) *akāṇḍe* 'suddenly'. *darbhāṅkureṇa caraṇaḥ kṣata ityakāṇḍe tanvī sthitā katicid eva padāni gatvā* (Śākuntala, 2. 13). 'Having gone only a few steps, the slender one suddenly stopped feigning that her foot was injured by a blade of darbha.'

(xvii) *āhosvit* 'or'. *āhosvit prasavo mamāpacaritair viṣṭambhito vīrudhām* (Śākuntala, 5. 9). 'Or is it that the flowering and fructifying of creepers has been withheld through my misdeeds?'

(xviii) *atīva* 'very much'. *bhaktās te 'tīva me priyāḥ* (Bh. G. 12. 20). 'Those devotees are very dear to me.'

(xix) *bata* 'a particle expressing compassion or sorrow'. *kva bata hariṇakānāṁ jīvitaṁ cātilolaṁ kva ca niśitanipātā vajrasārāḥ śarās te* (Śākuntala, 1. 10). 'Where, indeed, on the one hand, is the extremely frail life of fawns and where, on the other, are your sharpfalling shafts that have the hardness of adamant.' *tyajata mānamalaṁ bata vigrahair na punareti gataṁ caturaṁ vayaḥ* (Raghu, 9. 47). 'Give up your indignation excited by jealousy, away with your quarrels, the age fit for enjoyment when once departed will never reappear.'

(xx) *prabhṛti* 'from, beginning, etc.'

tadāprabhṛtyeva vanadvipānāṁ trāsārtham asminnaham adrikukṣau, vyāpāritaḥ śūlabhṛtā vidhāya siṁhatvamaṅkāgatasattvavṛtti. (Raghu, 2. 38). 'From that time I have been appointed by the trident-bearing God in this mountain valley to scare away wild elephants, after having transformed me into a lion the maintenance of whom is the animals that come within his grasp.'

(xxi) *tu* 'but, nevertheless, emphasis, difference'. *avaimi cainām anagheti kiṁ tu lokāpavādo balavān mato me,* (Raghu, 14. 40). 'I know her to be innocent but public reproach weighs higher in my consideration.' *sa sarveṣāṁ sukhānāṁ prāyo 'ntaṁ yayau, ekaṁ tu sutamukhadarśana-sukhaṁ na lebhe* (Kādambarī). 'He completely enjoyed all pleasures, but he did not enjoy the pleasure of seeing the face of a son.' *bhīmas tu pāṇḍavānāṁ raudraḥ* (Gaṇaratna). 'Bhīma indeed is the fiercest of the Pāṇḍavas.' *mṛṣṭaṁ payo mṛṣṭataraṁ tu dugdham* (Gaṇaratna). 'Water is pure, purer still is milk.'

(xxii) *nanu* 'surely, correctively, propitiatory expression, address, enquiry, to advance a contrary proposition'. *upapannaṁ nanu śivaṁ saptasvaṅgeṣu me* (Raghu, 1. 60). 'Prosperity is sure to reign in the seven departments of my state.' *nanu pade parivṛtya bhaṇa* (Mālavikā). 'I say, say (it) changing the words.' *nanu māṁ prāpaya patyur antikam* (Kumāra, 4. 32). 'Be pleased to take me to my husband.' *nanu mūrkhāḥ paṭhitam eva yuṣmābhis tatkāṇḍe* (Uttararāmacarita, 4). 'Ah fools, you have already learnt it in that chapter.' *nanu samāptakṛtyo gautamaḥ* (Uttararāmacarita, 4). 'Has Gautama accomplished his object?' *nanvacetanānyeva puruṣādiśarīrāṇyacetanānāṁ keśanakhādīnāṁ kāraṇāni, acetanānyeva ca vṛścikādiśarīrāṇyacetanānāṁ gomayādīnāṁ kāryāṇīti* (Śāṅkarabhāṣya on Brahmasūtra, 2. 1. 6). 'Is not a fact that the insentient bodies etc. of men and others are the sources of insentient hair, nails, etc. and the insentient bodies of scorpions etc. are produced from the insentient cow-dung etc.?'

(xxiii) *hi* 'for, indeed, for instance, only'. *kāmārtā hi prakṛtikṛpaṇāś cetanācetaneṣu* (Megha, 1. 5). '(The yakṣa made a request to the cloud) for, those afflicted by love are by nature incapable of discriminating between the sentient and the insentient.' *agnir ihāsti dhūmo hi dṛśyate* (Gaṇaratna). 'Here is fire, for smoke is being seen here.' *deva prayoga-pradhānaṁ hi nāṭyaśāstraṁ kim atra vāgvyavahāreṇa* (Mālavikā, 1).

'Indeed, my lord, the science of acting consists principally of representations; what is the use of oral discussion in this case?'

prajānām eva bhūtyarthaṁ sa tābhyo balim agrahīt,

sahasraguṇam utsraṣṭum ādatte hi rasaṁ raviḥ. (Raghu, 1. 18). 'It was for the welfare of his subjects alone, that he collected taxes from them. In this he resembled the sun, who draws up watery vapour only to pour forth thousandfold.' *mūḍho hi madanenāyāsyate* (Kādambarī). 'Only a fool is troubled by cupid.'

(xxiv) *nāma* 'called, truly, possibility, disguise, anger, wonder'. *astyuttarasyāṁ diśi devatātmā himālayo nāma nagādhirājaḥ* (Kumāra, 1. 1). 'In the north there is a divine soul, the king of mountains, who is called Himālaya.' *sūta vinītaveṣeṇa praveṣṭavyāni tapovanāni nāma.* (Śākuntala, 1). 'Charioteer, truly, penance-groves are to be entered in humble dress.' *atanuṣu vibhaveṣu jñātayaḥ santu nāma* (Śākuntala, 5. 8). 'When the wealth is in plenty, one may possibly have a number of relations.' *kārtāntiko nāma bhūtvā vastrāntapinaddhaśāliprastho bhuvaṁ babhrāma* (Daśakumāracarita, p. 159). 'He adopted the disguise of a fortune-teller and carrying with him a prastha of paddy bound up in his cloth, he travelled over the world.' *mamāpi nāma sattvair abhibhūyante gṛhāḥ* (Śākuntala, 6). 'How, even my house is infested by evil spirits!' *citram badhiro nāma vyākaraṇam adhyeṣyate* (Kāśikā 3. 3. 151). 'It is astonishing that the deaf will study grammar.'

(xxv) *iva* 'as, as if, somewhat, like (expressive of upamā)'. *chāyeva tāṁ bhūpatir anvagacchat* (Raghu, 2. 6). 'The lord of the earth followed her as her shadow.' *mṛgānusāriṇaṁ sākṣāt paśyāmīva pinākinam* (Śākuntala, 1). 'I behold, as it were, the Pināka-holder (Śiva) chasing the deer in a visible form.' *kaḍāra ivāyam* (Gaṇaratna.). 'He is somewhat tawny.' *sañcāriṇī dīpaśikheva rātrau* (Raghu, 6. 67). 'Like a moving flame of light at night.'

(xxvi) *iti* 'to indicate the meaning, to mark the conclusion, as for, because'. *tadanvaye śuddhimati prasūtaḥ śuddhimattaraḥ, dilīpa iti rājendur induḥ kṣīranidhāviva.* (Raghu, 1. 12). 'As the pure moon was produced in the pure milky ocean, in this pure line a purer soul was born, by name Dilīpa, who was an excellent king.' *iti prathamo 'ṅkaḥ* (Apte's Dictionary). 'Here ends the first act.' *nibhṛtam iti cintanīyaṁ bhavet. śīghram iti sukaram* (Śākuntala, 3). 'As for secretly, it must be considered. As for speedily, that can be done with ease.' *vaideśiko 'smīti pṛcchāmi* (Uttararāmacarita). 'I am a foreigner. Hence I am enquiring.'

(xxvii) *diṣṭyā* 'fortunately, to express congratulations'. *diṣṭyānurūpas te 'bhiniveśaḥ* (Śākuntala, 3). 'Fortunately, your choice is appropriate.' *diṣṭyā dharmapatnīsamāgamena putramukhadarśanena cāyuṣmān vardhate*

(Śākuntala, 7). 'The long-lived one is congratulated upon his reunion with his lawfully wedded wife and upon the sight of his son's face!'

(xxviii) *nu* 'a particle implying uncertainty, indeed'. *svapno nu māyā nu matibhramo nu kliṣṭaṁ nu tāvat phalam eva puṇyam* (Śākuntala, 6. 10). 'Whether it was a dream, or an illusion of magic, or an infatuation coming over the intellect, or a stock of merit, exhausted after having given that much of fruition.' *tato duḥkhataraṁ nu kim* (Bh. G. 2. 36)? 'What, indeed, can be more painful than this?'

(xxix) *astu* 'let it be, prohibition'. *evam astu* (Apte' s Dictionary). 'So be it.' *astu sāmnā* (Gaṇaratna.). 'Don't perform the propitiatory rite.'

(xxx) *akasmāt* 'suddenly, without cause'. *vijane vane gacchatas tasyābhimukhe 'kasmād vyāttānanaḥ pañcāsya upasthitaḥ* (Vyā. cand., IV, p. 295). 'When he was going in the lonely forest, suddenly a lion with an open mouth appeared before him.' *tvāṁ pratyakasmāt kaluṣapravṛttāvasty eva manyur bharatāgraje me* (Raghu, 14. 73). 'My wrath is against the elder brother of Bharata who, without any cause, has acted disgracefully towards you.'

(xxxi) *prasahya* 'forcibly'. *alakṣitābhyutpatano nṛpeṇa prasahya siṁhaḥ kila tāṁ cakarṣa* (Raghu, 2. 27). 'A lion feigned to seize her forcibly without his spring being noticed by the king.'

(xxxii) *yasmāt* 'because'. *avajānāsi māṁ yasmād atas te na bhaviṣyati matprasūtim anārādhya prajeti tvāṁ śaśāpa sā.* (Raghu, 1. 77). 'She cursed you by saying, "You will never have any issue without propitiating my offspring because you have treated me with disrespect."'

(xxxiii) *tasmāt* 'therefore'. *tasmāt yudhyasva bhārata* (Bh. G. 2. 36). 'Therefore, O descendant of Bharata, join the battle.'

(xxxiv) *yadi* 'if'. *yatne kṛte yadi na siddhyati ko 'tra doṣaḥ.* (Pañcatantra, 2. 138). 'If success is not gained even when effort has been made, then what is our fault?'

(xxxv) *kiñca* 'moreover, besides'. *kiñca kāvyasyopādeyatvam agnipurāṇe 'pyuktam* (Sāhityadarpaṇa, 1). 'Moreover, the usefulness of poetry is explained in the Agnipurāṇa too.'

(xxxvi) *yadyapi* 'although'. *yadyapyete na paśyanti lopopahatacetasaḥ, kulakṣayakṛtaṁ doṣaṁ mitradrohe ca pātakam.* (Bh. G. 1. 38). 'Although these people, with their hearts vitiated by greed, do not see the evil arising from destroying the family and the sin in hostility towards friends.'

(xxxvii) *purataḥ* 'in front'. *yaṁ yaṁ paśyasi tasya tasya purataḥ mā brūhi dīnaṁ vacaḥ* (Subhāṣitabhāṇḍāgāra, p. 226). 'Whomosever you see, do not speak piteously before him.'

(xxxviii) *kasmāt* 'why'. *acetanaṁ nāma guṇaṁ na lakṣayen mayaiva kasmād avadhīritā priyā* (Śākuntala, 6. 13). 'An inanimate thing may not possibly see merit; but why did I myself repudiate my beloved?'

(xxxix) *rahaḥ* 'in private'. *ataḥ parīkṣya kartayaṁ viśeṣāt saṅgataṁ rahaḥ* (Śākuntala, 5. 24). 'Therefore, one should form a union (only) after a careful examination, particulary one that is made in private.'

(xl) *upajoṣam* 'according to one's desire'. *upajoṣam vāsāṁsi paridhāya* (Bhāg. Pu., 8. 9. 15). 'Having put on the clothes of their choice.'

It is clear from the above treatment that some words are common to both the svarādi and cādi sets. However, it is to be kept in mind that the initial vowel of the words enlisted in the svarādi set has the property of high pitch (*udātta*), whereas in the words that are enlisted in the cādi class, it is the last vowel that has the property of high pitch. As such, the words which have both forms -- with the initial udātta vowel in one and the final udātta vowel in another -- are to be included in both the lists. Besides the words enlisted in cādi class, the words that have been explained in the sūtras from *prādayaḥ* Pā. 1. 4. 58 to *adhirīśvare* Pā. 1. 4. 97 are also designated as nipātas and hence are avyayas.[1]

Now Varadarāja defines the indeclinables that are not included in svarādi and cādi classes. The following sūtra describes the indeclinables that end in a taddhita affix.

(367) तद्धितश्चासर्वविभक्तिः । *taddhitaścāsarvavibhaktiḥ*. 1. 1. 38

लघु० - यस्मात् सर्वा विभक्तिर्नोत्पद्यते स तद्धितान्तोऽव्ययं स्यात् । *yasmāt sarvā vibhaktir notpadyate sa taddhitānto 'vyayaṁ syāt.*

Trans. : A derivative, ending in a taddhita affix, after which all the sup-affixes are not introduced, is designated as *avyaya*.

PP. *taddhitaḥ ca asarvavibhaktiḥ avyayam.*

Eluc. : The word *avyayam* is carried over from *svarādinipātam avyayam* Pā. 1. 1. 37 and with this word the sūtra becomes a complete sentence. The word *asarvavibhaktiḥ* is a bahuvrīhi compound which is analysed as follows : *sarvā* (*vacanatrayātmikā*) *vibhaktiḥ yasmān notpadyate saḥ taddhitāntaḥ* (*avyayasaṁjñaḥ syāt*). Here the word *sarva* is used in the sense of entirety as in the expression *sarvaḥ paṭo dagdhaḥ*. Consequently, the compound word *asarvavibhaktiḥ* comes to mean the derivative which does not take all the sup-endings. The word *taddhita*,

---

1. Cf. *atra svarādicādyor ākṛtigaṇatve 'pi yeṣāṁ nipātasvara iṣṭaḥ te cādiṣu anye svarādiṣu svaradvayabhājas tu ubhayatra bodhyāḥ*. BM, I, p. 487.

being an affix, means that which ends in a taddhita affix by virtue of the pratyayagrahaṇa paribhāṣā (Abhyankar, 23) although the use of the word *anta* in *suptiṅantaṁ padam* (14) precludes this metarule from functioning in saṁjñāvidhi. The reason why the word *taddhita* is taken to mean 'that which ends in that affix' is that the prescription of designating a taddhita affix as an avyaya does not serve any purpose. Thus the sūtra comes to mean that a derivative, which ends in a taddhita affix and which does not take all the sup-endings, is to be designated as *avyaya*.

लघु० – परिगणनं कर्तव्यम्। तसिलादयः प्राक्पाशपः। शस्प्रभृतयः प्राक् समासान्तेभ्यः। अम्। आम्। कृत्वोऽर्थाः। तसिवसी। नानाञौ। एतदन्तमव्ययम्। अत इत्यादि।
pariganaṇanaṁ kartavyam. tasilādayaḥ prākpāśapaḥ. śasprabhṛtayaḥ prāk samāsāntebhyaḥ. am. ām. kṛtvo 'rthāḥ. tasivasī. nānāñau. etadantam avyayam. ata ityādi.

Eluc. : The taddhita affixes in this category need to be enumerated.

1. The affixes prescribed in the sūtras from *pañcamyāstasil* Pā. 5. 3. 7 to *yāpye pāśap* Pā. 5. 3. 47 come under this category. Some of the secondary derivatives formed with taddhita affixes prescribed by some of these sūtras are : *itaḥ* (from here), *tataḥ* (from there), *ataḥ* (from this or that cause), *kutaḥ* (whence, why), *yataḥ* (from which place), *sarvataḥ* (from all sides), *paritaḥ* (on all sides), *abhitaḥ* (on all sides), *ubhayataḥ* (on both sides), *yatra* (where), *tatra* (there), *iha* (here, in this world), *sarvadā* (always), *kadā* (when), *yadā* (when), *tadā* (then), *etarhi* (now, at this time), *adhunā* (now), *idānīm* (now), *adya* (today), *yathā* (as, in the manner mentioned), *ittham* (in this manner), *katham* (in what way), etc.

2. The taddhita affixes prescribed in the sūtras from *bahvalpārthāc chaskārakādanyatarasyām* Pā. 5. 4. 42 prior to *samāsāntāḥ* Pā. 5. 4. 68 are also to be enlisted in this category. The words *bahuśaḥ* (repeatedly), *alpaśaḥ* (a little), *āditaḥ* (from the beginning), *pṛṣṭhataḥ*(from behind), *śuklī (bhavati)* (that which was not white becomes white), *agnisāt* (to the state of fire) etc. belong to this category and are to be designated as *avyayas* (indeclinables) by the present rule.

3. The words which end in the affixes *ām* and *am* respectively prescribed by *kimettiṅavyayaghādāmvadravyaprakarṣe* Pā. 5. 4. 11 *amu cacchandasi* Pā. 5. 4. 12, are also assigned the avyaya-designation. The respective illustrations are : (i) *pacatitarām* (he cooks relatively well), *pacatitamām* (he cooks the best), *uccaistarām* (relatively louder) and *uccaistamām* (loudest) (ii) *prataram* (relatively well) and *pratarām* (better) (cf. Rama Nath Sharma, IV, p. 670).

4. The *kṛtvasuc* affix and the affixes which convey the meaning conveyed by it belong to this category. These taddhita affixes are prescribed by *saṅkhyāyāḥ kriyābhyāvṛttigaṇane kṛtvasuc* Pā.5. 4. 17, *dvitricaturbhyaḥ suc* Pā. 5. 4. 18, *ekasya sakṛcca vibhāṣā* Pā. 5. 4. 19 and *bahordhā 'viprakṛṣṭakāle* Pā. 5. 4. 20. Their respective illustrations are *saptakṛtvaḥ* 'seven times', *triḥ* 'thrice' *sakṛt* 'once' and *bahudhā* 'many times'.

5. The affixes *tasi* and *vati* by *tasiśca* Pā. 4. 3. 113 *tena tulyaṁ kriyā cedvatiḥ* Pā. 5. 1. 115 are also enumerated in this category. *himavattaḥ* 'which is in the direction of the Himālayas' and *brāhmaṇavat* 'like a brāhmaṇa' respectively illustrate these two rules.

6. The affixes *nā* and *nāñ*, enjoined by the rule *vinañbhyāṁ nānāñau na saha* Pā. 5. 2. 27, complete the list of the indeclinables formed with the secondary affixes. The words, derived with these affixes, *vinā* and *nānā* are designated as *avyayas*. The phrases *vinā malayam* 'without Malaya mountain' and *nānā nārīm* 'without a woman' illustrate these two affixes respectively.

After discussing the derivatives which are formed with taddhita affixes and are assigned the avyaya designation, Varadarāja now starts to describe the words, formed with kṛt-affixes, which are to be assigned the avyaya designation.

(368) कृन्मेजन्तः । *kṛnmejantaḥ*. **1. 1. 39**

लघु० - कृद् यो मान्त एजन्तश्च तदन्तमव्ययं स्यात्। स्मारं स्मारम्। जीवसे। पिबध्यै।

kṛd yo.mānta ejantaś ca tadantam avyayaṁ syāt. smāraṁ smāram. jīvase. pibadhyai.

Trans. : Let a primary derivative which ends in a kṛt affix ending in the consonant *m* or in any one of vowels denoted by the abbreviatory term *ec* be designated as *avyaya*.

PP. *kṛt mejantaḥ avyayam.*

Eluc. : The word *avyayam* is carried over from *svarādinipātamavyayam* Pā. 1. 1. 37. The word *mejantaḥ* is a dvandva-seeded bahuvrīhi compound, which is analysed as follows : *m ca ec ca mecau* (itaretara-dvandva). *tau ante yasya sa = mejantaḥ*. Here Bhimasena Shastri remarks that the consonant *c* is not replaced by a guttural according to the rule *coḥ kuḥ* (305) since the term *mec* is construed as bha in the sūtra (*sautratvāt kutvābhāvaḥ*, Bhaimī, I, p. 576), whereas commenting on the sūtra *alpāctaram* (985), following Haradatta, he says that the retention of *c* as *c* is irregular (*ata eva nipātanāt svārthe tarap, kutvābhāvaś ca*, KP, II,

p. 145 and also cf. Bhaimī, IV, p. 237). So, here also for the sake of consistency the same ground may be accepted to account for the retention of *c* as *c* which is thereafter replaced by *j* (*jaś*) by *jhalāṁ jaśo 'nte* (67). The term *kṛt* denotes affixes which are other than *tiṅ* and are prescribed to be introduced after a verbal root in the governing domain of *dhātoḥ* Pā. 3. 1. 91. Since the term *kṛt* means an affix, in the present context it will mean a word that ends in a kṛt affix. Thus the meaning of the sūtra is as follows : A primary derivative, which ends in a kṛt affix ending in the consonant *m* or in any one of the vowels denoted by the abbreviatory term *ec*, is to be designated as *avyaya*.

Jñānendra Sarasvatī says that the consonant *m* and the vowels denoted by *ec*-pratyāhāra do not qualify a primary derivative (*kṛdanta*) since this is not enunciated in the sūtra but qualify the term *kṛt* because of its having been mentioned in the rule. In other words, only a primary derivative ending in a kṛt affix that ends in *m* or in a vowel denoted by *ec* qualifies for being designated as *avyaya* and not every primary derivative that ends in *m* or *ec*. Had this not been the case, then a primary derivative which ends either in *m* or in *ec* would have been designated as *avyaya*. To illustrate, the word *pratām* 'exhausted, tired' is a kṛdanta since this is derived from *pra* + *tam* + *kvip*. After the whole of *kvip* has been elided, the penultimate of the verbal root *tam* is lengthened by *anunāsikasya kvijhaloḥ kṅiti* (724) and we obtain the word *pratām* which is accepted as a kṛdanta according to the rule *pratyayalope pratyalakṣaṇam* (189). In case the consonant *m* is taken as an adjective of a kṛdanta derivate, then the word *pratām* will be an avyaya and as such it will have no declensional forms like *pratāmau*, *pratāmaḥ*. Similarly the word *lau* is also derived with the introduction of the affix *kvip* after *lū* + *ṇic* and we get the word *lau* through the following grammatical process (*lū* + *ṇic* + *kvip* --> *lau*+ *ṇic* + 0 {after the affix *kvip* has been wholly elided, vṛddhi takes place by *aco 'ñṇiti* (181) and we have *lāvi* by *eco 'yavāyāvaḥ* (22). Then *ṇic* is elided by *ṇeraniṭi* (528)} --> *lāv* --> {*lā ūṭh* by *cchvoḥ śūḍa...* (840) and vṛddhi takes place by *etyedhatyūṭhsu* (34) --> *lau*}. The word *lau* is accepted as a primary derivative by virtue of the rule *pratyayalope...* (189). Since this word ends in *au* which is a denotatum of *ec*-pratyāhāra, it would be treated as an avyaya and then the contingency of not having the declined form *lauḥ*, etc. would be incurred. It is to avoid such undesirable contingencies that the word *mejanta* is accepted as a qualifier of the term *kṛt* and not that of the kṛdanta.[1]

1. *atra mejanta ityetacchrutatvāt kṛta eva viśeṣaṇaṁ na tu kṛdantasyāśrutasya. anyathā pratāmau pratāmaḥ. lavamācaṣṭe ṇau kvipi ṇilope vasyoṭhi vṛddhau ca lauḥ. atrāpi prasajyeteti bhāvaḥ. bhavati hyetat pratyayalakṣaṇena kṛdantaṁ mejantaṁ ca śrūyate iti.* TB, I, p. 489.

The first illustration in the Laghu is *smāraṁ smāram*. The rule *ābhīkṣṇye ṇamul ca* (882) prescribes the affix *ṇamul* and we have *smṛ* + *ṇamul*. After the anubandhas have been elided the affix remains as *am* which ends in *m*. A vṛddhi vowel *ā* replaces the aṅga-final *ṛ* by *aco 'ñṇiti* (181) and the phoneme *r* is appended to it by *uraṇ raparaḥ* (29) and we get the form *smāraṁ* which is avyaya according to the present rule. Being kṛdanta, this gets the prātipadika designation. The sup-affix introduced after it is deleted by *avyayādāpsupaḥ* (371). The form *smāraṁ* is iterated by *nityavīpsayoḥ* (883) and we obtain the expression *smāraṁ smāram* 'remembering again and again'.

dhyāyaṁ dhyāyaṁ paraṁ brahma smāraṁ smāraṁ guror giraḥ,
siddhāntakaumudīvyākhyāṁ kurmaḥ prauḍhamanoramām.

Prauḍhamanoramā, invocatory verse.

'Contemplating on Parabrahman and remembering the sayings of my preceptor again and again, I compose the Prauḍhamanoramā, a commentary on the Siddhāntakaumudī.'

The affix *tumun*, which is prescribed by *tumuṇṇvulau kriyāyāṁ kriyārthāyām* (846) also remains as *tum* after the elision of the anubandhas : *paṭh* + *tumun* --> *paṭh* + *tum*. After the insertion of the augment *iṭ* by *ārdhadhātukasyeḍvalādeḥ* (400), we have the form *paṭhitum*. This is also assigned the avyaya designation by the present rule. Being kṛdanta, this word also gets the prātipadika designation. The sup-affix introduced after it is deleted by *avyayād āpsupaḥ* (371) and we have the form as it is. Ex. **ahaṁ paṭhituṁ vidyālayaṁ gacchāmi*. 'I go to school to study.'

The kṛt-affixes ending in *e, o, ai* and *au* are prescribed in the Vedas by the rules *tumarthe sesenase 'senksekasenadhyaiadhyainkadhyaikadhyain-śadhyaiśadhyaintavaitaveṅtavenaḥ* Pā. 3. 4. 9, *prayai rohiṣyai avyathiṣyai* Pā. 3. 4. 10, etc. The illustrations *jīvase* 'in order to live' and *pibadhyai* 'in order to drink' given in the Laghu are respectively formed with the affixes *ase* and *śadhyain*. Since they end in the kṛt-affixes ending in *e* and *ai*, they are assigned the avyaya designation. Being kṛdanta, they get the prātipadika designation and when the sup-affixes are introduced after them, they are deleted by *avyayād āpsupaḥ* (371).

(369) क्त्वातोसुन्कसुनः । *ktvātosunkasunaḥ*. 1. 1. 40

लघु॰ – एतदन्तमव्ययम् । कृत्वा । उदेतोः । विसृपः । *etadantam avyayam. kṛtvā. udetoḥ. visṛpaḥ.*

Trans. : The primary derivatives ending in the affixes *ktvā, tosun* and *kasun* are also designated as *avyayas*.

PP. *ktvātosunkasunaḥ avyayāni.*

Eluc. : The word *avyayam* is carried over from *svarādinipātam avyayam* Pā. 1. 1. 37 and is changed into *avyayāni* by the process of vacanavipariṇāma to agree with the itaretaradvandva which is in the plural. This compound is analysed as follows : *ktvā ca tosun ca kasun ca ktvātosunkasunaḥ*. Since it is no use assigning the avyaya designation to the affixes, tadantavidhi is resorted to by the pratyayagrahaṇa paribhāṣā and thus the sūtra means : The kṛdanta words which end in the affixes *ktvā, tosun* and *kasun* are designated as *avyayas*. The illustrations are : *paṭhitvā* 'having read', *kṛtvā* 'having done', *gatvā* 'having gone', etc. In these illustrations the affix *ktvā* is introduced by *samānakartṛkayoḥ pūrvakāle* (876) which prescribes the affix *ktvā* after one of two verbs that have the same agent. The affix is added to the verb whose action precedes that of the other. Here also, the purpose of assigning the avyaya designation is primarily to delete the sup-endings introduced after such indeclinables.

The other two affixes *tosun* and *kasun* are confined to the Vedas. These affixes are respectively illustrated in *purā sūryasyodetoḥ* 'before the rising of the sun' and *purā krūrasya visṛpaḥ* 'before the cruel one gets away.'

(370) अव्ययीभावश्च । *avyayībhāvaśca.* 1. 1. 41

लघु० – अधिहरि । *adhihari.*

Trans. : The avyayībhāva compound is also designated as *avyaya.*

PP. *avyayībhāvaḥ ca avyayam.*

Eluc. : The term *avyayam* is carried over from *svarādinipātam avyayam* Pā. 1. 1. 37. Thus the sūtra means : The avyayībhāva compound is also assigned the avyaya designation. The word *adhihari* is an avyayībhāva compound. The rule *avyayaṁ vibhaktisamīpasamṛddhi...* (904) enjoins that an indeclinable be compounded with a compatible inflected word in the sense of a case-ending etc. The avyayībhāva compound *adhihari* conveys the sense of *harau* which is in the locative singular. The word *adhihari,* being an avyayībhāva compound, gets the avyaya designation by the present rule. This word is also a prātipadika according to *kṛttaddhitasamāsāśca* (116). The sup-endings introduced after it are deleted by *avyayād āpsupaḥ* (371).

(371) अव्ययादाप्सुपः । *avyayādāpsupaḥ*. **2. 4. 82**

लघु० – अव्ययाद्विहितस्य आपः सुपश्च लुक् । तत्र शालायाम् । *avyayād vihitasya āpaḥ supaś ca luk. tatra śālāyām.*

Trans. : The affixes *āp* and *sup* enjoined after an avyaya are deleted.

PP. *avyayāt āpsupaḥ luk.*

Eluc. : The term *luk* is carried over from *ṇyakṣattriyārṣañito yūni luganiñoḥ* Pā. 2. 4. 58 into the present sūtra. The word *āp* stands for feminine affixes *ṭāp, ḍāp, cāp*, etc. and the abbreviatory term *sup* denotes all the nominal endings. The rule lays down that all these affixes, if enjoined after an avyaya, are to be replaced by luk (zero), which means that they are deleted. In the illustration *tatra śālāyām* 'in that apartment', the word *tatra* qualifies *śālāyām* which is in the feminine. As such, the affix *ṭāp* introduced after *tatra* by *ajādyataṣṭāp* (1243) is deleted according to the present rule since *tatra* is an avyaya by *taddhitaścāsarvavibhaktiḥ* (367). The NS edition reads *atha* as another illustration. The sup-affixes introduced are to be deleted by the present rule. (See supra p. 560 for explanation of this word at no. 80 in the svarādi class).

लघु० – सदृशं त्रिषु लिङ्गेषु सर्वासु च विभक्तिषु ।
वचनेषु च सर्वेषु यन्न व्येति तदव्ययम् ॥ गोपथब्राह्मण, 1. 1. 26

sadṛśaṁ triṣu liṅgeṣu sarvāsu ca vibhaktiṣu,
vacaneṣu ca sarveṣu yanna vyeti tadavyayam.
Gopathabrāhmaṇa, 1. 1. 26

Trans. The word which, remaining alike in the three genders, does not change in all the case-endings and in all numbers is called *avyaya*.

लघु० – वष्टि भागुरिरल्लोपम् अवाप्योरुपसर्गयोः ।
आपं चैव हलन्तानां यथा वाचा निशा दिशा ॥
वगाहः । अवगाहः । पिधानम् । अपिधानम् ।

vaṣṭi bhāgurirallopam avāpyorupasargayoḥ,
āpaṁ caiva halantānāṁ yathā vācā niśā diśā. vagāhaḥ, avagāhaḥ. pidhānam, apidhānam.

Trans. : The grammarian Bhāguri holds the view that the vowel *a* of the preverbs *ava* and *api* is elided. He also considers that the feminine affix *āp* be introduced after the feminine words that end in consonants, e. g. *vācā* 'speech', *niśā* 'night' and *diśā* 'space'.

Eluc. : The ancient grammarian Bhāguri holds the view that the vowel *a* of *ava* and *api* is elided. Words formed with these upasargas are *vagāhaḥ* 'bathing' and *pidhānam* 'covering' and the like. In these words, the vowel *a* of *ava* and *api* has been elided. Since other grammarians do not subscribe to this view, the elision of the vowel *a* is optional. Hence we have the alternative forms also : *avagāhaḥ* and *apidhānam*.

Bhāguri also considers that the feminine affix *āp* (*ṭāp*) be introduced after the feminine words that otherwise end in consonants. The three words that are given as illustrations are *vācā, niśā* and *diśā*. In Pāṇini's view there is no rule which prescribes a feminine affix after the nominal stems that end in consonants. So the alternative forms would be *vāc, niś* and *diś*.

Nāgeśa rejects the view of Bhāguri saying that this view is not available in the Mahābhāṣya. So far as the words *niś* and *diś* are concerned they will have the affix *ka* (= *a*) introduced by *igupadhajñāprīkiraḥ kaḥ* (784). Then there will be no difficulty in getting *ṭāp* introduced after them by *ajādyataṣṭāp* (1243). According to him the word *vācā* is corrupt.[1]

लघु० – इत्यव्ययानि । *ityavyayāni.*

Trans. : Here end the indeclinables.

---

1. *idaṁ bhāṣye na dṛśyate. niśdiśor igupadhalakṣaṇe ke 'ntatvād eva ṭāp. kvini dig ityapi..... tasmād vācetyasādhveveti śivam.* LS, pp. 589-90.

Bibliography

Texts

Aṣṭādhyāyībhāṣyaprathamāvṛtti: Brahmadattajijñāsu, 3 Parts [1985-1989], Third Edition, Ramlal Kapoor Trust, Sonepat, Haryana.

Bṛhaddhātukusumākaraḥ: (Ed.) Pt. Harekanta Mishra, Chaukhamba Surbharti Prakashan, Delhi 1995.

Gaṇaratnamahodadhi of Vardhamāna: (Ed.) J. Eggling, Motilal Banarsidass, Delhi 1963.

Kāśikā: (Ed.) Vijayapāla, Ramalal Kapoor Trust, Sonepat, Haryana 1997.

Kāśikāvṛtti of Vāmana and Jayāditya with the commentaries, Jinendrabuddhi's Nyāsa and Haradatta's Padamañjarī: (Eds.) Swami Dwarikadas Shastri and Pt. Kalikaprasad Shukla, 6 Vols. [1965-1967], Prachya Bharati Series 5, Varanasi.

Laghuśabdenduśekhara of Nāgeśa, with the commentaries Bhairavī (Sanskrit) *and Vaikuṇṭhī* (Hindi), 2 Vols., Chaukhamba Surbharati Prakashan, Varanasi 2006.

Laghusiddhāntakaumudī with the gloss of Vishvanath Shastri Prabhakar : Motilal Banarsidass, Delhi 1969.

Laghusiddhāntakaumudī, Śrīmadvidvadvaravaradācāryapraṇītā : Gita Press Gorakhpur, Vikram saṁvat 2060.

Laghusiddhāntakaumudī, Śrīvaradarājapaṇḍitaviracitā : Nirnayasagar Press, Mumbai 1925.

Laghusiddhāntakaumudī-Bhaimīvyākhyā : see Bhimsena Shastri.

Mahābhāṣyadīpikā of Bhartṛhari : see Bronkhorst, J.

Nyāyabhāṣyam on Gautama-nyāyasūtras with Prasannapadā commentary of Sudarśanācārya : (Ed.) Swami Dwarika Das Shastri, Sudhi Prakashana, Varanasi 1986.

Nyāyakośa : Mahamahopadhyaya Bhimacharya Jhalakikara, BORI, Poona 1978.

Paribhāṣāsaṅgrahaḥ: (Ed.) K. V. Abhyankar, BORI, Poona 1967.

The Paribhāṣenduśekhara of Nāgojibhaṭṭa with the commentary Tattvādarśa of Vāsudeva Shastri Abhyankar: Part I, (Ed.) K. V. Abhyankar, BORI, Poona 1962.

Patañjali's Vyākaraṇamahābhāṣya with Kaiyaṭa's Pradīpa and Nāgojibhaṭṭa's Uddyota: 5 Vols. [1962-63], edited and annotated by Vedavrata Snatak, Gurukula Jhajjar, Rohtak, Haryana.

Prauḍhamanoramā of M M. Bhaṭṭoji Dīkṣita (a commentary upon his Siddhāntakaumudī) with *its gloss Laghuśabdaratna by M M. Haridīkṣita with three commentaries — Bhairavī, Bhāvaprakāśa and Saralā* : (Ed.) Gopāla Śāstrī Nene, Kashi Sanskrit Series 125, Benares 1939.

Sārasiddhāntakaumudī of Varadarāja : (Ed. & Trans.) G. V. Devasthali, University of Poona, Poona 1968.

Vākyapadīya of Bhartṛhari Kāṇḍa II with the Commetary of Puṇyarāja and the ancient Vṛtti : (Ed.) K. A. Subramania Iyer, Motilal Banarsidass, Delhi 1983.

Vākyapadīya of Bhartṛhari with the Prakīrṇaprakāśa of Helārāja, Kāṇḍa III, Part I [1963], *Part II* [1973]: (Ed.) K. A. Subramania Iyer, Poona 1973.

The Vyākaraṇamahābhāṣya of Patañjali : 3 Vols. [I : 1965, II : 1965, III : 1972], (Ed.) F. Kielhorn, revised with critical notes by K. V. Abhyankar, BORI, Poona.

The Vyākaraṇamahābhāṣya of Patañjali with Kaiyaṭa's Bhāṣyapradīpa and Nāgeśabhaṭṭa's Bhāṣyapradīpoddyota : 6 Vols. [I: edited with notes and variants by Bhargavashastri Bhikaji Joshi, 2000; II : edited with notes and variants by Pt. Shivdatta Sharma, (reprint) 1991; III : edited by Pt. Shivdatta Sharma and Pt. Raghunath Kashinath Shastri, 2000; IV & V : edited by Shri Bhargava Shastri Joshi, 1991; VI : edited by Pt. Dadhiram Sharma, Chaukhamba Sanskrit Pratishthan, Delhi (reprint) 2000.

The Vyākaraṇamahābhāṣya with the commentaries Pradīpa, Uddyota and Vimarśa : Vol. I (Āhnikas 1-9), (Ed.) Vedavrata Snatak, Gurukul Jhajjar, Rohtak, Haryana 1963.

Vaiyākaraṇasiddhāntakaumudī of Bhaṭṭoji Dīkṣita with Bālamanoramā of Vāsudeva Dīkṣita and Jñānendra Sarasvatī's Tattvabodhinī : 4 Vols. [I : 1988, II : 1971, III : 1982, IV : 1976], (Eds.) Giridhara Sharma Chaturveda and Parameshvarananda Sharma Bhaskara, Motilal Banarsidass, Delhi.

Translations and Studies

Abhyankar, K. V. and J. M. Shukla : *A Dictionary of Sanskrit Grammar*, Oriental Institute, Baroda 1986.

Agrawal, V. S. : *India As known to Pāṇini*, University of Lucknow, Lucknow 1953.

Ballantyne, James, R. : *The Laghukaumudī of Varadarāja*, Motilal Banarsidass, Delhi 2005.

Bhatt, Vasantkumar : *Pāṇinīya Vyākaraṇa - Tantra Artha aur Sambhāṣaṇa Sandarbha*, L. D. Institute of Indology, Ahmedabad 2003.

Bhimasena Shastri : *Laghusiddhāntakaumudī-Bhaimīvyākhyā*, 6 Parts, [I : Fifth Edition, Delhi 2005; II : Fourth Edition, 2004; III : Third Edition, 2005; IV : Third Edition, 2004; V : Second Edition, 2006; VI: Bhaimi Prakashana, Second Edition, Delhi, 2005].

Bloomfield, Leonard : *Language*, Motilal Banarsidass, Delhi (reprint) 1963.

Bronkhorst, Johannes : *Mahābhāṣyadīpikā of Bhartṛhari, Āhnika* I, critically edited and translated, BORI, Poona 1987.

Cardona, George : *Pāṇini : His Work and its Traditions*, Second Edition, Motilal Banarsidass, Delhi 1997.

Charudeva Shastri : *Vyākaraṇacandrodaya*, 5 Vols. [I : *kāraka va samāsa*, reprint 1987; II : *kṛt va taddhita*, 1970; III : *tiṅanta*, reprint 1990; IV : *strīpratyaya, subanta, avyaya*, 1972; V : *śikṣā, saṁjñā, paribhāṣā, saṁhitā tathā liṅga*, 1973], Motilal Banarsidass, Delhi.

Chaturvedi, Mithilesh : *Vṛttisamuddeśa of Bhartṛhari's Vākyapadīya : A Study*, Shivalik Prakashan, Delhi 2001.

Joshi, S. D. and J. A. F. Roodbergen : *The Aṣṭādhyāyī of Pāṇini* with Translation and Explanatory notes, 13 Vols. [1991-2007], Sahitya Akademi, Delhi.

Joshi, S. D. and Saroja Bhate : *The Fundamentals of Anuvṛtti*, University of Poona, Pune 1984.

Junnarkar, P. B. : *An Introduction to Pāṇini*, 4 Vols. [I : Sri Gangadhareswar Trust, Rishikesh, 1977; II & III : Second Edition, Shanti S. Dighe, Shivaji Road, Baroda 1988; IV : Sri Gangadhareswar Trust, Rishikesh 1987].

Kanshi Ram : *Uṇādi-sūtras in the Sanskrit Grammatical Tradition*, Shivalik Prakashan, Delhi 2001.

Katre, S. M., (Tr.) : *The Aṣṭādhyāyī of Pāṇini*, Motilal Banarsidass, Delhi 1989.

— : *A Glossary of Grammatical Elements and Operations in Aṣṭādhyāyī*, Central Institute of Indian Languages, Mysore 1981.

Kielhorn, F.: *Paribhāṣenduśekhara of Nāgojibhaṭṭa*, Part II, translation and notes, Second Edition by K. V. Abhyankar, BORI, Poona 1960.

Kushwaha, M. S. : *Laghusiddhāntakaumudī*, Chaukhamba Vidyabhavan, Varanasi 1979.

Mimamsaka, Yudhishthira : *Saṁskṛta Vyākaraṇa Śāstra kā itihāsa* : Part I, Bharatiya Prachyavidyapratishthana, Ajmer, saṁvat 2020 (1963).

Misra, Vidya Niwas : *The Descriptive Technique of Pāṇini*, The Hague, Mouton 1966.

Naganatha Shastry, P. V. : *Bhaṭṭojidīkṣita's Vaiyākaraṇa Siddhānta Kaumudī : An Analysis in English*, 2 Vols. [I : 1974, II : 1983].

Pandeya, Radharamana : *Siddhātakaumudī-arthaprakāśikā*, Motilal Banarsidass, Delhi 1966.

Pawate, I. S. : *The Structure of the Aṣṭādhyāyī*, Amar Prakashan, Delhi 1987.

Sharma, Govind Prasad (Tr.) : *Laghusiddhāntakaumudī* (3 Parts), Chaukhamba Surbharati Prakashan, Varanasi 2007.

Sharma, Rama Nath : *The Aṣṭādhyāyī of Pāṇini*, 6 Vols. [I : 2002, II : 2000, III : 1995, IV: 1999, V : 2001, VI : 2003], Munshiram Manoharlal Publishers, Delhi.

Singh, Jag Dev : *Pāṇini : His Description of Sanskrit (An analytical study of the Aṣṭādhyāyī)*, Munshiram Manoharlal, Delhi 1991.

Sridharananda Shastri (Tr.) : *Laghusiddhāntakaumudī*, Motilal Banarsidass, Delhi 1969.

Staal, J. F. (Ed.) : *A Reader on the Sanskrit Grammarians*, Motilal Banarsidass, Delhi (reprint) 1985.

Vasu, S. C. : *The Aṣṭādhyāyī of Pāṇini*, edited and translated into English 2 Vols, Motilal Banarsidass, Delhi 1962.

— : *The Siddhāntakaumudī of Bhaṭṭojidīkṣita*, edited and translated into English, Second Edition, Motilal Banarsidass, Delhi 1962, (reprint) 2003.

Complete List of the sūtras of the Laghusiddhāntakaumudī

(1) halantyam. 1. 3. 3
(2) adarśanaṁ lopaḥ. 1. 1. 60
(3) tasya lopaḥ. 1. 3. 9
(4) ādirantyena sahetā. 1. 1. 71
(5) ūkālo 'jjhrasvadīrghaplutaḥ. 1. 2. 27
(6) uccairudāttaḥ. 1. 2. 29
(7) nīcairanudāttaḥ. 1. 2. 30
(8) samāhāraḥ svaritaḥ. 1. 2. 31
(9) mukhanāsikāvacano 'nunāsikaḥ. 1. 1. 8
(10) tulyāsyaprayatnaṁ savarṇam. 1. 1. 9
(11) aṇuditsavarṇasya cāpratyayaḥ. 1. 1. 69
(12) paraḥ sannikarṣaḥ saṁhitā. 1. 4. 109
(13) halo 'nantarāḥ saṁyogaḥ. 1. 1. 7
(14) suptiṅantaṁ padam. 1. 4. 14
(15) iko yaṇaci. 6. 1. 77
(16) tasminniti nirdiṣṭe pūrvasya. 1. 1. 66
(17) sthāne 'ntaratamaḥ. 1. 1. 50
(18) anaci ca. 8. 4. 47
(19) jhalāṁ jaś jhaśi. 8. 4. 53
(20) saṁyogāntasya lopaḥ. 8. 2. 23
(21) alo 'ntyasya. 1. 1. 52
(22) eco 'yavāyāvaḥ. 6. 1. 78
(23) yathāsaṁkhyamanudeśaḥ samānām. 1. 3. 10
(24) vānto yi pratyaye. 6. 1. 79
(25) adeṅ guṇaḥ. 1. 1. 2
(26) taparastatkālasya. 1. 1. 70
(27) ādguṇaḥ. 6. 1. 87
(28) upadeśe 'janunāsika it. 1. 3. 2
(29) uraṇ raparaḥ. 1. 1. 51
(30) lopaḥ śākalyasya. 8. 3. 19
(31) pūrvatrāsiddham. 8. 2. 1
(32) vṛddhirādaic. 1. 1. 1
(33) vṛddhireci. 6. 1. 88
(34) etyedhatyūṭhsu. 6. 1. 89
(35) upasargāḥ kriyāyoge. 1. 4. 59
(36) bhūvādayo dhātavaḥ. 1. 3. 1
(37) upasargādṛti dhātau. 6. 1. 91
(38) eṅi pararūpam. 6. 1. 94
(39) aco 'ntyādi ṭi. 1. 1. 64
(40) omāṅośca. 6. 1. 95
(41) antādivacca. 6. 1. 85
(42) akaḥ savarṇe dīrghaḥ. 6. 1. 101
(43) eṅaḥ padāntādati. 6. 1. 109
(44) sarvatra vibhāṣā goḥ. 6. 1. 122
(45) anekāl śitsarvasya. 1. 1. 55
(46) ṅicca. 1. 1. 53
(47) avaṅ sphoṭāyanasya. 6. 1. 123
(48) indre ca. 6. 1. 124
(49) dūrāddhūte ca. 8. 2. 84
(50) plutapragṛhyā aci nityam. 6. 1. 125
(51) īdūdeddvivacanaṁ pragṛhyam. 1. 1. 11
(52) adaso māt. 1. 1. 12
(53) cādayo 'sattve. 1. 4. 57
(54) prādayaḥ. 1. 4. 58
(55) nipāta ekājanāṅ. 1. 1. 14
(56) ot. 1. 1. 15
(57) saṁbuddhau śākalyasyetāv-anārṣe. 1. 1. 16

(58) maya uño vo vā. 8. 3. 33
(59) iko 'savarṇe śākalyasya hrasvaśca. 6. 1. 127
(60) aco rahābhyāṁ dve. 8. 4. 46
(61) ṛtyakaḥ. 6. 1. 128
(62) stoḥ ścunā ścuḥ. 8. 4. 40
(63) śāt. 8. 4. 44
(64) ṣṭunā ṣṭuḥ. 8. 4. 41
(65) na padāntāṭṭoranām. 8. 4. 42
(66) toḥ ṣi. 8. 4. 43
(67) jhalāṁ jaśo 'nte. 8. 2. 39
(68) yaro 'nunāsike 'nunāsiko vā. 8. 4. 45
(69) torli. 8. 4. 60
(70) udaḥ sthāstambhoḥ pūrvasya. 8. 4. 61
(71) tasmādityuttarasya. 1. 1. 67
(72) ādeḥ parasya. 1. 1. 54
(73) jharo jhari savarṇe. 8. 4. 65
(74) khari ca. 8. 4. 55
(75) jhayo ho 'nyatarasyām. 8. 4. 62
(76) śaścho 'ṭi. 8. 4. 63
(77) mo 'nusvāraḥ. 8. 3. 23
(78) naścāpadāntasya jhali. 8. 3. 24
(79) anusvārasya yayi parasavarṇaḥ. 8. 4. 58
(80) vā padāntasya. 8. 4. 59
(81) mo rāji samaḥ kvau. 8. 3. 25
(82) he mapare vā. 8. 3. 26
(83) napare naḥ. 8. 3. 27
(84) ādyantau ṭakitau. 1. 1. 46
(85) ṅṇoḥ kukṭuk śari. 8. 3. 28
(86) ḍaḥ si dhuṭ. 8. 3. 29
(87) naśca. 8. 3. 30
(88) śi tuk. 8. 3. 31
(89) ṅamo hrasvādaci ṅamuṇ nityam. 8. 3. 32
(90) samaḥ suṭi. 8. 3. 5
(91) atrānunāsikaḥ pūrvasya tu vā. 8. 3. 2
(92) anunāsikātparo 'nusvāraḥ. 8. 3. 4
(93) kharavasānayorvisarjanīyaḥ. 8. 3. 15
(94) pumaḥ khayyampare. 8. 3. 6
(95) naśchavyapraśān. 8. 3. 7
(96) visarjanīyasya saḥ. 8. 3. 34
(97) nṝn pe. 8. 3. 10
(98) kupvoḥ ⨯ka⨯ pau ca. 8. 3. 37
(99) tasya paramāmreḍitam. 8. 1. 2
(100) kānāmreḍite. 8. 3. 12
(101) che ca. 6. 1. 73
(102) padāntādvā. 6. 1. 76
* visarjanīyasya saḥ. 8. 3. 34
(103) vā śari. 8. 3. 36
(104) sasajuṣo ruḥ. 8. 2. 66
(105) ato roraplutādaplute. 6. 1. 113
(106) haśi ca. 6. 1. 114
(107) bho-bhago-agho-apūrvasya yo 'śi. 8. 3. 17
(108) hali sarveṣām. 8. 3. 22
(109) ro 'supi. 8. 2. 69
(110) ro ri. 8. 3 14
(111) ḍhralope pūrvasya dīrgho 'ṇaḥ. 6. 3. 111
(112) vipratiṣedhe paraṁ kāryam. 1. 4. 2
(113) etattadoḥ sulopo 'koranañsamāse hali. 6. 1. 132
(114) so 'ci lope cetpādapūraṇam. 6. 1. 134
(115) arthavadadhāturapratyayaḥ prātipadikam. 1. 2. 45
(116) kṛttaddhitasamāsāśca. 1. 2. 46
(117) svaujasamauṭchaṣṭābhyāmbhisṅebhyāmbhyasṅasibhyāmbhyasṅasosāmṅyossup. 4. 1. 2
(118) ṅyāpprātipadikāt. 4. 1. 1
(119) pratyayaḥ. 3. 1. 1
(120) paraśca. 3. 1. 2
(121) supaḥ. 1. 4. 103
(122) dvyekayordvivacanaikavacane. 1. 4. 22
(123) virāmo 'vasānam. 1. 4. 110

(124) sarūpāṇāmekaśeṣa ekavibhaktau. 1. 2. 64
(125) prathamayoḥ pūrvasavarṇaḥ. 6. 1. 102
(126) nādici. 6. 1. 104
(127) bahuṣu bahuvacanam. 1. 4. 21
(128) cuṭū. 1. 3. 7
(129) vibhaktiśca. 1. 4. 104
(130) na vibhaktau tusmāḥ. 1. 3. 4
(131) ekavacanaṁ sambuddhiḥ. 2. 3. 49
(132) yasmātpratyayavidhistadādi pratyaye 'ṅgam. 1. 4. 13
(133) eṅhrasvātsambuddheḥ. 6. 1. 69
(134) ami pūrvaḥ. 6. 1. 107
(135) laśakvataddhite. 1. 3. 8
(136) tasmācchaso naḥ puṁsi. 6. 1. 103
(137) aṭkupvāṅnumvyavāye 'pi. 8. 4. 2
(138) padāntasya. 8. 4. 37
(139) ṭāṅasiṅasāminātsyāḥ. 7. 1. 12
(140) supi ca.7. 3. 102
(141) ato bhisa ais. 7. 1. 9
(142) ṅeryaḥ. 7. 1. 13
(143) sthānivadādeśo 'nalvidhau. 1. 1. 56
(144) bahuvacane jhalyet. 7. 3. 103
(145) vā 'vasāne. 8. 4. 56
(146) osi ca. 7. 3. 104
(147) hrasvanadyāpo nuṭ. 7. 1. 54
(148) nāmi. 6. 4. 3
(149) ādeśapratyayayoḥ. 8. 3. 59
(150) sarvādīni sarvanāmāni. 1. 1. 27
(151) jasaḥ śī. 7. 1. 17
(152) sarvanāmnaḥ smai. 7. 1. 14
(153) ṅasiṅyoḥ smātsminau. 7. 1. 15
(154) āmi sarvanāmnaḥ suṭ. 7. 1. 52
(155) pūrvaparāvaradakṣiṇottarāparādharāṇi vyavasthāyāmasaṁjñāyām. 1. 1. 34
(156) svamajñātidhanākhyāyām. 1. 1. 35
(157) antaraṁ bahiryogopasaṁvyānayoḥ. 1. 1. 36
(158) pūrvādibhyo navabhyo vā. 7. 1. 16
(159) prathamacaramatayālpārdhakatipayanemāśca. 1. 1. 33
(160) jarāyā jarasanyatarasyām. 7. 2. 101
(161) dīrghājjasi ca. 6. 1. 105
(162) suḍanapuṁsakasya. 1. 1. 43
(163) svādiṣvasarvanāmasthāne. 1. 4. 17
(164) yaci bham. 1. 4. 18
(165) ā kaḍārādekā saṁjñā. 1. 4. 1
(166) āto dhātoḥ. 6. 4. 140
(167) jasi ca. 7. 3. 109
(168) hrasvasya guṇaḥ. 7. 3. 108
(169) śeṣo ghyasakhi. 1. 4. 7
(170) āṅo nā 'striyām. 7. 3. 120
(171) gherṅiti. 7. 3. 111
(172) ṅasiṅasośca. 6. 1. 110
(173) acca gheḥ. 7. 3. 119
(174) anaṅ sau. 7. 1. 93
(175) alo 'ntyāt pūrva upadhā. 1. 1. 65
(176) sarvanāmasthāne cāsambuddhau. 6. 4. 8
(177) apṛkta ekāl pratyayaḥ. 1. 2. 41
(178) halṅyābbhyo dīrghāt sutisyapṛktaṁ hal. 6. 1. 68
(179) na lopaḥ prātipadikāntasya. 8. 2. 7
(180) sakhyurasambuddhau. 7. 1. 92
(181) aco ñṇiti. 7. 2. 115
(182) khyatyātparasya. 6. 1. 112
(183) aut. 7. 3. 118
(184) patiḥ samāsa eva. 1. 4. 8
(185) bahugaṇavatuḍati saṅkhyā. 1. 1. 23
(186) ḍati ca. 1. 1. 25
(187) ṣaḍbhyo luk. 7. 1. 22
(188) pratyayasya lukślulupaḥ. 1. 1. 61

(189) pratyayalope pratyaya-lakṣaṇam. 1. 1. 62
(190) na lumatā 'ṅgasya. 1. 1. 63
(191) trestrayaḥ. 7. 1. 53
(192) tyadādīnāmaḥ. 7. 2. 102
(193) yū stryākhyau nadī. 1. 4. 3
(194) ambārthanadyorhrasvaḥ. 7. 3. 107
(195) āṇ nadyāḥ. 7. 3. 112
(196) āṭaśca. 6. 1. 90
(197) ṅerāmnadyāmnībhyaḥ. 7. 3. 116
(198) aci śnudhātubhruvāṁ yvor-iyaṅuvaṅau. 6. 4. 77
(199) eranekāco 'saṁyogapūrvasya. 6. 4. 82
(200) gatiśca. 1. 4. 60
(201) na bhūsudhiyoḥ. 6. 4. 85
(202) tṛjvatkroṣṭuḥ. 7. 1. 95
(203) ṛto ṅisarvanāmasthānayoḥ. 7. 3. 110
(204) ṛduśanaspurudaṁso 'nehasāṁ ca. 7. 1. 94
(205) ap-tṛn-tṛc-svasṛ-naptṛ-neṣṭṛ-tvaṣṭṛ-kṣatṛ-hotṛ-potṛ-praśāstṝṇām. 6. 4. 11
(206) vibhāṣā tṛtīyādiṣvaci. 7. 1. 97
(207) ṛta ut. 6. 1. 111
(208) rāt sasya. 8. 2. 24
(209) oḥ supi. 6. 4. 83
(210) varṣābhvaśca. 6. 4. 84
(211) nṛ ca. 6. 4. 6
(212) goto ṇit. 6. 1. 90
(213) auto 'mśasoḥ. 6. 1. 93
(214) rāyo hali. 7. 2. 85
(215) auṅa āpaḥ. 7. 1. 18
(216) sambuddhau ca. 7. 3. 106
(217) āṅi cāpaḥ. 7. 3. 105
(218) yāḍāpaḥ. 7. 3. 113
(219) sarvanāmnaḥ syāḍḍhrasvaśca. 7. 3. 114
(220) vibhāṣā diksamāse bahuvrīhau. 1. 1. 28
(221) ṅiti hrasvaśca. 1. 4. 6
(222) idudbhyām. 7. 3. 117
(223) tricaturoḥ striyāṁ tisṛcatasṛ. 7. 2. 99
(224) aci ra ṛtaḥ. 7. 2. 100
(225) na tisṛcatasṛ. 6. 4. 4
(226) striyāḥ. 6. 4. 79
(227) vā 'mśasoḥ. 6. 4. 80
(228) neyaṅuvaṅsthānāvastrī. 1. 4. 4
(229) vā "mi. 1. 4. 5
(230) striyāñca. 7. 1. 96
(231) ṛnnebhyo ṅīp. 4. 1. 5
(232) na ṣaṭsvasrādibhyaḥ. 4. 1. 10
(233) ato 'm. 7. 1. 24
(234) napuṁsakācca. 7. 1. 19
(235) yasyeti ca. 6. 4. 148
(236) jaśśasoḥ śiḥ. 7. 1. 20
(237) śi sarvanāmasthānam. 1. 1. 42
(238) napuṁsakasya jhalacaḥ. 7. 1. 72
(239) midaco 'ntyātparaḥ. 1. 1. 47
(240) adḍ ḍatarādibhyaḥ pañcabhyaḥ. 7. 1. 25
(241) ṭeḥ. 6. 4. 143
(242) hrasvo napuṁsake prāti-padikasya. 1. 2. 47
(243) svamornapuṁsakāt. 7. 1. 23
(244) iko 'ci vibhaktau. 7. 1. 73
(245) asthidadhisakthyakṣṇāmanaṅ-udāttaḥ 7. 1. 75
(246) allopo 'naḥ. 6. 4. 134
(247) vibhāṣā ṅiśyoḥ. 6. 4. 136
(248) tṛtīyādiṣu bhāṣitapuṁskaṁ puṁvad gālavasya. 7. 1. 74
(249) eca igghrasvādeśe. 1. 1. 48
(250) ho ḍhaḥ. 8. 2. 31
(251) dāderdhātorghaḥ. 8. 2. 32
(252) ekāco baśo bhaṣ jhaṣantasya sdhvoḥ. 8. 2. 37
(253) vā druha-muha-ṣṇuha-ṣṇihām. 8. 2. 33
(254) dhātvādeḥ ṣaḥ saḥ. 6. 1. 64

(255) igyaṇaḥ samprasāraṇam. 1. 1. 45
(256) vāha ūṭh. 6. 4. 132
(257) samprasāraṇācca. 6. 1. 108
(258) caturanaḍuhorāmudāttaḥ. 7. 1. 98
(259) sāvanaḍuhaḥ. 7. 1. 82
(260) am sambuddhau. 7. 1. 99
(261) vasusraṁsudhvaṁsvanaḍuhāṁ daḥ. 8. 2. 72
(262) saheḥ sāḍaḥ saḥ. 8. 3. 56
(263) diva aut. 7. 1. 84
(264) diva ut. 6. 1. 131
(265) ṣaṭcaturbhyaśca. 7. 1. 55
(266) raṣābhyāṁ no ṇaḥ samānapade. 8. 4. 1
(267) roḥ supi. 8. 3. 16
(268) śaro 'ci. 8. 4. 49
(269) mo no dhātoḥ. 8. 2. 64
(270) kimaḥ kaḥ. 7. 2. 103
(271) idamo maḥ. 7. 2. 108
(272) ido 'y puṁsi. 7. 2. 111
(273) ato guṇe. 6. 1. 97
(274) daśca. 7. 2. 109
(275) anāpyakaḥ. 7. 2. 112
(276) hali lopaḥ. 7. 2. 113
(277) ādyantavadekasmin. 1. 1. 21
(278) nedamadasorakoḥ. 7. 1. 11
(279) dvitīyāṭaussvenaḥ. 2. 4. 34
(280) na ṅisambuddhyoḥ. 8. 2. 8
(281) nalopaḥ supsvarasaṁjñātugvidhiṣu kṛti. 8. 2. 2
(282) na saṁyogādvamantāt. 6. 4. 137
(283) inhanpūṣāryamṇāṁ śau. 6. 4. 12
(284) sau ca. 6. 4. 13
(285) ekājuttarapade ṇaḥ. 8. 4. 12
(286) ho hanterñṇinneṣu. 7. 3. 54
(287) maghavā bahulam. 6. 4. 128
(288) ugidacāṁ sarvanāma-sthāne-'dhātoḥ. 7. 1. 70
(289) śvayuvamaghonāmataddhite. 6. 4. 133
(290) na samprasāraṇe samprasāraṇam. 6. 1. 37
(291) arvaṇastrasāvanañaḥ. 6. 4. 127
(292) pathimathyṛbhukṣāmāt. 7. 1. 85
(293) ito 't sarvanāmasthāne. 7. 1. 86
(294) tho 'nthaḥ. 7. 1. 87
(295) bhasya ṭerlopaḥ. 7. 1. 88
(296) ṣṇāntā ṣaṭ. 1. 1. 24
(297) nopadhāyāḥ. 6. 4. 7
(298) aṣṭana ā vibhaktau. 7. 2. 84
(299) aṣṭābhya auś. 7. 1. 21
(300) ṛtvigdadhṛksragdiguṣṇigañcuyujikruñcāṁ ca. 3. 2. 59
(301) kṛdatiṅ. 3. 1. 93
(302) verapṛktasya. 6. 1. 67
(303) kvinpratyayasya kuḥ. 8. 2. 62
(304) yujerasamāse. 7. 1. 71
(305) coḥ kuḥ. 8. 2. 30
(306) vraśca-bhrasja-sṛja-mṛja-yaja-rāja-bhrājacchaśāṁ ṣaḥ. 8. 2. 36
(307) viśvasya vasurāṭoḥ. 6. 3. 128
(308) skoḥ saṁyogādyorante ca. 8. 2. 29
(309) tadoḥ saḥ sāvanantyayoḥ. 7. 2. 106
(310) ṅe prathamayoram. 7. 1. 28
(311) tvāhau sau. 7. 2. 94
(312) śeṣe lopaḥ. 7. 2. 90
(313) yuvāvau dvivacane. 7. 2. 92
(314) prathamāyāśca dvivacane bhāṣāyām. 7. 2. 88
(315) yūyavayau jasi. 7. 2. 93
(316) tvamāvekavacane. 7. 2. 97
(317) dvitīyāyāñca. 7. 2. 87
(318) śaso na. 7. 1. 29
(319) yo 'ci. 7. 2. 89
(320) yuṣmadasmadoranādeśe. 7. 2. 86
(321) tubhyamahyau ṅayi. 7. 2. 95
(322) bhyaso bhyam. 7. 1. 30
(323) ekavacanasya ca. 7. 1. 32
(324) pañcamyā at. 7. 1. 31
(325) tavamamau ṅasi. 7. 2. 96

(326) yuṣmadasmadbhyāṁ ṅaso 'ś. 7. 1. 27
(327) sāma ākam. 7. 1. 33
(328) yuṣmadasmadoḥ ṣaṣṭhī-caturthī-dvitīyāsthayorvānnāvau. 8. 1. 20
(329) bahuvacanasya vasnasau. 8. 1. 21
(330) temayāvekavacanasya. 8. 1. 22
(331) tvāmau dvitīyāyāḥ. 8. 1. 23
(332) pādaḥ pat. 6. 4. 130
(333) aniditāṁ hala upadhāyāḥ kṅiti. 6. 4. 24
(334) acaḥ. 6. 4. 138
(335) cau. 6. 3. 138
(336) uda īt. 6. 4. 139
(337) samaḥ sami. 6. 3. 93
(338) sahasya sadhriḥ. 6. 3. 95
(339) tirasastiryalope. 6. 3. 94
(340) nāñceḥ pūjāyām. 6. 4. 30
(341) sānta mahataḥ saṁyogasya. 6. 4. 10
(342) atvasantasya cādhātoḥ. 6. 4. 14
(343) ubhe abhyastam. 6. 1. 5
(344) nābhyastācchatuḥ. 7. 1. 78
(345) jakṣityādayaḥ ṣaṭ. 6. 1. 6
(346) tyadādiṣu dṛśo 'nālocane kañ ca. 3. 2. 60
(347) ā sarvanāmnaḥ. 6. 3. 91
(348) naśervā. 8. 2. 63
(349) spṛśo 'nudake kvin. 3. 2. 58
(350) rvorupadhāyā dīrgha ikaḥ. 8. 2. 76
(351) numvisarjanīyaśarvyavāye 'pi. 8. 3. 58
(352) vasoḥ samprasāraṇam. 6. 4. 131
(353) puṁso 'suṅ. 7. 1. 89
(354) adasa au sulopaśca. 7. 2. 107
(355) adaso 'serdādu do maḥ. 8. 2. 80
(356) eta īd bahuvacane. 8. 2. 81
(357) na mu ne. 8. 2. 3
(358) naho dhaḥ. 8. 2. 34
(359) nahi-vṛti-vṛṣi-vyadhi-ruci-sahi-taniṣu kvau. 6. 3. 116
(360) yaḥ sau. 7. 2. 110
(361) apo bhi. 7. 4. 48
(362) ahan. 8. 2. 68
(363) vā napuṁsakasya. 7. 1. 79
(364) ācchīnadyornum. 7. 1. 80
(365) śapśyanornityam. 7. 1. 81
(366) svarādinipātamavyayam. 1. 1. 37
(367) taddhitaścāsarvavibhaktiḥ. 1. 1. 38
(368) kṛnmejantaḥ. 1. 1. 39
(369) ktvātosunkasunaḥ. 1. 1. 40
(370) avyayībhāvaśca. 1. 1. 41
(371) avyayādāpsupaḥ. 2. 4. 82
(372) laḥ karmaṇi ca bhāve cākarmakebhyaḥ. 3. 4. 69
(373) vartamāne laṭ. 3. 2. 123
(374) tiptasjhisipthasthamibvasmas-tātāñjhathāsāthāṁdhvamiḍvahimahiṅ. 3. 4. 78
(375) laḥ parasmaipadam. 1. 4. 99
(376) taṅānāvātmanepadam. 1. 4. 100
(377) anudāttaṅita ātmanepadam. 1. 3. 12
(378) svaritañitaḥ kartrabhiprāye kriyāphale. 1. 3. 72
(379) śeṣātkartari parasmaipadam. 1. 3. 78
(380) tiṅastrīṇi trīṇi prathama-madhyamottamāḥ. 1. 4. 101
(381) tānyekavacanadvivacanabahu-vacanānyekaśaḥ. 1. 4. 102
(382) yuṣmadyupapade samānādhi-karaṇe sthāninyapi madhyamaḥ. 1. 4. 105
(383) asmadyuttamaḥ. 1. 4. 107
(384) śeṣe prathamaḥ. 1. 4. 108
(385) tiṅśit sārvadhātukam. 3. 4. 113
(386) kartari śap. 3. 1. 68

(387) sārvadhātukārdhadhātukayoḥ. 7. 3. 84
(388) jho 'ntaḥ. 7. 1. 3
(389) ato dīrgho yañi. 7. 3. 101
(390) parokṣe liṭ. 3. 2. 115
(391) parasmaipadānāṁ ṇalatusus-thalathusaṇalvamāḥ. 6. 4. 88
(392) bhūvo vug luṅliṭoḥ. 6. 4. 88
(393) liṭi dhātoranabhyāsasya. 6. 1. 8
(394) pūrvo 'bhyāsaḥ. 6. 1. 4
(395) halādiḥ śeṣaḥ. 7. 4. 60
(396) hrasvaḥ. 7. 4. 59
(397) bhavateraḥ. 7. 4. 73
(398) abhyāse carca. 8. 4. 54
(399) liṭ ca. 3. 4. 115
(400) ārdhadhātukasyeḍvalādeḥ. 7. 2. 35
(401) anadyatane luṭ. 3. 3. 15
(402) syatāsī lṛluṭoḥ. 3. 1. 33
(403) ārdhadhātukaṁ śeṣaḥ. 3. 4. 114
(404) luṭaḥ prathamasya ḍāraurasaḥ. 2. 3. 85
(405) tāsastyorlopaḥ. 7. 4. 50
(406) ri ca . 7. 4. 51
(407) lṛṭ śeṣe ca. 3. 3. 13
(408) loṭ ca. 3. 3. 162
(409) āśiṣi liṅloṭau. 3. 3. 173
(410) eruḥ. 3. 4. 86
(411) tuhyostātaṅāśiṣyanyatara-syām. 7. 1. 35
(412) loṭo laṅvat. 3. 4. 85
(413) tasthasthamipāṁ tāntan-tāmaḥ. 3. 4. 101
(414) serhyapicca. 3. 4. 87
(415) ato heḥ. 6. 4. 105
(416) merniḥ. 3. 4. 89
(417) āḍuttamasya picca. 3. 4. 92
(418) te prāgdhātoḥ. 1. 4. 80
(419) āni loṭ. 8. 4. 16
(420) nityaṁ ṅitaḥ. 3. 4. 99
(421) anadyatane laṅ. 3. 2. 111
(422) luṅlaṅlṛṅkṣvaḍudāttaḥ. 6. 4. 71
(423) itaśca. 3. 4. 100
(424) vidhinimantraṇāmantraṇādhīṣṭa-saṁpraśnaprārthaneṣu liṅ. 3. 3. 161
(425) yāsuṭ parasmaipadeṣūdātto ṅicca. 3. 4. 103
(426) liṅaḥ salopo 'nantyasya. 7. 2. 79
(427) ato yeyaḥ. 7. 2. 80
(428) lopo vyorvali. 6. 1. 66
(429) jherjus. 3. 4. 108
(430) liṅāśiṣi. 3. 4. 116
(431) kidāśiṣi. 3. 4. 104
(432) kṅiti ca. 1. 1. 5
(433) luṅ. 3. 2. 110
(434) māṅi luṅ. 3. 3. 175
(435) smottare laṅ ca. 3. 3. 176
(436) cli luṅi. 3. 1. 43
(437) cleḥ sic. 3. 1. 44
(438) gātisthāghupābhūbhyaḥ sicaḥ parasmaipadeṣu. 2. 4. 77
(439) bhūsuvostiṅi. 7. 3. 88
(440) na māṅyoge. 6. 4. 74
(441) liṅnimitte lṛṅ kriyātipattau. 3. 3. 139
(442) ata ādeḥ. 7. 4. 70
(443) āḍajādīnām. 6. 4. 72
(444) astisico 'pṛkte. 7. 3. 96
(445) iṭa īṭi. 8. 2. 28
(446) sijabhyastavidibhyaśca. 3. 4. 109
(447) hrasvaṁ laghu. 1. 4. 10
(448) saṁyoge guru. 1. 4. 11
(449) dīrghaṁ ca. 1. 4. 12
(450) pugantalaghūpadhasya ca. 7. 3. 86
(451) asaṁyogālliṭ kit. 1. 2. 5
(452) nergadanadapatapadaghumā-syatihantiyātivātidrātipsātivapativahati-śāmyaticinotidegdhiṣu ca. 8. 4. 17
(453) kuhoścuḥ. 7. 4. 62
(454) ata upadhāyāḥ. 7. 2. 116
(455) ṇaluttamo vā. 7. 1. 91
(456) ato halāderlaghoḥ. 7. 2. 7

(457) ṇo naḥ. 6. 1. 65
(458) upasargādasamāse 'pi ṇopadeśasya. 8. 4. 14
(459) ata ekahalmadhye 'nādeśāderliṭi. 6. 4. 120
(460) thali ca seṭi. 6. 4. 121
(461) ādirñiṭuḍavaḥ. 1. 3. 5
(462) idito num dhātoḥ. 7. 1. 58
(463) tasmānnuḍ dvihalaḥ. 7. 4. 71
(464) vadavrajahalantasyācaḥ. 7. 2. 3
(465) hmayantakṣaṇaśvasajāgṛṇiśvyeditām. 7. 2. 5
(466) gupūdhūpavicchipaṇipanibhya āyaḥ. 3. 1. 28
(467) sanādyantā dhātavaḥ. 3. 1. 32
(468) āyādaya ārdhadhātuke vā. 3. 1. 31
(469) ato lopaḥ. 6. 4. 48
(470) āmaḥ. 2. 4. 81
(471) kṛñ cānuprayujyate liṭi. 3. 1. 40
(472) urat. 7. 4. 66
(473) dvirvacane 'ci. 1. 1. 59
(474) ekāca upadeśe 'nudāttāt. 7. 2. 10
(475) svaratisūtisūyatidhūñūdito vā. 7. 2. 44
(476) neṭi. 7. 2. 4
(477) jhalo jhali. 8. 2. 26
(478) kṛsṛbhṛvṛstudrusruśruvo liṭi. 7. 2. 13
(479) acastāsvat thalyaniṭo nityam. 7. 2. 61
(480) upadeśe 'tvataḥ. 7. 2. 62
(481) ṛto bhāradvājasya. 7. 2. 63
(482) akṛtsārvadhātukayordīrghaḥ. 7. 4. 25
(483) sici vṛddhiḥ parasmaipadeṣu. 7. 2. 1
(484) vā bhrāśabhlāśabhramukramuklamutrasitruṭilaṣaḥ. 3. 1. 70
(485) kramaḥ parasmaipadeṣu. 7. 3. 76
(486) pāghrādhmāsthāmnādāṇḍṛśyartisartiśadasadāṁ pibajighradhamatiṣṭhamanayacchapaśyarcchadhauśīyasīdāḥ. 7. 3. 78
(487) āta au ṇalaḥ. 7. 1. 34
(488) āto lopa iṭi ca. 6. 4. 64
(489) erliṅi. 6. 4. 67
(490) ātaḥ. 3. 4. 110
(491) usyapadāntāt. 6. 1. 96
(492) ādeca upadeśe 'śiti. 6. 1. 45
(493) vā 'nyasya saṁyogādeḥ. 6. 4. 68
(494) yamaramanamātāṁ sak ca. 7. 2. 73
(495) ṛtaśca saṁyogāderguṇaḥ. 7. 4. 10
(496) ṛddhanoḥ sye. 7. 2. 70
(497) guṇo 'rtisaṁyogādyoḥ. 7. 4. 29
(498) śruvaḥ śṛ ca. 3. 1. 74
(499) sārvadhātukamapit. 1. 2. 4
(500) huśnuvoḥ sārvadhātuke. 6. 4. 87
(501) lopaścāsyānyatarasyāṁ mvoḥ. 6. 4. 107
(502) utaśca pratyayādasaṁyogapūrvāt. 6. 4. 106
(503) iṣugamiyamāṁ chaḥ. 7. 3. 77
(504) gamahanajanakhanaghasāṁ lopaḥ kṅityanaṅi. 6. 4. 98
(505) gameriṭ parasmaipadeṣu. 7.2. 58
(506) puṣādidyutādyḷditaḥ parasmaipadeṣu. 3. 1. 55
(507) ṭita ātmanepadānāṁ ṭere. 3. 4. 79
(508) āto ṅitaḥ. 7. 2. 81
(509) thāsaḥ se. 3. 4. 80
(510) ijādeśca gurumato 'nṛcchaḥ. 3. 1. 36
(511) āmpratyayavatkṛño 'nuprayogasya. 1. 3. 63
(512) liṭastajhayoreśirec. 3. 4. 81

(513) iṇaḥ ṣīdhvaṁluṅliṭāṁ dho 'ṅgāt. 8. 3. 78
(514) dhi ca. 8. 2. 25
(515) ha eti. 7. 4. 52
(516) āmetaḥ. 3. 4. 90
(517) savābhyāṁ vāmau. 3. 4. 91
(518) eta ai. 3. 4. 93
(519) liṅaḥ sīyuṭ. 3. 4. 102
(520) jhasya ran. 3. 4. 105
(521) iṭo 't. 3. 4. 106
(522) suṭ tithoḥ. 3. 4. 107
(523) ātmanepadeṣvanataḥ. 7. 1. 5
(524) kamerṇiṅ. 3. 1. 30
(525) ayāmantālvāyyetnviṣṇuṣu. 6. 4. 55
(526) vibhāṣeṭaḥ. 8. 3. 79
(527) ṇiśridrusrubhyaḥ kartari caṅ. 3. 1. 48
(528) ṇeraniṭi. 6. 4. 51
(529) ṇau caṅyupadhāyā hrasvaḥ. 7. 4. 1
(530) caṅi. 6. 1. 11
(531) sanvallaghuni caṅpare 'naglope. 7. 4. 93
(532) sanyataḥ. 7. 4. 79
(533) dīrgho laghoḥ. 7. 4. 94
(534) upasargasyāyatau. 8. 2. 19
(535) dayāyāsaśca. 3. 1. 37
(536) dyutisvāpyoḥ samprasāraṇam. 7. 4. 67
(537) dyudbhyo luṅi. 1. 3. 91
(538) vṛdbhyaḥ syasanoḥ. 1. 3. 92
(539) na vṛdbhyaścaturbhyaḥ. 7. 2. 59
(540) na śasadadavādiguṇānām. 6. 4. 126
(541) tṝphalabhajatrapaśca. 6. 4. 122
(542) riṅ śayagliṅkṣu. 7. 4. 28
(543) uśca. 1. 2. 12
(544) hrasvādaṅgāt. 8. 2. 27
(545) liṭyabhyāsasyobhayeṣām. 6. 1. 17
(546) vacisvapiyajādīnāṁ kiti. 6. 1. 15
(547) ṣaḍhoḥ kaḥ si. 8. 2. 41
(548) jhaṣastathordho 'dhaḥ. 8. 2. 40
(549) ḍho ḍhe lopaḥ. 8. 3. 13
(550) sahivahorodavarṇasya. 6. 3. 112
(551) adiprabhṛtibhyaḥ śapaḥ. 2. 4. 72
(552) liṭyanyatarasyām. 2. 4. 40
(553) śāsivasighasīnāṁ ca. 8. 3. 60
(554) iḍattyartivyayatīnām. 7. 2. 66
(555) hujhalbhyo herdhiḥ. 6. 4. 101
(556) adaḥ sarveṣām. 7. 3. 100
(557) luṅsanorghasḷ. 2. 4. 37
(558) anudāttopadeśavanatitanotyādīnāmanunāsikalopo jhali kṅiti. 6. 4. 37
(559) abhyāsācca. 7. 3. 55
(560) hanterjaḥ. 6. 4. 36
(561) asiddhavadatrābhāt. 6. 4. 22
(562) ārdhadhātuke. 2. 4. 35
(563) hano vadha liṅi. 2. 4. 42
(564) luṅi ca. 2. 4. 43
(565) uto vṛddhirluki hali. 7. 3. 89
(566) laṅaḥ śākaṭāyanasyaiva. 3. 4. 111
(567) vido laṭo vā. 3. 4. 83
(568) uṣavidajāgṛbhyo 'nyatarasyām. 3. 1. 38
(569) vidāṅkurvantvityanyatarasyām. 3. 1. 41
(570) tanādikṛñbhya uḥ. 3. 1. 79
(571) ata utsārvadhātuke. 6. 4. 110
(572) daśca. 8. 2. 75
(573) śnasorallopaḥ. 6. 4. 111
(574) upasargaprādurbhyām astiryacparaḥ. 8. 3. 87
(575) asterbhūḥ. 2. 4. 52
(576) ghvasoreddhāvabhyāsalopaśca. 6. 4. 119
(577) iṇo yaṇ. 6. 4. 81
(578) abhyāsasyāsavarṇe. 6. 4. 78
(579) dīrgha iṇaḥ kiti. 7. 4. 69
(580) eterliṅi. 7. 4. 24
(581) iṇo gā luṅi. 2. 4. 45

(582) śīṅaḥ sārvadhātuke guṇaḥ. 7. 4. 21
(583) śīṅo ruṭ. 7. 1. 6
(584) gāṅ liṭi. 2. 4. 49
(585) vibhāṣā luṅlṛṅoḥ. 2. 4. 50
(586) gāṅkuṭādibhyo 'ñṇinṅit. 1. 2. 1
(587) ghumāsthāgāpājahātisāṁ hali. 6.4. 66
(588) liṅsicāvātmanepadeṣu. 1. 2. 11
(589) śala igupadhādaniṭaḥ ksaḥ. 3. 1. 45
(590) lugvā duhadihalihaguhām-ātmanepade dantye. 7. 3. 73
(591) ksasyāci. 7. 3. 72
(592) bruvaḥ pañcānāmādita āho bruvaḥ. 3. 4. 84
(593) āhasthaḥ. 8. 2. 35
(594) bruva īṭ. 7. 3. 93
(595) bruvo vaciḥ. 2. 4. 53
(596) asyativaktikhyātibhyo 'ṅ. 3. 1. 52
(597) vaca um. 7. 4. 20
(598) ūrṇotervibhāṣā. 7. 3. 90
(599) na ndrāḥ saṁyogādayaḥ. 6. 1. 3
(600) vibhāṣorṇoḥ. 1. 2. 3
(601) guṇo 'pṛkte. 7. 3. 91
(602) ūrṇotervibhāṣā. 7. 2. 6
(603) juhotyādibhyaḥ śluḥ. 2. 4. 75
(604) ślau. 6. 1. 10
(605) adabhyastāt. 7. 1. 4
(606) bhīhrībhṛhuvāṁ śluvacca. 3. 1. 39
(607) jusi ca. 7. 3. 83
(608) bhiyo 'nyatarasyām. 6. 4. 115
(609) artipipartyośca. 7. 4. 77
(610) udoṣṭhyapūrvasya. 7. 1. 102
(611) hali ca. 8. 2. 77
(612) śṝdṝprāṁ hrasvo vā. 7. 4. 12
(613) ṛcchayṝtām. 7. 4. 11
(614) vṝto vā. 7. 2. 38
(615) sici ca parasmaipadeṣu. 7. 2. 40
(616) jahāteśca. 6. 4. 116
(617) ī halyaghoḥ. 6. 4. 113
(618) śnābhyastayorātaḥ. 6. 4. 112
(619) ā ca hau. 6. 4. 117
(620) lopo yi. 6. 4. 118
(621) bhṛñāmit. 7. 4. 76
(622) dādhā ghvadāp. 1. 1. 20
(623) sthāghvoricca. 1. 2. 17
(624) dadhastathośca. 8. 2. 38
(625) ṇijāṁ trayāṇāṁ guṇaḥ ślau. 7. 4. 75
(626) nābhyastasyāci piti sārva-dhātuke. 7. 3. 87
(627) irito vā. 3. 1. 57
(628) divādibhyaḥ śyan. 3. 1. 69
(629) se 'sici kṛtacṛtacchṛdatṛda-nṛtaḥ. 7. 2. 57
(630) vā jṝbhramutrasām. 6. 4. 124
(631) otaḥ śyani. 7. 3. 71
(632) vibhāṣā ghrādheṭśācchāsaḥ. 2. 4. 78
(633) grahijyāvayivyadhivaṣṭivica-tivṛścatipṛcchatibhṛjjatīnāṁ ṅiti ca. 6. 1. 16
(634) radhādibhyaśca. 7. 2. 45
(635) masjinaśorjhali. 7. 1. 60
(636) dīṅo yuḍaci kṅiti. 6. 4. 63
(637) mīnātiminotidīṅāṁ lyapi ca. 6. 1. 50
(638) jñājanorjā. 7. 3. 79
(639) dīpajanabudhapūritāyipyāyi-bhyo 'nyatarasyām. 3. 1. 61
(640) ciṇo luk. 6. 4. 104
(641) janivadhyośca. 7. 3. 35
(642) ciṇ te padaḥ. 3. 1. 60
(643) sṛjidṛśorjhalyamakiti. 6. 1. 58
(644) svādibhyaḥ śnuḥ. 3. 1. 73
(645) stusudhūñbhyaḥ parasmai-padeṣu. 7. 2. 72
(646) vibhāṣā ceḥ. 7. 3. 58
(647) śarpūrvāḥ khayaḥ. 7. 4. 61
(648) ṛtaśca saṁyogādeḥ. 7. 2. 43

(649) śryukaḥ kiti. 7. 2. 11
(650) tudādibhyaḥ śaḥ. 3. 1. 77
(651) bhrasjo ropadhayo ram-anyatarasyām. 6. 4. 47
(652) anudāttasya cardupadha-syānyatarasyām. 6. 1. 59
(653) śe mucādīnām. 7. 1. 59
(654) lipisicihvaśca. 3. 1. 53
(655) ātmanepadeṣvanyatarasyām. 3. 1. 54
(656) tīṣasahalubharuṣariṣaḥ. 7. 2. 48
(657) sphuratisphulatyornirnivi-bhyaḥ. 8. 3. 76
(658) śadeḥ śitaḥ. 1. 3. 60
(659) ṝta iddhātoḥ. 7. 1. 100
(660) kiratau lavane. 6. 1. 140
(661) hiṁsāyāṁ prateśca. 6. 4. 141
(662) aci vibhāṣā. 8. 2. 21
(663) mriyaterluṅliṅośca. 1. 3. 61
(664) vija iṭ. 1. 2. 2
(665) rudhādibhyaḥ śnam. 3. 1. 78
(666) tṛṇaha im. 7. 3. 92
(667) śnānnalopaḥ. 6. 4. 23
(668) tipyanasteḥ. 8. 2. 73
(669) sipi dhāto rurvā. 8. 2. 74
(670) añjeḥ sici. 7. 2. 71
(671) bhujo 'navane. 1. 3. 66
* tanādikṛñbhya uḥ. 3. 1. 79
(672) tanādibhyastathāsoḥ. 2. 4. 79
(673) ye vibhāṣā. 6. 4. 43
(674) janasanakhanāṁ sañjhaloḥ. 6. 4. 42
* ata utsārvadhātuke. 6. 4. 110
(675) na bhakurchurām. 8. 2. 79
(676) nityaṁ karoteḥ. 6. 4. 108
(677) ye ca. 6. 4. 109
(678) samparibhyāṁ karotau bhūṣaṇe. 6. 1. 137
(679) samavāye ca. 6. 1. 138
(680) upātpratiyatnavaikṛtavākyā-dhyāhāreṣu ca. 6. 1. 139
(681) kryādibhyaḥ śnā. 3. 1. 81
(682) hinumīnā. 8. 4. 15
(683) stambhustumbhuskambhu-skumbhuskuñbhyaḥ śnuśca. 3. 1. 82
(684) halaḥ śnaḥ śānajjhau. 3. 1. 83
(685) jṝstambhumrucumlucugrucu-glucugluñcuśvibhyaśca. 3. 1. 58
(686) stanbheḥ. 8. 3. 67
(687) pvādīnāṁ hrasvaḥ. 7. 3. 80
(688) liṅsicorātmanepadeṣu. 7. 2. 42
(689) na liṅi. 7. 2. 39
(690) graho 'liṭi dīrghaḥ. 7. 2. 37
(691) satyāpapāśarūpavīṇātūlaśloka-senālomatvacavarmavarṇacūrṇacurādi-bhyo ṇic. 3. 1. 25
(692) ṇicaśca. 1. 3. 74
(693) acaḥ parasmin pūrvavidhau. 1. 1. 57
(694) ī ca gaṇaḥ. 7. 4. 97
(695) svatantraḥ kartā. 1. 4. 54
(696) tatprayojako hetuśca. 1. 4. 55
(697) hetumati ca. 3. 1. 26
(698) oḥ puyaṇjyapare. 7. 4. 80
(699) artihrīblīrīknūyīkṣmāyyātāṁ pug ṇau. 7. 3. 36
(700) tiṣṭhaterit. 7. 4. 5
(701) mitāṁ hrasvaḥ. 6. 4. 92
(702) dhātoḥ karmaṇaḥ samāna-kartṛkādicchāyāṁ vā. 3. 1. 7
(703) sanyaṅoḥ. 6. 1. 9
(704) saḥ syārdhadhātuke. 7. 4. 49
(705) ajjhanagamāṁ sani. 6. 4. 16
(706) iko jhal. 1. 2. 9
(707) sani grahaguhośca. 7. 2. 12
(708) dhātorekāco halādeḥ kriyā samabhihāre yaṅ. 3. 1. 22
(709) guṇo yaṅlukoḥ. 7. 4. 82
(710) nityaṁ kauṭilye gatau. 3. 1. 23
(711) dīrgho 'kitaḥ. 7. 4. 83
(712) yasya halaḥ. 6. 4. 49
(713) rīgṛdupadhasya ca. 7. 4.90
(714) kṣubhnādiṣu ca. 8. 4. 39
(715) yaṅo 'ci ca. 2. 4. 74

(716) yaṅo vā. 7. 3. 94
(717) supaḥ ātmanaḥ kyac. 3. 1. 8
(718) supo dhātuprātipadikayoḥ. 2. 4. 71
(719) kyaci ca. 7. 4. 33
(720) naḥ kye. 1. 4. 15
(721) kyasya vibhāṣā. 6. 4. 50
(722) kāmyacca. 3. 1. 9
(723) upamānādācāre. 3. 1. 10
(724) anunāsikasya kvijhaloḥ kṅiti. 6. 4. 15
(725) kaṣṭāya kramaṇe. 3. 1. 14
(726) śabdavairakalahābhrakaṇvameghebhyaḥ karaṇe. 3. 1. 17
(727) kaṇḍvādibhyo yak. 3. 1. 27
(728) kartari karmavyatihāre. 1. 3. 14
(729) na gatihiṁsārthebhyaḥ. 1. 3. 15
(730) nerviśaḥ. 1. 3. 17
(731) parivyavebhyaḥ kriyaḥ. 1. 3. 18
(732) viparābhyāṁ jeḥ. 1. 3. 19
(733) samavapravibhyaḥ sthaḥ. 1. 3. 22
(734) apahnave jñaḥ. 1. 3. 44
(735) akarmakācca. 1. 3. 45
(736) udaścaraḥ sakarmakāt. 1. 3. 53
(737) samastṛtīyāyuktāt. 1. 3. 54
(738) dāṇaśca sā ceccaturthyarthe. 1. 3. 55
(739) pūrvavat sanaḥ. 1. 3. 62
(740) halantācca. 1. 2. 10
(741) gandhanāvakṣepaṇasevanasāhasikyapratiyatnaprakathanopayogeṣu kṛñaḥ. 1. 3. 32
(742) anuparābhyāṁ kṛñaḥ. 1. 3. 79
(743) abhipratyatibhyaḥ kṣipaḥ. 1. 3. 80
(744) prādvahaḥ. 1. 3. 81
(745) parermṛṣaḥ. 1. 3. 82
(746) vyāṅparibhyo ramaḥ. 1. 3. 83
(747) upācca. 1. 3. 84
(748) bhāvakarmaṇoḥ. 1. 3. 13
(749) sārvadhātuke yak. 3. 1. 67
(750) syasicsīyuṭtāsiṣu bhāvakarmaṇorupadeśe 'jjhanagrahadṛśāṁ vā ciṇvadiṭ ca. 6. 4. 62
(751) ciṇ bhāvakarmaṇoḥ. 3. 1. 66
(752) tanoteryaki. 6. 4. 44
(753) tapo 'nutāpe ca. 3. 1. 65
(754) āto yuk ciṇkṛtoḥ. 7. 3. 33
(755) bhañjeśca ciṇi. 6. 4. 33
(756) vibhāṣā ciṇṇamuloḥ. 7. 1. 69
(757) karmavat karmaṇā tulyakriyaḥ. 3. 1. 87
(758) abhijñāvacane lṛṭ. 3. 2. 112
(759) na yadi. 3. 2. 113
(760) laṭ sme. 3. 2. 118
(761) vartamānasāmīpye vartamānavadvā. 3. 3. 131
(762) hetuhetumatorliṅ. 3. 3. 156
(763) dhātoḥ. 3. 1. 91
(764) vā 'sarūpo 'striyām. 3. 1. 94
(765) kṛtyāḥ. 3. 1. 95
(766) kartari kṛt. 3. 4. 67
(767) tayoreva kṛtyaktakhalarthāḥ. 3. 4. 70
(768) tavyattavyānīyaraḥ. 3. 1. 96
(769) kṛtyalyuṭo bahulam. 3. 3. 113
(770) aco yat. 3. 1. 97
(771) īdyati. 6. 4. 65
(772) poradupadhāt. 3. 1. 98
(773) etistuśāsvṛdṛjuṣaḥ kyap. 3. 1. 109
(774) hrasvasya piti kṛti tuk. 6. 1. 71
(775) śāsa idaṅhaloḥ. 6. 4. 34
(776) mṛjervibhāṣā. 3. 1. 113
(777) ṛhalorṇyat. 3. 1. 124
(778) cajoḥ ku ghiṇṇyatoḥ. 7. 3. 52
(779) mṛjervṛddhiḥ. 7. 2. 114
(780) bhojyaṁ bhakṣye. 7. 3. 69
(781) ṇvultṛcau. 3. 1. 133
(782) yuvoranākau. 7. 1. 1
(783) nandigrahipacādibhyo lyuṇinyacaḥ. 3. 1. 134

(784) igupadhajñāprīkiraḥ kaḥ. 3. 1. 135
(785) ātaścopasarge. 3. 1. 136
(786) gehe kaḥ. 3. 1. 144
(787) karmaṇyaṇ. 3. 2. 1
(788) āto 'nupasarge kaḥ. 3. 2. 3
(789) careṣṭaḥ. 3. 2. 16
(790) bhikṣāsenādāyeṣu ca. 3. 2. 17
(791) kṛño hetutācchīlyānulomyeṣu. 3. 2. 20
(792) pātrakuśākarṇīṣvanavyayasya. 8. 3. 46
(793) ejeḥ khaś. 3. 2. 28
(794) arurdviṣadajantasya mum. 6. 3. 67
(795) priyavaśe vadaḥ khac. 3. 2. 38
(796) anyebhyo 'pi dṛśyante. 3. 2. 75
(797) neḍvaśi kṛti. 7. 2. 8
(798) viḍvanoranunāsikasyā "t. 6. 4. 41
(799) kvip ca. 3. 2. 76
(800) supyajātau ṇinistācchīlye. 3. 2. 78
(801) manaḥ. 3. 2. 82
(802) ātmamāne khaśca. 3. 2. 83
(803) khityanavyayasya. 6. 3. 66
(804) karaṇe yajaḥ. 3. 2. 85
(805) dṛśeḥ kvanip. 3. 2. 94
(806) rājani yudhi kṛñaḥ. 3. 2. 95
(807) sahe ca. 3. 2. 96
(808) saptamyāṁ janerḍaḥ. 3. 2. 97
(809) tatpuruṣe kṛti bahulam. 6. 3. 14
(810) upasarge ca saṁjñāyām. 3. 2. 99
(811) ktaktavatū niṣṭhā. 1. 1. 26
(812) niṣṭhā. 3. 2. 102
(813) radābhyāṁ niṣṭhāto naḥ pūrvasya ca daḥ. 8. 2. 42
(814) saṁyogāderāto dhātoryaṇvataḥ. 8. 2. 43
(815) lvādibhyaḥ. 8. 2. 44
(816) halaḥ. 6. 4. 2
(817) oditaśca. 8. 2. 45
(818) śuṣaḥ kaḥ. 8. 2. 51
(819) paco vaḥ. 8. 2. 52
(820) kṣāyo maḥ. 8. 2. 53
(821) niṣṭhāyāṁ seṭi. 6. 4. 52
(822) dṛḍhaḥ sthūlabalayoḥ. 7. 2. 20
(823) dadhāterhiḥ. 7. 4. 42
(824) do dad ghoḥ. 7. 4. 46
(825) liṭaḥ kānajvā. 3. 2. 106
(826) kvasuśca. 3. 2. 107
(827) mvośca. 8. 2. 65
(828) laṭaḥ śatṛśānacāvaprathamāsamānādhikaraṇe. 3. 2. 124
(829) āne muk. 7. 2. 82
(830) videḥ śaturvasuḥ. 7. 1. 36
(831) tau sat. 3. 2. 127
(832) lṛtaḥ sadvā. 3. 3. 14
(833) ākvestacchīlataddharmatatsādhukāriṣu. 3. 2. 134
(834) tṛn. 3. 2. 135
(835) jalpabhikṣakuṭṭaluṇṭavṛṅaḥ ṣākan. 3. 2. 155
(836) ṣaḥ pratyayasya. 1. 3. 6
(837) sanāśaṁsabhikṣa uḥ. 3. 2. 168
(838) bhrājabhāsadhurvidyutorjipṝjugrāvastuvaḥ kvip. 3. 2. 177
(839) rāllopaḥ. 6. 4. 21
(840) cchvoḥ śūḍanunāsike ca. 6. 4. 19
(841) dāmnīśasayuyujastutudasisicamihapatadaśanahaḥ karaṇe. 3. 2. 182
(842) titutratathasisusarakaseṣu ca. 7. 2. 9
(843) artilūdhūsūkhanasahacara itraḥ. 3. 2. 184
(844) puvaḥ saṁjñāyām. 3. 2. 185
(845) uṇādayo bahulam. 3. 3. 1
(846) tumunṇvulau kriyāyāṁ kriyārthāyām. 3. 3. 10
(847) kālasamayavelāsu tumun. 3. 3. 167
(848) bhāve. 3. 3. 18
(849) akartari ca kārake saṁjñāyām. 3. 3. 19

(850) ghañi ca bhāvakaraṇayoḥ. 6. 4. 27
(851) nivāsacitiśarīropasamādhāneṣv-ādeśca kaḥ. 3. 3. 41
(852) erac. 3. 3. 56
(853) ṝdorap. 3. 3. 57
(854) ḍvitaḥ ktriḥ. 3. 3. 88
(855) ktrermamnityam. 4. 4. 20
(856) ṭvito 'thuc. 3. 3. 89
(857) yajayācayatavicchapraccha-rakṣo naṅ. 3. 3. 90
(858) svapo nan. 3. 3. 91
(859) upasarge ghoḥ kiḥ. 3. 3. 92
(860) striyāṁ ktin. 3. 3. 94
(861) ūtiyūtijūtisātihetikīrtayaśca. 3. 3. 97
(862) jvaratvarasrivyavimavām-upadhāyāśca. 6. 4. 20
(863) icchā. 3. 3. 101
(864) a pratyayāt. 3. 3. 102
(865) gurośca halaḥ. 3. 3. 103
(866) ṇyāsaśrantho yuc. 3. 3. 107
(867) napuṁsake bhāve ktaḥ. 3. 3. 114
(868) lyuṭ ca. 3. 3. 115
(869) puṁsi saṁjñāyāṁ ghaḥ prāyeṇa. 3. 3. 118
(870) chāderghe 'dvyupasargasya. 6. 4. 96
(871) ave tṝstrorghañ. 3. 3. 120
(872) halaśca. 3. 3. 121
(873) īṣadduḥsuṣu kṛcchrākṛcchrā-rtheṣu khal. 3. 3. 126
(874) āto yuc. 3. 3. 128
(875) alaṁkhalvoḥ pratiṣedhayoḥ prācāṁ ktvā. 3. 4. 18
(876) samānakartṛkayoḥ pūrvakāle. 3. 4. 21
(877) na ktvā seṭ. 1. 2. 18
(878) ralo vyupadhāddhalādeḥ saṁśca. 1. 2. 26
(879) udito vā. 7. 2. 56
(880) jahāteśca ktvi. 7. 4. 43
(881) samāse 'nañpūrve ktvo lyap. 7. 1. 37
(882) ābhīkṣṇye ṇamul ca. 3. 4. 22
(883) nityavīpsayoḥ. 8. 1. 4
(884) anyathaivaṁkathamitthaṁsu siddhāprayogaścet. 3. 4. 27
(885) prātipadikārthaliṅgaparimāṇa-vacanamātre prathamā. 2. 3. 46
(886) sambodhane ca. 2. 3. 47
(887) karturīpsitatamaṁ karma. 1. 4. 49
(888) karmaṇi dvitīyā. 2. 3. 2
(889) akathitaṁ ca. 1. 4. 51
* svatantraḥ kartā. 1. 4. 54
(890) sādhakatamaṁ karaṇam. 1. 4. 42
(891) kartṛkaraṇayostṛtīyā. 2. 3. 18
(892) karmaṇā yamabhipraiti sa sampradānam. 1. 4. 32
(893) caturthī saṁpradāne. 2. 3. 13
(894) namaḥsvastisvāhāsvadhālaṁ-vaṣaḍyogācca. 2. 3. 16
(895) dhruvamapāye 'pādānam. 1. 4. 24
(896) apādāne pañcamī. 2. 3. 28
(897) ṣaṣṭhī śeṣe. 2. 3. 50
(898) ādhāro 'dhikaraṇam. 1. 4. 45
(899) saptamyadhikaraṇe ca. 2. 3. 36
(900) samarthaḥ padavidhiḥ. 2. 1. 1
(901) prākkaḍārātsamāsaḥ. 2. 1. 3
(902) saha supā. 2. 1. 4
(903) avyayībhāvaḥ. 2. 1. 5
(904) avyayaṁ vibhaktisamīpa-samṛddhivyṛddhyarthābhāvātyayā-sampratiśabdaprādurbhāvapaścād-yathānupūrvyayaugapadyasādṛśya-sampattisākalyāntavacaneṣu. 2. 1. 6
(905) prathamānirdiṣṭaṁ samāsa upasarjanam. 1. 2. 43
(906) upasarjanaṁ pūrvam. 2. 2. 30
(907) avyayībhāvaśca. 2. 4. 18

(908) nāvyayībhāvādato 'mtvapañcamyāḥ. 2. 4. 83
(909) tṛtīyāsapatamyorbahulam. 2. 4. 84
(910) avyayībhāve cākāle. 6. 3. 81
(911) nadībhiśca. 2. 1. 20
(912) taddhitāḥ. 4. 1. 76
(913) avyayībhāve śaratprabhṛtibhyaḥ. 5. 4. 107
(914) anaśca. 5. 4. 108
(915) nastaddhite. 6. 4. 144
(916) napuṁsakādanyatarasyām. 5. 4. 109
(917) jhayaḥ. 5. 4. 111
(918) tatpuruṣaḥ. 2. 1. 22
(919) dviguśca. 2. 1. 23
(920) dvitīyā śritātītapatitagatātyastaprāptāpannaiḥ. 2. 1. 24
(921) tṛtīyā tatkṛtārthena guṇavacanena. 2. 1. 30
(922) kartṛkaraṇe kṛtā bahulam. 2. 1. 32
(923) caturthītadarthārthabalihitasukharakṣitaiḥ. 2. 1. 36
(924) pañcamī bhayena. 2. 1. 37
(925) stokāntikadūrārthakṛcchrāṇi ktena. 2. 1. 39
(926) pañcamyāḥ stokādibhyaḥ. 6. 3. 2
(927) ṣaṣṭhī. 2. 2. 8
(928) pūrvāparādharottaramekadeśinaikādhikaraṇe. 2. 2. 1
(929) ardhaṁ napuṁsakam. 2. 2. 2
(930) saptamī śauṇḍaiḥ. 2. 1. 40
(931) diksaṁkhye saṁjñāyām. 2. 1. 50
(932) taddhitārthottarapadasamāhāre ca. 2. 1. 51
(933) dikpūrvapadādasaṁjñāyāṁ ñaḥ. 4. 2. 107
(934) taddhiteṣvacāmādeḥ. 7. 2. 117
(935) gorataddhitaluki. 5. 4. 92
(936) tatpuruṣaḥ samānādhikaraṇaḥ karmadhārayaḥ. 1. 2. 42
(937) saṁkhyāpūrvo dviguḥ. 2. 1. 52
(938) dvigurekavacanam. 2. 4. 1
(939) sa napuṁsakam. 2. 4. 17
(940) viśeṣaṇaṁ viśeṣyeṇa bahulam. 2. 1. 57
(941) upamānāni sāmānyavacanaiḥ. 2. 1. 55
(942) nañ. 2. 2. 6
(943) nalopo nañaḥ. 6. 3. 73
(944) tasmānnuḍaci. 6. 3. 74
(945) kugatiprādayaḥ. 2. 2. 18
(946) ūryādicviḍācaśca. 1. 4. 61
(947) ekavibhakti cāpūrvanipāte. 1. 2. 44
(948) gostriyorupasarjanasya. 1. 2. 48
(949) tatropapadaṁ saptamīstham. 3. 1. 92
(950) upapadamatiṅ. 2. 2. 19
(951) tatpuruṣasyāṅguleḥ saṁkhyāvyayādeḥ. 5. 4. 86
(952) ahaḥsarvaikadeśasaṁkhyātapuṇyācca rātreḥ. 5. 4. 87
(953) rātrāhnāhāḥ puṁsi. 2. 4. 29
(954) rājāhaḥsakhibhyaṣṭac. 5. 4. 91
(955) ānmahataḥ samānādhikaraṇajātīyayoḥ. 6. 3. 46
(956) dvyaṣṭanaḥ saṁkhyāyāmabahuvrīhyaśītyoḥ. 6. 3. 47
(957) trestrayaḥ. 6. 3. 48
(958) paravalliṅgaṁ dvandvatatpuruṣayoḥ. 2. 4. 26
(959) prāptāpanne ca dvitīyayā. 2. 2. 4
(960) ardharcāḥ puṁsi ca. 2. 4. 31
(961) śeṣo bahuvrīhiḥ. 2. 2. 23
(962) anekamanyapadārthe. 2. 2. 24
(963) saptamīviśeṣaṇe bahuvrīhau. 2. 2. 35
(964) haladantātsaptamyāḥ saṁjñāyām. 6. 3. 9

(965) striyāḥ puṁvadbhāṣitapuṁskād-anūṅ samānādhikaraṇe striyām-apūraṇīpriyādiṣu. 6. 3. 34
(966) appūraṇīpramāṇyoḥ. 5. 4. 116
(967) bahuvrīhau sakthyakṣṇoḥ svāṅgāt ṣac. 5. 4. 113
(968) dvitribhyāṁ ṣa mūrdhnaḥ. 5. 4. 115
(969) antarbahirbhyāṁ ca lomnaḥ. 5. 4. 117
(970) pādasya lopo 'hastyādibhyaḥ. 5. 4. 138
(971) saṁkhyāsupūrvasya. 5. 4. 140
(972) udvibhyāṁ kākudasya. 5. 4. 148
(973) pūrṇādvibhāṣā. 5. 4. 149
(974) suhṛddurhṛdau mitrāmitrayoḥ. 5. 4. 150
(975) uraḥprabhṛtibhyaḥ kap. 5. 4. 151
(976) so 'padādau. 8. 3. 38
(977) iṇaḥ ṣaḥ. 8. 3. 39
(978) kaskādiṣu ca. 8. 3. 48
(979) niṣṭhā. 2. 2. 36
(980) śeṣādvibhāṣā. 5. 4. 154
(981) cārthe dvandvaḥ. 2. 2. 29
(982) rājadantādiṣu param. 2. 2. 31
(983) dvandve ghi. 2. 2. 32
(984) ajādyadantam. 2. 2. 33
(985) alpāctaram. 2. 2. 34
(986) pitā mātrā. 1. 2. 70
(987) dvandvaśca prāṇitūrya-senāṅgānām. 2. 4. 2
(988) dvandvāccudaṣahāntāt samāhāre. 5. 4. 106
(989) ṛkpūrabdhūḥpathām ānakṣe. 5. 4. 74
(990) akṣṇo 'darśanāt. 5. 4. 76
(991) upasargādadhvanaḥ. 5. 4. 85
(992) na pūjanāt. 5. 4. 69
(993) samarthānāṁ prathamādvā. 4. 1. 82
(994) aśvapatyādibhyaśca 4. 1. 84
(995) dityadityādityapatyuttara-padāṇṇyaḥ. 4. 1. 85
(996) halo yamāṁ yami lopaḥ. 8. 4. 64
(997) kiti ca. 7. 2. 118
(998) utsādibhyo 'ñ. 4. 1. 86
(999) strīpuṁsābhyāṁ nañsnañau bhavanāt. 4. 1. 87
(1000) tasyāpatyam. 4. 1. 92
(1001) orguṇaḥ. 6. 4. 146
(1002) apatyaṁ pautraprabhṛti gotram. 4. 1. 162
(1003) eko gotre. 4. 1. 93
(1004) gargādibhyo yañ. 4. 1. 105
(1005) yañañośca. 2. 4. 64
(1006) jīvati tu vaṁśye yuvā. 4. 1. 163
(1007) gotrādyūnyastriyām. 4. 1. 94
(1008) yañiñośca. 4. 1. 101
(1009) āyaneyīnīyiyaḥ phaḍhakha-chaghāṁ pratyayādīnām. 7. 1. 2
(1010) ata iñ. 4. 1. 95
(1011) bāhvādibhyaśca. 4. 1. 96
(1012) anṛṣyānantarye bidādibhyo 'ñ. 4. 1. 104
(1013) śivādibhyo 'ṇ. 4. 1. 112
(1014) ṛṣyandhakavṛṣṇikurubhyaśca. 4. 1. 114
(1015) māturutsaṁkhyāsaṁbhadra-pūrvāyāḥ. 4. 1. 115
(1016) strībhyo ḍhak. 4. 1. 120
(1017) kanyāyāḥ kanīna ca. 4. 1. 116
(1018) rājaśvaśurād yat. 4. 1. 137
(1019) ye cābhāvakarmaṇoḥ. 6. 4. 168
(1020) an. 6. 4. 167
(1021) kṣatrād ghaḥ. 4. 1. 138
(1022) revatyādibhyaṣṭhak. 4. 1. 146
(1023) ṭhasyekaḥ. 7. 3. 50
(1024) janapadaśabdāt kṣatriyād añ. 4. 1. 168
(1025) kurunādibhyo ṇyaḥ. 4. 1. 172
(1026) te tadrājāḥ. 4. 1. 174
(1027) tadrājasya bahuṣu tenaivā-striyām. 2. 4. 62

(1028) kambojālluk. 4. 1. 175
(1029) tena raktaṁ rāgāt. 4. 2. 1
(1030) nakṣatreṇa yuktaḥ kālaḥ. 4. 2. 3
(1031) lubaviśeṣe. 4. 2. 4
(1032) dṛṣṭaṁ sāma. 4. 2. 7
(1033) vāmadevāḍḍyaḍḍyau. 4. 2. 9
(1034) parivṛto rathaḥ. 4. 2. 10
(1035) tatroddhṛtamamatrebhyaḥ. 4. 2. 14
(1036) saṁskṛtaṁ bhakṣāḥ. 4. 2. 16
(1037) sā 'sya devatā. 4. 2. 24
(1038) śukrād ghan. 4. 2. 26
(1039) somāṭ ṭyaṇ. 4. 2. 30
(1040) vāyvṛtupitruṣaso yat. 4. 2. 31
(1041) rīṅ ṛtaḥ. 7. 4. 27
(1042) pitṛvyamātulamātāmaha-pitāmahāḥ. 4. 2. 36
(1043) tasya samūhaḥ. 4. 2. 37
(1044) bhikṣādibhyo 'ṇ. 4. 2. 38
(1045) inaṇyanapatye. 6. 4. 164
(1046) grāmajanabandhubhyastal. 4. 2. 43
(1047) acittahastidhenoṣṭhak. 4. 2. 47
(1048) isusuktāntāt kaḥ. 7. 3. 51
(1049) tadadhīte tadveda. 4. 2. 59
(1050) na yvābhyāṁ padāntābhyāṁ pūrvau tu tābhyāmaic. 7. 3. 3
(1051) kramādibhyo vun. 4. 2. 61
(1052) tadasminnastīti deśe tannāmni. 4. 2. 67
(1053) tena nirvṛttam. 4. 2. 68
(1054) tasya nivāsaḥ. 4. 2. 69
(1055) adūrabhavaśca. 4. 2. 70
(1056) janapade lup. 4. 2. 81
(1057) lupi yuktavadvyaktivacane. 1. 2. 51
(1058) varaṇādibhyaśca. 4. 2. 82
(1059) kumudanaḍavetasebhyo ḍmatup. 4. 2. 87
(1060) jhayaḥ. 8. 2. 10
(1061) mādupadhāyāśca matorvo 'yavādibhyaḥ. 8. 2. 9
(1062) naḍaśādāḍḍvalac. 4. 2. 88
(1063) śikhāyā valac. 4. 2. 89
(1064) śeṣe. 4. 2. 92
(1065) rāṣṭrāvārapārād ghakhau. 4. 2. 93
(1066) grāmādyakhañau. 4. 2. 94
(1067) nadyādibhyo ḍhak. 4. 2. 97
(1068) dakṣiṇāpaścātpurasastyak. 4. 2. 98
(1069) dyuprāgapāgudakpratīco yat. 4. 2. 101
(1070) avyayāttyap. 4. 2. 104
(1071) vṛddhiryasyācāmādistad-vṛddham. 1. 1. 73
(1072) tyadādīni ca. 1. 1. 74
(1073) vṛddhācchaḥ. 4. 2. 114
(1074) gahādibhyaśca. 4. 2. 138
(1075) yuṣmadasmadoranyatarasyāṁ khañ ca. 4. 3. 1
(1076) tasminnaṇi ca yuṣmākāsmākau. 4. 3. 2
(1077) tavakamamakāvekavacane. 4. 3. 3
(1078) pratyayottarapadayośca. 7. 2. 98
(1079) madhyānmaḥ. 4. 3. 8
(1080) kālāṭṭhañ. 4. 3. 11
(1081) prāvṛṣa eṇyaḥ. 4. 3. 17
(1082) sāyañciramprāhṇeprage 'vyayebhyaṣṭyuṭyulau tuṭ ca. 4. 3. 23
(1083) tatra jātaḥ. 4. 3. 25
(1084) prāvṛṣaṣṭhap. 4. 3. 26
(1085) prāyabhavaḥ. 4. 3. 39
(1086) sambhūte. 4. 3. 41
(1087) kośāḍḍhañ. 4. 3. 42
(1088) tatra bhavaḥ. 4. 3. 53
(1089) digādibhyo yat. 4. 3. 54
(1090) śarīrāvayavācca. 4. 3. 55
(1091) anuśatikādīnāṁ ca. 7. 3. 20
(1092) jihvāmūlāṅguleśchaḥ. 4. 3. 62

(1093) vargāntācca. 4. 3. 63
(1094) tata āgataḥ. 4. 3. 74
(1095) ṭhagāyasthānebhyaḥ. 4. 3. 75
(1096) vidyāyonisambandhebhyo vuñ. 4. 3. 77
(1097) hetumanuṣyebhyo 'nyatarasyāṁ rūpyaḥ. 4. 3. 81
(1098) mayaṭ ca. 4. 3. 82
(1099) prabhavati. 4. 3. 83
(1100) tadgacchati paṭhidūtayoḥ. 4. 3. 85
(1101) abhiniṣkrāmati dvāram. 4. 3. 86
(1102) adhikṛtya kṛte granthe. 4. 3. 87
(1103) so 'sya nivāsaḥ. 4. 3. 89
(1104) tena proktam. 4. 3. 101
(1105) tasyedam. 4. 3. 120
(1106) tasya vikāraḥ. 4. 3. 134
(1107) avayave ca prāṇyoṣadhivṛkṣebhyaḥ. 4. 3. 135
(1108) mayaḍvaitayorbhāṣāyāmabhakṣyācchādanayoḥ. 4. 3. 143
(1109) nityaṁ vṛddhaśarādibhyaḥ. 4. 3 .144
(1110) gośca purīṣe. 4. 3. 145
(1111) gopayasoryat. 4. 3. 160
(1112) prāgvahateṣṭhak. 4. 4. 1
(1113) tena dīvyati khanati jayati jitam. 4. 4. 2
(1114) saṁskṛtam. 4. 4. 3
(1115) tarati. 4. 4. 5
(1116) carati. 4. 4. 8
(1117) saṁsṛṣṭe. 4. 4. 22
(1118) uñchati. 4. 4. 32
(1119) rakṣati. 4. 4. 33
(1120) śabdadarduraṁ karoti. 4. 4. 34
(1121) dharmaṁ carati. 4. 4. 41
(1122) śilpam. 4. 4. 55
(1123) praharaṇam. 4. 4. 57
(1124) śīlam. 4. 4. 61
(1125) nikaṭe vasati. 4. 4. 73
(1126) prāgghitādyat. 4. 4. 75
(1127) tadvahati rathayugaprāsaṅgam. 4. 4. 76
(1128 dhuro yaḍḍhakau. 4. 4. 77
* na bhakurchurām. 8. 2. 79
(1129) nauvayodharmaviṣamūlamūlasītātulābhyastāryatulyaprāpyavadhyānāmyasamasamitasaṁmiteṣu. 4. 4. 91
(1130) tatra sādhuḥ. 4. 4. 98
(1131) sabhāyā yaḥ. 4. 4. 105
(1132) prāk krītācchaḥ. 5. 1. 1
(1133) ugavādibhyo yat . 5. 1. 2
(1134) tasmai hitam. 5. 1. 5
(1135) śarīrāvayavādyat. 5. 1. 6
(1136) ātmanviśvajanabhogottarapadāt khaḥ. 5. 1. 9
(1137) ātmādhvānau khe. 6. 4. 169
(1138) prāgvateṣṭhañ. 5. 1. 18
(1139) tena krītam. 5. 1. 37
(1140) tasyeśvaraḥ. 5. 1. 42
(1141) paṅktiviṁśatitriṁśaccatvāriṁśatpañcāśatṣaṣṭisaptatyaśītinavatiśatam. 5. 1. 59
(1142) tadarhati. 5. 1. 63
(1143) daṇḍādibhyo yat. 5. 1. 66
(1144) tena nirvṛttam. 5. 1. 79
(1145) tena tulyaṁ kriyā cedvatih. 5. 1. 115
(1146) tatra tasyeva. 5. 1. 116
(1147) tasya bhāvastvatalau. 5. 1. 119
(1148) ā ca tvāt. 5. 1. 120
(1149) pṛthvādibhya imanijvā. 5. 1. 122
(1150) ra ṛto halāderlaghoḥ. 6. 4. 161
(1151) ṭeḥ. 6. 4. 155
(1152) igantācca laghupūrvāt. 5. 1. 131
(1153) varṇadṛḍhādibhyaḥ ṣyañ ca. 5. 1. 123
(1154) guṇavacanabrāhmaṇādibhyaḥ karmaṇi ca. 5. 1. 124
(1155) sakhyuryaḥ. 5. 1. 126
(1156) kapijñātyorḍhak. 5. 1. 127

(1157) patyantapurohitādibhyo yak. 5. 1. 128
(1158) dhānyānāṁ bhavane kṣetre khañ. 5. 2. 1
(1159) vrīhiśālyorḍhak. 5. 2. 2
(1160) haiyaṅgavīnaṁ saṁjñāyām. 5. 2. 23
(1161) tadasya saṁjātaṁ tārakādibhya itac. 5. 2. 36
(1162) pramāṇe dvyasajdaghanañmātracaḥ. 5. 2. 37
(1163) yattadetebhyaḥ parimāṇe vatup. 5. 2. 39
(1164) kimidambhyāṁ vo ghaḥ. 5. 2. 40
(1165) idaṅkimorīśkī. 6. 3. 90
(1166) saṁkhyāyā avayave tayap. 5. 2. 42
(1167) dvitribhyāṁ tayasyāyajvā. 5. 2. 43
(1168) ubhādudātto nityam. 5. 2. 44
(1169) tasya pūraṇe ḍaṭ. 5. 2. 48
(1170) nāntādasaṁkhyādermaṭ. 5. 2. 49
(1171) ti viṁśaterḍiti. 6. 4. 142
(1172) ṣaṭkatikatipayacaturāṁ thuk. 5. 2. 51
(1173) dvestīyaḥ. 5. 2. 54
(1174) treḥ samprasāraṇaṁ ca. 5. 2. 55
(1175) śrotriyaṁśchando 'dhīte. 5. 2. 84
(1176) pūrvādiniḥ. 5. 2. 86
(1177) sapūrvācca. 5. 2. 87
(1178) iṣṭādibhyaśca. 5. 2. 88
(1179) tadasyāstyasminniti matup. 5. 2. 94
(1180) tasau matvarthe. 1. 4. 19
(1181) prāṇisthādāto lajanyatarasyām. 5. 2. 96
(1182) lomādipāmādipicchādibhyaḥ śanelacaḥ. 5. 2. 100
(1183) danta unnata urac. 5. 2. 106
(1184) keśādvo 'nyatarasyām. 5. 2. 109
(1185) ata iniṭhanau. 5. 2. 115
(1186) vrīhyādibhyaśca. 5. 2. 116
(1187) asmāyāmedhāsrajo viniḥ. 5. 2. 121
(1188) vāco gminiḥ. 5. 2. 124
(1189) arśa ādibhyo 'c. 5. 2. 127
(1190) ahaṁśubhayoryus. 5. 2. 140
(1191) prāgdiśo vibhaktiḥ. 5. 3. 1
(1192) kiṁsarvanāmabahubhyo 'dvyādibhyaḥ. 5. 3. 2
(1193) pañcamyāstasil. 5. 3. 7
(1194) ku tihoḥ. 7. 2. 104
(1195) idama iś. 5. 3. 3
(1196) an. 5. 3. 5
(1197) paryabhibhyāṁ ca. 5. 3. 9
(1198) saptamyāstral. 5. 3. 10.
(1199) idamo haḥ. 5. 3. 11
(1200) kimo 't. 5. 3. 12
(1201) kvāti. 7. 2. 105
(1202) itarābhyo 'pi dṛśyante. 5. 3. 14
(1203) sarvaikānyakiṁyattadaḥ kāle dā. 5. 3. 15
(1204) sarvasya so 'nyatarasyāṁ di. 5. 3. 6
(1205) idamo rhil. 5. 3. 16
(1206) etetau rathoḥ. 5. 3. 4
(1207) anadyatane rhilanyatarasyām. 5. 3. 21
(1208) etadaḥ. 5. 3. 5
(1209) prakāravacane thāl. 5. 3. 23
(1210) idamasthamu. 5. 3. 24
(1211) kimaśca. 5. 3. 25
(1212) atiśāyane tamabiṣṭhanau. 5. 3. 55
(1213) tiṅaśca. 5. 3. 56
(1214) taraptamapau ghaḥ. 1. 1. 22
(1215) kimettiṅavyayaghādāmvadravyaprakarṣe. 5. 4. 11
(1216) dvivacanavibhajyopapade tarabīyasunau. 5. 3. 57
(1217) praśasyasya śraḥ. 5. 3. 60

(1218) prakṛtyaikāc. 6. 4. 163
(1219) jya ca. 5. 3. 61
(1220) jyādādīyasaḥ. 6. 4. 160
(1221) bahorlopo bhū ca bahoḥ. 6. 4. 158
(1222) iṣṭhasya yiṭ ca. 6. 4. 159
(1223) vinmatorluk. 5. 3. 65
(1224) īṣadasamāptau kalpabdeśya-deśīyaraḥ. 5. 3. 67
(1225) vibhāṣā supo bahuc purastāttu. 5. 3. 68
(1226) prāgivātkaḥ. 5. 3. 70
(1227) avyayasarvanāmnāmakac prāk ṭeḥ. 5. 3. 71
(1228) ajñāte. 5. 3. 73
(1229) kutsite. 5. 3. 74
(1230) kiṁyattado nirdhāraṇe dvayorekasya ḍatarac. 5. 3. 92
(1231) vā bahūnāṁ jātiparipraśne ḍatamac. 5. 3. 93
(1232) ive pratikṛtau. 5. 3. 96
(1233) tatprakṛtavacane mayaṭ. 5. 4. 21
(1234) prajñādibhyaśca. 5. 4. 38
(1235) bahvalpārthācchaskārakād-anyatarasyām. 5. 4. 42
(1236) kṛbhvastiyoge sampadya-kartari cviḥ. 5. 4. 50
(1237) asya cvau. 7. 4. 32
(1238) vibhāṣā sāti kārtsnye. 5. 4. 52
(1239) sātpadādyoḥ. 8. 3. 111
(1240) cvau ca. 7. 4. 26
(1241) avyaktānukaraṇāddvyajavarā-rdhādanitau ḍāc. 5. 4. 57
(1242) striyām. 4. 1. 3
(1243) ajādyataṣṭāp. 4. 1. 4
(1244) ugitaśca. 4. 1. 6
(1245) ṭiḍḍhāṇañdvayasajdaghnañ-mātractayapṭhakṭhañkañkvarapaḥ. 4. 1. 15
(1246) yañaśca. 4. 1. 16
(1247) halastaddhitasya. 6. 4. 150
(1248) prācāṁ ṣpha taddhitaḥ. 4. 1. 17
(1249) ṣidgaurādibhyaśca. 4. 1. 41
(1250) vayasi prathame. 4. 1. 20
(1251) dvigoḥ. 4. 1. 21
(1252) varṇādanudāttāttopadhātto naḥ. 4. 1. 39
(1253) voto guṇavacanāt. 4. 1. 44
(1254) bahvādibhyaśca. 4. 1. 45
(1255) puṁyogādākhyāyām. 4. 1. 48
(1256) pratyayasthātkāt pūrvasyāta idāpyasupaḥ. 7. 3. 44
(1257) indravaruṇabhavaśarvarudra-mṛḍahimāraṇyayavayavanamātulā-cāryāṇāmānuk. 4. 1. 49
(1258) krītāt karaṇapūrvāt. 4. 1. 50
(1259) svāṅgāccopasarjanādasaṁ-yogopadhāt. 4. 1. 54
(1260) na kroḍādibahvacaḥ. 4. 1. 56
(1261) nakhamukhāt saṁjñāyām. 4. 1. 58
(1262) pūrvapadāt saṁjñāyāmagaḥ. 8. 4. 3
(1263) jāterastrīviṣayādayopadhāt. 4. 1. 63
(1264) ito manuṣyajāteḥ. 4. 1. 65
(1265) ūṅutaḥ. 4. 1. 66
(1266) paṅgośca. 4. 1. 68
(1267) ūrūttarapadādaupamye. 4. 1. 69
(1268) saṁhitaśaphalakṣaṇavāmā-deśca. 4. 1. 70
(1269) śārṅgaravādyaño ṅīn. 4. 1. 73
(1270) yūnastiḥ. 4. 1. 77

Index of the sūtras of the Laghusiddhāntakaumudī (Vol. I)

[Figures refer to page numbers]

Index of the vārttikas and paribhāṣās (Vol. I)

[(P) indicates paribhāṣā]

Index of Declined Words

The numbers refer to the pages where declensional forms begin. Abbreviations – m : masculine, f : feminine, n : neuter. They are given where they are required.

Index of Indeclinables